The Pilot's Manual

PM 2

Ground School

The Pilot's Manual **PM 2**

Ground School

All the aeronautical knowledge required to pass the FAA exams and operate as a Private and Commercial Pilot

Fifth Edition

Foreword by Barry Schiff

AVIATION SUPPLIES & ACADEMICS
NEWCASTLE, WASHINGTON

The Pilot's Manual Volume 2: Ground School
Fifth Edition

Aviation Supplies & Academics, Inc.
7005 132nd Place SE
Newcastle, Washington 98059-3153
asa@asa2fly.com | www.asa2fly.com

(Originally published by Center for Aviation Theory, 1990–1998)

None of the material in this book supersedes any operational documents or procedures issued by the Federal Aviation Administration, aircraft and avionics manufacturers, flight schools, or the operators of aircraft.

ASA-PM-2D
ISBN 978-1-64425-051-8

Additional formats available:
Kindle ISBN 978-1-64425-053-2
eBook ePub ISBN 978-1-64425-052-5
eBook PDF ISBN 978-1-64425-054-9
eBundle ISBN 978-1-64425-055-6 (print + eBook PDF download code)

Printed in the United States of America
2024 2023 2022 2021 2020 10 9 8 7 6 5 4 3 2 1

Graphics and cover: Rob Loriente
Photographs: Rob Fox (main cover photo)

Acknowledgments:
The publishers would like to thank the Federal Aviation Administration (FAA), the National Weather Service (NWS), Allied Signal Aerospace, Bendix/King (a division of Allied Signal Aerospace), Cessna Aircraft Company, Department of the Air Force, Environment Protection Authority (Vic. Australia), Flight Data Center, Wilkes-Barre PA, General Aviation Manufacturer's Association (GAMA), Narco Avionics, Piper Aircraft Corporation, II Morrow, Inc.

Also, to the many students, instructors, and FAA personnel whose comments have helped in developing and refining the material in this manual.

Contents

Personal Progress Table

Aerodynamics

Text	Review

The Airplane

Text	Review

Airplane and Pilot Performance

Text	Review

Weather

Text	Review

Flight Operations

Text	Review

Appendices

Foreword

When it was time to take my private pilot written examination in 1955, my flight instructor handed me a pocket-size booklet. It was published by the Civil Aeronautics Administration (FAA's predecessor) and contained 200 true/false questions (including answers).

"Study these well," he cautioned with a wink, "because the test consists of 50 of these." As I flipped through the dozen or so pages, my anxiety about the pending examination dissolved into relief. Nothing could be easier, I thought. One question, for example, stated "True or False: It is dangerous to fly through a thunderstorm." Really. (I passed the test with flying colors—but so did everyone else in those days.)

The modern pilot, however, must know a great deal more to hurdle today's more challenging examinations. This has resulted in a crop of books developed specifically to help pilots pass tests. Unfortunately, some do little else, and the student's education remains incomplete.

An exciting exception is *The Pilot's Manual* series. These voluminous manuals provide far in excess of that needed to pass examinations. They are chock-full of practical advice and techniques that are as useful to experienced pilots as they are to students.

The *Pilot's Manuals* are a refreshingly creative and clever approach that simplifies and adds spice to what often are regarded as academically dry subjects. Reading these books is like sitting with an experienced flight instructor who senses when you might be having difficulty with a subject and patiently continues teaching until confident that you understand.

Barry Schiff
Los Angeles

Barry Schiff has over 26,000 hours in more than 300 types of aircraft. He is retired from Trans World Airlines, where he flew everything from the Lockheed Constellation to the Boeing 747 and was a check captain on the Boeing 767. He earned every available FAA category and class rating (except airship) and every possible instructor's rating. He also received numerous honors for his contributions to aviation. An award-winning journalist and author, he is well known to flying audiences for his many articles published in some 90 aviation periodicals, notably *AOPA Pilot*, of which he is a contributing editor. ASA publishes several Barry Schiff titles.

About the Editorial Team

David Robson QTP

David Robson is a career aviator having been nurtured on balsa wood, dope (the legal kind) and tissue paper, and currently holds an ATP certificate with instructor ratings. He served as a fighter pilot and test pilot for the Royal Australian Air Force, completed a tour in Vietnam as a forward air controller flying the USAF O-2A and was a member of the Mirage formation acrobatic team, the Deltas. After retiring from the Air Force, he became a civilian instructor and lecturer for the Australian Aviation College, and editor for Aviation Safety Digest, which won the Flight Safety Foundation's international award. He was awarded the Australian Aviation Safety Foundation's Certificate of Air Safety.

Richard Coffey

Richard Coffey is a commercial pilot and flight instructor with instrument, multi-engine, and sea plane privileges. He has also been an aviation writer and editor since 1976 and is the author of the Skylane Pilot's Companion (1996). He has written for Airports Services Management magazine, Aviation Consumer, Aviation Safety and IFR magazines. He regularly flies Cessna 210s and 182s, although he has a weakness for older Beech Bonanzas and has owned an M model.

Dr. Dale DeRemer

Dr. DeRemer was recognized as "Seaplane Pilot of the Year" by the Seaplane Pilots Association, and inducted into the EAA-NAFI Flight Instructor Hall of Fame. He was named "Professor Emeritus of Aviation" by the University of North Dakota College of Aerospace Sciences after 20 years of teaching aviation subjects at the university level. During his career, he has served as corporate pilot, agricultural pilot and chief pilot for his own and other companies. He has logged over 20,000 hours total time in general aviation aircraft of many types. Dale holds ATP, CFI-A, CFI-H, CFI-I, and MEI licenses with single- and multi-engine land and sea, rotorcraft-helicopter, and instrument ratings.

James Johnson

James Johnson is the Director of Aviation Training for ASA. He has accumulated many years of aviation industry experience, from flight and ground instruction to working within corporate flight departments. James received a B.S. in Aeronautics with minors in Aviation Safety and Airport Management from Embry-Riddle Aeronautical University. He holds certificates for Commercial Pilot, Advanced Ground, and Instrument Instructor, as well as Remote Pilot sUAS.

Jeanne MacPherson

Bureau Chief, Safety and Education for the Montana Aeronautics Division of Helena, Jeanne is also the Chief Pilot and Mountain Flight Instructor. She coordinates air search for the State of Montana and coordinates Mountain Search Pilot Clinics, Flight Instructor

Refresher Clinics, Winter Survival, Density Altitude Clinics, Aviation Education Workshops, and Aviation Careers Programs. Jeanne is a Young Eagles Flight Leader (EAA) and has flown over 2,900 students; she is the recipient of the 2003 EAA Freedom of Flight Award, 2002 Women in Aviation Educator of the Year Award, and 2000 FAA Aviation Educator of the Year for the Northwest Region.

Dennis Newton

Dennis Newton holds ATP and CFI certificates, and is an FAA-Designated Engineering Representative Flight Test Pilot for both small and transport airplanes. A few of Mr. Newton's past achievements include meteorologist, weather research pilot, and engineering test pilot; he has also served as a consultant to government and industry on icing certification and flight testing. Dennis Newton is the author of numerous papers and aviation magazine articles on icing and other weather topics. He holds a B.S. in Engineering and an M.S. in Meteorology. Mr. Newton is also a member of the American Institute of Aeronautics and Astronautics, and the Society of Experimental Test Pilots.

Dr. Phil Poynor

Phillip J. Poynor, J.D., FAA/Industry 2001 Flight Instructor of the Year, holds an ATP pilot certificate, has been captain qualified on Part 135 carriers, and has taught courses on Air Carrier Operations and Advanced Systems for many years at three major aviation colleges. Phil is an attorney with a practice limited to aviation matters. He was a staff attorney in the flight operations department of a major, international airline. He began his flying career over 38 years ago and has been instructing for more than 30 years. Phil received the Excellence in Pilot Training Award from the National Air Transportation Association in 1998 and the Chancellor's Award for Excellence in Teaching from SUNY in 1994. He currently volunteers as Vice President—Government and Industry Affairs for the National Association of Flight Instructors, for which he is also an emeritus member of the Board of Directors.

Barry Schiff

Barry Schiff has over 26,000 hours in more than 300 types of aircraft. He is retired from Trans World Airlines, where he flew everything from the Lockheed Constellation to the Boeing 747 and was a check captain on the Boeing 767. He earned every available FAA category and class rating (except airship) and every possible instructor's rating. He also received numerous honors for his contributions to aviation. An award-winning journalist and author, he is well known to flying audiences for his many articles published in some 90 aviation periodicals, notably AOPA Pilot, of which he is a contributing editor.

Warren Smith

James Warren Smith is the Vice President of Flight Operations and Chief Pilot for the Flightstar Corporation located in Savoy, IL. With over 8,000 hours flown and over 3,000 hours of flight training given, Warren currently flies a Falcon 900 internationally and serves as a Designated Pilot Examiner (DPE) for the FAA. Warren has been a certificated flight instructor (CFI) for over 20 years and has served as the chief flight instructor for several 141 flight schools. In addition, Warren has served as Chairman of the National Air Transportation Association (NATA) Flight Training Committee dealing with flight training issues on a national level.

Jackie Spanitz

As General Manager of ASA, Jackie Spanitz oversees maintenance and development of more than 1,000 titles and pilot supplies in the ASA product line. Ms. Spanitz has worked with airman training and testing for over 25 years, including participation in the Airman Certification Standards development committees. Jackie holds a B.S. in Aviation Technology from Western Michigan University, a M.S. in Aeronautical Science from Embry-Riddle Aeronautical University and Instructor, Commercial, and Remote Pilot certificates. She is the author of *Guide to the Flight Review* and the technical editor for ASA's *Test Prep* and *FAR/AIM* series.

Richard Taylor

Richard L. Taylor is an award-winning author of many articles and 14 aviation books. He retired from the Air Force Reserve as a major, having earned Command Pilot status. Now associate professor emeritus, Taylor was director of flight operations and training and taught at all levels of the flight curriculum at the Ohio State University. He is the founder and editor of The Pilot's Audio Update, a monthly audio tape cassette service published continuously since 1978. Taylor has accumulated nearly 13,000 hours of pilot time in a wide variety of aircraft including gliders, helicopters, amphibians, turboprops, jets, and most general aviation light airplanes. He remains active in accident investigation and as an aviation consultant in Dublin, Ohio.

Dr. Mike Wiggins

Mike Wiggins has been with Embry-Riddle Aeronautical University for over 27 years. He is currently a tenured professor in the Aeronautical Science Department and the director of the newly created campus Center for Teaching and Learning, having taught in the classroom, been a member of the ERAU Flight Department, and active with the National Intercollegiate Flying Association (NIFA). He holds a Doctorate in Education from Oklahoma State University, a Masters Degree in Business Administration, and a Bachelor of Science Degree in Aeronautical Science from Embry-Riddle Aeronautical University. He holds an ATP certificate with Boeing 757 and 767 type-ratings, and flight instructor and ground instructor certificates.

Tom Wild

Thomas Wild is a full professor at Purdue University who holds an Aviation Maintenance Technician certificate with Inspection Authorization. He is also a Designated Mechanics Examiner, and a Flight Engineer. With numerous awards for his contributions to education, Tom has been teaching aviation technology at Purdue University for more than 25 years. He is the Managing Editor for the ATEC Journal, has written many articles, textbooks, and conducted seminars for the industry. He is a past member of the Board of Directors for Professional Aviation Maintenance Association (PAMA).

Introduction

You are about to become a flyer, and join the worldwide family of pilots. To do this safely, you need some knowledge, and the aim of *The Pilot's Manual* is to introduce you to this knowledge in an easy-to-follow manner that is both practical and thorough, so that you will fly the airplane confidently and pass the FAA Knowledge Exams with flying colors.

You will learn to be a safe pilot, to take off and fly in the vicinity of your home airport, and to navigate around the country without getting lost or tangled up with thunderstorms and airliners.

The Pilot's Manual has been written not only to help you to pass the FAA Knowledge Exams, but also for you to keep on your bookshelves as a ready reference containing items of practical importance to a pilot. The team involved in producing *The Pilot's Manual* includes many very experienced pilots from a wide range of backgrounds—flight instructors, ground instructors, mountain-flying experts, professors of aviation, meteorologists, FAA inspectors, examiners, air force pilots, naval aviators, airline pilots, and others. The accumulated knowledge between these covers is yours for the taking!

Ground School is divided into five sections and introduces you to:

- *aerodynamics*—the basic principles of flight and airplane design;
- *the airplane*—the piston engine, airplane systems and flight instruments;
- *airplane and pilot performance*—the factors which affect takeoff and landing performance, climbing and the cruise, how to safely load your airplane, and basic physiology so that you can maximize your personal performance;
- *weather*—the main processes of weather and how to interpret charts and forecasts; and
- *flight operations*—the Federal Aviation Regulations (to keep everyone safe), the basic principles of navigation, charts, airspace and airports, flight planning, and radio navigation.

This manual is designed for both the Private and Commercial Pilot. The main body of each chapter contains the knowledge required for the Private Pilot Certificate, with review questions. The questions highlight important points and give you practice at typical Knowledge Exam questions.

Additional Commercial Pilot Certificate knowledge, with review questions is included. It is not necessary for the prospective Private Pilot to read these additions, but we hope, when you see how straightforward they are, you will be encouraged to further your aviation knowledge at some stage and take the Commercial Pilot Knowledge Exam. If you plan to go straight to Commercial, this book is ideal for you.

Note. Additions intended only for students studying for their CPL are indicated by a blue line across the top of the relevant text and the letters "CPL" on the outer margin. Subsequent pages are also indicated in this way when appropriate. The end of a CPL-only section is indicated with the text "End CPL" in the outer margin (and a blue line underneath the text should that text fall mid-page).

A Few Points on Studying

Keep your study periods short and intense. Quietness, good lighting, and a clear and fresh mind are important to efficient study. Leisure is important too. Occasional walks and breaks for relaxation are beneficial to study, as is a day a week away from it all.

Make your own notes and summaries as you read through our text. The summary that you prepare is a most important aid to your learning. We suggest you work your way through the manual chapter-by-chapter, making your own notes and completing each set of review questions as you go. The reviews are not difficult because the knowledge required is in the text. The review questions are designed to give you confidence in your own knowledge and ability while giving you practice for the Private or Commercial Knowledge Exams.

The FAA Knowledge Exams consist of multiple-choice questions which are quick and easy to process. However, multiple-choice questions are not a good learning aid as they present you with a choice of answers, some of which are wrong. To continually read incorrect statements is confusing, so in our reviews we question you in a more positive manner, while retaining some multiple-choice questions in the examination style for your practice.

Our advice when working multiple-choice questions is, prior to reading through the selection of possible answers, think in your own mind what the answer might be. Then read through the choices and quite often you will find the answer you already have in mind is among them. If not, then proceed to eliminate the incorrect statements.

Please note that if you are preparing for the Commercial Knowledge Exam you should complete both the private and commercial reviews.

Note. Italics are used throughout the text to highlight significant terms and concepts.

Conclusion

The Pilot's Manual: Ground School is designed to develop an in-depth understanding of the main facets of aviation. Not only will it help you pass the Knowledge Exams easily, it will also provide an excellent basis for becoming a competent and safe pilot, regardless of whether you plan to use your skills for personal recreation and travel, or in a full-fledged career as a flight instructor or with the airlines.

Best wishes for success in your Knowledge Exams and practical flying.

Aerodynamics

1. **Forces Acting on an Airplane**
2. **Stability and Control**
3. **Aerodynamics of Flight**

Forces Acting on an Airplane 1

Like all things, an airplane has *weight*, the force of gravity that acts through the center of the airplane in a vertical direction toward the center of the earth. While the airplane is on the ground, its *weight* is supported by the force of the ground on the airplane, which acts upward through the wheels.

During the takeoff roll, the task of supporting the weight of the airplane is transferred from the ground to the wings (and vice versa during the landing). While in level flight, the weight of the airplane is supported by the *lift* force, which is generated aerodynamically by the flow of air around the wings. In addition, as the airplane moves through the air it will experience a retarding force known as *drag*, which, unless counteracted, will cause the airplane to decelerate and lose speed.

In steady (unaccelerated) straight-and-level flight, the drag (or retarding force) is neutralized by the *thrust* (figure 1-2). In most smaller airplanes, thrust is produced by the engine–propeller combination; in pure-jet airplanes, the thrust is produced by the gas efflux, without the need for a propeller.

Figure 1-1 Drag counteracted by thrust.

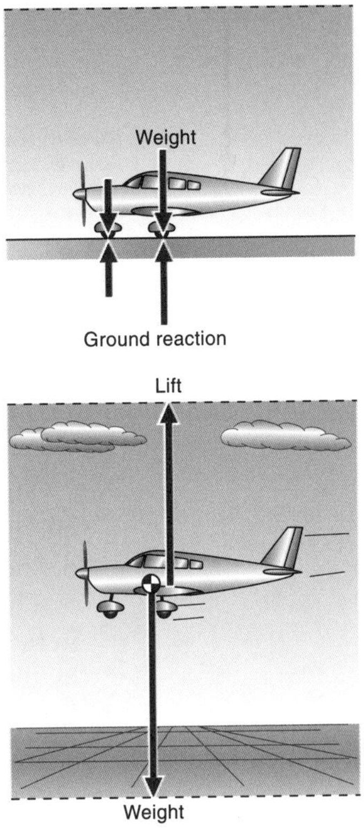

Figure 1-2
The airplane is supported by the ground, and in the air by lift.

In figure 1-3, the forces are equal and opposite, canceling each other out, so that the resultant force acting on the airplane is zero, and it will neither accelerate nor decelerate. In this situation the airplane is in a state of *equilibrium*:

- *weight* is equal to *lift*, and acts in the opposite direction; and
- *drag* is equal to *thrust*, and acts in the opposite direction.

During steady (unaccelerated) flight the four main forces are in equilibrium and the airplane will continue in level flight at the same speed.

For the type of airplane you are likely to be flying during your training, the amount of the lift (and therefore the weight) during cruise flight will be approximately 10 times greater than the drag (and thrust). This relationship of lift to drag is very important and is referred to as the *lift/drag ratio*. The L/D ratio in this case is 10 to 1.

If the airplane is to accelerate in level flight, the thrust must exceed the drag; if the airplane is to be slowed down in level flight, the thrust must be less than the drag. A state of equilibrium does not exist during acceleration or deceleration.

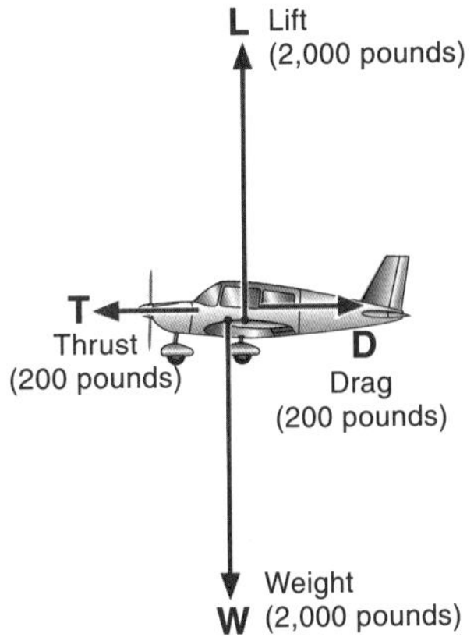

Figure 1-3 The four main forces are in equilibrium during unaccelerated flight.

Gravitational Force (Weight)

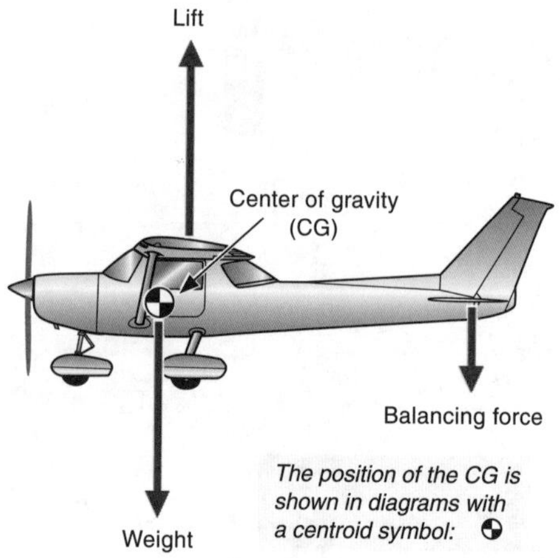

Figure 1-4
Weight acts downward through the center of gravity (CG).

Gravity is the downward force attracting all bodies vertically toward the center of the earth. The name given to the gravitational force is *weight*, and for our purposes it is the total weight of the loaded airplane. This weight is called *gross weight*, and it may be considered to act as a single force through the *center of gravity* (CG).

The CG is the point of balance. Its position depends on the weight and position of the various parts of the airplane and the load that it is carrying. If the airplane were supported at its center of gravity, the airplane would be balanced.

The weight of an airplane varies depending on the load it has to carry (cargo, baggage, passengers) and the amount of fuel on board. Airplane gross weight will gradually decrease as the flight progresses and fuel is burned off. The magnitude of the weight is important and there are certain limitations placed on it—for instance, a maximum takeoff weight will be specified for the airplane. Weight limitations depend on the structural strength of the components making up the airplane and the operational requirements the airplane is designed to meet.

The balance point (center of gravity) is very important during flight because of its effect on the stability and performance of the airplane. It must remain within carefully defined limits at all stages of the flight.

The location of the CG depends on the weight and the location of the load placed in the airplane. The CG will move if the distribution of the load changes, for instance by transferring load from one position to another by passengers moving about or by transferring fuel from one tank to another. The CG may shift forward or aft as the aircraft weight reduces in flight, such as when fuel burns off or parachutists jump out.

CPL

Wing Loading

Both weight and balance must be considered by the pilot prior to flight. If any limitation is exceeded at any point in the flight, safety will be compromised. (A detailed study of weight and balance appears in chapter 11.) A useful means of describing the load that the wings carry in straight-and-level flight (when the lift from the wings supports the weight of the airplane) is *wing loading*, which is simply the weight supported per unit area of wing.

$$\text{Wing loading} = \frac{\text{weight of the airplane}}{\text{wing area}}$$

Example 1-1

An airplane has a maximum certificated weight of 2,600 pounds and a wing area of 200 square feet. What is its wing loading at maximum weight?

$$\text{Wing loading} = \frac{\text{weight}}{\text{wing area}} = \frac{2{,}600}{200} = 13 \text{ pounds/square foot}$$

End CPL

Airflow and Airfoils

An airfoil is a surface designed to lift, control, and propel an airplane. Some well-known airfoils are the wing, the horizontal stabilizer (or tailplane), the vertical stabilizer (or fin), and the propeller blades. A wing is shaped so that as the air flows over and under, a pressure difference is created—lower pressure above the wing and higher pressure below the wing—resulting in the upward aerodynamic force known as lift. The wing also bends the free stream of air, creating downwash. The total reaction has a vertical component to lift the aircraft or change its flight path, and it has a rearward component, drag, which resists the movement of the wing through the air.

The airplane's control surfaces—ailerons, elevator, and rudder—form part of the various airfoils. You can move these to vary the shape of each airfoil and the forces generated by the airflow over it. This enables you to maneuver the airplane and control it in flight. These control surfaces also operate based on Newton's Third Law of Motion, which says that every action has an equal and opposite reaction. By deflecting the free stream of air that flows over them, control surfaces cause the airplane to roll, yaw or pitch as the reaction.

The wing shape can also be changed by extending the flaps to provide better low-speed airfoil characteristics for takeoff and landing.

Figure 1-5
Airfoil shape.

Figure 1-6
Left aileron.

Airflow Around an Airfoil

The pattern of the airflow around an airplane depends on the shape of the airplane and its attitude relative to the airflow. There are two airflow types: streamline flow and turbulent flow.

Laminar Flow

If successive molecules or particles of air follow the same steady path in a flow, then this path can be represented by a line called a *streamline*. There will be no flow across the streamlines, only along them. There is no turbulence or mixing, hence the name *laminar* (layered) flow. At any fixed point on the streamline, each particle of air will experience the same speed and pressure as the preceding particles of air when they passed that particular point. These values of speed and pressure may change from point to point along the streamline. A reduction in the speed of streamline flow is indicated by wider spacing on the streamlines, while increased speed is indicated by decreased spacing of the streamlines. The existence of streamline flow is very desirable around an airplane because streamlined flow offers the least drag.

Figure 1-7
Vertical stabilizer and rudder.

Figure 1-8
Wing flaps.

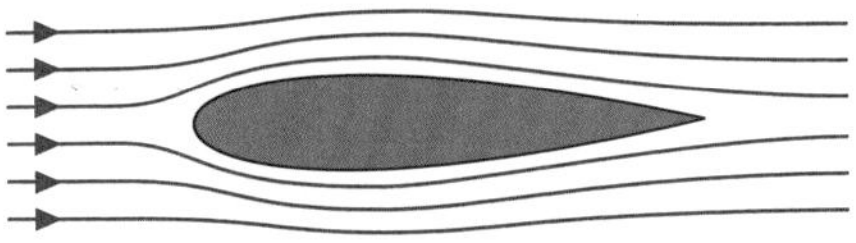

Figure 1-9 Laminar flow.

Turbulent Flow

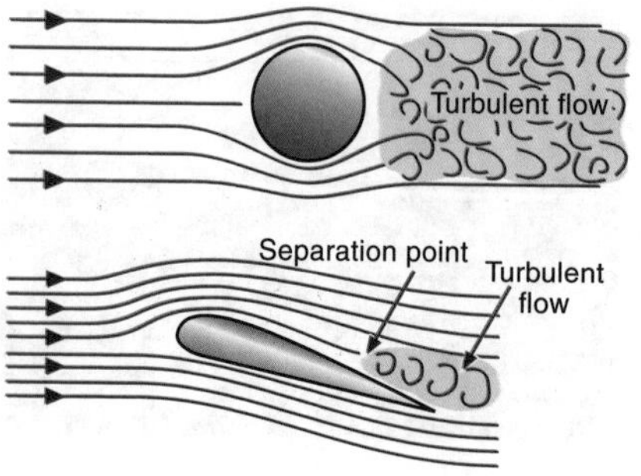

Figure 1-10 Turbulent flow.

In turbulent flow, the airflow does not follow a streamlined pattern. Succeeding particles of air may travel a path quite different to the preceding parcels of air. This turbulent flow is also known as unsteady flow, vortices or eddying, and is an undesirable feature in most phases of flight. The point where the airflow around a surface becomes turbulent is called the *transition point.* The point where the turbulence is so severe that the airflow separates from the surface of an airfoil is known as the *separation point* (see figure 1-10).

The wing of an airplane pushes and induces the air downwards and forwards, because of its shape, angle of attack, and speed. The reaction is an upward/rearward force called the *total reaction.* The upward component of this reaction lifts the airplane (i.e. it overcomes gravity), and the rearward force (drag) is the force that must be overcome by the engine and propeller.

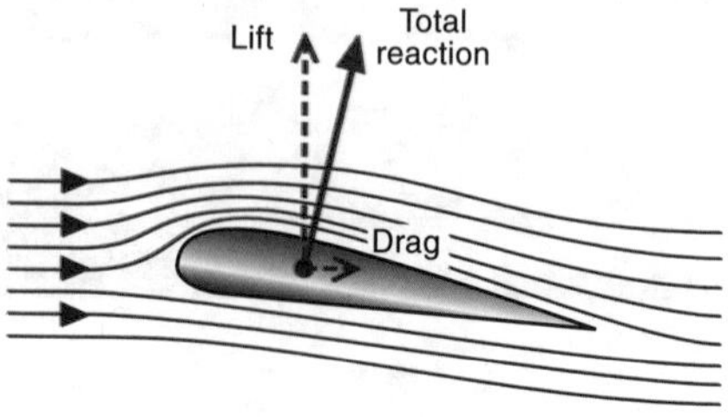

Figure 1-11 Total reaction.

How the wing generates the action and total reaction has been a subject of theoretical debate for many years. You may hear theorems of lift due to:

- Bernoulli's principle (pressure inequalities);
- circulation theory (vortices); and
- Coanda effect (downwash).

The end result of these is that the passage of the wing causes downwash, and the reaction causes lift and drag (Newton's third law). The most common explanation of lift is given by Bernoulli's principle, but this theorem is by no means the whole story.

Energy and Pressure

There are two types of mechanical energy:

- potential energy (due to height—for example, the pressure in a faucet is a function of the relative height of the water tank); and
- kinetic energy (due to speed).

Energy management is the process of controlling and monitoring aircraft altitude and airspeed.

The sum of potential energy and kinetic energy when combined is mechanical energy, which is a direct measure of the total energy available to the aircraft (for the purposes of this textbook).

Flight controls (specifically the throttle and elevator) play a significant role in the management of aircraft mechanical energy. You can think of the throttle as the total energy controller and the elevator as the total energy distribution controller. The throttle is used to set engine thrust to match the total energy demanded for a specific flight profile (vertical flight path and airspeed) and the elevator is used to set the vertical pitch to maintain the distribution of total energy for that profile.

An airplane at 10,000 feet has the potential to dive and accelerate. An airplane at low altitude and high speed has the capacity to zoom up to a higher altitude. Thus any body has a total bank of energy that can be exchanged as speed or height (with some losses in the exchange process).

For a gas, mass equates to density and energy equates to pressure. The pressure forces exerted by air are caused by:

- static pressure (a function of height); and
- dynamic pressure (due to speed).

Static pressure is caused by gravity. The stack of air molecules in the earth's atmosphere causes the lower molecules to be squashed (less volume, greater density) and the upper molecules to be relaxed (more volume, less density). *Dynamic pressure* is caused by air moving against an object (wind and turbulence) or by an object trying to move through the air.

The forces experienced by an aircraft are a combination of static and dynamic pressure. If the aircraft is stationary, it experiences only static atmospheric pressure (and any dynamic pressure due to wind). Static pressure is equal in all directions—up, down, and all around. As soon as the airplane moves through the air, the static and dynamic pressures change, while the total pressure remains constant. Thus for any place on the aircraft when the dynamic pressure increases, the static pressure drops. If the dynamic pressure reduces, the static pressure increases. This is reflected around an airfoil, as shown in figure 1-12.

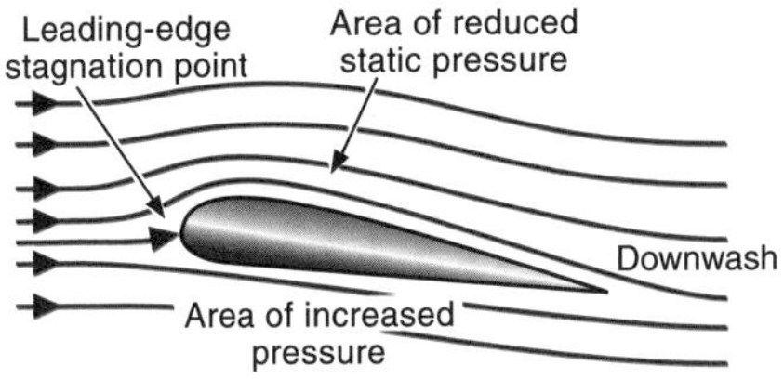

Figure 1-12
Pressure around an airfoil.

The dynamic pressure of a parcel of air moving relative to an object is a function of its density. This density (and velocity) generates a force on any object that tries to move through it. This force, when calculated per unit of surface area, is called *dynamic pressure*. If you hold your hand up in a strong wind or out of the window of a moving automobile, air pressure is felt because of the air striking your hand and flowing around it. This pressure is dynamic pressure—pressure caused by the relative movement between your hand and the air.

Dynamic pressure (represented by the symbol "q.") involves *air density* (mass per unit volume) which is denoted by the Greek letter *rho* (ρ). The more dense the air, the greater the dynamic pressure:

$$\text{Dynamic pressure (q)} = \tfrac{1}{2}\rho \times \text{velocity-squared} = \tfrac{1}{2}\rho V^2$$

The strength of dynamic pressure therefore depends on:

- the *velocity* (speed in a particular direction) of the body relative to the air; and
- the *density* of the air.

Bernoulli's Principle

Bernoulli's principle is the easiest non-mathematical way to understand the production of lift (and drag) by an airfoil.

The production of the lift force by an airfoil may be explained by *Bernoulli's principle*—also known as the *venturi effect*. Daniel Bernoulli (1700–82) was a Swiss scientist who discovered this effect. A fluid in steady motion has a total energy. Air is a fluid, and if we assume it to be incompressible, it behaves as a so-called "ideal" fluid. Bernoulli's principle states that for an ideal fluid the total energy in steady streamline flow remains constant. Therefore:

$$\begin{matrix}\text{Potential} \\ \text{energy}\end{matrix} + \begin{matrix}\text{kinetic} \\ \text{energy}\end{matrix} = \text{constant total energy}$$

Total energy in a steady streamline flow remains constant.

Within any steady streamline flow the total energy content will always remain constant, but the relative proportions of pressure energy and kinetic energy can vary. If kinetic energy increases because of a greater speed of flow, then potential energy will decrease accordingly. This is explained by Bernoulli as fluid flowing through a tube.

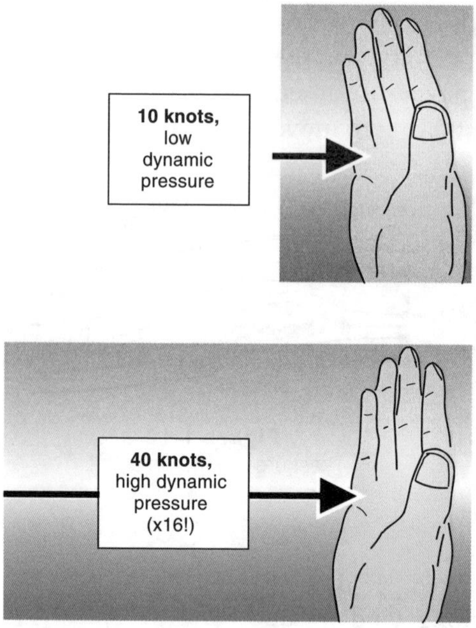

Figure 1-13
Dynamic pressure increases with airspeed.

The mass flow (total energy) is constant. If the opening is restricted (like the nozzle in a garden hose), the velocity is increased.

The faster an automobile drives or the stronger the wind blows, the stronger the dynamic pressure that you feel on your hand. This is because of the greater number of air molecules that impact per second.

Note. It is the *relative velocity* of the airplane and the airflow that matters. The force is the same whether it is the airplane moving through the air or the air is flowing over the airplane.

At the same speed, the denser the air, the more molecules per second that will strike your hand and so the greater the dynamic pressure. Density changes with altitude and temperature.

Note. Bernoulli's principle may be used to explain many aspects of aerodynamics, but only if it is assumed that air is incompressible. At the private- and commercial-pilot level, such an assumption is valid because we are mainly concerned with airplanes that operate at relatively slow speeds and at altitudes below 10,000 feet. At higher speeds and altitudes, compressibility of air must be accounted for, but this is only applicable when you are studying at the Airline Transport Pilot (ATP) level.

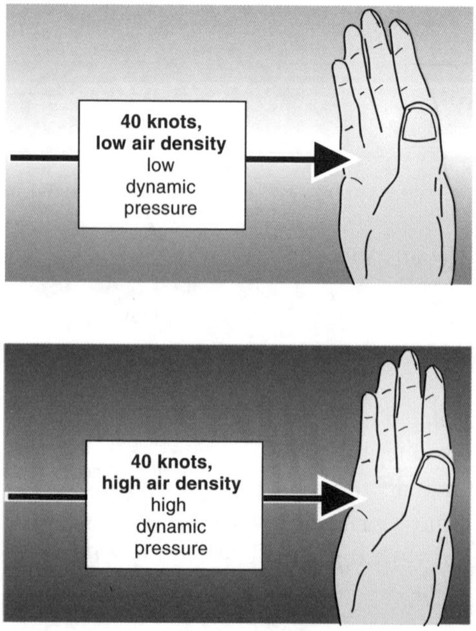

Figure 1-14
Dynamic pressure is greater in dense air.

Lift and Thrust

Pressure is force per unit area—pounds per square inch (psi). This force around an airplane is significant. Static pressure alone acts on all sides of the airplane and thus cancels itself, until we use dynamic pressure and the resultant differences in static pressure to our advantage. It is an imbalance of forces that allows the airplane to fly. The propeller causes reduced static pressure ahead and increased static pressure behind. The force is called *thrust* and drives the airplane forward. The airfoil section of the wing accelerates the air; this causes a downwash and a change in static pressure between the lower and upper surfaces. This is sufficient to carry the aircraft and to maneuver it (change its flight path). The control surfaces cause the change in flight path.

Airspeed

Dynamic pressure (q) and the term $\frac{1}{2}\rho V^2$ are very important in aviation. The airspeed indicator shows *indicated airspeed* (IAS), which is not a real speed but a measure of dynamic pressure. Since dynamic pressure is related to air density, the real speed of the airplane relative to the airflow can only be calculated if the change in density due to altitude or temperature is recognized. This corrected speed is known as *true airspeed* (TAS or V). Although indicated airspeed is of most concern to you when flying, you will need to calculate true airspeed for measuring time, fuel, and distance.

Airfoils

All parts of the airplane contribute positively or negatively to the total forces of lift and drag, but it is the *airfoil* of the wing that is specifically designed to provide the lift needed to support the weight of the airplane in flight. If a thin, flat metal plate is oriented parallel to a streamline airflow, it causes virtually no alteration to that airflow, and consequently experiences no reaction (aerodynamic force). If, however, the plate is inclined with respect to the airflow, it will experience a reaction that tends to both lift it up and drag it back. This is the same effect that you feel if you hold your hand out the window of a moving vehicle. The amount of reaction depends on the relative speed and the angle between the flat plate (or your hand) and the airstream.

Because of the angle of the plate to the airflow, the straight-line streamline flow of the air is disturbed. A slight *upwash* is created in front of the plate, causing the air to flow through a more constricted area, almost as if there was an invisible venturi above the plate. As it passes through this constricted area, the air speeds up. The velocity increase produces a decrease in static pressure (Bernoulli's principle).

The static pressure above the plate is now lower than the static pressure beneath the plate, causing a net upward and rearward reaction. After passing the plate there is a *downwash* of the airstream. Note that if the angle of the flat plate to the airflow becomes too large, the streamline airflow breaks down resulting in less lift and more drag. See figure 1-15.

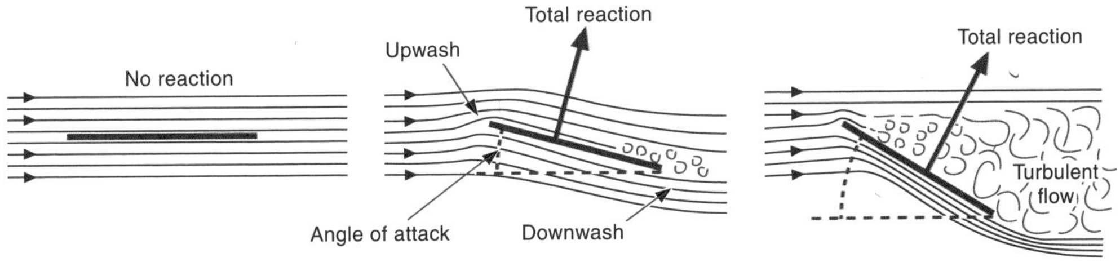

Figure 1-15 Airflow can lift a flat plate (but not efficiently).

The reaction, or aerodynamic force, on the plate caused by its disturbance of the airflow has two components:

- one at right angles to the relative airflow, known as *lift*; and
- one parallel to the relative airflow, opposing the relative motion, known as *drag*.

Airfoil Shape

A flat plate is not the ideal airfoil shape because it breaks up the streamline flow, causing eddying (turbulence), with a loss of lift and a great increase in drag. In addition, it is difficult to construct a thin, flat wing (no strength, no internal structure).

Figure 1-16 Examples of various airfoil shapes.

A cambered airfoil surface not only generates more lift and less drag compared to a flat plate, it is also easier to construct in terms of structural strength. Airfoils can have many cross-sectional shapes. Airplane designers choose the shape with the best aerodynamic characteristics to suit the role of the airplane.

Camber

Camber is curvature. Aviation pioneers, such as Wilbur and Orville Wright, experimented with different curved (cambered) shapes and found that the degree of curvature, the point of maximum curvature, and the ratio of thickness to length were critical. Later designers found that the shape of the upper curvature was more important than the lower curvature, and therefore they could have a thicker, lighter, stronger wing with internal storage capacity for fuel and structure with no aerodynamic penalty. Thick wings with a large camber have a good lifting ability, making them suitable for low-speed flight. The position of greatest camber is usually about 30 percent back from the wing leading edge. As camber increases, the airflow path lengthens, resulting in the airflow speeding up, static pressure reducing and lift and drag increasing.

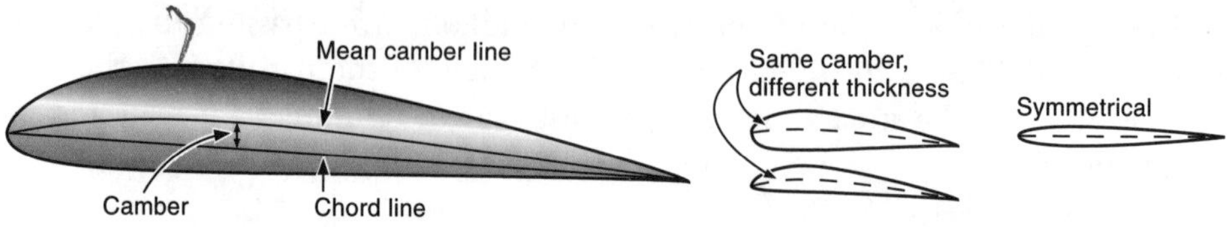

Figure 1-17 A cambered airfoil with internal structure.

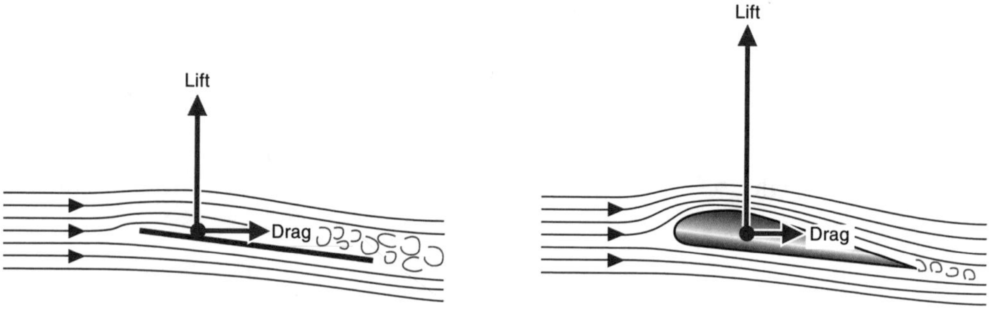

Figure 1-18 More camber, more lift, less drag.

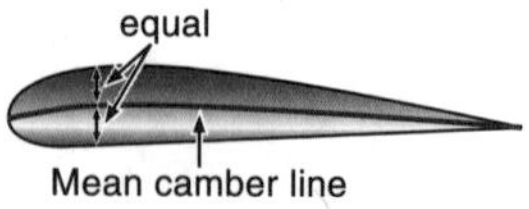

Figure 1-19 Mean camber line.

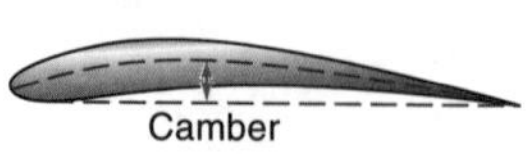

Figure 1-20 Camber.

Wings with less camber give a better cruise performance but a higher takeoff and landing speed (and distance). Aircraft and airfoil design is a compromise to suit customers' requirements.

Mean Camber Line

The mean camber line is the line drawn halfway between the upper and lower surfaces of the airfoil cross-section. This line gives a picture of the average curvature of the airfoil.

Camber

The camber is the maximum distance between the mean camber line and the chord line.

Chord Line

The chord line is the straight line joining the leading edge and the trailing edge of the airfoil or, in other words, the straight line joining the ends of the (curved) mean camber line.

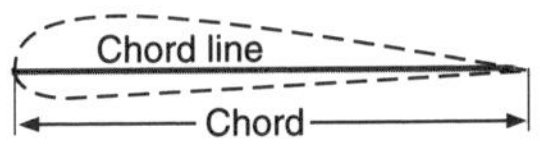

Figure 1-21
Chord line.

The Chord

The length of the chord line is called the chord of the wing. It varies from the wing root to the wing tip, so we use the average (mean) chord.

Aerodynamic Forces

In normal flight, the static pressure over most of the upper surface of the airfoil is slightly reduced when compared with the normal static pressure of the airflow well away from the airfoil. The static pressure beneath much of the lower surface of the airfoil is greater than that on the upper surface, because a greater number of air molecules are impacting the airfoil's lower surface and the airflow is being slowed down. This pressure difference is the origin of the *total aerodynamic force* exerted on the airfoil, with the greater contribution coming from the upper surface.

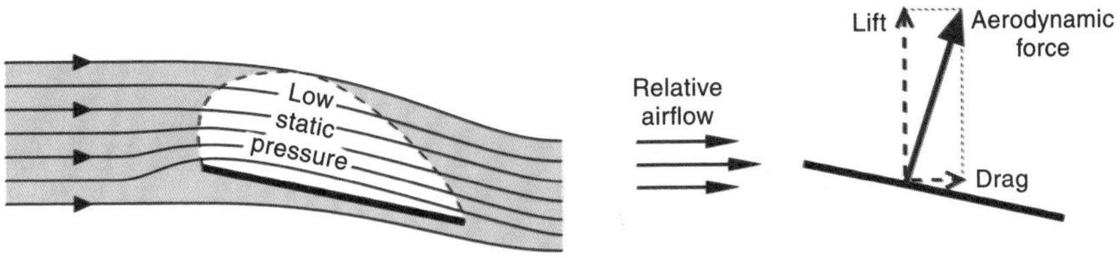

Figure 1-22 The production of lift and drag.

In the same way that the total weight of an airplane can be considered to act through a single point—the center of gravity—the aerodynamic forces on an airfoil can be considered to act through a single point known as the *center of pressure* (CP) or center of lift.

It is convenient for us to consider the aerodynamic force (*total reaction*) in its two components: lift and drag:

- *lift* is the sum total of the components of the aerodynamic force at right angles, or perpendicular, to the relative airflow; and
- *drag* is the total of the component of the aerodynamic force parallel to the relative airflow and opposing motion.

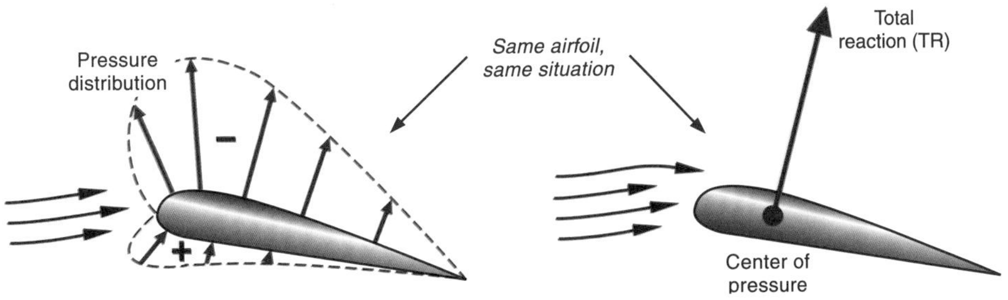

Figure 1-23 The aerodynamic force acts through a point on the wing called the center of pressure.

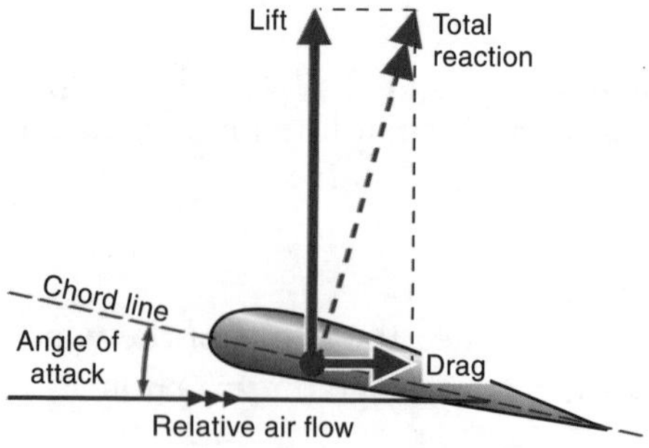

Figure 1-24 Relative airflow (measured relative to the "free-stream" airflow).

The *center of pressure* is the point through which the equivalent single force (TR) would act to cause the same effect as all the component forces distributed over the wing.

The *relative airflow*, or *relative wind*, refers to the relative motion between a body and the remote (free stream) airflow—that is, the airflow far enough away from the body not to be disturbed by it. The relative airflow is the direction opposite to the flight path of the airplane.

The *angle of attack* is the angle between the chord line of an airfoil or wing and the remote relative airflow. It is represented by the Greek letter α (alpha).

Note the following.

1. Do not confuse the *pitch attitude* of the airplane (relative to the horizontal) with the angle of attack of the airfoil (relative to the remote airflow). See figures 1-25 and 1-26.

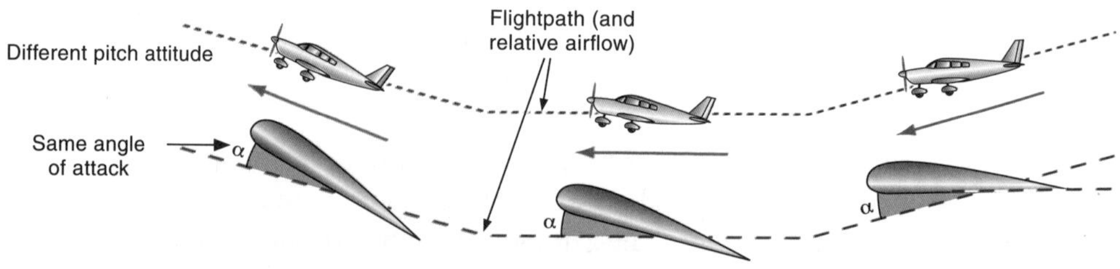

Figure 1-25 Same angle of attack, but different pitch attitudes.

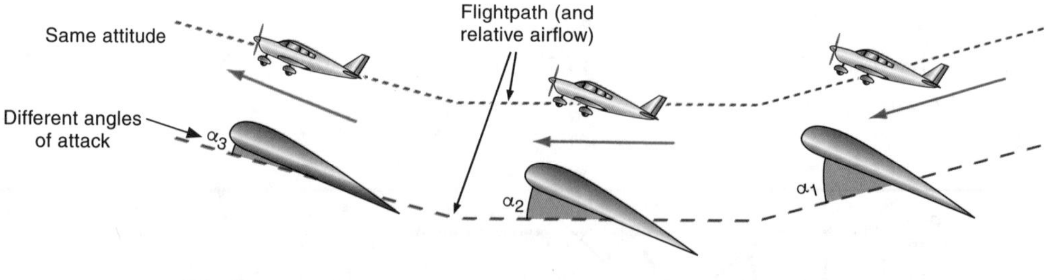

Figure 1-26 Same pitch attitude, but different angles of attack.

2. Do not confuse angle of attack with *angle of incidence*—the angle at which the wing is mounted onto the fuselage, relative to the longitudinal axis. The angle of incidence is fixed at construction (figure 1-27), while the angle of attack changes in flight.

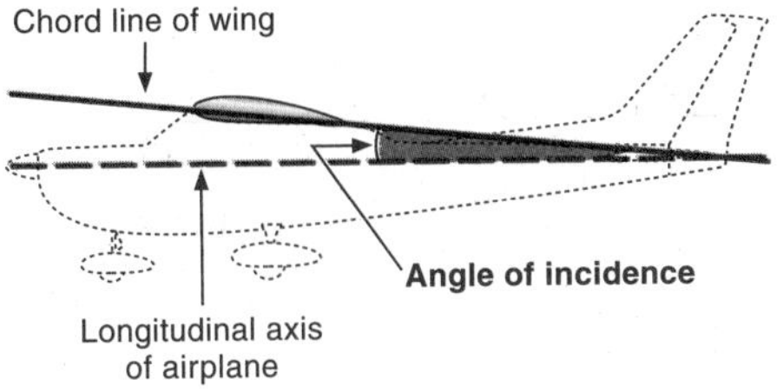

Figure 1-27 The angle-of-incidence is fixed during design and construction.

Lift and Drag from a Typical Wing

CPL

The amount of lift that a wing can produce depends on:
- the lifting efficiency of the wing (angle of attack, shape, airfoil section, camber, and flaps);
- dynamic pressure; and
- wing area.

$$\text{Lift} = \text{lifting efficiency of the wing and its angle of attack} \times \text{dynamic pressure} \times \text{surface area}$$

$$L = C_L \times \tfrac{1}{2}\rho V^2 \times S$$

The equation shows that for constant lift, a reduction in airspeed must be countered by an increased lifting ability of the wing (increase in angle of attack). Conversely as airspeed is increased, to maintain level flight the pilot will need to lower the airplane's nose to reduce the angle of attack and decrease the wing's lifting ability. Also notice that if the lifting ability and area of the wings remain constant, and the airspeed doubles, the lift will increase four times (two squared).

The drag depends on the shape, angle of attack, and smoothness, the square of the true airspeed:

$$\text{Drag} = \text{shape} \times \text{dynamic pressure} \times \text{surface area}$$

$$D = C_D \times \tfrac{1}{2}\rho V^2 \times S$$

Experimentally, it can be shown that the aerodynamic force, and therefore the lift, depends on:
- wing shape (airfoil section and flap position);
- angle of attack;
- air density (ρ);
- velocity—true airspeed ($V \times V$, or V^2); and
- wing surface area (S).

Velocity of the airflow and air density (ρ) are combined in the expression for *dynamic pressure*: $\frac{1}{2}\rho V^2$, which is related to *indicated airspeed*. Putting this together with the wing surface area (S) we obtain the equation:

$$\text{Lift} = (\text{some efficiency factor}) \times \tfrac{1}{2}\rho V^2 \times S$$

We use the efficiency factor to cover the other variables, especially the wing shape and the angle of attack. This factor is called the *coefficient of lift* (C_L), which is really the lifting ability of the wing at that particular angle of attack. Therefore:

$$\text{Lift} = C_L \times \tfrac{1}{2}\rho V^2 \times S$$

Apart from the extension of flaps, the wing shape is fixed, and any change in C_L can only be caused by a change in angle of attack. At cruise speed, most of the lift is due to dynamic pressure, as the angle of attack is low. To fly slowly, the dynamic pressure is low, and so a high angle of attack is needed to generate the same lift. This interrelationship between angle of attack and airspeed is very important.

Lift depends on the angle of attack and indicated airspeed.

By using the equation:

$$L = C_L \times \tfrac{1}{2} \times \rho V^2 \times S$$

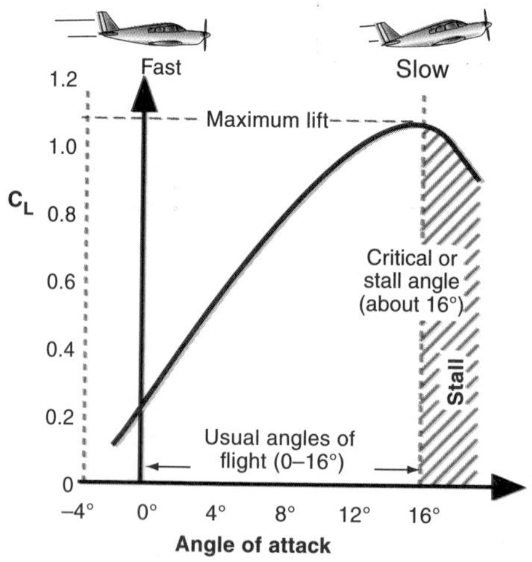

Figure 1-28
Coefficient of lift versus angle of attack; each angle of attack produces a particular C_L value.

and measuring L, V, ρ, and S, we can calculate the value of C_L and develop a graph or curve of C_L versus angle of attack, known as the *lift curve* (figure 1-28), or C_L/α curve.

For a given wing, the angle of attack is the major controlling factor in the distribution of the static pressure around the wing. This determines the lift force that is generated. The actual value of C_L will therefore differ according to the angle of attack.

Each airfoil shape has its own particular lift curve which relates its C_L to angle of attack. We will consider an average cambered wing like that found on a typical training airplane such as a Cessna 172:

- at 0° angle of attack the cambered wing creates some lift and has a positive C_L;
- at about -4° angle of attack the lift is zero; and
- as the angle of attack increases, the C_L increases proportionally up to about 12° or 13° angle of attack and then falls off as the airflow separates before the stall.

At higher angles of attack, the curve starts to lean over, until at the stall angle (about 16° in this case) the C_L begins to decrease. This occurs when the airflow is unable to remain streamline over the wing's upper surface, separates from the wing surface, and breaks up into eddies. Notice that the maximum C_L (the maximum lifting ability of the wing) occurs immediately prior to the stall.

CPL

Lift from a Symmetrical Airfoil

An equally symmetrical airfoil is chosen for a surface that has to generate positive or negative forces. Typical symmetrical airfoils are the vertical stabilizer and some horizontal stabilizers. The mean camber line of a symmetrical airfoil is a straight line because both surfaces have identical curvature. Therefore the chord line and mean camber line are identical.

The lift curve for a symmetrical airfoil will give a $C_L = 0$ (and zero lift) at 0° angle of attack, see figure 1-30. This is because the streamlines follow mirror-image paths and therefore the airflow on both sides of the airfoil has the same velocity and static pressure. The center of pressure will *not* move as the angle of attack of a symmetrical airfoil is increased (whereas it moves forward on a cambered airfoil).

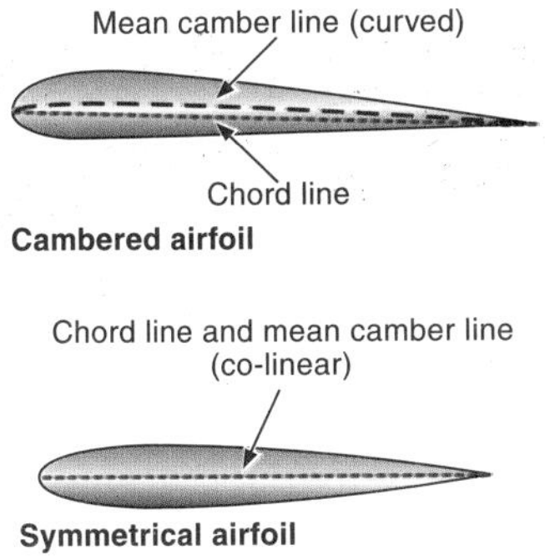

Figure 1-29
A cambered and a symmetrical airfoil.

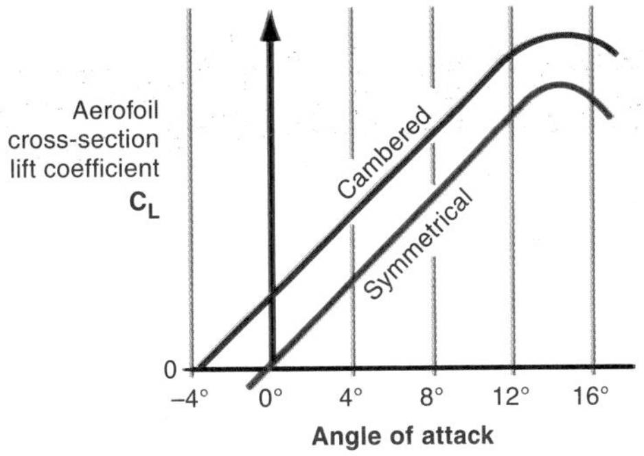

Figure 1-30
Lift curve for a symmetrical airfoil.

Changing Wing Area

Another factor that can alter lift is the wing area, S. If we could increase S, then we would obtain the same lift at a slower air-speed. Some flaps, such as Fowler flaps, increase the wing area as they are extended. Other basic flaps simply change the cross-section of the wing as they are extended. All flaps cause changes in lift and drag, and consequently have an effect on the value of the L/D ratio. Some flaps create slots that enhance the airflow and improve efficiency at low speed.

End CPL

Pressure Distribution and CP Movement

Bernoulli's principle links a decrease in static pressure with an increase in velocity, which means a decreasing static pressure goes hand-in-hand with an accelerating airflow. The shape of the airfoil and its angle of attack determine:

- the acceleration of the airflow above and below the wing; and
- the distribution of the static pressures over the surface and the lifting ability of the airfoil.

If we reduce speed while flying straight-and-level, and we progressively increase the angle of attack, two important things occur.

1. The lifting ability of the wing increases, allowing the wing to produce the same amount of lift (required to counteract the weight) at a lower airspeed.
2. The center of pressure (CP) moves forward—the furthest forward is about ⅕ of the chord (20 percent) back from the wing leading edge.

At normal cruise speeds (about 4° angle of attack), the CP is located approximately ⅓ of the chord back from the wing's leading edge. As the angle of attack increases with the reduction in airspeed, the CP moves forward until a point is eventually reached where the airflow over the wing upper surface cannot follow the curved surface, but separates and becomes turbulent, and produces significantly less lift. This is known as the *critical* or *stall* angle of attack. At the critical angle of attack—about 16° where the streamline airflow over the wing upper surface breaks down—the CP moves rearward.

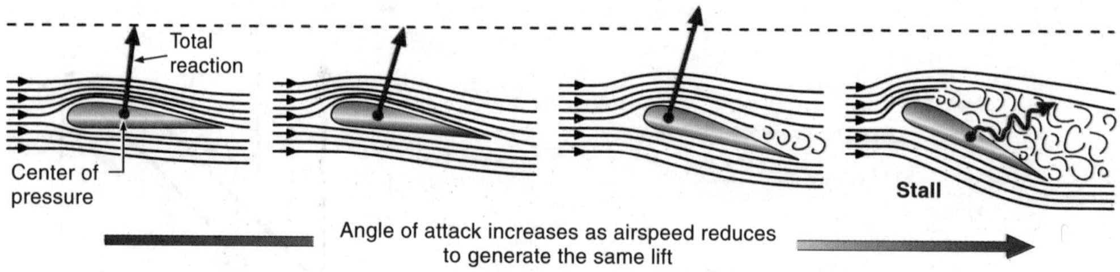

Figure 1-31
The size of the aerodynamic force and the CP position change at various angles of attack.

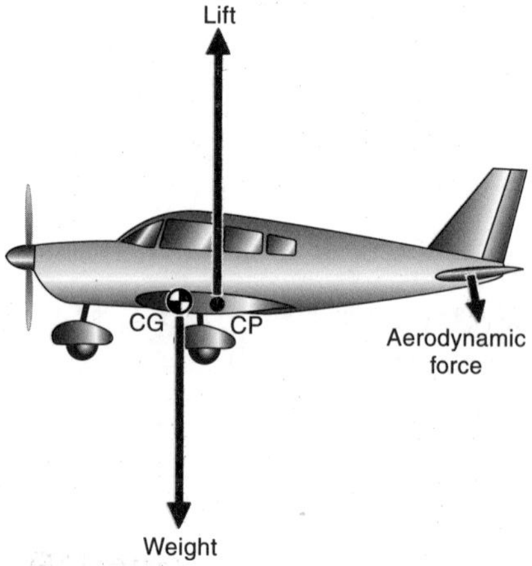

Figure 1-32
The elevator keeps the attitude constant.

Changes in the size and location of the aerodynamic force produce a different *moment* (or *rotating effect*) in the pitching plane of the airplane, (this means that the airplane will want to rotate nose-up or nose-down to a new pitch attitude). The extent of this pitching moment depends on both the size of the aerodynamic force and the distance between the CP and the CG. You can normally neutralize this moment, and prevent the airplane from pitching nose-up or nose-down, by varying the aerodynamic force generated by the *horizontal stabilizer.* This is achieved by the forward and rearward movement of the control column, which controls the elevator (see also chapter 2).

Past the stall angle, the significant rearward movement of the CP and the changed airflow over the horizontal stabilizer cause a nose-down pitching moment, and the nose of the airplane will drop, even with the control column held fully back (nose-up). This is a good safety feature because the nose-drop reduces the angle of attack below the stall angle. With appropriate stall recovery actions by the pilot, the angle of attack will remain below the critical (or stall) angle.

Contamination of the Wings

Any contamination or damage to a wing, especially to its main lifting surface (the upper third rearward from the leading edge), will disrupt the smooth airflow over the airfoil and cause it to separate from the wing at a lower angle of attack than usual. This will cause decreased lift, increased drag, and may make it difficult, or even impossible, for the airplane to become airborne on takeoff.

If there is *frost*, *ice*, or any other *contamination* (such as the remains of insects or a build-up of salt from sea-spray, for example) on the wings, remove this contamination before flying.

Frost on a wing disturbs the airflow, reduces its lifting ability, and can prevent an airplane from becoming airborne.

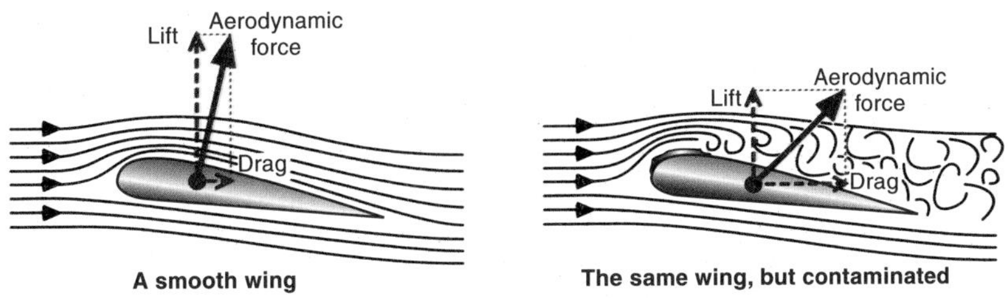

Figure 1-33
Contamination on the wings can seriously affect the lifting characteristics.

Drag

Drag is the aeronautical term for the air resistance experienced by the airplane as it moves through the air. It acts in the opposite direction to the motion of the airplane, and is the enemy of flight. Streamlining of shapes, flush riveting, polishing of surfaces and many design features are all attempts to reduce the drag force.

The function of the *thrust* produced by the propeller is to overcome the *drag*. The lower the drag, the less the thrust required to counteract it. The advantages of a lower thrust requirement are obvious: smaller (and possibly fewer) engines, lower fuel flow, less strain on the engine(s) and associated structures, and lower operating costs.

Drag opposes motion.

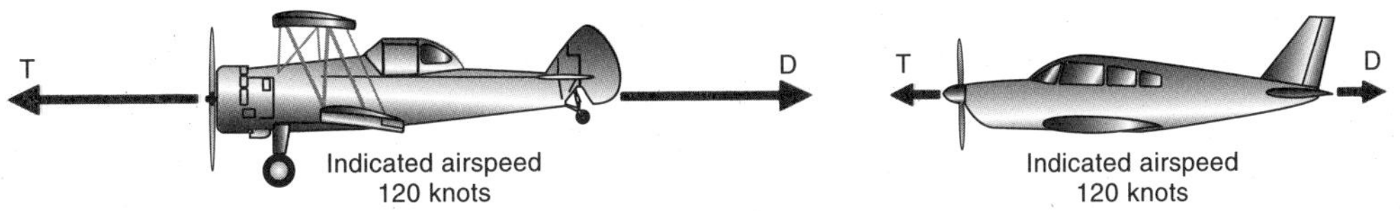

Figure 1-34 Low drag requires only low thrust to counteract it.

Total Drag

The total drag is the sum total of the various drag forces acting on the airplane. A convenient way of studying these various types of drag forces is to break them up into two basic groups.

Total drag is the sum of induced drag and parasite drag.

1. Those drag forces not directly associated with the development of lift—known as *parasite drag*, which includes form drag, skin friction and interference drag. (Form drag and skin friction are sometimes classified together under the name *profile drag*.)
2. Those drag forces associated with the production of lift, known as *induced drag* (manifested as vortices at the trailing edge of the wing and especially at the wing-tips).

Parasite Drag

Parasite drag comprises *skin friction, form drag*, and *interference drag*.

Skin-Friction

Friction forces between an object and the air through which it is moving produce skin-friction drag. The magnitude of this component of parasite drag depends on:

- the surface area of the airplane—the whole surface area of the airplane experiences skin-friction drag as it moves through the air;
- roughness on a surface (including ice-accretion)—flush riveting and polishing are attempts to smooth the surface and reduce skin-friction drag; and
- airspeed—an increase in airspeed increases skin-friction drag.

Form Drag

When the airflow actually separates from the airfoil, disturbing the streamline flow and forming eddies, a turbulent wake is formed which increases drag. This is form drag.

Perhaps the easiest way to distinguish form drag from skin-friction drag is to consider a flat plate in two different attitudes relative to the airflow. At zero degrees angle of attack, the drag is all skin friction. When the flat plate is perpendicular to the airflow, the drag is all form drag.

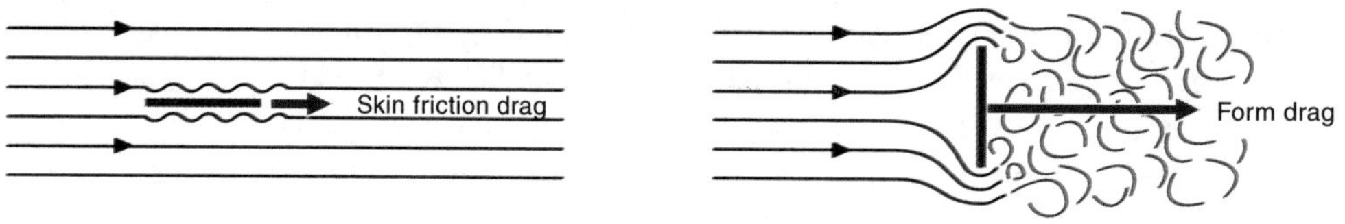

Figure 1-35 Skin friction and form drag.

The point at which the streamline airflow separates from the airfoil and becomes turbulent is known as the *separation point*. As the wing's angle of attack increases, the separation point moves forward and the turbulent wake becomes deeper. The size of the wake (caused by an airfoil, or indeed the entire aircraft) indicates the magnitude of the form drag—the larger the wake the greater the form drag.

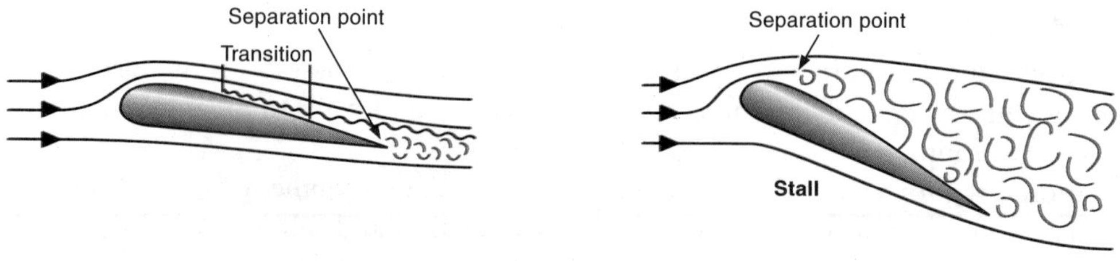

Figure 1-36 A stalled wing increases form drag substantially.

Streamlining reduces form drag by decreasing the curvature of surfaces. This delays the separation of the airflow, and thereby reduces the size of the turbulent wake. The designer may choose an airfoil of different *fineness ratio* (wing thickness/chord) to achieve better streamlining.

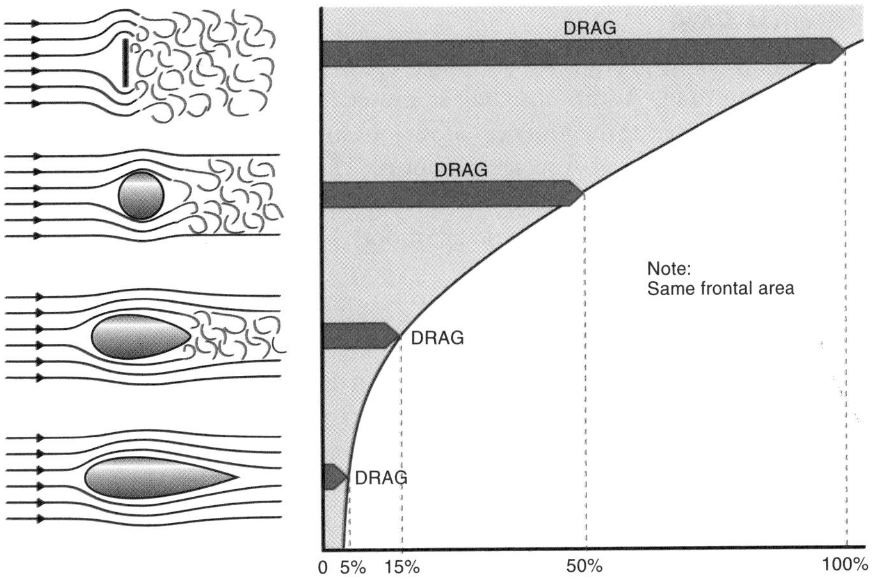

Figure 1-37 Streamlining, especially behind the shape, greatly reduces form drag.

Streamlining of other parts of the airframe can be achieved by adding *fairings*—parts of the external surface of an airplane that encourage streamline flow, thereby reducing eddying and decreasing drag (figure 1-38).

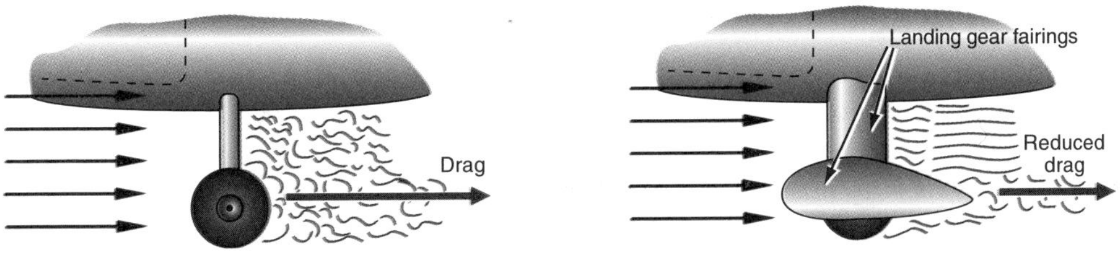

Figure 1-38 Streamlining reduces form drag.

Remember, streamlining may be ineffective if ice is allowed to form (figure 1-39).

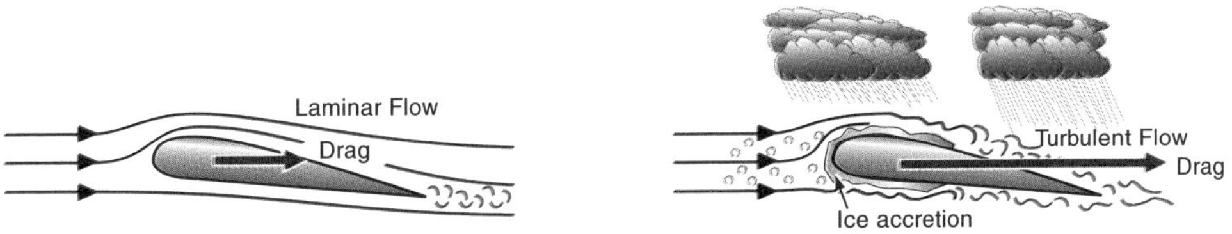

Figure 1-39 Ice accretion on the airframe will increase drag.

Interference Drag

The total parasite drag produced by an airplane is greater than the sum of the skin friction and form drag. Additional drag is caused by the mixing, or interference of airflows, which converge at the junction of various surfaces, such as at the wing-fuselage junctions and the tail section-fuselage junctions. This additional drag is referred to as interference drag. As it is not directly associated with the production of lift, interference drag is a component of parasite drag. Smooth fairings at surface junctions reduce interference drag.

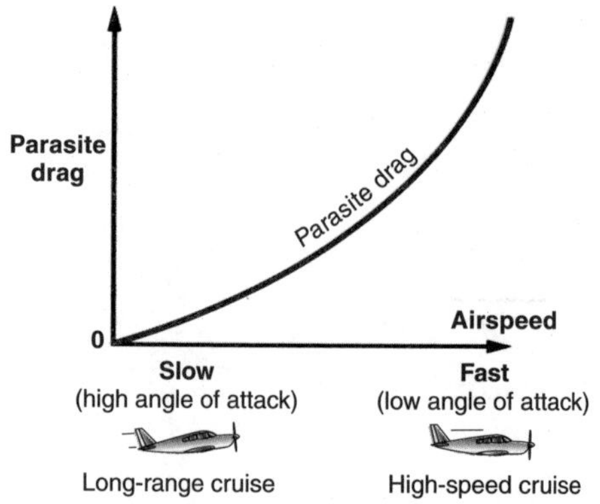

Figure 1-40
Parasite drag increases with airspeed.

Parasite Drag versus Airspeed

At zero airspeed there is no relative motion between the airplane and the air. Therefore there is no parasite drag. As the airspeed increases, the skin friction, form drag, and interference drag (which together make up parasite drag) all increase.

Airspeed has a powerful effect on parasite drag. Doubling the airspeed gives four times (2-squared, or $2 \times 2 = 4$) the parasite drag, while tripling the airspeed would give $3 \times 3 = 9$ times the parasite drag. Parasite drag is therefore of greatest significance at high speeds and is small at low speeds. However, there is another form of drag called induced drag, which increases with reducing airspeed (increasing angle of attack). An airplane flying at a speed just above the stall may have only 25 percent of its total drag caused by parasite drag, with most of the total drag caused by induced drag.

Induced Drag

Induced drag occurs when lift is produced and is closely related to the angle of attack.

By definition lift is said to act at right angles to the remote free stream of air. It is the vertical component of the total reaction. At lower airspeeds, the angle of attack is higher, and the total vector is tilted rearwards. The increasing horizontal component is induced drag. It is an unavoidable cost for the generation of lift.

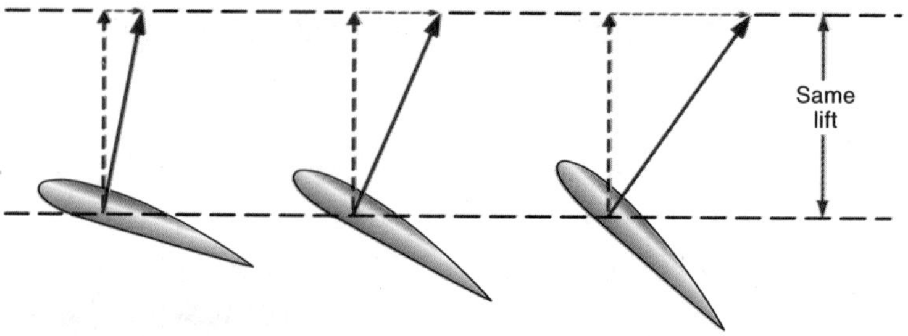

Figure 1-41 Induced drag increases as angle of attack increases.

Vortices

To produce lift, the static pressure on the upper wing surface will be less than that on the lower wing surface. The air flowing over the bottom surface of the wing tends to flow outward as well as rearward. The air flowing over the top surface of the wing has a lower pressure and tends to flow inward, toward the aircraft fuselage, as well as rearward.

When the two flows meet at the trailing edge they are flowing across, or at different angles to each other and a sheet of *trailing-edge vortices* rotating clockwise (when viewed from the rear) is formed. At the wingtips, where the spanwise flow is greatest, the strongest vortices are formed. These are known as *wingtip vortices*. A vortex is a whirling or twisting flow of air or some other fluid. Wingtip vortices are also discussed under *Wake Turbulence* on page 220.

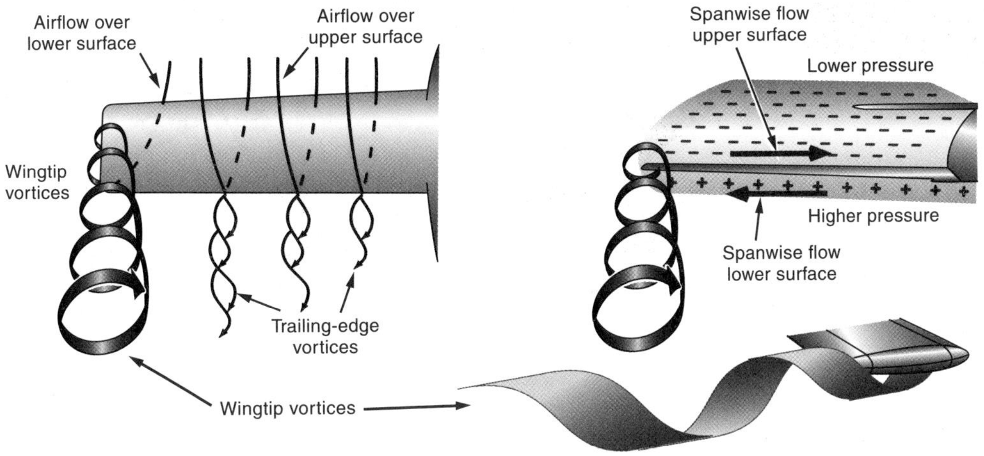

Figure 1-42 The production of lift creates wingtip vortices and induced drag.

Angle of Attack

The greater the lift produced, the greater the induced drag. Induced drag is therefore most significant when the wing is at high angles of attack, such as during low-speed flight or maneuvering. Near the stall speed in level flight, induced drag could account for 75% of the total drag (parasite drag making up the rest), yet at high speed in level flight the induced drag might provide only 1% of the total drag.

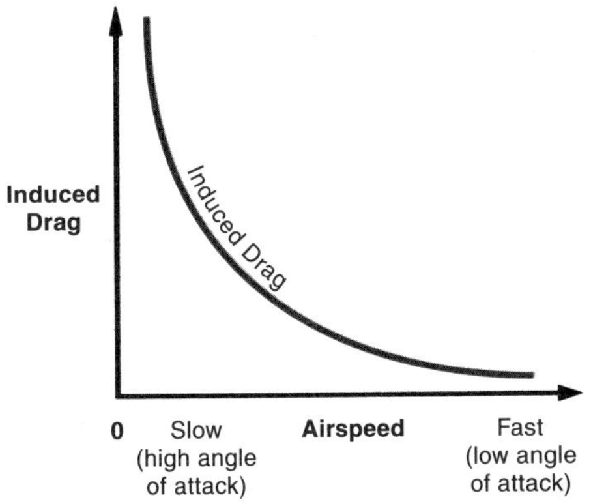

Figure 1-43 Induced drag is greatest at low speeds and high angles of attack.

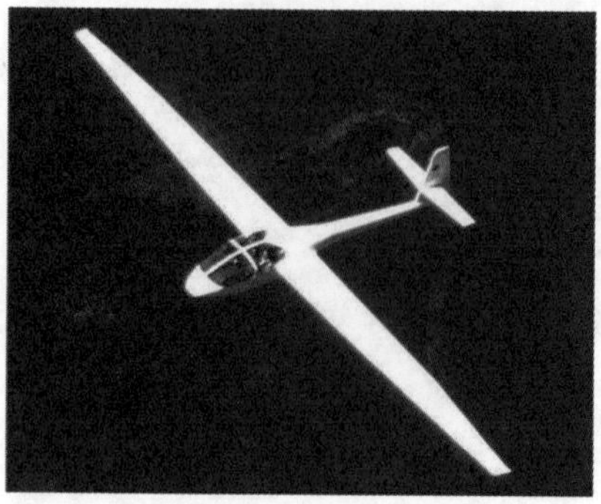

Figure 1-44
High aspect ratio.

Wing Design

Induced drag is affected by the span-to-chord ratio, known as the *aspect ratio.* Wings with a high aspect ratio (such as those on sailplanes) produce significantly less induced drag than short, stubby wings.

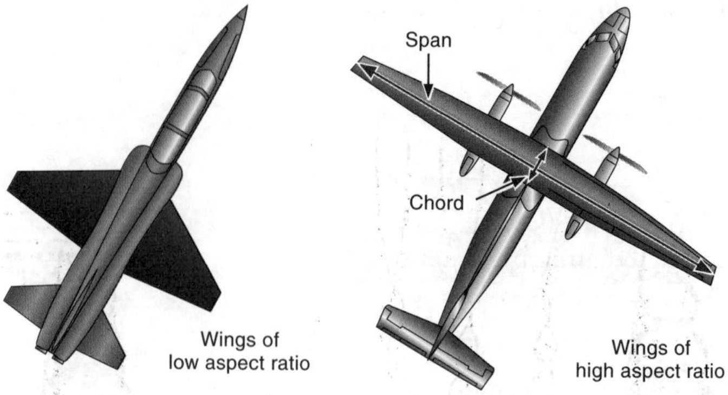

Figure 1-45 Aspect ratio.

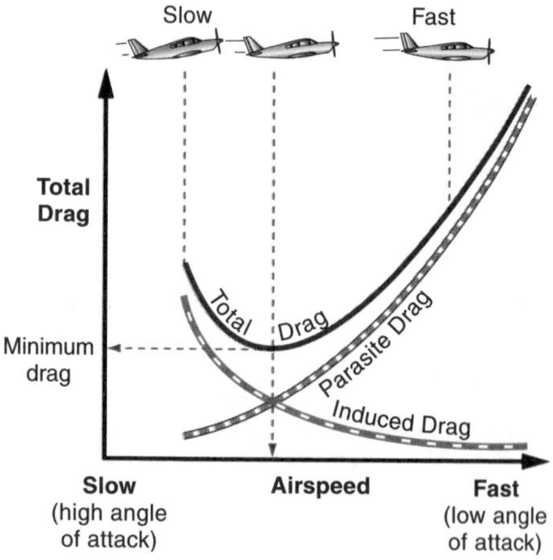

Figure 1-46
Total drag versus airspeed.

The Total Drag on an Airplane

Total drag is the total of all the drag forces. As we have seen, total drag has two components:

- *parasite drag*; and
- *induced drag.*

If we combine the graphs of parasite and induced drag as they vary with airspeed, we end up with a graph that illustrates the variation of total drag with airspeed (for a given airplane in level flight at a particular weight, configuration, and altitude). This total drag graph (figure 1-46) of drag versus airspeed (angle of attack) illustrates an extremely important relationship. It is a summary of all we need to know about drag.

The parasite drag increases with speed. The induced drag decreases as the speed increases. The graph shows how induced drag is predominant at low speed, while at high speed the parasite drag predominates. The total drag is least at the point where the parasite drag and the induced drag are equal. Many aspects of airplane performance are related to this *minimum drag speed.*

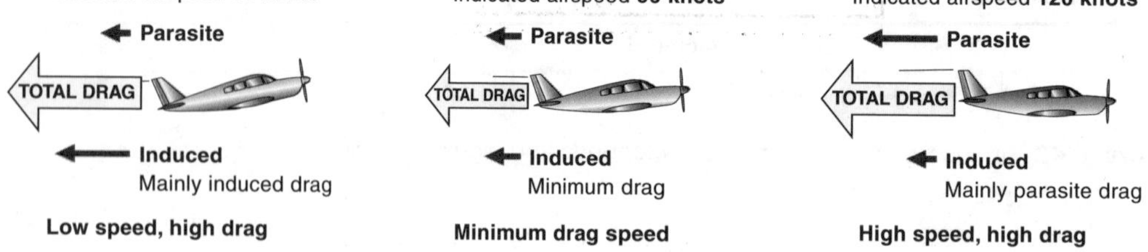

Figure 1-47 Minimum drag speed.

Drag from an Airfoil

At low speeds the total drag from the airfoil is high (because of induced drag) and at high speeds the total drag is high (because of parasite drag). A formula (similar to that for lift) can be developed for the drag produced by an airfoil:

$$\text{Drag} = C_D \times \tfrac{1}{2}\rho V^2 \times S$$

Where:

- *coefficient of drag* (C_D) represents shape and angle of attack;
- $\tfrac{1}{2}\rho V^2$ is dynamic pressure; and
- S is the size of the object.

A *drag curve* for the airfoil relating C_D to angle of attack can be developed. This is useful for comparison with the lift curve (C_L versus angle of attack). Note that at high angles of attack near the stall angle, the coefficient of drag for an airfoil is high and is a large factor in the formula:

$$D = C_D \times \tfrac{1}{2}\rho V^2 \times S$$

At low angles of attack, as during normal cruise, the coefficient of drag for the airfoil is small, but the airspeed (V) is high, which has a large effect in the formula. This is why the drag force (D) is high at both extremes of angle of attack (and airspeed). In between these extremes is an angle of attack (and airspeed) where the drag force is a minimum. The minimum C_D for a typical airfoil occurs at a small positive angle of attack.

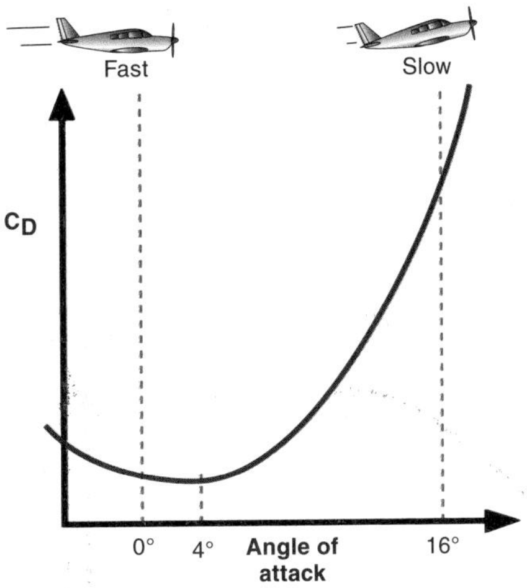

Figure 1-48
Coefficient of drag versus angle of attack.

CPL

Design Features that Minimize Induced Drag

Induced drag increases as the difference in pressure above and below the wing increases. This causes greater spanwise flow and larger vortices at the wingtips and trailing edges. In the history of airplane development, designers have made great advances in reducing induced drag by decreasing the amount of spanwise flow close to the wingtips. Design features to achieve this include the following (see figure 1-49):

- tapered or elliptical-shaped wings;
- wings of high aspect ratio (high span/chord ratio, as evident on sailplanes);
- wing washout (built-in twist that causes a lower angle of attack at the wingtips compared with near the wing root); and
- winglets (upper and lower wingtip extensions—as seen on Boeing 737 MAX or Diamond DA-42 aircraft).

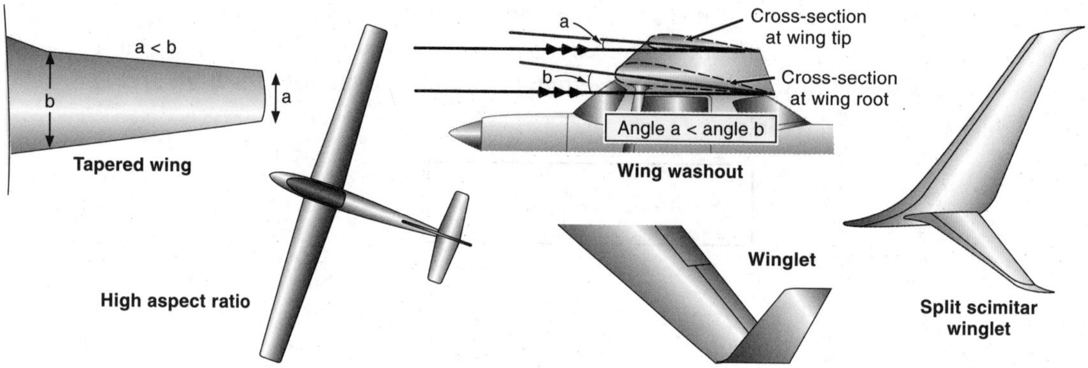

Figure 1-49 Design features that minimize induced drag.

End CPL

Lift/Drag Ratio

The *lift curve* shows a steady increase in the coefficient of lift as the angle of attack is increased, up to the stall angle, beyond which C_L decreases.

The *drag curve* shows that drag is least at small positive angles of attack and increases either side as angle of attack is increased or decreased. As the stall angle is approached

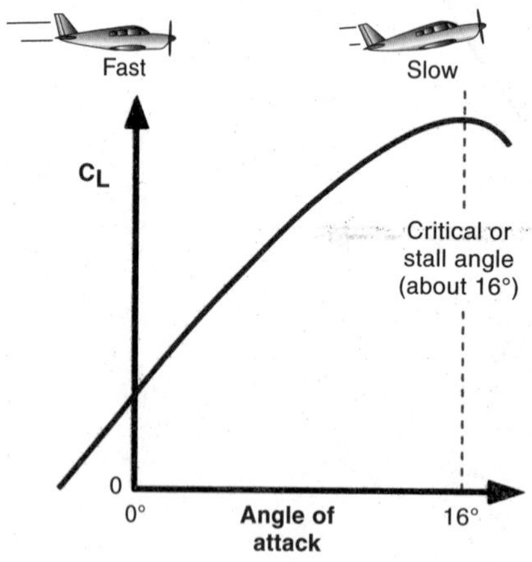

Figure 1-50 C_L versus angle of attack.

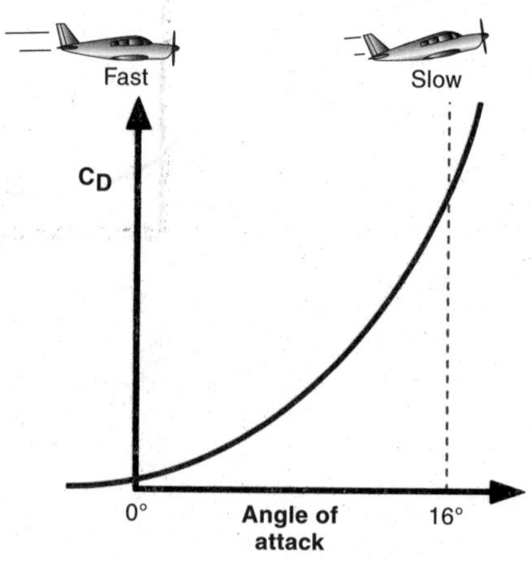

Figure 1-51 C_D versus angle of attack.

the drag increases at a greater rate. At the stall the separation of streamline airflow and the formation of a turbulent wake causes a large increase in drag.

To determine the performance and efficiency of an airfoil at a particular angle of attack (and airspeed), both the lift and the drag need to be considered. The size of lift compared to drag is the *lift/drag ratio* and is very important.

The most efficient angle of attack is the angle that gives the maximum or best lift/drag ratio, typically 10:1. In most airplanes you do not have an instrument to indicate angle of attack, but the airspeed indicator is a good guide because airspeed is related to angle of attack. High angles of attack in steady flight are associated with low airspeeds (and vice versa).

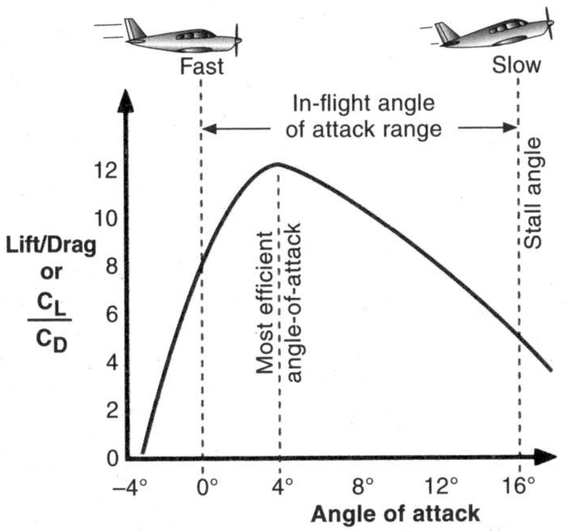

Figure 1-52 Lift/drag ratio versus angle of attack.

The angle of attack (and airspeed) for the best lift/drag ratio gives the required lift (to counteract the weight) for the minimum cost in total drag. At any other angle of attack there is a greater cost in terms of increased drag to obtain the same lift.

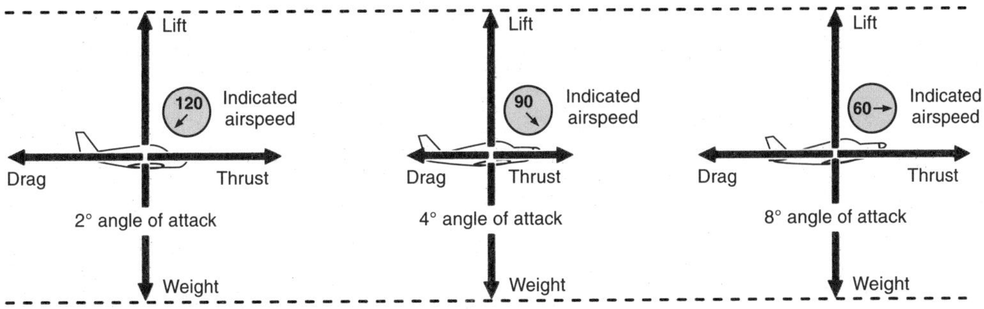

Figure 1-53 Same lift at a different cost in total drag.

In steady flight drag is counteracted by thrust. If the lift required to counteract the weight is obtained at the minimum cost in drag, then thrust can be kept to a minimum with the resulting benefits—smaller powerplant, better economy through lower fuel and maintenance costs, and so on.

Minimum drag means maximum L/D.

The L/D ratio is greatest when the drag is least—this occurs at about 4° angle of attack. For a propeller-driven airplane some important in-flight performance characteristics are obtained at the best L/D ratio, such as the maximum cruise range and the maximum power-off glide range.

Variation of the L/D Ratio with Angle of Attack

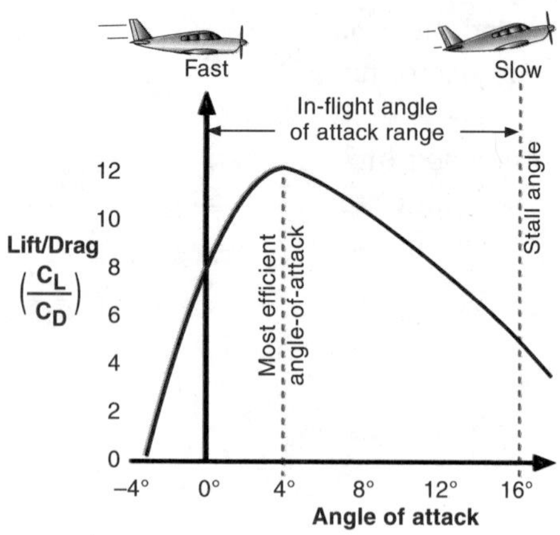

Figure 1-54
Lift/drag ratio versus angle of attack.

Lift is the benefit you obtain from an airfoil and drag is the price you pay for it. Efficiency is measured by how much lift you can gain for what cost of drag. If you require 2,400 pounds of lift and the cost is 200 units of drag from the airfoil, then $L/D = 2{,}400/200 = 12$, which means the lift is 12 times greater than the drag from the airfoil. If the 2,400 pounds of lift come with 400 units of drag from the airfoil, then the lift/drag ratio $= 2{,}400/400 = 6$ (the wing is much less efficient).

An airfoil has the greatest lifting ability (C_L) at a high angle of attack, just prior to the stall angle of attack—approximately 16° (figure 1-54). Unfortunately, near the stall angle, the airfoil generates a lot of induced drag. The minimum C_D occurs at a fairly low angle of attack, in this case at about 0° angle of attack. Unfortunately, at low angles of attack, the lifting ability (C_L) of the wing is low. Neither of these situations (high angle of attack or low angle of attack) is really satisfactory, because the ratio of lift to drag at these extreme angles of attack is low. What is required is the greatest lifting ability compared with the drag at the same angle of attack.

To find the *lift/drag ratio* we can divide the two equations:

$$\frac{\text{Lift}}{\text{Drag}} = \frac{C_L \times \frac{1}{2}\rho V^2 \times S}{C_D \times \frac{1}{2}\rho V^2 \times S} = \frac{C_L}{C_D}$$

For any angle of attack we can calculate the L/D ratio by dividing C_L by C_D. Developing a curve for L/D versus angle of attack shows that L/D increases rapidly up to about 4° angle of attack, where the lift is typically between 10 to 15 times the drag, depending on the airfoil used. At angles of attack higher than about 4° the L/D ratio decreases steadily. Even though the C_L is still increasing, the C_D increases at a greater rate. At the stall angle of attack the L/D ratio for this particular airfoil is about 5.

The curve shown in figure 1-54 clearly shows the specific angle of attack at which the L/D ratio is a maximum, and this angle of attack is where the airfoil is most efficient—it gives the required lift for the minimum cost in drag. In most airplanes you do not have an instrument to indicate angle of attack, but you can read airspeed, which is related to angle of attack. High angles of attack in steady flight are associated with lower airspeeds (and vice versa).

The angle of attack (and airspeed) for the best lift/drag ratio gives the required lift (to counteract the weight) for the minimum cost in drag. At any other angle of attack there is a greater cost in terms of increased drag to obtain the same lift.

End CPL

Wing Flaps

The type of wing flaps fitted to most airplanes are those mounted on the trailing edge of the main wings. They serve two purposes: to increase the lifting ability of the wing, and to increase drag:

- sometimes it is desirable to fly slowly, for instance when taking off and landing. The usual method to do this safely is to use the flaps to *increase the lifting ability* of the wing, enabling it to produce the required lift at a lower airspeed; and
- at other times it is useful to have *increased drag*—to help reduce the airspeed, or to increase the rate of descent and allow a steeper descent angle without increasing the airspeed.

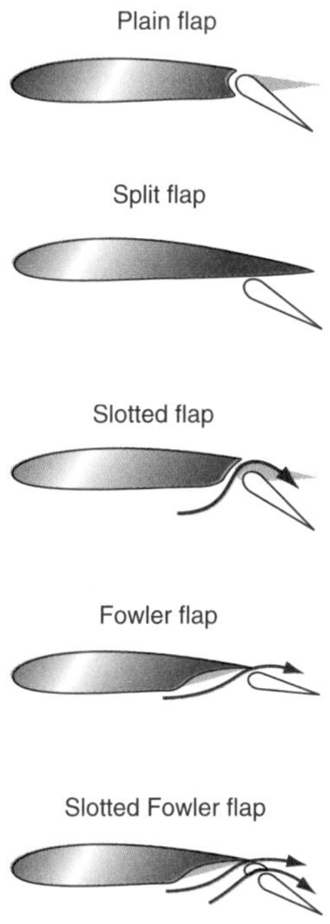

Figure 1-55 Common types of wing flaps.

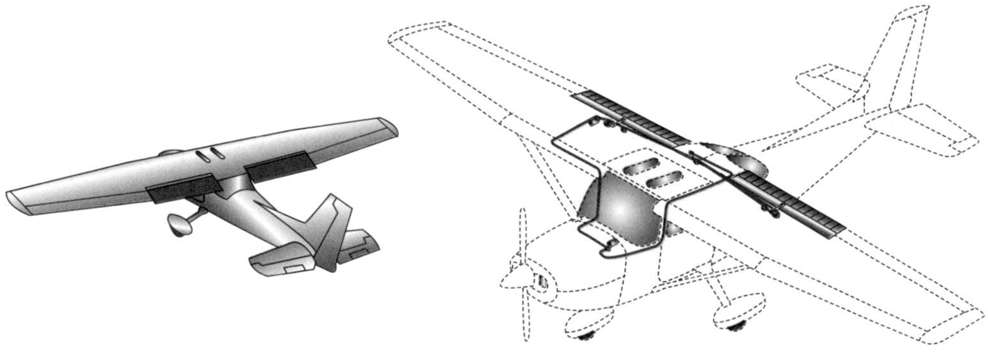

Figure 1-56 Typical flap installation—a Cessna wing-flap system.

In straight-and-level flight the weight is counteracted by the lift:

lift =	lifting ability of the wing	×	dynamic pressure	×	wing area
L =	C_L	×	$\frac{1}{2}\rho V^2$	×	S

Wing flaps allow the pilot to change the basic airfoil shape to one which has an increased lifting ability (and also an increased wing area, in the case of Fowler flaps), enabling the required lift to be generated at much lower speeds.

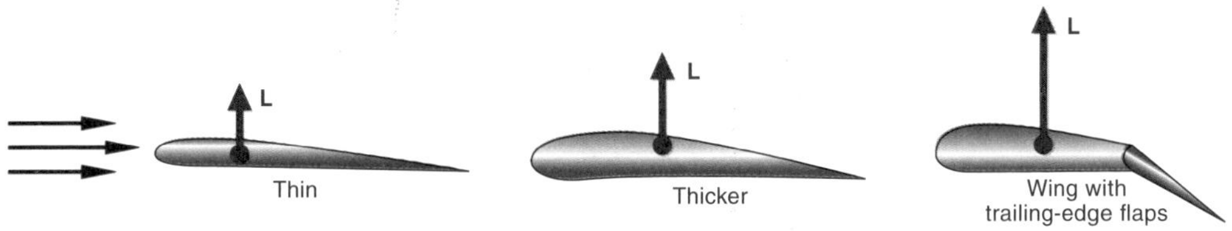

Figure 1-57 Same airspeed: increased camber and/or wing flaps give higher lift.

When the wing is near the stall angle of attack, the required lift with flaps extended will be generated at a much lower airspeed. When the stall angle is finally reached, the airspeed is much lower than that for flaps up. This means that all the other speeds which are factored from the stall speed, such as takeoff speed, approach speed, and landing speed, can be lower—a safer situation that allows shorter takeoff and landing distances.

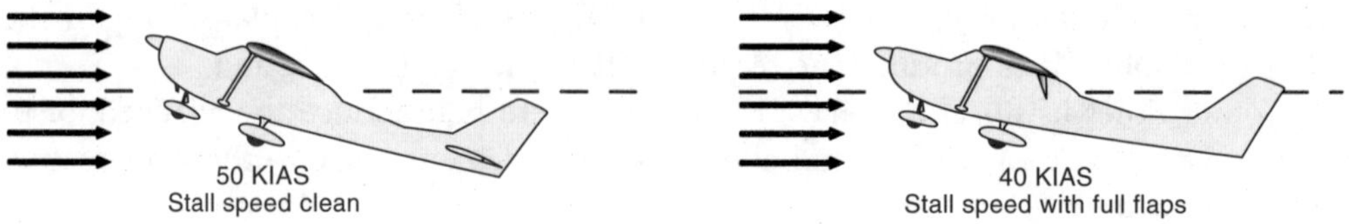

Figure 1-58 Flaps lower the stall speed (and nose attitude).

Lift/Drag Ratio

Trailing-edge flaps decrease the lift/drag ratio, and reduce glide range.

When the flaps are extended the lift increases, but so too does the drag. When we consider the angle of attack giving the best lift/drag ratio, the drag increase is proportionately greater than the lift increase, therefore the lift/drag (L/D) ratio decreases once the flaps are extended. As a result of a lower L/D ratio, the airplane will not glide as far with flaps lowered as it would when *clean* (flaps up)—nor will it climb at as steep an angle. Also, if you cruise with flaps lowered, more fuel will be required to travel the same distance.

Think of the trailing-edge flaps at their early extension as *lift* flaps (when the lifting ability of the wings is increased significantly for a moderate cost in drag), and when fully extended as *drag* flaps. The latter stages of trailing-edge flap extension give only a small increase in lifting capability for a large increase in drag. In both cases the L/D ratio will reduce, however the L/D ratio will decrease greatly with full flaps extended. When the flaps are extended, because the drag increases, the speed will decrease unless power is added or the rate of descent increased—or both.

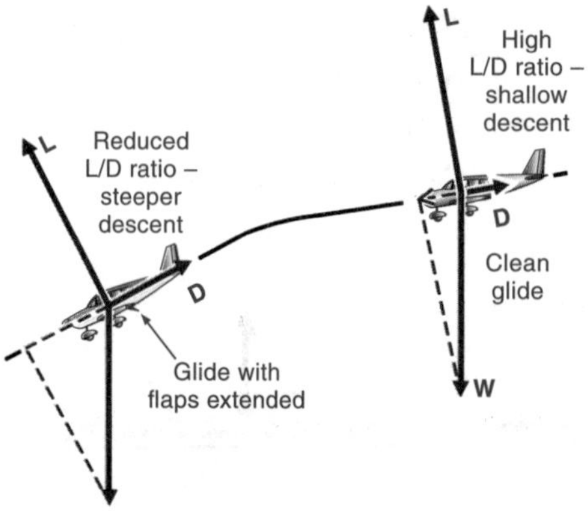

Figure 1-59 Effect of flaps on lift/drag ratio.

Approach

When flaps are extended the L/D ratio reduces, which enables the pilot to make a steeper approach without increasing airspeed.

Takeoff and Landing

One of the main functions of flaps, as previously stated, is to provide the same lift at a lower airspeed. This not only reduces takeoff and landing speeds (which is safer), but also shortens the length of runway required.

Ballooning

The initial effect of lowering the trailing-edge flaps is to produce an increased aerodynamic force because of the increased camber. With flaps extended, a lower pitch attitude is required to decrease the angle of attack, and prevent a short-lived climb called a *balloon*. It is only short-lived because the increased drag soon slows the airplane down, reducing the aerodynamic force. Conversely, raising the flaps can cause the airplane to *sink*, unless you raise the pitch attitude.

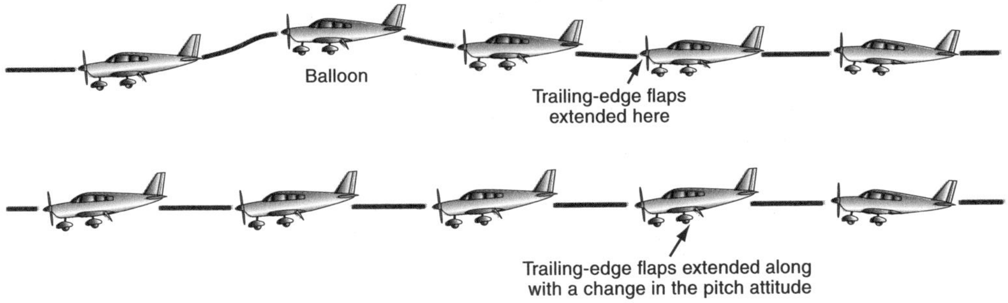

Figure 1-60 Lowering the flaps can cause the airplane to balloon unless you simultaneously adjust the pitch attitude.

Pitch Attitude

Because the increased camber resulting from extending the trailing-edge flaps occurs at the rear of the wing, the center of pressure moves rearward as the flaps are extended. The resultant pitching effect will vary between airplane types. Elevator pressure will be required to hold the desired pitch attitude, but you can trim this steady pressure off.

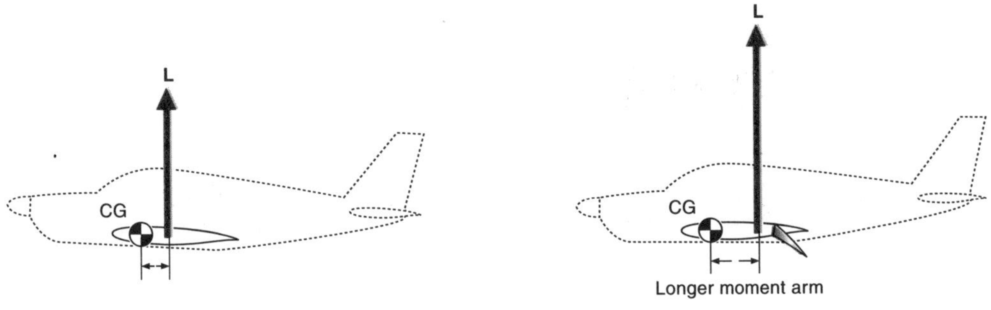

Figure 1-61 Extending the flaps may cause the nose to pitch.

Changing Wing Area

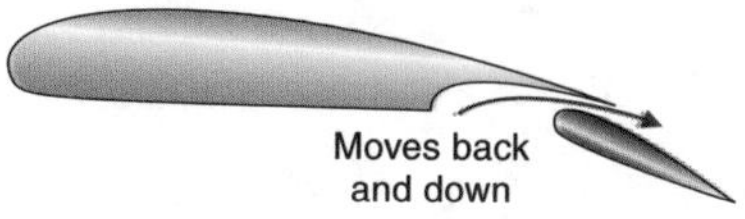

Figure 1-62 A Fowler flap.

Increasing the wing area allows the same lift to be produced at an even lower airspeed. Some flaps, such as Fowler flaps (which extend rearward as well as downward), increase the wing area as they are extended. Other less complex flaps simply change the cross-section of the wing, increasing camber, as they are extended. All types of flaps change lift and drag, and consequently have an effect on the value of the L/D ratio.

Leading-Edge Devices

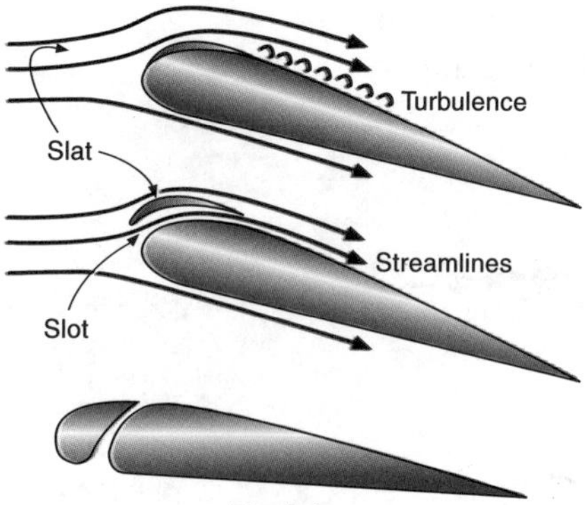

Figure 1-63
Slats and slots delay the stall.

At high angles of attack, the airflow separates from the wing's upper surface and becomes turbulent. This leads to a stalled condition that destroys much of the lifting ability of the wing.

Some airplanes have leading-edge devices that allow some of the high energy air from beneath the wing to flow through a slot and over the upper surface of the wing, thereby delaying separation and the stall, allowing the airplane to fly at a higher angle of attack and a lower airspeed. This can be achieved with *slats* which form part of the upper leading edge of the wing in normal flight, but can be extended forward and/or down to form a slot.

Some wings have fixed *slots* built in to the wing leading edge, but this is less common because they generate high drag at cruise speeds. On a high performance airplane this would be unacceptable, so the more complicated extendable slat would be fitted.

Spoilers

Spoilers increase drag and reduce the L/D ratio.

Most advanced jet transports and most gliders have *spoilers* on the upper surfaces of their wings. These are hinged control panels which, when extended, disturb the airflow over the upper lift-producing part of the wing, thereby decreasing lift and increasing drag. Pilots use spoilers to reduce airspeed and/or steepen the descent path without increasing airspeed. On large jet airplanes, pilots deploy the spoilers after touchdown to dump the lift and get all of the weight onto the wheels, thus making the wheel brakes more effective.

Thrust

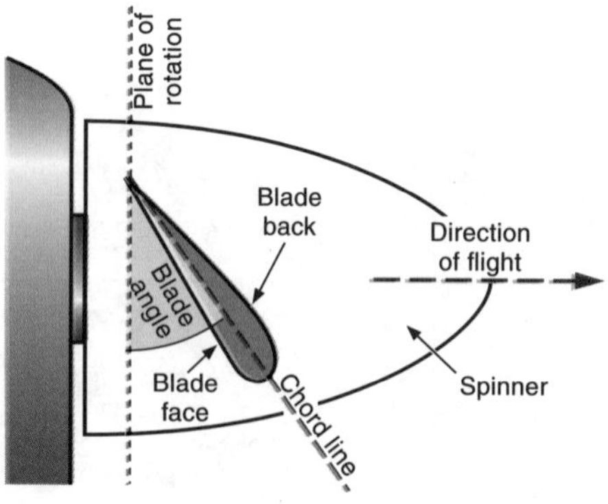

Figure 1-64 Propeller terminology.

Thrust is one of the four main forces that act on an airplane. To maintain a steady straight-and-level speed, the thrust must equal the total drag of the airplane. To accelerate the airplane in level flight, thrust must be greater than drag; conversely, to decelerate in level flight, thrust must be less than drag.

A piston engine uses a propeller to convert the power output of the engine into thrust. Engine power is transmitted by a shaft to the propeller as *torque* or *turning effect.* This power is used to rotate the propeller, which converts most of the torque supplied by the engine into an aerodynamic force called *thrust.*

The propeller blades are *airfoils* that generate aerodynamic forces in a similar way to other airfoils, such as the wings, by modifying the airflow around them. Notice how the cross-section of a propeller blade resembles the cross-section of a wing.

As the propeller blade rotates through the air, the acceleration of the airflow over the front cambered surface of the blade causes a reduced static pressure ahead of the blade (Bernoulli's principle). The result is a forward thrust force on the propeller blade which pulls the airplane along. Air density affects the efficiency of a propeller, as it does a wing. In addition, the less dense the air, the less the mass of air accelerated rearward, and the less effective the propeller, such as at high altitudes or on very hot days.

Consider just one *blade section*, or *blade element* as it is sometimes called, at some radial distance from the hub or the centerline of the propeller rotation. The blade section is an airfoil and it has a leading edge, a trailing edge, a chord line, and a camber just like any other airfoil.

The angle which the chord line of a propeller section makes with the plane of rotation is called the propeller *blade angle*. As we shall soon see, the blade angle varies from a large angle at the root near the hub, and gradually becomes less toward the propeller tip. However, the rotating blade creates not only thrust but also many unbalanced forces. These are considered later in this chapter.

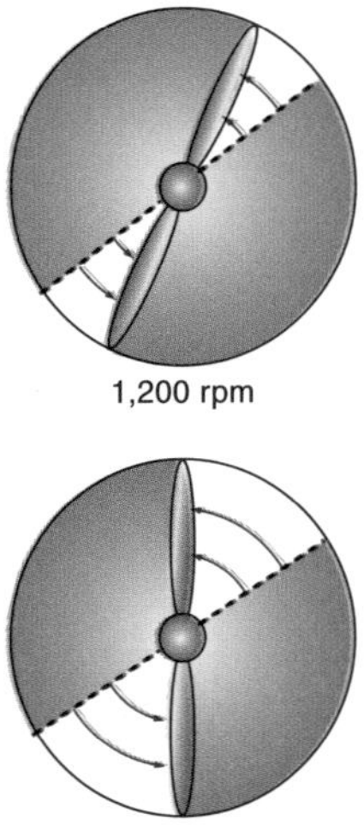

Figure 1-65 The speed of the blade section depends on the radius and RPM.

Propeller Motion

Rotational Velocity

If the airplane is stationary, the motion of the propeller section under consideration is purely rotational. The further out along the blade the section is, the faster its rotational velocity. Also, the higher the RPM (revolutions per minute) of the propeller, the faster the rotational velocity of the section.

Forward Velocity

As the airplane moves forward in flight, the propeller section will have a forward velocity as well as its rotational velocity. When this forward motion is combined with the rotational velocity, the overall *resultant velocity* of the propeller blade section through the air is obtained, as shown in figure 1-66. The angle between the resultant velocity (and therefore relative airflow) of the propeller blade and the plane of rotation is called the *helix angle* or the *pitch angle* or the *angle of advance*.

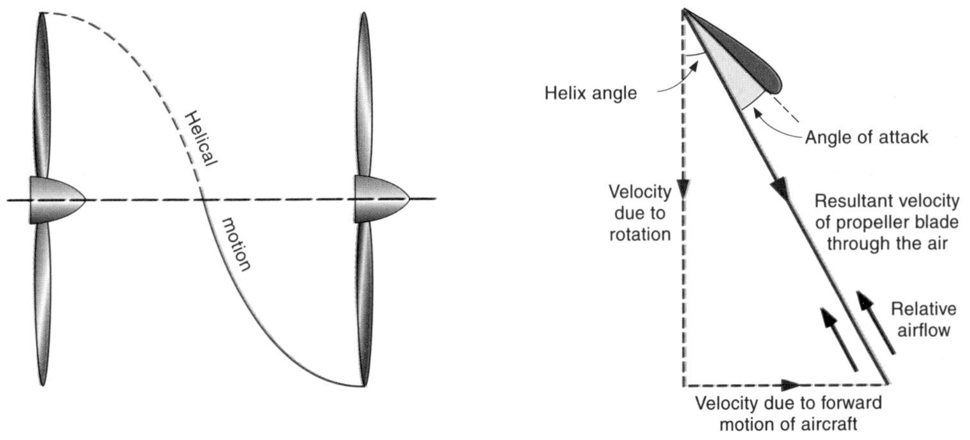

Figure 1-66 Each propeller blade-section follows its own path.

Helical Motion

Each propeller blade section follows a corkscrew path through the air—called a *helix*—as a result of the combined rotational and forward velocities. The easiest way to picture it is to consider the helix as the path which the trailing edge of the propeller section follows.

The blade section experiences a relative airflow directly opposite its own path through the air. The angle between the chord line of the propeller blade section and the relative airflow is its *angle of attack*. Notice that the angle of attack plus the helix angle (pitch angle) make up the blade angle.

When the airplane is in flight each propeller blade section will have the same forward velocity component. What will differ, however, is the rotational component of velocity—the further each blade section is from the propeller shaft the faster it is moving. If the blade angle was the same along the whole length of the propeller (which we know is not the case), then the angle of attack would be different at all points.

For a propeller with the same blade angle along its length, the angle of attack would vary with distance from the propeller shaft, causing thrust to be produced in an inefficient manner.

A propeller has blade twist to maintain the same angle of attack along the length of the blade.

Like all airfoils, there is a most efficient angle of attack. If the propeller is designed to be most efficient at a certain airspeed of the airplane and RPM of the propeller, then the designer will aim to have this most efficient angle of attack along the whole length of the propeller blade when it is operating under the design airspeed and RPM conditions. To achieve this, the blade angle at the hub needs to be much greater than the blade angle at the tip. This is known as *blade twist* or *helical twist*.

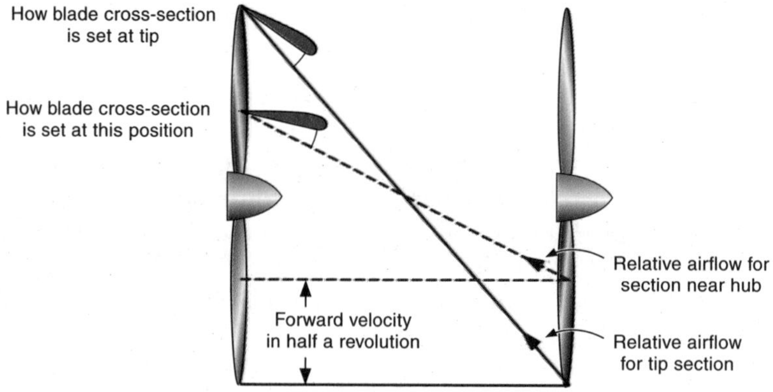

Figure 1-67 The propeller blade angle is made progressively larger from tip to hub to provide efficient angles of attack along its full length.

Forces on a Propeller Blade

When considering a wing, the total aerodynamic force is resolved into a lift component perpendicular to the relative airflow, and a drag component parallel to the relative airflow. For a propeller airfoil, however, each blade section has a different oriented relative airflow because of the different rotational velocities. It would therefore be complicated to resolve the aerodynamic forces into components parallel and perpendicular to the relative airflow. Therefore when considering the forces on a propeller blade it is much more convenient to resolve the total reaction into two components:

- one in the plane of rotation called *propeller torque* (which is resistance to motion in the plane of rotation); and
- another in the direction perpendicular to the plane of rotation called *thrust*.

For a wing, drag must be overcome to provide lift. For a propeller, the propeller torque must be overcome or balanced by the engine for the propeller to provide thrust. Opening the throttle increases the engine power, overcomes the propeller torque, causes the propeller to rotate faster and generate more thrust.

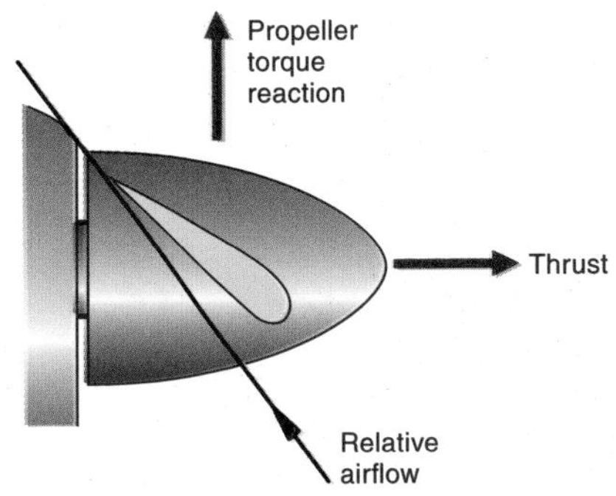

Figure 1-68
Forces on a propeller blade.

Propeller Efficiency

An efficient propeller can convert a lot of the power produced by the engine (the brake horsepower) into thrust (that is, to thrust horsepower). A less-efficient propeller converts less of the engine power (brake horsepower or BHP) to thrust (thrust HP). Therefore:

$$\text{Propeller efficiency} = \frac{\text{thrust horsepower}}{\text{brake horsepower}}$$

Variation of Propeller Efficiency

Only part of the propeller blade is capable of producing thrust efficiently—this usually lies at some distance from the hub between 60 and 90 percent of the blade radius, with the greatest useful thrust produced at approximately 75 percent of the blade radius. Reference to blade angle, angle of attack, and so on, will refer to this most effective part of the propeller blade.

Now consider a well-designed fixed-pitch propeller blade. The term *fixed-pitch* means that the blade angle is fixed and unable to be changed, as on most training airplanes. If the propeller RPM is constant, then the direction of the relative airflow and the angle of attack will be determined by the forward speed.

As the forward airspeed increases, the angle of attack of a fixed-pitch propeller turning at a constant RPM will decrease. At some high forward speed, the angle of attack of the blades will be such that little or no thrust will be produced. For a given RPM, there will only be one airspeed at which the fixed-pitch propeller will operate at its most efficient angle of attack.

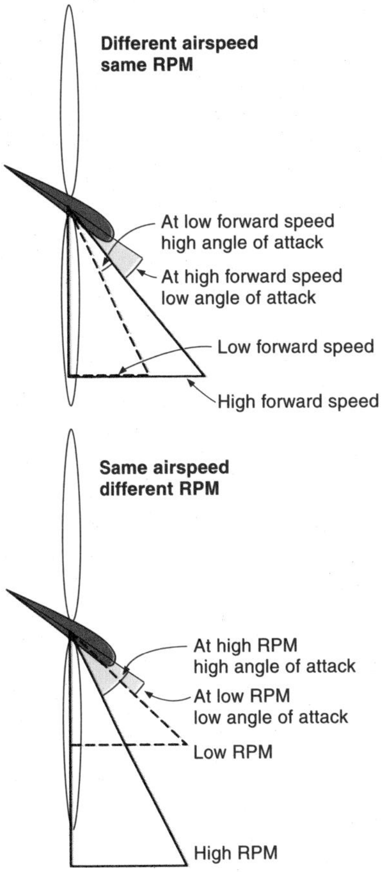

Figure 1-69
Fixed-pitch propeller—the angle of attack varies with forward speed and RPM.

The designer chooses a fixed-pitch propeller whose most efficient airspeed/RPM combination fits the tasks for which the airplane is designed. For an airplane whose primary purpose is to lift heavy loads off short runways and operate at low airspeeds, a low-pitch propeller (small blade angle) is most suitable. Airplanes designed for agricultural spraying or fire-bombing are typical examples. For an airplane whose primary purpose is cruising long distances at high speeds, a propeller of higher pitch (large blade angle) is more suitable.

A fixed-pitch propeller is most efficient at only one airspeed and RPM.

Although the fixed-pitch propeller can be designed for a specific role, its maximum efficiency is limited to just one airspeed/RPM combination. Faster or slower than this speed/RPM, propeller efficiency will reduce markedly. The constant-speed propeller overcomes this problem by varying the blade angle so that it operates at an efficient angle of attack at any airspeed. Most pilots will fly constant-speed propeller airplanes early in their careers.

Variable-Pitch Propellers

An early development in improving propeller efficiency was the two-pitch propeller, which enabled the pilot to select a low pitch for takeoff and low-speed operations, and a high pitch for the higher airspeeds on the cruise and descent. More recently, the automatic *constant-speed propeller* was developed, with a blade angle that could take up any position between two in-flight limits at the *low* and *high* pitch ends of its range. This allows the propeller blade to maintain its most efficient angle of attack at all airspeed/RPM combinations.

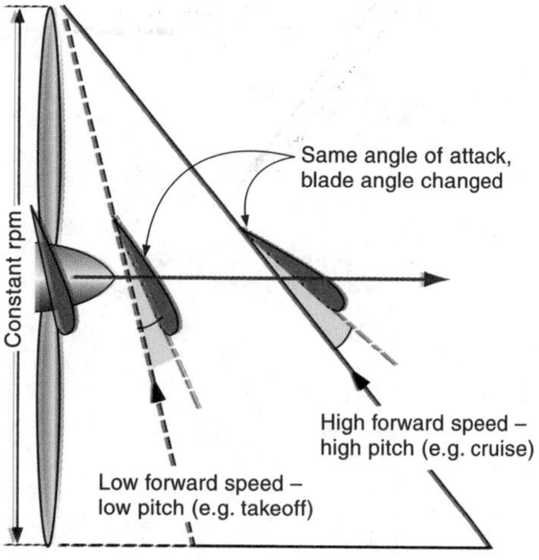

Figure 1-70 A constant-speed propeller maintains an efficient angle of attack over a wide speed/RPM range.

At low airspeeds, the blade angle needs to be small for the angle of attack to be optimum. This is known as *fine pitch*. As the forward speed increases, the blade angle needs to increase toward *coarse* pitch for the angle of attack to remain optimum. The device used to achieve this is the *governor*, whose function is to regulate the propeller RPM to that selected by the pilot. It does this by automatically adjusting the blade angle so that the RPM is maintained irrespective of the airspeed and the power delivered by the engine, hence the term constant-speed propeller.

The pilot sets the recommended RPM for the operation (climb, cruise, or descent) with the propeller control. The aim is to have the propeller working close to its best angle of attack and maximum efficiency throughout its operating range, as advised by the manufacturer's operating procedures. In the extreme case of low engine power, the blade angle will reduce until it reaches the minimum limit, known as the low-pitch stop. From then on, the propeller acts as a fixed-pitch propeller, with further power reductions causing a drop in RPM because the governor cannot reduce the blade angle any further to maintain the RPM.

Takeoff

Fine pitch is used for takeoff so that the blade angle of the constant-speed propeller is at a small angle of attack. This enables the propeller to operate at maximum RPM as the throttle is advanced to the takeoff position, and so enable the engine to deliver maximum power.

Cruise

The throttle is mid-range and the propeller is set to medium pitch (low RPM) for best cruise fuel consumption.

Approach and Landing

When the airspeed and power are low, as on approach to land, the propeller blades are hard against the fine-pitch stop, and the RPM changes with throttle movements. However, in case a go-around is necessary, it is good airmanship to advance the prop control to high RPM on final approach so that the propeller can quickly and efficiently achieve maximum thrust when the throttle is advanced.

Constant-Speed Propeller Controls

The pitch-changing mechanism is usually operated hydraulically by governor-regulated oil pressure. In contrast to fixed-pitch propellers, where the throttle alone is used to control RPM with a constant-speed propeller there are two controls:

- the *propeller control* to control propeller RPM; and
- the *throttle* to control the manifold pressure in the engine.

The desired power is achieved by selecting certain combinations of propeller RPM and manifold pressure (see also chapter 5).

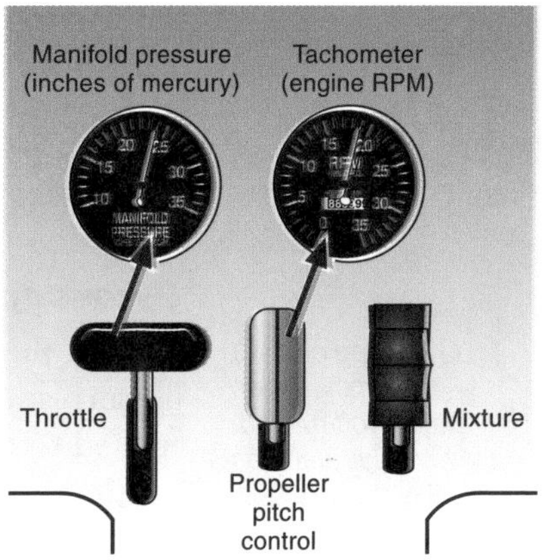

Figure 1-71
Constant-speed propeller controls.

Advantages of the Constant-Speed Propeller

A constant-speed (or variable-pitch) propeller enables the propeller to be at its most efficient angle of attack over a wide range of RPM and airspeed. In comparison, a fixed-pitch propeller only operates efficiently under the one set of RPM and airspeed conditions.

A constant-speed propeller is efficient over a range of RPM and airspeed conditions.

More complex constant-speed propellers used in multi-engine or turbine airplanes have other significant features, including:

- *beta range*, which is a range of very low pitch angles that reduce thrust and produce more drag for ground operations;
- *reverse thrust*—some propeller mechanisms can rotate the blades into reverse (or negative) pitch, which results in the propeller's thrust acting backwards; and
- *feathering*—on multi-engine airplanes, propellers can be feathered in flight to stop a windmilling prop, reduce drag, and prevent further engine damage following an engine failure.

Unbalanced Effects of Propellers—Left Turning Tendencies

Slipstream Effect

A clockwise-rotating propeller (as seen from the cockpit) will impart a clockwise rotation to the slipstream as it flows back over the airplane, following a corkscrew path. This causes an asymmetric airflow over the vertical stabilizer and rudder. In the case of a single-engine airplane at high power, the slipstream will strike the left of the vertical stabilizer at an angle of attack, generating an aerodynamic force which pushes the tail to the right and makes the airplane *yaw left*. Some airplanes have an *offset vertical stabilizer* to help overcome this effect. It is most noticeable at high power and low airspeed.

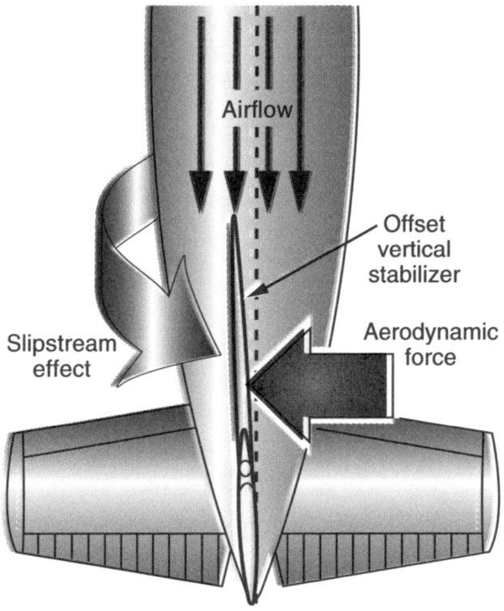

Figure 1-72 An offset fin helps counteract propeller-slipstream effect.

Propeller Torque Effect

If the propeller rotates clockwise (when viewed from behind), the torque reaction will tend to rotate the airplane counterclockwise, which means the airplane will *roll left*. This effect is most pronounced under conditions of high power and high propeller RPM, and at low airspeeds when fixed-pitch propeller blades have a large angle of attack—for example, during takeoff.

On the takeoff ground run, the tendency to roll left is absorbed by the left mainwheel, which will have to support more load. This will increase the friction force, tending to slow it down, and consequently the airplane will *yaw left*. Notice that on the ground run this effect yaws the airplane in the same direction as the slipstream effect. Use right rudder to keep straight. A high-powered airplane, such as a P-51 Mustang, can roll uncontrollably if full power is applied suddenly at low airspeed (e.g. for a go-around).

Gyroscopic Effect

Gyroscopic effect is significant on the takeoff run in a tailwheel airplane as the tail is raised.

Early in the takeoff run of a tailwheel airplane, the tail is lifted off the ground to place the airplane into a low drag and flying attitude. As the tail is being raised, a force is applied to the rotating propeller to tilt the rotating propeller disc forward. Because a rotating body tends to resist any attempt to change its plane of rotation, when such a change is imposed on it, a *gyroscopic precession* will be superimposed. See chapter 7 for more on gyroscopic precession.

Gyroscopic effect causes any force applied to a spinning object to be displaced 90° in the direction of rotation. The action of *raising the tail* of the airplane on the takeoff run is like applying a forward force to the top of the rotating propeller disc. Gyroscopic precession causes an equivalent force to be applied 90° degrees in the direction of propeller rotation. With clockwise rotation, there will appear to be a force acting on the right side of the rotating propeller disc, causing the airplane to *yaw left*. The direction of yaw depends on the direction of propeller rotation. Right rudder must be applied to counteract this effect.

The extent of the gyroscopic effect depends on the propeller's *moment of inertia*. The moment of inertia depends on the mass of the propeller, how the mass is distributed along the blades, and how fast the propeller is rotating. It also depends on how fast you try to change the plane of rotation—if you raise the tail quickly, the tendency to yaw left will be greater.

Raising the tail of a high-powered airplane like a P-51 Mustang on takeoff produces a much greater gyroscopic effect than raising the tail of a Piper Cub.

Asymmetric Propeller Blade Effect (P-Factor)

P-factor is present at high angles of attack (low airspeed) and high power.

P-factor occurs for tailwheel airplanes on takeoff and for all airplanes when flying at high angles of attack (low speeds). During the first part of a tailwheel airplane's takeoff run, the tail is still on the ground, the propeller shaft is inclined upward, and the plane of propeller rotation is not vertical. Because the airplane is moving horizontally, the down-going propeller blade has a greater angle of attack than the up-going blade. In addition, the down-going blade also travels further (and therefore faster) through the air than the up-going blade.

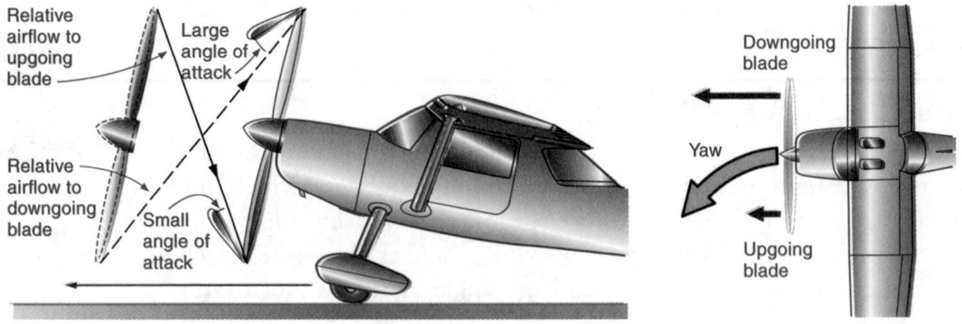

Figure 1-73 The down-going propeller blade produces more thrust when the airplane is in a nose-high attitude, causing P-factor.

These two effects (greater angle of attack and higher blade velocity) combine to produce more thrust on the down-going half of the propeller disc than on the up-going half and the airplane will *yaw left*. P-factor is strongest at high power settings and high angles of attack, both on the ground and in flight. In normal cruise flight, the P-factor is insignificant because the up-going and down-going propeller blades produce similar amounts of thrust when the angle of attack is low.

Summary

On the takeoff ground run, the above four effects cause the airplane to *yaw left*. You can remain on the runway centerline by counteracting the yaw with right rudder. However, be cautious if there is any crosswind from the left. During flight, an increase in power will cause the airplane to yaw left due to slipstream effect and roll left due to the torque reaction. In addition, when flying slowly at a high angle of attack the airplane will yaw further left because of asymmetric blade effect.

Prevent unwanted yaw with rudder.

CPL

Pitch

Earlier in the chapter reference was made to "low pitch" and "high pitch" in constant-speed propellers. In summary, low pitch is associated with a small blade angle and slow flight, while high pitch is associated with a large blade angle and fast flight.

However, *pitch* is not a blade angle but a distance—the distance the propeller moves forward in one complete revolution. Normally during flight at low speeds you *select* low pitch to ensure the propeller is at the most efficient angle of attack. However the pitch (distance moved forward in one revolution) would have been small whether "low" or "high" pitch had been selected.

Propeller Efficiency

There is a certain amount of slippage as a propeller blade moves through the air and pulls the airplane along, in the same way as a swimmer's hands or a rower's oars slip backward through the water. A propeller will therefore not advance as far through "fluid" air as a corkscrew would through a solid cork, where there is no slippage.

Propeller efficiency is the ratio of thrust horsepower (propeller) to brake horsepower (engine).

Geometric pitch is how far the propeller would theoretically advance in one revolution with no slippage. *Effective pitch* is how far the propeller *actually* advances through the air in one revolution. It is equal to geometric pitch minus propeller slippage. A propeller is more efficient in dense air than in thin air, because there is less slippage.

As a result of propeller slippage through the air, not all of the power generated by the engine will be converted to thrust by the propeller. We describe this as *propeller efficiency*, the ratio of useful power output (from the propeller) to actual power output (from the engine). Typical propeller efficiency varies between 50 percent and 85 percent lift-to-weight, depending on slippage.

End CPL

Review 1
Forces Acting on an Airplane

Four Forces in Flight

1. Which force produced by the wings sup-ports the airplane in flight?
2. Which force is produced by the engine–propeller?
3. Which force resists the motion of the airplane through the air?
4. Lift and weight are generally how much greater than thrust and drag in straight-and-level flight at a constant airspeed?
5. What relationships exist between lift and weight, and between thrust and drag, when the airplane is flying straight-and-level at a constant airspeed?

Airfoil Lift

6. Which surface is designed to create an aerodynamic lifting force as air flows over it?
7. What do you call a steady airflow around an airfoil in which succeeding parcels of air follow each other?
8. Where on an airfoil does the smooth boundary-layer flow separate from the airfoil surface and become turbulent?
9. Static pressure in the air is exerted in which direction(s)?
10. Which pressure is caused by motion?
11. What is total pressure energy the sum of?
12. In streamline flow, if dynamic pressure increases, what happens to the static pressure?
13. What does the expression "$\frac{1}{2}\rho V^2$" represent?
14. What line is drawn half-way between the upper and lower surfaces of the wing to give an indication of its curvature?
15. The wing shape and the angle of attack determine the profile that the airfoil presents to the airflow. What else do they determine?
16. True or false? The forces acting on an airfoil in flight, as a result of the changes in static pressure around it, may be considered to act through the center of pressure.
17. Describe how the relative airflow relates to the flight path of an airplane.
18. Define the term *angle of attack.*
19. If the angle of attack is gradually increased in normal cruise flight, what will happen to the lifting ability of the wing?
20. On a wing, the force of lift acts perpendicular to and the force of drag acts parallel to the:
    a. chord line.
    b. flight path.
    c. longitudinal axis.
21. What does the angle of attack of a wing control directly?
22. What happens to the center of pressure as the angle of attack is gradually increased in the normal flight range?
23. True or false? Beyond the stall angle of attack, the lifting ability of the wing decreases significantly and the center of pressure moves rearward on the wing.
24. How will frost on the wings of an airplane affect takeoff performance?

Drag

25. What is drag?
26. True or false? If drag can be kept low, thrust can be kept low.
27. Describe the two basic groups of total drag.
28. True or false? As airspeed increases, drag caused by skin friction decreases.
29. How can form drag be reduced?
30. True or false? The spanwise flow of air on the upper wing surface is toward the wing root.
31. When is the formation of wingtip vortices and induced drag greatest?
32. When is the total drag at a minimum?
33. Why is the thrust requirement greater at high speeds and low angles of attack?
34. True or false? Minimum drag means minimum thrust to maintain airspeed.
35. What does the lift/drag ratio describe?

Wing Flaps

36. What effect does extending the flaps have on the camber of the wing?
37. Aside from lift, what do trailing-edge flaps increase?
38. The percentage increase in drag usually exceeds that in lift when the flaps are extended. Do flaps therefore increase the *lift/drag* ratio?
39. True or false? The extension of flaps on a glide approach allows a steeper approach path at a constant speed.
40. True or false? With flaps extended, the nose attitude of the airplane is higher.
41. True or false? Slots increase the angle of attack at which the wing stalls by delaying the separation of the smooth airflow over the upper surface of the wing.

Thrust from the Propeller

42. What does a propeller convert engine torque into?
43. True or false? At high altitudes, when the air is less dense, a propeller will be more efficient.
44. Why is a propeller blade twisted?
45. True or false? A fixed-pitch propeller is efficient at only one set of RPM and airspeed conditions.
46. True or false? A constant-speed propeller has a variable pitch angle and is efficient over a wide range of RPM and airspeed conditions.
47. As the forward speed of an airplane with a fixed-pitch propeller increases, with the RPM remaining constant, the angle of attack of the propeller blades:
    a. decreases as forward speed increases.
    b. increases as forward speed increases.
    c. remains unaltered as forward speed increases.
48. In an airplane with a clockwise rotating propeller, what does P-factor, or asymmetric blade effect cause the airplane to do?
49. During the takeoff roll in a single-engine airplane, the left tire will carry more load. Why?
50. When is torque effect greatest in a single-engine airplane?
51. How can you keep the airplane tracking straight down the runway during the takeoff roll in a single-engine airplane?

Commercial Review

52. If airflow velocity increases, what happens to the static pressure?
53. Write down the lift formula and identify each term.
54. When the angle of attack of a symmetrical airfoil is increased, what will happen to the center of pressure?
55. Define *wing loading* in straight-and-level flight.
56. An airplane weighs 3,000 pounds and has a wing area of 150 square feet. What is its wing loading?
57. An airplane has burned off 150 pounds of fuel.
    a. What does it now weigh?
    b. What is its wing loading?
58. What sort of wings help minimize the formation of wingtip vortices and induced drag?
59. True or false? A high aspect ratio wing has a short span and a long chord.
60. Does a wing with washout have a lower angle of attack at the wingtip?
61. If you require 3,000 pounds of lift to support the airplane and the drag is 250 pounds, what is the L/D ratio?

Refer to figure 1-46 (page 22) for questions 62 and 63.

62. The total drag is greater when flying faster than the minimum-drag airspeed. Why?
63. The total drag is greater when flying slower than the minimum-drag airspeed. Why?
64. True or false? Propeller efficiency is affected by propeller slippage.
65. Which ratio describes propeller efficiency?
66. You are flying an airplane with a constant-speed propeller. What would you select for high-speed cruise compared with takeoff?
67. What does a constant-speed propeller automatically adjust?

Refer to figure 1-74 for questions 68 to 70.

Note. The graphs here apply to a military fighter with swept wings. The angles of attack at which L/D and C_L are maximum are therefore higher than those you would expect for a training airplane.

68. At 4° angle of attack, what is:
a. the C_L?
b. the C_D?
c. the ratio C_L/C_D?
d. the L/D?

69. **a.** The airpseed for the best L/D ratio occurs at what percentage of angle of attack?
b. What is the L/D at this point?

70. **a.** What is the L/D at 2° angle of attack on the low-airspeed side?
b. What percentage of angle of attack on the high-airspeed side is this the same as?

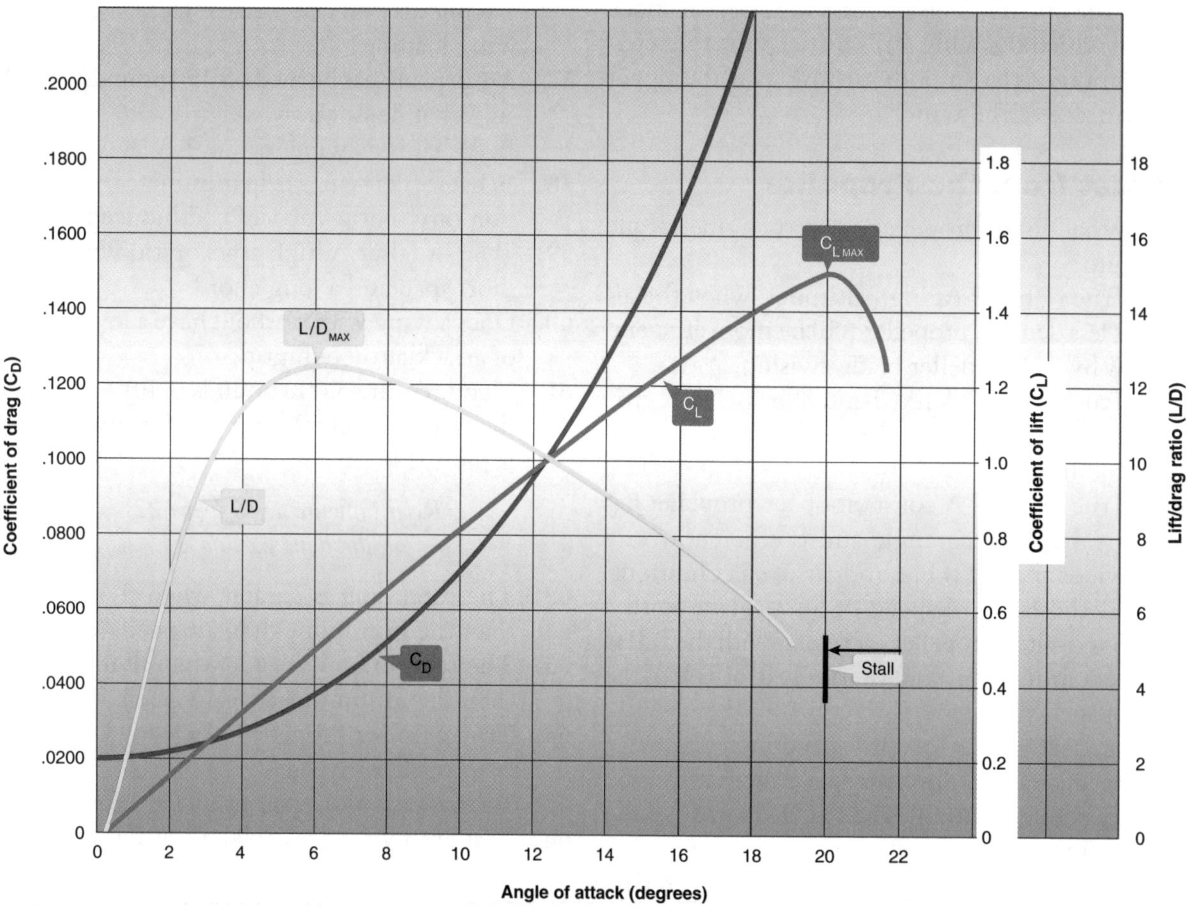

Figure 1-74 Questions 68 to 70.

Answers are given on page 685.

Stability and Control 2

Stability

Stability describes the initial response and subsequent behavior of an aircraft when it is disturbed from its trimmed condition by atmospheric effects, such as wind gusts or thermals. There are two stages:

- the initial response, which is called *static stability*; and
- the subsequent behavior, which is called *dynamic stability*.

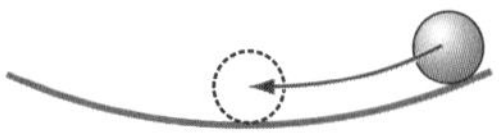

Figure 2-1
Tends to return to center.

Static Stability

If an aircraft tends to return to its trimmed condition, it has positive static stability or is statically stable, like a marble in a saucer (figure 2-1). If an aircraft has neutral static stability, it will tend to stay in its new condition, like a marble on a flat surface (figure 2-2). If an aircraft has negative static stability, it is unstable and will diverge further when disturbed, like a marble on a convex dish (figure 2-3).

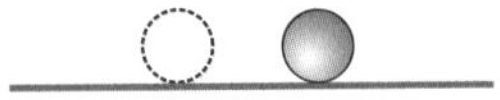

Figure 2-2
No tendency to return.

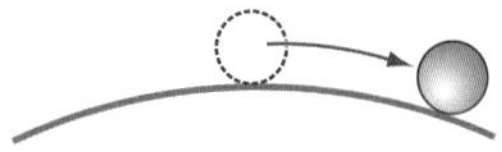

Figure 2-3
Tends to diverge.

Dynamic Stability

Dynamic stability describes the behavior of the aircraft after the disturbance. An aircraft is subject to many external forces. These are balanced in trimmed, steady flight. When the aircraft is disturbed, the forces change, and the dominant ones determine the behavior. An aircraft that is dynamically stable will experience an oscillation that is quickly damped.

An aircraft with neutral dynamic stability will follow a continuing, undamped oscillation.

An aircraft that is dynamically unstable will have increasingly divergent oscillation.

Figure 2-4
Damped oscillation—dynamically stable.

Figure 2-5
Undamped oscillation—dynamically neutral.

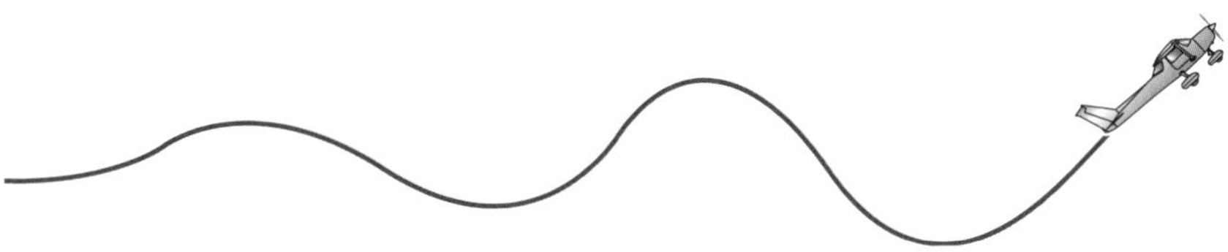

Figure 2-6
Divergent oscillation—dynamically unstable.

Stability and Maneuverability

There is a trade-off between stability and maneuverability.

An airplane with some positive stability is much easier to fly than an unstable airplane that shows a tendency to diverge from the trimmed flight attitude. The stability must not be so great, however, as to require unacceptably high control forces for maneuvering. An unstable airplane is difficult, if not impossible, to fly because of the continual need to apply control corrections. A stable airplane can almost be flown hands-off and only requires guidance rather than second-to-second control inputs by the pilot. The designer must achieve a compromise between stability and maneuverability, bearing in mind the qualities most desirable for the airplane's planned use. For instance, a passenger airplane would require more stability, whereas a fighter requires greater maneuverability.

Our examples so far have been drawn from the pitching plane, but stability in the other planes and about the other axes is just as important.

Airplane Equilibrium

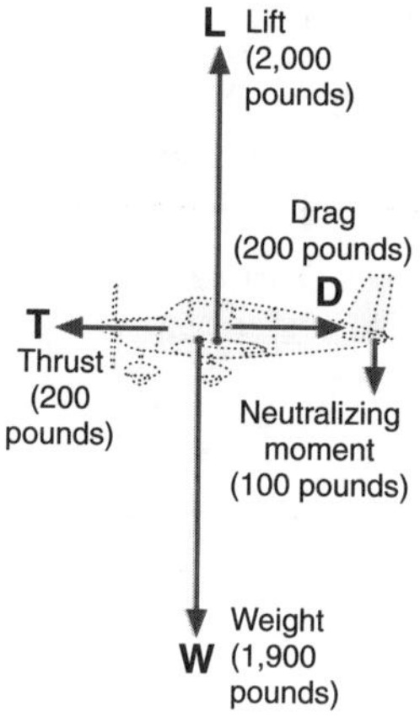

Figure 2-7
Lift counteracts weight, thrust counteracts drag in straight-and-level flight (moments neutralized by stabilizers and trim). Total weight includes download on the tail.

An airplane is in a state of *equilibrium* when the sum of all forces and moments is zero. This means it will fly in a straight line at a steady airspeed. The airplane is *in trim* if all the moments in pitch, roll and yaw are zero.

As explained in the previous chapter, four main forces act on an airplane in flight: lift, weight, thrust and drag. For the airplane to remain in equilibrium in steady straight-and-level flight, the opposing forces must be equal so that they balance out, leaving an overall force of zero acting on the airplane.

Therefore:

- lift is equal to weight and acts in the opposite direction; and
- thrust is equal to drag and acts in the opposite direction.

There is usually a considerable difference between the two pairs of forces, with lift and weight being much greater in magnitude than thrust and drag in normal flight. For example, lift and weight may each be 2,000 pounds, with thrust and drag each 200 pounds (that is, a lift/drag ratio of $2{,}000/200 = 10{:}1$). The weight will gradually decrease as fuel is burned off, meaning that the lift required will also decrease. Thrust and drag will vary considerably depending on the angle of attack and airspeed.

Pitching Moments

The positions of the lift force acting through the center of pressure (CP), and the weight force acting through the center of gravity (CG), are not constant in flight. The basic CG position is established when the airplane is loaded, but will move as passengers or crew move around (noticeable in airliners as flight attendants walk down the cabin), if unsecured freight moves, and as fuel burns off. The CP changes position according to the angle of attack (and therefore airspeed).

A couple is a pair of equal, parallel forces acting in opposite directions which tends to cause rotation because the forces are acting along different axes.

Under most conditions of flight the CP and CG are not at the same point. The outcome is that the opposing forces of lift and weight, even though approximately equal in magnitude, will set up a *couple*, causing a nose-down pitching moment if the lift (CP) is behind the weight (CG), or a nose-up pitching moment if the CP is in front of the CG.

The different lines of action of the thrust force and the drag force produce another couple, causing a nose-up pitching moment if the drag line is above the thrust line, or a nose-down pitching moment if it is below the thrust line.

The pitching moments from the two couples should neutralize each other in level flight so that there is no *residual* (remaining) moment that would cause the airplane to pitch nose-up or nose-down.

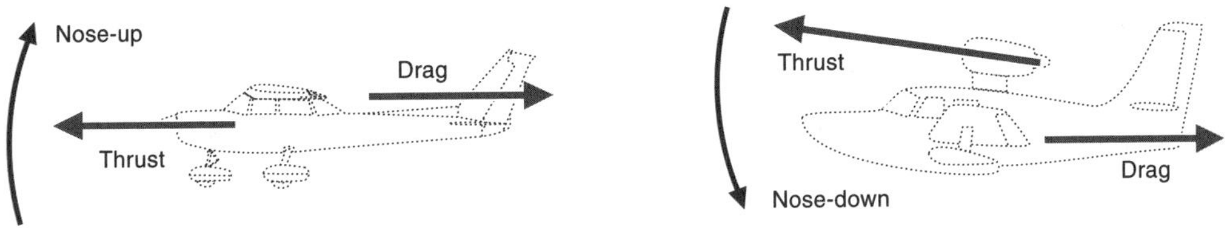

Figure 2-8 Thrust and drag form a pitching couple.

Ideally, the lines of action of the two couples are designed to be as shown in figure 2-9. With this arrangement the thrust–drag couple produces a nose-up pitching moment which approximately cancels the nose-down pitching moment of the lift–weight couple, and little or no elevator deflection or trim is required.

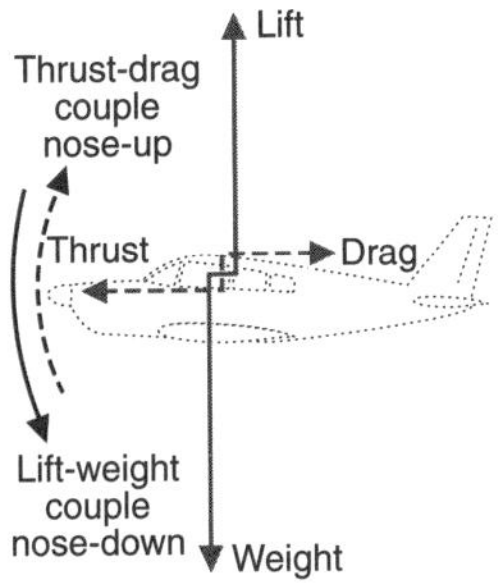

Figure 2-9 The lift–weight couple and the thrust–drag couple may be balanced.

There is a very good reason for the lift–weight couple to have a nose-down pitching moment balanced by the thrust–drag nose-up pitching moment. If thrust is lost after engine failure, the thrust–drag nose-up couple is weakened and therefore the lift–weight couple will pitch the airplane nose-down, without any action by the pilot. The airplane will then assume a glide attitude without a tendency to lose flying speed.

It is rare to have the sum of moments exactly zero. The force generated by the horizontal stabilizer and elevator provides the final balancing force.

The Horizontal Stabilizer

The horizontal stabilizer counteracts the residual pitching moments from the two main couples. It is simply an airfoil that can generate an aerodynamic force by being positioned at an angle of attack relative to the local airflow. The lift component of the aerodynamic force can act upward or downward as required by the pilot, and because of this the horizontal stabilizer usually has a symmetrical section.

If the residual moment from the four main forces is nose-down (as is most common), the horizontal stabilizer provides an aerodynamic force with a downward component on the tail section, which generates a nose-up pitching moment to balance the nose-down moment.

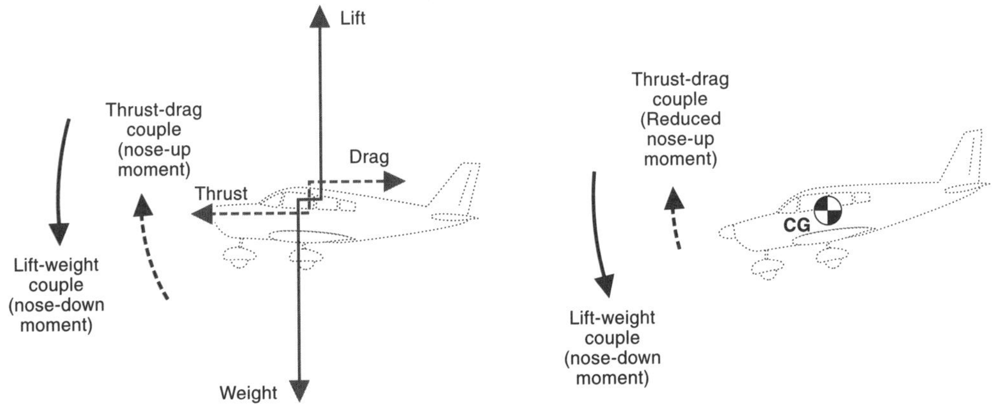

Figure 2-10 Following a loss of thrust the lift–weight couple pitches the airplane nose-down.

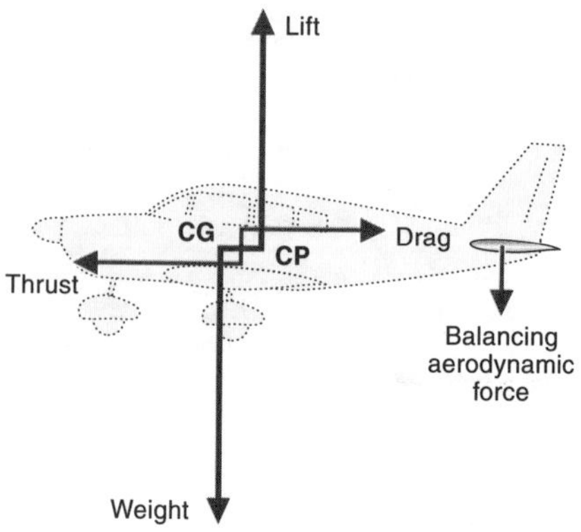

Figure 2-11
The horizontal stabilizer provides the final balancing moment.

Because the horizontal stabilizer is situated some distance from the center of gravity, its moment arm is quite long. The aerodynamic force provided by the horizontal stabilizer therefore needs only to be small to have a significant pitching effect. Consequently its size and aerodynamic capabilities are small compared with the wings.

Many airplanes are designed to operate most efficiently at cruise speed. By designing the couples to be at least in approximate equilibrium during the cruise, only small balancing aerodynamic forces are required from the horizontal stabilizer, thereby minimizing drag. Generally an airplane's center of pressure is designed to be aft of the center of gravity, with the horizontal stabilizer producing a small downward aerodynamic force.

The airplane will also pitch whenever the engine power setting is altered, because the speed of the slipstream over the horizontal stabilizer will change. When power is reduced, the slipstream over the horizontal stabilizer weakens, reducing the downward force and causing the nose to pitch down. Conversely, if the power is increased the slipstream over the horizontal stabilizer strengthens, increasing the downward force and causing the nose to pitch up. Therefore whenever power is changed you will need to retrim.

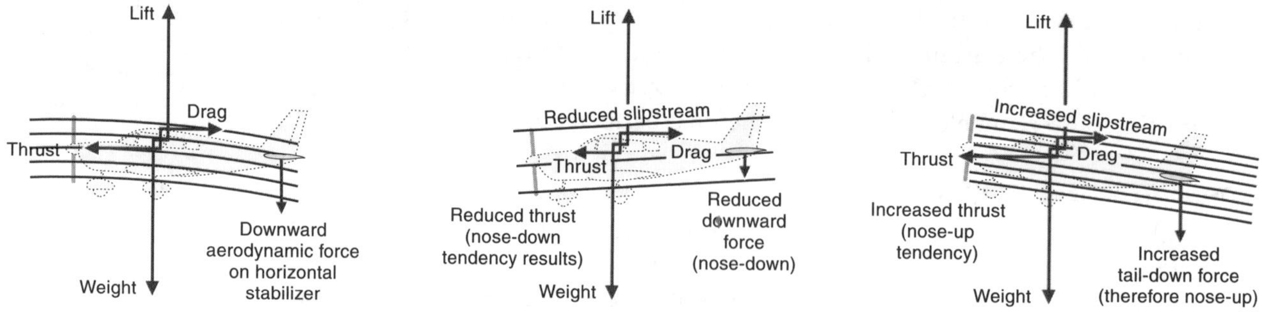

Figure 2-12 Propeller slipstream affects the force generated by the horizontal stabilizer.

Angular Movement

We may consider the motion of the airplane to occur about each of three reference axes. Each axis passes through the center of gravity and is mutually perpendicular, or at right angles, to the other two.

The *longitudinal axis* runs from front to rear through the center of gravity. Movement around the longitudinal axis is known as rolling. Stability around the longitudinal axis is known as *lateral stability*, because it is concerned with movement in the lateral or rolling plane. See figure 2-14. The *lateral axis* passes through the center of gravity across the airplane from one side to the other. Movement around the lateral axis is called pitching (nose-up or nose-down). Stability around the lateral axis is called *longitudinal stability*, because it is concerned with stability in the longitudinal or pitching plane. See figure 2-15. The *vertical axis* passes through the center of gravity and is perpendicular (normal) to the other two axes. Movement around the vertical axis is called yawing. Stability around the vertical axis is *directional stability*, because it is concerned with stability in the directional or yawing plane. See figure 2-16.

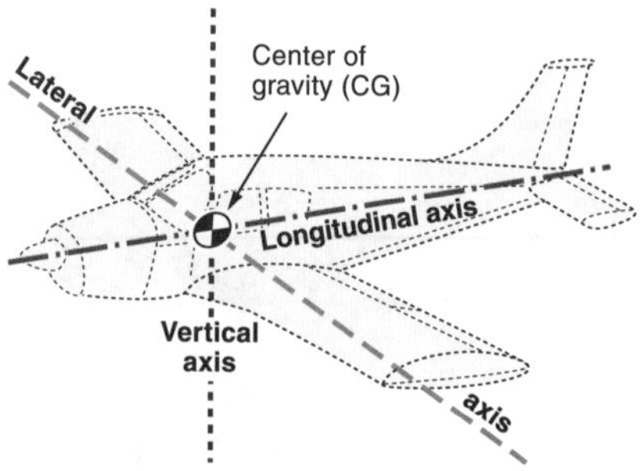

Figure 2-13
Angular movement can occur about three axes.

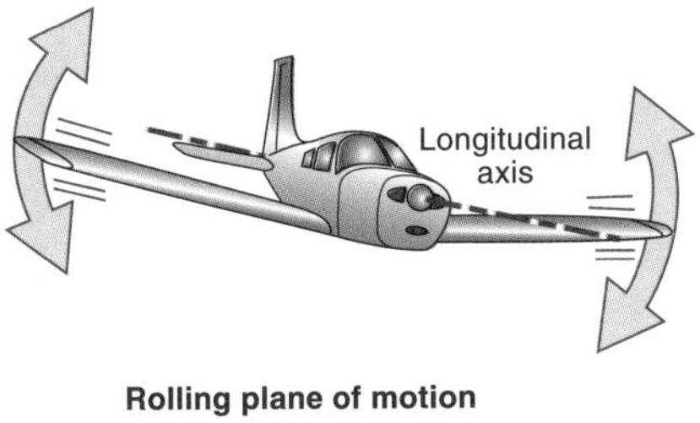

Figure 2-14
Rolling about the longitudinal axis.

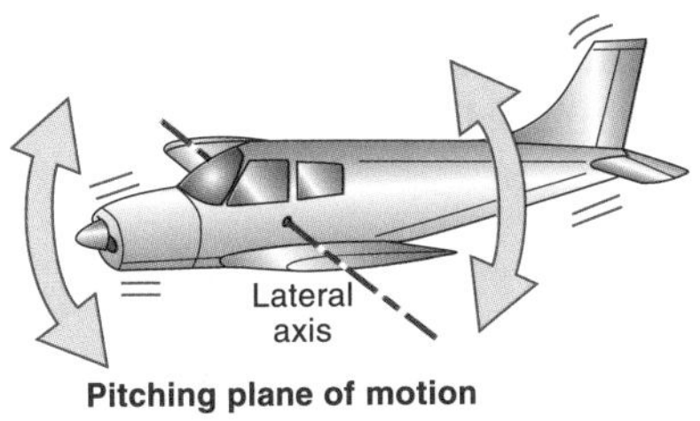

Figure 2-15
Pitching about the lateral axis.

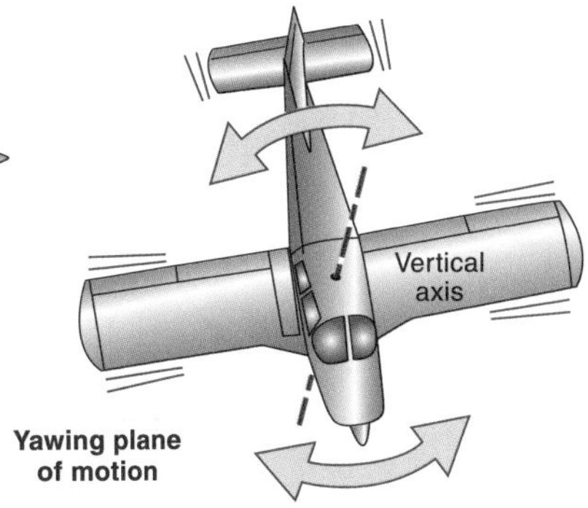

Figure 2-16
Yawing about the vertical axis.

Longitudinal Stability

Longitudinal stability is in the pitching plane and occurs about the lateral axis. To be longitudinally stable, an airplane must have a natural tendency to return to the same attitude in pitch after any disturbance. A longitudinally stable airplane tends to maintain the trimmed condition of flight and is therefore easy to fly in pitch.

The position of the center of gravity (CG) and the size of the horizontal stabilizer determines an airplane's longitudinal stability characteristics.

Let us consider a situation that is constantly occurring in flight, referring to figure 2-17. If a disturbance, such as a gust (1), changes the attitude of the airplane by pitching it nose-up, the airplane, because of its inertia, will initially continue on its original flight path and therefore present itself to the relative airflow at an increased angle of attack (2). This will cause the horizontal stabilizer to produce a greater upward force (or decreased downward force) than before the disturbance. The increased aerodynamic force acting about the CG will produce a nose-down pitching moment, causing the airplane to return to its original trimmed condition (3).

As shown in figure 2-18, the horizontal stabilizer has a similar stabilizing effect following an uninvited nose-down pitch. In this way changes in the horizontal stabilizer's aerodynamic force lead to longitudinal stability.

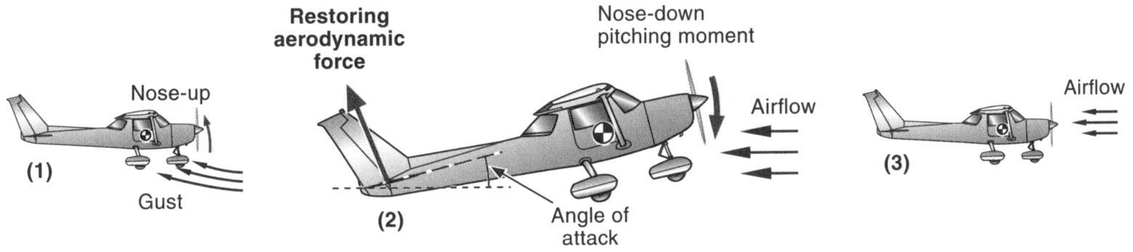

Figure 2-17
Longitudinal stability following an uninvited nose-up pitch.

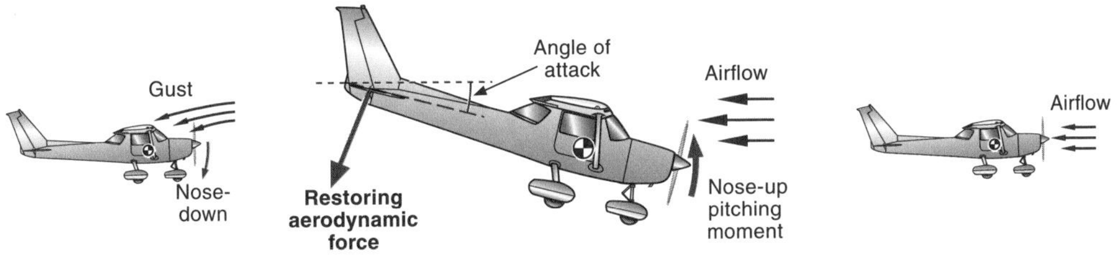

Figure 2-18
Longitudinal stability following an uninvited nose-down pitch.

A good example of the stabilizing effect of a horizontal stabilizer is the flight of a dart or an arrow through the air, where the tail feathers act as a horizontal stabilizer to maintain longitudinal stability.

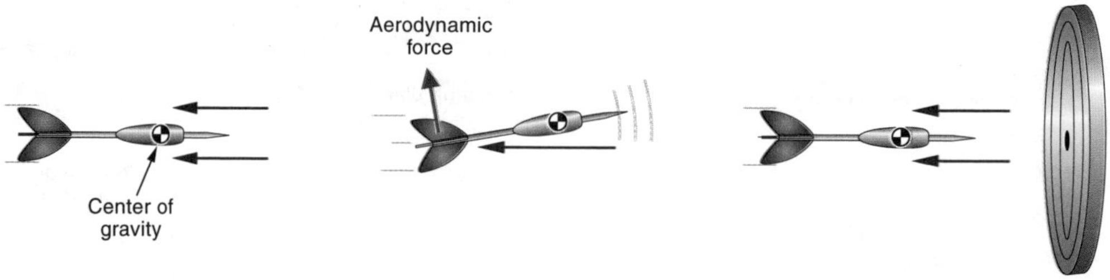

Figure 2-19 Longitudinal stability is provided by the tail feathers of a dart.

The CG and Longitudinal Stability

The longitudinal stability of an airplane is determined by the size of the horizontal stabilizer and its distance from the airplane's CG. The pilot has a lot of control over the CG position when the airplane is being loaded. The further forward the CG, the greater the moment arm of the horizontal stabilizer, and therefore the greater the leverage effect of the horizontal stabilizer aerodynamic force, and the greater the horizontal stability.

Limits are laid down for the range within which the CG must be located for safe flight. You must always load your airplane so that the actual CG position falls within the allowable CG range. If the CG is *behind* the legally allowable aft (rear) limit, the restoring moment of the horizontal stabilizer in pitch may be insufficient for satisfactory longitudinal stability, and the airplane may be difficult, or even impossible to control. The further *forward* the CG, the greater the longitudinal stability.

Also, the more stable the airplane, the greater the control force you must exert to maneuver it, which can become tiring. If the CG is even further forward, beyond the allowable limit, the elevator may not be sufficiently effective at low speeds to flare the nose-heavy airplane for landing.

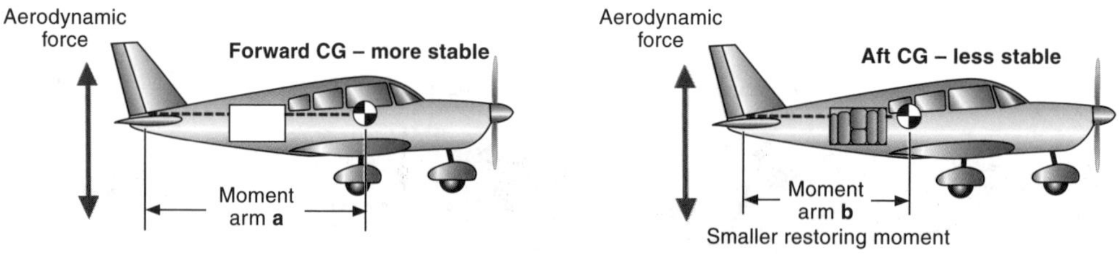

Figure 2-20 A forward CG—greater longitudinal stability.

Design Considerations

Tailplane design features are very important to longitudinal stability. Horizontal stabilizer area, distance from the center of gravity, aspect ratio, angle of incidence, and *longitudinal dihedral* are considered by the designer. The aim is to generate a restoring force that is effective because of a long moment arm, leading to an airplane that is longitudinally stable.

At high angles of attack the wing may shield the horizontal stabilizer or cause the airflow over it to be turbulent, decreasing longitudinal stability.

Note. *Longitudinal dihedral* is the difference between the angle of incidence of the wing and the normally smaller angle of incidence of the horizontal stabilizer.

Directional Stability

Directional stability of an airplane is its natural tendency to recover from a disturbance in the yawing plane about the vertical axis. It refers to an airplane's ability to weathercock or weathervane its nose into any airflow from the side.

If the airplane is disturbed from its straight path by the nose or tail being pushed to one side (yawed) by turbulence or by the pilot, then, because of its inertia, the airplane will initially keep moving in the original direction.

The airplane will now be moving somewhat sideways through the air, with its side surfaces, or keel surfaces, exposed to the relative wind.

The vertical stabilizer is a symmetrical airfoil. As it is now positioned at an angle of attack to the relative airflow, it will generate a sideways aerodynamic force that acts about the CG and yaws the airplane back to its original position.

The position of the CG and size of the vertical stabilizer (fin) determine the directional stability. The greater the vertical stabilizer area and keel surface area behind the CG, and the greater the moment arm, the greater the directional stability of the airplane. Therefore, the further *forward* the CG, the greater the directional stability.

As well as being caused by turbulence, a yawing effect will also result from power changes, which cause changes in the slipstream over the vertical stabilizer and can lead to large changes in rudder requirements.

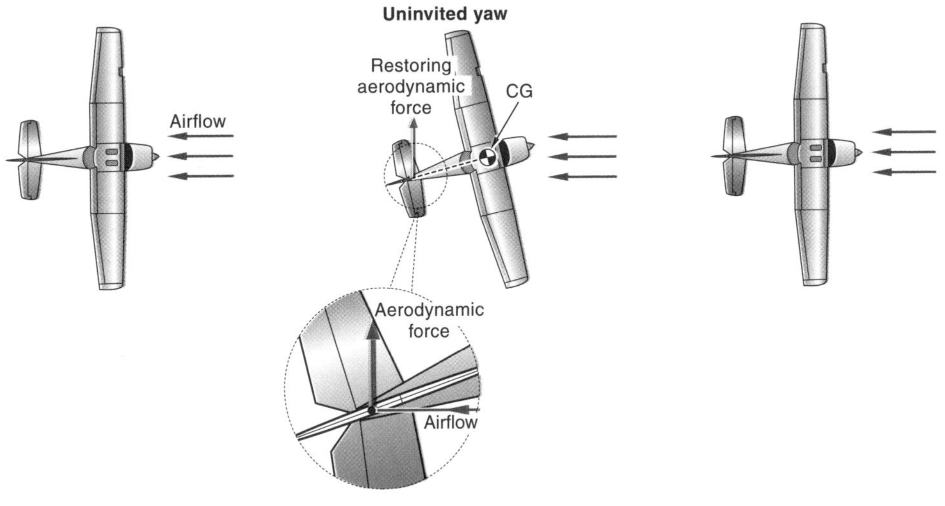

Figure 2-21 Directional stability following an uninvited yaw.

Lateral Stability

Lateral stability is the natural ability of the airplane to recover from a disturbance in the lateral plane (that is, rolling about the longitudinal axis) without any pilot input.

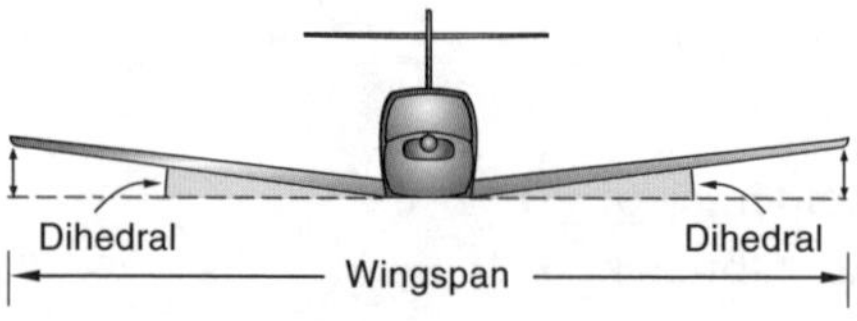

Figure 2-22
Wing dihedral.

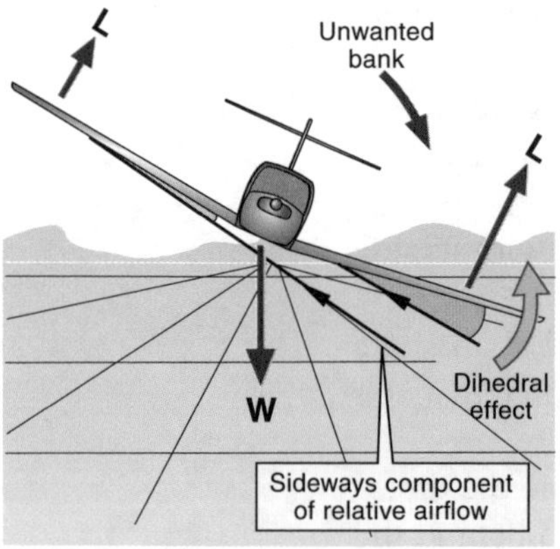

Figure 2-23
Dihedral corrects an uninvited roll.

Wing Dihedral

The wings can add lateral stability to an airplane if they have *dihedral*—a design feature where each wing is inclined upward from the fuselage to the wingtips. When an airplane is disturbed in roll, the lift force is inclined and causes the airplane to *sideslip*. This sideslip combines a sideways and downward motion, which results in the relative airflow having a small upward and sideways component, as shown in figure 2-23.

As the airplane sideslips, the lower wing, because of its dihedral, will meet the upcoming relative airflow at a larger angle of attack and produce increased lift. The upper wing will meet the relative airflow at a smaller angle of attack and will produce less lift. The upper wing may also be shielded somewhat by the fuselage, causing even less lift to be generated. The rolling moment so produced will tend to return the airplane to its original wings-level position.

Negative dihedral, or *anhedral* (where the wing is inclined downward from the fuselage) has a destabilizing effect and is used when an airplane would otherwise be too stable (more difficult to maneuver).

Wing Sweepback and Lateral Stability

The wing can increase lateral stability if it has sweepback. As the airplane sideslips following a disturbance in roll, the lower sweptback wing generates more lift than the upper wing. This is because in the sideslip the lower wing presents more of its span to the airflow than the upper wing. Therefore the lower wing generates more lift and tends to restore the airplane to a wings-level position.

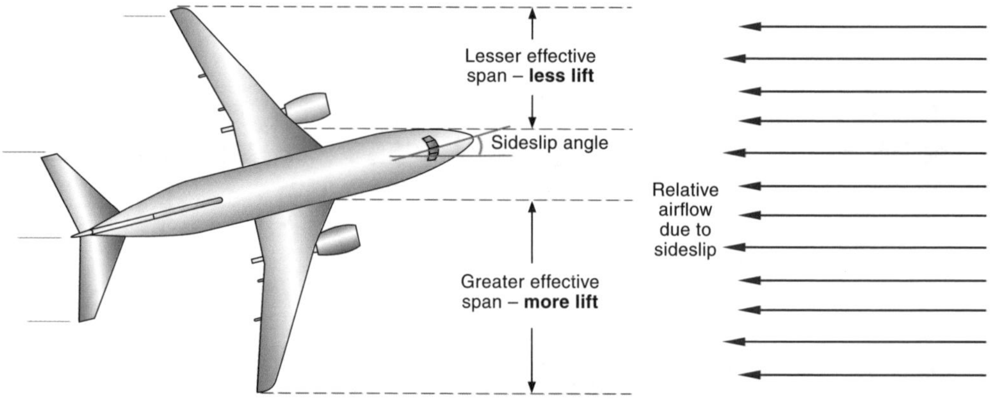

Figure 2-24 Sweepback corrects uninvited roll.

High Keel Surfaces and Low CG

In the sideslip that follows a disturbance in roll, a high sideways drag line caused by high keel surfaces (high vertical stabilizer, a T-tail high on the vertical stabilizer, or high wings) and a low CG will give a restoring moment tending to raise the lower wing and return the airplane to the original wings-level position. See figure 2-25.

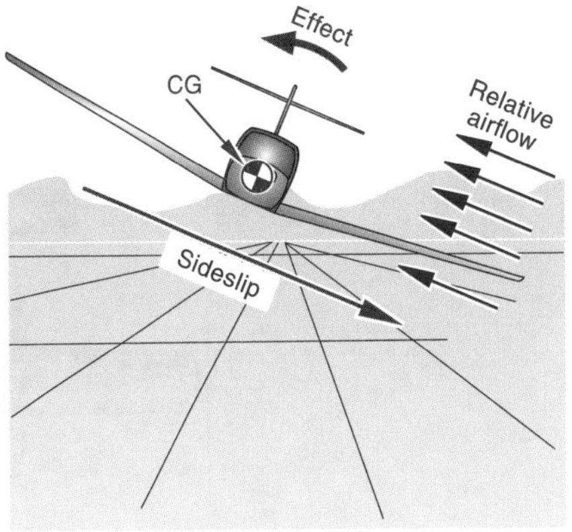

Figure 2-25
High keel surfaces and a low CG correct uninvited roll.

High-Wing Airplanes

If a wind gust causes a wing to drop, the lift force is tilted, and the airplane will sideslip. The airflow striking the upper keel surfaces, including the high wings, will tend to return the airplane to the wings-level condition.

The increased stability of a high-wing airplane also comes from the pendulum effect when the airplane rolls. The CG is displaced from vertically beneath the CP and so a couple is established which tends to roll the airplane wings-level. Conversely, a low wing, below the airplane's CG, will be unstable. This is apparent when observing the difference in dihedrals of high- and low-wing airplanes.

High-wing airplanes have more lateral stability (by virtue of their wing position) than low-wing airplanes. If the high wing also has sweepback, it may require zero or even negative dihedral to achieve the required lateral stability. The McDonnell Douglas C-17, Lockheed C-141 Starlifter and British Aerospace 146 regional airliner are examples of high-wing airplanes with negative dihedral.

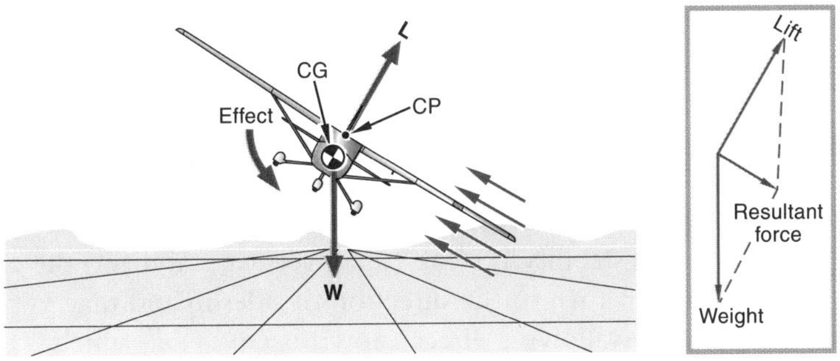

Figure 2-26 A high wing tends to level the wings.

Lateral and Directional Stability Together

Roll Followed by Yaw

A roll is always followed by yaw. For lateral stability it is essential to have the sideslip that the disturbance in roll causes. This sideslip exerts a force on the side or keel surfaces of the airplane, which, if the airplane is directionally stable, will cause it to yaw its nose into the relative airflow. The roll causes a yaw in the direction of the sideslip and the airplane will turn further from its original heading in the direction of the lower wing.

Note this interesting consequence: the greater the directional stability of the airplane, the greater the tendency to turn away from the original heading in the direction of the lower wing when the airplane is banked.

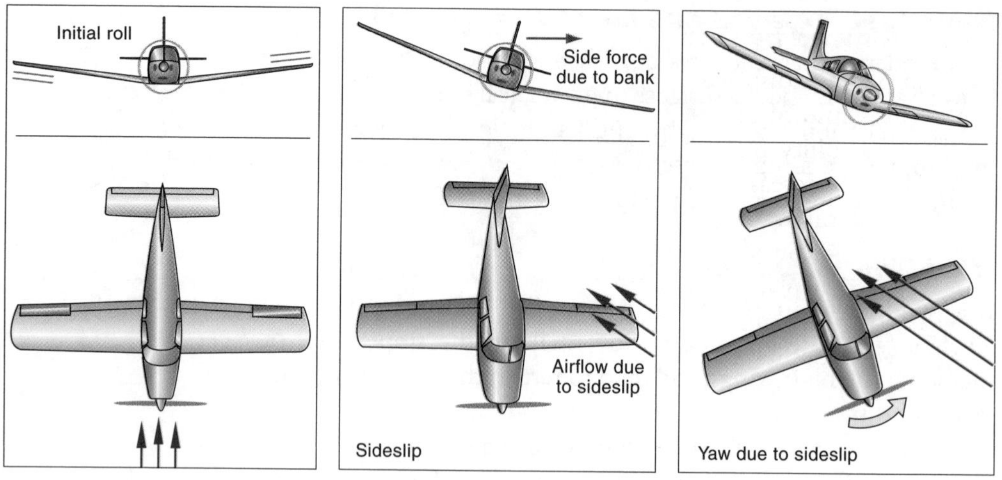

Figure 2-27 Roll causes yaw.

The lateral stability characteristics of the airplane, such as those resulting from wing dihedral, cause the lower wing to produce increased lift and to return the airplane to the wings-level position. There are two effects in conflict here.

1. The directionally stable characteristics (large vertical stabilizer) want to steepen the turn and drop the nose farther.
2. The laterally stable characteristics (dihedral) want to level the wings.

If the first effect wins, with directional stability overriding lateral stability, (large vertical stabilizer and no dihedral), then the airplane will tend to bank farther into the sideslip, toward the lower wing, with the nose continuing to drop, until the airplane is in a spiral dive (and all this without any input from the pilot). This is called *spiral instability*.

Most airplanes are designed with only weak positive lateral stability and have a slight tendency toward spiral instability. This is preferable to Dutch roll (see figure 2-28).

If the lateral stability (dihedral) is stronger, the airplane will right itself to wings-level, and if the directional stability is weak (small vertical stabilizer) the airplane may have shown no tendency to turn in the direction of sideslip and may even turn away from the sideslip, causing a wallowing effect known as *Dutch roll*, which is best avoided.

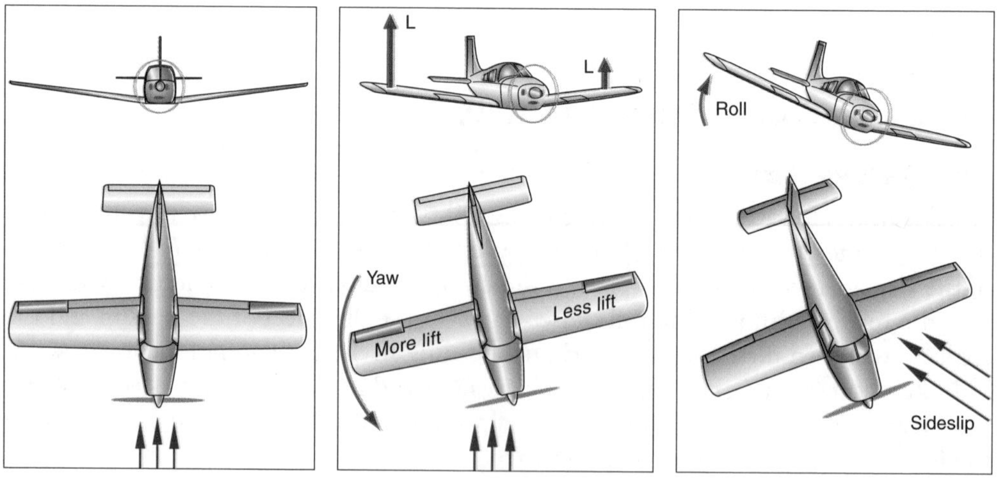

Figure 2-28 Yaw causes roll.

Yaw Followed by Roll

If the airplane is displaced in yaw, it will initially continue in the original direction of flight because of its inertia, and therefore enter a sideslip. This sideslip will cause the lateral stability features of the airplane's wing such as dihedral, sweepback, or a high-wing, to increase lift on the forward wing and decrease lift on the trailing wing. This causes a rolling moment that will tend to raise the forward wing, resulting in the airplane rolling toward the trailing wing and away from the sideslip. Yaw causes roll.

Also, as the airplane is actually yawing, the outer wing will move faster and produce more lift than the inner wing, giving a tendency to roll toward the inner wing. The aircraft then sideslips due to bank. The airplane's inherent directional stability (from the vertical stabilizer) will tend to weathercock or yaw the airplane in the direction of the sideslip.

Stability on the Ground

On the ground, the center of gravity (CG) of an airplane must lie somewhere in the area between the three wheels at all times. The farther away the CG is from any one wheel, the less the tendency for the airplane to tip over that wheel.

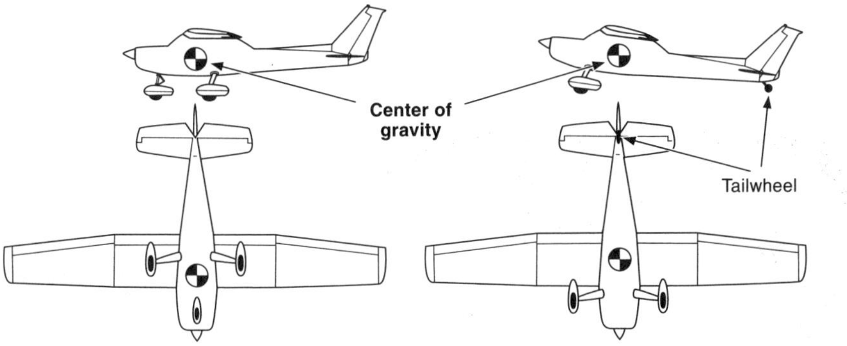

Figure 2-29 The CG must remain within the area bounded by the wheels.

A low CG and widely spaced wheels reduces the tendency for the airplane to tip over on the ground when turning, braking the airplane, or when applying high power on takeoff.

A low thrust-line reduces the tendency for an airplane to pitch over on its nose when high power is applied (especially with brakes on). High keel surfaces and dihedral allow crosswinds to have a greater destabilizing effect.

You move in a straight line on the ground by using the rudder pedals to maintain directional control and using the control wheel to prevent any crosswind from lifting the upwind wing. This is covered in chapter 9.

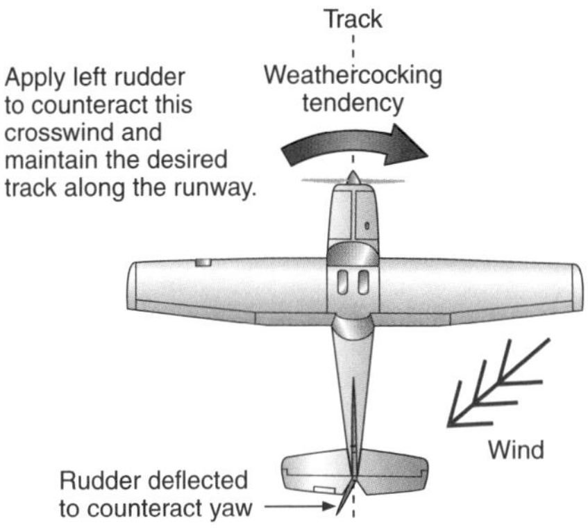

Figure 2-30 A destabilizing crosswind.

Control

All airplanes have a flight control system to allow the pilot to maneuver the airplane in flight about each of the three axes. Airplanes normally have three *primary control* circuits, each one is equipped with its own control surface(s):

- *elevators* for longitudinal (pitch) control, operated by forward and rearward movement of the control wheel or stick;
- *ailerons* for lateral (roll) control, operated by rotation of the control wheel or by sideways movement of the control stick; and
- *rudder* for directional (yaw) control, operated by movement of the two interconnected rudder pedals.

Ideally, each set of control surfaces should produce a moment about only one axis, but in practice *secondary* moments about other axes are often produced as well. For example, if an airplane yaws it will then start to roll.

The control surfaces work by deflecting airflow and changing the pressure distribution over the whole airfoil, not just over the control surface itself. The effect is to change the aerodynamic force produced by the total airfoil—control surface combination. The effectiveness of moving these control surfaces will partially determine the airplane's maneuverability. As mentioned earlier, an airplane with too much stability is very resistant to change and has poor maneuverability. Excessive stability opposes maneuverability.

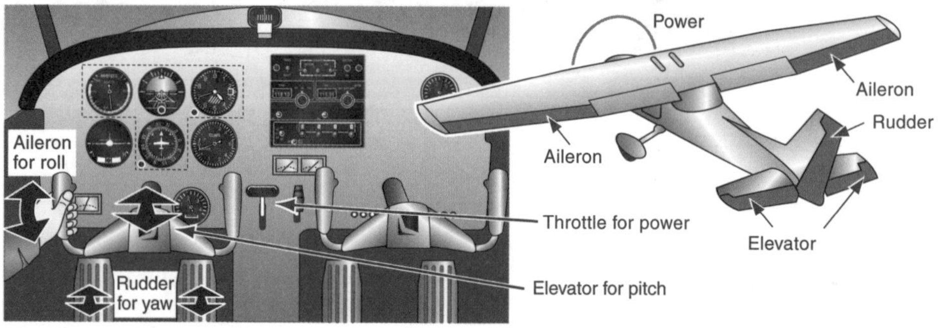

Figure 2-31 The primary flight controls: elevator, ailerons, and rudder.

The Elevator

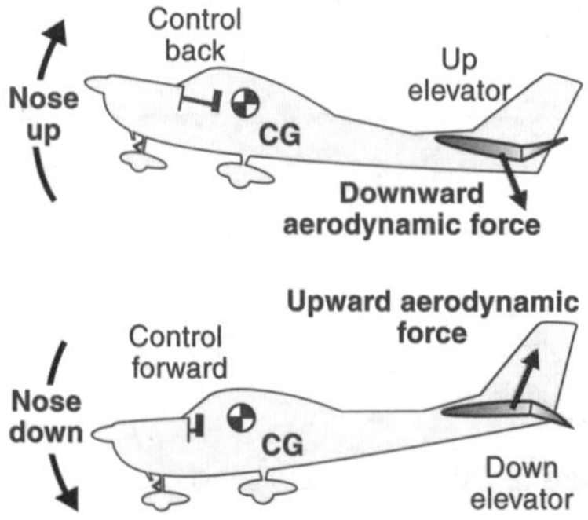

Figure 2-32
The elevator is the primary pitching control.

The pilot controls the elevator by forward and rearward movement of the control column. A forward movement of the control column moves the elevator down which has the effect of pushing the nose of the airplane down. Rearward movement of the control column moves the elevator up, which has the effect of pulling the nose of the airplane up. These movements will become logical and instinctive to you.

When the control wheel is moved forward, the elevator moves down and the horizontal stabilizer section becomes cambered so that it provides an upward aerodynamic force. This creates an upward force on the tail section of the airplane and a moment about the airplane's CG that moves the nose down. A further effect of pitching the nose down with the elevator is a gradual increase in airspeed. When the control wheel is pulled back, the elevator moves up and an extra downward aerodynamic force is produced by the horizontal stabilizer airfoil, causing the nose of the airplane to move up. The strength of the tail moment depends on the force produced by it and the length of the moment arm between it and the CG.

CG Position

If the CG is too far forward, the airplane will be too longitudinally stable. If the CG is too far aft the airplane will be longitudinally unstable.

To retain satisfactory handling characteristics and elevator effectiveness throughout the airplane's entire speed range, the position of the CG must be kept within the prescribed range. If the *CG is too far forward*, the airplane will be too longitudinally stable because of the long moment arm to the horizontal stabilizer. Even with the control column pulled fully back there will be insufficient up-elevator to reach the high angles of attack and low speeds sometimes required in maneuvers such as flying slowly, taking off and landing. Therefore, the *forward allowable CG limit* is determined by the amount of pitch control available from the elevator. The *aft (rear) limit of the CG* is determined by the requirement for longitudinal stability.

Usually, the most critical situation for a nose-up requirement is in the flare and landing. A forward CG makes the airplane nose-heavy and resistant to changes in pitch. This may make it difficult to raise the nose during a landing, especially since the elevator will be less effective because of the reduced airflow over it due both to the slow landing speed and weak propeller slipstream (low power).

The Stabilator

Some designers combine the horizontal stabilizer and elevator into one airfoil and have the whole tailplane movable. A combined horizontal stabilizer/elevator combination is called a *stabilator*. Other terms include all-moving tail, all-flying tail and slab tail. When the control column is moved the entire slab moves. Forward movement of the control column increases the angle of attack of the stabilator, thereby generating a force that causes the tail to rise). Some airplanes have a V-tail (butterfly tail), which combines the functions of the elevator and rudder.

Figure 2-33
A butterfly tail (early Beech Bonanza model).

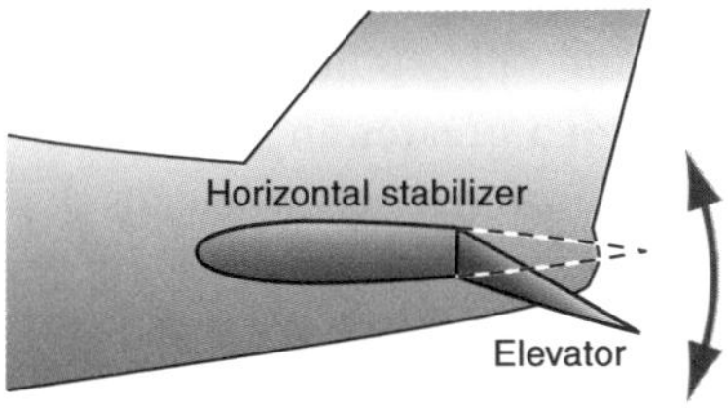

Figure 2-34
Seperate horizontal stabilizer and elevator.

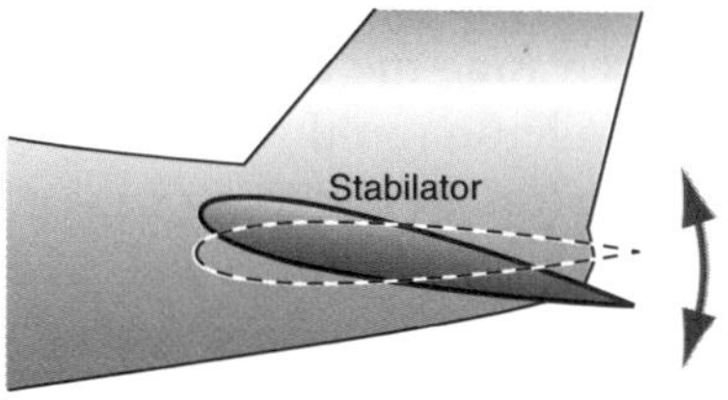

Figure 2-35
Stabilator.

The Ailerons

The primary control in roll is provided by the ailerons.

The ailerons are positioned on the outboard trailing edges of the wings. The ailerons act in opposing senses, one goes up as the other goes down, so that the lift generated by one wing increases and the lift generated by the other wing decreases. The pilot operates the ailerons with rotation of the control wheel or sideways movement of the control stick. A resultant rolling moment is exerted on the airplane. The magnitude of this rolling moment depends on the distance the ailerons are from the airplane's CG (fixed at construction), and the magnitude of the differing lift forces (determined by the degree of aileron deflection and airspeed). Note that the aileron on the up-going wing is deflected downward. Conversely, the aileron on the down-going wing is deflected upward.

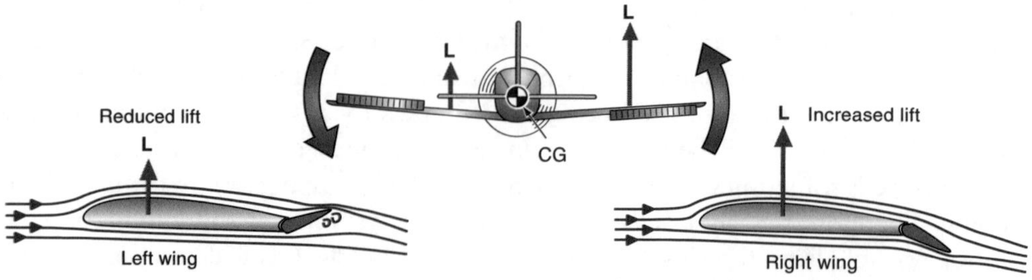

Figure 2-36 The ailerons—one up, one down—provide a rolling moment.

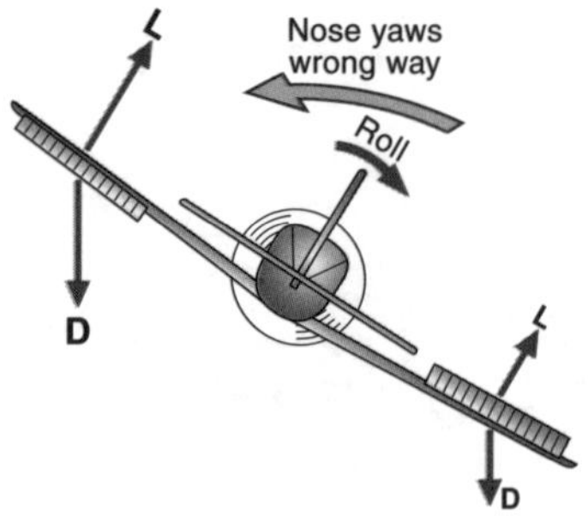

Figure 2-37 The rising wing has increased aileron drag, causing adverse yaw effect.

Adverse Yaw Effect

Adverse yaw effect is caused by differential aileron drag. Deflecting an aileron down causes an effective increase in the camber of that wing section and an increase in the effective angle of attack. The lift from that wing increases, but unfortunately so does the drag. As the other aileron rises, the effective camber of that wing section is decreased and its angle of attack is less, therefore lift and drag from that wing are decreased. The differing lift causes the airplane to bank one way, but the differential aileron drag causes it to yaw the other way. This is known as *aileron drag* or *adverse yaw effect* and is mainly a low airspeed problem that you would most notice during a turn entry at low speed shortly after takeoff or on final approach.

Adverse yaw effect can be reduced by differential ailerons, Frise-type ailerons, or interconnecting the rudder to the ailerons.

Differential ailerons overcome adverse yaw effect.

Differential Ailerons. Differential ailerons are designed to minimize adverse yaw effect by increasing the drag on the down-going wing. This is achieved by deflecting the upward aileron (on the descending wing) through a greater angle than the down-going aileron (on the up-going wing). The greater aileron deflection means that drag is increased on the down-going wing, reducing (but not eliminating) the adverse yaw. The remaining unwanted yaw can be removed with rudder.

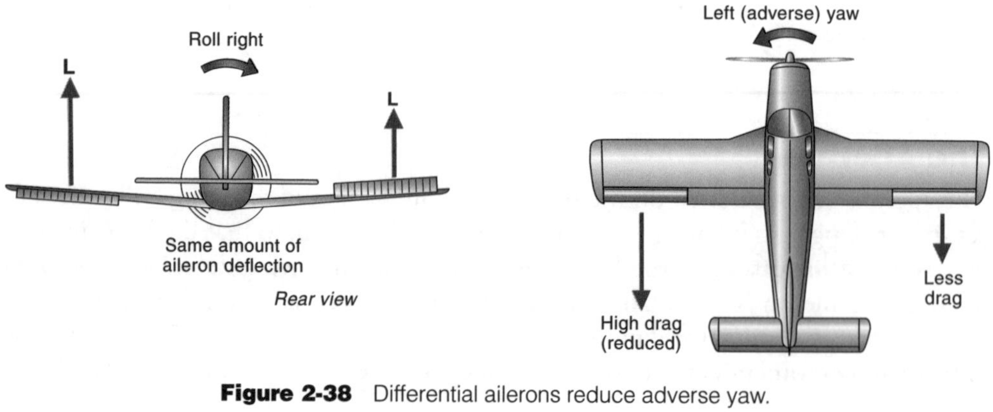

Figure 2-38 Differential ailerons reduce adverse yaw.

Frise-Type Ailerons. Frise-type ailerons are shaped so that the drag from the descending wing is increased. The leading edge of the Frise aileron on the down-going wing protrudes into the airstream beneath wthe wing causing increased drag on the down-going wing. The leading edge of the up-going aileron does not protrude into the airstream, causing no extra drag. Frise-type ailerons also can be designed to operate differentially, thereby combining both effects.

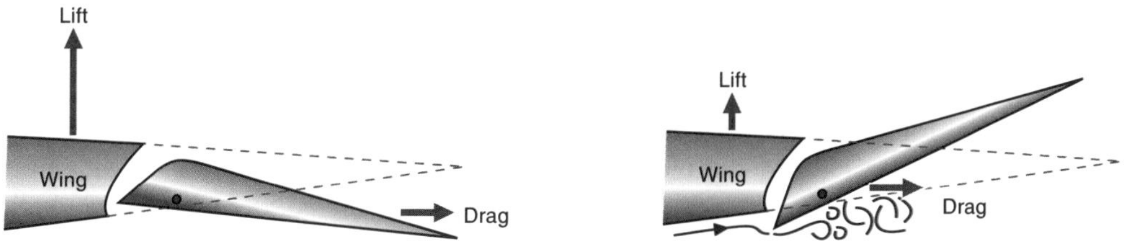

Figure 2-39 Frise-type ailerons equalize aileron drag and reduce adverse yaw.

Interconnected Ailerons and Rudder. Interconnected ailerons and rudder cause the rudder to move automatically and yaw the airplane into the bank, opposing the adverse yaw from the ailerons. The primary effect of the ailerons is to roll the airplane, and the secondary effect is to yaw it. The primary effect of the rudder is to yaw the airplane, and the secondary effect is to roll it. Using the rudder to neutralize adverse yaw, with the ailerons deflected and the airplane rolling is one of the most important elements of airplane control by the pilot.

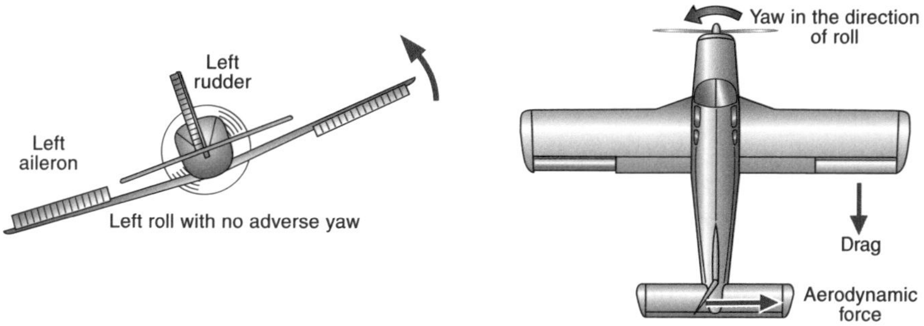

Figure 2-40 Aileron/rudder interconnect can reduce adverse yaw.

The Rudder

To control and eliminate unwanted yaw, the airplane has a rudder. The rudder does not turn the airplane, it yaws it, which by itself, does not cause any change in flight path direction. By pushing the left rudder pedal, the rudder will move left. This alters the vertical stabilizer–rudder airfoil section and a sideways aerodynamic force is created that moves the tail to the right and yaws the airplane to the left about the vertical axis. Left rudder—the airplane yaws left.

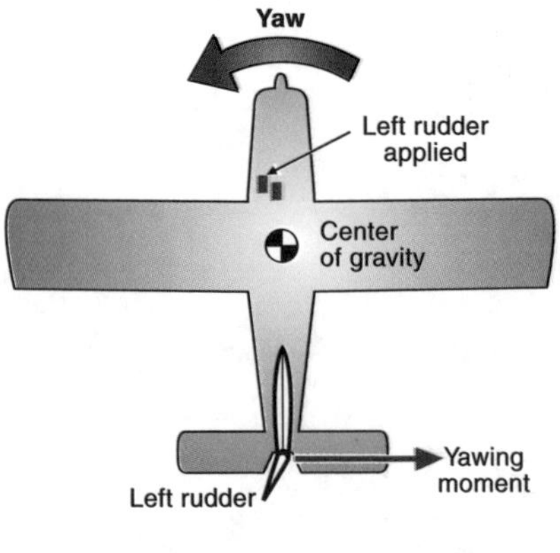

Figure 2-41 Left rudder pressure—the nose yaws left.

Rudder effectiveness increases with airspeed, so large rudder deflections at low airspeeds and small deflections at high airspeeds are required to gain the same effect. In propeller-driven airplanes, any propeller *slipstream* flowing over the rudder increases rudder effectiveness.

Yaw Is Followed by Roll

The primary effect of rudder is to yaw the airplane. This causes the outer wing to speed up, generate increased lift, and cause the airplane to roll.

When it has begun to yaw, the airplane will continue on its original flight path for a brief period because of inertia. Any dihedral on the forward wing will cause it to be presented to the airflow at a greater angle of attack and therefore generate more lift. Consequently, having first yawed the airplane, the secondary effect of the rudder is to cause a roll.

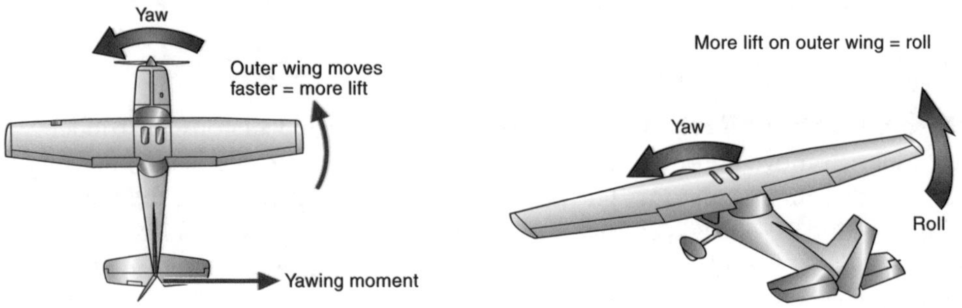

Figure 2-42 Yaw is followed by roll.

Control Effectiveness

The size and shape of a control surface and its moment about the center of gravity primarily determine its effectiveness. Since the size and shape are fixed by the designer, and the CG (with the airplane loaded within limits) only moves a small amount, they can all be considered constant.

The variables in control effectiveness are *airspeed* and *control deflection*. For a given amount of control deflection, if the airspeed is doubled, the effect is squared ($2 \times 2 = 4$), so it quadruples. If the airspeed is halved, the same control surface deflection is only one-fourth as effective. Therefore, at low airspeeds, achieving a nominal change in attitude requires a much greater control-surface deflection but the forces are lighter (often referred to as *sloppy controls* or *less powerful controls*).

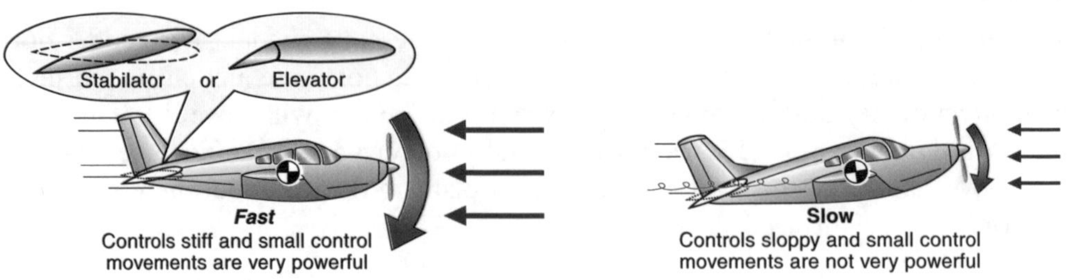

Figure 2-43 The controls are more powerful with increased airflow.

Slipstream Effect

Any factor that increases the speed of the airflow over a control surface will make it more effective. Such an increase in airflow does not necessarily have to be achieved by an increase in the airplane's forward speed. For instance, with high engine power set, the propeller slipstream (or *propwash*) of a single-engine airplane will flow strongly back over the empennage, making the elevators and rudder more effective, even at low airspeeds.

Approaching the stall with power on, the elevator and rudder will be more effective than the ailerons, because of the propeller slipstream flowing over them. The slipstream helps when taxiing single-engine tailwheel airplanes because power application increases rudder effectiveness.

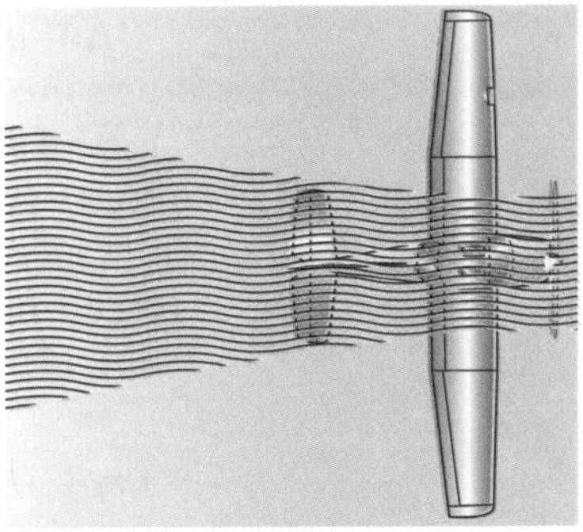

Figure 2-44 The slipstream only affects the elevator and rudder.

Control Forces Felt by the Pilot

When a control surface is deflected, the aerodynamic force produced by the control surface itself opposes its own deflection. This causes a moment to act on the control surface about its hinge line trying to return the control surface to its original faired (streamlined) position, and the pilot must overcome this to maintain the selected position. The pilot feels this as *stick force.*

Aerodynamic Balances

The *stick force* (the amount of control force a pilot feels) depends on the turning moment at the hinge line of the control surface and the means by which the control wheel is linked to the control surface. If the control surface is hinged at its leading edge and trails from this position in flight, the stick forces required will be high, especially in heavy or fast airplanes. These forces can be made smaller by the designer adding an *aerodynamic balance,* which reduces the stick load on the pilot.

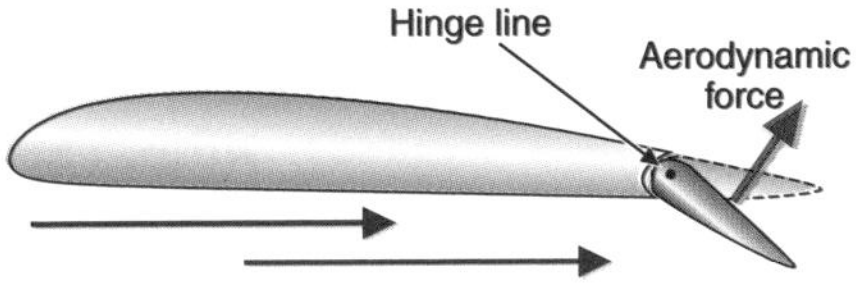

Figure 2-45
Hinge moment at the control surface.

The designer may use an *inset hinge,* a *horn balance,* or a *balance tab* to provide an aerodynamic force during control surface deflection that partially balances or reduces the hinge moment. The aerodynamic balance of a control surface is designed to reduce the control forces required from the pilot. The designer, however, must be careful not to over-balance the controls, otherwise the pilot will lose the important sense of feel.

An aerodynamic balance on a control reduces the stick load on the pilot.

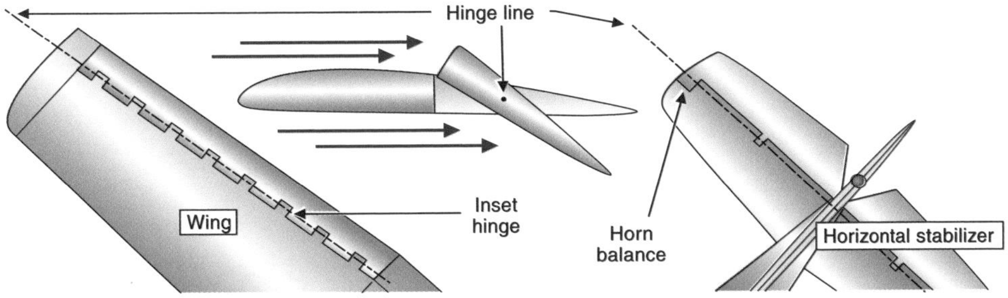

Figure 2-46 Inset hinge balance (at left) and horn balance (at right).

An *inset hinge* reduces the distance from the hinge line to the control's center of pressure, which reduces the moment that the pilot feels as stick load. In addition, the part of the control ahead of the hinge protrudes into the airflow causing a balancing moment which assists the pilot by reducing the stick load.

On conventional tailplanes, the elevator may have a *balance tab* incorporated. It is mechanically connected to the elevator by a linkage that causes it to move in the opposite direction.

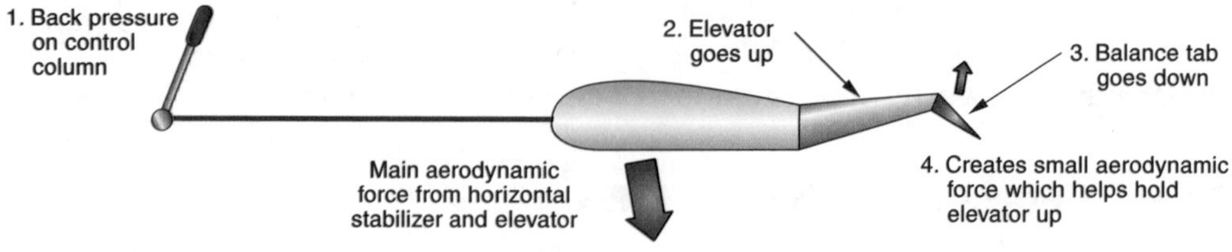

Figure 2-47 The balance tab.

If the pilot exerts back pressure on the control wheel, the elevator is raised and the balance tab goes down. The elevator balance tab unit now generates a small upward aerodynamic force that acts to hold the elevator up, thereby reducing the control effort required from the pilot.

> **Note.** The balance tab acts automatically as the elevator moves. This movement should be checked during the preflight inspection by moving the elevator one way and noting that the tab moves the other way.

Anti-Balance Tab

An anti-balance tab increases the control force on the pilot to prevent overcontrolling.

Airplanes fitted with a stabilator often have an *anti-balance tab* (sometimes referred to as an *anti-servo tab*) to increase control forces at higher airspeeds to reduce possible over-stress when maneuvering. Because of their combined function, stabilators have a much larger area than elevators and so produce a more powerful response to control input. Small movements can produce large aerodynamic forces. To prevent you from moving the stabilator too far and overcontrolling the airplane (especially at high airspeeds), stabilators are often designed with anti-balance tabs.

An anti-balance tab moves in the *same* direction as the stabilator's trailing edge and generates an aerodynamic force that makes it harder to move the stabilator further, as well as providing feel for the pilot.

Figure 2-48 Anti-balance tab on stabilator.

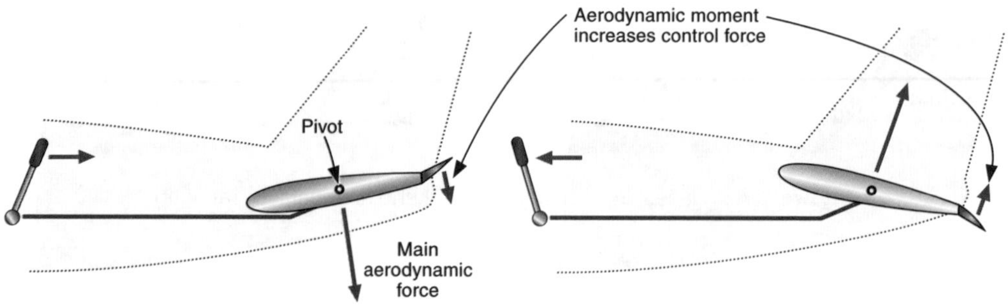

Figure 2-49 The anti-balance tab opposes further control deflection and provides feel.

Correct operation of the anti-balance tab can be checked during the preflight inspection by moving the trailing edge of the stabilator and noting that the anti-balance tab moves in the same direction.

Trim Tabs

Trim tabs are designed to remove the stick load on the pilot.

An airplane is "in trim" in pitch, roll, or yaw when it maintains a constant attitude without the pilot having to exert any steady pressure on the particular control surface. An airplane that you have trimmed properly is far more pleasant to fly than an untrimmed airplane. It requires control inputs only to maneuver and not to maintain an attitude or heading. The function of the *trim tab* is to reduce the moment at the hinge line of the control surface to approximately zero, so that the present condition of flight can be maintained hands-off.

Almost all airplanes have an elevator trim, many light single-engine and all multi-engine airplanes have a rudder trim, and more sophisticated airplanes also have an aileron trim. Trim tabs can differ in complexity. Some are metal strips that can only be altered on the ground, or springs that can apply a load to the control column. Other trim tabs can be operated from the cockpit by the pilot, usually by a trim wheel or trim handle (this may be mechanical or electrical). Airplanes with stabilators may have the elevator trim incorporated so that trimming moves the entire slab.

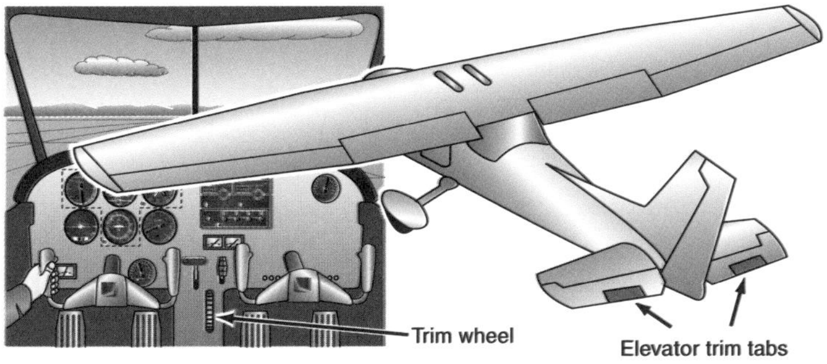

Figure 2-50 An elevator trim tab.

Mass Balancing

A mass balance prevents flutter.

At high speeds some control surfaces have a tendency to flutter. This is a vibration that results from the changes in pressure distribution over the surface as its angle of attack is altered. If part of the airframe structure starts to vibrate—control surfaces are particularly susceptible to this—then these oscillations can quickly reach structurally damaging proportions. To avoid this flutter, the designer may need to alter the mass distribution of the surface.

The *mass balance* is placed forward of the hinge line to bring the CG of the control surface up to the hinge line or even slightly ahead of it. On the inset hinge or horn balance this mass can easily be incorporated in that part ahead of the hinge line, but on others the mass must be placed on an arm that extends forward of the hinge line. The distribution of mass on control surfaces is an important design consideration. The aim of mass balancing is not for the control to be balanced in the sense of remaining level, but to alter the mass distribution of the control to avoid flutter or vibration.

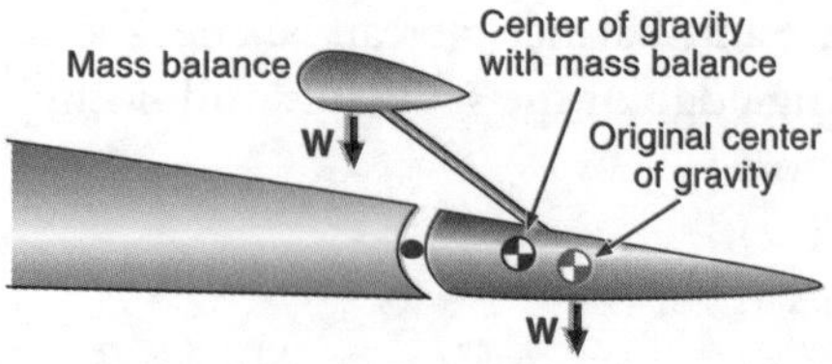

Figure 2-51 A mass balance moves the control's CG forward to prevent flutter.

Control on the Ground

Directional control on the ground is achieved by use of the rudder, nosewheel steering (which may be connected to the rudder pedals), power, and brakes. Airflow over the rudder increases its effectiveness. Use of the controls on the ground is covered in chapter 9.

Review 2
Stability and Control

Stability

1. Following a disturbance, an airplane that returns to its original position unassisted by the pilot is said to be inherently stable. Is this sort of airplane easier to fly?
2. If the center of pressure is behind the center of gravity, what sort of pitching moment will the lift–weight couple have?
3. If the thrust line is lower than the drag line, what sort of pitching moment will the thrust–drag couple have?
4. In questions 2 and 3, if there was a sudden loss of thrust, what would the nose do?
5. Where is the center of pressure in relation to the center of gravity in most training airplanes?
6. What sort of aerodynamic force does the horizontal stabilizer produce?
7. When power is reduced, what will the reduced propeller slipstream and reduced downwash over the horizontal stabilizer cause the nose to do?
8. Longitudinal stability refers to the motion of the airplane about its:
   a. longitudinal axis.
   b. lateral axis.
   c. vertical axis (sometimes called the *normal axis*).
9. What is rotation about the lateral axis known as?
10. What is rotation about the vertical axis known as?
11. What is the most important factor contributing to longitudinal stability?
12. Is longitudinal stability greater with a forward CG?
13. True or false? An airplane loaded with the CG too far aft will be stable at slow speeds, but if stalled will be difficult to recover.
14. Will a forward CG location cause an airplane to be more unstable at high speeds?
15. How can aircraft directional stability be improved?
16. If the airplane is loaded incorrectly so that the CG is forward of the allowable range, the elevator force required to flare the airplane for landing will be:
    a. the same as usual.
    b. greater than usual.
    c. less than usual.
17. If a wing has dihedral or sweepback, which sort of stability is increased?
18. If an airplane is yawed, it will sideslip. What will the dihedral cause it to do?

Control

19. What primary control provides pitch?
20. Nose movement up and down occurs in which plane?
21. Nose movement involves angular movement around its CG as well as which axis?
22. In order to raise the nose and lower the tail of the airplane, which direction does the trailing edge of the elevator move in?
23. What are the consequences of loading the airplane incorrectly with:
    a. the center of gravity forward of the forward limit?
    b. with the center of gravity behind the aft limit?
24. What primary control provides roll?
25. Rolling is angular motion about which axis running through the CG?
26. In which direction does the pilot move the control column to make the right wing rise?
27. True or false? At normal flight speeds, for the right wing to rise, the right aileron will go down and the left aileron will go up.
28. True or false? If differential ailerons are used to counteract the effect of adverse yaw effect, one aileron will rise by an amount the same as the other aileron is lowered.
29. Does the area below the wing have higher static pressure than the area above the wing?
30. Yawing occurs about which axis that passes through the CG?

31. An airplane is banking left for a left turn. What effect will the extra drag on the right aileron have?
32. How can adverse yaw effect be reduced?
33. What primary control provides yaw?
34. Yawing increases the speed of the outer wing. Does this cause its lift to increase? If so, what does this lead to?
35. Yaw also generates a sideslip. Will the dihedral on the more forward wing cause it to rise?
36. At high airspeeds, are the control surfaces more effective than at low airspeeds?
37. Does slipstream from the propeller over the rudder and elevators increase their effectiveness?
38. What is the purpose of *aerodynamic balance*?
39. Give three examples of *aerodynamic balance*.
40. If the stabilator is moved in the preflight external inspection, the anti-balance tab should:
    - **a.** move in the same direction.
    - **b.** move in the opposite direction.
    - **c.** not move.
41. If the elevator is moved in the preflight external inspection, the balance tab should:
    - **a.** move in the same direction.
    - **b.** move in the opposite direction.
    - **c.** not move.
42. What is mass balance used for?

Commercial Review

43. What is the term for the initial tendency of an airplane to return to its original attitude after being disturbed?
44. How can longitudinal dynamic instability in an airplane be identified?
45. If airplane attitude remains in a new position after the control column is pressed forward and released, the airplane is said to display:
    - **a.** negative longitudinal static stability.
    - **b.** neutral longitudinal dynamic stability.
    - **c.** positive longitudinal static stability.
    - **d.** neutral longitudinal static stability.
46. If airplane attitude oscillates about its original position before gradually settling down after the control column is pressed forward and released, the airplane is said to display:
    - **a.** positive dynamic stability.
    - **b.** neutral static stability.
    - **c.** negative dynamic stability.
    - **d.** neutral dynamic stability.
47. The longitudinal stability of an airplane is determined by:
    - **a.** the location of the CG with respect to the center of pressure.
    - **b.** the effectiveness of the horizontal stabilizer, rudder and rudder trim tab.
    - **c.** the relationship of thrust and lift to weight and drag.
    - **d.** the dihedral, sweepback angle, and the keel effect.
48. An airplane remains in a new attitude after the control column is pressed forward and released. The airplane displays:
    - **a.** neutral longitudinal static stability.
    - **b.** positive longitudinal static stability.
    - **c.** neutral longitudinal dynamic stability.

Answers are given on page 686

Aerodynamics of Flight 3

Straight-and-Level Flight

Relationship Between Attitude, Angle of Attack, and Airspeed

In steady straight-and-level flight, lift equals weight and thrust equals drag.

In straight-and-level flight, there is a fixed relationship between attitude, angle of attack, and indicated airspeed. At high speed, the dynamic pressure is high, and the required value of lift can be generated at a small angle of attack. In level flight, this is reflected by a lower nose attitude. At lower airspeeds, the dynamic pressure is reduced, and the loss of lift must be compensated by increasing the angle of attack. The pitch attitude is directly affected also. At low airspeed, the value of the dynamic pressure reduces significantly, and the angle of attack must increase disproportionately. At the minimum level flight speed, the pitch attitude is at its highest. With this increase in angle of attack, there is an associated increase in induced drag, and to sustain a very slow airspeed, the power also has to be increased. Extending the flaps allows a slower speed and a reduced pitch attitude.

For straight-and-level flight at constant weight, the lift required will be constant. For a given airfoil, each angle of attack has a particular lifting ability. At low speed a high angle of attack (high lifting ability) is needed to maintain altitude, while at high speed only a small angle of attack (low lifting ability) is required. Since we are considering level flight, the pilot *sees* the angle of attack as the pitch attitude of the airplane relative to the horizon—nose-up at low speeds and approximately nose-level at high speeds.

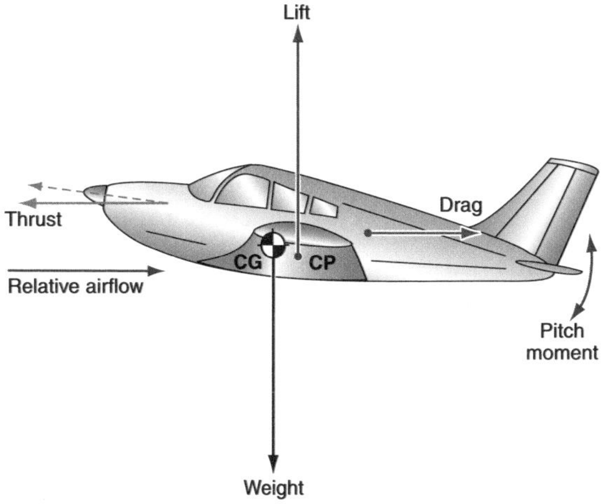

Figure 3-1
Balance of forces and moments.

The Effect of Weight

In flight the weight gradually decreases as fuel is burned off. If the airplane is to fly level, the lift produced must gradually decrease as the weight decreases. If there is a sudden decrease in weight, say by parachutists jumping out, then to maintain straight-and-level flight the lift must also decrease. In chapter 1 we said that if the airplane wing shape and area are kept constant by not using the flaps, then lift depends only on angle of attack and airspeed. Therefore to reduce lift either angle of attack or airspeed must be reduced.

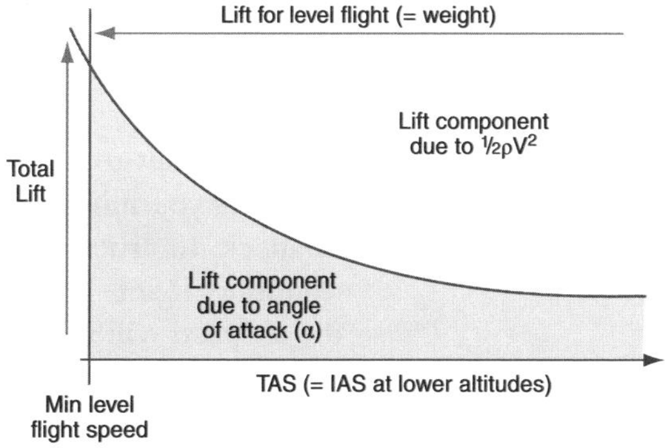

Figure 3-2
Indicated airspeed varies inversely with angle of attack.

Suppose that an airplane is flying at a particular angle of attack, say at that for the best L/D ratio (about 4°). As weight gradually decreases, lift must also be reduced to remain equal to weight. If lift is to be reduced without altering the angle of attack, the airspeed must gradually be reduced. The power (thrust) will also need to be reduced because drag will decrease as lift decreases.

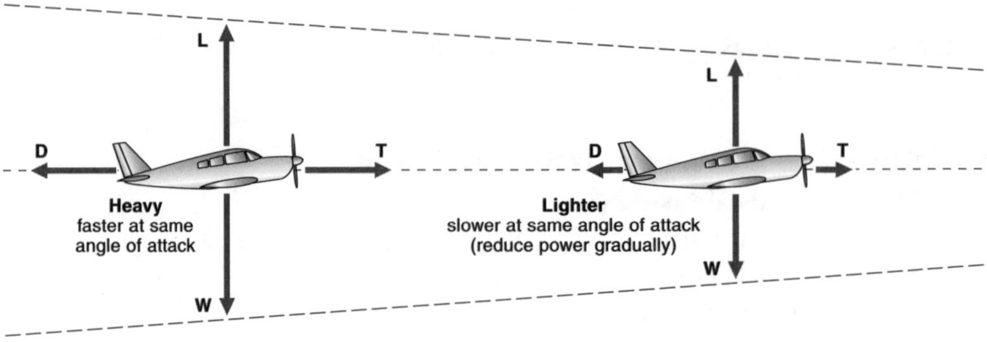

Figure 3-3 At a constant angle of attack, a lighter airplane must fly slower.

If the power (thrust) is kept constant and you want to maintain altitude as the weight decreases, the lift must be decreased by lowering the angle of attack. The speed will then increase until the thrust produced by the engine–propeller is equal to the drag (which increases as the speed increases). This is the normal technique for the cruise in small training airplanes.

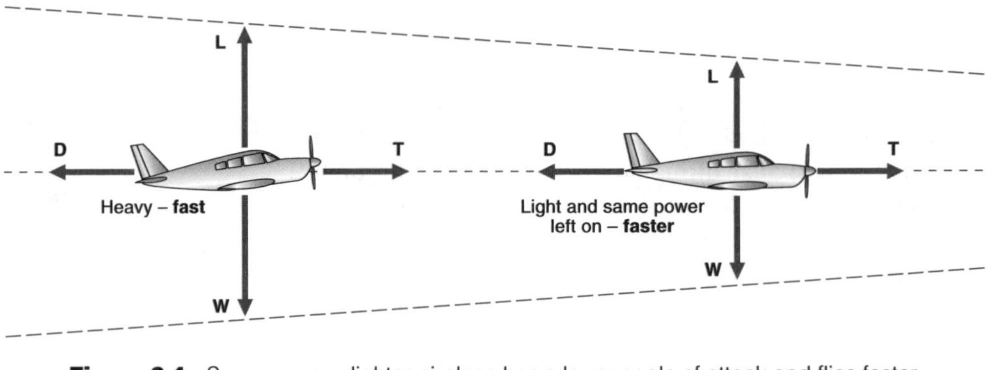

Figure 3-4 Same power—lighter airplane has a lower angle of attack and flies faster.

If you want to keep the speed constant and maintain altitude, then as the weight decreases you must reduce the lift produced, and you do this by decreasing the angle of attack. In cruise flight this will mean less drag, and therefore the power required from the engine–propeller is less. If the power is not reduced as the weight decreases, the airspeed will increase.

If your aim is to maintain a constant airspeed without reducing power, then you would need to slightly raise the nose to avoid the airspeed increasing. The airplane would then commence a climb and gradually a new set of equilibrium conditions (balance of forces) would establish themselves for a steady climb—no longer level flight. (This is covered in the next part of this chapter where we deal with *climbing and descending*.)

A very practical relationship to remember is that:

Power + attitude = performance (flight path + speed)

If you have excess power, you can adjust the pitch attitude so that altitude is maintained and airspeed increases; or you can maintain the pitch attitude and airspeed and accept a rate of climb.

Performance in Level Flight

CPL

As the thrust required for steady (unaccelerated) straight-and-level flight is equal to the drag (thrust equals drag), the thrust-required curve is identical to the familiar drag curve (figure 3-5).

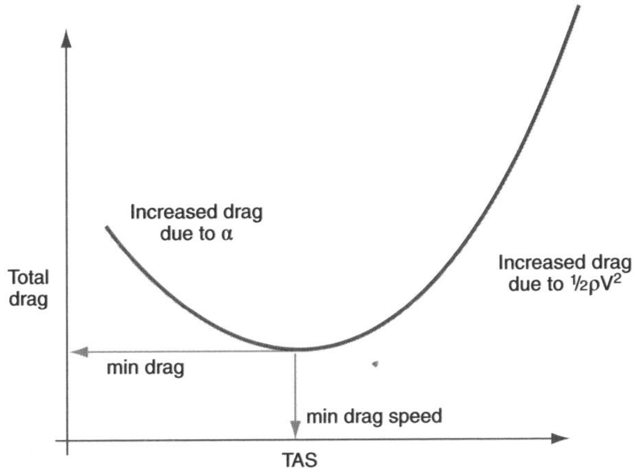

Figure 3-5 The thrust-required or drag curve.

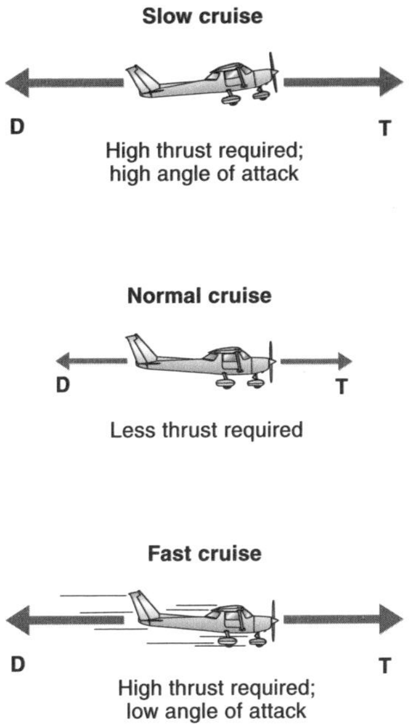

Figure 3-6
Both low speed and high speed require high thrust.

Points to be noted from the thrust-required or drag curve are:

- high thrust is required at high speeds and low angles of attack to overcome what is mainly *parasite* drag;
- minimum thrust is required at the minimum drag speed (which is also the best L/D ratio speed, since lift equals weight in straight-and-level flight and drag is at its minimum value); and
- high thrust is required at low speeds and high angles of attack to overcome what is mainly *induced* drag (caused in the production of lift).

The engine and propeller combination is a power producer (rather than a thrust producer like a jet engine). The fuel flow (in gallons per hour) of an engine–propeller combination is a function of power produced (rather than thrust produced). Power is defined as the *rate* of doing work, or the speed at which an applied force moves a body. Therefore the power required for flight depends on the product of:

- thrust required; and
- flight velocity (true airspeed or TAS).

$$\text{Power} = \text{thrust} \times \text{TAS}$$

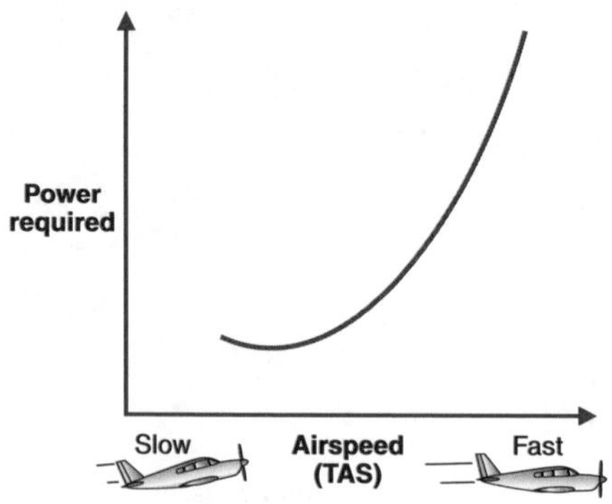

Figure 3-7
The power-required curve.

We can develop a power-required curve from the thrust-required curve (shown previously) by multiplying:

$$\text{Thrust required at a point on curve} \times \text{the TAS at that point}$$

The graph of power required to maintain steady straight-and-level flight is easy to understand if you take it slowly. If you want to fly at a particular velocity (TAS) then, by reading up from that TAS on the velocity axis, the power curve will tell you the power that the engine–propeller must deliver. This power supplies sufficient thrust to balance the drag and maintain the airspeed in straight-and-level flight.

These graphs may not be published for your airplane, and practically you would not refer to them. To achieve the minimum drag airspeed in straight-and-level flight, set the attitude for the selected airspeed (different airspeeds require different angles of attack) and adjust the power to maintain this speed.

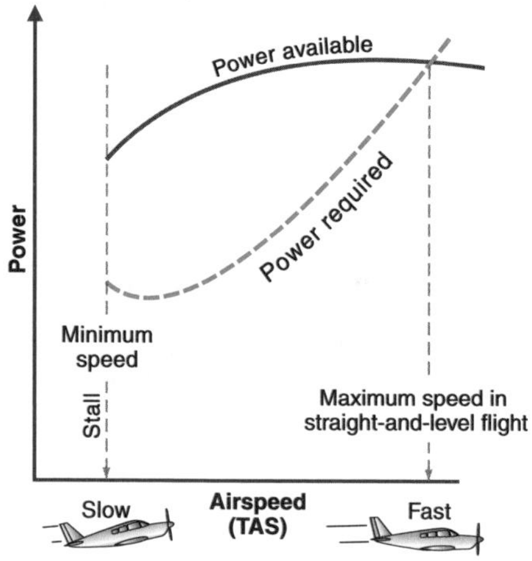

Figure 3-8
Maximum level-flight speed.

Maximum Level-Flight Speed

If maximum power is applied, the airplane will accelerate and the drag will increase (mainly parasite drag). When the drag equals the thrust produced by the engine–propeller, the airplane will stop accelerating, and it will have reached its maximum level-flight speed.

Minimum Level-Flight Speed

At low speeds (slower than the minimum drag speed), higher power from the engine–propeller is required to provide thrust to counteract the higher drag (mainly induced drag).

The minimum level-flight speed is usually not determined by the power capabilities of the powerplant, but rather by the aerodynamic capabilities of the airplane. For most light airplanes, as airspeed reduces, the stall angle is reached, or some condition of instability or loss of control effectiveness occurs prior to any power limitation of the powerplant. This is the reason that the lines on the graph at left stop on the low-speed side before they meet.

Maximum Range Speed

Maximum range speed occurs at the TAS where drag is at a minimum and the L/D ratio maximum.

For propeller-driven airplanes maximum range in still air is achieved at the TAS which allows:
- maximum *distance* for a given fuel burn-off (ratio of distance to fuel burn-off); or conversely; and
- minimum fuel burn-off for a given air distance.

As stated above the *maximum range* speed is achieved when the ratio of distance to fuel burn-off is maximum. This occurs when *drag is minimum*. On the drag curve (figure 3-9) the maximum range speed will occur at the minimum drag point—which, as explained earlier—is also the point for the maximum L/D ratio. Both the engine and propeller are most efficient at low altitude where the air is more dense. However, for the same IAS, TAS increases with altitude; therefore, a greater distance can be covered at altitude.

To achieve the maximum ratio of distance to fuel burn-off, a compromise is required and the airplane should be flown at *full-throttle altitude* (about 4,000 to 7,000 feet altitude) for maximum range. Ask your flight instructor how to achieve full-throttle altitude for your airplane engine type.

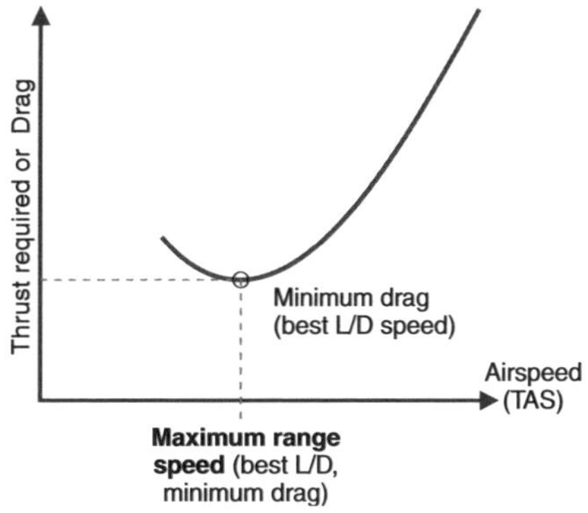

Figure 3-9 Graph of drag versus TAS.

Maximum Endurance Speed

Endurance refers to the *time* an airplane is airborne. The length of time airborne depends on the amount of fuel in the tanks and the rate at which it is used. Maximum endurance means:

- the maximum *time* in flight for given amount of fuel (ratio of time to fuel used); or
- a given time in flight for the minimum amount of fuel.

Maximum endurance speed occurs at the TAS where power is at a minimum.

In both cases, for maximum endurance the rate of fuel use, which is known as *fuel flow*, must be *minimum*.

It is appropriate to fly at maximum endurance speed when the speed over the ground is not significant, for instance, when:

- holding overhead or near an airport waiting to land; or
- carrying out a search in a specific area.

The speed for *maximum endurance* occurs when the ratio of time to fuel used is maximum and fuel flow is minimum. For a propeller-driven airplane this occurs when *power is minimum*. At low altitude, because the engine and propeller are more efficient, fuel flow will be least. Therefore endurance is greatest at *low altitude*.

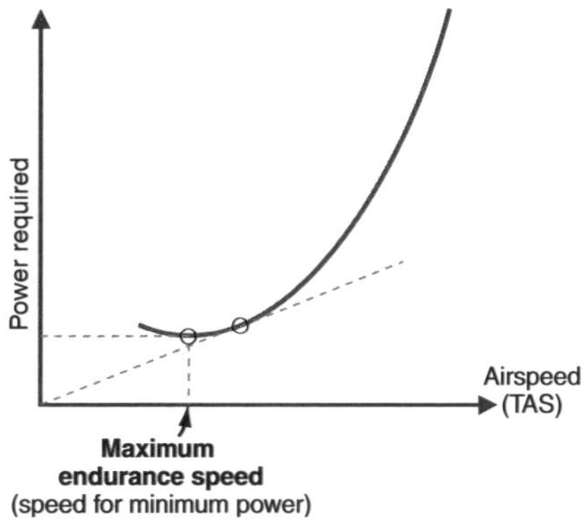

Figure 3-10 Graph of power versus TAS.

Speed Stability

Higher Speed Range

An increase in airspeed increases the total drag, as can be seen from the drag curve, mainly because of an increase in parasite drag. This drag increase is not counteracted by the thrust from the propeller, so the airplane slows down.

A decrease in airspeed from a gust decreases the total drag (due mainly to a decrease in parasite drag) and the thrust, which now exceeds the drag, causes the airplane to accelerate back to its original speed.

In the normal flight range (above the minimum drag speed) you do not need to be very active on the throttle since the airplane is *speed stable* and, following any disturbance, tends to return to its original equilibrium airspeed without further control inputs.

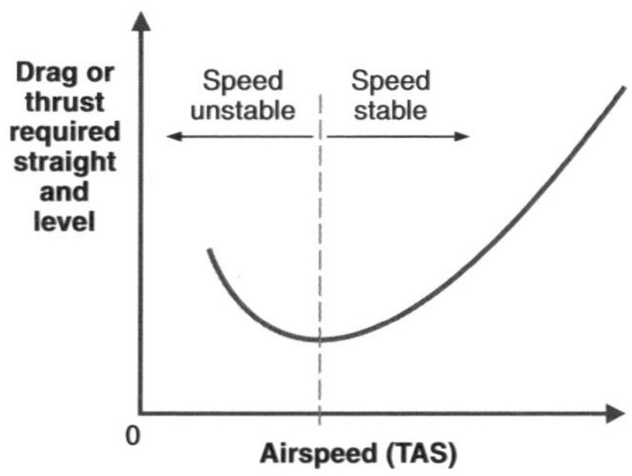

Figure 3-11 Speed stability.

CPL

Lower Speed Range

At low airspeeds, when pitch is toward the stall angle of attack, it is a different matter. If a gust causes airspeed to decrease, the total drag increases (because of an increase in induced drag) and drag now exceeds thrust, causing the airplane to slow down even further unless you respond with more power.

If a gust causes airspeed to increase, the total drag decreases (because of a decrease in induced drag), and drag is now less than thrust, causing the airplane to accelerate further away from the original speed unless you react by reducing power. Therefore, at low speeds near the stall angle you need to be fairly active with the throttle to maintain the required low speed accurately.

Straight-and-Level Flight at Altitude

At any altitude, if the airplane is in steady straight-and-level flight the lift must counteract the weight.

$$\text{Lift} = C_L \times \tfrac{1}{2}\rho V^2 \times S$$

As altitude is increased, air density, ρ, decreases. One way to generate the required lift and compensate for the decreased density, ρ, is to increase the true airspeed (V) so that the value of $\frac{1}{2}\rho V^2$ remains the same as before. This means that the decrease in density with altitude can be compensated for with an increase in V (the TAS).

To produce the same lift as altitude increases, fly at the same indicated airspeed (true airspeed increases).

The term $\frac{1}{2}\rho V^2$ (dynamic pressure) is related to the indicated airspeed which you can read in the cockpit on the airspeed indicator. If $\frac{1}{2}\rho V^2$ remains the same, the indicated airspeed (IAS) remains the same and lift remains the same. (A further explanation of the difference between IAS and TAS is given on page 166.) Therefore as altitude increases the airplane has the same lift at the same IAS, but an increased TAS.

Note. As altitude increases the indicated stall speed also remains the same and the true stall speed increases.

Only at lower altitudes and slower airspeeds can we go straight from IAS to TAS without considering calibration and compression effects.

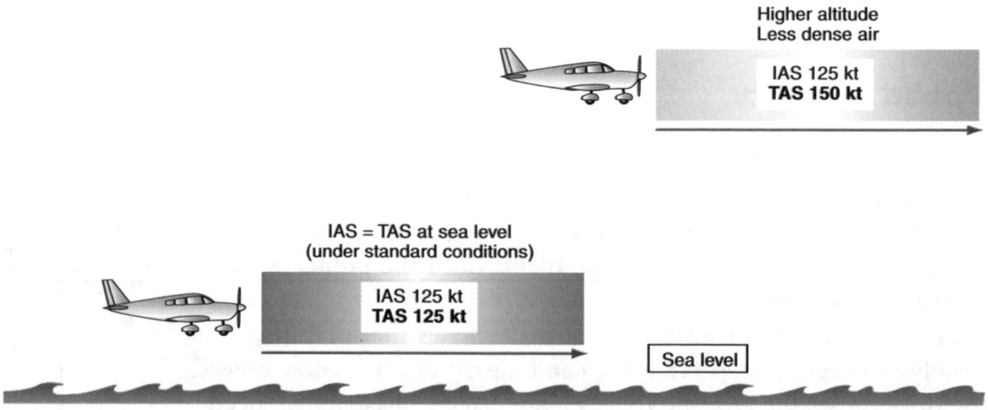

Figure 3-12 Same IAS (and lift) at a high altitude means higher TAS.

End CPL

Climbs

As an airplane climbs, it gains potential energy (the energy of position, in this case because of altitude). There are two ways an airplane can do this:

- by making a zoom climb; or
- by a steady, long-term climb.

Zoom Climb

A zoom climb exchanges the kinetic energy of motion for potential energy by exchanging high velocity for an increase in altitude. Therefore, kinetic energy *reduces* while potential energy *increases*, and (kinetic + potential) energy remains the same. It is only a transient (temporary) process, as the velocity cannot be decreased below flying speed. Of course, the greater the speed range of the airplane the greater the capability of the zoom. For example, a jet fighter being pursued at high speed can gain altitude rapidly with a zoom, or an aerobatic glider that converts the kinetic energy of a dive into potential energy at the top of a loop. An airplane can zoom as long as it is above its stall speed.

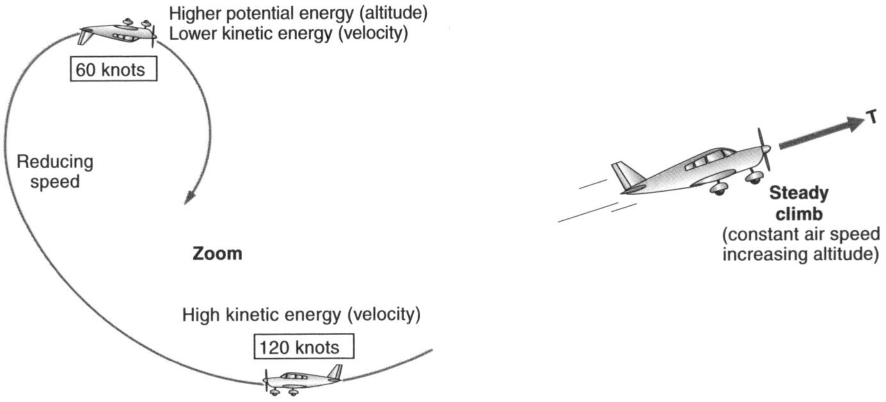

Figure 3-13 A zoom and a steady climb.

Steady Climb

In a steady climb, kinetic energy remains *constant* while potential energy increases. This increase in (kinetic + potential) energy is provided by the additional fuel which is burned in the engine during the climb. It is the steady climb that is of importance in day-to-day flying. To enter a steady climb, raise the nose (which temporarily increases the angle of attack) and add power. The airplane quickly settles into a steady climb.

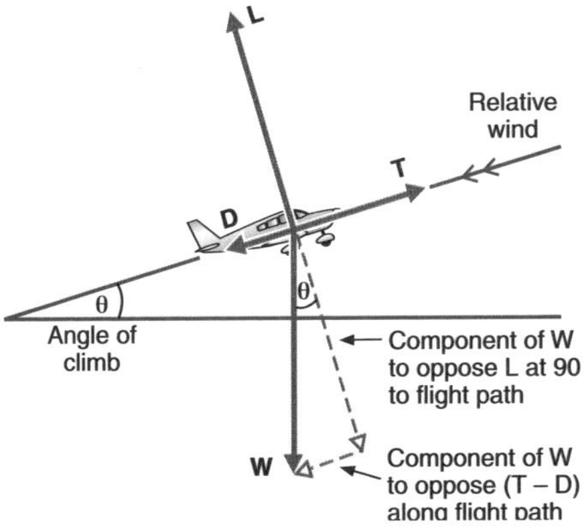

Figure 3-14 The four forces in equilibrium in a steady climb.

Forces in the Climb

In a steady en route climb the thrust force acts in the direction of flight, directly opposite to the drag force. The lift force acts perpendicular to the relative wind and is no longer vertical. The weight force acts vertically, but note how, in the climb, it has a component that acts in the direction opposing flight.

If you maintain a *steady climb* at a constant indicated airspeed, the engine–propeller must supply sufficient thrust to:

- overcome the drag force; and
- help lift the weight of the airplane at a vertical speed (known as rate of climb).

In a steady climb there is no acceleration. The forces are in equilibrium, with the up forces equaling the down forces, and the forward forces equaling the rearward forces. Consequently, the resultant force acting on the airplane is zero.

Types of Climb

There are three types of climb, each with a different purpose.

Maximum Angle Climb

A maximum angle climb is used to clear obstacles, as it gains the greatest altitude for a given *horizontal distance*. By definition it is the steepest climb (maximum gradient) and is flown at a relatively slow airspeed, referred to as V_X. Because the slow airspeed results in reduced cooling and higher engine temperatures, it should only be used for short periods while clearing obstacles.

Maximum Rate Climb

A *maximum rate climb* is used to reach cruise altitude as quickly as possible, as it gains the greatest altitude in a given *time*. Best rate of climb speed is known as V_Y. The airspeed is faster than V_X at sea level and is usually somewhere near the speed for the optimum lift/drag ratio. It is a shallower climb than the maximum angle climb. Rate of climb is a vertical velocity and is indicated on the vertical speed indicator (VSI) in feet per minute (FPM).

Cruise Climb

A *cruise climb* is a compromise climb that allows for a higher groundspeed (to expedite your arrival at the destination) as well as allowing the airplane to gain altitude and reach the cruise altitude without too much delay. It also allows for better engine cooling because of the faster speed, and better forward visibility because of the lower pitch attitude. The cruise climb is the shallowest climb at a higher airspeed compared with V_X and V_Y. For most airplanes it is the *normal climb*.

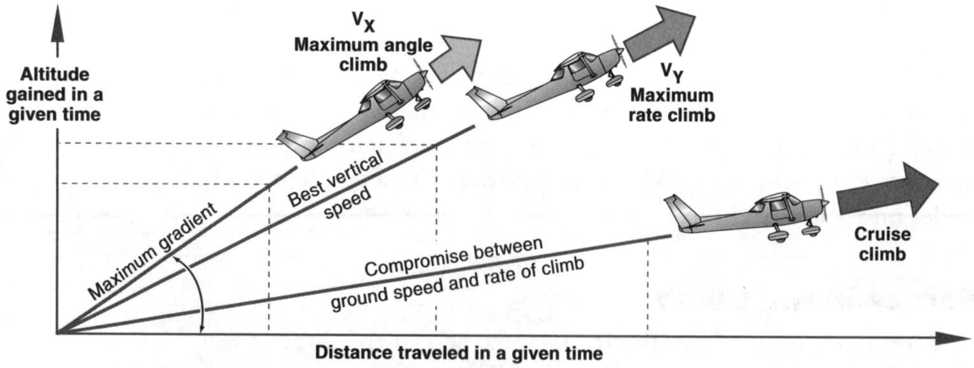

Figure 3-15 Maximum angle climb, maximum rate climb, cruise climb; use the one that suits the situation.

Climb Speed

Refer to your Pilot's Operating Handbook for the various climb speeds for your particular airplane. Typically, the best angle-of-climb speed V_X is about 10–15 knots less than the best rate-of-climb speed V_Y at sea level for single-engine airplanes.

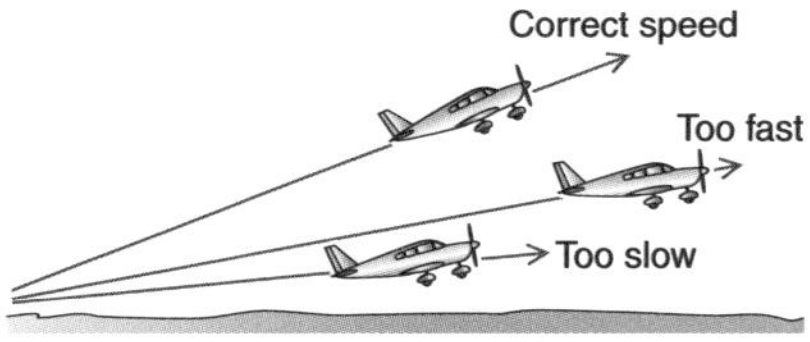

Figure 3-16
Fly at the correct climb speed for best performance.

Climb Performance

Performance in the climb, be it angle or rate of climb, will:

- decrease when power is decreased;
- decrease when airplane weight is increased;
- decrease when temperature increases because of lower air density;
- decrease if you fly at the incorrect speed (either too fast or too slow); and
- decrease as altitude increases because of lower air density.

The power available from the engine and propeller decreases with altitude. The climb performance, rate of climb, and angle of climb capabilities all decrease with altitude.

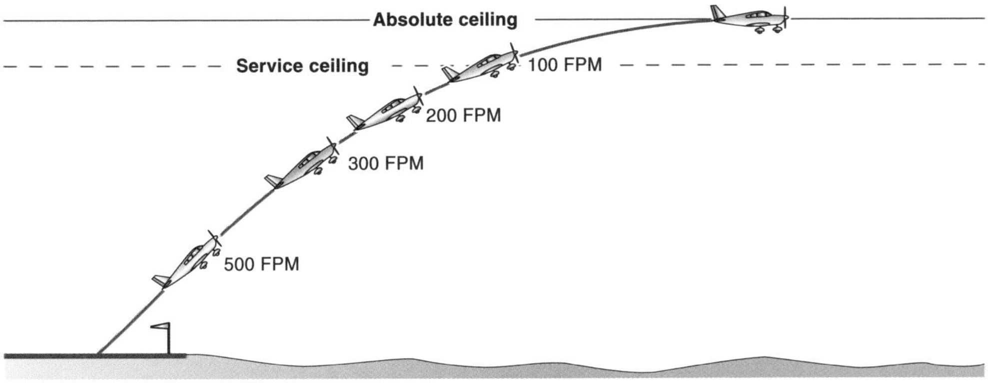

Figure 3-17 Climb performance decreases with altitude.

The altitude at which climb performance falls close to zero and a steady climb can no longer be maintained is called *ceiling*. The *service ceiling* is the altitude at which the steady rate of climb has fallen to just 100 feet per minute (FPM). The *absolute ceiling* is the slightly higher altitude at which the steady rate of climb achievable at climbing speed is zero. It is therefore almost impossible to climb to the absolute ceiling, and the speed you maintain at this altitude is at the point where V_X and V_Y meet, as V_X increases and V_Y decreases with altitude.

The airplane's Pilot's Operating Handbook normally contains a table or graph with climb performance information, see figure 3-18.

MAXIMUM RATE OF CLIMB

SAMPLE ONLY
Not to be used in conjunction with flight operations or flight planning.

CONDITIONS:
Flaps Up
Full Throttle

NOTE:
Mixture leaned above 3,000 feet for maximum rpm.

WEIGHT LBS	PRESS ALT FT	CLIMB SPEED KIAS	RATE OF CLIMB – FPM			
			−20°C	0°C	20°C	40°C
1,670	S.L.	67	835	765	700	630
	2,000	66	735	670	600	535
	4,000	65	635	570	505	445
	6,000	63	535	475	415	355
	8,000	62	440	380	320	265
	10,000	61	340	285	230	175
	12,000	60	245	190	135	85

Climbing IAS for best rate of climb decreases with altitude.

Rate of climb decreases with altitude increase.

Rate of climb decreases with temperature increase.

Figure 3-18 A typical climb performance table.

The Effect of a Steady Wind on Climbing

A headwind increases climb gradient—a tailwind reduces it. Wind does not affect rate of climb, but does affect angle of climb over the ground.

Because rate of climb is a vertical velocity and wind normally acts horizontally, rate of climb is not affected by a steady wind. Angle of climb through the air also is not affected by a steady wind. However, if we consider the angle (or gradient) of climb over the ground—the airplane's flight path—a headwind increases the effective climb gradient over the ground and a tailwind decreases it. T*aking off into a headwind* has obvious advantages for obstacle clearance—it improves your clearance of obstacles on the ground.

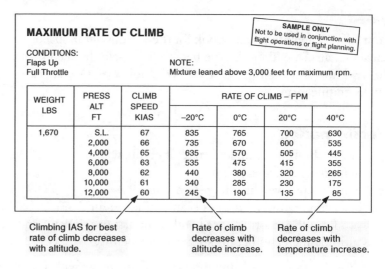

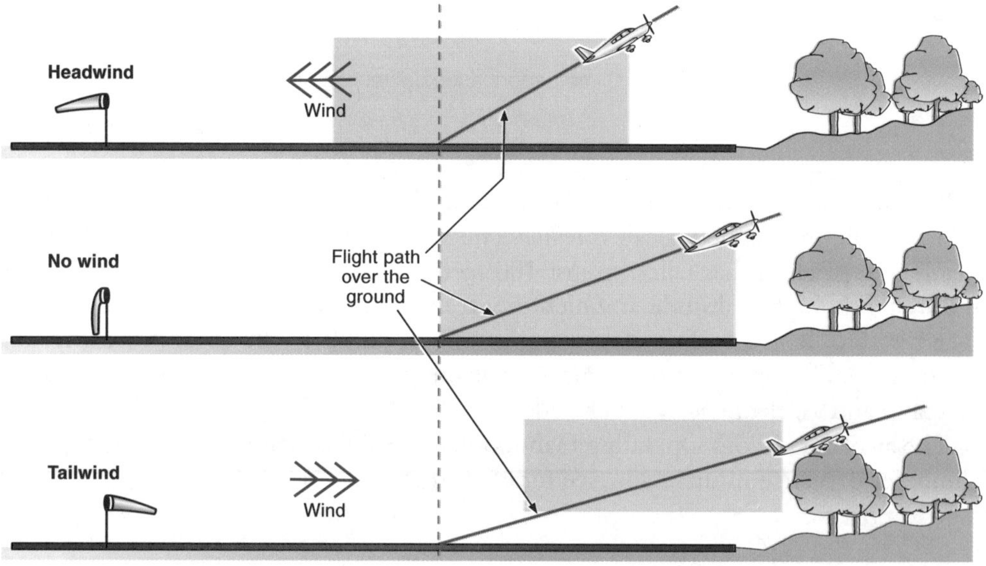

Figure 3-19 Wind affects the flight path achieved over the ground.

Angle of Climb

Angle of climb depends on excess thrust.

The angle of climb (climb gradient) depends directly on the excess thrust (the thrust force in excess of the drag force). The angle of climb therefore increases when thrust increases or drag decreases. When a maximum angle of climb is required, you use full power, climb at the correct speed for maximum excess thrust, and ensure the airplane is in a low drag configuration with flaps and gear up (as indicated by the POH). This is a very important consideration for the climb out after takeoff. Flaps for takeoff decrease the takeoff run prior to liftoff, but once in flight the angle of climb may be less because of the higher drag with flaps down.

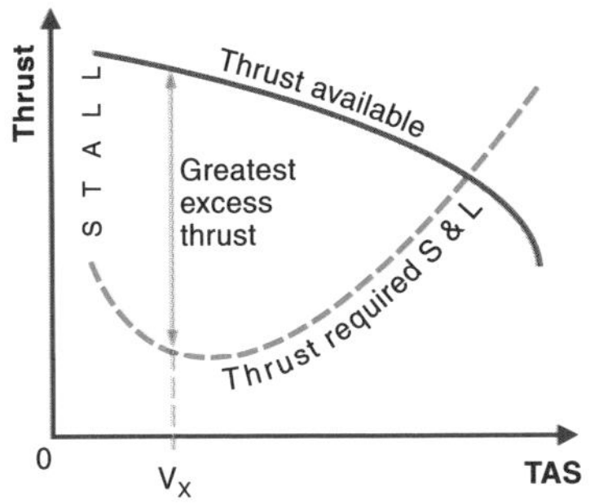

Figure 3-20 "Thrust required" and "thrust available" versus TAS.

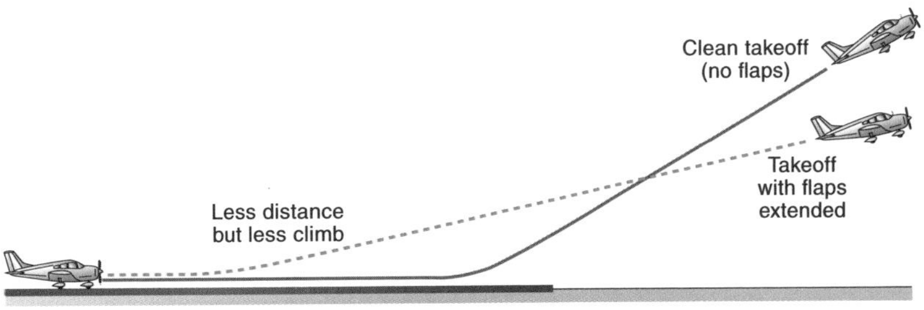

Figure 3-21
Climb gradient may be less with flaps extended.

Rate of Climb

Rate of climb depends on excess power.

The *rate of climb* depends directly on the *excess power* (power is the rate of doing work which equals thrust velocity). Rate of climb increases when power increases or the product of drag and TAS reduces. The maximum rate of climb usually occurs at a speed somewhere near that for the maximum *lift/drag* ratio, and is faster than the speed for maximum angle of climb (gradient). The maximum rate of climb speed will give the greatest altitude gain in the shortest amount of time.

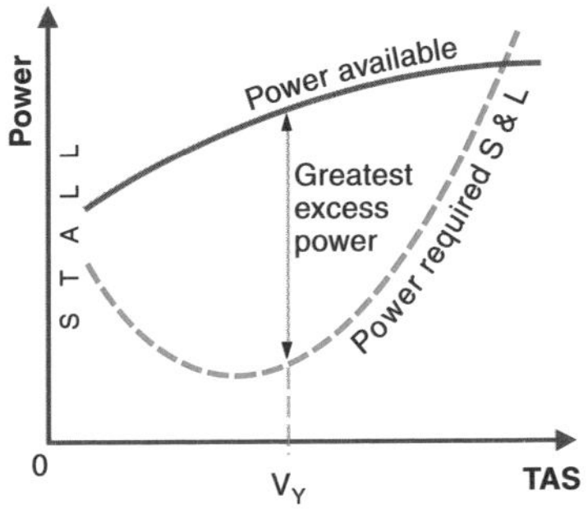

Figure 3-22
"Power required" and "power available" versus TAS.

Factors Affecting Climb Performance

Power

If full power is not used in a climb, the power (and thrust) *available* decreases, which decreases the excess power and excess thrust and therefore the rate and angle of climb. During the initial climb it is important that you ensure that the correct climb power is set and maintained.

Weight

Compared to a light airplane, a heavy airplane requires more lift and therefore produces more drag. Thrust and power *required* for straight-and-level flight is therefore increased, and excess thrust and excess power is decreased.

A heavier airplane weight therefore reduces angle and rate of climb.

CPL

Air Density

When temperature, humidity, or airplane altitude increase, the air density reduces. This causes the piston engine to produce less power and the propeller to produce less thrust. This reduction in thrust and power *available* results in excess thrust and excess power decreasing.

A reduction in air density therefore reduces angle of climb and rate of climb.

Incorrect Airspeed

If you fly faster or slower than the recommended speeds (V_X and V_Y), excess thrust and excess power decrease, decreasing the angle and rate of climb respectively.

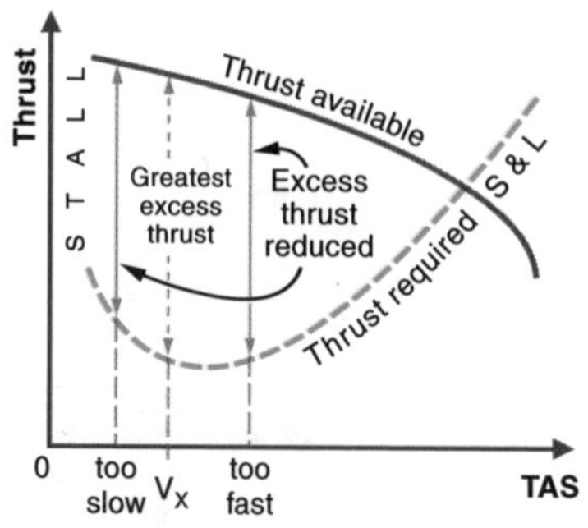

Figure 3-23
Flying the incorrect airspeed reduces excess thrust and angle of climb.

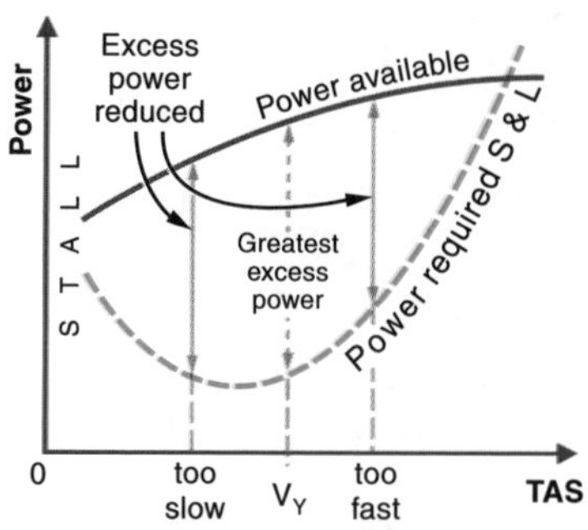

Figure 3-24
Flying the incorrect airspeed reduces excess power and rate of climb.

End CPL

Descent

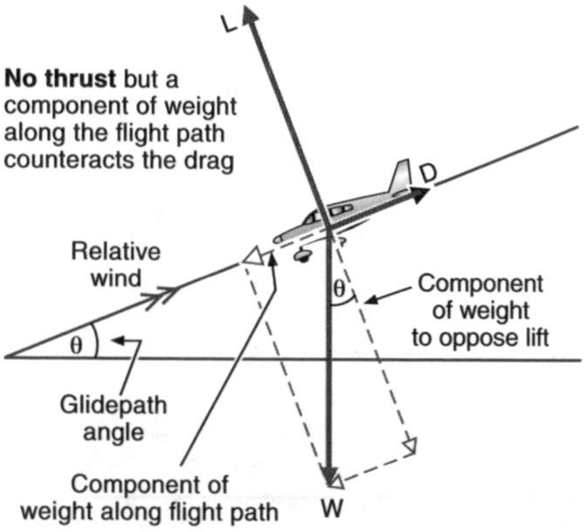

Figure 3-25
In a glide descent, a component of weight counteracts the drag.

In a steady glide lift, weight and drag are in equilibrium.

If an airplane is in a glide descent, with no thrust being produced by the engine and propeller, only *three* of the four main forces will be acting on the airplane: *weight*, *lift*, and *drag*. In a steady glide these three forces are in equilibrium as the resultant force acting on the airplane is zero. Suppose that the airplane is in steady straight-and-level flight and the thrust is reduced to zero. The drag force is no longer opposed with an equal and opposite force, and will therefore decelerate the airplane—unless a descent is commenced where the component of the weight force acting in the direction of the flight path is sufficient to counteract the drag. This effect allows the airplane to maintain airspeed by descending and converting potential energy because of its altitude into kinetic energy (motion).

Resolving the forces in the direction of the flight path shows that a component of the weight force acts along the flight path in a descent, counteracting drag and contributing to the airplane's speed. The airspeed in the descent remains constant when this component of weight is equal and opposite to the drag.

Resolving the forces vertically, you can see that, in a glide descent, the weight is counteracted by the total aerodynamic force, which is the resultant of the lift and drag. Notice that the greater the drag force, the steeper the glide. The shallowest glide is obtained at the maximum lift/drag ratio when, for the required lift, the drag is least:

- *if the L/D ratio is high*, the angle of descent is shallow—a flat glide angle—and the airplane will glide a long distance; and
- *if the L/D ratio is low* (a poor situation), with a lot of drag being produced for the required lift, then the airplane will have a large angle of descent—a steep glide angle—and the airplane will therefore not glide very far.

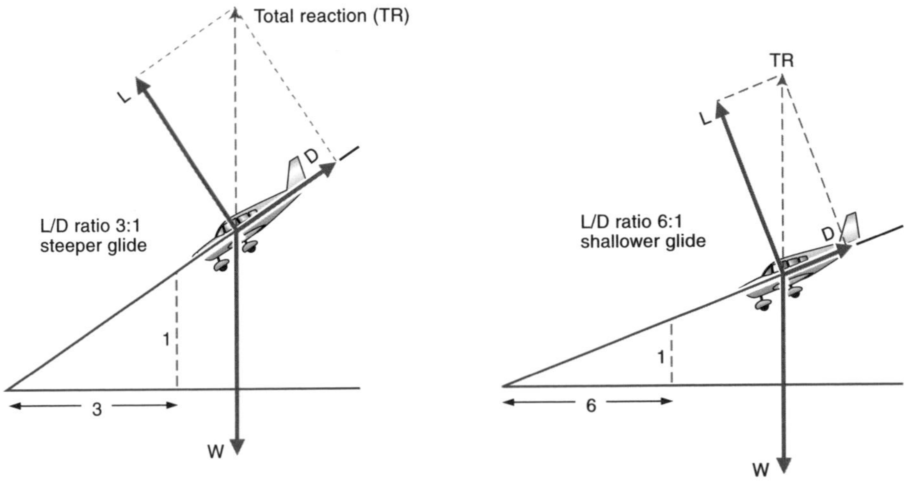

Figure 3-26 A smaller L/D ratio (increased drag) results in a steeper glide.

Two points can be made here:

1. an aerodynamically efficient airplane is one which can be flown at a high lift/drag ratio. It is capable of gliding further for the same loss of altitude compared with an airplane that is flown with a lower L/D ratio; and
2. the same airplane will glide furthest through still air when it is flown at the angle of attack (and airspeed) that gives its maximum L/D ratio. This angle of attack is usually about 4°.

Because you cannot read angle of attack in the cockpit, flying at the recommended best glide or descent speed (listed in the Pilot's Operating Handbook) ensures that the airplane is somewhere near this most efficient angle of attack to achieve the best glide angle.

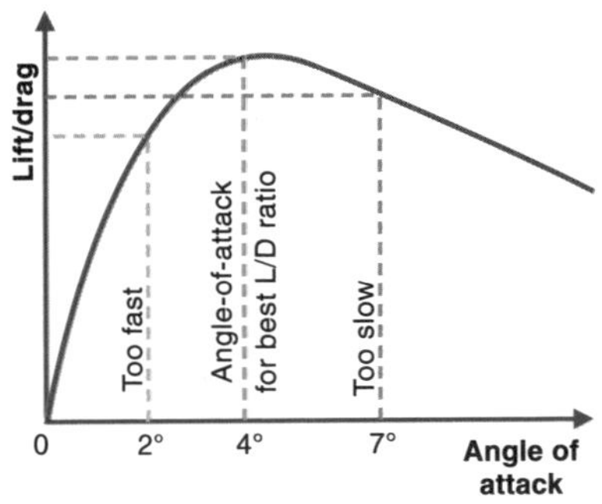

Figure 3-27
Angle of attack versus L/D ratio.

Factors Affecting Glide Angle

Airspeed

The wrong airspeed (too fast or too slow) steepens the glide angle.

To glide the furthest in still air, fly at the recommended airspeed (and therefore angle of attack) that gives the maximum lift/drag ratio. This may be deceptive for the pilot because the nose attitude may be quite high, but the airplane is descending steeply.

If you are gliding at the recommended airspeed and it looks like you will not reach the selected point, do not raise the nose to increase the glide distance. It will not work!

The higher nose attitude may give the appearance of stretching the glide, but in fact it will decrease your glide distance.

The best glide speed reduces as weight decreases.

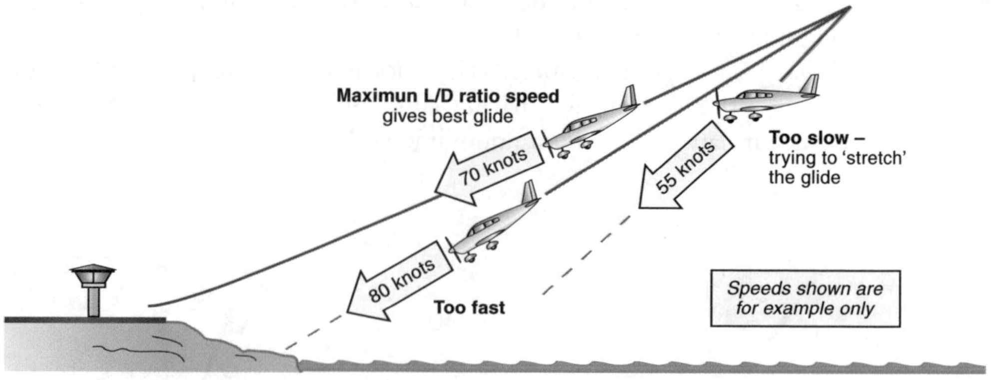

Figure 3-28 The flattest glide is achieved at the maximum L/D ratio.

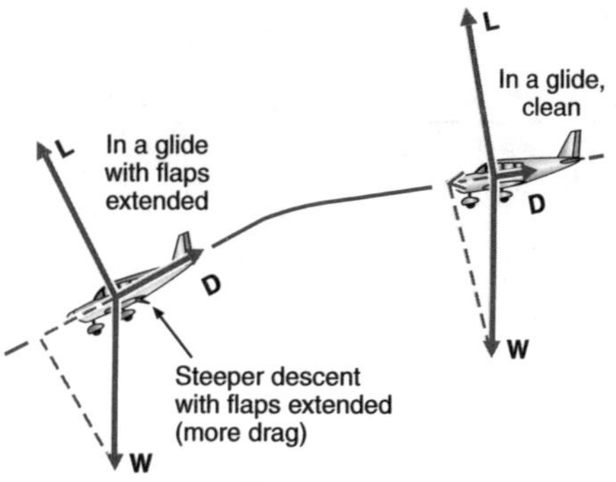

Figure 3-29
Steeper glide angle with flaps extended.

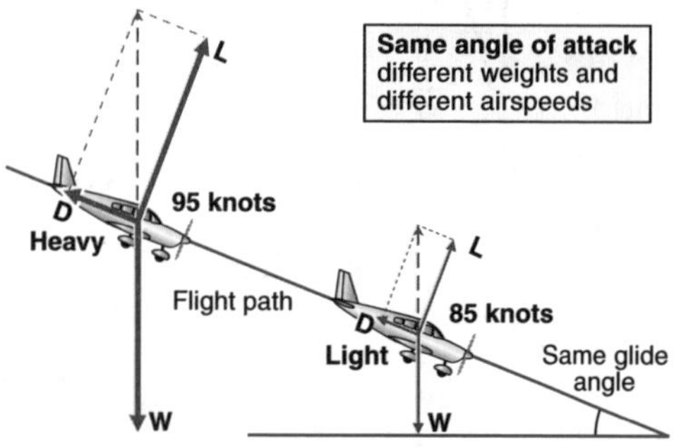

Figure 3-30
The best glide angle is the same at all weights (maximum L/D) but the airspeed must be lower at lower weights.

Flap Setting

Flaps increase the drag more than the lift and consequently the L/D ratio is lower. This gives a steeper glide.

Weight

If the airplane weight reduces, you can achieve the best glide angle by flying a slightly slower glide speed. By maintaining the angle of attack for the maximum L/D ratio (and therefore for the best glide), the airspeed will be lower but the glide angle the same. This also means that the rate of descent for the airplane when it is lighter will be less—it will glide the same distance through the air, but take longer to reach the ground because of the reduced airspeed.

The recommended glide speed (stated in the Pilot's Operating Handbook) is based on *maximum gross weight*. The variation in weight for most training airplanes is not large enough to significantly affect the glide if the recommended glide speed is used at all times—even though, theoretically, a slightly lower glide speed could be used when lightly loaded.

The recommended glide speed in your Pilot's Operating Handbook is suitable for all permissible weights of your light training airplane.

Glide Distance over the Ground

A headwind reduces the glide distance over the ground—a tailwind increases it.

A headwind reduces the glide distance over the ground, even though it does not affect the glide distance through the air, nor does it affect the rate of descent:

- *glide angle* means relative to the *air mass* and is not affected by wind; and
- *flight path* means relative to the *ground* and is affected by wind.

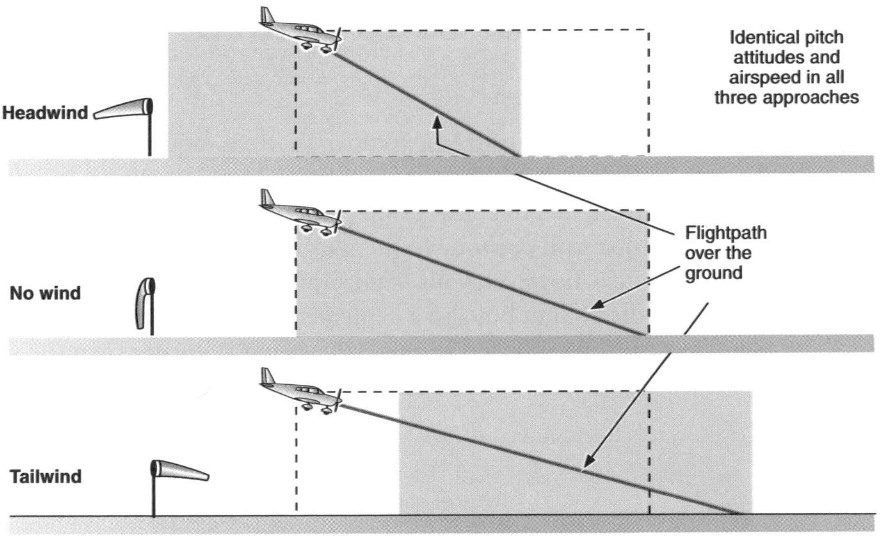

Figure 3-31 More ground is covered gliding with a tailwind and less with a headwind.

Wind does not affect rate of descent.

The airplane "sees" only the air in which it is flying. In the case illustrated in figure 3-31, we can see three identical glides through an air mass—same airspeed, same nose attitude, same angle of attack, same rate of descent (therefore same time taken to reach the ground) in all three cases. The only difference is that the air mass is moving over the ground in three different ways and carrying the airplane with it. The ground distance covered differs. A tailwind increases the glide distance over the ground, even though it does not affect the glide distance relative to the air mass or the rate of descent.

Still Air Glide Distance

Figure 3-32 shows the forces acting in a glide. You will see that the glide distance is furthest when the L/D ratio is at its maximum value. If the L/D ratio is 5:1, the airplane will glide 5 times as far as it will descend. If you are 1 nautical mile (NM) high (about 6,000 feet), you will glide for about 5 NM. If you are at about 12,000 feet (2 NM), you will glide approximately 10 NM. An airplane with a L/D ratio of 12:1 will glide 12 times as far in still air as it will descend.

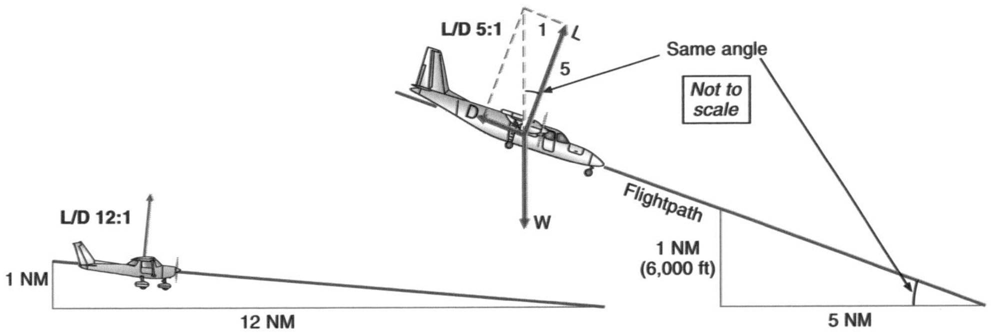

Figure 3-32 "Air distance/altitude" is the same ratio as "lift/drag"

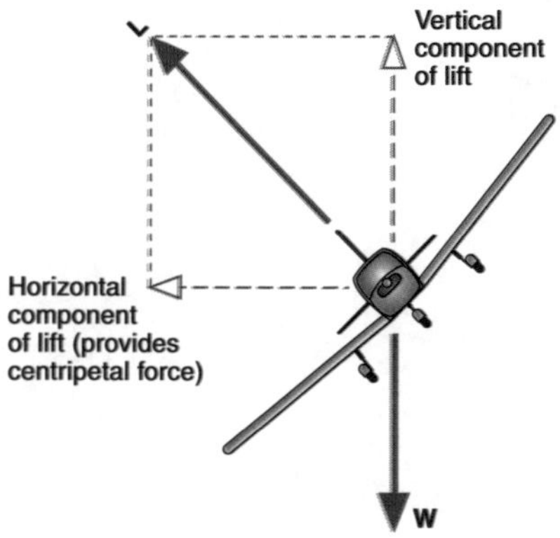

Figure 3-33
By banking, the tilted lift force has a horizontal component which provides the centripetal force.

Turning and Load Factor

Forces in a Turn

For an object such as an airplane to turn, a force is required that acts toward the center of the turn. This turning force is known as the *centripetal force*. Holding a string tied to a heavy object such as a stone, your hand supplies a lift force equal and opposite to the weight of the stone. If you swing the stone in a circle, however, your hand supplies not only a vertical force to counteract the weight but also a centripetal force to keep the stone turning. The total force exerted through the string is greater than the weight of the stone, and you will feel the increase in effective weight.

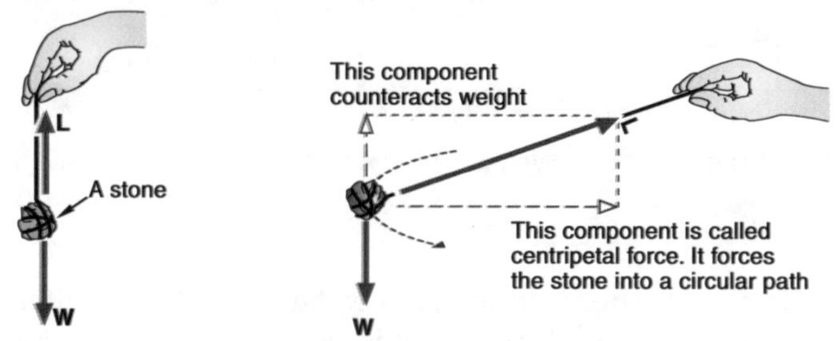

Figure 3-34 The centripetal force pulls a body into a turn.

To turn an airplane, a centripetal force (toward the center of the turn) needs to be generated. This can be done by banking the airplane and tilting the lift force so that it has a sideways component.

Flying straight-and-level, the lift force from the wings counteracts the weight of the airplane. If you turn the airplane, the wings still need to supply a vertical force to counteract the weight (unless you want to descend) plus the centripetal force toward the center of the turn to keep the turn going. Consequently, the lift force in a level turn must be greater than the lift force when flying straight-and-level. To develop this increased lift force at the same airspeed, the angle of attack must be increased by applying back pressure on the control column.

The steeper the bank angle in a level turn, the greater the lift force required. Note that you select the bank angle using the *ailerons* (to roll the airplane) and *elevator* to increase the angle of attack (and increase lift) to produce the centripetal force required to turn the airplane and maintain the selected altitude.

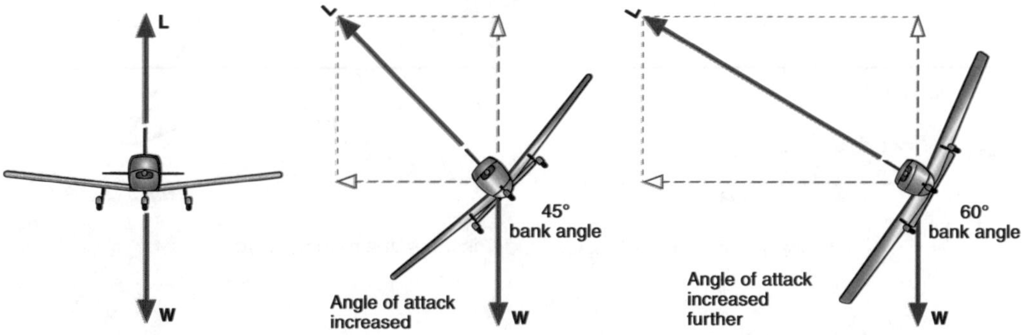

Figure 3-35 The steeper the bank, the greater the lift force required from the wings.

The stability designed into the airplane, together with adverse yaw effect, may resist it turning, and the application of a little rudder (left rudder for a left turn and vice versa) helps bring the tail around and yaw the nose into the turn, aligning the fuselage with the turning flight path—therefore the rudder is used to *coordinate* the turn by controlling yaw. You, of course, are forced into the turn along with the airplane and feel this as an increase in the force exerted by the seat; it feels like an *apparent* increase in your weight—the centrifugal reaction.

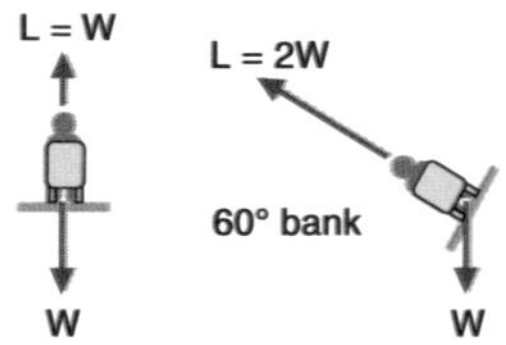

Figure 3-36
The steeper the bank angle, the greater the g-forces.

Load Factor

The load factor on the wings is increased in a turn. Flying straight-and-level, the wing produces a lift force *equal* to the weight and L = W. The load factor is said to be 1. You experience a force from the seat equal to normal weight, and feel it as "1g."

In a banked turn of 60°, the wings produce a lift force equal to *double* the weight and L = 2W. This means the loading on the wings is doubled when compared with straight-and-level flight, or each square foot of wing has to produce twice as much lift in a 60° banked turn as it does in straight-and-level flight. You experience a force from the seat equal to twice your weight. This is 2g and the load factor is 2. This is true for all 60° banked turns, irrespective of airspeed, rate of turn, or weight of the airplane.

The *load factor* is the ratio of the lift force produced by the wings compared with the weight force of the airplane.

$$\text{Load factor} = \frac{\text{lift}}{\text{weight}} = \frac{\text{wing loading in maneuver}}{\text{wing loading straight-and-level}}$$

At bank angles beyond 60°, the lift force generated by the wings must increase greatly so that its vertical component can counteract the weight, otherwise altitude will be lost. Increased lift from the wings means increased wing loading and an increased load factor. We can show this in a curve of load factor versus bank angle.

Note the following:

- in a 30° banked turn you will experience 1.15g load factor. The wings will produce 15% more lift than when straight-and-level, and you will feel 15% heavier;
- at 60° bank angle, the load factor is 2. The wings have to produce a lift force equal to double the weight to maintain altitude. The g-force is 2g, you will feel twice as heavy, and the wing will have to support double the weight;
- a 70° bank, the load factor is 3;
- a utility category airplane has a maximum allowable positive load factor of 4.4g, which is reached at approximately 77° bank angle (a normal category airplane is limited to 3.8g); and
- in a 90° banked turn, the lift force is horizontal, and, even if of infinite size, would have no vertical component to counteract the weight. Therefore altitude cannot be maintained in a coordinated turn at 90° bank angle (unless extreme excess thrust is used).

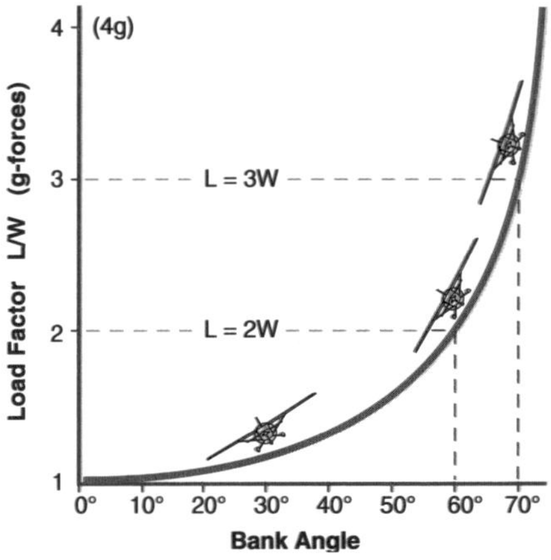

Figure 3-37
Load factor versus bank angle.

For those who are interested in a mathematical explanation, the load factor in a turn can be calculated from 1 divided by the cosine of the bank angle, or $\frac{1}{\cos\theta}$.

The maximum weights permitted to be carried in a particular airplane (or compartments within an airplane) take into account load factor. A normal category airplane is stressed to 3.8g. If the baggage compartment is approved for 220 lb, then it will not be overstressed provided 3.8g is not exceeded.

Load Factor in a Turn

Load factor increases as bank angle increases.

In straight-and-level flight, the wings support a load that is the weight of the airplane. In a banked turn of 60°, the load factor is 2, and now each wing has to support twice the load that it did in straight-and-level. Wing loading is the load supported by the wings divided by their area. For example, an airplane weighing 2,500 pounds (lb) with a wing area of 200 square feet has a wing loading of 12.5 lb/sq. feet in level flight. In a 60° banked turn the load factor is 2. Therefore the load that the wings are supporting is 2,500 × 2 = 5,000 lb:

$$\text{Wing Loading} = \frac{\text{load}}{\text{wing area}} = \frac{5{,}000}{200} = 25 \text{ lb/square foot}$$

Like load factor, wing loading in a turn depends only on the bank angle. But wing loading is not only of concern for structural strength, it also affects minimum landing speeds: the smaller the wing, the higher the wing loading and the faster the minimum landing speed.

Thrust in a Turn

In a turn, extra thrust is required to maintain airspeed.

In a turn, increased lift from the wings is required to provide the centripetal force and to maintain altitude. This is achieved by applying back pressure on the control column to increase the angle of attack.

The steeper the bank angle, the greater the angle of attack and back pressure required. As we saw in our discussion on drag, an increase in the angle of attack will lead to an increase in the induced drag. If a constant airspeed is to be maintained in a level turn, an increase in thrust to counteract the increased drag in a turn is required (typically 50 RPM for a fixed-pitch propeller or ½ in. Hg manifold pressure for an airplane with a constant-speed propeller). In practice, however, the power is usually kept constant in medium turns and you accept a reduction in airspeed of approximately 5 knots. If extra thrust is not added, the airspeed will decrease in a level turn. If required, airspeed could be maintained by allowing the airplane to lose altitude, trading potential energy for kinetic energy.

Steep Turns

A steep turn is one in which the bank angle exceeds 45° and airspeed is maintained by applying a significant increase in power. It is a high-performance maneuver that requires good coordination and positive control. A steep level turn requires a significant increase in lift so that:

- a strong horizontal component exists to pull the airplane into the turn; and
- the vertical component is sufficient to support the weight and allow altitude to be maintained.

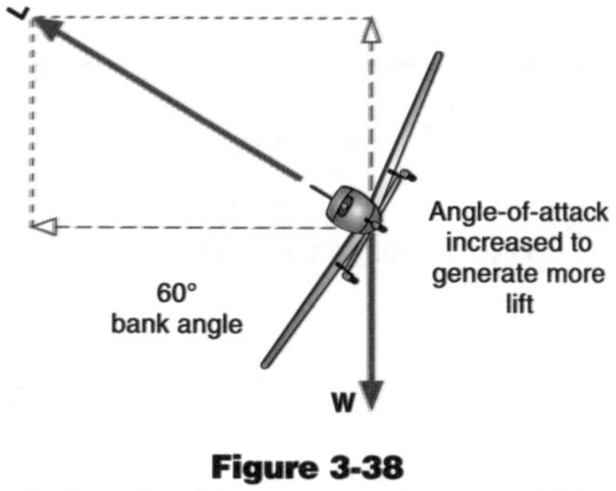

Figure 3-38
A steep level turn requires increased lift.

Firm *back pressure* is needed on the control column to increase the lift force, and *increased power* is required to overcome the tendency to lose airspeed because of the increased drag. Ailerons must be used to maintain the selected bank angle as accurately as possible.

The Stall in a Turn

In a turn, the angle of attack has to be greater than at the same speed in straight-and-level flight, to create the additional lift needed to turn the airplane as well as support its weight. This means that the stall angle of attack will be reached at a higher speed in a turn—the steeper the bank angle, the higher the airspeed at which the stall angle of attack is reached:

- at 30° bank angle, the stall speed is increased by 7% over the straight-and-level stall speed;
- at 45° bank angle, the stall speed is increased by 19%;
- at 60° bank angle, the stall speed is increased by 41%; and
- at 75° bank angle, the stall speed is increased by 100%, or doubled.

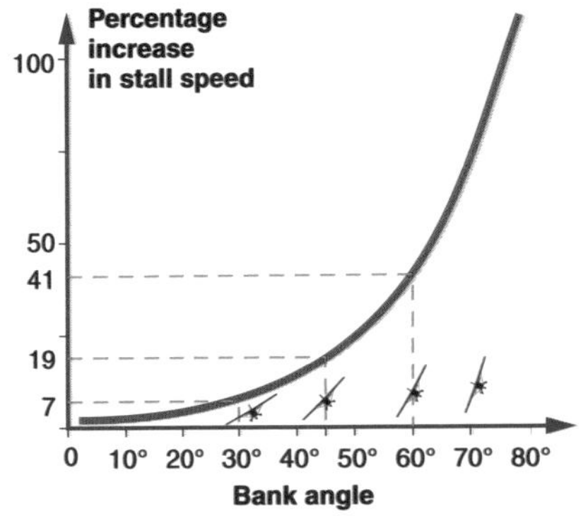

Figure 3-39
Percentage increase in stall speed versus bank angle.

For example, if your airplane stalls at 50 knots straight-and-level, then in a 60° banked turn it will stall at 71 knots (141% of 50 knots) which is a significant increase. In steep turns, you may feel the onset of the stall buffet because the margin between your speed and the stall speed has decreased.

Note. The stall speed increases by the square root of the load factor.

Rate of Turn

The rate of turn of an airplane in degrees per second is important. Instrument flying usually requires *standard-rate* turns of *3°/second*. This means that the airplane turns through:

- 180° in 1 minute; and
- 360° in 2 minutes.

A standard-rate turn at a higher airspeed requires a steeper bank angle.

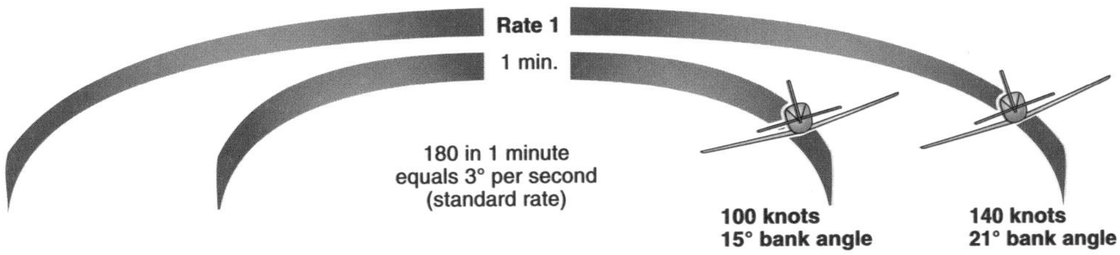

Figure 3-40 A standard-rate turn requires a steeper bank angle at a higher airspeed.

An easy way to estimate the bank angle (in degrees) required for a standard-rate turn is:

⅒ of the airspeed in knots, plus ½ the answer

For example, at 140 knots, for a standard-rate turn, bank angle is $\frac{140}{10} + \frac{1}{2}\left(\frac{140}{10}\right) = 14 + 7 = 21°$.

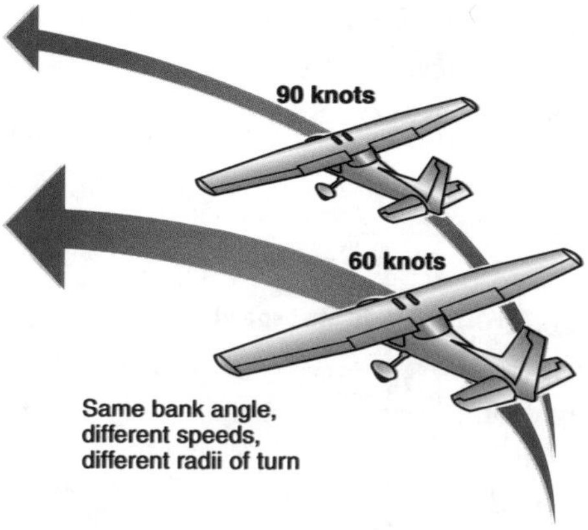

Figure 3-41 Turning performance is increased at low airspeeds.

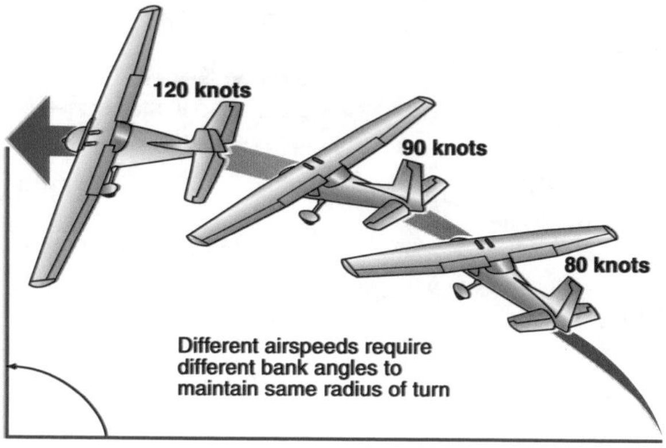

Figure 3-42 Constant-radius turn.

Turn Performance

Constant-Angle Turn

An airplane in a 30° banked turn travels around different circular paths depending on its airspeed. At low speed the turn is tighter (the radius of turn is smaller) than at high speed, see figure 3-41.

At a constant bank angle, the slower airplane has an increased rate of turn. This is because the radius of turn decreases by the square of airspeed. Therefore although the airplane is flying through the air at a slower speed than the faster airplane, its radius of turn is much smaller, and the overall rate of turn is greater.

In summary, if the bank angle is kept constant and the speed reduced, the radius of the turn will decrease and rate of turn increase.

Constant-Radius Turn

To fly a turn of the same radius at a higher speed requires a greater bank angle.

CPL

Constant-Speed Turn

At a constant airspeed, the greater the bank angle, the tighter the turn (the smaller the radius of turn) and the greater the rate of turning (in degrees per second). Note that, if airspeed and bank angle are kept constant, the turn radius (and rate) will remain the same regardless of airplane weight.

If bank angle remains constant and airspeed doubles, the turn radius must increase four times. Similarly if airspeed remains constant and the turn radius is reduced, bank angle must increase.

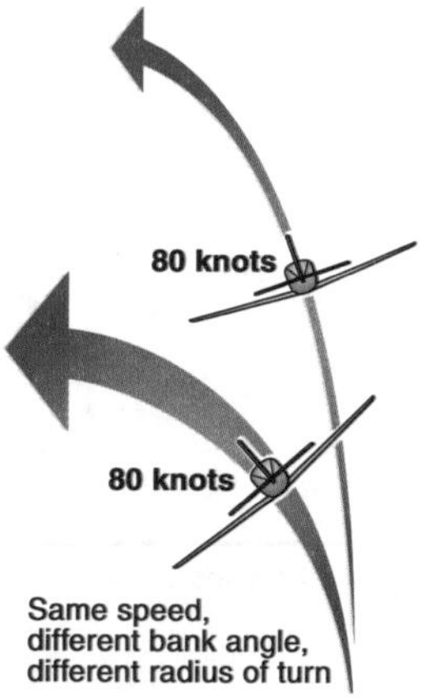

Figure 3-43 A steeper bank angle at constant speed increases turn performance.

Flaps and Turning

If flaps are lowered before a level turn, the stall speed decreases allowing the airplane to turn at a slower airspeed. This has the advantage of allowing a smaller turn radius at the same bank angle but increases drag and decreases the limit load factor in many cases.

End CPL

Stalling

A wing stalls when it reaches the *stall*, or *critical* angle of attack, which is the point where the smooth airflow breaks down and becomes turbulent, thereby considerably reducing the lift generated. You can induce a stall on purpose by increasing the angle of attack using back pressure on the control column.

A stall occurs at the critical angle of attack.

It is very easy both to prevent a stall, simply by ensuring that the critical angle of attack (about 16°) is not approached, and to recover from a stall, by easing the nose forward to decrease the angle of attack. Sometimes you want to approach the stall, for instance during the final stages of a landing.

Ideally the airflow around an airfoil would be streamlined. In flight however, the streamlined flow breaks away (or separates) at some point from the airfoil surface and becomes turbulent. At low angles of attack this separation point is toward the rear of the wing and the turbulence is not significant. At higher angles of attack the separation point moves forward. As the angle of attack is increased, a critical angle is reached beyond which the separation point suddenly moves well forward causing a large increase in the turbulence over the wing.

The separation of the airflow from the wing's upper surface and breakdown of the streamlined flow reduces the magnitude of the low static pressure above the wing, greatly reducing the lift developed by the wing. Conversely, as the angle of attack increases the small aerodynamic force produced by the airflow striking the wing's lower surface increases slightly. The overall effect however, is a marked decrease in lift and the airplane loses altitude. This reduction in the wing's lifting ability is shown in figure 3-44.

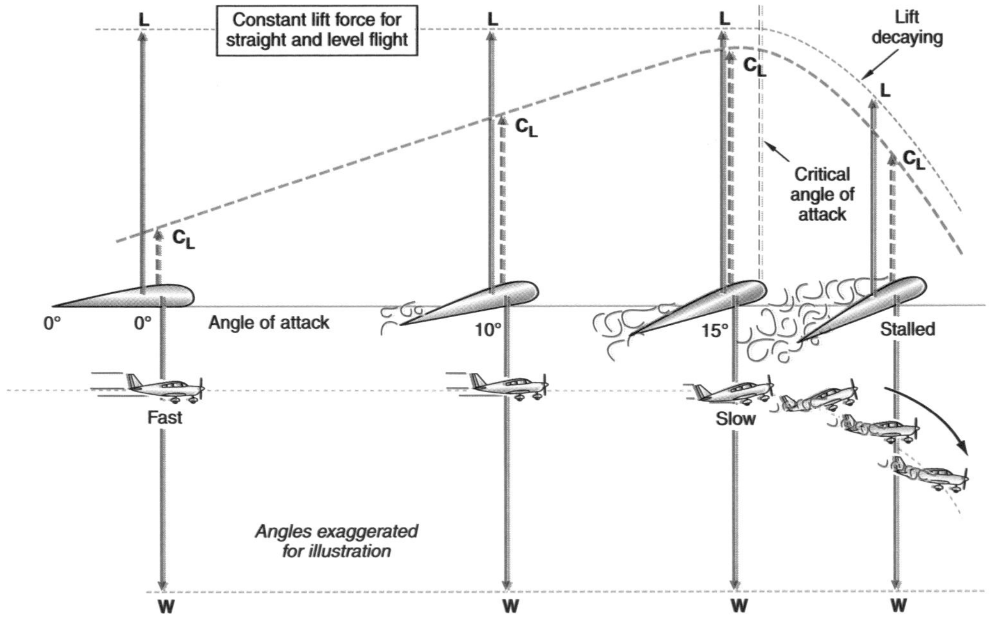

Figure 3-44 An airfoil reaches its maximum lifting ability at the critical angle of attack.

Recognition of the Stall

Approaching the stall angle of attack, the streamlined flow breaks down over parts of the wing and turbulent air flows back over the horizontal stabilizer. The airframe may shake or *buffet* as a result, known as *pre-stall buffet* or *control buffet*. Many airplanes have

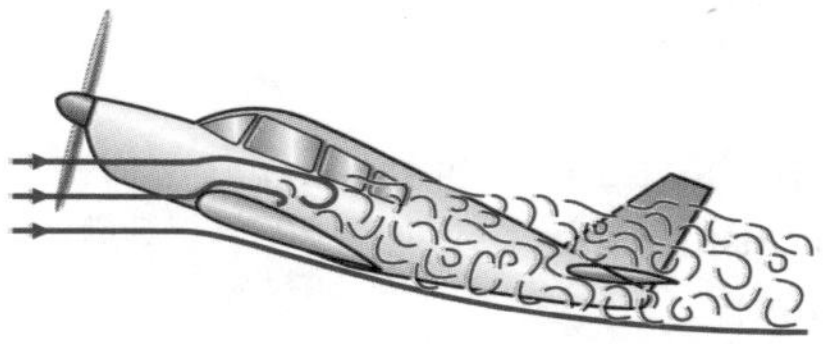

Figure 3-45 Turbulent flow over the horizontal stabilizer.

stall warning devices such as a buzzer or horn that sounds to warn the pilot that the wing is approaching the stall angle.

At the stall, the decrease in lift causes the airplane to *sink*. The rearward movement of the center of pressure causes the *nose to drop*.

Recovery from the Stall

To recover from a stall reduce the angle of attack by lowering the nose.

To recover from a stall, the angle of attack must be reduced. This is achieved by releasing the back pressure on the control column and allowing the nose to come down. If the airspeed is low, which is often the case, full power should also be applied to increase the airspeed as quickly as possible. Stall recovery should be initiated at the first indication of an impending stall.

Stall and Angle of Attack

For most training airplanes, the stall angle of attack is about 16°. This stalling or critical angle of attack is always the same regardless of airspeed, weight, loading, position of the center of gravity, load factor in maneuvers, altitude, and so on. The wing stalls at a particular angle of attack, and not at a particular airspeed.

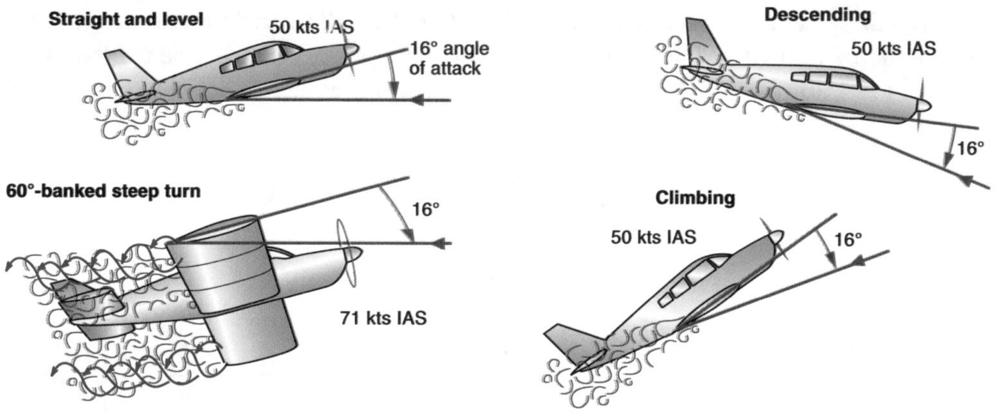

Figure 3-46 The stall occurs at the same stall angle in all phases of flight, but not necessarily at the same speed.

Factors Affecting Stall Speed

A specific airfoil stalls at a particular angle of attack; however, the stall may occur, for example, at:

- 50 knots straight-and-level for an airplane at maximum gross weight;
- 45 knots straight-and-level when it is light;
- 44 knots straight-and-level with flaps and gear down;
- 70 knots in a 60° banked turn; and
- 80 knots if you experience 3g pulling out of a dive.

Note. Do not bother learning these figures as they are only examples.

There is, however, some connection between *angle of attack* and *indicated airspeed.* Their relationship depends on:

- lift produced by the airfoil;
- load factor;

- bank angle;
- weight;
- power; and
- flap setting (which changes the airfoil's shape and lifting ability).

Load Factor

Stall speed increases with load factor.

If the wing has to produce increased lift to maneuver the airplane at a particular airspeed, for instance in a turn or pulling out of a dive, then you will apply back pressure on the control column to increase the angle of attack. Lift will be increased, causing an increased load factor, and you will feel an increase in your g-loading.

Stalling occurs at a critical angle of attack—not at any particular airspeed.

An increased angle of attack in maneuvers will bring the wing closer to the critical or stall angle, even though the airspeed has not changed, and, in the extreme case, if you increase the angle of attack to the critical angle, the wing will stall even though the airspeed is well above the 1g straight-and-level stall speed.

In *airfoil lift* (chapter 1) we saw that lift depends on angle of attack and airspeed squared. If lift depends on airspeed-squared then, conversely, airspeed is related to the square root of lift. This means that the actual stall speed when the critical angle of attack is reached depends on the square root of the lift being produced.

If lift is increased by a factor of four in an aggressive maneuver, the stall speed will be doubled. If the straight-and-level 1g stall speed is 50 knots, then when pulling 4g the wing will stall at 100 knots. Note that 4g is outside the load limits for most training airplanes.

If the load factor is doubled, for instance in a 60° banked turn, you will feel 2g (double your normal weight), and the stall speed will be 1.4 times greater (the square root of 2 is approximately 1.41), which is approximately 71 knots (1.41 × 50). This is illustrated in figures 3-47 and 3-48.

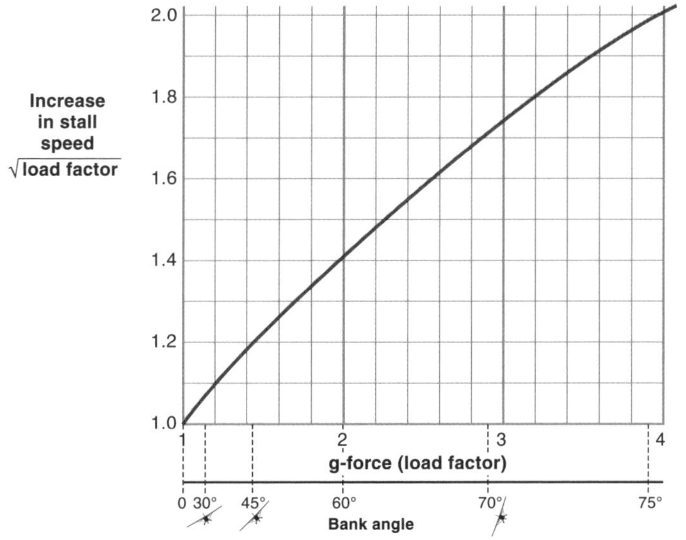

Examples

1. At 2g (load factor 2) the stall speed increases by 1.41, and at 3g by 1.73 times the level stall speed for the airplane.
2. In a 60° bank turn the load factor is 2 and the stall speed increase is by 1.41.

Figure 3-47
Stall speed increases with load factor.

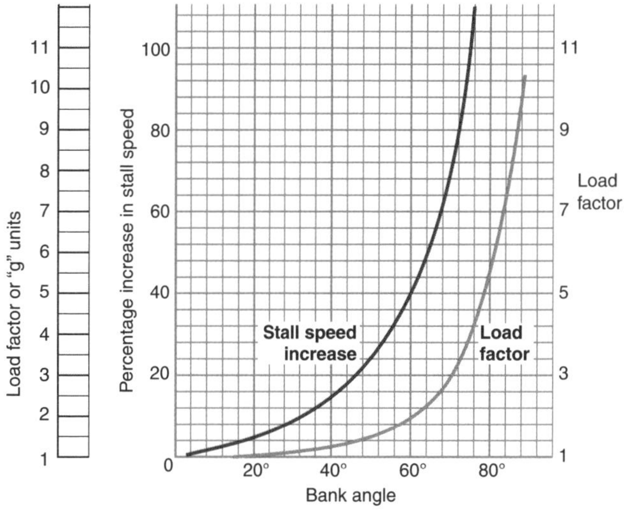

Figure 3-48
Relationship between stall speed, load factor and bank angle.

Because the stall angle is reached in maneuvers at higher speeds than when flying under 1g conditions, these are known as *accelerated stalls*. Stall speed will be increased any time lift from the wings is increased, which will occur in turns, when pulling out of dives, in gusts, and in turbulence.

Weight

Stall speed increases with weight (stall angle of attack stays the same).

In straight-and-level flight, sufficient lift must be generated to balance the weight. The heavier the airplane, the greater is the lift force required. Because the stall speed varies with the square root of lift, an increase in airplane weight increases the stall speed—but does not affect the stall angle of attack.

If the weight decreases 20% to only 0.8 of its original value, then the stall speed will decrease to 0.9 times its original value (0.9 is the square root of 0.8).

If the stall speed at maximum gross weight (say 2,000 pounds) was stated in the Pilot's Operating Handbook to be 50 knots, then at 1,600 pounds (only 80% of the maximum weight), the stall speed is only 90% of the original stall speed which is 45 knots. Conversely, an increase in weight increases the stall speed.

The Pilot's Operating Handbook states various stall speeds. V_S is the minimum steady-flight speed at which the airplane is controllable or stall speed, in straight-and-level flight, with the power off, at *maximum allowable gross weight*. Remember that whenever your airplane weighs less than its maximum weight it will stall at a speed slightly *below* that specified in the Pilot's Operating Handbook.

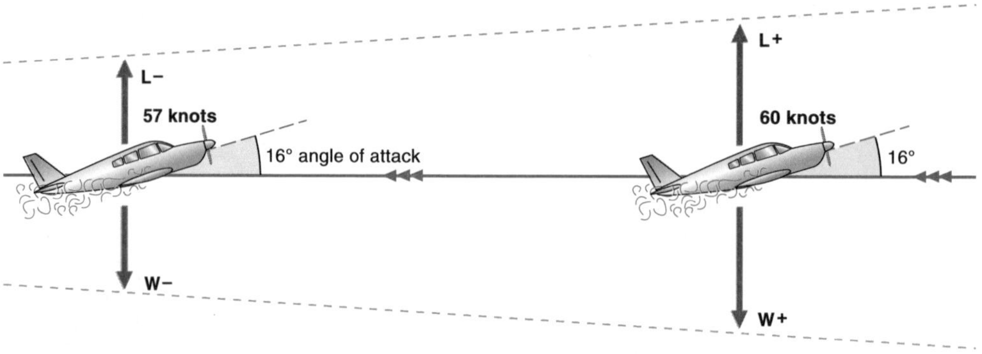

Figure 3-49 Stall speed is a function of weight.

Power

Stall speed is lower in a power-on stall.

With full power on, the strong slipstream passes over the inner section of each wing as well as the empennage. The separation of the airflow from the upper surface of the inner section of each wing is thereby delayed, so a more positive stall occurs at a *lower* indicated airspeed, compared with power off.

In addition, as the stall angle is approached with power on, the high nose attitude allows the thrust to have a vertical component that will partially support the weight. Therefore, the wings are off-loaded a little and less lift is required from them. Less lift means a lowered stall speed.

Because the slipstream encourages the generation of lift from the inner parts of the wing, the outer sections of the wing may stall first. Any uneven production of lift from the outer sections of the two wings will lead to a rapid roll called a *wing drop*. If a wing does drop close to the stall, do not correct by putting the aileron on the dropped wing down. In other words, do not try lifting the wing with aileron.

This will further increase the lower wing's effective angle of attack resulting in the wing becoming more stalled and dropping further. If a wing drops close to the stall, correct with rudder (the secondary effect of rudder is roll). Be aware rudder input yaws the airplane, increasing the angle of attack on the dropped wing.

A power-on stall may be more definite and accompanied by a wing drop.

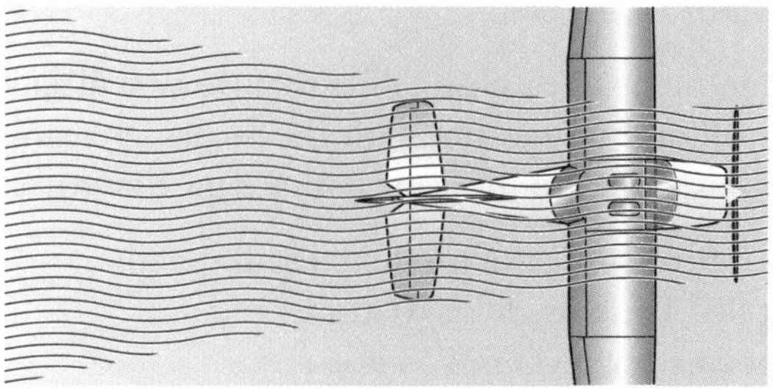

Figure 3-50 Slipstream can lower stall speed.

Altitude

The stall angle of attack will be reached (straight-and-level) at the same stall indicated airspeed irrespective of altitude. If the airplane has a 1g stall speed of 45 knots indicated airspeed (KIAS) at 1,000 feet MSL, its 1g stall speed at 5,000 feet MSL will also be 45 KIAS.

Stall indicated airspeed does not vary with altitude.

Ice, Frost, and Other Wing Contamination

Ice accretion has two effects:

- ice increases weight, so the stall speed is increased; and
- much more significantly, ice accretion, frost, or other contamination on the wings (particularly the front half of the upper surface where most of the lift is generated) disrupts the airflow over the wing, decreasing its lifting ability, and causes early separation of the airflow from the wing.

Ice, frost, or other wing contamination increases stall speed.

The early separation of the airflow results in the breakdown of streamlined flow at angles of attack well below the normal stall angle, and stalling occurs at higher speeds. In addition, the higher stall speeds result in the takeoff speed increasing above the normal takeoff speed, and the takeoff distance increasing at an unknown rate. Ice can prevent an airplane from becoming airborne.

> **Note.** Any ice or frost at all, even if only the texture of very fine sandpaper, should be removed from the wing prior to flight, as should insects and salt from the wing leading edges.

Flaps

Extending flaps gives us a new airfoil shape with increased camber and an *increased lifting ability*. This enables the wings to support the same load at a lower speed, and the airspeed can decrease to a lower value before the stall angle is reached.

Flaps reduce the stall speed.

The reduction of stall speeds is the main advantage of flaps. It makes for safe flight at lower speeds—very useful for takeoffs, landings (shorter fields) and low speed searches. Also, extending the flaps allows lower nose attitudes—not only is visibility increased, but also the stall angle will be reached at a lower nose attitude.

The stall with flaps extended may be accompanied by a wing drop, especially with power on. Use rudder to correct the wing drop, not aileron. Because of the increased drag with flaps extended, any speed loss, especially with power off, could be quite rapid, with little advance warning to the pilot of an impending stall.

In the stall with flaps down, turbulence over the horizontal stabilizer may cause very poor control from the elevator, known as *blanketing* of the elevator. Some training airplanes have a T-tail with the horizontal stabilizer high on the fin to avoid any such blanketing of the elevator in the stall.

Note. Some airplane manuals publish tables that show stall speed at various bank angles with power off and power on, with the airplane clean, and also with the airplane in the landing configuration (gear and flaps down).

For example from figure 3-51, the predicted stall speed:

- clean, power off at 30° bank angle is 70 knots; and
- gear/flaps down, power on, level is 47 knots.

Stall Speeds					
Gross Weight 2,750 lb		Bank Angle			
		Level	30°	45°	60°
Power		Gear and Flaps Up			
On	mph	62	67	74	88
	kt	54	58	64	76
Off	mph	75	81	89	106
	kt	65	70	77	92
		Gear and Flaps Down			
On	mph	54	58	64	76
	kt	47	50	56	66
Off	mph	66	71	78	93
	kt	57	62	68	81

SAMPLE ONLY not to be used for flight operations or flight planning

Increasing bank angle increases stall speed

Adding power reduces stall speed

Extending flaps reduces stall speed

Figure 3-51 Examples of stall speeds in different situations.

Stall Warning Devices

Most airplanes are equipped with a device such as a horn, flashing red light, or whistle to warn of an impending stall. Such artificial devices are only secondary to the aerodynamic *stall warnings* that you must learn to recognize, such as stall buffet, decreasing speed, and less effective controls. If a stall recovery is initiated at the sound of the stall horn, it is known as an *impending stall recovery*.

Wing Design and Stall Characteristics

Stalling first at the wing root is preferable to stalling first at the wingtip.

If there is an uneven loss of lift from the outer sections of the wings near the tips, caused by one of them stalling first, then a strong rolling moment is set up because of the long moment arm from the outer sections of the wing to the CG. Also, the ailerons become less effective because of the disturbed airflow around them.

Stalling at the wing roots is preferable because it allows the control buffet over the horizontal stabilizer (because of the turbulent air from the inner sections of the wing) to be felt, while the outer sections of the wings are still producing lift and the ailerons should still be effective. An uneven loss of lift on the inner sections, if one wing stalls before the other, does not have as great a rolling moment compared with when the outer sections of the wing stall first.

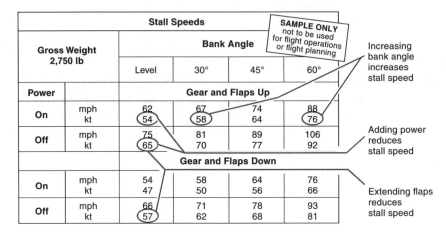

A *rectangular* wing, compared with other wing planforms, has a tendency to stall first at the wing root, and so provide adequate stall warning to the pilot while the ailerons are still effective. This is one reason why rectangular wings are common in basic training airplanes.

Stalling at the wing root first can also be achieved with a lower angle of incidence (and therefore a lower angle of attack) at the wingtip when compared with the wing root, which is known as *washout*. This means that the wing root reaches the stall angle prior to the wingtip. (Washout also helps to reduce the induced drag from wingtip vortices.) On other airplanes, small metal plates can be placed at the inboard leading edges to encourage the early onset of the stall at the wing root.

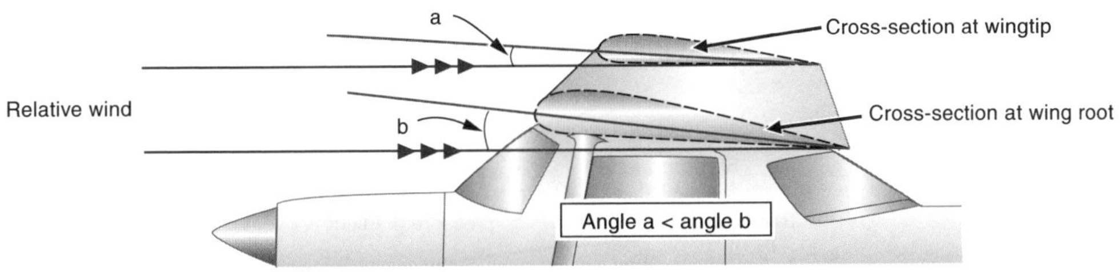

Figure 3-52 Built-in washout causes the wingtip to stall later than the root.

The Boundary Layer

CPL

We said earlier in this chapter that a wing stalls when it exceeds the critical angle of attack and the airflow separates from the wing's surface. To understand why this occurs it is important to study the boundary layer. The *boundary layer* is the thin (1/12- to 3/4-inch) layer of air next to the wing's surface. Because of the air's viscosity, or stickiness, the speed of the air in the boundary layer is reduced below that of the main airflow.

In the boundary layer the air closest to the surface is slowest. As the distance from the surface increases the relative speed of the air increases until it reaches that of the main airflow (free-stream flow). You may have noticed when watching water flow down a dam spillway that at the top the flow is thin and laminar, and then at some point it becomes thicker and turbulent. Figures 3-53 and 3-54 show how flow (in this case water) has two types, *laminar* and *turbulent*, separated by a transition point or region.

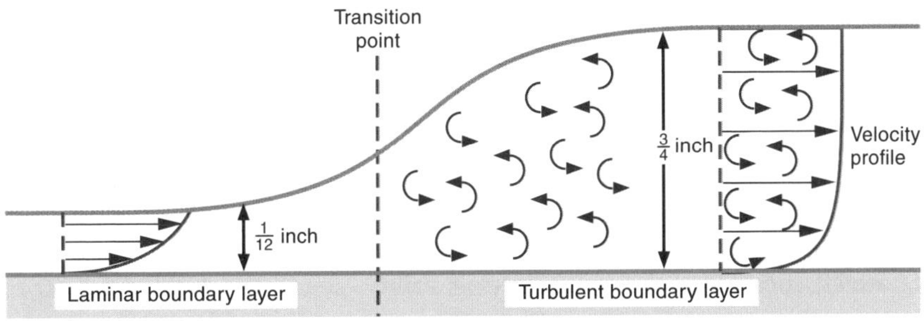

Figure 3-53 The boundary layer over a flat surface.

CPL

The Adverse Pressure Gradient

Over a curved surface such as a wing, however, there is an additional factor that affects the boundary layer. As the airflow is fastest at the point of maximum curvature, the static pressure there is lowest. Further aft the airflow's speed decreases and the static pressure, although still low, increases. This difference in static pressure causes a pressure gradient which acts in the opposite direction to the airflow. This is called an *adverse pressure gradient.*

Close to the wing's surface the air is moving slowest and therefore has less kinetic energy to overcome this adverse pressure gradient. As the air in the boundary layer moves aft it slows, and at some point the adverse pressure gradient will be strong enough to stop it. This is the *separation point.* Note that aft of the separation point *flow reversal* occurs, where the air close to the wing is actually moving forward against the main flow.

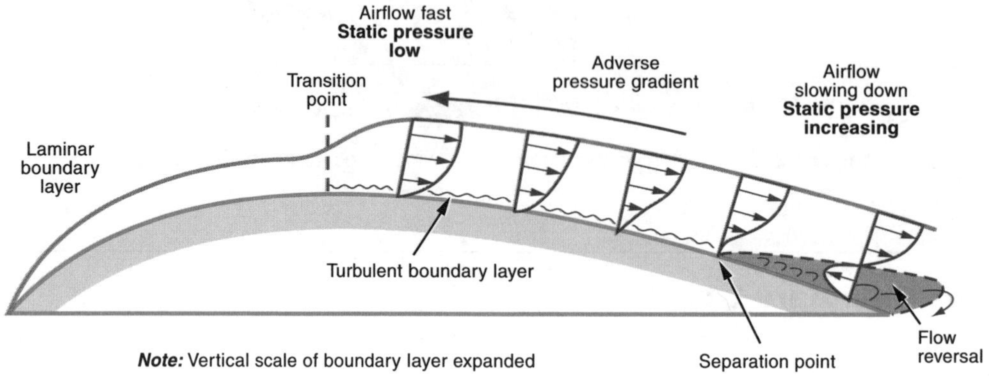

Figure 3-54 The boundary layer over the wing's upper surface.

Separation and the Stall

As the angle of attack increases, the static pressure at the point of maximum curvature becomes even lower. The adverse pressure gradient now strengthens and the separation point moves further forward until the point is reached where the wing stalls.

Wing Contamination and Slats

If the adverse pressure gradient were kept constant, and the speed of the boundary layer altered, the separation point would also move. Ice, frost, and other contamination on the wing slow down the speed of the thin boundary layer causing the separation point to move forward and the wing to stall at a lower angle of attack (which reduces the wing's lifting ability).

Slats, which introduce high-speed air into the boundary layer near the leading edge, delay the forward movement of the separation point, allowing the wing to fly at higher angles of attack, increasing the wing's lifting ability (see figure 1-63, page 30).

End CPL

The Spin

A spin is a condition of stalled flight in which the airplane follows a spiral descent path. As well as the airplane being in a stalled condition, and yawing, one wing is producing more lift than the other, which results in a roll. The dropping wing is more deeply stalled than the other, and the greater drag from this wing results in further yaw, further roll, and autorotation develops. Upward pitching of the nose will also occur. You can induce a spin on purpose by yawing an airplane that is stalled, or just on the point of stalling.

To spin, an airplane must first be stalled.

In a spin, the airplane is in motion about all three axes. In other words, lots of things are happening in a spin! The airplane is:

- stalled;
- rolling;
- yawing;
- pitching;
- slipping; and
- rapidly losing altitude at a low airspeed (close to the stall speed).

In a spin the wings will not produce much lift, since they are stalled. The airplane will accelerate downward until it reaches a vertical rate of descent where the greatly increased drag, now acting upward, counteracts the weight. The altitude loss will be rapid as the airplane spins downward around the vertical spin axis but, because of the high angle of attack and the stalled condition, the airspeed in the spin will be quite low and fluctuating.

Characteristics of a developed spin include a *low airspeed* (which does not increase until recovery action is initiated), and a *high rate of descent*.

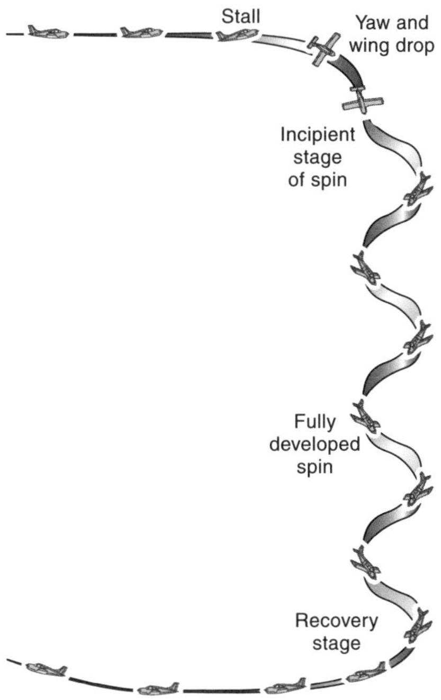

Figure 3-55
The flight path in a spin.

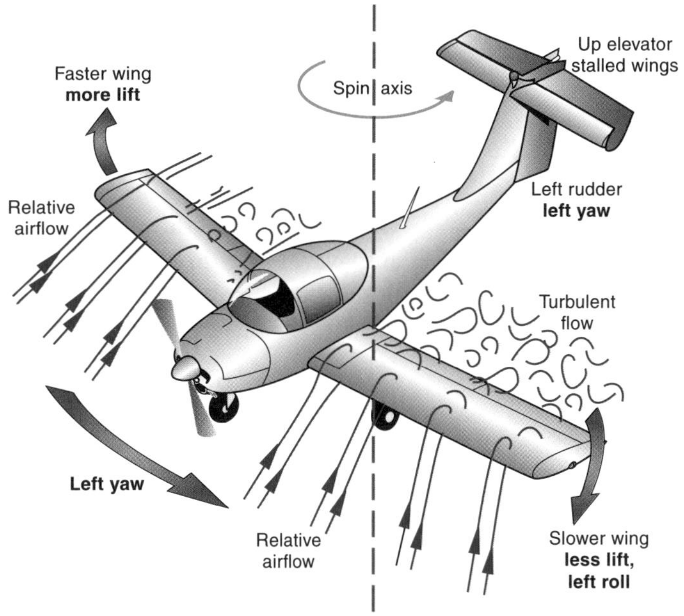

Figure 3-56
The airplane in a stable spin to the left.

Spin Recovery

To recover from a spin, you must ensure power is off, oppose the yaw, and unstall the wings. First note yaw direction and apply full opposite rudder, and then move the control column forward to unstall the wings by decreasing the angle of attack. Once the airplane has stopped spinning, ease the airplane out of the dive and resume normal flight.

Misuse of Ailerons

On some airplanes, misuse of the ailerons can cause a spin.

Trying to raise a dropped wing with opposite aileron may have the *reverse* effect when the airplane is near the stall. If, as the aileron goes down, the stall angle of attack is exceeded, the wing may drop quickly instead of rising, resulting in a spin.

The application of aileron after a spin has developed may aggravate the spin. Discuss the spin characteristics of your particular airplane with your flight instructor.

The Spiral Dive

Do not confuse a spin (low airspeed and stalled) with a spiral dive (high airspeed and not stalled).

A maneuver that must not be confused with a spin is the spiral dive, which can be thought of as a steep turn that has gone wrong. In a spiral dive the nose attitude is low, and the rate of descent is high, but neither wing is stalled and the airspeed is high and rapidly increasing. A spiral dive is really just a steep descending turn. However, because the pilot may be disoriented it is often mistaken for a spin. The high and increasing airspeed indicates that the airplane is in a spiral dive rather than a spin (when the airspeed would fluctuate at a low value).

Recovery from a spiral dive is simple. Roll wings level and pull gently out of the dive. Beware of overstressing the airplane by pulling too quickly out of the dive—remember the controls will be very effective because of the high airspeed.

CPL

Autorotation

The two main features of the autorotation that occurs when a wing drops in stalled flight are:

- auto-roll—the more-deeply stalled dropping wing will generate even less lift, and so will want to keep dropping, causing the airplane to continue rolling; and
- auto-yaw—the dropping wing will generate increased drag, and want to yaw the nose of the airplane in the same direction as the roll.

If a wing drops in flight, perhaps from a gust or perhaps intentionally by the pilot's actions, the relative airflow will strike it more from below, and so its angle of attack will be greater. The rising wing, conversely, will have its angle of attack temporarily reduced.

In normal flight, at fairly low angles of attack well away from the stall, the increased angle of attack of the dropping wing causes it to develop more lift. Conversely, the reduced angle of attack of the rising wing reduces its lift. The natural tendencies of the airplane in normal flight are therefore for the airplane to roll wings level.

In stalled flight, however, the increased angle of attack on the dropping wing causes it to be even more stalled, and develop even less lift. The result is that the dropping wing in a stalled condition continues to drop, and the rolling motion tends to continue. This occurs without any movement of the ailerons, so this characteristic may be thought of as *auto-roll*.

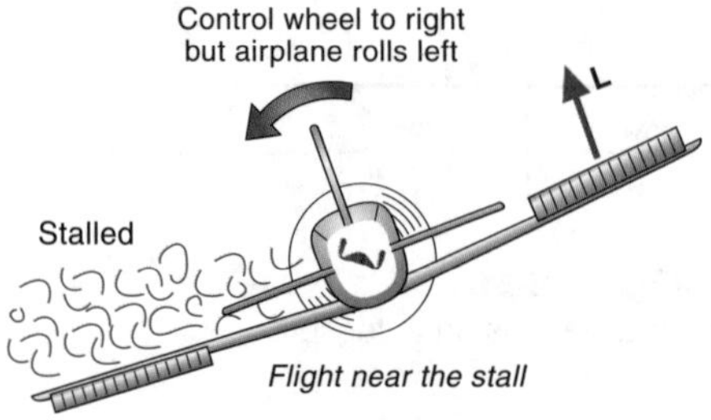

Figure 3-57
Close to the stall, reduced lift and increased drag on a dropping wing cause autorotaion.

The *auto-roll* effect can be illustrated on the familiar *lift curve*, which shows lift increasing with angle of attack, but only up to the critical stall angle of attack beyond which lift decreases.

In normal flight, when lift on a wing increases, so does drag. In stalled flight, however, as we can see from the *drag curve* above, a dropping wing that is stalled not only experiences reduced lift, causing it to continue rolling (auto-roll), it also experiences increased drag which tends to yaw it in the direction of roll (auto-yaw).

In addition, the yawing motion in the same direction as the roll *increases* the rolling tendency because the outside wing is traveling faster. This makes the rolling-yawing cycle self-sustaining, or automatic, in that the increased rolling velocity sustains or even increases the difference in the angle of attack on the two wings, strengthening the roll-yaw tendency. This natural tendency to *continue* rolling and yawing in the same direction when in the stalled condition is known as *autorotation*. Autorotation is the basis of the spin.

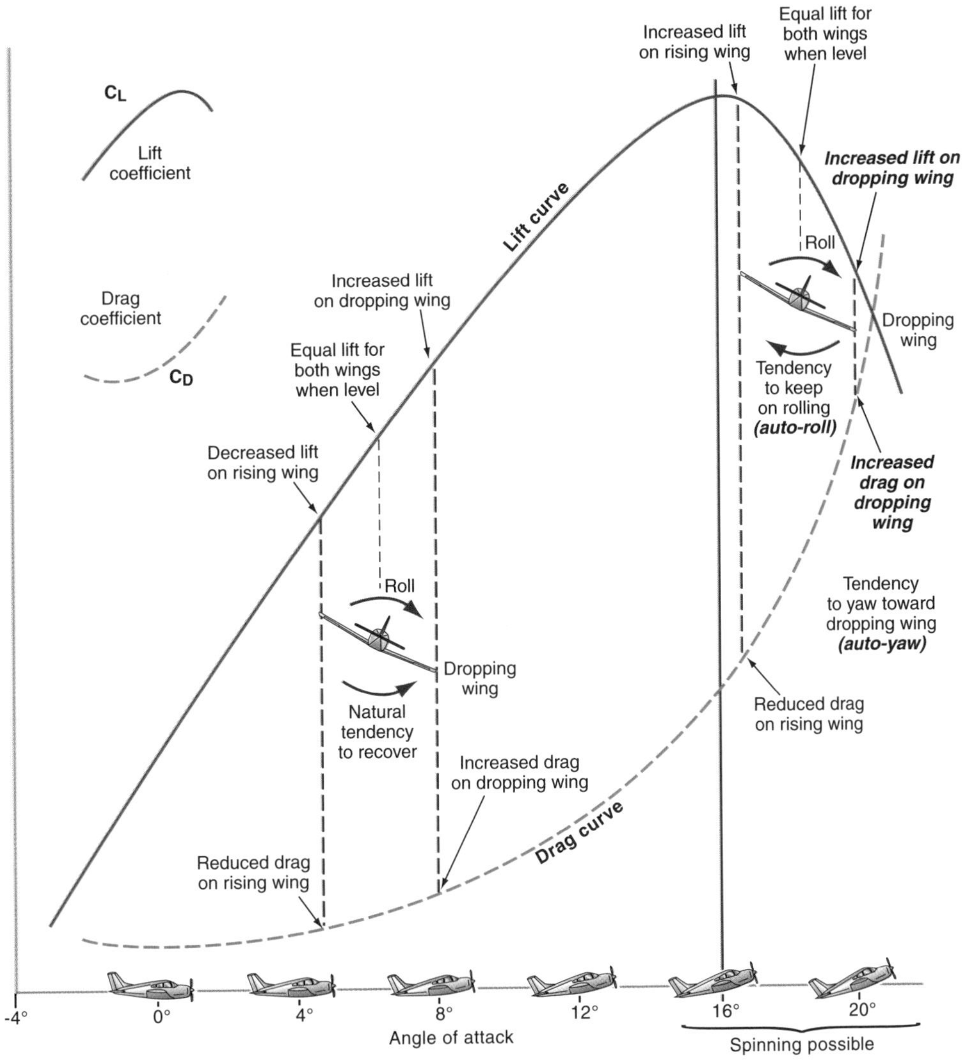

Figure 3-58 Lift and drag effects on a dropping wing.

CPL

Rate of Rotation

The flatness of the spin determines the rate of rotation. If the airplane adopts a higher nose attitude and the spin flattens:

- the rate of rotation decreases; and
- the rate of descent decreases (caused by increased drag from the higher angle of attack).

A spinning ice skater moves her arms in and out from her body to alter the rate of rotation. The same effect occurs in an airplane. In a steep nose-down attitude, the mass of the airplane is close to the spin axis and the rate of rotation is high. If the spin flattens, some of the airplane's mass is distributed further from the spin axis and the rate of rotation decreases.

If the nose pitches up and down in the spin, the rate of rotation varies, becoming slower when the spin is flatter and faster when the nose position is steeper. Since the nose is purposely lowered in the recovery from a spin, you can expect a temporary increase in the rate of rotation until the recovery is complete.

A rearward CG makes a spin recovery more difficult.

A *rearward CG* encourages a flatter spin and it is more difficult to lower the nose in the recovery. This applies to straight stalls as well as spins, and is a very important reason for ensuring that you never fly an airplane loaded outside its approved weight-and-balance limits.

Conversely, a *forward CG* normally results in a steeper spin with a higher rate of descent and a higher rate of rotation. It may make recovery much easier and, in fact, may even prevent a spin occurring.

Spin Direction

Spin direction is determined by the direction of yaw. This can be found from the airplane in the turn coordinator. Do not use the inclinometer to determine direction of yaw as it will indicate the same regardless of turn direction depending on where it is mounted.

End CPL

Review 3
Aerodynamics of Flight

Straight-and-Level Flight

1. In steady straight-and-level flight:
   a. lift is greater than drag and thrust equals weight.
   b. weight equals lift and drag equals thrust.
   c. lift equals weight and thrust is greater than drag.
2. In steady-state flight, what is the sum of the opposing forces acting on an airplane?
3. If indicated airspeed is decreased, what needs to happen to the angle of attack for the airplane to remain in straight-and-level flight?
4. What are low indicated airspeeds associated with?
5. There is a decrease in aircraft weight. You want straight-and-level flight to continue, so lift is decreased. How is this achieved?
6. Why is ice or frost on the wings hazardous?

Climb and Descent

7. Are the four main forces in equilibrium in a steady climb when the airplane is not accelerating or decelerating?
8. An airplane will clear obstacles by a greater margin at the:
   a. best angle-of-climb speed.
   b. best rate-of-climb speed.
   c. cruise-climb speed.
9. What is the rate of climb (FPM) for an airplane that climbs 700 feet in 2 minutes?
10. During the transition from straight-and-level flight to a climb, the angle of attack is:
    a. increased but lift is decreased.
    b. increased but lift remains the same.
    c. increased and lift is momentarily increased.
11. What rate of climb is needed to climb 1,200 feet in 2 minutes?
12. An airplane will reach a given altitude in the minimum time if it climbs at the:
    a. best angle-of-climb speed.
    b. best rate-of-climb speed.
    c. cruise-climb speed.
13. What instrument depicts rate of climb?
14. True or false? The angle of climb of the same airplane carrying the pilot and three passengers will be less than the angle of climb when only the pilot is on board.
15. What is absolute ceiling?
16. If the airplane is climbing into a headwind after takeoff, the climb angle relative to the ground obstacles on the ground will be:
    a. the same.
    b. steeper.
    c. shallower.
17. Climb performance reduces if:
    a. weight, altitude, and temperature decrease.
    b. weight, temperature, and altitude increase.
    c. power and weight increase.
18. What is weight counteracted by for an airplane to be in equilibrium in a steady glide?
19. What effect will adding power while maintaining the same airspeed have on the rate and angle of descent?
20. True or false? If flaps are lowered, the drag increases and the descent becomes shallower.
21. True or false? Flying faster than the correct descent speed flattens the descent angle through the air.
22. If the same angle of attack is maintained, will a heavily loaded airplane glide further compared with when it carries a light load?
23. What adjustment to airspeed must be made for an airplane with a light load to glide the same distance as when it is heavy?
24. If you have a rate of descent of 500 FPM, how long will it take you to descend 3,000 feet in a 20-knot headwind?
25. An airplane is flown in a glide at an airspeed where the L/D ratio is 8:1. How many feet air distance will this airplane glide for each 1,000 feet of altitude lost?
26. How much altitude would an airplane lose in gliding 1 statute mile in still air at an airspeed that provides an L/D ratio of 10:1 (1 statute mile is 5,280 feet)?

Turning and Load Factor

27. What is load factor?

28. What sort of force is required for an airplane to turn?

29. What is the force in question 28 provided by?

30. True or false? To maintain airspeed in a turn, the pilot must apply power to overcome the increased parasite drag.

31. The load factor in a turn depends on:
- **a.** bank angle.
- **b.** airspeed.
- **c.** bank angle and airspeed.

Refer to figure 3-37 (page 79) for questions 32 to 34.

32. In a 60° banked turn at a constant altitude:
- **a.** what is the load factor?
- **b.** the wings must generate a force equal to how many times the weight of the airplane?

33. If an airplane weighs 3,300 pounds, what is the approximate "load" (in pounds) that the airplane structure is required to support in a 30° banked turn while maintaining altitude?

34. If an airplane weighs 5,400 pounds, what is the approximate "load" (in pounds) that the airplane structure is required to support in a 55° banked turn while maintaining altitude?

Stalling and Spinning

35. What can the turbulent airflow over the horizontal stabilizer cause if the wings stall?

36. What is the stall angle on a typical light training airplane (degrees angle of attack)?

37. An airplane wing can be stalled:
- **a.** only when the nose is high and the airspeed is low.
- **b.** at any airspeed and in any flight attitude, provided that the critical angle of attack is reached.

38. Indicated stall speed is affected by changes in:
- **a.** temperature.
- **b.** density.
- **c.** altitude.
- **d.** load factor.

39. True or false? At higher weights, the airplane will stall at a higher angle of attack.

40. Washout designed into a wing causes which section of the wing to stall first?

41. If the airplane approaches the stall angle with a lot of power on, the slipstream adds a lot of kinetic energy to the airflow so separation and stalling is delayed. Is the stall speed with power on the same as the power-off stall speed?

42. In what flight condition must an aircraft be placed in order to spin?

43. During an approach to a stall, an increased load factor caused by turning or turbulence will make the airplane:
- **a.** stall at a higher airspeed.
- **b.** have a tendency to spin.
- **c.** more difficult to control.

44. How does frost and ice affect the lifting surfaces of an airplane on takeoff?

Commercial Review

45. Describe maximum-range cruise airspeed and maximum-endurance airspeed.

46. The lower the fuel flow in gallons per hour, the greater the what?

47. True or false? The maximum-range airspeed is the airspeed where minimum drag occurs.

48. As weight decreases, what happens to the maximum range airspeed, which is the airspeed for minimum drag?

49. When is an airplane *speed stable*?

50. What is the rate of climb (FPM) for an airplane that climbs 250 feet in 30 seconds?

51. What does rate of climb depend on?

52. What does angle of climb depend on?

53. Is climb performance better on a hot day than on a cold day?

Refer to figure 1-74 (page 40) for questions 54 to 57.

54. How would you achieve the best glide range in this airplane?

55. What lift/drag ratio will the airplane have if it is flown at an angle of attack of 10°?

56. If the airplane glides at an angle of attack of 10°, how many feet will it descend in one statute mile?

57. How much altitude will this airplane lose in 3 miles of gliding at an angle of attack of 8°?

58. What adjustment needs to be made to the bank angle in order to:
  a. increase rate of turn at a constant airspeed?
  b. decrease radius of turn at a constant airspeed?

59. What adjustment needs to be made to the airspeed in order to:
  a. increase rate of turn at a constant bank angle?
  b. reduce radius of turn at a constant bank angle?

60. What would happen to the rate of turn if radius of turn is reduced?

61. If bank angle is kept constant but airspeed in the turn is varied, what will happen to the wing loading?

62. In a turn, what do wing loading and load factor depend on?

63. You are turning though 120° at standard rate.
  a. How long would the turn take?
  b. What bank angle would be required to achieve this at 100 knots?

64. A normal category airplane is stressed to 3.8g. If a baggage compartment weight limit is 80 lb, what is the maximum baggage weight you can put in the compartment if you intend to fly up to 3g?

65. *Refer to figure 3-51 (page 88)* Determine the stall speed in KIAS at gross weight 2,750 pounds under the following conditions:
  a. gear and flaps up, wings level, power on.
  b. gear and flaps up, 30° bank angle, power on.
  c. gear and flaps up, 45° bank angle, power off.
  d. gear and flaps down, 30° bank angle, power off.

66. What should the pilot do to simultaneously increase rate of turn and decrease turn radius?

67. While maintaining a constant bank angle and altitude in a coordinated turn, an increase in airspeed will:
  a. decrease the rate of turn resulting in a decreased load factor.
  b. decrease the rate of turn resulting in no change in load factor.
  c. increase the rate of turn resulting in no change in load factor.

68. Turbulent air can cause an increase in stall speed by:
  a. abrupt increases in the angle of attack and load factor.
  b. abrupt decreases in the angle of attack and load factor.
  c. abrupt increases in weight.

69. It is more difficult to recover from a stall or spin when the airplane is loaded with:
  a. a forward center of gravity.
  b. a mid-range center of gravity.
  c. an aft center of gravity.

70. Which is true regarding the use of flaps during turns?
  a. The addition of flaps increases stall speed.
  b. The addition of flaps decreases stall speed.
  c. In any given degree of bank, the addition of flaps has no effect on stall speed.

71. A rectangular wing, as compared to other wing shapes, has a tendency to stall first at the:
  a. wingtip, providing adequate stall warning.
  b. wing root, providing adequate stall warning.
  c. wing root, providing inadequate stall warning.

Answers are given on page 686.

The Airplane

4. **Airframe**
5. **Engine**
6. **Systems**
7. **Flight Instruments**

Airframe 4

Airplane Components

The major components of an airplane are:
- the fuselage;
- the wings;
- the empennage (tail section);
- the flight controls;
- the landing gear (or undercarriage); and
- the engine and propeller.

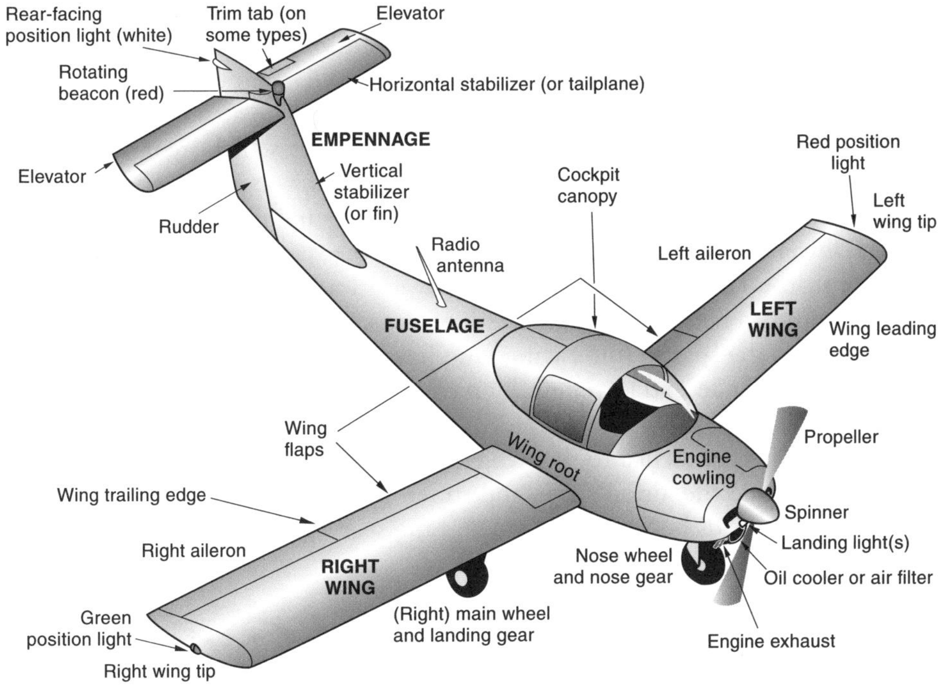

Figure 4-1 Features of a modern training airplane.

Fuselage

The fuselage is the body of the airplane to which the wings, empennage, engine and landing gear are attached. It contains a cabin with seats for the pilot and passengers plus cockpit controls and instruments. It may also contain a baggage compartment.

The fuselage of many modern training airplanes is of *semi-monocoque* construction, a light framework covered by a skin (usually aluminum) that absorbs much of the stress. It is a combination of the best features of a *strut-type* structure, in which the internal framework absorbs almost all of the stress, and a *monocoque* structure which, like an eggshell, has no internal structure and the stress is carried entirely by the skin.

Figure 4-2 Fuselage.

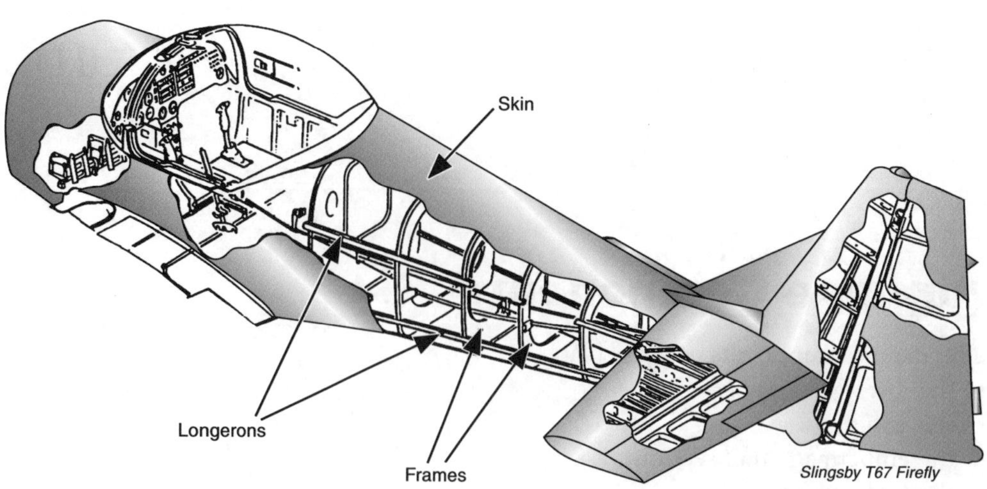

Figure 4-3 Typical semi-monocoque construction.

Wings

The wings are designed to cope with the flight loads of lift and drag. They also may support other external devices such as engines (on multi-engine airplanes) and flaps.

Wings generally have one or more internal *spars* which are attached to the fuselage and extend to the wingtips. The spars carry the major loads, which are upward bending because of the lift, and downward bending because of wing-mounted engines and fuel.

The wings in most airplanes also contain *fuel tanks* installed between the curved upper and lower surfaces. This is an efficient use of the space available, and the weight of the fuel in the tanks also provides a downward force on the wing structure that reduces the upward bending effect of the lift forces.

Figure 4-4 Wing strut.

In addition to the spar(s), some wings also have external *struts* connecting them to the fuselage to provide extra strength by transmitting some of the wing loads to the fuselage.

Ribs, roughly perpendicular to the wing spar(s), assisted by stringers running parallel to the spars, provide the airfoil shape and stiffen the skin which is attached to them. The ribs transmit loads between the skin and the spar(s).

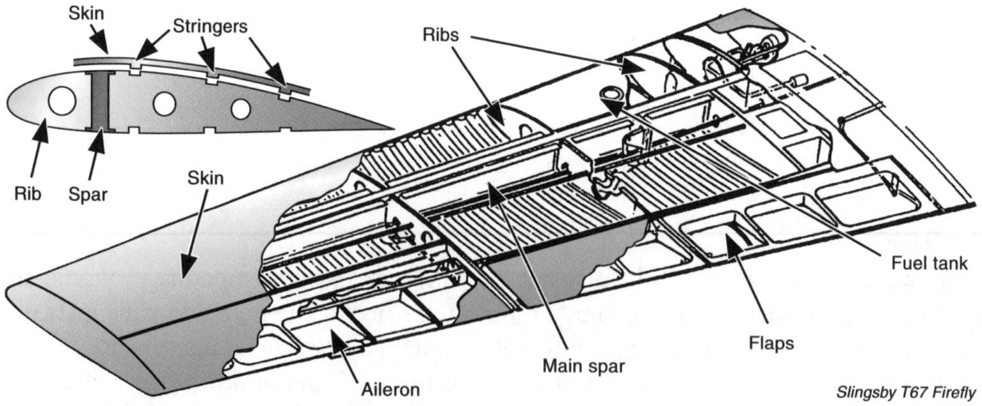

Figure 4-5 Components of a wing.

Monoplanes are designed with a single set of wings placed so that the airplane is known as a high-wing, low-wing, or mid-wing monoplane. Biplanes, such as the Pitts Special, are designed with a double set of wings. The Cessna 172 is a high-wing monoplane; the Piper Warrior is a low-wing monoplane.

Figure 4-7 Biplane.

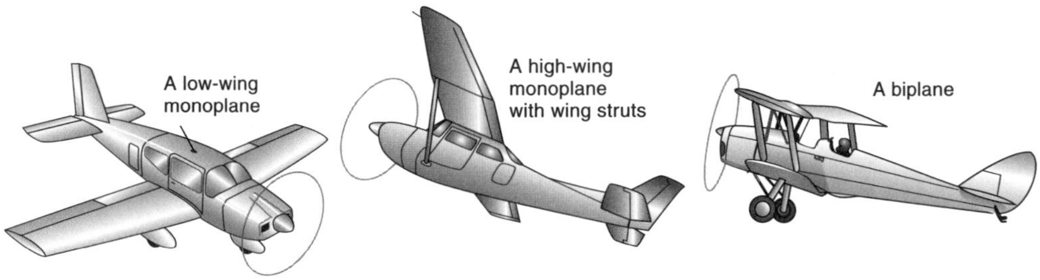

Figure 4-6 Low-wing monoplane, high-wing monoplane, and biplane.

Figure 4-8 Empennage.

Empennage

The empennage is the tail section of the airplane. It is generally constructed like the wings and consists of a fixed *vertical stabilizer* (or fin) to which is attached a movable *rudder*, and a fixed *horizontal stabilizer* with a movable *elevator* hinged to its trailing edge.

There are variations in design, some airplanes have a stabilator (all-moving tailplane), others have a *ruddervator* (combined rudder and elevator) in the form of a butterfly tail, and yet others have a high T-tail, with the horizontal stabilizer mounted on top of the vertical stabilizer.

Figure 4-9 V-tail.

Flight Controls

The main flight control surfaces are the *elevator*, *ailerons* and *rudder*. They are operated from the cockpit by moving the control wheel and rudder pedals. In a typical airplane, movement of the control wheel or rudder pedals operates an internal system of cables and pulleys that then moves the relevant control surface. Turnbuckles may be inserted in the cables to allow the cable tension to be adjusted by qualified personnel.

There are usually stops to protect the control surfaces from excessive movement in flight and on the ground. Stops in the flight control system may be installed to limit control wheel movement.

Figure 4-10 Aileron.

Figure 4-11 Conventional landing gear.

Landing Gear

The landing gear (or undercarriage) supports the weight of the airplane when it is on the ground, and may be of either the tricycle type (with a nosewheel) or the tailwheel type. Most tricycle landing gear airplanes are equipped with *nosewheel steering* through the rudder pedals, and almost all airplanes have *mainwheel brakes*.

Mainwheels

The mainwheels carry most of the load when the airplane is on the ground, especially during the takeoff and landing, and so are more robust than the nosewheel (or tailwheel). They are usually attached to the main airplane structure with legs in the form of:

- a very strong spring leaf of steel or fiberglass;
- struts and braces; or
- an oleo strut.

Figure 4-12 Spring-steel strut.

Figure 4-13 Retractable gear.

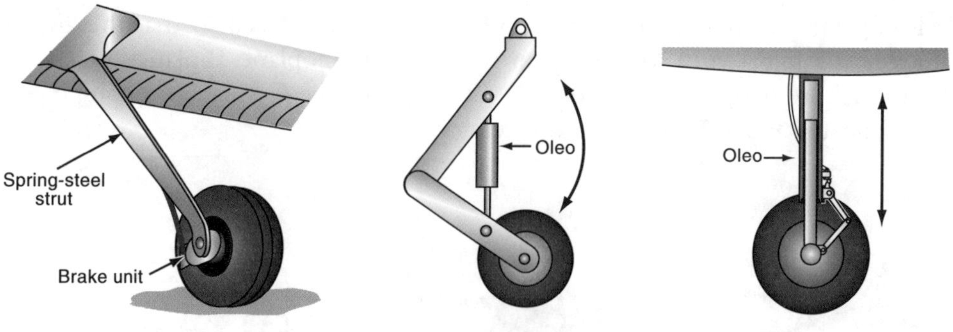

Figure 4-14 Various types of landing gear.

A squat switch is used on airplanes with retractable landing gear to prevent the wheels from being inadvertently raised when the airplane is on the ground. With the weight of the airplane pressing down on the wheel struts, the squat switch opens the gear circuit so electricity will not flow to the hydraulic gear pump, even if the gear handle is placed in the up position.

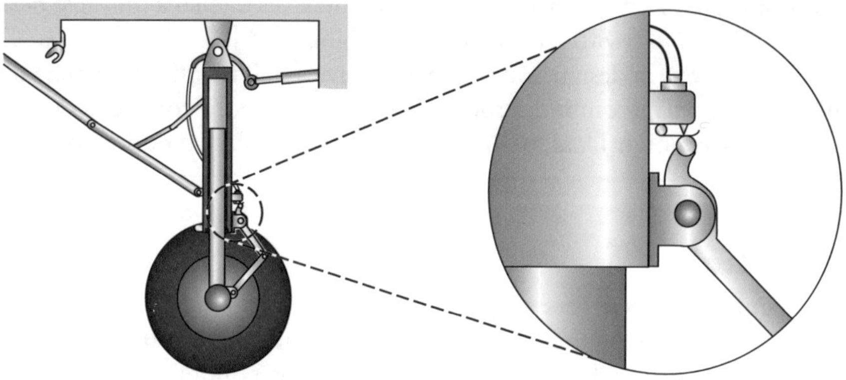

Figure 4-15 Micro-switch (squat switch).

The *oleo strut* acts as a shock absorber, and is of telescopic construction, with a piston that can move within a cylinder against an opposing pressure of compressed air. The piston is attached to the wheel by an oleo strut and the cylinder is attached to the airframe.

The greater the load on the strut, the more the air is compressed by the piston. While the airplane is moving along the ground, the load will vary, and so the strut will move up and down as the compressed air absorbs the loads and shocks, preventing jarring of the main airplane structure.

Special oil is used as a *damping agent* to prevent excessive in-and-out telescoping movements of the oleo strut and to damp its rebound action.

When the airplane is stationary, a certain length of polished oleo strut should be visible (depending to some extent on how the airplane is loaded), and this should be checked in the preflight external inspection. Items to check are:

- correct extension when supporting its share of the airplane's weight;
- the polished section of the oleo strut is clean of mud or dirt (to avoid rapid wearing of the seals during the telescoping motion of the strut); and
- there are no fluid leaks.

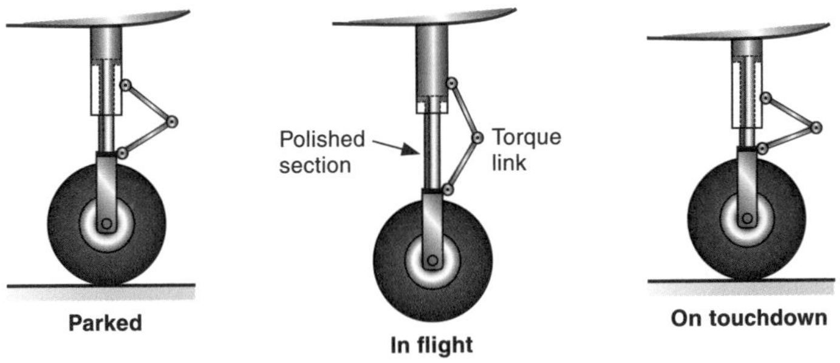

Figure 4-16 The oleo strut.

Nosewheel

The nosewheel is usually of lighter construction than the mainwheels and is usually attached to the main structure of the airplane near the engine firewall. A *torque-link* is used on nosewheel assemblies to correctly align the nosewheel with the airframe. It links the cylinder assembly attached to the airplane structure with the nosewheel assembly, and is hinged to allow for the telescopic extension and compression of the oleo.

Most airplanes have *nosewheel steering*, achieved by moving the rudder pedals which are attached by control rods or cables to the nosewheel assembly, thereby allowing the pilot greater directional control when taxiing.

Some airplanes have *castoring nosewheels* which are free to turn, but are *not* connected by controls to the cockpit. The pilot can turn the airplane by using the rudder when it has sufficient airflow over it (from either slipstream or airspeed) or with differential braking of the mainwheel brakes.

Nosewheel oleo struts are prone to *nosewheel shimmy*, an unpleasant and possibly damaging vibration set up when the nosewheel oscillates a few degrees either side of center as the airplane moves along the ground. To prevent this, most nosewheel assemblies are equipped with a *shimmy damper*, a small piston-cylinder unit that dampens out the oscillations and prevents the vibration. If nosewheel shimmy does occur, it could be because the shimmy damper is insufficiently pressurized or the torque link has failed.

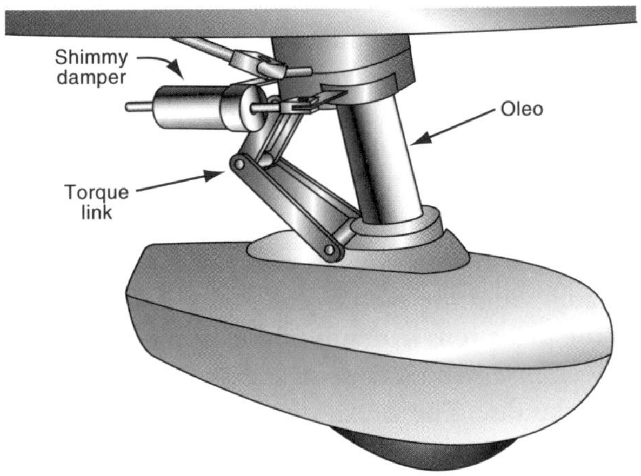

Figure 4-17 Shimmy damper.

Tires

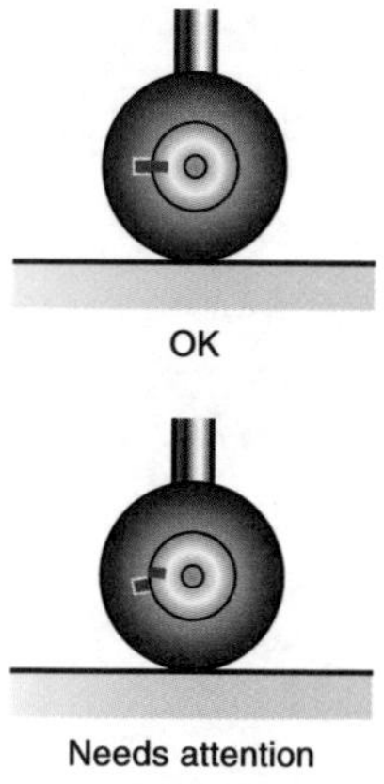

Figure 4-18 Creep marks on the tire and wheel flange enable visual checks for creep.

Airplane tires must be inflated to the correct pressure for them to function as designed. Vibration during taxiing, uneven wear and burst tires may result from a pressure that is too high; damage to the tire structure and a tendency for the tire to creep with respect to the rim can occur if pressure is too low. Correct *inflation* is important in achieving a good service life from a tire. Aircraft tires are unique in that they have to withstand ballooning pressures on each landing.

Creep can occur in normal operations because of the stresses during landing, when a stationary tire is forced to rotate on touching the ground and has to "drag" the wheel around with it, and will also occur when the airplane is braking or turning.

To monitor creep, there are usually paint marks on the wheel flange and on the tire which should remain aligned. If any part of the two creep marks is still in contact, that amount of creep is acceptable, but if the marks are separated, then the inner tube may suffer damage and the tire should be inspected and serviced. This may require removal and reinstallation, or replacement.

Tire *strength* comes from its carcass which is built up from casing cords and then covered with rubber. The ply rating is a measure of its supposed strength. Neither the rubber sidewalls nor the tread provide the main strength of the tire; the sidewalls protect the sides of the tire carcass, and the rubber tread provides a wearing surface at the contact points between the tire and the runway.

Shallow cuts or scores in the sidewalls or on the tread, or small stones embedded in the tread, will not be detrimental to tire strength. However, any large cuts (especially if they expose the casing cords) or bulges (that may be external indications of an internal casing failure) should cause you to reject the tire prior to flight. The condition of the tires should be noted during the preflight external inspection, especially with respect to:

- inflation;
- creep;
- wear, especially flat spots caused by skidding;
- cuts, bulges (especially deep cuts that expose the casing cords); and
- damage to the structure of the sidewall.

Wheel Brakes

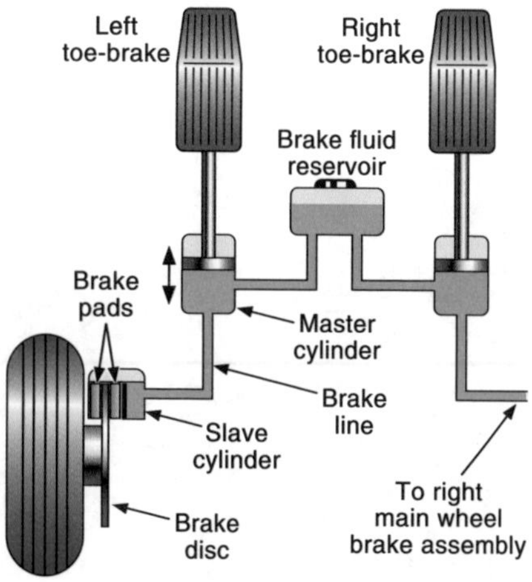

Figure 4-19 Typical simple hydraulic braking system.

Most training airplanes are equipped with *disc brakes* on the mainwheels. These are hydraulically operated by the *toe brakes* which are situated on top of the rudder pedals. Pressing the left toe brake will slow the left mainwheel down and pressing the right toe brake will slow the right mainwheel down. Used separately, they provide differential braking, which is useful for maneuvering on the ground. Used together, they provide normal straight-line braking.

A typical system consists of a separate master cylinder containing hydraulic fluid for each brake. As an individual toe brake is pressed, this toe pressure is hydraulically transmitted via the master cylinder to a *slave cylinder* which closes the brake friction pads (like calipers) onto the brake disc. The brake disc, which is part of the wheel assembly, then has its rotation slowed down.

Most airplanes have a *parking brake* (usually hand-operated, sometimes in conjunction with the toe-brakes) that will hold the pressure on the wheel brakes and can be used when the airplane is parked.

During the preflight external inspection, you should check the brakes to ensure that they will function when you need them, ensuring that:

- there are no leaks of hydraulic brake fluid from the brake lines;
- the brake discs are not corroded or pitted;
- the brake pads are not worn-out; and
- the brake assembly is firmly attached.

A severely corroded or pitted disc will cause rapid wear of the brake pads, as well as reducing their effectiveness, and, in an extreme case, the disc may even fail structurally. Fluid leaks from the brake lines or cylinders indicate a faulty system that may provide no braking at all when it is needed. Any brake problems should be rectified prior to flight.

Following a satisfactory external inspection, you should still test the brakes immediately after the airplane first moves, by closing the throttle and gently applying toe brake pressure. *Brake wear* can be minimized by judicious use of the brakes during ground operations.

Engine and Propeller

The engine is usually mounted on the front of the airplane, and separated from the cockpit by a *firewall*. In most training airplanes, the engine drives a *fixed-pitch propeller*, although more advanced airplanes will have a *constant-speed propeller* with blades whose pitch can vary. The engine and its attachments are considered in detail in the next few chapters.

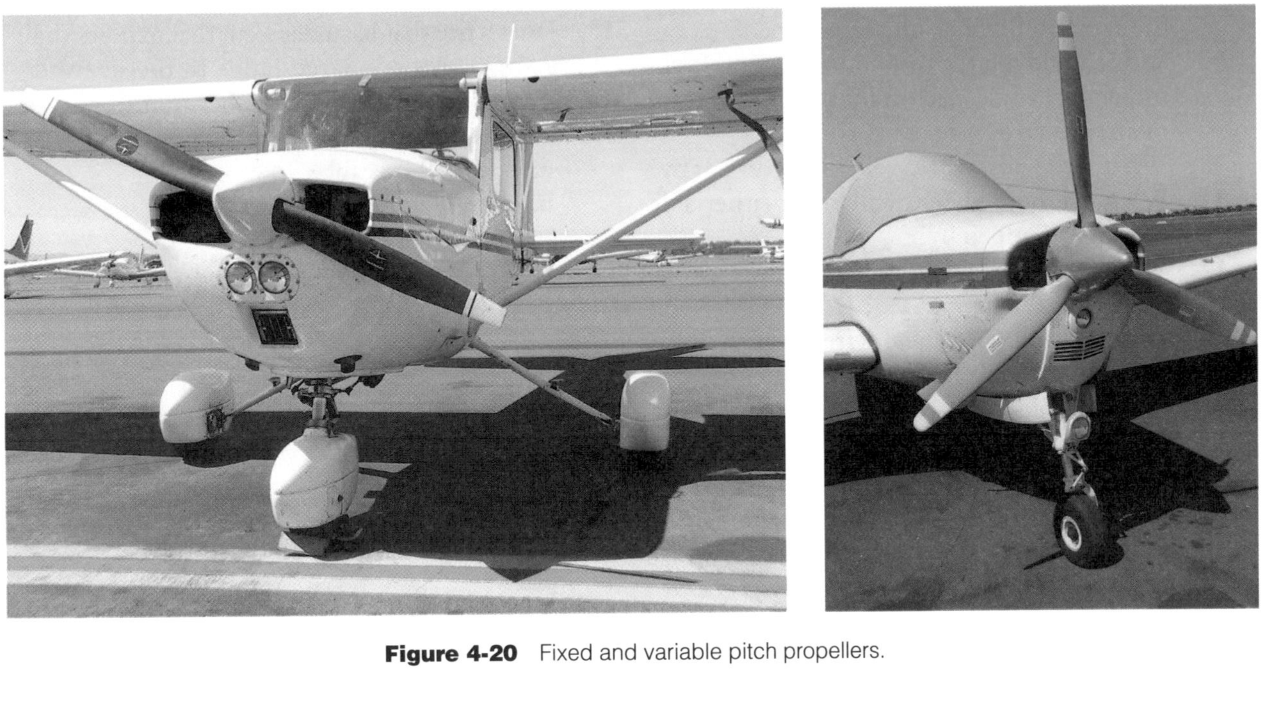

Figure 4-20 Fixed and variable pitch propellers.

Review 4
Airframe

1. What is the main structural component of the wing?
2. Name the four major components of the empennage.
3. What is the airfoil shape of the wing surface formed by?
4. What sort of airplanes are designed with only one pair of wings?
5. What is the most usual form of fuselage construction in training airplanes, in which the skin covers a light structure and carries much of the stress?
6. Does a cracked or severely corroded landing gear strut found during your preflight inspection need to be inspected by a qualified maintenance technician before the airplane flies?
7. What is the agent used to dampen the rebound action in the oleo strut following a shock?
8. True or false? The oleo strut will only extend the same in flight as on the ground.
9. Why should mud or dirt noticed in a preflight inspection be cleaned off the polished section of an oleo strut prior to taxiing?
10. What is the nosewheel held in alignment by?
11. What are nosewheel oscillations either side of center damped by?
12. What is the relative movement between a tire and a wheel flange called?
13. What type of nosewheel is free to turn but is not connected to the cockpit by any control rods or cables for turning?
14. Nosewheel steering in light airplanes is usually operated by:
    a. control rods or cables operated by the rudder pedals.
    b. a steering wheel.
    c. the brakes.
15. A castoring nosewheel can be made to turn:
    a. by a steering wheel.
    b. with differential braking.
16. If a tire has moved so that the creep marks are out of alignment, then:
    a. the tire is serviceable.
    b. the tire should be inspected and possibly reinstalled or replaced.
    c. tire pressure should be checked.
17. Does a tire that has some shallow cuts in the sidewalls and a number of small stones embedded in its tread need to be rejected for further flight?
18. Does a tire that has a deep cut that exposes the casing cords or a large bulge in the sidewall need to be rejected for further flight?
19. Most light airplane braking systems are:
    a. operated by cables.
    b. operated pneumatically.
    c. operated hydraulically.

Answers are given on page 687.

Engine 5

Airplanes can be powered by a variety of engines, and the two fundamental types are *reciprocating* or *piston engines* and *gas turbines* (jets). The jet engine will not be considered in this manual. The piston engine can be designed in various ways, many of which are suitable for airplanes. Older engine types often had the cylinders arranged *radially* around the crankshaft, for example the radial powerplants in the Stearman, Douglas DC-3, North American T-6, de Havilland Canada Beaver and Cessna 195.

The de Havilland Canada Beaver and the Grumman Ag-Cat are two types with radial engines that are still in use today. These engines have an excellent power/weight ratio in the high power range required for operations such as agricultural spraying.

Figure 5-1 Radial engine.

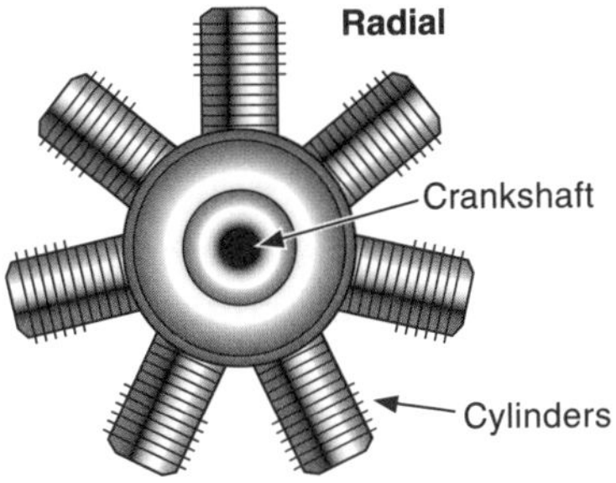

Figure 5-2 Radial engine.

Some airplanes have *in-line engines*, where the cylinders are arranged in one line—the same basic design as in many automobiles. Some of the earliest airplanes had upright, in-line engines, with the cylinder head at the top of the engine and the crankshaft/propeller shaft at the bottom, but this caused some design problems. Raising the thrust line to a suitable position, put the cylinders and the main body of the engine in a very high position. This obscured the pilot's vision and prevented effective streamlining.

Figure 5-3 Inverted in-line engine.

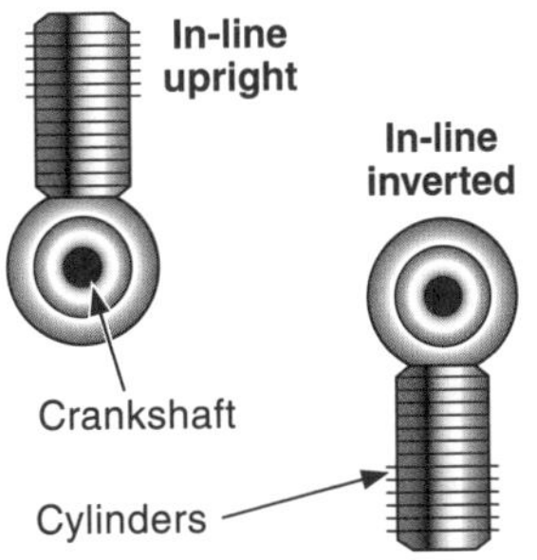

Figure 5-4 In-line engine and inverted in-line engine.

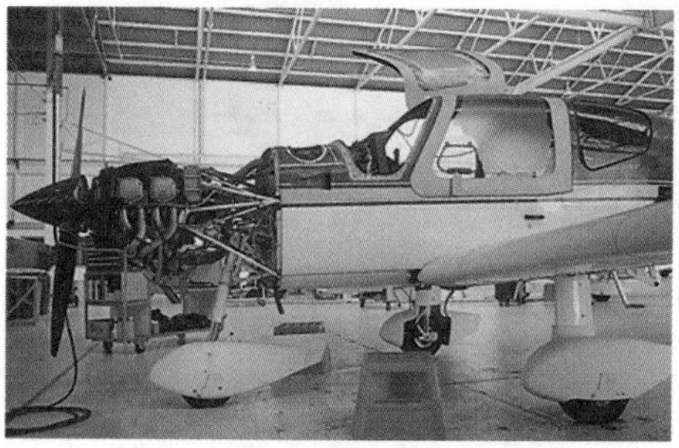

Figure 5-5
Horizontally opposed engine.

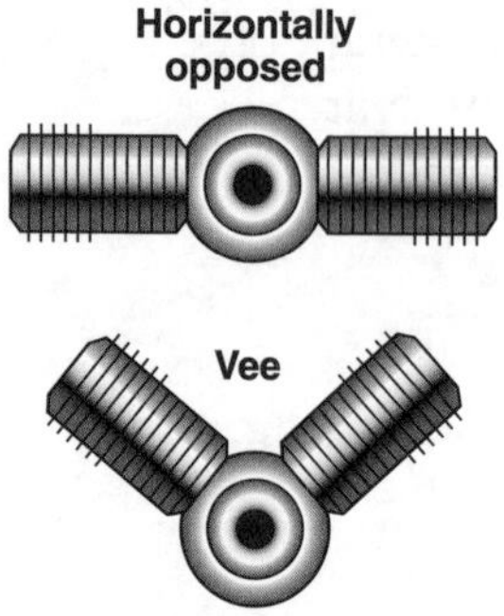

Figure 5-6
Horizontally opposed engine and vee configuration.

Another problem was the ground clearance of the propeller, requiring long struts for the mainwheels. The easiest way to solve this problem was to invert the engine and have the crankshaft/propeller shaft at the top of the engine. Many airplanes have these *inverted* in-line engines. There are other possibilities, such as V-engines and H-engines (V and H describes the layout of the cylinders).

The usual powerplant found in the modern light airplane is the *reciprocating engine*, with the cylinders (4, 6 or 8 of them) laid out in a *horizontally opposed* manner.

Basic Principles

The reciprocating engine has a number of cylinders within which pistons move back and forth (hence the name reciprocating engine). In each cylinder a fuel/air mixture is burned, and the heat energy causes gases to expand and push the piston down the cylinder. A two-stage energy-conversion process is therefore involved, whereby chemical energy (in the fuel) is initially converted to heat energy in the cylinder, and then finally converted to mechanical energy by the action of the piston.

The piston is connected by a rod to a crankshaft, which it turns. This connecting rod, or conrod, converts the back-forth motion of the piston into a rotary motion of the crankshaft, which transmits the power generated by the engine to the propeller. Light airplanes with fixed-pitch propellers (and most with constant-speed propellers) have the propeller directly attached to the crankshaft, in which case the crankshaft is also the propeller shaft. The propeller produces the thrust force necessary for powered flight.

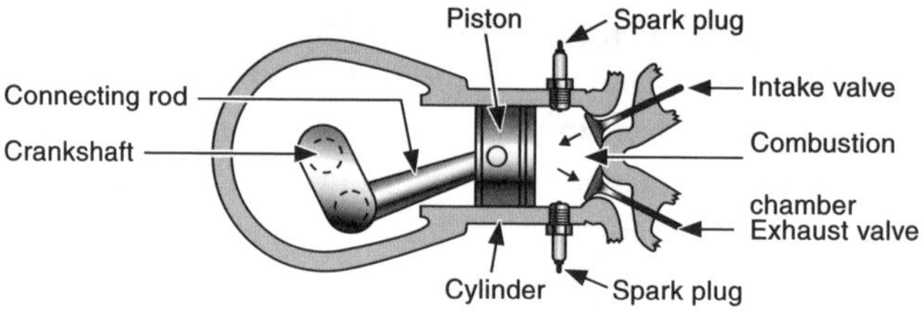

Figure 5-7 Parts of a typical reciprocatig engine.

Four-Stroke Engine Cycle

A complete cycle of this type of piston engine comprises four strokes of the piston traveling within the cylinder, hence the name *four-stroke engine*. The German engineer, Nikolaus Otto, developed this engine, so the four-stroke cycle is also known as the *Otto cycle*. The four strokes are:

1. *intake* (or induction);
2. *compression*;
3. *power* (or expansion); and
4. *exhaust*.

In the *intake* (or *induction*) stroke, the fuel/air mixture is "sucked" or induced to flow into the top of the cylinder. The piston, moving from the top to the bottom of the cylinder, decreases the pressure in the cylinder by increasing the volume of the space between the piston and the top of the cylinder. The decreased pressure draws air in through the induction system and, as the air passes through the carburetor prior to reaching the cylinder, fuel is metered into the airflow to provide a fuel/air mixture. A charge of this fuel/air mixture of gases is drawn into the cylinder during each induction stroke via the intake manifold and the temporarily open intake valve. The *intake manifold* is a pipe system distributing from a single input (the carburetor) to multiple outlets which are fed to the cylinder inlet ports.

Early in the *compression stroke*, the intake valve is closed and the piston moves back toward the top (or the head) of the cylinder. This increases the pressure of the fuel/air mixture, and because of the compression, the temperature of the fuel/air mixture rises.

As the piston is completing the compression stroke well before it reaches top center, the fuel/air mixture is ignited by an electrical discharge between the electrodes of a spark plug and a controlled burning commences. This causes the gases to expand rapidly and exert a strong pressure on the piston. The piston, which has now passed the top of its stroke, is pushed back down the cylinder in the *power stroke*.

Just prior to the completion of the power stroke, the exhaust valve opens and then, as the piston returns to the top of the cylinder in the *exhaust stroke*, the burnt gases are forced out of the cylinder to the atmosphere via the exhaust manifold, a pipe system that collects gases from the cylinder outlets and feeds them through an exhaust pipe to the atmosphere. As the piston is approaching the cylinder head again, while the last of the burnt gases is being exhausted, the intake valve opens in preparation for the next induction stroke. And so the cycle continues.

In a single-cylinder Otto-cycle engine involving four strokes of the piston (down—*induction*, up—*compression*, down—*power*, up—*exhaust*), only one stroke provides power for each two rotations of the crankshaft (which carries the power to the propeller).

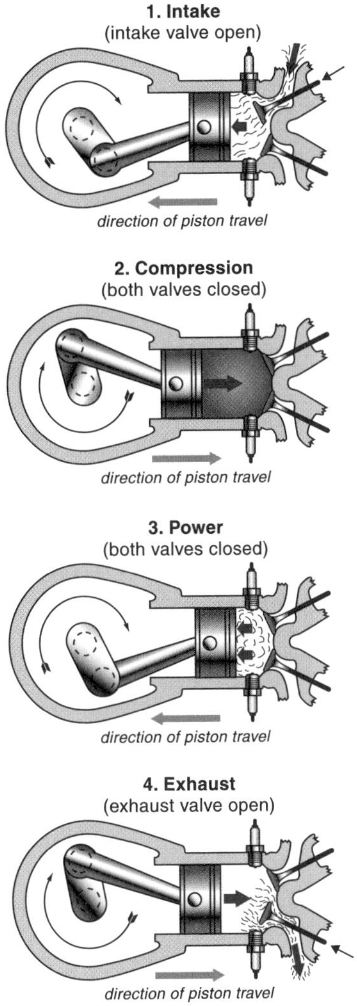

Figure 5-8
The four strokes of a reciprocating engine.

The four-stroke cycle comprises intake, compression, power and exhaust.

To increase the power developed by the engine and to allow smoother operation, the engine has a number of cylinders whose power strokes occur at different positions during the revolution of the crankshaft. The spacing of these power strokes is equal, so that evenly spaced impulses are imparted to the crankshaft. So, in a full Otto cycle of a six-cylinder engine, the crankshaft would, in two revolutions, receive the power from six different power stokes—one per cylinder.

An engine with four cylinders (common in light airplanes) would receive four impulses of power in two revolutions of the crankshaft. The more evenly these impulses of power from each of the cylinders are spread, the more efficient the transfer of power, the smoother the running of the engine and the less the vibration.

Valves and Valve Timing

The intake valve, through which the fuel/air mixture is taken into the cylinder, and the exhaust valve, through which the burned gases are exhausted, must open and close at the correct times during the four-stroke cycle of each piston. To achieve this, there is a *camshaft*, which is usually gear-driven by the crankshaft of the engine. The camshaft operates rocker arms and push rods which push the appropriate valve open (against spring pressure) at what has been determined by the design engineers to be the most suitable moment in the cycle.

A typical engine speed while cruising is *2,400 revolutions per minute* (RPM). Since the intake valve and exhaust valve of each cylinder must each open and close once during the four piston strokes of each complete cycle, the camshaft must rotate at half-crankshaft speed. At an engine speed of 2,400 RPM, each valve will have to open and close 1,200 times—1,200 times in 60 seconds means 20 times a second—quite amazing!

Power is increased by increasing the amount of fuel/air mixture entering the cylinder by extending the time of the intake stroke using valve lead and valve lag.

The power that the engine can develop depends on how much fuel/air mixture can be induced through the intake valve during the intake stroke, which, as we have seen, is extremely short. Opening the intake valve just prior to the piston reaching the top of its stroke, or *top dead center* (TDC), and not closing it until the piston has gone just past *bottom dead center* (BDC) following the induction stroke, allows maximum time for the intake of the fuel/air mixture to occur. This is called *valve lead* and *valve lag*.

Similarly, the exhaust valve opens just prior to the piston reaching bottom-dead-center on the power stroke and remains open until a little after the piston passes top-dead-center for the exhaust stroke and commences the induction stroke.

Notice that, for a brief period at the start of the induction stroke, the burned gases are still being exhausted through the still-open exhaust valve while a fresh charge of fuel/air is commencing induction through the just-opened intake valve. This brief period when both the intake and the exhaust valves are open together is called *valve overlap*.

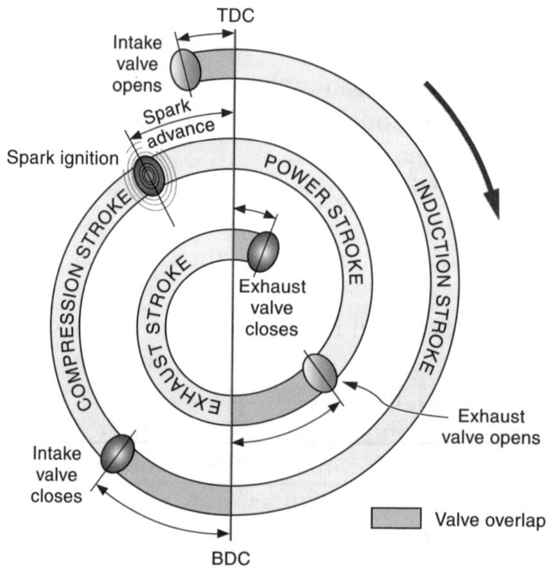

Figure 5-9 Typical valve timing in the four-stroke cycle.

Ignition

A high voltage (or high tension) spark occurs in the cylinder just prior to the piston reaching top-dead-center, shortly before commencing the power stroke. This slightly advanced spark is to enable a controlled flame front to start moving through the fuel/air mixture that has been compressed in the cylinder. The purpose of the ignition system is to provide this correctly timed spark.

Most airplane engines have *dual* (and independent) *ignition* systems running in parallel with one another, with the magneto of each ignition system supplying one of the two *spark plugs* per cylinder.

Dual ignition is safer and results in improved fuel combustion.

A dual ignition system:

- improves engine performance;
- is safer, in the event of failure of one ignition system; and
- results in more even and more efficient fuel combustion.

The necessary high-tension electrical current for the spark plugs comes from self-contained generation and distribution units called the *magnetos*. Each of the dual ignition systems has its own magneto which is mechanically driven by the engine.

The magneto consists of a magnet that is rotated (within the magneto housing) near a conductor which has a coil of wire wound around it. The rotation of the magnet induces an electrical current to flow in the coil. Around this primary coil is wound a secondary coil of many more turns of wire, which transforms the primary voltage into a much higher voltage. This arrangement of primary and secondary coils is known as a transformer. The higher voltage is fed to each spark plug at the appropriate time, causing a spark to jump between the two electrodes. This spark ignites the fuel/air mixture.

The timing of the spark is critical. The magneto has a set of *breaker points* which are forced open and closed by a small cam that is part of the rotating magnet-shaft connected indirectly to the crankshaft. The points are in the circuit of the primary coil and, when they open, the electrical current in the primary coil stops flowing. This sudden collapse of the primary current (aided by a condenser or capacitor placed across the points) induces a high voltage in the secondary coil. The spark plug is in the circuit of the secondary coil and the large voltage (up to approximately 20,000 volts) across its electrodes causes a spark to jump between them.

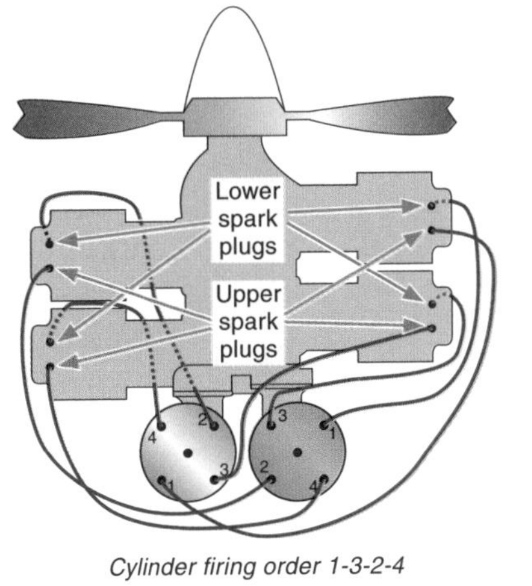

Figure 5-10
A typical ignition system.

As each cylinder is operating out of phase with the others, the current must be distributed by the distributor to each spark plug at the correct moment (generally 20°–25° before top center).

Each cylinder fires once in every two revolutions of the crankshaft and the distributor has a *finger* (distributor rotor) which is geared to the crankshaft in such a way that it turns only once for every two turns of the crankshaft. Therefore the distributor finger turns once in every complete four-stroke cycle. Once during each turn of the distributor finger it transfers the high-tension secondary current to each cylinder, in the correct firing order of the cylinders.

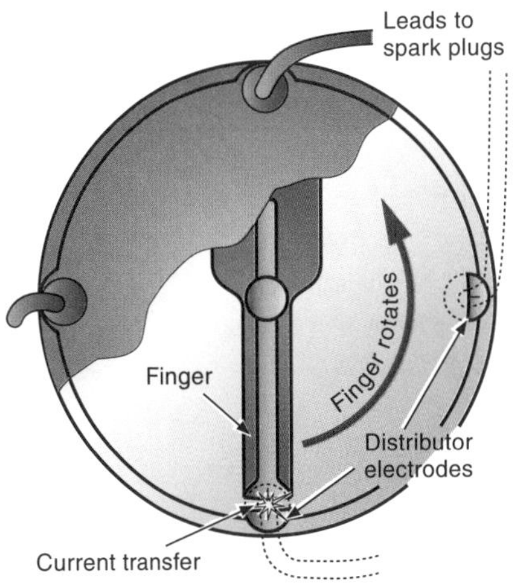

Figure 5-11
Distributor finger.

Separate leads to each of the spark plugs belonging to each ignition system (one per cylinder) emanate from different electrodes of the distributor case. These leads are often bound together, forming an *ignition harness*. Leakage of current from the ignition harness will lead to rough running. One item of the preflight inspection is a visual check for chafing and heat cracking of those parts of the ignition harness easily seen. While the engine is running, the magneto is a completely self-sufficient source of electrical energy and it operates independently of all the other electrical power sources. All it needs is mechanical energy from the engine to rotate the magnet.

Starter

Most modern training airplanes have an *electric starter motor* that is powered by the battery and activated by turning the ignition key to the *start* position.

Starting the engine causes a very high current to flow between the battery and the starter motor, and this requires heavy-duty wiring. If the ignition switch in the cockpit was directly connected to the starter circuit, heavy-duty wiring to the cockpit switch would be required.

Such an arrangement would have a number of disadvantages, including the additional weight of the heavy cable, a significant loss of electrical energy over the additional length, and high electrical currents through the cockpit environment (which would introduce an unnecessary fire risk). To avoid these disadvantages, the starter circuit connecting the battery to the starter motor is remotely controlled from the cockpit using a solenoid-activated switch.

Moving the ignition key to *start* causes a small current to flow through the starter key circuit point A to B and energize a *solenoid* (an electromagnet with a movable core). The energized solenoid operates a heavy-duty switch that closes the heavy-duty circuit between the battery and starter motor. High current flows through this circuit, activating the starter motor which turns the engine over (point C to D).

Electric starters often have an associated *starter warning light* in the cockpit that glows while the starter is engaged. It should extinguish immediately when the starter is released. If by any chance the starter relay sticks (so that electrical power is still supplied to the starter motor even though the starter switch has been released from the *start* position) the warning light will remain on. The engine should be stopped (mixture control to *idle cut-off*) to avoid damage to the engine and/or starter motor.

Only one spark per cylinder is necessary for start-up, so when the ignition key is in the *start* position, the right magneto system is automatically de-energized and only the left magneto system provides a high-tension supply to the spark plugs. (For this reason, only the left magneto is equipped with an impulse coupling, a device which aids the starting

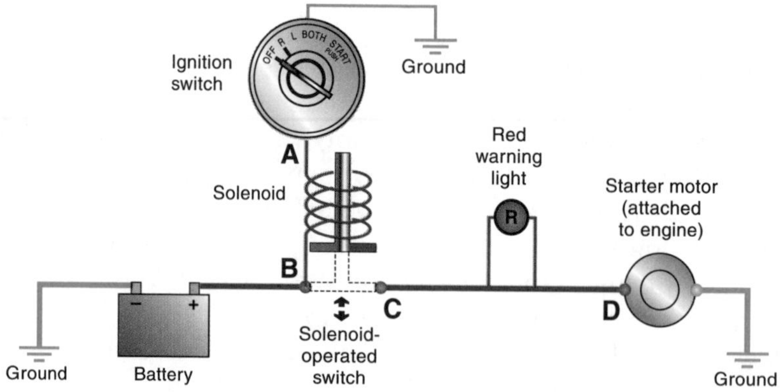

Figure 5-12 The electric starter system.

process—see below.) After start-up, switching the ignition key to *both* activates the right magneto system as well, and the engine now runs with dual ignition in each cylinder.

Older airplanes with the starter switch separate to the magneto switches should have only the left magneto switch *on* for start-up. Once the engine is started, you should switch the other magneto on as well.

There are two design limitations of magnetos that significantly affect starting an engine.

1. When the starter motor turns the engine over, the engine rotates comparatively slowly (approximately 120 RPM as against 800 RPM at idle speed). Because the magneto rotates at half crankshaft speed (to supply one spark per cylinder every two revolutions of the crankshaft), magneto speed at start-up is very slow, up to about 60 RPM. To generate a spark of sufficiently high voltage to ignite the fuel/air mixture requires a magneto speed of about 100–200 RPM, so some device must be incorporated in the system to overcome this slow magneto speed when starting the engine.
2. When the engine is running (800–2,700 RPM is a typical operating range) the spark occurs at a fixed number of degrees *prior* to the piston reaching top-dead-center at the commencement of the power stroke. This is known as *spark advance*. On start-up, with only very low revs occurring, unless the spark is *retarded* (delayed) until the piston is at or past top-dead-center, ignition of the gases could push the piston down the cylinder prematurely, causing the crankshaft to turn in the wrong direction. This is called *kick-back*.

To overcome these two difficulties special devices have been developed for installation in the magneto; the most common in small airplane engines is the *impulse coupling*.

Impulse Coupling

Impulse coupling generates a high voltage and retards the ignition timing to start the engine.

The impulse coupling initially delays the magnet from rotating as the engine is turned over. Energy from the initial part of the engine rotation is stored by winding up a coiled spring. When a certain amount of energy is stored, the coupling releases, and the spring accelerates the magnet rapidly. This generates a current of sufficient strength to create a spark across the electrodes of the spark plug. It also retards the spark sufficiently to allow the burning fuel/air mixture to drive the crankshaft in the correct direction. Once the engine is started and is running at its usual RPM, the magneto's driveshaft accelerates away from the coiled spring, which has no further effect. The spark is then produced normally (by the engine rotating the magnet), and the timing is no longer retarded but operates normally, with the spark occurring just prior to commencement of the power stroke.

Notice that, as the impulse coupling does not depend on any electrical power source, the engine can be started by swinging the propeller. (This should only be done by trained and qualified personnel.) If you use an electric starter powered by the airplane battery to start the engine then, once the engine is running, disconnecting the battery will not stop the engine. It will, however, prevent the battery from being recharged.

Figure 5-13 The ignition switch in the cockpit.

Ignition Switch

There are two separate ignition systems for safety in the event of failure of one of them, as well as for more efficient burning of the fuel/air mixture with two sparks in the cylinder instead of one. Older airplanes often have separate switches for each magneto, while most modern airplanes have rotary switches operated by the ignition key. With these, you can select either the left system *L*, the right system *R*, or *BOTH*. BOTH is selected for normal engine operation. Airplanes with a separate starter button are usually started on the left magneto.

The engine will run on just one magneto, but not as smoothly as on two, and with a slight drop in RPM. With one spark instead of two, there will be only one flame-front advancing through the fuel/air mixture in the cylinder instead of two. This increases the time for full combustion to occur and decreases the efficiency of the burning.

If *L* is selected, only the left magneto system supplies a spark. The *R* magneto is grounded to the airframe, which means its primary current runs to ground and no spark is generated. Switching from *BOTH* to *L* should cause a drop in RPM and possibly slightly rougher running. If a slight drop in RPM does not occur, then either the *R* system is still supplying a spark or else the *R* magneto was not working previously when *BOTH* was selected. The pilot will normally check both left and right magneto systems in this way as part of the pre-takeoff power check, switching from *BOTH* to *L*, noting the RPM drop and returning to *BOTH*, when the RPM originally set should be regained. Then the pilot will switch from *BOTH* to *R*, noting the RPM drop, and back to *BOTH*.

Comparisons are made between the two RPM drops, which should be within certain limits (see the Pilot's Operating Handbook for your particular airplane). Some typical figures are: check at 1,600 RPM on *BOTH*, magneto drop 125 RPM maximum on either *L* or *R*, with a difference between these two drops not to exceed 50 RPM.

Always treat a propeller as live.

Remember that placing the ignition switch to *OFF* grounds the primary winding of the magneto system so that it no longer supplies electrical power. This means that with a particular magneto's ignition switch *OFF*, the system is supposed to be grounded and unable to supply a spark. The magneto ground wire is called a *p-lead*. With a loose or broken wire, or some other fault, switching the ignition to *OFF* may not ground both of the magnetos. Therefore, a person moving the propeller could inadvertently start the engine, even though the ignition is switched off. It *has* happened, often with fatal results, and is still happening.

If the ignition switch is momentarily switched off and the engine continues to run, this indicates that the system is not grounded, which is a dangerous situation.

The pilot has no visual method of checking that the magneto systems, although switched off, are actually de-activated. Just before shutting an engine down, some pilots do a system function test at idle RPM, checking *BOTH*, *L*, *R*. This is followed by a dead-cut, where the ignition is switched to *OFF* (a sudden loss of power should be apparent) and rapidly back to *BOTH* to allow the engine to run normally. The engine is then shut down normally using the idle cut-off function of the mixture control. Some manufacturers/instructors advise against a dead-cut check as it may damage the engine. Refer to your Pilot's Operating Handbook. During a preflight power check, if there is no drop in speed while checking the magnetos, the magneto may be hot. A hot magneto is one that cannot be turned off by the ignition switch.

Exhaust System

The burnt gases leave the engine cylinders and are carried out to the atmosphere via the exhaust system. It is important that there is no leakage of exhaust gas into the cabin because it contains carbon monoxide, a colorless and odorless gas that is difficult to detect, but can cause loss of consciousness and death.

The Oil System

Oil lubricates, clears, and cools and seals.

The purpose of the oil system is to circulate oil around the engine, to:

- lubricate the moving parts so that they can move smoothly;
- prevent high temperatures by reducing friction between the moving parts;
- provide a seal between the cylinder walls and the pistons, increasing the effectiveness of the expanding gases in the combustion process;

Figure 5-14
Oil check.

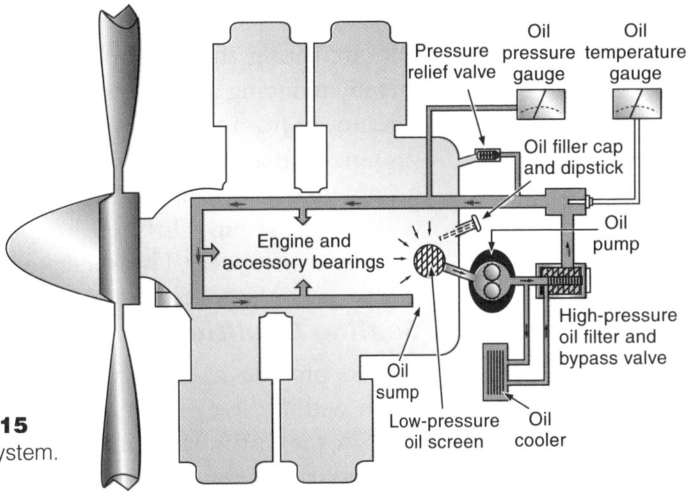

Figure 5-15
A typical oil system.

- assist in cooling the engine by carrying some of the heat generated by combustion away from the pistons; and
- carry away contaminants which are then removed in an oil filter.

Sufficient quantity of oil of the correct grade is absolutely essential. An oil dipstick to check oil quantity is generally found under a small cowl above the engine, along with an oil filling point if more oil is required. Always check that the oil filler cap has been firmly replaced prior to flight. Indication of correct operation of the oil system is provided in the cockpit by an *oil pressure gauge*, an *oil temperature gauge*, and, in some aircraft, a *cylinder-head temperature gauge*.

The Functions of Engine Oil

Friction

Oil reduces friction.

If a small film of oil separates two metal surfaces, it will allow them to slide over each other without actually touching. There will be only low friction forces and consequently, high temperatures will not be generated in the metal. The metallic friction will be replaced by internal friction in the lubricating oil, which will heat up to some extent. Engine components subjected to high loads, such as the bearings at either end of the connecting rods and the crankshaft (or *big end*) bearings, need to be cushioned by a layer of oil so that the mechanical shock on them is reduced. Without oil there would be high friction forces, causing very high temperatures to develop quickly in the metal, with extreme wearing of the metal surfaces and, very likely, subsequent mechanical failure.

Cooling

Oil cools the hot sections of the engine.

The pistons absorb a lot of heat from the combustion chamber and are cooled by oil splashed or sprayed onto them from below. Lubrication and cooling of the bearings and pistons is the main function of the oil system.

Heat generated by internal friction in the oil and the heat absorbed from the hot sections of the engine is removed by the oil continually being circulated. The hot oil is carried away and cooled in a component known as the *oil cooler*, which is exposed to the airflow.

Removal of Contaminants

Oil carries away contaminants.

Oil circulating through an engine can carry away dirt and other foreign material, thereby reducing abrasive wear on the moving parts of the engine. This contamination is removed from the oil as it passes through the *oil filter*. If the filter is not kept clean (by correct maintenance or replacement at the recommended service intervals) it may become blocked, causing dirty oil to bypass the filter and circulate within the engine's lubrication system. Dirty oil has poorer cooling and lubricating qualities, which can cause excessive wear. This increased wear rate will shorten the life of the engine.

Sealing Qualities

Oil provides a seal.

Oil also provides a seal between the cylinder walls and the pistons as they move up and down within the cylinders, preventing the compressed gases (burning fuel/air) escaping past the piston rings into the crankcase, and so increasing the effectiveness of the compressed gases in forcing the piston down the cylinder.

Oil Properties

Excessively high temperatures affect the lubricating qualities of oil, impairing its effectiveness, so keep an eye on the oil temperature gauge.

Oil must have appropriate *viscosity* over the operating temperature range of the engine—it must flow freely, but not be too thin. An oil of high viscosity (thickness) flows slowly; an oil of low viscosity flows more easily. High temperatures make oil less viscous and cause it to flow more freely. The oil must remain sufficiently viscous under the wide range of operating temperatures and bearing pressures found in aviation engines.

The owner or operator of the airplane may decide to use an oil of lower viscosity than normal in a severely cold climate. Likewise, an oil of higher viscosity could be used if the airplane is to be operated in a continually hot climate. Be aware of the oil grade being used and *do not mix oil grades*. The oil must also have a sufficiently *high flash point* and fire point to ensure that it will not vaporize excessively or catch fire easily. It must also be chemically stable and not change its state or characteristics.

Use only recommended type and grade of oils. Do not mix grades.

Maintenance

Since the same oil in an engine is continually circulated, over a period of time it will become contaminated because the filters cannot clean it perfectly. Chemical changes will also occur in the oil in the form of:

- oxidation caused by contamination from some of the byproducts of the fuel combustion in the engine; and
- absorption of water that condenses in the engine when it cools after shutdown.

Consequently the *oil must be changed at regular intervals*, as required by the maintenance schedule.

The airplane's Pilot's Operating Handbook will usually show the oil grade as an SAE rating (Society of Automotive Engineers), but commercial aviation oil has a *commercial aviation number* which is *double* the SAE rating:

- 80 grade oil—SAE 40; and
- 100 grade oil—SAE 50.

There are different types of oils designed for different operating conditions. Use only the correct type of oil as directed in the Pilot's Operating Handbook and *do not use turbine (jet) oil in piston engines.*

A Typical Oil System

After doing its work in the engine, the oil gathers in the *sump*, which is a reservoir attached to the lower part of the engine casing:

- a *wet sump* engine has a sump attached to it in which the oil is stored. Most light aircraft engines are wet sump engines; and
- a *dry sump* engine has scavenge pumps that scavenge the oil from the sump attached to the lower part of the engine casing and pump it back into the oil tank, which is separate from the engine. It is usual to have a dry sump on aerobatic airplanes for continuous lubrication in extreme attitudes. Radial engines have dry sump oil systems.

There is usually an *engine-driven oil supply pump* that supplies oil from the sump or the tank through oil lines, passages and galleries to the moving parts of the engine. Within the oil pump is a spring-loaded *oil pressure relief valve*. If the pressure set on the pressure relief valve is exceeded, it will open and relieve the pressure by allowing oil to be returned to the pump inlet.

An *oil pressure gauge* in the cockpit indicates the oil pressure provided by the oil pump. The oil pressure sensor is situated after the oil pump and before the oil does its work in the engine.

Oil filters and screens are placed in the system to remove any foreign matter such as dirt or carbon particles in the circulating oil. The oil filters should be inspected and replaced at regular intervals, as required in the maintenance schedule. The foreign matter collected may give an indication of the condition of the engine—for instance, small metal particles might indicate an impending engine failure. Within the oil filter housing is the *oil filter bypass valve*. This permits the oil to bypass the filter in the event of the filter becoming clogged. Dirty and contaminated oil is preferable to no oil at all.

Because the oil absorbs engine heat, the cooling that occurs in the sump is often insufficient, so most engines have an *oil cooler*. The oil is pumped from the sump through the oil filter to the oil cooler. If the oil is already cool, a thermally operated valve allows it to bypass the oil cooler, as further cooling is unnecessary. If the oil is hot (as it is when the engine has warmed-up), the thermally operated valve directs the oil through the cooler. Should the cooler become blocked, a *pressure bypass valve* allows the oil to bypass the cooler. The oil cooler is usually positioned in the system so that the oil cools a little in the sump and then passes through the oil cooler for further cooling just prior to entering the main parts of the engine.

As part of your *daily/preflight inspection* you should check the condition of the oil cooler for freedom from insects, birds' nests and other contamination, to ensure free air passages and any oil leakage or fatigue cracks.

There is an *oil temperature gauge* in the cockpit. It is connected to a temperature probe that senses the temperature of the oil after the oil has passed through the oil cooler and before its use within the hot sections of the engine. Also, some airplanes have a *cylinder-head temperature* (CHT) *gauge* to provide another indication of engine temperature, this time in the cylinder head.

Malfunctions in the Oil/Lubrication System

Incorrect Oil Type

The *incorrect type of oil* will possibly cause poor lubrication, poor cooling, and engine damage. Oil temperature and oil pressure indications may be abnormal. For instance, mixing detergent and mineral oils can lead to engine damage.

Incorrect Oil Quantity

The *oil level* should be checked and corrected if necessary prior to flight. There will be an *oil dipstick* in the tank for this purpose. The dipstick is calibrated to show maximum and minimum oil quantities. If the oil quantity is below the minimum, then you will find that the oil overheats and/or the oil pressure is too low or fluctuates. If the oil quantity is too great, then the excess oil may be forced out through various parts of the engine, such as the front shaft seal. The oil quantity needs to be checked before each flight, as it gradually decreases because of:

- being burned with the fuel/air mixture in the cylinders;
- loss as a mist or spray through the oil breather; and
- leaks.

Low Oil Pressure

At normal power a low oil pressure may indicate an impending engine failure caused by:

- insufficient oil;
- lack of oil because of a failure in the oil system;
- a leak in the oil tank or oil lines;
- failure of the oil pump;
- a problem in the engine, such as failing bearings; or
- the oil pressure relief valve (PRV) stuck open.

Where an indication of low or fluctuating oil pressure occurs and is associated with a rise in oil temperature while in flight—play it safe and land as soon as possible, as it could indicate a serious problem in the lubrication system.

High Oil Temperature

Too little oil being circulated will also be indicated by a high oil temperature, therefore a rising oil temperature may indicate a decreasing oil quantity. Prolonged operation at excessive cylinder head temperatures will also give rise to a high oil temperature indication. This would be most likely to occur in situations of high power, low airspeed (climbing), especially in high ambient air temperatures.

Gradual Loss of Oil

Lack of oil will cause an engine seizure and an immediate loss of power.

If the engine is gradually losing oil, the oil temperature will gradually rise as less oil is available for cooling and lubricating the engine. If oil is lost, the oil pressure will probably be maintained, until the oil quantity reaches a critically low level. This may be indicated by rapidly rising oil temperature with a sudden drop in oil pressure occurring just before engine seizure.

If you suspect a problem concerning oil, then you should plan a landing before the time you estimate the oil problem will become serious. This is a matter of judgment, especially if the choice of nearby landing areas is not great.

Faulty Oil Pressure Gauge

Sometimes of course, the oil pressure gauge may be faulty. A low oil pressure indication may be recognized as a faulty indication—and not a genuine low pressure—by noting that the oil temperature remains normal over a period of time. Keep your eye on both gauges.

High Oil Pressure

A pressure relief valve in the system should ensure that the oil does not reach an unacceptably high oil pressure. A high oil pressure may cause some part of the system to fail, rendering the whole oil system inoperative.

The Cooling System

The engine cooling system is designed to keep the engine temperatures within those limits designed by the manufacturer. The burning of the fuel/air mixture in the engine's cylinders, and the friction of its moving parts, results in the engine heating up. Engine temperatures are kept within acceptable limits by:

- the oil that circulates within the engine;
- expulsion of much heat energy in the exhaust gases; and
- the air cooling system that circulates fresh air around the engine compartment.

Most modern light airplane engines are *air-cooled* by exposing the cylinders and their cooling fins to an airflow. The fins increase the exposed surface area to allow better cooling.

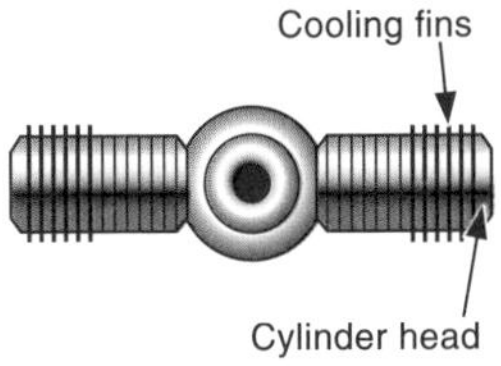

Figure 5-16
Cooling fins.

As the airflow passes around a cylinder it may become turbulent and break away in such a manner that uneven cooling occurs, forming local poorly cooled hot-spots. To avoid this uneven cooling, cowling ducts at the front of the engine capture air from the high-pressure area behind the propeller, and then baffles distribute it as evenly as possible around the cylinders. After cooling the engine, the air flows out holes at the bottom rear of the engine compartment.

Air cooling is least effective at high power and low airspeed, for instance on takeoff or go-around. The high power produces a lot of heat, and the low airspeed provides a reduced cooling airflow. At high airspeed and low power, for instance on descent, the cooling might be too effective.

Some airplanes have movable cooling *cowl flaps* that can be operated (electrically or manually) from the cockpit, giving the pilot more control over the cooling of the engine. Open cowl flaps permit more air to escape from the engine compartment. This causes increased airflow over and around the engine. The open cowl flaps cause parasite drag to increase.

Cowl flaps are normally open for takeoff, partially open or closed on climb and cruise, and closed during a power-off descent. They will be open on final in readiness for a go-around, when high power at a low airspeed will be required. Cowl flaps should be open when taxiing to help dissipate the engine heat.

The deciding factor for the pilot in where to position the cowl flaps is the cylinder head temperature, or the anticipated cylinder head temperature, and this may be indicated in the cockpit by a *cylinder-head temperature* (CHT) *gauge*.

Excessive engine temperatures may be caused by:

- high power (greater heat generation);
- low airspeed (less air cooling);
- incorrect fuel (lower-than-specified grade);
- a too-lean mixture (no excess fuel to evaporate and cool the cylinders); or
- a low oil level.

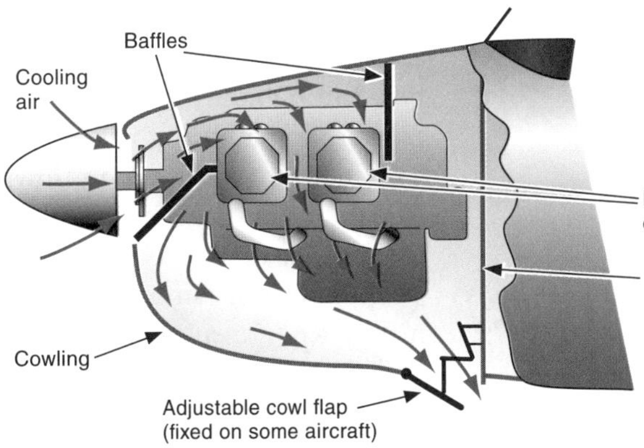

Figure 5-17 Cowl flaps and engine cooling.

Monitor CHT and adjust engine cooling if necessary.

You should monitor the cylinder-head temperature gauge throughout the flight, and also on the ground when air-cooling will be poor.

Note. The Pilot's Operating Handbook will give advice on satisfactory temperatures.

Figure 5-18
The cowls direct cooling air.

If excessive cylinder-head temperatures are noted in flight, the cooling of the engine can be improved by:

- opening the cowl flaps fully (to allow greater airflow around the engine);
- making the mixture richer (extra fuel has a cooling effect in the cylinders because more fuel is evaporated, so a rich mixture cools better than a lean mixture);
- reducing the engine power (so that less heat is produced); or
- increasing the airspeed (for greater air cooling).

Just how you achieve the latter two is a matter of judgment. In a climb, you could increase speed by reducing the rate of climb. In a cruise (straight-and-level) at normal cruise speeds, you could maintain the power and increase the airspeed by commencing a descent, unless terrain prevents this.

Other factors influencing engine cooling and over which the pilot has little control during flight include:

- the condition of the oil cooler; and
- the outside air temperature.

A dirty and inefficient oil cooler will not allow the best cooling of the circulating oil. The oil, if warmer than optimum, will be unable to carry as much heat away from the engine, and its viscosity and lubricating qualities will be reduced, which will lead to higher engine temperatures.

Obviously, warm air will not cool the engine as well as cool air.

Note. On some airplanes the propeller *spinner* is part of the airflow director for the cooling air, so these airplanes should *not* be operated without the spinner installed. If you find yourself in such a situation, refer to the Flight Manual or a technician to establish what is allowable for your airplane.

The Carburetor

The carburetor mixes fuel with air.

Gasoline needs to be mixed with oxygen in the correct ratio to burn properly. The correct *fuel/air* ratio is about 1 part of fuel to 12 parts of air by *weight*. The device commonly used to mix fuel with air in an engine is called the *carburetor*.

The carburetor works on the principle that the airflow through the throat of the carburetor will have its pressure reduced by the venturi effect. This causes the fuel to flow through the main metering jet and into the airstream, because of the atmospheric pressure in the float chamber being greater. The fuel vaporizes and mixes with the air. The fuel/air mixture then flows through to the cylinders in preparation for burning. The pilot can vary the airflow using the *throttle lever* in the cockpit. The fuel/air mixture can be varied, if necessary, using the *mixture control*.

Vary the fuel/air mixture with the mixture control.

Combustion can occur in the cylinders when the fuel/air ratio is between approximately 1:8 (*rich mixture*) and 1:20 (*lean mixture*). The ideal or chemically correct mixture of fuel/air is one in which the fuel and the oxygen are perfectly matched so that, after burning, all of the fuel and all of the oxygen have been used. The chemically correct mixture may be referred to as the *ccm* or the *stoichiometric* mixture.

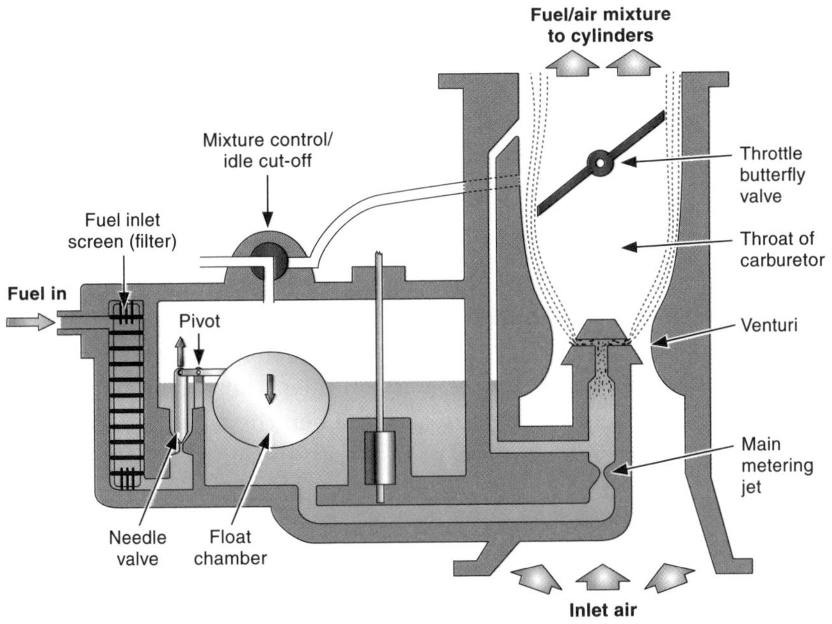

Figure 5-19 Cross-section of a simple float-type carburetor.

If the mixture is rich, there is *excess* fuel and, after burning, some unburned fuel will remain. If the mixture is lean, there is a *shortage* of fuel in the sense that, after all of the fuel has burned, there will still be some oxygen remaining.

A simple carburetor, like that in figure 5-19, has a venturi through which the amount of airflow is controlled by a *throttle valve* (or *butterfly*). The venturi has fuel jets positioned in it so that the correct amount of fuel by weight is metered into the airflow. The butterfly valve is controlled with the throttle lever in the cockpit.

It is important that you move the throttle smoothly so that unnecessary stress is not placed on the many moving parts in the engine. To open or close the throttle fully should take about the same time as a "1-2-3" count.

A simple float-type carburetor has a small chamber that requires a certain level of fuel. If the level is too low, the float-valve opens and allows more fuel from the fuel tanks to enter. This is happening continually as fuel is drawn from the float chamber into the venturi of the carburetor. The air pressure in the float chamber is atmospheric, while the air pressure near the metering jet is reduced by the venturi effect.

The acceleration of the airflow through the carburetor venturi causes a decreased static pressure (Bernoulli's principle—increased velocity, decreased static pressure). The higher atmospheric pressure in the float chamber forces fuel through the main metering jet into the venturi airflow. The faster the airflow, the greater the differential pressure and the greater the quantity of fuel discharged to the airflow. Therefore the *weight* of fuel that flows through the carburetor is controlled by the airflow through the carburetor venturi.

Accelerator Pump

When you fully open the throttle, the butterfly valve is fully opened and does not restrict the airflow through the venturi. The airflow therefore increases. If the throttle is opened quickly, the airflow initially increases at a rate greater than the fuel flow, producing an insufficiently rich mixture. This would cause a lag in the production of

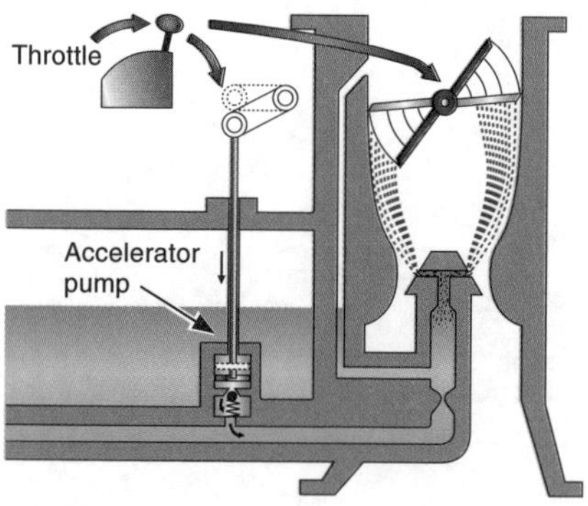

Figure 5-20 The accelerator pump.

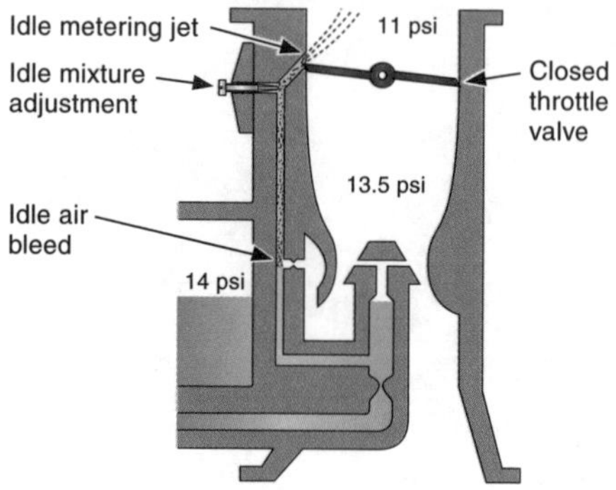

Figure 5-21 The idling system.

power if it were not for the *accelerator pump*. The accelerator pump is therefore used to prevent a weak-cut when the throttle is rapidly opened. The accelerator pump is a small plunger within the float chamber, connected to the throttle linkage so that it gives an extra spurt of fuel as the throttle is opened.

Idling System

When the engine is idling with the butterfly valve almost closed, the pressure differential between the venturi and the float chamber is not great enough to force fuel through the main jet. To allow for this, there is a small *idling jet* with an inlet near the butterfly valve, where a small venturi effect is caused when the valve is almost closed. This provides sufficient fuel to mix with the air to keep the engine idling at low RPM.

Fuel/Air Mixture Control

The *fuel/air ratio* is the ratio between the weight of fuel and the weight of air mixed together and entering the cylinders where the combustion process is to occur. The carburetor is the device used to mix the fuel and the air, and it is designed in its most basic form to function best under mean sea level conditions at standard temperature +15°C (59°F).

Under other conditions when the air density is significantly less, such as at high altitudes or with high temperatures, the basic operation of the carburetor must be modified by the pilot to maintain a suitable fuel/air ratio.

Using the Mixture Control for Climbs and Descents

As altitude is gained in a climb, the volume of air flowing through the carburetor remains the same, but the weight of air is less because of its lower density (fewer molecules in the same volume). The same weight of fuel is drawn into the airstream, however, which means that the fuel/air mixture is now richer with fuel. This may lead to rough running, fouling of the spark plugs, increased fuel consumption, and a loss of power (loss of RPM for a fixed-pitch propeller and loss of manifold pressure for a constant-speed propeller).

A *mixture control* is provided to keep the fuel/air ratio roughly constant. To return to a correct mixture, you can reduce the amount of fuel entering the carburetor venturi by moving the mixture control back out slightly toward lean. This moves a small needle in the carburetor which restricts the fuel flow through the main metering jet, thereby *leaning* the mixture, or making it less rich. The mixture control in the cockpit is usually a red knob. It should be moved smoothly and gradually, to avoid leaning the mixture too far and perhaps even stopping the engine by starving it of fuel. When climbing above approximately 5,000 feet MSL, if rough running is present, the mixture should only be leaned sufficiently to return the engine to smooth running. Normally, an engine is leaned if less than 75 percent power is being used.

Conversely, as an airplane descends the air becomes more dense, and so the weight of air in each charge increases while the weight of fuel remains the same. This causes the fuel/air mixture to become leaner. The correct procedure on descent is to move the mixture control in toward the *RICH* position, which (for a given throttle position)

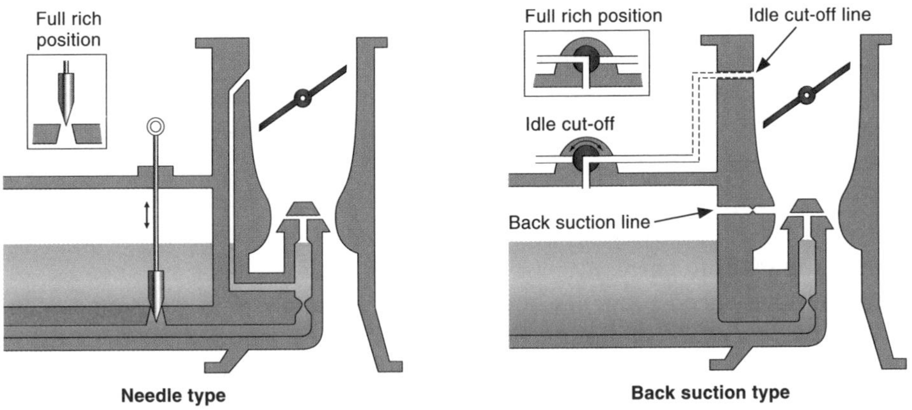

Figure 5-22 Mixture control systems.

will provide additional fuel to match the increased weight of air. Since most descents are made with low power set from cruise altitude until reaching pattern altitude at the destination airport, it is common practice to move the mixture control to the rich position at the top of descent, or to progressively richen the mixture (if descending from high altitude), so that the mixture control is correctly positioned for the approach and landing phase, when full power should be available in case of a go-around.

The mixture control is usually in *FULL RICH* for takeoff, unless you are operating at a high-elevation airport, possibly with high temperatures, where the air density as a consequence is very low (see below). Usually, the mixture remains in *FULL RICH* for the climb, unless it is an extended climb to altitudes in excess of 5,000 feet MSL.

As you climb with the mixture in *FULL RICH* the resulting excess fuel as the fuel/air mixture gradually becomes richer acts as a cooling agent for the cylinder walls and piston tops to help prevent abnormal combustion. Some of the more sophisticated engines require leaning during the climb, but for training airplanes this is not generally the case.

Using the Mixture Control at Cruise Altitude

On the cruise, and with cruise power set, you should consider leaning the mixture to regain a more chemically correct fuel/air ratio. This ensures more efficient burning of the gases in the cylinders, more efficient operation of the engine (slightly higher RPM for a fixed-pitch propeller) and better fuel economy. In some light airplanes correct leaning on the cruise can reduce the fuel consumption by over 25 percent compared with full rich, allowing greatly improved range and endurance performance.

The mixture should be slightly on the rich side of the chemically correct mixture, provided the cruise power setting is less than 75 percent of maximum continuous power (MCP).

Normal cruise for most airplanes is about 55–65 percent MCP, and so leaning the mixture is advisable.

At high power settings (in excess of 75 percent) a full-rich mixture is necessary to provide excess fuel as a coolant. The Pilot's Operating Handbook contains information on how to achieve the best power mixture and how to achieve the best economy mixture.

To lean the mixture, slowly move the mixture control toward the lean position. As a chemically correct fuel/air ratio is regained, the RPM for a fixed-pitch propeller will increase. Eventually, with further leaning, the RPM will decrease slightly and the engine will show signs of rough running. The mixture control should then be gently pushed back in a small amount to regain the best RPM (indicating a chemically correct mixture) and smoother running. The mixture control is then moved further in to a slightly richer position to ensure that the engine is operating on the rich side of the chemically correct mixture. This must be repeated when either cruise altitude or power-setting is changed.

Some airplanes are equipped with an *exhaust gas temperature* (EGT) *gauge* which indicates peak EGT when there is a chemically correct mixture, and this can assist you in leaning the mixture correctly.

For a constant-speed propeller, the leaning is normally done with reference to a *fuel flow gauge* (to obtain minimum fuel flow for smooth running) or the exhaust gas temperature gauge. Refer to your Pilot's Operating Handbook.

The principles of leaning the mixture apply to both carburetor-equipped and fuel-injected engines (to be discussed shortly).

> **Note.** Above 5,000 feet density altitude, a normally aspirated (not turbocharged) engine *cannot* achieve more than 75 percent maximum continuous power (even at full throttle).

Using the Mixture Control for Takeoff and Landing

During takeoff (and landing, when high power may be required in case of a go-around), the mixture control should normally be in *FULL RICH.*

In conditions where the air density is very low, however, such as at a very high elevation airport with high outside air temperatures (say 6,000 feet MSL and 100°F), you should consider if there is a need to lean the mixture. The reduced air density, sometimes referred to as a *high density altitude*, may result in too little air for the normal fuel flow, and an excessively fuel-rich mixture. When the engine runs too rich it is unable to provide its best power for takeoff.

An excessively rich mixture may be indicated on the ground by slightly rough running that is made worse during the carburetor heat check, when hot and even less-dense air enters the carburetor, starving the engine of air and further richening the fuel/air mixture.

You should discuss leaning the mixture for high density altitude takeoffs with your flight instructor, and refer to the Pilot's Operating Handbook.

Rich and Lean Mixtures

The mixture is usually slightly rich to protect against abnormal combustion and overheating in the cylinders. These damaging events are more likely to occur at power settings above 75 percent maximum continuous power than at the normal cruise power settings (55–65 percent), when leaning is advisable.

An over-rich mixture will cause a loss of power, rough running, high fuel consumption, fouling of the spark plugs and formation of lead deposits (from unburned fuel) on the piston heads and valves. The extra fuel in a rich mixture causes cooling within the cylinders by its evaporation which absorbs some of the heat produced in the combustion chamber. A lean mixture will therefore have higher cylinder head temperatures.

Too rich a mixture is preferable to too lean a mixture.

An excessively lean mixture will cause excessively high cylinder head temperatures, leading to abnormal combustion (detonation). The pilot is then faced with a loss of power and quite possibly complete engine failure. If you suspect that conditions are conducive to detonation, richen the mixture and check engine temperatures. A high cylinder head temperature could be an indication of detonation. Too rich is preferable to too lean.

Idle Cut-Off (or Idle Cut-Out)

The *idle cut-off* position of the mixture control is the normal means of shutting the engine down. In a typical system, when the mixture control is moved fully out to the idle cut-off position by the pilot, a small needle moves to cut off the fuel flow between the float chamber and the venturi. The supply of fuel to the fuel jets is then cut off.

The engine will continue running until all of the fuel/air mixture in the inlet manifold and the cylinders is burned. This leaves no combustible fuel/air mixture anywhere in the system, which would not be the case if the engine was stopped simply by turning the ignition *OFF*.

Abnormal Combustion

There are two kinds of abnormal combustion and both should be avoided:

- detonation—explosive combustion; and
- preignition—early ignition ahead of the spark.

Detonation

Detonation is the instantaneous, explosive combustion of the unburned charge in the cylinder.

Correct progressive burning of the fuel/air mixture should occur as the flame-front advances through the combustion chamber. This causes an increase in pressure which smoothly forces the piston down the cylinder in the power stroke.

When a gas is compressed, it experiences a rise in temperature. You can feel this if you hold your hand over a bicycle pump outlet during the compression stroke. If the pressure and the temperature rise is too great for the fuel/air mixture in the cylinders, the burning will not be progressive, but explosive, spontaneous combustion of the unburned charge after normal spark ignition.

This explosive increase in pressure is called *detonation* and can cause severe damage to the pistons, valves and spark plugs, as well as causing a decrease in power and quite possibly complete engine failure. Detonation cannot normally be detected by a pilot, although an indication of excessively high cylinder head temperature is a warning that conditions conducive to detonation may exist.

Detonation can be caused by:

- a lower fuel grade than recommended;
- a time-expired fuel;
- an over-lean mixture;
- excessive manifold pressure;
- an over-heated engine; or
- excessive temperature of the air which is passing through the carburetor.

If detonation conditions are expected, for instance by an excessively high cylinder head temperature:

- richen the mixture;
- reduce pressures in the cylinders (throttle back); or
- increase airspeed to assist in reducing cylinder head temperatures.

Preignition

Preignition is the uncontrolled firing of the fuel/air charge before the spark ignition.

Preignition, while involving a progressive combustion of the fuel/air mixture, is an ignition that commences before the spark from the plug. This early ignition (or preignition) can be caused by a hot-spot in the cylinder (from a carbon or lead deposit) becoming red-hot and igniting the mixture before the spark plug fires, causing peak pressures in the cylinder at the wrong point in the cycle. The results of preignition are:

- rough running;
- possibly back-firing;
- a sudden rise in the cylinder head temperature;
- possible engine damage such as a burnt piston, broken cylinder head, scuffed cylinder wall, and damage to valves and spark plugs; and
- cross-firing ignition leads or bad magneto distribution.

Preignition can be caused by:
- carbon or lead deposits in the cylinder;
- using high power when the mixture is too lean (no extra fuel for cooling); or
- overheated or wrong heat range spark plugs (possibly as a result of detonation).

Preignition may occur in one cylinder only, where a hot-spot exists, whereas detonation will normally occur in all cylinders. Preignition is a function of the condition of a particular cylinder or cylinders (such as a hot spot) whereas detonation is a function of the fuel/air mixture that is being supplied to all cylinders (too lean and/or too hot).

Both detonation and preignition can be prevented, provided the correct fuel is used, good magneto maintenance and inspection, and the operating limitations of the engine are observed. This information is available to you in the Pilot's Operating Handbook.

Carburetor Ice

The expansion of the air as it accelerates through the carburetor venturi causes it to drop in temperature. Even quite warm air can cool to below zero and, if it contains moisture, ice can form. This will seriously degrade the functioning of the carburetor, even to the point of stopping the engine! The first sign of carburetor ice in an airplane equipped with a fixed-pitch propeller is a loss of RPM.

Fuel-injected engines do not have a carburetor and are less susceptible to ice.

Impact Ice

Impact ice will occur when water droplets, which are below freezing point (in the intake air), contact the metal surfaces of the inlet air scoop and duct to the carburetor, immediately forming ice. (This can happen even in a fuel-injected system as well as in a normal carburetor system.)

Impact ice can occur when the outside air temperature is near or below zero, or if the inlet surfaces themselves are below zero and the airplane is in visible moisture such as cloud, rain or sleet. This may be the case if the airplane is on descent from high altitudes, where the temperature is below the freezing level, into areas of visible moisture.

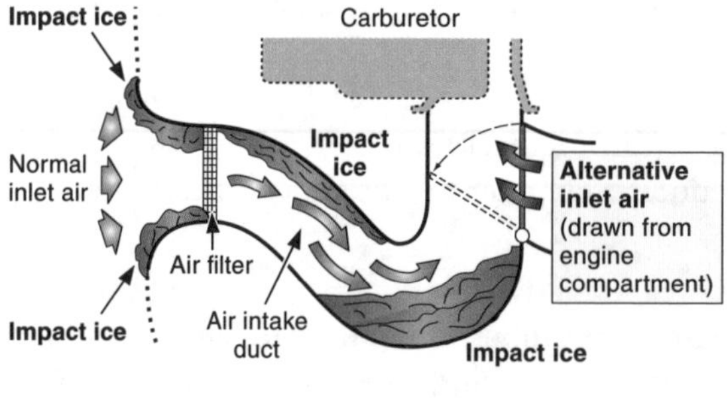

Alternative inlet air

In systems with float-type carburetors this is manual **carburetor heat** air.

In fuel-injection systems this is **alternate air**, usually supplied automatically if normal inlet is blocked by ice.

Note: As carburetor heat/alternate air is not filtered its use on the ground must be kept to a minimum.

Figure 5-23 Impact ice.

Fuel Ice

When fuel is introduced into the carburetor airstream, the temperature of the resulting fuel/air mixture is lowered substantially because of the latent heat absorption that occurs during fuel vaporization. You can feel this effect when water or perspiration evaporates off your skin on a hot day.

Fuel ice will form downstream of the metering jet in the throat of the carburetor if the temperature of the fuel/air mixture drops to between 0°C to -8°C (32°F to 16°F). The water will precipitate from the incoming air (if it is moist) and freeze onto any surface it encounters, such as the inlet manifold walls and the throttle butterfly valve. This ice will seriously restrict the airflow and thus reduce the engine's power output.

Fuel ice can occur in ambient air temperatures well above freezing, even as high as 30°C (85°F) when the relative humidity exceeds about 50 percent.

> **Note.** Fuel ice is sometimes called refrigeration ice, since it is caused by the vaporizing of a liquid—the same process that is used in most refrigerators.

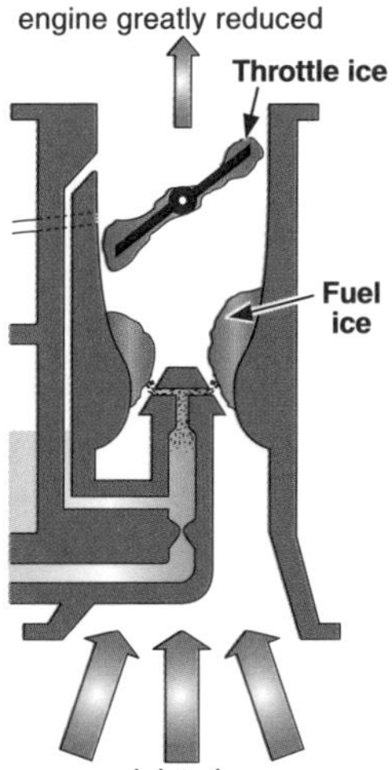

Figure 5-24
Throttle and fuel ice.

Throttle Ice

As the fuel/air mixture accelerates past the throttle valve, there is a decrease in static pressure and a consequent drop in temperature. This process can cause ice to form on the throttle valve. The acceleration and resulting temperature drop is greatest at small throttle openings because the throttle butterfly restricts the airflow at these low power settings, creating a substantial pressure drop. Therefore, there is a greater likelihood of carburetor ice at low throttle settings.

Formation of Carburetor Ice

Both fuel ice and throttle ice can occur even when the *outside* air temperature is high. Any time the outside air temperature is within the approximate range (20°F to 70°F) and especially if the relative humidity is high, you should remain alert for signs of carburetor ice, caused by cooling in the carburetor venturi.

Carburetor ice is most likely when the temperature is between –10°C to +20°C (20°F to 70°F) and relative humidity is high.

> **Note.** Visible moisture is not necessary for the formation of throttle ice.

All of this carburetor ice can have a very serious effect on the running of the engine. The size and shape of the carburetor passages are altered by the ice, the airflow is disturbed, and the fuel/air mixture ratio is affected. These factors all lead to rough running, a loss of power and possibly a total stoppage of the engine unless prompt corrective action is taken.

Typical symptoms of carburetor ice formation are:

- a power loss (a drop in RPM for a fixed-pitch propeller, and a drop in manifold pressure for a constant-speed propeller), resulting in poorer performance (a loss of airspeed or a poorer rate of climb); and
- rough running.

Carburetor Heat

Most modern airplanes have a carburetor heat system to prevent and remove carburetor ice. This usually involves heating the induction air prior to intake into the carburetor by passing the air close to the (hot) exhaust system of the engine. The density of this *heated air* passing through the carburetor will be less, therefore making the fuel/air mixture too rich. The initial effect of applying carburetor heat will be to decrease the power from the engine (seen as an initial drop in RPM for a fixed-pitch propeller or an initial drop in manifold pressure for a constant-speed propeller), possibly by as much as 10–20 percent.

The *carburetor heat control* is usually located near the throttle in the cockpit. By pulling it fully out, heated air is passed into the carburetor. It is usual, if carburetor ice is suspected, to apply full carburetor heat. As the hot air passes through the carburetor venturi, it will melt the ice. If there has been a large ice build-up in the carburetor, the engine may run extremely roughly, especially as the melted ice (now water) passes through the cylinders along with the fuel/air mixture, but this roughness will quickly disappear.

When the ice clears from the carburetor, the engine will begin running smoother and there will be an increase in power. The RPM of a fixed-pitch propeller will rise as the ice clears, as will the manifold pressure of a constant-speed propeller. Following this, carburetor heat may be removed and cold air again used, at which time there will be a further slight increase in power.

If carburetor ice re-forms, then this operation will have to be repeated. Full carburetor heat must be re-applied until the carburetor ice melts. You may find that, under some conditions, full carburetor heat is required not only to remove carburetor ice, but also to prevent it from re-forming.

Some engines have a *carburetor air temperature gauge*, which may be used to keep the carburetor air temperature out of the icing range. It may allow you to use only partial carburetor heat to prevent further formation of ice once the initial ice has been removed with full carburetor heat. If carburetor ice still forms, immediately re-apply full carburetor heat to remove it, and then try a higher setting of partial heat to prevent its formation.

Caution. Partial use of carburetor heat may raise the temperature of the induction air into the temperature range which is most conducive to the formation of carburetor ice, thereby increasing the risk of ice build-up rather than decreasing it. Monitor the engine power gauges and be alert for any rough running.

On descent with low power, particularly in high humidity, it is usual to apply carburetor heat to ensure that no carburetor ice forms or is present. The small throttle butterfly openings needed for low power increase the chance of carburetor ice forming.

On short final approach to land, the carburetor heat is usually returned to *COLD*, just in case full power is required in the event of a go-around.

Avoid using carburetor heat on the ground because the hot air is taken from around the engine exhaust manifold (in most airplanes) and, unlike the normal inlet air, is unfiltered. This will avoid introducing dust and grit into the carburetor and the engine itself, which could lead to unnecessary wear and damage.

Fuel Injection Systems

Many sophisticated engines have fuel directly metered into the induction manifold and then into the cylinders without using a carburetor. This is known as *fuel injection.*

A venturi system is still used to create the pressure differential. This is coupled to a *fuel control unit* (FCU), from which metered fuel is piped to the *fuel manifold unit* (fuel distributor). From here, a separate fuel line carries fuel to the *discharge nozzle* in each cylinder head, or into the inlet port prior to the inlet valve. The mixture control in the fuel injection system controls the idle cut-off.

With fuel injection, each individual cylinder is provided with a correct mixture by its own separate fuel line. (This is unlike the carburetor system, which supplies the same fuel/air mixture to all cylinders. This requires a slightly richer-than-ideal mixture to ensure that the leanest-running cylinder does not run too lean.)

The advantages of fuel injection include:

- freedom from fuel ice (no suitable place for it to form);
- more uniform delivery of the fuel/air mixture to each cylinder;
- improved control of fuel/air ratio;
- fewer maintenance problems;
- instant acceleration of the engine after idling with no tendency for it to stall; and
- increased engine efficiency.

Starting an already hot engine that has a fuel injection system may be difficult because of vapor locking in the fuel lines. Electric boost pumps that pressurize the fuel lines can help alleviate this problem. Having very fine fuel lines, fuel injection engines are more susceptible to any contamination in the fuel such as dirt or water. Correct fuel management is imperative! Know the fuel system of your particular airplane. Surplus fuel provided by a fuel injection system will pass through a *return line* which may be routed to only one of the fuel tanks. If the pilot does not remain aware of where the surplus fuel is being returned to, it may result in uneven fuel loading in the tanks or fuel being vented overboard (thus reducing flight fuel available).

Correct fuel management is imperative! Know the fuel system of your airplane!

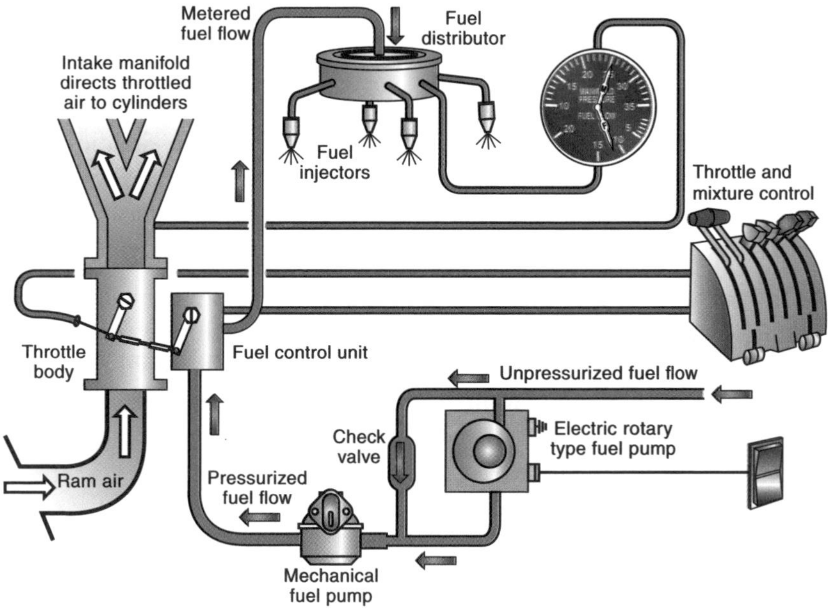

Figure 5-25 Typical fuel injection system.

Engine Operation

Starting the Engine

Ensure that adequate *safety precautions* are always taken prior to engine start:

- prior to start, position the aircraft so that it is clear of obstructions, other aircraft, open hangar/workshop doors, and fueling installations;
- set the parking brakes on, or chock the mainwheels, to avoid the embarrassing and dangerous situation of the airplane commencing its own taxiing. Chocking the nosewheel is *not* advisable because of its proximity to the propeller and the consequent risk to a person walking into the rotating propeller when removing a nosewheel chock;

Figure 5-26 Check propeller is clean.

- be aware of the location of firefighting equipment—just in case of fire. Ensure no open flames, cigarettes or fuel spillages in the vicinity; and
- most importantly *check* the immediate area is clear of people and then *warn* any nearby persons (especially those you may not be able to see) of the impending danger of a spinning propeller by making a loud warning call of *"clear!"* or *"clear prop!"* The aircraft red rotating beacon should be turned on just prior to starting the engine. Be prepared to discontinue the start immediately if a problem develops or if someone approaches the danger area near the propeller.

Figure 5-27
RPM and MAP gauges.

Your first action after starting the engine should be to adjust for proper RPM and check for the desired indications on the engine gauges, especially the oil pressure gauge which should show an increase within 30 seconds.

If it is necessary to handprop an airplane engine (an extremely hazardous procedure) it is important that a competent pilot be at the airplane controls and that the person turning the propeller has sufficient training.

Starting a Cold Engine

Figure 5-28
Starting.

Starting in cold conditions usually requires some *priming* (providing an initial charge of fuel to the cylinders). Many aircraft have a priming pump (electrical or manual) in the cockpit for this purpose—it is used only prior to startup, and should be locked at all other times.

Know the procedures recommended in your Pilot's Operating Handbook. These differ from airplane-to-airplane, engine-to-engine and situation-to-situation. You should understand the reasons why a certain procedure is recommended and when it is appropriate to vary it slightly. An over-primed (flooded) engine or restarting a hot engine, for example, will require different techniques to starting a cold engine in a cold climate.

> **Note.** On start-up of a cold engine, the oil pressure should normally rise within 30 seconds, to ensure adequate lubrication of the engine and its moving parts. If the oil pressure rise is not indicated within this time, shut down the engine to avoid possible damage. If the engine is warm, the oil pressure should rise more quickly. In cold climates, it is normal for the oil pressure rise to take up to 60 seconds—*see* your Pilot's Operating Handbook.

Starting an Engine That Has Been Over-Primed

Most over-primed engines will start more easily with the mixture control in *idle cut-off* so that no more fuel enters the cylinders until the engine has actually started. When the mixture in the cylinders reaches the right balance as air-only is drawn in, the engine should fire, at which stage the mixture control should be moved quickly to *full rich* to provide a continuing fuel supply.

If the engine does *not* fire, the rotations may have cleared the cylinders of fuel. Therefore move the mixture control to rich to allow fresh fuel to be drawn into the cylinders. This technique applies to both carbureted and fuel-injected engines. Refer to your Pilot's Operating Handbook.

Starting a Hot Engine

Usually a hot carbureted engine will start satisfactorily using the normal procedure for a cold engine if you do not prime it or pump the throttle.

When starting a hot fuel-injected engine, the hot air and vapor in the very narrow fuel lines may cause a vapor lock and prevent the flow of any fuel. To prevent this, switch on the fuel boost pumps. This will pressurize the fuel lines up to the fuel control unit, removing any vapor in that part of the system. Leave the mixture control in *idle cut-off* so that fuel does not reach the cylinders but is recycled back into the tank.

Some engines require the throttle to be opened for the boost pumps to work in *high*. After 15 to 20 seconds, the narrow fuel lines to the fuel injectors should have been purged of vapor and be full of fuel. Because a small amount of fuel will probably have found its way into the fuel nozzles near the cylinders, a start can be made without priming (with throttle at idle or open about ½ inch).

Stopping the Engine

A brief *cooling period* at 1,000 RPM is usually recommended to allow gradual cooling. During this time check for any abnormal indications and perform a systems check of the ignition system for *off*.

Most engines are shut down from a low power position (usually 1,000 RPM) by moving the mixture control to *idle cut-off*, thus allowing the cylinders to be purged of fuel. All switches are usually moved to *off*.

It is a good practice to:

- leave the mixture control in the idle cut-off position; and
- leave the throttle in the closed position in case someone turns the propeller and firing occurs because the magneto system is still *live*.

Changing Power Settings with a Constant-Speed Propeller

Change RPM with the propeller control. Change MP with the throttle.

While almost all training airplanes have a *fixed-pitch propeller* whose RPM is controlled with the throttle, more advanced airplanes which you may soon fly are equipped with a *constant-speed propeller* with blades that can vary their pitch angle.

The controls in the cockpit for a constant-speed propeller are:

- the *propeller control* (or pitch knob) to control *RPM*; and
- the *throttle* to control fuel flow and *manifold pressure (MP)*.

The pilot selects the desired RPM of the engine and propeller using the *propeller control* (also known as the *pitch control* or *RPM control*). The propeller blades will then automatically change their pitch angle or blade angle to absorb the power available and maintain the selected RPM. For instance, if you have selected a cruise RPM of 2,400 with the propeller control and then move the throttle to increase manifold pressure from 22 to 23 in. Hg, the propeller pitch will increase to absorb the extra power by increasing the blade angle and providing increased thrust.

Conversely, if power is reduced, the propeller blade angle will reduce to maintain RPM. The constant-speed unit in the propeller operates automatically—usually the blade movement to a new pitch angle is hydraulically operated by a governor sensitive to RPM.

There is a mechanical limit to how far the propeller pitch or blade angle can reduce, known as the *low-pitch stop*. With the blades back on the low-pitch stop, the propeller will behave like a fixed-pitch propeller.

Never exceed the recommended manifold pressure.

The pilot selects the desired power with various combinations of RPM and manifold pressure. *Manifold pressure* is the pressure in the intake manifold of the engine, and is normally measured in inches of mercury (in. Hg). Manifold pressures higher than those recommended by the manufacturer can lead to high cylinder pressures and possibly detonation, and must be avoided. This can occur if high manifold pressures are set at low RPM.

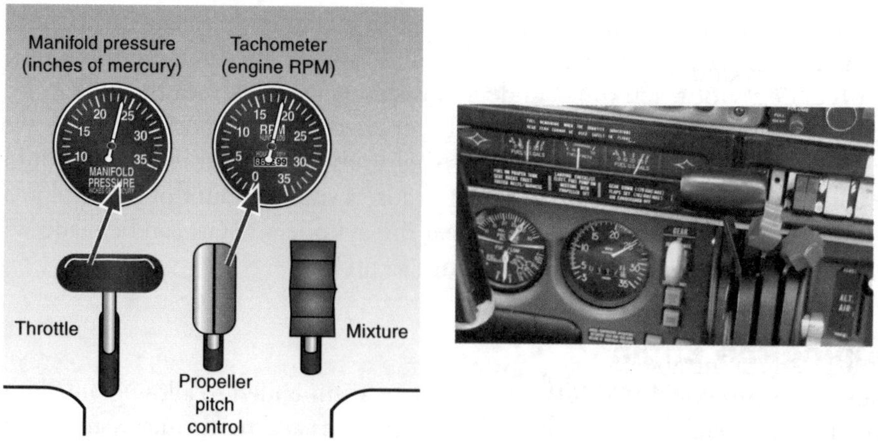

Figure 5-29 With a constant-speed propeller, the propeller control controls RPM and the throttle determines the manifold pressure.

Increasing Power

When increasing power increase RPM before MP.

To avoid high MP and low RPM:

- *first increase RPM* with the propeller control. The MP will drop automatically as a result of less time per cycle being available for the fuel/air mixture to be induced into the cylinder, hence a smaller charge in the cylinder for combustion; and
- *then increase MP* to desired value with the throttle.

Decreasing Power

When decreasing power reduce MP before RPM.

To avoid high MP and low RPM:

- *first reduce MP* with the throttle; and
- *then reduce RPM* with the propeller control. The MP will rise a little automatically—as a result of more time for cycle for the fuel/air mixture to be induced into the cylinder, hence a larger charge in the cylinder for combustion. After the reduction of RPM, some minor readjustment of MP will be necessary.

Air pressure falls by about 1 in. Hg per 1,000 feet as altitude is gained, and so will the manifold pressure in an unsupercharged engine if you do not adjust it with the throttle. In this situation the RPM would remain the same, but the power would reduce gradually. Superchargers and turbochargers are used in more sophisticated engines to boost the air pressure to the engine, thereby increasing the power available at altitude.

> **Note.** The propeller governor that controls RPM is operated by engine oil, which is another very good reason for regular oil changes. Dirty oil could have an adverse effect on propeller operation.

Engine Handling

At all times, follow recommended procedures found in the manufacturer's handbook. This will ensure correct operation of the engine, avoid spark plug fouling and over-stressing the engine components, and achieve best fuel economy. Know the manufacturer's engine limitations and do not exceed them.

When the engine is operating, you should monitor the *oil temperature gauge* (and the *cylinder-head temperature gauge* if installed). An abnormally high engine oil temperature could indicate insufficient oil in the engine. High engine temperatures, either in the air or on the ground, will cause:

- loss of power;
- excessive oil consumption; and
- possible permanent internal engine damage.

In flight, you could consider cooling the engine by opening the air-cooling cowl flaps (if installed), richening the mixture, reducing power, or lowering the nose and increasing airspeed.

Avoid running the engine *on the ground* for prolonged periods if possible but, if unavoidable, face the aircraft into wind for better cooling and, if they are installed, open the cowl flaps. If the limiting red-line temperatures are approached during ground operations, consider taxiing clear of the runway and shutting the engine down to allow cooling.

Prevent *spark-plug fouling* by avoiding operating the engine at very low RPM for long periods. At low idling RPM, deposits can form on the spark plugs which will increase their electrical conductivity and may lead to misfiring.

Advance and retard the throttle smoothly.

Misuse of controls can lead to de-tuning of engine crankshaft counterweights and engine damage. Opening the throttle by ramming it forward can produce an incorrect fuel/air mixture in the carburetor and cause the engine to cut-out, or encourage detonation. Rough handling of the throttle can also cause de-tuning of the crankshaft counterweights, which will permanently reduce the efficiency of the engine as a power-producer. As a guide you should take about three seconds to open the throttle from idle to full. Similarly when reducing power, do so slowly.

On a prolonged descent at low power, it is good airmanship to smoothly open the throttle for brief periods to avoid the engine becoming too cool. Closing cowl flaps, if installed, also helps. This will avoid a sudden temperature shock to the engine when it is returned to high power at the end of the descent.

Use the mixture control correctly. A too-lean mixture at high power and low altitudes can cause detonation. It is usual to lean the mixture when cruising at altitude, depending on the manufacturer's recommendations. On a very hot day, even at only 1,000 feet MSL the atmosphere may have a density altitude of several thousand feet, and leaning may be required for efficient operation (*see* chapter 8).

Rough Running

The Engine

Engine rough running can be continuous or intermittent. If the engine starts running roughly, immediately refer to the engine instruments to see if they indicate the cause. In all cases, follow the procedures laid down in the Pilot's Operating Handbook. A thorough knowledge of these is essential.

Figure 5-30
Engine checks.

Rough running can be caused by:

- *an inadequate fuel supply*—check the fuel quantity gauge and if it indicates empty immediately select another tank. If the gauges show sufficient fuel suspect low fuel pressure caused by a blocked filter and switch on the fuel boost pumps to ensure a steady fuel pressure;
- *carburetor ice*—the formation of ice in the carburetor causes a loss of power and possibly rough running. Remember that carburetor ice can form when the outside air temperature is as high as 70°F if the humidity is high enough;

- *an incorrect mixture*—if the mixture is not leaned correctly, a prolonged climb will gradually lead to a richening of the mixture as the air density falls, with consequent rough running. A prolonged descent will require the pilot to move the mixture control towards the rich position;
- *a faulty magneto*—if you suspect a faulty magneto is causing the engine to run roughly, select a low cruise power, and then check each magneto individually by switching the other one off. If the engine runs smoothly on one particular magneto, but roughly on both or on the other magneto, then select the single magneto system that gives smoother running. Consideration should be given to landing at the nearest suitable airport, the airplane engine will still operate satisfactorily on only one ignition system, but a failure of the second magneto would leave you with none; or
- *a faulty ignition system*—fouling of the spark plugs can cause faulty ignition. Sometimes this can be cured by leaning the mixture to raise the temperature and perhaps burn the residue off the plug, or by changing the power setting. Leakage of the *ignition current*, which can sometimes occur around the ignition leads could be the cause, however this cannot be remedied in flight. This leakage may be worse at high altitude/high power settings and in wet weather.

The Propeller

An out-of-balance propeller can cause vibration.

Vibration or rough running usually indicates a problem or impending problem. An out-of-balance propeller can cause vibration.

If the vibration is caused by a damaged propeller, possibly an out-of-balance propeller due to nicks, then a change of RPM or a change of airspeed should reduce the vibration. This, of course, is only a temporary remedy and the nicks should be repaired on landing. Nicks in the propeller blade degrade its performance considerably and are liable to cause cracks which can ultimately lead to blade failure in flight, with disastrous results. Propeller nicks and other damage should be brought immediately to the attention of a maintenance technician.

If the vibration does not diminish, but worsens, it could indicate that the bolts attaching the propeller to the shaft are loosening. In this case, shutting down the engine is advisable. If you suspect this defect in a single-engine airplane, a landing as soon as possible (a forced landing, if necessary) should be contemplated. Ice on the propeller blades may also cause vibration.

Cross-Checking Engine Instruments

If one engine instrument indicates a problem, verify this, if possible, by checking against another instrument. For instance, an oil pressure gauge that suddenly shows zero could indicate that all the oil has been lost out of the system, or it could be just a faulty gauge. Cross-reference to the oil temperature gauge should establish the fault. A normal oil temperature would indicate sufficient oil is still circulating, whereas a rapidly increasing oil temperature would indicate that loss of oil has occurred.

If you are in flight, a serious loss of oil will mean an engine shutdown, so in a single-engine airplane you should prepare to land as soon as possible. With a faulty gauge, the engine will continue to operate normally.

Taxiing

Do not taxi over rough ground because the propeller could hit long grass, obstructions or the ground, damaging the propeller and possibly bending the engine crankshaft, a very costly lack of common sense.

Avoid engine runups or taxiing on stony or gravel surfaces where possible. The strong airflow and vortices around a propeller pick up stones, damaging the propeller and airframe and hitting other aircraft and people. Good airmanship involves looking after your airplane and thinking of others.

Emergencies

Engine Failure in Flight

Due to improved manufacturing and operating procedures, mechanical engine failure is becoming a rare event, but *fuel starvation* as a cause of engine stoppage is not as uncommon as it should be. Fuel starvation will of course stop an engine and can be caused by:

- insufficient fuel;
- mishandling of the fuel tank selection;
- incorrect use of the mixture control;
- ice forming in the carburetor; or
- contaminated fuel (such as water in the fuel).

If the *mixture control* is left in *lean* for descent (instead of being moved to *rich*), the fuel/air mixture will gradually become more and more lean as the airplane descends into denser air, possibly resulting in the engine stopping. *Carburetor ice* can also be a problem, especially on descent when the engine is idling and not producing much heat. *Electrical failure* in both magneto systems will also cause the engine to stop.

In all these cases, the airflow past the airplane may cause the propeller to windmill and turn the engine over, even though it is not producing power.

Mechanical failure, such as the break-up of pistons or valves, will probably be accompanied by mechanical noise and the engine and propeller may be unable to rotate. In such cases any attempt to restart the engine is not advisable.

Irrespective of whether you decide to glide down for a landing or attempt to restart the engine, you must ensure that flying speed is maintained.

Some obvious items to be considered in an attempted engine restart are:

- a fuel problem:
  - change fuel tanks;
  - fuel pump on (if installed);
  - mixture *rich*;
  - primer locked;
- an ignition problem:
  - check magneto switches individually (*both–left–right*). If the engine operates on one magneto as a result of a fault in the other magneto system, then operate using the one good ignition system, otherwise return to *both*; or
- an icing problem:
  - carburetor heat *full hot*.

Engine Fire In Flight

Engine fire is also a rare event, but you should always be prepared to cope with it. The firewall at the back of the engine is designed to protect the structural parts of the airframe from damage and the cockpit occupants from injury if a fire breaks out in the engine bay, provided the fire is extinguished without delay.

To check for the presence of fire, the pilot should yaw the nose left and look rearward and to the left for any trailing smoke.

The initial reaction to an engine fire in flight should be as per the Pilot's Operating Handbook. This usually involves turning off the fuel (fuel selector *off* or mixture control to *idle cut-off*) and allowing the engine to run itself dry of fuel and stop. The engine and induction system will then be purged of fuel and the fire should extinguish. At this point, the ignition should be switched off and a forced landing carried out.

Throughout any emergency procedure in flight, remember that your main task is to *fly the airplane* (maintain flying speed and avoid collisions)—and the secondary task is to resolve the emergency.

Engine Fire on Startup

If a fire starts in the engine air intake during startup, a generally accepted procedure to minimize the problem is:

- *continue cranking* the engine with the starter (to keep air moving through);
- move the mixture control to *idle cut-off* (to remove the source of fuel); and
- *open the throttle* (to maximize the airflow through the carburetor and induction system, and purge the system of fuel).

The fire will probably go out, but if it does not, then further action would be taken:

- fuel—*off*;
- switches—*off*;
- brakes—*off*; and
- evacuate the airplane, taking the fire extinguisher.

You should refer to the Pilot's Operating Handbook for the correct procedure for your particular airplane.

Review 5

Engine

The Engine

1. Name the four strokes of a piston engine commencing with the stroke intake.
2. Is the intake valve open during most of the compression stroke?
3. Is the exhaust valve open during most of the compression stroke?
4. Is the intake valve open during most of the exhaust stroke?
5. Is the exhaust valve open during most of the exhaust stroke?
6. What is the period when both intake and exhaust valves are open simultaneously known as?
7. How is the fuel/air mixture ignited in the cylinder?
8. If one of the magneto switches is turned to OFF, should there be an engine RPM drop?
9. True or false? Switching the ignition OFF connects the magneto systems to ground.
10. If a magneto ground wire comes loose in flight, will the engine stop?
11. The spark plugs in a piston engine are provided with a high energy (or high tension) electrical supply from:
    a. the battery at all times.
    b. the magnetos.
    c. the battery at start-up, then the magnetos.
12. What is the most probable reason an engine continues to run after the ignition switch has been turned off?
13. If the ground wire between the magneto and the ignition switch becomes disconnected, the engine:
    a. will not operate on one magneto.
    b. cannot be started with the switch in the BOTH position.
    c. could accidentally start if the propeller is moved with fuel in the cylinder.
14. Because of the very low revs as you start the engine, the spark needs to be delayed. How is this done automatically in some magnetos?

Carburetor and Fuel Injection

15. Describe the principle of a simple carburetor.
16. What is the fuel/air ratio?
17. How does the pilot control the fuel/air ratio?
18. What remains following combustion of a rich mixture?
19. What remains following combustion of a lean mixture?
20. What carburetor device ensures that sufficient fuel is fed to the cylinders when idling at low RPM?
21. What is meant by the term *best-power mixture*?
22. As air density decreases, the weight of fuel introduced into the cylinder needs to be reduced to match the decreased weight of air. How is this done?
23. What can an over-rich mixture cause?
24. For takeoff at a sea level airport on a cool day, the mixture control should normally be:
    a. full rich.
    b. lean.
    c. in idle cut-off.
25. True or false? The extra fuel in a rich mixture causes extra heating in the cylinders by its evaporation.
26. If no leaning is made with the mixture control as the flight altitude increases:
    a. the volume of air entering the carburetor decreases and the amount of fuel decreases.
    b. the density of air entering the carburetor decreases and the amount of fuel increases.
    c. the density of air entering the carburetor decreases and the amount of fuel remains constant.
27. The correct procedure to achieve the best fuel/air mixture when cruising at altitude is to move the mixture control toward LEAN until the engine RPM:
    a. drops to a minimum value.
    b. reaches a peak value.
    c. passes through a peak value at which point the mixture control is returned to a slightly richer position.

28. If a pilot suspects that the engine (with a fixed-pitch propeller) is detonating during climb-out after takeoff, the initial corrective action to take would be to:
    a. lean the mixture.
    b. lower the nose slightly to increase air-speed.
    c. apply carburetor heat.
29. What are hot-spots in a combustion chamber likely to cause?
30. How is carburetor ice formed?
31. What is the remedy for suspected carburetor ice?
32. What is one of the first indications of carburetor ice forming in an airplane equipped with a fixed-pitch propeller?
33. Hotter air entering the engine after carburetor heat is applied will be less dense, which means that less air by weight for the same weight of fuel enters the cylinders. Will applying carburetor heat therefore result in a richer mixture?
34. What is the effect of leaving the carburetor heat on while taking off?
35. Does the principle of leaning the mixture by reducing the fuel flow to match the lower density air as altitude is gained apply to fuel-injected engines?
36. True or false? The the pressure drop (and consequent temperature drop) near the throttle butterfly is greatest at small throttle openings, causing a greater likelihood of carburetor ice forming.
37. The presence of carburetor ice in an aircraft equipped with a fixed-pitch propeller can be verified by applying carburetor heat and:
    a. noting an increase in RPM, then a gradual decrease in RPM.
    b. noting a decrease in RPM, then a constant RPM indication.
    c. noting a decrease in RPM, then a gradual increase in RPM.
38. While cruising at 9,500 feet MSL, the fuel/air mixture is properly adjusted. What will occur if a descent to 4,500 feet MSL is made without readjusting the mixture?
39. What is detonation?
40. How is detonation caused?
41. What is the uncontrolled firing of the fuel/air charge in advance of normal spark ignition known as?
42. Which condition is most favorable to the development of carburetor icing?
    a. Any temperature below freezing and a relative humidity of less than 50 percent.
    b. Between 32°F and 50°F and low humidity.
    c. Between 20°F and 70°F and high humidity.
43. Why would you normally avoid using carburetor heat during ground operations?
44. With regard to carburetor ice, float-type carburetor systems in comparison to fuel injection systems are generally considered to be:
    a. more susceptible to icing.
    b. equally susceptible to icing.
    c. susceptible to icing only when visible moisture is present.

The Oil System

45. What is the function of oil?
46. True or false? Oil grades may be mixed.
47. How are impurities in the oil removed?
48. What might you observe with too little oil?
49. If the oil filter becomes blocked, what happens to the unfiltered oil?
50. True or false? Dirty and contaminated oil is better than no oil at all.

The Cooling System

51. What is the function of cooling fins?
52. For internal cooling, reciprocating aircraft engines are especially dependent on:
    a. a properly functioning thermostat.
    b. air flowing over the exhaust manifold.
    c. the circulation of lubricating oil.
53. What action can a pilot take to aid in cooling an engine that is overheating during a climb?
54. Excessively high engine temperatures will:
    a. cause damage to heat-conducting hoses and warping of the cylinder cooling fins.
    b. cause loss of power, excessive oil consumption, and possible permanent internal engine damage.
    c. not appreciably affect an aircraft engine.

Engine Operation

55. When is the engine fuel primer used?
56. What should the pilot monitor when an engine is started up?
57. If the engine is cold prior to start-up, it should be shut down if the oil pressure does not rise within how many seconds after start-up?
58. Prior to takeoff, should you check each of the two ignition systems with a magneto check?
59. How is power indicated:
    - **a.** for a fixed-pitch propeller?
    - **b.** for an engine equipped with a constant-speed propeller?
60. True or false? A fixed-pitch propeller achieves its best efficiency at only one airspeed and RPM.
61. True or false? A constant-speed propeller, with cruise RPM selected, automatically adjusts its blade angle to absorb the power available.
62. How should you increase power with a constant-speed propeller?
63. How should you decrease power with a constant-speed propeller?
64. For an engine equipped with a constant-speed propeller:
    - **a.** what is fuel flow and consequently power output controlled by?
    - **b.** what is the power output registered on?
65. In an airplane with a constant-speed propeller, which of the following procedures should be used?
    - **a.** When power is decreased, reduce RPM before manifold pressure.
    - **b.** When power is increased, increase RPM before manifold pressure.
    - **c.** When power is increased or decreased adjust manifold pressure before RPM.
66. As altitude is gained when climbing in an airplane equipped with a constant-speed propeller:
    - **a.** what will happen to the RPM?
    - **b.** what will happen to the manifold pressure unless you adjust the throttle?
67. True or false? If you are cruising at 8,000 feet MSL, you will achieve better fuel efficiency by leaning the mixture.
68. When operating a constant-speed propeller:
    - **a.** avoid high RPM setting with high manifold pressures.
    - **b.** avoid low RPM settings with high manifold pressures.
    - **c.** always use a rich mixture with high RPM settings.
69. A de-tuning of engine crankshaft counterweights is a source of overstress that may be caused by:
    - **a.** rapid opening and closing of the throttle.
    - **b.** carburetor ice forming on the throttle valve.
    - **c.** operating with an excessively rich fuel/air mixture.
70. What does "leaning the mixture" mean?
71. The usual method of shutting an engine down is to:
    - **a.** switch the magnetos off.
    - **b.** move the mixture to idle cut-off.
    - **c.** switch the master switch off.
72. Explain your answer to question 71 and state why the other alternatives are incorrect.
73. If the oil quantity gauge suddenly drops to zero in flight, which gauge should you check immediately?
74. The oil temperature gauge shows a rapid increase in temperature.
    - **a.** What should you suspect?
    - **b.** What actions should you consider?
75. If the oil temperature gauge and the cylinder head temperature gauge are both reading higher than their normal operating range, a possible cause is:
    - **a.** an over-rich mixture and too much power.
    - **b.** a too-lean mixture and too much power.
    - **c.** fuel with a higher-than-specified fuel rating.

Answers are given on page 687.

Systems 6

The Fuel System

The function of a fuel system is to store fuel and deliver it to the carburetor (or fuel injection system) in adequate quantities at the proper pressures. It should provide a continuous flow of fuel under positive pressure for all normal flight conditions, including:

- changes of altitude;
- changes of attitude; and/or
- sudden throttle movements and power changes.

Fuel is stored in *fuel tanks*, which are usually installed in the wing. A sump and a drain point at the lowest point of the tank allows heavy impurities (such as water or sediment) to gather, be inspected and drained off. The tanks often contain *baffles* to prevent the fuel surging about in flight—especially during large attitude changes or uncoordinated maneuvers, or in turbulence.

The fuel supply line (tube) inlet is higher than the sump to prevent impurities (water or sludge) from entering the fuel lines to the carburetor, even though there is a *fuel filter* in the line to remove any small impurities from the fuel as it passes down the supply line. Because the fuel enters the supply line through a standpipe at the bottom of the tank, there will always be some *unusable fuel* in the tanks.

The top of the fuel tank is vented to the atmosphere so that the air pressure above the fuel in the tank remains the same as outside as altitude is changed. Reduced pressure in the tank caused by ineffective venting could reduce the rate of fuel flow to the engine and also cause the fuel tanks to collapse inward. *Fuel vents* should be checked in the preflight external inspection to ensure that they are not blocked or damaged.

An *overflow drain* prevents excessive pressure building up if fuel volume increases because the full tanks have been warmed in the sun.

A high-wing airplane with the tanks in the wings will generally allow the fuel to be *gravity-fed* to the carburetor without the need for a *fuel pump*. If there is no carburetor as with a fuel injection system, then electric *boost pumps* are necessary.

In a low-wing airplane, the tanks, being lower than the engine, need a fuel pump to lift the fuel to the carburetor. Prior to start-up, an electric auxiliary (boost) pump is used to prime the fuel lines and to purge any vapor from them. Once the engine is started, the engine-driven mechanical fuel pump takes over. Pump function can be monitored on the fuel pressure gauge.

All engines have an engine-driven fuel pump.

For many airplanes, the Pilot's Operating Handbook recommends that the electric fuel pump be switched on for critical maneuvers such as the takeoff, landing and low flying. This prevents fuel starvation in the event the engine-driven mechanical fuel pump fails.

Some engines (such as those in low-wing airplanes) also have an electric auxiliary fuel boost pump.

It is important that the fuel strainer drain valve in a low part of the fuel system is checked closed during the preflight external inspection. If it is not closed, the engine-driven fuel pump may not be able to draw sufficient fuel into the engine (sucking air instead), and the engine may be starved of fuel unless the electric fuel pump is used.

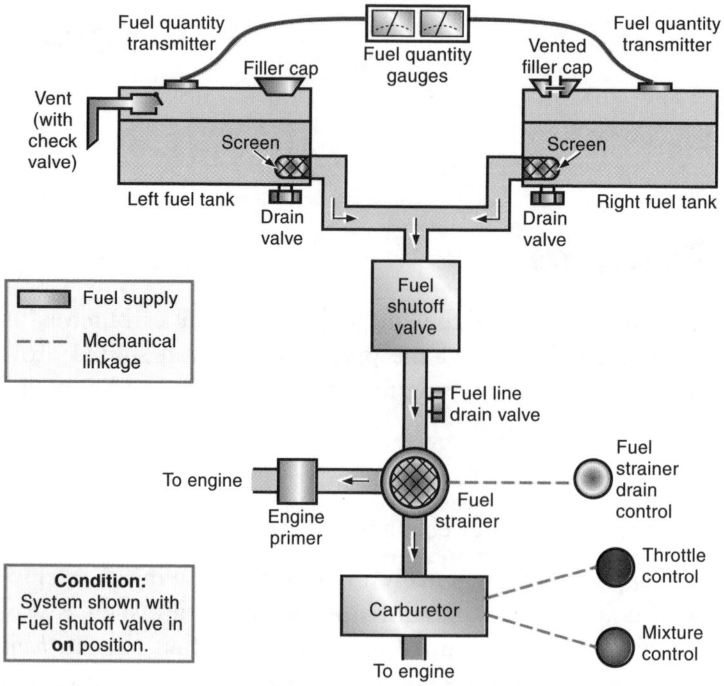

Figure 6-1 Simple carburetor fuel system.

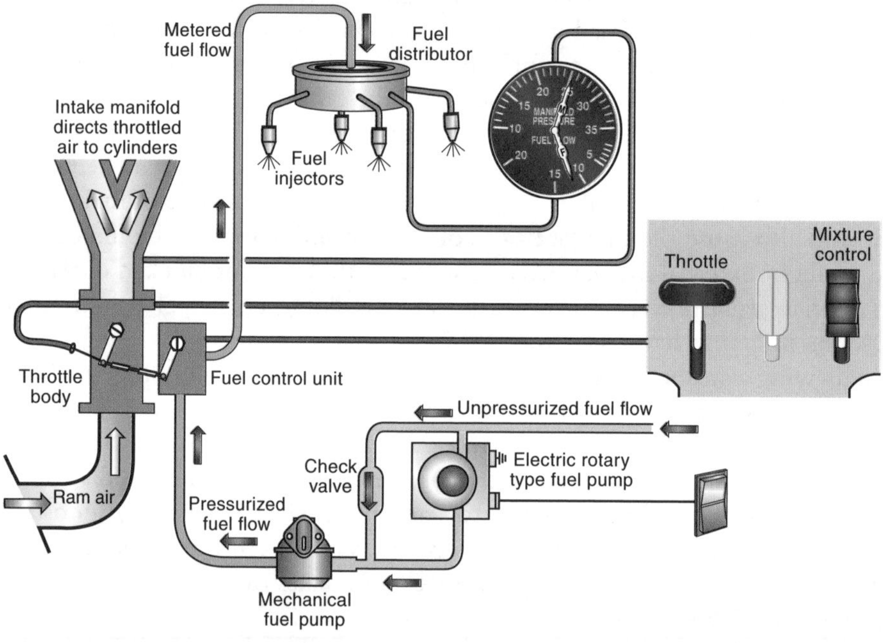

Figure 6-2 Typical fuel injection system.

The Priming Pump

A priming pump sends fuel directly into the engine prior to start-up.

The fuel primer is a hand-operated pump in the cockpit which the pilot uses to pump fuel into the induction system of the engine in preparation for engine start-up. This fuel does not pass through the carburetor, but is hand-pumped directly into the inlet manifold just before the cylinders.

Priming the engine is especially useful when starting a cold engine on a cold day, when the fuel in the carburetor is reluctant to vaporize.

The primer must be locked when the engine is running to avoid excessive fuel being drawn through the priming line into the cylinders, especially at low power settings, which could stop the engine if the fuel/air mixture is too rich.

Fuel Selection

Know your fuel system and always select a tank that contains fuel.

A fuel line runs from each tank to a selector valve in the cockpit, which the pilot uses to select the tank from which fuel will be taken or to shut the fuel off. Incorrect fuel tank selection can result in fuel starvation, and has been the cause of many accidents—so study your Pilot's Operating Handbook very closely on this matter. The sounds of silence while you still have fuel in one tank, but not the tank that you have incorrectly selected, can be very loud indeed! You should not run a tank dry in flight before switching tanks, because the fuel pump may draw air into the fuel lines, causing a vapor lock which may stop the fuel flow, even from another tank, into the engine. Once a vapor lock has formed, it may be very difficult to restart the engine.

It is advisable when changing tanks to switch on the electric auxiliary or booster fuel pump (if installed) to guarantee fuel pressure to the carburetor, and then to positively monitor the fuel pressure as the tanks are changed. Any sudden and unexpected loss of power should bring two possible causes immediately to mind:

- lack of fuel to the engine; or
- carburetor icing.

If the cause is incorrect fuel selection, your actions should include:

- close the throttle (to avoid a sudden surge of power as the engine restarts);
- set the mixture control to full-rich;
- turn the electric fuel pump on; and
- check fuel tank selection and tank quantity—change tanks if necessary.

If the cause of the engine problem is carburetor ice, then apply full carburetor heat. Refer to your Pilot's Operating Handbook for the correct actions to be taken in the event of any power loss.

Fuel Boost Pumps (or Auxiliary Pumps)

The reasons for installing *electric fuel boost pumps* are to:

- provide fuel at the required pressure to the carburetor or to the fuel metering unit of a fuel injection system;
- purge the fuel lines of any vapor to eliminate the possibility of a vapor lock;
- prime the cylinders of fuel-injected engines for start-up; and
- supply fuel if the engine-driven pump fails.

If an electric fuel pump is installed, it is usual to also have a *fuel pressure gauge* to monitor its operation.

Fuel Gauges

Most light airplanes have fuel gauges in the cockpit, which may be electrical, so the master switch will have to be *on* for them to register. Some older airplanes have direct-reading fuel gauges which do not require electrical power.

Do not rely on the fuel gauges—they can be inaccurate. Always check the contents of the fuel tanks visually before takeoff.

It is good airmanship not to rely on the fuel gauges, since they can read quite inaccurately, especially when the airplane is not straight-and-level. Always carry out a visual check of the contents in the fuel tanks during the preflight external inspection by removing the fuel caps, visually checking the contents of the tanks, and then replacing the caps securely.

The fuel consumption rate specified in the Pilot's Operating Handbook assumes *correct leaning of the mixture* which, if not done, could lead to a fuel burn around 20% in excess of the 'book-figures,' and the fuel gauges consequently reading much less than expected because of excessive fuel burn.

Fueling

For safety during fueling, the airplane should be positioned well away from other airplanes and from buildings, the engine should not be running, and the ignition switches should be in the *off* position and the parking brake should be on. The location of any firefighting equipment should be noted in case it is needed. A *no-smoking* rule should be enforced and passengers should be kept well clear.

Before fueling, the airplane must be electrically grounded to minimize the risk of fire.

To prevent the possibility of a spark of static electricity igniting the fuel vapor that is present in any fueling operations, you should connect ground wires between the airplane, the fueling equipment and the ground to ensure that they are all at the same electrical potential. This should be done before you start fueling—even before you remove the fuel caps, when fuel vapor could be released into the atmosphere.

Figure 6-3 Fueling from a tanker.

Fuel Grades

AVGAS (AViation GASoline) comes in various grades to cater for different types of piston engines. These different grades of AVGAS are *color-coded* to aid you in checking that the correct fuel is on board. Normal fuel for light airplanes is blue-colored 100LL (low lead) or green-colored 100/130 octane.

Do not use jet fuel (kerosene) in piston engines. AVGAS decals on fueling equipment have a red background with white letters.

The most important thing is to ensure that you are loading the correct fuel type into the airplane tanks. Jet fuel (kerosene) is required for gas turbine engines (jets) and AVGAS for piston engines. Jet fuel is straw-colored or clear, has a distinctive smell, and must not be used in piston engines.

Figure 6-4 Fuel grades.

The *fueling equipment* has color-coded labeling:

- jet-fuel decals have a black background with Jet-A written in white letters; and
- AVGAS decals have a red background with white letters, (100/130 or AVGAS).

There are additional small labels on the fuel hoses or nozzles colored the same as the fuel grade, for both AVGAS and jet fuel.

Fuel should possess *anti-detonation* (or anti-knock) qualities, which are described by their *grade* (octane rating or performance number). The higher the grade, the greater the compression that the fuel/air mixture can take without detonating. High grade fuels have a higher lead content, which improves their anti-detonation qualities.

The higher grade indicates the power possible (compared with the standard reference fuel) before a rich mixture would detonate, and the lower grade indicates the power possible before the same fuel leaned-out would detonate. Certain engines require certain fuel—make sure you know which one your engine requires and use it, and make sure that the fuel already in the tanks is the same as that being loaded.

If you use fuel of a *lower* grade than specified, or fuel that is date-expired, excessive engine temperatures and detonation may occur, especially at high power settings, with a consequent loss of power and possible engine damage. If you use fuel of a *higher* grade than specified, the spark plugs can be fouled by lead deposits, and also the exhaust valves and their sealing faces can be eroded during the exhaust cycle.

> **Note.** A *higher* grade of fuel than specified is usually less dangerous than using a lower grade. If the recommended grade of fuel is not available, you could consider using the next higher grade of fuel on a short term basis, but not a lower grade. Refer to the manufacturer's handbook and your flight instructor.

Auto Gasoline

AVGAS comes in batches with tight quality control. Ordinary auto gasoline from the gas station does *not* have such tight quality control and has different burning characteristics to AVGAS. In an airplane engine, auto gasoline would cause a lower power output, lead fouling of the spark plugs and a strong possibility of detonation. Auto fuel is more volatile and vaporizes more readily than AVGAS, which might cause vapor locks in the fuel system and starve the engine of fuel.

Do not use auto gasoline in an airplane engine unless it is specifically authorized by the manufacturer and in accordance with an FAA Supplemental Type Certificate (STC).

Fuel Checks

Fuel must be checked for water and other contaminants.

Fuel which is about to be loaded should be checked first for contamination. The most common contamination is water. It can leak into ground fuel tanks, and from there be loaded into the fuel truck and into the tanks of an airplane.

Fuel naturally contains a small amount of water and this can condense with a drop in temperature, contaminate the fuel system, block the fuel passages in the carburetor, and possibly cause a loss of engine power. There are certain *fuel test pastes* and *fuel test papers* available which react when water is present, and the fueling agent will use these on a regular basis to guarantee the purity of the fuel in his storage tanks.

Other impurities besides water can also cause problems in the fuel. Rust, sand, dust and micro-organisms can cause problems just like water. Filtering or straining the fuel should indicate the presence of these and hopefully remove them prior to fueling.

Be especially careful when fueling from drums because they may have been standing for some time. Always check drum fuel with water-detection paste, for date of expiration, and for correct grade of fuel. Additionally, it is a good idea to check the release note for the fuel. Filter the fuel through a chamois cloth prior to loading into the airplane tanks if the drum pump has no filter.

Water, because it is more dense than fuel, will tend to gather at the low points in the airplane fuel system. After fueling has been completed, a small quantity of fuel should be drained from the bottom of each tank and from the *fuel strainer drain valve* to check for impurities, especially water, which will sink to the bottom of the glass. Fuel drains are usually spring-loaded valves at the bottom of each fuel tank, and the fuel strainer drain is usually found at the lowest point in the whole fuel system.

There is usually a drop in air temperature overnight and, if the space above the fuel in the airplane's fuel tanks is large, the fuel tank walls will become cold and there will be a lot more condensation than if the tanks were full of fuel. The water, as it condenses, will accumulate at the bottom of the fuel tanks.

Full fuel tanks minimize condensation in low temperatures.

If the tanks are kept full when the airplane is not being used for some days, or overnight if low temperatures are expected, condensation will be minimized. However, the disadvantages of fueling overnight include:

- if the airplane has a takeoff weight restriction the following day, it may have to be partially defueled to reduce the weight or adjust the balance; and
- if the tanks are full and the temperature rises, the fuel will expand and some could overflow from the tank, creating a possible fire hazard on the tarmac. This is an operational choice—check with your flight instructor.

It is good practice to carry out a check for water in the airplane fuel system:

- prior to the first flight of the day;
- following each fueling; and
- any time you suspect fuel contamination.

In general terms, if you find a large quantity of water in the tanks, the following procedures should be included in your actions:

- the maintenance technician should be informed;
- drain the tanks until all the water has been removed;
- rock the wing to allow any other water to gravitate to the fuel strainer drain valve; and
- drain off more fuel and check for water at *all* drain points.

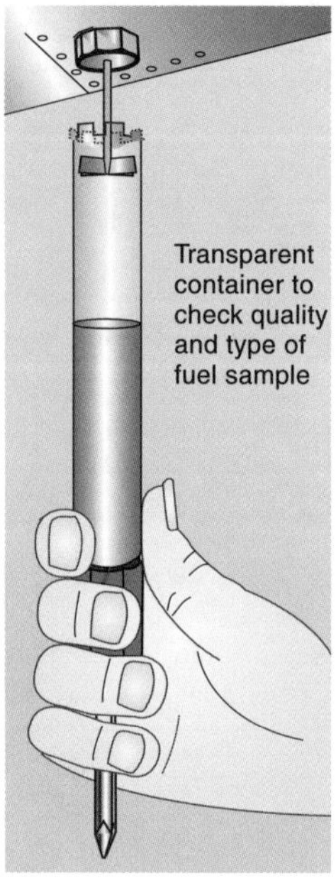

Figure 6-5
Fuel drains are located at the lowest point of the fuel tanks.

Fuel Management

Ensure that the airplane has the correct grade of fuel on board and that it is free of impurities. Ensure that sufficient fuel for the flight plus an adequate reserve is on board. Do not rely only on the fuel gauges as they are often inaccurate. Calculate the fuel required and be sure to check the tanks visually prior to flight for sufficient fuel. Remember that some of the fuel in the tanks will be unusable fuel. Carry out a fuel drain if required or if you think it is advisable.

Ensure that there are no leaks, that fuel caps are replaced, and that tank vents are clear and unobstructed. Fuel tank caps are usually on the upper surface of the wing, which is a low pressure area in normal flight. *Fuel can be siphoned out very quickly in flight if the tank caps are not secured.* With high-wing airplanes especially, where the tank caps are not visible easily from the ground or when in flight, extra care should be taken.

Fuel planning and good management are vital tasks.

Be familiar with, and follow, the procedures recommended in the Pilot's Operating Handbook for your airplane. Understand the fuel system, especially the functioning of the fuel selector valves. When selecting a new tank, ensure that the selector valve is moved firmly and positively into the correct detent.

Do not change tanks unnecessarily immediately prior to takeoff or landing, or at low altitude. If possible, verify prior to takeoff that fuel is being drawn from the appropriate tank(s). If operation is possible from more than one tank at the one time, this is usually preferred for operations near the ground. If boost pumps are installed, their use for takeoff is generally advised.

When changing tanks, check that there is fuel in the tank about to be selected; if an electric fuel pump is installed, switch it on and if a fuel pressure gauge is installed, monitor fuel pressure during and after the transfer, and when you switch off the electric boost pump.

Figure 6-6
Fuel check.

The Electrical System

A typical modern light airplane has a *direct current* (DC) electrical system. The electric current is produced by an *alternator* when the engine is running, or from a *battery or external power source* when the engine is not running.

The current runs through wires and the *bus bar* to the electrical unit requiring power, does its work there and then runs to ground through a *ground wire* attached to the airplane structure (which is the return path of the electrical current).

Typical Electrical Systems

The Pilot's Operating Handbook for each airplane will contain a diagram of its electrical system and the services to which electrical power is supplied. It is good airmanship to be aware of what powers the vital services and instruments in your particular airplane. Electrical systems vary greatly between airplanes, but certain important services that may be powered electrically include:

- some, or all, gyroscopic flight instruments (turn coordinator, attitude indicator, and heading indicator)—a common arrangement is electrically powered turn coordinator with vacuum-driven attitude indicator and heading indicator to reduce the possibility of all gyroscopic instruments failing simultaneously (note that the pitot-static instruments—airspeed indicator, altimeter, vertical speed indicator—are not electrically powered);
- the fuel quantity indicators, and perhaps an oil temperature gauge, or carburetor air temperature gauge;
- the starting system;
- landing lights, beacon, strobe, cabin lights, instrument lights; and
- radios.

Check the electrical system diagram for your particular airplane. A schematic diagram of a typical light airplane electrical system follows.

The Bus Bar

The *bus bar* is the main conductor and the distribution center in the electrical system. Electrical power is supplied to the bus bar by the alternator (or generator) and a battery, from where it is distributed to the circuits and electrical components that require power.

The Battery

The battery provides emergency power and electrical power for engine start.

The *battery* provides the initial electrical power to turn the engine over and start it with an *electric starter motor*, and also provides back-up or emergency electrical power at all times. Once the engine is running, it is self-sustaining and no longer needs electrical power from the battery. In fact the alternator (or generator), which is driven by the engine, provides current to recharge the battery after the engine has been started.

Most light airplanes have a *lead-acid battery* that creates an electrical current (measured in amps) by a chemical reaction between lead plates immersed in weak *sulfuric acid* that acts as an electrolyte. To prevent corrosion from any spillage of the acid, the battery is usually housed in its own compartment. The battery needs to be vented to exhaust the hydrogen and oxygen formed when it is being charged.

The battery is classified according to the voltage across its terminals (usually 12 or 24 volts) and its capacity to provide a current for a certain time (amp-hours). For instance, a 30 amp-hour battery is capable of steadily supplying a current of 1 amp for 30 hours (or 6 amps for 5 hours; 3 amps for 10 hours).

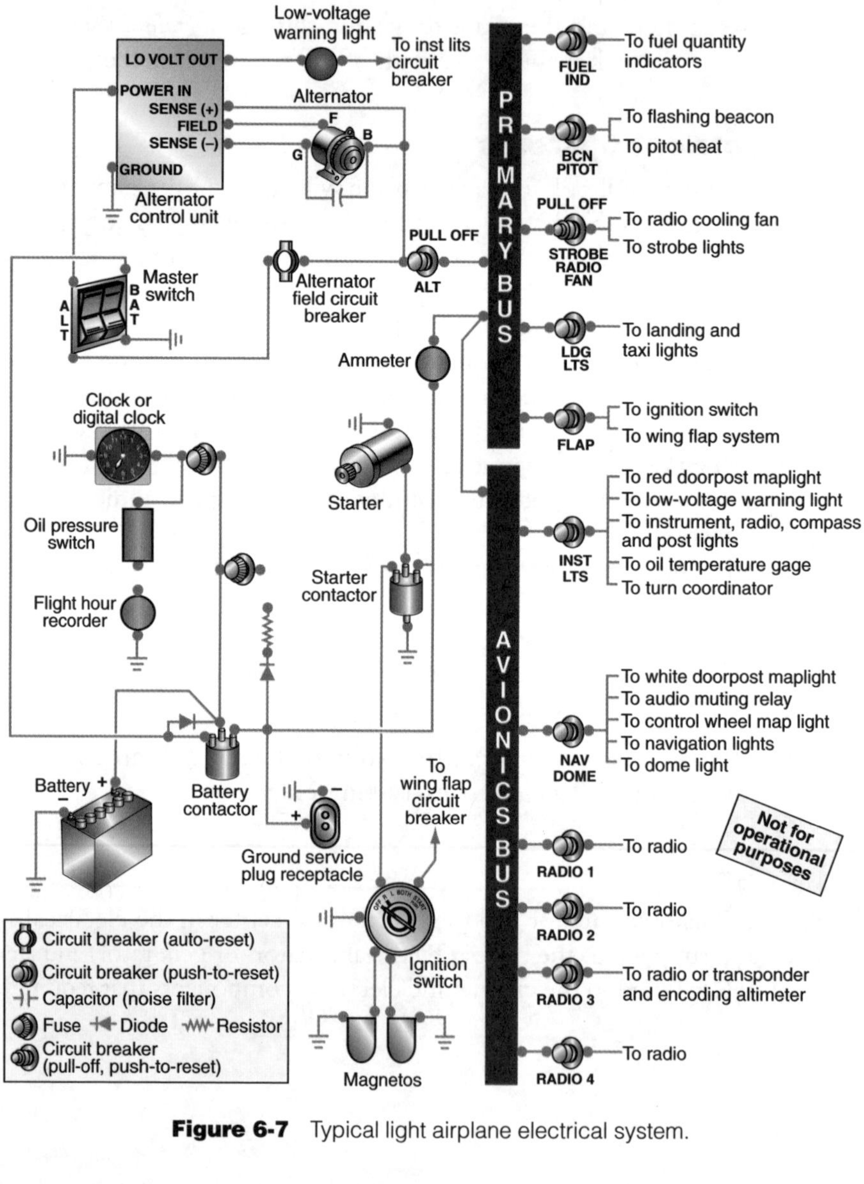

Figure 6-7 Typical light airplane electrical system.

If its electrical energy is depleted, as it is in an engine start, the battery needs to be recharged. This normally occurs after the engine is running, when the battery absorbs power produced by the alternator. The largest current draw on the battery is during start-up, when it supplies electrical power to the starter motor to turn the engine over, so the greatest rate of battery recharging will normally occur immediately after the engine is started.

The battery should recharge after engine start.

The electrolytic level in the battery should be checked periodically, to ensure that the plates are covered. If the level is well below the top of the plates, the battery will not retain its full charge for very long, and the ammeter will indicate a high charging rate in flight. Leaks, connections and security of the battery should also be checked. This is carried out in the regular maintenance schedule by the maintenance technician.

Do not start a flight with an uncharged (flat) battery—it could result in you having no electrical power in flight if the engine-driven alternator fails. If the battery is flat, replace it or have it recharged before flight. Do not start the engine with radios and other unnecessary electrical equipment switched on. Large voltage fluctuations when the starter is engaged may severely damage sensitive electronic circuits. Turn on this ancillary electrical equipment after the engine is started, and after you have checked that the alternator is charging the battery. For the same reasons, turn off ancillary electrical equipment before shutting down the engine.

The Alternator

The electrical power in most modern light airplanes is usually supplied by an *alternator*. On older airplanes, the electrical power may be produced by a *generator*.

Both alternators and generators initially produce *alternating current* (AC)—an electric current that flows in alternate directions. Since most airplanes require *direct current* (DC)—electric current that flows in only one direction—the AC has to be rectified to DC. The AC within the alternator is rectified into DC electronically with diodes, whereas within the generator an electromechanical device known as the commutator performs this function. Also, the diodes in the alternator prevent any reverse current flow out of the battery, whereas a generator requires a reverse current relay.

As well as providing the power for lights, radios, and other services, a very important function of the generator/alternator is to recharge the battery so that it is ready for further use. Most airplane electrical systems are direct current of 14 or 28 volts. Note that these voltages are marginally higher than the battery voltages to allow the battery to be fully recharged by the electrical system.

The Advantages of an Alternator

Alternators:

- are lighter than generators because alternators do not contain as heavy electromagnets and casings, and have a simpler and lighter brush assembly;
- have a relatively constant electrical voltage output, even at low RPM; and
- are easier to maintain (because of their simpler brush assembly and the absence of a commutator).

The Disadvantage of an Alternator

Unlike a generator, an alternator requires an initial current from the battery to set up a magnetic field, which is necessary before the alternator can produce an electrical current. Therefore an airplane with an alternator must have a serviceable battery. A

An aircraft with an alternator must have a serviceable battery.

flat battery must be replaced or recharged. If the propeller is hand propped to start the engine, the alternator will *not* come on-line unless the battery has at least some residual voltage. The advantages of an alternator outweigh this disadvantage.

Voltage Regulator

The correct output voltage from the generator/alternator is maintained by a *voltage regulator*, over which the pilot has no direct control.

Overvoltage Protector

Some airplanes have *overvoltage protectors* (or overvoltage relays). Refer to your Pilot's Operating Handbook for information.

The Ammeter

The *ammeter* measures the electrical current (amps) flowing into or out of the battery. (In some airplanes a *voltmeter* is provided to measure the electromotive force available to deliver the current.) There are two quite distinct types of ammeter presentation and you should understand exactly what this important instrument is telling you.

Left-Zero Ammeter

A *left-zero* ammeter measures only the output of the alternator or generator. It is graduated from zero amperes on the left end of the scale and increases in amperes to the right end of the scale, or it may be shown as a percentage of the alternator's rated load.

As the left-zero ammeter indicates the electrical load on the alternator, this type of ammeter can be referred to as a *loadmeter*:

- with the battery switch on and the engine not running, or, with the engine running and the alternator switch *off*, the ammeter will show zero; and
- if the engine is started and the alternator is turned *on*, the ammeter will then show the *alternator output*.

During start-up, the battery discharges electrical power, so immediately after start-up the ammeter indication will be quite high during the initial battery recharging.

When the battery is fully charged, and the alternator is operating, the ammeter should show a reading slightly above the zero graduation if all the other electrical circuits are switched off. As these extra circuits are switched on (lights, radios), the ammeter reading will increase. *If the ammeter reading drops to zero* in flight, it probably means an alternator failure. Some electrical systems have a red warning light that illuminates when the alternator fails to supply electrical power. You should be familiar with the procedures for electrical failure in your Pilot's Operating Handbook, which may allow you to restore electrical power.

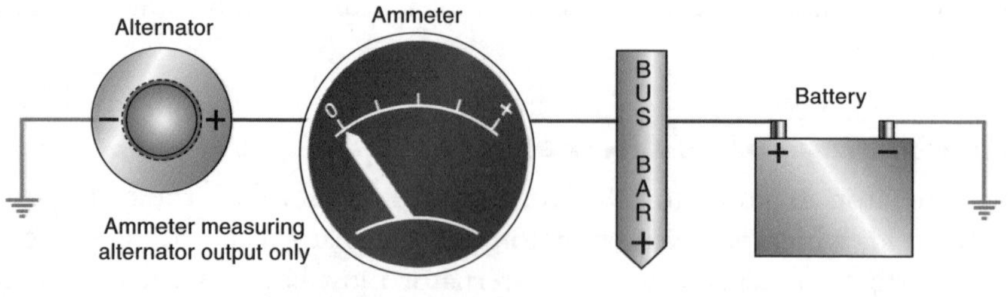

Figure 6-8 The left-zero ammeter.

Generally, it is advisable to reduce electrical load to a minimum if the alternator fails, since only the battery will be supplying electrical power. Land as soon as practicable to have the problem corrected.

Center-Zero Ammeter

The *center-zero* ammeter measures the flow of current (amperage) into and out-of the battery:

- current into the battery is *charge*, with the ammeter needle deflected right of center;
- current out of the battery is *discharge*, with the ammeter needle deflected left of center;
- no current flow either into or out of the battery is shown by the needle being in the center-zero position;
- with the battery switch *on* and no alternator output, the ammeter will indicate a *discharge* from the battery, because the battery is providing current for the electrical circuits that are switched on. The ammeter needle is to the left (discharge) side of center-zero;
- with the alternator on and supplying electrical power, if the electrical load required to power the circuits switched on is less than the capability of the alternator, the ammeter will show a *charge*, because there will be a flow of current to the battery; and
- if the alternator is *on*, but incapable of supplying sufficient power to the electrical circuits, the battery must make up the balance and there will be some flow of current from the battery. The ammeter will show a discharge. If this continues, the battery could be drained or "flattened." In this case, reduce the load on the electrical system by switching off unnecessary electrical equipment until the ammeter indicates a charge, (a flow of current from the alternator into the battery).

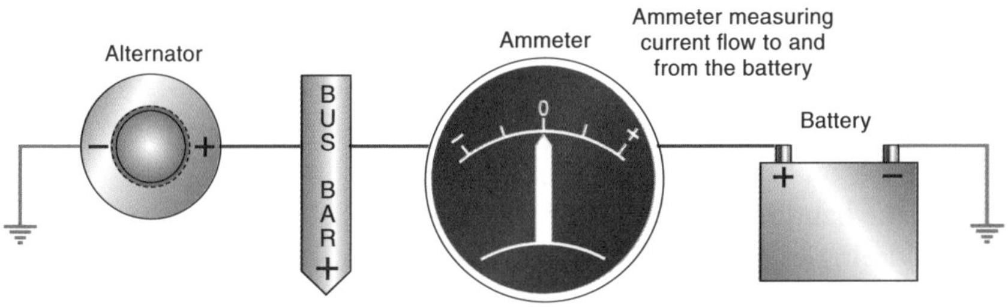

Figure 6-9 The center-zero ammeter.

The Master Switch

The *master switch* (or battery switch/alternator switch) controls all of the airplane's electrical system, with one very important exception—it does not control the ignition system which gets electrical power directly from the engine-driven magneto. This statement is not completely true if the airplane has an electric clock, which will draw a very small amount of electrical power at all times whether the master switch is on or not.

The master switch needs to be on for any other electrical system to receive power or for the battery to be recharged when the engine is running. It should be turned *off* after stopping the engine, to avoid the battery discharging by powering electrical equipment connected to it.

In airplanes with an alternator installed, the master switch is a *split switch* (with two halves that can be switched on and off separately):

Figure 6-10 The master switch (battery switch/ alternator switch).

- one half for operating the *battery switch* (or master relay for the electrical systems), which connects battery power to the bus bar (electrical load distribution point or bar); and
- the other half, the *alternator switch*, for energizing the alternator. It connects the alternator field to the bus bar, thus providing the alternator with battery power.

Both switches must be *on* for normal operation of the electrical system. If either switch has to be turned *off* due to malfunction in flight then you should consider terminating the flight as soon as possible. They can be switched on separately, but only the alternator can be switched off separately—switching the battery *off* will automatically switch the alternator off as well.

Fuses, Circuit Breakers and Overload Switches

Fuses, circuit breakers and *overload switches* are provided to protect electrical equipment from current overload. If there is an electrical overload or short-circuit, a fuse-wire will melt or a *circuit breaker* (CB) will pop out and break the circuit so that no current can flow through it. It may prevent the circuit from overheating, smoking or catching fire.

Only reset a circuit breaker once.

It is normal procedure (provided there is no smell or other sign of burning or overheating) to reset a circuit breaker once only, by pushing it back in or resetting it.

If a circuit breaker pops again, you can be fairly sure there is an electrical problem, and so it should not be reset a second time.

A fuse wire should not be replaced more than once.

Similarly, a fuse-wire should not be replaced more than once (with the correct amperage first checked on the replacement fuse-wire). Spare fuses of the correct type and rating should be available in the cockpit.

Do not replace a blown fuse with one of a higher rating.

Do not replace a blown fuse with one of a higher rating (15 amp is a higher rating than 5 amp), as this may allow excessive current to flow through the electrical circuit that it is supposed to protect. An electrical fire could result.

Overload switches are combined *on-off* switches and *overload protectors*. Overload switches will switch themselves off if they experience an electrical overload. The pilot can switch them back on like a resettable circuit breaker.

Some airplane handbooks recommend a delay of a minute or two prior to resetting, to allow for cooling of the possibly overloaded circuit. If you detect fire, smoke, or a burning smell, then caution is advised. Resetting the circuit breaker or replacing the fuse in such cases is not advisable.

Relays

A *relay* is a device in an electrical circuit that can be activated by a current or voltage to cause a change in the electrical condition of another electrical circuit.

Instead of having high currents and heavy wiring running to where the switches are in the cockpit (with consequent current losses and fire danger from arcing), a low amperage current operated by a switch in the cockpit can be used to close a remote relay and complete the circuit for a much higher amperage circuit in the engine compartment, the starter motor for example.

A relay is usually operated on the *solenoid* principle. A solenoid is a metal bar or rod with a coil of wire wound around it. If a current passes through the coil, it establishes a magnetic field that can move the metal rod, which can then perform some mechanical task, such as making or breaking a contact in another electrical circuit.

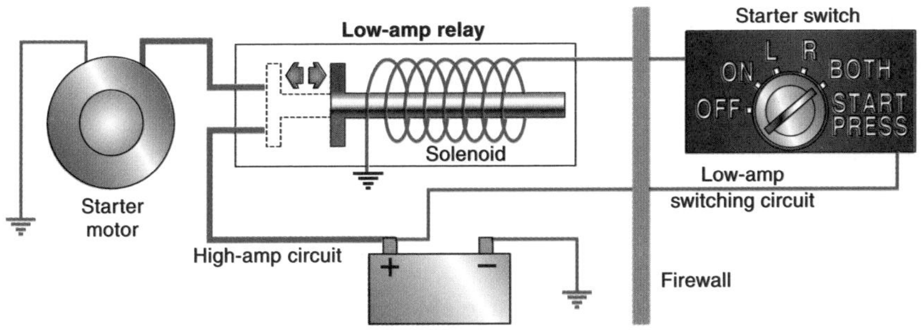

Figure 6-11 Low-amp relay circuit activates high-amp starter circuit.

A typical relay consists of a contact held open by a spring, thereby interrupting an electrical circuit. Around the stem of the relay is wound a coil of wire. If a current is made to pass through this coil, a magnetic field is set up that will move the relay to the closed position, thereby completing the circuit and allowing current to flow in it.

The current that activates the relay is in a completely different circuit to the relay. Occasionally a relay will stick even though its activating current has been removed, and an unwanted current will flow through the circuit. Many electric starters have an associated red warning light that will stay illuminated to warn the pilot of the starter relay sticking and the starter motor still operating even though the starter has been selected to *off*. (In this situation, the engine could be stopped by starving it of fuel—mixture control to *idle cut-off*.)

External Power Sockets or Ground Servicing Receptacle

The more sophisticated light airplanes and most large airplanes have provision for a suitable external power source to be plugged into the airplane's electrical system. The external power source provides ground power over an extended period when the engine or engines are not running or conserves the airplane battery during an engine start.

On some airplane types external power can be plugged in but will not connect in to the airplane electrical system. A small current from the battery is needed to operate the relay that connects the plugged-in external power to the airplane circuit, hence a serviceable battery is required to use external power. There are other systems that operate differently to this, so refer to your Pilot's Operating Handbook. Ensure a ground power unit (GPU) of the correct voltage is used. (Connecting a 28V GPU on a 12 volt airplane will severely damage the radios and other electrical equipment.)

Electrical Malfunctions

An electrical overload will normally cause a fuse-wire to melt or a circuit breaker to pop. This protects the affected circuit. Allow two minutes to cool and, if no indication of smoke, fire, or a burning smell, replace the fuse or reset the circuit breaker—*but reset once only*. If the circuit breaker pops or the fuse melts again—do not reset or replace a second time.

The ammeter should be checked when the engine is running to ensure that the alternator is supplying sufficient current (amps) for the electrical services and to recharge the battery. The ammeter usually indicates the rate at which current is flowing into the battery and recharging it.

With the engine running, the ammeter can indicate two faults.

1. Insufficient current to charge the battery.
2. Too much current.

With insufficient current from the alternator, or none at all, nonessential electrical equipment should be switched off to conserve the battery, and thought should be given to making an early landing. Most airplane batteries cannot, on their own, supply all electrical equipment for a long period.

With too much current and an excessive charge rate, the battery could overheat and the electrolyte (which may be sulfuric acid) begin to evaporate, possibly damaging the battery. If the cause of the excessive current is a faulty voltage regulator, equipment such as the radio could be adversely affected. Many airplanes have an overvoltage sensor that would, in these circumstances, automatically shut-down the alternator and illuminate a red warning light in the cockpit to alert the pilot.

Note. Operations of an alternator-powered electrical system with a partially charged battery that is unable to turn the engine over are not recommended for the above reasons.

If the alternator fails (indicated in most airplanes by either the ammeter indication dropping to zero and/or a red warning light), the battery will act as an emergency source of electrical power. To extend the period for which the battery can supply power following failure of the alternator, the electrical load should be reduced. This can be done by switching off nonessential services such as unnecessary lights and radios. Consideration should be given to terminating the flight at a nearby suitable airport while electrical power is still available.

The Vacuum System

The gyroscopes in the flight instruments may be spun electrically or by a stream of high-speed air directed onto buckets cut into the perimeter of the rotor. The vacuum system (which sucks this high-speed air into the gyro instrument cases and onto the gyro rotors, causing them to spin very fast) needs a little explaining.

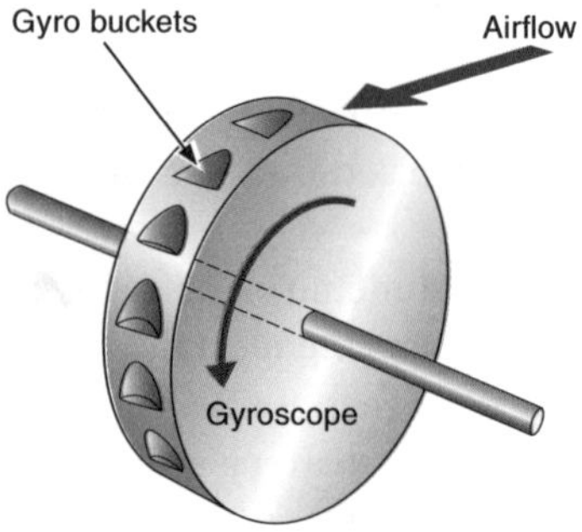

Figure 6-12
Gyroscope buckets.

The Engine-Driven Vacuum Pump

Most modern vacuum systems use an engine-driven vacuum suction pump. Some airplanes are equipped with an electrically driven system. The vacuum suction pump evacuates the cases of the gyroscopic-driven instruments creating a partial vacuum (low pressure). The required suction is typically 4.5 to 5.4 inches of mercury, which creates a pressure 4.5–5.4 in. Hg *less* than atmospheric, indicated in the cockpit on a suction gauge.

Filtered air is continuously drawn in at high speed through a nozzle directed at the gyro buckets, causing the gyro to spin at high speed, often in excess of 20,000 RPM. This air is continuously being sucked out by the suction pump and exhausted into the atmosphere.

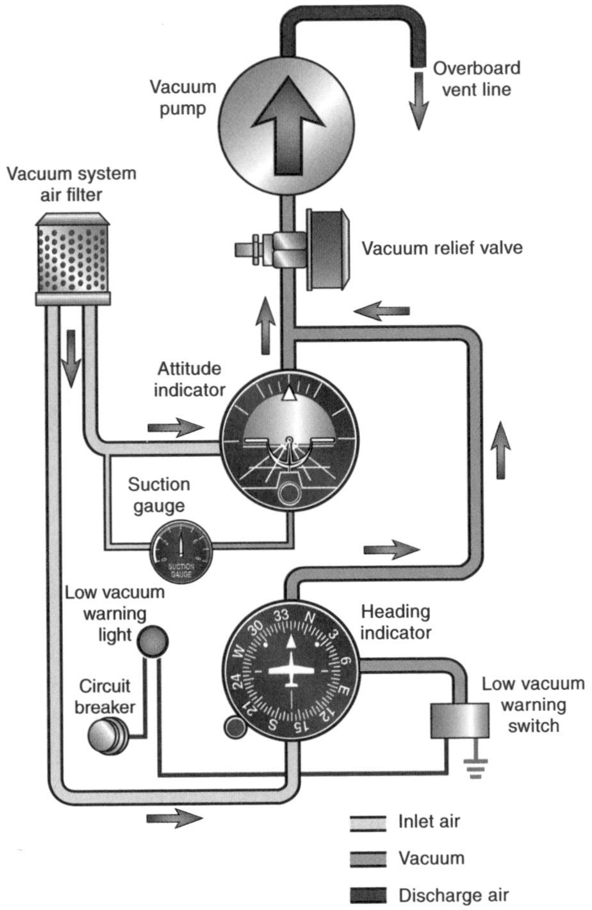

Figure 6-13 A typical vacuum system.

The effects of various malfunctions in the vacuum system are summarized below:

- if the air filter blocks, or the vacuum system fails, the reduced airflow may allow the gyroscopes to gradually run down and the vacuum-operated instruments will eventually indicate erratically or incorrectly, or respond slowly. A lower suction will be indicated on the gauge;
- failure of the vacuum pump will be indicated by a zero reading on the suction gauge. It may be that the gyroscopes have sufficient speed to allow the instruments to read correctly for a minute or two before the gyros run down following failure of the vacuum pump;
- a zero reading on the suction gauge could also mean a failure of the gauge (rather than a failure of the vacuum pump), in which case the instruments should continue to operate normally; and
- if the vacuum pressure is too high, the gyro rotors may spin too fast and suffer mechanical damage. To prevent this, a vacuum relief valve (or vacuum regulator) in the system will admit air from the atmosphere to reduce the excessive suction.

When the gyros are not being used, they should normally be *caged* (if provision is made to do this). Caging a gyro locks it in a fixed position. Caging the gyros is also recommended in the Pilot's Operating Handbook of some airplanes when performing aerobatic maneuvers.

Vacuum Provided by a Venturi Tube

Some airplanes (especially older ones) have their vacuum system operated by a *venturi tube*. This is a shaped tube on the outside of the airframe, which replaces the engine-driven vacuum pump. When air flows through the venturi tube, and speeds up because of the shape of the venturi, the static pressure decreases (Bernoulli's principle). This low pressure area, if connected to the gyro instrument cases, will draw air through each instrument via an internal filter and spin the gyroscopes, as in the engine-driven system.

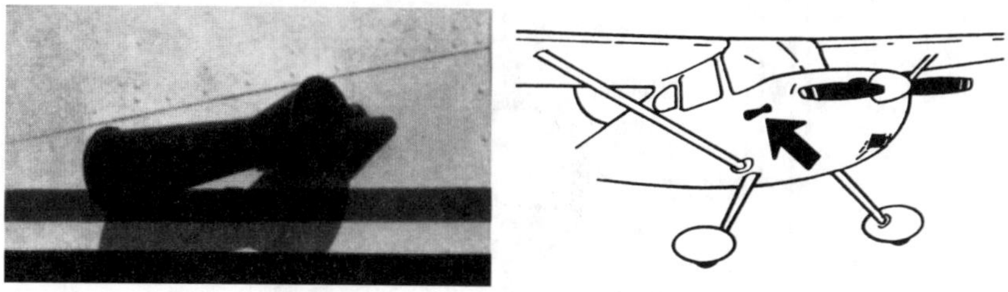

Figure 6-14 A typical venturi tube.

Before the venturi-powered vacuum system can work there must be an appreciable airflow through the venturi tube. This is normally created by the forward motion of the airplane through the air with sufficient airflow being provided at flying speeds. It may be several minutes after takeoff before the gyroscopes are spinning fast enough for the instrument indications to be reliable. This is a significant disadvantage compared with the engine-driven system. Other disadvantages are the increased drag caused by the externally mounted venturi-tube, and the possibility of ice affecting it (like in a carburetor, where the reduced pressure causes a reduced temperature).

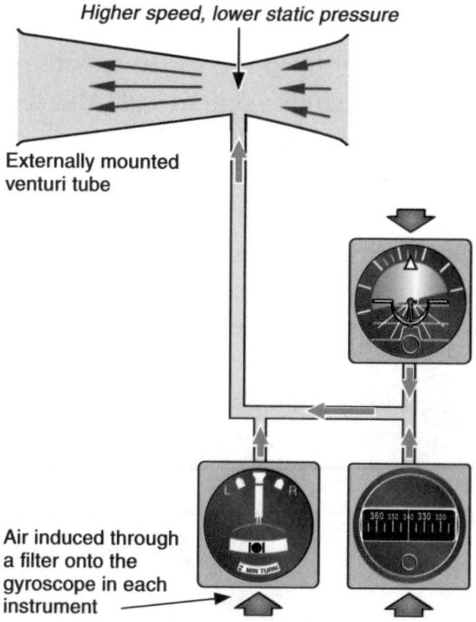

Figure 6-15
Air flowing through a venturi tube can create a "suction", and power a vacuum system.

Review 6
Systems

The Fuel System

1. What are the functions of an auxiliary fuel boost pump?
2. What type of fuel can be substituted in an aircraft if the recommended octane is not available?
3. Why should you *not* use fuel of a lower grade than specified?
4. Should auto gasoline be used in an airplane engine?
5. When should fuel be checked for contamination, especially water?
6. True or false? Water tends to collect at the highest points in the fuel system.
7. How is aviation gasoline distinguished from aviation turbine fuel (kerosene)?
8. What color is 100/130 fuel?
9. What color is 100 LL (low lead) fuel?
10. Filling the fuel tanks after the last flight of the day is considered a good operating procedure because this will:
    a. force any existing water to the top of the tank away from the fuel lines to the engine.
    b. prevent expansion of the fuel by eliminating airspace in the tanks.
    c. prevent moisture condensation by eliminating airspace in the tanks.
11. What color are AVGAS fueling equipment decals?
12. What color are jet fuel equipment decals?
13. If you allow a fuel tank to run dry in flight before changing tanks, what do you run the risk of?

The Electrical System

14. What is the source for normal in-flight electrical power?
15. Where does the initial current required to activate the alternator come from?
16. A distribution point for electrical power to various services is called a:
    a. circuit breaker.
    b. distributor.
    c. bus bar.
17. What is the function of the battery?
18. What does a center-zero ammeter do?
19. What does a left-zero ammeter do?
20. True or false? Immediately after start-up, the ammeter indication will be high while the battery is recharging.
21. What do fuses and circuit breakers protect against?
22. A fully charged battery rated at 15 amp-hours is capable of providing 5 amps for how many hours without recharging?
23. Which of the following would normally be electrically powered?
    a. ASI.
    b. Altimeter.
    c. VSI.
    d. AI.
    e. Turn coordinator.
    f. HI.
    g. Fuel quantity gauges.
    h. Engine RPM gauge.
    i. Oil temperature gauge.

The Vacuum System

24. The vacuum pump, if installed on a modern airplane, is most likely to be:
    a. electrically driven.
    b. engine-driven.
    c. hydraulically driven.
25. How are air-driven gyro rotors prevented from spinning too fast?
26. True or false? Insufficient suction may cause gyroscopic instruments (such as the artificial horizon or the heading indicator) to indicate incorrectly, erratically, or respond slowly.

Answers are given on page 688.

Flight Instruments 7

The first impression most people have of an airplane cockpit is of the number of instruments. However when you analyze the instrument panels of even the largest jet transport airplanes, you will find that the instrumentation is not all that complicated. In fact, the basic instruments will be very similar to those found in the smallest training airplane.

Airplane flight instruments fall into three basic categories:

- pressure instruments—which use variations in air pressure;
- gyroscopic instruments—which use the properties of gyroscopic inertia; and
- magnetic instruments—which use the earth's magnetic field.

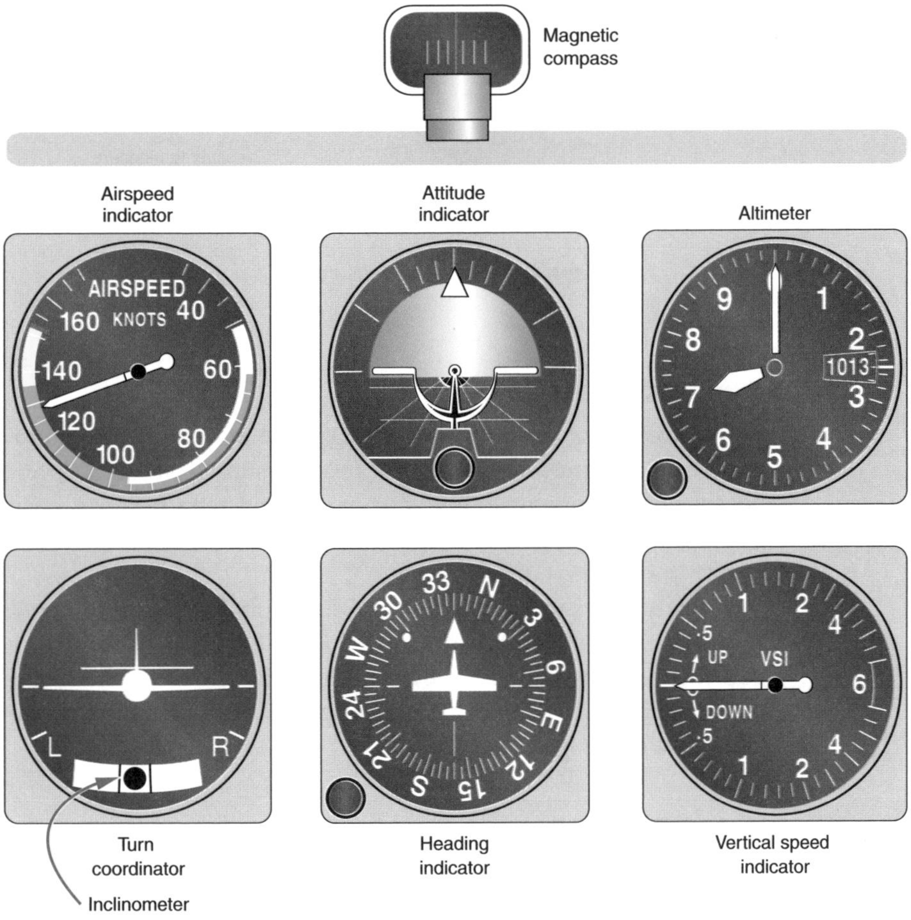

Figure 7-1 The flight instruments.

Pressure Instruments

The basic flight instruments that inform the pilot of airspeed (airspeed indicator), altitude (altimeter) and rate of change of altitude (vertical speed indicator) are *pressure instruments*.

Static Pressure

At any point in the atmosphere static pressure is exerted equally in all directions. It is the result of the weight of all the air molecules above that point pressing down. As its name implies, static pressure does not involve relative movement of the air. Static pressure is measured on the surface of an airplane through a *static vent* or *static port* (see figure 7-4, page 163).

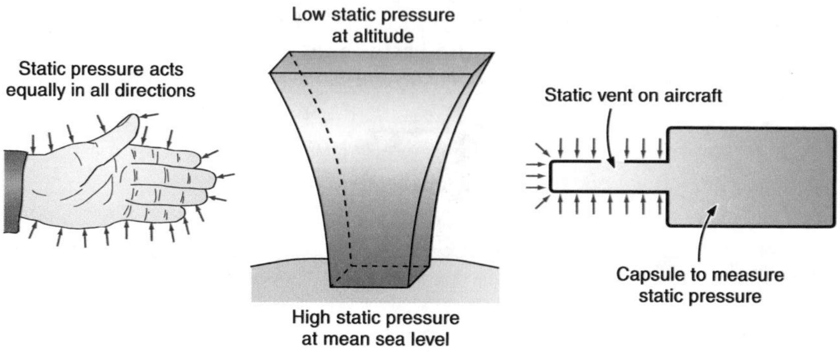

Static pressure acts equally in all directions
Low static pressure at altitude
High static pressure at mean sea level
Static vent on aircraft
Capsule to measure static pressure

Figure 7-2 Static pressure.

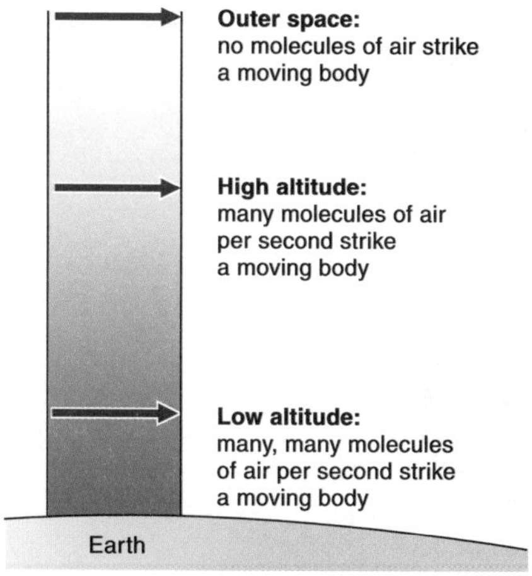

Outer space: no molecules of air strike a moving body
High altitude: many molecules of air per second strike a moving body
Low altitude: many, many molecules of air per second strike a moving body
Earth

Figure 7-3
Dynamic pressure depends on air density.

Dynamic Pressure

If you hold your hand up in a strong wind or out of the window of a moving automobile, you feel extra pressure (over static pressure) because of the air impacting your hand. This extra pressure, over and above the static pressure is called dynamic pressure, the pressure that results from relative movement.

Dynamic pressure is expressed as $\frac{1}{2}\rho V^2$ and therefore depends on the air's density (ρ) and relative speed (V). The faster the airflow or the denser the air, the stronger the dynamic pressure, because of the greater number of air molecules that impact per second. Dynamic pressure is also known as *impact pressure*.

Total Pressure

In chapter 1 we looked at Bernoulli's principle and noted that the total air pressure equals static pressure plus dynamic pressure:

Static pressure	+ dynamic pressure	= total pressure
measured by static vent	$\frac{1}{2}\rho V^2$	measured by pitot tube

From this equation dynamic pressure can be found by subtracting the static pressure (measured by the static vent) from the total pressure (measured by the pitot tube). Although the airspeed indicator (ASI) indicates dynamic pressure, it is calibrated to read in units of speed (usually knots) rather than in units of pressure.

The Pitot-Static System

Three flight instruments make use of pressure readings:
- the *altimeter* which converts static pressure to altitude;
- the *vertical speed indicator* which relates the rate of change of static pressure to a rate of climb or descent; and
- the *airspeed indicator* which relates the difference between total pressure and static pressure to the indicated airspeed.

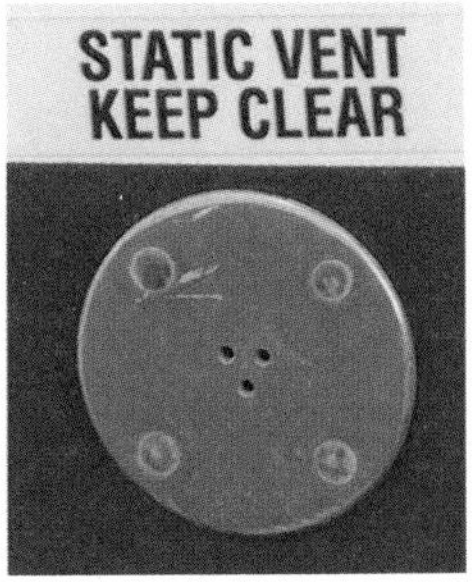

Figure 7-4
Static vent.

The *pitot tube* mounted on the airplane is the source of total pressure and the airplane's static vent is the source of static pressure. There are two common arrangements of the pitot-static sensing system:
- a combined pitot-static head; or
- a pitot tube (possibly on the wing) and a static vent (or two) on the side of the fuselage.

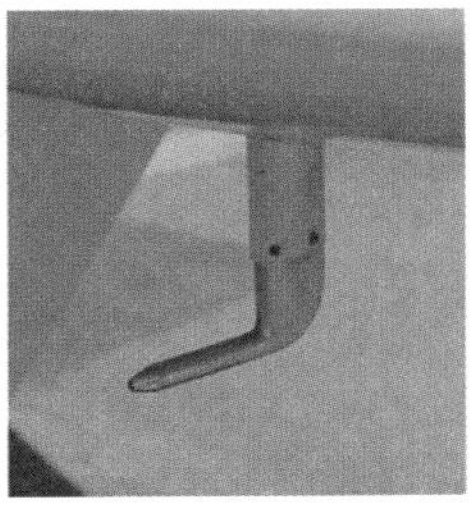

Figure 7-5
Pitot head.

The pitot tube must be positioned where the free airflow is not greatly disturbed by changes in static pressure, often forward of, or beneath the outer section of one wing. Otherwise the airspeed indicator system will suffer from significant errors. In addition, pitot heaters are sometimes provided as a precaution against ice blocking the pitot tube. They usually consist of electrical elements built into the pitot tube, and are operated by a switch from the cockpit.

Some airplanes have two *static vents*, one on each side of the fuselage, so that the reading for static pressure, when averaged, is more accurate, especially if the airplane is slipping or skidding.

There is often an *alternative static source* that can measure pressure inside the cabin, in case of ice or other matter obstructing the external vents. Cabin pressure is usually slightly less than the external atmospheric pressure and will cause the instrument readings to be slightly in error when the alternate static source is being used.

It is vital that the pitot tube and static vent(s) are not damaged or obstructed, otherwise false readings from the relevant flight instruments could degrade the safety of the flight. They should be carefully checked in the preflight external inspection. The pitot

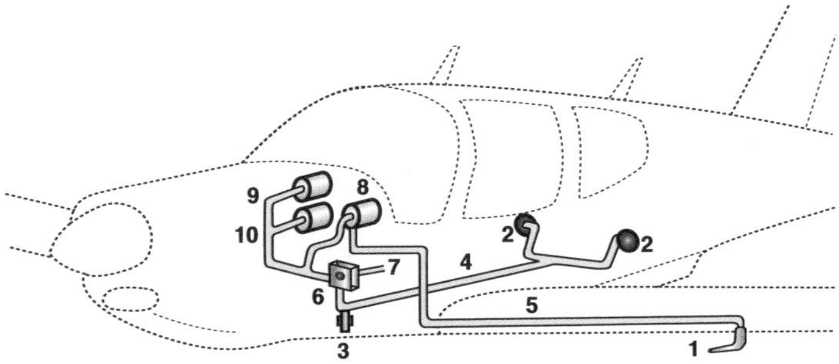

1. Pitot tube
2. Static vents
3. Static drain
4. Static line
5. Pitot line
6. Alternate static selector
7. Alternate static pressure
8. Airspeed indicator
9. Altimeter
10. Vertical speed indicator

Figure 7-6 Typical pitot-static installation.

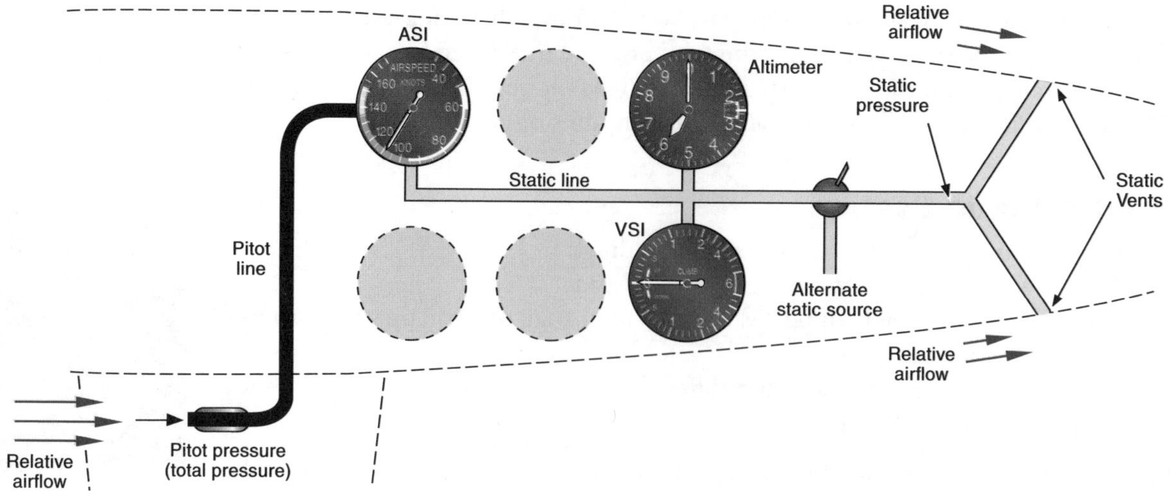

Figure 7-7 The pitot-static system.

cover, used to prevent water or insects accumulating in the tube, should be removed. They should not be tested by blowing in them, since very sensitive instruments are involved.

Airspeed Indicator (ASI)

The airspeed indicator displays indicated airspeed (IAS), which is related to dynamic pressure. We can find dynamic pressure by subtracting the static vent measurement from the pitot tube measurement. This is easily done by having a diaphragm with total pressure from the pitot tube being fed onto one side of it and static pressure from the static line being fed onto the other side of it. The diaphragm and pointer connected to it will move according to the difference between the total pressure and the static pressure.

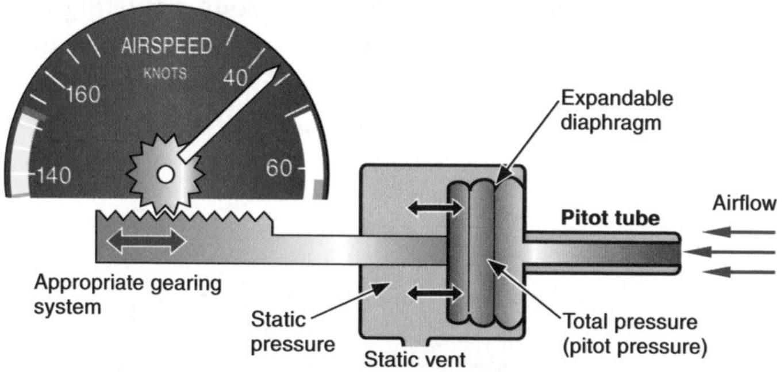

Figure 7-8 The airspeed indicator measures dynamic pressure.

As airspeed increases, the dynamic pressure increases, but the static pressure remains the same. The difference between the total pressure (measured by the pitot tube) and the static pressure (measured by the static vent or static port) gives us a measure of the dynamic pressure (which is related to indicated airspeed). This difference between total and static pressures causes the diaphragm to reposition itself, and the pointer to indicate a higher airspeed.

Color Coding on the Airspeed Indicator

To assist the pilot, ASIs in modern airplanes have certain speed ranges and certain specific speeds marked according to a conventional color code:

- the *green arc* denotes the *normal-operating speed range*, from stall speed V_{S1} at maximum gross weight (flaps up, wings level) up to V_{NO} (normal-operating limit speed or maximum structural cruise speed) which should not be exceeded except in smooth air. Operations at indicated airspeeds in the green arc should be safe in normal flying conditions. The maximum airspeed to use in turbulence is V_A or V_B (specified in the Pilot's Operating Handbook);
- the *yellow arc* denotes the *caution range*, which extends from V_{NO} (normal-operating limit speed) up to V_{NE} (the never-exceed speed). The airplane may be operated at indicated airspeeds in the caution range *only in smooth air*, and then only with small control inputs;
- the *white arc* denotes the *flaps operating range*, from stall speed at maximum gross weight in the landing configuration V_{S0} (full flaps, landing gear down, wings level, power-off) up to V_{FE} (maximum flaps-extended speed); and
- the *red radial line* denotes V_{NE}, the *never-exceed speed*. It is the maximum speed at which the airplane may be operated.

Figure 7-9 ASI coding.

One important speed not marked on the airspeed indicator is the maneuvering speed (V_A)—the maximum speed at which the limit load factor can be imposed (either by gusts or by full control deflection) without overstressing or causing structural damage.

Note. ASI markings refer to indicated airspeed (IAS) and not true airspeed (TAS). Where weight is a factor in determining limit speeds, such as stall speeds, the value marked is for the maximum gross weight situation.

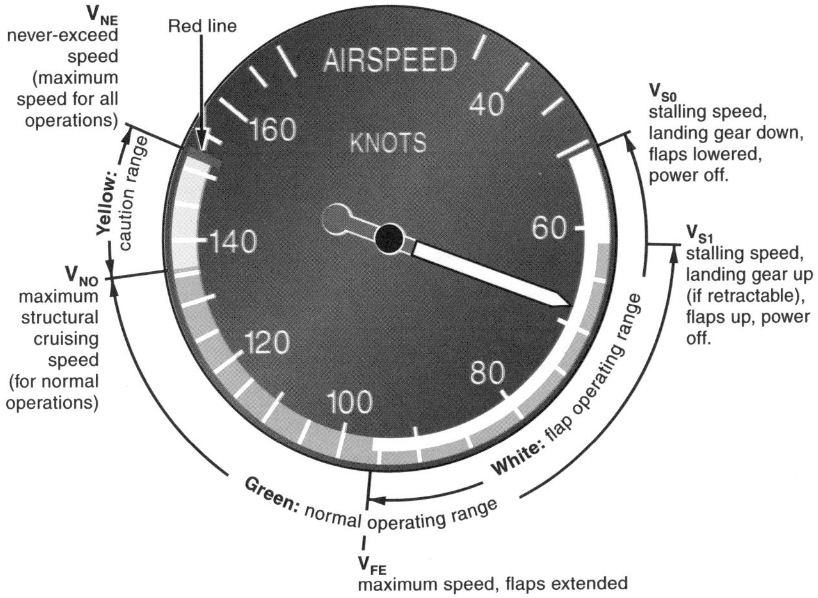

Figure 7-10 The airspeed indicator.

Indicated Airspeed (IAS) and True Airspeed (TAS)

The fact that indicated airspeed (IAS) and true airspeed (TAS) are usually different seems to worry many student pilots, but it need not. IAS is closely related to dynamic pressure ($\frac{1}{2}\rho V^2$), and is of aerodynamic importance.

Indicated airspeed (IAS) is important aerodynamically.

When we discuss the flight performance of the airplane—lift, drag, stall speed, takeoff speed, maximum speeds and climb speeds—we talk in terms of *indicated airspeed* (IAS). The indicated airspeed is vital performance information for the pilot, as the aerodynamic qualities of the airplane depend on it.

True airspeed (TAS) is important for navigation.

The *true airspeed* (TAS) is the actual speed of the airplane relative to the air. TAS (or V) is important for navigational purposes, to describe speed through the air (TAS). By incorporating wind, we can calculate speed over the ground.

True Airspeed Usually Exceeds Indicated Airspeed

In a climb it is usual for the pilot to maintain the same indicated airspeed. As the airplane gains altitude it climbs into less dense air because air density (ρ) decreases with increasing altitude.

For IAS to remain the same, the value of dynamic pressure ($\frac{1}{2}\rho V^2$) must remain constant. Because air density (ρ) decreases with increasing altitude, a constant IAS ($\frac{1}{2}\rho V^2$) can only be maintained by increasing the value of V (TAS). Therefore, climbing to a higher altitude with the airspeed indicator showing a constant IAS, will mean TAS is gradually increasing. You can calculate true airspeed from indicated airspeed, pressure altitude and temperature using a flight computer (see chapter 24).

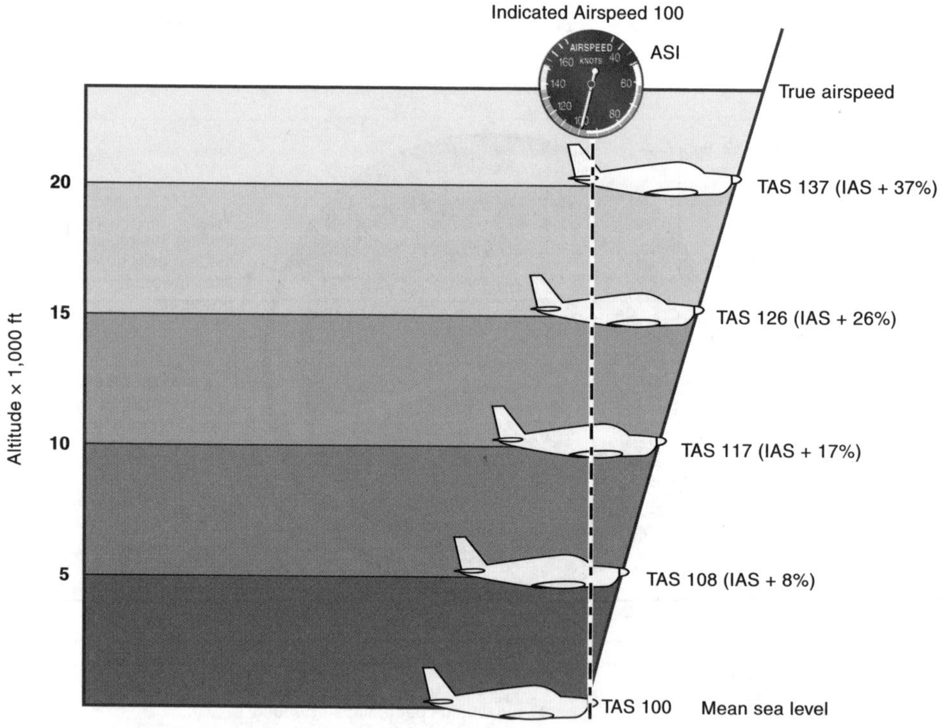

Figure 7-11 With IAS constant, TAS increases with increase in altitude.

On hot days and at high airports, to generate sufficient lift for takeoff the airplane must be accelerated to a higher V (TAS) to compensate for the decreased air density. (IAS shown on the ASI will remain the same.) This, coupled with possible reduced performance from the engine–propeller, will mean a longer takeoff distance—this is discussed in detail in chapter 9.

ASI Errors Caused by a Blocked Static Vent

If the static vent(s) become blocked the ASI will read low in a climb, and high in a descent.

A blockage or ice buildup in either the static vent(s) or pitot tube will cause the pressure to be trapped in that particular line to the pressure instruments. If you are climbing and the static vent ices over, then the static pressure trapped in the line will be higher than the actual static pressure at the altitude the airplane has climbed to. The measured difference between pitot (total) pressure and static pressure will be less than actual and the ASI will read low, (show a lower indicated airspeed than actual).

On a descent, the reverse would be the case, a blocked static vent would cause the ASI to read high, (show an indicated airspeed higher than actual). This is a dangerous situation if the pilot does not recognize it and reduces speed, because the airplane will actually be flying at a lower speed than indicated.

ASI Errors Caused by a Blocked Pitot Tube

A blocked pitot tube will cause the ASI to read high in a climb, and low in a descent.

If the pitot tube becomes blocked, say by ice, the total pressure trapped in the pitot tube (which remains constant) will be fed to the ASI, to be compared to the varying static pressure from the static vent. Therefore in a climb, the outside static pressure reduces, hence the airspeed indicator will read higher than it should. Conversely, on descent below the altitude where icing occurred, it will read a lower airspeed than it should.

Altimeter

Unlike an automobile, an airplane must be navigated and its position known in three dimensions, not only left and right (or west and east), but also up and down. The altimeter is the most important instrument for *vertical navigation* and *vertical separation* between yourself and the ground or other aircraft. You must use it correctly and understand exactly what it is telling you.

Figure 7-12
Altimeter.

A very important reference point for vertical navigation and for charts is *mean sea level* (MSL), the average height of the sea surface calculated from hourly tide readings taken over many years. The altimeter relates the static pressure at the level of the airplane to a height in the *International Standard Atmosphere* (ISA), a theoretical "average" atmosphere which acts as a convenient hypothetical yardstick. The main purpose of the International Standard Atmosphere is to calibrate altimeters. Standard pressure at mean sea level (MSL) is 29.92 inches of mercury. (Its metric (SI) equivalent is 1,013.2 hectopascals, usually written 1,013 hPa.)

Atmospheric pressure reduces by approximately 1 in. Hg for each 1,000 feet gain in altitude.

Atmospheric pressure reduces by approximately 1 in. Hg (one inch of mercury) for each 1,000 feet gain in altitude in the lower levels of the atmosphere (up to about 5,000 feet).

The altimeter converts this reduction in atmospheric pressure to a gain in altitude. For instance, if the pressure falls by 0.45 in. Hg, the altimeter will indicate a gain in altitude of 450 feet.

How the Altimeter Works

The altimeter contains sealed, but expandable, aneroid capsules that are exposed within the instrument case to the current static pressure that enters through the static port. As the airplane climbs and static pressure decreases, the sealed capsules expand and drive pointers, via a mechanical linkage, around the altimeter scale. These indicate the increased height above the selected pressure level. There may be a short time lag before changes in altitude are actually indicated on the altimeter.

Unfortunately for altimeters, the real atmosphere existing at a particular place and time can differ significantly from the standard atmosphere. Atmospheric pressure at MSL will vary from place-to-place and from time-to-time as weather pressure patterns move across the country. If an altimeter is to measure altitude from any particular level, such as mean sea level (MSL), then it must be designed so that the appropriate MSL pressure setting can be selected.

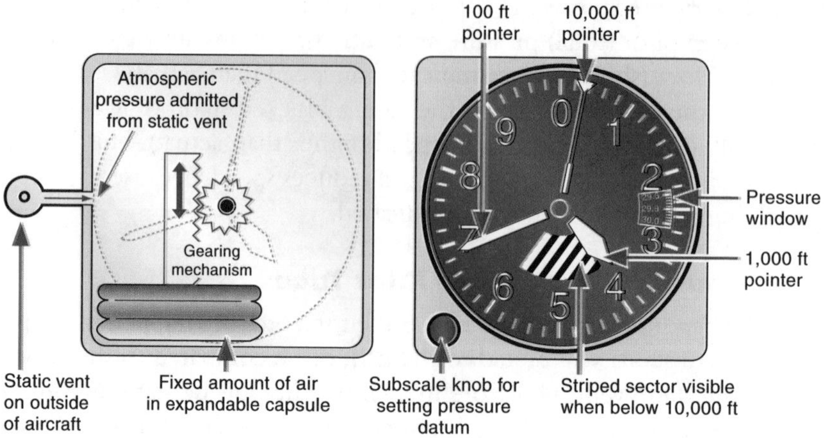

Figure 7-13 The altimeter is a pressure-sensitive instrument.

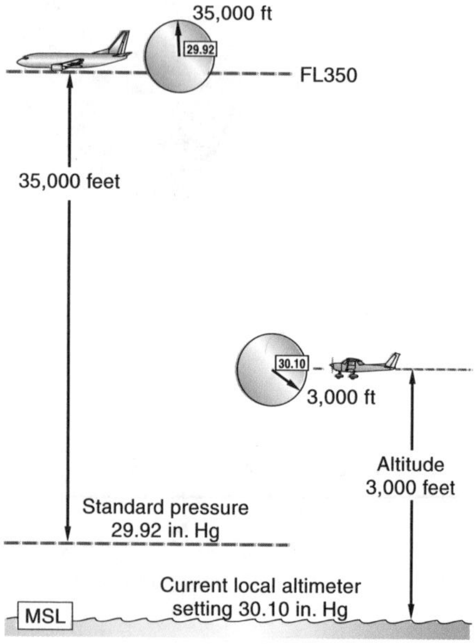

Figure 7-14
The altimeter measures height above the pressure level set in the pressure window.

The Pressure Window

The altimeter incorporates a small adjustable pressure subscale that allows the pilot to select the pressure level from which altitude will be measured. This subscale is known as the *pressure window* or *Kollsman window*. If you want to measure the altitude of the airplane above the 29.92 in. Hg standard pressure level, then you set 29.92 in the pressure window.

If you want to measure the height of the airplane above the 30.10 in. Hg pressure level, then you set 30.10 in the pressure window. If 30.10 in. Hg happens to be the current MSL barometric pressure, then the altimeter will be indicating the altitude of the airplane above sea level.

For flight operations in the United States below 18,000 feet MSL, the level from which height is measured is mean sea level (MSL). Although 29.92 inches of mercury is standard MSL pressure, the existing MSL pressure will usually differ, often significantly, from this value.

The MSL pressure at a particular place and time is called the *local altimeter setting* and, when this is set in the pressure window, the altimeter will display what is known as the *indicated altitude*.

When the setting in the pressure window is changed by winding the pressure setting knob, the altimeter needle will also move around the dial. This is because it measures height above the selected pressure level and the selected level is being changed. A one inch decrease in pressure in the lower levels of the atmosphere indicates approximately 1,000 feet gain in altitude. Therefore, increasing the setting in the pressure window will increase the altimeter reading. This can be remembered as "Wind on inches, wind on altitude."

Pressure Settings Above 18,000 feet MSL

When flying in the United States at or above 18,000 feet MSL, standard pressure (29.92 in. Hg) should be set in the pressure window. Above 18,000 feet MSL there is adequate terrain clearance above the highest mountains, so vertical separation from other aircraft is the main concern. Having a common setting of 29.92 in. Hg gives all high-flying aircraft a common pressure level from which their flight level is measured, avoiding any conflict caused by altimeter settings from different geographic locations.

With standard pressure 29.92 set, the altimeter indicates *pressure altitude*. It is usual to remove the last two zeros of a pressure altitude and refer to it as a *flight level*. For example, an altimeter reading 21,000 feet with 29.92 in. Hg set, is referred to as FL210 (flight level two one zero).

Different Altimeter Presentations

You must be able to interpret the altimeter reading correctly since it provides absolutely vital information. Lives have been lost in the past because pilots have misread the altimeter by 10,000 feet. Learn how to interpret the altimeter pointers correctly! The most common altimeter presentation consists of *three pointers* of varying shapes and sizes:

- the pointer with a long, fine needle and a splayed tip indicates 10,000s of feet. If it is on 1 (or just past it), it is indicating 10,000 feet. This pointer is particularly easy to misread. Note that some altimeters have a very short, medium thickness 10,000 feet pointer, rather than the usual long, fine needle;
- the short, fat pointer indicates 1,000s of feet. It will move once around the dial for a change of 10,000 feet. If it is on 4 (or just past it), it is indicating 4,000 feet. To reinforce that the airplane is below 10,000 feet, a striped sector is visible which gradually becomes smaller as 10,000 feet is approached; and
- the long, medium-thickness pointer indicates 100s of feet. It will move once around the dial for each 1,000 feet change in altitude. If it is on 7, it means 7 × 100 = 700 feet.

All taken together, the altimeter shown in figure 7-15 reads 4,700 feet.

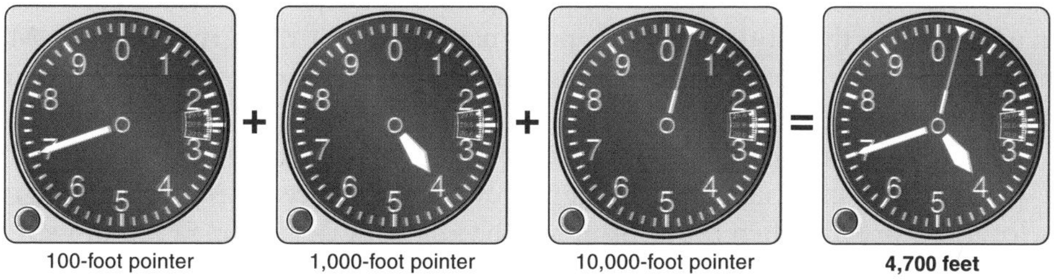

Figure 7-15 Altimeter presentation.

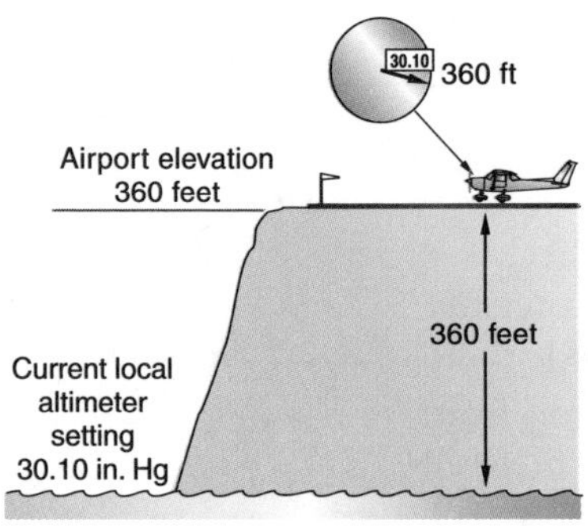

Figure 7-16
On the ground, the altimeter should read airport elevation.

Check Altimeter Accuracy on the Ground

The altimeter uses air pressure to measure altitude above (or below) the reference pressure level selected in the pressure window. The only place you can check the accuracy of an altimeter is while the airplane is on the ground at an airport where the elevation is accurately known. With the local altimeter setting in the pressure window, the altimeter should indicate approximate airport elevation (to within ±75 feet).

During this check, allow for the fact that the published airport elevation is the height above MSL of the highest point on any of the usable runways. If you have any doubts about the accuracy of the altimeter, refer it to an appropriately rated repair station for evaluation and possible correction. The only place you can check the accuracy of the altimeter is on the ground at an airport where the elevation is known.

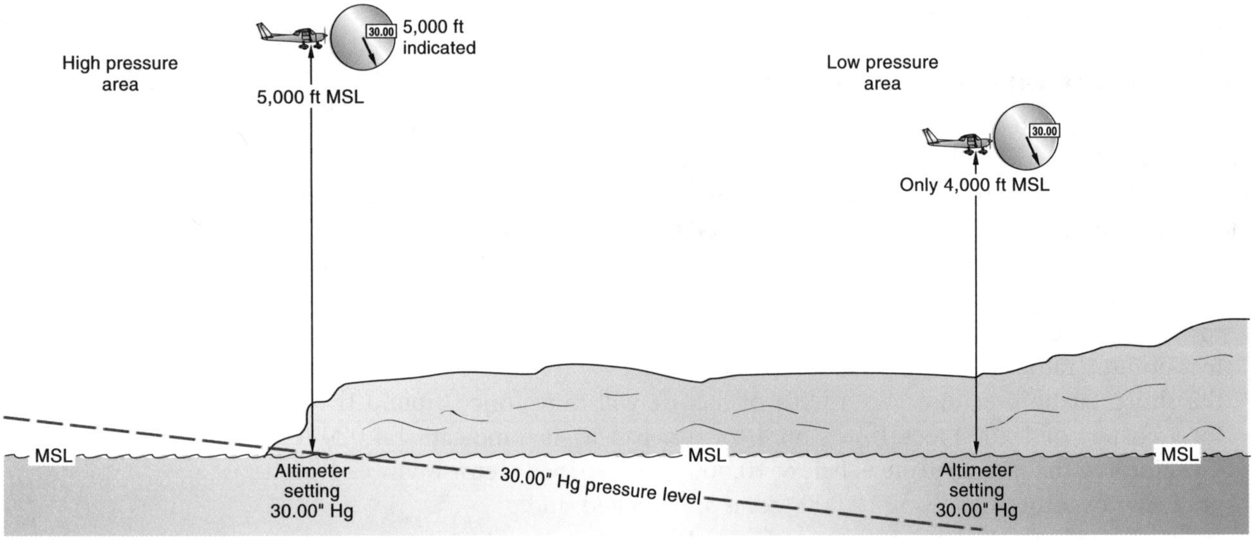

Figure 7-17 Always update your altimeter setting.

Whenever the current local altimeter setting is set in the pressure window, the altimeter will indicate the altitude—the approximate height of the airplane above MSL. This will enable the pilot to fly at an altitude that is well separated vertically both from terrain and other aircraft.

"From high to low— look out below!"

If you are flying at a constant indicated altitude from a high-pressure area toward a low-pressure area, and you neglect to set the lower altimeter settings periodically given by a local FSS or ATC, then the airplane will be gradually descending even though the altimeter reading is not changing. This could be dangerous. Remember, "From high to low look out below!"

Note. The pilot reads indicated altitude on the altimeter. For the reading to be correct, the altimeter setting must be correct.

Altimeter Errors

A number of errors are evident in altimeters.

Instrument Errors. Imperfections in the design, manufacture, installation, and maintenance of the individual altimeter will cause errors.

Instrument Lag. Because the altimeter takes a second or two to respond to rapid pressure changes, the indicated altitude will lag behind the actual altitude.

Position Error. Poor design may place the static vent in a position where the static pressure is not representative of the free atmosphere in that vicinity, resulting in an inaccurate altimeter reading.

Blockages of the Static Vent. If ice or insects (or anything) block the static vent completely, then that static pressure will remain fixed in the line to the altimeter. A constant altitude will be indicated, even though the airplane may be changing altitude.

If ice forms over the static vent on a climb-out, the altimeter will continue to read the altitude at which the static vent froze over, and not indicate the higher altitude that the airplane is actually at.

Similarly on a descent, a blocked static vent will cause the altimeter to indicate a constant altitude which is higher than the actual altitude, a dangerous situation.

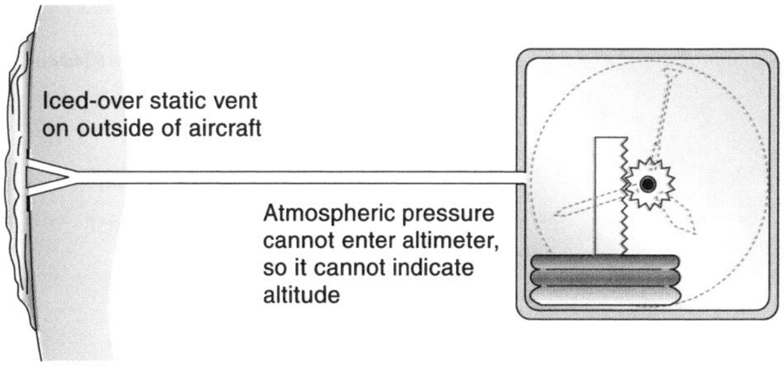

Figure 7-18
A blocked static vent—altimeter indication constant regardless of airplane altitude.

Temperature Error. The altimeter is calibrated to read the height above the pressure level selected in the pressure window as if the characteristics of the existing atmosphere (temperature, density and humidity) are identical to the International Standard Atmosphere. Since this is rarely the case, the altimeter indication will differ by some extent from the real or true altitude. Normally, this does not present a problem, since all airplanes in the one area will have their altimeters affected identically, and so vertical separation between aircraft will not be affected.

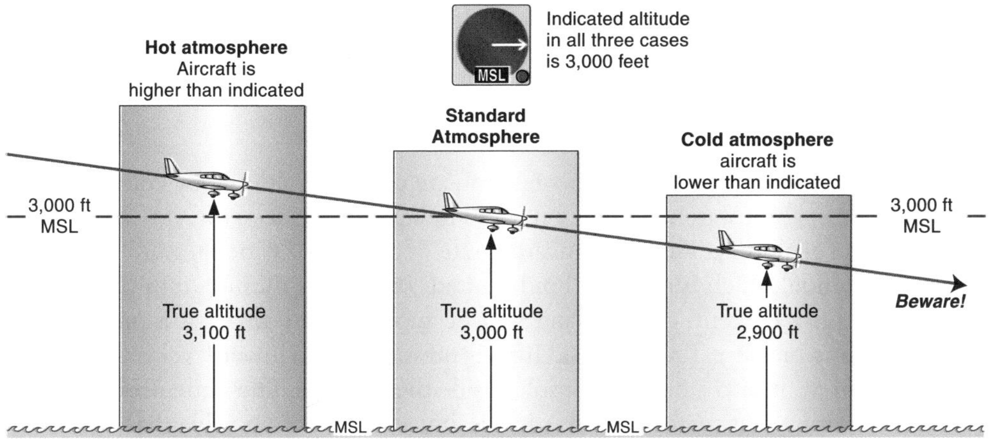

Figure 7-19 Temperature error often causes indicated altitude to differ from true altitude.

While the temperature error is of little significance for most flight operations, it may occasionally require some consideration during precision instrument approaches.

The altimeter in warmer air will read low.

In very warm air, the density will be less than standard and the pressure levels will be expanded. Therefore a given pressure level will be higher in a warm atmosphere compared with the standard atmosphere. After climbing a *true* 1,000 feet, the altimeter will sense less than 1,000 feet difference in pressure in the thinner air and will *indicate* a climb of less than 1,000 feet, and the altimeter will read low. This is easily remembered as *hi–lo* (higher temperature than standard—lower altimeter reading).

An altimeter in colder air will read high — "from high to low, look out below."

Conversely, in air colder than ISA, the altimeter will indicate higher than the airplane actually is, a hazardous situation. Remember *lo–hi* (lower temperature than standard—higher altimeter reading) or the saying "from high to low, look out below."

Altitude Measurement

Indicated Altitude. Indicated altitude is what you read on your altimeter when the *local altimeter setting* is set in the pressure window, as is the case when you are operating at or below 18,000 feet MSL in the United States. Indicated altitude is approximate height above MSL.

Pressure Altitude. Pressure altitude is what you read on your altimeter when *standard pressure* (*29.92 in. Hg* or *1,013.2 hPa*) is set in the pressure window, as is the case when you are operating above 18,000 feet MSL in the United States.

True Altitude. True altitude is the actual altitude above MSL, and cannot be determined in flight by the altimeter alone. It is rarely required in flight. True altitudes of airports, mountains, radio masts, and so on are measured by survey and shown on charts. The difference between indicated and true altitude is usually no more than 100 feet.

Absolute Altitude. Absolute altitude means height above ground level or *height AGL*. To determine this, you need to know both airplane altitude MSL and ground elevation.

Density Altitude. Density altitude is one means of describing air density, and is used in performance calculations. It is computed from pressure altitude and air temperature (see chapter 8).

Encoded Altitude. Encoded altitude is not seen by the pilot, but by the radar controller—the aircraft's encoding altimeter sends altitude information to the aircraft's transponder which transmits position and altitude information to radar stations.

Vertical Speed Indicator (VSI)

Figure 7-20
VSI.

While you can form some idea of how fast you are changing altitude by comparing the altimeter against a stopwatch, the vertical speed indicator provides a direct readout of the rate of change of altitude. The VSI converts a rate of change of static pressure to a rate of change of altitude, which is expressed in hundreds of feet per minute (fpm or ft/min).

If you begin a descent, the airplane will be moving into air with a progressively increasing static pressure. The new and higher pressure at the lower level is fed directly from the static vent into a flexible capsule inside the VSI case. The same pressure is also fed into the casing that surrounds this capsule, but via a metering valve that introduces a slight delay to the increase in pressure. This means there is a small differential pressure within the instrument. The capsule therefore expands and drives a pointer around the VSI scale (graduated in fpm) to indicate a rate of descent, such as 500 fpm. It will take some seconds before a stabilized rate is indicated, because of the inherent lag in the VSI.

If the *static vent* became iced-over or *blocked*, then the two pressure areas (inside the capsule and surrounding it) would equalize and the VSI would read zero, even though the airplane's altitude might be changing.

Figure 7-21 The vertical speed indicator.

Gyroscopic Instruments

Gyroscopes

A gyroscope is basically a rotating wheel, mounted so that its axis is free to move in one or more directions. A characteristic of rotating masses, such as gyroscopes, is their tendency to maintain their original alignment in space despite what goes on around them, a property referred to as *rigidity in space*. This means that a gyro is able to remain stable in space while the airplane in which it is mounted moves around it. Gyroscopes are therefore useful as the basis for indicators that show direction and attitude.

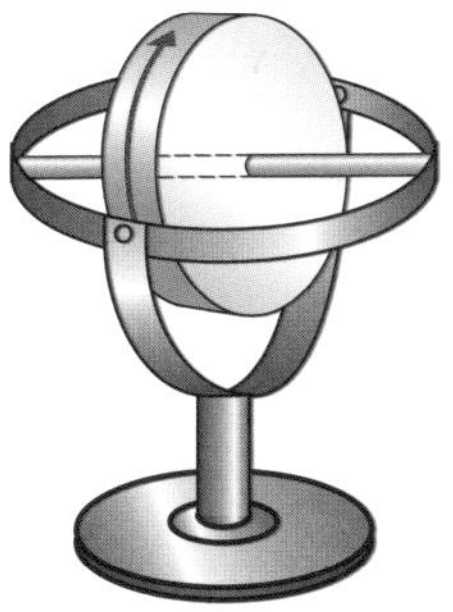

Figure 7-22
Gyroscopes are rotating masses.

The degree of rigidity of a gyroscope depends on the mass of the rotor, the speed at which it is rotating, and the radius at which the mass is concentrated. A large mass concentrated near the rim and rotating at high speed provides the greatest directional rigidity.

A gyroscope has another characteristic called *precession*. If a force is applied to the gyroscope, the change in direction brought about by the force is not in line with the force, but is displaced 90° in the direction of rotation. This gyroscopic effect is quite common (you use it every time you lean your bicycle over to turn a corner).

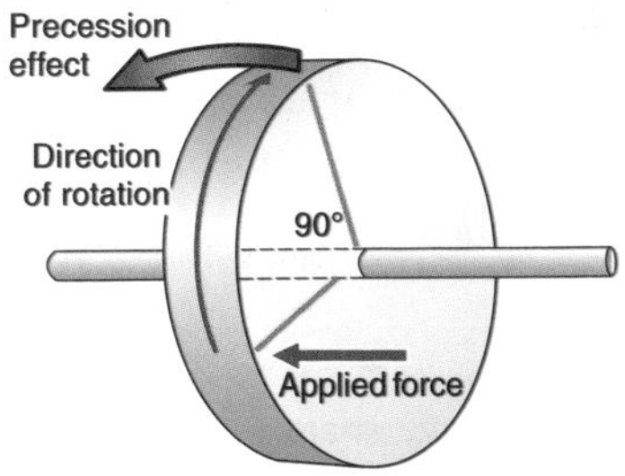

Figure 7-23
Gyroscopic precession.

There are various ways of mounting a gyroscope on one or more axis of rotation (*gimbals*), depending on the information required from that gyroscopic instrument. Gyroscopes are used in the turn coordinator/turn indicator, the attitude indicator and the heading indicator.

Vacuum-Driven Gyroscopes

Many gyroscopes are operated by a vacuum system which draws high-speed air through a nozzle and directs it at the gyro rotor blades. A vacuum pump that draws air through is generally preferable to a pressure pump that blows

Figure 7-24 Suction (vacuum) gauge.

air through, since the air may pick up contaminants such as oil from the pressure pump which could affect the very sensitive rotor.

The amount of suction is shown on a gauge in the cockpit and is approximately 4.5 to 5.4 inches of mercury, which is 4.5 to 5.4 in. Hg *below* atmospheric pressure. If the *numerical* vacuum reading is too small, the airflow will be reduced, the rotor(s) will not be up-to-speed, and the gyros will be unstable or will only respond slowly. If the numerical vacuum reading is too high, the gyro rotors may spin too fast and be damaged.

The vacuum in most airplanes is provided by an engine-driven vacuum pump, but some older airplanes may have the vacuum provided by an externally mounted venturi-tube (making the gyroscopic instruments unusable until after several minutes at flying speed following takeoff).

Electrically Driven Gyroscopes

When the electrical master switch first goes on, you will probably hear the electrically driven gyroscope(s) start to spin up. They should self-erect and red power-failure warning flags (if provided on the instrument face) should disappear.

If the master switch is left on, when the engine is shut down on the ground, these instruments will be drawing power from the battery and the battery will gradually discharge. So ensure that there is no power to the electrically driven gyroscopes when leaving the airplane for any length of time.

Errors in Gyroscopic Instruments

If the gyroscope is not up-to-speed, the instrument may indicate erratically, respond only slowly to changes in attitude and/or heading, or indicate incorrectly.

Check for a *red power-failure warning flag* on *electrically driven* instruments, and check for correct *suction* on *vacuum-driven* instruments. In many airplanes the attitude indicator and the heading indicator are driven by suction, but the turn coordinator is driven electrically. This guards against the loss of all three instruments simultaneously.

Check that the heading indicator is aligned with the magnetic compass during steady straight-and-level flight. Check that the attitude indicator, if it has a caging (locking) device, has been uncaged. Do this in steady straight-and-level flight or in a level attitude on the ground.

Turn Coordinator/Turn Indicator

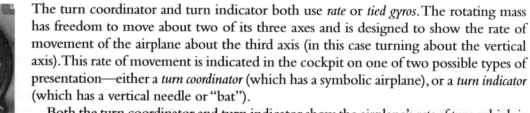

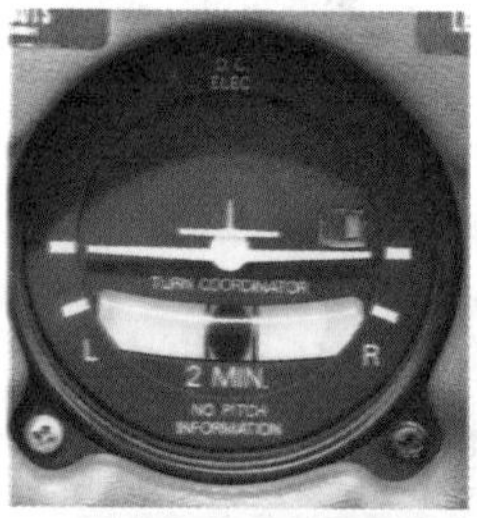

Figure 7-25 Turn coordinator.

The turn coordinator and turn indicator both use *rate* or *tied gyros*. The rotating mass has freedom to move about two of its three axes and is designed to show the rate of movement of the airplane about the third axis (in this case turning about the vertical axis). This rate of movement is indicated in the cockpit on one of two possible types of presentation—either a *turn coordinator* (which has a symbolic airplane), or a *turn indicator* (which has a vertical needle or "bat").

Both the turn coordinator and turn indicator show the airplane's *rate of turn*, which is not bank angle. However, because the gyro in the turn coordinator is mounted slightly differently to that in the turn indicator, the *turn coordinator* will also show *roll rate*. It will respond when an airplane banks, even before the turn actually commences. Note that the symbolic airplane on the turn coordinator (even though it resembles that on an attitude indicator) does not give pitch information.

If the airplane is turning to the left, the gyroscope will experience a turning force, (see figure 7-27). However this force will precess through a further 90° in the direction of rotation and will cause the gyro to tilt. The greater the turning force, the greater the tendency to tilt.

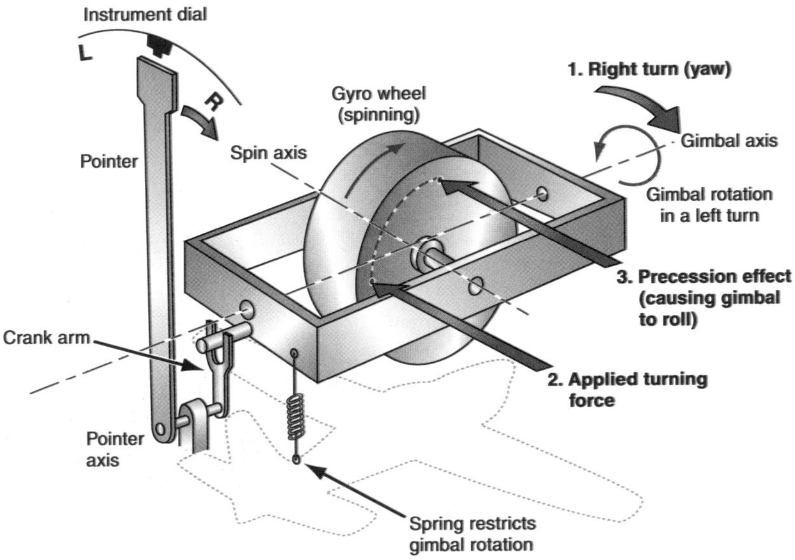

Figure 7-27 Workings of the turn indicator.

Figure 7-26
The modern turn coordinator (top), and the older turn indicator, each indicating standard-rate turns to the left.

The tilting of the gyroscope stretches a spring, which makes the gyro precess with the airplane turn until the rates match up, when further tilt ceases. A pointer moved by the action of the gimbal tilting indicates the rate of turn against a scale. The scale is graduated to show a *standard-rate* turn of 3° per second. You can check the accuracy of the turn indicator by timing yourself through a steady indicated standard rate turn of 180° and see if it takes 60 seconds (3° per second).

The gyroscope may be rotated at high speed by an electric motor, or it may be spun by a small jet of air generated by a vacuum system, and directed at small "buckets" cut into the edge of the gyro wheel. Preflight checks for the serviceability of the turn coordinator should include:

- a check of the gyro rotation speed (whirring sound and no failure flags if electrically driven, correct vacuum if pressure-driven); and
- correct indications in a turn while taxiing ("turning left, skidding right—turning right, skidding left"), and, if in any doubt, a timed turn in flight.

Attitude Indicator (AI)

As the airplane changes its attitude, the *earth gyro* that is the basis of the attitude indicator (AI) retains its alignment (rigidity) at right angles to the earth's surface. This means that the airplane moves around the gyro rotor of the attitude indicator which has a vertical spin axis. Attached to the gyroscope is a picture of the horizon, around which the airplane (and the instrument panel) moves. The attitude of the airplane relative to the real horizon is symbolized by the artificial horizon line attached to the gyro and a small symbolic airplane attached to the instrument dial. This small model airplane is referred to as the miniature airplane or index airplane.

Figure 7-28
Attitude indicator.

The attitude indicator shows *pitch attitude* and *bank angle*. Pitch attitude is indicated by the position of the center dot of the miniature airplane relative to the artificial horizon. Bank attitude is indicated by the relationship of the wings of the miniature airplane to the artificial horizon.

The AI shows a picture of the airplane's attitude, but tells you nothing about the performance of the airplane. For instance, a nose-high attitude could occur in a steep climb or in a stalled descent—to know the performance of the airplane you need to refer to the airspeed indicator, altimeter, and vertical speed indicator.

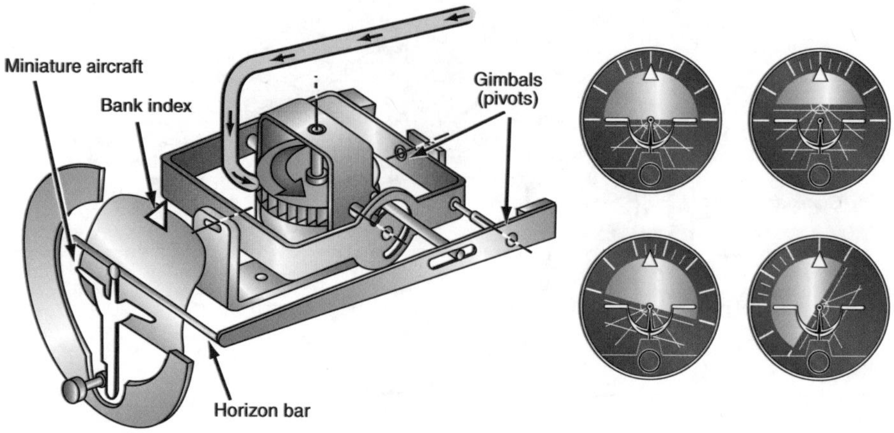

Figure 7-29 The attitude indicator displays pitch attitude and bank angle.

You should always check the power source of the attitude gyro. Some attitude indicators, especially the vacuum-driven ones, have limits of pitch and bank which, if exceeded, may cause the gyro to tumble and give erroneous readings. The miniature airplane should be aligned with the artificial horizon on the instrument when the airplane is in straight-and-level flight or on the ground. The small knob at the base of the AI adjusts the miniature airplane alignment. Some older types of gyroscope need to be caged when not being used. The attitude indicator is also called the *artificial horizon* and *gyro horizon*.

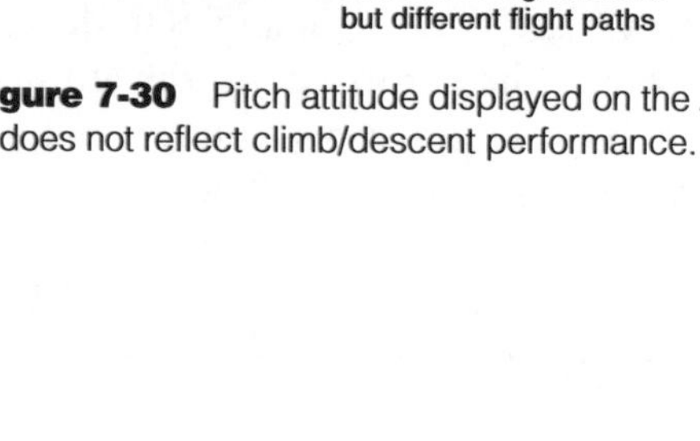

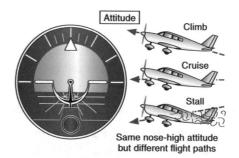

Figure 7-30 Pitch attitude displayed on the AI does not reflect climb/descent performance.

Heading Indicator (HI)

The magnetic compass is the primary indicator of direction in most airplanes. It is, however, difficult to read in turbulence and subject to acceleration and turning errors, making it a difficult instrument to fly by accurately. The heading indicator (HI) is a gyroscopic instrument that you should keep aligned with the magnetic compass in flight. Although it takes its directional reference from the compass, it is not subject to the same acceleration and turning errors. This makes accurate turns and a constant heading possible.

Figure 7-31
The heading indicator.

There are mechanical factors present in the HI (mainly friction) that will cause it to drift off its original alignment with magnetic north because of gyroscopic precession. This is called mechanical drift. In addition, because the airplane is flying over a rotating earth, a line in space from the airplane to north will steadily change. This causes apparent drift. Both mechanical and apparent drift can be corrected by simply realigning the HI with the magnetic compass periodically, as described below.

You should check the power source of the HI prior to flight and, when taxiing, check the correct turn indications on the HI ("turning right, heading increases—turning left, heading decreases"). The HI has a *slaving knob* that enables the pilot to realign the HI with the magnetic compass, correcting for both mechanical drift and apparent drift. This should be done every 10 or 15 minutes. Some older heading indicators have to be uncaged after realigning with the magnetic compass. Advanced airplanes have HI gyros that are aligned automatically.

Manually Aligning HI with Magnetic Compass

To manually align the heading indicator with the magnetic compass:

- choose a reference point directly ahead of the airplane, aim for it and fly steadily straight-and-level;
- keep the nose precisely on the reference point, and then read the magnetic compass heading (when the compass is steady);
- maintain the airplane's heading toward the reference point and then refer to the HI, adjusting its reading (if necessary) to that taken from the magnetic compass; and
- check that the airplane has remained steadily heading toward the reference point during the operation (if not, repeat the procedure).

Inclinometer (Coordination Ball)

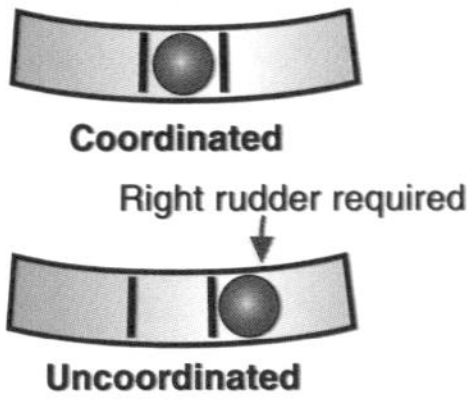

Figure 7-32
The coordination ball.

The coordination ball is a simple device that is usually incorporated into the turn coordinator/turn indicator. It is a useful mechanical device that indicates the direction of the g-forces—the combined effect of the earth's gravity force and any turning force. It has no power source. It is also known as the inclinometer, the slip-skid indicator, the balance ball, or the coordination ball.

The coordination ball is simply a small ball, free to move like a pendulum bob, except that it moves in a curved cylinder filled with damping fluid. In straight flight it should appear at the lowest point in the curved cylinder (like a pendulum bob hanging straight down), and the airplane is said to be coordinated, or in balance.

In a *skid*, the ball will move to one side in the same way as a pendulum bob would swing out, and you will feel a force pushing you outward. In a *slip*, the ball will fall to one side, and you will feel as if you are falling inward.

In a coordinated turn, you will feel no sideways forces, nor will the ball, which should remain centered. Any sideways force (either a *slip* in toward the turn or a *skid* out away from the turn) will be shown by the coordination ball and felt by you.

Figure 7-33
The coordination ball.

For coordinated flight, "Step on the ball."

If the ball is out to the right, apply right rudder pressure to center it. Use same-side rudder pressure to center the ball. Some instructors say, "Step on the ball."

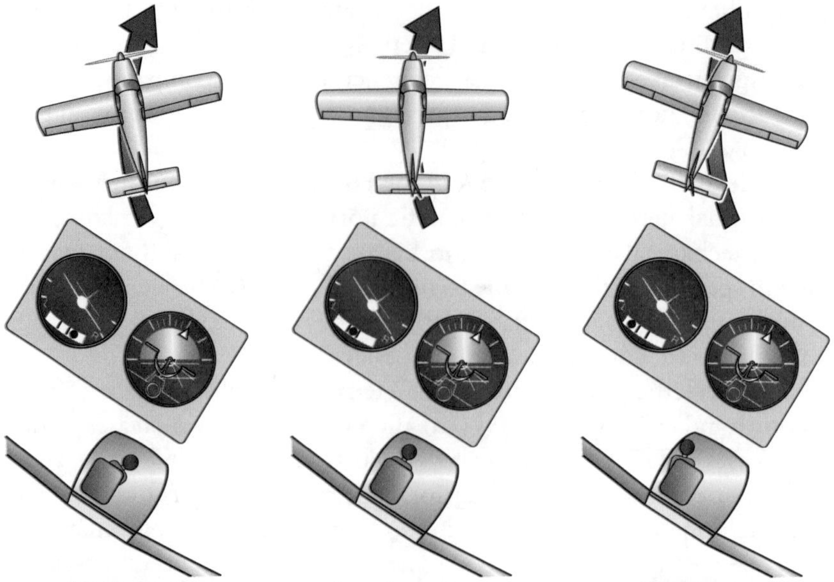
Slipping turn
Pilot slips into turn – more right rudder required to balance the turn
Coordinated turn
Skidding turn
Pilot skids out of turn – too much right rudder has been applied

Figure 7-34 Slipping turn; more right rudder required (left). A comfortable and coordinated turn (center). A skidding turn (right).

Angle of Attack Indicator (AOA)

The purpose of an AOA indicator is to give the pilot better situation awareness pertaining to the aerodynamic health of the airfoil. This can also be referred to as stall margin awareness. More simply explained it is the margin that exists between the current AOA that the airfoil is operating at, and the AOA at which the airfoil will stall (critical AOA). See figure 7-35.

Speed by itself is not a reliable parameter to avoid a stall. An airplane can stall at any speed. Angle of attack is a better parameter to use to avoid a stall. For a given configuration, the airplane always stalls at the same angle of attack, referred to as the critical AOA. This critical AOA does not change with:

- weight;
- bank angle;
- temperature;
- density altitude; and
- center of gravity.

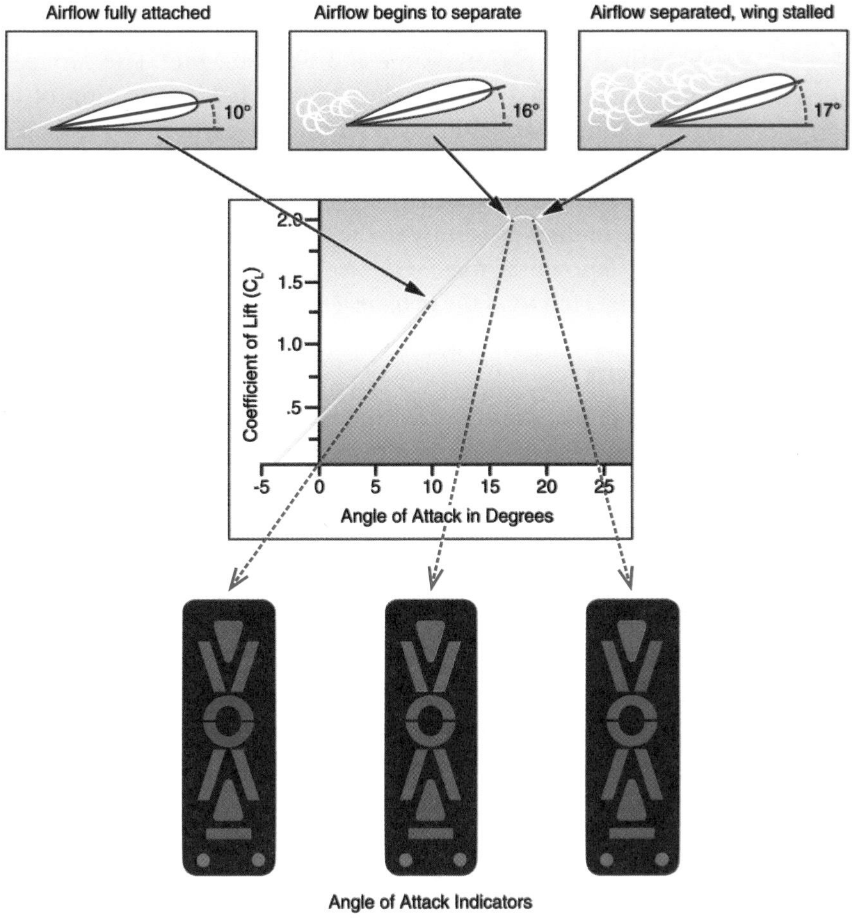

Figure 7-35 Critical angle of attack, stall, and angle of attack indicators.

An AOA indicator can have several benefits when installed in General Aviation aircraft, not the least of which is increased situational awareness. Without an AOA indicator, the AOA is "invisible" to pilots. These devices measure several parameters simultaneously and determine the current angle of attack providing a visual image to the pilot of the current AOA along with representations of the proximity to the critical AOA. These devices can give a visual representation of the energy management state of the airplane. The energy state of an airplane is the balance between airspeed, altitude, drag, and thrust and represents how efficiently the airfoil is operating.

The Magnetic Compass

In most light airplanes, the magnetic compass is the primary source of direction information, to which other direction indicators are aligned. In steady straight-and-level flight, the reference line of the magnetic compass indicates the *magnetic heading* of the airplane. Magnetic compass readings will not be accurate while the airplane is accelerating or turning, or when entering a climb or descent, nor will they be accurate if magnetic objects are placed near the compass.

Figure 7-36
Magnetic compass.

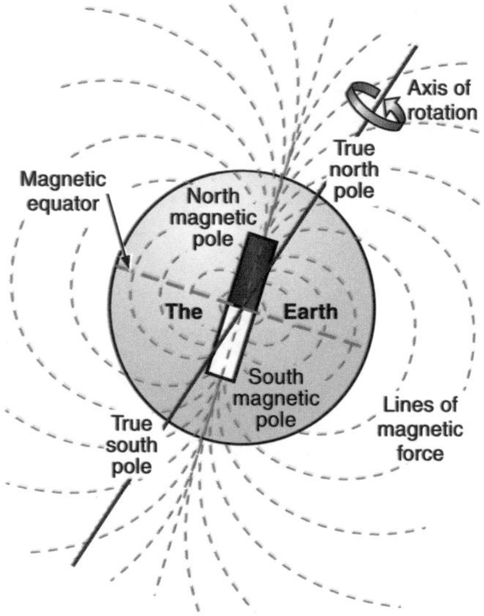

Figure 7-37
The earth has a magnetic field.

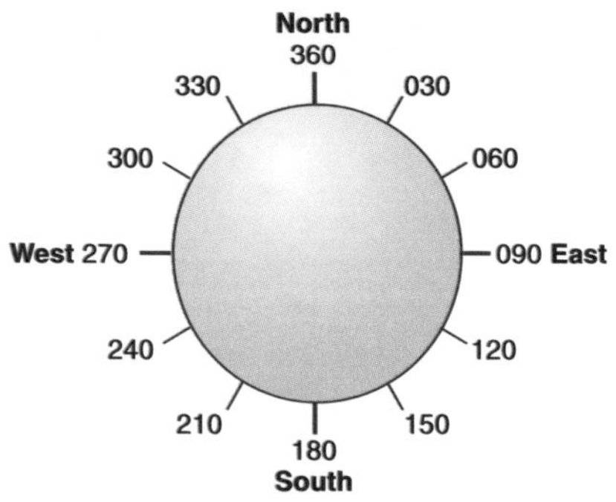

Figure 7-38 Direction.

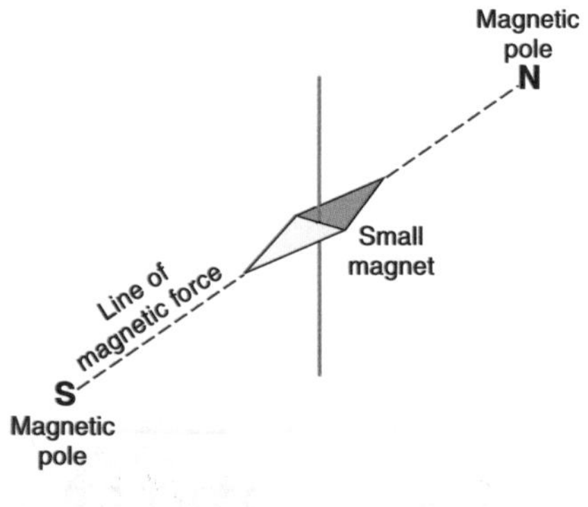

Figure 7-39 A simple bar magnet.

The Earth's Magnetic Field

The earth acts like a very large and weak magnet. The surface of the earth is surrounded by a weak magnetic field, consisting of lines of magnetic force that begin deep within the earth near Hudson Bay in Canada and flow toward a point deep within the earth near South Victoria Land in Antarctica.

Because of their proximity to the north and south geographical poles which are known as *true north pole* and *true south pole*, the magnetic poles are referred to as the *north magnetic pole* and the *south magnetic pole*.

Direction

There are two common ways to describe direction: using the cardinal points of north, south, east, and west; or by using a graduated circle of 360 degrees going clockwise from true or magnetic north.

Direction is almost always expressed as a three-figure group such as 251, 340, or 020. The only exception is runway direction, where the numbers are rounded off to the nearest 10°. A runway bearing 247° magnetic would be referred to as RWY 25, and its reciprocal, bearing 067°M, would be RWY 7.

A bar magnet that is freely suspended horizontally will swing so that its axis points roughly north–south. The end of the magnet that points toward the earth's *north magnetic pole* is called the north-seeking pole of the magnet.

Magnetic Variation

The latitude-longitude grid shown on charts is based on *true* north and *true* south. Our small compass magnet, however, does not point exactly at true north but at the north magnetic pole. The angular difference between true north and magnetic north at any particular point on the earth is called *variation*. If the magnet points slightly east of true north, then the variation is said to be east. If the compass points to the west of true north, then the variation is west. Magnetic variation is the same for all aircraft in a given vicinity.

Isogonic Lines

On charts, as well as the lines forming the latitude-longitude grid, there are dashed lines joining places that have the same magnetic variation, known as *isogonic lines* or *isogonals*.

For example, the 10° east isogonic line is drawn through all the places having a variation of 10°E. If you are anywhere on this line, magnetic north will be 10° east of true north. As you can see from the left inset in figure 7-40, a magnetic heading of 105° will correspond to a true heading of 115°. The line joining places where the variation is zero is called the *agonic line*.

Variation east, magnetic least; variation west, magnetic best.

Two easy ways to remember the relationship between true and magnetic are:

- "variation east, magnetic least; variation west, magnetic best"; and
- "east is least; west is best."

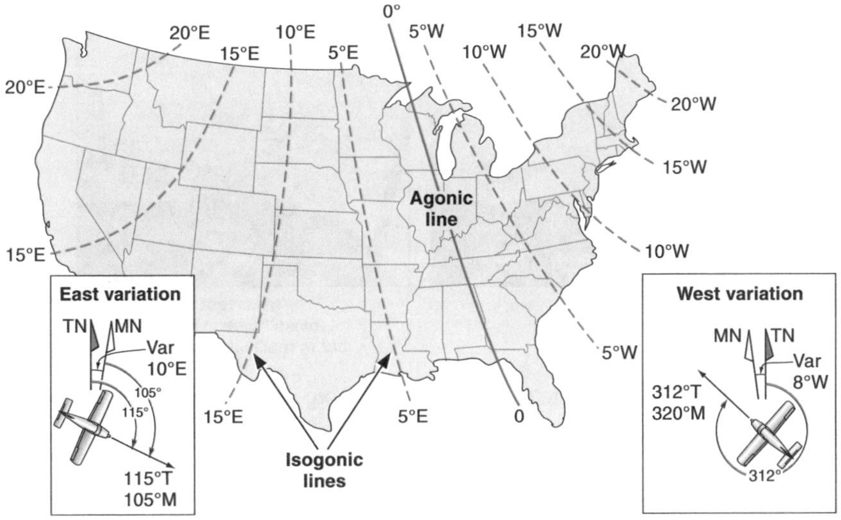

Figure 7-40 Variation is the angle between true and magnetic; isogonic lines join places of equal magnetic variation.

Example 7-1

If the magnetic variation in your area is 10° east and your airplane is heading 295 on the magnetic compass, what is your true heading?

Variation east, magnetic least: so 295°M is 295 + 10 = 305°true.

Example 7-2

If your compass indicates due east, and the magnetic variation where you are is 4° west, what is your heading related to true north?

Variation west, magnetic best: so 090 − 4 = 086° true.

Deviation

Unfortunately, the magnet in each compass is affected not only by the magnetic field of the earth, but also by any other magnetic field it is exposed to. Metal airframe components, the rotating parts of an engine, and electrical equipment all generate their own magnetic fields. The combined effect of these fields in a particular airplane on its magnetic compass is called *deviation*. Deviation causes the compass to deviate, or deflect, from precisely indicating magnetic north. The precise deviation can only be established once the compass is installed in the particular airplane, and test measurements made with the airplane on different headings.

DEVIATION CARD

FOR	N	30	60	E	120	150
STEER	001	031	060	089	118	149

FOR	S	210	240	W	300	330
STEER	181	213	242	271	301	330

ON ☒ RADIOS ☐ NO

Figure 7-41
Deviation card.

In each airplane is a small placard, known as the *deviation card*, which shows the pilot the corrections to be made to the compass reading to obtain the magnetic direction. This correction usually involves only a few degrees and is an easy mental calculation to do in flight.

The deviation card is filled out by a mechanic to reflect the deviation present when the compass was tested. If any other magnetic influences are introduced into the airplane at a later time, they will not be allowed for, even though they may significantly affect the compass. Therefore, ensure that no metal or magnetic materials are placed anywhere near the compass. Many pilots have become lost as a result of random deviations in the compass readings caused by these extraneous magnetic fields.

Do not place these cockpit items near the magnetic compass: headphones, ferrous metals, portable radios, calculators, or books with metal binders.

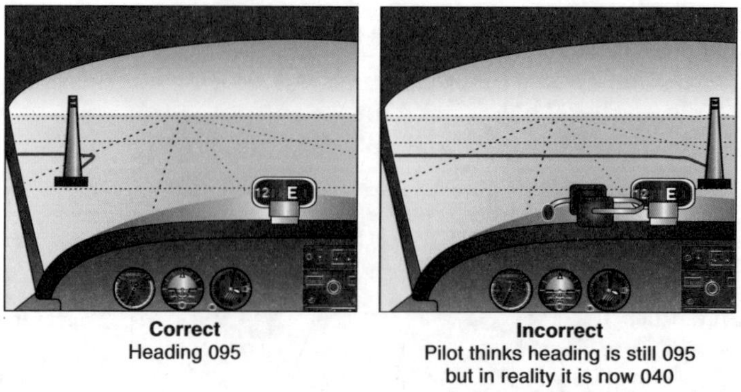

Figure 7-42 Keep foreign objects away from the magnetic compass.

Compass Construction and Serviceability

The modern airplane has a direct-reading compass, usually filled with a liquid in which a float partially supporting a bar magnet is pivoted. The liquid supports some of the weight, decreases the friction on the pivot and, most importantly, dampens the oscillations of the magnet and float during flight. This allows the compass to give a steadier indication and makes it easier to read.

Attached to the pivot is the combined magnet and compass card. The compass card is graduated in degrees and can be read against a reference line which is attached to the bowl of the compass, and therefore to the rest of the airplane. Remember that it is the airplane that turns around the magnet, while the magnet continues to point to magnetic north at all times.

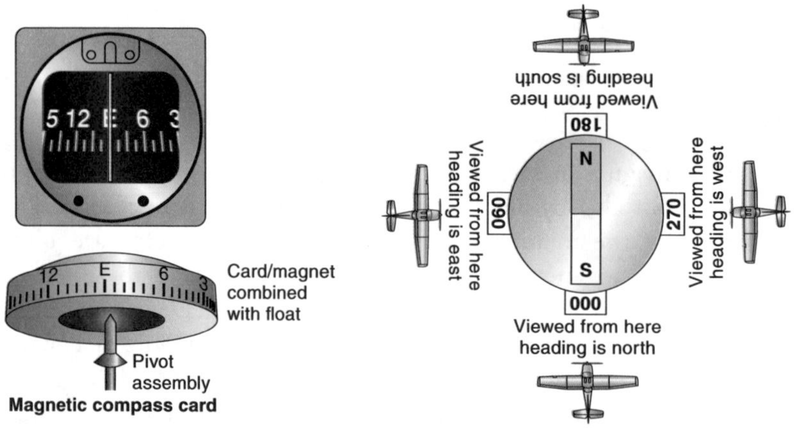

Figure 7-43 The magnetic compass.

Pilot Serviceability Checks

During preflight, you should check that the compass is securely installed and can be easily read. The liquid in which the magnet is suspended should be free of bubbles and should not be discolored. The glass should not be broken, cracked or discolored, and it should be secure. Then locate the position of the compass deviation card in the cockpit.

When you are taxiing out prior to takeoff, check the compass is working correctly by turning the airplane left and right and note the response of the magnet. In addition, before takeoff cross-check the compass reading with the runway direction. Runway 18 will point approximately 180° magnetic.

Figure 7-44 Always cross-check compass direction.

Magnetic Dip and Compass Errors

Near the magnetic equator, the lines of magnetic force are parallel to the surface of the earth. As the magnetic poles are approached, the lines of magnetic force dip toward them and any magnet bar will also try to dip down and align itself with these lines of force. The angle of dip, called *magnetic dip*, is approximately 70° in the United States. Magnetic dip is zero at the magnetic equator and increases to 90° at the magnetic poles.

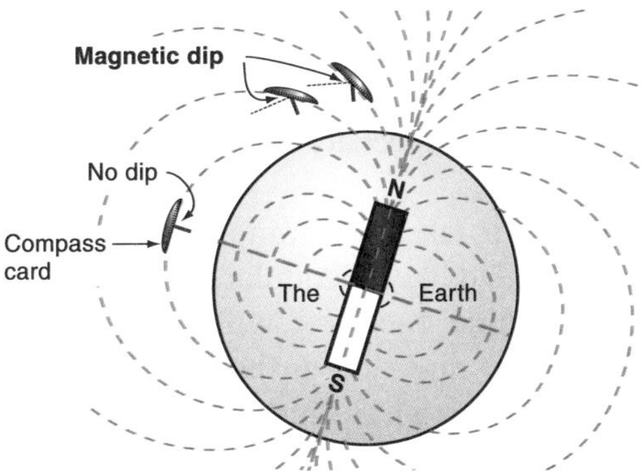

Figure 7-45 Magnetic dip is strongest nearest the poles.

Magnetic Dip Effect

The earth's *magnetic field* can be resolved into two components: a horizontal one parallel to the surface of the earth (which is used to align the compass with magnetic north), and a vertical component, which causes the compass magnet to dip down.

At the magnetic equator, the horizontal component of the earth's magnetic field is at its strongest and so the magnetic compass is very stable and accurate.

However, at higher latitudes, the horizontal component parallel to the surface of the earth is weaker, making the compass magnet less effective as an indicator of horizontal direction. At latitudes higher than 60° north or south, the magnetic compass is not very reliable.

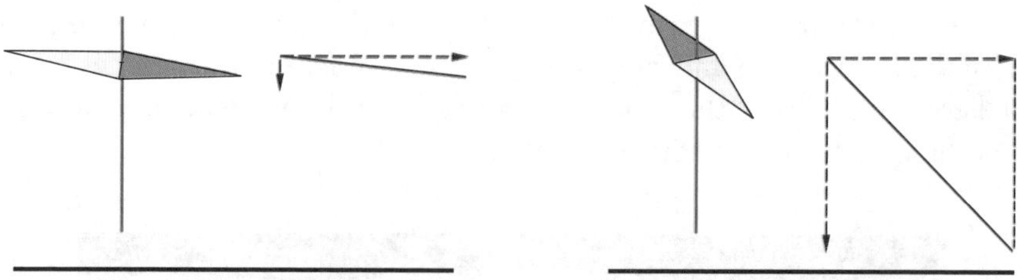

Figure 7-46 Dip is caused by the vertical component of the earth's magnetic field.

Compass Design to Minimize Dip Effect

To keep the magnet as close to horizontal as possible, the airplane compass is cleverly designed so that the point from which the magnet is suspended is well above its center of gravity. As the magnet aligns itself with the earth's magnetic field, the more it tries to dip down, the further out its center of gravity is displaced. This sets up a balancing couple which reduces the remaining dip, which is known as residual dip, to less than 5° from the horizontal.

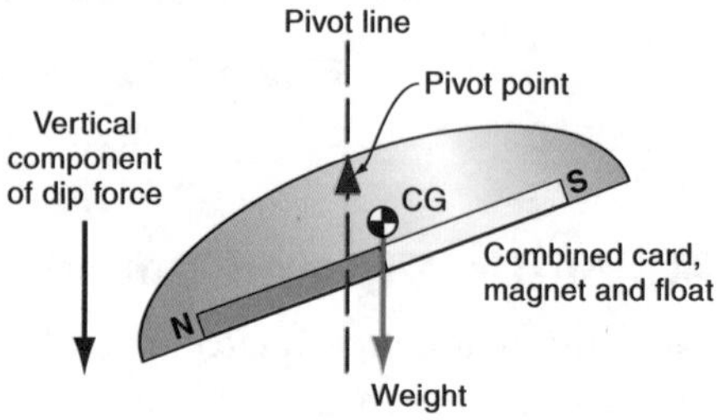

Figure 7-47 Magnet suspension.

Acceleration Errors

If you change airspeed, either by accelerating or decelerating, transient indication errors occur with a magnetic compass, especially on easterly and westerly headings. They disappear after the speed stabilizes.

As the airplane accelerates, it takes the compass and the pivot along with it. The compass magnet, being suspended like a pendulum, is left behind because of its inertia. Its weight, not being directly under the pivot, will cause the compass magnet to swing away from the correct magnetic direction as the pivot accelerates away. The compass card attached to the magnet rotates a little and indicates a new direction, even though there has been no change in direction.

Once a new steady speed is maintained, the magnet will settle down and the compass will read correctly once again.

Accelerating East or West

Accelerating toward the east or west, the center of gravity of the magnet, near the south-seeking end, is left behind. This swings the compass card so that it indicates an *apparent turn to the north.* After acceleration is completed you should allow the compass to settle down before adjusting the airplane heading (if necessary).

Decelerating East or West

Decelerating toward the east or west, the pivot slows down with the rest of the airplane and the center of gravity of the magnet, because of its inertia, tries to advance. The compass card rotates to indicate an *apparent turn to the south.*

Accelerating North and South

Accelerating and decelerating (toward the north or south) will *not* cause apparent turns, because the pivot and the CG of the magnet will lie in the same N–S line as the acceleration or deceleration. On other headings, the acceleration errors will be greater the closer you are to due east or west.

> **Note.** These effects are valid only for the Northern Hemisphere. In the Southern Hemisphere, the effects are reversed. Also, the closer to the magnetic poles you are, the greater the effect because the dip is greater. Magnetic dip is the major source of compass indication errors.

Remember: acceleration and deceleration errors on easterly and westerly headings in the Northern Hemisphere may be summarized by the mnemonic "A N D S." Accelerate—apparent turn North; Decelerate—apparent turn South. The situation in the Southern Hemisphere is reversed.

When accelerating or decelerating on an easterly or westerly heading, use: "A N D S:" Accelerate—apparent turn North; Decelerate—apparent turn South.

Turning Errors

Turning is also an acceleration, because of the change in direction. In a turn, a centripetal force acts on the compass pivot, which is attached to the airplane, and accelerates it toward the center of the turn. The compass magnet (and compass card), being suspended like a pendulum, is left behind because of inertia. This leads to a transient error in the direction indicated by the compass, which will gradually disappear after the wings have been leveled. The result is that when turning through north the compass lags behind.

Turning Through North

For example, when turning from 310° to 040° you should level the wings at about 020°, before reaching 040°. This is because once the airplane stops turning the compass reading will continue rotating for a few seconds because of the lag.

Turning Through South

When turning through south the compass heading turns ahead of the airplane. If you turn from 130° to 210° you should level the wings at about 230°. Once the compass settles down it should read 210°.

Remember: Turning errors of the magnetic compass may be summarized by the mnemonic "U N O S:" Undershoot heading through North; Overshoot heading through South.

When turning onto a heading use: "U N O S:" Undershoot heading through North; Overshoot heading through South.

> **Note.** Do not align the heading indicator with the magnetic compass if you are changing speed or direction, or entering a climb or descent, as the magnetic compass will be experiencing acceleration or turning errors. When aligning the heading indicator with the compass keep the wings level and maintain a constant speed.

A magnetic compass only reads accurately in straight unaccelerated flight.

One of the advantages of a heading indicator is that it is not subject to turning or acceleration errors. However its accuracy depends on it being correctly aligned with magnetic north.

Review 7
Flight Instruments

Pressure Instruments

1. How is static pressure measured?
2. What does the pitot tube collect?
3. Why are electrical pitot heaters fitted in airplanes?
4. What does the VSI measure?
5. Which pressure(s) does the ASI use?
6. The pitot tube/static vent provides total or impact pressure for which instrument(s)?
7. Will the altimeter be affected if the pitot tube becomes clogged, but the static vents remain clear?
8. Will the airspeed indicator be affected if the pitot tube becomes clogged, but the static vents remain clear?
9. Which instrument(s) will be affected if the static vents become clogged?
10. If a static vent ices over, what will the altimeter show during a climb?
11. What color arc on the ASI indicates the following:
    - **a.** the caution airspeed range of an airplane?
    - **b.** the normal-operating airspeed range of an airplane?
    - **c.** the normal flap-operating range of an airplane?
12. Which color on the ASI identifies the never-exceed speed?
13. Which color on the ASI identifies the power-off stalling speed with wing flaps and landing gear in the landing configuration?
14. With wings-level and full flaps extended, what is stall speed indicated as on the ASI?
15. Where is stall speed, with wings-level and no flaps extended, indicated on the ASI?
16. Is it permissible to fly at speeds in the yellow caution range in smooth air?
17. True or false? The maximum flaps-extended speed corresponds to the high-speed end of the green arc.
18. Is the altimeter a pressure instrument?

Refer to figure 7-48 for questions 19 to 21.

19. What is the caution range of the airplane?
20. What is the full flap operating range for the airplane?
21. What is the maximum flaps-extended speed?

Figure 7-48 Airspeed indicator.

22. What is standard MSL pressure? Give your answer in both in. Hg. and hectopascals.
23. If 30.05 is set in the pressure window, what will the altimeter indicate when the airplane is in flight?
24. If the current altimeter setting is set in the pressure window, what will the altimeter indicate when the airplane is in flight?
25. If the current airport altimeter setting is set in the pressure window, what will the altimeter indicate when the airplane is on the runway?
26. What is absolute altitude?
27. What is density altitude?
28. What must you set in the pressure window of the altimeter prior to takeoff and landing?

29. What is usually set in the pressure window when cruising below 18,000 feet in the United States? Explain why this is done.

Refer to figure 7-49 for question 30.

30. What is the altitude depicted by:
   a. altimeter A?
   b. altimeter B?
   c. altimeter C?
31. You are departing from an airport where you cannot obtain an altimeter setting. You should:
   a. set 29.92 in. Hg in the pressure window of the altimeter.
   b. set the altimeter to read field elevation.
   c. set the altimeter to read zero.
32. If a pilot changes the altimeter setting from 30.11 to 29.96, what is the approximate change in indication?
33. You change the setting in the pressure window of an altimeter from 29.92 to 29.98. What will happen to the indicated altitude?
34. The current altimeter setting is 30.32 in. Hg. If an airplane is flying at an altitude of 6,500 feet MSL, what is its approximate pressure altitude?
35. What does a cruising level of FL230 signify?
36. True or false? If you fly from an area of high pressure into an area of low pressure without adjusting the altimeter setting while maintaining a constant indicated altitude, the airplane will be at the indicated altitude.
37. On warmer than standard days, the pressure and density levels are raised. What effect does this have on the indicated altitude in relation to true altitude?
38. What conditions are required for the pressure altitude to be equal to the true altitude?
39. Under what conditions will true altitude be higher than indicated altitude?
40. True or false? The altimeter will indicate a lower altitude than actually flown (true altitude) when the air temperature is lower than standard.
41. If the outside air temperature increases during a flight at constant power and at a constant indicated altitude, what will happen to the true altitude?
42. What does an encoding altimeter send electronic altitude information to?

Gyroscopic Instruments

43. Is the miniature airplane of an AI adjustable?
44. During a turn to the left, where will the left wing of the miniature airplane appear in relation to the horizon bar of the AI?
45. What sort of information does the turn indicator give?
46. What sort of information does the turn coordinator give?
47. Does the turn coordinator give pitch information?
48. Most turn coordinators have markings to indicate a standard-rate turn left or right. What is standard rate (° per second)?
49. What should the gyroscopic heading indicator be regularly realigned with?
50. The vacuum pump operates which instruments?
51. Slip or skid is indicated on which instrument?

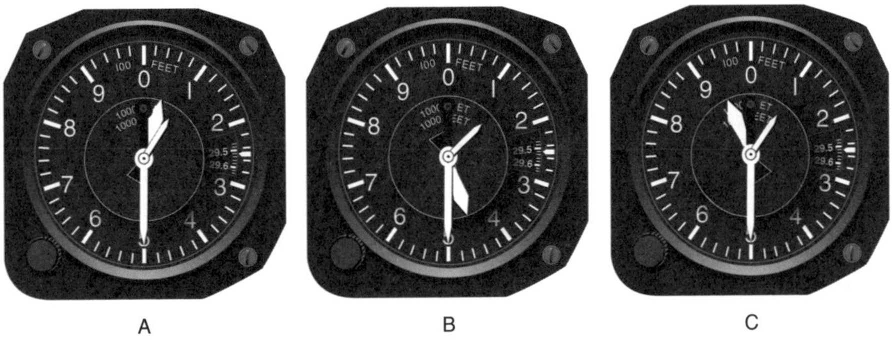

Figure 7-49 Altimeter presentation.

52. Failure of the electrical supply to an electrically driven attitude indicator may be indicated by:
   a. a low ammeter reading.
   b. a red warning flag.
   c. low suction.
53. Some airplanes have an electrically driven turn coordinator with the other gyroscopic instruments being vacuum-driven. Why?
54. Which instrument provides direct pitch attitude information?
55. Which instrument provides rate of turn information?
56. To receive accurate indications during flight from a heading indicator, the instrument must be:
   a. set prior to flight on a known heading.
   b. calibrated on a compass rose at regular intervals.
   c. periodically realigned with the magnetic compass as the gyro precesses.

Magnetic Compass

57. The earth rotates about its axis. This axis intersects the surface of the earth at which points?
58. The lines of magnetic force surrounding the earth flow to which points on the earth?
59. What is the difference between true north and magnetic north at any point on earth called?
60. Is the difference between true north and magnetic north constant over the earth?
61. If a perfect magnetic compass points 10° to the right of true north at a particular point on earth, what is the magnetic variation?
62. Your airplane is headed due east (090° true or TH 090). What will the compass indicate (MH) if magnetic variation at that position on earth is:
   a. 10° east?
   b. 4° east?
   c. 5° west?
63. What do you call lines drawn on charts joining places of equal magnetic variation?
64. What line joins places where the variation is zero (i.e. where the directions to true north and magnetic north coincide)?
65. How would you depict a heading of magnetic south?
66. How would you depict a heading of southwest?
67. What is magnetic variation the result of?
68. What is deviation in a magnetic compass caused by?
69. Deviation varies with which factor(s)?
70. During flight, the indications of a magnetic compass are accurate:
   a. in straight-and-level unaccelerated flight.
   b. if the airspeed is constant, even in turns.
   c. in straight-and-level flight, even if accelerating.
71. What does the reference line of the magnetic compass indicate?
72. Runway 32 at a particular airport could have a bearing of approximately:
   a. 032°M.
   b. 322°M.
   c. 032°T.
73. Acceleration errors for a magnetic compass occur on which headings?
74. You are heading MH 010 in the Northern Hemisphere and want to make a left turn to a heading of MH 300. What should you do?
75. You are heading MH 210 in the Northern Hemisphere, and want to make a left turn to MH 160. What should you do?
76. What affects the amount of magnetic dip?
77. Turning and acceleration errors of the magnetic compass will be greater in Alaska than in Florida. Why?
78. In the Northern Hemisphere, a magnetic compass may initially indicate a turn toward the east if:
   a. it decelerates while on a southerly heading.
   b. it accelerates while on a northerly heading.
   c. it turns left from a northerly heading.
79. During flight, when are the indications of a magnetic compass accurate?
80. In the Northern Hemisphere, a magnetic compass will normally indicate a turn toward the north if:
   a. a right turn is entered from an east heading.
   b. a left turn is entered from a west heading.
   c. the aircraft is accelerated while on an east or west heading.

Answers are given on page 689

Airplane and Pilot Performance

Airplane Performance Factors 8

Airworthiness

When a new type or model of airplane is designed and built, the manufacturer applies for and, after suitable tests on the original test airplanes have been passed, is granted a Certificate of Type Approval. This document is issued to the manufacturer by the aviation authority in the country of manufacture (Federal Aviation Administration (FAA) in the United States).

Engineering and safety requirements, reliability and many other factors are considered in detail, and many inspections and flight tests are carried out prior to the issue of a Type Certificate. Once it is obtained, the manufacturer commences production and a new airplane type comes onto the market. The pilot does not see the Type Certificate, which is retained by the manufacturer.

The airworthiness requirements for airplanes are specified in the Federal Aviation Regulations. A large number of documents are involved in the airworthiness system, but those of most immediate importance to the individual pilot are the:

- Certificate of Registration (Part 91);
- Certificate of Airworthiness (Part 91); and
- Approved Flight Manual (Part 91).

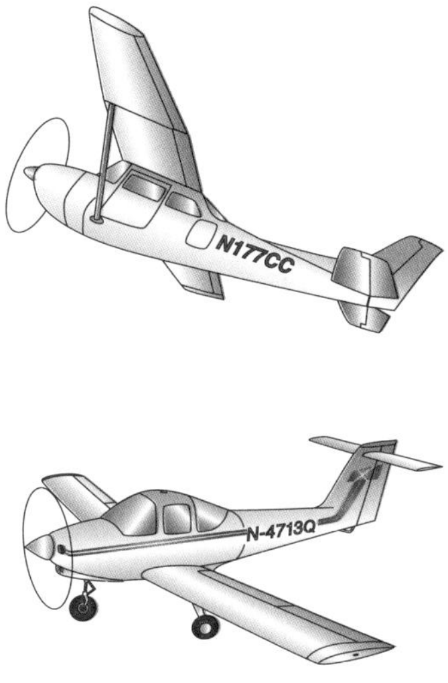

Figure 8-1 Examples of airplane registrations.

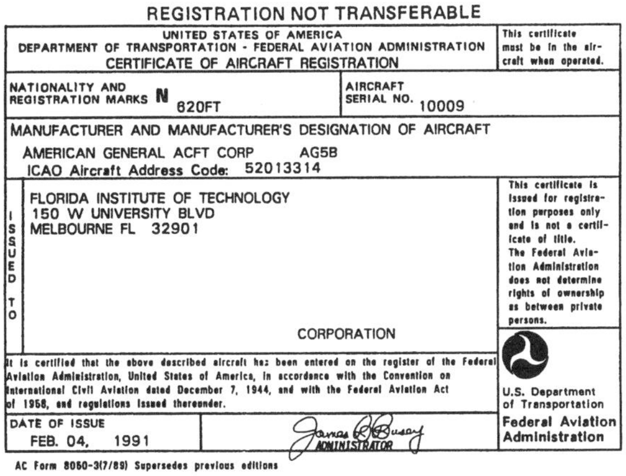

REGISTRATION NOT TRANSFERABLE

UNITED STATES OF AMERICA
DEPARTMENT OF TRANSPORTATION - FEDERAL AVIATION ADMINISTRATION
CERTIFICATE OF AIRCRAFT REGISTRATION

This certificate must be in the aircraft when operated.

NATIONALITY AND REGISTRATION MARKS N 620FT

AIRCRAFT SERIAL NO. 10009

MANUFACTURER AND MANUFACTURER'S DESIGNATION OF AIRCRAFT
AMERICAN GENERAL ACFT CORP AG5B
ICAO Aircraft Address Code: 52013314

ISSUED TO
FLORIDA INSTITUTE OF TECHNOLOGY
150 W UNIVERSITY BLVD
MELBOURNE FL 32901

CORPORATION

This certificate is issued for registration purposes only and is not a certificate of title. The Federal Aviation Administration does not determine rights of ownership as between private persons.

It is certified that the above described aircraft has been entered on the register of the Federal Aviation Administration, United States of America, in accordance with the Convention on International Civil Aviation dated December 7, 1944, and with the Federal Aviation Act of 1958, and regulations issued thereunder.

DATE OF ISSUE
FEB. 04, 1991

ADMINISTRATOR

U.S. Department of Transportation
Federal Aviation Administration

AC Form 8050-3(7/89) Supersedes previous editions

Figure 8-2 Certificate of Registration.

UNITED STATES OF AMERICA
DEPARTMENT OF TRANSPORTATION—FEDERAL AVIATION ADMINISTRATION
STANDARD AIRWORTHINESS CERTIFICATE

1 NATIONALITY AND REGISTRATION MARKS	2 MANUFACTURER AND MODEL	3 AIRCRAFT SERIAL NUMBER	4 CATEGORY
N620FT	American General Aircraft AG-5B	10009	Normal Utility

5 AUTHORITY AND BASIS FOR ISSUANCE
This airworthiness certificate is issued pursuant to the Federal Aviation Act of 1958 and certifies that as of the date of issuance the aircraft to which issued has been inspected and found to conform to the type certificate therefor to be in condition for safe operation, and has been shown to meet the requirements of the applicable comprehensive and detailed airworthiness code as provided by Annex 8 to the Convention on International Civil Aviation, except as noted herein
Exceptions

None

6 TERMS AND CONDITIONS
Unless sooner surrendered, suspended, revoked, or a termination date is otherwise established by the Administrator this airworthiness certificate is effective as long as the maintenance, preventative maintenance and alterations are performed in accordance with Parts 21, 43, and 91 of the Federal Aviation Regulations, as appropriate and the aircraft is registered in the United States

DATE OF ISSUANCE	FAA REPRESENTATIVE	DESIGNATION NUMBER
12-20-90	Emil F. Miehlke	CE-51

Any alteration, reproduction, or misuse of this certificate may be punishable by a fine not exceeding $1,000 or imprisonment not exceeding 3 years, or both. THIS CERTIFICATE MUST BE DISPLAYED IN THE AIRCRAFT IN ACCORDANCE WITH APPLICABLE FEDERAL AVIATION REGULATIONS.

FAA Form 8100-2 (8-82) U.S. GOVERNMENT PRINTING OFFICE: 1988-0-562-105

Figure 8-3 Certificate of Airworthiness.

Certificate of Registration

The Federal Aviation Regulations require that an American-owned or operated airplane be on the Register of Aircraft. When this is done for an individual airplane, the FAA issues a Certificate of Registration to the owner. The airplane is given a registration number to follow the letter "N," which is the United States nationality marking, for example, N4713P, and this must be displayed prominently on the airplane in specific sizes and positions. Examples of other aircraft nationality markings are: "D-" for Germany (Deutschland), "F-" for France and "G-" for Great Britain.

The Certificate of Registration must be carried and prominently displayed in the airplane. Before flight you should verify that the airplane is registered.

Certificate of Airworthiness

The Certificate of Airworthiness is issued by the FAA for an individual airplane. This may be American or an American approval of a foreign certificate. The Certificate of Airworthiness is normally granted for an unlimited period—its validity being subject to regular inspections. However, in some cases, the Certificate of Airworthiness may be issued for only a specified period. It should be carried in the airplane and prominently displayed.

The Certificate of Airworthiness is issued by the FAA for an individual airplane to operate in a particular category, provided it complies with the appropriate airworthiness requirements. Categories and their authorized purposes include transport, experimental, normal, limited, utility, restricted, acrobatic, and provisional.

A private pilot is likely to fly airplanes in the following categories, which are defined in Part 23 of the Federal Aviation Regulations:

- *normal category*—below 12,500 pounds and non-acrobatic maneuvers limited to stalls (but not whip stalls), lazy eights, chandelles and steep turns of 60°. Typical limit load factors are +3.8g and -1.52g;
- *utility category*—same as for a normal category, plus limited acrobatics (aerobatics), which may include spins. Typical limit load factors are +4.4g and -1.76g. Note that some airplanes in the normal category may be allowed to operate in the utility category within certain specified weight-and-balance limits, usually with fuel/passenger restrictions; and
- *aerobatic category*—airplanes in this category are fully aerobatic, but may have some limitations based on flight test results. Typical limit load factors are +6.0g and -3.0g.

Never intentionally carry out inappropriate maneuvers for the category of your airplane—structural damage or destruction is a very real possibility. The Certificate of Airworthiness has other documents associated with it, in particular, the approved Flight Manual.

Approved Flight Manual (AFM)

The Flight Manual for each airplane must be approved by the FAA. The AFM comes in various forms, including the Pilot's Operating Handbook (POH) for modern airplanes, and the Owner's Manual for older aircraft. These documents must contain the latest valid information for the airplane.

The information in the Flight Manual is presented in a standard format, as given in table 8-1.

The pilot must comply with all of the requirements, procedures, and limitations with respect to the operation of the airplane as set out in its approved Flight Manual. Placards placed in the cockpit will often reflect the Flight Manual limitations, and have the same status.

1.	General Section;
2.	Limitations Section;
3.	Emergency Procedures;
4.	Normal Procedures;
5.	Performance;
6.	Weight and Balance;
7.	Description and Operation of the Airplane and its Systems;
8.	Handling, Service and Maintenance; and
9.	Supplements (optional systems and equipment not provided with the standard airplane).

Table 8-1
Sections of the Flight Manual.

Maintenance

The owner or operator of an airplane is responsible for maintaining it in an airworthy condition. Specific FAA requirements for maintenance may be found in Parts 91 and 43 of the Federal Aviation Regulations.

Airframe Limitations

Weight Limitations

The gross weight (GW) of the airplane is subject to certain limitations. Some of the limitations are structural in nature, as the airplane is designed and built to perform certain tasks and carry certain loads, up to a maximum. Other limitations stem from the performance limitations of the airplane—certain conditions of temperature, pressure, runway conditions, and wind, may limit allowable weights for takeoff, landing and so on.

Maximum Takeoff Weight (MTOW)

This is a structural limitation. The MTOW is the maximum gross weight, according to the Flight Manual and approved weight-and-balance documents, at which that airplane is permitted to takeoff. The takeoff weight (TOW) for a particular takeoff must not exceed the structural MTOW or the weight as limited by airplane performance and runway considerations.

Maximum Landing Weight (MLW)

This is also a structural limitation. The MLW is the maximum gross weight, according to the Flight Manual and approved weight-and-balance documents at which that airplane is permitted to land.

> **Note.** The landing weight (LW) for a particular landing should not exceed the structural MLW or the weight as limited by airplane performance and runway considerations. The MLW is usually less than the MTOW because of the greater stresses expected in landing compared with taking off.

Maximum Zero Fuel Weight (MZFW)

Although not generally applicable to light airplanes, you should be aware that most large airplanes have a *structurally limited zero fuel weight* (MZFW). This limit is imposed to ensure that stresses on the wing caused by the upward lift forces in flight are not excessive. The fuel load carried in the wing tanks exerts a downward force which helps to relieve these stresses. Any load above MZFW *must* be usable fuel in the wings.

Maximum Ramp Weight

The *maximum ramp weight* is the maximum gross weight permitted prior to taxiing. It may exceed the *maximum takeoff weight* by the taxi fuel allowance. While this is not specified for many light airplanes, you may come across it.

Speed Limitations

The airplane should only be flown in a specific operating speed range, limited by certain high and low speeds. Sometimes *aerodynamic* considerations provide the reason for the limit (the stall speed V_S is the lower speed limit), and sometimes *power* considerations limit the speeds, (the maximum speed on the cruise is limited by the amount of power available to overcome the increasing parasite drag).

More important are the structural speed limitations. There might be sufficient power available for a very high speed cruise or dive, but the airframe may not be designed to withstand these stresses. The speed limitations range from the structural limit of the never-exceed speed (V_{NE}) on the high side to the aerodynamic limit of stall speed (V_S) on the low side. Within these extreme limits are other more cautious limits, such as the normal-operating limit speed (V_{NO}), and the stall buffet.

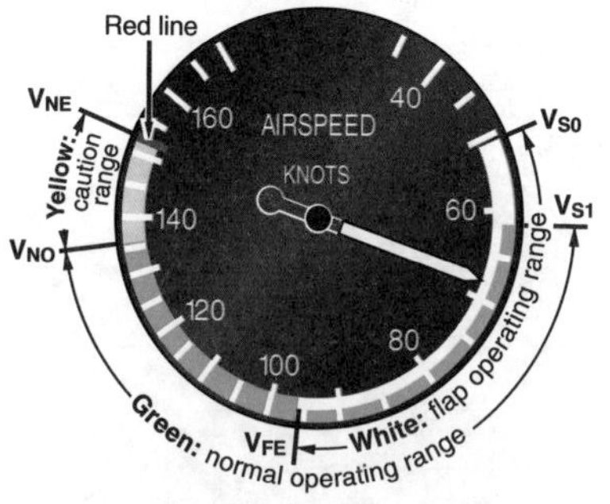

V_{S0}	Stall speed at max weight, landing gear down, flaps down, power off
V_{S1}	Stall speed at max weight, landing gear up (if retractable), flaps up, power off
V_{FE}	Maximum speed, flaps extended
V_{NO}	Maximum structural cruising speed (for normal operations)
V_{NE}	Never-exceed speed (max speed, all ops.)

Figure 8-4
Color coding on the airspeed indicator.

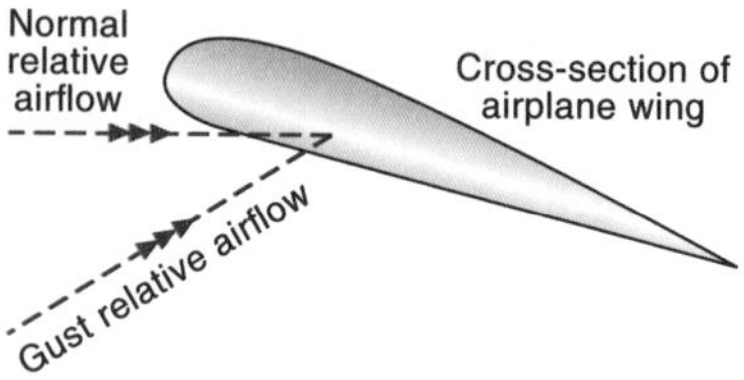

Figure 8-5
Gusts can increase or decrease the angle of attack, cause high wing loadings, or cause the wing's critical angle of attack to be exceeded (stall).

The Never-Exceed Speed—V_{NE}

V_{NE} is the absolute maximum speed at which the airplane may be flown. It is indicated on the airspeed indicator (ASI) by a red line. Any gusts or maneuvering at speeds approaching V_{NE} may cause unacceptable load factors leading to airframe deformation and failure. A sensible pilot would not allow the airplane to approach this speed under normal operations.

The Normal-Operating Limit Speed—V_{NO}

V_{NO} is known as the normal-operating limit speed, or the maximum structural cruising speed, and is the maximum speed at which the airplane should be flown under normal operating conditions. You should not exceed V_{NO}, because while it may be safe in smooth air, any gusts could overstress the airframe.

The normal-operating speed range is indicated on the ASI by a green arc. Above V_{NO} (normal-operating limit speed) is a yellow or orange caution arc, extending to the limiting red line at V_{NO}.

The Maneuvering Speed—V_A or V_{MAN}

When the pilot is maneuvering the airplane, the control surfaces (ailerons, elevators and rudder), the wings and the empennage are all subjected to increased loading. Maneuvering speed (V_A) is the maximum speed for maneuvers at which full application of the primary flight controls cannot overstress the airframe. This is because below V_A the airplane will always stall before the limiting load factor is reached. V_A is not marked on the airspeed indicator. Note that the airplane Flight Manual may specify varying speeds for V_A because, at light weights, V_A is slower than at higher weights. See figure 8-8 (page 196).

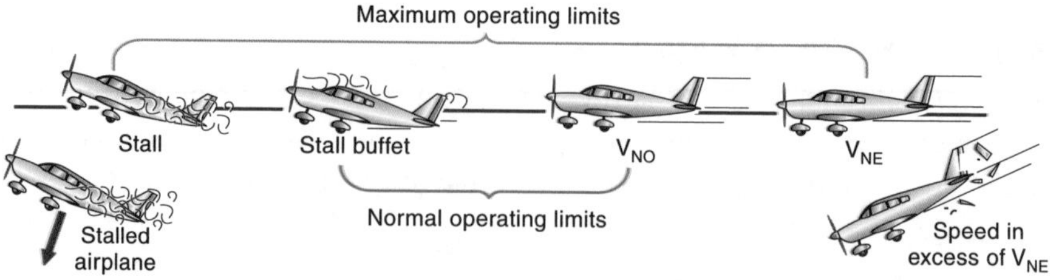

Figure 8-6 The speed range of an airplane.

Flying in Turbulence

Turbulent air or gusts can change the direction of the local relative airflow and the angle of attack almost instantaneously. Flying slowly (at a high angle of attack), an upward gust could increase the angle of attack causing the wing to stall. Flying slowly through gusts therefore decreases the stresses on the airplane, but exposes it to the possibility of a stall. Flying fast through turbulence gives a bumpier ride and puts more stress (higher load factors) on the structure that could exceed the structural load factor limits.

The *turbulence-penetration speed* (V_B or V_{TURB}), or the rough-air speed (V_{RA}), are the recommended target speeds for flying through turbulence. They are compromise speeds to avoid the stall on the low-speed side and excessive wing loading on the high-speed side. Not every airplane Flight Manual will specify a V_B or V_{RA}. In this event, you should use the maneuvering speed (V_A) to avoid structural damage. V_{NO} should not be exceeded in turbulence.

Other Maximum Speeds Specified

As the flaps are lowered, drag increases and the airframe is subjected to extra stresses and so a maximum flaps-extended speed (V_{FE}) is usually specified. For airplanes with retractable landing gear (also known as retractable undercarriage) one or two speed limitations will be specified according to system design. The maximum speed for operating (extending or retracting) the landing gear (V_{LO}) may be slower than the airspeed at which you may fly with the gear extended (V_{LE}). This is because, while the landing gear is extending and retracting, some gear doors may open outward into the airstream and be subjected to air loads. With those systems in which the doors close again once the gear is extended, the faster airspeed V_{LE} is permitted. Also, the landing gear system may include small locking devices which strengthen the landing gear structure when it is fully extended.

Load Factor Limitations

In straight-and-level flight, the airframe is subjected to 1g forces. You also experience a force of 1g exerted on your body by the seat, equal and opposite to your weight. This force, both on the airframe and you, will change in maneuvers. Any maneuvering, such as turning, pulling out of a dive, or performing aerobatics will increase or decrease this load on the airplane structure and you. For example, a 60° banked turn increases the structural load to 2g, and pulling out of a dive at a fast airspeed could easily achieve a load factor of 3 or 4g.

It is important when recovering from the more unusual flight attitudes (steep turns, steep dives, spiral dives) that you avoid pulling excessive "g", because this may overstress the airframe.

As well as the static load factor or g-forces, there are dynamic strength considerations, such as dynamic instability of the airplane in high-speed flight, flutter in the control surfaces, which, if allowed to develop, can lead to structural failure.

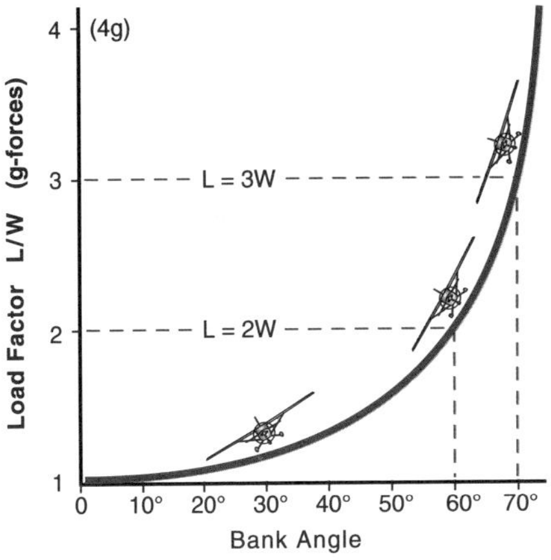

Figure 8-7
Load factor versus bank angle.

The Velocity/Load Factor or V-G Diagram

The V-G diagram illustrates the flight operating strength of an airplane. Limit load factors and limit speeds are specified by the FAA for different airplane categories, within which the airplane must be operated. Taken beyond these limits, the airplane may suffer structural damage or even structural failure. As can be seen in figure 8-8, the amount of excess load (in excess of 1g) that can be imposed on the wings without causing structural damage depends on airspeed. The high-speed limit is V_{NE}, the never-exceed speed, and the low-speed limit is the stall. The stall speed is affected by the load factor, occurring at higher speeds when g's are being pulled.

Above V_A you should avoid making any abrupt or large control movements.

Full backward movement of the control column will increase the g-loading but, at low speeds, the stall occurs before the limit load factor is reached. At speeds above V_A, however, the wing is at a small angle of attack, and so lots of excess lift is available by pulling the control column back. This could cause the limit load factor to be exceeded, therefore you must not apply full back stick at high speeds.

Gusts also cause changes in the load factor and care should be taken when flying in turbulence. V_{NO}, the normal-operating limit speed, should not be exceeded except in very smooth air, when V_{NE} becomes the absolute limit.

The limit load factor should never be intentionally exceeded, because of the risk of structural damage. The load factor at which the structure will actually break is called the ultimate load factor and it is greater than the limit load factor.

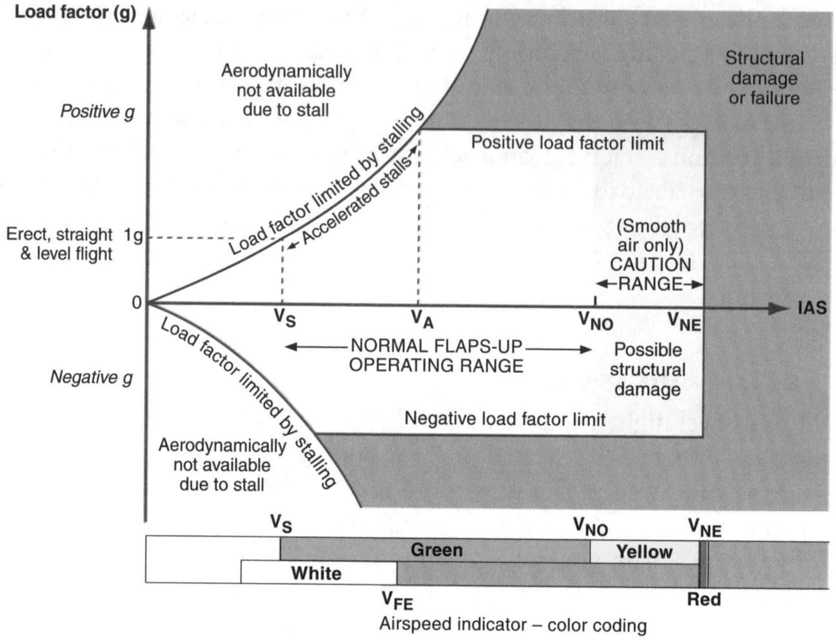

Figure 8-8 A typical V-G diagram related to ASI markings.

Checks Following Excessive Stress on the Airframe

While you must not knowingly exceed the airframe limitations, excessive stress can be caused by unexpected severe turbulence or a particularly heavy landing. In both cases, the wing structure may be heavily loaded and, in the case of a heavy landing, the landing gear and the areas to which it is attached to the airframe will have been heavily loaded.

One of the responsibilities of being a pilot is to ensure that following pilots will be presented with an airworthy airplane. The occurrence of heavy stress must be referred to an aviation maintenance technician (AMT). There could be damage not immediately apparent to you during an inspection, quite apart from those items already mentioned.

For this reason, if an airplane has been overstressed, you must ensure that an AMT carries out an inspection prior to the next flight.

Many light airplanes are of semi-monocoque construction, where the loads are carried, not only by the internal structure, but also by the skin. Damage to either of these will weaken the overall structure. In carrying out an inspection, the AMT will look for indications of stress on the airframe, the main external items being:

Structural damage can exist even without external indications. If you overstress an airplane you must ensure an AMT checks it.

- distortion of the structure;
- cracks;
- popped or sheared rivets; and
- wrinkles in the skin, especially in the areas surrounding the main structural attachments for the engine, wing, wing struts, landing gear attachments, and tailplane.

Severe overload can distort or break the wings and associated struts or braces. In the case of a heavy landing, checks of the landing gear and the areas surrounding its attachment points would be made, for example, the engine firewall to which a nosewheel may be attached.

Air Density

Pressure and temperature are extremely important factors in the operation of airplanes, and affect both the performance of the airframe and the engine. The critical element is air density, which decreases as pressure falls and temperature rises. On a hot day, the air is less dense and the performance capabilities of the airplane will be reduced. Similarly, if the pressure is low (for example, on takeoff at an airport of high elevation), the air will be less dense, and airplane performance will suffer. Of the two factors, temperature has the most effect.

Figure 8-9
Performance reduces when air density reduces.

The *power* delivered by the engine depends on the weight of the fuel/air charge—the less dense the air, the lower the power-producing capability of the engine.

The *aerodynamic qualities* of the airframe depend on air density. If air density decreases, then aerodynamic qualities decrease, and the airplane will have to move faster through the air to create the same aerodynamic forces. High temperatures and low pressures (at altitude) cause a decrease in air density, as does high humidity (moisture content).

Factors Affecting Air Density

Altitude

The earth is surrounded by an atmosphere of gases held near the earth by gravity. The pressure that this atmosphere exerts at any point on the earth depends on the weight of the air pressing down from above. Since gravity compresses the molecules of air closest to the earth, the air density and therefore the pressure decreases with altitude. Since both engine and aerodynamic performance depend on air density, airplane performance is poorer at high altitudes.

Performance reduces as altitude increases.

Temperature

Heating of an air mass to a higher temperature causes it to expand and its density to decrease, resulting in a reduction in both engine and aerodynamic performance. Airplane performance is therefore poorer on hot days. Temperature generally decreases with altitude (the nominal standard rate is approximately 2°C/1,000 feet). Although cooling of an air mass increases its density, the effect of this, as altitude is gained, is not as great as that of the decreased pressure—the overall effect is still a decrease of density at higher altitudes.

Performance reduces as air temperature increases.

Humidity

Performance reduces as humidity increases.

The mixture of gases that we call *air* consists mainly of nitrogen (78%), oxygen (21%), and water vapor. The other 1% consists of argon, carbon dioxide and other gases.

The presence of water vapor in the air is called *humidity*. Because water molecules are very light, a high humidity will cause the air density to be slightly less, but no account of this effect is taken in performance charts. You should be aware, however, that high humidity will cause reduced performance that is *not* allowed for on the performance charts.

Just how much water a parcel of air can hold depends on its temperature—warm air is able to hold more water than cold air. If a parcel of air is holding 70% of its maximum capacity of water vapor, then it has a relative humidity of 70%. As it cools, its capacity to hold water vapor becomes less and, even though the actual amount of water does not change, the relative humidity increases.

Relative humidity is defined as the amount of water vapor present in a parcel of air compared to the maximum amount that it can support (when saturated) at the same temperature. High relative humidity means poorer airplane performance.

The Standard Atmosphere

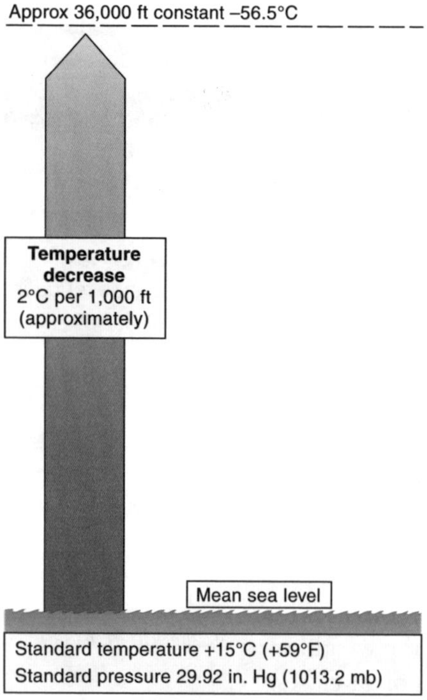

Figure 8-10
The standard atmosphere.

The continual changes in temperature and pressure which take place in the atmosphere make major difficulties for engineers and meteorologists, who need a fixed standard reference for calculations such as airplane performance, instrument calibration, and determination of cloud heights. As a result a *standard atmosphere* has been derived with specific values of temperatures and pressures. The important values for pilots are as follows:

- a surface temperature of 59°F (15°C) and a surface pressure of 29.92 inches of mercury (1,013.2 millibars—mb) at sea level; and
- a temperature lapse rate of approximately 2°C per 1,000 feet up to approximately 36,000 feet, where the temperature of -56.6°C is assumed to remain constant up to approximately 80,000 feet. (See also chapter 13.)

Note. It is still common practice to use °F for surface temperatures, but °C are used almost exclusively for temperatures aloft.

The standard atmosphere described above is essentially the same as that established by the International Civil Aviation Organization (ICAO). The ICAO Standard Atmosphere (always referred to as ISA) is in general use throughout the world, and you will find reference to both it and the standard atmosphere during your aviation career. For instance, you may be told that on a "standard day" a takeoff run of 2,000 feet is required. Similarly, you may be told that the temperature deviation is "ISA+10°C" or "10° warmer than standard."

Pressure Altitude

The standard mean sea level pressure is 29.92 in. Hg, and this decreases at about 1 inch of mercury per 1,000 feet increase in altitude (up to about 5,000 feet). At 2,000 feet, the standard pressure will have decreased by approximately 2 in. Hg, (from 29.92 in. Hg to 27.92 in. Hg). If the point where your airplane is located has a pressure of 27.92

in. Hg, then we say it has a pressure altitude of 2,000 feet, which means it is 2,000 feet above the 29.92 in. Hg pressure level.

Pressure altitude is the altitude in the standard atmosphere above the 29.92 in. Hg pressure level at which the pressure equals that of the point under consideration.

The easiest way to read pressure altitude in the cockpit is to set 29.92 in the pressure window—the altimeter will then indicate pressure altitude. Knowing the pressure altitude allows us to compare the airplane performance against a known standard.

Example 8-1

An airplane is flying at 5,000 feet with altimeter setting 30.34. How can you find the pressure altitude in flight? (See figure 8-11.)

Answer: The altimeter measures altitude above or below the particular pressure level set in the pressure window. To quickly estimate pressure altitude, simply wind 29.92 into the pressure window. Winding off inches, winds off altitude.

Pressure altitude can also be estimated (using a decrease of 1 in. Hg per 1,000 feet gain in altitude), or found using the pressure altitude conversion factors on a density altitude chart (see figure 8-15).

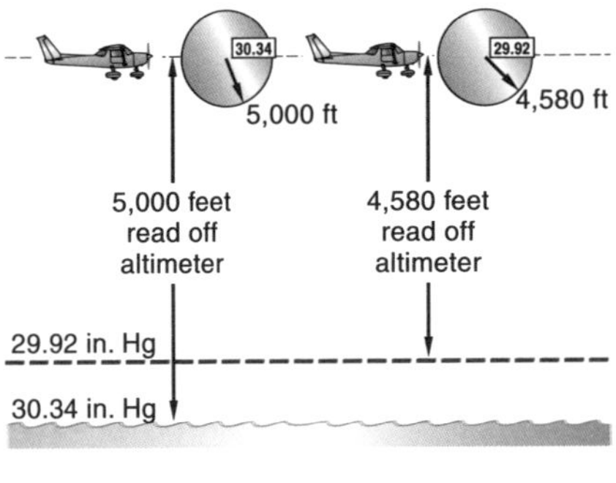

Figure 8-11 Example 8-1.

Example 8-2

If local altimeter setting is 29.42 in. Hg, find the pressure altitude of an airport with an elevation of 20 feet (figure 8-12).

Answer: Since pressure decreases with altitude, the standard pressure level of 29.92 in. Hg must be below sea level. To find pressure altitude (altitude above the standard 29.92 in. Hg level), we first find the altitude difference between MSL (with a setting of 29.42) and the 29.92 in. Hg level. The 0.5 in. Hg difference is equivalent to $(0.5 \times 1{,}000) = 500$ feet. The airport is a further 20 feet above this, therefore it is 520 feet above the 29.92 in. Hg pressure level. The pressure altitude is 520 feet.

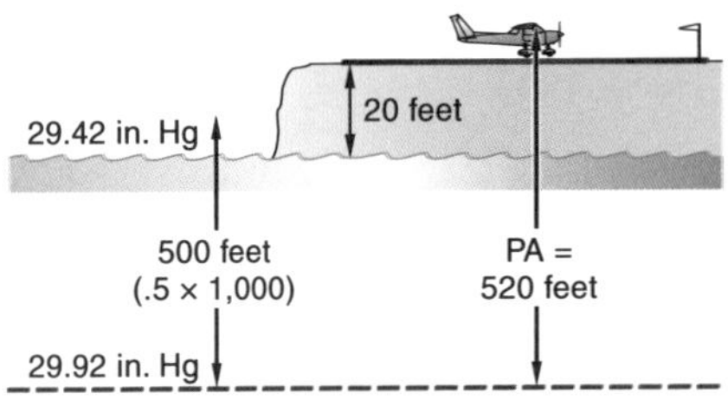

Figure 8-12 Example 8-2.

Example 8-3

The altimeter setting is 30.50 in. Hg at an airport with an elevation of 20 feet. Find the pressure altitude of the airport (figure 8-13).

Answer: The standard pressure level of 29.92 in. Hg must be above MSL on this particular day. The pressure difference of 0.58 in. Hg $(30.5 - 29.92)$ means that the altitude difference is about $(0.58 \times 1{,}000) = 580$ feet. From figure 8-13 we can see that the airport is 560 feet below the standard 29.92 in. Hg pressure level. Thus, its pressure altitude is -560 feet.

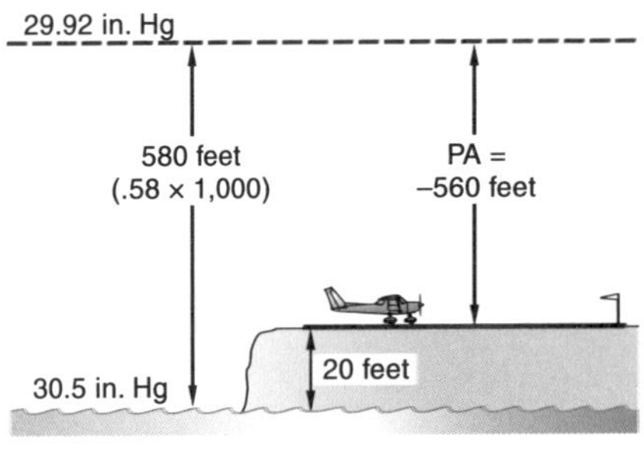

Figure 8-13 Example 8-3.

More Accurate Calculation of Pressure Altitude

As an alternative to estimating pressure altitude by using the approximation of 1 in. Hg per 1,000 feet change in altitude, the pressure altitude data given in the density altitude chart in figure 8-15 can be used. This will give a more accurate answer than the approximations used in examples 8-2 and 8-3 above.

In figure 8-15, to the right of the chart, there are two columns. The left-hand column shows the altimeter settings, and the right-hand column the pressure altitude conversion factor, which is the correction (in feet) which must be added or subtracted from the indicated altitude, which is based on the local altimeter setting to obtain pressure altitude. For example, with a local altimeter setting of 28.80 in. Hg, you would add 1,053 feet to the indicated altitude to obtain the pressure altitude. Similarly, if the altimeter setting was 30.40 in. Hg, you would have to subtract 440 feet.

For in-between altimeter settings that are not tabulated, such as 29.45 in. Hg, you will need to interpolate, or estimate, the in-between number. In this case, the correction number lies halfway between the 485 for 29.4 and the 392 for 29.5. The difference in altitude is (485 − 392) = 93, half of this is 47 which we can add to 392 (or subtract from 485) to give +439 feet correction.

Example 8-4

Using the same data as in example 8-3, find the pressure altitude using figure 8-15.

From the chart, the pressure altitude conversion factor for an altimeter setting of 30.50 in. Hg is -531 feet. Field elevation is 20 feet, so pressure altitude is: 20 − 531 = -511 feet (compared with -560 feet using the approximation of 1 in. Hg = 1,000 feet).

Temperature

The higher the temperature the lower the air density—and the poorer the airplane performance. Standard (ISA) sea level temperature is +15°C and it falls at approximately 2°C per 1,000 feet gain in altitude:

- at 1,000 feet in the ISA, the temperature will have fallen to +13°C;
- at 2,000 feet in the ISA, the temperature will have fallen to +11°C; and
- at 3,000 feet in the ISA, the temperature will have fallen to +9°C.

To Calculate ISA (Standard) Temperature

ISA temperature in °C at any altitude = 15 − (2 × number of thousands of feet).

Example 8-5

$$\text{ISA at 9,000 feet} = 15 - (2 \times 9) = 15 - 18 = -3°\text{C}$$

Example 8-6

$$\text{ISA at 13,500 feet} = 15 - (2 \times 13.5) = 15 - 27 = -12°\text{C}$$

Note. Temperature is usually expressed in °C. To allow for occasions when you have to use a performance chart that is still using °F, standard MSL temperature is +59°F (the equivalent of +15°C) and the temperature lapse rate is approximately 3.6°F/1,000 feet.

Example 8-7

$$\text{ISA in °F at 9,000 feet} = 59 - (3.6 \times 9) = 59 - 32.4 = -26.6°\text{C}$$

Fahrenheit and Celsius Conversions

There are two main temperature scales used in aviation at present. If you are flying in foreign countries, it may be necessary to convert from one to the other. The Fahrenheit and Celsius scales both use the boiling point and freezing point of water as set temperatures—the difference between them is 180°F or 100°C as shown in figure 8-14.

Each 1°C is larger than 1°F by a ratio of $^{180}/_{100}$ or $^{9}/_{5}$. The starting point of both scales is the freezing point of water, 0°C or 32°F. These can be combined into one relationship connecting °F and °C:

$$F = \tfrac{9}{5}C + 32 \qquad C = \tfrac{5}{9}(F - 32)$$

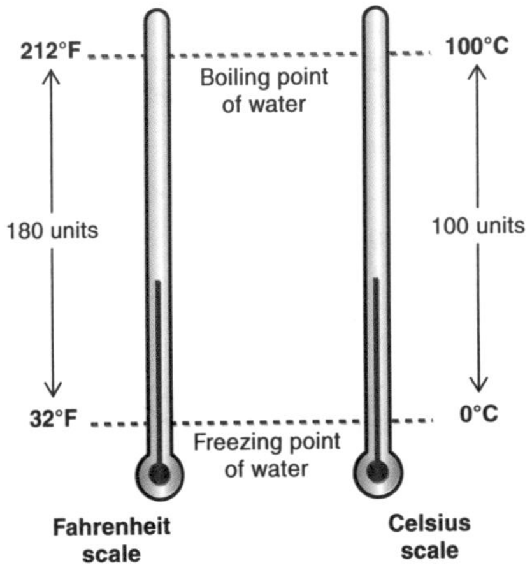

Figure 8-14
Comparing the Fahrenheit and Celsius temperature scales.

Example 8-8

Convert 20°C to °F: °F = ($^{9}/_{5}$ × 20°C) + 32 = 36 + 32 = 68°F.

To reverse the relationship, simply subtract 32 from both sides and then multiply both sides by $^{5}/_{9}$ to obtain °C = $^{5}/_{9}$ (°F – 32). For example, to convert 68°F to °C: °C = $^{5}/_{9}$ (68°F – 32) = $^{5}/_{9}$ × 36 = 20°C.

Note. In practice, the easiest method of converting temperatures is to use the flight computer (see chapter 24).

To Calculate Deviations from ISA (Standard) Temperature

Temperature at an altitude is often expressed as an ISA deviation, which is the difference between the standard, or ISA, temperature at that altitude and the actual temperature at that altitude. For instance, at 9,000 feet the ISA temperature is -3°C. If the actual temperature at 9,000 feet today happens to be -8°C, the actual temperature is 5°C colder than the ISA temperature, which is described as ISA – 5.

Example 8-9

Express an actual temperature of +16°C at a pressure altitude of 3,000 feet as an ISA deviation.

ISA at 3,000 feet = 15 – (2 × 3) = 15 – 6 = +9°C

16°C at 3,000 feet is 7° warmer than the ISA temperature +9°C = ISA+7

Density Altitude

Airplane and engine performance depend on air density. It is impracticable for you to have the equipment necessary to measure air density, so we use two pieces of information already available in the cockpit and on which air density depends—pressure altitude and temperature.

By considering pressure altitude and temperature, we are really considering density. Most performance charts allow us to enter with pressure altitude and temperature, therefore there is usually no need to calculate density directly.

The term density altitude is simply one means of describing air density—it is the altitude in the standard atmosphere that has an identical density as the air we are considering. If temperature or pressure are nonstandard (which is almost always the case), then density altitude will differ from the airplane's true altitude MSL:

- the lower the pressure, the higher the density altitude; and
- the higher the temperature, the higher the density altitude.

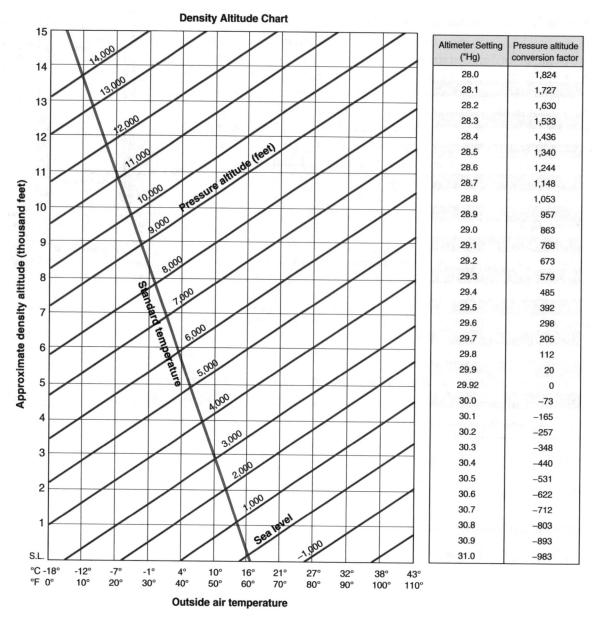

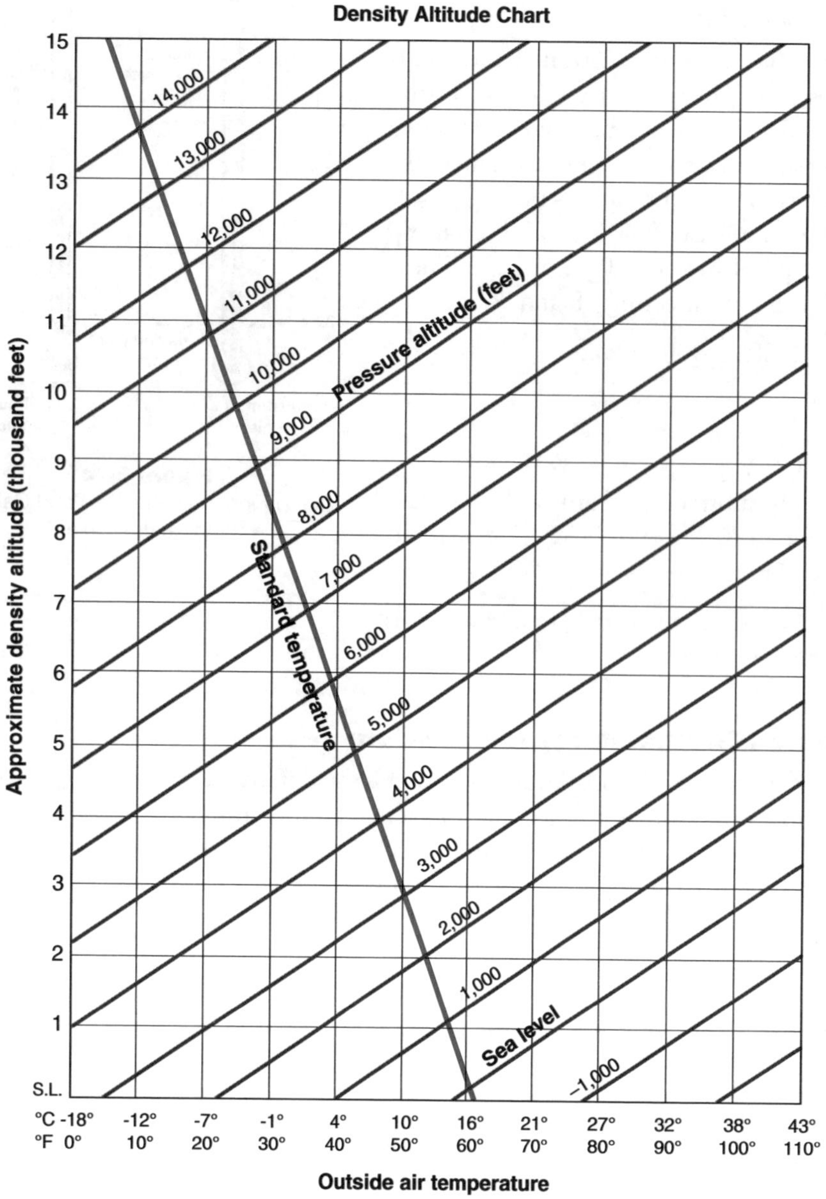

Altimeter Setting ("Hg)	Pressure altitude conversion factor
28.0	1,824
28.1	1,727
28.2	1,630
28.3	1,533
28.4	1,436
28.5	1,340
28.6	1,244
28.7	1,148
28.8	1,053
28.9	957
29.0	863
29.1	768
29.2	673
29.3	579
29.4	485
29.5	392
29.6	298
29.7	205
29.8	112
29.9	20
29.92	0
30.0	–73
30.1	–165
30.2	–257
30.3	–348
30.4	–440
30.5	–531
30.6	–622
30.7	–712
30.8	–803
30.9	–893
31.0	–983

Figure 8-15 Density altitude chart.

To Calculate Density Altitude

The main reason for calculating density altitude is to determine airplane performance—and you may allow for its effect unknowingly if you enter performance charts or graphs with pressure altitude and temperature. Sometimes however, you need to calculate density altitude specifically, and this is done in two steps.

1. Determine pressure altitude as discussed previously, by:
  - **a.** setting 29.92 in pressure window and reading altimeter;
  - **b.** by using the 1 in. Hg/1,000 feet approximation; or
  - **c.** by using the tabulated pressure altitude conversion factor.

2. Adjust pressure altitude for temperature by:
   a. mental arithmetic (each deviation of 1°C above the temperature in the standard atmosphere, or ISA, will increase density altitude by approximately 120 feet, or 70 feet for each 1°F deviation); or
   b. graph (see density altitude chart in figure 8-15); or
   c. light computer (see chapter 24).

Example 8-10

Using the density altitude chart in figure 8-15. What is the density altitude if the altimeter reads 5,000 feet with 28.30 in. Hg in the pressure window, and the true outside air temperature is 90°F?

1. Pressure altitude = 5,000 + 1,533 (from table) = 6,533 feet.
2. Enter graph at bottom with 90°F and proceed up to your estimate of the 6,533 feet (say 6,500 feet) sloping pressure altitude line, and then read across horizontally from this intersection to obtain the answer: 10,000 feet density altitude.

Indicated Airspeed and Performance

Indicated airspeed is not affected by changes in density.

As density altitude increases TAS increases for a constant IAS.

We stated earlier that indicated airspeed (shown on the airspeed indicator in the cockpit) is related to dynamic pressure, which is dependent on air density and velocity ($\frac{1}{2}\rho V^2$).

Therefore, to create the same aerodynamic forces that are required, for instance, to achieve takeoff, you need to fly the airplane at the same indicated airspeed regardless of density altitude. The consequence of this is that if air density ρ is low, then V (true airspeed) must be greater. Therefore when air density is low, to achieve the required indicated airspeed, the true speed of the airplane through the air must be greater. This leads to longer takeoff and landing distances at high elevation airports and/or under high temperature conditions.

Review 8

Airplane Performance Factors

Airworthiness

1. Can a POH be approved by the FAA as an approved Flight Manual for an airplane?
2. Refer to your own POH. Which section(s) of the POH include(s) the following?
   - **a.** Maximum takeoff weight for the airplane.
   - **b.** Emergency procedures, such as for engine failure immediately after takeoff.
   - **c.** Takeoff and landing performance charts or tables.
   - **d.** Descriptions of the airplane fuel system, or any other system.
   - **e.** A particular area navigation (RNAV) system, which is an option that does not come with the basic airplane.
3. If the operational category of an airplane is listed as "utility," it means that this airplane could be operated in which maneuvers?
4. Who is primarily responsible for maintaining an aircraft in an airworthy condition?

Airframe Limitations

5. At speeds in excess of the maneuvering speed (V_A), the pilot should avoid abrupt or large control movements. Why?
6. Define the following:
   - **a.** maximum landing weight;
   - **b.** never-exceed speed; and
   - **c.** turbulence-penetration speed.
7. What is V_{NE} represented on the airspeed indicator by?

Refer to figure 8-16 for questions 8 and 9.

8. What does the horizontal dashed line from point C to point E represent?
9. The vertical line from point D to point G is represented on the airspeed indicator by the maximum speed limit of which arc?

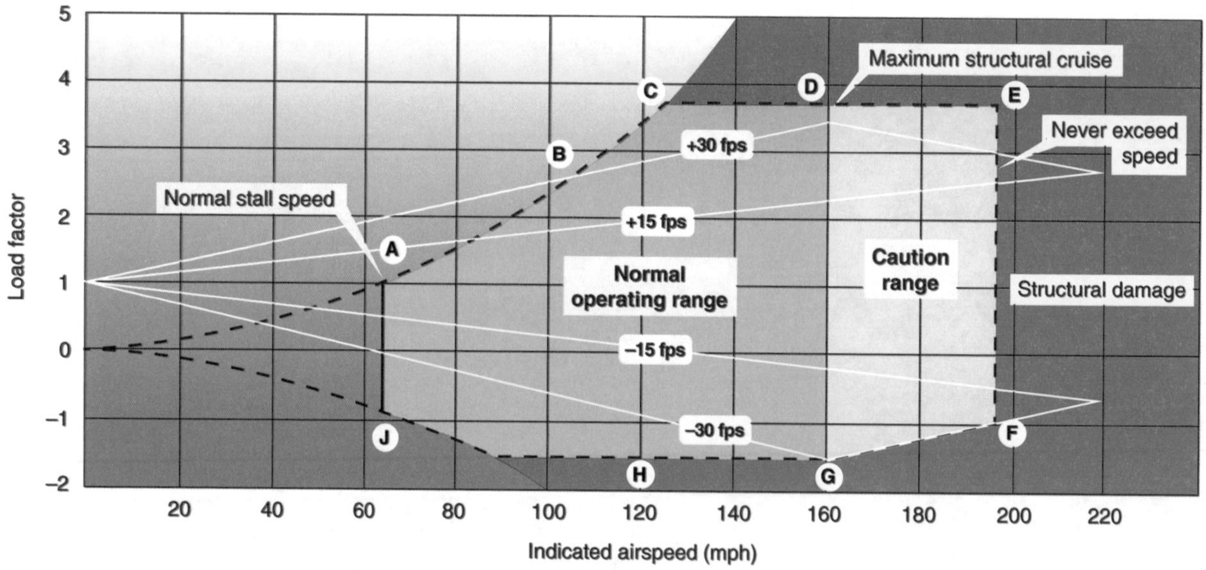

Figure 8-16 Velocity versus G-loads or V-G diagram.

Air Density

10. Performance tables and graphs are based on what sort of altitude?
11. Air density may be accounted for by considering which two things?
12. Does a water molecule weigh more than the average "air molecule"?
13. In less dense air at high pressure altitudes, is more air processed by the propeller than at sea level?
14. Does less dense air at high pressure altitudes increase propeller efficiency?
15. Describe a quick method of determining pressure altitude when you are in the cockpit.
16. What are the standard values for mean sea level temperature and pressure?
17. Which of the following would increase the density altitude at a given airfield?
    a. An increase in barometric pressure.
    b. An increase in ambient temperature.
    c. A decrease in relative humidity.
18. Estimate the approximate pressure altitude of an airport with elevation 3,000 feet MSL if the altimeter setting is 28.90 in. Hg.
19. Which combination of atmospheric conditions will reduce airplane takeoff and climb performance?
    a. Low temperature, low relative humidity, and low density altitude.
    b. High temperature, low relative humidity, and low density altitude.
    c. High temperature, high relative humidity, and high density altitude.
20. Express +9°C at 7,000 feet as an ISA deviation.

Refer to figure 8-15 (page 202) for questions 21 to 29.

21. What is the pressure altitude at an airport with elevation 3,563 feet MSL if the altimeter setting is 29.96 in. Hg?
22. The indicated altitude is 1,380 feet with an altimeter setting of 28.22 in. Hg. What is the pressure altitude?
23. What is the pressure altitude at an airport with elevation 3,000 feet MSL if the altimeter setting is 29.60 in. Hg?
24. From the density altitude chart, what is the density altitude if the pressure altitude is 5,000 feet and the temperature is:
    a. 42°F (i.e. standard temperature at 5,000 feet).
    b. 50°F.
    c. 4°C.
    d. 21°C.
25. What is the effect of a temperature increase from -1°C to +16°C on the density altitude if the pressure altitude remains at 5,000 feet?
26. What is the effect on the density altitude of a temperature decrease and a pressure altitude decrease from +4°C and 3,000 feet to -7°C and 2,500 feet?
27. Determine the density altitude for the following conditions:

Altimeter setting	29.25 in. Hg
Runway temperature	+27°C
Airport elevation	5,250 feet

28. What is the effect of a temperature increase from 25 to 50°F on the density altitude if the pressure altitude remains at 5,000 feet.
    a. 1,200-foot increase.
    b. 1,400-foot increase.
    c. 1,650-foot increase.
29. What is the effect of a temperature decrease and a pressure altitude increase on the density altitude from 90°F and 1,250 feet pressure altitude to 60°F and 1,750 feet pressure altitude.
    a. 500-foot increase.
    b. 1,300-foot decrease.
    c. 1,300-foot increase.

For questions 30 to 32, calculate the density altitude and cross-check your answers using figure 8-15 (page 202) and your flight computer.

30. Determine the density altitude given:

Indicated altitude	5,000 feet
Pressure setting	28.30 in. Hg
Temperature	ISA +10°C

31. Calculate density altitude given:

Pressure altitude	15,000 feet
True air temperature	-35°C

32. Calculate density altitude given:

Pressure altitude	15,000 feet
True air temperature	–5°C

Answers are given on page 690.

Takeoff and Landing Performance 9

Takeoff Performance

Figure 9-1
Takeoff is a critical phase.

Takeoff and landing are perhaps two of the most labor intensive tasks involved in piloting an airplane, and they start long before the wheels leave the ground.

Takeoffs involve much more than smooth piloting skills; they involve careful planning and preparation. A very smooth takeoff is of little value if the airplane, once airborne, is faced with obstacles impossible to avoid. The takeoff performance of the airplane needs to be matched to the runway and the surrounding obstacles prior to actually taking off.

Definitions

The *ground roll* is the distance an airplane will travel on the takeoff run, from a standing start until it leaves the ground. The *takeoff distance* is the distance established on a paved, level, dry runway for the airplane to clear a 50-foot obstacle from a standing start, at maximum takeoff power. The *takeoff safety speed* (TOSS), which provides a 20% margin over the stall speed, should be achieved by the 50-foot point.

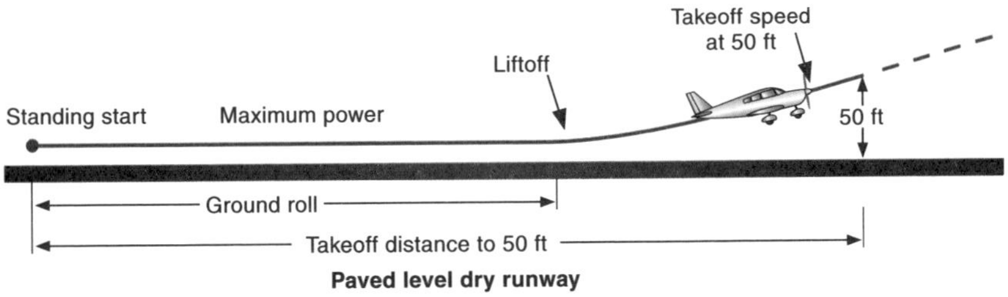

Figure 9-2 Takeoff distance.

Factors Affecting Takeoff Performance

Weight

A heavier airplane results in a greater takeoff distance.

A heavier airplane will require an increased ground run and takeoff distance to clear a 50-foot obstacle because of the slower airplane acceleration and increased takeoff speed. In addition, the greater weight on the wheels during the ground run increases the friction, further reducing acceleration and increasing the distance to reach a set takeoff speed.

Increased Takeoff Speed

A heavier airplane will have a higher stall speed. Because the liftoff speed is related to the stall speed, any increase in stall speed also means an increase in liftoff speed. After liftoff, the greater weight will also reduce the airplane's climb performance (rate of climb and angle of climb) and so the distance required for the initial climb to 50 feet above the runway will be greater. This climb is still part of the takeoff distance, hence there is a corresponding increase in the takeoff distance extracted from the performance chart.

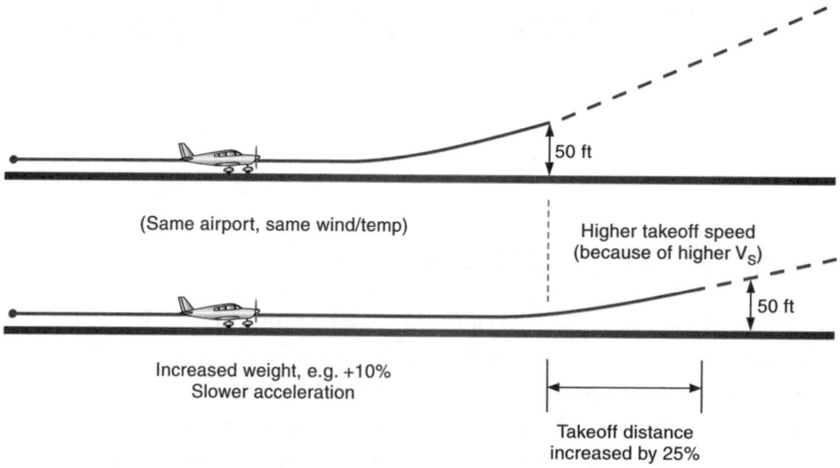

Figure 9-3 Increased weight decreases takeoff performance.

The overall effect of a 10% increase in weight may be to increase the takeoff distance by 25%.

Air Density

One cause of an increase in density altitude is a decrease in air density. This results in a longer ground run and takeoff distance to clear a 50-foot obstacle. A decrease in air density can be caused by a number of factors.

A high airport elevation results in decreased airplane and engine performance.

A *lower air pressure* will decrease the density and this can occur as a result of a different ground-level ambient pressure or as a result of a higher airport elevation. This effect is covered by pressure altitude, which relates the actual pressure experienced by the airplane to a level in the standard atmosphere that has an identical pressure. High-elevation airports lead to longer takeoff distances.

High temperatures decrease airplane and engine performance.

A *higher air temperature* will also decrease the air density, reducing airplane and engine performance.

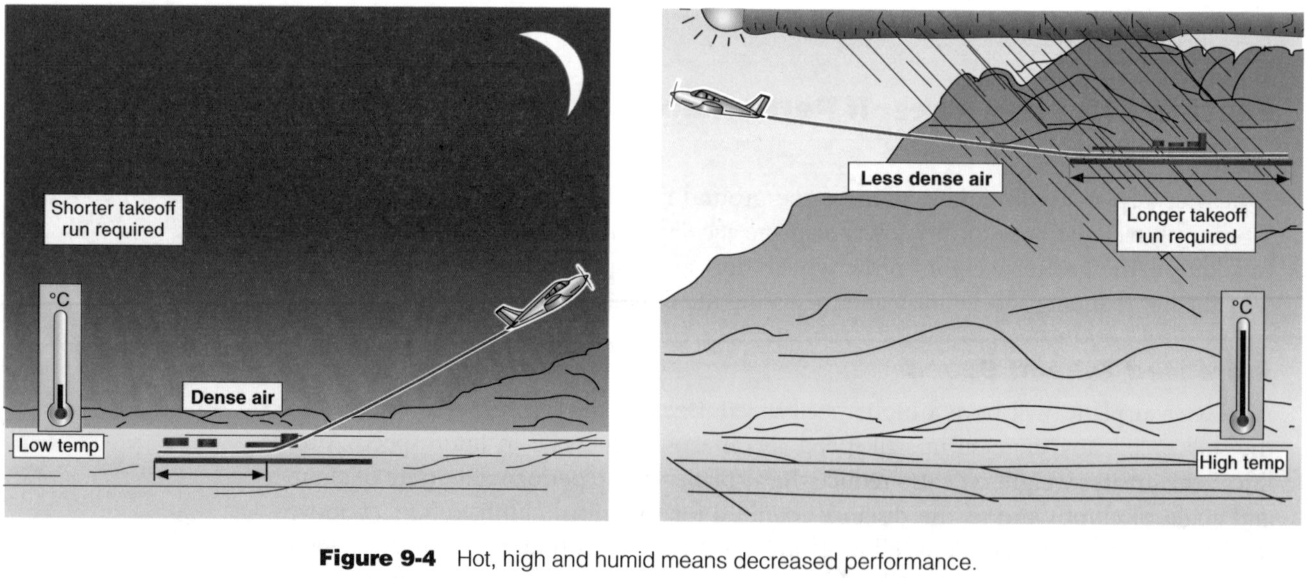

Figure 9-4 Hot, high and humid means decreased performance.

If the air density decreases, the engine–propeller combination will not produce as much power and so the takeoff distance will increase. In addition to the power-producing performance of the engine–propeller decreasing, the aerodynamic performance of the airplane will also decrease as air density becomes less.

To produce the required lift force (L = Lifting ability $\frac{1}{2}\rho V^2 \times S$), a decrease in air density (ρ) means that for the same required indicated airspeed, an increase in the velocity (true airspeed, V) is required and a longer takeoff distance will result. Not only does a lower air density affect the aerodynamic performance of the airframe (controlled by $\frac{1}{2}\rho V^2$), it also decreases the weight of the fuel/air mixture in the engine cylinders, causing a decrease in engine power.

Headwinds and Tailwinds

A headwind reduces the takeoff distance.

A headwind reduces the ground roll and takeoff distance to clear a 50-foot obstacle. For flight, the airplane requires a certain speed relative to the air in which it is flying. An airplane stopped at the end of the runway and facing into a 20-knot headwind is already 20 knots closer to the liftoff indicated airspeed, compared with the no-wind situation.

In a *headwind* takeoff the airplane therefore reaches liftoff indicated airspeed at a lower groundspeed, and so less ground run is required. Once in the air, the angle or gradient relative to the ground is increased by a headwind, making for better obstacle clearance.

In a *tailwind*, the effect is to lengthen the ground run and to flatten the climb-out. Tailwinds in excess of 5 knots are normally not considered suitable for takeoff. Obviously, a takeoff into the wind shows better airmanship.

Crosswinds

The airplane must not be taken off in a *crosswind* that exceeds the maximum crosswind limit for the airplane. Directional control is a problem. The aerodynamic force from the

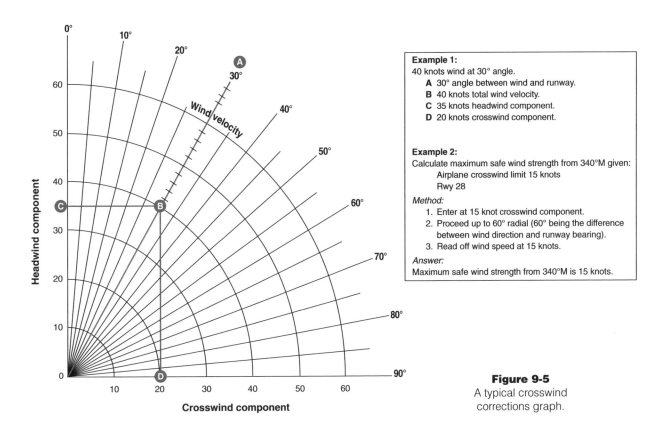

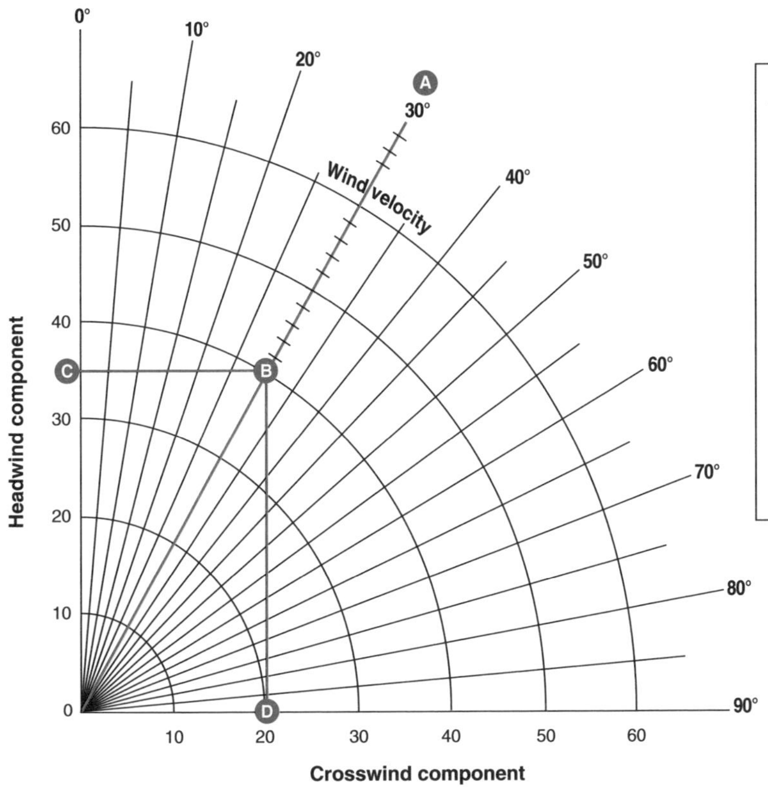

Example 1:
40 knots wind at 30° angle.
- **A** 30° angle between wind and runway.
- **B** 40 knots total wind velocity.
- **C** 35 knots headwind component.
- **D** 20 knots crosswind component.

Example 2:
Calculate maximum safe wind strength from 340°M given:
Airplane crosswind limit 15 knots
Rwy 28

Method:
1. Enter at 15 knot crosswind component.
2. Proceed up to 60° radial (60° being the difference between wind direction and runway bearing).
3. Read off wind speed at 15 knots.

Answer:
Maximum safe wind strength from 340°M is 15 knots.

Figure 9-5
A typical crosswind corrections graph.

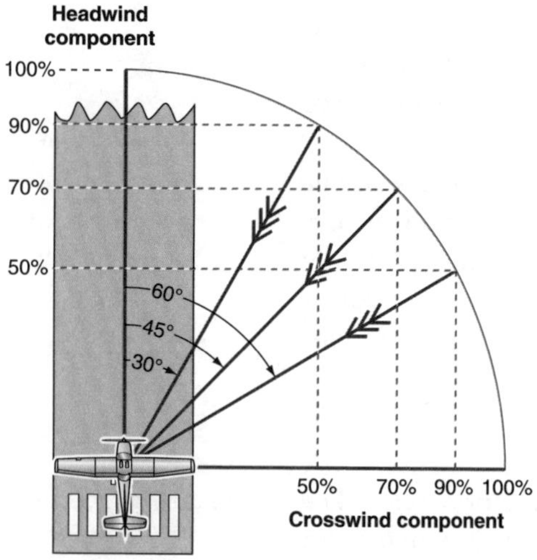

Figure 9-6 Estimating crosswind and headwind components.

rudder is potentially not sufficient to overcome the effect of the keel surfaces wanting to weathercock the airplane into the wind. Lateral control is an additional problem, because the crosswind will generally try to lift into the upwind wing, which then has to be held down with aileron.

In calculating the strength of a crosswind component we will consider a 10-knot wind blowing from various directions. The approximate values of headwind and crosswind are:

- if the wind is 30° off the runway heading, then the crosswind component is ½ the wind strength;
- if the wind is 45° off the runway heading, then the crosswind component is ⅔ the wind strength;
- if the wind is 60° off the runway heading, then the crosswind component is 9/10 the wind strength; and
- if the wind is 90° off the runway heading, then it is all crosswind.

Note. Flight computers have the facility for calculating crosswind (and head/tail wind components), see chapter 24. Sometimes a *crosswind corrections graph* is provided in the Pilot's Operating Handbook.

Runway Surface

The length of the ground roll, at any given weight, will vary in response to the friction caused by the runway surface during the takeoff roll. A dry hard-paved runway causes the least amount of friction, and so this type of surface may serve as a datum, or reference surface, on takeoff performance charts. A runway with a short dry-grass surface, based on firm subsoil, has only a marginally higher retarding effect.

Poor runway surfaces increase takeoff ground run.

Soft ground or long grass (especially if wet) will reduce the acceleration, and this will result in a greater takeoff distance by as much as 25%. Gravel is considered to have the same effect as a short dry-grass surface. Pools of water on any type of runway surface can significantly retard the acceleration, and takeoff under such conditions requires very careful consideration. Soft, wet ground or a soft, sandy surface might make acceleration to the liftoff speed impossible, no matter what runway length is available.

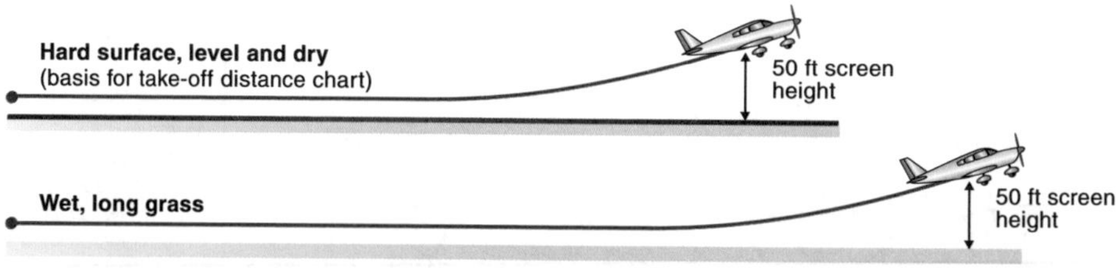

Figure 9-7 Poor surfaces may increase the ground run.

Flaps

The use of small flap settings decreases the ground run.

The use of small flap settings decreases the length of the ground run. Flaps have the effect of lowering the stall speed, which reduces the liftoff speed. Provided that the flap setting used for takeoff is small (so that the drag is not greatly increased), the slower liftoff speed after a shorter ground run may enable a shorter runway to be used.

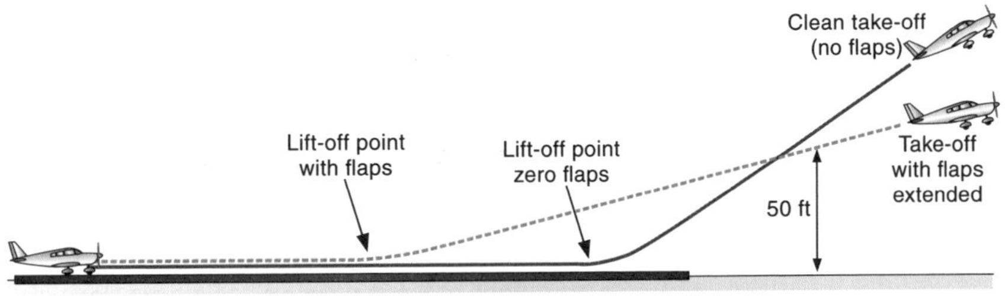

Figure 9-8 Use of takeoff flaps reduces the ground run.

If the ground surface is rough, using a small flap setting for takeoff will allow you to get off the ground sooner.

Notice we have used the words "ground run" rather than "takeoff distance to clear a 50-foot obstacle." While the ground run will be less when small flap settings are used, the takeoff distance to clear a 50-foot obstacle may not be reduced significantly. This is because flaps, as well as increasing lift, increase drag, thus reducing the excess thrust and thereby the angle of climb. This is the main reason for only using small flap settings for takeoff. A larger flap setting, even though it might reduce the stall speed, would greatly increase the aerodynamic drag during the ground run, causing a slower acceleration and then, once airborne, would significantly degrade the climb-performance.

We cannot generalize too much in our statements here, as the precise effect of the use of flaps on the takeoff of a particular airplane depends on many things, including the flap setting, the engine–propeller combination and the airspeed flown. You must become familiar with your own airplane type.

Runway Slope

Takeoff distance is calculated for a level runway, and some takeoff charts allow for the effect of runway slope. A downslope of 2-in-100 or 2% down will allow the airplane to accelerate faster and so will decrease the ground roll. An upslope of 2-in-100 or 2% up will make it more difficult for the airplane to accelerate and so the ground roll will be greater. A 2% upslope may increase the takeoff distance to 50 feet by approximately 20%.

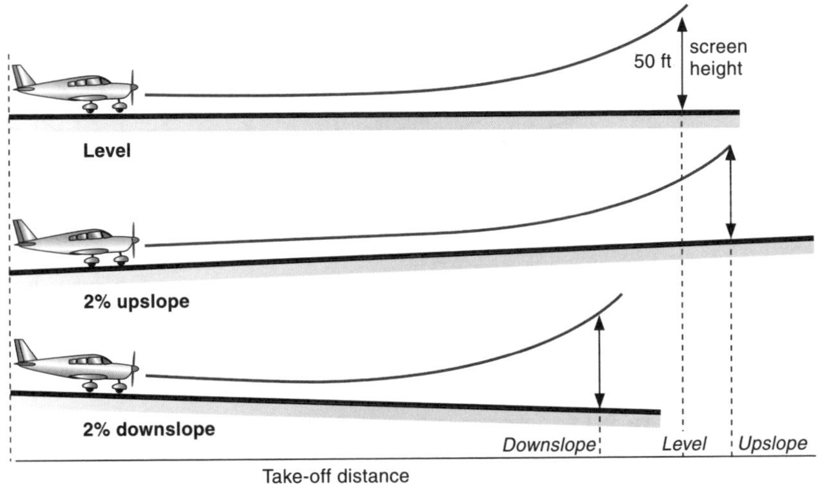

Figure 9-9 An upward-sloping runway will increase the ground roll and takeoff distance to 50 feet.

Note. Runway slope is calculated using the elevations at either end. Therefore a runway with downslope may have a hump (involving upslope) somewhere along its length.

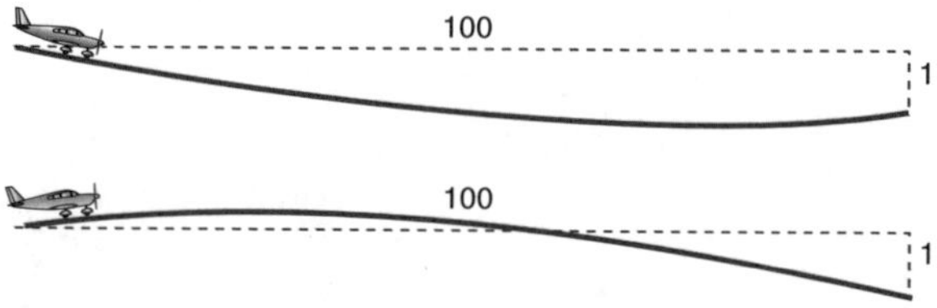

Figure 9-10
Each of these runways has a downslope of 1%.

The Takeoff Distance Graph

Many manufacturers present performance data in the form of graphs and tables. When using performance graphs, it is important to be certain to comply with the associated conditions stated in the graph or make the recommended adjustments to the performance based on not complying with the associated conditions (if applicable). The most common is the graph, and an example is shown in figure 9-11. This performance graph has been prepared for a full-throttle takeoff with flaps up. Using this graph you can apply corrections for:

- air density (using temperature, and pressure altitude);
- airplane takeoff weight; and
- headwind or tailwind component (note that the tailwind must not exceed 10 knots).

Example:

OAT	15°C (59°F)
Pressure altitude	5,650 ft
Takeoff weight	2,950 lbs
Headwind comp.	9.0 kts
Ground roll	1,375 ft
Total distance over 50 ft obstacle	2,300 ft
Takeoff speed at:	
Lift-off	66 kts (76 mph)
50 ft	72 kts (83 mph)

Weight	Takeoff speed			
	Lift-off		50 ft	
	kts	MPH	kts	MPH
2,950	66	76	72	83
2,800	64	74	70	81
2,600	63	72	68	78
2,400	61	70	66	76
2,200	58	67	63	73

Associated conditions:

Power	Full throttle 2,600 rpm
Mixture	Lean to appropriate fuel pressure
Flaps	Up
Landing gear	Retract after positive climb established
Cowl flaps	Open

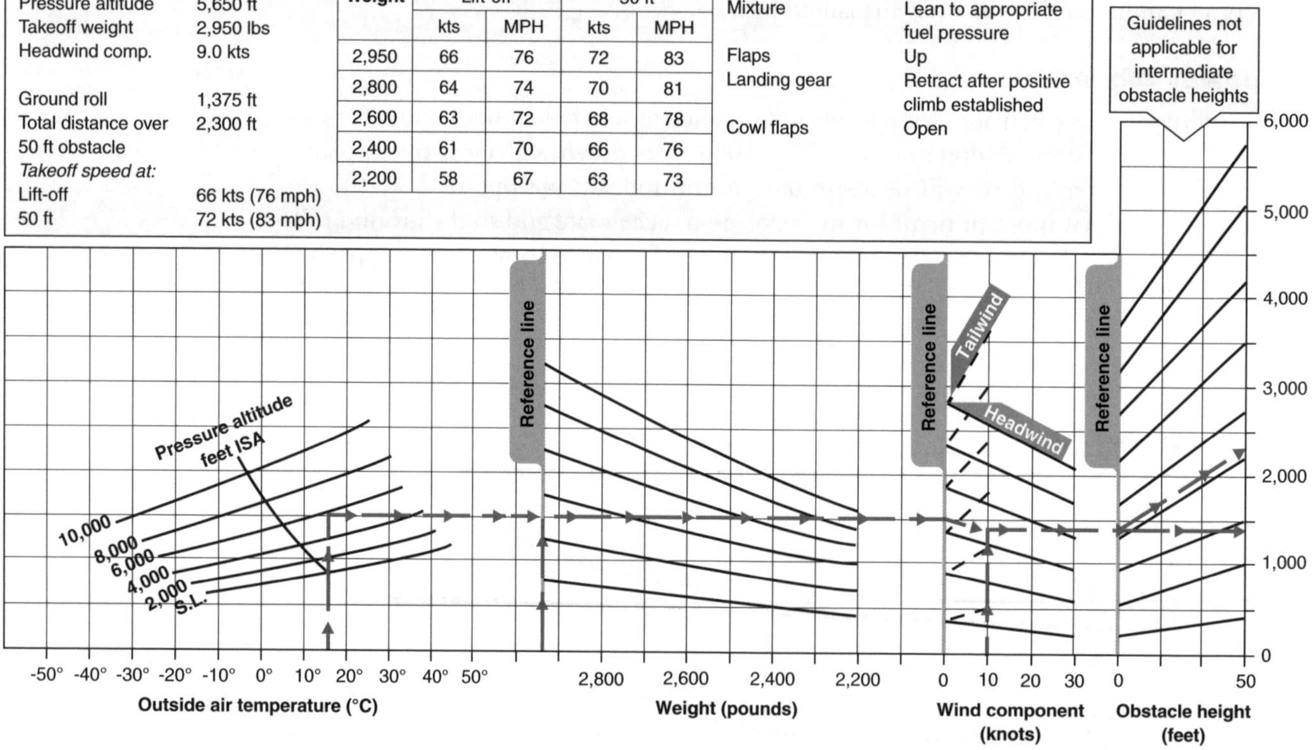

Figure 9-11 Takeoff distance graph.

A takeoff performance graph allows you to determine:

- the takeoff distance from the starting point to a point 50 feet above the runway;
- the length of the ground roll prior to liftoff; and
- the liftoff speed and takeoff speed at 50 feet.

1. The air density correction is made in the first (left) section of the graph where you enter at the bottom with *temperature*, and move up to the appropriate *pressure altitude* line. Then move horizontally to the right until you meet the reference line. The higher the pressure altitude and/or temperature, the longer the takeoff distance.

   Note. The line sloping upward to the left intersects the pressure altitude lines at standard temperature for those altitudes, eliminating the need for you to calculate the numerical figure for temperature if it is given to you as standard.

2. The *airplane weight correction* is made in the next section of the graph. If the airplane is at maximum takeoff weight of 2,950 pounds (represented by the reference line), then you continue straight across horizontally; if not, you should follow the guidelines down to the right until you intersect a line drawn upward from the weight, from which point you should move horizontally right to the next reference line.
3. The *wind correction* section of the graph comes next. This allows you to correct for a headwind, which will shorten the takeoff distance, or a tailwind, which will increase the takeoff distance. Follow the appropriate guidelines (up for a tailwind, down for a headwind) until you meet the wind component line drawn up from the bottom. Then move horizontally across to the final reference line. This last section of the graph allows you to determine:
   a. the *ground roll* (from starting point to just on liftoff at 0 feet above the runway) shown at the reference line; and
   b. the *takeoff distance* to 50 feet from the starting point on the runway, by following the guidelines up to the right to the 50 feet line.
4. The *liftoff speed* and the *takeoff speed* at 50 feet are found in a small table above the graph. At 2,800 pounds takeoff weight, for instance, you would lift the wheels off at 64 knots and fly away from the ground at a rate that allows you to reach 70 knots by 50 feet above the runway.

   Note. It is possible to use this graph somewhat in reverse if you have a short runway and wish to determine the maximum takeoff weight permitted. This would be known as the *performance-limited takeoff weight*. You would enter the graph from the left and the right with the known information, following the same pattern of lines until the left line and right line intersect in the weight section. Then drop a vertical line to find the maximum permissible weight.

Different Presentations of Performance Data

CPL

You must become familiar with the various methods of presentation of data. Refer to the performance documents for the airplane you are flying.

Although the takeoff and landing charts in the Commercial Pilot Knowledge Test are not identical to those used in the Private Pilot Knowledge Test, the same principles apply. The commercial review at the end of the chapter includes questions on the commercial knowledge takeoff and landing charts to test your understanding and to increase your confidence.

End CPL

Landing Performance

The total *landing distance* is the distance established from a point where the airplane is 50 feet over the runway threshold (assumed to be a paved, level dry runway) to the point where the airplane reaches a full stop, assuming a steady, full flaps approach, with power off at 50 feet and maximum braking once the wheels are on the ground.

Note. This is the certification technique—you are not required to carry out all landings and stops exactly like this in practice.

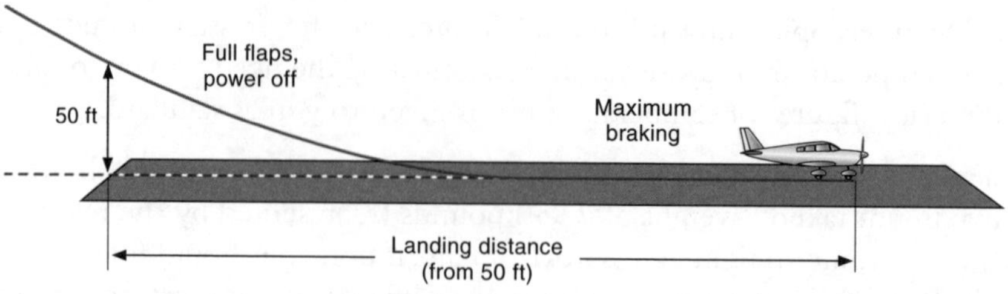

Figure 9-12 Landing distance.

Factors Affecting Landing Performance

Weight

A heavier airplane will need a greater landing distance.

A heavier airplane will need a greater ground roll and total landing distance. A heavier weight has a number of effects:

- the stall speed is increased, so the approach speed must be greater; and
- the higher approach speed results in the airplane possessing greater kinetic energy ($\frac{1}{2}\rho V^2$) which has to be absorbed by the brakes, increasing the length of the landing run. (There will, however, be a slight increase in the retarding friction force because of the extra weight on the wheels.)

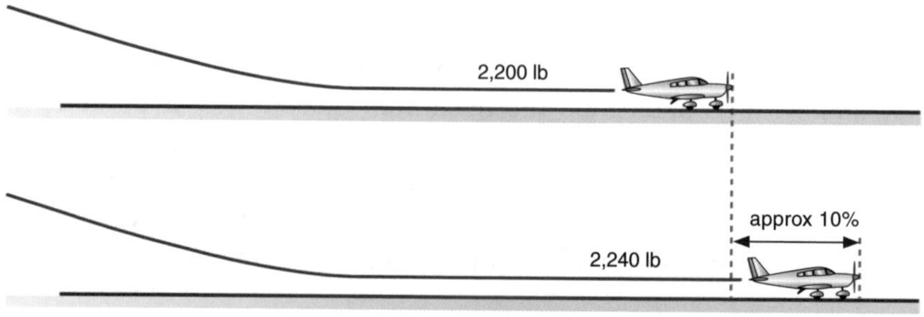

Figure 9-13 A 10% increase in weight requires a 10% increase in landing distance (approximately).

Air Density

An increased density altitude results in a longer landing distance.

An increased density altitude results in a longer landing distance. Low ambient pressure, high elevation and high ambient temperatures decrease the air density (ρ), giving a higher density altitude.

A decreased air density (ρ) means an increased V (TAS) is needed to provide the same lift force. Even though you see the same indicated airspeed ($\frac{1}{2}\rho V^2$) in the cockpit, the true airspeed is higher in air of lower density.

At high density altitudes the true airspeed will be greater than for lower density altitudes, and the touchdown groundspeed will be higher. Therefore the amount of kinetic energy to be dissipated in the ground roll is greater—hence a longer ground run and total landing distance is required.

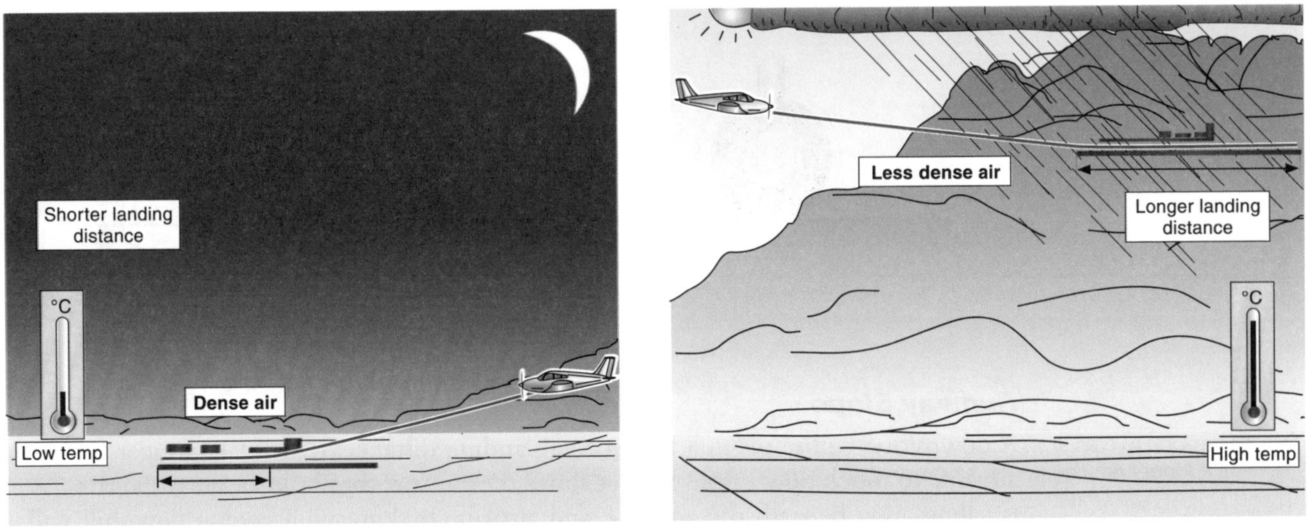

Figure 9-14 High temperatures and high altitudes result in a longer landing distance.

The Effect of Wind

A headwind reduces the landing distance because the groundspeed is reduced by the headwind for the same true airspeed (V). A tailwind means that the groundspeed will exceed the true airspeed, and so the touchdown speed relative to the ground is higher and a longer landing distance will be required.

A headwind reduces the ground run and landing distance.

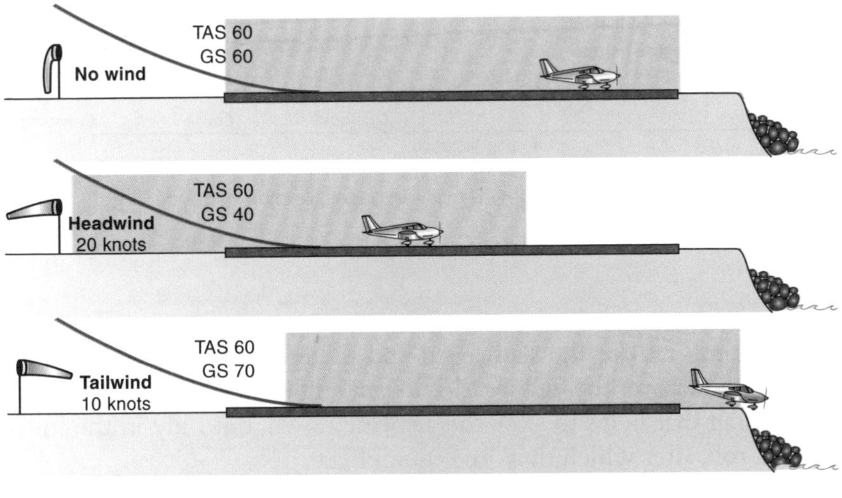

Figure 9-15 Headwind reduces landing distance.

Runway Surface

Figure 9-16 Consider runway surface.

Smooth, wet, or loose runway surfaces will not allow good braking to occur and so the landing distance required will be longer. On a wet surface, hydroplaning may occur, which will greatly increase the stopping distance. Conversely a runway with long grass has increased friction and will reduce the landing distance.

Hydroplaning is the phenomenon of a tire skating along on a thin film of water and not rotating, even though it is free to do so. Wheel braking therefore has no effect. Friction forces are practically zero.

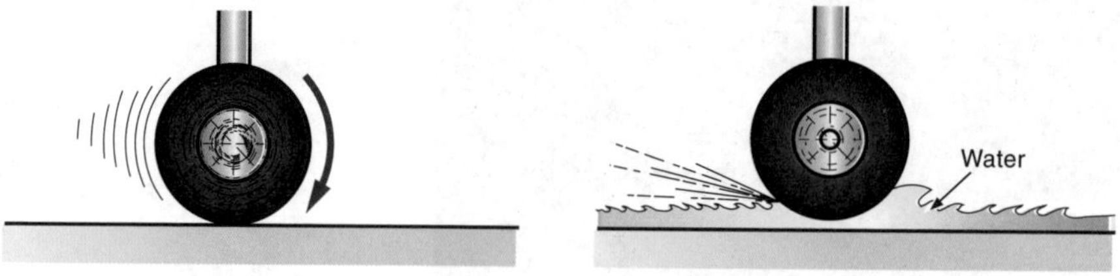

Figure 9-17 Hydroplaning.

Runway Slope

A downslope will result in a longer landing distance.

A downslope will result in a longer total landing distance. It will take longer for the airplane to touch down from 50 feet above the runway threshold, because the runway is falling away beneath the airplane, and airplane braking while going downhill will not be as effective as on a level or upward sloping runway.

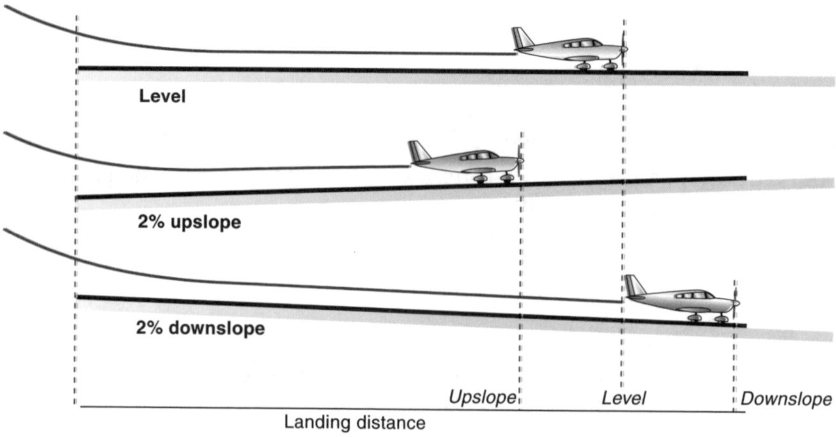

Figure 9-18 Downslope increases landing distance.

Flaps

Increased flap settings decrease the landing distance.

Higher flap settings reduce the stall speed and therefore the approach speed, which provides a 30% buffer over the stall speed, is lower. High flap settings also give additional aerodynamic drag that helps to slow the airplane down, but only in the initial stages of the landing roll, after which they lose their effect.

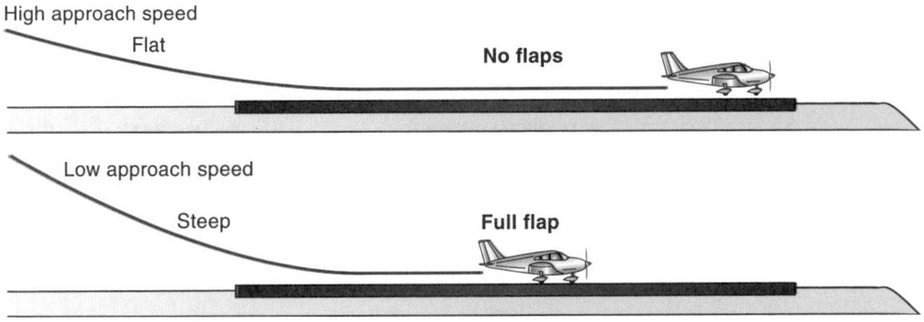

Figure 9-19 Increased flaps—slower and steeper.

Fast Approach Speeds

The landing performance charts are based on *specified approach speeds*. If you approach for a landing at a speed higher than that specified, the landing distance will exceed that predicted by the chart. This is because of the greater kinetic energy of the airplane and the tendency of the airplane to float at the round-out because of ground effect (see page 224).

The Landing Distance Graph

Many manufacturers present performance data in the form of a graph, rather than a table of figures. The landing performance graph in figure 9-20 is an example.

This graph has been prepared for a flaps-down landing, on a paved, level, dry surface, followed by maximum braking. However in normal practice it is not good airmanship to use maximum braking on every landing, since uncomfortable stops for the passengers and excessive brake wear will occur. Only use maximum braking when necessary on short runways. The landing performance graph allows you to apply corrections for:

- air density (using temperature and pressure altitude);
- airplane landing weight; and
- headwind or tailwind component (tailwind must not exceed 10 knots).

The landing performance graph allows you to determine:

- total landing distance from an obstacle 50 feet above runway threshold;
- ground roll; and
- approach speed.

First the air density correction is made in the left-hand section of the graph where you enter at the bottom with *temperature* and move up to the appropriate *pressure altitude* line. Then mark a horizontal line to the reference line. The higher the pressure altitude and/or temperature, the longer the final distances.

The *airplane weight correction* is then made by starting at the point on the reference line where the air density line intersected it, and moving parallel to the guidelines that slope down to the right until you intersect the airplane weight line drawn up from the bottom. At this point mark a horizontal line across to the next reference line. The lower the weight, the shorter the final distances.

Note that for maximum takeoff weight 2,950 pounds, which is represented by the first reference line, you would not need to follow the guidelines down but just keep moving across horizontally to the second reference line.

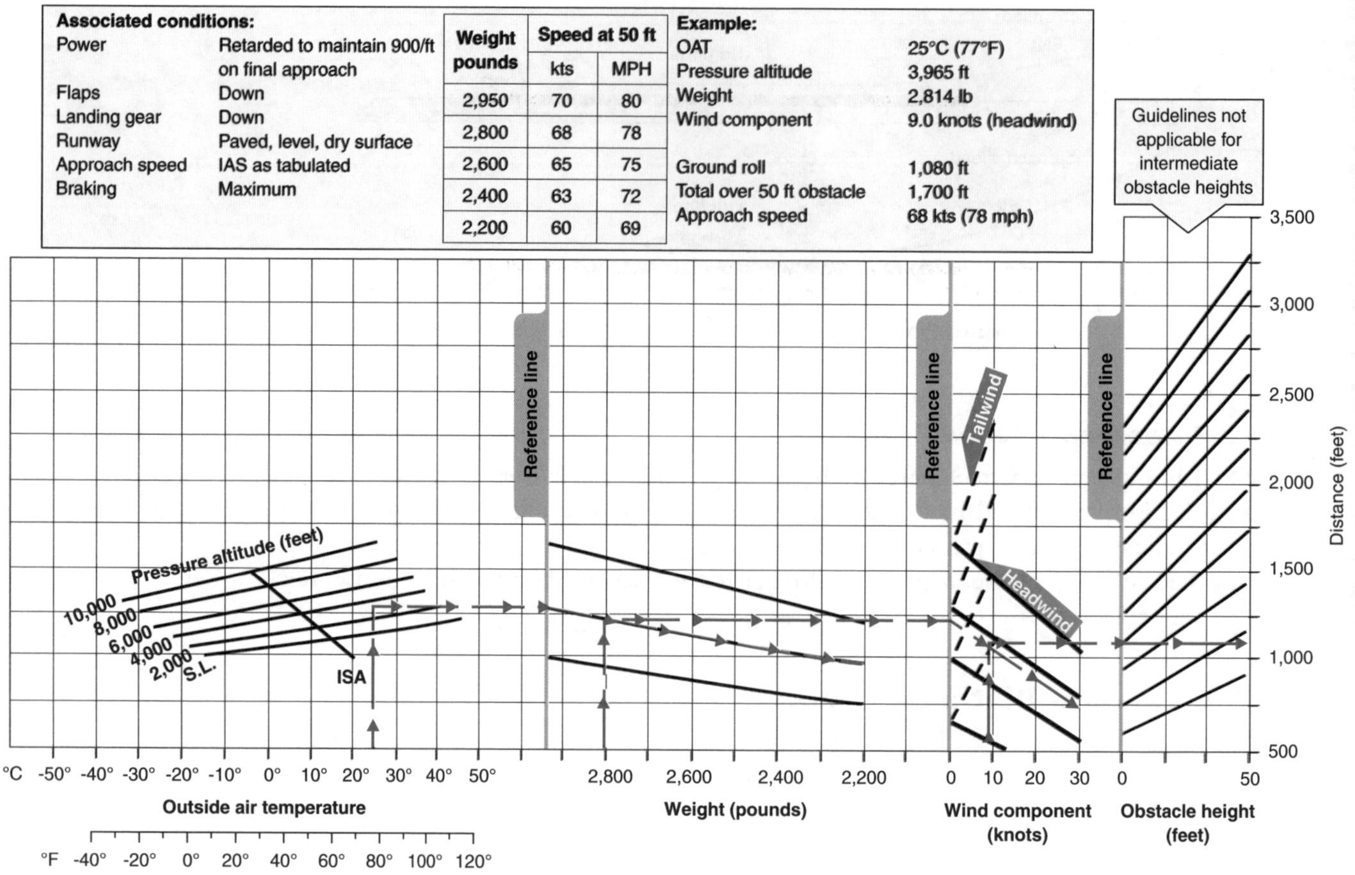

Figure 9-20 Landing distance graph.

The *wind correction* part of the graph allows you to correct for either a headwind (which will shorten the landing distance) or a tailwind (which will increase the landing distance). Follow the appropriate guidelines (up for a tailwind, down for a headwind) until you meet the wind component line drawn up from the bottom. Then move horizontally across to the final reference line.

This last section of the graph allows you to determine:

a. the *ground roll*, where your line intersects the reference line (which is marked as 0 feet); and

b. the total *landing distance from 50 feet*, by following the guidelines up to the right (marked 50 feet) to give a significantly greater distance, since much of the landing from 50 feet consists of air distance before the wheels touch down.

The *approach speed* is shown in a small table above the graph. At 2,800 pounds for instance, you would approach with flaps down at 68 knots.

The graph can also be used in reverse if you have a *short runway* and wish to determine the maximum landing weight permitted. The steps are:

1. as before, enter from the left with temperature and pressure altitude, then from the reference line move down the guidelines to mark a so far unknown weight;

2. enter from the far right with runway length. Following the original pattern, move to the left down the guidelines to the reference line. Next move horizontally across to intersect with the appropriate headwind or tailwind line, and follow the guidelines up to the reference line. Then move horizontally across to the left until you intersect the line you marked in during (1); and

3. from this intersection point, drop a line vertically to give you the maximum permissible weight, known as the *performance-limited landing weight.*

The Landing Distance Table

Some manufacturers present performance data in the form of a table, rather than a graph. The landing performance table in figure 9-21 is an example. This table has been prepared for a 40° flaps landing, power off, on a dry and level hard-surface runway with zero wind, at specific pressure altitudes at standard temperatures. Both the total distance to land from 50 feet over the runway threshold, and the ground roll, are published. For instance, at pressure altitude 2,500 feet and standard temperature 50°F, the landing distance from 50 feet is 1,135 feet and the ground roll is 470 feet.

When the pressure altitude is between the values given in the table, you will need to interpolate to find the landing distance and ground roll.

For example, the pressure altitude 6,250 feet is halfway between the published pressure altitudes 5,000 feet and 7,500 feet, so the distances will also be halfway between the published figures. To find the "landing distance from 50 feet", take the 5,000 feet pressure altitude figure of 1,195 feet, and to this add one-half of the *difference* between it and the figure for 7,500 feet pressure altitude (1,255 − 1,195 = 60 feet, ½ of 60 = 30), to give an answer of *1,225 feet* (1,195 + 30). Ground roll is 495 + ½ of (520 − 495) = 495 + 12.5 = 507.5, say *508 feet.*

Once the ground roll and landing distance to clear a 50-foot obstacle have been found for a given pressure altitude, apply the following corrections, if applicable:

- headwind component;
- high temperatures (60°F above standard); and
- a dry grass runway (instead of a hard surface).

Landing Distance

Flaps lowered to 40°—Power off
Hard Surface Runway—Zero wind

Gross weight (pounds)	Approach speed, IAS (mph)	At sea level & 59°F		At 2,500 feet & 50°F		At 5,000 feet & 41°F		At 7,500 feet & 32°F	
		Ground roll	Total to clear 50 feet OBS	Ground roll	Total to clear 50 feet OBS	Ground roll	Total to clear 50 feet OBS	Ground roll	Total to clear 50 feet OBS
1,600	60	445	1,075	470	1,135	495	1,195	520	1,255

Notes:
1. Decrease the distances shown by 10% for each 4 knots of headwind.
2. Increase the distance by 10% for each 60°F temperature increase above standard.
3. For operation on a dry, grass runway, increase distance (both "ground roll" and "total to clear 50 feet obstacle") by 20% of the "total to clear 50 feet obstacle" figure.

Figure 9-21 Landing distance table.

Headwind Component Correction

For each 4 knots of headwind, you may reduce the distances by 10%. You can calculate this 10% and then subtract, but a faster method is simply to take 90% of the distance, by multiplying it by 0.9. For a headwind of 12 knots (3 × 4 knots), you may reduce the distance by 30%, or multiply it by 0.7. If the airport is at sea level then the corrected distance would be 1,075 × 0.7 = 752.5, say *753 feet.*

High Temperature Correction

For extremely high temperatures (at least 60°F above the standard temperature for that altitude) you should increase the distance by 10%. If the OAT at 5,000 feet was 105°F (more than 60°F above standard at 6,250 feet altitude), the corrected distance would now be 1,195 × 1.1 = 1,315 feet (increasing by 10% is the same as multiplying by 1.1).

Dry Grass Runway Correction

On this surface both the ground roll and landing distance must be increased by 20% of the total distance to land from 50 feet. The logic for this is that the retarding effect of the grass does not occur before touchdown, hence the same increase for both distances.

At 2,500 feet for example, the correction for a dry grass surface is 20% of 1,135 feet = 227 feet. Therefore, the corrected landing distance from 50 feet = 1,135 + 227 = 1,362 feet, and the corrected ground roll is 470 + 227 = 697 feet.

Wake Turbulence

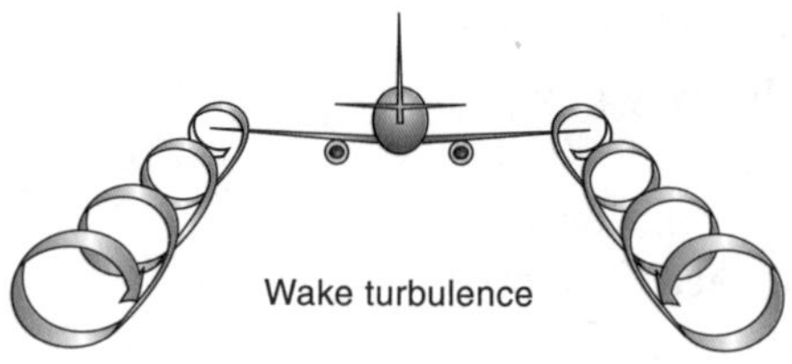

Figure 9-22
Wake turbulence from a large, slow-flying airliner.

As a wing produces lift, the higher static pressure area beneath the wing causes an airflow around the wingtip to the lower pressure area above. The greater the difference in pressure, the greater the flow around the wingtips. (We suggest that you reread the section on induced drag (page 20) to refresh your memory.) At the high angles of attack necessary to produce the required lift force at low speeds, very large and strong trailing vortices are formed. High angles of attack are required when an airplane is heavy and flying slowly (particularly if flaps are not extended). As a large and heavy airplane is rotated for takeoff or flared for landing, the angle of attack is also large. The trailing wingtip vortices formed at these high angles of attack can be strong enough to rapidly roll a following airplane if it flies into them. This hazardous trail of wingtip vortices behind an airplane is known as *wake turbulence.*

The main danger from wake turbulence is loss of control because of induced roll.

The wake turbulence behind a Boeing 747 can significantly affect a 737 and cause a lighter airplane to become uncontrollable. The induced rolling motion may exceed the rolling capability of the airplane affected, making it impossible for the pilot to hold the wings level. The rolling effect will be greatest when the affected airplane is aligned with the flight path of the airplane generating the vortices.

To avoid wake turbulence accidents and incidents, Air Traffic Control may delay the operation of light airplanes on runways behind heavy jets for up to five minutes to allow the vortices to drift away and dissipate.

Every pilot should have an awareness of wake turbulence because the Air Traffic Control procedures may occasionally provide insufficient separation from the wingtip vortices behind another airplane. Remember that pilots have the ultimate responsibility for the safety of their airplanes—so learn to visualize the formation and movement of invisible wingtip vortices. Recent research also suggests wake turbulence (from

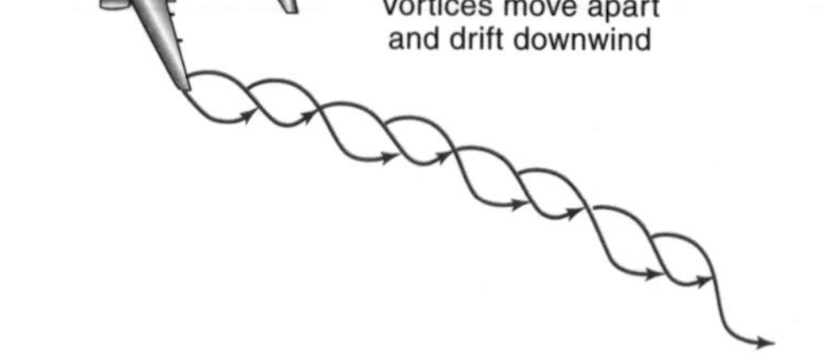

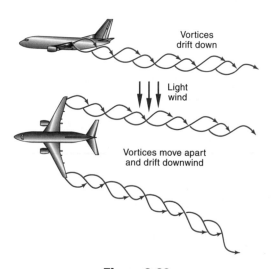

Figure 9-23
Wingtip vortices slowly lose height, move apart and drift downwind.

about 500 feet down) has the ability to descend, strike the ground, and then "bounce" back up to about 250 feet (or more) above the surface. This is important because it is also drifting and can drift across the landing approach path of another unrelated runway, causing problems for pilots who think they are being safe by going to another runway.

Wingtip vortices tend to *lose height* slowly (typically at approximately 500 fpm), slowly *move apart* and drift *downwind*. To be able to avoid these invisible danger areas, you must visualize the movement of the vortices and take steps to avoid them.

Helicopters also produce wake turbulence. The helicopter blades act as a wing to produce lift and, as the helicopter proceeds, a trail of wingtip vortices will be left behind, just the same as for a fixed-wing aircraft. The heavier and slower the helicopter, the stronger the wake turbulence behind it.

Avoiding Wake Turbulence

The main aim of wake-turbulence avoidance is to avoid passing through it at all. This is accomplished by flying *above* and *upwind* of the flight path of the aircraft producing wake turbulence.

Avoid wake turbulence by flying above and upwind of the path of other aircraft.

Takeoff

When taking off behind a large airplane which has itself just taken off, commence your takeoff at the end of the runway so that you will become airborne in an area well before where the heavy airplane rotated, or to where its vortices may have drifted with the wind. If in doubt, delay your takeoff. Once airborne, maneuver to avoid the vortices in flight by turning away from where you think the wake turbulence is.

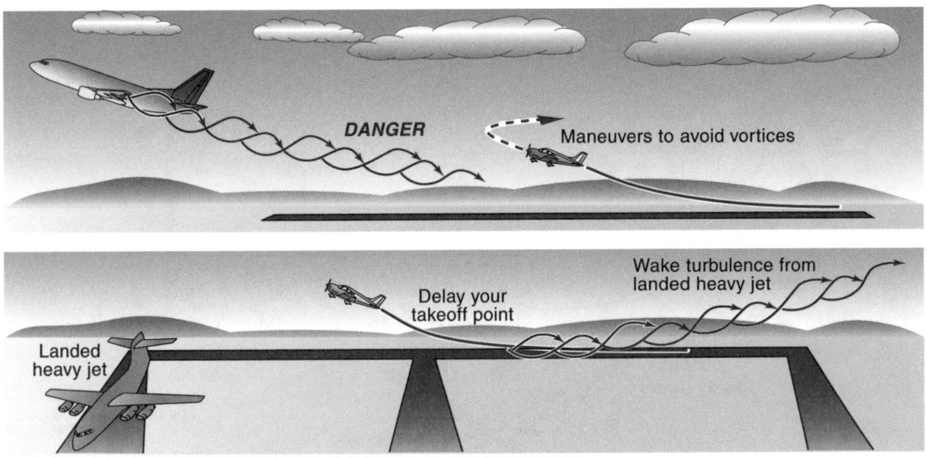

Figure 9-24 Avoid wake turbulence on your takeoff.

When taking off after a heavy airplane has landed, plan to become airborne well past the point where it flared and landed.

If a heavy airplane has taken off on a different runway and you expect to be airborne prior to the intersection of the runways, check to ensure that the heavy airplane was still on the ground and hasn't rotated until well past the intersection, before you commence your takeoff. This is because unless an airplane is flying (or rotated for takeoff) and therefore producing lift, it will not be producing wake turbulence.

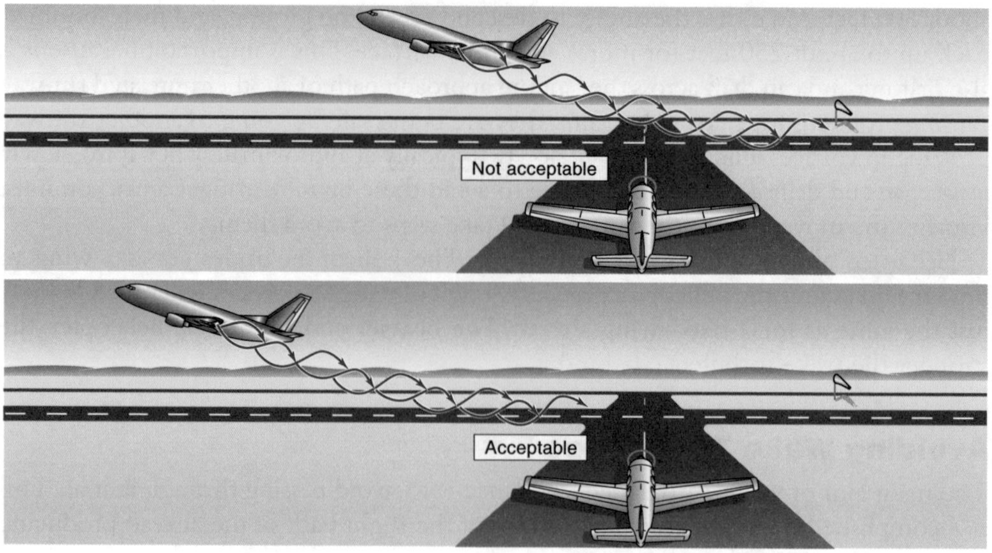

Figure 9-25 Awareness of wake turbulence for your takeoff.

In the Traffic Pattern

Avoid flying below and behind large airplanes. Fly a few hundred feet above them, a thousand feet below them or upwind of them. Calm days, where there is no turbulence to break up the vortices, are potentially the most dangerous.

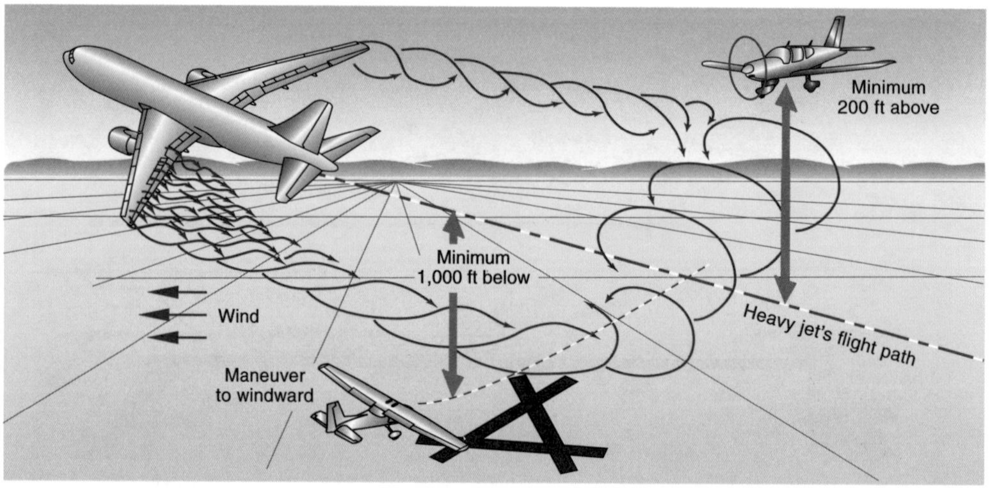

Figure 9-26 Avoidance of wake turbulence in the traffic pattern area.

Figure 9-27 Beware wake turbulence.

Approach to Land

When following a preceding landing airplane, fly above the approach path of the heavy airplane and land well beyond his touchdown point. This is usually possible in a light airplane landing on a long runway where heavy airplanes are landing. Be very cautious in light, quartering tailwinds, which may drift the vortices of the preceding airplane forward into your touchdown zone.

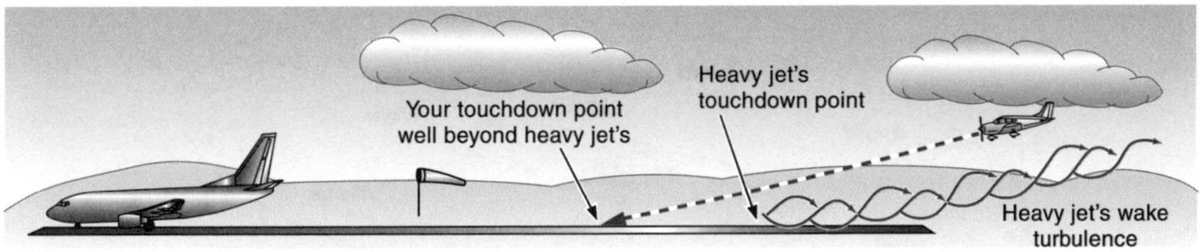

Figure 9-28 Avoidance of wake turbulence on approach.

If a preceding heavy airplane has discontinued its approach and gone around, its turbulent wake will be a hazard to a following airplane. You must consider changing your flight path in these circumstances.

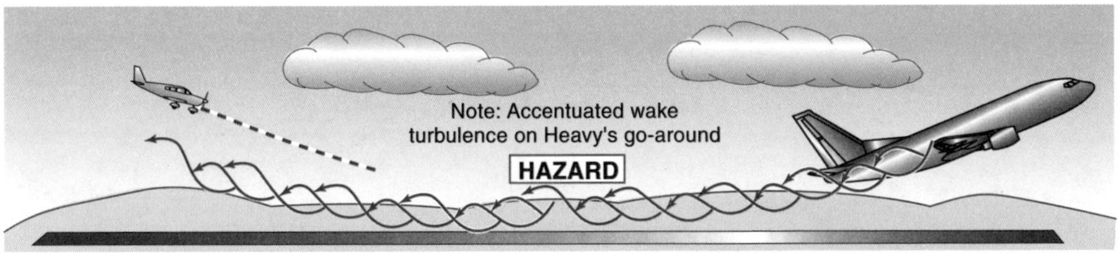

Figure 9-29 Making an approach behind a heavy airplane that has gone around.

Jet Blast

Do not confuse wake turbulence (wingtip vortices, see figure 9-22) with jet blast, which is the high velocity air exhausted from a jet engine. Jet blast can be dangerous to a light airplane taxiing on the ground behind a jet, so always position your airplane when taxiing or when stopped to avoid any potential jet blast.

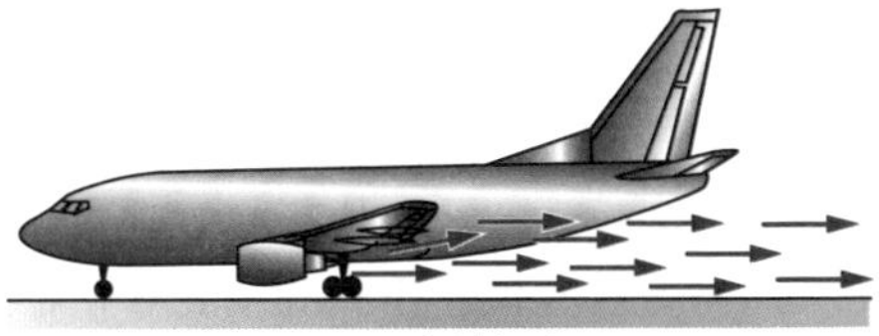

Figure 9-30 Jet blast.

Helicopter Rotor Downwash

Helicopters produce wake turbulence. The helicopter blades act as a wing to produce lift, and as the helicopter proceeds, a trail of wingtip vortices will be left behind, just the same as for a fixed-wing aircraft. The heavier and slower the helicopter, the stronger the wake turbulence behind it. A helicopter hovering near the runway is a hazard to small aircraft.

Rotor downwash from a hovering or taxiing helicopter can be hazardous up to a radius of approximately three times the rotor diameter.

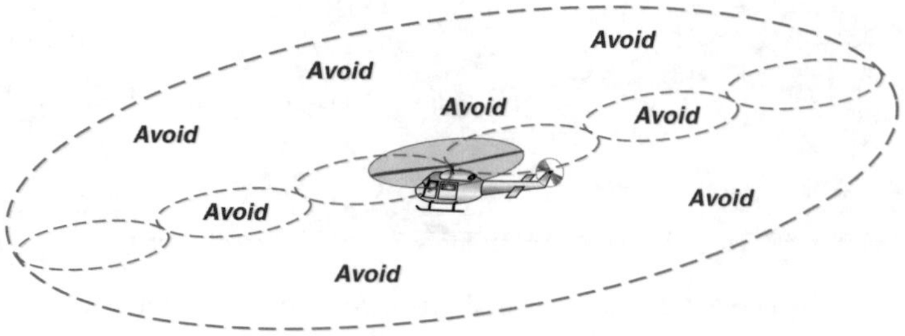

Figure 9-31 Beware rotorwash.

Small aircraft need to exercise care when behind helicopters that are departing, landing, or are in forward flight.

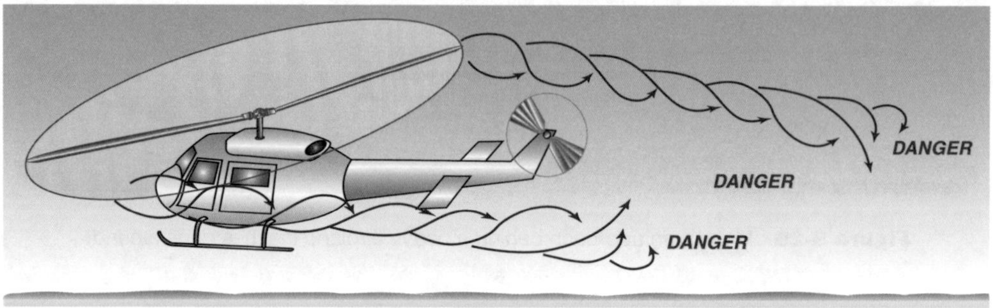

Figure 9-32 Rotorwash.

Ground Effect

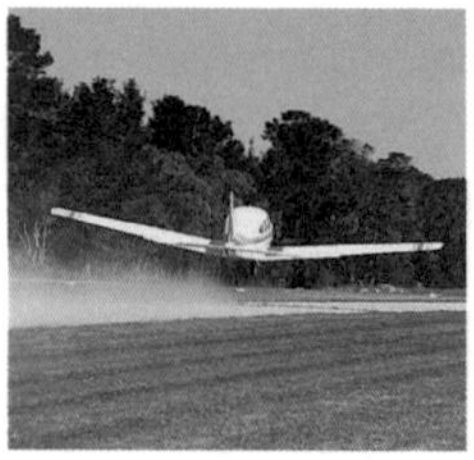

Figure 9-33 Ground effect.

An airplane's flight characteristics change when it is very close to the ground or any other surface, because:

- it can fly at a slower speed than when it is at altitude; and
- it can fly at the same speed using less thrust than when it is at altitude.

This increased performance of an airplane flying just above a surface is known as *ground effect*. Ground effect is greatest when the aircraft is just airborne and least when the aircraft is at an altitude above the ground approximately one wingspan's distance. In part one, we considered the airplane to be flying well away from the ground. There was no restriction to the downwash of the airflow behind the wings, nor to the upwash ahead of the wings. There was also no restriction to the formation of wingtip vortices.

When the wing is just above the ground, the ground modifies the downwash and the angle is reduced, thus reducing the effect on the local average relative wind. In other words, the relative wind angle about the wing will be closer to the remote free stream. This keeps drag at a minimum and the wingtip vortices at a minimum.

As the aircraft gradually climbs and increases its altitude above the ground, the downwash angle steepens and increases the induced drag, all without an aircraft attitude change. When at one wingspan's height above the ground, ground effect ceases to affect the downwash or wingtip vortices and induced drag is at its maximum.

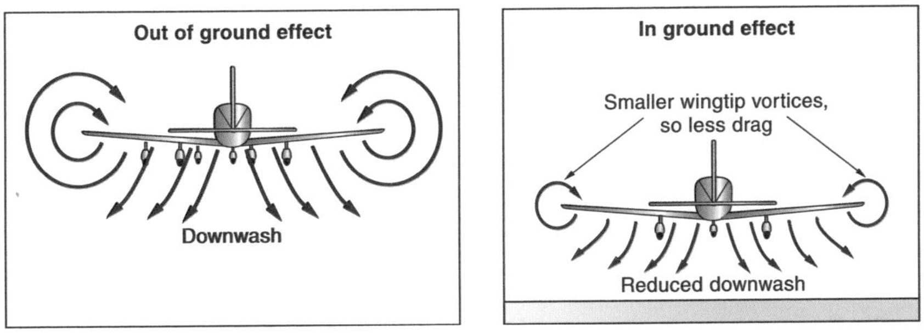

Figure 9-34 Near the ground, the upwash and downwash are restricted and the formation of wingtip vortices is restricted.

Reduced Drag

Ground effect limits the size of wingtip vortices which reduces induced drag.

In chapter 1 we divided the total drag on an airplane into two main types: *induced drag*, which is a by-product of the production of lift, and *parasite drag*, which is not directly associated with the production of lift. Wingtip vortices, and trailing vortices behind the trailing edge, are the major cause of induced drag. So when a nearby surface, such as the ground, restricts their formation, the induced drag will be less, and therefore the total drag on the airplane will be less.

You are aware that, in level flight, drag is counteracted by thrust. The reduction in drag when near the ground or water means that the same airspeed can be maintained using less thrust. Therefore, under-powered airplanes may be able to maintain flying speed while in ground effect, even if they cannot maintain that speed in free air, well away from the ground.

Ground effect becomes noticeable when the airplane is at a height above the surface of less than one wingspan. The effect is greater the closer the wing is to the surface.

Ground Effect During Landing

On an approach to land, as the airplane enters ground effect at about one wingspan's height, the pilot will experience a floating sensation—a result of the extra lift (from the increased lifting ability of the wing) and the slower deceleration (because of less drag).

In most landings there is no desire to maintain speed—indeed the aim is to lose speed. It is therefore usually important at flare height and in ground effect to ensure that the power is throttled back, especially considering the reduction in drag because of ground effect.

Excess speed at the beginning of the landing flare and the better flyability of an airplane in ground effect may incur a considerable *float* distance prior to touchdown. This is not desirable, especially on short landing strips.

Ground Effect on Takeoff

As the airplane climbs out of ground effect on takeoff the lifting ability of the wing will decrease for the same airplane pitch attitude. In addition the induced drag will increase because of the greater wingtip vortices and line vortices. Thus the airplane will not perform as well in free air as it will in ground effect. You will feel a sagging in climb-out performance as the airplane flies out of ground effect. You will need to increase the angle of attack to generate the same lift as you fly out of ground effect, and either increase thrust to overcome the additional induced drag or accept a reduced climb performance.

It pays to bear this in mind if you are ever operating on very short runways, or runways which finish on the edge of a cliff (or aircraft carrier). Ground effect may allow the airplane to become airborne before reaching the recommended takeoff speed. Once away from the takeoff surface the climb performance will be less—a good reason for not forcing the airplane to become airborne at too low a speed. It might manage to fly in ground effect, but it will be unable to climb out of it.

Windshear

The study of windshear and its effect on airplanes, and what protective measures can be taken to avoid potentially dangerous results, is still in its infancy and much still remains to be learned. What is certain is that every airplane and every pilot will be affected by windshear—usually the light windshears that occur in everyday flying, but occasionally a moderate windshear that requires positive recovery action from the pilot. On rare occasions, severe windshears can occur from which a recovery may even be impossible. A little knowledge can help you understand how to avoid significant windshear, and how best to recover from a windshear encounter.

Windshear Terminology

Windshear is a change in wind speed and/or wind direction.

A *windshear* is defined as a change in wind direction and/or wind speed in space. This includes updrafts and downdrafts. Any change in the wind velocity (be it a change in speed or in direction) as you move from one point to another is a windshear. The stronger the change and the shorter the distance within which it occurs, the stronger the windshear.

Updrafts and *downdrafts* are the vertical components of wind. The most hazardous updrafts and downdrafts are usually those associated with a thunderstorm.

The term *low-level windshear* is used to specify any windshear occurring along the final approach path prior to landing, along the runway and along the takeoff/initial climb-out flight path. Windshear near the ground (below 3,000 feet) is often the most critical in terms of safety for the airplane.

Turbulence is eddy motions in the atmosphere which vary both with time and from place to place.

The Effects of Windshear on an Airplane

So far our studies have considered an airplane flying in still air or a steady wind. However, an actual air mass does not move in a totally steady manner—there will be gusts and updrafts and changes of wind speed and direction, which the airplane will encounter as it flies through the air mass. These windshears will have a *transient effect* on the flight path of an airplane. Even when the wind is relatively calm on the ground, it is not unusual for the light and variable surface wind to suddenly change into a strong and steady wind at a level only a few hundred feet above the ground. If we consider an airplane making an approach to land in these conditions, we can see the effect the windshear has as the airplane passes through the shear.

An airplane flying through the air will have a certain *inertia* depending on its mass and its velocity relative to the ground. Its inertia makes it resistant to change. If the airplane has an airspeed of 80 knots and the headwind component is 30 knots, then the inertial speed of the airplane over the ground is (80 − 30) 50 knots.

When the airplane flies down into the calm air, the headwind component reduces reasonably quickly to, say, 5 knots. The inertial speed of the airplane is still 50 knots, but the new headwind of only 5 knots will mean that its airspeed has suddenly dropped back to 55 knots. The normal reaction is to add power and/or to lower the nose to regain airspeed, and to avoid undershooting the desired flight path. The stronger the windshear, the greater the changes in power and attitude that will be required. Any fluctuations in wind will require adjustments by the pilot, and this is why you have to work so hard sometimes, especially when approaching to land.

In gusty wind conditions, a power-on approach and landing should be used so that the engine can respond more quickly when required. In addition, if turbulence is encountered during the approach to land you should increase the airspeed to slightly above the normal approach speed to allow for sudden changes in indicated airspeed.

In gusty conditions, use a power-on approach and landing and consider adding a few knots to the approach speed.

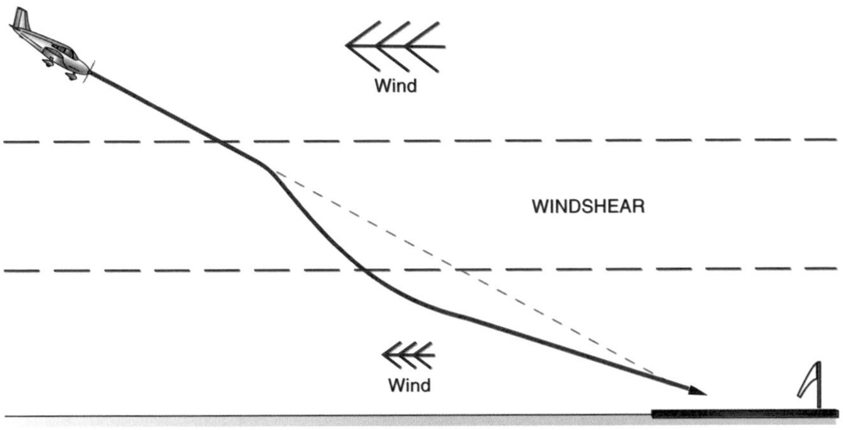

Figure 9-35
A typical windshear situation—calm on the ground with a wind at altitude.

Overshoot and Undershoot Effect

The effects of windshear on an airplane's flight path depend on the nature and location of the shear, as follows.

Overshoot Effect

Overshoot effect is caused by a windshear that results in the airplane flying above the desired flight path and/or an increase in indicated airspeed. The nose of the airplane may also tend to rise. Overshoot effect may result from flying into an increasing headwind, a decreasing tailwind, from a tailwind into a headwind, or an updraft.

Undershoot Effect

Undershoot effect is caused by a windshear that results in an airplane flying below the desired flight path and/or a decrease in indicated airspeed. The nose of the airplane may also tend to drop. Undershoot effect may result from flying into a decreasing headwind, an increasing tailwind, from a headwind into a tailwind, or into a downdraft.

The actual effect of a windshear depends on:

- the nature of the windshear;
- whether the airplane is climbing or descending through that particular windshear; and
- the direction in which the airplane is proceeding.

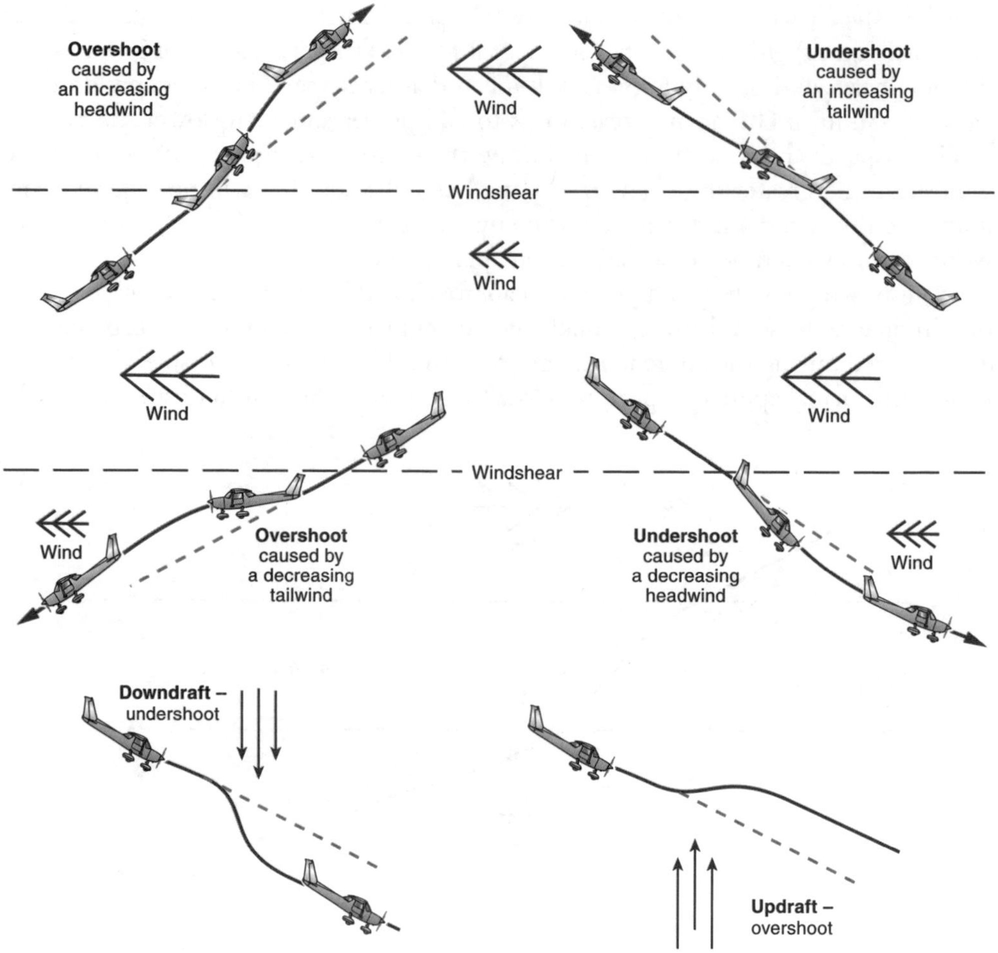

Figure 9-36 Six common windshear situations.

Windshear Reversal Effect

Windshear reversal effect is caused by a windshear which results in the initial effect on the airplane being reversed as the airplane proceeds further along the flight path. It is an overshoot effect followed by undershoot, or undershoot followed by overshoot effect, as appropriate.

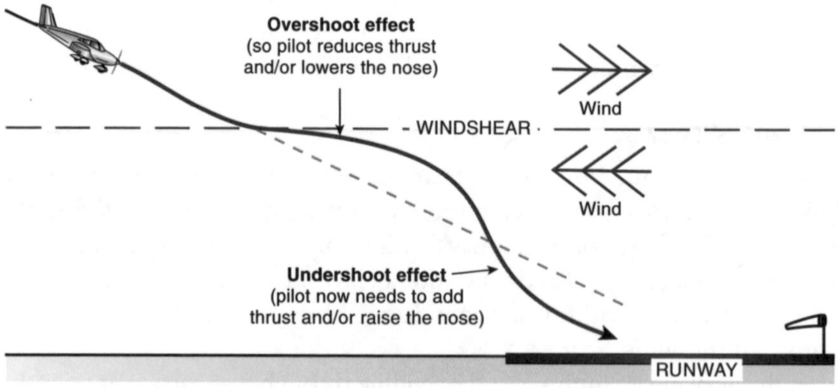

Figure 9-37 Windshear reversal effect.

Windshear reversal effect is a very common phenomenon that pilots often experience on approach to land, when things are usually happening too fast to analyze exactly what is taking place in terms of wind. The pilot can, of course, observe undershoot and overshoot effect and react accordingly with changes in pitch attitude and/or power to maintain the desired flight path and airspeed.

Crosswind Effect

Crosswind effect is caused by a windshear that requires a rapid change of airplane heading to maintain a desired track (not uncommon in a crosswind approach and landing because the crosswind component changes as the ground is neared). On crosswind landings, at the moment of touchdown the direction of the airplane's motion and its longitudinal axis must be parallel to the runway. If this is not the case the airplane will skip sideways on landing imposing large side loads on the landing gear.

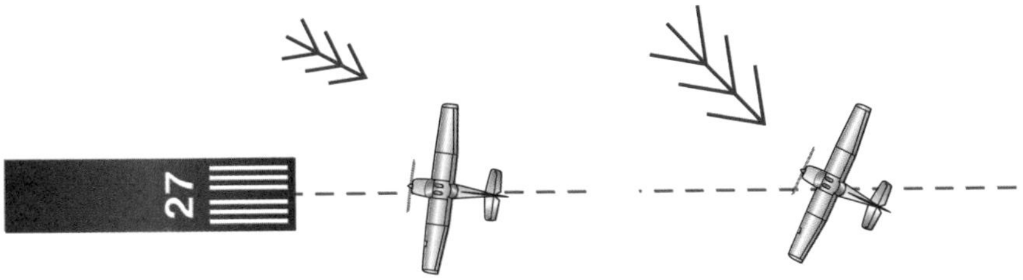

Figure 9-38 Crosswind effect.

The Causes of Windshear

There are many causes of windshear. They include: obstructions and terrain features which disrupt the normal smooth wind flow; localized vertical air movements associated with thunderstorms, cumulonimbus and large cumulus clouds; low-level temperature inversions; and sea breezes. These will be discussed in the Weather section.

Review 9

Takeoff and Landing Performance

Takeoff Performance

Refer to figure 9-5 (page 209) for questions 1 to 4.

1. In crosswind conditions, should the headwind or tailwind component be applied when calculating the takeoff or landing distances?
2. There is a 20-knot wind at 30° off the runway heading. What is the crosswind component?
3. What is the crosswind component for a landing on Runway 18 if the tower reports the wind as 220° at 30 knots?
   - **a.** 19 knots.
   - **b.** 23 knots.
   - **c.** 30 knots.
4. The airplane has a crosswind limit of 12 kt.
   - **a.** What is the maximum wind strength you can tolerate from 30° off the runway direction (such as runway 18 with the wind from 150°)?
   - **b.** What headwind component would this wind give you?

Refer to the takeoff distance performance graph in figure 9-11 (page 212) for questions 5 to 14.

5. What effect does each of the following have on takeoff distance?
   - **a.** An increase in pressure altitude.
   - **b.** An uphill runway slope.
   - **c.** An increase in headwind component.
6. How is takeoff distance measured?
7. What flap setting is indicated in the graph?
8. What is the maximum pressure altitude allowed for in the graph?
9. What is the maximum takeoff weight for the airplane in the graph?
10. What is the liftoff speed and the takeoff speed at 50 feet if the takeoff weight is 2,400 pounds? (Give your answer in knots.)
11. What is ISA (standard) temperature at 10,000 feet? (Give your answer in both °C and °F.)
12. Given a true OAT of 100°F, a pressure altitude of 2,000 feet, a takeoff weight of 2,750 pounds, and the headwind component is calm, determine:
    - **a.** the total distance for a takeoff to clear a 50-foot obstacle.
    - **b.** the ground roll distance.
    - **c.** the takeoff speeds.
13. Given standard temperature, a pressure altitude of 4,000 feet, a takeoff weight of 2,800 pounds, and headwind component is calm, determine:
    - **a.** takeoff distance.
    - **b.** ground roll.
    - **c.** liftoff speed.
    - **d.** speed at 50 feet.
    - **e.** OAT in both °C and °F.
14. If OAT is 90°F, pressure altitude is 2,000 feet, takeoff weight is 2,500 pounds, and there is a 20-knot headwind component, determine the approximate ground roll distance required for takeoff.

Landing Performance

Refer to the landing distance graph in figure 9-20 (page 218) for questions 15 to 18.

15. What flap setting is indicated on the graph?
16. Conditions are OAT 90°F, pressure altitude 4,000 feet, weight 2,800 pounds, and tailwind 10 knots. Determine:
    - **a.** the landing distance from over a 50-foot obstacle.
    - **b.** the expected ground roll.
    - **c.** the approach speed at 50 feet.
17. Given the following data, determine the total distance required to land:

OAT	90°F
Pressure altitude	3,000 feet
Takeoff weight	2,900 pounds
Headwind component	10 knots
Obstacle	50 feet

18. Given the following data, determine the approximate distance required to land.

OAT	32°F
Pressure altitude	8,000 feet
Takeoff weight	2,600 pounds
Headwind component	20 knots
Obstacle	50 feet

Refer to the landing distance performance table in figure 9-21 (page 219) for questions 19 to 24.

19. What flap setting is indicated on the table?
20. Conditions are sea level, standard temperature (59°F), and headwind 4 knots. What is:
    a. the total landing distance over a 50-foot obstacle?
    b. the approximate ground roll?
21. Conditions are elevation 2,500 feet, 48°F, and headwind 8 knots. What is:
    a. the total landing distance over a 50-foot obstacle?
    b. the approximate ground roll?
22. Conditions are pressure altitude 3,750 feet, headwind 12 knots, and temperature standard. What is:
    a. the total landing distance over a 50-foot obstacle?
    b. the approximate ground roll?
23. Conditions are pressure altitude 1,250 feet, headwind 12 knots, temperature 55°F, and dry grass runway. What is:
    a. the total landing distance over a 50-foot obstacle?
    b. the approximate ground roll?
24. Given the following, determine the approximate distance required to land over a 50-foot obstacle.

Pressure altitude	5,000 feet
Headwind component	8 knots
Temperature	41°F
Runway	Hard surface

Wake Turbulence

25. The air beneath a wing of an airplane in flight tends to leak around the wingtip and into the lower static pressure area above the wing.
    a. What does this leave a trail of?
    b. What kind of turbulence does this trail cause?
26. Wingtip vortices tend to drift in which direction(s)?
27. The greatest vortex strength occurs when the generating aircraft is:
    a. light, dirty (flaps down), and fast.
    b. heavy, dirty, and fast.
    c. heavy, clean (flaps up), and slow.
28. A large airplane generating turbulence. Where in relation to its flight path is wake turbulence most likely to be encountered?
29. You are departing behind a heavy airplane. How do you avoid its wake turbulence?
30. How can a pilot minimize the hazard of wingtip vortices during a takeoff made behind a departing large jet airplane?
31. A heavy jet airplane has landed on the runway you intend to use for takeoff and there is a light headwind blowing. When should you become airborne in relation to its touchdown point?
32. What procedure should you follow to avoid wake turbulence if a large jet crosses your course from left to right approximately 1 mile ahead and at your altitude?
33. Vortices created by a helicopter:
    a. only descend downward in the prop-wash.
    b. do not exist.
    c. trail behind it and descend gradually, like from fixed-wing aircraft.

Ground Effect

34. What is ground effect?
35. An airplane leaving the ground will:
    a. experience a reduction in ground friction and require a slight power reduction.
    b. experience an increase in induced drag.
    c. require a lower angle of attack to maintain the same lift coefficient.
36. If the same angle of attack is maintained in ground effect as when out of ground effect, lift will:
    a. increase, and induced drag will decrease.
    b. decrease, and parasite drag will increase.
    c. increase, and induced drag will increase.
37. When can ground effect cause floating during a landing?

38. After climbing out of ground effect immediately after takeoff, the induced drag will:
   a. increase, leading to decreased performance capability.
   b. decrease, leading to increased performance capability.
   c. stay the same, leading to the same performance capability.
39. Ground effect is most likely to result in:
   a. settling to the surface abruptly during landing.
   b. becoming airborne before reaching recommended takeoff speed.
   c. an inability to become airborne even though airspeed is sufficient for normal takeoff needs.

Windshear

40. What is windshear?
41. What is the "overshoot effect"?
42. What is "windshear reversal effect"?
43. A sudden decrease in headwind will cause the airplane to briefly show a loss of airspeed equal to the decrease in wind velocity. On approach to land, could this be more dangerous than an increase in headwind?
44. Which type of approach and landing is recommended during gusty wind conditions?
   a. A power-on approach and landing.
   b. A power-off approach and a power-on landing.
   c. A power-on approach and a power-off landing.
45. When turbulence is encountered during the approach to a landing, what action is recommended and for what primary reason?
   a. Increase the airspeed slightly above normal approach speed to attain more positive control.
   b. Decrease the airspeed slightly below normal approach speed to avoid over-stressing the airplane.
   c. Increase the airspeed slightly above normal approach speed to penetrate the turbulence as quickly as possible.

Commercial Review

Refer to the obstacle takeoff graph in figure 9-39 for questions 46 to 52.

46. What flap setting is indicated in the graph?
47. How is the ground roll calculated?
48. If the takeoff distance is 2,000 feet, what is the ground roll?

ASSOCIATED CONDITIONS:

POWER — TAKEOFF POWER SET BEFORE BRAKE RELEASE
FLAPS — 20°
RUNWAY — PAVED, LEVEL, DRY SURFACE
TAKEOFF SPEED — IAS AS TABULATED

NOTE: GROUND ROLL IS APPROX 73% OF TOTAL TAKEOFF DISTANCE OVER A 50 FT OBSTACLE

EXAMPLE:

OAT	75 °F
PRESSURE ALTITUDE	4,000 FT
TAKEOFF WEIGHT	3,100 LB
HEADWIND	20 KNOTS
TOTAL TAKEOFF DISTANCE OVER A 50 FT OBSTACLE	1,350 FT
GROUND ROLL (73% OF 1,350)	986 FT
IAS TAKEOFF SPEED	
LIFT-OFF	74 MPH
AT 50 FT	74 MPH

WEIGHT (LB)	IAS TAKEOFF SPEED (ASSUMES ZERO INSTR ERROR)			
	LIFT-OFF		50 FEET	
	MPH	KNOTS	MPH	KNOTS
3,400	77	67	77	67
3,200	75	65	75	65
3,000	72	63	72	63
2,800	69	60	69	60
2,600	66	57	66	57
2,400	63	55	63	55

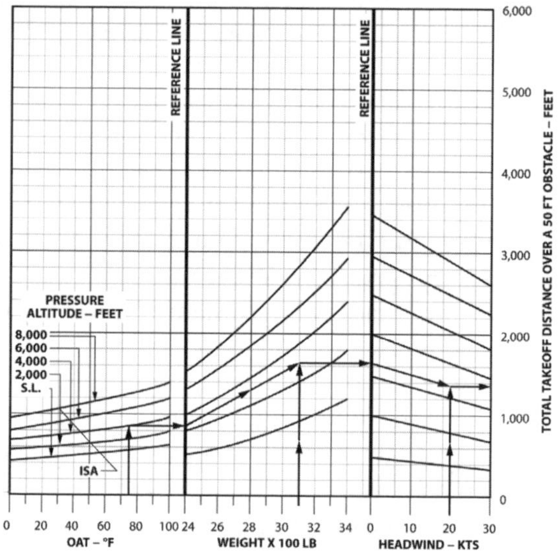

Figure 9-39 Obstacle takeoff graph.

49. Given an OAT of 75°F, a pressure altitude of 6,000 feet, a takeoff weight of 2,900 pounds and a headwind component of 20 knots, determine:

a. the total distance required for a takeoff to clear a 50-foot obstacle.

b. the ground roll distance.

c. the liftoff speed and the required takeoff speed at 50 feet.

50. What is the liftoff speed and takeoff speed at 50 feet for a takeoff weight of 3,100 pounds?

51. What is the total takeoff distance over a 50-foot obstacle given the following?

Temperature	30°F
Pressure altitude	6,000 feet
Weight	3,300 pounds
Headwind	20 knots

52. What is the ground roll required for takeoff over a 50-foot obstacle given the following?

Temperature	100°F
Pressure altitude	4,000 feet
Weight	3,200 pounds
Headwind	Calm

Refer to the landing distance chart in figure 9-40 for questions 53 to 57.

53. What flap setting is indicated in the chart?

54. What is the approach speed at maximum weight?

55. This chart applies to what type of runway surface?

56. Determine the approximate ground roll given the following:

Temperature	50°F
Pressure altitude	Sea level
Weight	3,000 pounds
Headwind	10 knots

ASSOCIATED CONDITIONS:

POWER	AS REQUIRED TO MAINTAIN 800 FT/MIN DESCENT ON APPROACH
FLAPS	DOWN
RUNWAY	PAVED, LEVEL, DRY SURFACE
APPROACH SPEED	IAS AS TABULATED

NOTE: GROUND ROLL IS APPROX 53% OF TOTAL LANDING DISTANCE OVER A 50 FT OBSTACLE.

EXAMPLE:

OAT	75 °F
PRESSURE ALTITUDE	4,000 FT
LANDING WEIGHT	3,200 LB
HEADWIND	10 KNOTS
TOTAL LANDING DISTANCE OVER A 50 FT OBSTACLE	1,475 FT
GROUND ROLL (53% OF 1,475)	782 FT
IAS TAKEOFF SPEED	87 MPH IAS

WEIGHT (LB)	IAS APPROACH SPEED (ASSUMES ZERO INSTR ERROR)	
	MPH	KNOTS
3,400	90	78
3,200	87	76
3,000	84	73
2,800	81	70
2,600	78	68
2,400	75	65

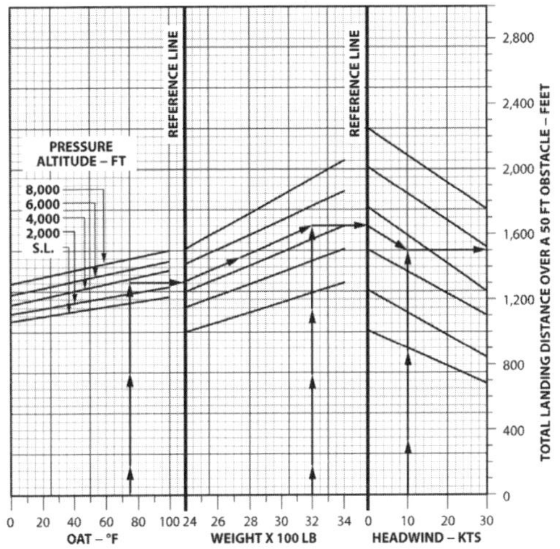

Figure 9-40 Normal landing chart.

57. What is the total landing distance over a 50-foot obstacle given the following?

Temperature	80°F
Pressure altitude	4,000 feet
Weight	2,800 pounds
Headwind	24 knots

Answers are given on page 691

En Route Performance 10

En route performance is an important consideration, especially in high-performance airplanes. The incorrect selection of power settings, cruise speed, and cruise altitudes can significantly affect the efficiency and economics of operating your airplane.

While you are required to extract only cruise performance data for the Private Pilot FAA Knowledge Exam, we recommend that, at some stage, you read through the commercial pilot sections of this chapter that include climb performance data, as well as different presentations of cruise performance data. The additional knowledge gained will lead to improved practical operation of your airplane.

Note. The Commercial Pilot Knowledge Exam requires that you have a knowledge of climb performance as well as cruise performance, and that you can apply some basic navigation and flight planning knowledge, such as wind effect increasing or decreasing your groundspeed.

Cruise Altitude and Power Setting

Figure 10-1
Cruising.

Choice of *cruise altitude* depends on:
- distance to destination;
- terrain;
- airplane gross weight;
- weather (visibility and cloud base);
- wind at various altitudes; and
- ATC and airspace requirements.

To level off at cruise altitude leave climb power set until the airplane has accelerated to the desired cruise speed in level flight. The power is then reduced to *cruise power*, and the mixture is *leaned* as recommended in the Pilot's Operating Handbook.

The cruise speed maintained is determined by the power set.

The cruise speed maintained is determined by the power set. Cruise power settings are usually specified as a percentage of *maximum continuous power* (MCP). Typical cruise figures are in the range of 55%–75% MCP (or 55–75% BHP, where BHP means brake horsepower). It is possible, of course, to set higher power for cruise, even 100% MCP as the name maximum continuous power implies, but the consequences will be very high fuel consumption and increased engine wear.

Lean the mixture for best fuel consumption.

After cruise power is set, you should lean the mixture according to the procedures in the Pilot's Operating Handbook. Most engine manufacturers recommend that you lean the mixture only when the power setting is 75% MCP or less—full rich is used at higher power settings. Usually you would lean for *best power*, so that there is a slight excess of fuel compared with the chemically correct mixture. This will give the best speed at that power setting, and the small amount of excess fuel will help cool the cylinders. Correct leaning procedure is important for long engine life.

From a performance point of view, the engine–propeller combination is most efficient at the altitude where the desired percentage power is obtained with the throttle fully open, known as the full-throttle altitude.

Indicated and Outside Air Temperature

As airspeed increases the IOAT will be slightly higher than the actual outsider air temperature.

The temperature shown in the cockpit on the outside air temperature gauge is the *indicated outside air temperature* (IOAT). As airspeed increases, air moving past the outside-air-temperature probe will be compressed. When air is compressed, it warms, and this will cause a slight increase in the temperature detected and displayed in the cockpit.

The actual temperature of the outside air is called the *outside air temperature* (OAT) and also can be obtained from a weather forecast or report. When operating high-speed airplanes a correction factor can be applied to the IOAT to obtain OAT.

Although you will find both IOAT and OAT in performance tables and graphs, in the Private and Commercial Knowledge Exams, it is normal to find a simple reference to "temperature" in the question setting.

Presentation of Performance Data

Manufacturers present performance data in different ways, the most common being tables and graphs. The following examples are typical of the data for Piper and Cessna airplanes.

Piper Warrior Performance Data

To use the graph in figure 10-2, simply enter with the temperature and pressure altitude, move across to the desired percentage power and then down to find the cruise TAS.

> **Note.** On the graph in figure 10-2, at higher cruise altitudes, the maximum power available in terms of percentage MCP is limited by the full throttle position.

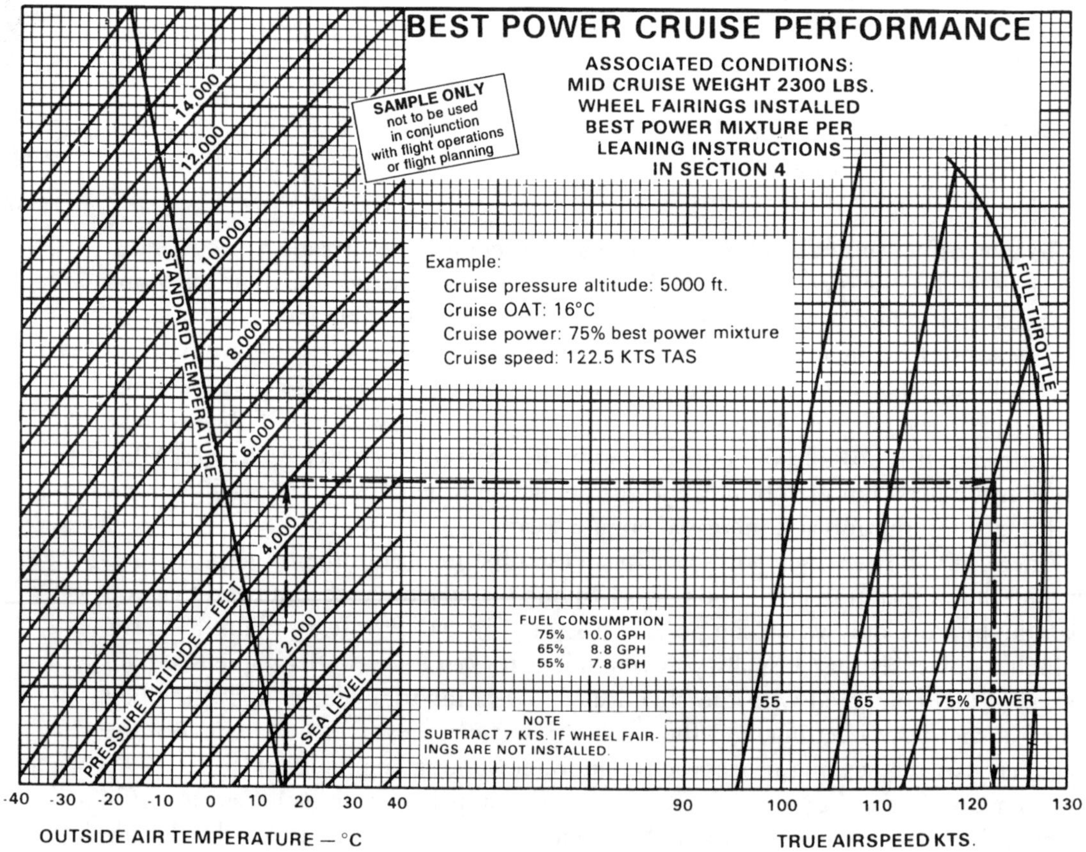

Figure 10-2 Cruise performance graph for a Piper Warrior (PA-28-161).

Cessna 172 Performance Data

To use the table in figure 10-3, simply extract the figures. For instance, at 4,000 feet pressure altitude at standard temperature and with 2,400 RPM set, you would be cruising at 65% BHP and would achieve 108 knots true air speed (KTAS) with a fuel flow/consumption of 7.3 gph.

> **Note.** All performance graphs and tables will have various notes printed on them, giving details of the conditions that apply and information governing use of the data. You should pay particular attention to these notes, and be aware that they will be different for each graph or table.

SECTION 5
PERFORMANCE

CESSNA
MODEL 172P

CRUISE PERFORMANCE

CONDITIONS:
2400 Pounds
Recommended Lean Mixture (See Section 4, Cruise)

NOTE:
Cruise speeds are shown for an airplane equipped with speed fairings which increase the speeds by approximately two knots.

PRESSURE ALTITUDE FT	RPM	20°C BELOW STANDARD TEMP			STANDARD TEMPERATURE			20°C ABOVE STANDARD TEMP		
		% BHP	KTAS	GPH	% BHP	KTAS	GPH	% BHP	KTAS	GPH
2000	2500	---	---	---	76	114	8.5	72	114	8.1
	2400	72	110	8.1	69	109	7.7	65	108	7.3
	2300	65	104	7.3	62	103	6.9	59	102	6.6
	2200	58	99	6.6	55	97	6.3	53	96	6.1
	2100	52	92	6.0	50	91	5.8	48	89	5.7
4000	2550	---	---	---	76	117	8.5	72	116	8.1
	2500	77	115	8.6	73	114	8.1	69	113	7.7
	2400	69	109	7.8	65	108	7.3	62	107	7.0
	2300	62	104	7.0	59	102	6.6	57	101	6.4
	2200	56	98	6.3	54	96	6.1	51	94	5.9
	2100	51	91	5.8	48	89	5.7	47	88	5.5
6000	2600	---	---	---	77	119	8.6	72	118	8.1
	2500	73	114	8.2	69	113	7.8	66	112	7.4
	2400	66	108	7.4	63	107	7.0	60	106	6.7
	2300	60	103	6.7	57	101	6.4	55	99	6.2
	2200	54	96	6.1	52	95	5.9	50	92	5.8
	2100	49	90	5.7	47	88	5.5	46	86	5.5
8000	2650	---	---	---	77	121	8.6	73	120	8.1
	2600	77	119	8.7	73	118	8.2	69	117	7.8
	2500	70	113	7.8	66	112	7.4	63	111	7.1
	2400	63	108	7.1	60	106	6.7	58	104	6.5
	2300	57	101	6.4	55	100	6.2	53	97	6.0
	2200	52	95	6.0	50	93	5.8	49	91	5.7
10,000	2600	74	118	8.3	70	117	7.8	66	115	7.4
	2500	67	112	7.5	64	111	7.1	61	109	6.8
	2400	61	106	6.8	58	105	6.5	56	102	6.3
	2300	55	100	6.3	53	98	6.0	51	96	5.9
	2200	50	93	5.8	49	91	5.7	47	89	5.6
12,000	2550	67	114	7.5	64	112	7.1	61	111	6.9
	2500	64	111	7.2	61	109	6.8	59	107	6.6
	2400	59	105	6.6	56	103	6.3	54	100	6.1
	2300	53	98	6.1	51	96	5.9	50	94	5.8

Figure 10-3 Cruise performance table for a Cessna 172P.

Performance Data used for the Private Pilot Knowledge Exam

The table of *cruise power settings* used in the Private Pilot Knowledge Exam is shown in figure 10-4. It is based on an airplane gross weight of 2,800 pounds with 65% maximum continuous power set, or full throttle at higher altitudes. Enter this table on the left-hand side with *pressure altitude*, and *temperature* using either ISA deviation at the top of the table when planning, or with IOAT when in flight. Note that you will see that the IOAT values are slightly higher than the OAT. For instance at sea level, the ISA temperature is +15°C, whereas the IOAT for a TAS of 150 knots is +17°C. Now you can find:

- *power setting* to achieve 65% MCP in terms of *RPM* and *manifold pressure* (MP);
- fuel flow in gallons per hour (gph), with the expected fuel pressure gauge indication in pounds per square inch (psi); and
- *true airspeed* (TAS) in knots or miles per hour (MPH).

For example, at 4,000 feet pressure altitude with standard temperature (ISA), you can extract:

a. power setting 2,450 RPM, MP 20.7 in. Hg;
b. fuel flow 11.5 gph (expected fuel pressure 6.6 psi); and
c. TAS 156 knots (or 180 MPH).

Cruise Power Settings
65% maximum continuous power (or full throttle), 2800 pounds

	ISA -20°C (-36°F)								STANDARD DAY (ISA)								ISA +20°C (+36°F)							
PRESS. ALT.	IOAT		ENG. SPEED	MAN. PRESS.	FUEL FLOW PER ENGINE		TAS		IOAT		ENG. SPEED	MAN. PRESS.	FUEL FLOW PER ENGINE		TAS		IOAT		ENG. SPEED	MAN. PRESS.	FUEL FLOW PER ENGINE		TAS	
FEET	°F	°C	RPM	IN HG	PSI	GPH	KTS	MPH	°F	°C	RPM	IN HG	PSI	GPH	KTS	MPH	°F	°C	RPM	IN HG	PSI	GPH	KTS	MPH
SL	27	-3	2,450	20.7	6.6	11.5	147	169	63	17	2,450	21.2	6.6	11.5	150	173	99	37	2,450	21.8	6.6	11.5	153	176
2,000	19	-7	2,450	20.4	6.6	11.5	149	171	55	13	2,450	21.0	6.6	11.5	153	176	91	33	2,450	21.5	6.6	11.5	156	180
4,000	12	-11	2,450	20.1	6.6	11.5	152	175	48	9	2,450	20.7	6.6	11.5	156	180	84	29	2,450	21.3	6.6	11.5	159	183
6,000	5	-15	2,450	19.8	6.6	11.5	155	178	41	5	2,450	20.4	6.6	11.5	158	182	79	26	2,450	21.0	6.6	11.5	161	185
8,000	-2	-19	2,450	19.5	6.6	11.5	157	181	36	2	2,450	20.2	6.6	11.5	161	185	72	22	2,450	20.8	6.6	11.5	164	189
10,000	-8	-22	2,450	19.2	6.6	11.5	160	184	28	-2	2,450	19.9	6.6	11.5	163	188	64	18	2,450	20.3	6.5	11.4	166	191
12,000	-15	-26	2,450	18.8	6.4	11.5	162	186	21	-6	2,450	18.8	6.1	10.9	163	188	57	14	2,450	18.8	5.9	10.6	163	188
14,000	-22	-30	2,450	17.4	5.8	10.5	159	183	14	-10	2,450	17.4	5.6	10.1	160	184	50	10	2,450	17.4	5.4	9.8	160	184
16,000	-29	-34	2,450	16.1	5.3	9.7	156	180	7	-14	2,450	16.1	5.1	9.4	156	180	43	6	2,450	16.1	4.9	9.1	155	178

Note:
1. Full throttle manifold pressure settings are approximate.
2. Shaded area represents operation with full throttle.

Figure 10-4 Airplane power setting table used in the Private Knowledge Exam.

Interpolation

Often the figures you require lie somewhere between the tabulated figures, and so you must interpolate.

Press alt	IOAT °C	TAS kt	IOAT °C	TAS kt
6,000	−15	155	+5	158

Table 10-1
Extract of table for interpolation.

Example 10-1

Refer to figure 10-4. The IOAT at 6,000 ft is -5°C, what is the TAS? From table 10-1, you can see that at 6,000 ft, an IOAT of -15°C gives a TAS of 155 knots and +5° gives 158 knots. Since -5°C is halfway between -15 and +5°C, the TAS is:

$$155 + \left(\frac{158 - 155}{2}\right) = 155 + 1.5 = 156.5 \text{ knots}$$

Fuel Consumption

Once the flight distance has been measured and the TAS and fuel flow found from the performance graph or chart, the fuel consumption for the flight can be calculated:

- first find the flight time by dividing the flight distance by the TAS. For example, to cover 240 nautical miles (NM) at 90 KTAS will take $^{240}/_{90}$ = 2.67 hours; and
- find the fuel consumption by multiplying the flight time by the fuel flow. For example, if the fuel flow was 6.6 gph over 2.67 hours the fuel consumption would be 6.6 × 2.67 = 17.6 gallons.

Note. These calculations can be done either on an electronic calculator or on a flight computer (see chapter 24).

Example 10-2

Referring to figure 10-4, what is the expected fuel consumption for a 420 NM flight in no-wind conditions at 65% MCP under the following conditions? Specify the power settings.

Pressure altitude	6,000 feet
Forecast temperature	–15°C
Wind	calm

First find which ISA column to use. ISA at 6,000 feet is [15 – (6 × 2)] = 3°C. Therefore -15°C is equivalent to ISA–18°C. This is closest to ISA–20°C, so we can extract:

- power setting: 2,450 RPM, MP 19.8 in. Hg;
- TAS 155 knots; and
- 11.5 gph.

1. Time calculation: $\text{Time} = \frac{\text{distance}}{\text{TAS}} = \frac{420}{155} = 2.71 \text{ hours}$

2. Fuel calculation: Fuel = time × fuel flow = 2.71 × 11.5 = 31.2 gallons.

Effect of Wind in Cruise

Normally during cruise, there is a wind that will affect the distance covered over the ground. If there is a headwind, the air in which the airplane is flying will be moving backward over the ground and therefore in a given time the ground distance covered, measured in nautical air miles (NM), will decrease. Conversely a tailwind will increase the ground distance covered in a given time. However the distance flown through the air, measured in nautical miles (NM), will remain the same.

Because the effect of wind will alter the time to cover a set ground distance, such as between two airports, it will also affect the amount of fuel required. A strong headwind will increase your flight time and fuel consumption, a hazardous situation if you had planned your fuel requirements without wind.

Example 10-3

Using the information in example 10-2, what will be the flight time and fuel consumption if there is now a 30-knot headwind?

1. $\text{Time} = \frac{\text{ground distance}}{\text{ground speed}} = \frac{420}{(\text{KTAS} - \text{headwind})} = \frac{420}{(155 - 30)} = 3.36 \text{ hours}$

2. Fuel = time × fuel flow = 3.36 × 11.5 = 38.7 gallons.

Climb Performance

There are three types of climb that you may use at the start of a cross-country flight:

1. the *maximum angle of climb* at speed V_X allows you to gain the maximum altitude in the shortest *distance*. It is normally used only immediately after the takeoff to provide a steep climb gradient over any obstacles, after which the airplane's nose is lowered slightly and the airspeed allowed to increase to normal climb speed. Since this type of climb is only of short duration, no performance tables (in terms of fuel flow and distance covered) are provided;
2. the *maximum rate of climb* at speed V_Y allows you to gain the maximum altitude in the shortest *time*. This climb speed is used when you want to reach cruise altitude as quickly as possible. Performance charts or tables, such as that shown in figure 10-6, are provided, since this type of climb may be prolonged and used all the way up to cruise altitude. The important figures from a flight planning point of view are the time, fuel and distance to top of climb. A wind will not affect the time, fuel and air distance to reach the required altitude, but it will affect the *ground* distance covered; and
3. the *normal climb* at the specified climb speed is somewhat faster than the maximum rate climb speed, and is sometimes called a *cruise* climb. Performance tables or charts are provided.

For all climb types the fuel required from start-up to cruise altitude will be the climb fuel plus a fuel allowance for start, taxi and takeoff.

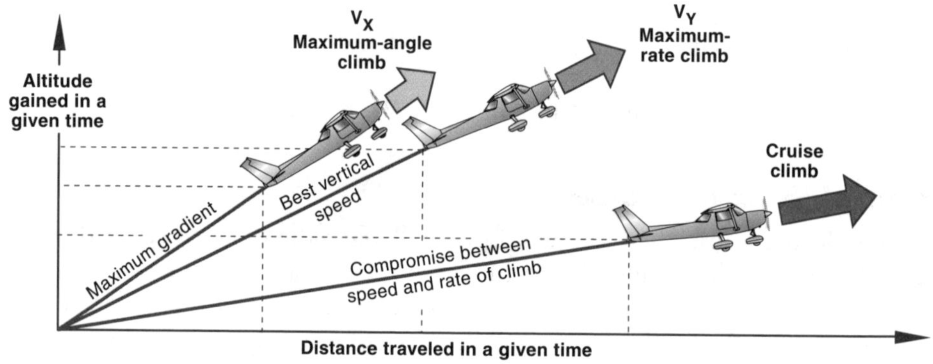

Figure 10-5 The three different types of climb.

Maximum Rate of Climb

Figure 10-6 shows a maximum rate of climb performance table. To see how simple it is to use, follow this explanation. Consider a *maximum rate climb* from a sea level airport to 8,000 feet under ISA conditions, with a takeoff weight of 3,700 pounds.

Under standard conditions, it should take 12 minutes to climb from MSL to 8,000 feet, and you will cover 23 nautical miles (NM). Fuel used on the climb will be 24 pounds (plus the 16 pounds for start-up, taxi and takeoff, making a total of 40 pounds used from start-up to top of climb). Initial rate of climb will be approximately 700 fpm, decreasing to approximately 665 fpm by 4,000 feet MSL, and 625 fpm as you approach 8,000 feet MSL.

WEIGHT LBS	PRESS ALT FT	RATE OF CLIMB FPM	FROM SEA LEVEL		
			TIME MIN	FUEL USED POUNDS	DISTANCE NM
4000	S.L.	605	0	0	0
	4000	570	7	14	13
	8000	530	14	28	27
	12,000	485	22	44	43
	16,000	430	31	62	63
	20,000	365	41	82	87
	S.L.	700	0	0	0
3700	4000	665	6	12	11
	8000	625	12	24	23
	12,000	580	19	37	37
	16,000	525	26	52	53
	20,000	460	34	68	72
	S.L.	810	0	0	0
	4000	775	5	10	9
3400	8000	735	10	21	20
	12,000	690	16	32	31
	16,000	635	22	44	45
	20,000	565	29	57	61

CONDITIONS:
Flaps Up
Gear Up
2600 RPM
Cowl Flaps Open
Standard Temperature

SAMPLE ONLY
not to be used in conjunction with flight operations or flight planning

NOTES:
1. Add 16 pounds of fuel for engine start, taxi and takeoff allowance.
2. Increase time, fuel and distance by 10% for each 10°C above standard temperature.
3. Distances shown are based on zero wind.

PRESS ALT	MP	PPH
S.L. TO 17,000	35	162
18,000	34	156
20,000	32	144
22,000	30	132
24,000	28	120

Figure 10-6 Climb performance table.

If the temperature is *warmer than standard*, climb performance will be poorer (see Note 2), with time, fuel, and air distance all increasing. Rate of climb will be poorer. Under ISA+10°C conditions, time, fuel and air distance must be increased by 10% to 110% of the ISA figures—we can calculate these by multiplying the tabulated figures by 1.1 to obtain the following:

If temperature is *colder than standard*, use the tabulated figures.

Figure 10-7
Maximum angle climb.

$$12 \text{ minutes} \times 1.1 = 13.2$$
$$23 \text{ NM} \times 1.1 = 25.3 \text{ NM}$$
$$24 \text{ lb} \times 1.1 = 26.4 \text{ gallons}$$

Remember. A *headwind* will reduce the ground distance covered on the climb. For instance, an average 30-knot headwind acting for the estimated 9 minutes of climb would have an effect of $-30 \times \frac{9}{60} = -4.5$ NM, with 14.3 NM becoming $14.3 - 4.5 = 9.8$ NM. (This method is quicker than working out the TAS and then finding the groundspeed.) Conversely, a *tailwind* will increase the ground distance covered.

Climbing from a High-Elevation Airport

The technique for calculating a climb to cruise altitude following takeoff from a high-elevation airport is:

- determine the climb figures from sea level to cruise pressure altitude; and
- subtract the climb figures for an imaginary climb from sea level to airport pressure altitude.

CPL

Example 10-4

Using figure 10-6, determine the climb figures for a maximum rate climb to 12,000 feet pressure altitude where the temperature is +1°C from an airport with pressure altitude 4,000 feet. There is a 20-knot headwind on the climb. Airplane weight is 3,700 pounds.

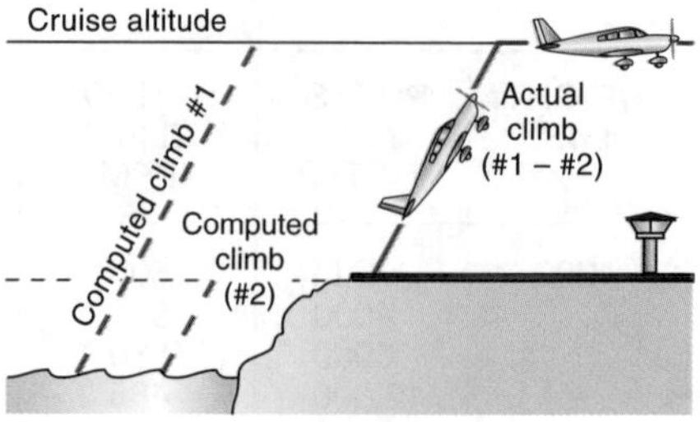

Figure 10-8 Climb to cruise altitude from a high-elevation airport.

First find the ISA deviation. At 12,000 feet, ISA = 15 − (2 × 12) = -09°C. Therefore +1°C is equivalent to ISA+10°C. A temperature correction will therefore be required.

The answer is: 14 minutes, 44 lb, 29 NM, 26 NM.

Note. Fuel has been rounded-up to the next whole gallon to be on the safe side.

	Time (minutes)	Fuel (lb)	Distance (NM)
Climb from sea level to 12,000 ft (#1)	19	37	37
Climb from sea level to 4,000 ft (#2)	6	12	11
Climb from 4,000 to 12,000 ft (#1–#2)	13	25	26
Correction for temperature deviation ISA+10°C, so increase figres by 10%, i.e. multiply by 1.1)	14 (14.3)	28 (27.5)	29 (28.6)
Startup, taxi, takeoff allowance	–	16	–
Totals	14 min	44 lb	29 NM
		Wind effect: −20 × (9 ÷ 60) =	-3
			26 NM

The Cruise or Normal Climb

Figure 10-9 shows a typical climb performance chart. To use this chart, enter with the temperature at the cruise level and read vertically up to the pressure altitude at the top of climb. Then move horizontally until reaching the fuel, time, and distance curved lines, and read vertically down to determine fuel, time, and distance.

Next, enter with the temperature at the start of climb and read vertically to the departure pressure altitude. Then move horizontally to extract the fuel, time, and distance values as before. The difference between the two sets of figures is the actual climb data. See the example on the chart.

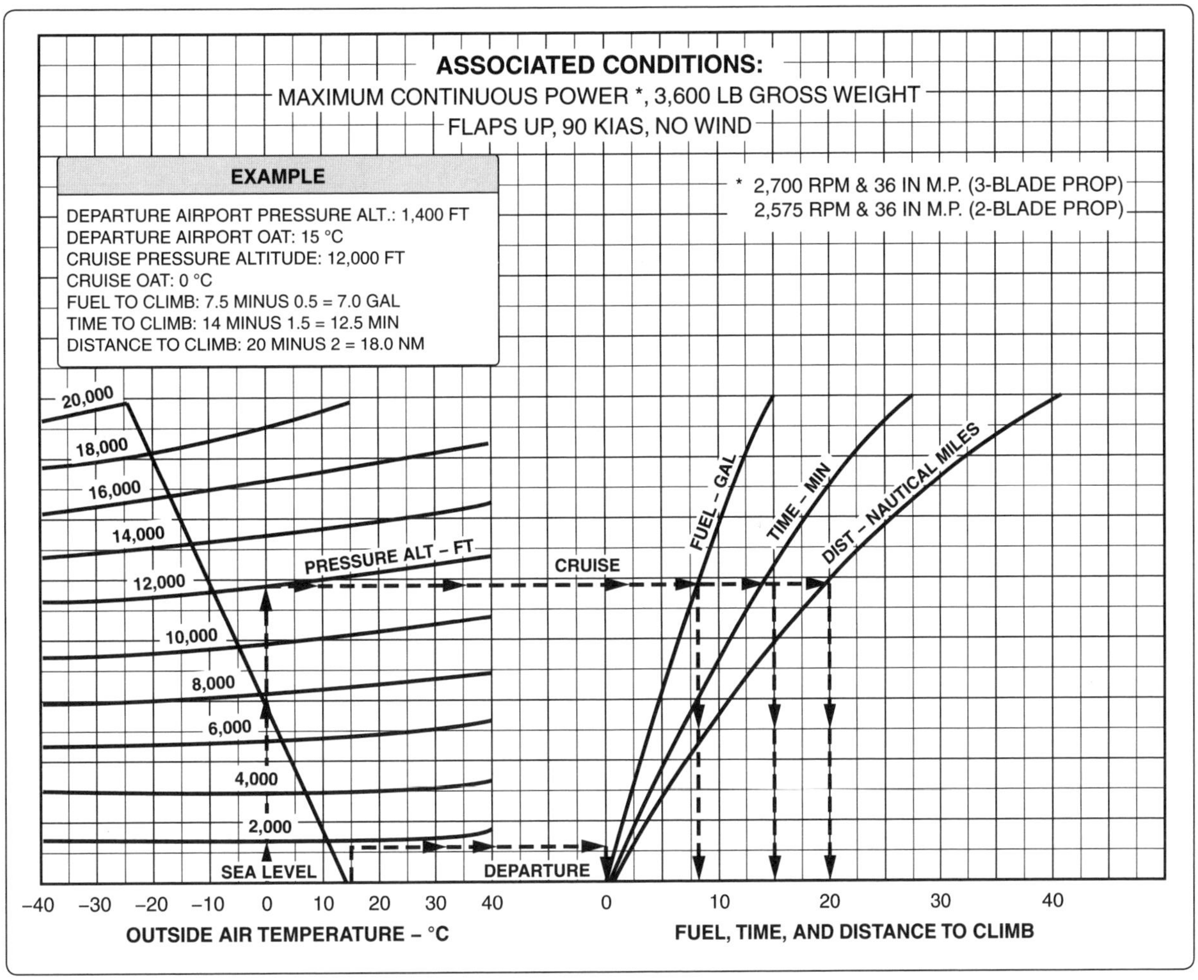

Figure 10-9 A climb performance chart.

Cruise Performance

This part of the chapter looks at the cruise in greater depth. If it has been a while since you read chapter 3, we suggest you review range and endurance (see pages 65-67).

Fuel Reserves

Fuel reserves for Visual Flight Rules (VFR) flights are specified in the Federal Aviation Regulations, Part 91. Reserve fuel is designed not to be used. It is a safety reserve, available for unplanned situations, such as unexpected closure of your destination airport due to a runway obstruction, or unforecast poor weather. Reserve fuel is fuel in your tanks that you should not plan on using—think of it as an emergency reserve.

The reserves specified in Part 91 are:

- VFR day reserve: 30 minutes at normal cruising speed; and
- VFR night reserve: 45 minutes at normal cruising speed.

CPL

Specific Range

Specific range is the distance traveled per unit of fuel burned. It may be expressed in various units, such as NM/pound or NM/gallon for specific range.

$$\text{Specific range} = \frac{\text{nautical miles}}{\text{fuel}} = \frac{\text{nautical miles/time}}{\text{fuel/time}} = \frac{\text{airspeed}}{\text{fuel flow}}$$

$$\underset{\text{(air)}}{\text{Specific range}} = \frac{\text{TAS}}{\text{fuel flow}} \quad \text{and} \quad \underset{\text{(ground)}}{\text{specific range}} = \frac{\text{GS}}{\text{fuel flow}}$$

Example 10-5

With a given power setting, you can achieve 150 KTAS with a fuel flow of 9 gallons per hour (gph). Calculate specific air range. Also calculate specific ground range if a headwind of 30 knots exists.

$$\underset{\text{(air)}}{\text{Specific range}} = \frac{\text{150 KTAS}}{\text{9 gph}} = \text{16.7 NM/gallon}$$

$$\underset{\text{(ground)}}{\text{Specific range}} = \frac{\text{120 knots GS}}{\text{9 gph}} = \text{13.3 NM/gallon}$$

Flying for Range

Normal cruise speed takes into account time-to-destination as well as fuel burn. However sometimes you will want to keep fuel used over a given flight distance as low as possible, which reduces fuel costs. This is achieved by flying at the correct speed for maximum range and keeping fuel burn to a minimum.

The maximum range speed occurs where the wing is most efficient, which occurs at the airspeed for *minimum drag*. Maximum range airspeed for most airplanes is considerably slower than normal cruise speed, and typically requires about 45% MCP. As weight reduces with fuel burn, the maximum range airspeed also reduces.

Efficiency during cruise requires that you *lean* the fuel/air mixture correctly according to procedures specified in the Pilot's Operating Handbook. *To achieve maximum range:*

- keep airplane gross weight to a reasonable minimum;
- fly at full-throttle altitude if possible (throttle butterfly fully open, causing less restriction to the airflow through the carburetor);
- use the correct power setting and airspeed (usually the highest recommended "high MP/low RPM" combination for maximum engine efficiency);
- lean the mixture as recommended in the Pilot's Operating Handbook;
- avoid use of carburetor heat if possible; and
- minimize drag (ensure in-trim, gear up and flaps up).

Wind Effect on Range

The maximum range airspeed in no-wind conditions is illustrated in figure 10-10. A *tailwind* will increase the range over the ground, and this range can be further increased by flying a little slower than the no-wind maximum range airspeed, which gives the wind more time to carry the airplane farther. Conversely, a *headwind* will reduce the range over the ground, but this reduction can be minimized by flying a little faster than the no-wind maximum airspeed, giving the wind less time to act on the airplane. Typical increases or decreases in airspeed for strong wind conditions are 5%.

Whereas specific air range is nautical air miles per unit of fuel, specific ground range is nautical *ground* miles per unit of fuel. Best range will be achieved at the airspeed that provides the best specific ground range—the maximum number of nautical ground miles per pound of fuel burned.

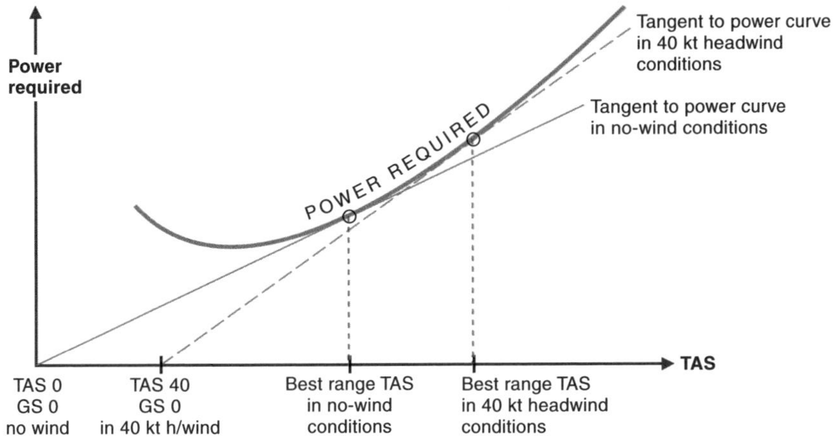

Figure 10-11 Graphical explanation of increased best-range TAS for strong winds.

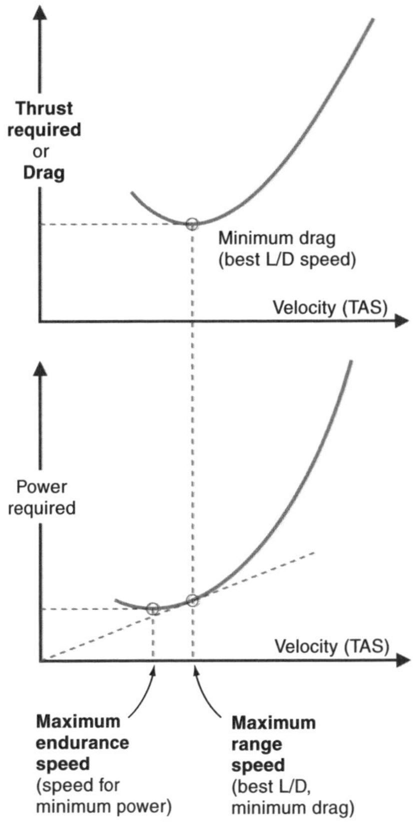

Figure 10-10 Maximum-endurance speed and maximum-range speed.

Example 10-6

Some typical cruise performance figures extracted from figure 10-13 (page 249), for a particular airplane type at 6,000 feet and standard temperature are shown below. Consider the effect of an 80-knot headwind on specific ground range at these power settings.

% BHP	RPM	MP	KTAS	pph (lb per hr)	SAR (TAS/pph)	W/C	GS	SGR (GS/pph)
75% BHP	2,500	24	171	95	1.80	–80	91	0.96
63% BHP	2,400	22	159	79	2.01	–80	79	1.00
48% BHP	2,200	20	138	62	2.22	–80	58	0.94

In no-wind conditions, specific air and ground range will be the same, and best range performance in the above case is 2.22 NM/lb, obtained at the low speed of 138 KTAS.

You can see that an 80-knot headwind has a very significant effect on specific ground range, reducing it to only 0.94 NM/lb at speed 138 KTAS. Note that the maximum specific ground range of 1.00 NM/lb is achieved at the higher speed of 159 KTAS in strong headwind conditions.

CPL

Flying for Endurance

Occasionally you might want to remain in flight for the longest time possible without any consideration of the distance covered, for instance when holding over a fix and waiting for an ATC clearance to proceed. The airspeed at which you would hold is known as the *best endurance airspeed*. To achieve this you need to keep the fuel flow as low as possible. Fuel consumption of a piston engine depends on the power it produces. Therefore, for best endurance, you should select an indicated airspeed near the *minimum power speed* from the performance charts. Best endurance airspeed is slower than best range airspeed (see figure 10-10).

At the appropriate endurance IAS, the power required is lowest at *low altitudes*—so, for maximum endurance in a piston-engine airplane, fly at a low (but safe) altitude at the speed for minimum power.

End CPL

Review 10

En Route Performance

Cruise Altitude and Power Setting

Refer to the cruise power setting table in figure 10-4 (page 238) for questions 1 to 10.

1. What true airspeed can you expect with 65% maximum continuous power at 8,000 feet pressure altitude with a temperature of 20°C below standard?
2. What true airspeed can you expect with 65% maximum continuous power at 9,500 feet pressure altitude with a temperature of ISA -20°C? Give your answer in knots and mph.
3. To achieve 65% maximum continuous power at 4,000 feet pressure altitude with 2,450 RPM set, what would be the manifold pressure, if the temperature was ISA –20°C?
4. Which of the following is the approximate manifold pressure setting with 2,450 RPM to achieve 65% maximum continuous power at 7,000 feet with a temperature of 36°F higher than standard:
   a. 20.9 in. Hg.
   b. 20.8 in. Hg.
   c. 21.0 in. Hg.
5. You are cruising at 10,000 feet pressure altitude on a standard day (ISA temperatures) with 65% maximum continuous power.
   a. What fuel flow in gph can you expect?
   b. What true airspeed in knots would you expect to achieve?
6. You are cruising at 11,000 feet pressure altitude on a standard day (ISA temperatures) with 65% maximum continuous power.
   a. What fuel flow in gph can you expect?
   b. What true airspeed in knots would you expect to achieve?
7. Which of the following is the approximate true airspeed a pilot will expect with 65% maximum continuous power at 9,500 feet with a temperature of 36°F below standard?
   a. 178 mph.
   b. 181 mph.
   c. 183 mph.
8. Given the following, what is the expected fuel consumption for a 500 NM flight?

Pressure altitude	4,000 feet
Temperature	+29°C
Manifold pressure	21.3 in. Hg
Wind	calm

9. Given the following, what is the expected fuel consumption for a 450 NM flight?

Pressure altitude	12,000 feet
IOAT	–6°C
Manifold pressure	18.8 in. Hg
Headwind	10 knots

10. Given the following, what is the expected fuel consumption for a 1,000 NM flight?

Pressure altitude	8,000 feet
Indicated temperature	–19°C
Manifold pressure	19.5 in. Hg
Wind	calm

Commercial Review

11. As altitude is gained, rate of climb:
    a. increases.
    b. decreases.
    c. stays the same.
12. What is ISA+10°C equivalent to (in °C) at 6,000 feet pressure altitude?
13. True or false? A headwind will not affect the amount of fuel burned in the climb to a given altitude.
14. True or false? Higher gross weights will not affect climb performance.
15. Fuel flow is 54 pounds/hr at 210 KTAS. Express fuel consumption in NM/pound.
16. Fuel flow is 6.6 gph at 161 KTAS. Give:
    a. fuel consumption in NM/gallon.
    b. specific ground range in 30-knot headwind conditions.
    c. specific ground range in 30-knot tailwind conditions.
17. Which maximum range factor decreases as weight decreases?
    a. Maximum range altitude.
    b. Maximum range airspeed.
    c. Maximum range angle of attack.

Refer to figure 10-12 for questions 18 to 22.

NORMAL CLIMB – 110 KIAS

CONDITIONS:
Flaps Up
Gear Up
2500 RPM
30 Inches Hg
120 PPH Fuel Flow
Cowl Flaps Open
Standard Temperature

NOTES:
1. Add 16 pounds of fuel for engine start, taxi and takeoff allowance.
2. Increase time, fuel and distance by 10% for each 7 °C above standard temperature.
3. Distances shown are based on zero wind.

WEIGHT LBS	PRESS ALT FT	RATE OF CLIMB FPM	FROM SEA LEVEL		
			TIME MIN	FUEL USED POUNDS	DISTANCE NM
4000	S.L.	605	0	0	0
	4000	570	7	14	13
	8000	530	14	28	27
	12,000	485	22	44	43
	16,000	430	31	62	63
	20,000	365	41	82	87
	S.L.	700	0	0	0
3700	4000	665	6	12	11
	8000	625	12	24	23
	12,000	580	19	37	37
	16,000	525	26	52	53
	20,000	460	34	68	72
	S.L.	810	0	0	0
	4000	775	5	10	9
3400	8000	735	10	21	20
	12,000	690	16	32	31
	16,000	635	22	44	45
	20,000	565	29	57	61

Figure 10-12 Fuel, time, and distance to climb table.

18. Describe the following for a normal climb in this airplane:
- **a.** power set (RPM and MP);
- **b.** indicated airspeed for flaps up and gear up;
- **c.** cowl flap configuration; and
- **d.** fuel allowance for engine start, taxi, and takeoff.

19. Under ISA+14°C conditions, you would need to increase the climb figures by 20%. How is this best achieved?

20. With reference to figure 10-12, from SL to 12,000 feet under ISA conditions for an airplane weighing 4,000 pounds, give the:
- **a.** climb figures (minutes, pounds, NM) in no-wind conditions.
- **b.** climb figures if there is an average tailwind component of 24 knots.
- **c.** fuel required from engine start through to top of climb.

21. Calculate the fuel burn from engine start at a sea level airport to top of climb at pressure altitude 14,000 feet under ISA conditions for an airplane with gross weight 4,000 pounds.

22. Given the following using a normal climb, how much fuel would be used from engine start to a pressure altitude of 12,000 feet:

Aircraft weight	3,700 pounds
Airport pressure altitude	4,000 feet
Temperature at 4,000 feet	21°C

Refer to figure 10-13 (page 249) for questions 23 to 27.

23. What would be the fuel flow given 6,000 ft pressure altitude, ISA+10°C, 2,400 RPM power setting, and 23 in. Hg MP?

24. Given the following, describe the maximum available flight time:
- **a.** with no reserves.
- **b.** with VFR night reserve.

Pressure altitude	6,000 feet
Temperature	–17°C
Power	2,300 RPM, 23" Hg
Usable fuel available	370 lb

25. Given the following, describe the maximum available flight time:
- **a.** with no reserves.
- **b.** with VFR night reserve.

Pressure altitude	6,000 feet
Temperature	–17°C
Power	2,400 RPM, 23" MP
Usable fuel available	505 lb

26. Given the following power settings, what cruise performance (KTAS and fuel flow in lb/hr) can you expect at 6,000 ft pressure altitude and ISA (i.e. 3°C)? (Calculate the distances in NM per 1 lb of fuel burned.)
- **a.** 2,550 RPM, 22 MP.
- **b.** 2,500 RPM, 22 MP.
- **c.** 2,400 RPM, 22 MP.
- **d.** 2,300 RPM, 22 MP.

27. Given the following, describe the maximum available flight time:

a. with no reserves.

b. with VFR night reserve.

Pressure altitude	6,000 feet
Temperature	+3°C
Power	2,300 RPM, 22" MP
Usable fuel available	465 lb

Refer to figure 10-14 for questions 28 to 31.

28. What flight time is available, allowing for VFR day fuel reserve, under the following conditions if the mixture is leaned correctly?

Pressure altitude	18,000 feet
Temperature	–21°C
Power	2,400 RPM, 28" MP
Usable fuel available	425 lb

29. What flight time is available, allowing for VFR night fuel reserve, under the following conditions if the mixture is leaned correctly?

Pressure altitude	18,000 feet
Temperature	–41°C
Power	2,500 RPM, 26" MP
Usable fuel available	318 lb

30. Given the following, calculate the available flight time, allowing for VFR day fuel reserve, if the mixture is leaned correctly:

a. for the tabulated figures.

b. for "best fuel economy" as mentioned in the note in figure 10-14.

Pressure altitude	18,000 feet
Temperature	–1°C
Power	2,200 RPM, 20" MP
Usable fuel available	344 lb

PRESSURE ALTITUDE 6,000 FEET

CONDITIONS:
Recommended Lean Mixture
3800 Pounds
Cowl Flaps Closed

		20 °C BELOW STANDARD TEMP -17 °C			STANDARD TEMPERATURE 3 °C			20 °C ABOVE STANDARD TEMP 23 °C		
RPM	MP	% BHP	KTAS	PPH	% BHP	KTAS	PPH	% BHP	KTAS	PPH
2550	24	---	---	---	78	173	97	75	174	94
	23	76	167	96	74	169	92	71	171	89
	22	72	164	90	69	166	87	67	167	84
	21	68	160	85	65	162	82	63	163	80
2500	24	78	169	98	75	171	95	73	172	91
	23	74	166	93	71	167	90	69	169	87
	22	70	162	88	67	164	85	65	165	82
	21	66	158	83	63	160	80	61	160	77
2400	24	73	165	91	70	166	88	68	167	85
	23	69	161	87	67	163	84	64	164	81
	22	65	158	82	63	159	79	61	160	77
	21	61	154	77	59	155	75	57	155	73
2300	24	68	161	86	66	162	83	64	163	80
	23	65	158	82	62	159	79	60	159	76
	22	61	154	77	59	155	75	57	155	72
	21	57	150	73	55	150	71	53	150	68
2200	24	63	156	80	61	157	77	59	158	75
	23	60	152	76	58	153	73	56	154	71
	22	57	149	72	54	149	70	53	149	67
	21	53	144	68	51	144	66	49	143	64
	20	50	139	64	48	138	62	46	137	60
	19	46	133	60	44	132	58	43	131	57

Figure 10-13 Cruise performance table.

PRESSURE ALTITUDE 18,000 FEET

CONDITIONS:
4000 Pounds
Recommended Lean Mixture
Cowl Flaps Closed

NOTE
For best fuel economy at 70% power or less, operate at 6 PPH leaner than shown in this chart or at peak EGT.

		20 °C BELOW STANDARD TEMP -41 °C			STANDARD TEMPERATURE -21 °C			20 °C ABOVE STANDARD TEMP -1 °C		
RPM	MP	% BHP	KTAS	PPH	% BHP	KTAS	PPH	% BHP	KTAS	PPH
2500	30	---	---	---	81	188	106	76	185	100
	28	80	184	105	76	182	99	71	178	93
	26	75	178	99	71	176	93	67	172	88
	24	70	171	91	66	168	86	62	164	81
	22	63	162	84	60	159	79	56	155	75
2400	30	81	185	107	77	183	101	72	180	94
	28	76	179	100	72	177	94	67	173	88
	26	71	172	93	67	170	88	63	166	83
	24	66	165	87	62	163	82	58	159	77
	22	61	158	80	57	155	76	54	150	72
2300	30	79	182	103	74	180	97	70	176	91
	28	74	176	97	70	174	91	65	170	86
	26	69	170	91	65	167	86	61	163	81
	24	64	162	84	60	159	79	56	155	75
	22	58	154	77	55	150	73	51	145	65
2200	26	66	166	87	62	163	82	58	159	77
	24	61	158	80	57	154	76	54	150	72
	22	55	148	73	51	144	69	48	138	66
	20	49	136	66	46	131	63	43	124	59

Figure 10-14 Cruise performance table.

31. In order to achieve 76% power at 18,000 ft under ISA conditions with 2,500 RPM set with the propeller control:

a. what manifold pressure would you set with the throttle?

b. what true airspeed could be expected?

c. what fuel flow could be expected?

Refer to figure 10-15 for questions 32 to 36.

32. How much fuel is consumed for a takeoff and climb at 70% power for 10 minutes?

33. Allowing for 45 minutes reserve (calculated at cruise rate), what flight time is available if the usage fuel on board is 47 gallons and you set 55% cruise (lean) power?

34. You have 65 gallons of usable fuel. Power setting is 55% best power level flight. How much flight time would be available with a 30 minute reserve remaining?

35. With 38 gallons of fuel aboard cruising (lean) at 55% power and a 45 minute fuel reserve, how much flight time is available?

36. You cruise with 75% best power level flight set. What is the fuel flow in gallons/hour?

37. Fuel flow is 80 lb/hr at 160 KTAS. Express fuel consumption in NM/lb.

38. Fuel flow is 6.6 gph at 161 KTAS.

a. Express fuel consumption in NM/lb.

b. What is SGR with a 30-knot headwind?

c. What is SGR with a 30-knot tailwind?

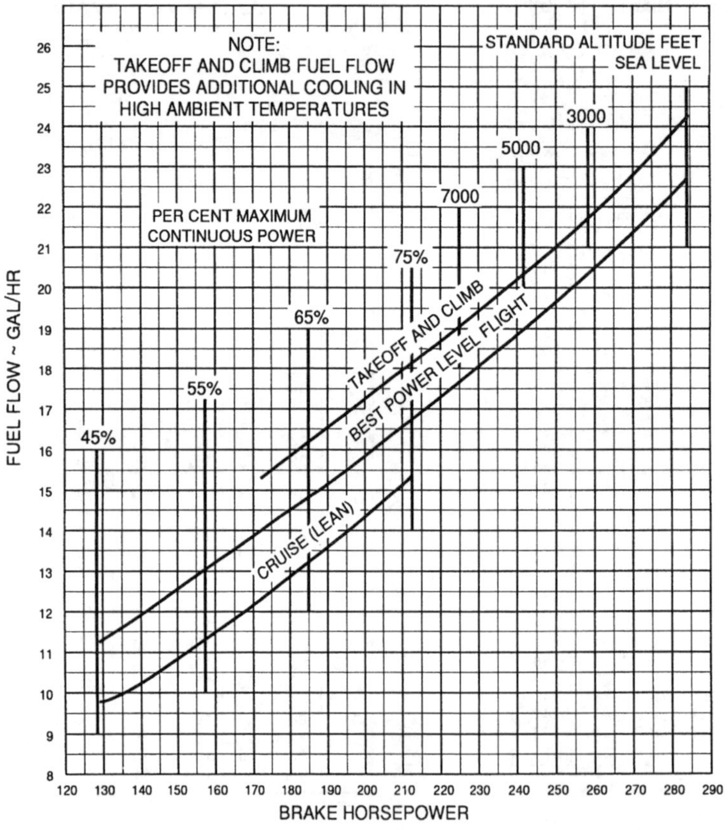

Figure 10-15 Fuel consumption versus brake horsepower graph.

Answers are given on page 692.

Weight and Balance 11

Airframe Limitations

An airplane must only be flown within certificated limits of weight and balance to ensure that it remains controllable, performs adequately and is not overstressed. Correct weight and balance means:
- maximum allowable weight is not exceeded; and
- center of gravity (CG) is within a specified range.

Figure 11-1
Load carefully.

Weight

The main force created to counteract the weight and allow the airplane to be maneuvered is lift. In straight-and-level flight the lift will be approximately equal to the weight. In certain maneuvers it may considerably exceed the weight—increased lift means an increase in wing loading and load factor (see pages 79–80).

For instance, in a 2g maneuver such as a 60° banked turn, where the load factor is 2, the load on the wings is double the weight. If the airplane weighs 3,000 pounds, the wings will be carrying a load of 6,000 pounds.

Figure 11-2
Consider fuel quantity and balance.

The heavier an airplane is, the poorer its performance will be. In particular, it will have:
- a higher stall speed;
- a higher takeoff speed and a longer takeoff run;
- poorer climb performance (poorer climb angle and climb rate);
- a lower cruising level;
- less maneuverability;
- higher fuel consumption, and less range and endurance;
- reduced cruise speed for a given power setting;
- a higher landing speed and a longer landing distance; and
- greater braking requirements when stopping.

This is not to suggest that following a takeoff at maximum permissible weight, the airplane will not perform perfectly safely; it simply draws attention to the effect of weight on performance.

On the other hand, if the airplane is actually *overweight*, that is, above any weight limitations imposed by the manufacturer, then not only will it perform poorly but it will also be difficult to control. If turbulence is encountered, or other than gentle maneuvers performed, the resulting wing loading may be so great that structural damage will result.

Never fly an overloaded airplane!

On a more mundane (but possibly expensive) level, operating an overloaded airplane may render your insurance invalid. Besides the limiting weights of maximum takeoff weight, maximum landing weight, maximum zero fuel weight and maximum ramp weight discussed in chapter 8, for weight-and-balance purposes we need to take account of the following weights.

Figure 11-3
Weight and balance affect all aspects of airplane performance.

Empty Weight

The *empty weight* of an airplane is a precise, measured weight for that particular airplane. It is included in its weight-and-balance documents as the licensed empty weight.

The empty weight includes:

- the airframe and the powerplant;
- all permanently installed operating equipment (such as radios); and
- all nondrainable fluids (including unusable fuel, hydraulic fluid, and undrainable oil—see note below).

Note. For some airplanes, the certificated empty weight specifically includes full oil. You should check this point carefully in all your weight-and-balance problems—if full oil is *not* included, then you must add its weight and moment.

Items that the empty weight does *not* include are:

- pilot(s) and their equipment and baggage;
- passenger(s);
- baggage, cargo and temporary ballast added for balance; and
- full oil (unless specifically included).

If the airplane has new equipment installed (such as a new GPS receiver), then a qualified person should amend the empty weight and the empty-weight CG position and moment in the weight-and-balance documents.

Gross Weight (GW)

The *gross weight* is the actual total weight of the airplane and its contents at any particular time. In other words, gross weight is the empty weight plus pilot(s), payload (passengers and cargo), added ballast and fuel load.

The gross weight should not exceed the maximum weight permissible for any particular maneuver. On *takeoff*, it must not exceed the structural maximum takeoff weight or the performance-limited takeoff weight; on *landing*, gross weight must not exceed the structural maximum landing weight or the performance-limited landing weight. If you wish to operate the airplane in the utility category, rather than in the normal category, you must ensure that the lower maximum permissible gross weight for the utility category is not exceeded.

The Weight of Fuel and Oil

Note the following:

- one gallon of AVGAS weighs 6 pounds (lb);
- one liter of AVGAS weighs 1.56 lb (0.71 kg); and
- one gallon of oil weighs 7.5 pounds (so 8 quarts or 2 gallons weighs 15 pounds).

Caution. Be careful when ordering fuel in foreign countries—some places measure fuel quantity in units such as liters rather than US gallons.

Other Weight Limitations

There may be other weight restrictions specified in your airplane's weight-and-balance documents or on placards in the airplane—for instance, a maximum baggage compartment load, or a maximum zero fuel weight (ZFW).

Be familiar with you airplane's weight limitations.

The more familiar you are with the weight limitations applicable to your airplane, the easier weight-and-balance problems will become. In the following table, we show the important data for the loading of any airplane, and you should consider using this for any airplane you fly.

MTOW (structural)	=________ lb
MLW (structural)	=________ lb
Empty weight	=________ lb (with/without oil)
Maximum fuel load	=________ gal =________ lb
Taxi allowance	=________ lb
Maximum number of passengers	=________ gal =________ lb
Maximum baggage compartment load	=________ lb
Maximum fuel ________ gallons (total)	Mains ________ gal = ________ lb Aux ________ gal = ________ lb

Table 11-1 Typical loading table.

Note. In most small airplanes, it is *not* possible to carry both a full fuel load and a full passenger-and-baggage load and remain within the maximum permissible gross weight.

Balance

The Moment of a Force

The *moment* of a force is its *turning effect*, and it depends on two things:

- the *size* (magnitude) of the force; and
- its moment *arm*, which is the distance from the point at which the force is applied to the pivot point (or fulcrum).

If the force being applied (weight) is measured in pounds (lb) and the arm is in inches (in.), then the moment is expressed in *pound-inches* (lb-in), or *inch-pounds* (in-lb).

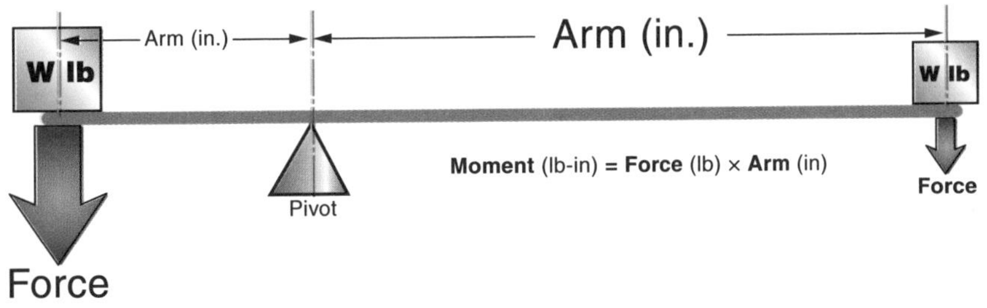

Figure 11-4 Force, arm and moment.

We are all familiar with the effect of a lever—the longer the lever arm, the smaller the force required to achieve the same turning effect. In the case of an airplane, we are not trying to rotate it, but to balance it—to stop it rotating or pitching. This is like a balanced beam, where the moments trying to turn it clockwise are perfectly balanced by the moments wanting to turn it counterclockwise.

We can see in figure 11-5 that the same turning effect (moment) is achieved by placing half the original weight at double the distance. For instance:

- a 2 pound weight, with an arm of 10 inches, has a moment of $2 \times 10 = 20$ lb-in; and
- a 1 pound weight, with an arm of 20 inches, has a moment of $1 \times 20 = 20$ lb-in.

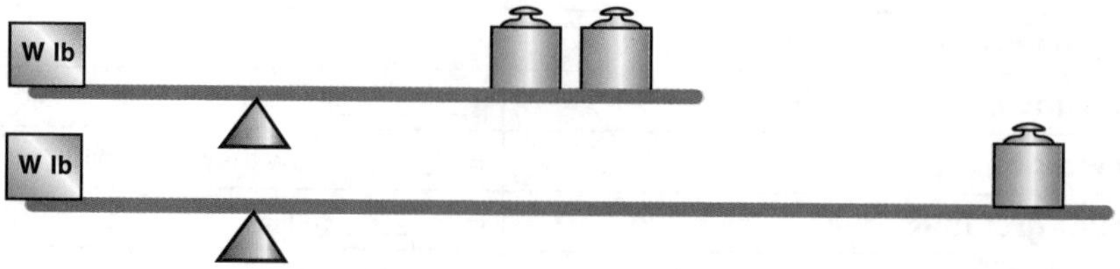

Figure 11-5 Balancing (or turning) moment depends on weight and moment arm.

Balancing a Loaded Beam (or Airplane)

To balance a beam, we need to provide a supporting force at its central position.

To balance a loaded beam (or airplane), we need to provide a supporting force at the point where the total weight may be considered to be concentrated, and where the counterclockwise turning moments are balanced by the clockwise turning moments. This position is called the *center of gravity* (CG). The magnitude of the supporting force will need to equal the total weight. For a beam, the supporting force may be provided by a pivot or by a rope; for an airplane, the supporting force is provided by the lift.

In this case you have probably already estimated the position of the CG to be closer to the 6 pounds weight, in fact about 10 inches from it. If the supporting force is provided at this CG position, the beam will balance.

For an airplane to be in balance, its CG must lie somewhere near the point where the lift is produced by the wings.

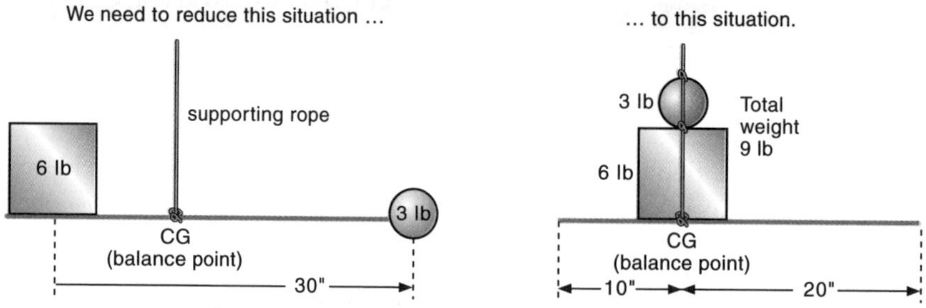

Figure 11-6 Finding the total weight and CG position.

Finding the Position of the CG

To calculate the position of the CG (rather than just estimate it), we need to calculate the total moment—the sum of the turning effects of the individual weights. Then we find the position (CG arm) where a *single* weight (equal to the sum of the individual weights) will have the same total moment. The CG arm can be found using the equation:

$$\text{Total weight} \times \text{CG arm} = \text{total moment}$$

The CG position remains the same regardless of the datum position.

To do this we need to know the individual moment arms as measured from an appropriate datum. It does not matter which point we choose as the datum—the results for the CG position will always be the same. We will take time out to illustrate this important point. By convention, moment arms to the left of the chosen datum are negative; arms to the right of the datum are positive.

Conclusion

Refer to figures 11-7, 11-8 and 11-9. The choice of datum makes no difference to the results for CG position.

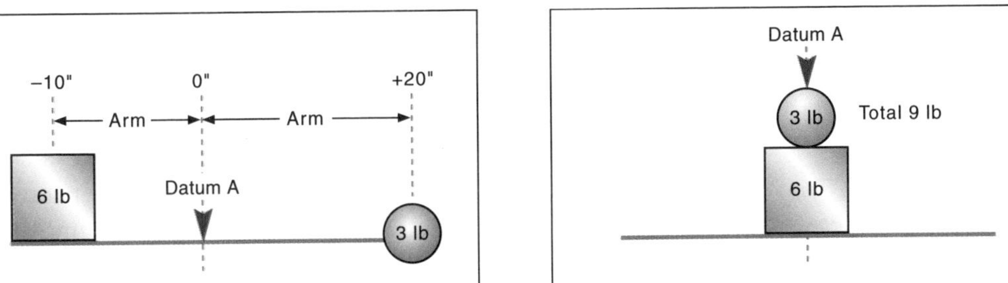

	Weight		Arm		Moment
	6 lb	×	−10 in	=	−60 lb-in
	3 lb	×	+20 in	=	+60 lb-in
Totals	**9 lb** total weight				**0 lb-in** total moment

Total Weight		CG Arm		Total Moment
9 lb	×	CG arm	=	0 lb-in

Therefore CG arm = $\frac{0 \text{ lb-in}}{9 \text{ lb}}$ = 0" from datum, i.e. CG is at Datum A, which is 10" from the left end of the beam, as expected.

Figure 11-7 Using the estimated CG position as datum.

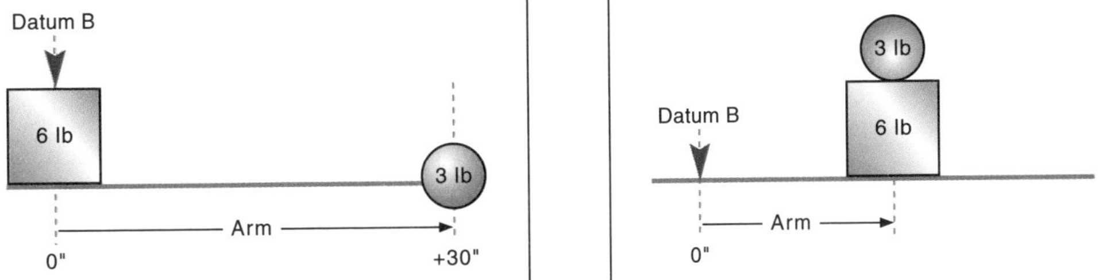

	Weight		Arm		Moment
	6 lb	×	0 in	=	0 lb-in
	3 lb	×	30 in	=	90 lb-in
Totals	**9 lb** total weight				**90 lb-in** total moment

Total Weight		CG Arm		Total Moment
9 lb	×	CG arm	=	90 lb-in

Therefore CG arm = $\frac{90}{9}$ = 10" from datum, i.e. CG is +10" from Datum B, which places the CG 10" from the left end of the beam, the same position as calculated before.

Figure 11-8 Using another datum, the left end of the beam.

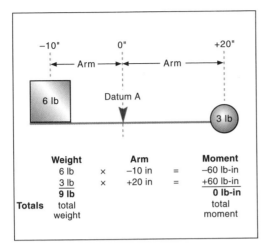

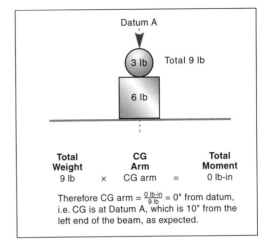

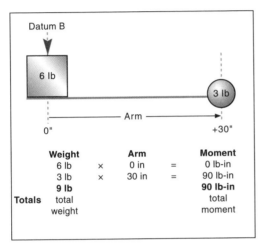

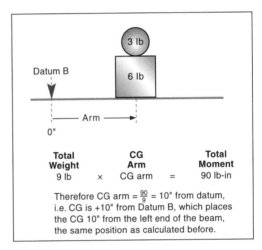

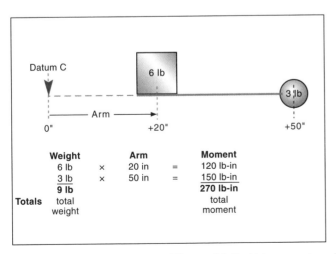

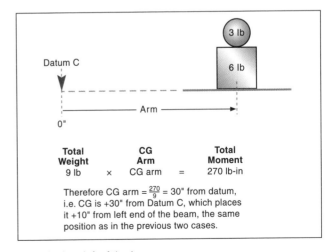

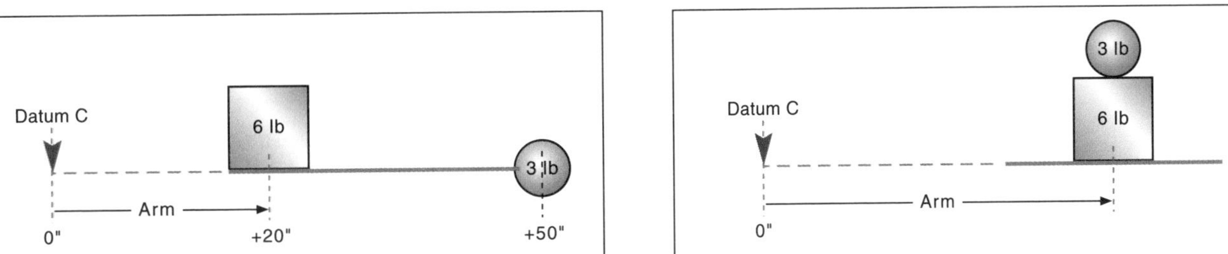

	Weight		Arm		Moment
	6 lb	×	20 in	=	120 lb-in
	3 lb	×	50 in	=	150 lb-in
Totals	**9 lb** total weight				**270 lb-in** total moment

Total Weight		CG Arm		Total Moment
9 lb	×	CG arm	=	270 lb-in

Therefore CG arm = $\frac{270}{9}$ = 30" from datum, i.e. CG is +30" from Datum C, which places it +10" from left end of the beam, the same position as in the previous two cases.

Figure 11-9 Using an external datum, 20 inches left of the beam.

Airplane Datums

In the case of airplanes, the manufacturer specifies a datum point in the weight-and-balance data supplied. Some manufacturers choose the nose of the airplane as the datum; others choose the firewall behind the engine; and others choose an external point along the extended longitudinal axis, ahead of the nose. The datum point for your particular airplane will be stated in its weight-and-balance documents.

The position of the datum is often referred to as "station zero" (or STA 0). Other positions may be specified relative to the station zero datum—for instance, a point 40 inches aft of the datum is called "STA 40." If the datum is behind the nose, then all weights forward of this datum will have a negative arm and a negative moment. The advantage of having a datum at or forward of the nose is that all moments are positive, making the calculations easier.

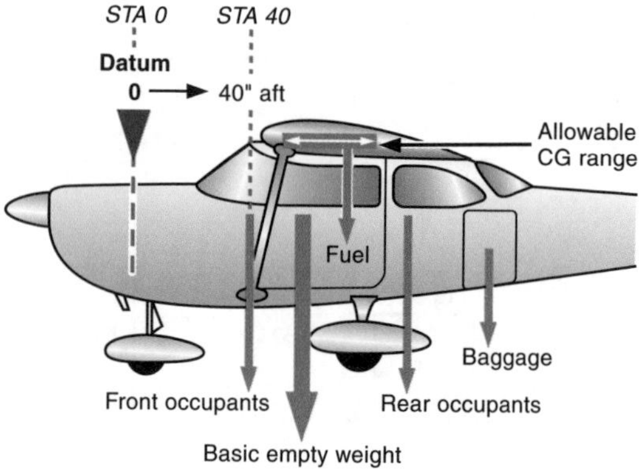

Figure 11-10
The datum can be at any convenient point on the longitudinal axis.

Effect of CG Position on Airplane Handling

The CG of an airplane is on the longitudinal axis and must lie within a specified range for the airplane to be controllable and to fly safely (and legally). The main supporting force in flight counteracting the total weight of the loaded airplane is the lift generated by the wings. It is considered to be concentrated at the center of pressure (CP), usually situated somewhere on the forward section of the wing—its position varies depending on angle of attack and other factors. A small balancing force (usually downward) is provided by the horizontal stabilizer.

If loaded with the CG *well forward*, the horizontal stabilizer has a long moment arm, the airplane will be very stable longitudinally, and resist any pitching moment. The forward position of the CG is limited to ensure that the elevator has sufficient turning moment to overcome the nose-heaviness and excessive longitudinal stability, ensuring that you are able to rotate the airplane for takeoff and flare it for landing at relatively low airspeeds.

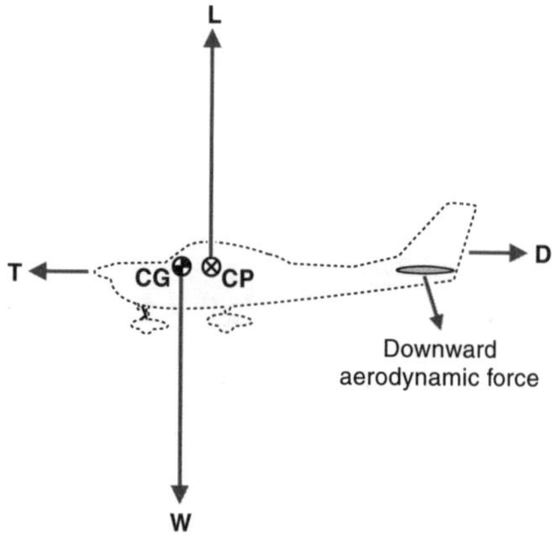

Figure 11-11
Final balance is provided by the horizontal stabilizer.

If the CG *is well aft*, the airplane will be tail-heavy and less stable longitudinally, because of the shorter moment arm from the CG to the CP. The aft position of the CG is limited to ensure that the airplane remains sufficiently stable so that a reasonably steady nose position can be held without excessive and frequent control movements being necessary, and so that the elevator-feel experienced through the control column remains satisfactory.

If the CG is too far aft, the airplane might not recover from a spin.

With a CG that is too far aft, the airplane will be very tail-heavy, will be difficult to control, and tend to stall and/or spin more easily—a situation from which it may be more difficult (or even impossible) to recover.

A Simple Layout for Weight-and-Balance Calculations

The CG is the position through which all of the weights, combined into a gross weight (or total weight), may be considered to act. The total weight should have the same turning moment as the sum of the individual moments.

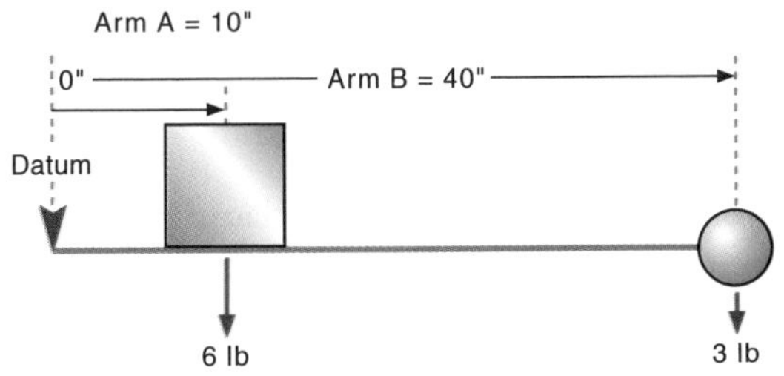

Figure 11-12 The actual situation.

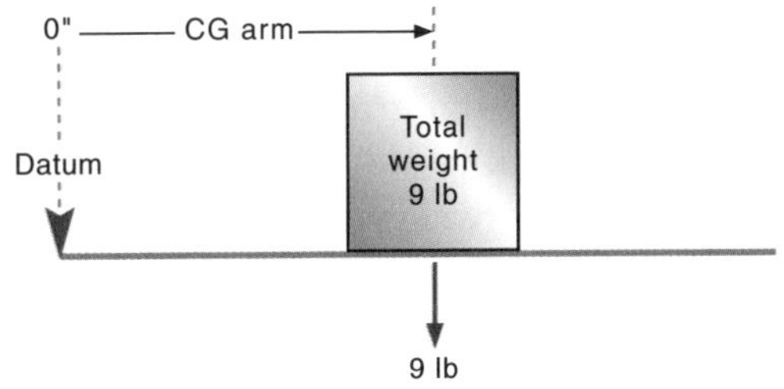

Figure 11-13 The modified situation.

$$\text{Sum of individual moments} = \text{total moment} = \text{total weight} \times \text{its moment arm}$$

$$(6 \times 10) + (3 \times 40) = 180 \text{ lb-in} = 9 \text{ pounds} \times \text{CG arm}$$

The CG position can now be found by dividing the total moment by the total weight.

$$\text{CG arm} = \frac{\text{total moment}}{\text{total weight}} = \frac{180 \text{ lb-in}}{9 \text{ lb}} = 20 \text{ inches}$$

Therefore the CG position is 20 inches aft of the datum. This can be neatly laid out in tabular form, which is the way we do many of our airplane weight-and-balance problems.

	Weight (lb)	Arm (in)	Moment (lb-in)
	6	10	60
	3	40	120
Totals	9	20 CG position	180

Take particular note when doing these problems that you *cannot add the individual arms* to obtain the location of the CG. This answer can be found only by dividing the sum of all the moments by the total weight.

To help you visualize the method by which you can solve this type of problem, the figure below shows the pattern of the steps to be taken—and this pattern can be applied to almost all airplane weight-and-balance problems.

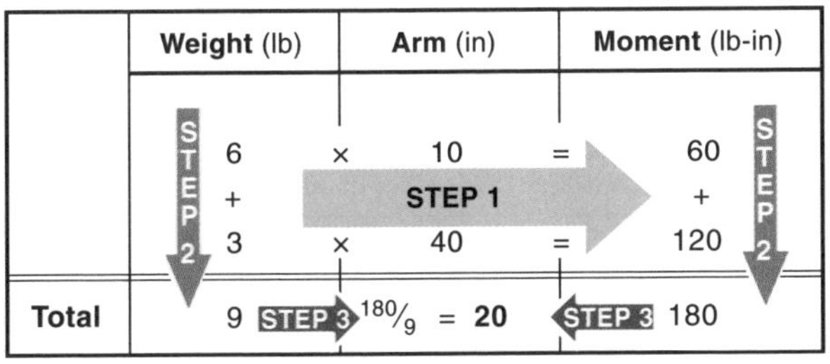

To find the CG position:

1. calculate the individual moments;
2. calculate the total weight and the total moment; and
3. find the CG arm: $\frac{\text{total moment}}{\text{total weight}}$

Figure 11-14 How to find CG position.

Finding the CG for a Loaded Airplane

Using a tabulated layout, like that suggested above, will make all airplane weight-and-balance problems easy to do, and easy to check.

Example 11-1

Given the following information regarding a loaded airplane, calculate total moment and CG position:

- maximum gross weight 2,400 pounds;
- CG limits are 35 inches forward limit and 47.3 inches aft limit;
- empty weight 1,200 pounds acting at position 40 inches aft of the datum;
- pilot and passenger in front seat (arm 36 inches) 300 pounds;
- passengers in rear seat (arm 72 inches) 400 pounds;
- baggage in baggage compartment (arm 100 inches) 35 pounds;
- fuel 30 gallons (arm 50 inches); and
- oil 8 quarts (arm − 10 inches).

Note the following:

1. oil is obviously in front of the datum, since it has a negative arm (it may be that the datum on this airplane is the firewall behind the engine);
2. a calculator will help you in these weight-and-balance problems;
3. using the tabular form provided in most POHs will keep things neat; and
4. a diagram of the airplane is not necessary, but we show one here to help you visualize the situation.

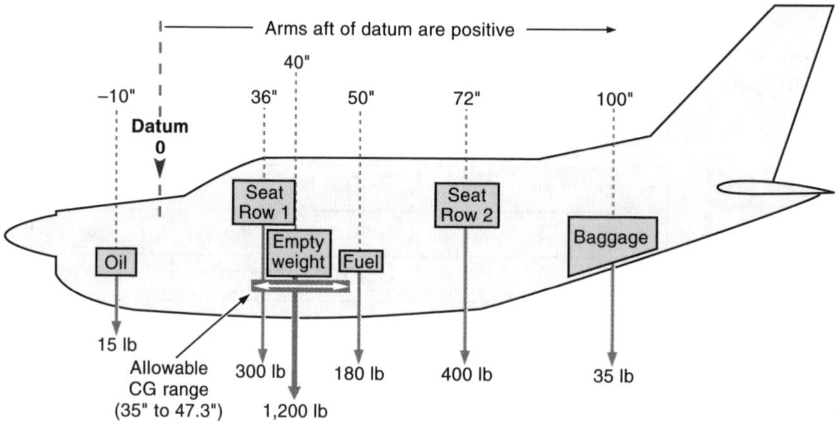

Figure 11-15 The loaded airplane.

Item	**Weight** (lb)	**Arm** (in)	**Moment** (lb-in)
Empty weight	1200	40	48000
Pilot + front passenger	300	36	10800
Rear passengers	400	72	28800
Baggage	35	100	3500
Fuel: 30 gal (× 6 lb)	180	50	9000
Oil: 8 qt (2 gal × 7.5 lb)	15	−10	−150
Totals	2130	**46.9**	99950

Figure 11-16 Flow chart of CG calculation.

Total moment (99,950 lb-in) = total weight (2,130 pounds × CG arm)

Therefore:

$$\text{CG arm} = \frac{99{,}950 \text{ lb-in}}{2{,}130 \text{ lb}} = 46.9 \text{ in aft of datum}$$

With every weight-and-balance problem, you should always check that:
- no weight limit is exceeded; and
- the CG is within limits.

For this airplane, maximum gross weight is 2,400 pounds, so 2,130 pounds is OK. Center of gravity limits are 35 inches forward limit and 47.3 inches aft limit, which means the CG must lie between 35 and 47.3 inches aft of the datum, so 46.9 inches is OK. Therefore this airplane is loaded correctly.

Figure 11-17 Consider passenger distribution.

Weight and/or CG Outside Limits

If the airplane was shown to be loaded incorrectly, then you would have to reorganize the loading so that it is within the weight and CG limits:
- if the airplane is *too heavy*, then you must remove some of the load, which is baggage, passenger(s) or fuel (make your choice!); and
- if the airplane is *out of balance*, with the CG outside the specified limits, then you must move the CG position. There are three ways in which this can be done:
  1. *shift the load*—for example, move the CG forward by moving baggage forward from the baggage compartment to an empty seat (where you would need to restrain it);
  2. *remove some of the load*—for example, move the CG forward by removing some baggage from the baggage compartment, or by leaving one of the rear passengers behind; or
  3. *add ballast*—for example, move the CG aft by adding ballast to the baggage compartment.

Later in this chapter we will show how to ensure that the CG position is within the allowable CG range, and that it remains between the forward and aft limits throughout the flight as fuel is used.

Index Units

When calculating the weight and balance of an airplane, the moments are often quite large numbers, such as 28,800 lb-in. The size of these numbers can be reduced, for instance by dividing them by 1,000 to give *moment/1,000* and 28,800 lb-in would therefore equal 28.8 index units, where 1 index unit = 1,000 lb-in.

In some cases, you will see the moment divided by 100 to give *moment/100* and 28,800 lb-in would then equal 288 index units, where 1 index unit = 100 lb-in.

Example 11-2

If you are given moment/1,000 = 93.2 lb-in/1,000, then the moment = 93,200 lb-in (found by multiplying the index unit by 1,000 in this case).

Example 11-3

If you are given moment/100 = 1,617 lb-in/100, then the moment = 161,700 lb-in (found by multiplying the index unit by 100 in this case).

Graphical Presentation of Weight-and-Balance Data

To eliminate the need to calculate moments or index units, some airplane manufacturers provide a small loading graph that you can use to find the moment in index units. Enter with the weight in pounds on the left-hand side of the graph, move across horizontally to the appropriate guideline (for front seat position, fuel position, and so on), and then vertically down to read off the moment in index units (in this case moment/1,000).

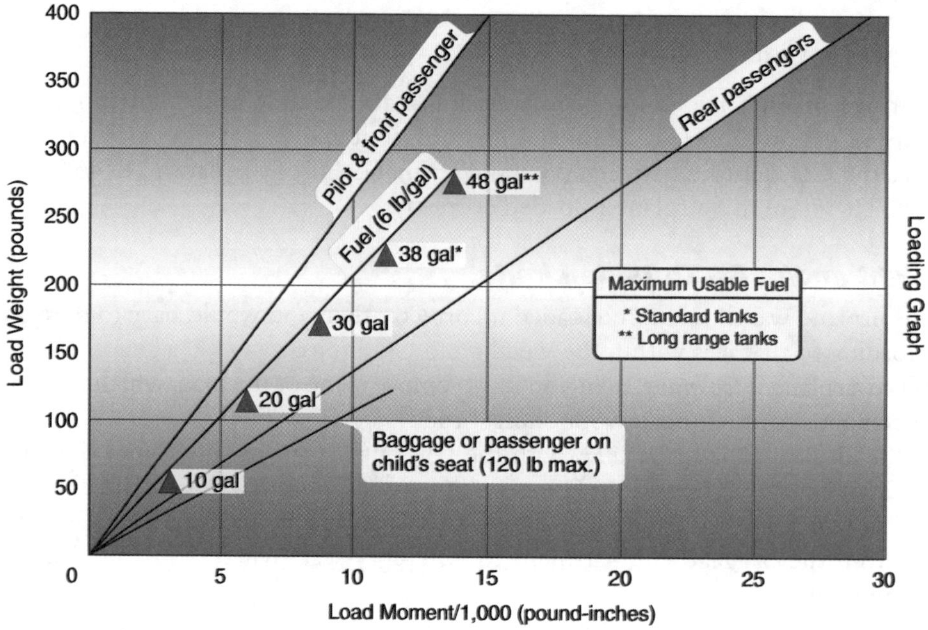

Notes:
1. Lines representing adjustable seats show the pilot or passenger CG on adjustable seats positioned for an average occupant. Refer to the Loading Arrangements diagram for forward and aft limits of occupant CG range.
2. Engine Oil: 8 qt = 15 lbs at -0.2 Moment/1,000
3. The empty weight of this airplane does not include the weight of the oil.

Figure 11-18 Graphical weight-and-balance data. See the following table for calculations.

	Sample Loading Problem	Weight (lb)	Mom/1,000 (lb-in./1,000)
1	Basic empty weight (includes unusable fuel and full oil)	1463	56.9
2*	Usable fuel (35 gallons)	210	10.0
3	Pilot and front passenger	390	14.5
4	Rear passenger	260	19.0
5	Baggage area 1	54	5.0
6**	Baggage area 2	–	–
7	Ramp weight and moment	2377	105.4
8	Fuel allowance for start, taxi and runup	–7	–0.3
9***	Takeoff weight and moment	2370	105.1

Note that given figures are entered in white boxes. Calculated figures are in blue boxes.

**35 gal @ 6 lb/gal = 210 lb. Enter loading graph with 210 lb, go across fuel line, and then read down to get 10.0 mom/1,000*

***Add items 1 to 6*

****Plot on CG Moment envelope Graph in figure 11-19*

Having found the total weight and moment, we can check figure 11-19:

- the weight is outside acceptable limits; and
- the airplane is balanced correctly.

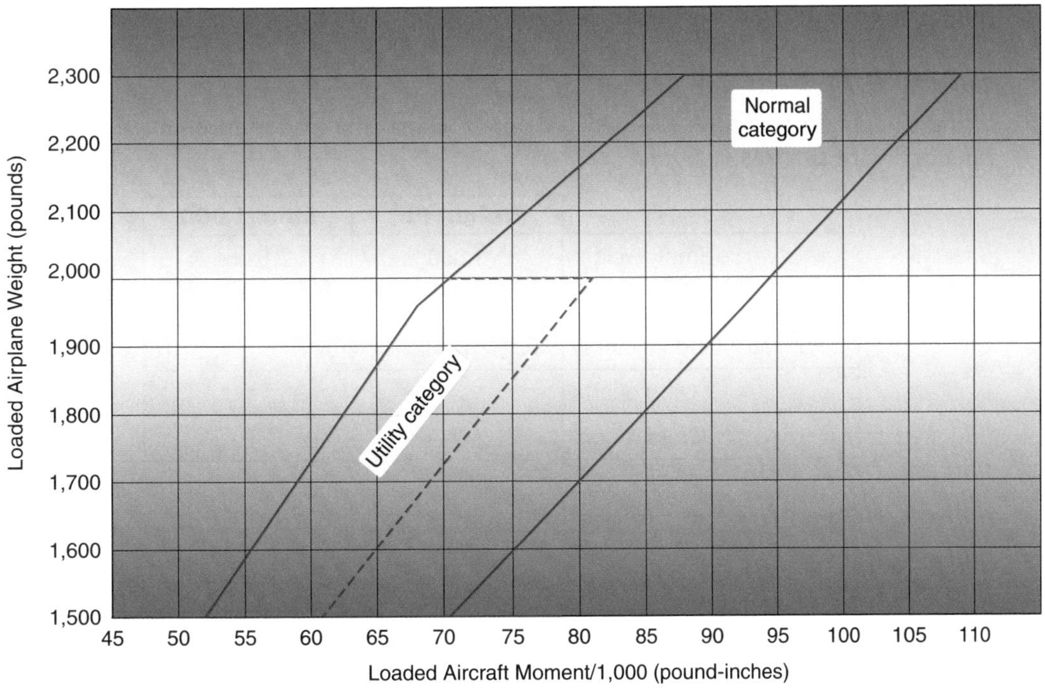

Figure 11-19 Cessna 172 weight-and-balance data.

The maximum weight is specified in figure 11-19: 2,300 pounds for normal category operations; and 2,000 pounds for utility category operations:

- the total weight should not exceed the specified maximum weight;
- if the total moment lies within the CG moment envelope (figure 11-18), then the airplane is in balance with the CG within limits (even though you may not have calculated the actual position of the CG, but only the total moment); or
- if the center of gravity lies within the CG limits (figure 11-19), then the airplane is in balance—but finding the CG involves the extra calculation:

$$\text{CG position} = \frac{\text{total moment}}{\text{total weight}}$$

Using the graph in figure 11-19 avoids the need to calculate the CG position. To illustrate this point, notice that total weight 2,300 pounds and total moment 109,000 pound-inches places the airplane on the extreme limit of the CG moment envelope. If you go ahead and calculate the CG position for this case, you will get:

$$\text{CG position} = \frac{109{,}000 \text{ lb-in}}{2{,}300 \text{ lb}} = 47.4 \text{ inches}$$

This puts you at the extreme limit of the CG limits graph, which is the same message in a slightly different form.

Weight and Balance for the Private Knowledge Exam

The airplane weight-and-balance graphs used in the Private Pilot Knowledge Exam are used in exactly the same way as the Cessna 172 weight-and-balance data. The following example uses these graphs, shown in figure 11-20.

Example 11-4

Using the graphs in figure 11-20, determine the airplane loaded moment and aircraft category with the following data.

	Weight (lb)	Mom/1,000
Empty weight	1,350	51.5
Pilot and front passenger	340	
Full fuel (standard tanks)	Full (38 gallons)	
Oil, 8 quarts		
Gross weight		

Answer: 74.8 pound-inches, utility category.

1. Fill in the table as far as possible.

	Weight (lb)	Mom/1,000 (lb-in/1,000)
Empty weight	1,350	51.5
Pilot and front passenger	340	12.5
Full fuel (standard tanks)	228	11
Oil, 8 quarts	15	-0.2
Gross weight	*1,933*	*74.8*

Read the notes carefully. The bottom note states that the empty weight does not include oil and therefore it must be considered separately. Note 2 gives the oil's weight and moment index units. (Do not omit the minus in the index unit.) The maximum usable fuel in standard tanks is shown in the top graph and is 38 gallons at 6 lb/gal. The fuel therefore weighs 38 × 6 = 228 lb and has an index unit of 11 pound inches. Similarly, to find pilot and front passenger index unit move horizontally across at 340 lb until you meet the pilot and front passenger line and then vertically down to read off the moment index of 12.5.

2. Add up the gross weight and its index unit. Then using the bottom center of gravity moment index, plot the gross weight and moment index unit to discover it falls within the envelope in the utility category.

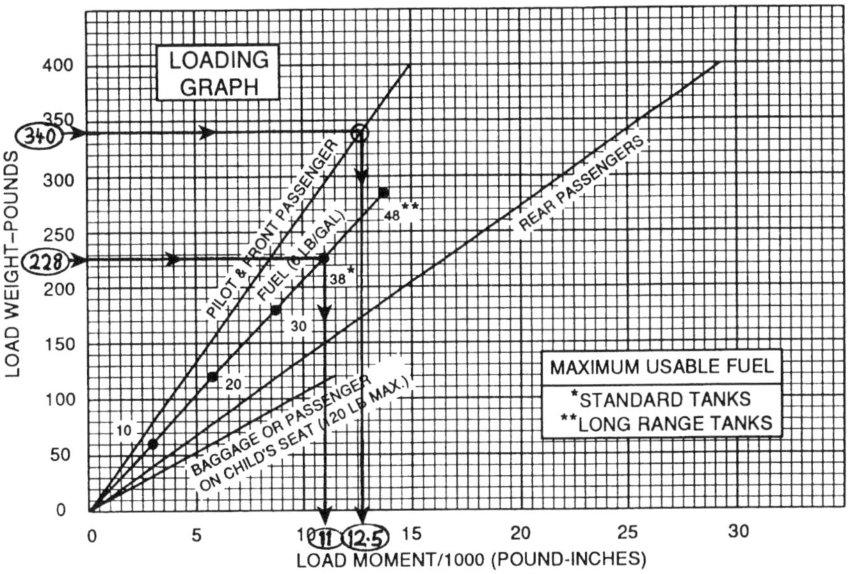

NOTES: (1) Lines representing adjustable seats show the pilot or passenger center of gravity on adjustable seats positioned for an average occupant. Refer to the Loading Arrangements diagram for forward and aft limits of occupant CG range.

(2) Engine Oil: 8 Qt. =15 Lb at –0.2 Moment/1000. ← Oil

NOTE: The empty weight of this airplane does not include the weight of the oil.

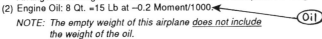

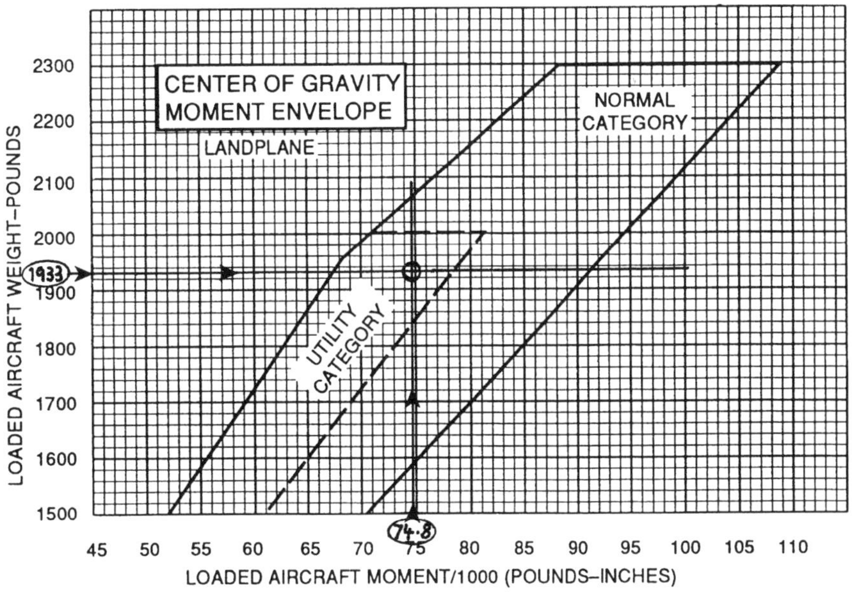

Figure 11-20
Loading and CG envelope charts.

Tabular Presentation of Weight-and-Balance Data

Some manufacturers present their weight-and-balance data, not in graphical form, but in the form of tables as shown in figures 11-21 and 11-22. From figure 11-21, the empty weight is 2,015 pounds (the ⋆ indicating that full oil, 10 quarts, has been included in the empty weight), with an empty weight moment of 1,554 mom/100 (155,400 lb-in). Since full oil is included here, there is no need to consider it separately in your calculations.

Useful Load Weights and Moments

Baggage or 5th seat occupant	
ARM 140	
Weight	Moment/100
10	14
20	28
30	42
40	56
50	70
60	84
70	98
80	112
90	126
100	140
110	154
120	168
130	182
140	196
150	210
160	224
170	238
180	252
190	266
200	280
210	294
220	308
230	322
240	336
250	350
260	364
270	378

Occupants			
Front seats ARM 85		Rear seats ARM 121	
Weight	Moment/100	Weight	Moment/100
120	102	120	145
130	110	130	157
140	119	140	169
150	128	150	182
160	136	160	194
170	144	170	206
180	153	180	218
190	162	190	230
200	170	200	242

Usable fuel		
Main wing tanks ARM 75		
Gallons	Weight	Moment/100
5	30	22
10	60	45
15	90	68
20	120	90
25	150	112
30	180	135
35	210	158
40	240	180
44	264	198

Auxiliary wing tanks ARM 94		
Gallons	Weight	Moment/100
5	30	28
10	60	56
15	90	85
19	114	107

Oil*		
Quarts	Weight	Moment/100
10	19	5

*Included in basic empty weight.

Empty weight ~2,015
MOM/100 ~1,554

Moment limits vs weight

Moment limits are based on the following weight and center of gravity limit data (landing gear down).

Weight condition	Forward CG limit	AFT CG limit
2,950 lb (takeoff or landing)	82.1	84.7
2,525 lb	77.5	85.7
2,475 lb or less	77.0	85.7

Figure 11-21 Loading and CG limits in tabular format.

Figure 11-21 allows you to extract the moment (as an index unit) for a series of weights at each station, without having to multiply the weight by the arm. This tabular presentation saves time and is sufficiently accurate.

Moment Limits vs Weight (Continued)

Weight	Minimum Moment/100	Maximum Moment/100
2,100	1,617	1,800
2,110	1,625	1,808
2,120	1,632	1,817
2,130	1,640	1,825
2,140	1,648	1,834
2,150	1,656	1,843
2,160	1,663	1,851
2,170	1,671	1,860
2,180	1,679	1,868
2,190	1,686	1,877
2,200	1,694	1,885
2,210	1,702	1,894
2,220	1,709	1,903
2,230	1,717	1,911
2,240	1,725	1,920
2,250	1,733	1,928
2,260	1,740	1,937
2,270	1,748	1,945
2,280	1,756	1,954
2,290	1,763	1,963
2,300	1,771	1,971
2,310	1,779	1,980
2,320	1,786	1,988
2,330	1,794	1,997
2,340	1,802	2,005
2,350	1,810	2,014
2,360	1,817	2,023
2,370	1,825	2,031
2,380	1,833	2,040
2,390	1,840	2,048

Weight	Minimum Moment/100	Maximum Moment/100
2,400	1,848	2,057
2,410	1,856	2,065
2,420	1,863	2,074
2,430	1,871	2,083
2,440	1,879	2,091
2,450	1,887	2,100
2,460	1,894	2,108
2,470	1,902	2,117
2,480	1,911	2,125
2,490	1,921	2,134
2,500	1,932	2,143
2,510	1,942	2,151
2,520	1,953	2,160
2,530	1,963	2,168
2,540	1,974	2,176
2,550	1,984	2,184
2,560	1,995	2,192
2,570	2,005	2,200
2,580	2,016	2,208
2,590	2,026	2,216
2,600	2,037	2,224
2,610	2,048	2,232
2,620	2,058	2,239
2,630	2,069	2,247
2,640	2,080	2,255
2,650	2,090	2,263
2,660	2,101	2,271
2,670	2,112	2,279
2,680	2,123	2,287
2,690	2,133	2,295

Weight	Minimum Moment/100	Maximum Moment/100
2,700	2,144	2,303
2,710	2,155	2,311
2,720	2,166	2,319
2,730	2,177	2,326
2,740	2,188	2,334
2,750	2,199	2,342
2,760	2,210	2,350
2,770	2,221	2,358
2,780	2,232	2,366
2,790	2,243	2,374
2,800	2,254	2,381
2,810	2,265	2,389
2,820	2,276	2,397
2,830	2,287	2,405
2,840	2,298	2,413
2,850	2,309	2,421
2,860	2,320	2,428
2,870	2,332	2,436
2,880	2,343	2,444
2,890	2,354	2,452
2,900	2,365	2,460
2,910	2,377	2,468
2,920	2,388	2,475
2,930	2,399	2,483
2,940	2,411	2,491
2,950	2,422	2,499

Figure 11-22 CG limits.

Finding the Moment Index for an Item

To find the mom/100 for any item, there are two ways to proceed. For example, find the mom/100 for a pilot weighing 180 pounds in the front seats.

a. *Using tabular data*: from front-seat table, enter with 180 pounds and extract 153 mom/100.

b. *Mathematically*: moment = weight 180 lb × arm 85 in. = 15,300 lb-in, or 153 mom/100.

Nontabulated Weights

For nontabulated weights, it will be necessary to interpolate when using the tabular data. For example, find the mom/100 for a passenger weighing 177 pounds in the rear seat. There are several ways of interpolating, as follows:

- for a difference of 10 pounds between 170 pounds and 180 pounds, there is a mom/100 difference of 12. A moment/100 difference of 12 for 10 pounds = 1.2 per pound—therefore, for 7 pounds = 7 × 1.2 = 8.4 mom/100, plus the 206 gives 214 mom/100; or
- for a difference of 7 pounds between 170 pounds and 177 pounds, there will be a mom/100 difference of 7/10 of 12 = 8.4 (say 8), and for a weight of 177 pounds, the mom/100 = 206 + 8 = 214.

Note. For nontabulated weights, or for weights outside the table, it is easier to use the mathematical method to find the moment index.

$$\text{Moment} = \text{weight 177 pounds} \times \text{arm 121 inches}$$
$$= 21{,}417 \text{ lb-in, or } 214.7 \text{ mom/100}$$

Weight-Shift Calculations

If, after calculating the weight and balance, you find that the CG is outside the limits of the CG range, it will be necessary to *shift* some weight to bring the CG position back within limits.

Note. The tabulated method shown here does not require the use of a formula. Some instructors prefer to use a formula for weight-shift and weight-change problems. We discuss the formula method at the end of this chapter in the section for commercial pilots.

Example 11-5

You have calculated the total weight to be 4,000 pounds with the CG located at 100 inches aft of datum. What is the new CG position if you shift 50 pounds of baggage from the rear baggage area at station 200 to the forward baggage area at station 50?

	Weight (lb)	Arm (in)	Moment (lb-in)
Original totals	4,000	100	400,000
Rear baggage out	–50	200	–10,000
Forward baggage in	+50	50	+2,500
New totals	*4,000*	*98.13*	*392,500*

Answer: 98.13 inches aft of datum. Remember: *Moment* ÷ *Weight* = *Arm*. You cannot add the arm values to derive total arm.

Example 11-6

You have calculated the total weight to be 4,000 pounds with the CG located 100 inches aft of datum. You wish to move the CG to 98 inches aft of datum, by shifting some baggage from the rear baggage area at station 200 to the forward baggage area at station 50. How much should you shift (to the nearest pound)?

Answer: 53.3 lb. Assume that you shift "w" lb.

	Weight (lb)	Arm (in)	Moment (lb-in)
Original totals	4,000	100	400,000
Rear baggage out	–w	200	–200w
Forward baggage *in*	+w	50	+50w
New totals	*4,000*	*98*	*400,000 - 150w*

$$\text{CG position} = \frac{\text{total moment}}{\text{total weight}}$$

$$98 = \frac{400{,}000 - 150\text{ w}}{4{,}000}$$

Multiply both sides of the equation by 4,000:

$$4{,}000 \times 98 = 400{,}000 - 150\text{ w}$$

$$392{,}000 = 400{,}000 - 150\text{ w}$$

$$150\text{ w} = 400{,}000 - 392{,}000 = 8{,}000$$

$$\therefore \text{w} = \frac{8{,}000}{150} = 53.5\text{ lb}$$

You should do a quick check as follows:

$$\text{New moment (lb-in)} = 400{,}000 - 150\text{ w}$$

$$\text{therefore new moment} = 400{,}000 - (150 \times 53.3) = 392{,}005$$

$$\text{therefore new arm} = \frac{392{,}005}{4{,}000\text{ (wt)}} = 98\text{ inches}$$

Weight-Change Calculations

Having calculated the weight and balance, you may decide to *change* the weight, perhaps because the airplane is overweight (reduce the load), perhaps because the airplane is below maximum weight (you can add extra load), or perhaps because the CG is out of limits and you want to shift it (by removing weight or adding ballast). You can work out a formula to assist in this calculation, but the simplest approach is to follow your now-familiar tabular pattern.

Example 11-7

Your airplane total weight is 4,100 lb with the CG located at 100 inches aft of datum. Maximum permissible weight is 4,000 lb, so you decide to remove 100 lb of baggage from the baggage compartment at station 200. What is the new CG position?

Answer: 97.5 inches aft of datum.

Item	**Weight** (lb)	**Arm** (inches)	**Moment** (lb-inches)
Original totals	STEP 2 ↓ 4100	100 STEP 1 →	410000 STEP 2 ↓
Baggage change	–100	200	–20000
Revised totals	4000 STEP 3 →	97.5	← STEP 3 390000

Figure 11-23 Flow chart of calculation.

Example 11-8

You have calculated the total weight to be 2,400 lb with the CG located at 73.5 inches, which is 1.5 inches outside the aft limit of 72 inches. Maximum permissible weight is 2,400 lb and the airplane is fully loaded, with no possibility of shifting the load. What is the minimum baggage (to the next pound) you must remove from station 150 to bring the CG within limits for takeoff?

Answer: 47 lb. Set up the table and assume you remove "w" lb of baggage.

	Weight (lb)	Arm (in)	Moment (lb-in)
Original totals	2,400	73.5	176,400
Baggage change	–w	150	–150w
Revised totals	*2,400 – w*	*72.0*	*176,400 – 150w*

$$\text{New CG position } 72.0 = \frac{\text{total moment}}{\text{total weight}}$$

$$72.0 = \frac{176{,}400 - 150\text{ w}}{2{,}400 - \text{w}}$$

Multiplying both sides by (2,400 – w) (note that the (2,400 w) cancels out on side of the equation):

$$72 \times (2{,}400 - \text{w}) = 176{,}400 - 150\text{ w}$$
$$172{,}800 - 72\text{ w} = 176{,}400 - 150\text{ w}$$
$$150\text{ w} - 72\text{ w} = 176{,}400 - 172{,}800$$
$$78\text{ w} = 3{,}600$$
$$\text{w} = \frac{3{,}600}{78} = 46.15$$

To the next pound to be on the safe side, this is 47 lb.

Weight-Shift/Change Calculations

A more usual occurrence is for there to be a change in both the location and weight of passengers, fuel or baggage.

Example 11-9

You have calculated the TOW to be 2,800 lb, with the CG moment at 2,296 mom/100 index units. Before departure you are advised that a passenger weighing 180 lb and seated at STA 85.0 will not be traveling, and will be replaced by another person weighing 200 lb and carrying 40 lb of luggage. This passenger will be seated at STA 85.0 and the accompanying luggage stowed at STA 140.0. Calculate the new CG moment in index units, and how far the CG has moved forward or aft.

	Weight (lb)	Arm (in)	Moment (lb-in)
TOW	2,800	82.0	2,296
Passenger OUT	–180	85.0	–153
New totals	2,620	–	2,143
Passenger IN	+200	85.0	+170
Baggage IN	+40	140.0	+56
New TOW	*2,860*	*82.83*	*2,369*

Answer: The new mom/100 = 2,369, and the CG has moved (82.83 – 82.0) = 0.83 inches aft.

CG Movement

The center of gravity moves during flight as fuel is used.

Up to this point, we have ignored the fact that during flight, the gross weight of the airplane decreases as fuel is used. This change in weight will cause the position of the CG to move gradually. The amount of movement of the CG will depend on the location, and therefore the moment arm of the fuel tanks. The airplane designer ensures that the fuel tanks are positioned so that their effective arms, when full and empty, are not much displaced from the fore-and-aft CG limits of the airplane.

To be precise in your weight-and-balance calculations, you should confirm that the CG position (or total moment) is within limits throughout the flight. This is done by checking that the CG is within limits at both the *takeoff weight* (TOW) and *zero fuel weight* (ZFW).

> **Note.** If you considered weight and balance at the landing weight (rather than at the zero fuel weight), and found that the CG was right on the rear limit, then any further fuel burn-off (say for an emergency diversion) may take you out of the CG envelope. Therefore, it is better to consider the moment at the ZFW, rather than at the LW. Despite this, you may be asked in the Knowledge Exam to compute the weight and balance at landing, and some airplane loading data may require it (see the note on figure 11-26).

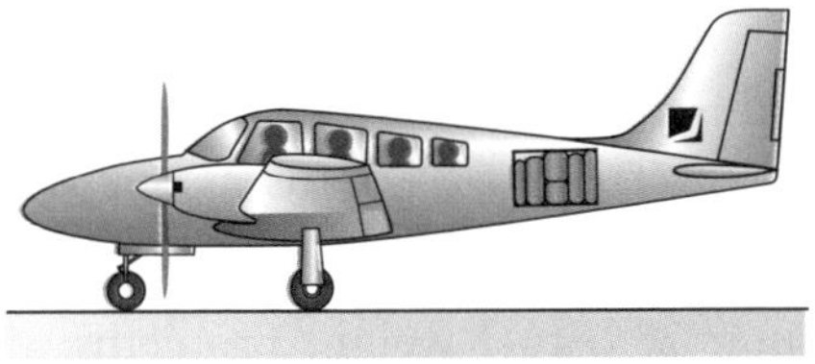

Figure 11-24 Zero fuel weight.

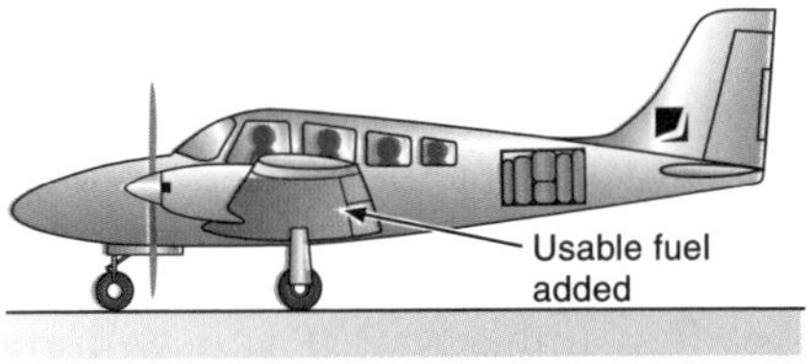

Figure 11-25 Gross weight.

Example 11-10

You have calculated the loaded weight and moment of your airplane to be 3,400 lb and 180 lb-in/1,000. The fuel on board is 60 gallons. Is the airplane loaded satisfactorily? If not, offer a suggestion. (Refer to the graphs in figure 11-26.)

Answer:

	Weight (lb)	Mom/1,000 (lb-in/1,000)
Takeoff weight	3,400	180 (OK—just within limits)
Fuel: 60 gal	–360	–15.5 (Moment from top graph)
Zero fuel weight	*3,040*	*164.5 (NOT OK—outside limits)*

At takeoff, the total moment is right on the rear limit. As fuel burns off, however, the CG moment position on the graph will move toward the ZFW CG moment position, which is *outside limits*. Therefore this flight should *not* commence unless the airplane is loaded differently—a solution could be to shift passengers or baggage forward if possible. Then you should recalculate the weight and balance to confirm within limits.

Suppose you decide to move a 150 lb passenger from a rear seat to an empty center seat. Total weight will be unchanged, but the moment for this passenger will change from 15.0 in the rear seat to 10.7 in the center seat, a decrease of 4.3 lb-in/1,000. Now recalculate the weight and balance.

	Weight (lb)	Mom/1,000 (lb-in/1,000)
Original TOW and Moment	3, 400	180
Adjustment—move 150 lb passenger from rear to center	0	–4.3
New TOW Moment	3,400	175.7 (OK—within limits)
Fuel: 60 gal	–360	–15.5 (OK—within limits)
Now ZFW and Moment	*3,040*	*160.2*

To help in deciding how much weight you have to move in order to bring the ZFW within the CG limits, you can easily establish the required minimum change in moment from the graph. In this example we find:

ZFW 3,040, actual moment	164.5 mom/1,000
for ZFW 3,040, limiting rear moment	160.5
therefore minimum *change required in moment* =	*4.0 mom/1,000*

Since 164.5 is outside the rear limit, this required change must be forward. Moving from the rear seat to the center gives a moment change of 4.3; this is slightly more than the minimum and is therefore acceptable.

Note. It is unlikely that you will encounter zero fuel weight problems until operating a twin-engine aircraft.

Example 11-11

State if the CG is within the allowable CG envelope for the following load configuration. (See figure 11-26.)

Empty weight (oil included)	2,260 lb
Empty weight moment	93.2 lb-in/1,000
Pilot + front seat passenger	380 lb
Center passengers	240 lb
Aft passengers	220 lb
Baggage	120 lb
Fuel	75 gal

Note. A convenient way to tabulate your answer is to calculate the ZFW and moment (without fuel) and then add the fuel weight and moment to find the takeoff weight and moment.

Answer: Yes, the CG is within limits throughout the flight.

	Weight (lb)	Mom/1,000 (lb-in/1,000)
Empty weight	2,260	93.2
Pilot and front seat passenger	380	14.0
Center passengers	240	17.0
Aft passengers	220	22.0
Baggage	120	16.5
ZFW	3,220	162.7 (OK)
Fuel: 75 gal	450	19.2
Total weight	*3,670*	*181.9 (OK)*

Note for Commercial Students. The weight-and-balance graphs used in the Commercial Knowledge Exam are shown in figure 11-34 (page 280). Practice questions using these graphs are in the commercial review at the end of the chapter.

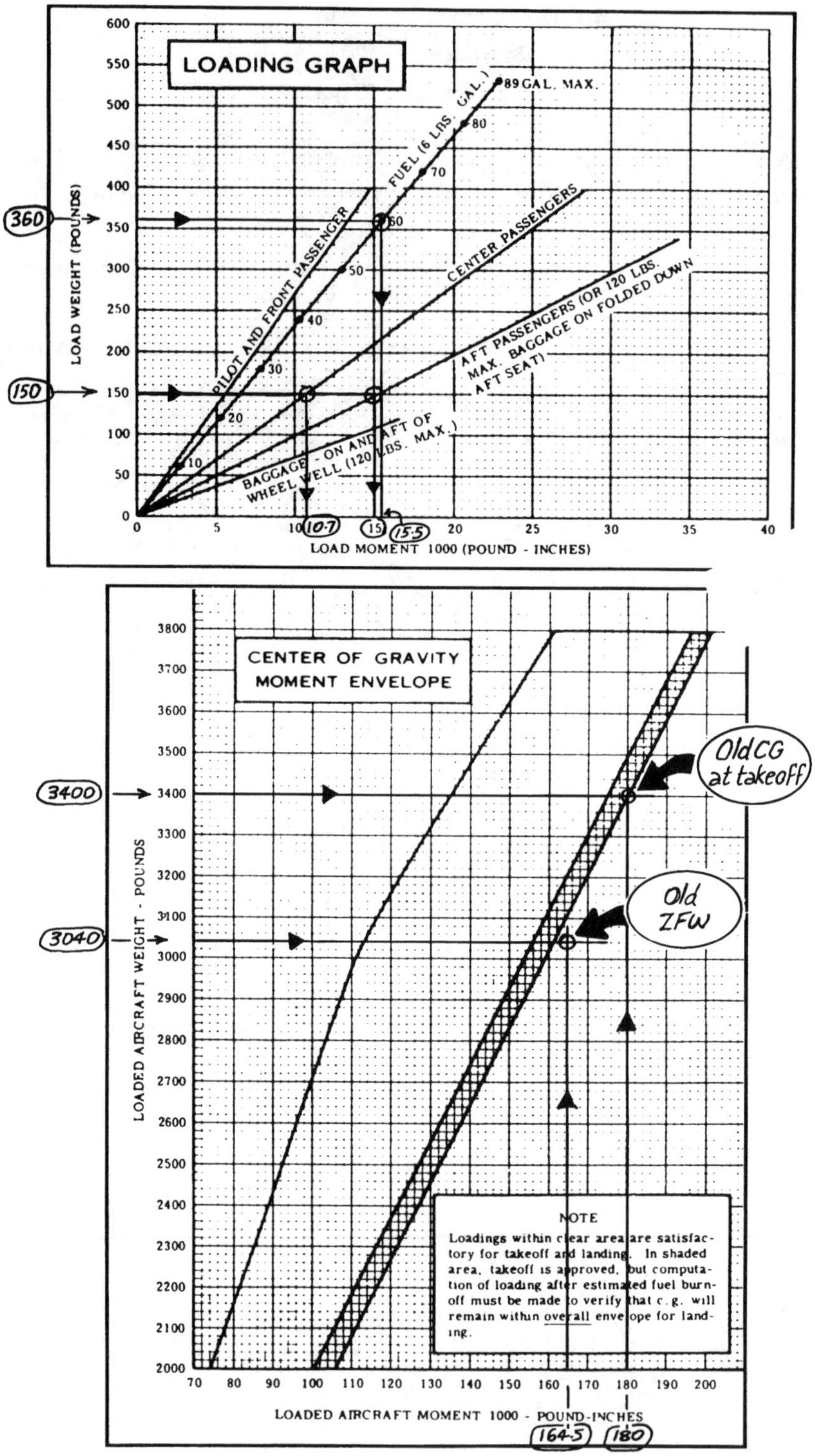

Figure 11-26 Example 11-11.

Weight-Shift and Weight-Change by Formula

Weight-shift and weight-change problems may be easily solved using our standard tabulated layout, without the need to remember any formulas. Some pilots, however, prefer to use a formula for these problems, and so we now include this method, which is based on:

Any change in individual moments = the change in total moments.

Weight Shift

Suppose weight "w" is shifted from the aft baggage compartment to the forward baggage compartment (figure 11-27). This will have the effect of shifting the CG forward. Since weight is shifted (not changed), airplane gross weight remains the same.

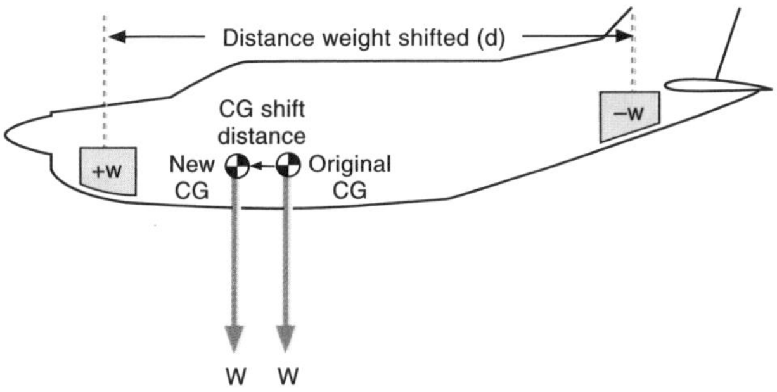

Figure 11-27 Shifting weight forward moves the CG forward.

Change in individual moments = change in total moment

Therefore:

Weight shifted × distance shifted = airplane GW CG shift

Example 11-12

Your loaded airplane weighs 4,000 lb with CG at station 91.0. How much baggage must be shifted from the rear baggage area (station 150) to the forward baggage area (station 30) in order to move the CG to station 89.0?

$$\begin{aligned} \text{Weight shifted} \times \text{distance shifted} &= \text{GW} \times \text{CG shift} \\ \text{w} \times (150 - 30) &= \text{GW} \times (91.0 - 89.0) \\ \text{w} \times 120 &= 4{,}000 \times 2 \\ \text{w} &= \frac{4{,}000 \times 2}{120} = 66.7 \text{ lb} \end{aligned}$$

CPL

Weight-Change

If weight "w" is added to the forward bag-gage compartment (figure 11-28), it will have the effect of shifting the CG forward, as will removing weight from aft of the CG. Conversely, reducing weight ahead of the CG will shift the CG rearward, as will adding weight aft. Weight added to shift the CG is known as *ballast*.

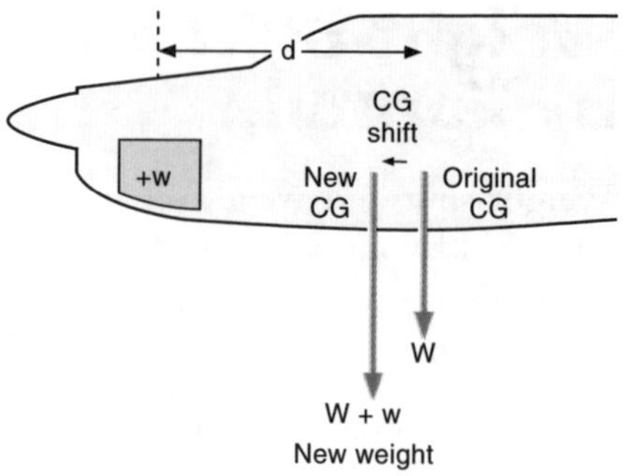

Figure 11-28 Adding weight forward moves the CG forward.

Change in individual moments = change in total moment

Therefore:

Weight shifted × distance shifted = new GW CG shift

Example 11-13

Your airplane weighs 4,000 lb with the CG located at station 85.0. The fuel tanks are at station 84.0, and the fuel consumption is 10 gph. What is the CG position after 2 hours of flight?

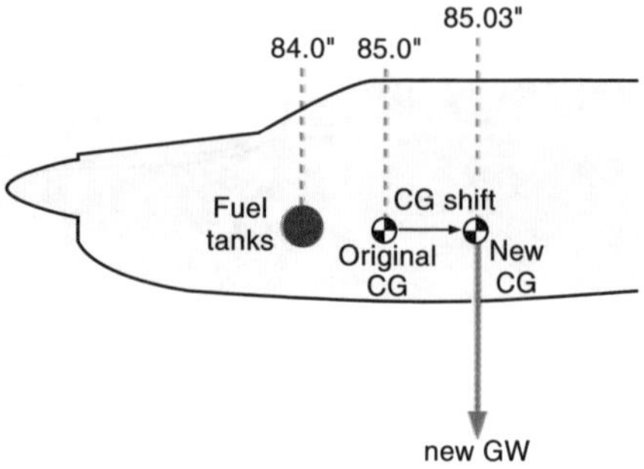

Figure 11-29 Removing weight forward of the CG, shifts the CG aft.

Answer:

$$\text{Fuel burn} = 2 \text{ hours @ } 10 \text{ GPH}$$
$$= 20 \text{ gallons}$$
$$20 \times 6 \text{ lb} = 120 \text{ lb}$$

Therefore:

$$\text{New GW} = 4{,}000 - 120 = 3{,}880 \text{ lb}$$

As the fuel forward of the CG reduces, the CG will move aft:

$$\text{Change in individual moments} = \text{change in total moment}$$
$$120 \times 1.0 = 3{,}880 \times \text{CG shift}$$
$$\text{CG shift} = \frac{120 \times 1.0}{3{,}880} = 0.03$$

Therefore, new position of CG is:

(85.0 + 0.03) = 85.03 inches aft of the datum (figure 11-29).

Mean Aerodynamic Chord

The mean aerodynamic chord (MAC) is the chord of an imaginary rectangular wing that has the same aerodynamic characteristics as the actual wing. In effect, this replaces the actual wing (which may have a quite different and more complicated plan form) for calculation purposes with a theoretical simplified, rectangular average wing. The

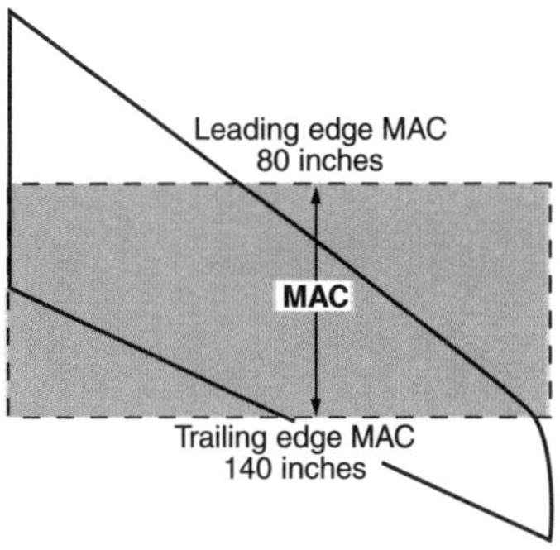

Figure 11-30
A typical
mean aerodynamic chord.

MAC is the chord of this theoretical rectangular wing and its main use is as a reference for longitudinal stability characteristics (such as balance). The MAC of the airplane illustrated in figures 11-30 and 11-31 is:

- length of MAC 60.00 inches; and
- location of leading edge of MAC 80.00 inches aft of reference datum.

This concept of MAC is used by designers when they determine stability characteristics of the airplane, bearing in mind that any turning moments generated by the lift–weight and thrust–drag couples will have to be balanced by a force (usually downward) from the horizontal stabilizer.

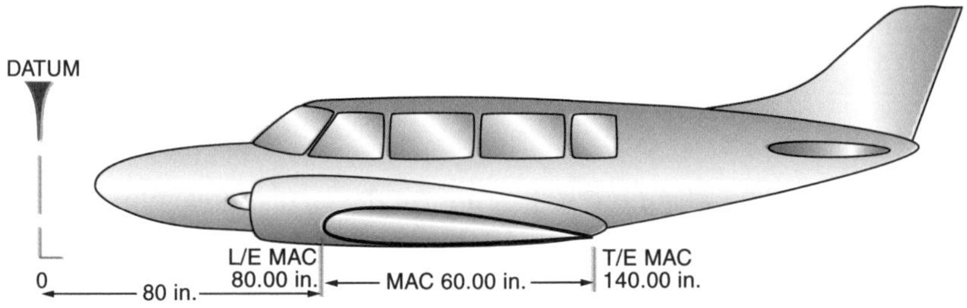

Figure 11-31 MAC in relation to the airplane.

Calculating CG Position as a "Percentage MAC"

The greatest forces acting on an airplane are weight and lift. It is important that the distance between them is not too great to ensure that their turning moment is kept within limits. Since the lift force will act somewhere along the mean aerodynamic chord, it is common for the CG to be specified as a position on the MAC, usually as a percentage aft of the MAC leading edge.

$$\text{CG position as \% MAC} = \frac{\text{distance aft of MAC leading edge}}{\text{MAC}} \times \frac{100}{1} \text{ \% MAC}$$

Example 11-14

Convert a CG of 100.00 inches aft of reference datum to a percentage MAC. CG at 100.00 inches aft of datum is (100.00 – 80.00) = 20.00 inches aft of the MAC leading edge.

$$\text{\% MAC} = \frac{\text{distance aft of MAC leading edge}}{\text{MAC}} \times \frac{100}{1}$$

$$= \frac{20.00}{60.00} \times \frac{100}{1} = 33.3\% \text{ MAC}$$

Note. The center of pressure (CP), through which the lift force may be considered to act, is, for most airplanes in normal flight, somewhere on the forward half of the wing chord. The CG (through which the weight force may be considered to act) should be forward of the CP so that, if power fails, the nose will drop.

CPL

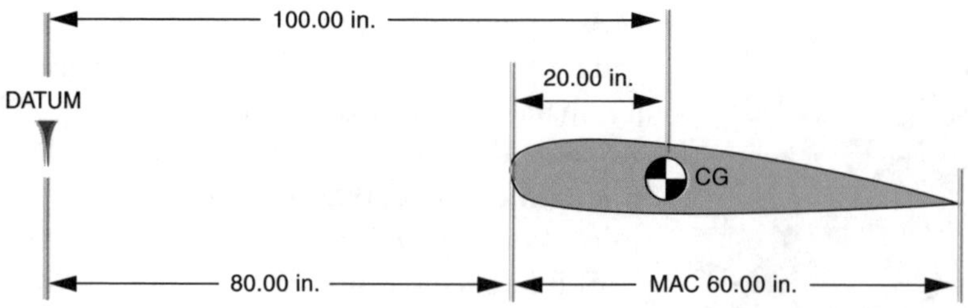

Figure 11-32
Example 11-14.

Relating the Allowable CG Range to the MAC

The weight-and-balance documents for a certain airplane specify the position and length of the mean aerodynamic chord (MAC leading edge 219.0 inches aft of datum; length of MAC 190.0 inches), which allows us to relate the allowable CG range to the MAC.

For this airplane, at all weights, the *aft CG limit* is 268.0 inches, which is (268.0 − 219.0) = 49.0 inches aft of the MAC leading edge:

$$\% \text{ MAC} = \frac{49.0}{190.0} \times \frac{100}{1} = 25.79\% \text{ MAC}$$

However the *forward CG limit* often depends on the airplane weight. Below a certain low weight, the forward CG limit is at 240.0 inches, which is (240.0 − 219.0) = 21.0 inches aft of the MAC leading edge:

$$\% \text{ MAC} = \frac{21.0}{190.0} \times \frac{100}{1} = 11.05\% \text{ MAC}$$

At the maximum gross weight, the forward CG limit is 256.0 inches, which is (256.0 − 219.0) = 37.0 inches aft of the MAC leading edge:

$$\% \text{ MAC} = \frac{37.0}{190.0} \times \frac{100}{1} = 19.47\% \text{ MAC}$$

Between these weights the forward limit progressively moves aft as weight increases. These are quite typical figures, in that the CG range for most conventional airplanes lies somewhere between 10% and 30% MAC. Provided that the CG lies within the CG limits for that particular gross weight, the in-flight stability and control characteristics of the airplane will be acceptable.

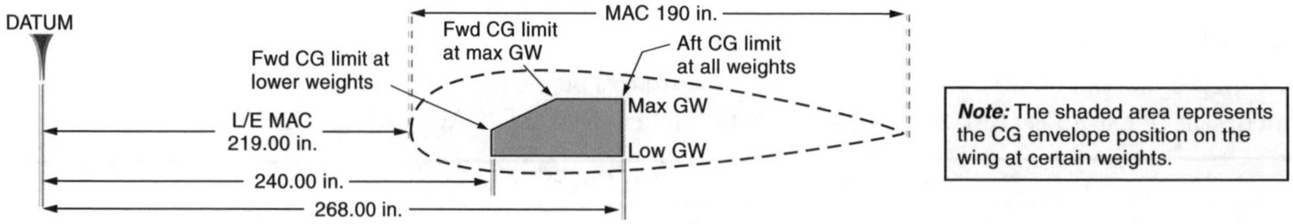

Figure 11-33 The CG range related to MAC.

The allowable CG range is quite restricted (28.0 inches maximum, covering only some 15% of the forward part of the MAC) because the lift and weight forces are so large. Small movements in the position of the CG or the center of pressure will produce large alterations of turning moments, because of the magnitude of the forces involved.

End CPL

Review 11
Weight and Balance

Weight and Balance

1. What term describes the maximum allowable gross weight permitted for takeoff?
2. True or false? A short runway may not allow you to land at the MLW (structural) but at a lighter performance-limited landing weight.
3. True or false? Landing weight = takeoff weight minus fuel burn-off.
4. The empty weight of an airplane includes which of the following items:
   a. airframe.
   b. powerplant.
   c. permanently installed equipment.
   d. full fuel.
   e. unusable fuel.
   f. full oil.
   g. unusable oil.
   h. hydraulic fluid.
   i. pilots.
   j. passengers.
   k. baggage.
5. How many pounds do the following weigh:
   a. one gallon of AVGAS?
   b. 26 gallons of AVGAS?
6. An aircraft is loaded 110 pounds over maximum certificated gross weight. If fuel (AVGAS) is drained to bring the aircraft weight within limits, how much fuel should be drained?
7. True or false? If the CG is located at the rear limit, the airplane will be very stable longitudinally.
8. True or false? The longer the moment arm from the CG, the greater the turning effect of a given force.
9. The CG of an aircraft may be determined by:
   a. dividing total arms by total moments.
   b. dividing total moments by total weight.
   c. multiplying total weight by total moments.
10. If 1 index unit = 100 lb-in, what is the moment for 176 index units?
11. If all index units are positive when computing weight and balance, the location of the datum would be at the:
    a. centerline of the mainwheels.
    b. nose, or out in front of the airplane.
    c. centerline of the nose or tailwheel, depending on the type of airplane.
12. Given the following data, what is the maximum amount of fuel (in pounds and gallons) that you can carry if the maximum takeoff weight is 2,400 lb? Tank capacity is 50 gallons. (*No need to consider CG position.*)

Empty weight	1,432 lb
Front seat occupants	320 lb
Rear seat occupants	340 lb
Baggage	20 lb
Oil	8 qt 15 lb

13. Given the following data, what is the maximum weight of baggage that can be carried when the airplane is loaded for a takeoff that is performance-limited to 2,910 lb, because of a high elevation airport and high temperatures? (*No need to consider balance.*)

Basic empty weight (incl. full oil)	2,015 lb
Front seat occupants	369 lb
Rear seat occupants	267 lb
Fuel (36 gal)	—

14. Where is the CG located in the following situation? (No mention of oil, so assume full oil in empty weight.)
    a. 92.44.
    b. 94.01.
    c. 119.8.

	Wt (lb)	Arm (in)	Mom (lb-in)
Empty weight	1,495.0	101.4	151,593.0
Pilot and passengers	380.0	64.0	—
Fuel (30 gal usable)	—	96.0	—

Weight-and-Balance Calculations

Use the loading graphs in figure 11-20 (page 263) for questions 15 to 17.

15. Given the following data:
   a. calculate the loaded index units (moments/1,000) of the airplane.
   b. determine in which category you may operate it.

	Weight (lb)	Mom/1,000
Empty weight	1,350	51.5
Pilot and front passenger	310	—
Rear passengers	96	—
Fuel (38 gal)	—	—
Oil (8 qt)	—	–0.2

16. Given the following data:
   a. calculate the loaded moment (normal category).
   b. determine if it is within limits.
   c. determine where the CG is.

	Weight (lb)	Mom/1,000
Empty weight	1,350	51.5
Pilot and front passenger	380	—
Fuel (48 gal)	—	—
Oil (8 qt)	—	—

17. What is the maximum amount of fuel that may be in the tanks when the airplane is loaded as given below:
   a. 24 gallons.
   b. 32 gallons.
   c. 40 gallons.

	Weight (lb)	Mom/1,000
Empty weight	1,350	51.5
Pilot and front passenger	340	—
Rear passengers	310	—
Baggage	45	—
Oil (8 qt)	—	—

Use the tables in figures 11-21 and 11-22 (pages 264 and 265) for questions 18 to 20.

18. Calculate the maximum weight of baggage that can be carried when the airplane is loaded as follows:

Front seat occupants	387 lb
Rear seat occupants	293 lb
Fuel	35 gal

19. Given the following:
   a. determine the weight.
   b. determine the balance.
   c. calculate if the CG and weight of the airplane are within limits.

Front seat occupants	350 lb
Rear seat occupants	325 lb
Baggage	27 lb
Fuel	35 gal

20. Is the following weight and balance within limits?

Front seat occupants	415 lb
Rear seat occupants	110 lb
Baggage	32 lb
Fuel	63 gal

Weight–Shift Calculations

Refer to figures 11-21 and 11-22 (pages 264 and 265) for questions 21 to 25.

21. Which action can adjust the airplane's weight to the maximum gross weight and the CG located within limits for takeoff, when it is loaded as given below?
   a. Drain 12 gallons of fuel.
   b. Drain 9 gallons of fuel.
   c. Transfer 12 gallons of fuel from the main tanks to the auxiliary tanks.

Front seat occupants	425 lb
Rear seat occupants	300 lb
Fuel (main tanks)	44 gal

22. On landing, the front passenger (180 lb) departs the airplane. A rear passenger (204 lb) moves to the front passenger position. What effect does this have on the CG if the airplane weighed 2,690 lb and the mom/100 was 2,260 prior to the passenger transfer?
   a. CG moves forward approx. 3 inches.
   b. Weight changes, but CG is unaffected.
   c. CG moves forward approx. 0.1 inch.

23. With the following loading:
   a. can you carry 100 lb of baggage (if not, what action could be taken to carry it)?
   b. what is the final CG position?

Pilot	180 lb
2 passengers on rear seats	2 x 170 lb
Minimum fuel required	30 gal

24. What effect does a 35 gal fuel burn have on the weight and balance, if the airplane weighs 2,890 lb and the mom/100 is 2,452 at takeoff?
  a. Weight reduced by 210 lb, and CG is aft of limits.
  b. Weight reduced by 210 lb, and CG is unaffected.
  c. Weight reduced to 2,680 lb, and CG moves forward.

25. Given the following:
  a. can you take off under the following conditions and, if not, what ballast must be added in the baggage locker?
  b. calculate the landing weight and CG location (*assume auxiliary fuel used first*).

Pilot & passenger (front)	300 lb
Passenger (rear)	180 lb
Baggage	60 lb
Fuel (44 mains + 15 aux)	59 gal
Planned fuel burn-off to landing	35 gal

Commercial Review

26. Calculate the position of the CG for the following weights at the given locations.

Weight A	165 lb at 135 in. aft of datum.
Weight B	125 lb at 115 in. aft of datum.
Weight C	75 lb at 85 in. aft of datum.

27. Determine the CG under these conditions.

Empty weight	857 lb, arm +29.07 in.
Pilot (fwd seat)	145 lb, arm –45.30 in.
Passenger (aft seat)	175 lb, arm +1.60 in.
Ballast	15 lb, arm –45.30 in.

Refer to figure 11-34 (page 280) for questions 28 and 29.

28. Given the following, is the airplane loaded within limits?
  a. Yes, the weight and CG is within limits.
  b. No, the weight exceeds the maximum allowable.
  c. No, the weight is acceptable, but the CG is aft of the aft limit.

Empty weight (oil included)	1,271 lb
Empty weight moment	102.04 lb-in/1,000
Pilot + copilot	400 lb
Rear seat passenger	140 lb
Cargo	100 lb
Fuel	37 gal

29. Given the following, will the CG remain within limits after 30 gallons of fuel have been used in flight?
  a. Yes, the CG will remain within limits.
  b. No, the CG will be located aft of the CG limit.
  c. Yes, but the CG will be located in the shaded area of the CG envelope.

Empty weight (oil is included)	1,271 lb
Empty weight moment (in-lb/1,000)	102.04
Pilot and copilot	360 lb
Cargo	340 lb
Fuel	37 gal

Solve questions 30 and 31 using the tabular method.

30. The airplane is loaded to a gross weight of 5,000 lb, with three pieces of luggage in the rear baggage compartment. The CG is 98 inches aft of datum, which is 2 inches aft of the permissible rear limit. If you move two pieces of luggage weighing a total of 100 lb from the rear baggage compartment (145 inches aft of datum) to the front compartment (45 inches aft of datum), what is the new CG?

31. Determine the position of the CG after 1 hour 45 minutes of flight time, given the following data:

Total weight	4,037 lb
CG location station	67.8
Fuel consumption	14.7 gph
Fuel tanks	station 68.0

Obtain the solutions to questions 32 to 34 by formula.

32. Given the following data, after 1 hour 30 minutes of flight time, the CG would be located at station:
  a. 67.79.
  b. 68.79.
  c. 70.78.

Total weight	4,137 lb
CG location station	67.8
Fuel consumption	13.7 gph
Fuel tanks station	68.0

an airplane loaded with a ramp weight 0 lb and having a CG of 94.0, approxi- how much baggage would have to be from the rear baggage area at station 180, to the forward baggage area at station 40, in order to move the CG to 92.0?

a. 52.14 lb.

b. 62.24 lb.

c. 78.14 lb.

34. Using the *Moment Limit versus Weight* table in figure 11-22 (page 265), express the fwd (minimum) and rear (maximum) CG limits as % MAC for an airplane with a gross weight of 2,700 lb. The leading edge of the MAC is 75 inches aft of the datum, and the length of the MAC is 40 inches.

35. Given the following, what minimum weight must be added as ballast in the rear baggage compartment (120 inches aft of datum), to bring the CG within limits?:

Total weight	2,017 lb
CG location	58.5 in. aft of datum
CG limits	between 60 and 68 in. aft of datum

36. The leading edge of the MAC is 75 inches aft of the datum, and the length of the MAC is 40 inches. What are the CG limits expressed in inches aft of datum if the MAC limits are forward 13.75% and rear 25.07%?

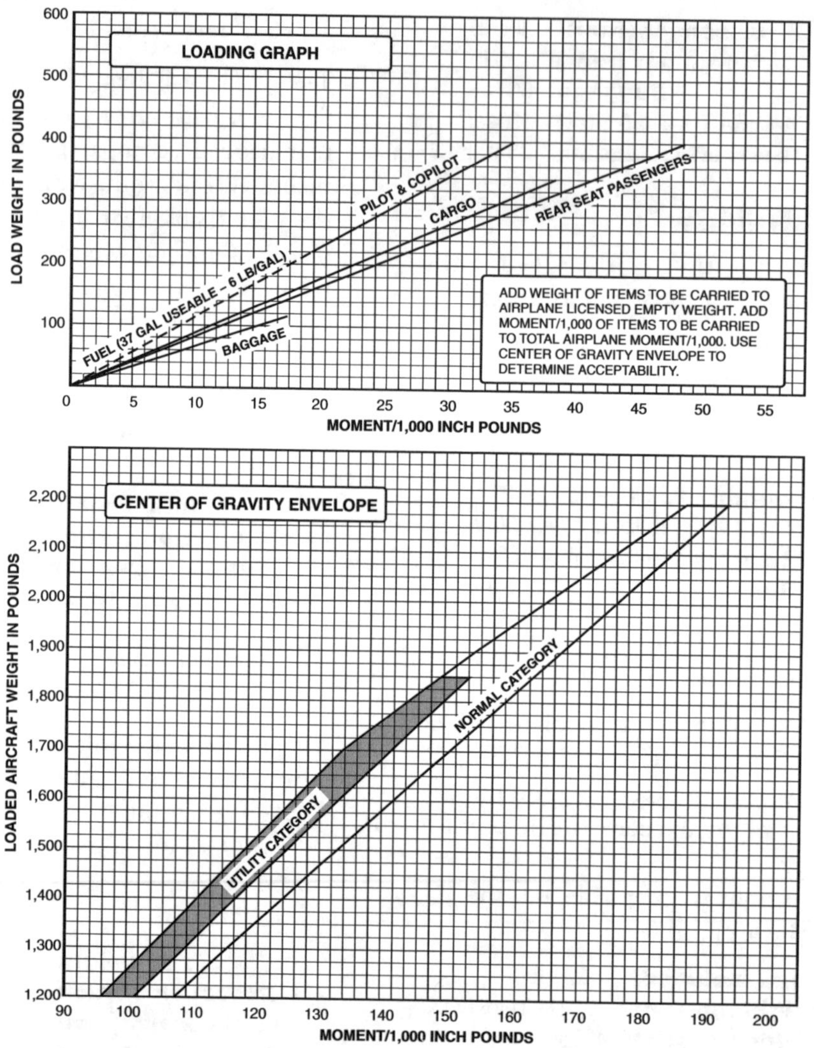

Figure 11-34 Commercial Knowledge Exam weight-and-balance graphs.

Answers are given on page 693

The Human in the Cockpit 12

Human factors, as it relates to flying an aircraft, is the interaction between the pilot, the flying environment, and the aircraft. The area defined by human factors is complex and is where most errors occur. To safely operate an aircraft, you need to develop an awareness of not only the physiological aspect of flying, but also those that influence workload and fatigue, decision making, and situational awareness. It is vital that you, as a pilot, understand and appreciate how these factors affect your everyday flying.

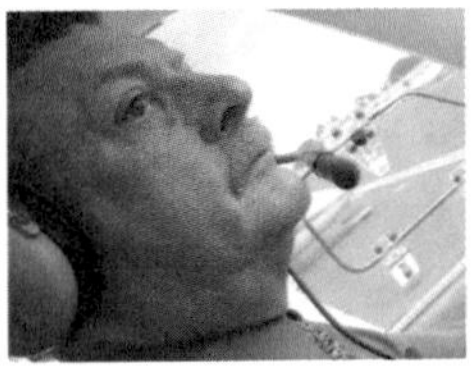

Figure 12-1 The pilot is human.

This chapter will discuss the following elements of the human in the cockpit:

- the physical pilot;
- the flight environment;
- health and well-being;
- vision and visual illusions;
- hearing and balance;
- situational awareness; and
- decision making.

The Physical Pilot

Circulatory System

The circulatory, or cardiovascular, system moves blood around the body, carrying oxygen and nutrients to the cells, and takes away waste products such as carbon dioxide. Blood is composed of plasma that carries red and white blood cells, or corpuscles. The red blood cells contain the iron-rich pigment hemoglobin, the principal function of which is to transport oxygen around the body. The white blood cells, of which there are various types, protect the body against foreign substances and are involved in the production of antibodies. The antibodies attack any substance that the body regards as foreign or dangerous. Platelets in the blood function to form clots when necessary to stop loss of blood from an injury.

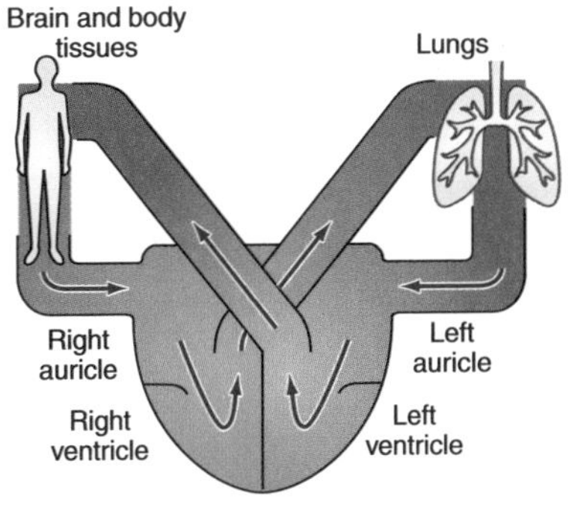

Figure 12-2 Circulatory system.

Heart

The heart is a muscular pump, about the size of a closed fist, that is divided into two sides, each with two chambers. The muscles of the heart contract in a double-action pulse, forcing blood through the one-way heart valves and through the network of arteries. This pump stroke causes a pressure pulse which can be felt at various parts of the body where the arteries are near the surface (such as the wrist and the side of the neck). Blood pressure is a measure of the pressure of the blood against the walls of the main arteries. It is necessary for the blood to be continuously replenished with oxygen, which it gives out to the tissues, and at the same time rid itself of the carbon dioxide that it acquires.

Circulation

On long flights you may be seated and stationary for very long periods. You can improve circulation by contracting and relaxing your stomach diaphragm as well as the leg and buttock muscles. Without the physical demand of activity, the heart will go into a dormant mode and the circulation slows down. This leads to sleepiness and loss of concentration. The muscles atrophy and you could suffer cramps. It is important to change your seating position and, if possible, exercise individual muscles by stretching and straightening the joints, and occasionally shaking a leg or twisting to improve circulation.

Respiratory System

The process of respiration brings oxygen into the body and removes carbon dioxide. The body has a permanent need for oxygen; it is used in the energy-producing burning process that goes on in every cell of the body tissues. The body is unable to store oxygen permanently and hence the need for continuous breathing. Any interruption to breathing lasting more than a few minutes may lead to permanent physical damage, especially of the brain, and to possible death.

Flight Environment

Atmosphere

Air is made up of 21% oxygen, 78% nitrogen, and 1% carbon dioxide and other inert gases.

The earth is surrounded and protected by a life-giving layer called the atmosphere. The atmosphere consists of a transparent mixture of gases that we call air. The atmosphere is held to the earth by the force of gravity and, because air is compressible, it packs in around the earth's surface. As altitude is gained, the air thins with fewer and fewer molecules in the same volume, but the percentage of each of the components of the air does not change. Total air pressure falls with altitude, as does the partial pressure of each of the gases in the air. (Total air pressure is a sum of all of the partial pressures.)

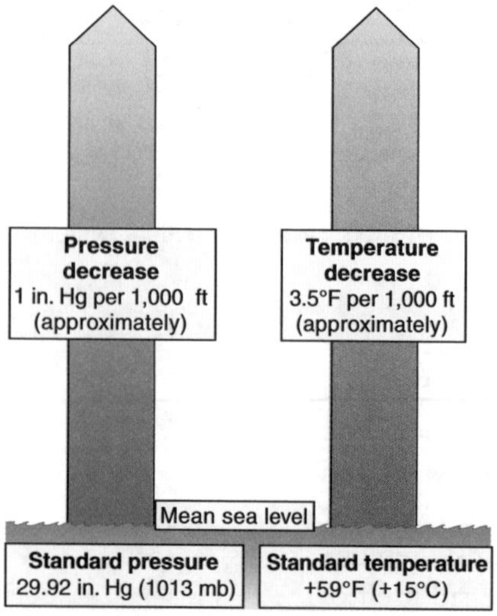

Figure 12-3 Standard atmosphere.

The International Standard Atmosphere

So that we have a common reference, scientists have agreed on average atmospheric conditions called the *International Standard Atmosphere* (ISA) or, simply, standard atmosphere. Like the "average" person, it never exists, but it is an essential yardstick used for comparisons, especially of aircraft performance. The standard atmosphere is as follows:

- sea level temperature: 59°F (15°C);
- lapse rate: -3.5°F (-2°C) per 1,000 feet;
- freezing level (32°F/0°C): 7,500 feet;
- sea level pressure: 29.92 in. Hg (1,013.2 hectopascals);
- tropopause: 36,080 feet; and
- temperature at the tropopause: -56°C.

Flying at Altitude

The human body is designed to function in the lower levels of the atmosphere, where the air is fairly dense. Aircraft may operate at quite high altitudes where the air density is very low, exposing the pilot to possible oxygen deficiency and other problems such as low ambient temperatures. There are three major effects of altitude on the human body brought about by pressure changes:

- lower external pressure causes gases inside body cavities to expand;
- lower oxygen pressure causes hypoxia; and
- dissolved gases form bubbles in the blood, also due to decreased external pressure.

Hypoxia

Hypoxia is a condition in which oxygen concentration in the tissues is less than normal. Total absence of oxygen is called *anoxia*. Hypoxia is a lack of oxygen and may be caused by:

- a lack of oxygen in the air (called *hypoxic hypoxia*);
- a partial pressure of oxygen that is too low; or
- an inability of the blood to carry oxygen (called *anaemic hypoxia*) due to a medical condition (anaemia) or to carbon monoxide poisoning in the blood (from, say, a faulty engine exhaust system or smoking cigarettes).

Hypoxic hypoxia is an insufficient amount of oxygen available to the body. As altitude increases pressure decreases and the body is less able to uptake oxygen from the atmosphere.

Hypemic hypoxia is an oxygen deficiency in the blood. Blood is unable to absorb and transport sufficient amounts of oxygen to the cells within the body. Most commonly occurs due to CO poisoning.

Stagnant hypoxia results when oxygen-rich blood from the lungs is unable to flow to the tissues and cells in the body essentially becoming stagnant or non-flowing. Examples a leg or arm "falls asleep".

Histotoxic hypoxia occurs when the cells or tissues in the body are unable to effectively use the oxygen-rich blood being transported to them. Often caused by alcohol or drugs.

Air pressure and density decrease with altitude; approximately 18,000 feet is where atmospheric pressure is at 50% of sea level (1,000 mb versus 500 mb). As an airplane climbs, the density of the air in which it is flying gradually reduces. The less dense the air, the lower the mass of oxygen taken into the lungs in each breath. In addition, the lower partial pressure of oxygen at altitude (i.e. fewer percentage of molecules), further reduces the amount of oxygen that will diffuse across the alveoli membranes into the bloodstream. A high cabin altitude therefore means less oxygen will be transported around the body, and less energy will be generated (including in the brain). Hypoxia is subtle and it sneaks up on you, like the effects of that extra glass of wine. Rapid rates of ascent can allow higher altitudes to be reached before severe symptoms occur. In these circumstances, unconsciousness may occur before any or many of the symptoms of hypoxia appear. At 9,000 feet, the partial pressure of oxygen in the air is about *half* that at sea level.

The initial symptoms of hypoxia may hardly be noticeable to the sufferer, and in fact they often include feelings of euphoria. The brain is affected quite early, so a false sense of security and well-being may be present. Physical movements will become clumsy, but the pilot may not notice this. Difficulty in concentrating, faulty judgment, moodiness, drowsiness, indecision, giddiness, physical clumsiness, headache, deterioration of vision, high pulse rate, blue lips and fingernails (cyanosis), and tingling of the skin may all follow, ending in loss of consciousness. Throughout all of this pilots will probably feel euphoric and as if doing a great job.

In this oxygen-deficient condition, a pilot is less able to think clearly and perform physically. The body attempts to compensate by increasing the pulse rate, and the rate and depth of ventilation. Pilots between 25 and 50 years who are in good physical condition and regularly exposed to low oxygen levels have a higher tolerance. Above about 8,000 feet cabin altitude, the effects of oxygen deprivation may start to become apparent in some pilots, especially if the pilot is active or under stress. At 10,000 feet, most people can still cope with the diminished oxygen supply, but above 10,000 feet supplementary oxygen is required (i.e. oxygen supplied through a mask), if a marked deterioration in performance is not to occur. At 14,000 feet without supplementary oxygen, performance will be very poor and, at 18,000 feet, the pilot may become unconscious. This will occur at lower altitudes if the pilot is a smoker, or is unfit or fatigued.

Avoid hypoxia by using supplemental oxygen at high cabin altitudes (above 10,000 feet).

In general terms, 10,000 feet is considered to be the critical cabin altitude above which flight crew should wear an oxygen mask (5,000 feet at night). The effects of oxygen deprivation are very personal in that they may differ from person to person and become apparent at different cabin altitudes. Some people are more resilient than others; however, the event of oxygen deprivation will eventually produce the same effects. For instance, night vision will generally start to deteriorate at a cabin altitude of above 4,000 feet.

Susceptibility to hypoxia is increased by anything that reduces the oxygen available to the brain, such as a high cabin altitude (of course), high or low temperatures, illness, stress, fatigue, physical activity, or smoke in the cockpit. The reduction of the oxygen-carrying capacity of the blood by smoking has the same effect as increasing the cabin altitude by 4,000–5,000 feet and this effect intensifies as the airplane climbs to higher altitudes. The preference of hemoglobin for carbon monoxide, as opposed to oxygen, means that a person who has been smoking has less oxygen circulating than would have been the case had CO not been absorbed. The onset of symptoms of hypoxia will occur at a lower altitude in that person. However, a smoker is acclimated to being hypoxic and may be more tolerant—to a degree.

Tolerance to hypoxia can be reduced by a loss of blood, as is the case after a person has made a blood donation. It is therefore recommended that active pilots do not donate blood. Should you decide you do want to give blood, it is recommended not to fly for 24 hours afterward.

Time of Useful Consciousness. If a person is deprived of an adequate supply of oxygen, unconsciousness will ultimately result. The cells of the brain are particularly sensitive to a lack of oxygen, even for a brief period. Total cessation of the oxygen supply to the brain results in unconsciousness in six to eight seconds and irreversible damage ensues if the oxygen supply is not restored within four minutes. The time available for pilots to perform useful tasks without a supplementary oxygen supply, and before severe hypoxia sets in, is known as the *time of useful consciousness* (TUC), or *effective performance time* (EPT). TUC/EPT reduces with increasing altitude.

Altitude above sea level	Sudden failure of oxygen supply	
	Moderate activity	Minimal activity
18,000 feet	20 minutes	30 minutes
22,000 feet	5 minutes	10 minutes
25,000 feet	2 minutes	3 minutes
28,000 feet	1 minute	1½ minutes
30,000 feet	45 seconds	1¼ minutes
35,000 feet	30 seconds	45 seconds
40,000 feet	12 seconds	15 seconds

Table 12-1 Time of useful consciousness (effective performance time).

Barotrauma

Another effect of increasing cabin altitude is that gases trapped in parts of your body—such as the stomach, intestines, sinuses, middle ear, or in a decaying tooth—will want to expand as external pressure decreases. Either they will be able to escape into the atmosphere, or they may be trapped and possibly cause pain known as *barotrauma.* Pain is most severe on ascent with teeth and intestines and on descent with ears and sinus. Foods such as legumes and leafy greens known to produce gas should be avoided when flying.

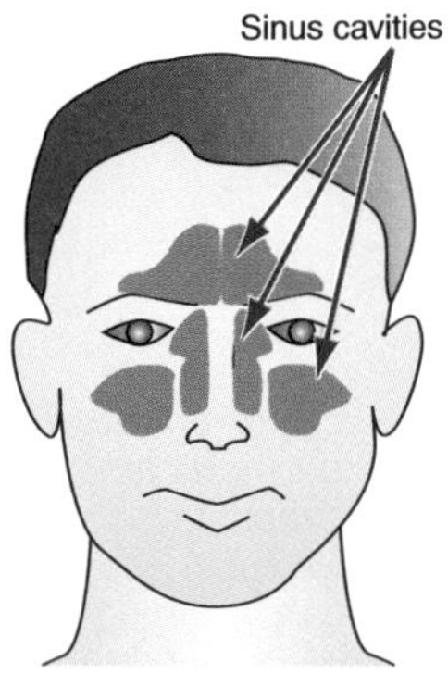

Figure 12-4
Sinus cavities in the skull.

Barotrauma of the Ears. You hear sound because waves of air pressure move a membrane within your ear (eardrum). The cavity behind the eardrum has a small tube (the Eustachian tube) that is open through the nose and allows air pressure on the inside to be balanced with outside air pressure. If you have a head cold or sinusitis, this tube can become restricted or even totally blocked. If this is the case, as the aircraft climbs, the air inside the ear easily escapes through the tube because that is the normal direction of fluid movement. However, when you descend again, you end up in a situation where the air on the outside of the drum is at a higher pressure than the air inside. It may collapse the tube. Because of this restriction, air cannot pass through to balance the pressure and so the eardrum is pushed in. This can be painful or even damaging. The pressure can usually be helped to equalize and open the Eustachian tube by swallowing, chewing, or by blowing with the mouth and nose held shut.

Decompression Sickness (The Bends)

Gas bubbles in the body will cause great pain and some immobilization in the shoulders, arms and joints. This serious complaint is known as *decompression sickness* or *the bends.* The remedy is to subject the body to a region of high pressure for a lengthy period of time (in a *recompression* chamber, for example), and then gradually return it to normal pressures over a period of hours or days. In an aircraft, the best you can do if the bends is suspected is to descend to a low altitude, where air pressure is greater. Even landing may not provide a sufficient pressure increase to remedy the problem, in which case seek medical assistance without delay. Sometimes low altitude pressure will cause nitrogen to form bubbles; however, this is unlikely below 18,000 feet.

Decompression sickness can follow scuba diving.

Scuba Diving. Decompression sickness can result from flying after scuba diving. When the body is deep under water it is subjected to strong pressures, and certain gases, such as nitrogen, are absorbed into the blood under pressure, because the air cylinders have to be pressurized above the local water pressure so the lungs can inhale increasing the partial pressure of nitrogen. The deeper and longer the dive, the more this absorption occurs. If the pressure on the body is then reduced too quickly—say, by rapidly returning to the surface from a great depth or, even worse, by then flying in an airplane at high cabin altitudes—the gases (especially nitrogen) will come out of the blood solution and form bubbles in the bloodstream and tissues, especially the joints. (You can see the same effect caused by a sudden reduction in pressure when the top is removed from carbonated drinks and bubbles of gas come out.)

Rules regarding scuba diving and flying vary slightly from country to country. The current Diver's Alert Network's recommendation is that you do not fly for 12 hours after any single dive without decompression stops. A greater surface interval is needed after multiple dives or dives with decompression stops. Ask your instructor for advice.

Figure 12-5
Do not fly within 24 hours of scuba diving.

Decompression stops are necessary if a dive is deeper than 33 feet. At this depth, the pressure is twice that at sea level, and the amount of nitrogen dissolved increases appreciably.

Snorkeling will not cause decompression sickness as you are not taking in air under pressure. The risk of suffering decompression sickness increases with the depth to which you dive, the rate at which you resurface, how soon after you fly, how high you fly, how quickly the cabin altitude increases, your age, obesity, fatigue, and reexposure to decompression within 24 hours.

Hyperventilation

Hyperventilation is an involuntary and inappropriate increase in breathing rate, and is usually a symptom of psychological distress.

Hyperventilation occurs when the body over breathes due to some psychological distress such as fear or anxiety (gasping for breath). It is most likely to occur with inexperienced pilots in new situations. It is a self-perpetuating cycle, in which a feeling of breathlessness and dizziness develops—one is unable to catch one's breath and so one becomes more stressed—and continues even if the triggering influence is removed.

Carbon Monoxide Poisoning

Engine smells in the cabin are warning that carbon monoxide may be present.

Carbon monoxide is produced during combustion. It is present in engine exhaust gases and in cigarette smoke, both of which can sometimes be found in the cockpit. Its entry into the cockpit may be from a faulty heating system. Carbon monoxide is a colorless, odorless, tasteless and poisonous gas for which hemoglobin in the blood has an enormous affinity. If carbon monoxide molecules are inhaled, then the hemoglobin will transport them in preference to oxygen, causing the body and the brain to suffer oxygen starvation, even though oxygen is present in the air. Hence, the first cigarette can cause light-headedness. Carbon monoxide poisoning is insidious and can be ultimately fatal. Recovery, even on pure oxygen, may take several hours.

Figure 12-6
CO detectors can alert pilots to danger.

Susceptibility to carbon monoxide poisoning increases as the cabin altitude increases because there is already an oxygen deficiency. Many cabin heating systems use warm air from around the engine and exhaust manifold as their source of heat. Any leaks in the engine exhaust system can allow carbon monoxide to enter the cabin in the heating air and possibly through open windows and cracks. To minimize the effect of any carbon monoxide that enters the cockpit in this way, fresh air should always be used in conjunction with cabin heating. Regular checks and maintenance of the aircraft are essential. Even though carbon monoxide is odorless, it may be associated with other exhaust gases that do have an odor. Engine smells in the cabin are a warning that carbon monoxide may be present. Symptoms of carbon monoxide poisoning include the following:

- headache, dizziness and nausea;
- deterioration in vision;
- impaired judgment;
- personality change;
- impaired memory;
- slower breathing rate;
- cherry-red complexion;
- loss of muscular power;
- convulsions; and
- coma and eventually death.

Carbon monoxide poisoning is serious and can be fatal!

If carbon monoxide is suspected in the cabin, carry out the following actions:

- shut off the cabin heat;
- stop all smoking;
- increase the supply of fresh air through vents (except exhaust ones) and windows; and
- land as soon as possible.

Many operators place carbon monoxide detectors in the cockpit. The most common type contains crystals that change color when carbon monoxide is present. These detectors are inexpensive and are a wise investment, but they do have a limited life, so check the expiration date. If the detector is date-expired, it is not reliable. Indeed, the crystal-type detector may not be as reliable as first thought. Increasingly, the more costly, but more effective, electronic detectors are being recommended. Be aware that carbon monoxide is not the only toxic chemical to which you may be exposed in aircraft operations (agricultural pilots especially). Vapors and fumes from fuels and lubricants, poorly packed dangerous goods, and other products of combustion may produce a range of symptoms including skin, eye and lung irritation, dizziness, drowsiness, confusion and loss of consciousness.

Dehydration

Dehydration is not only associated with hot days and intense sporting activities when you don't drink enough. It is also a problem when sitting relatively still when flying. As you climb, the atmosphere becomes less dense and is much colder. Both decreased density and temperature means less water is available in the atmosphere. So just by breathing, you are going to lose moisture from your lungs at a greater rate than you would at sea level. On large aircraft, the pressurization and air conditioning tend to reduce the moisture content of the air still further. Aircraft manufacturers incorporate humidifiers in these systems to keep the cabin environment comfortable. On any flight of more than an hour or so and especially in summer, always carry drinking water and sip it regularly. Don't wait until you are thirsty. Dehydration can quickly affect the brain's ability to function rationally.

Condition	Cause/ Altitude	Common Symptoms	Notes	Actions
Hypoxia	Rare below 10,000 feet.	Euphoria, visual disturbances, dizziness, light-headedness, confused thinking, apprehension, sense of well-being.	May be unaware of condition due to decreased partial pressure of oxygen.	Descend. Use oxygen. 10,000–33,700 feet—air-oxygen mix. 33,700–40,000 feet—100% oxygen.
Hyper-ventilation	Anxiety. Any altitude.	Light-headedness, dizziness, tingling, numbness, visual disturbances, confused thinking, tremors, faintness.	Overbreathing reduces carbon dioxide level in the blood.	Control breathing rate. Breathe into hand or bag. If above 10,000 feet, suspect hypoxia.
Carbon monoxide poisoning	Faulty exhaust heating. Smoking. Any altitude.	Headache, breathlessness, sluggishness, impaired judgment, feeling of warmth, cherry-red skin.	Hemoglobin has greater affinity for CO than for oxygen. (Smoking makes night vision poor.)	Immediate fresh air. Oxygen. Land and seek medical attention.
Decompres-sion sickness	Flying after diving. Unlikely below 18,000 feet.	Headache, pain (joints), paralysis, choking, skin irritation.	Nitrogen forms bubbles in lungs (chokes), joints (bends), skin (creeps), central nervous system (paralysis).	Do not fly for 4 hours for dives less than 30 feet; wait longer if deeper dive.
Dehydration	Workload. Radiant heat. Perspiration.	Darker urine, dryness.	Carry drinking water in the cockpit. Cover exposed skin.	Sip water regularly in-flight.

Table 12-2 Summary of symptoms.

Health and Well-Being

General Health and Well-Being

The effects of flight on the human body and mind are representative of an average human in good health. Obviously, ill physical or psychological health adversely affects all of your capabilities, capacities, stamina, concentration, memory, and tolerances to the stresses of flight.

Health Indicators

You are the result of two primary influences: heredity (*nature*) and environment (*nurture*). One of the most reliable indicators of general health is the parentage from which you are born. If your parents were healthy and lived long lives then all you need to worry about are the environmental factors.

Blood Pressure

There are two levels of blood pressure:
- *systolic*, which is when the heart pumps (should be around 120 mm Hg); over
- *diastolic*, which is when it pauses (should be around 80 mm Hg).

The resting (diastolic) blood pressure is a good indicator of potential problems. High blood pressure can pertain with no apparent, underlying cause. It can be controlled with medication. If identifiable, the cause of the high blood pressure (*hypertension*) should also be addressed, whether it be physical or psychological.

Cholesterol

Cholesterol is formed by the body in response to dietary intake. There are two levels of cholesterol in the blood:
- low-density lipoprotein (LDL), which is related to animal fats; and
- high-density lipoprotein (HDL), which is related to exercise.

The former is not good and should be controlled by diet and exercise.

Obesity

You should maintain a reasonable degree of physical fitness. It allows better physical and mental performance during flight, and, in the long term, improves your chances of a long and healthy life. Physical fitness helps pilots cope better with stress, fatigue, and the reduced availability of oxygen. Diseases that have been directly related to obesity include osteoarthritis, hypertension (and risk of cardiovascular problems), and gout.

Medical Fitness

Disqualifying Illnesses

Disqualifying illnesses are conditions likely to restrict or deny the issue of a medical certificate either temporarily or permanently. They include heart attack, stroke, diabetes, kidney stones and ulcers.

Debilitating Illnesses

Migraines and Headaches. Headaches can be compromising due to stress, pain, distraction and reduced attention. Migraine headaches are due to the constriction of the arteries in a particular part of the brain. They can be totally incapacitating if accompanied by vision impairment, nausea, vomiting, oversensitivity to light and sound, and severe pain. Rarely, migraine attacks are accompanied by temporary, partial paralysis (one arm or one side of the body). They seem to be triggered by allergic reactions to certain foods such as cheese or chocolate, by stress, or by the removal of stress. Many are short lived and may be related to temporary circumstances, but do seek medical advice. There are treatments that are sometimes, but not always, effective. Heredity seems to be a significant factor in your susceptibility to migraine attacks.

Viruses/Colds/Flu/Middle-Ear Infections. Each eardrum has ambient pressure from the atmosphere or cabin on one side and air pressure in the middle ear on the other side, the middle ear being connected to ambient air via the Eustachian tube. During a climb, atmospheric pressure decreases and the differential pressure across the eardrum forces out the eardrum, as well as causing air to flow from the middle ear through the Eustachian tubes into the throat. In this way, the pressure differential is equalized. Any prevention of this equalization process is hazardous because of the pain and the potential to perforate the membrane of the eardrum.

Most pressurized aircraft have a low rate of climb (500 feet per minute or less) for the cabin and cockpit, allowing adequate time for pressure equalization to occur through the Eustachian tubes. This means that ear problems during the climb are generally not serious. During descent, however, difficulties with the ears may be more serious due to high rates of descent and problems with pressure equalization within the middle ear (the air finds it easier to escape through the collapsed tubes during the climb but cannot pass through the collapsed tube during the descent).

Further, the greatest proportional pressure differential occurs at lower altitudes and so the first few thousand feet on the way up and the last few on the way down are the difficult ones. Although the cockpit may be kept at 5,000 feet, the pressure change is very significant. Moreover, a depressurization with blocked Eustachian tubes could be overwhelming. High rates of descent worsen the situation. Pain in the ears can be debilitating, and there is a danger of the eardrums collapsing inward as the external pressure builds up, giving rise to a loss of hearing that may be permanent. In extreme cases, the balance mechanisms could be affected—a situation known as *pressure vertigo*. Blocked ears can sometimes be cleared by holding the nose and blowing hard (a technique known as the *Valsalva maneuver*), by chewing, swallowing or yawning. It is best not to risk flying with a head cold if you have difficulty clearing your ears. Problems can also arise in the sinuses, the cavities in the skull connected by narrow tubes to the nasal/throat passages. Blockages can cause severe pain, equivalent to the most severe headache, such that you cannot concentrate on flying.

Gastroenteritis. Gastrointestinal disorders are the most common cause of in-flight incapacitation. They may result from an improperly prepared meal (food poisoning), impure drinking water, or infection. Onset may be almost immediate following consumption of the food or drink, or it may not become evident for some hours. Even then, onset may be very sudden. The stomach pains, nausea, diarrhea and vomiting that accompany food poisoning can make it physically impossible to perform pilot duties. Some of the reflexes are uncontrollable (projectile vomiting and diarrhea, sometimes simultaneously). A wise precaution is never to have the same meal as your crew.

For the day prior to flight, avoid foods that are associated with food poisoning, including shellfish, fish, mayonnaise, creams, overripe and thin-skinned fruits, uncooked foods such as salads and raw foods, and old, tired food (e.g. food that has been cooked, then stored for some time or reheated several times). If you suspect that some symptoms of food poisoning are present or forthcoming, don't take a chance—don't fly. After the event, you will be dehydrated and weak—very weak indeed. You should not fly for at least 72 hours after the last symptoms of even a mild case of food poisoning. Gastroenteritis, flu, food poisoning, and dysentery can leave you sitting on the toilet and vomiting simultaneously. You cannot possibly fly with those symptoms. You are literally and totally incapacitated.

Cardiovascular Diseases. Diseases affecting the heart and circulatory system include the following:

- *thrombosis*—a *coronary thrombosis* is caused by blood clots (*embolisms*) obstructing the flow of blood to the heart. The heart muscle may go into irregular spasms (*fibrillation*);
- *myocardial infarction* (*heart attack*)—sudden blockage may result in the death of heart tissue;
- *angina*—part of the heart may be deprived of oxygen by a reduced blood flow when demand is increased. It is felt as pain in the chest, neck, shoulders and arm, especially the left, that comes and goes with exercise. If untreated, angina causes heart inefficiency and gradual or sudden heart failure;
- *arteriosclerosis*—the arteries can be blocked by fats, often as a the result of high cholesterol due to poor diet and lack of exercise;
- *aneurism*—a bursting of an artery, generally in the brain; and
- *stroke*—the blood flow in some part of the brain may be interrupted, leaving loss of sensation or paralysis in any part of the body but commonly on one side of the face.

Cardiovascular risk factors, in order of priority, appear to be: family history of heart disease, smoking, high blood pressure, high cholesterol, obesity, lack of exercise, diabetes and stress. Excessive alcohol consumption may also be an influence, but moderate consumption may actually be beneficial in controlling stress and cholesterol. All the above factors relate to inheritance or lifestyle, and pilots particularly need to manage the latter.

The normal electrocardiogram, or resting ECG, is a sensor that measures the heartbeat at 12 locations. It is carried out while the body is resting to check whether there is a deficiency in the action of the heart muscle. It is a here-and-now indicator that shows congenital or preexisting defects, but it cannot predict future problems.

Physical and Mental Fitness

Exercise

Keeping fit takes some effort, and this effort must be continually maintained for fitness to be retained; but it can also be good fun and very recreational. Walking, jogging, digging in the garden, cycling, swimming, in fact anything that steadily raises your pulse rate, will improve your fitness. If you are grossly unfit or obese, then allow yourself several diet-conscious months with moderate exercise that is gradually increased, and consider medical supervision. It might seem like a long haul, but the quality of life and your self-esteem will improve along with your fitness.

Fatigue and Sleep Deprivation

Fatigue, tiredness and sleep deprivation can lower a pilot's mental and physical capacity quite dramatically. Fatigue can become deep-seated and chronic. If personal, psychological or emotional problems are not resolved, they prevent deep rest and good sleep over a prolonged period. Chronic fatigue won't be cured until the problems are resolved, or at least are being addressed, and the person can relax and unwind. You should prohibit yourself from flying if the distress is distracting.

Do not fly when fatigued. It shows poor judgement.

Short-term fatigue can be caused by overwork, mental stress, an uncomfortable body position, a recent lack of sleep, living-it-up a little too much, lack of oxygen or lack of food.

Stress

Stress is part of our lifestyle. It is inevitable but manageable. Management of stress is relatively easy, once learned. You have to learn a way that best suits you. You need to find the particular technique that tickles your own fancy. The objective is not to confront stress head on. Like a kite it will climb against the wind and become even more challenging. The idea is to defuse it—to divide it into bite-size chunks—and remind yourself that it is temporary. It will pass and there is a future. Alcohol doesn't defuse stress: it defers it and then it is added to the next day's lot.

Stress management includes the following:
1. *Identifying hazardous attitudes.*
2. *Learning to modify your behavior.*
3. *Recognizing and coping with stress.*
4. *Developing a method to assess risks.*
5. *Using all your resources.*
6. *Being able to evaluate your performance.*

Coping/defusing techniques include:

- *exercise/sports*—physical demands that take your mind off mental problems are good for you. Physical demand that also requires mental concentration is even better; for example, golf, skiing or sailing are more diverting and therefore relaxing than jogging;
- *fresh air*—the wide world around you keeps everything in perspective and reinforces your hope and realization that you are both small and large in the scheme of things;
- *diversions/hobbies*—the mental and manipulative occupation of hobbies are a marvellous relaxant as their appeal usually claims one's total concentration; and
- *relaxation therapy and meditation*—these use the same technique of mental occupation and diversion so the build-up of stress is deflated by inattention. It is not the same as lying in the sun and snoozing as the brain dwells on the problem. They are effective and easy to learn techniques for focusing the single-channel processor of the conscious mind on a trivial routine symbol.

Diet and Nutrition

We are what we eat. Diet concerns what you eat, how much and in what proportions. It receives much attention in the media these days because in western society our dietary intake is poorly managed: too much animal fat, too much processed sugar, too few vegetables, cereals and fruit. In all, too much quantity and too little exercise. The suggested eating pattern is to have smaller, more varied servings often, rather than larger servings less frequently. Snacks, such as fruit, muesli bars and cereals, keep the hunger at bay and avoid the temptation to eat a large meal too quickly. Eating slowly allows the digestive system to process the food and to feel satisfied with a lesser quantity.

Water is best. Drink lots of it. Don't wait until you feel thirsty. The color of your urine should be light straw or paler. Any darker means potential dehydration. Too much fruit juice can cause bowel problems and also adds calories. Mineral-enriched health drinks are for athletes. Use them for severe exercise; otherwise, drink water. Avoid too much of the sugary soft drinks, as they make you even thirstier.

Tea and Coffee. Caffeine is a drug and stimulant. Coffee contains the most, especially espresso. Caffeine increases the pulse rate, prevents sleep, increases urination and therefore fluid loss (it is a *diuretic*), causes headaches and increases the level of stress. It may wake you up but it won't let you rest. There are also withdrawal symptoms when you stop consuming it.

Dependencies

Alcohol

Do not fly under the influence of alcohol.

Even small quantities of alcohol in the blood can impair one's performance, in addition to the danger of relieving anxiety so that the person believes he or she is performing marvelously. Alcohol severely affects a person's judgment and abilities. Reduced oxygen worsens the effect. Alcohol is a depressant. It lowers the body's natural sensitivities, cautions and fears (shown as overconfidence) and, at the same time, it lowers capabilities—a deadly combination as demonstrated by the road accident statistics. It also represses social mores and allows emotions, that would otherwise be controlled, to run free, such as aggression, anger, passion, violence, showing-off and taking risks. In some personalities, it causes depression and low self-esteem.

It takes time for the body to remove alcohol. As a general rule, a pilot must not fly for at least 8 hours after drinking small quantities of alcohol and increase this time if greater quantities are consumed. After heavy drinking, alcohol may be present in the blood 24 hours later. Sleep will not speed up the removal process; in fact, it slows the body processes down and the elimination of alcohol may take even longer. Exercise is better. Having coffee, soup or water between drinks only helps if they are taken *instead* of an alcoholic beverage. Otherwise, the body receives the same total amount of alcohol in the same time, so it takes the same time for it to be discarded and for its effects to be removed.

Tobacco

Smoking is detrimental to good health, both in the short term and long term. Smoking also significantly decreases a pilot's capacity to perform by reducing the amount of oxygen carried in the blood, replacing it with the useless, poisonous byproducts of cigarette smoke. A pilot does not have to be the active smoker to suffer the effects. Second-hand smoke is also detrimental.

Drugs and Medication

Recreational drugs such as marijuana, cocaine and LSD must never be mixed with flying. Persons who are dependent on such drugs are not permitted to hold a pilot certificate.

All drugs affect the body (as well as the disease they are taken to combat). They may be incompatible with flying. Sedatives, and their side effects, are a prime example of this, also antihistamines. Some drugs may have long *half-lives*; that is, their concentration stays too high for too long, e.g. certain sleeping pills. Other drugs, called potentiating agents, change or exaggerate the effect of other drugs taken in combination with them, especially alcohol. Until cleared by a doctor, it is safest to assume that *any* drug or medication will temporarily ground you. *Don't accept or use non-prescribed drugs.*

There are several thousand medications currently approved by the U.S. Food and Drug Administration (FDA), not including over the counter (OTC) drugs. Virtually all medications have the potential for adverse side effects in some people. Additionally, herbal and dietary supplements, sport and energy boosters, and some other "natural" products are derived from substances often found in medications that could also have adverse side effects. While some individuals experience no side effects with a particular drug or product, others may be noticeably affected. The FAA regularly reviews FDA and other data to assure that medications found acceptable for aviation duties do not pose an adverse safety risk. Drugs that cause no apparent side effects on the ground can create serious problems at even relatively low altitudes. Even at typical general aviation altitudes, the changes in concentrations of atmospheric gases in the blood can enhance the effects of seemingly innocuous drugs that can result in impaired judgment, decision-making, and performance. In addition, fatigue, stress, dehydration, and inadequate nutrition can increase an airman's susceptibility to adverse effects from various drugs, even if they appeared to tolerate them in the past. If multiple medications are being taken at the same time, the adverse effects can be even more pronounced.

Some of the most commonly used OTC drugs, antihistamines and decongestants, have the potential to cause noticeable adverse side effects, including drowsiness and cognitive deficits. The symptoms associated with common upper respiratory infections, including the common cold, will often suppress a pilot's desire to fly, and treating symptoms with a drug that causes adverse side effects only compounds the problem. Particularly, medications containing diphenhydramine (e.g., Benadryl®) are known to cause drowsiness and have a prolonged half-life, meaning the drugs stay in one's system for an extended time, which lengthens the time that side effects are present.

Another important consideration is that the medical condition for which a medication is prescribed may itself be disqualifying. The FAA will consider the condition in the context of risk for medical incapacitation, and the medication as well for cognitive impairment, and either or both could be found unacceptable for medical certification.

Toxic Substances

Some pilots will come in contact with toxic substances—fuel additives, cleaning agents, aerial agriculture sprays and powders, defoliants, compressed gases and extinguishants. Don't ever take shortcuts. Observe the special precautions and protections required for each. If in doubt, don't fly.

Vision and Visual Illusions

Eyes provide the brain with a visual image of the environment. Each eye acts as a natural and very sophisticated digital camera. Its basic function is to collect light rays reflected from an object, using the lens to focus these rays into an image on a screen (the retina), and then converting this image into electrical signals that are sent via the optic nerve to the brain. This is how you *see.* The brain matches the image to previously stored data so you recognize (*perceive*) the object. The connection of the optic nerve to the brain is so close and integral, and the importance of the messages sent to the brain is so dominant, that the eyes can almost be considered an extension of the brain.

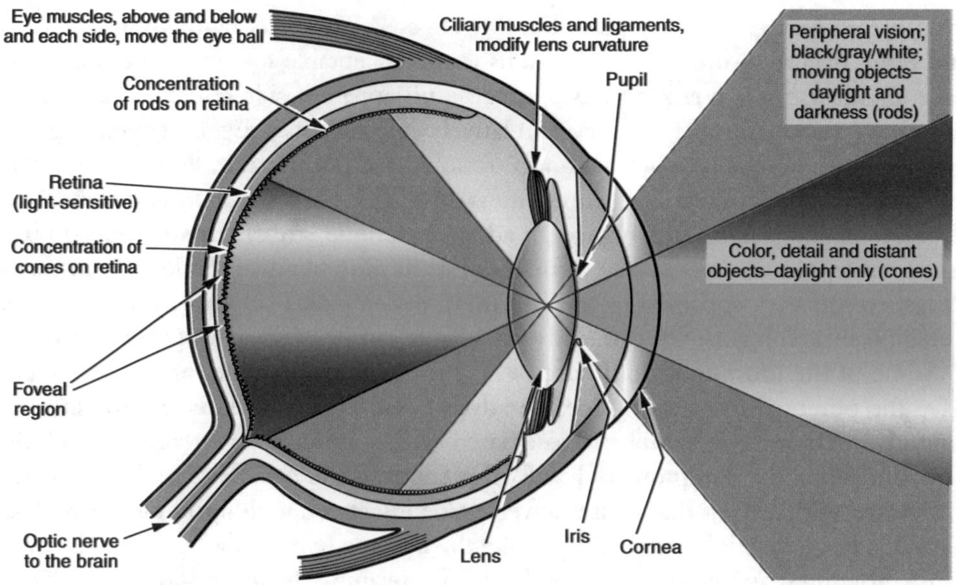

Figure 12-7 Structure of the eye.

Binocular Vision

Binocular vision describes the process whereby optical information is received and processed from two eyes. To track a moving object with both eyes, they need to move in harmony, and this means coordinated control of the two sets of muscles by the brain. In a fatigued person, this coordination sometimes fails, and the result is quite different images from each eye resulting in double vision.

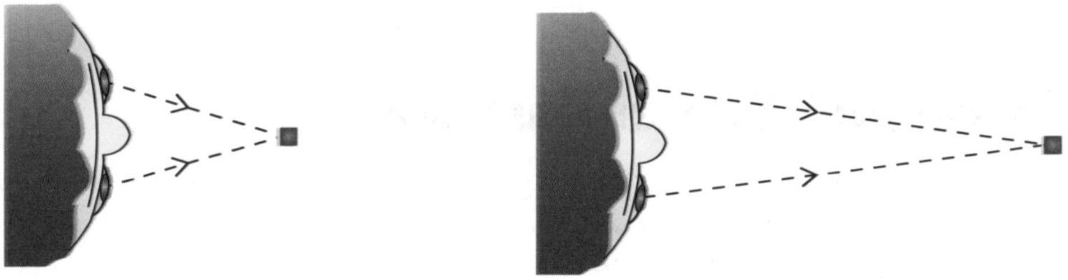

Figure 12-8 Binocular vision.

Blind Spot

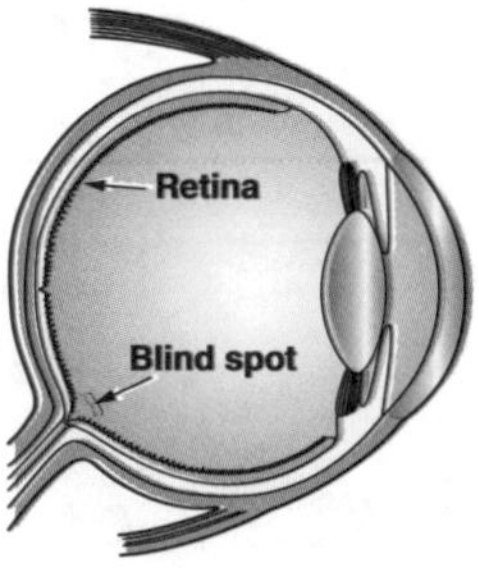

Figure 12-9 Blind spot.

Absolute distance can only be judged by triangulation (the convergence of sight lines) and this is the prime reason for binocular vision. The other reason is to compensate for the blind spot in each eye. The blind spot is the small area on the retina of the eye where the nerve fibers from the light-sensitive cells (rods and cones) on the retina lead into the optic nerve. At this point, there is no coating of light-sensitive cells, and hence any light falling here will not register; that is, it is literally a blind spot. However, it is not possible for an image to fall on the blind spot of both eyes simultaneously because it will be in different relative position for each. Even when an image falls on the blind spot of one eye, and is therefore not registered, the brain will receive a message from the other eye and so the object will still be seen.

You can observe the existence of the blind spot in each eye by viewing figure 12-10. Hold the page at arm's length, cover your right eye, and then with your left eye focus on the airplane on the right. It will be clearly recognizable as a biplane because it will be focused on your retina. Move the page closer and as you still focus on the biplane, you will notice that the helicopter will eventually disappear. Its image has fallen on the position on the retina occupied by the optic nerve. In practice you must be careful when you are scanning the sky that another aircraft is not blocked from view by the magnetic compass or some part of the windshield structure. If it is blocked from the view of both eyes, you will not see it at all; if it is blocked from the view of only one eye, you will lose the blind-spot protection provided by binocular vision.

Rods and cones are the nerve endings that feed the optic nerve.

Figure 12-10 Example of blind spot.

Vision Limitations

Rods and cones are the endings of the optic nerve. As an extension of the brain, they will be affected by anything that affects the brain. With a shortage of oxygen (hypoxia), or an excess of alcohol, medication, or other drugs, sight is one of the first senses to suffer. High positive g-loadings, as in strenuous aerobatic maneuvers, will force the blood into the lower regions of the body and temporarily starve the brain and eyes of blood, leading to a grayout (black-and-white tunnel vision) or unconsciousness (blackout).

Vision Defects

With normal vision, the lens focuses an inverted image of the object on the rear of the eyeball (the retina). The shape of the lens changes to adjust for the distance of the object from the lens to ensure the visual data is focused on the retina. Inability to focus may result naturally from a lens that has become less flexible with age, or it may result from a lens or eyeball that is not shaped correctly. In almost all cases, artificial lenses in the form of spectacles or contact lenses can be made to correct the specific deficiency and restore sharp vision, just like the focus of a camera. Since good eyesight is essential for safe flight, professional assistance is required whenever there is a problem.

Visual Acuity (Clarity or Focus of What We See)

Visual acuity is the ability of the eye to see clearly and sharply. Perfect visual acuity (focus) means that the eye sees the object exactly as it is, clearly and without distortion, no matter how distant the object is. The degree of visual acuity varies between different people and also between the two eyes of any one person, as well as for the single eye at different times. This depends upon whether the person is fatigued, suffering hypoxia (lack of oxygen), or under the influence of alcohol or some other drug. To describe differences in visual acuity, the standard is considered to be what a normal eye is capable of seeing clearly at a particular distance. The eye test chart usually has lines of letters readable for a normal eye from 120, 80, 60, 40, 30, 20 and 16 feet respectively.

The standard testing distance between the eye and the eye chart is 20 feet; the normal eye is capable of clearly seeing letters of a certain size at this distance. If another eye at 20 feet cannot read the 20-foot line clearly, and can only identify letters on the chart that a normal eye can see clearly at 30 feet, then the abnormal eye is said to have 20/30 vision. This is compared with the 20/20 vision of the so-called normal eye. As a rule of thumb, pilots should be able to read a car license plate at a distance of approximately 130 feet.

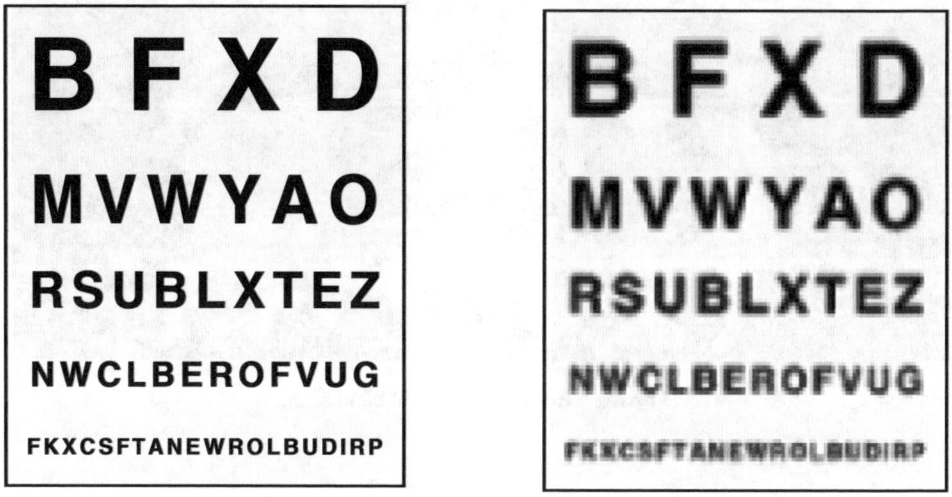

Figure 12-11 An eye chart seen with 20/20 vision and 20/30 vision.

Perfect visual acuity within the individual eye occurs when the image is focused sharply by a high-quality cornea and lens onto the central foveal region of a healthy retina, where the cone receptors predominate. The cone receptors are very sensitive to small details and send very sharp, colorful images to the brain. Light rays that are focused on the retina away from the central foveal region in areas where there are not so many cone receptors but more rod receptors will not be seen as clearly nor will they be in color. Visual acuity (focus) will therefore be less for these images. To illustrate the difference between central and peripheral vision, look at the words on this page. You must move your eyes so that the image of the word that you want to read falls on the central foveal region. While you can clearly read the word you are looking at right now, you will not be able to read words some distance away from it—up, down, or sideways from it—unless you move your eyeball so that the image of that word falls on the central high visual acuity area of the retina.

Color Vision

Colors are detected in the central foveal region of the retina by the cone receptors, which are only active in fairly bright light. There are some eyes that cannot distinguish any colors at all, even in bright light. Males are more susceptible to color blindness. Defective color vision shows up as difficulty in distinguishing between red and green. It may cause problems during night flying, as well as in poor visibility, with the white, red and green navigation lights of other aircraft used for recognition, with red or green taxiway or threshold lighting, and also with visual light signals from the control tower used in a radio-failure situation instead of radio voice messages (an uncommon event nowadays).

Night Vision

Cockpit lighting should be dimmed at night.

Adaptation of the Eyes to Darkness. At night, there are some special considerations regarding vision. Your attention during night flying is both inside and outside the cockpit. It takes the eyes some minutes to adapt to a dark environment, as experienced when walking into a darkened cinema stumbling over other patrons in an attempt to find an empty seat. As mentioned, night vision is susceptible to hypoxia: it is affected by cabin altitudes above 4,000 feet. The time it takes for the eyes to adapt depends, to a large extent, on the contrast between the brightness of light previously experienced and the degree of darkness of the new environment. Conversely, when the lights are turned on at the end of a movie the opposite effect takes place. Whereas the cones, concentrated in the central region of the retina, adjust quickly to variations in light intensity (about seven minutes to return to normal), the rods (which are most important for night vision) take some 30 minutes to adapt fully to darkness. In dim light, the cones become less effective, or even totally ineffective, and there is a chemical change in the rods to increase their sensitivity. Thus we adapt more quickly to brightening lights rather than dimming light.

Adapt your eyes to darkness before night flying by avoiding bright lights for at least 30 minutes before flight.

Protecting Night Vision. It is a common misconception that, at night, you are using your night vision in the cockpit or looking at the runway. When you are looking at something that is well illuminated, you are using normal vision. The night fighter pilots of World War II sat blindfolded in darkened rooms and used red cockpit lighting (and ate carrots) so they could look for other aircraft or ground features not illuminated due to the blackout. The only equivalent situation for today would be when you are looking for ground features like lakes or coastlines or the shadows of hills on a moonlit night; otherwise, you use normal vision. The disadvantage of red lighting is that red lines or tints on maps do not show up.

Keep the internal lighting to an acceptably low level to minimize reflections and to allow best transmission of light through the transparencies. It's the same as other natural processes; the transmission depends on the energy difference—outside to in. More light outside and less light inside provides best transmission of light through the windows. Even wear a dark-colored shirt for night flying as the traditional white pilot's shirt adds considerably to the reflections off the face of the instrument glass. Avoid brilliant lights as they temporarily reduce the sensitivity of the eyes to less well-lit objects. Be especially careful of viewing sunsets and then trying to see down-sun at the darkened earth. Exposure to glare and bright sunlight should be avoided before night flights, possibly by wearing sunglasses. Vision is also affected by reduced oxygen levels and so, at night in an unpressurized aircraft, avoid smoking and use supplemental oxygen (recommended above 5,000 feet).

Protection of Vision

Safety Glasses. A pilot's vision is precious. Always wear eye protection for sports, when using tools, or when gardening.

Sunglasses. When flying into a rising or setting sun or above cloud layers, the pilot is exposed to very high intensity light coming from all angles. The eyes are protected from light coming from above by the forehead, eyebrows, eyelashes, and strong upper eyelids, they are not so well protected from light coming from below. Bright sunlight reflected from cloud tops, for instance, can be particularly bothersome because of this lack of natural protection. In conditions of glare, it is advisable to protect your eyes by using high quality sunglasses that reduce glare but not your visual acuity. The contrast between the glare of a very bright outside environment and the darker cockpit interior may also make it difficult for the eyes to adjust quickly enough to read instruments and charts inside the cockpit. Sunglasses should be impact resistant, having thin metal frames. They should transmit 10 to 15% of the light, filtering out damaging ultraviolet rays. They should not be worn in decreased light.

When landing directly facing the sun, 100% of your vision can be lost at the moment of flare. Even when the sun is 40° to the side, vision is reduced by 42%.

Visual Scanning

Scanning by Day

The central (foveal) region of the retina provides the best vision, and in full color but only during reasonable daylight. Objects are best seen by day if you can focus their image on the foveal region, and you do this by looking directly at them. The most effective method of scanning for other aircraft for collision avoidance during daylight hours is to use a series of short, regularly spaced eye movements to search each 10° sector of the sky. Systematically focusing on different segments of the sky for short intervals is a better technique than continuously sweeping the sky. This is sometimes called the *saccade/fixation cycle*, where the saccade or movement takes about one-third of a second.

Figure 12-12 Methodical scan.

Relative Movement. If there is no apparent relative motion between you and another aircraft, you may be on a collision course, especially if the other aircraft appears to be getting bigger and bigger in the windshield. Due to the lack of movement across your windshield, an aircraft on a collision course with you will be more difficult to spot than one that is not on a collision course.

Any relative movement of an object against its background usually makes it easier to notice in your peripheral vision. The image of the other aircraft may not increase in size much at first, but, shortly before impact, it would rapidly increase in size. The time available for you to avoid a collision may be quite brief, depending upon when you see the other aircraft and the rate of closure.

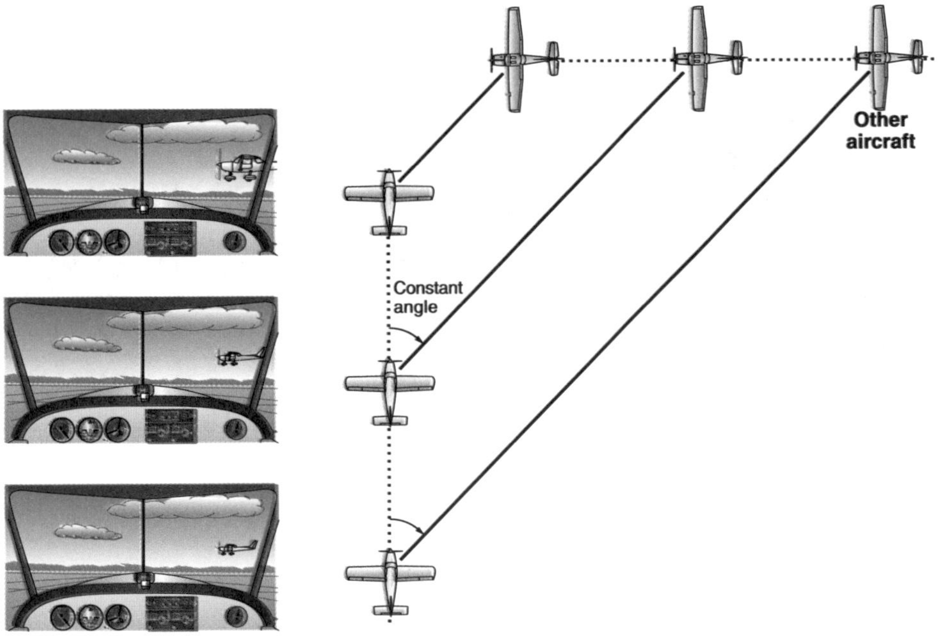

Figure 12-13 Constant relative position = collision course.

If you are flying at 100 knots and it is flying at 500 knots in the opposite direction, the rate of closure is 600 knots, i.e. ten nautical miles per minute. If you spot the other aircraft at a distance of one nautical mile, you only have 1⁄10 of a minute (six seconds) to potential impact. If you are a vigilant pilot and spot it at 3 nautical miles you have eighteen seconds in which to act.

In hazy or low-visibility conditions, your ability to see other aircraft and objects with edges that might be blurred will be diminished and, if you can see them, they may appear to be further away than their actual distance. You might be closer than you think.

In hazy conditions, objects may be closer than they appear.

Empty-Field Myopia. When trying to search for other aircraft in an empty sky, the natural tendency of a resting eye is to focus at about six feet. Consequently, distant aircraft may not be noticed. To avoid this empty-field myopia, you should focus on any available distant object, such as a cloud or a landmark, to lengthen your focus. If the sky is empty of clouds or other objects, then focus briefly on a relatively distant part of the airplane like a wing tip as a means of lengthening your focus. Having spotted an airplane in an otherwise empty sky, be aware that it could be closer to you than it appears to be, because you have no other object with which to compare its size.

Specks. A small, dark image formed on the retina could be a distant aircraft, or it could be a speck of dirt or dust, or an insect spot, on the windshield. Specks, dust particles, a scratch, or an insect on the windshield might be mistaken for a distant airplane. Simply moving your head will allow you to discriminate between marks on the windshield and distant objects.

Figure 12-14 Specks?

Scanning by Night

At night, scan slowly using your peripheral vision.

The central (foveal) region of the retina containing mainly cones is not as effective at night, causing an area of reduced visual sensitivity in your central vision. Peripheral vision, provided by the rods in the outer band of the retina, is more effective albeit color blind. An object at night is more readily visible when you are looking to the side of it by ten or twenty degrees, rather than directly at it. Color is not perceived by the rods, and so your night vision will be in shades of gray. Objects will not be as sharply defined (focused) as in daytime foveal vision.

The most effective way to use your eyes during night flight is to scan small sectors of sky more *slowly* than in daylight to permit off-center viewing of objects in your *peripheral vision*, and to deliberately focus your perception (mind) a few degrees from your visual center of attention (that is, *look at* a point but *look for* objects around it).

Since you may not be able to see the aircraft shape at night, you will have to determine its direction of travel making use of its visible lighting:

- the flashing red beacon;
- the red navigation light on the left wing tip;
- the green navigation light on the right wing tip; and
- a steady white light on the tail.

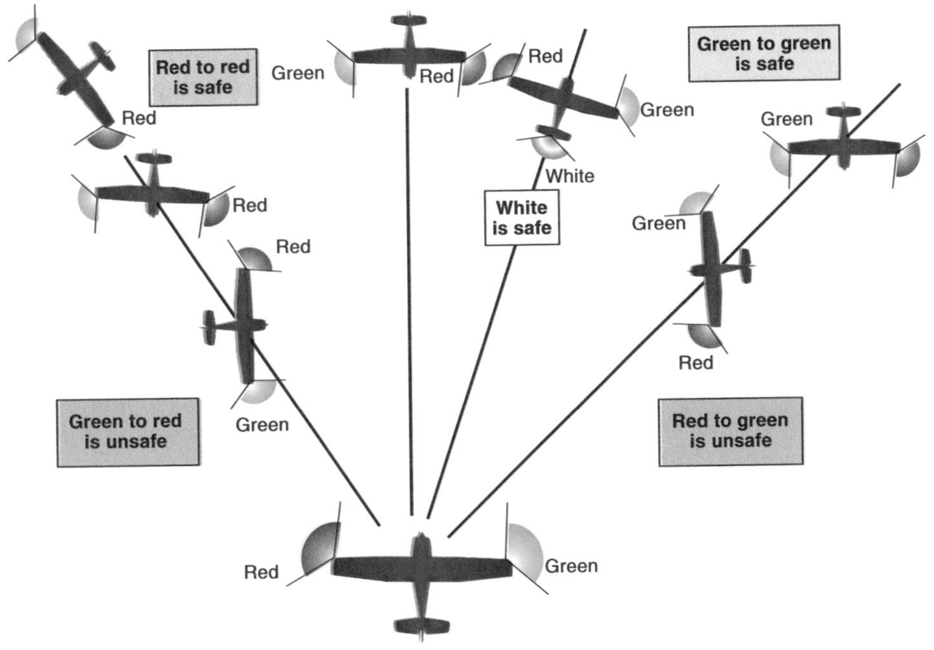

Figure 12-15 Position lights.

Visual Judgment on Approach

The eyes and brain use many clues and stored images of known objects to help in judging distance, size and height. The relative size and relative clarity of objects give clues to their relative distances: a bigger object is assumed to be nearer than a smaller one and a more clearly defined object nearer than a blurry one. When the object is near, binocular vision (the slightly different images of a nearby object relative to its background seen by each eye) assists in depth perception.

Texture also assists in depth perception: the more visible the texture, the closer the object appears to be. On final approach as you near the aim point, the surface texture will appear to flow outward in all directions from the point on which you are focused.

This is one means by which you can visually maintain the flight path to the aim point: adjust the attitude and heading so that the point from which the texture appears to be moving outward remains the desired aim point.

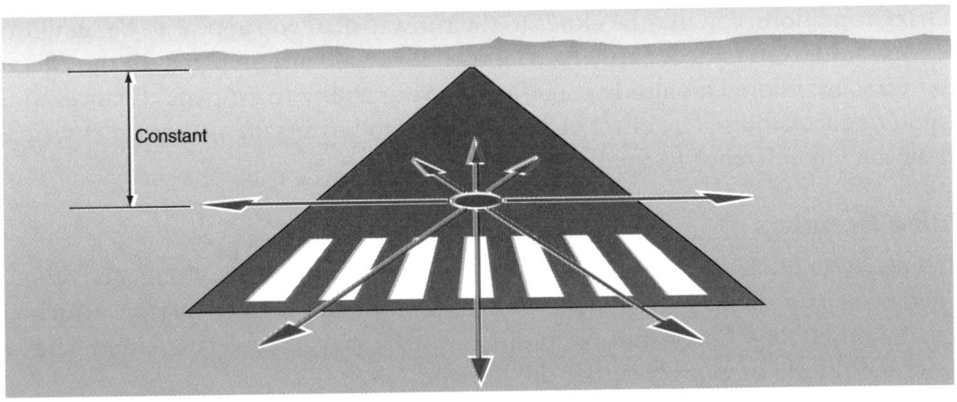

Figure 12-16 Aim point.

Texture is also used for the estimation of height; for instance, as you approach flare height for a landing, the actual texture of the runway or the grass passing by the cockpit becomes increasingly noticeable. Relative motion also aids in depth perception. Near objects generally appear to pass by faster than more distant objects. This helps a visual pilot estimate height above the runway before and during the flare: the closer the airplane is to the runway, the faster the runway surface and the surrounding environment appears to pass by.

Depth perception can be difficult in hazy or misty conditions, where edges are blurred, colors are muted, and light rays may be refracted unusually. This gives the impression of greater distance, an impression reinforced by the fact that we often have to look at distant objects through a smoggy or hazy atmosphere. This illusion is referred to as *environmental perspective*. In hazy conditions, the object might be closer than it seems; in very clear conditions, the object might be further away than it seems. On hazy days, you might touch down earlier than expected; on very clear nights, you might flare a little too soon.

Visual Illusions

Sometimes what we perceive in our brain (what we think we see) is not actual because images sent from the eyes can sometimes be misinterpreted by the brain.

Autokinesis

The visual illusion of autokinesis (self-motion) can occur at night if you stare continuously at a single light against a generally dark background. It will appear to move, perhaps in an oscillating fashion, after only a few seconds of staring at it, even though in fact it is stationary. You could lose spatial orientation if you use it as your single point of reference. The more you try to concentrate on it, the more it may appear to oscillate. You can guard against autokinesis at night by maintaining movement of your eyes in normal scanning, and by monitoring the flight instruments frequently to ensure correct attitude.

Unless you have a distant object in view at night, your eyes will tend to focus at a point about three to six feet ahead of you, especially if you are an older person, and you may miss sighting distant objects. This empty-field myopia or night myopia (short-sightedness) can be combated by searching for distant lights and focusing briefly on them. Beware also of false horizons at night (see later in this chapter).

Haze

On hazy days, objects are closer than they appear. On clear days, objects may be further away than they appear.

In hazy conditions, you may be closer to the runway than you appear to be, an illusion that may lead to an unnecessarily hard landing if you are not prepared for the effect of haze on your vision. This also has an effect on your ability to estimate distances to the airport or checkpoints. The effect of haze over featureless terrain or over water virtually eliminates any reference to the horizon.

False Horizons

Sloping layers of cloud by day, angled lines on the ground, lights along a coastline at night, or areas of lights by night can present a pilot with a false horizon, which can be very misleading. This is not uncommon with a ragged, lowering cloud base and associated drizzle or rain obscuring the horizon.

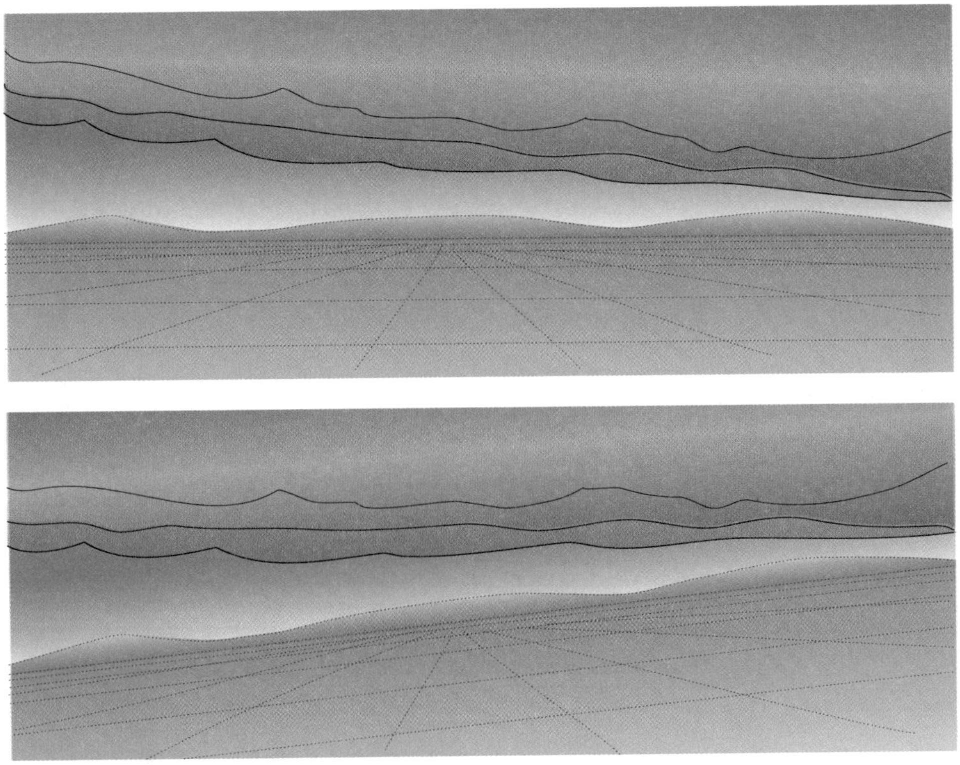

Figure 12-17 False horizon.

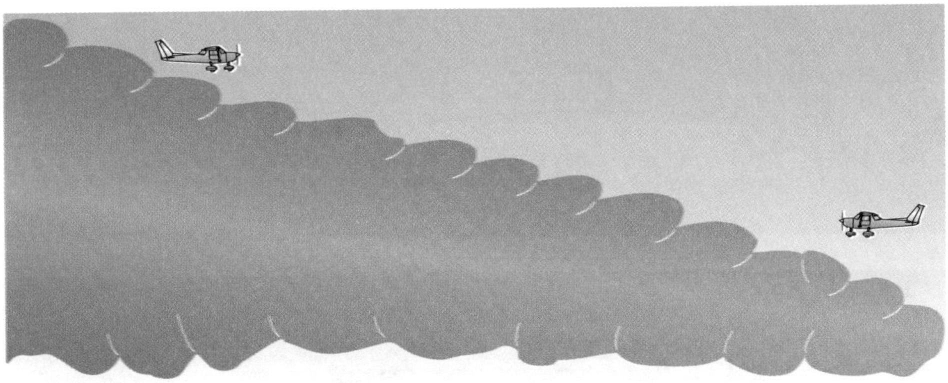

Figure 12-18 False level.

Visual Illusions in the Pattern

Visual Estimation Of Height. A pilot flying a right traffic pattern may get the impression that the aircraft is higher than normal. This illusion could occur to a pilot who has developed the habit of visually judging pattern altitude and position by relating the position of the runway lights to some feature of the aircraft, such as a particular position in a side window. Such a rule of thumb that worked satisfactorily for the more typical left patterns could lead a pilot to descend lower to achieve the same picture when making right traffic patterns. Like most habits, such a practice could happen unconsciously.

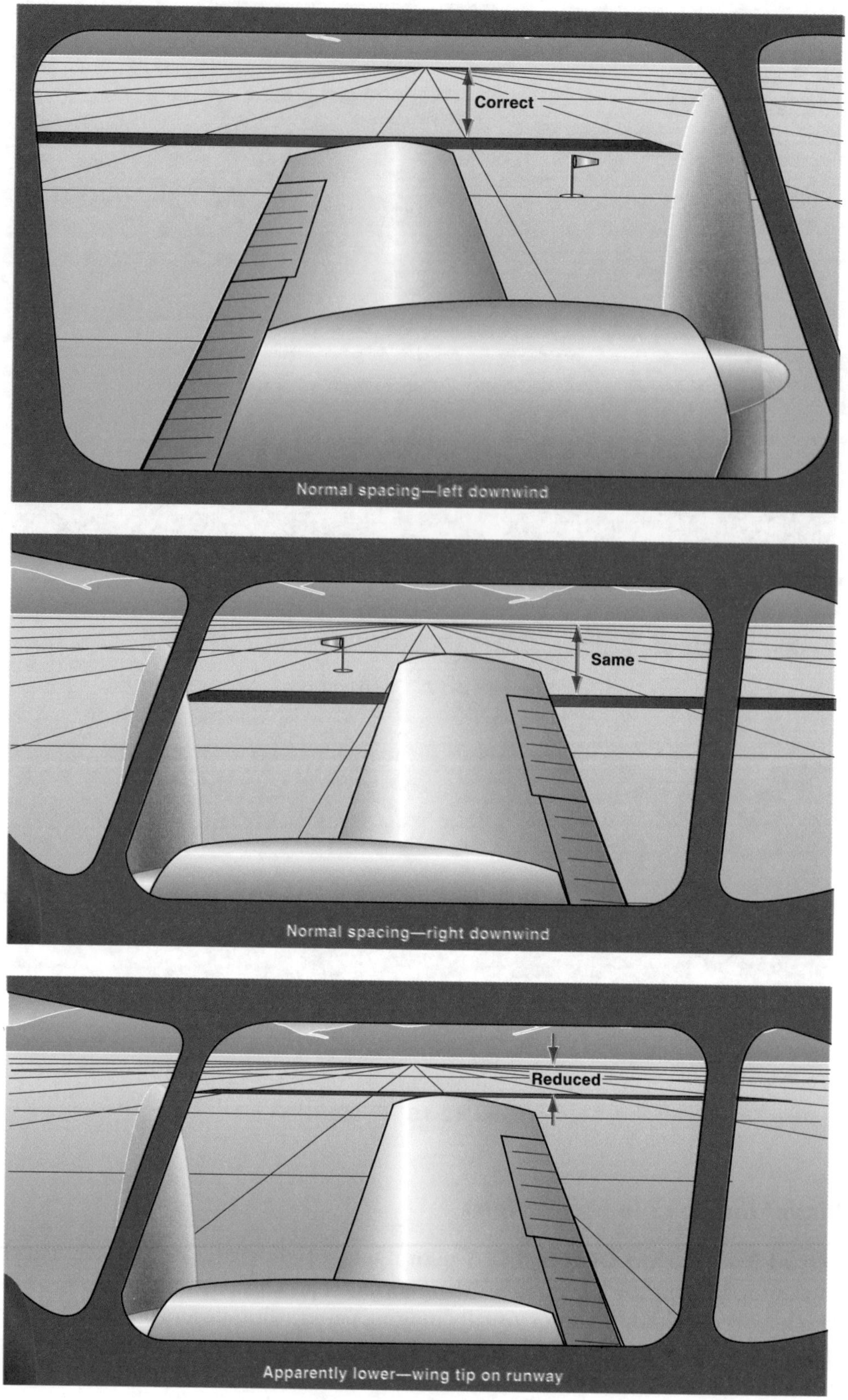

Figure 12-19 Downwind spacing in the traffic pattern.

Visual Illusions on Approach

Runway Slope. Most runways are of standard width and on flat ground. On every approach, you should try to achieve the same flight path angle to the horizontal, to which your eyes will become accustomed, allowing you to make consistently good approaches along an acceptable approach slope merely by keeping your view of the runway through the windshield in a standard perspective.

When approaching a sloping runway, however, the perspective will be different. A runway that slopes upward will look longer, and you will feel that you are high on slope, when in fact you are right on slope. The tendency will be for you to go lower or make a shallower approach.

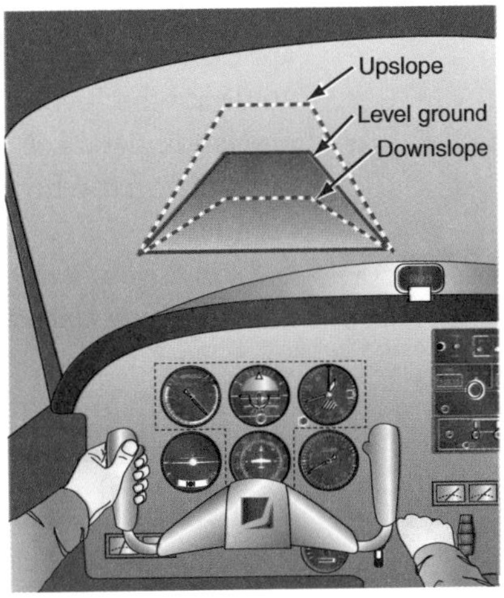

Figure 12-20 Runway slope.

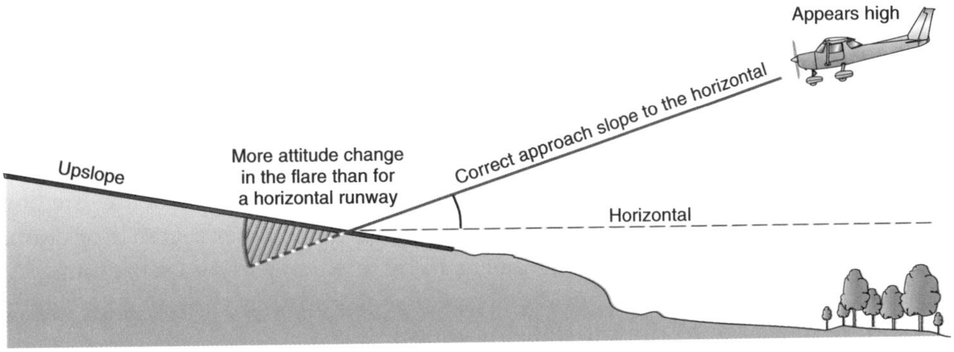

Figure 12-21 Upsloping runway.

A runway that slopes downward will look shorter, and you will feel that you are low when in fact you are on the correct path. The tendency will be for you to go higher and make a steeper approach.

If you know the runway slope, you can allow for it in your visual estimation of whether you are high or low on approach.

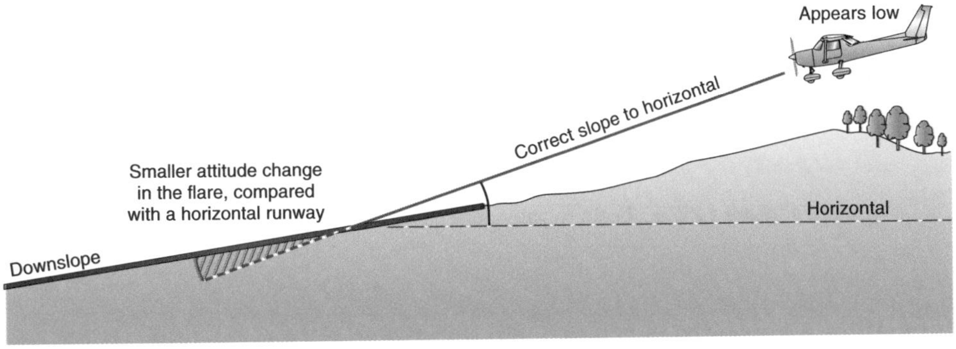

Figure 12-22 Downsloping runway.

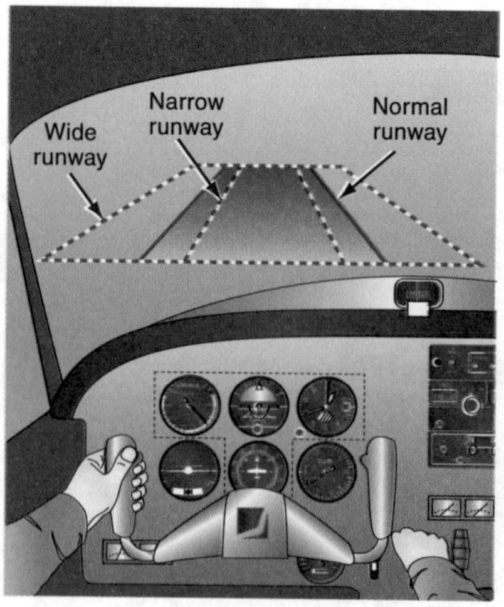

Figure 12-23
Runway width.

Runway Width. A runway that is wider than usual will appear to be closer than it really is. Conversely, a runway that is narrower than usual will appear to be further away than it really is. A wide runway, because of the angle at which you view it peripherally in the final stages of the approach and landing, will also cause an illusion of being too low, and you may flare and hold off too high as a result. This may lead to "dropping in" for a heavy landing.

Conversely, a narrow runway will cause an illusion of being too high, and you may delay the flare and make contact with the runway earlier (and harder) than expected. If you know that the runway is wider or narrower than what you are familiar with, then you can allow for this in your visual judgment of flare height.

Night Approach. A powered approach is preferred. Power gives the pilot more precise control, a lower rate of descent and a shallower approach path. The approach to the aim point should be stabilized as early as possible (constant airspeed, path, attitude, thrust and configuration). Use all the available aids, such as the runway lighting and a visual approach slope indicator (VASI).

If the runway edge lighting is the only aid, correct tracking and slope is achieved when the runway perspective is the same as in daylight. On centerline, the runway will appear symmetrical.

Guidance on achieving the correct approach slope is obtained from the apparent spacing between the runway edge lights and the distance of aim point below the horizon. If the aircraft is low, the runway lights will appear to be closer together or closing. If above slope, the runway lights will appear to be further apart and separating. VASI will provide correct indications, but the perspective provided by runway edge lighting may be misleading due to runway slope or width.

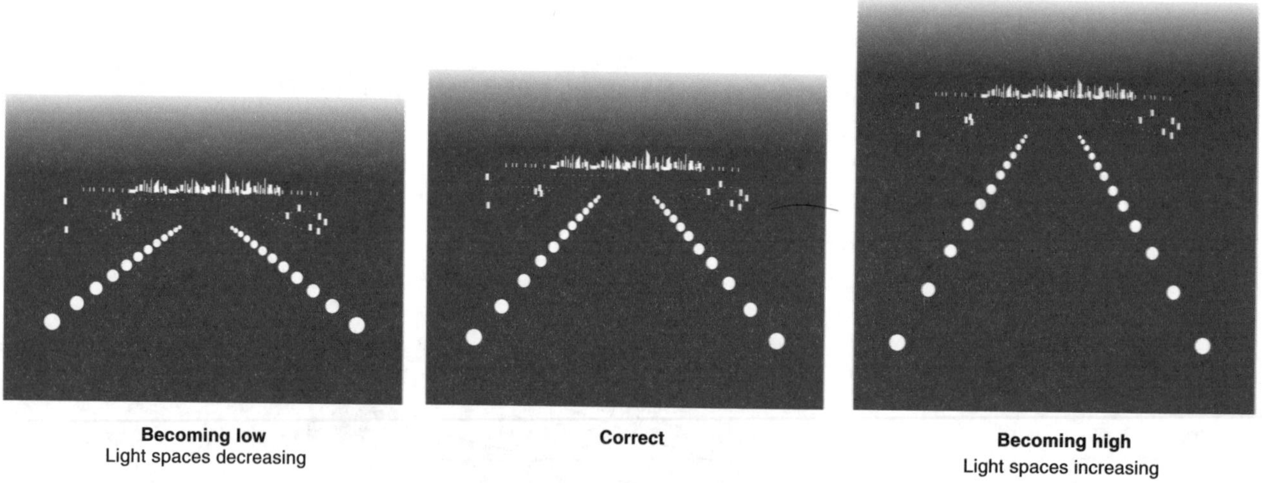

Figure 12-24 Night runway aspect.

Black-Hole Approach. Flying an approach to a runway with no other visible references can often be difficult. This can occur when approaching a runway on a dark night where the only lights visible are the runway edge lights, with no town lights or street lights to be seen, and no indication of the nature of the surrounding terrain. This is what is known as a *black-hole approach*. Alternatively, there could be city lights in the area beyond the airfield but no visual cues near the threshold. Black-hole approaches also occur on tropical atolls, at remote desert airfields, or on approaches to runways that are surrounded by water.

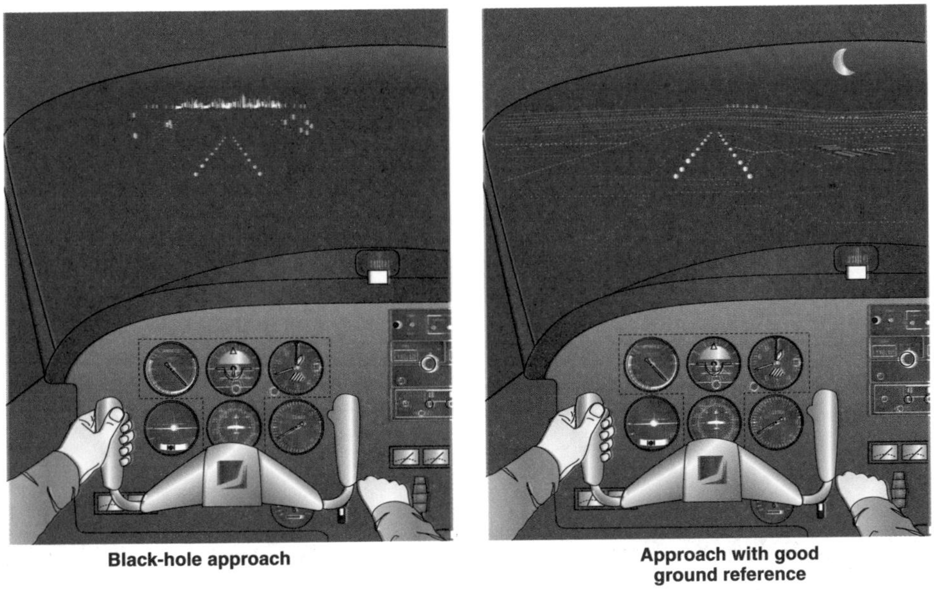

Figure 12-25 Black-hole approach.

The tendency is to think that you are higher than in fact you are, resulting in an urge to fly down and to fly a shallower approach—to sink into the abyss, the black hole.

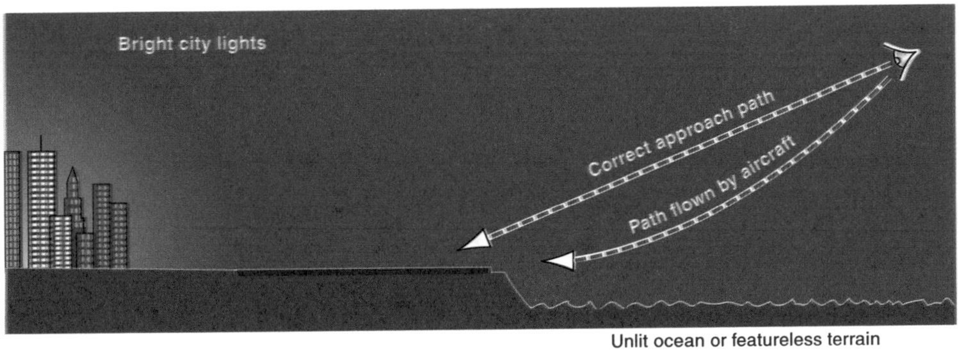

Figure 12-26 Black hole with high-contrast illumination.

The worst black-hole problem of all is to be found in remote airfields on a dark night (say, under cloud) where there is no other light source or any ground texture, and autokinesis might generate an impression of movement when there is none. Rely on the instruments, not your eyes, to maintain horizontal and vertical navigation plots.

If VASI is not available, crosscheck the vertical speed indicator (VSI) to ensure that the rate of descent is proportional to the approach speed (V_{REF}). As a guide, the rate of descent should be close to five times the groundspeed for a 3° approach. The glidepath is approximately 300 feet of altitude AGL for every mile from the runway, i.e., you should be at 900 feet AGL if you are on a three-mile final. Target an altitude of 300 feet one mile from the runway with a rate of descent of approximately 450 feet per minute with a 90-knot approach speed (use DME or GPS distance from the threshold, if available, to better plan descents).

Similar situations to a black-hole approach arise in conditions where the ground is covered with snow, making it featureless (white-out approach). The lack of a horizon and details around the runway threshold make depth and slope perception much more difficult.

Normal perspective   Obscured approach

Figure 12-27 Reduced visibility.

A variety of atmospheric and terrain conditions may produce visual illusions on approach. When you encounter such situations, anticipate and compensate for them.

Situation	**Illusion**	**Result**	
Upslope runway or terrain	Greater height	Lower approaches	**Shallower**
Narrower-than-usual runway	Greater height	Lower approaches	
Featureless terrain	Greater height	Lower approaches	
Rain on the windshield	Greater height	Lower approaches	
Haze	Greater height	Lower approaches	
Downslope runway or terrain	Less height	Higher approaches	**Steeper**
Wider-than-usual runway	Less height	Higher approaches	
Bright runway and approach lights	Less distance	Higher approaches	

Table 12-3 Visual illusion on approach.

Hearing and Balance

The ears provide two senses: hearing and balance. Hearing allows you to perceive sounds and to interpret them; the sense of balance lets you know which way is up and whether you are accelerating or not. Balance is the next most important sense for a pilot after vision.

Sound is defined as energy that you can detect with your ears. It is often very useful and pleasant, as with voice messages and music; however, excessive sound may be annoying and fatiguing, and can even lead to damage within the ear. Irregular, unwanted and unpleasant sound is called noise and is best filtered out. Sound signals are caused by pressure waves traveling through the air, and these cause the eardrum to vibrate. The inner ear converts these pressure vibrations into electrical signals that are sent via the auditory nerve to the brain where they are interpreted.

Similarly, balance and acceleration signals from the balance mechanism in the inner ear pass to the brain as electrical signals for interpretation. The interpretation is sometimes tricky in the case of an airborne pilot, since the brain is accustomed to the person generally being upright and slow moving on the earth's surface.

Figure 12-28 Ears aren't only for hearing.

Structure of the Ear

The ear is divided into three areas: the outer, middle, and inner ear.

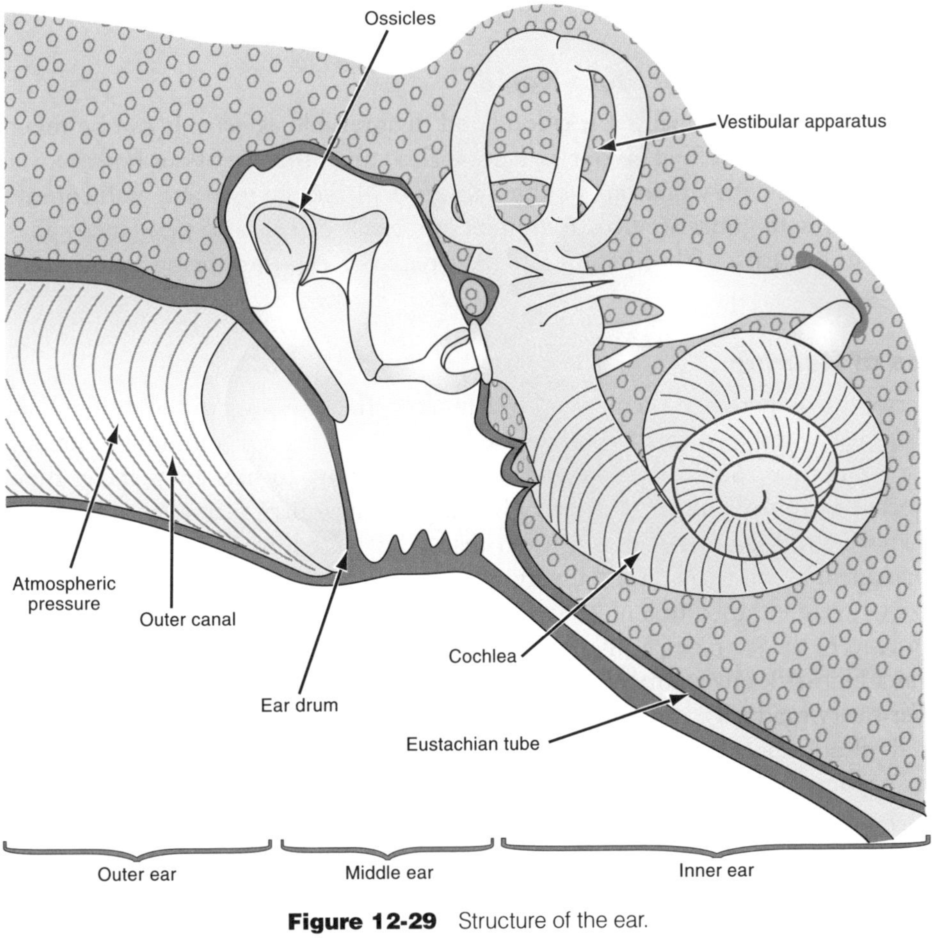

Figure 12-29 Structure of the ear.

Hearing

The ear is never switched off. Loud or particular noises to which you have a conditioned response can always stir you from the deepest sleep. A quiet room is essential for sound sleep. It is also interesting to note that you can extract messages important for you out of a noisy background; for instance, a radio message directed at you, the sound of your own child on a crowded beach, or your own name mentioned in a distant conversation can all be discerned. This is known as the *cocktail party effect*.

The region of the middle ear has much to do with your sensations of movement and balance. It is for that reason that people with middle-ear infections often lose their sense of balance. Furthermore, disturbed signals from these sensors lead to a feeling of nausea. In extreme cases, *vertigo*, the total loss of balance with massive and disturbing disorientation, results. The comments that follow apply to the hearing aspects of the ear; balance is discussed later in the chapter.

Sound is what you hear, and each sound can be defined by the following qualities:

- *frequency* or *pitch*, which is the number of pressure waves per second (or hertz, Hz) that the sound source produces. Perfect human hearing is in the range of 20 Hz to 20,000 Hz, and voices use the frequency range 500 Hz to 3,000 Hz;
- *loudness* or *intensity*, which is the strength or amplitude of the pressure waves, measured in decibels (dB), a logarithmic scale where an increase of 20 dB signifies an increase in intensity of ten times. (20 dB is ten times as loud as 0 dB, the threshold of hearing; 40 dB is ten times louder again, i.e. 100 times as loud as 0 dB; 60 dB is 1,000 times as loud as 0 dB and 100 times as loud as 20 dB); and
- *duration*, which is how long the sound lasts.

Fatigue and Damage From Noise

Unwanted sound, especially if it is loud and disagreeable, is *noise*. It can be mentally fatiguing through its effect on our ears, but it also affects the rest of our body, especially if it is associated with vibration as is often the case. Noise can interfere with communications, and with concentration. Extreme noise levels can also do permanent physical damage to our ears, with duration and recurrence of exposure being as important as loudness.

Loss of Hearing

A person can experience a temporary hearing loss after exposure to noise. The noise of an engine, for instance, may no longer be heard after a while even though the engine noise is still there. Some factory workers lose the ability to hear frequencies they are subjected to all day long. A temporary hearing loss may disappear after a few hours.

Exposure to high noise levels (greater than 80 dB) for long periods can also lead to a permanent hearing loss, especially in the high-frequency range. This is a risk area for pilots who are exposed to a noisy work environment for long periods. Put it together with visits to the car races, noisy night clubs, plus a top set of speakers at home and you are in a high-risk environment from the point of view of your hearing.

Very, very gradually, and imperceptibly, a person can lose the ability to hear certain sounds clearly, speech becomes more difficult to comprehend and radio communications become more difficult. Sudden, unexpected loud noises (greater than 130 dB), such as an explosion or the sound of an impact, can cause damage to hearing, possibly even physical damage to the eardrum or to the small and delicate ossicles.

Level (dB)	Situation
130	Standing near a jet aircraft (noise becoming painful).
120	Standing near a piston-engine aircraft (noise becoming uncomfortable). Several hours per day for three months could lead to deafness.
110	Maximum recommended for up to thirty minutes' exposure.
100	Maximum recommended for two hours' exposure.
90	Maximum recommended for eight hours' exposure (a working day).
80	Standing near heavy machinery. Above 80 dB for long periods can lead to temporary or permanent hearing loss.
60	Loud street noise, trucks, etc.
50	Conversation in a noisy factory.
40	Office noise.
30	Quiet conversation.
20	Whispering.
0	The threshold of hearing.

Table 12-4 Noise levels of typical sounds.

Aircraft Type	Takeoff	Cruise	Landing
Aero Commander 680	102	92	83
Beechcraft A36	97	86	75
Cessna 172	94	89	75
Piper Pawnee	103	102	89
Bell 206	91	92	89

Table 12-5 Indicative cockpit noise levels (decibels).

Hearing loss can also result from:

- problems in the conduction of the sound due to a blocked outer canal (ear wax), or fluid or pressure problems in the middle ear, e.g. barotrauma or damaged ossicles (known as *conductive hearing loss*);
- loss of sensitivity of the hair cells in the cochlea due to exposure to noise, infection, or age (known as a *sensory* or *noise-induced hearing loss*);
- *presbycusis*, a natural loss of hearing ability with increasing age, especially in the higher frequencies (down about 5% by age 60 and 10% by age 70); and
- excessive use of alcohol or medications.

Precautions for Minimizing Hearing Loss. A noise-induced hearing loss may develop gradually over a period of years without the person noticing. It is something that cannot be reversed, hence the need for prevention rather than cure. As a pilot, you are lucky in that you will have regular audiometry tests that can be compared over the years to look for any gradual loss of hearing, especially in the higher frequencies. Wear hearing protection when in noisy areas. A good noise-canceling headset is highly recommended for the cockpit, and earplugs or earmuffs for when you are moving around outside the aircraft. Earplugs can reduce noise by about 20 dB, and good earmuffs by about 40 dB. The radio headset, especially if it is well sealed, will block out background noise. Unprotected, close exposure to jet-engine noise can be hazardous to the balance mechanism in the ears also, which is another reason to wear hearing protection on the tarmac.

Balance

The sense of balance makes it possible for you to remain upright. The most powerful reference is visual. If you can see, you can tell directly whether you are vertical (if there is a vertical or horizontal reference). If you close your eyes, things are not so easy. Try standing on one leg and closing your eyes.

The secondary sensing mechanisms are those devices (other than vision) from which your brain might be sent orientation messages. The secondary signals are very feeble indeed, compared to visual cues. They really only supplement visual perception. In other words, they can only make sense in partnership with the vastly more powerful visual picture. These sensory mechanisms were designed for three-dimensional orientation but not three-dimensional motion or accelerations. However, if you have no visual horizon, these other sensors will supply fall-back information, but it is not totally reliable.

In the absence of a powerful visual cue, your system will crave orientation signals and accord them equal weight. The secondary sensing mechanisms will be sensed very strongly indeed, but they are always misleading. You cannot rely on any of them. You must never use them to judge your flight path. You can only guard against that by knowing what they will try to tell you, and by becoming familiar with their illusive signals. To be confident and competent in cloud requires training, experience and recency in cloud or in a motion simulator.

Spatial Orientation

Avoid spatial disorientation by looking outside or by looking at the flight instruments. Do not rely on body signals.

Orientation is the ability to determine your position and alignment in space. It is usually achieved by a combination of three senses:
- vision, the most powerful sense;
- balance, the *vestibular* sense (gravity, acceleration, and angular acceleration); and
- "seat-of-the-pants" (bodily feel or the *proprioceptive* sense).

The brain uses all information that it has available to assemble a picture. If there are conflicting signals, vision is given first priority. In most situations, each of the three senses reinforce the others; however, in flight, this is not always the case. Each of these senses can sometimes have its messages misinterpreted by the brain. Not knowing your attitude (i.e. which way is up) is *spatial disorientation*. When you are denied external vision, and flying is solely by reference to the instruments, a range of false sensations can be perceived. Hence, the need to rely totally on your flight instruments (but also scan to check that they agree with each other).

Human Balance Mechanism: The Vestibular Apparatus

The balance mechanism is designed to keep you upright—i.e. vertical and balanced—while standing or moving without input from the eyes. In the absence of visual references, the inner ear can sense what it believes is vertical by two means:
- sensing tilt angle; and
- sensing tilting motion (backward/forward or left/right).

The angle of tilt is sensed by the equivalent of a pendulous mass (which senses gravity as vertical) and the tilting motion by the fluid-filled semicircular canals.

Sensing Gravity (Verticality)

Your body can sense accelerations (g-forces).

Gravity is detected by sensory hairs in a sac filled with gelatinous material, commonly known as the *otolithic organ* or *utricle*. The sac's outer membrane is studded with small crystals of calcium carbonate. These are called *otoliths* and give the organ its name.

The otolithic organ has a resting position when the head is upright. The brain interprets the message sent from the small hairs at this time as *up*; that is, the sac is affected by a 1g force directly downward. If the head is tilted to one side, or forward or backward, then the otoliths act as weights moving the sac under the force of gravity and taking up a new position, thus bending the hairs, which sends a different signal to the brain.

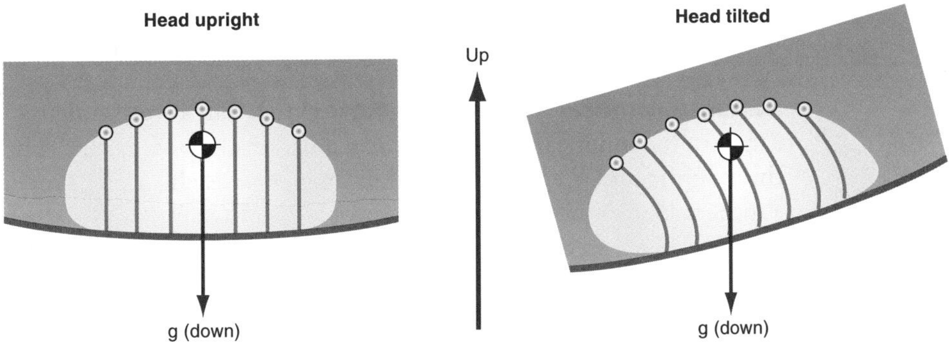

Figure 12-30 Sensing vertical.

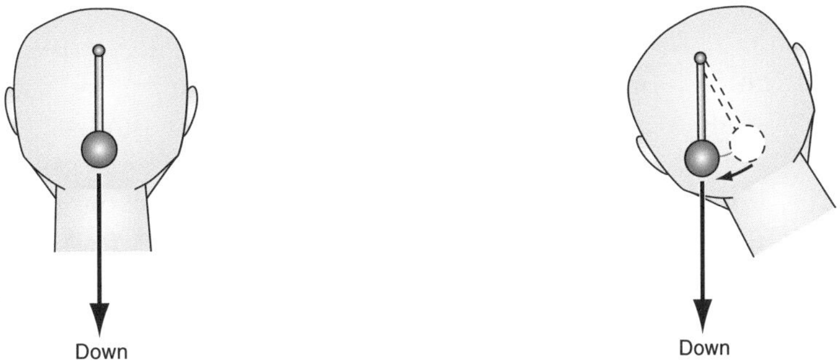

Figure 12-31 Pendulous effect.

The otolithic organ detects the direction of g-forces but cannot distinguish their origin; that is, it cannot tell whether it is the force of gravity or a centripetal force pulling you into a coordinated turn. You must remember that the body was designed for fairly slow motion on the face of the earth, with a consistent 1g force of gravity exerted on it, and not for the three-dimensional forces you experience in flight (or zero g for that matter). In a turn, it will recognize the direction of the total load factor as a false vertical.

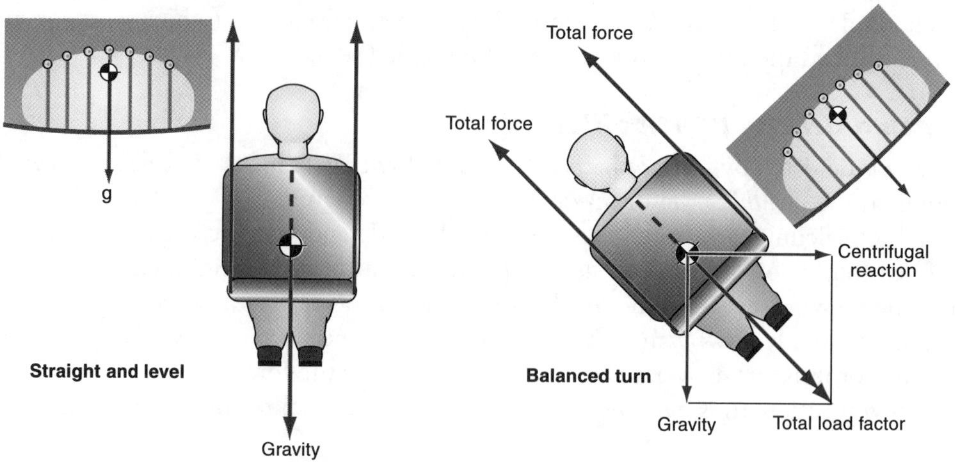

Figure 12-32 Apparent vertical—straight and turning flight.

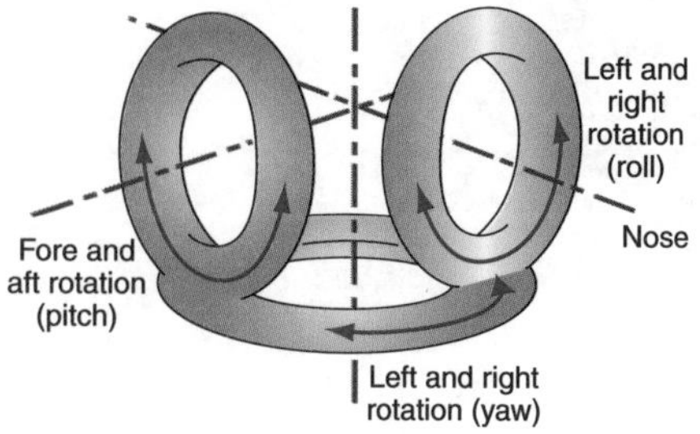

Figure 12-33 Semicircular canals.

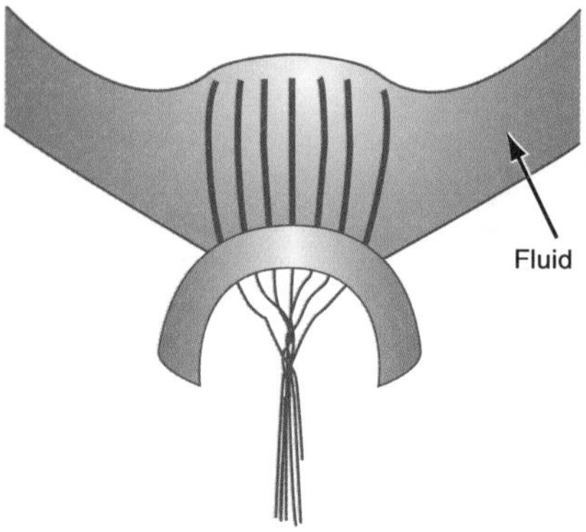

Figure 12-34 Cupula.

Sensing Angular Movement (Rotation). The three semicircular canals of the inner ear—the vestibular apparatus—contain fluid. These three semicircular canals are at right angles to each other (they are orthogonal) like the pitch, roll and yaw planes of an airplane, and therefore they can detect angular accelerations (change in the rate of rotational speed) in pitch, roll and yaw.

The *cupula* is a saddle-shaped chamber at the base of each canal as depicted in the diagram opposite. It has a cluster of fine hairs that protrudes into the fluid. Movement in the fluid is sensed by these hairs. Nerve endings at their base send corresponding signals to the brain for interpretation (perception).

The semicircular canals are *not* designed to detect linear changes in motion or linear acceleration, because the upper and lower volumes of fluid are self-canceling. For example, if the fluid at the top of the semicircular canal tries to move counterclockwise around the canal due to an acceleration forward, then the fluid at the bottom will try to move around clockwise to the same degree. The net effect is no relative movement of the fluid and the sensory hairs of the cupula will remain straight.

The vestibular apparatus senses angular acceleration by recognizing changes in rotary motion due to the lag of the viscous fluid. During angular acceleration, the relevant semicircular canal moves around a mass of fluid that lags. This lag in the fluid bends the sensory hairs to send a signal to the brain that the head is rolling, yawing or pitching (three dimensions—three channels—three canals). Once the rate of roll steadies—that is, there is no more angular acceleration—the fluid will catch up with the surface of the semicircular canals, straightening the sensory hairs of the cupula. This means you will detect the entry to the roll but not its continuing steady state. Similarly, you will sense the opposite acceleration as you stop the roll (decelerate) at the required bank angle.

In flight, the sensory mechanisms are suppliers only of crude and potentially deceptive messages (compared to the direct orientation

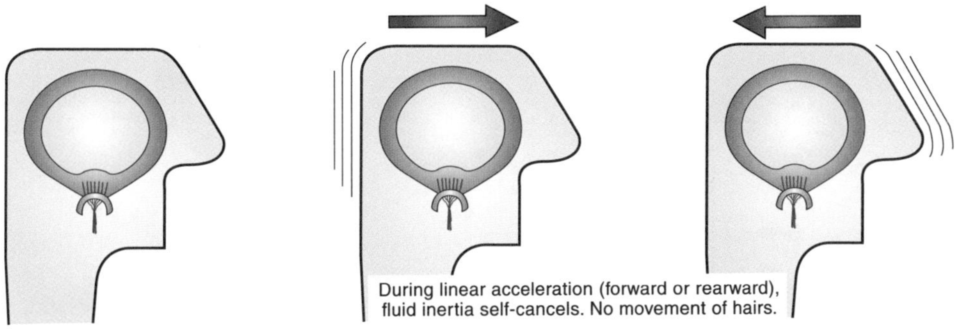

During linear acceleration (forward or rearward), fluid inertia self-cancels. No movement of hairs.

Figure 12-35 Linear acceleration.

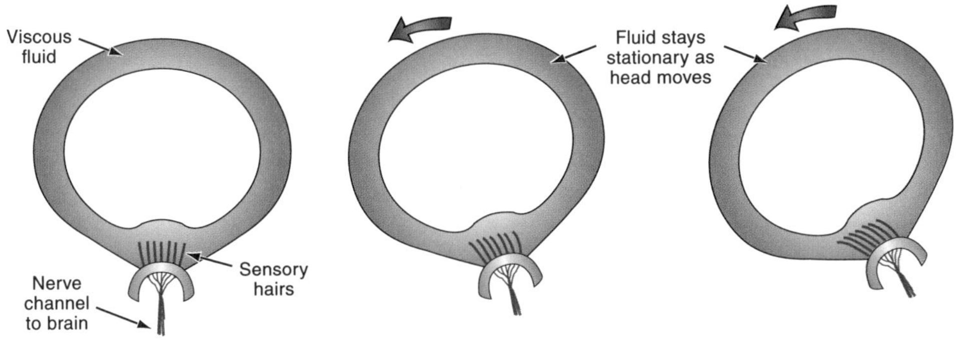

Figure 12-36 Angular acceleration—rotation.

images flowing through the sight channel). As is the case with any stimulus or sensation, there is a threshold below which movement will not be detected. For example, you will sense a rapid change in roll rate, but not a gentle one. In reality, you do not necessarily detect the angular acceleration that commences the roll as a rolling sensation. You may feel the entry into the roll as a rolling sensation if the roll is rapid enough. Similarly, you may sense the rotary deceleration that stops the roll at the selected bank angle. You may also sense rolling signals from adjustments to the control input while adjusting either roll rate or angle of bank. However, in many flight regimes, your control inputs will be so gentle that you will not detect any rolling sensation at all. The potential for confusion is serious.

Sensations in Turning Flight. In a balanced turn, a full glass of water on top of the instrument panel will remain unspilled; it will remain level with respect to the glass. It is as if the weight of the fluid is acting through the aircraft's vertical axis. It is. The apparent weight is the result of gravity and centrifugal reaction.

Your body will also sense up and down as acting in that same axis. There will no longer be any rolling sensation, nor is there any other sensation source other than seat-of-the-pants. In other words, once you are established in a turn, you will feel that you are in straight and level flight. And that feeling will be the same regardless of the bank angle, except that the load factor is increased. When you bring together this feeling of certainty of where down is and the sensation of rolling, things can become very confusing, a condition generally known as *the leans*. The leans can profoundly interfere with your mental equilibrium, but only if you let them.

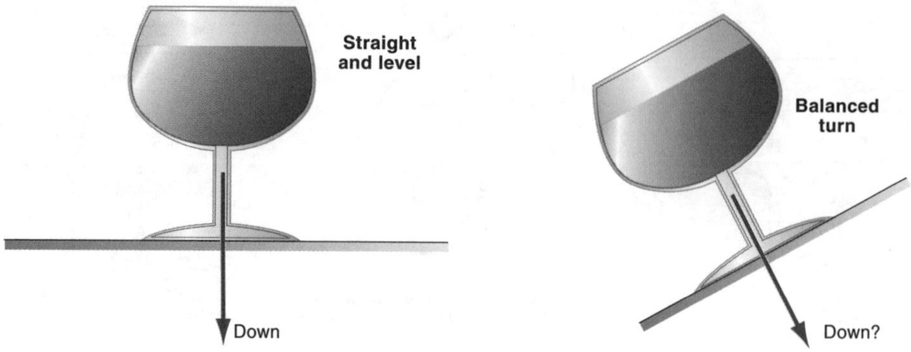

Figure 12-37 Sensed vertical.

Disorientation and Illusions

The Leans

Let's look at another situation. If the turn entry is very gentle, it is not sensed by the semicircular canals, but the stop-roll deceleration is detected. The end result is quite discomforting:

- the gentle onset of roll into the turn is not perceived;
- next, no sensation is available during the steady-state roll;
- but, when the stop-roll control movements are made briskly, the angular deceleration that stops the roll and establishes the bank angle is felt—strongly;
- however, it is felt as a roll to the left; and
- as there is no canceling sensation available, the sensation of rolling—continuous rolling—persists, though it will slowly dissipate as the fluid stops moving and the sensory hairs get to stand up straight again.

In entering this turn, the only sensation perceived was the stop-roll angular deceleration. The signal sent to your brain is read as a roll to the left. With no corresponding canceling sensation, it will be a sensation of continuously rolling. When you then roll out of the turn, and the rollout is briskly commenced (enough to be detected), you will then experience the sensation that the left-roll movement has become faster.

Perception of rapid roll rates can quickly produce strong sensations of disorientation. You can get the leans from turn entries or exits. That is:

- you might be wings level and yet absolutely convinced you are rolling into or established in a turn; or
- equally, you can be in the turn and certain that your wings are level.

Slow rates of roll (or movement around the other two axes) will not be detected. Brisk control inputs will induce sensations, and the brisker, the stronger. A common leans scenario is the following:

- you slowly let a wing drop then suddenly notice the wing-low condition;
- you spontaneously and rapidly roll to wings level (and perhaps be looking down at a map or over your shoulder for the runway after a night takeoff); and
- you feel a strong rolling sensation.

Nose-Up Pitch Illusion of Linear Acceleration

The otoliths are tiny weights on the membrane enclosing the utricle sac and its sensing hairs. When you tilt your head back, or lean backward, the weights cause the sac to slump in that direction. The corresponding sensor-hair movement tells your brain that your vertical axis is now inclined rearward.

The same sensation is caused by linear acceleration. Under acceleration, the sac lags behind, and sensor hairs send a message of tilting backward. This sensation of the nose rising as you accelerate is known as the *somatogravic illusion* (*somato* meaning originating in the body, *gravic* meaning sense of gravity). The greater the acceleration, the stronger the feeling. Obviously, it is not a problem when there are clear visual cues, but it can have very serious consequences when there are few, or none, as on a dark night. The forward acceleration through takeoff and then to climb speed will be sensed as backward tilt or, rather, as a higher nose-attitude and pitch-up than actually exists. There is a temptation to lower the nose with sometimes fatal consequences.

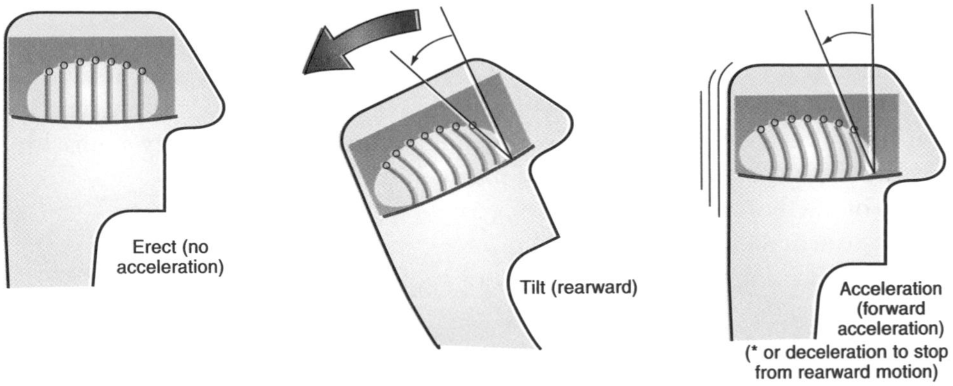

Figure 12-38 Rearward tilt or acceleration?

Nose-Down Pitch Illusion of Linear Deceleration

There is a converse to the somatogravic illusion, but not as serious, as it is less likely to happen near the ground. Deceleration in flight is sensed as tilting forward. It is particularly noticeable in higher performance aircraft when reducing thrust and extending the speed brakes. If the aircraft is already descending, the deceleration will be sensed as a steepening descent.

Again, if there is clear visual reference, the sensation is hardly noticeable. If the horizon is less clear, then they are more powerful. Fly attitude as depicted on your flight instruments.

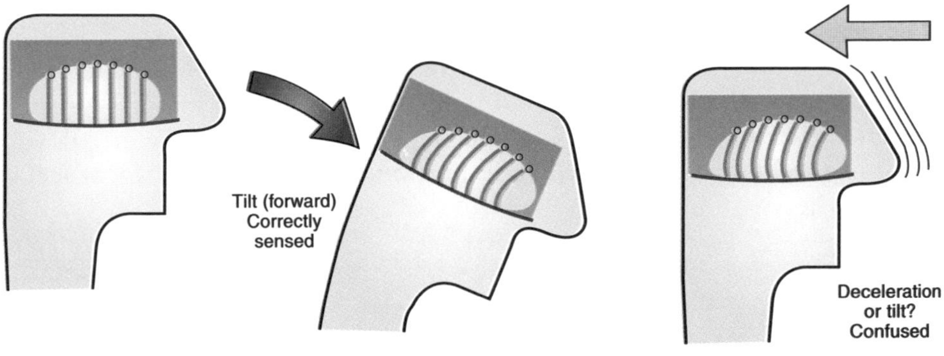

Figure 12-39 Forward tilt or deceleration?

Motion Sickness

Motion sickness is usually caused by the balance mechanisms of the inner ear being overstimulated by motion. This can be caused by turbulence, or maneuvers such as steep turns or spins, in which forces other than the normal will be experienced, especially if there is no clear horizon. A hot, smelly cockpit does not help. Psychological aspects can also play a role in the onset of motion sickness. Anxiety, in particular, will make the condition worse by causing the sufferer to lose control over where he or she looks and focuses attention. Visual scanning is likely to become purposeless, random or fixed.

The visual channel is, by far, the most powerful spatial orientation reference. If the messages coming in through non-visual channels—the balance organs—are accorded priority, the sensory confusion causing airsickness will predominate. If the airsick person focuses on the horizon, the visual messages will be given a chance to assert their authority and to tone down the strength of the signals coming from other sources.

Many pilots have experienced airsickness, especially early in their training when stress levels are higher, and unusual attitudes and g-forces are encountered perhaps for the first time, so do not be discouraged if you experience it occasionally.

To avoid airsickness:

- anticipate and avoid areas of turbulence, known from weather forecasts and any local effects such as the side of hills (if not a local, seek the views of someone who is);
- eat lightly before flight, but do eat something (don't fly on an empty stomach);
- fly the airplane smoothly, gently and maintain trim and balance;
- focus on the horizon as much as you can;
- avoid maneuvers involving unusual g-forces; and
- ventilate the cabin with a good supply of cool, fresh air.

If turbulence is encountered:

- fly at best speed;
- relax, don't fight, and maintain attitude;
- occupy a potentially airsick passenger in the flight, especially with looking outside the airplane into the distance or at the horizon;
- as a last resort, recline the airsick passenger's seat to reduce the effect of the vertical accelerations and keep an airsickness bag handy; and
- land as soon as is reasonably possible (if necessary).

Load Factor

Speed has relatively little effect on the human body, whereas acceleration or deceleration may produce pronounced effects ranging from the fatiguing characteristics of flight to a complete collapse of the cardiovascular system. In aviation, acceleration is usually expressed in multiples of the acceleration due to gravity of 32.2 fps^2 (9.81 m/s^2) and is represented by the symbol g.

The brain and eyes need a continuous supply of oxygen. They have little storage capacity, so strong or prolonged g-forces, which reduce the supply, lead to reduced visual acuity, loss of color vision, loss of sight and even unconsciousness. When the acceleration is centripetal, as in turn or pitching maneuvers, it is felt by the pilot as an increase in weight. In a 60°-banked level turn, you will experience +2g, or feel you are twice as heavy.

All parts of the body are affected by g-force. The blood, for instance, will also get heavier. It therefore is harder to pump and circulate, and tends to pool in the legs and lower abdomen. At higher load factors of, say, +3.5g and upward, this can produce physiological symptoms.

Reduced blood circulation diminishes the transport of oxygen and sugar to the head. That is manifested as less blood supply and reduced local blood pressure. As there is very little stored oxygen and sugar in the head (as opposed to muscles, which have some storage capacity), the reduced blood supply can cause an immediate effect.

The first to notice anything is the eyes. As the eyeballs must remain balls—as opposed to being squashed by surrounding tissue—they are inflated to positive internal pressure (they feel hard to the touch.) A side-effect of this necessary condition is that blood flow to the eyes, and the oxygen and sugar supply it carries, is inhibited. It's an uphill slope.

If g-force is reducing the blood pressure in the head, then the eyes will be affected first because of this pressure gradient. The supply of oxygen and sugar is necessary to process sight signals. As g increases, sight becomes affected, with color vision the first to go. If you are not used to high load factors, this stage of the phenomenon might occur at +3.5 to +4.5g. It is called *grayout.* All images are seen as shades of gray and white.

If the g keeps building, the field of view will begin to shrink, starting from the sides. This limiting vision effect is called tunnel vision. Still increasing g-forces will lead to total loss of vision, or blackout. At this point, the pilot is temporarily blind, though still conscious. Further g increase will inevitably lead to insufficient oxygen and sugar supply to keep the brain functioning—loss of consciousness.

So far, we have only talked about positive g—the plane is the right way up. If the aircraft is inverted, the effect of negative g is not only uncomfortable, it is potentially dangerous. It's one thing for large amounts of blood under higher pressure to be accumulating in the legs and lower abdomen, surrounded by tough and flexible muscle. To have that happening in the head around all that delicate machinery is another thing altogether.

Most pilots, once they have accommodated to aerobatic maneuvering, can withstand up to negative 2.5g. If, however, you push beyond that, you will encounter the phenomenon called *redout.* When you red out, the impression is of total loss of sight, because a red veil is in the way. The reason for it is that your lower eyelid muscles have evolved to match the human bodies needs. As we mostly stand erect, blinking requires the lower eyelid to move only upward. Gravity will organize the return journey. There is no corresponding muscle group to "unblink" the lower eyelid. So if you are inverted, and push to a certain negative g limit, the lower eyelid will drop, covering the pupil, and you cannot force it out of the way.

Many pilots will never experience any of these g-related phenomena. However, some will go on to learn aerobatic maneuvers, or to fly military jets capable of high g-forces in turns and maneuvering. For those who do, there is an especially insidious potential trap: *g-induced loss of consciousness* or *g-loc.*

We saw earlier how positive g-force brings on a sequence of sight-related changes before getting to the point of unconsciousness—grayout, tunnel vision, blackout. As all of these occur while conscious, they can be controlled and relieved. Relaxing the back pressure on the controls will bring nearly instantaneous relief from the degraded sight condition. Indeed, in the case of blackout, the reaction to diminish the g-force by easing the control forces is nearly reflexive. However, g-loc occurs with high rates of onset of g where the warning symptoms are overruled.

As the graph in figure 12-40 shows, the grayout to blackout phenomena acts as a threshold or warning of unconsciousness. It enables forewarning and the chance to reduce the control pressure. There is appreciable delay before the effects are felt and therefore time to return to normal. That is what happens at the normal rate of g onset.

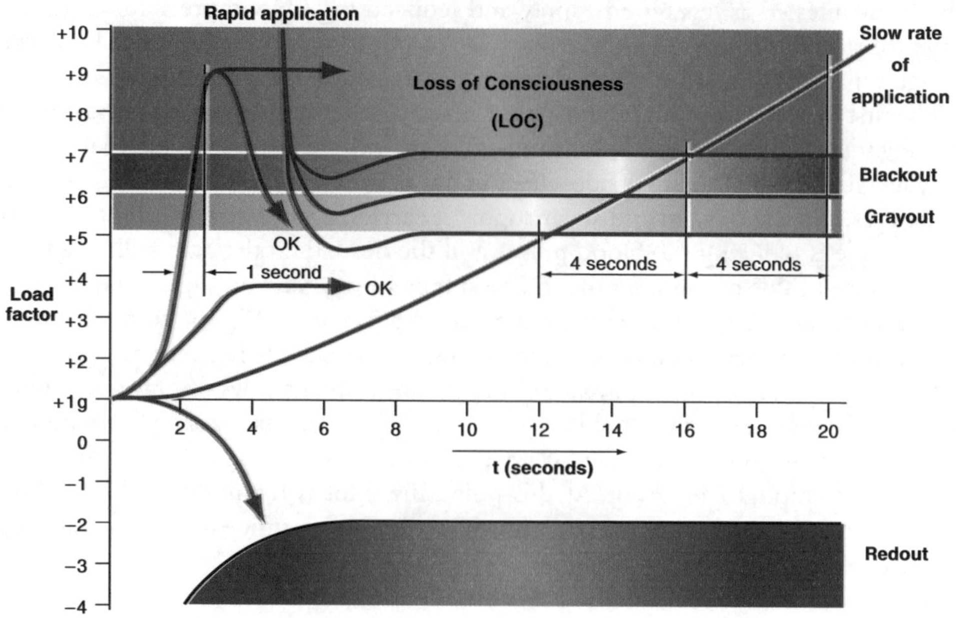

Figure 12-40 Physical response to load factor.

If, however, the rate of onset of g is rapid, the warning signals of degraded sight will be bypassed. The pilot will become instantly unconscious. If you blackout, you will, intuitively relax the control pressure to reduce the g, and immediately regain full sight and you remain conscious throughout. However, if you lose consciousness, it takes at least 15 seconds to recover. Loss of consciousness is a debilitating experience. Think of the last time you saw someone faint: recall how disoriented and incapable they were during the ensuing period. Momentary loss of consciousness in an aircraft can never be safe. Being out of control for 15 seconds will often prove fatal. However, only aerobatic aircraft have the structure and control power for flight capable of causing g-loc.

Coping With High Load Factors

Your personal resistance to g-forces is highest not only if you are physically fit but also toughened—hardened by regular exposure. Serious exercise is a good idea for all pilots, but it is especially so for those who want to be good at aerobatics. On the other hand, no matter how fit you are, there will be times in your life (or day) when your resistance levels are down, like when recovering from illness, tired after a long day, under domestic stress or suffering work problems.

A-loc

Another term that has been recently coined is *a-loc*. A-loc is *almost* loss of consciousness due to g. The reason for the differentiation is that, even if the pilot does not lose consciousness, there is a temporary period of confusion and even euphoria, where the pilot either does not recognize, or does not care about, the seriousness of the situation. It is momentary, but it is believed to have caused some otherwise unexplained pilot lack-of-response during recovery from high-g maneuvers.

Situational Awareness

We tend to think of piloting an airplane as a physical skill. However, there is more to it—much more. Aircraft control, the manipulation of controls to achieve a desired performance, is important, but it is only one element of the pilot's total task. The pilot must assemble information, interpret the data, assess its importance, make decisions, act, communicate, correct and continuously reassess. We call this total process *piloting*. But let's start with the control process so that, once the aircraft is under control, we can be sensitive to and more aware of the bigger picture.

Where am I, where am I going, when will I get there, with how much fuel, at what time, what will the weather be like, how well is the aircraft performing, how tired am I, how well are the passengers, how do I get to the town after I land, how to avoid weather, how to avoid airspace, what calls I have to make . . . this is situational awareness. It is a total appreciation of where you are at, where you want to be and how best to get there safely and on time.

How You Process Information

The main feature of your brain, as a central decision-maker, is that it can only function as a *single-channel* computer, which means that you can consider only one problem at a time. Conscious decisions are therefore not made simultaneously, but sequentially. They are placed in a queue according to a priority—but not always logically.

How the brain processes information is fascinating. There are six fundamental stages:

- *stimulation* and *sensation* where sensors receive a signal;
- *perception* for recognition, classification and remembering;
- *analysis* to work out what to do (make a decision);
- *action* for doing something (or nothing);
- *feedback* to check results; and
- *correction* to achieve acceptable standards of accuracy.

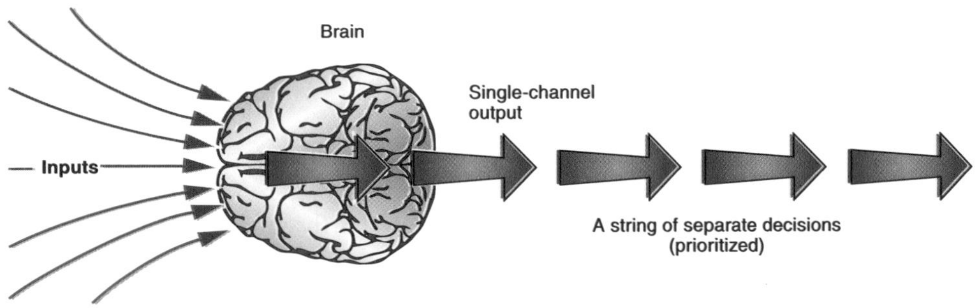

Figure 12-41 Single-channel processing.

Assembling the Big Picture

The pilot's task involves two processes:

- being in *control* of the airplane; and
- being in *command* of the situation.

Situational awareness is the process whereby the pilot gathers data from his or her own senses via sight, hearing, smell, taste, touch, and feel. For a pilot, the eyes and ears are the primary sensors—although control feel and "seat-of-the-pants" are important cues for aircraft control. In addition to direct sight and sound, the eyes and ears are used to gather information from the instruments, radios, and NAVAIDs so that the pilot can build and maintain an awareness of position, time, fuel, weather, traffic, and aircraft status. From these data, the pilot can prioritize the importance of the information, anticipate trends, assess the need for urgency, and make decisions. The primary task of being the pilot-in-command is decision making. The quality of the decision depends upon the quality, completeness, and timeliness of the data—and is affected by pilot aptitude, training, fatigue, stress, and personality.

The process of assembling data, making a decision, acting and correcting is called the pilot's *control loop*.

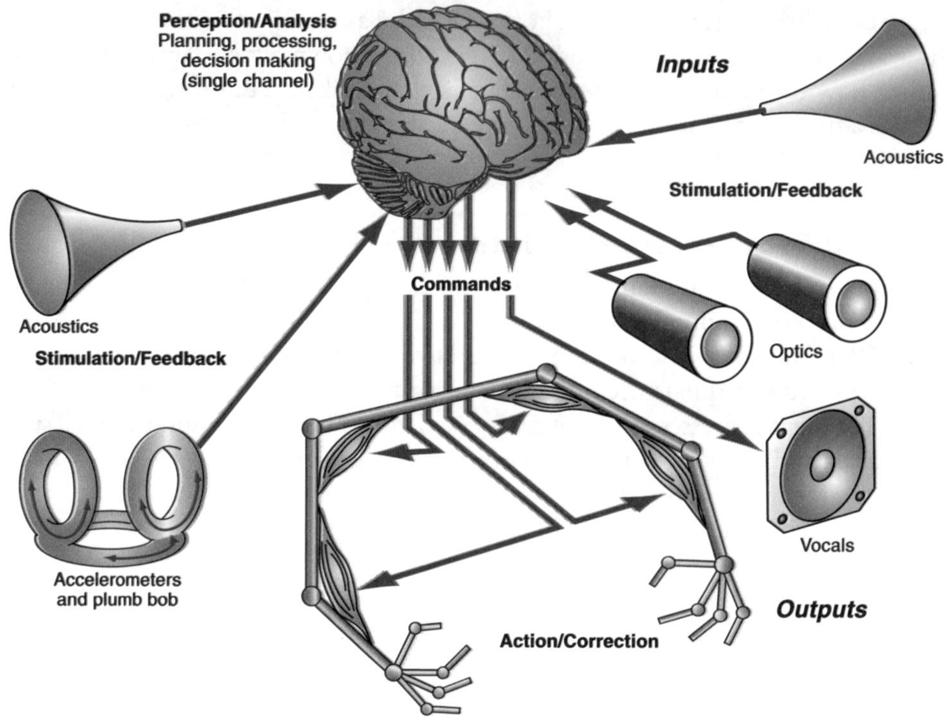

Figure 12-42 The pilot's central role in the control loop.

Flying as a Learned Set of Skills

While a student pilot is concentrating on learning to fly safely and accurately, the central decision-maker will be almost fully occupied. There will be very little spare capacity for other tasks such as navigation and radio calls—or even listening to the instructor. Once the student has learned the motor skills and practiced them until they are second nature, flying the airplane will occur with little conscious thought. In this case, a string of activities is run autonomously in the brain, leaving the central decision-maker available for higher-level decisions. Strings (or sets) of skills are often initiated by the central decision-maker. You might make a decision to get up and walk toward the door, but once this decision has been made, the central decision-maker can drop out of the picture temporarily and let the motor program run the activity. As well as initiating the activity, the central decision-maker will also return to monitor the motor program from time to time, to check that the proper skill sequence is in use, and to check progress and decide when to stop.

Figure 12-43
The primary pilot-airplane interface.

If skills are not used regularly, they deteriorate, and an activity that was once run automatically by a single thought may now have to be managed by conscious decision-making. This will occupy the central decision-maker and, as a result, you can expect a temporary deterioration in the performance of other tasks. Professional pilots returning from a holiday break notice this, as do musicians and others who have to perform skilled tasks. We can certainly *do* more than one thing at a time, thanks to skill programming, but we can only *think* about one thing at a time.

Response Time

The time it takes for any initial stimulus to be perceived, considered, and acted upon can take between a fraction of a second and several seconds, depending upon the complexity of the decision to be made, the action to be taken and the acceptability of the degree of deviation. In a control loop, such as an autopilot, this is known as the *gain*—high gain means a quick response to any deviation, and low gain is a sluggish response. High gain is less tolerant of deviations but can mean a rough ride and so autopilots have a soft-ride or half-bank mode for less disturbances and a more comfortable flight.

Responding to a stimulus often requires a series of sequential decisions to be made: this of course needs time due to the single-channel nature of the brain's central decision-maker. On approach to land, for instance, the landing gear has been selected down and a horn unexpectedly sounds.

Some of the decisions that now need to be made are the following:

- *establish a safe flight path*—in this case, a go-around is essential to gain time and place you into a position where you can sort out the problem. Continuing with the approach is pushing you to a higher workload, with more critical demands on time;
- *silence the horn to remove the distraction*—the horn has been heard and the warning has been noted;
- *what does the horn mean?*—is it landing gear not down, or something else? It means that the landing gear has been selected down, but is not actually down;
- *radio call*—declare emergency to tower, ATC or other traffic; and
- carry out checklist items.

Throughout the decision-making process following a very simple unexpected event, you must continue to switch attention through the tasks of aviating, navigating, and communicating to allocate priorities and to trigger skilled responses. In a situation like that above, you removed the pressure of time by deciding to make a missed approach, and then allowing the learned skill to fly the aircraft. Once the safe response was seen to be in progress, the conscious mind then established the next priority. Time was thus made available to solve the problem. In other situations, you may not have that luxury—e.g. in a takeoff that is rejected at a high speed on a limiting runway. This will require a split-second decision and immediate actions. If the pilot of a large aircraft suspects a problem during the takeoff run, especially as the decision speed is approached, there is only two seconds to decide what to do: *stop or go?* Stopping may not be possible if a tire has blown and reduced the wheel-braking capability. Continuing the takeoff may not be possible if the problem is with the flight controls, or if the problem is multiple engine failure due to bird strikes. The enormous pressure of limited time between input and a necessary decision can sometimes lead to a faulty decision and response.

The risk of making a poor decision, no decision, or an incorrect response is minimized by maintaining a high level of knowledge, and by practicing a maneuver frequently so that it becomes a conditioned response. The decision/response is thus based on the probability of the best course of action and accepting the smallest odds. Simulators can play a big role here, particularly when practicing critical maneuvers.

Mental Workload

Best performance is achieved by a combination of high levels of skill, knowledge, and experience (consistency and confidence), and with an optimum degree of arousal. Skill, knowledge and experience depend upon the training of the pilot; the degree of arousal depends not only upon the pilot's flying ability but also upon other factors, such as the design of the cockpit, air traffic control, as well as upon the environment, motivation, personal life, weather, and so on. Low levels of skill, knowledge and experience, plus a poorly designed cockpit, bad weather, and poor controlling will lead to a high mental workload and a poor performance. If the mental workload becomes too high, decision making will deteriorate in quality, or maybe not even occur. This could result in concentrating only on one task (sometimes called *tunnel vision*) with excessive or inappropriate load-shedding. You can raise your capability by studying and practicing, and by being fit, relaxed and well rested.

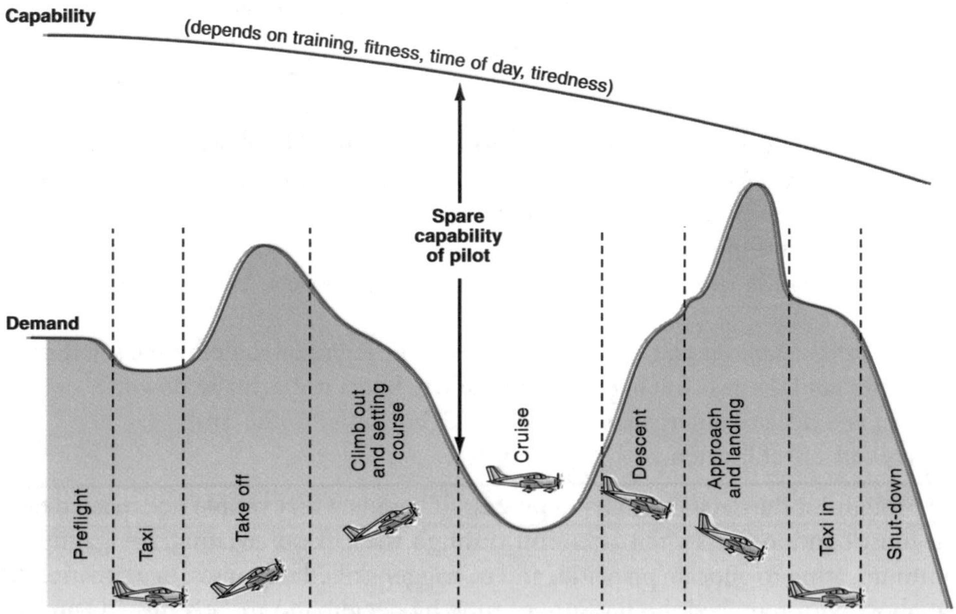

Figure 12-44 Reserve capability.

The pilot's tasks need to be analyzed so that at no time do they demand more of the pilot than the average, current and fit pilot is capable of delivering. There should always be some reserve capacity to allow for handling unexpected abnormal and emergency situations. At the aircraft design stage, the pilot is taken to be of an average standard. On this basis, skills and responses are established during testing so that the aircraft can be certificated as compliant. But there is some argument that the specimen should not be the average pilot, because half of the pilot population would be below this standard.

The legislators establish the minimum acceptable standards for licensing but the marginal pilot, who maintains only the minimum required standard, is not really of an acceptable standard. You can each ensure that you are at an acceptable standard by honestly reviewing the demand that the aircraft and the flight placed upon you. If your capabilities, mental or physical, were stretched at all, then you need more practice, more study or more training—at least in those aspects that challenged you. Many pilots feel that, under normal conditions, they should be able to operate at only 40–50% of capacity, except during takeoffs and landings, when that might rise to 70%. This leaves some capacity to handle abnormal situations.

Aeronautical Decision Making

The essential, fundamental role of the pilot is to make decisions—reliably, safely and timely. But fortunately or unfortunately, pilots are only human.

Figure 12-45
Make conscious decisions.

Information Processing

The decision-making process is one of assembling data, assessing its importance and urgency, making the optimum decision (based on experience and training) and then taking the appropriate action. The quality of this action reflects the pilot's aptitude, skill, discipline, training and recent experience (on the aircraft type, in those conditions and for the particular phase of flight). The quality of the decision depends very much on having complete and recent data (such as position, weather and traffic) for both existing conditions and the likely trends. This big picture is called *situational awareness.* Then there is the dimension that must have a high priority in the pilot's mind: the "fourth dimension."

The Fourth Dimension

An airplane operates in four dimensions:

- three-dimensional space; and
- time.

Everything in flight is changing, and the rate of change varies enormously. Learning to fly is very much a process of being conditioned to the rate at which things happen.

The other aspect of time is that it is finite. You run out of fuel, daylight and clear weather. You become tired. You may have limited time and space in which to make a decision or to maneuver the aircraft.

Thus situational awareness for a pilot is knowing more than where you are. It is knowing the aircraft's position, environment and status, all in the context of time—time gone, time to go and time available.

Emotions in Decisions

Emotion plays a significant, often a dominant role, in the decision-making process. We often decide on the basis of what we want to happen rather than what is most likely to happen. What we hope instead of what is likely. What we expect can also be ambitious or cautious, especially if we have pushed the boundaries and got away with it previously. Thus decisions also depend on personality and confidence. What are the chances I wrongly perceive rather than correctly know what the odds really are? Do I by nature err on the positive side or the negative? And in terms of safety, the negative is not a bad thing. It is cautious and survival-oriented rather than goal/success oriented. *I made it!* You must learn to make as much of a song-and-dance about sensible, reserved decisions and actions, as you do about taking a risk and getting away with it.

Decisions and Stress

Internal Stressors

Keep stress down by: avoiding high risk flights; knowing your personal limits; staying proficient in your aircraft; concentrate on flying the aircraft, first and foremost.

Decisions not taken cause stress. While you are deciding, and are under pressure to decide, the level of stress can become unreasonable. Avoiding a decision also causes stress because you know that ultimately the problem will have to be addressed. It won't go away. The solution is to make the decision and go for it. Stress is relieved by action, either fight or flight.

External Stressors

External pressures have a significant effect on your decisions. You have human wants, needs and fears: wanting to please, wanting to impress friends or siblings, wanting to earn more money or be promoted, needing to be loved, needing to be noticed, needing to be rewarded, fearing criticism or ridicule, fearing to lose a job, or fearing injury. A completely rational decision is made in isolation and such decisions can often only be made retrospectively: what you should have decided rather than what you did decide. Accident investigations are largely of this ilk because they do not—cannot—know the pressures under which the particular decision was made. We can rationalize why the pilot should have made the correct decision when we read the accident report. It's obvious. What is not obvious is the emotional strings attached to that decision. Making correct decisions sometimes takes considerable courage or, to use the old term, *moral fortitude*.

Destination Obsession

Destination obsession (also known as "get-there-itis") is getting there, today, at all costs. It seems not to be the result of a conscious, foolish decision, but more likely delaying a decision to turn back and land until it is no longer safe to do so. Illusions and misinterpretation of the seriousness of the deteriorating situation complicate the decision.

Low Cloud, Pressing On

The problem with pilots pressing on under lowering cloud is well-known within the aviation industry, and yet it just doesn't go away. (Fatal accidents continue to occur due to this problem.) The solution to the problem is elusive. The process involved obviously affects judgment of distances—distance from cloud and height above the terrain. Incredibly visual meteorological conditions (VMC) do not require a visual horizon!

True we can estimate the horizontal by perceiving the vertical—by looking down—but this is not always reliable. What if the terrain is not level?

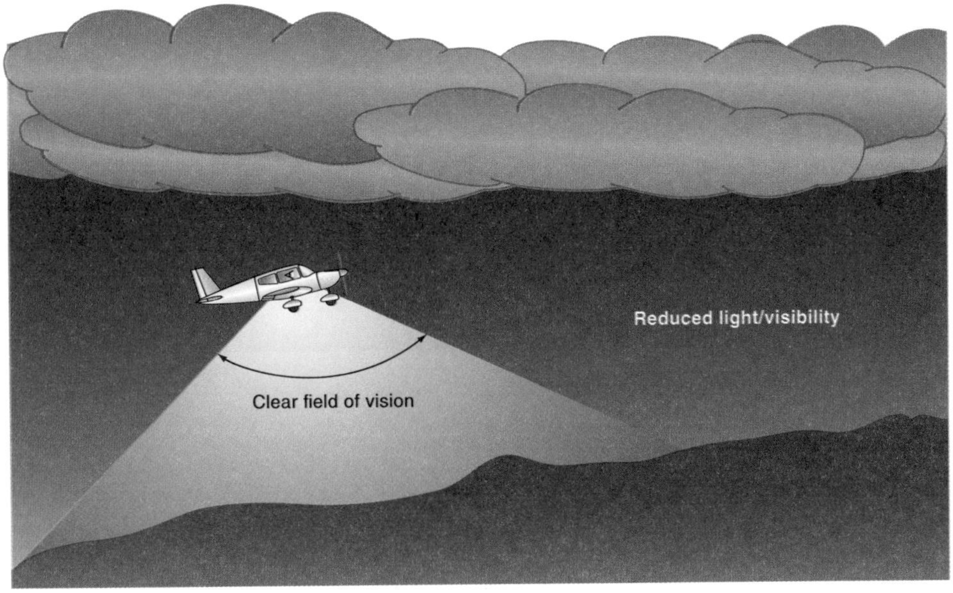

Figure 12-46 Limited cone of vision.

With fewer cues available, those that can be read are given greater importance. They appear more pronounced, more compelling in their meaning. They invite greater reliance on what they are telling you. The main effect will be to deny a proper and accurate assessment of height above terrain, distance from obstacles and cloud and you have a false appreciation of level attitude.

With restricted forward visibility, your judgment of height and distance will be so distorted as to be next to useless. You could become very close to the trees or ground without realizing. But, by then, it's far too late. We've all heard news reports of aircraft engine noise low overhead, often for long periods before the actual crash.

All of which adds up the unsurprising conclusion that most, if not all, pilots who do go on too far under cloud have no idea how low they are actually flying until they hit something—or wind up in the "soup" itself, blind in cloud. The destination obsession affecting their decision making and distorting their judgment must have been very powerful indeed. Moreover, there is one more influence: *visual illusion.*

Many aircraft that have crashed under cloud into rising terrain having stalled while under full power. With the limited field of view, there is a tendency to use the ground as reference for level flight. The closer you get to the ground without a strong nose attitude vs. horizon reference, the more prone will you be to seeing the fuselage being parallel to the earth's surface as an indication of level flight. As the slope increases, therefore, so will the climb angle, until the inevitable stall.

It's the same phenomenon as not being able to judge height, anymore—too few visual clues available to make a correct assessment. The further you go pressing on, the less you'll appreciate just how close you are to the cloud and the tree tops. But, of course, you should never have got there in the first place. Unfortunately pilots do.

Figure 12-47 Rising terrain—false horizontal.

Personality and Matters of Choice

One of our defences against being discomforted by situations like these is the confidence that, "It won't happen to me." On the other hand, most of us do know people who we would rate as more-likely-than-most to do such a thing. Thus, the idea that some types are more prone to taking higher risks than others is not especially controversial. The sort or type of person is usually defined by a hazardous attitude.

Five Hazardous Attitudes

The FAA defines five types of hazardous mental attitudes for pilots. They include:

- *antiauthority (don't tell me!).* People who don't like others to tell them what to do are often resentful of wise advice and prone to disregarding the rules. *The antidote to antiauthority is: Follow the rules; they are usually right;*
- *impulsivity (do something, quickly!).* People who don't stop to think before they act are impulsive. They often do the first thing that comes to mind. *The antidote is: Not so fast. Think first;*
- *invulnerability (it won't happen to me).* We all know accidents happen, but some feel it could never happen to them. They are far more likely to take chances and risks. *The antidote is: It could happen to me;*
- *macho (I can do it).* Now, here's a person with something to prove and he or she will probably take risks to show off. *The antidote is: Taking chances is foolish;* and
- *resignation (what's the use?).* Resigned pilots figure that the flight went well because they were lucky. If the flight goes poorly, however, it isn't their fault, there's nothing they can, or will do to change things. *The antidote to this attitude is: I'm not helpless. I can make a difference.*

Formal Decision-Making Processes

Pilots must assess the risks involved in any flight. Good judgement and decision-making skills can be learned.

You can learn to make better decisions by itemizing the correct decision-making process:

1. identify the decision to be made or problem to be solved;
2. collect relevant information;
3. generate alternatives;

4. analyze alternatives;
5. decide the most acceptable alternative;
6. action the alternative; and
7. monitor the outcome: if satisfactory, proceed; if not, repeat steps 2–7.

While this may seem to be time consuming, it gives structure and method to the process and ensures no jumping to conclusions. Most airlines use these steps in crew resource management (CRM), decision making and training. It is a valid way to make decisions and to check if your normal process covers all options. But there is another important element: how much time you have to make the decision.

The other problem is not making a decision, i.e. deferring the decision until it is too late. You are forced into a situation where there is no decision to make. You are then committed with no escape route.

There is a well-known model for decision making based on the mnemonic DECIDE. This model implies the decision is a reaction to circumstances, a situation or a change in events. A better way to make decisions is to anticipate—to be *pro*active rather than *re*active. Have the decision made before it is needed—on standby—like you practice emergency procedures so you can anticipate a decision point and have most of the work done.

D Detect a change.

E Estimate the need to react.

C Choose an outcome.

I Identify actions.

D Do the necessary action.

E Evaluate the effect.

Crises? Decisions should ideally not be made under duress—in a crisis situation. They should be made under controlled conditions and be stored—ready for use. A different model is based on the mnemonic ACTION:

A Anticipate and assess the possible scenarios.

C Consider actions and outcomes.

T Time—if available, immediate decision or nominate decision point (go/no-go point) and criteria.

I Implement decision—make a control input, transmission etc.

O Observe the result and correct—fine tune.

N Nominate the next milestone, decision point or potential hazard.

Figure 12-48
In-flight decisions must be decisive.

Many problems are due to no decision or a delayed decision. Decisions are easy to defer. Deferring decisions is only acceptable if a nominated decision point is made and adhered to.

Prior to each and every flight, all pilots must do a proper physical self-assessment to ensure safety. A great mnemonic is IMSAFE, which stands for Illness, Medication, Stress, Alcohol, Fatigue, and Emotion.

For the Medication component of IMSAFE, pilots need to ask themselves, "Am I taking any medicines that might affect my judgment or make me drowsy? For any *new* medication, OTC or prescribed, you should wait at least 48 hours after the first dose before flying to determine you don't have any adverse side effects that would make it unsafe to operate an aircraft. In addition to medication questions, pilots should also consider the following:

- don't take any unnecessary or elective medications;
- make sure you eat regular, balanced meals;
- bring a snack for both you and your passengers for the flight;
- maintain good hydration—bring plenty of water;
- ensure adequate sleep the night prior to the flight; and
- stay physically fit.

Additionally, you should wait at least five maximal dosing intervals, the time between recommended or prescribed dosing, (e.g., a dosing interval of 5 to 6 hours would require you to wait 30 hours) before flying after taking any medication that has potentially adverse side effects (e.g., sedating or dizziness). Observing the recommended dosing interval doesn't eliminate the risk for adverse side effects because everyone metabolizes medications differently. However, five times the dosing interval is a reasonable rule of thumb.

Assembling What-If's

Sesame Street (Envisioning Outcomes)

A fabulous episode of Sesame Street involved a child who was encouraged to imagine outcomes before crossing the road:

- what if I run onto the road without warning . . . ?
- what if I run out in front of a school bus . . . ?
- what if I run across the road and trip . . . ?
- what if I cross without looking in both directions . . . ?

This is exactly the what-if attitude a pilot needs to develop.

Choosing the Best Option

Priorities

The first priority must surely be to arrive safely, but we often neglect that or compromise it for "must arrive today," "must get to a meeting on time," "must land before dark," "haven't time to top off the tanks, complete a fuel check, complete an engine run-up check," etc.

Bets and Betters

We endlessly evaluate bad decisions but what about some examples of good decisions? It is better to spend a cold night in a sleeping bag in a tent under the wing of the airplane than flying into deteriorating weather and impacting terrain. It is better to arrive late, even the next day or next week, than not at all.

If you have to be there, have an alternative plan: "I will leave early enough so that if the weather deteriorates over the mountains, I can land at . . . and take the bus and pick up the airplane on the way home."

It's better to accept the rebuke, criticism and complaints of a passenger or employer by refusing to overload the airplane or exceed the CG limits than crash on takeoff. Saying "I told you so" is no consolation in the eddying seconds of the flight as you inevitably impact the trees. (Incidentally, they expect you to protect them from themselves.) It is better to land and leave your family safely on the ground rather than risk injuring all of them because you have to get to a business meeting. But then shouldn't you also stay on the ground with them? It is better to pay several hundred dollars for taxis and hotel rooms at an unplanned stop than miss your daughter's wedding and have them attend your hospital bed instead. It is better to be called a chicken than to be decimated and burned in the wreck of an airplane that stalled and spun trying to attempt a low pass after takeoff. It is better to go around and accept the extra time and expense than land when the runway is occupied or when your threshold speed is too high. You bet!

On Def Ears

Two common situations lead to dangerous situations. They are:
- deference; and
- deferral.

Deference is when you relinquish the decision to someone or allow their views to dominate such as when you avoid discussion and possible conflict, or when you want to please by saying what they want to hear or doing what they want to do despite your inner feelings that this option is perhaps risky. Deferral is avoiding making a decision—until later perhaps until its too late. This is the reason you have to set your own milestones, gates and go/no-go points and stick to them.

Figure 12-49
Go or no-go.

Choosing When to Implement a Decision

As important as the decision is the timing (when to implement it). But when is the right time?
- Immediately?
- Before sunset?
- Before reaching the point of no return (PNR)?
- Before becoming fatigued?
- Before becoming stressed due to weather or terrain?

Mostly a decision is needed now. But there are some occasions when a gate or milestone can be set. For example:
- I will proceed until the PNR, but at that point, if I have any doubts about the weather at the destination, I will turn back. (The decision is already made and the criteria set. The decision point is also set—it is non-negotiable);
- I will maintain minimums until overhead the airfield and if I cannot see the runway lights I will divert to the alternate. (I will not descend);
- I will continue while I can maintain safe terrain clearance. I have a defined horizon and I have at least a 500-foot vertical separation from cloud. If I lose the horizon, if I feel squeezed between ground and cloud, I will immediately turn right (least risk); and
- I will continue until an intermediate landing point and if I do not reach there by a certain time, which guarantees I will reach the ultimate destination by sunset, I will land.

Review 12

The Human in the Cockpit

Am I Fit to Fly?

1. You have consumed a small amount of alcohol. You should not fly for at least how many hours?
2. What is Hypothermia?
3. The FAA prescribes a method for evaluating risk and reducing stress. What is it?
4. List at least two ways you can keep your stress levels down when planning a flight or during a flight.

Respiration

5. What is hypoxia?
6. What is hyperventilation?
7. What effect does hyperventilation have on the body?
8. What is the main cause of hyperventilation?
9. Name a common symptom of hyperventilation.
10. Why is a faulty exhaust system potentially dangerous?
11. Susceptibility to carbon monoxide poisoning increases as:
    a. air pressure increases.
    b. altitude decreases.
    c. altitude increases.

Balance

12. What is spatial disorientation?
13. What should you rely on in order to interpret airplane attitude in poor visibility conditions?
14. To best overcome the effects of spatial disorientation, a pilot should:
    a. rely on body sensations.
    b. increase the breathing rate.
    c. rely on aircraft instrument indications.

Vision

15. The retina contains rods and cones. Describe where each are located in the eye.
16. True or false? Cones are most effective at night.
17. Are rods color-sensitive?
18. What is your peripheral vision provided by?
19. What is the most effective method of scanning for other aircraft in daylight?
20. True or false? In daylight, other aircraft are most clearly seen in your central vision.
21. Another aircraft remains in view in the same position in your windshield. Is there a possibility that you are on a collision course?
22. True or false? At night, other aircraft are most clearly seen in your central vision.
23. The most effective method of scanning for other aircraft for collision avoidance during nighttime hours is to use:
    a. regularly spaced concentration on the 3, 9, and 12 o'clock positions.
    b. a series of short, regularly spaced eye movements to search each 30° sector.
    c. peripheral vision by slowly scanning small sectors and utilizing off-center viewing.
24. How can you determine if another aircraft is on a collision course with your aircraft?
25. Is it possible for other objects to be closer than they appear to be in hazy conditions?
26. If you are exposed to bright lights prior to flight, how long is it recommended you wait before undertaking a night flight?
27. During a night flight, you observe a steady red light and a flashing red light ahead and at the same altitude. What is the general direction of movement of the other aircraft?
28. What illusion can an upward sloping runway give?
29. What illusion can a narrow runway give?

Answers are given on page 697.

Weather

Heating Effects in the Atmosphere 13

The Atmosphere

The earth is surrounded by a mixture of gases held to it by the force of gravity. This mixture of gases we know as *air*, and the space it occupies around the earth we call the *atmosphere*. The atmosphere is of particular importance to pilots because it is the medium in which we fly.

Air Density

Air density decreases with altitude.

The force of gravity attracts the air molecules toward the surface of the earth, causing them to squeeze closer together in the lower levels of the atmosphere than at higher altitudes. The number of molecules in a cubic foot of air at 18,000 feet altitude is only one-half that at sea level where the air is much more dense.

Air density is important to pilots because:

- the airplane's lift force is generated by the flow of air around the wings;
- engine power is generated by burning fuel and air; and
- we need to breathe air in order to live.

If the air is more dense:

- the required airfoil lift force can be generated at a lower true airspeed (V);
- greater engine power is available because of the greater mass of each fuel/air charge taken into the cylinders; and
- breathing is easier, since a greater mass of oxygen is taken into the lungs during each breath.

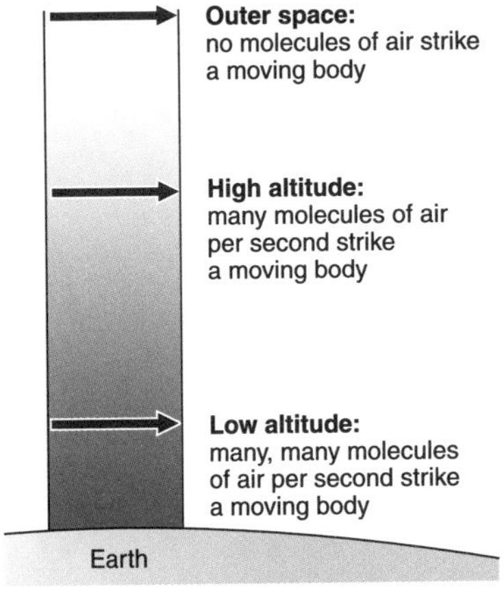

Outer space:
no molecules of air strike a moving body
High altitude:
many molecules of air per second strike a moving body
Low altitude:
many, many molecules of air per second strike a moving body
Earth

Figure 13-1
The density of air decreases as altitude is gained.

The Subdivision of the Atmosphere

The atmosphere is divided into layers based on temperature—the *troposphere*, the *stratosphere*, the *mesosphere* and the *thermosphere*. Most flying occurs in the troposphere, although high-flying jets may cruise in the stratosphere—the boundary between the two regions is known as the *tropopause*.

Most flying occurs in the troposphere.

The temperature usually falls with a gain in altitude in the troposphere until the tropopause is reached, above which it remains somewhat constant at a fairly low value (typically -57°C). The rate of change of temperature with altitude is called the *temperature lapse rate*.

The earth spins on its axis, carrying the atmosphere with it and tends to throw the air in the lower part of the atmosphere to the outside. This, plus strong heating in tropical areas, causes the troposphere to extend further into space above the equator than above the poles. The tropopause occurs at an altitude of about 20,000 feet over the poles, and at about 60,000 feet over the equator. It is higher in each region in summer than in winter. On average, the tropopause is assumed to occur at approximately 36,000 feet.

Most weather occurs in the troposphere, including clouds, precipitation (rain, snow, and so on), and wind—especially the vertical air currents that cause the strong vertical development of convective clouds. Sometimes this vertical development is so strong that large thunderstorm clouds, known as *cumulonimbus*, burst through the tropopause into the stratosphere. Because almost all flight occurs in the troposphere and the lower levels of the stratosphere, we concentrate on these areas in this manual.

Differences Between the Troposphere and Stratosphere

Significant differences between the troposphere and the stratosphere include:

- temperature decreases with altitude in the troposphere, with an abrupt change in temperature lapse rate at the tropopause, above which it is constant;
- a marked vertical movement of air in the troposphere, with warm air rising and cool air descending on both large and small scales, whereas there is little vertical movement of air in the stratosphere; and
- almost all the water vapor in the atmosphere is contained in the troposphere, and so cloud formation rarely extends beyond the tropopause.

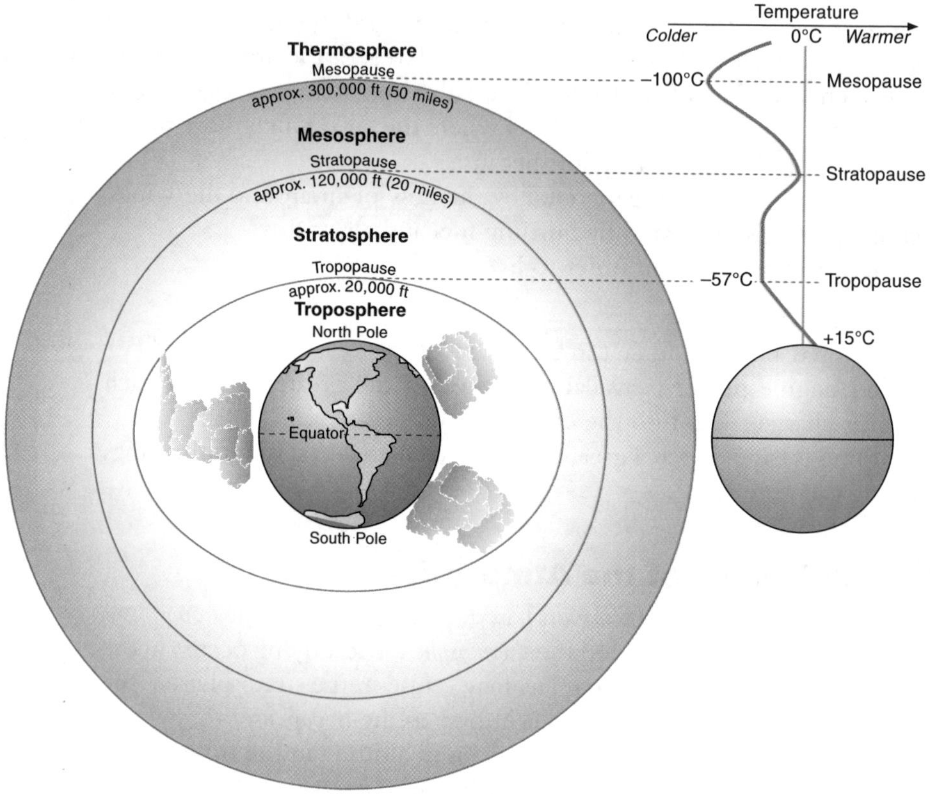

Figure 13-2 The subdivision of the atmosphere is based on temperature.

Air Is a Mixture of Gases

In its dry state, air is a mixture of atmospheric gases—the two main constituents are nitrogen (78%) and oxygen (21%). The remaining (1%) gases include argon, neon, helium and carbon dioxide. See table 13-1.

Air in the troposphere nearly always contains some *water vapor*, varying from almost zero to 5% by volume. This is most important, because it is water vapor that condenses to form clouds from which we get the precipitation (rain, snow, hail, and so on) that is vital to life on earth. As the content of water vapor in a parcel of air increases, the other gases decrease proportionately.

Gas	Volume (%)
Nitrogen	78%
Oxygen	21%
Other gases (argon, carbon dioxide, neon, helium, etc.)	1%
Total	100%

Table 13-1 The composition of air.

Maritime and Continental Air Masses

Maritime air is more moist than continental air.

Air over an ocean (known as *maritime air*) will absorb moisture from the body of water and will, in general, contain more water vapor than the air over a continent (known as *continental air*), particularly if the land mass consists largely of desert areas. In other words, a maritime air mass is more moist than a continental air mass. An air mass moving in across the United States from over the Caribbean Sea, for instance, is likely to carry more moisture than an air mass originating in continental Canada.

The Standard Atmosphere

In chapter 8 we briefly discussed the standard atmosphere and its values. To refresh your memory, these are repeated below:

- mean sea level (MSL) pressure is 29.92 in. Hg;
- mean sea level temperature is +15°C (or 59°F); and
- temperature lapse rate is 1.98°C (3.5°F)/1,000 feet up to approximately 36,000 feet above which temperature is assumed to remain constant at -56.5°C.

Note. For forecasting purposes, pressure is usually expressed in *hectopascals* (hPa), and the standard MSL pressure is 1,013.2 hPa. You will see pressure plotted as lines (isobars) on weather charts to indicate places of the same surface pressure.

The Actual Atmosphere

The actual atmosphere differs from the ISA.

The actual atmosphere can differ from the standard atmosphere in many ways, and in reality almost always does. The pressure at sea level varies from day-to-day, indeed from hour-to-hour, and the temperature fluctuates between wide extremes at all levels.

The variation of ambient pressure throughout the atmosphere—both horizontally and vertically, is of great significance to pilots as it affects the operation of the altimeter, as well as causing wind.

One difference between the actual atmosphere and the theoretical standard atmosphere, which is very important for high-flying jet pilots, is that the real tropopause is much higher over equatorial latitudes than over polar latitudes. This means that weather, such as cumulonimbus clouds, will typically exist to higher levels in tropical regions. Also, the tropopause is not a continuous sheet, but has some breaks in it, within which high-speed jet stream tubes of wind blowing from west to east develop.

Heat Exchange Processes

The Sun

The sun radiates energy and heats the earth.

The main source of energy on earth is the sun, which radiates electromagnetic energy in the form of infrared radiation, light rays, radio waves, ultraviolet radiation, and so on. We experience this solar radiation as *heat* and *light*.

The wavelengths of solar radiation are such that a large percentage penetrates the earth's atmosphere and is absorbed by the earth's surface, causing its temperature to increase. How much the surface temperature rises depends on its nature—land shows a greater temperature rise than water for the same amount of solar energy. The earth's surface, in turn, heats the air closest to it and if that parcel of air is warmer than the surrounding air, it will rise.

All weather processes result from, or are accompanied by a heat exchange.

Heat exchanges and temperature variations in the atmosphere create air movements within the atmosphere, resulting in changes in the weather.

Seasonal Variations

The earth orbits around the sun once every year and, because the earth's axis is tilted, this gives rise to the four seasons (see figure 13-3). The solar radiation received at a place on earth is more intense during its summer than in winter, when its surface is presented to the sun at a more oblique angle.

Solar Heating

Heating from solar radiation is greatest in the tropics.

Solar radiation is like a flashlight beam that produces more intense light on a perpendicular surface than on an oblique surface. Since solar radiation strikes tropical regions from directly overhead, or almost so, right through the year, the heating is quite intense. In contrast, the sun's rays strike polar regions of the earth at an oblique angle and, during winter (the northern summer is shown in figure 13-4), they do not strike the polar regions at all.

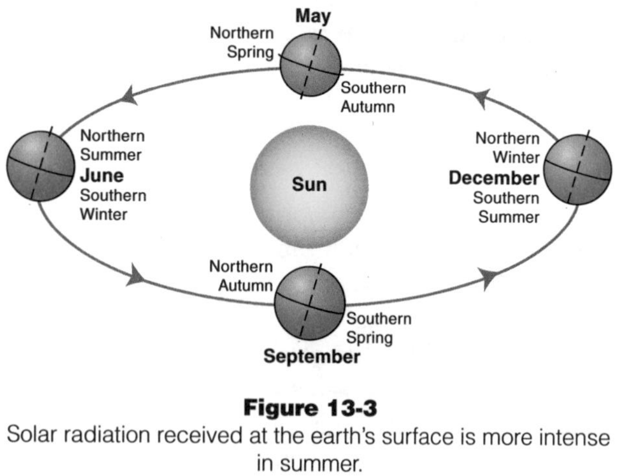

Figure 13-3
Solar radiation received at the earth's surface is more intense in summer.

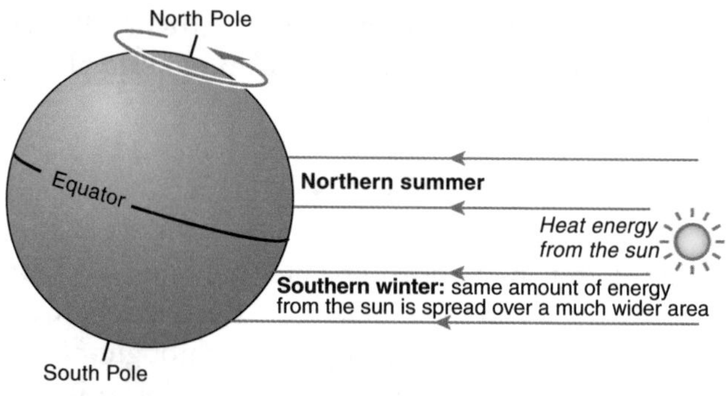

Figure 13-4
Surface heating is greatest in the tropics and least at high latitudes.

Terrestrial Re-Radiation

Heat energy in the earth's surface is re-radiated into the atmosphere but, because its wavelength is longer than solar radiation, it is more readily absorbed in the atmosphere, especially by water vapor and carbon dioxide. It is this absorption of heat from the earth that is the main heat exchange that causes weather. In summary:

- solar radiation penetrates the atmosphere and heats the earth's surface; then
- the earth re-radiates this energy and heats the lower levels of the atmosphere; this indirect heating of air by solar heating causes thermals.

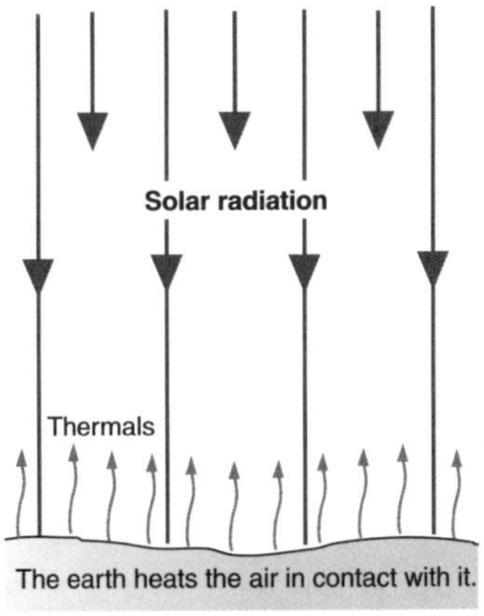

Figure 13-5
Indirect heating of the atmosphere by the sun.

General Circulation

Large vertical circulations of air occur in the troposphere caused by unequal heating of the different regions of the earth. The tropics for instance, receive much more energy than the polar regions. The surface air in the tropics becomes very warm, causing it to expand and rise. This thermally induced vertical motion is called *convection*. The rising air leaves behind an area of lower pressure near the surface known as the *equatorial trough*. New surface air moves as a result of the pressure differential that has been created, and replaces the air that has risen. (These surface winds flowing into the equatorial trough are the trade winds, which were so important to sailing ships in the old days.) Meanwhile, the tropical air rising above the equatorial trough cools as it rises, and spreads out in the upper atmosphere.

In contrast, the cooler air over the polar regions sinks, causing a higher pressure at the surface and spreads out, moving toward areas of lower pressure. This sinking polar air together with the rising air in warmer regions creates a large scale *general circulation* pattern in the troposphere. You would expect the general circulation to be a single large cell in each hemisphere, but an effect produced by the earth's rotation—known as the *Coriolis effect*—leads to *three* main circulation cells existing over each hemisphere of the earth:

- the polar cell;
- the mid-latitude cell; and
- the tropical (or Hadley) cell.

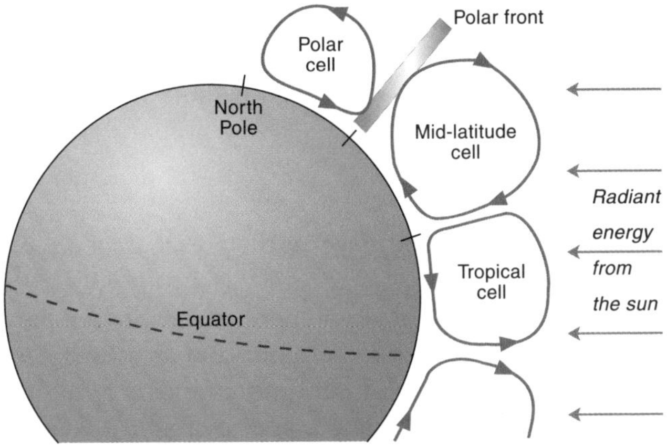

Figure 13-6
The general circulation pattern.

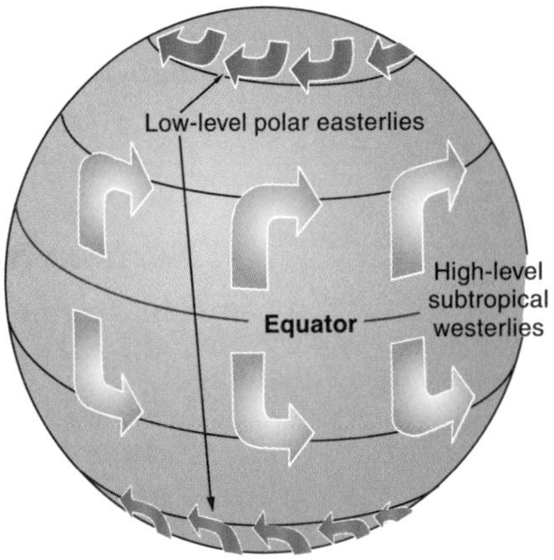

Figure 13-7
The north—south flow of air is blocked at latitudes around 60° and 30°.

The cold surface air moving southward from the north polar region is "left behind" by the rotation of the earth, effectively turning right and becoming easterly by about latitude 60°. Further southward movement of the surface air is blocked. As this air is warmed, it rises, spreads out, and so the *polar circulation cell* is formed.

Meanwhile, the warm upper air flowing out from the equator "moves ahead" of the rotating earth, effectively turning right and becoming westerly by about latitude 30°. Further movement is blocked because, as this air cools, it subsides (descends) to form the subtropical high-pressure belt at about latitude 30°. Surface air diverges from this area and forms the *tropical circulation cell.* Note that the Coriolis force (from earth rotation) causes air movement to turn right in the Northern Hemisphere and left in the Southern Hemisphere. The Coriolis force will be further explained in chapter 14.

Most weather occurs in the mid-latitudes. In this area, the rising air spreading out in the upper levels of the troposphere near latitude 60° and the descending air spreading out in the lower levels near latitude 30° cause an intermediate or *mid-latitude circulation cell* between latitudes 30° and 60°. Sometimes large masses of very cold polar air break through the barrier near 60° and move toward the equator, and sometimes large masses of warm air move from the tropics into this area—the result being that the mid-latitudes have moving storms and ever-changing weather.

The generalized circulation is an idealized version of the real situation of constantly changing large masses of cold and warm air pushing their way around, responding to pressure differentials caused by uneven surface heating.

The situation in the Southern Hemisphere, with its great ocean areas, is less complicated than in the Northern Hemisphere, where the large continental land masses with their uneven surface heating and cooling cause many variations and complicated weather patterns.

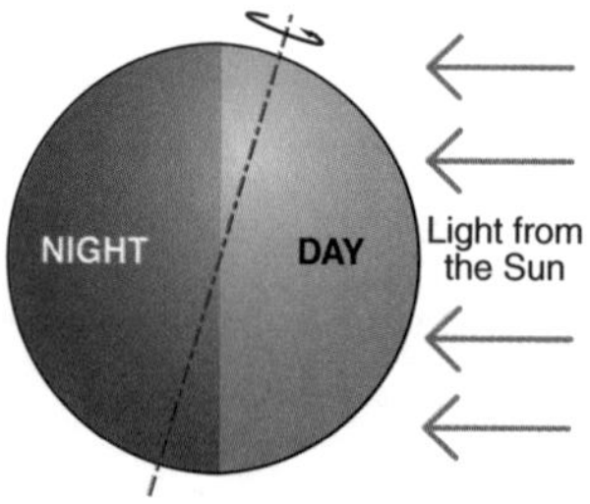

Figure 13-8
The earth's rotation causes day and night.

Local Heating and Cooling

Daily variations in heating are caused by the earth's rotation. The earth makes one complete rotation on its axis every 24 hours, causing the *apparent* motion of the sun across the sky, and day and night on earth. Solar heating of the earth's surface occurs only by day, but terrestrial re-radiation of heat energy from the earth occurs continually, both day and night. The net result is that the earth's surface heats up by day, reaches its maximum temperature about mid-afternoon (3:00 p.m.) and cools by night, reaching its minimum temperature typically an hour after sunrise. This continual heating and cooling on a daily basis is called the *diurnal variation* of temperature—a typical daily pattern of heating and cooling that is most extreme in desert areas and more moderate (in some cases almost nonexistent) over the oceans.

Surface Heating

The heating of various surfaces and the temperatures that they reach depends on a number of factors:

- *the specific heat of the surface*—water requires more heat energy to raise its temperature by one degree Fahrenheit than does land, therefore land areas will heat more quickly during the day than sea (and also cool more quickly at night). Compared with the sea, land is warmer by day and cooler by night. Scientifically we say that water has a higher *specific heat* than land;
- *the reflectivity of the surface*—if the solar radiation is reflected by a surface, it is not absorbed. There is less heating of reflective surfaces, such as snow and water compared with absorbent surfaces, such as plowed fields; and

- *the conductivity of the surface*—heat energy does not readily pass through soil into the lower levels, whereas ocean currents carry heat energy with them, causing the sea to be heated to a greater depth than a land surface.

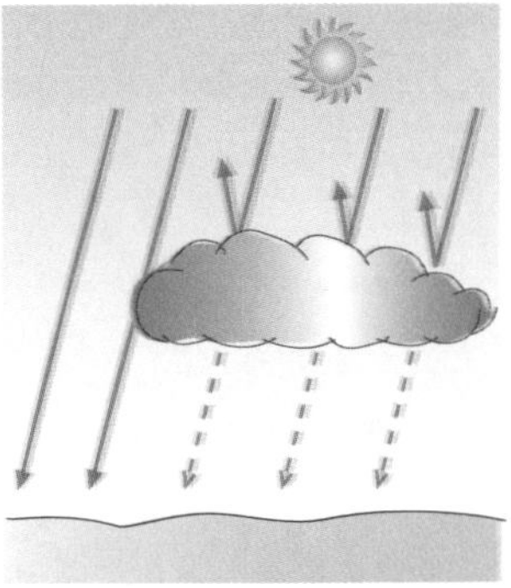

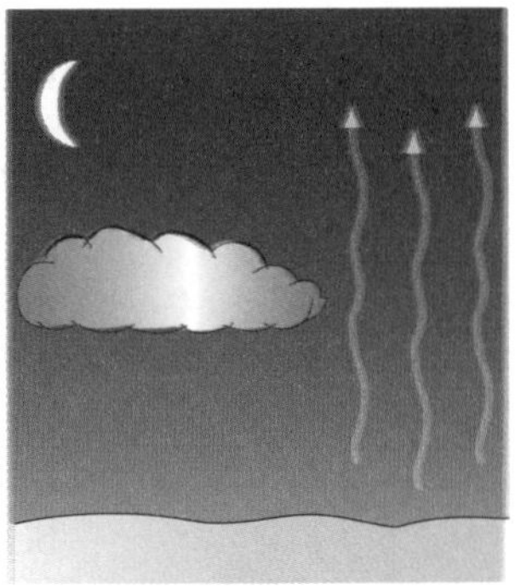

Figure 13-9
Clouds reduce surface heating by day and cooling by night.

Cloud Cover

Cloud coverage by day prevents some of the solar radiation penetrating to the earth's surface, resulting in reduced heating of the earth and lower temperatures on cloudy days compared with sunny days. By night, however, cloud cover causes the opposite effect and prevents some of the heat energy escaping from the earth's surface. The atmosphere beneath the clouds experiences less cooling, and so cloudy nights are not as cool as clear nights.

The Transfer of Heat Energy

Heat energy may be transmitted from one body to another, or redistributed within the one body by a number of means, including the following:

- *radiation*—all bodies transmit energy in the form of electromagnetic radiation, the higher the temperature of the body, the shorter the wavelength of the radiation. Radiation from the sun is therefore of shorter wavelength than the much cooler re-radiation from the earth;
- *absorption*—any body in the path of radiation will absorb some of its energy. How much is absorbed depends on both the body and the radiation. A rocky desert area will absorb more solar radiation than snow-covered mountains;
- *conduction*—heat energy may be passed or conducted within the one body, or from one body to another in direct contact with it, by conduction. Iron is a good conductor of heat. Wood is not a good conductor, nor is air. A parcel of air heated by contact with the earth's surface will not transfer this heat energy to neighboring parcels of air. It will, however, carry its heat energy if it moves—a very significant factor in the development of weather systems;
- *convection*—a mass of air that is heated at the earth's surface will expand, become less dense, and rise, carrying its heat energy higher into the atmosphere, a process known as *thermal convection*. A small mass of rising air is called a *thermal*. These are common over open terrain on sunny afternoons with light winds; and

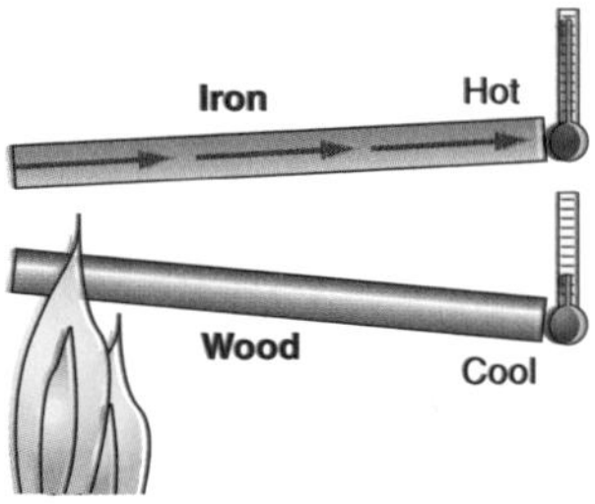

Figure 13-10
Some things are good conductors of heat; others are not.

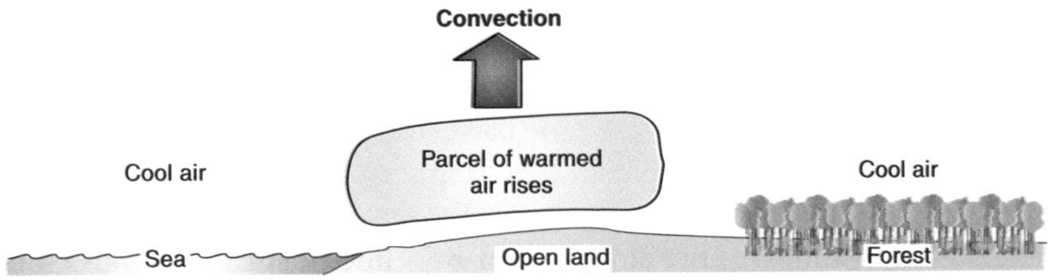

Figure 13-11 Convection.

- *advection*—the horizontal motion of air is known as advection. An air mass moving horizontally by advection, for instance the surface air moving in to replace air that has risen by convection, will of course bring its heat energy and moisture content with it. Advection is simply another term for winds.

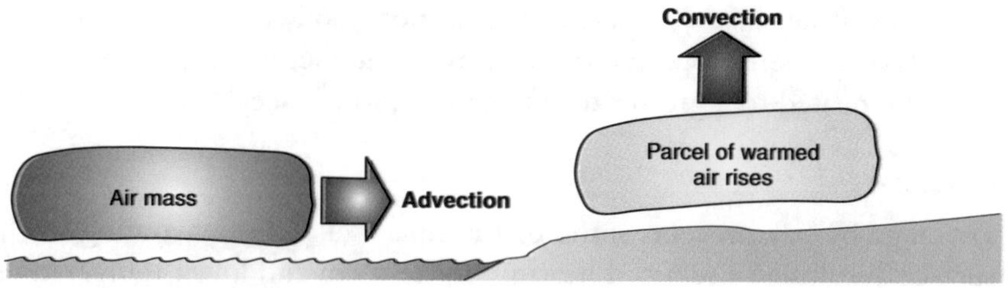

Figure 13-12 Advection is the horizontal transfer of air and heat energy. Convection is the vertical transfer of air and heat energy.

Local Air Movements

The Sea Breeze by Day

Circulation patterns can be large scale, like the general circulation pattern just discussed—or they can be on a small scale, like sea breezes and land breezes.

Sea breezes occur on sunny afternoons after the land has warmed. The land heats the surface air in contact with it, causing it to rise, and to leave behind a localized area of low pressure. Cool air from over the sea moves in, lowering the temperature on the beach, and a small circulation pattern is set up. The vertical extent of a sea breeze is usually only 1,000 or 2,000 feet.

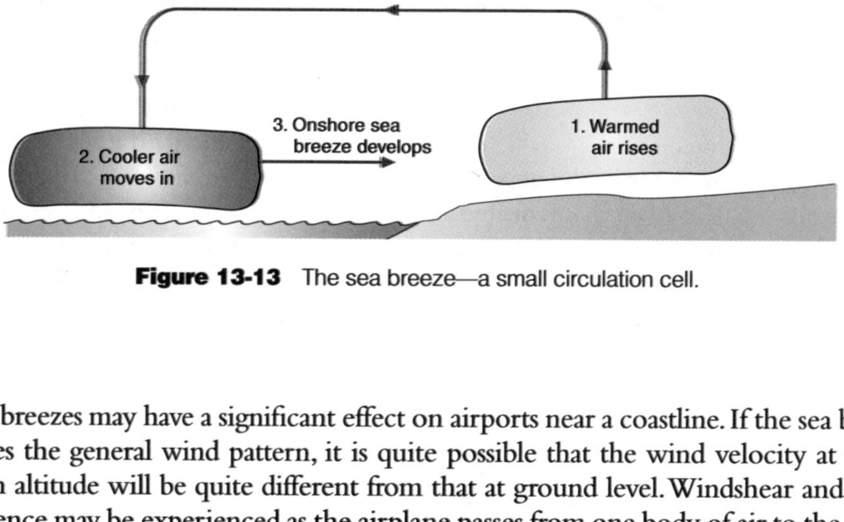

Figure 13-13 The sea breeze—a small circulation cell.

Sea breezes may have a significant effect on airports near a coastline. If the sea breeze opposes the general wind pattern, it is quite possible that the wind velocity at traffic pattern altitude will be quite different from that at ground level. Windshear and some turbulence may be experienced as the airplane passes from one body of air to the other. Also, a sea breeze may carry a sea fog inland, causing visibility problems for pilots.

Sometimes you can determine the position of the sea breeze front over the land by the differences in visibility either side of it, or by a line of small cumulus clouds if the warm inland air moving upward at the cold sea breeze front is moist enough to form clouds.

The Land Breeze by Night

By night, the land cools more quickly than the sea, causing the air above it to cool and subside (descend). The air over the sea is warmer and will rise. A small *land breeze* circulation pattern is set up, with surface air moving out to sea and upper air moving inland. The land breeze may reach maximum strength just after dawn when the land is at its minimum temperature.

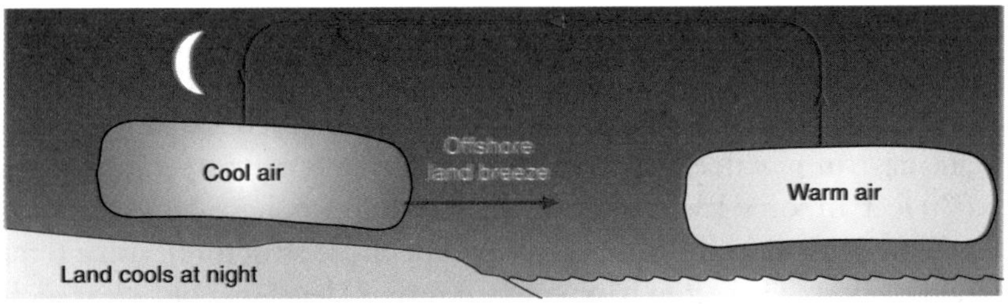

Figure 13-14 The land breeze blows offshore at night.

Sometimes a land breeze holds a sea fog offshore early in the day but, as the land warms, the land breeze dies out and a sea breeze develops, bringing the sea fog inland and causing visibility problems at coastal airports.

Katabatic Winds

Katabatic winds blow down mountain slopes and valleys at night.

During night time the earth's surface loses heat energy through terrestrial radiation and cools down, particularly on clear, cloudless nights. The air in contact with the surface then cools down.

Air that is cooled by contact with a mountain slope at night becomes denser than air at the same altitude but further from the slope. The cooler parcels of air start to flow down the slope and into the valleys, creating what is called a ***katabatic wind***, a ***mountain wind***, or a ***drainage wind*** flowing down and out of the valleys. In certain areas, katabatic winds can build up during the night and, by sunrise, be flowing down the slopes of large mountains and into the valleys at speeds in excess of 30 knots.

As you will see in the next chapter, air that is descending becomes warmer and drier, and so what starts out as a cool katabatic wind may become relatively warm as it flows down mountain slopes.

Anabatic Winds

Anabatic winds drift up mountain slopes by day.

Solar heating of a mountain slope causes the air mass in contact with it to become warmer than air at the same altitude but further from the slope, decreasing its density and causing it to flow up the slope. This local upslope wind is known as an ***anabatic wind***, or as a ***valley wind*** since it flows up and out of valleys. Uphill flow is opposed by gravity, so the anabatic wind, which flows up the slope, is generally a weaker wind than the nighttime downslope katabatic wind.

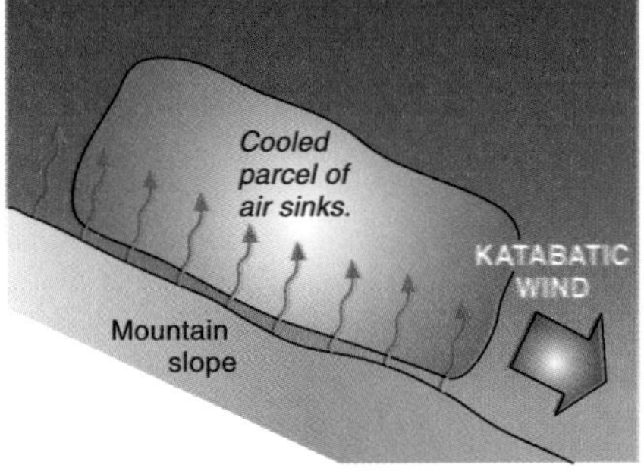

Figure 13-15 The katabatic wind.

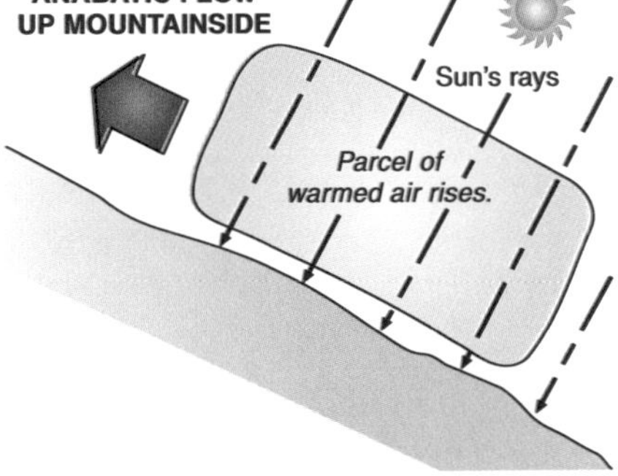

Figure 13-16 The anabatic wind.

Temperature Inversions

Temperature normally decreases with altitude. In the standard atmosphere the temperature is assumed to decrease by approximately 1.98°C for each 1,000 feet climbed in a stationary air mass. In practice, we can assume a decrease, or temperature lapse rate, of 2°C per 1,000 feet. In some layers of air in the actual atmosphere, however, air temperature may increase with altitude (an inverted temperature structure), and a temperature *inversion* is said to exist. This often happens near ground level on cold, clear nights when the earth's surface loses heat by terrestrial radiation and cools down. The air near the ground is cooled by conduction, and tends to sink and not mix with air at the higher levels. This leads to the air at ground level being cooler than the air at altitude, and a temperature inversion will exist.

Air that has no tendency to rise is called *stable air*, as is the case in a temperature inversion, and this generally means smooth flying conditions. Visibility may be a problem, however, because there will be no upward convective currents to carry particles in the air away, so any fog, haze, smoke, smog or low clouds will stay beneath the inversion layer and restrict visibility.

A phenomenon known as *windshear* (in which the wind strength or direction changes from place-to-place) may exist at the upper boundary of the inversion if there are overlying strong winds. An airplane may experience an airspeed change or some turbulence as it flies through the inversion level from one air mass to another. (Windshear is covered in chapter 17.)

Over desert areas, the upper level of an inversion can sometimes be identified by a layer of dust with clear air above it. Inversions also occur at altitude in warm fronts, when a warm current of air overruns a lower colder layer. A danger for pilots in this situation is freezing rain, which is liquid rain falling out of warmer air above into below-freezing air beneath, where it can quickly form a great deal of ice on an airplane's structure.

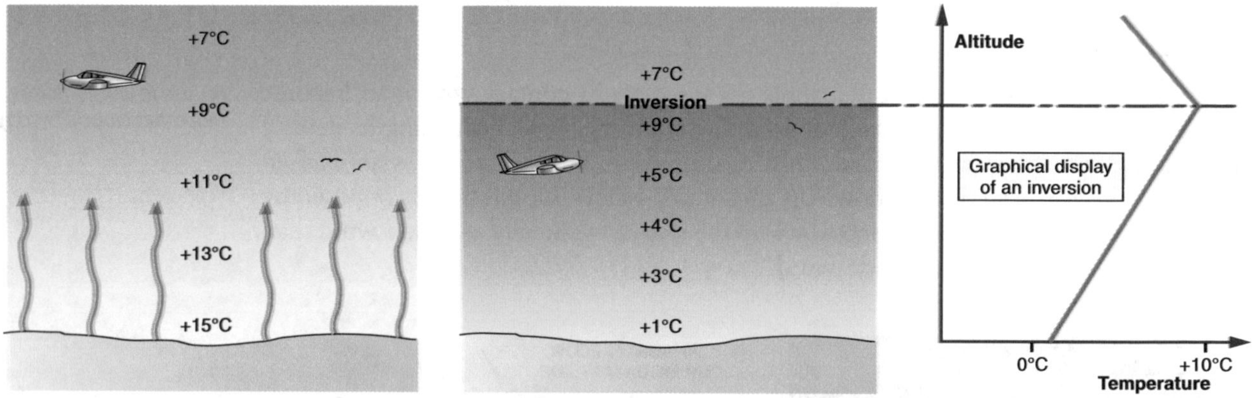

Figure 13-17 Normal temperature situation (left) and a temperature inversion.

Review 13
Heating Effects in the Atmosphere

The Atmosphere

1. The atmosphere is divided into four layers. What are these divisions based on?
2. Which layer of the atmosphere, in which weather occurs, is closest to the earth?
3. **a.** What is the second layer of the atmosphere called?
   b. What is the boundary between this layer and the troposphere called?
4. Which feature is associated with the tropopause?
5. What are the main gases that form the atmosphere and their approximate proportions?
6. Most of the water vapor in the atmosphere is contained in which layer of the atmosphere?
7. As altitude is gained in the troposphere, temperature generally:
   a. increases.
   b. decreases.
   c. stays the same.
8. What is a body of air over an ocean referred to as?
9. Define "temperature lapse rate."
10. What are the standard temperature and pressure values for sea level?

Heat Exchange Process

11. Where is the heating of the earth greatest?
12. What is every physical process of weather accompanied by or the result of?
13. What is terrestrial radiation?
14. True or false? The sea heats more rapidly than land, but cools less rapidly than land.
15. How does cloud coverage affect the heating of the earth's surface?
16. How does cloud coverage reduce the cooling of the earth's surface?
17. What is:
    a. radiation?
    b. conduction?
    c. convection?
    d. advection?
18. What does the development of thermals depend on?
19. True or false? A sea breeze blows onshore during the late afternoon.
20. A sea breeze front can sometimes be identified by a line of which type of clouds just inland?
21. Convective circulation patterns associated with sea breezes are caused by:
    a. warm, dense air moving inland from over the water.
    b. water absorbing and radiating heat faster than the land.
    c. cool, dense air moving inland from over the water.
22. Define "katabatic wind."
23. Define "anabatic wind."
24. Are upslope winds usually weaker than downslope winds? If so, why?
25. What is meant by the term "inversion?"
26. What is meant by the term "temperature inversion?"
27. A ground-based inversion is most likely to form on:
    a. clear nights.
    b. cloudy nights.
28. Will the air beneath a ground-based inversion:
    a. be stable?
    b. tend to rise?
29. Describe the likely flying conditions beneath an inversion.

Answers are given on page 698

Wind 14

What Is Wind?

The term *wind* refers to the flow of air over the earth's surface. This flow is almost completely horizontal, with only about one one-thousandth of the total flow being vertical.

Despite being only a small proportion of the overall flow of air in the atmosphere, vertical airflow is extremely important to weather and to aviation, since it leads to the formation of clouds. Some vertical winds are so strong, like those in or below a cumulonimbus stormcloud, that they are a hazard to aviation and can destroy airplanes.

In general, however, the term wind is used in reference to the horizontal flow of air. It is pressure differences in the atmosphere (usually resulting from temperature differences) that causes winds.

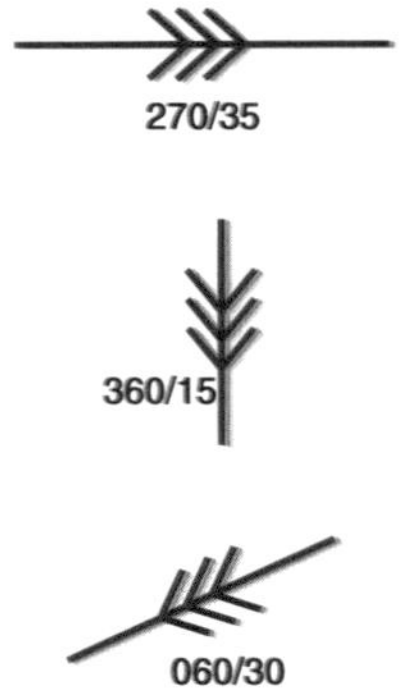

Figure 14-1
Examples of wind velocity (three barbs show the wind vector).

How Wind Is Described

Both the direction and strength of a wind are significant and are expressed thus:

- *wind direction* is the direction *from* which the wind is blowing and is expressed in degrees, measured clockwise from north; and
- *wind strength* is expressed in knots (abbreviated kt, the same unit as your airspeed).

If wind direction is written, it's true. If spoken, it's magnetic.

Direction and strength together describe the *wind velocity*, which is usually written in the form 27035 or 270/35—in other words, a wind blowing from 270° at a strength of 35 knots. Meteorologists relate wind direction to *true* north, so all winds that appear on forecasts are expressed in degrees true (°T). Thus 34012KT on a forecast or observation means a wind strength of 12 knots from a direction of 340°T.

Airport runways, however, are described in terms of their *magnetic* direction, so when an airplane lines up on a runway for takeoff, its magnetic compass and the runway direction should agree, at least approximately.

The wind direction relative to the runway direction is extremely important when taking off and landing. For this reason, winds passed to the pilot by the Tower have direction expressed in degrees *magnetic*. This is also the case for the recorded messages on the automatic terminal information service (ATIS) that a pilot can listen to on the radio at some airports.

Veering and Backing

A wind whose direction is changing in a clockwise direction is called a *veering* wind. For example, following a change from 080/20 to 120/25, the wind is said to have veered. A wind the direction of which is changing in a counterclockwise direction is called a *backing* wind. A change from 210/15 to 140/15 is an example of a wind that has backed.

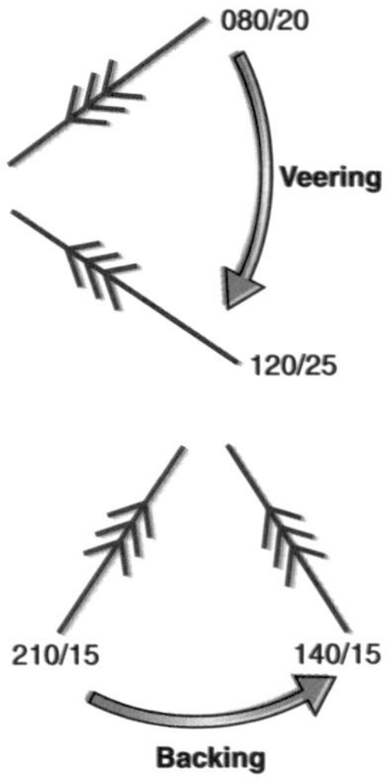

Figure 14-2
A veering wind (top) and a backing wind.

What Causes a Wind to Blow?

A change in velocity (speed and/or direction) is called acceleration. Acceleration is caused by a force (or forces) being exerted on an object, be it an airplane, an automobile or a parcel of air.

The combined effect of all the forces acting on a body is known as the net (or resultant) force, and determines the acceleration of the body. If all of the forces acting on a parcel of air balance each other so that the resultant force is zero, then the parcel of air will not accelerate, but will continue to move in a straight line at a constant speed (or stay still). A steady wind velocity is known as *balanced flow*.

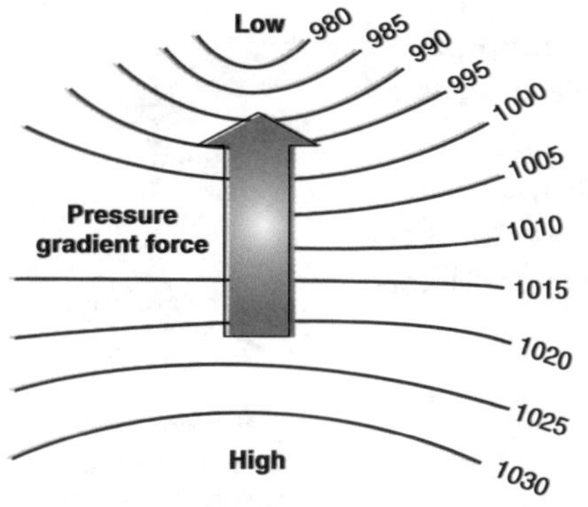

Figure 14-3 The pressure-gradient force starts a parcel of air moving.

The Pressure-Gradient Force

The force that is usually responsible for starting the movement of a parcel of air is known as the *pressure-gradient force*. This acts to move air from areas of *high* pressure to areas of *low* pressure. Places on the earth's surface where the air pressure is the same are shown on weather charts by lines called *isobars*. The pressure-gradient force acts at right angles to the isobars, in the direction from high to low pressure. Strong pressure gradients are indicated by closely spaced isobars.

If the pressure gradient force was the only force acting on a parcel of air, it would continue to accelerate toward the low pressure, getting faster and faster, and eventually the high and low pressure areas would disappear. This, of course, does not occur, and the reason is that there is another force acting on the air. This force, which is created by the earth's rotation, is known as the Coriolis effect.

The Coriolis Effect

The *Coriolis effect* was named after G. G. de Coriolis, the French mathematician who discovered the effect in the 19th century. It results from the passage of air across the rotating earth's surface. Imagine a parcel of air that is stationary over point A on the equator, as shown in figure 14-4. It is in fact moving with point A as the earth rotates on its axis from west to east. Now, suppose that a pressure gradient exists, with a high pressure at point A and a low pressure at point B, directly north of A. The parcel of air at A starts moving toward B, but still with its motion toward the east due to the earth's rotation.

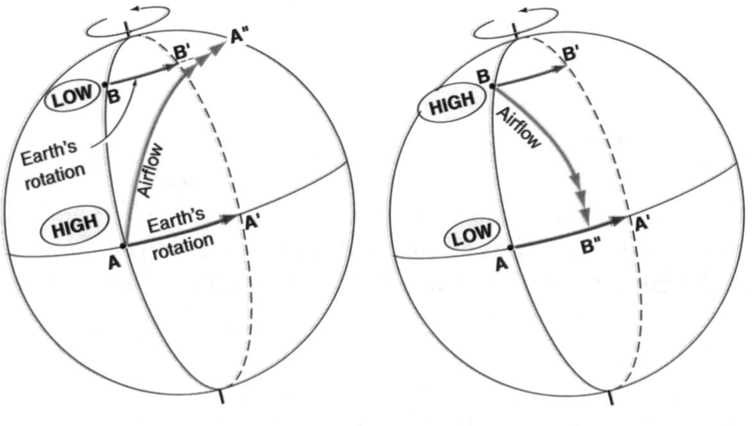

Figure 14-4 The Coriolis effect acts toward the right in the Northern Hemisphere.

The further away from the equator a position is, the less the easterly motion of the earth's surface (compare A—A' with B—B' in figure 14-4). Consequently, the further away from the equator it is, the more it will lag behind the easterly motion of the parcel of air. In figure 14-4, point B will have only moved to B', but the parcel of air will have moved to A". To an observer standing on the earth's surface, the parcel of air will *appear* to have turned to the right.

If the parcel of air was being accelerated (by a pressure-gradient force) in a southerly direction from a high-pressure area toward a low-pressure area near the equator, the earth's rotation toward the east would "get away from it" and so the air movement, or wind, would appear to turn right also—point A having moved to A', but the airflow only reaching B" to the west.

The faster the airflow, the greater the Coriolis effect—if there is no air movement, then there is no Coriolis effect. The effect is also greater in regions near the poles, where changes in latitude cause more significant changes in the speed at which each point on the earth is moving toward the east. In the Northern Hemisphere, the Coriolis effect causes the wind to curve to the *right*; in the Southern Hemisphere, the situation is reversed and it deflects the wind to the *left*.

Note. Throughout the rest of this chapter, the discussion will only consider the Northern Hemisphere. The effects will be reversed in the Southern Hemisphere.

The Geostrophic Wind

The two influences on a moving airstream are:

- the pressure-gradient force (the *initiating* force); and
- the Coriolis effect (the *deviating* influence).

The pressure-gradient force starts the air moving and the Coriolis effect turns it right (in the Northern Hemisphere). This curving of the airflow over the earth continues until the pressure-gradient force is counterbalanced by the Coriolis effect, resulting in a wind flow that is steady and blowing in a direction parallel to the isobars. This balanced flow is called the *geostrophic wind*.

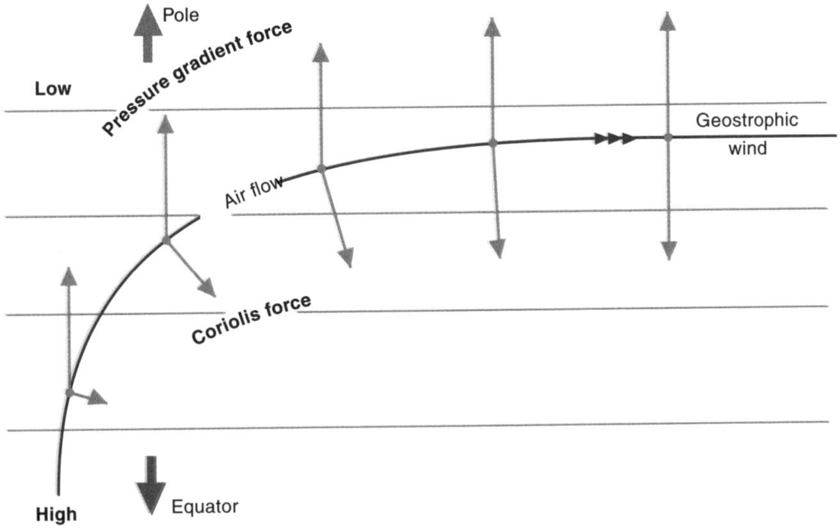

Figure 14-5 Balanced flow occurs parallel to the isobars—the geostrophic wind.

The geostrophic wind is important to a weather forecaster because it flows in a direction parallel with the isobars, with the low pressure on its left, at a speed that is directly proportional to the spacing of the isobars (that is, proportional to the pressure gradient). This enables a reasonable estimate of wind direction and strength—the closer the isobars, the stronger the wind.

It is the Coriolis effect that causes the air movement created by the pressure gradient to not flow directly from a high to a low pressure area.

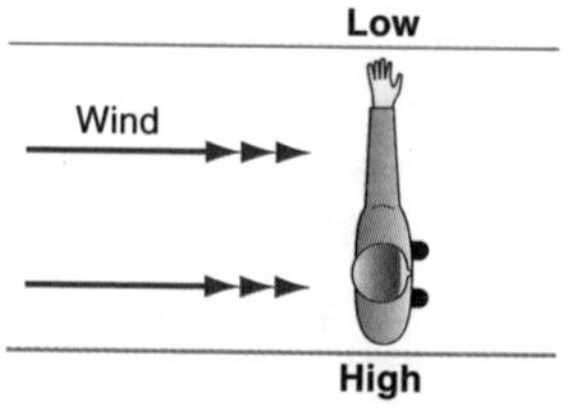

Figure 14-6
Buys Ballot's law.

Buys Ballot's Law

Buys Ballot was a Dutchman who noticed that (in the Northern Hemisphere):

if you stand with your back to the wind the low pressure will be on your left.

Flying from High to Low

If an airplane in the Northern Hemisphere is experiencing *right drift*, the wind is from the left and therefore, according to Buys Ballot's law, the airplane is flying toward an area of lower pressure. Low pressure often has poor weather associated with it, such as low cloud, rain and poor visibility in showers.

When flying towards an area of lower pressure the altimeter will over-read unless the pilot periodically resets the lower altimeter settings in the pressure window. This is not a healthy situation—beware below.

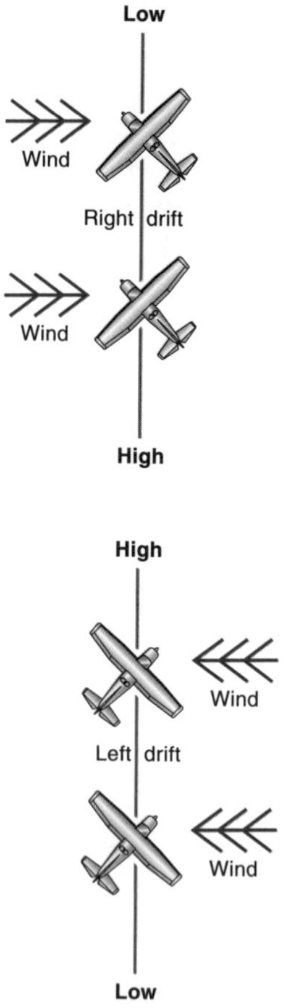

Figure 14-7
Pressure areas can be identified by the direction of wind drift.

Flying from Low to High

If an airplane is experiencing *left drift,* the wind is from the right and so, according to Buys Ballot's law, it is flying toward an area of higher pressure. High pressure often indicates a more stable atmosphere and generally better weather (although fog or poor visibility may occur).

The Gradient Wind

Isobars (the lines joining places of equal pressure) are usually curved. For the wind to flow parallel to these isobars, the airflow must be accelerated toward the center of the pressure pattern to cause it to deviate from its straight path. In the same manner as a stone when being swung on a string is pulled into the turn by a force, a curving airflow must have a resultant (or net) force acting on it to pull it into the turn. The resultant wind flow around the *curved* isobars is called the *gradient wind.*

In the Northern Hemisphere, the gradient wind flows clockwise around high-pressure areas (known as *anticyclonic motion*) and counterclockwise around low pressure areas (known as *cyclonic motion*).

For a wind that is blowing around a low (in the Northern Hemisphere), the net force results from the pressure-gradient force being greater than the Coriolis effect, thereby pulling the airflow in toward the low. For a wind that is blowing around a high, the net force results from the Coriolis effect being greater than the pressure-gradient force.

Since the Coriolis effect increases with speed, it follows that, with equally spaced isobars, the wind speed around a high will be greater than around a low.

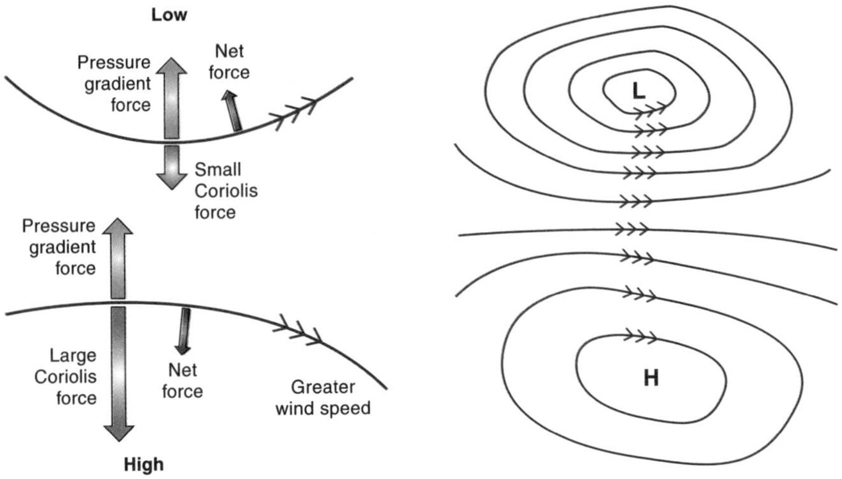

Figure 14-8 Wind flow is clockwise around a high and counterclockwise around a low in the Northern Hemisphere.

The Surface Wind

The surface wind is important to pilots because of the effect it has on takeoff and landing. The surface wind is measured at 30 feet above level (from the control tower) or in a clear area, where windsocks and other wind indicators are usually situated.

In the *friction layer* up to about 2,000 feet AGL, surface friction slows the wind down—a lower wind speed means less Coriolis effect and less deviation of the wind, so that the surface wind will tend to cross the isobars and flow out from a high and in to a low. The rougher the surface is, the greater the slowing-down. Friction forces will be least over oceans and flat desert areas, and greatest over hilly or city areas with many obstructions.

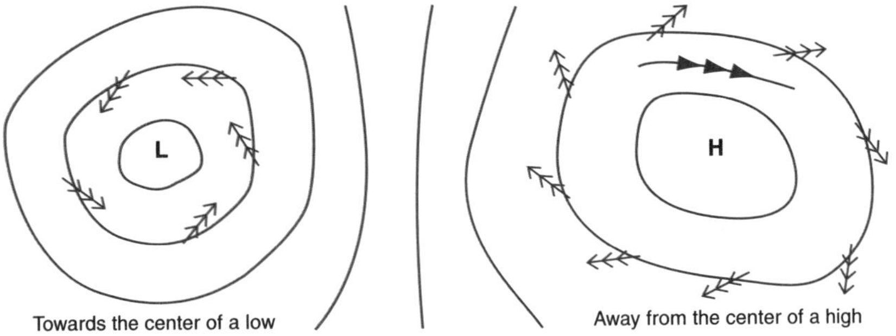

Figure 14-9 Friction causes the surface wind to weaken in strength and back in direction.

A reduced wind speed results in a reduced Coriolis effect (since the Coriolis effect depends on speed). So, the pressure-gradient force will have a more pronounced effect in the lower levels, causing the wind to flow *in* toward low-pressure areas and *out* from high-pressure areas, rather than parallel to the isobars. In other words, the surface wind tends to "back" counterclockwise compared with the gradient wind.

For example, a strong southwesterly gradient wind at 5,000 feet AGL *backs* (change direction counterclockwise) to become a less-strong southerly wind at the surface, caused by friction between the wind and the surface causing the air movement to slow down, thereby reducing the Coriolis effect. In the Northern Hemisphere:

- surface winds associated with *low-pressure* areas flow inward at an angle to the isobars in a *counterclockwise* manner; and
- surface winds associated with *high-pressure* areas flow outward at an angle to the isobars in a *clockwise* manner.

Since there is less surface friction over oceans, the surface wind may slow to about two-thirds of the gradient wind strength and the backing may only be about 10°. Over land surfaces, where friction is greater, the surface wind may slow to just one-third of the gradient wind strength, with its direction some 30° back from the gradient flow at altitude.

Friction due to the earth's surface decreases rapidly with altitude and is almost negligible above 2,000 feet AGL. The turbulence due to wind flow over rough ground also fades out at about the same level.

Daily Variation

During the day, heating of the earth's surface by the rays of the sun, and the consequent heating of the air in contact with it, will cause *vertical* motion in the lower levels of the atmosphere. This promotes mixing of the various layers of air and consequently the effect of the gradient wind at altitude will be brought *closer* to the earth's surface.

The surface wind by day will resemble the gradient wind more closely than the surface wind by night—that is, the day surface wind will be seen as a stronger wind that has veered clockwise compared with the night surface wind.

Day—
veer and increase.
Night—
slack and back.

During the night, mixing of the layers decreases. The gradient wind will continue to blow at altitude, but its effects will not be mixed with the airflow at the surface to such an extent as during the day. The night wind at surface level will drop in strength and the Coriolis effect will weaken—that is, compared with the day wind, the night wind will drop in strength and back counterclockwise in direction (figure 14-10).

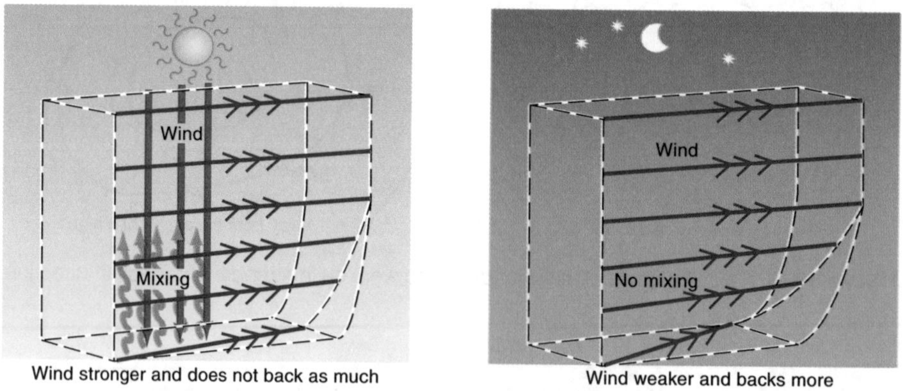

Figure 14-10 The daily variation of wind.

Wind in the Tropics

In tropical areas, pressure gradients are generally fairly weak and so will not cause the air to flow at high speeds. Local effects, such as land and sea breezes, may have a stronger influence than the pressure gradient.

The Coriolis effect that causes the air to flow parallel to the isobars is very weak in the tropics since the distance from the earth's axis remains fairly constant. The pressure gradient force, even though relatively weak, will dominate and so the air will tend to flow more from the high-pressure areas to the low-pressure areas across the isobars, rather than parallel to them.

Instead of using isobars (that join places of equal pressure) on tropical weather charts, it is more common to use:

- *streamlines* to indicate wind direction, which will be outdrafts from high-pressure areas and indrafts to low-pressure areas; in combination with
- *isotachs*, which are dotted lines joining places of equal wind strength.

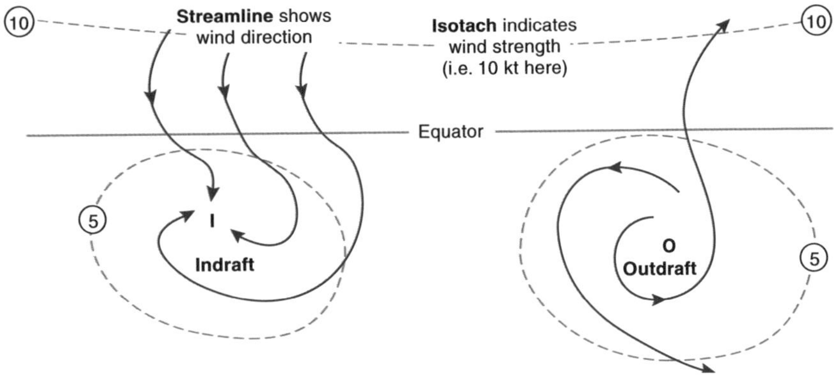

Figure 14-11 Streamline/isotach analysis chart.

High-Level Weather

CPL

The Tropopause

The tropopause is characterized by a sudden change in the temperature lapse rate.

High-level weather applies near to and above the *tropopause*, which is the border between the troposphere and the stratosphere. The tropopause varies in altitude from about 20,000 feet over the poles to 55,000–65,000 feet over the equator. In mid-latitudes, it is approximately 36,000 feet, which is its assumed level in the standard atmosphere.

Temperatures and winds vary significantly near the tropopause, with temperature above the tropopause no longer decreasing with altitude. Knowledge of these can assist you in achieving an efficient and comfortable flight.

Jet Streams

A *jet stream* is a strong narrow current of air with horizontal motion, typically located in the upper troposphere or in the stratosphere. A jet stream looks similar to the shape of a ruler, with dimensions typically 1 NM deep, 100 NM wide, and 1,200 NM long. To be called a jet stream, the wind speeds must exceed 60 knots.

We have seen that the tropopause is not one continuous sheet, but descends from the equator to the poles in a number of steps. These steps in the tropopause are like horizontal line breaks and coincide with the *Hadley cells* found in the general circulation pattern. Each step has an intense temperature (thermal) gradient that will in turn mean there is a strong thermal wind component. As a consequence the upper winds will become very strong. These tubes of strong wind between the tropopause steps are called jet streams and are associated with narrow bands of windshear and severe turbulence.

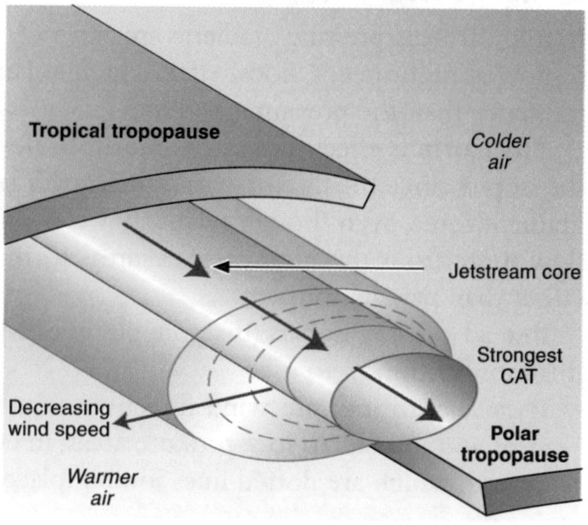

Figure 14-12 A jet stream.

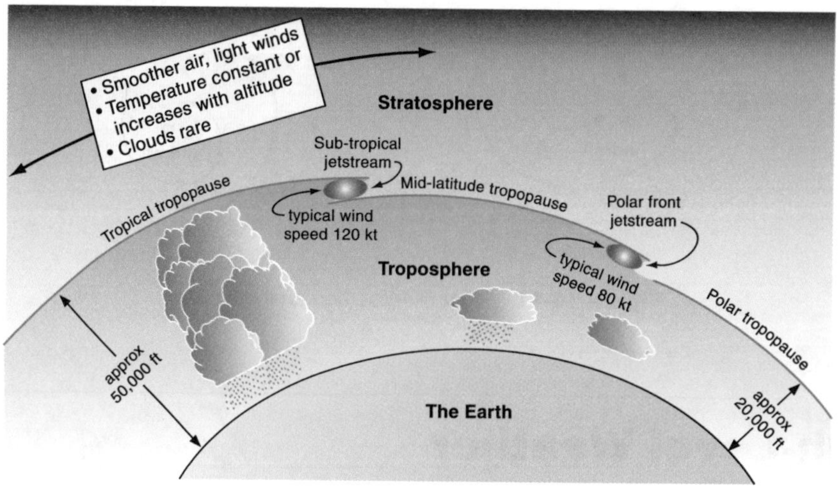

Figure 14-13 Jet stream winds flow in the breaks in the tropopause.

In the winter months in the Northern Hemisphere the general circulation pattern moves further south (along with the sun), and the jet streams increase in strength. The position of the jet stream over North America varies, but it is (in general terms) further south and stronger in winter, and moves further north in summer and is somewhat weaker.

The position of the jet stream and its associated clear air turbulence (CAT) can sometimes be visually identified by long streaks of high-level cirrus clouds (see next chapter). A jet stream is typically, 5,000 feet thick and associated with a deep low-pressure trough situated in the upper atmosphere near the tropopause. It may run in a curved path for thousands of miles around the earth at high altitude basically from west to east, but its path may meander quite a bit. By definition, the wind strength in a jet stream is *60 knots* or greater, with the strongest winds existing in the core of the jet stream tube. It is possible sometimes for a second and third jet stream to form.

High-flying jets often take advantage of the strong winds in the core of the jet stream when they are flying from west to east, perhaps giving a tailwind of 100 knots or more (and avoid the jet stream when flying from east to west).

Note. Flying conditions near jet streams are covered in Chapter 18.

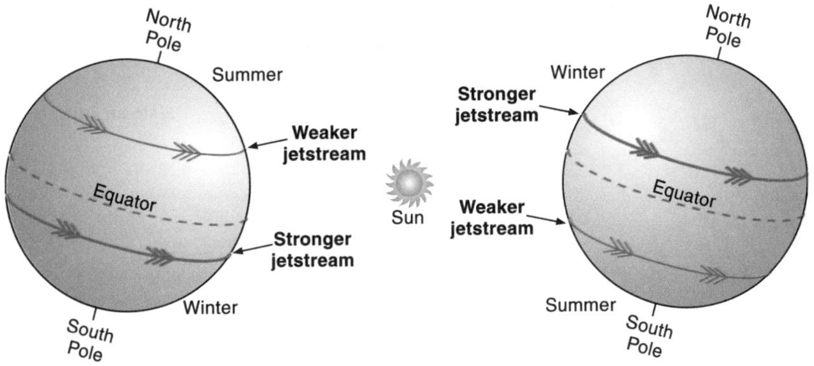

Figure 14-14 The position of jet streams varies with the season.

How a Jet Stream Forms

Wind velocity changes with altitude because of uneven temperatures in the horizontal. A warm air mass alongside a cold air mass (as is the case at the polar front) will be less dense and have relatively expanded pressure levels. Even though the pressures may be the same at ground level in the two air masses (in other words, with no pressure gradient), the pressure at altitude in the warm air mass will be greater than that at the same level in the cold air mass. A pressure-gradient force will exist and a wind will be initiated. In general, the higher the altitude in the troposphere, the steeper the pressure gradient and the stronger the wind.

Once the jet stream starts to flow, the Coriolis effect turns it to the right (in the Northern Hemisphere). In the situation illustrated (see figure 14-15), the wind will flow "out" of the page (that is, from west to east—as a westerly wind), and will be stronger at higher altitudes in the troposphere. If you look at weather charts and winds-aloft forecasts, you will often see westerlies that increase with altitude.

At the tropopause temperature stops decreasing. Since the polar tropopause is lower than the mid-latitude tropopause, temperature above it will stop decreasing with altitude, whereas temperature will continue decreasing in the "warm" air mass until its tropopause is reached, by which time it may be significantly colder than the "cold" air mass at the same level.

As well as the temperature gradient reversing with altitude, the pressure gradient will also start to reverse, and so the westerlies will start to weaken with increasing altitude above the tropopause, and may even become easterlies at great altitudes. The westerly winds reach their maximum intensity in the break between the two tropopause sheets, often blowing in a narrow jet stream tube at speeds well in excess of 100 knots.

CPL

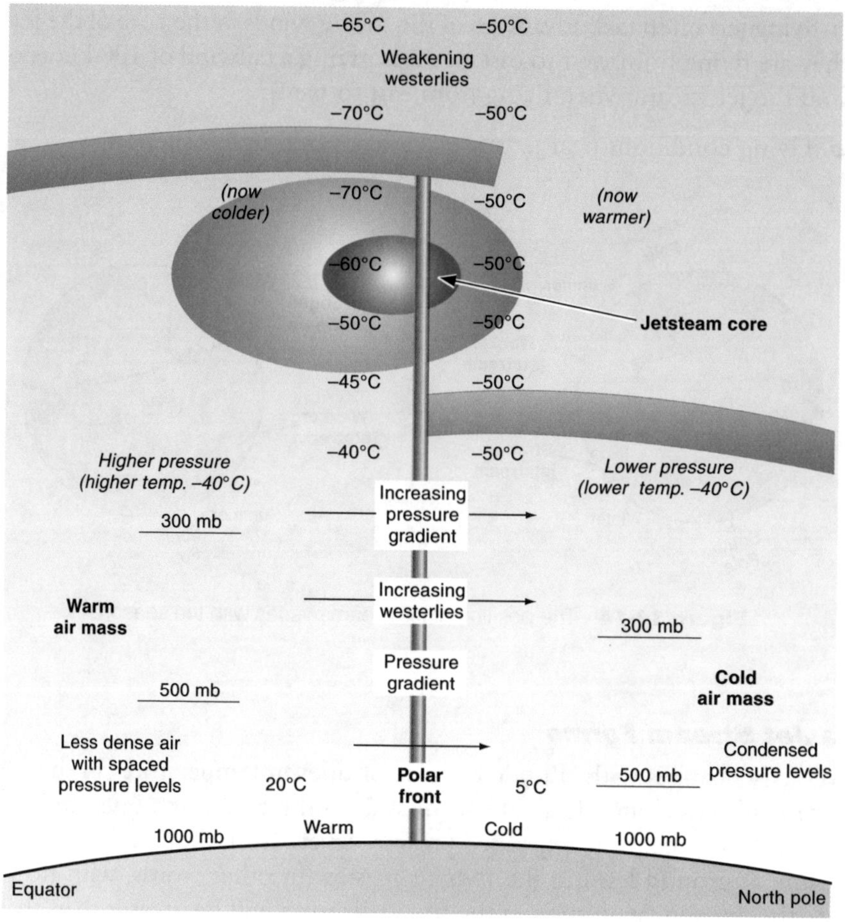

Figure 14-15 The polar front brings cold air down from polar regions.

Clear Air Turbulence

Turbulence can also be expected at high altitudes in the vicinity of any jet stream. Turbulence above 15,000 feet AGL that is not associated with cumuliform clouds is known as *clear air turbulence* (CAT). If there is a change in wind strength of more than about *6 knots per 1,000 feet* of altitude change, then moderate or stronger clear air turbulence is probable.

End CPL

Review 14
Wind

1. What causes wind?
2. The driving force that initiates a wind is the:
   a. pressure gradient force.
   b. Coriolis force.
3. The pressure gradient force acts:
   a. parallel to the isobars.
   b. perpendicular to the isobars.
4. True or false? The stronger the pressure gradient, the stronger the wind.
5. True or false? A wind initially tends to flow from a low pressure area to a high pressure area before it is turned by the Coriolis force.
6. In the Northern Hemisphere, the wind is deflected to the:
   a. right by Coriolis force.
   b. right by surface friction.
   c. left by Coriolis force.
7. Why does the wind have a tendency to flow parallel to the isobars above the friction level?
8. What causes air to flow counterclockwise around a low-pressure area in the Northern Hemisphere?
9. Are surface winds usually weaker than winds at 2,000 feet AGL? If so, why?
10. True or false? The surface winds associated with a high-pressure area in the Northern Hemisphere flow outward in a clockwise manner.
11. Compared with the gradient wind that flows parallel to the isobars, the surface wind tends to:
    a. veer clockwise.
    b. back counterclockwise.
12. The wind at 5,000 feet AGL is southwesterly while the surface wind is southerly. What is this difference in direction primarily due to?

Commercial Review

13. Why does surface wind tend to flow across the isobars towards the lower pressure?
14. True or false? When the isobars are close together, the pressure gradient force is greater and wind velocities are stronger.
15. Define jet stream.
16. What is the average altitude of the tropopause in mid-latitudes?
17. Where are jet streams usually found?
18. What are upper-level jet streams often associated with?
19. True or false? The jet stream is generally weaker and further south in the summer compared with in the winter.
20. During the winter months in the middle latitudes, the jet stream shifts toward the:
    a. north and speed decreases.
    b. south and speed increases.
    c. north and speed increases.
21. You can expect greater turbulence:
    a. in a curving jet stream.
    b. in a straight jet stream.
22. A strong windshear can be expected:
    a. in the jet stream front above a core having a speed of 60 to 90 knots.
    b. if the 5°C isotherms are spaced between 7° and 10° of latitude.
    c. on the low-pressure side of a jet stream core where the speed at the core is stronger than 110 knots.
23. A common location of clear air turbulence is:
    a. in an upper trough on the polar side of a jet stream.
    b. near a ridge aloft on the equatorial side of a high-pressure flow.
    c. south of an east/west oriented high-pressure ridge in its dissipating stage.
24. The jet stream and associated clear air turbulence can sometimes be visually identified in flight by:
    a. dust or haze at flight level.
    b. long streaks of cirrus clouds.
    c. a constant outside air temperature.

Answers are given on page 698

Clouds and Thunderstorms 15

Clouds

Clouds and thunderstorms present some of the biggest challenges to pilots of all levels. Do you fly through them? Do you fly around them? That all depends on what kind of clouds you've encountered. A cloud is a visible aggregate of minute particles of water and/or ice in free air. The effect of clouds on aviation, particularly on flight, makes them an important topic in training as the VFR pilot is required to plan for and fly in visual meteorological conditions (VMC). Low *stratus* clouds formed in stable atmospheric conditions can sit low over the ground, possibly even on the ground as fog, and cause an instrument-rated pilot to divert to an alternate destination. Towering cumulus clouds form in unstable conditions which allows moist air to rise and cool, and these can develop into one of the greatest hazards to an airplane, cumulonimbus clouds and thunderstorms.

The Naming of Clouds

Clouds may take on numerous different forms, many of which continually change. They are classified into four families according to height and named individually according to their nature. It is important to understand cloud classification because meteorological forecasts and reports use this system to give you a picture of the weather.

Clouds belong to one of four families depending on height. They are:

- *high-level clouds* with a base above approximately 20,000 feet, and composed mainly of ice crystals in the below-freezing upper atmosphere (cirrus, cirrocumulus, cirrostratus);
- *middle-level clouds* with a base above approximately 6,500 feet (altocumulus, altostratus, nimbostratus);
- *low-level clouds* with a base below approximately 6,500 feet (stratocumulus, stratus, fair weather cumulus, nimbostratus); and
- *clouds with extensive vertical development* (towering cumulus, cumulo-nimbus).

Clouds are named according to the following types:

- *cirriform* (or fibrous)—consisting mainly of ice crystals;
- *cumuliform* (or heaped)—formed by unstable air rising and cooling;
- *stratiform* (or layered)—formed by the cooling of a stable layer;
- *nimbus* (or rain-bearing), and *fractus* (fragmented);
- *castellanus* (common base with separate vertical development, often in lines); and
- *lenticularis* (lens-shaped, often formed in strong winds over mountains).

Nimbostratus, for example, means stratified clouds from which rain is falling. Altocumulus is middle-level heaped clouds. Cumulus fractus is fragmentary cumulus clouds. Cirrostratus is high-level stratified clouds consisting of ice crystals. Standing lenticular altocumulus clouds are lens-shaped, middle-level clouds standing in the one position, usually over a mountain range in strong winds. Nimbostratus is a hybrid cloud in terms of classification since its base can be low level or middle level, and it can have great vertical depth. Sometimes nimbostratus is 10,000 or even 15,000 feet thick, making it very dark when seen from underneath and capable of causing heavy rain for many hours.

Flying in clouds presents the qualified instrument-rated pilot with considerations such as poor visibility and the risk of icing—not a great risk in the high-level cirriform clouds consisting of ice crystals, but very great in clouds of extensive vertical development which may contain large supercooled water drops that will freeze on contact with a cold airplane.

Moisture in the Atmosphere

Clouds are formed when water vapor in the atmosphere condenses into water droplets. Below freezing temperatures, the droplets often freeze rapidly into ice crystals. The cloud is then said to be glaciated. Water vapor is taken up into the atmosphere mainly by *evaporation* from the oceans and other bodies where water is present, or by *sublimation* directly from solid ice when the air overlies a frozen surface.

The Three States of Water

Water in its vapor state is not visible, but when the water vapor condenses to form water droplets we see it as cloud, fog, mist, rain or dew. Frozen water is also visible as high-level clouds, snow, hail, ice or frost. Water exists in three states—gas (vapor), liquid (water) and solid (ice).

Under certain conditions water can change from one state to another, *absorbing* heat energy if it moves to a higher energy state (from ice to water to vapor) and *giving off* heat energy if it moves to a lower energy state (vapor to water to ice). This heat energy is known as *latent heat* and is a vital part of any change of state. The absorption or emission of latent heat is important in meteorological processes such as cloud formation, and evaporation of rain (virga).

The three states of water, the names of the various transfer processes and the absorption or giving-off of latent heat are shown in figure 15-1.

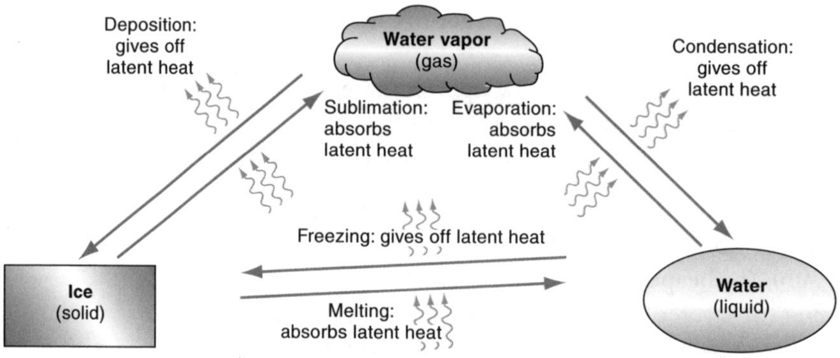

Figure 15-1 The three states of water.

Relative Humidity

The amount of water vapor present in the air depends on the amount of evaporation, which will be greater over wet surfaces such as oceans and flooded ground than over a desert or continent. The actual amount of water vapor in the air, known as *absolute humidity*, is not as important as whether the air can support that water vapor or not. When a parcel of air is supporting as much water vapor as it can, it is said to be *saturated* and have a *relative humidity of 100%.*

Air supporting less than its full capacity of water vapor is said to be *unsaturated*, and will have a relative humidity of less than 100%. In clouds and fog, the relative humidity is 100% and the air is saturated; over a desert, relative humidity might be only 20%.

Dewpoint Temperature

Clouds are formed when air is cooled to its *dewpoint* temperature, and the excess water vapor condenses as liquid water. The droplets may then freeze into ice crystals, depending on temperature. If the cloud remains liquid at below freezing temperatures, it is said to be *supercooled* and will present structural icing possibilities until it glaciates. The cooling of a parcel of air can occur by various means, such as:

- rising air cooling adiabatically as it expands; or
- air flowing over, or lying over, a cooling surface.

How much water vapor a particular parcel of air can support depends on the air temperature—warm air is able to support more water vapor than cold air. If the temperature of the air falls, it is capable of holding less water vapor, and so will move closer to being saturated—its relative humidity will rise. The relative humidity increases greatly with a decrease in temperature.

The temperature at which the relative humidity reaches 100%, and the excess water vapor starts to condense into water droplets, is known as the *dewpoint temperature*. Condensation may be delayed if there are insufficient condensation nuclei in the air, or conversely, certain types of condensation nuclei may induce condensation shortly before 100% relative humidity is reached. Typical condensation nuclei are small particles of hygroscopic (water-soluble) dust, salt, and so on. Clouds form when the water vapor actually condenses.

A parcel of air that has a temperature higher than its dewpoint is unsaturated. This means its relative humidity is less than 100%, since it is capable of holding more moisture at its current temperature. The closer the actual temperature of the air to its dewpoint, the closer it is to being saturated. In other words, as the temperature/dewpoint spread reduces with a fall in air temperature, the relative humidity increases.

At its *dewpoint*, the air will be fully saturated—its relative humidity will be 100%. If it becomes cooler than its dewpoint, then the excess water vapor will condense as visible water droplets (or if in contact with some surface in sub-freezing temperatures below the frost point, it may deposit on the surface as ice crystals).

The actual value of the dewpoint temperature for a particular parcel of air varies, depending on the amount of water vapor it contains. If the air is moist (for instance over a tropical ocean), the dewpoint temperature may be quite high, say +25°C; if the air is dry, the dewpoint temperature may be quite low.

If the air temperature falls to a dewpoint temperature which is above freezing, the water vapor will condense as liquid water droplets and become visible as clouds, fog or dew; if the dewpoint is below freezing, the excess water vapor may wind up as ice crystals (for example, high-level cirriform clouds, or frost on the ground on a below freezing night). If the air in which clouds form is unable to support the water droplets (if they become too large and heavy), then the drops will fall as precipitation (rain, hail or snow).

Adiabatic Processes

The *temperature* of a gas depends on the number and energy of its molecules striking the measuring surface of a thermometer. In *adiabatic* processes, temperature can change as a result of pressure changes, even though heat energy is neither added to nor taken from the system. Expanding a gas and decreasing its pressure causes a lowering of temperature, because fewer molecules will collide with the measuring surface. Conversely, compressing a gas and increasing its pressure will raise its temperature because more molecules will collide with the measuring surface. Placing your finger over the outlet of a bicycle pump illustrates that compressing air increases its temperature.

Also, air that has been compressed and stored at room temperature will cool when it is released to the atmosphere and allowed to expand.

A common adiabatic process that involves the expansion of a gas and its cooling is when a parcel of air rises in the atmosphere. This can be initiated by the heating of the parcel of air over warm ground, causing it to expand and become less dense than the surrounding air, hence it will rise. A parcel of air can also be forced aloft as it blows over a mountain range, or as it is lifted over a front.

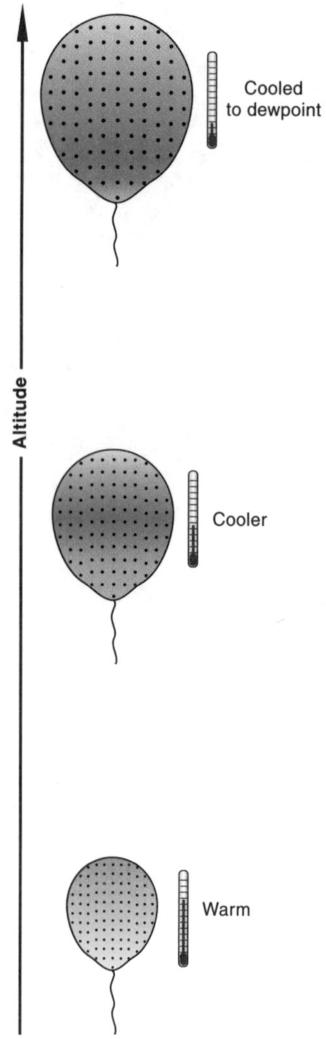

Figure 15-2
As air rises and expands, it cools adiabatically.

Unsaturated air will cool adiabatically at about 3°C/1,000 feet as it rises and expands. This is known as the *dry adiabatic lapse rate* (DALR). Air that is 12°C at ground level will cool adiabatically to 9°C if it is forced up to 1,000 feet AGL, and to 6°C at 2,000 feet AGL, and so on, provided it does not reach saturation point. Cooler air can support less water vapor, so, as the parcel of air rises and cools, its relative humidity will increase. At the altitude where its temperature is reduced to the dewpoint temperature (that is, relative humidity reaches 100%), water will start to condense and form cloud.

Above this altitude, the now-saturated air will continue to cool as it rises but, because latent heat will be given off as the water vapor condenses into the lower energy liquid state, the cooling will not be as great. The rate at which saturated air cools as it rises is known as the *saturated adiabatic lapse rate* (SALR) and may be assumed to have a value of approximately half the DALR (1.5°C/1,000 feet). Air that is say 5°C inside a cloud will, if it is forced 1,000 feet higher, cool adiabatically to 3.5°C.

Note. At higher levels in the cloud where there is less water vapor to condense into water (since most of this has already occurred), there will be less latent heat given off and so SALR will increase.

The Formation of Clouds

Which Cloud Type Forms?

The structure or type of cloud that forms depends mainly on the *stability* of the air before lifting occurs. *Moist air* that is unstable will continue rising, forming cumulus-type cloud with significant vertical development and turbulence, whereas moist air that is stable has no tendency to continue rising and so will form stratus-type clouds with little vertical development and little or no turbulence. Some stratiform clouds, such as nimbostratus, can however form in a very thick layer. *Dry air* that is forced to rise, but does not cool to its dewpoint temperature, will not form clouds. As long as a parcel of air given vertical movement is *warmer* than its surroundings, it will continue to rise. This is known as an *unstable* parcel of air. Its characteristics are:

- turbulence in the rising air;
- the formation of cumuliform clouds (heaped clouds);
- showery rain from these clouds, if there is precipitation; and
- good visibility between the showers (caused by the rising air carrying any obscuring particles away).

The type of cloud which forms depends on stability of the air.

If the rising parcel of air is cooler than the ambient air around it, then it will stop rising because its density will be greater than the surroundings. An atmosphere in which air tends to remain at the one level, or to sink, is called a stable atmosphere.

Characteristics of stable air are:

- the formation of *stratiform* clouds (layer-type) with little vertical development and steady, if any, precipitation;
- poor visibility if there are any obscuring particles; and
- possibly smooth flying conditions with little or no turbulence.

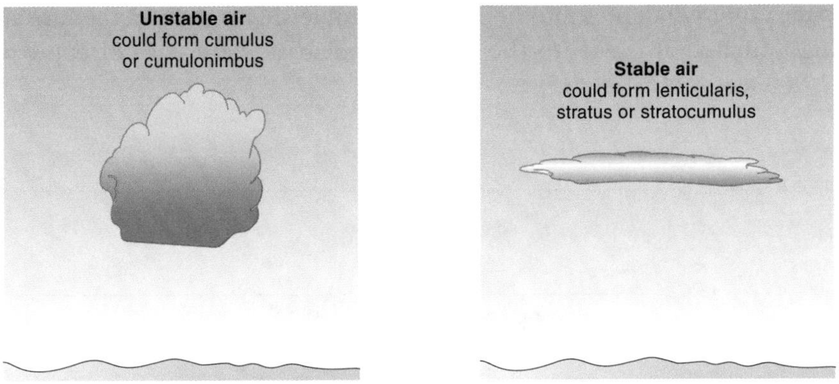

Figure 15-3 Cumuliform clouds form in unstable conditions; stratiform clouds form in stable conditions.

The rate of temperature change as altitude is gained in the surrounding atmosphere (that is, in the air that is not rising) is called the *environmental lapse rate* (ELR), the *ambient lapse rate* or the *actual lapse rate*. Its relationship to DALR and SALR is the main factor in determining the levels of the bases and tops of the clouds that form. A great decrease in ambient air temperature with altitude (that is, a high ELR) encourages warm air to keep rising (that is, an unstable situation) and form clouds of great vertical development. A lesser ELR may indicate a stable situation. The actual environmental lapse rate varies from time-to-time and from place-to-place.

The stability in the atmosphere depends on the ambient lapse rate.

Clouds Formed by Convection Due To Heating

Cold air moving over or lying over a warm surface will be warmed from below, and so become less stable. It will tend to rise, causing turbulence and good visibility. If the air is moist and unstable, cumuliform clouds will develop as the air ascends and cools adiabatically to its dewpoint temperature.

The ascending unsaturated air will cool at the dry adiabatic lapse rate of 3°C/1,000 feet. The closer the air temperature is to the dewpoint, the lesser height it has to rise before condensing to form clouds. The dewpoint decreases at about 0.5°C/1,000 feet, which means that the air temperature/dewpoint spread will decrease at approximately 2.5°C/1,000 feet in rising unstable air.

For working in degrees Fahrenheit, the DALR for unsaturated air is 5.4°F and the dewpoint lapse rate is approximately 1°F, so they converge at approximately 4.4°F/1,000 feet (which is the same as 2.5°C/1,000 feet).

$$\text{Cloud base in thousands of feet} = \frac{\text{air temperature} - \text{dewpoint}}{4.4°\text{F (or } 2.5°\text{C)}}$$

If the temperature at a given level is 17°C and the dewpoint is 12°C—a temperature/dewpoint spread of 5°C, then as the air rises this spread will decrease by approximately 2.5°C/1,000 feet. The temperature and dewpoint will have the same value at an altitude approximately ($5/2.5 = 2$) 2,000 feet higher.

The cloud base of the air in the above example will form at a level 2,000 feet higher than the given level, and if the air is still unstable, it will continue to rise and form a cumuliform cloud. Because the air is now saturated, latent heat will be given off as more water vapor condenses into liquid water droplets. This reduces the rate at which the rising saturated air cools to the saturated adiabatic lapse rate of approximately 1.5°C/1,000 feet.

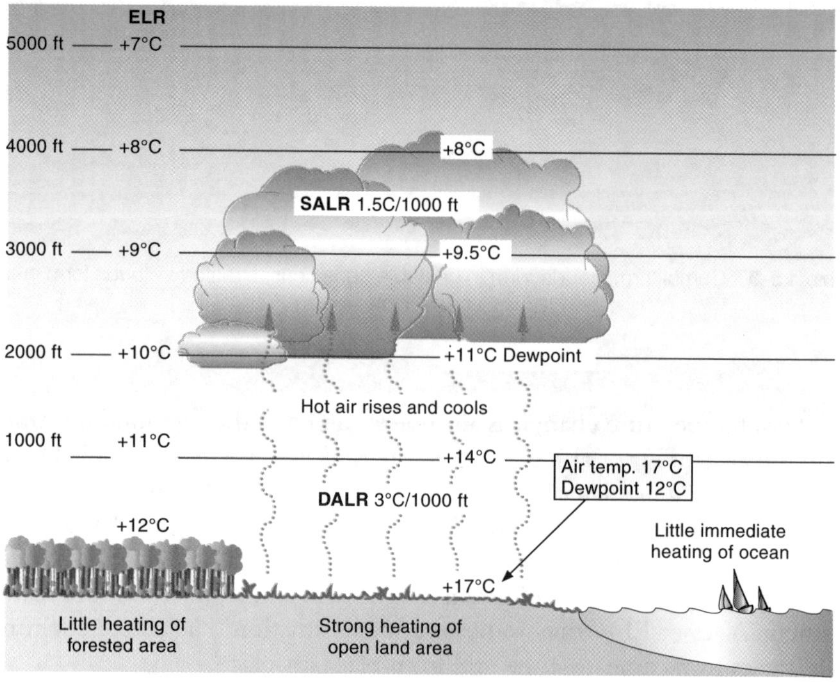

Figure 15-4
The temperature processes involved in the formation of a cumulus cloud.

Example 15-1

What is the approximate base MSL of clouds if the temperature at 3,000 feet MSL is 68°F and the dewpoint is 46°F?

$$\text{Cloud base in thousands of feet} = \frac{68 - 46}{4.4} = \frac{22}{4.4} = 5$$

$$\text{therefore the cloud base MSL} = 3{,}000 \text{ ft MSL} + 5{,}000 \text{ ft}$$
$$= 8{,}000 \text{ ft MSL}$$

Clouds Formed by Orographic Uplift

Air flowing over mountains rises and is cooled adiabatically. If it cools to below its *dewpoint temperature*, then the water vapor will condense and clouds will form.

Descending on the other side of the mountains, however, the airflow will warm adiabatically and, once its temperature exceeds the dewpoint for that parcel of air, the water vapor will no longer condense. The liquid water drops will now start to vaporize, and the clouds will cease to exist below this level.

The altitude at which the cloud base forms depends on the moisture content of the parcel of air and its dewpoint. The cloud base may be below the mountain tops, or well above them, depending on the situation. Having started to form, the clouds may sit low over the mountain as stratiform clouds (in stable air), or (if the air is unstable) may rise to high levels as cumulus clouds.

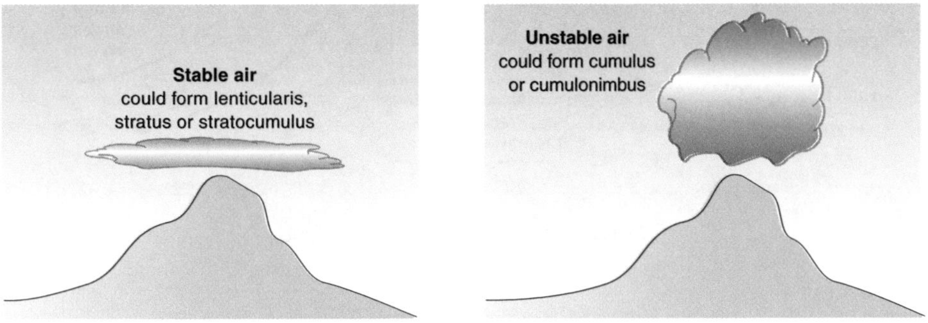

Figure 15-5 Orographic uplift can lead to cloud formation.

An almond or lens-shaped cloud that forms as a *cap* over a mountain is known as a lenticular cloud. It will remain more or less stationary while the air flows through it, possibly at speeds of 50 knots or more. Mount Shasta in northern California invariably has a lenticular cap cloud.

Sometimes, when an airstream flows over a mountain range and there is a stable layer of air above, standing waves occur. Clouds may form in the crest of the lee waves, and a rotor or roll cloud may form at a low altitude. The presence of standing lenticular altocumulus clouds is a good indicator that strong *turbulence* exists.

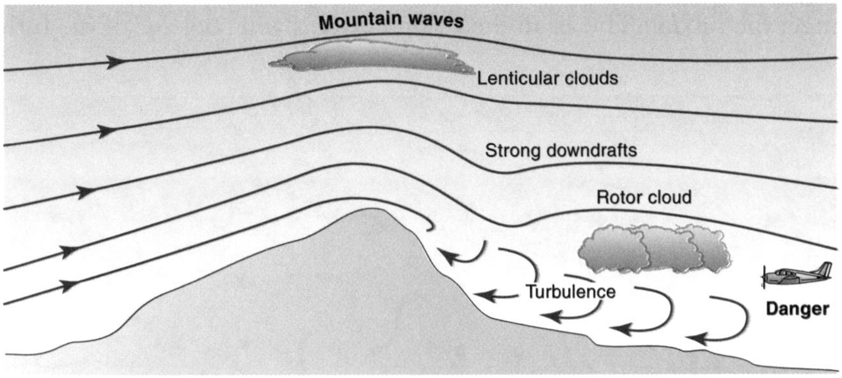

Figure 15-6 Lenticular cloud cap (left), and mountain waves.

The Föhn (or Chinook) Wind Effect. If the air rising up a mountain range is moist enough to have a high dewpoint temperature and is cooled down to it before reaching the top of the mountain, then cloud will form on the windward side. If any precipitation occurs, moisture will be removed from the airflow and, as it descends on the lee side of the mountain, it will therefore be drier. The dewpoint temperature will be less and so the cloud base will be higher on the lee side of the mountain.

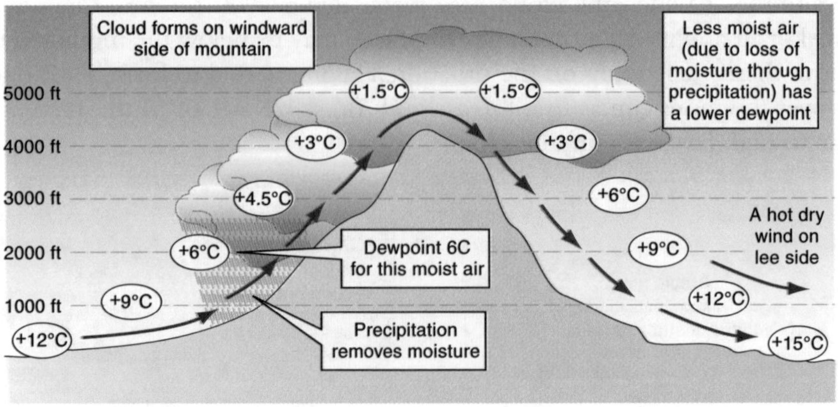

Figure 15-7 The Föhn wind effect.

As the dry air beneath the cloud descends, it will warm at the dry adiabatic lapse rate of 3°C/1,000 feet, which is at a greater rate than the rising air cooled inside the cloud (saturated adiabatic lapse rate: 1.5°C/1,000 feet). The result is a *warmer* and *drier wind* on the lee side of the mountains. This very noticeable effect is seen in many parts of the world, for example the *föhn* (pronounced "fern") wind in Switzerland and southern Germany, from which this effect gets its name, the *chinook* wind which blows down the eastern slope of the Rocky Mountains, and the *Santa Ana* wind which blows from the east or northeast in southern California.

Clouds Formed by Turbulence and Mixing

As air flows over the surface of the earth, frictional effects cause variations in local wind strength and direction. Eddies are set up which cause the lower levels of air to mix—the stronger the wind and the rougher the earth's surface, the larger the eddies and the stronger the mixing. The air in the rising currents will cool and, if the turbulence

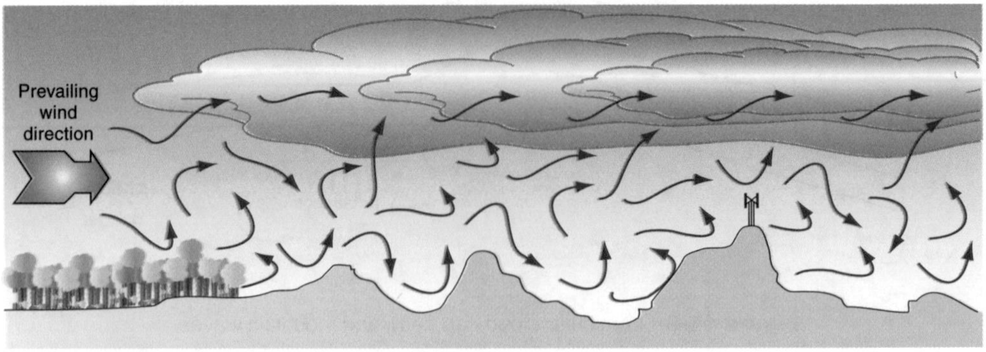

Figure 15-8 Formation of turbulence clouds.

extends to a sufficient height, it may cool to the dewpoint temperature, water vapor will condense to form liquid water droplets and clouds will form.

The descending air currents in the turbulent cloud layer will warm and, if the air's dewpoint temperature is exceeded, the liquid water droplets that make up the clouds will return to the water vapor state. The air will dry out and clouds will not exist below this altitude. With turbulent mixing, stratiform clouds may form over quite a large area, possibly with an undulating base. They may be continuous stratus or broken stratocumulus.

Clouds Formed by Widespread Ascent

Clouds can be formed by the widespread ascent of an air mass.

When two large masses of air of differing temperatures meet, the warmer and less dense air will flow over (or be undercut by) the cooler air. As the warmer air mass is forced aloft it will cool and, if the dewpoint temperature is reached, clouds will form. The boundary layer between two air masses is called a *front*.

Widespread lifting can also result from latitudinal pinching of an air mass as it moves to higher latitudes and has to crowd into a smaller area.

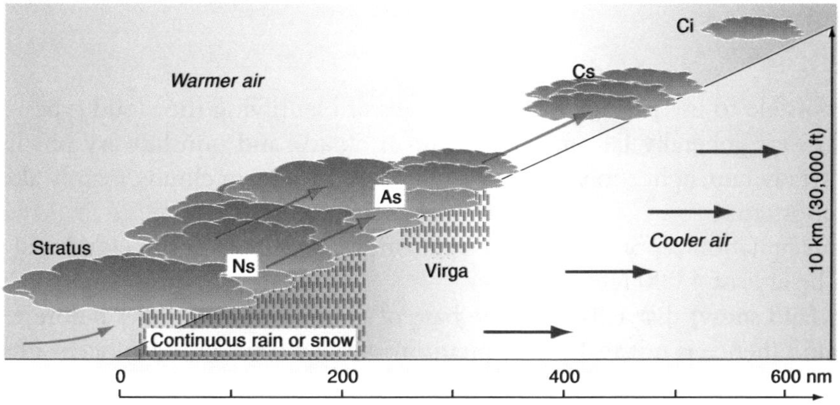

Figure 15-9 Cloud formation resulting from widespread ascent.

Precipitation from Clouds

Precipitation refers to falling water that finally reaches the ground, including:

- *rain* consisting of liquid water drops;
- *drizzle* consisting of fine water droplets;
- *snow* consisting of branched and star-shaped ice crystals;
- *hail* consisting of small balls of ice;
- *freezing rain* or *drizzle*—liquid drops or droplets which freeze on contact with a cold surface (such as the ground or an aircraft in flight); and
- *dew, frost* or *ice*.

Intermittent or continuous precipitation (which often starts and finishes gradually, perhaps over a long period) is usually associated with stratiform clouds—for example, fine drizzle or snow from stratus and stratocumulus, heavy continuous rain or snow from nimbostratus, and steady rain from altostratus.

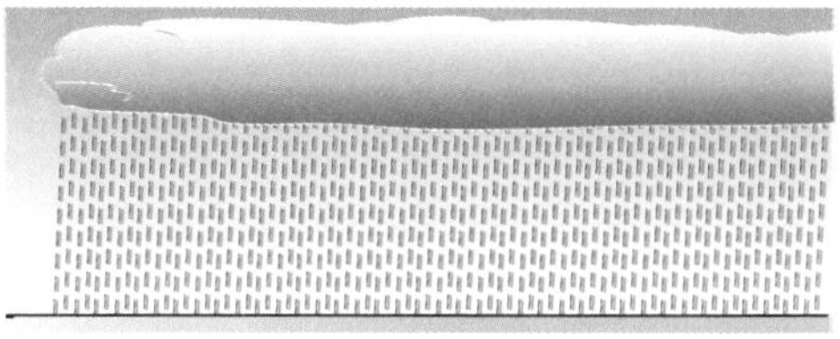

Figure 15-10
Nonshowery (steady) precipitation falls from stratiform clouds.

Rain or snow showers are associated with cumuliform clouds, and very heavy rain may fall from cumulonimbus storm clouds. The strong updrafts in these clouds carry the water droplets up to cooler levels where the condensation process continues and the drops grow in size and weight before they fall.

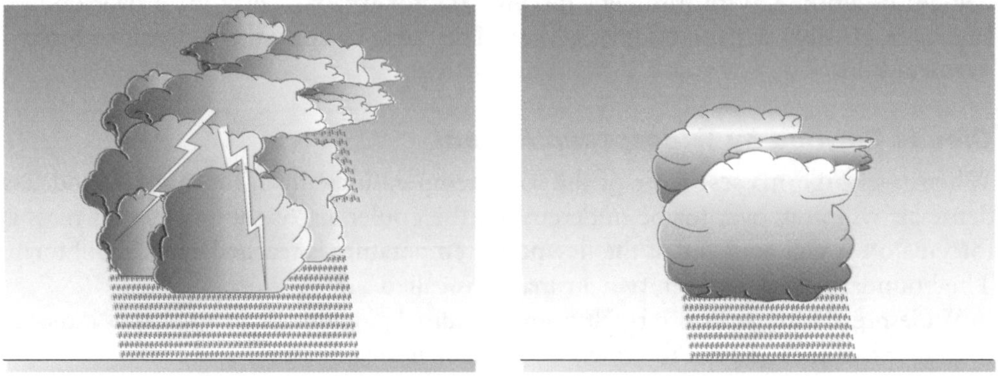

Figure 15-11 Rain showers fall from cumuliform clouds.

It is possible to use precipitation as a means of identifying the cloud type—rain or snow showers generally fall from cumuliform clouds, and nonshowery precipitation such as steady rain, light snow or drizzle falls from stratiform clouds, mainly altostratus and nimbostratus.

For precipitation reported to be of light or greater intensity, the cloud will usually have to be at least 4,000 feet thick.

Rain (and snow) that falls from the base of clouds but evaporates before reaching the ground (hence is not really precipitation) is called *virga*. This can occur in areas of low humidity, often over deserts. One extremely important consequence of virga is that the evaporation of the rain absorbs latent heat from the air, creating a very cool and invisible parcel of air that may sink, or even plummet, quite rapidly toward the ground. This can sometimes result in a *microburst* or *downburst*, which are forms of downflow, usually beneath thunderstorms, that have brought many aircraft to grief.

Sometimes the only indications of a microburst are high-level virga and a ring of dust blown up on the ground. Examine the microburst sequence which is included in the color section in this chapter. Microbursts are covered later in this chapter.

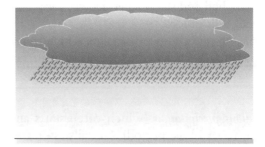

Figure 15-12 Virga.

Thunderstorms

A *thunderstorm* is one or more cumulonimbus clouds accompanied by sudden electrical discharges known as *lightning*, which cause a sharp rumbling sound known as *thunder*. Thunderstorms generate spectacular weather which may be accompanied by lightning, thunder, heavy rain showers, and sometimes hail, squalls and tornados.

For a thunderstorm to develop there must be deep instability, high moisture content and a trigger action.

Thunderstorms are *only* associated with cumulonimbus clouds, and there may be several thunderstorm cells within the one cloud mass. Thunderstorms constitute a *severe hazard* to the aviator and must be avoided.

Lightning and Thunder

Lightning is simply a discharge of *static electricity* that has built up in the cloud. The air along the path that the lightning follows experiences intense heating, causing it to expand violently. The speed of this "expansion" is faster than the local speed of sound, which produces the familiar clap of thunder. By definition, all thunderstorms have lightning—since it is the lightning which causes the thunder.

Conditions Necessary for Thunderstorm Development

Three conditions are necessary for a thunderstorm to develop, and they are:

- *deep instability* in the atmosphere, so that once the air starts to rise it will continue to rise (for example, a steep unstable lapse rate with warm air in the lower levels of the atmosphere and cold air in the upper levels);
- a *high moisture* content, so that clouds can readily form; and
- a *trigger action* (or catalyst or lifting force) to start the air rising, possibly caused by:
  - a front forcing the air aloft;
  - a mountain or other terrain forcing the air aloft (orographic ascent);
  - convective ascent from strong heating of air in contact with the surface;
  - heating of the lower layers of a cold polar air mass as it moves by advection to warmer latitudes, causing convective ascent and known as a *cold stream thunderstorm*;
  - advection of upper cold air over warm air beneath, which will then rise;
  - less-dense moist air (for example, from the Gulf of Mexico) moving up and over drier and denser continental air; or
  - cooling of the tops of large clouds at night by radiation which will cause the lower warmer air to rise (for example, thunderstorms in tropical areas at night or in the early mornings).

The Life Cycle of a Thunderstorm

The Cumulus Stage

When moist air rises, it is cooled until its dewpoint temperature is reached. Then the water vapor starts to condense out as liquid droplets, forming clouds. Latent heat is given off in the condensation process, and so the rising air cools at a lesser rate, with the release of large amounts of latent heat energy driving along the formation of the storm cloud. At this early cumulus stage in the formation of a thunderstorm, there are strong, warm *updrafts* over a diameter of one or two miles, with no significant downdrafts.

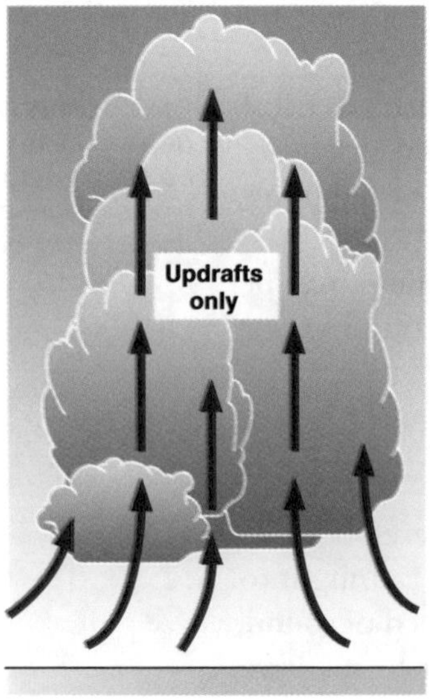

Figure 15-13
The cumulus stage in the development of a thunderstorm.

Air is drawn horizontally into the cell at all levels and causes the updraft to become stronger with altitude. The temperature inside the cloud is higher than the outside environment (because of the release of latent heat during the condensation), and the cloud continues to build to greater and greater heights. This growth often occurs at such a rate that an airplane cannot outclimb the growing cloud.

The strong, warm updrafts carry the water droplets higher and higher, to levels often much higher than the freezing level, where they may freeze or continue to exist as liquid water droplets in a supercooled state. Water condensation occurs, and the liquid droplets coalesce to form larger and larger drops. The cumulus stage as a thunderstorm forms typically lasts 10 to 20 minutes and is characterized by continuous updrafts. If the cumulus cloud develops into a towering cumulus 25,000 feet high in only 10 minutes, then the average updraft strength exceeds 2,000 FPM.

The Mature Stage

The water drops eventually become too large and too heavy to be supported by the updrafts, even though the updrafts may be in excess of 6,000 FPM, and so start to fall. As the drops fall in great numbers inside the cloud, they drag air along with them causing strong downdrafts. Often the first lightning flashes and the first rain from the cloud base will occur at this stage. Rain commencing to fall from the base of a cumulonimbus cloud to the surface is an indication that the thunderstorm has entered the mature stage, and it is in this stage that the thunderstorm reaches its greatest intensity. The descending air warms adiabatically, but the cold drops of water slow down the rate at which this occurs, resulting in *cool downdrafts* in contrast to the *warm updrafts* which are also present. Heavy rain or hail may fall from the base of the cloud at this stage; falls are generally heaviest for the first five minutes. The strong wind currents associated with the thunderstorm may throw *hailstones* well out from the core of the storm, possibly several miles, where they may fall in clear air.

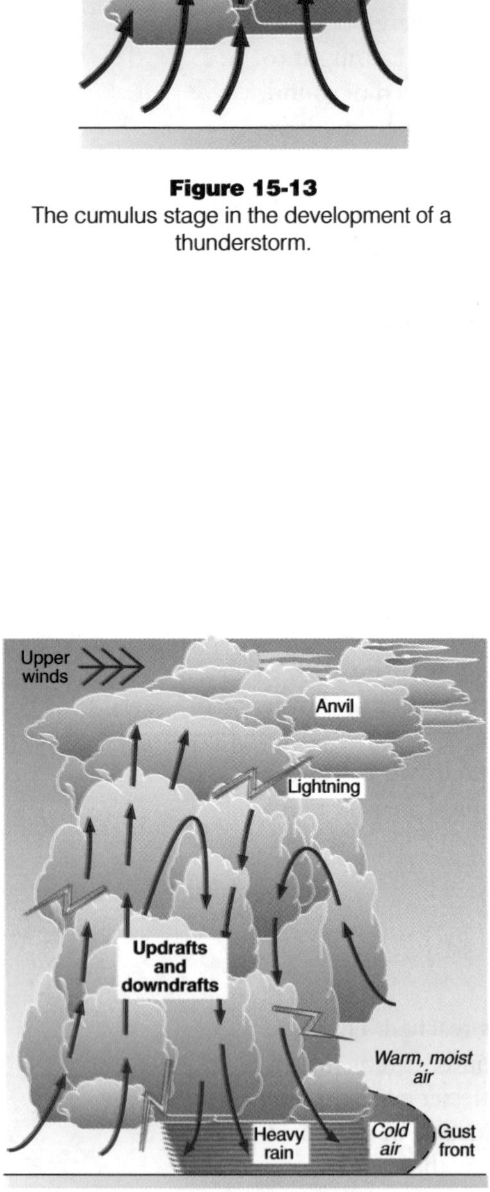

Figure 15-14
The mature stage of a thunderstorm.

The top of a mature storm cloud may reach as far up as the tropopause, which is perhaps 30,000 feet MSL in temperate latitudes and 50,000 feet MSL in the tropics. The storm cloud may now have the typical shape of a cumulonimbus, with the top spreading out in an *anvil* shape in the direction that the upper winds are blowing. Extremely large cumulonimbus with strong vertical development can sometimes push through the tropopause and into the stratosphere. Over the Midwestern plains, some thunderstorms reach well over 50,000 feet MSL.

The violent updrafts and downdrafts (which are very close to each other in a mature thunderstorm) cause extremely strong windshear and turbulence, which can result in structural failure of the airframe. The rapidly changing direction from which the airflow strikes the wings could also cause a stall, so intentionally flying into a mature cumulonimbus cloud is very foolhardy. As the cold downdrafts flow out of the base of the cloud at a great rate, they change direction and begin to flow horizontally as the ground is approached. Strong windshear and turbulence occur—causing the demise of many aircraft, large and small.

The outflowing cold air will undercut the inflowing warmer air and, like a mini cold front, a gusty wind and a sudden drop in temperature may precede the actual storm.

Squalls may occur at the surface—a squall is defined as a sudden increase in wind speed of at least 15 knots that lasts more than one minute, with a peak of at least 20 knots. A *gust* is less dramatic than a squall and is defined as a brief increase in wind speed of at least 10 knots. A *roll cloud* may also develop at the base of the main cloud where the cold downdrafts and warm updrafts pass, indicating possible extreme turbulence.

The mature stage of a thunderstorm typically lasts between 20 and 40 minutes, and is characterized by updrafts and downdrafts, and by precipitation. There is so much water falling through the cloud toward the end of the mature stage that it starts to wash out the updrafts.

The Dissipating Stage

The cold downdrafts gradually cause the warm updrafts to weaken, thereby reducing the supply of warm, moist air to the upper levels of the cloud. The cool downdrafts continue (since they are colder than the ambient air surrounding the cloud) and spread out over the whole cloud, which starts to collapse from above. The dissipating stage of a thunderstorm is characterized by *downdrafts* only. Eventually the temperature inside the cloud warms to reach that of the environment, and what was once a towering cumulonimbus cloud may collapse into stratiform cloud.

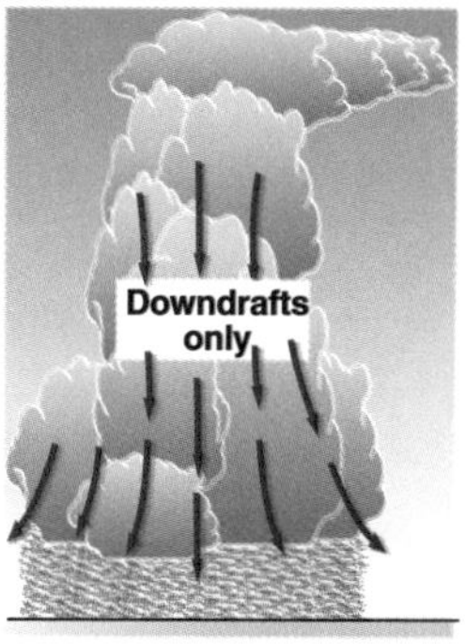

Figure 15-15 Thunderstorm dissipating.

Severe Thunderstorms

Sometimes severe thunderstorms develop; these contain more than one storm cell, and have a prolonged mature stage of updrafts and downdrafts, with very strong windshears resulting. The cells within the one large storm may be at different stages in their life cycle. Strong winds aloft may cause the updrafts to slope. The rain and resulting downdrafts will be well-separated from the sloping updrafts, and so will not affect the updrafts and the moisture they are carrying up to the upper levels of the clouds. This can lead to the development of very large cumulonimbus clouds and *supercell* thunderstorms.

The strong downdrafts, on approaching the ground, tend to spread out in all directions, with the forward edge in front of the cloud forming a gust front. As the gust front advances, air is forced aloft and new storm cells can form.

Embedded Thunderstorms

Sometimes cumulonimbus clouds are embedded in a general cloud layer and, unlike many isolated and scattered thunderstorms, may not be detected by a pilot flying visually below the clouds or by an instrument-rated pilot flying without weather radar.

The presence of embedded thunderstorms might be indicated to a pilot flying visually beneath the cloud base by heavy rain showers. In general, however, you should not fly into or under a cloud mass containing embedded thunderstorms unless you have thunderstorm detection equipment.

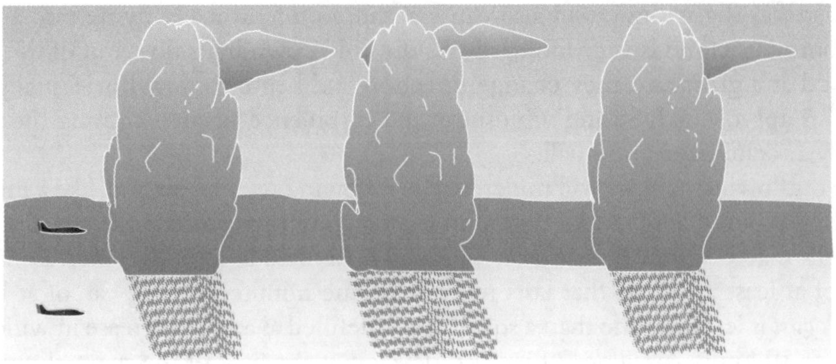

Figure 15-16 Embedded thunderstorms can be a hazard to aviation.

Squall Lines

The most severe flying conditions, such as heavy hail and destructive winds, may be produced in a *squall line*, which is a nonfrontal band of very active thunderstorms, possibly in a long line that requires a large detour to fly around. This line of thunderstorms (sometimes more than one line) can form in the relatively warm air ahead of a cold front, and can be quite fast moving. A squall line may contain a number of severe steady-state thunderstorms, destructive winds, heavy hail, and tornados. It can present a most intense hazard to aircraft.

Icing

The most critical icing levels for airplanes inside a cumulonimbus cloud is from the freezing level (0°C) up to an altitude where the temperature is -15°C, the range where it is most likely to encounter supercooled water drops (freezing rain). If possible, avoid this temperature band inside clouds. However, liquid water has been observed in thunderstorms at temperatures as low as -40°C. Thus no level in a thunderstorm above the freezing level can be safely considered to be icing free.

Hailstones

Large hailstones often form inside cumulonimbus clouds as water adheres to already formed hailstones and then freezes, leading to even larger hailstones. In certain conditions hailstones can grow to the size of an orange. Heavy hail can damage the skin of an airplane and damage its windshield. Almost all cumulonimbus clouds contain hail, with most of it melting before reaching the ground where it falls as rain. Strong air currents can sometimes throw hailstones out of the storm for a distance of several miles. On cold days, with freezing level at or near ground level, hail will fall from the cloud and reach the ground before melting.

Lightning Strikes

Lightning strikes can cause damage to electrical equipment in the airplane and to the airplane skin and antennas. It can also temporarily blind pilots, especially if flying at night in a darkened cockpit with their eyes adjusted to the darkness. A good precaution against this is to turn up the cockpit lights when in the vicinity of thunderstorms. Lightning strikes seem to be most likely when flying in or near to cumulonimbus clouds at altitudes near the freezing level (plus or minus 5°C—that is, within about 2,500 feet of the freezing level).

Turbulence

Turbulence in the vicinity of a thunderstorm that causes large changes in attitude, altitude and airspeed, with the aircraft occasionally out of control for a moment, and causing you to experience severe pulling from the seat belt for about three quarters of the time, would be described as *continuous severe turbulence*.

Downbursts and Microbursts

Strong downdrafts that spread out near the ground are known as *downbursts*. A very strong downburst not exceeding two nautical miles in diameter is called a *microburst*. Most aircraft do not have the performance capability or the structural strength to combat the extremely strong downdrafts, turbulence and windshear in downbursts and microbursts, and can be destroyed. *Avoid downbursts and microbursts at all costs*. Downbursts and microbursts are mainly associated with cumulonimbus (thunderstorm) clouds, but they may also occur with smaller clouds, such as cumulus, or with clouds from which *virga* is falling.

Virga is rain that falls from high clouds and evaporates before it reaches the surface. In the process of evaporating, latent heat is absorbed from the surrounding air and a cold parcel of air is formed beneath the cloud; this may plummet earthward as a downburst or a microburst. It can sometimes be detected by eye as a ring of dust blown up where the microburst hits the ground and spreads out, or by sudden reversals of direction on a windsock. In extreme cases, microbursts have been known to blow hundreds of trees down in a radial pattern, and to blow trains off the rails. Microbursts and downbursts may appear very suddenly and may or may not last very long. A typical life cycle lasts about 15 minutes from when the very strong shaft of downdrafts first strikes the ground. The wind spreads out horizontally in all directions, usually with the horizontal winds increasing in strength for the first 5 minutes and peak wind strength lasting 2–4 minutes.

Even though one airplane might make an approach satisfactorily underneath a large cloud, a following aircraft may not. There are a number of accidents to illustrate this. Always be on the lookout for large clouds with a bulging undersurface, for virga, or for any other indication of downbursts or microbursts.

Note. Operational factors relating to thunderstorms and microbursts are covered in chapter 17.

Figure 15-17 Some types of microbursts.

Tornados and Water Spouts

A strongly growing large cumuliform cloud may "suck" air into it as an updraft. These strong updrafts may commence from just beneath the base of the cloud, or they may commence well below the cloud base from near the ground, from where they may raise objects or, if over a water surface, cause a water spout.

Tornados and water spouts are rotating funnels of air of small diameter. The central pressure will be much lower than in the surrounding air, creating a vortex of wind with speeds possibly exceeding 150 knots.

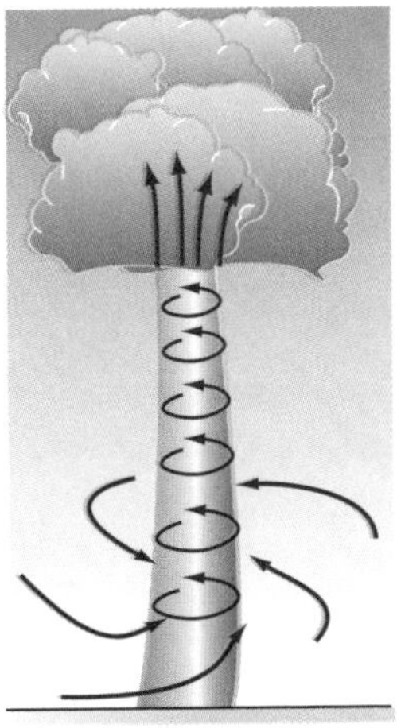

Figure 15-18 A tornado.

CPL

Lifted Index

The *lifted index* of a parcel of air is a measure of its stability. The lifted index is calculated by:

a. theoretically lifting the parcel of air from the surface to the 500-millibar pressure level, and calculating its temperature based on cooling adiabatically by expansion; then

b. subtracting this calculated value from the *actual* temperature of the air already at the 500 millibar pressure level.

$$\text{Lifted index} = \begin{array}{c}\text{air temperature}\\ \text{at 500 mb level}\end{array} - \begin{array}{c}\text{theoretical temperature}\\ \text{at 500 mb level if the}\\ \text{surface air is raised}\end{array}$$

If the "lifted" parcel of air has a temperature less than that existing in the actual air at the 500 mb pressure level, then the parcel would have no tendency to keep rising, and the lifted index would have a positive value—a *positive* lifted index indicates *stable* air.

If the lifted air is warmer than the environmental air, then it will tend to keep on rising, and the lifted index would have a negative value—a *negative* lifted index indicates *unstable* air.

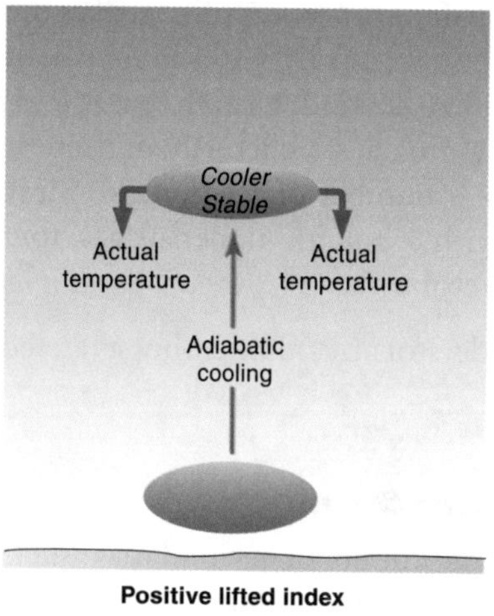

Figure 15-19 Positive lifted index.

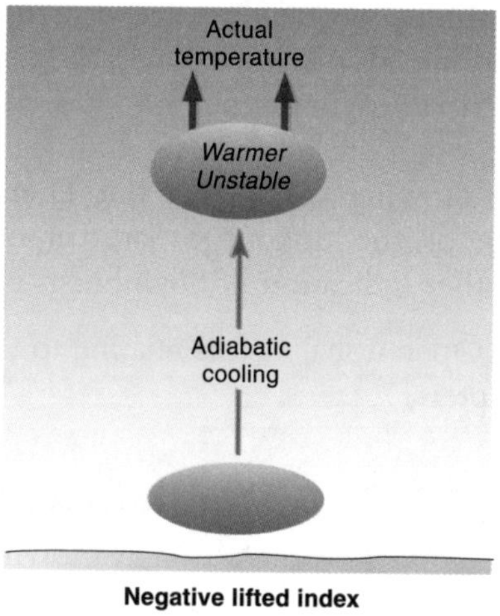

Figure 15-20 Negative lifted index.

End CPL

High-Level Clouds

Cirrus (Ci)

Cirrus clouds are detached clouds in the form of white, delicate filaments, or white or mostly white patches or narrow bands. These clouds have a fibrous appearance, or a silky sheen, or both. Their formation processes consist of widespread lifting, and they are composed of ice crystals.

Figure 15-21 Fibrous cirrus.

Figure 15-22 Dense cirrus with a silky sheen.

Figure 15-23 Cirrus with hooks caused by jet stream wind.

Cirrostratus (Cs)

Cirrostratus clouds are transparent, having a whitish cloud veil of fibrous or smooth appearance which totally or partly covers the sky, generally producing halo phenomena. They are formed by widespread lifting and are composed of ice crystals.

Figure 15-24 Cirrostratus—halo is visible.

Cirrocumulus (Cc)

Cirrocumulus clouds are thin, with a white layer, sheet or patch of cloud without shading composed of very small elements in the form of grains, ripples, etc., merged or separate, and more or less regularly arranged. Most of the elements have an apparent width of less than one degree. They are formed through turbulence or perturbations in cirrus or cirrostratus clouds and are composed of ice crystals.

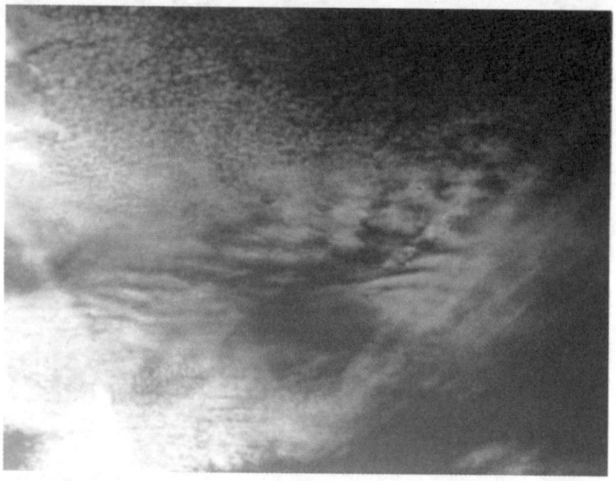

Figure 15-25 Cirrocumulus in grains—note halo to the left, indicating presence of ice crystals.

Figure 15-26
Cirrocumulus formed in ripples.

Middle-Level Clouds

Altostratus (As)

Altostratus clouds are a greyish or bluish cloud sheet or layer of striated, fibrous or uniform appearance, totally or partly covering the sky and having parts thin enough to reveal the sun at least vaguely, as if through ground glass. Altostratus does not show halo phenomena. They are formed through widespread lifting and may contain supercooled water droplets if not glaciated.

Figure 15-27
Thin altostratus—sun visible as through ground glass.

Figure 15-28
Thick, opaque altostratus—bluish grey, giving light rain.

Altocumulus (Ac)

Altocumulus clouds are white or grey, or both white and grey, patches, sheets or layers of cloud, generally with shading—composed of laminae, rounded masses, rolls, etc.—which are sometimes partly fibrous or diffuse and which may or may not be merged. Most of the regularly arranged small elements usually have an apparent width of between one and five degrees. They are formed through turbulence perturbations, thermal convection, orographic lifting, and the spreading of cumulus clouds. They often contain supercooled water droplets.

Figure 15-29 Broken layer of altocumulus—in rounded elements, formed by turbulence.

Figure 15-30 Sheet of altocumulus in rolls—formed in the shear between wind layers.

Figure 15-31
Lenticular (lens-shaped) altocumulus—formed in the crest of mountain waves; expect strong turbulence.

Figure 15-32
Altocumulus resulting from the spreading out of cumulus tops under a stable layer.

Figure 15-33 Altocumulus floccus—Ac in the form of "wool tufts." Both Ac castellanus and Ac floccus indicate instability and moisture in the middle troposphere, with the possibility of thunderstorms forming.

Figure 15-34 Altocumulus castellanus—"castles in the air."

Low-Level Clouds

Stratocumulus (Sc)

Stratocumulus clouds are grey or whitish, or both grey and whitish patches, sheets or layers of cloud, which almost always have dark parts composed of tessellations, rounded masses, rolls, etc., and are non-fibrous (except for virga), and which may or may not be merged. Most of the regularly arranged small elements have an apparent width of more than five degrees. They are formed through turbulence perturbations, orographic lifting and the spreading of cumulus clouds. They are generally composed of water droplets and may be supercooled above the freezing level.

Figure 15-35 Stratocumulus in a continuous layer, base around 2,000 ft AGL.

Figure 15-36 Stratocumulus in a broken layer, base around 4,000 ft AGL.

Stratus (St)

Stratus clouds generally comprise a grey cloud layer with a fairly uniform base, which may give drizzle, ice prisms or snow grains. When the sun is visible through the cloud, its outline is clearly discernible. Stratus does not show halo phenomena, except possibly at very low temperatures. Sometimes stratus appears in the form of ragged patches. These clouds are formed through radiation cooling coupled with turbulence and through orographic lifting. They are composed of water droplets at above-freezing temperatures and may be supercooled or glaciated above the freezing level.

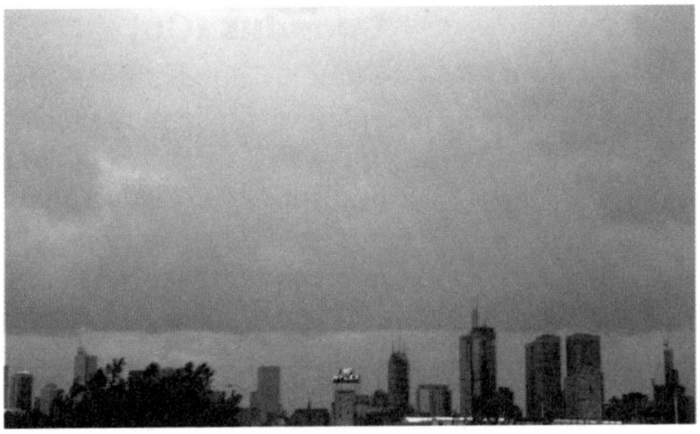

Figure 15-37 Broken stratus (stratus fractus) formed by the breaking up of a stratus layer.

Figure 15-38 stratus with a low base.

Figure 15-39 Edge of stratus sheet, base around 300 ft AGL (altostratus above).

Nimbostratus (Ns)

Nimbostratus clouds comprise a grey cloud layer, often dark, and their appearance is rendered diffuse by more or less continuously falling rain or snow, which in most cases reaches the ground. They are thick enough to blot out the sun. They are formed through widespread lifting and are composed of water drops and droplets. They may be supercooled above the freezing level, but if snowing are generally glaciated.

Figure 15-40 Nimbostratus.

Cumulus (Cu)

Cumulus clouds are detached clouds, generally dense and with sharp outlines, developing vertically in the form of rising mounds, domes or towers, of which the bulging upper part often resembles a cauliflower. The sunlit parts of these clouds are a most brilliant white. Their base is relatively dark and nearly horizontal. Sometimes cumulus is ragged. They are formed through thermal convection and are composed of water drops and droplets, and are often supercooled above the freezing level.

Figure 15-41 Cumulus of medium development.

Figure 15-42 Congested towering cumulus.

Cumulonimbus (Cb)

Cumulonimbus clouds are heavy and dense with a considerable vertical extent in the form of a mountain or huge towers. At least part of their upper portion is usually smooth, or fibrous or striated, and nearly always flattened. This part often spreads out in the shape of an anvil or vast plume. These clouds are formed through extreme thermal convection. They are composed of water drops and droplets below the freezing level, supercooled water drops and droplets above the freezing level and ice crystals at the top.

Figure 15-43 Cumulonimbus cloud in the early mature stage, starting to flatten at the top.

Figure 15-44
Line of cold-stream thunderstorms.

Figure 15-45
Classic, fully developed thunderstorm.

Figure 15-46
Mature Cb cloud, entering dissipating stage.

Figure 15-47 A heavy rain shower from a storm cell within a cumulonimbus cloud accompanying a cold front.

Figure 15-48
Lightning from an evening thunderstorm.

Figure 15-49
Tornadoes—to be avoided!

Frontal Activity

Figure 15-50 Weather associated with passage of a cold front.

Clouds Formed by Orographic Lifting

Figure 15-51
Clouds formed by broad lifting of moist, stable air.

Figure 15-52
Stationary caps on the peaks.

Inversion Effects

Figure 15-53 Sign of an Inversion in the early morning.

Microbursts

Figure 15-54 Photo sequence showing the development of a potentially destructive microburst.

Figure 15-55 A Wet microburst emanating from the base of a cumulonimbus cloud.

Summary of Cloud Types

	Cloud Type	Definition	Formation Processes	Composition
High-Level Cloud	Cirrus (Ci)	Detached clouds in the form of white, delicate filaments, or white or mostly white patches or narrow bands. These clouds have a fibrous (hair-like) appearance, or a silky sheen, or both.	Widespread lifting.	Ice crystals.
	Cirrostratus (Cs)	Transparent, whitish cloud veil of fibrous (hair-like) or smooth appearance, totally or partly covering the sky, and generally producing a halo phenomenon.	Widespread lifting.	Ice crystals.
	Cirrocumulus (Cc)	Thin, white layer, sheet or patch of cloud without shading, composed of very small elements in the form of grains, ripples, etc., merged or separate, and more or less regularly arranged. Most of the elements have an apparent width of less than one degree.	Turbulence or perturbations in Ci or Cs.	Ice crystals.
Medium-Level Cloud	Altostratus (As)	Greyish or bluish cloud sheet or layer of striated, fibrous or uniform appearance, totally or partly covering the sky, and having parts thin enough to reveal the sun at least vaguely, as if through ground glass. Altostratus does not show halo phenomena.	Widespread lifting.	Supercooled water droplets predominate unless glaciated.
	Altocumulus (Ac)	White or grey, or both white and grey patch, sheet or layer of cloud, generally with shading, composed of laminae, rounded masses, rolls, etc., which are sometimes partly fibrous or diffuse, and which may or may not be merged. Most of the regularly arranged small elements usually have an apparent width of between one and five degrees.	Turbulence perturbations, thermal convection, orographic lifting, spreading of Cu.	Often contain supercooled water droplets.
Low-Level Cloud	Nimbostratus (Ns)	Grey cloud layer, often dark, the appearance of which is rendered diffuse by more or less continuously falling rain or snow, which in most cases reaches the ground. It is thick enough to blot out the sun.	Widespread lifting.	Water drops and droplets; may contain supercooled drops and droplets above the freezing level.
	Stratocumulus (Sc)	Grey or whitish, or both grey and whitish, patch, sheet or layer of cloud which almost always has dark parts composed of tessellations, rounded masses, rolls, etc., which are non-fibrous (except for virga), and which may or may not be merged. Most of the regularly arranged small elements have an apparent width of more than five degrees.	Turbulence perturbations, orographic lifting, spreading of Cu.	Water droplets. May be supercooled above the freezing level.
	Stratus (St)	Generally grey cloud layer with a fairly uniform base, which may give drizzle, ice prisms or snow grains. When the sun is visible through the cloud, its outline is clearly discernible. Stratus does not show halo phenomena, except possibly at very low temperatures. Sometimes stratus appears in the form of ragged patches.	Radiation cooling coupled with turbulence, orographic lifting.	Water drops and droplets below the freezing level; may be supercooled or glaciated above the freezing level.
	Cumulus (Cu)	Detached clouds, generally dense and with sharp outlines, developing vertically in the form of rising mounds, domes or towers, of which the bulging upper part often resembles a cauliflower. The sunlit parts of these clouds are a most brilliant white. Their base is relatively dark and nearly horizontal. Sometimes cumulus is ragged.	Thermal convection.	Water drops and droplets below the freezing level; may be supercooled or glaciated above the freezing level.
	Cumulonimbus (Cb)	Heavy and dense cloud, with a considerable vertical extent, in the form of a mountain or huge towers. At least part of its upper portion is usually smooth, or fibrous or striated, and nearly always flattened. This part often spreads out in the shape of an anvil or vast plume.	Extreme thermal convection.	Water drops and droplets below the freezing level; supercooled water drops and droplets above freezing level; ice crystals at the top.

Computerized Weather Displays

Throughout the United States and many other parts of the world, weather presentations are becoming increasingly sophisticated and useful, thanks to the advent of high-quality data from weather satellites and the use of computer-enhancement techniques.

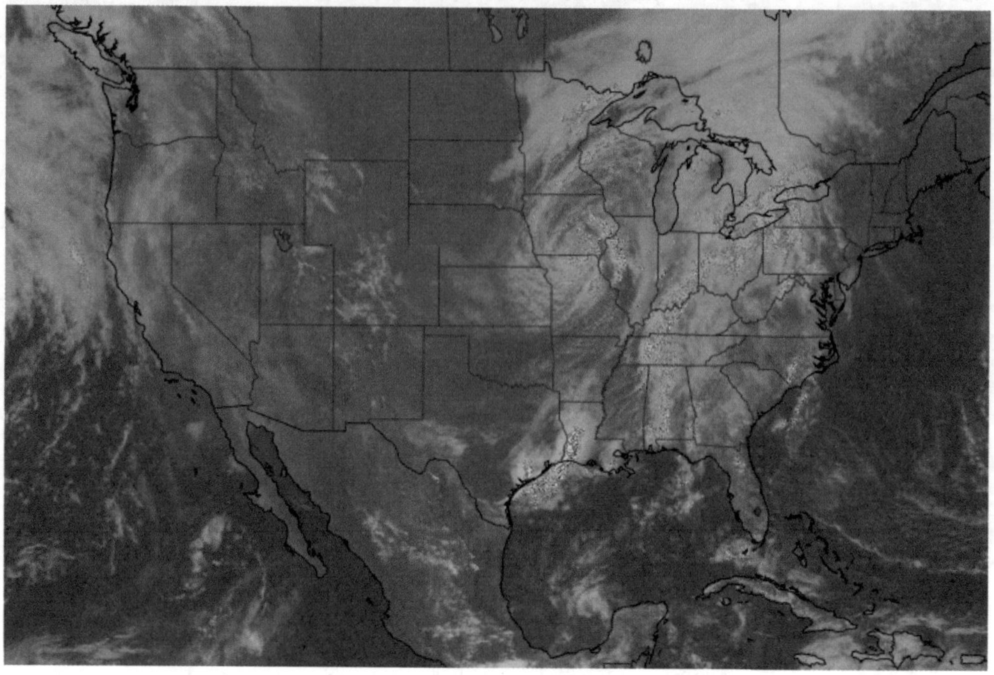

Figure 15-56 Example of NOAA Aviation Weather Overview with satellite, visible fog, and radar imagery overlay.

Review 15
Clouds and Thunderstorms

Clouds

1. When do clouds, fog, or dew form?
2. Clouds are divided into four families. What are these divisions based on?
3. Name the four families of clouds.
4. What are clouds with a base below approximately 6,500 feet known as?
5. What do the suffix "*-nimbus*" and the prefix "*nimbo-*" mean?
6. Clouds broken into fragments are often identified by which suffix?
7. What are the processes by which moisture is added to unsaturated air?
8. What is evaporation?
9. What is sublimation?
10. What does the amount of water vapor that air can hold largely depend on?
11. What is meant by the term dewpoint?
12. If air in contact with the ground cools to its dewpoint temperature, which is above freezing, the excess water vapor will condense. What will be formed?
13. Describe the conditions necessary for frost to form.
14. What sort of conditions are associated with stratiform cloud?
15. Convective turbulence is indicated by which cloud type?
16. Give the following (°C/feet):
    - **a.** dry adiabatic lapse rate.
    - **b.** saturated adiabatic lapse rate.
    - **c.** ambient lapse rate in the standard atmosphere for air that is not rising or sinking.
17. If a stable airmass is forced to ascend a mountain slope, what type of cloud is most likely to develop?
18. If an unstable air mass is forced upward, what type of clouds can be expected?
19. There is an unstable cold air mass moving over a warm surface.
    - **a.** What type of cloud can this give rise to?
    - **b.** What will the flying conditions be like?
    - **c.** What sort of visibility can be expected?
20. What are high-level clouds mainly composed of?
21. Which clouds have the greatest turbulence?
22. How do flying conditions above fair weather cumulus clouds compare to conditions below them?
23. What are the features of lenticular cloud?
24. What is virga?
25. Will evaporating rain cause the air temperature to increase?
26. Are strong downdrafts possible beneath virga?
27. What is a microburst?
28. On average, temperature and dewpoint in rising unsaturated air converge by how many degrees for each 1,000 feet of height gained? (Give your answer in both °C and °F.)
29. What is the approximate cloud base of cumulus clouds if the temperature at 1,000 feet MSL is 70°F and the dewpoint is 48°F?
30. The surface air temperature at an airport is 82°F and the dewpoint is 38°F.
    - **a.** What is the cloud base AGL if the air is unstable and convective cumuliform cloud develops?
    - **b.** If the airport has an elevation 1,500 feet MSL, what is the approximate cloud base MSL?

Thunderstorms

31. Thunderstorms are associated with which cloud type?
32. Do all thunderstorms have lightning?
33. What three conditions are necessary for the formation of thunderstorms?
34. What is meant by the term "unstable lapse rate?"
35. Name the three stages of a typical thunderstorm.
36. What is the main characteristic of each of the following stages of a thunderstorm?
    - **a.** The cumulus stage.
    - **b.** The mature stage.
    - **c.** The dissipating stage.

37. Rain is falling from the base of a storm cloud. What does this indicate?
38. During which stage do thunderstorms reach their greatest intensity?
39. What are embedded thunderstorms?
40. The most hazardous flying conditions associated with a thunderstorm are due to which of the following:
    a. lightening.
    b. static electricity.
    c. windshear.
    d. turbulence.
    e. hail.
    f. reduced visibility.
41. What is a squall line?

Commercial Review

42. As the temperature/dewpoint spread reduces, what happens to the relative humidity?
43. What is the approximate base of cumulus clouds if the temperature at 2,000 feet MSL is 70°F and the dewpoint is 52°F?
44. What height AGL would you expect the bases of convective-type cumuliform cloud to form if the METAR for the airport indicates temperature 89°F and dewpoint 45°F?
45. What is an unstable parcel of air?
46. What determines the structure or type of clouds formed as a result of air being forced to ascend?
47. What sort of air does a negative lifted index indicate?
48. When conditionally unstable air with high-moisture content and very warm surface temperature is forecast, one can expect what type of weather?
49. Hail is most likely to be associated with which cloud type?
50. Which combination of weather-producing variables would likely result in cumuliform-type clouds, good visibility, and showery rain?
51. How does airborne weather radar identify areas of possible turbulence?
52. If airborne weather radar is indicating an extremely intense thunderstorm echo, this thunderstorm should be avoided by a distance of at least:
    a. 20 miles.
    b. 25 miles.
    c. 30 miles.
53. Two storms are causing intense weather radar echoes. What is the minimum distance that should exist between these two storms before any attempt is made to fly between them? Explain the reason for this minimum distance.
54. If there are no echoes showing on an airborne weather radarscope, are you guaranteed that good flying conditions exist?
55. The formation of predominantly stratiform or predominantly cumuliform clouds is dependent on the:
    a. source of lift.
    b. stability of the air being lifted.
    c. temperature of the air being lifted.
56. From which measurement of the atmosphere can stability be determined?
57. What visible signs indicate extreme turbulence in thunderstorms?
    a. Base of the clouds near the surface, heavy rain, and hail.
    b. Low ceiling and visibility, hail and precipitation static.
    c. Cumulonimbus clouds, very frequent lightning, and roll clouds.
58. The most severe weather conditions, such as destructive winds, heavy hail, and tornados, are generally associated with:
    a. fast-moving warm fronts.
    b. slow moving warm fronts.
    c. squall lines and steady-state thunderstorms.
59. What minimum distance should exist between intense radar echoes before any attempt is made to fly between these thunderstorms?
    a. 20 miles.
    b. 30 miles.
    c. 40 miles.

Answers are given on page 699.

Air Masses and Frontal Weather 16

Air Masses

An air mass is a large parcel of air with fairly consistent properties (such as temperature and moisture content) throughout. It is usual to classify an air mass according to:

- its origin;
- its path over the earth's surface; and
- whether the air is diverging or converging.

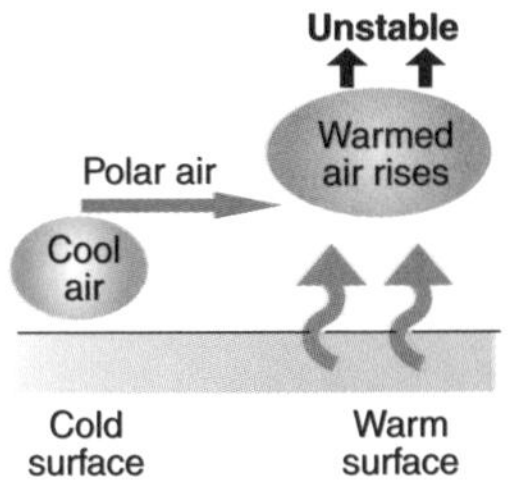

Figure 16-1
Polar air warms and becomes unstable.

Origin and Path

A *polar* air mass originating in the polar regions will, of course, be very cold. A *tropical* air mass originating from near the equator will be very warm. *Maritime air* flowing over an ocean will absorb moisture and tend to become saturated in its lower levels; *continental air* flowing over a land mass will remain reasonably dry since little water is available for evaporation. Polar air flowing toward the lower latitudes will be warmed from below and so become unstable. Conversely, tropical air flowing to higher latitudes will be cooled from below and so become more stable (figures 16-1 and 16-2).

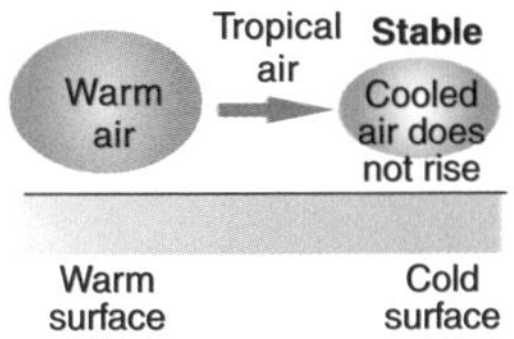

Figure 16-2
Tropical air cools and becomes stable.

> **Note.** Air masses in the polar and tropical regions usually overlie a surface long enough to take on its properties (heat and moisture), whereas air masses in the mid-latitude areas are constantly being disturbed by weather and so do not have such definite characteristics.

Divergence or Convergence

An upper air mass influenced by the *divergence* of air flowing out of a high-pressure system at the earth's surface will slowly sink (known as subsidence) and become warmer, drier and more stable. An upper air mass influenced by *convergence* as air flows into a low-pressure system at the surface will be forced to rise slowly, becoming cooler, moister

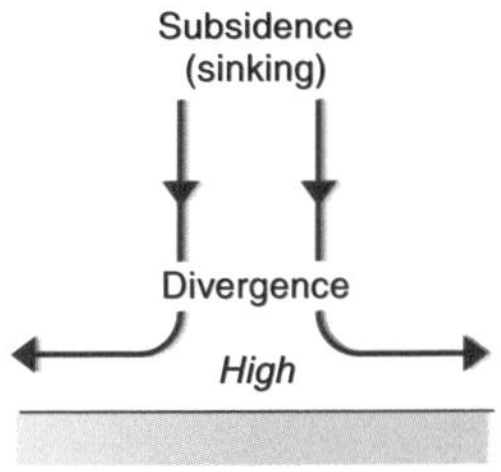

Figure 16-3
Subsiding air, resulting from divergence, is stable.

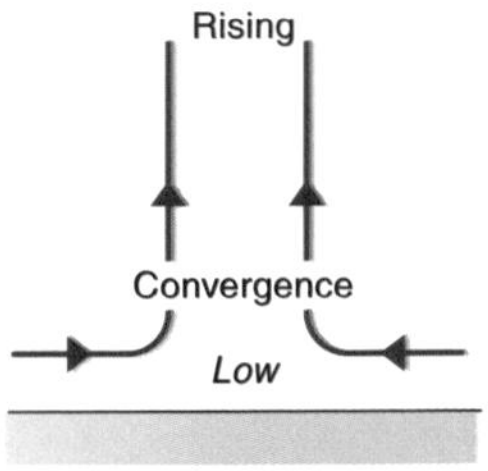

Figure 16-4
Rising air, resulting from convergence, is unstable.

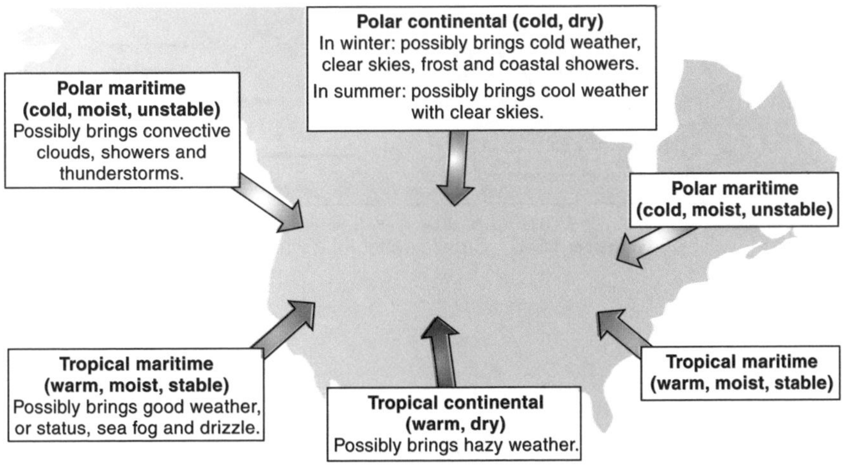

Figure 16-5 Air masses that affect North America.

and less stable. The sources of most air masses that affect North America are shown below, classified by temperature and moisture level. Note that the polar continental air mass from Canada can be modified by the addition of moisture over the Great Lakes.

Frontal Weather

Air masses have different characteristics, depending on their origin and the type of surface over which they have been passing. Because of these differences there is usually a distinct division between adjacent air masses. The boundary between two adjacent air masses is called a *front*, and there are two basic types—cold fronts and warm fronts.

Frontal activity describes the interaction between the air masses, as one mass replaces the other. When a front passes a point on the earth, or when you fly through a front, there is always a wind change and a temperature change (which may be large or small). The term *frontal zone* refers to the area affected by the front.

The Warm Front

If two air masses meet so that the warmer air replaces the cooler air at the surface, a *warm front* is said to exist. The boundary at the earth's surface between the two air masses is represented on a weather chart by a line with semicircles pointed in the direction of movement. The slope formed in a warm front, as the warm air slides up over the cold air, is fairly shallow and so the cloud that forms in the (usually quite stable) rising warm air is likely to be stratiform. In a warm front the frontal air at altitude is actually well ahead of the frontal line shown at ground level on the weather chart. The cirrus clouds could be some 600 miles ahead of the surface front, and rain could be falling up to approximately 200 miles ahead of it. The slope of the warm front is typically 1 in 150, much flatter than a cold front, and has been exaggerated in figure 16-6.

Rain falling into the cooler air beneath the surface of the warm front may cause precipitation-induced fog. If the air beneath the front is below freezing, freezing rain from the warmer air above may cause severe icing on an airplane.

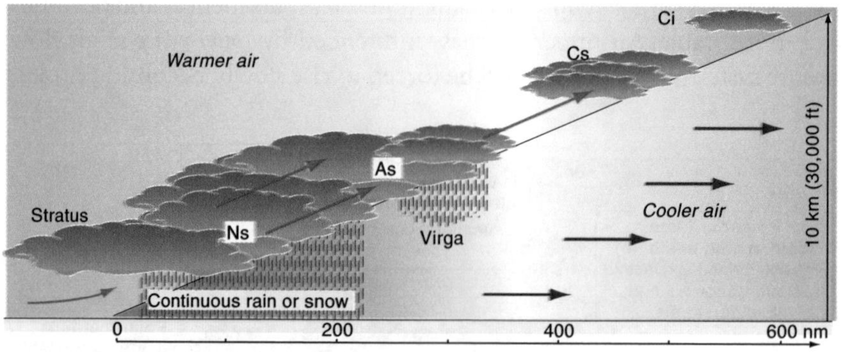

Figure 16-6 Cross section of a warm front.

Observation from the Ground

As a warm front gradually passes, an observer on the ground may first see high cirrus clouds, which will slowly be followed by a lowering base of cirrostratus, altostratus and nimbostratus. Rain may be falling from the altostratus and possibly evaporating before it reaches the ground (virga) and from the nimbostratus. The rain from the nimbostratus may be continuous until the warm front passes and may, by adding moisture to the cold air beneath the front, cause fog. Visibility may be quite poor.

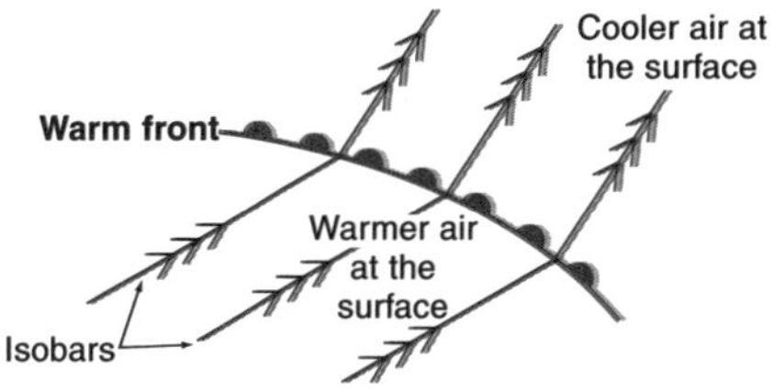

Figure 16-7
Depiction of a warm front on a weather chart.

The *atmospheric* (or barometric) *pressure* will normally fall continuously as the warm front approaches, and, as it passes, either stop falling or fall at a lower rate. The *air temperature* will rise as the warm air moves in over the surface. The warm air will hold more moisture than the cold air, and the dewpoint temperature in the warmer air will be higher. Relative humidity will decrease, and any frontal fog may dissipate. There is always a wind change as a front passes. In the Northern Hemisphere, the *wind direction* will *veer* (a clockwise change of direction) as the warm front passes. Behind the warm front, and after it passes, there is likely to be stratus clouds; the visibility may still be poor. Weather associated with a warm front may extend over several hundred miles.

The general characteristics of a warm front are:
- lowering stratiform clouds;
- increasing rain, with the possibility of poor visibility and fog;
- possible low-level windshear before the warm front passes;
- falling atmospheric pressure that slows down or stops;
- winds veering (clockwise change of direction); and
- rising air temperature.

Observation from the Air

What a pilot sees, and in which order, will depend on the direction of flight. You may see a gradually lowering cloud base if in the cold sector underneath the warm air and flying toward the warm front, with steady rain falling. If the airplane is at subzero temperatures, the rain may freeze and form ice on the wings, thereby decreasing their aerodynamic qualities. The clouds may be as low as ground level (that is, hill fog) and sometimes the lower layers of stratiform clouds can conceal cumulonimbus and thunderstorm activity. Visibility may be quite poor. There will be a wind change either side of the front and a change of the airplane's heading may be required to maintain course.

The Cold Front

If a cooler air mass undercuts a mass of warm air and displaces it at the surface, a *cold front* is said to occur. The slope between the two air masses in a well-developed cold front is much steeper than a warm front, and typically about 1 in 50. This is due to surface friction tending to slow down the fast-moving cold air near ground level, and the frontal weather may occupy a band of only 30 to 50 miles.

The boundary between the two air masses at the surface is shown on weather charts as a line with barbs pointing in the direction of travel of the front. The cold front moves quite rapidly, with the cooler frontal air at altitude lagging behind that at the surface. The air that is forced to rise with the passage of a cold front is *unstable* and so the clouds that form are cumuliform in nature—for example, cumulus and cumulonimbus. Severe weather hazardous to aviation, such as thunderstorm activity, squall lines, severe turbulence and windshear, may accompany the passage of a cold front. Low-level windshear and turbulence is possible at an airport at or just after a cold front passes.

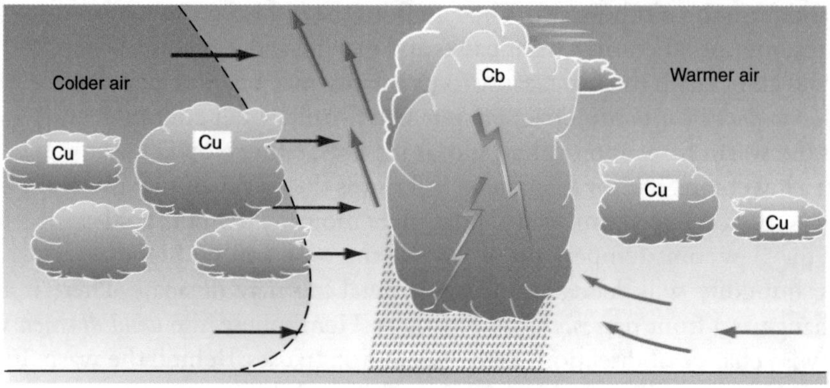

Figure 16-8 Cross section of a cold front.

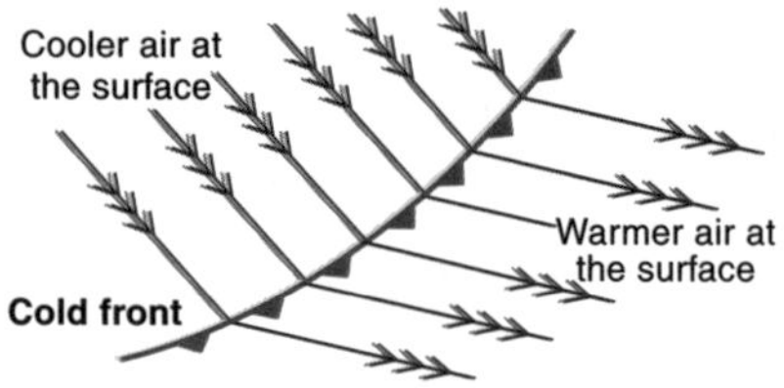

Figure 16-9
Depiction of a cold front on a weather chart.

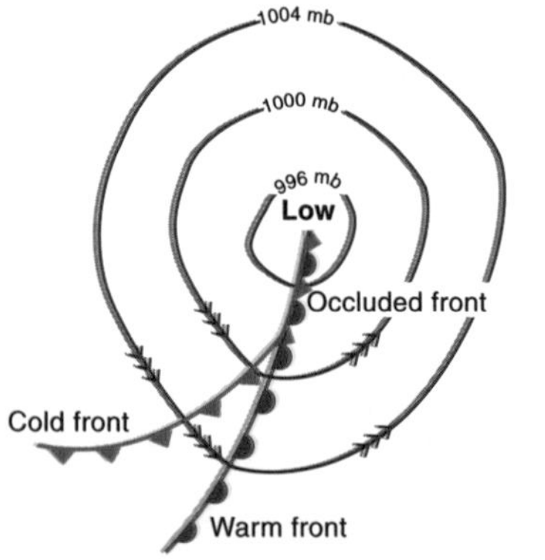

Figure 16-10
Depiction of an occluded front on a weather map.

Observation from the Ground

The atmospheric pressure will fall as a cold front approaches and the change in weather with its passage may be quite pronounced. Prior to the cold front arriving, there may be middle-level altostratus or altocumulus present. Accompanying the front, there may be cumulus and possibly cumulonimbus clouds with heavy rain showers, thunderstorm activity and squalls, with a sudden drop in temperature and a veering wind direction as the front passes. The cooler air mass will contain less moisture than the warm air, and so the dewpoint temperature after the cold front has passed will be lower. Once the cold front has passed, the pressure may rise rapidly.

The general characteristics of a cold front are:

- cumuliform cloud—cumulus, cumulonimbus;
- often a sudden drop in temperature, and a lower dewpoint temperature;
- possible low-level windshear as or just after the front passes;
- a veering of the wind direction (same as for a warm front); and
- a falling pressure that rises once the front is past.

Observation from the Air

Flying through a cold front may require diversions to avoid weather. There may be thunderstorm activity, violent winds (both horizontal and vertical) from cumulonimbus clouds, squall lines, windshear, heavy showers of rain or hail, and severe turbulence. Icing could be a problem. Visibility away from the showers and the clouds may be quite good, but it is still a good idea for a pilot to consider avoiding the strong weather activity that accompanies many cold fronts. A squall line may form ahead of the front.

The Occluded Front

Because cold fronts usually travel much faster than warm fronts, it often happens that a cold front overtakes a warm front, creating an *occlusion* (or occluded front). This may happen in the final stages of a frontal depression (which is discussed shortly). Three air masses are involved and their vertical passage, one to the other, will depend on their relative temperatures. Because the air circulating around the northern side of a low is closer to the pole, it is more likely to be modified to a lower temperature than the more-southerly air. Therefore, it is common for a cold front to occur in the southwest sector of a low (and a warm front in the eastern sector). The occluded front is depicted on charts by a line with alternating barbs and semicircles pointing in the direction of motion of the front.

The clouds that are associated with an occluded front will depend on what clouds are associated with the individual cold and warm fronts. It is not unusual to have cumuliform clouds from the cold front as well as stratiform clouds from the warm front. Sometimes the stratiform clouds can conceal thunderstorm activity, a situation known as embedded thunderstorms. Severe weather can occur in the early stages of an occlusion as unstable air is forced upward, but this period is often short.

Flight through an occluded front may involve encountering intense weather, as both a cold front and a warm front are involved, with a warm air mass being squeezed up between them. The wind direction will be different either side of the front.

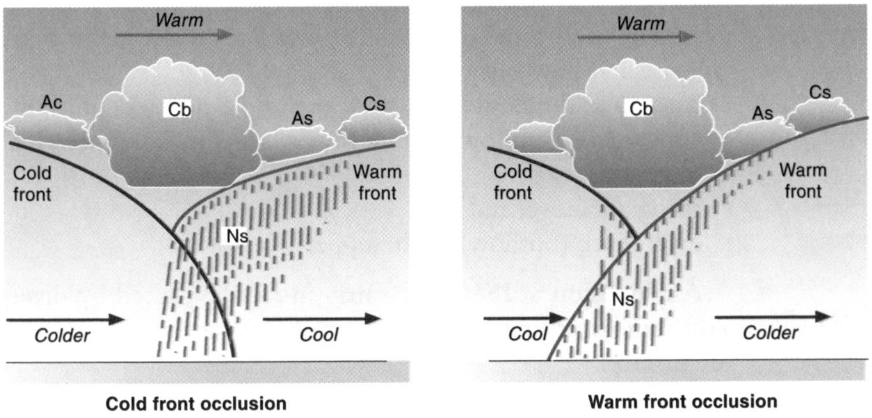

Figure 16-11 Cross sections of occluded fronts.

The Stationary Front

A front that is not moving—or moving very slowly at, say, less than 5 knots—is called a *stationary front*; it may influence the weather in that area for a period of days. Winds may be blowing behind each side of the front (perhaps in opposite directions) and within the frontal zone, and the weather may be a mixture of both cold front and warm front weather, although any thunderstorm activity will probably be less than in a fast-moving cold front.

A stationary front is depicted on weather charts by a line with barbs on one side and semicircles on the other.

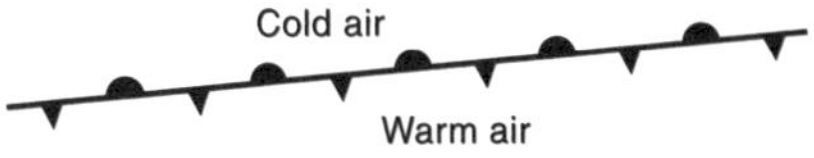

Figure 16-12
Depiction of a stationary front.

The Development and Decay of Fronts

The development of a front as one air mass overtakes or confronts another, or when strong temperature differences develop within an air mass, is called *frontogenesis*. The decay or dissipation of a front, as the frontal energy is expended and the temperature and pressure differences diminish, is called *frontolysis*.

Areas of Low Pressure

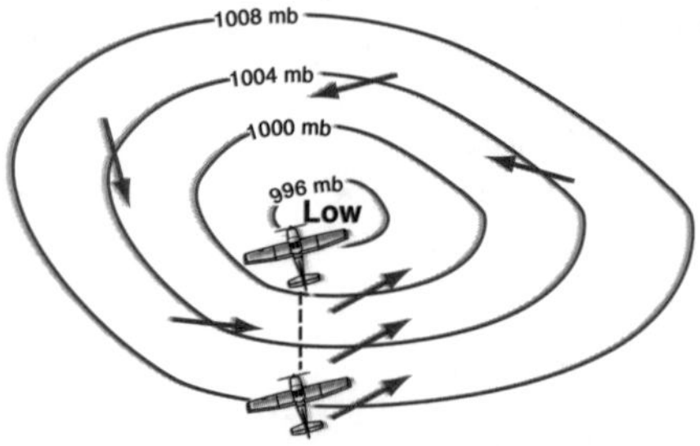

Figure 16-13
A depression or low-pressure system.

A *depression* or *low* is a region of low pressure at the surface, the pressure rising as you move away from its center. A low is depicted on a weather chart by a series of concentric isobars joining places of equal sea level pressure, with the lowest pressure in the center. In the northern hemisphere, winds circulate counterclockwise around a low. Flying toward a low, an airplane will experience right drift.

Depressions generally are more intense than highs, being spread over a smaller area and with a stronger pressure gradient (change of pressure with distance). The more intense the depression, the "deeper" it is said to be. Lows move faster across the face of the earth than highs and do not last as long. Because the pressure at the surface in the center of a depression is lower than in the surrounding areas, there will be an inflow of air, known as *convergence*, with the wind strength increasing toward the center of the low. The air above the depression will rise and flow outward.

The three-dimensional pattern of airflow near a depression is:

- convergence (inflow) in the lower layers in a counterclockwise direction;
- rising air above; and
- divergence (outflow) in the upper layers.

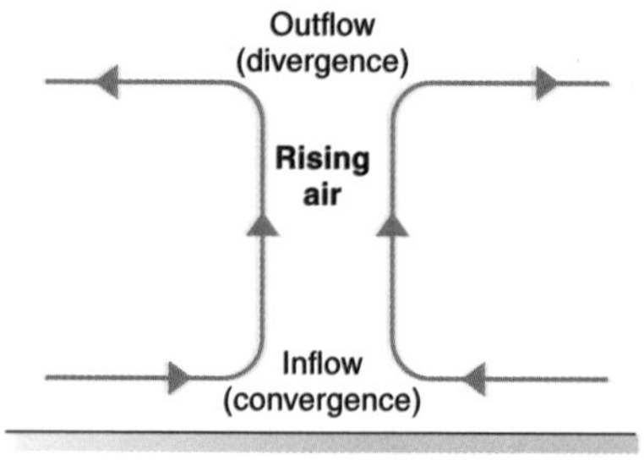

Figure 16-14
The three dimensional flow of air near a low.

A depression at the surface may in fact be caused by divergence aloft removing air faster than it can be replaced by convergence at the surface.

Weather Associated with a Depression

In a depression, the rising air will be cooling and so clouds will tend to form. Instability in the rising air may lead to quite large vertical development of cumuliform clouds accompanied by rain showers. Good visibility (except in the showers), may be expected since the vertical motion will tend to carry away all the particles suspended in the air. Some turbulence can be expected.

Troughs of Low Pressure

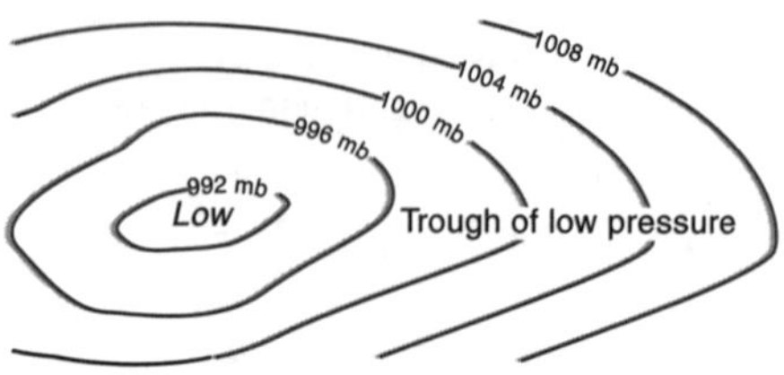

Figure 16-15 A trough.

A V-shaped extension of isobars from a region of low pressure is called a *trough*. Air will flow into it at the surface (convergence) and rise. If the air is unstable, weather similar to that in a depression or a cold front will occur—for example, cumuliform cloud, possibly with cumulonimbus and thunderstorm activity. The trough may in fact be associated with a front. Less prominent troughs, possibly more U-shaped than V-shaped, will generally have less severe weather.

The Wave or Frontal Depression

The boundary between two air masses moving (relative to one another) side by side is often distorted by the warmer air bulging into the cold air mass, with the bulge moving along like a wave. This is known as a *frontal wave*.

The leading edge of the bulge of warm air is a warm front and its rear edge is a cold front. The pressure near the tip of the wave falls sharply and so a depression forms, along with a warm front, a cold front, and possibly an occlusion. It is usual for the cold front to move faster across the surface than the warm front, but even then, the cold front moves only relatively slowly. Frontal waves can also form on a stationary front.

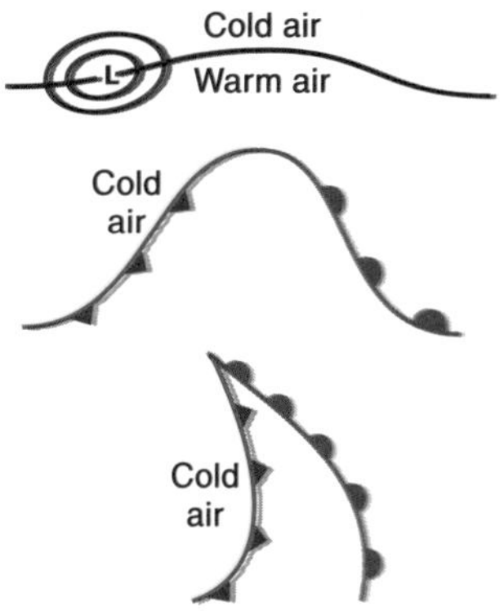

Figure 16-16
The frontal depression.

The Hurricane or Tropical Revolving Storm

Hurricanes are intense cyclonic depressions that can be both violent and destructive. They originate over warm tropical oceans at about 10°–20° latitude during certain periods of the year, but often move into the mid-latitudes, especially in the eastern United States, which is threatened by such storms from the Atlantic, the Gulf of Mexico and the Caribbean. Hurricanes also form in the Pacific off the west coast of Mexico, but rarely threaten the mainland United States or Hawaii. They do sometimes, however, bring heavy clouds and rain to the southwestern United States. Occasionally, weak troughs in these tropical areas develop into intense depressions. Air converges in the lower levels, flows into the depression and then rises—the warm, moist air forming large cumulus and cumulonimbus clouds. The very deep depression may be only quite small (200–300 miles in diameter) compared to the typical depression in temperate latitudes, but its central pressure can be extremely low. See figure 16-17.

Tropical revolving storms are best avoided by all aircraft.

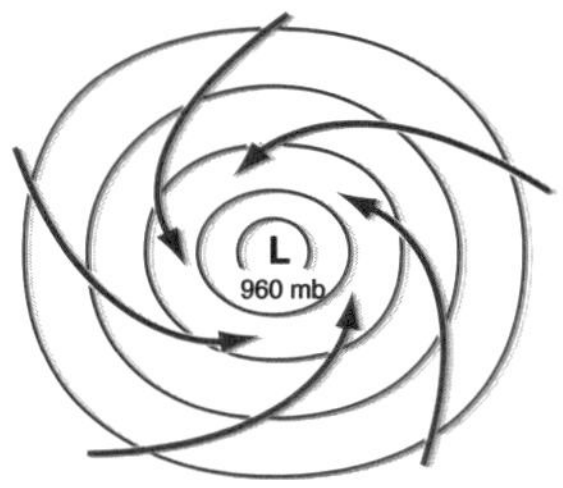

Figure 16-17
A hurricane or tropical revolving storm.

Winds in hurricanes can exceed 100 knots, with heavy showers and thunderstorm activity becoming increasingly frequent as the center of the storm approaches. Despite the strong winds, hurricanes move quite slowly and usually only dissipate after encountering a land mass, which gradually weakens the depression through surface friction. They are then usually classified as tropical storms.

The *eye* of a hurricane is often only some 10 NM in diameter, with light winds and broken cloud. It is characterized by very warm subsiding air. Once the eye has passed, a very strong wind from the opposite direction will occur. In the northern hemisphere, if an aircraft is experiencing pronounced right drift due to a strong wind from the left, the eye of the hurricane is ahead. In addition to the term hurricane, the tropical revolving storm is also known by other names in different parts of the world, such as *tropical cyclone* in Australia and the South Pacific, and *typhoon* in the South China Sea.

Subsiding air is very stable.

Areas of High Pressure

An *anticyclone* or *high* is an area of high pressure at the surface surrounded by roughly concentric isobars. Highs are generally greater in extent than lows, but with a weaker pressure gradient and slower moving, although they are more persistent than lows and last longer. In the Northern Hemisphere, the wind circulates clockwise around the center of a high. Flying toward a high an aircraft will experience left drift.

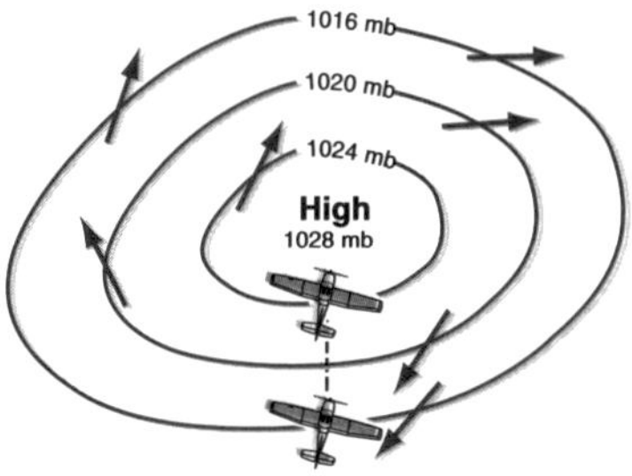

Figure 16-18
The anticyclone or high.

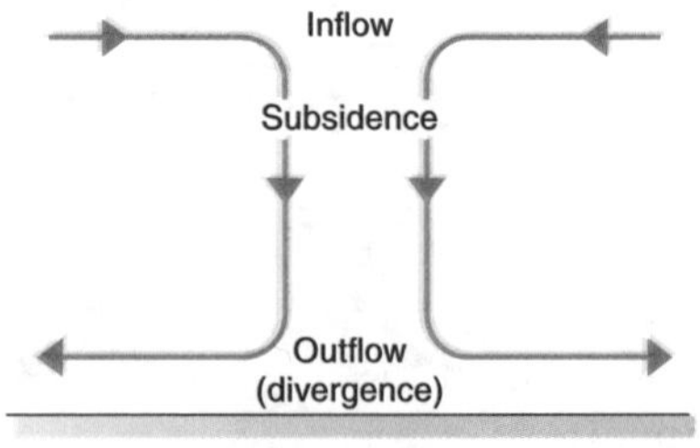

Figure 16-19
The three-dimensional flow of air near a high.

The *three-dimensional flow* of air associated with an anticyclone is:

- an outflow of air from the high-pressure area in the lower layer of the atmosphere (divergence) in a clockwise direction; with
- slow subsidence of air over a wide area from above; and
- an inflow of air in the upper layers (convergence).

The high-pressure area at the surface originates when the convergence in the upper layers adds air faster than the divergence in the lower layers removes it.

Weather Associated with a High

The subsiding air in a high-pressure system will be warming as it descends. Cloud will tend to disperse as the dewpoint temperature is exceeded and the relative humidity decreases. It is possible that the subsiding air may warm sufficiently to create an *inversion*, with the upper air that is descending warming to a temperature higher than that of air beneath it, and possibly causing stratiform clouds to form (stratocumulus, stratus) and/or trapping smoke, haze and dust beneath it. This can happen in winter in some parts of the country, leading to rather gloomy days with poor flight visibility. In summer, heating by the sun may disperse the clouds, leading to a fine but hazy day.

Subsidence inversions associated with an area of high pressure can be very strong indeed, causing phenomena such as the smog and gloom common in Los Angeles. If the sky remains clear at night, which is often the case with high-pressure systems, greater cooling of the earth's surface by radiation heat-loss may lead to the formation of radiation fog. If the high pressure is situated entirely over land, the weather may be dry and cloudless but, with any air flowing in from the sea, extensive stratiform clouds in the lower levels can occur, possibly leading to steady precipitation. In stable air, there is usually little or no turbulence.

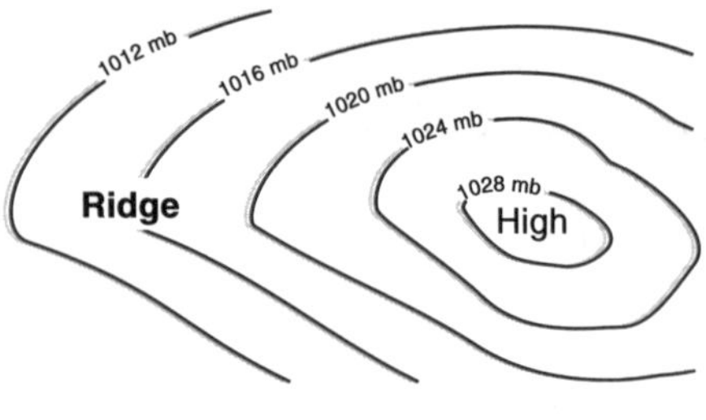

Figure 16-20 A ridge.

A Ridge of High Pressure

Isobars which extend out from a high-pressure system in a U-shape indicate a ridge of high pressure (like a ridge extending from a mountain). Weather conditions associated with a ridge are, in general, similar to the weather found with anticyclones.

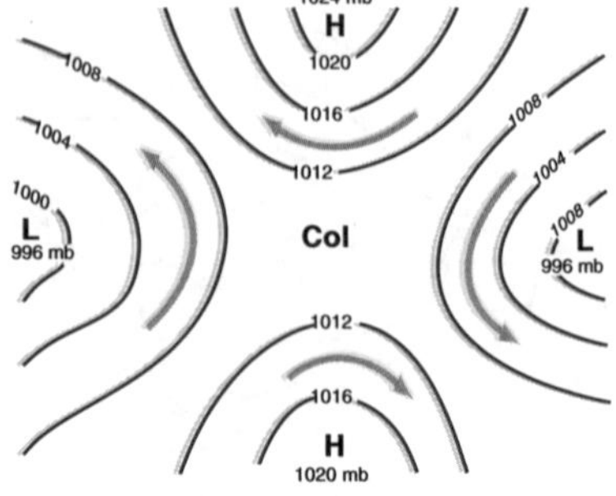

Figure 16-21 A col.

A Col

The area of almost constant pressure (and therefore indicated by a few very widely spaced isobars) that exists between two highs and two lows is called a *col*. It is like a saddle on a mountain ridge. Light winds are often associated with cols, with fog a possibility in winter and high temperatures in summer possibly leading to showers or thunderstorms.

Review 16

Air Masses and Frontal Weather

1. What is an air mass?
2. True or false? A polar maritime air mass will be cold and dry.
3. A polar air mass moving toward the warmer mid-latitudes will tend to warm from below. Will it become less stable as a result?
4. Does unstable air tend to sink?
5. If unstable air contains sufficient moisture, what sort of clouds will form?
6. True or false? A polar continental air mass will be cold and dry.
7. True or false? A tropical continental air mass will be warm and moist.
8. True or false? A tropical maritime air mass will be warm and moist.
9. Is it possible for a polar continental air mass moving down from Canada to have its moisture content modified by the Great Lakes?
10. What is the boundary layer between two different air masses referred to as?
11. Which weather phenomenon will always occur when flying across a front:
    - **a.** a change in wind direction.
    - **b.** a change in type of precipitation.
    - **c.** a change in stability of the airmass.
12. Steady precipitation preceding a front is an indication of:
    - **a.** stratiform clouds with moderate turbulence.
    - **b.** cumuliform clouds with little or no turbulence.
    - **c.** stratiform clouds with little or no turbulence.
13. What sort of change will usually occur whenever a front passes?
14. What is a warm front?
15. What is a cold front?
16. Compare cold and warm fronts in terms of slope and movement.
17. As a cold front forces warm air aloft, what sort of clouds are likely to develop?
18. What is an occluded front?
19. What is a stationary front?

Commercial Review

20. What is a high-pressure area or ridge?
21. What is a low-pressure area or trough?
22. The general circulation of air associated with a high-pressure area in the Northern Hemisphere is:
    - **a.** outward, downward, and clockwise.
    - **b.** outward, upward, and counterclockwise.
    - **c.** inward, downward, and counterclockwise.
23. When flying into a low-pressure area in the Northern Hemisphere, the wind direction and velocity will be from the:
    - **a.** left and decreasing.
    - **b.** left and increasing.
    - **c.** right and decreasing.
24. Which is true for a cold front occlusion?
    - **a.** Air ahead of the warm front is colder than the air behind the overtaking cold front.
    - **b.** The air ahead of the warm front is warmer than the air behind the overtaking cold front.
    - **c.** The air ahead of the warm front has the same temperature as the air behind the overtaking cold front.
25. Which in-flight hazard is most commonly associated with warm fronts?
    - **a.** Advection fog.
    - **b.** Radiation fog.
    - **c.** Precipitation-induced fog.
26. What are ice pellets encountered during flight normally evidence of?
27. A weather chart shows a particular front as a line with barbs on one side and semicircles on the other. What sort of front does this indicate?
28. Squall lines often develop ahead of which sort of front?
29. What sort of fronts do frontal waves normally form on?
30. With a cold front, when is the most critical period for low-level windshear above an airport?

Answers are given on page 700.

Operational Weather Factors 17

Icing

Icing can be hazardous to aviation.

Ice accretion on an airplane structure or within the engine induction system can significantly reduce flight safety by causing the following:

- *adverse aerodynamic effects*—ice build-up on the airframe structure can modify the air-flow pattern around airfoils (wings, propeller blades, and tail surfaces), leading to a serious loss of lift and an increase in drag; ice/snow or frost has a thickness and/or roughness similar to medium or coarse sandpaper, and on the leading edge and upper surface of a wing it can reduce lift by as much as 50%, and increase drag also by as much as 50%. Thicker accumulations with irregular shapes can more than double the drag;
- *a loss of engine power*, or complete stoppage, if ice blocks the engine air intake (in subzero temperatures) or carburetor ice forms (in moist air up to +25°C or +80°F);
- *a weight increase* and a *change in the CG position* of the airplane, as well as unbalancing of the various control surfaces and the propeller, perhaps causing severe vibration and/or control difficulties;
- blockage of the pitot tube and/or static vent, producing *errors* in the cockpit *pressure instruments* (airspeed indicator, altimeter, vertical speed indicator);
- *degradation in radio communications* and *navigation* (if ice forms on the antennas); and
- *loss of visibility* (if ice forms on the windshield).

The possibility of icing conditions can be determined from weather forecasts and prognostic (forecast) charts, but the most accurate information on icing conditions, both current and forecast, can be obtained from PIREPs (pilot reports), SIGMETs (weather advisories which warn of conditions that could be dangerous to all aircraft) and AIRMETs (which warn of hazards primarily for small aircraft). As a VFR (Visual Flight Rules) pilot, you will only be flying in VMC (visual meteorological conditions), however the following section is provided for your general information. It will be important later during your instrument flight training.

Structural Icing

For ice to form on the aircraft structure, two conditions must be satisfied:

- there must be *visible moisture* (clouds); and
- the temperature must be *at or below freezing* (0°C or +32°F).

Aerodynamic cooling can lower the temperature of the airplane structure below that of the surrounding air by a few degrees. This makes it possible for ice to form on the structure even though the ambient air temperature is still a few degrees above freezing—so be on the watch for structural icing when the air temperature is below about +5°C (+41°F) and you are flying in visible moisture.

The ambient temperature usually decreases in the atmosphere as you climb. The altitude where the temperature has fallen to 0°C (+32°F) is known as the *freezing level*, and it is possible to estimate this level, at least approximately.

The rate at which temperature falls with altitude (the lapse rate) depends on a number of variables, but the standard (average) lapse rate is a temperature decrease of approximately 2°C for every 1,000 feet of altitude gained. For instance, if the air temperature is +8°C at 5,000 feet MSL, then you would need to climb approximately 4,000 feet for the temperature to fall to 0°C, and so the freezing level in this case is at 9,000 feet MSL. However, since lapse rate conditions are often not standard when icing conditions are present, the standard lapse rate should not be used to make tactical decisions about climbing or descending to escape icing.

In general terms, the worst continuous icing conditions are usually found near the cloud tops in heavy stratified clouds or in rain, with icing likely down to temperatures of about -10°C, but rarely at much colder temperatures where the droplets in the clouds are already frozen. In cumuliform clouds with strong updrafts, however, large water droplets may be carried to high altitudes making structural icing a possibility up to very high altitudes and much colder temperatures.

Clear Ice

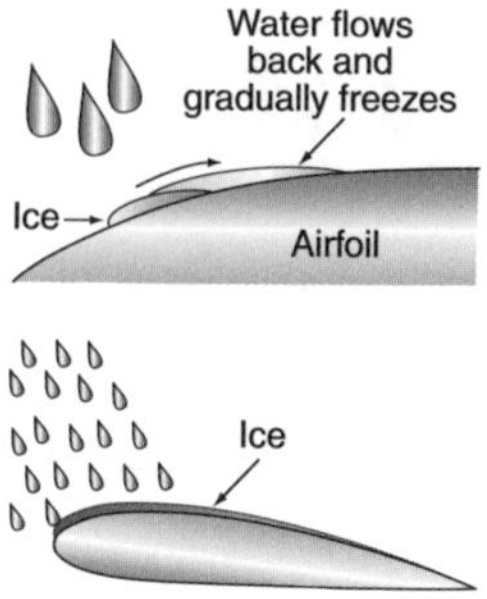

Figure 17-1
Clear ice formed from large, supercooled water drops.

Clear ice is the most dangerous form of structural icing. It is also called rain ice. It is most likely to form when you are flying through *freezing rain*, which consists of raindrops that spread out and freeze on contact with the cold airplane. It is possible for liquid water drops to exist in the atmosphere at temperatures well below the normal freezing point of water 0°C (+32°F), possibly at -20°C (-4°F) or even lower. These are known as *supercooled* drops, and can occur when rain falls from air warmer than 0°C into a subzero layer of air beneath. Supercooled drops are in an unstable state, and will freeze on contact with a subzero surface such as the skin of an airplane, or the propeller blades. Each drop will freeze gradually because of the latent heat released in the freezing process, which allows part of the water drop to spread backward before it freezes. The slower the freezing process, the greater the spread-back of the water before it freezes. The spread-back is greatest at temperatures just below freezing. The result is a sheet of solid, clear, glazed ice with very little air enclosed.

Clear ice is a major hazard to flight safety.

Clear ice can alter the aerodynamic shape of airfoils quite dramatically and reduce or destroy their effectiveness. Along with the increased weight, this creates a major hazard to flight safety. The surface of clear ice is smooth, usually with undulations and lumps. It is very tenacious but, if it does break off, it could be in large chunks capable of doing damage.

A good indication to a pilot that *freezing rain* may exist at higher altitudes is the presence of ice pellets, formed by rain falling from warmer air and freezing on the way down through colder air. Wet snow, however, indicates subzero temperatures at some higher altitude, and warmer air at your level. The snow which formed in the subzero air above is now melting to form wet snow as it passes through your level.

Rime Ice

Rime ice is the most usual form of icing.

Rime ice occurs when tiny, supercooled liquid water droplets freeze on contact with a surface whose temperature is below-freezing. Because the drops are small, the amount of water remaining after the initial freezing is insufficient to coalesce into a continuous sheet before freezing. The result is a mixture of tiny ice particles and trapped air, giving a rough, opaque, crystalline deposit that is fairly brittle. Rime ice often forms on leading edges and can affect the aerodynamic qualities of an airfoil or the airflow into the engine intake. It does cause a significant increase in weight.

Mixed Ice

Rain falling from clouds may consist of drops of many sizes. A mixture of clear ice (from large drops) and rime ice (from small drops) may result. This is known as *mixed ice.*

Frost

Frost occurs when moist air comes in contact with a subzero surface. The water vapor, rather than condensing to form liquid water, changes directly to ice in the form of frost. This is a white crystalline coating that can be very tenacious and difficult to scrape off, but which should always be removed before takeoff is attempted.

Frost can form in clear air when the airplane is parked in subzero temperatures or when the airplane flies from below-freezing temperatures into warmer moist air—for example, on descent, or when climbing through a temperature inversion (where temperature increases with altitude). Although frost is not as dangerous as clear ice, it can obscure vision through a cockpit window and can possibly affect the lifting characteristics of the wings, which can be extremely serious. Although frost does not alter the basic aerodynamic shape of the wing (like clear ice does), frost can disrupt the smooth airflow over the wing, causing early separation of the airflow from the upper surface of the wing and a consequent loss of lift.

Frost on the wings during takeoff may disturb the airflow sufficiently to prevent the airplane from becoming airborne at its normal takeoff speed, or prevent it from becoming airborne at all.

Frost remaining on the wings is dangerous, especially during takeoff.

Structural Icing and Cloud Type

Cumulus-type clouds nearly always consist predominantly of liquid water droplets at temperatures down to about -10°C (+14°F) and if the convective lifting is particularly energetic they may remain supercooled to about -20°C (-4°F), below which the cloud generally partially or completely glaciates. Newly formed parts of the clouds will tend to contain more liquid drops than in mature parts. The risk of airframe icing is severe in these clouds in the range 0°C to -10°C (+32°F to +14°F), and moderate to severe in the range -10° to -20°C (+14°F to -4°F). The risk of structural icing decreases rapidly below these temperatures, with only a small chance of structural icing below -40°C.

Since there is a lot of vertical motion in convective clouds, the composition of the clouds may vary considerably at the one level, and the risk of icing may exist throughout a wide altitude band in (and under) the clouds. Updrafts will tend to carry the water droplets higher and increase their size. If significant structural icing does occur, it may be necessary to descend into warmer air.

Stratiform clouds usually consist entirely or predominantly of liquid water drops down to about -10°C (+14°F), with a risk of structural icing. If significant icing is a possibility, it may be advisable to fly at a lower level where the temperature is above 0°C, or at a higher level where the temperature is colder than -10°C. The greater risk of icing in stratiform clouds is generally near the top of the cloud deck. In certain conditions, such as stratiform clouds associated with an active front or with orographic uplift, the risk of icing is increased at temperatures lower than usual; continuous upward motion of air generally means a greater retention of liquid water in the clouds.

Raindrops and drizzle from any type of clouds will freeze if they meet an airplane whose surface is below 0°C, with a severe risk of clear ice forming the bigger the water droplets are. You need to be cautious when flying in rain at freezing temperatures. This could occur for instance when flying in the cool sector underlying the warmer air of a warm front from which rain is falling.

High-level clouds, such as cirrus, with their bases above 20,000 feet, are usually composed of ice crystals which will not freeze onto the airplane, and so the risk of structural icing is only slight in these clouds.

Structural icing is most likely to accumulate rapidly on an airplane in conditions of *freezing rain*, for instance when flying in below-freezing air underneath the surface of a warm front from which rain is falling.

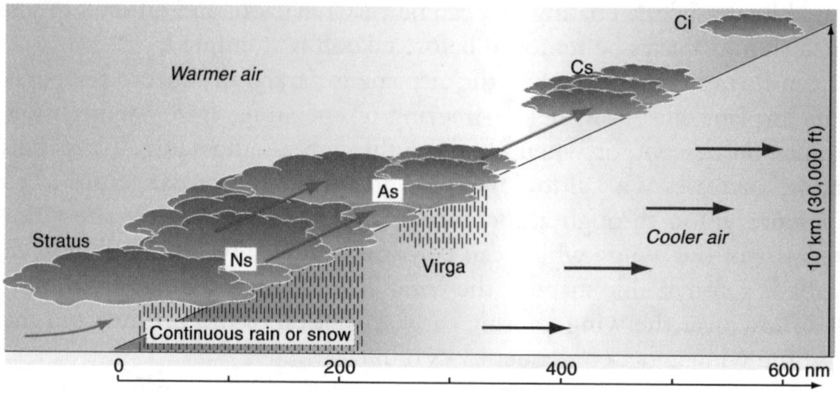

Figure 17-2 Danger area beneath a warm front.

Carburetor Icing

When the air is moist carburetor ice can form in air temperatures as high as 25°C!

Ice can form in the carburetor and induction system of an engine in moist air with outside air temperatures as high as +25°C (+80°F). It will disturb or prevent the flow of air and fuel into the engine, causing it to lose power, run roughly and perhaps even stop. Most airplanes whose engines have carburetors are fitted with a carburetor heat control that can direct hot air from around the engine into the carburetor, instead of the ambient air. The hot air can melt the ice and prevent further ice from forming. The correct method of using carburetor heat for your airplane will be found in the Pilot's Operating Handbook. Carburetor ice is covered in more detail in chapter 5.

Engine Intake Icing

Structural icing near the engine air intake at subzero temperatures can restrict the airflow into the induction system and cause problems. Some aircraft have an *alternate air system* in case this occurs.

Instrument Icing

Icing of the pitot-static system can affect the readings of the pressure-operated flight instruments (the airspeed indicator, altimeter, and VSI). If the airplane has a pitot heater, then use it when appropriate.

Warning!

An ice-laden airplane may be incapable of flight.

Ice of any type on the airframe or propeller, or in the carburetor and induction system, deserves your immediate attention. Wings contaminated by ice prior to takeoff will lengthen the takeoff run because of the higher speed needed to fly—a dangerous situation! Ice or frost on the leading edge and upper forward area of the wings (where the majority of the lift is generated) is especially dangerous. Flight into known icing conditions is not authorized and extremely hazardous if the aircraft is not certified for flight into known icing.

Cold Weather Operations

In extreme cold-weather conditions you should check the engine crankcase breathing lines, to ensure that vapors from the crankcase have not frozen and blocked the breathing lines with ice. You should also consider preheating the cockpit and the engine to ensure that the electronic instruments and the engine are at normal temperatures before start-up. On start-up the time for the oil pressure to rise will be longer. The engine should be shut down if the oil pressure has not risen within 60 seconds.

After takeoff from a slushy runway in below-freezing conditions, you should consider cycling the gear up and down several times shortly after takeoff to ensure that any ice formed is broken off and blown away, and not freezing the landing gear in the up position, if in accordance with the manufacturer's recommended procedures.

Visibility

Visibility is the greatest distance you can see and identify objects—it is a measure of how transparent the atmosphere is to the human eye. The actual visibility is very important to a pilot, and strict visibility requirements are specified for visual flight operations. Slant visibility may be quite different from horizontal visibility. A runway clearly visible through stratus, fog or smog from directly overhead an airport might be impossible to see when you are trying to join final approach. It is essential that you conduct your VFR flight only in visual meteorological conditions (VMC). Instrument flight training will introduce you to reduced visibility operations.

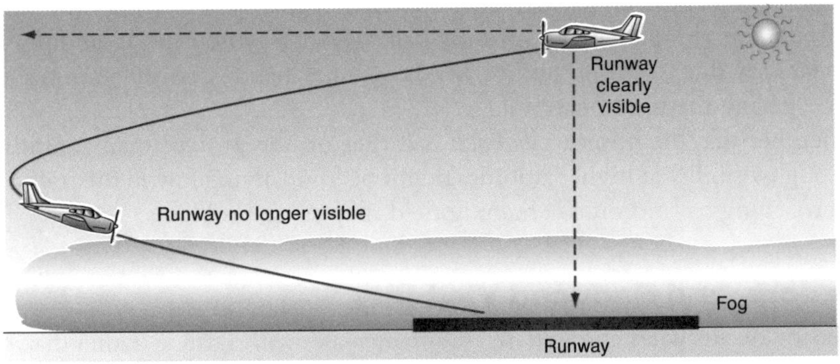

Figure 17-3 Slant visibility may be severely reduced by fog, smog or stratus.

Particles in the Air

Visibility can be reduced by particles suspended in the air.

On a perfectly clear day visibility can exceed 100 miles, however this is rarely the case since there are always some particles suspended in the air, preventing all of the light from a distant object reaching your eyes. Rising air (unstable air) may carry these particles up and blow them away, leading to good visibility; stable air that is *not* rising, however, will keep the particles in the lower levels, which may result in poor visibility.

Particles that restrict visibility include:

- minute particles so small that even very light winds can support them;
  - dust or smoke, causing haze;
  - liquid water or ice, producing mist, fog, or clouds;
- larger particles of sand, dust or sea spray which require stronger winds and turbulence for the air to hold them in suspension; and
- precipitation (rain, snow, hail), the worst visibility being associated with very heavy rain or with large numbers of small particles—for example, thick drizzle or heavy, fine snow.

Unstable air that is rising may cause cumuliform clouds to form, with poor visibility in the showers falling from them, but good visibility otherwise, since the rising unstable air will carry the obscuring particles away. As well as causing good visibility, the rising unstable air may cause bumpy flying conditions.

Rain or snow will of course reduce the distance that you can see, as well as possibly obscuring the horizon and making it more difficult for you to keep the wings level or hold a steady bank angle in a turn. Poor visibility over a large area may occur in mist, fog, smog, stratus, drizzle or rain. As well as restricting visibility through the atmosphere, heavy rain may collect on the windshield and further restrict your vision, especially if the airplane is flying fast. If freezing occurs on the windshield, either as ice or frost, vision may be further impaired.

Strong winds can raise dust or sand from the surface and, in some parts of the world, visibility may be reduced to just a few feet in *dust* and *sandstorms*. *Sea spray* often evaporates after being blown into the atmosphere, leaving small salt particles suspended in the air that can act as condensation nuclei. The salt particles attract water and can cause condensation at relative humidities as low as 70%, restricting visibility much sooner than would otherwise be the case. Haze produced by sea salt often has a whitish appearance, and may often be seen along ocean coastlines. The position of the sun can also have a significant effect on visibility. Flying with the sun behind you where you can see the sunlit side of objects, visibility may be much greater than when flying into the sun. As well as reducing visibility, flying into the sun may also cause *glare*. If landing into the sun is necessary due to strong surface winds or other reasons, consideration should be given to altering the time of arrival.

Remember that the onset of *darkness* is earlier on the ground than at altitude and, even though visibility at higher altitudes might be good, flying low in the traffic pattern and approaching to land on a darkening field may cause problems.

Inversions and Reduced Visibility

An inversion occurs when the air temperature increases with altitude (rather than decreases, which is the usual situation). A temperature inversion can act as a blanket, stopping vertical convection currents—air that starts to rise meets warmer air and so ceases rising. In other words, temperature inversions are associated with a *stable* layer of air. Particles suspended in the lower layers will be trapped there causing a rather dirty layer of smoke, dust, or pollution, particularly in industrial areas. These small particles may act as condensation particles or nuclei, and encourage the formation of fog if the relative humidity is high, the combination of smoke and fog being known as *smog*. There is usually an abundance of condensation nuclei in industrial areas as a result of the combustion process (factory smoke, car exhausts, and so on)—hence the poor visibility often found over these areas. Similar poor visibility effects below inversions can be seen in rural areas if there is a lot of pollen, dust or other matter in the air.

Inversions can occur by cooling of the air in contact with the earth's surface overnight, or by subsidence associated with a high pressure system as descending air warms. The most common type of ground-based inversion is produced by terrestrial radiation on a clear, relatively still, night. This often leads to poor visibility in the lower levels the following morning caused by fog, smoke or smog.

Flying conditions beneath a low-level inversion layer are typically smooth air (because the air is stable and not rising), with poor visibility, haze, fog, smog or low clouds.

Because there is little or no mixing of the air above and below an inversion, the effect of any upper winds may not be carried down beneath the inversion. This may cause a quite sharp *windshear* as an airplane climbs or descends through the inversion.

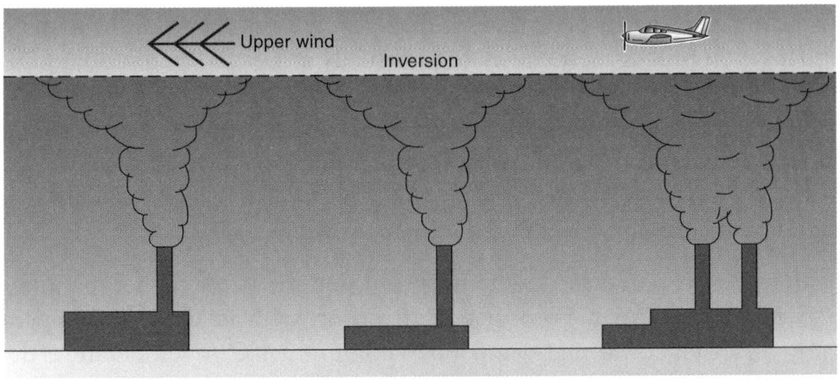

Figure 17-4 Reduced visibility and smooth flying conditions will usually be encountered beneath an inversion, and possible windshear passing through it.

Condensation

Visibility for a pilot can be dramatically reduced when invisible water vapor in the air condenses as visible water droplets and forms clouds or fog (fog simply being a cloud layer reaching ground level). The amount of water vapor which a parcel of air can hold depends on its temperature—warm air being able to carry more water vapor than cold air. Warm air passing over a water surface, such as an ocean or a lake, is capable of absorbing much more water vapor than cooler air.

If the moist air is then cooled, say by being forced aloft and expanding or by passing over or lying over a cooling surface, it eventually reaches a point where it can no longer carry all of its invisible water vapor and is said to be saturated. The temperature at which *saturation* occurs is called the *dewpoint temperature* (or simply *dewpoint*) of that parcel of air. Any further cooling will most likely lead to the excess water vapor condensing out as visible water droplets and forming *fog* or *clouds*, a process encouraged by the presence of dust or other condensation nuclei in the air. If the air is extremely clean, with very few condensation nuclei, the actual condensation process may be delayed until the temperature falls some degrees below the dewpoint.

Air carrying a lot of water vapor, for instance warm air after passing over an ocean or large lake, will have a high dewpoint temperature compared with the relatively dry air over an arid desert. Moist air may only have to cool to a dewpoint of +25°C (+77°F) before becoming saturated, whereas less moist air may have to cool to +5°C (+41°F) before reaching saturation point. Extremely dry air may have to cool to a dewpoint temperature of -5°C (+23°F) before becoming saturated.

Clouds or fog form when the invisible water vapor condenses in the air as visible water droplets.

The closeness of the actual air temperature to the dewpoint of the air—often contained in surface aviation weather reports—is a good indication of how close the air is to saturation and the possible formation of clouds or fog. If the water vapor condenses on contact with a surface such as the ground or an airplane that is below the dewpoint of the surrounding air, then it will form *dew* (or *frost*, if the temperature of the collecting surface is below freezing).

The reverse process to condensation may occur in the air if its temperature rises above the dewpoint, causing the water droplets to evaporate into water vapor and, consequently, the fog or clouds to disperse.

Fog

Fog is of major concern to pilots because it severely restricts vision near the ground. The condensation process that causes fog is usually associated with cooling of the air either by:

- an underlying cold ground or water surface (causing *radiation* or *advection fog*);
- interaction of two air masses (causing *frontal fog*);
- adiabatic cooling of a moist air mass moving up a slope (causing *upslope fog*); or
- very cold air overlying a warm water surface (causing *steam fog*).

The closer the temperature/dewpoint spread, and the faster the temperature is falling, the sooner fog will form. For instance, an airport with an actual air temperature of +6°C early on a calm, clear night, and a dewpoint of +4°C (a temperature/dewpoint spread of 2°C) is likely to experience fog when the temperature falls 2°C or more from its current +6°C.

Radiation Fog

Radiation fog forms when air is cooled to below its dewpoint temperature by losing heat energy as a result of radiation. Conditions suitable for the formation of radiation fog are:

- a *cloudless night*, allowing the land to lose heat by radiation to the atmosphere and thereby cool, also causing the air in contact with the ground to lose heat (possibly leading to a temperature inversion);
- *moist air* and a *small temperature/dewpoint spread* (a high relative humidity) that only requires a little cooling for the air to reach its dewpoint temperature, causing the water vapor to condense onto small condensation nuclei in the air and form visible water; and
- *light winds* (5–7 knots) to promote mixing of the air at low level, thereby thickening the fog layer.

These conditions are commonly found with a high-pressure system.

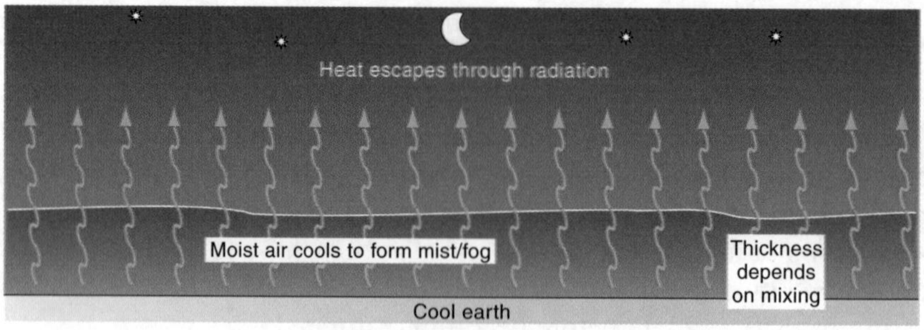

Figure 17-5 Radiation fog.

Air is a poor conductor of heat, so that if the wind is absolutely calm, only the thin layer of air 1–2 inches thick actually in contact with the surface will lose heat to it. This will cause dew or frost to form on the surface itself, instead of fog forming in the air above it. *Dew* will form at temperatures above freezing, and *frost* will form at below freezing temperatures. This may inhibit the formation of radiation fog by removing moisture from the air. After dawn, however, the dew may evaporate and fog may form.

If the wind is stronger than about 7 knots, the extra turbulence may cause too much mixing and, instead of radiation fog right down to the ground, a layer of stratus may form above the surface.

The temperature of the sea remains fairly constant throughout the year, unlike that of the land, which warms and cools quite quickly on a diurnal (daily) basis. Radiation fog is therefore much more likely to form over land, which cools more quickly at night, than over the sea.

Figure 17-6 The wind strength will affect the formation of dew/frost, mist/fog, or stratus.

The *dispersal* of radiation fog depends on the heating of the air. As the earth's surface begins to warm up again some time after sunrise, the air in contact with it will also warm, causing the fog to gradually dissipate. It is common for this to occur by early or mid-morning. Possibly the fog may rise to form a low layer of stratus before the sky fully clears. If the fog that has formed overnight is thick, however, it may act as a blanket, shutting out the sun and impeding the heating of the earth's surface after the sun has risen. As a consequence, the air in which the fog exists will *not* be warmed from below and the radiation fog may last throughout the day. An increasing wind speed could create sufficient turbulence to drag warmer and drier air down into the fog layer, causing it to dissipate.

Note. Haze caused by particles of dust or pollen in the air cannot, of course, be dissipated by the air warming—haze needs to be blown away by a wind.

Advection Fog

A warm, moist air mass moving across a colder surface will be cooled from below. If its temperature is reduced to the dewpoint temperature, then fog will form. Since the term advection means the horizontal flow of air, fog formed in this manner is known as *advection fog*, and can occur quite suddenly, day or night, if the right conditions exist, and can be more persistent than radiation fog.

For instance, a warm, moist maritime airflow over a cold land surface can lead to advection fog forming over the land. In winter, moist air from the Gulf of Mexico moving north over cold ground often causes advection fog extending well into the south-central and eastern United States.

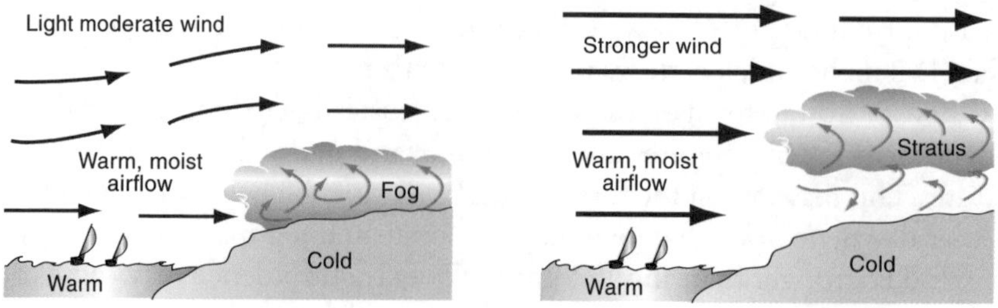

Figure 17-7 Fog or stratus caused by advection.

Advection fog depends on a wind to move the relatively warm and moist air mass over a cooler surface. Unlike radiation fog, the formation of advection fog is *not* affected by overhead cloud layers, and can form with or without clouds obscuring the sky. Light to moderate winds will encourage mixing in the lower levels to give a thicker layer of fog, but winds stronger than about 15 knots may cause stratus clouds rather than fog. Advection fog can persist in much stronger winds than radiation fog.

Sea fog is a type of advection fog, and may be caused by:

- tropical maritime air moving toward the pole over a colder ocean or meeting a colder air mass; or
- an airflow off a warm land surface moving over a cooler sea, affecting airports in coastal areas. Advection fog is common in coastal regions of California during summer.

Upslope Fog

Moist air moving up a slope will cool adiabatically and, if it cools to below its dewpoint temperature, fog will form. This is known as *upslope fog*. It may form whether there is cloud above or not. If the wind stops, the upslope fog will dissipate. Upslope fog is common on the eastern slopes of the Rockies and the Appalachian mountains. Both upslope fog and advection fog need wind (but radiation fog does not).

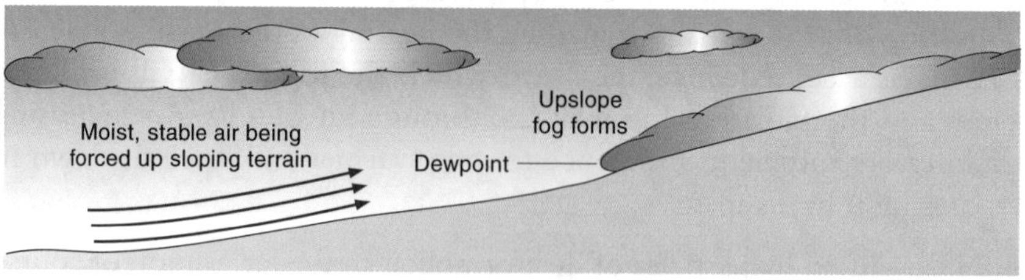

Figure 17-8 Upslope fog.

Frontal Fog

Frontal fog forms from the interaction of two air masses in one of two ways:

- clouds that extend down to the surface during the passage of a weather front (forming mainly over hills and consequently called *hill fog*); and
- air that becomes saturated by the evaporation from rain that has fallen—known as *precipitation-induced fog*.

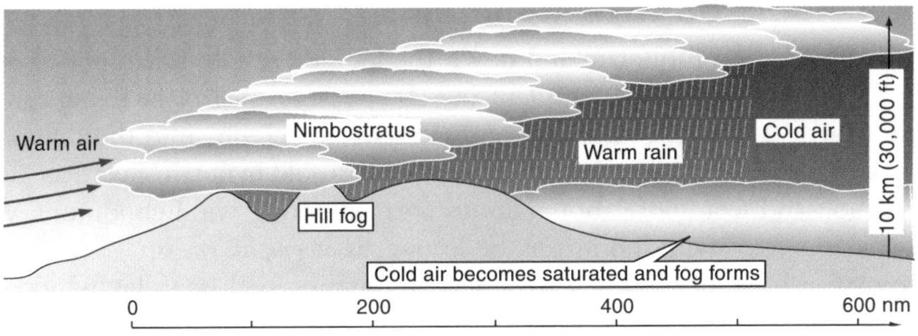

Figure 17-9 Fog associated with a warm front.

These conditions may develop in the cold air ahead of a warm front (or an occluded front), the prefrontal fog possibly being very widespread. Rain or drizzle falling from relatively warm air into cooler air may saturate it, forming precipitation-induced fog which may be thick and long-lasting over wide areas. Precipitation-induced fog is most likely to be associated with a warm front, but it can also be associated with a stationary front or a slow-moving cold front.

Steam Fog

Steam fog can form when cool air blows over a warm, moist surface (a warm sea or wet land), cooling the water vapor rising from the moist surface to below its dewpoint temperature. Steam fog over polar oceans is sometimes called *arctic sea smoke*. It forms in air more than 10°C (20°F) colder than water, and can be very thick and widespread, causing serious visibility problems for shipping. Low-level turbulence and the risk of severe icing can be present in steam fog.

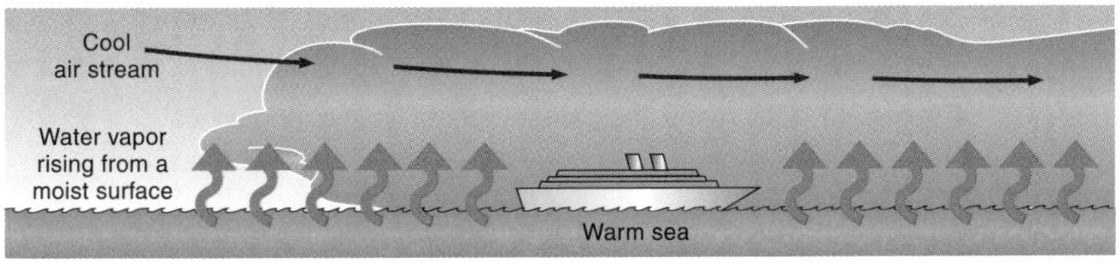

Figure 17-10 Steam fog.

Turbulence

Localized Friction Effects

The surface wind may bear no resemblance to the gradient wind at 2,000 feet AGL and above if it has to blow over and around obstacles such as hills, trees, and buildings. The wind will form turbulent eddies, the size of which will depend on both the size of the obstructions and the wind strength. This is known as *frictional turbulence* or *mechanical turbulence*.

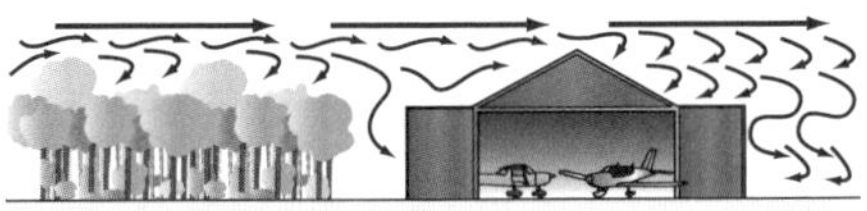

Figure 17-11
Friction and obstacles affect the surface wind.

Winds Associated with Mountains

Winds that flow over a mountain and down the lee side can be hazardous to aviation, not only because the air may be turbulent, but also because an airplane flying toward the mountain from the downwind or lee side will have to "climb" into the downflowing winds even to maintain altitude. For this reason, you should maintain a vertical clearance of several thousand feet above mountainous areas in strong wind conditions. Weather phenomena associated with mountains are known as *orographic effects*.

There may also be local wind effects near mountains, such as valley winds and the katabatic winds that flow down cool slopes at night and in the morning (as explained in chapter 13).

Large mountains or mountain ranges cause an effect on the wind that may extend well above ground level resulting in *mountain waves*, possibly with associated *lenticular clouds*. These clouds are continuously forming and dissipating as they stand over the mountain, and do not appear to move. This may lead you to think that there is little or no wind present—definitely *not* the case.

The up-currents and down-currents associated with mountain waves can be quite strong, and can extend for 30 or 40 miles downwind of the mountains.

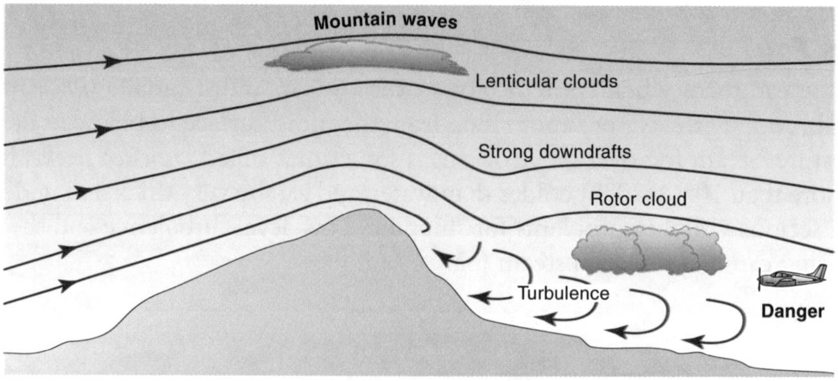

Figure 17-12 Avoid flying near mountains in strong winds.

Flying in Turbulence

Some degree of turbulence is almost always present in the atmosphere and pilots quickly become accustomed to slight turbulence. Moderate or severe turbulence, however, is uncomfortable and can even overstress the airplane.

Vertical gusts increase the wing's angle of attack, causing an increase in the lift generated at that particular airspeed and therefore an increased load factor. Of course, if the angle of attack is increased beyond the critical angle, the wing will stall; this can occur at a speed well above the published 1g stall speed (known as an accelerated stall).

The load factor (or g-force) is a measure of the stress on the airplane and each category of airplane is built to take only certain load factors. It is important that these load factors are not exceeded. One means of achieving this is to fly the airplane at the turbulence-penetration speed (V_B) which is usually slower by some 10–20% than normal cruise speed, but not so slow as to allow the airplane to stall, remembering that in turbulence the airplane may stall at a higher indicated airspeed than that published.

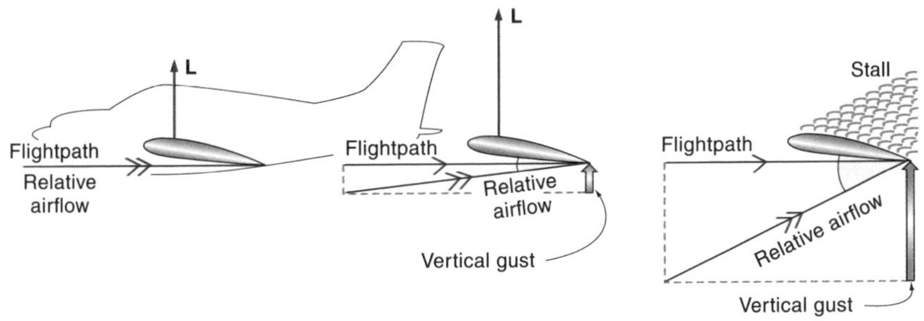

Figure 17-13 Vertical gusts increase the angle of attack, and will increase the load factor and/or stall the wings.

When encountering turbulence:

- fasten the seat belts;
- maintain the level flight attitude for the desired flight phase (climb, cruise or descent), using whatever aileron movements are needed to retain lateral control, but be fairly gentle on the elevator to avoid over-stressing the airframe structurally through large changes in angle of attack and lift, and be prepared to accept variations in altitude; and
- use power to maintain speed, aiming to have the airspeed fluctuate around the selected turbulence penetration speed, which may require reducing power; the airspeed indicator will probably be fluctuating and so will be less useful than normal.

Turbulence Avoidance

It is obviously better to avoid turbulence, and to some extent this is possible. Avoid flying underneath, in or near thunderstorms where changes to airflow can be enormous. Avoid flying under large cumulus clouds because of the large updrafts that cause them. Avoid flying in the lee of hills when strong winds are blowing, since they will tumble over the ridges and possibly be quite turbulent as well as flowing down and into valleys at a rate which your airplane may not be able to out-climb. Avoid flying at a low level over rough ground when strong winds are blowing.

Clear Air Turbulence

Turbulence can also be expected at high altitudes in the vicinity of any *jet streams* (tubes of strong wind flowing for many hundreds or thousands of miles, usually from west to east). Turbulence above 15,000 feet AGL that is not associated with cumuliform clouds is known as clear air turbulence (CAT). If there is a change in wind strength of more than about *6 knots per 1,000 feet* of altitude change, then moderate or stronger clear air turbulence is likely to exist.

Flying Conditions Near Jet Streams

Flying conditions can be smooth *in* a jet stream, but turbulence can be expected on its edges where it meets with slower moving air—so *clear air turbulence* (CAT) is always a possibility near a jet stream. CAT is likely to be greatest on the edges of the jet stream core, especially on the cold polar side of the jet stream where there may be strong windshear, strong curvature in the airflow, and cold air moving in by advection associated with sharply curving strong upper-level troughs. A strong windshear can be expected on the low-pressure side of a jet stream core if speed at the core is greater than 110 knots. A curving jet stream associated with a deep upper-level trough will create the greatest turbulence, especially during the winter months when the jet stream wind speeds are greater.

If encountering CAT associated with a jet stream at high altitude, it is good airmanship to report it, and also to determine from other pilot reports (PIREPs) if smooth flight is being achieved at other levels. You might fly out of the CAT by climbing or descending several thousand feet, or by moving some miles laterally from the jet stream.

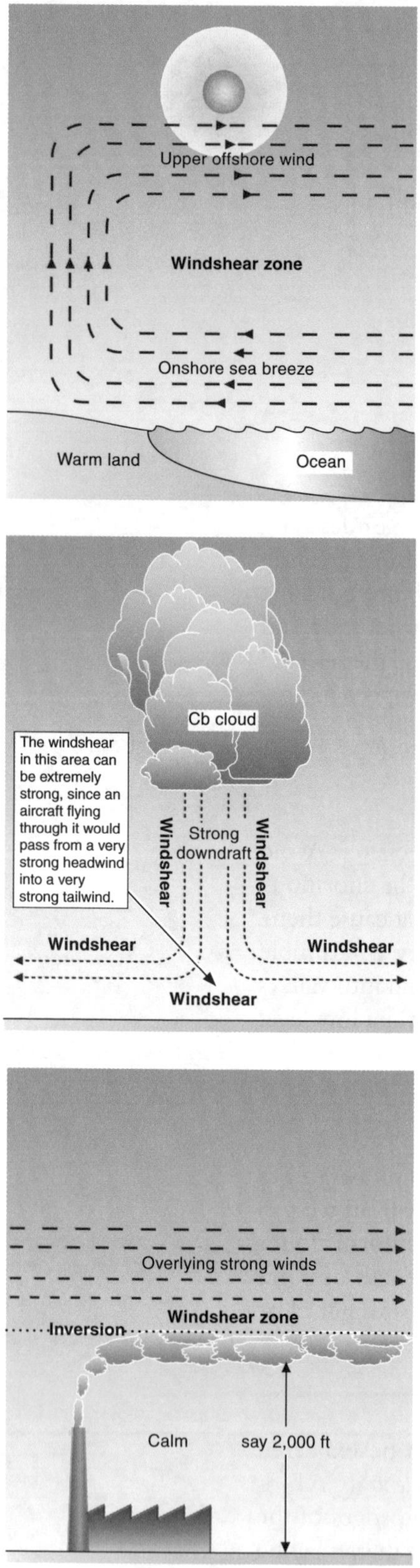

Figure 17-14
Windshear is a change of wind speed and/or direction between places.

Windshear, Thunderstorms, and Microbursts

A theoretical discussion of windshear, thunderstorms and microbursts is covered in chapter 15. This section deals with the operational effects these potentially dangerous phenomenon can cause.

Windshear

A windshear is defined as a change in wind direction and/or speed in space. A windshear is a *changing* wind. This can mean a wind whose *speed* alters as you climb or descend to a different level. It can mean a wind whose *direction* changes from place to place or it can mean an updraft or a downdraft that an airplane has to fly through. Windshear is generally understood to mean a wind change within a short distance or a short space of time. Windshear affects the flight path and the airspeed of an airplane and can be a hazard to aviation. It can be present at any level in the atmosphere, and can exist in both a horizontal and vertical direction. Windshear is commonly experienced at high altitudes near a jet stream as clear air turbulence (CAT), near frontal zones, and at low levels associated with low-level temperature inversions, in or near thunderstorms or showers.

Some windshear is usually present to some extent as an airplane approaches the ground for a landing, because of the different speed and direction of the surface wind compared to the wind at altitude. Low-level windshear can be more pronounced at night or in the early morning when there is little mixing of the lower layers—for instance, when a temperature inversion exists with calm winds on and near the ground and overlying winds of 25 knots or greater.

When climbing or descending through a windshear zone, you should be alert for sudden airspeed changes. Flying into a suddenly decreasing headwind on approach, for instance, would cause a sudden loss of airspeed. You would counter this with appropriate changes of power and attitude. This is covered in chapter 9. Windshear can also be expected when a sea breeze or a land breeze is blowing, or when you are flying in the vicinity of a thunderstorm or a front. Cumulonimbus clouds have enormous updrafts and downdrafts associated with them, and the effects can be felt up to 10 or 20 miles away from the actual cloud. These downdrafts can be so strong as to be classified as microbursts.

Thunderstorms

Do *not* land or take off if there is an active thunderstorm approaching the airport. Sudden wind changes, severe turbulence and windshear are possible. Avoid thunderstorms in flight by at least 10 miles and, in severe situations, by 20 miles. If you are passing downwind of them, you should perhaps increase this distance even further. Use your weather radar, if available, otherwise detour visually, making use of heavy rain showers, towering clouds, lightning and roll clouds as indicators of where mature storm cells are likely to be.

Remember that embedded thunderstorms may be obscured from sight by the general cloud layers, so avoid areas where embedded cumulonimbus clouds are forecast, unless you are equipped with serviceable thunderstorm detection equipment. Also avoid areas with six-tenths or more of thunderstorm coverage. Any thunderstorm with tops of 35,000 feet or higher should be regarded as extremely hazardous. When flying in the area of thunderstorms:

- fasten the seat belts and shoulder harnesses, and secure any loose objects;
- turn up the cockpit lights at night to lessen the danger of temporary blindness from nearby lightning; and
- do not fly under thunderstorms, because you may experience severe turbulence, strong downdrafts, microbursts, heavy hail and windshear.

If you cannot avoid flying through or near a thunderstorm:

- plan a course that will take minimum time through the hazardous area;
- establish a power setting for the recommended turbulence penetration speed;
- turn on pitot heat (to avoid loss of airspeed indication), carburetor heat or jet-engine anti-ice (to avoid power loss) and other anti-icing equipment (to avoid airframe icing). The most critical icing band within a cloud is from the freezing level (0°C) up to an altitude where the temperature is about -20°C, which is the temperature band where supercooled water drops are most likely. However, supercooled water drops have been observed in thunderstorms down to much lower temperatures, possibly as low as -40°C;
- maintain your heading by keeping the wings level with ailerons, and do not make sudden changes in pitch attitude with the elevators because sudden changes in pitch attitude may overstress the airplane structure. It may be advisable to disconnect the autopilot, or at least its altitude-hold and speed-hold functions, to avoid the autopilot making sudden changes in pitch attitude (causing additional structural stress) and sudden changes in power (increasing the risk of a power loss);
- avoid turns if possible, as this increases g-loading—continue heading straight ahead and avoid turning back once you have penetrated the storm, as a turn will increase stress on the airframe and also increase the stall speed. Maintaining the heading will most likely get you through the storm in minimum time;
- allow the airspeed to fluctuate in the turbulence, avoiding rapid power changes;
- monitor the flight and engine instruments, avoiding looking out of the cockpit too much to reduce the risk of temporary blindness from lightning; and
- use thunderstorm detection equipment. If the equipment is weather radar, manage the antenna tilt effectively so as not to over-scan or under-scan thunderstorm activity at other levels.

Note. You may sometimes experience *St. Elmo's fire*, a spectacular static electricity discharge across the windshield, or from sharp edges or points on the airplane's structure, especially at night. St. Elmo's fire is not dangerous.

Microbursts

An aircraft entering the area of a microburst within 1,000–3,000 feet AGL will first encounter an increasing headwind. The aircraft will initially maintain its inertial speed over the ground (its groundspeed) and the increased headwind will cause it to have a higher airspeed, therefore increased performance. It will tend to fly above the original flight path. Then the aircraft will enter the downburst shaft and will be carried earthward in the strong downward air current—a dramatic loss of performance.

As the aircraft flies out of the downburst shaft (hopefully), the situation is not greatly improved. It will fly into an area of increasing tailwind. As the aircraft will tend to maintain its inertial groundspeed initially, the increasing tailwind will cause the airspeed to decay—a reduced airspeed, resulting in reduced aircraft performance.

Even with the addition of full power and suitable adjustments to pitch attitude by the pilot, the airplane may struggle to maintain a safe airspeed and flight path. Traversing some small, strong microbursts safely may be beyond the performance capabilities of any aircraft. Figures 17-15 and 17-16 depict the likely effect on an aircraft encountering a microburst under a thunderstorm on approach and after takeoff.

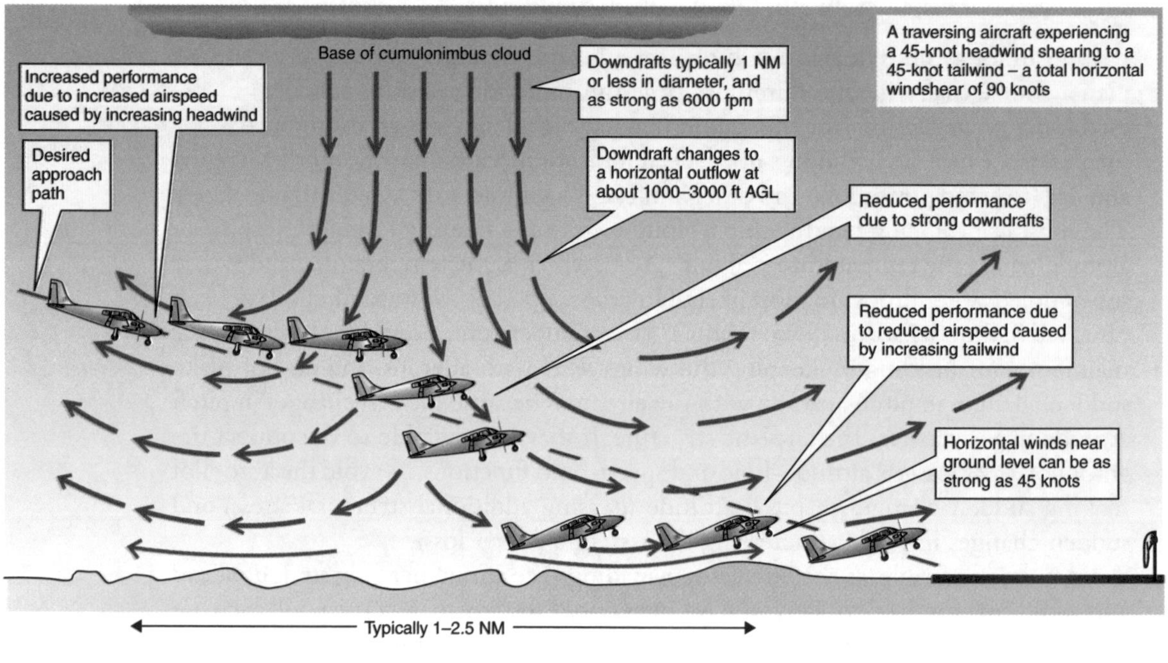

Figure 17-15 The dangers of a microburst on approach to land.

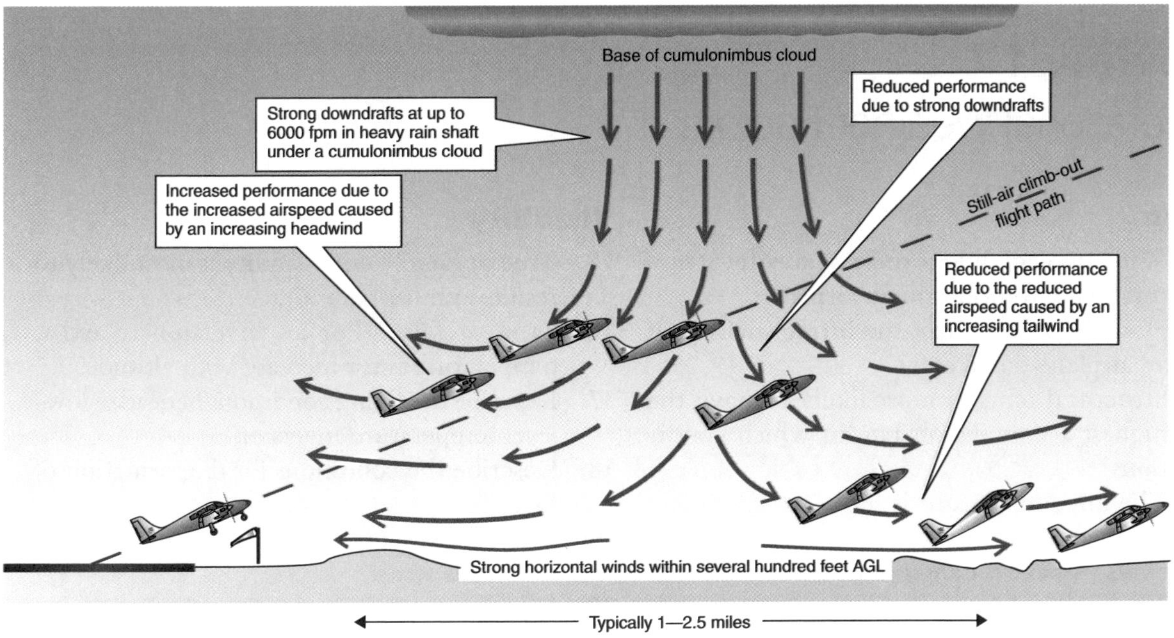

Figure 17-16 The dangers of a microburst after takeoff.

Review 17

Operational Weather Factors

Icing

1. What two conditions must be met for structural icing to occur on an airplane?
2. How does frost affect the lifting surfaces of an airplane on takeoff?
3. Structural icing is most likely to have the highest accumulation rate in which conditions?
4. The air temperature is +6°C at 1,500 feet MSL, and a standard temperature lapse rate exists. What is the approximate freezing level?
5. Name one in-flight condition necessary for structural icing to form.
6. Which family of clouds is least likely to contribute to structural icing on an airplane?
7. Why is frost considered hazardous to flight?
8. Which control in the cockpit is used to protect you against carburetor icing?
9. Which instruments are likely to give faulty indications in the following situations?
   a. Ice has formed over the pitot tube.
   b. Ice has formed over the static vents.
10. Which is true regarding preheating an aircraft during cold weather operations?
    a. The cabin area as well as the engine should be preheated.
    b. The cabin area should not be preheated with portable heaters.
    c. Hot air should be blown directly at the engine through the air intakes.
11. True or false? The outside air temperature does not need to be below freezing for carburetor icing to occur.
12. True or false? The ambient air temperature does not need to be below freezing for carburetor icing to occur.
13. It is necessary for you to take off from a slushy runway. How can you minimize the freezing of landing gear mechanisms?
14. During preflight in cold weather, why should crankcase breather lines receive special attention?

Visibility

15. True or false? Poor visibility is most likely to result with unstable air.
16. True or false? For an inversion to exist, temperature must increase with altitude.
17. Describe the flying conditions beneath a low-level temperature inversion.
18. Describe the conditions for the formation of fog.
19. Why is the possibility of fog increased in industrial areas?
20. Which situation is most conducive to the formation of radiation fog?
    a. Warm, moist air over low, flat land areas on clear, calm nights.
    b. Moist, tropical air moving over cold, offshore water.
    c. The movement of cold air over much warmer water.
21. If the temperature/dewpoint spread is small and decreasing, and the temperature is 62°F, what type of weather is most likely to develop?
22. What is smog?
23. In what situation is advection fog most likely to form?
24. True or false? There does not need to be a wind in order for advection fog to form.
25. True or false? Moist air moving up a slope will cool adiabatically and may form upslope fog if its temperature reaches the dewpoint temperature.
26. Low-level turbulence can occur and icing can become hazardous in which type of fog?

Turbulence

27. When turbulence causes changes in altitude and/or attitude but aircraft control remains positive, what should it be reported as?
28. What is the minimum vertical windshear value critical for probable moderate or greater turbulence?

29. What are some of the important characteristics of windshear?
30. What is one of the most dangerous features of mountain waves?
31. What is the presence of standing lenticular altocumulus clouds a good indication of?
32. The wind at 5,000 feet AGL is southwesterly while the surface wind is southerly. What is this difference in direction primarily due to?
33. A pilot can expect a windshear zone in a temperature inversion whenever the wind speed at 2,000 to 4,000 feet above the surface is at least:
    a. 10 knots.
    b. 15 knots.
    c. 25 knots.
34. True or false? Windshear can be associated with speed at any level in the atmosphere.
35. With a warm front, what is the most critical period for low-level windshear above an airport?
36. Hazardous windshear is commonly encountered near the ground during periods:
    a. when the wind velocity is stronger than 35 knots.
    b. of strong low-level temperature inversion.
    c. following frontal passage.

Commercial Review

37. Which situation would most likely result in freezing precipitation?
    a. Rain falling from air which has a temperature of 32°F or less into air having a temperature of more than 32°F.
    b. Rain falling from air which has a temperature of 0°C or less into air having a temperature of 0°C or more.
    c. Rain falling from air which has a temperature of more than 32°F into air having a temperature of 32°F or less.
38. True or false? Advection fog can form suddenly during the day or night.
39. Precipitation-induced fog is most commonly associated with:
    a. warm fronts.
    b. cold fronts.
    c. stationary fronts.
40. Conditions favorable to the formation of a surface-based temperature inversion are:
    a. clear, cool nights with calm or light wind.
    b. an area of unstable air rapidly transferring heat from the surface.
    c. broad areas of cumulus clouds with smooth, level bases at the same altitude.
41. Fog produced by frontal activity is a result of saturation due to:
    a. nocturnal cooling.
    b. adiabatic cooling.
    c. evaporation of precipitation.
42. Advection fog has drifted over a coastal airport during the day. What may tend to dissipate or lift this fog into low stratus clouds?
    a. Night time cooling.
    b. Surface radiation.
    c. Wind 15 knots or stronger.
43. With respect to advection fog, which statement is true?
    a. It is slow to develop, and dissipates quite rapidly.
    b. It forms almost exclusively at night or near daybreak.
    c. It can appear suddenly during day or night, and it is more persistent than radiation fog.
44. Which in-flight hazard is most commonly associated with warm fronts?
45. Ice pellets encountered during flight at any altitude are normally evidence of:
    a. snow at a higher altitude.
    b. freezing rain at a higher altitude.
    c. a thunderstorm at a higher altitude.
46. True or false? Ice pellets encountered during flight normally mean there is a layer of colder air above.
47. What sort of structural ice is most likely if you fly through a large cumulus cloud at a temperature of -3°C?

Answers are given on page 700.

Weather Reports and Forecasts 18

Weather conditions vary from place to place and from time to time. It is good airmanship (common sense) that you make yourself aware of the weather that you are likely to encounter en route. You can do this by making your own observations to a limited extent but, for flights away from the local airport, you should obtain weather reports and forecasts.

Weather that has actually been observed is contained in weather *reports*. Weather that is expected to occur at some time in the future is contained in weather *forecasts* or shown graphically on *prognostic charts*.

Reports and forecasts are available before flight by telephone (call 1-800-WX-BRIEF) or through various websites including aviationweather.gov and 1800wxbrief.com. While airborne reports and forecasts are also available from Flight Service by contacting 122.2 MHz or by using a Remote Communications Outlet (RCO) frequency, shown on sectional charts and in the Chart Supplement U.S. Additionally, airborne weather can be obtained from the automatic terminal information service (ATIS), automated observation systems (AWOS and ASOS), and through the use of automatic dependent surveillance – broadcast (ADS-B) or flight information system broadcast (FIS-B) weather products.

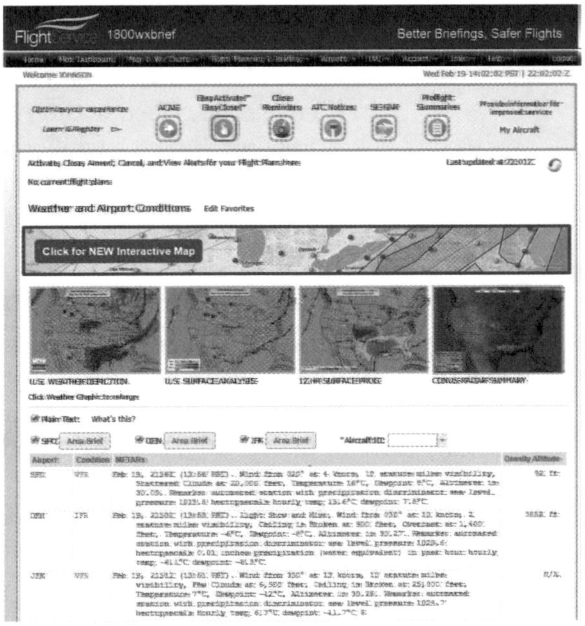

Figure 18-1
1800wxbrief.com customizable pilot dashboard.

Obtaining a Weather Briefing

Obtaining Weather from the FAA

In the United States, the primary method of obtaining a weather briefing is by contacting Flight Service on the ground by calling 1-800-WX-BRIEF or visiting online at 1800wxbrief.com. Flight Service is contracted through Leidos Flight Services for all areas of the United States except Alaska, which is still handled by the FAA.

Although numerous websites exist for accessing weather information, it is important to note differences exist—not only in site navigation but in chart names. Site maps are most useful in these instances.

When you call for a briefing, you can request a standard, outlook, or abbreviated weather briefing; listen to recorded route forecasts; or requests whatever additional information you need. The same information available by telephone is available through the online portal.

Additionally, weather and forecasts can be obtained online through the National Weather Service at aviationweather.gov. Leidos Flight Service also has an automated voice service where weather information can be accessed through Google Assistant or Amazon Alexa. Information provided through this service includes airport METARs and TAFs, aviation forecasts discussions, and adverse conditions updates. For more information about automated voice service visit 1800wxbrief.com.

Pilot Responsibility

The pilot is responsible for obtaining needed weather data.

The growing use of recorded briefings and computer briefings means that you must assume more responsibility for interpreting weather data than in the past. It also means you are less likely than in the past to be able to talk face-to-face or by telephone with a meteorologist or briefer who can help you understand the reports and forecasts.

You must learn how to read and understand coded forecasts and the various kinds of weather charts of reports and forecasts. One key to weather reports and forecasts is *Aviation Weather Services*, a document published by the Federal Aviation Administration and National Weather Service as FAA Advisory Circular AC 00-45. The U.S. METAR code is described in the *Federal Meteorological Handbook* (FMH) *No. 1 "Surface Observations and Reports,"* while the U.S. TAF code procedures used by the National Weather Service are described in the *Weather Service Operations Manual*, Chapter D-31. These are available online at faa.gov.

The Big Picture from the Media

TV, newspaper, and internet weather information can provide you with an overall "big picture."

Before obtaining a specific briefing for a flight, you can get a good idea of general weather trends—the big picture—from newspaper, online, and television weather programs. The Weather Channel, which is available on cable television systems across the country, broadcasts nothing but weather reports and forecasts, including segments specifically for pilots, 24 hours a day and available at weather.com. Local television stations give detailed reports and forecasts for their viewing areas on evening news shows. These usually include moving satellite pictures, live local radar images and maps that give you a good idea of the national picture for the coming day. Many of these local weather shows are presented by knowledgeable weathercasters using sophisticated graphics, and watching them is a good way to further your weather education.

Specific Aviation Briefings

Specific aviation weather briefings provide more specific weather information; see AIM.

No matter how good the information you receive from a newspaper, television, or the internet, both common sense and the regulations require that you obtain a specific briefing for a flight to a destination away from your takeoff point. Use Flight Service to obtain a weather briefing either by telephone or online.

When you call, first tell the briefer you want a standard, outlook, or abbreviated flight weather briefing and give the briefer the following information: you are a pilot, whether the flight will be VFR or IFR, the aircraft's N number, the aircraft type, your departure point, your proposed route, your destination, the altitude you plan to fly at, the estimated time of departure, and your estimated time en route. This information will enable the briefer to give you the information you need as a pilot. By providing your aircraft's N number, the FAA will have a record that you obtained a weather briefing for your intended flight.

If you obtain your weather briefing online you will be required to provide the same basic information as you would over the phone. You will be able to save specific routes in the system so you can easily recall them at a later time to obtain a weather route briefing on a different day. This option works well for pilots who may fly the same routes on a weekly or monthly basis.

Standard Weather Briefing

A "standard briefing" is a full briefing.

The standard briefing should follow the items specified in the FAA's *Flight Service Handbook*. If the briefer follows the standard format, you will receive all the needed information, but there is always a slight chance that the briefer might not give you a complete briefing. Also, if you are using a personal computer to gather weather information, you need some way to ensure that you receive all the needed data. For these reasons, you should have a form like the one shown below. If you fill in all of the blanks and complete the Pilot's Weather Checklist, you will be assured of getting a complete briefing every time.

Pilots Weather Checklist					
	Synopsis and area WX		Destination WX forecast		Temperature/dewpoint spread
	Adverse WX, including SIGMETs/AIRMETs		Winds & temperatures aloft forecast		Better WX area forecast
	Current en route WX		PIREPs, including top levels		Alternate airport WX forecast
	Forecast en route WX		Freezing levels		NOTAMs

Table 18-1 The weather checklist.

A good weather briefing should include at least the following:

- *adverse conditions*—information about any conditions that could be a hazard to your flight, such as thunderstorms, low ceilings, poor visibility, icing;
- *weather synopsis*—a brief statement explaining the causes of the weather. This should include the locations and movements of highs, lows, and fronts;
- *severe weather warnings*—includes AIRMETs, SIGMETs and Convective SIGMETs, and ATC weather advisories;
- *freezing levels*—to aid in predicting any possibility of icing conditions en route;
- *current weather*—if you are leaving within two hours, reports of the current weather along your route should be included;
- *an en route forecast*—the briefer should summarize the expected en route conditions in a logical order; this is departure, climb-out, en route and arrival;
- *destination terminal forecast*—this will be the forecast for one hour before your expected arrival time until an hour later;
- *winds aloft*—a summary of the forecast winds aloft at and near your planned cruise level. The briefer can also supply the expected temperatures; and
- *notices to airmen* (NOTAMs)—current NOTAMs for your route will be provided, but you have to ask for information about military training routes and NOTAMs that have been published. Only Flight Service Stations, not National Weather Service offices, can supply NOTAMs.

Other Types of Briefings

In addition to standard briefings, an FSS can offer two other kinds of briefings. When your planned departure is six or more hours away you should ask for an *outlook briefing*. It will include general information about expected weather trends that should help your planning. You need to ask for a more complete briefing later on, when it is closer to your takeoff time. When you need to update a previous briefing or to supplement mass-disseminated data or recorded data received by telephone or radio, you should ask for an *abbreviated briefing*. Tell the briefer the type of previous information you received and when you received it.

An "outlook briefing" is useful 6 or more hours before the flight. An "abbreviated briefing" is an update of, or supplement to, information you already have.

Updating Your Weather Information In Flight

Weather information can be updated in flight using Flight Service (122.2 MHz).

Once you are in the air you can update weather information by contacting Flight Service on 122.2 MHz as well as other charted frequencies. This frequency is the same all over the U.S. and used for the exchange of weather information. The information should flow two ways. In addition to receiving updated information, you should give Flight Service pilot weather reports, known as PIREPs. Since weather observation stations are often far apart, PIREPs are an important source of information for what is going on between stations. They give other pilots information which meteorologists usually cannot obtain from satellite photos and other sources, such as how turbulent the air is. For aircraft equipped with ADS-B In receivers with the ability to receive data over 978 MHz (UAT) free in-flight weather is available through FIS-B. FIS-B broadcasts a wide range of aviation weather related products including, METARs and TAFs, SIGMETs, convective SIGMETs, AIRMETs, NEXRAD, D-NOTAMs, FDC-NOTAMs, PIREPs, and winds and temperatures aloft forecast.

Weather Reports

You should start your briefing by finding out what the current weather is along your planned route and what it has been doing the last few hours. When you have a good idea of the current conditions, you are ready to look at forecasts of what the weather is expected to be doing at the time of your flight.

Weather Depiction Charts

The weather depiction chart or Ceiling & Visibility Chart is a good place to begin. These charts give a broad-brush snapshot of the actual weather and areas of clouds and precipitation. They are good charts for determining general weather conditions (IFR or VFR) on which to base your flight planning.

Weather depiction charts are prepared from METAR reports. They give a broad overview of flying conditions at the valid time of the chart, allowing you to determine general weather conditions quite readily, and so provide a good starting point when flight planning. More specific information, however, does need to be obtained from forecasts, prognostic charts, and the latest pilot, radar and METAR reports to augment the general information shown on weather depiction charts.

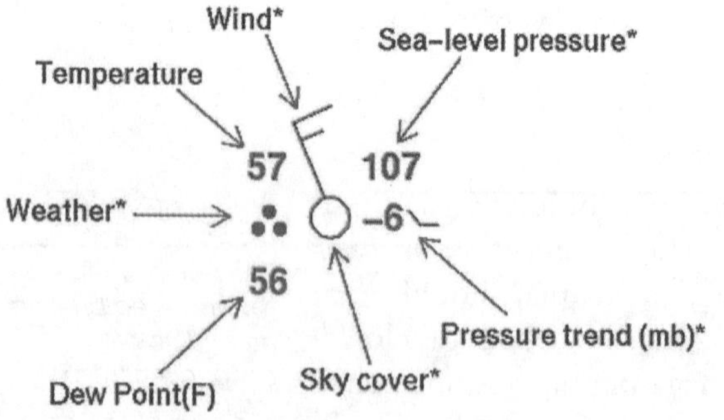

Figure 18-2 A station model.

Weather depiction charts show:

- areas of IFR, marginal VFR (MVFR), and VFR conditions, as determined by cloud base and visibility; and
- sky cover, cloud height, or ceiling, weather (including types of precipitation or obstructions to vision) and reduced visibilities as observed at various stations.

At each station:

- sky cover is shown in the station circle (with "M" indicating missing data);
- cloud height or ceiling above ground level (AGL) is shown under the station circle in hundreds of feet (when the total sky cover is few or scattered, the height shown on the weather depiction chart is the base of the lowest layer);

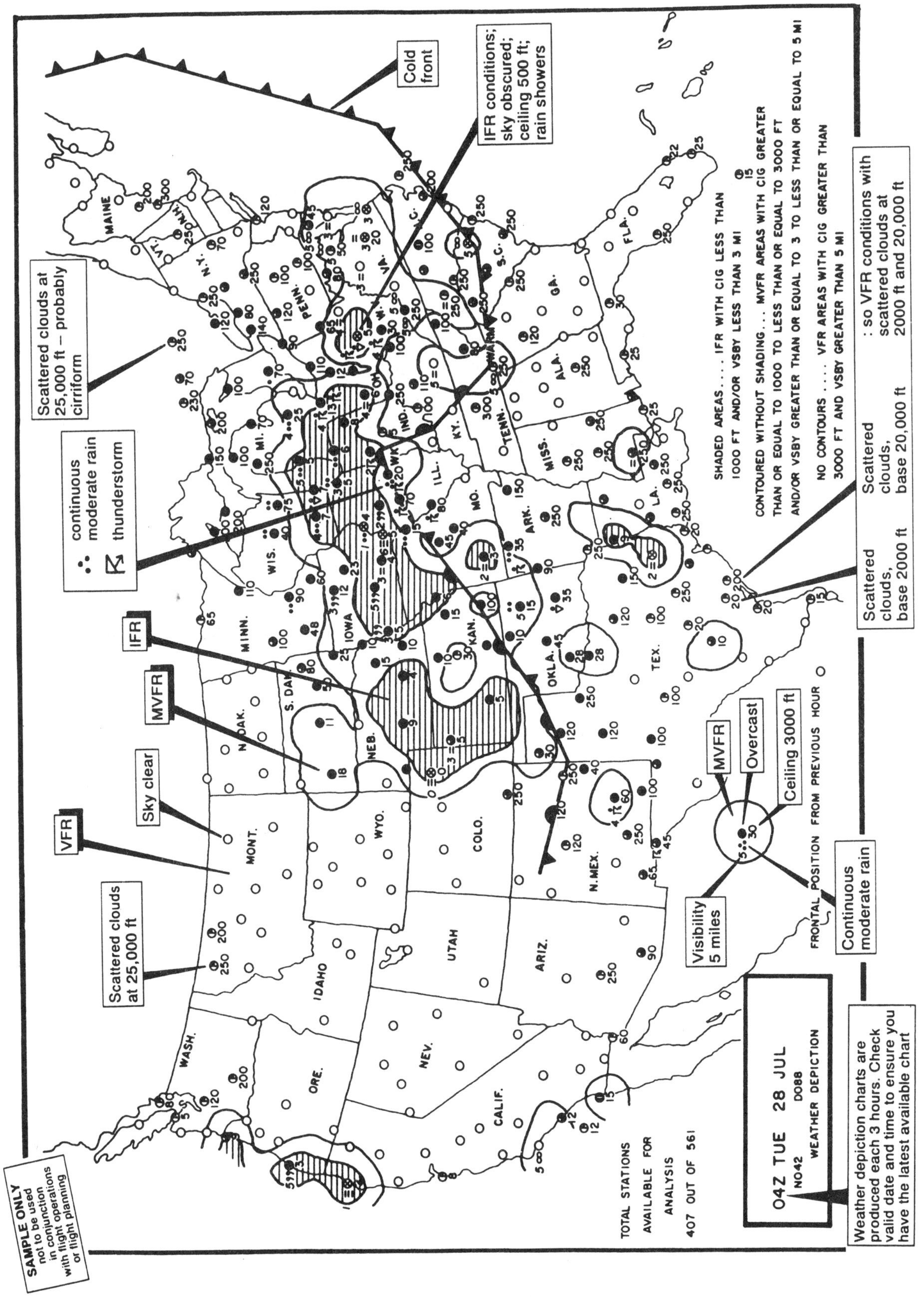

Figure 18-3 A typical weather depiction chart.

- weather and obstructions to vision symbols are shown left of the station circle; and
- visibility (if 6 miles or less) is shown to the left of the symbols for weather and obstructions to vision.

For example, rain is indicated by small black dots to the left of the station circle—a single dot representing intermittent rain, two dots side-by-side representing continuous rain, and three dots arranged in a triangle representing continuous moderate rain. Fog is indicated by two or three horizontal lines, arranged one above the other—three lines: visibility is less than ¼ mile; two lines it is ¼ mile or greater (and a visibility value would usually be added to the left of the fog symbol).

Surface Analysis Charts

The surface analysis chart, also known as the surface weather chart, provides an overview of the *observed* situation at the surface (ground level), and this allows you to:
- locate the position of pressure systems and fronts at ground level; and
- overview surface winds, temperatures, dewpoints, visibility problems and total sky cover at chart time.

Note. The surface analysis chart does not show cloud heights or tops (even though it shows total sky cover in the small station model circle), nor does it show the expected movement of weather pressure systems (even though it shows their position at chart time).

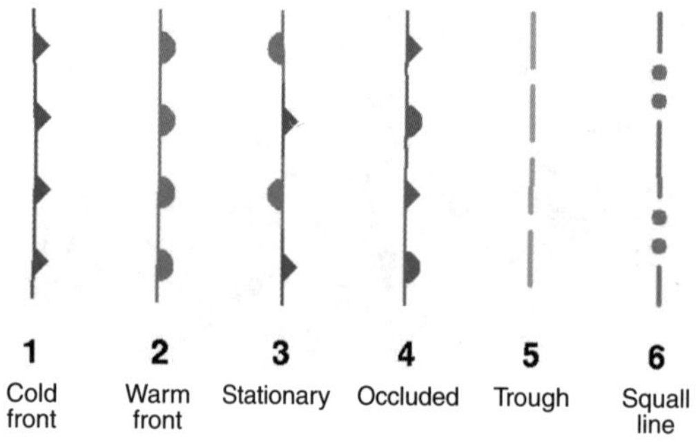

Figure 18-4
Some symbols on surface analysis charts.

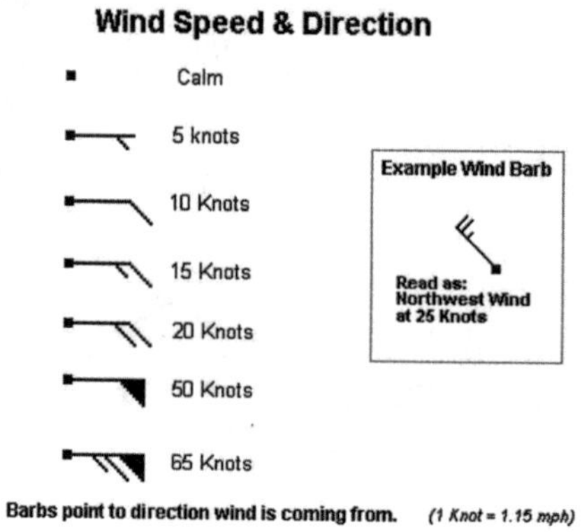

Figure 18-5
Wind speed and direction.

The National Weather Service (NWS) prepares these charts from observations taken at many weather stations, and the validity time of the chart in *Coordinated Universal Time* (UTC, or Zulu) corresponds to the time of observation. When using surface analysis charts, you should remember that weather moves and conditions change, so what is portrayed on the chart at its validity time may have changed.

The actual chart may appear to be a bit jumbled, but the main features are shown below. The information for each station is set out in standard format, known as a *station model*. Detailed decoding information is available at Flight Service Stations and in FAA weather publications such as AC 00-45.

The closer the isobars are, the stronger the pressure gradient and so the higher the winds. If the pressure gradient is weak, sometimes dashed isobars are spaced 4 mb apart.

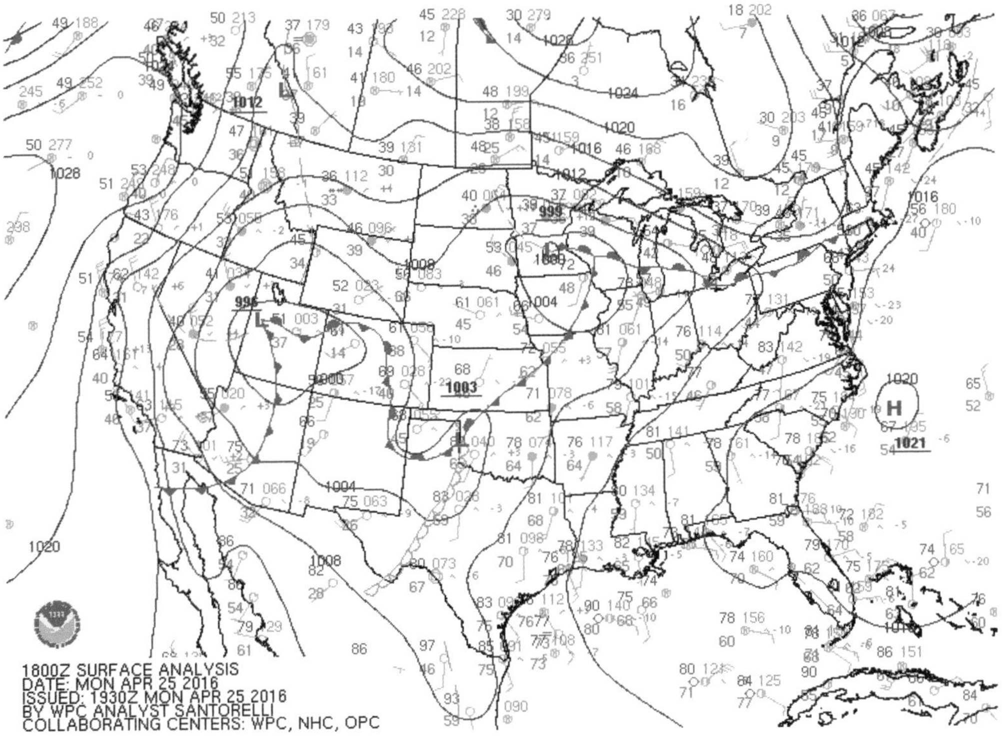

Figure 18-6
Surface analysis—North American continent.

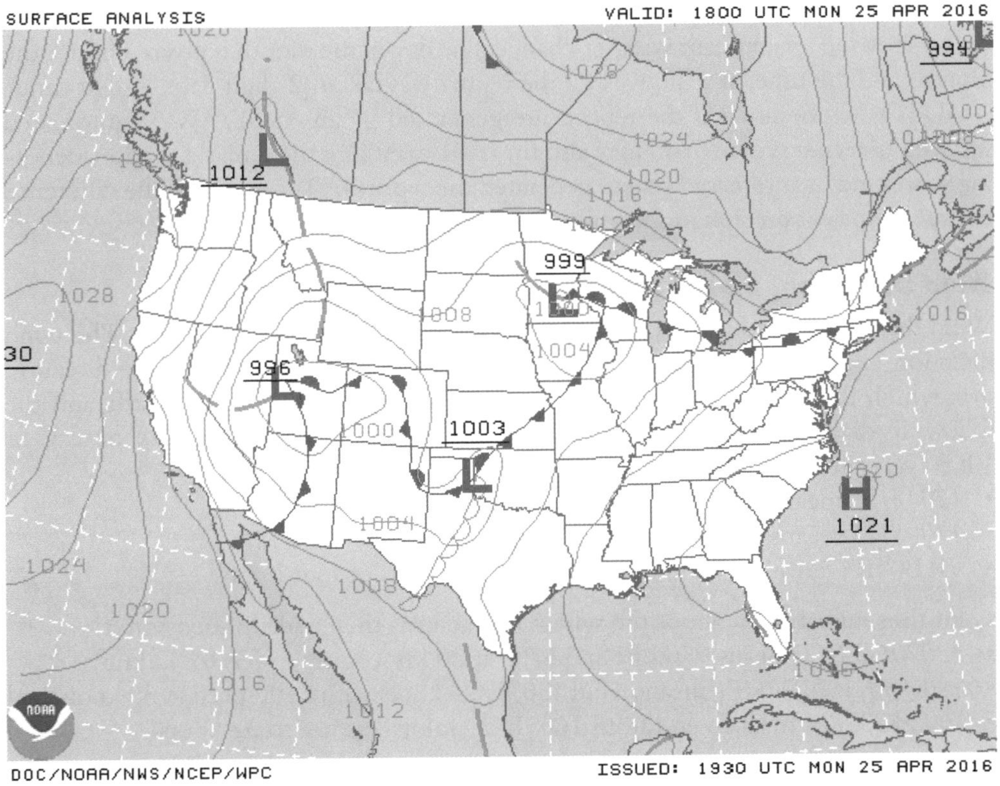

Figure 18-7
Extract from a typical surface analysis chart.

Aviation Routine Weather Reports (METAR/SPECI)

Your best source of information about the current weather or past weather at a particular airport is the hourly aviation routine weather reports, known as METAR reports. The SPECI acronym roughly translates as "Aviation Selected Special Weather Report." At weather stations all over the world, observers note the weather about five or ten minutes before the end of each hour and transmit their observations. The coded reports follow a format that makes them relatively easy to translate once you understand the system.

There are a few differences, worldwide, in how the reports are coded. In the U.S., winds are reported in knots, cloud layer heights and runway visual range in feet, visibility in statute miles and altimeter settings in inches of mercury. In other parts of the world, metric measurements and hectopascals are used. Temperatures throughout the world are reported in degrees Celsius.

While the METAR code uses some non-English words for some weather phenomena, the U.S. standard for METAR was developed in a cooperative effort. Some of the coding groups (such as GR for hail or FU for smoke) are based on French words, but many English abbreviations have been adopted. For example, the international abbreviations for *fog* and *rain* are FG and RA, respectively. A METAR observation will contain some or all of the following elements in the following order.

Station Designator

"K" identifies U.S. Stations.

The station designator is the standard 4-letter or combination letter and number code for the station. For example, KLAX for Los Angeles, KMDW for Chicago Midway.

Type and Time of Report

METAR is for a scheduled hourly observation. *SPECI* is an unscheduled special observation showing a significant weather change. The day of the month is given (but not the month) and the time, in Zulu (UTC) the report was taken (2-digit date, 4-digit time).

AUTO will be listed if the reports are generated by an ASOS/AWOS automated surface observing system. You may also find A01 or A02 in the remarks section, denoting what kind of automated system generated the report (A01 cannot tell the difference between types of precipitation, while A02 can).

Wind Direction, Speed and Character

Wind direction, speed and character follow the date and time of the report. The wind direction and speed is given together, the first three digits representing the direction *from* which the wind is blowing in tens of degrees referenced to *true* north, and the following digits representing speed. Winds are listed in degrees (i.e. 220) or as V or VRB (variable):

- *12015KT* means wind from 120 degrees true (°T) at 15 knots;
- *19008KT* means a wind from 190°T at 8 knots; and
- VRB04KT means a wind from variable directions of four knots.

Further information about the wind's character is then added if necessary:

- *32020G32KT* means wind from 320°T at 20 knots gusting (G) to 32 knots;
- *18024PKWND39KT* means wind 180°T/24 knots with peak speed to 39 knots; and
- 16020G32KT means wind from 160°T/20 knots gusting to 32 knots.

Visibility

The visibility is given next. Visibility is listed in statute miles, or quarters of statute miles (i.e. 3/4SM). *Runway visibility* is the horizontal distance a pilot can expect to see along a runway from a specific point on that runway. Runway visual ranges are listed as R23/3000FT (RVR runway 23 is 3,000 ft).

Visibility is the greatest distance, in statute miles or fractions thereof, at which objects can be seen and identified through at least 180 degrees of the horizon:

- 8 means visibility 8 statute miles;
- 1/2 means visibility ½ statute mile; and
- 11/2 means visibility 1½ statute miles.

Significant Weather, Sky Condition, and Ceiling

Any thunderstorms or other significant weather is listed here, followed by the sky condition and any ceiling. The weather is reported in a specific order:

- intensity;
- proximity;
- descriptor;
- precipitation;
- obstruction to visibility; and
- other.

Some *weather symbols*, which are used regardless of visibility, are given in table 18-2. *Precipitation* is measured as light (–), moderate (no sign) and heavy (+).

Some *obstructions to vision symbols* are given in table 18-3. If there is no weather and no obstructions to vision, then no entries will appear in the report.

RA+FG means heavy rain (RA+) as weather and fog (FG) as an obstruction to vision. Clouds are listed as:

- amount;
- height;
- (type); or
- vertical visibility.

Scattered layers of clouds are listed if the sky is covered by 3/8 to 4/8 (octas) of clouds. A broken layer is 5/8 to 7/8 coverage. Heights of clouds AGL are reported in hundreds of feet; add two zeros to read the height. The height AGL of the base of the layer preceding the sky-cover designator is also shown:

- *SCT140* means a scattered layer with the base at 14,000 feet AGL;
- *SCT006 SCT15CU* means two layers, a scattered layer at 600 feet AGL and a second higher layer of cumulous clouds at 1,500 feet AGL with the *total* sky cover of that layer and all layers beneath it not exceeding SCT;
- *SKC* means sky clear with, of course, no base being reported. In an automated report this will be CLR;
- *OVC008* means a ceiling 800 feet AGL overcast;
- *BKN070 OVC150* means a ceiling 7,000 feet AGL of broken cloud and another layer base 15,000 feet AGL with it and all layers beneath it adding up to overcast; and
- *VV005* means indefinite ceiling 500 feet AGL and sky obscured; *ceiling* is the height AGL of the lowest layer of clouds or obscuring phenomena aloft that is reported as BKN or OVC and not classified as thin, or the vertical visibility into surface-based obscuring phenomena that hides all the sky.

TS	Thunderstorm
+TS	Severe thunderstorm
RA	Rain
SH	Rain shower
DZ	Drizzle
FZRA	Freezing rain
FZDZ	Freezing drizzle
GR	Hail
PL	Ice pellets
SN	Snow
SNSH	Snow shower
SP	Snow pellets
SG	Snow grains
IC	Ice crystals

Table 18-2
Weather symbols.

DS	Dust storm
SS	Sand storm
BLSN	Blowing snow
BLPY	Blowing spray
DZ	Drizzle
FG	Fog
BR	Mist
HZ	Haze
VA	Volcanic ash
SG	Snow grains

Table 18-3
Obstructions to vision symbols.

Temperature and Dewpoint

Temperature and dewpoint are given in degrees *Celsius*, separated from each other by a slash (/):

- *23/20* means a temperature of 23°C and dewpoint 20°C; and
- *7/M09* means temperature 7°C and dewpoint minus 9°C.

Altimeter Setting

Following the temperature and dewpoint spread is the altimeter setting in inches of mercury. Only the last three digits are transmitted and the decimal point is omitted on METAR depiction charts; the pilot must add a 2 or a 3 to bring it close to 30 inches (normal sea level pressures are in the range 28.00 to 31.00 inches of mercury). In coded text, the 2 or 3 are not omitted, and the decimal point is omitted:

- *A2995* means an altimeter setting of 29.95 inches; and
- *A3013* means an altimeter setting of 30.13 inches.

Remarks and Coded Data

If included, the Remarks and Coded Data follow the altimeter group:

- the remarks in SLP013 means the Sea Level Pressure in hectopascals (1,001.3, in this case); and
- the remarks in T01760158 breaks down the temperature and the dewpoint spread at this station to the nearest ⅒ degree Celsius—T for temperature, 0 for positive (1 if negative), 17.6 degrees Celsius temperature, 15.8 degrees Celsius dewpoint.

Note. Any information that is missing in a METAR/SPECI report will simply be left out of the report. For this reason, take care when decoding the reports.

1. Type of Report	METAR or SPECI is included in all reports, and is separated from the element following it by a space.
2. The Station Identifier	This denotes where the report was taken from. Station identifiers are always given in four-letter ICAO code (KLAX, for example).
3. The Date and Time of the Report	The day of the month is shown first, followed by Zulu time of the report.
4. Modifier	If used, this tells if report is automated (AUTO).
5. Wind	Wind is reported as the full three-digit true direction, to the nearest 10°. (Note that ATC towers and ATIS report wind as magnetic.)
6. Visibility	Visibility is reported in statute miles. Runway visual range (RVR) is reported in feet.
7. Weather and Obstructions to Visibility	These are reported in the format: intensity/proximity/descriptor/precipitation/obstruction to visibility/other.
8. Sky Conditions	These are reported by their amount, height above ground level and type. Cloud coverage is categorized in eighths, or octas. SKC, sky clear, is just what it says. FEW is 0–2 octas coverage, SCT is 3–4 octas coverage, BKN is 5–7 octas coverage and OVC is 8 octas, or total coverage. Indefinite ceilings may be listed as VV (giving vertical visibility in feet).
9. Temperature and Dewpoint	These are reported in degrees Celsius. This is sometimes found in the Remarks section of a METAR.
10. Altimeter Setting	Given in inches of mercury—consists of A followed by four digits. Just add a decimal point in the middle to decode.
11. Remarks	If included, these follow the altimeter setting. Some stations will note the sea level pressure (SLP) in hectopascals to the nearest tenth here. Temperature and dewpoint, coded as 9 characters, may also be listed, as well as other temperatures. Remarks are best decoded with the aid of a decoder card (see illustration).

Table 18-4 Summary of METAR/SPECI reports.

Example 18-1

Decode the following METAR report, using the decoder illustrated.

```
METAR KFMY 141647Z VRB05KT 10SM SKC 30/16 A3003
```

This breaks down into:

1	2	3	4	5	6	7	8	9
KFMY	141647Z	VRB05KT	10SM	SKC	30/16	A3003		

1. KFMY is Fort Myers, Florida.
2. The report was taken the 14th day of the month, at 16:47 Zulu.
3. The wind direction is variable at 5 knots.
4. The visibility is 10 miles.
5. The sky is clear.
6. The temperature is 30°C and the dewpoint is 16°C.
7. The altimeter setting is 30.03 in. Hg.

That was a nice day in Fort Myers, Florida.

Example 18-2

Next, decode a more complicated report:

```
METAR KMCO 141653Z 23006KT 10SM FEW040 27/14 A3004 RMK
A02 SLP170 T02720144
```

This breaks down into:

1	2	3	4	5	6	7	8	9
KMCO	141653Z	23006KT	10SM	FEW040	27/14	A3004	RMK A02 SLP170 T02720144	

1. The report is from Orlando International Airport, Florida.
2. The day is the 14th, the time is 16:53Z.
3. The wind is from 230 degrees, at 6 knots.
4. The visibility is 10 statute miles or better.
5. There are a few clouds (0–2/8 coverage) at 4,000 feet.
6. The temperature is 27°C and the dewpoint 14°C, not close enough for you to have to worry about fog at the present time.
7. The altimeter is 30.04 in. Hg.
8. The remarks tell us that an automated observation (AWOS) that can determine precipitation (AO2) was used. We also see that the sea level pressure is 1,017.0 hPa and the temperature/dewpoint spread is a + 27.2°C and 14.4°C, respectively.

Another typical METAR/SPECI weather report is:

```
SPECI KTPA 141056Z 35003KT 6SM BR SCT250 21/18 A2998 RMK
AO2 SLP152 TO2060183
```

This decodes to: "Special weather observation for Tampa International Airport at the 14th day of the month, 10:56Z. The wind is 350 at 3 knots. There is 6 miles visibility with mist. There are scattered clouds (3/8–4/8 coverage) at 25,000 feet. The temperature is 21°C and the dewpoint is 18°C. The weather was taken by an automated observer capable of noting precipitation. The sea level pressure is 1,015.2, and the precise temperature/dewpoint spread is +20.6°C/+18.3°C."

Key to Aerodrome Forecast (TAF) and Aviation Routine Weather Report (METAR)

TAF KPIT 091730Z 0918/1024 15005KT 5SM HZ FEW020 WS010/31022KT
FM091930 30015G25KT 3SM SHRA OVC015
TEMPO 0920/0922 1/2SM +TSRA OVC008CB
FM100100 27008KT 5SM SHRA BKN020 OVC040
PROB30 1004/1007 1SM -RA BR
FM101015 18005KT 6SM -SHRA OVC020
BECMG 1013/1015 P6SM NSW SKC

Note: Users are cautioned to confirm ***DATE*** and ***TIME*** of the TAF.
For example FM**10**0000 is 0000Z on the **10th**. Do not confuse with ***1000Z!***

METAR KPIT 091955Z COR 22015G25KT 3/4SM R28L/2600FT TSRA OVC010CB 18/16 A2992 RMK SLP045 T01820159

Forecast	Explanation	Report
TAF	Message type: TAF: routine or TAF AMD: amended forecast; METAR: hourly; SPECI: special or TESTM: noncommissioned ASOS report	**METAR**
KPIT	ICAO location indicator	**KPIT**
091730Z	Issuance time: ALL times in UTC "Z", 2-digit date, 4-digit time	**091955Z**
0918/1024	Valid period: Either 24 hours or 30 hours. The first two digits of EACH four-digit number indicate the date of the valid period, the final two digits indicate the time (valid from 18Z on the 9th to 24Z on the 10th).	
	In U.S. **METAR**: CORrected ob; or AUTOmated ob for automated report with no human intervention; omitted when observer logs on.	**COR**
15005KT	Wind: 3-digit true-north direction, nearest 10 degrees (or VaRiaBle); next 2–3 digits for speed and unit, KT (KMH or MPS); as needed, Gust and maximum speed; 00000KT for calm; for **METAR**, if direction varies 60 degrees or more, Variability appended, e.g., 180V260	**22015G25KT**
5SM	Prevailing visibility: In U.S., Statute Miles and fractions; above 6 miles in **TAF** Plus6SM. (Or, 4-digit minimum visibility in meters and as required, lowest value with direction.)	**3/4SM**
	Runway Visual Range: R; 2-digit runway designator Left, Center, or Right as needed; "/"; Minus or Plus in U.S., 4-digit value, FeeT in U.S. (usually meters elsewhere); 4-digit value Variability, 4-digit value (and tendency Down, Up or No change)	**R28L/2600FT**
HZ	Significant present, forecast and recent weather: See table (on reverse side)	**TSRA**
FEW020	Cloud amount, height and type: SKy Clear 0/8, FEW >0/8-2/8, SCaTtered 3/8-4/8, BroKeN 5/8-7/8, OVerCast 8/8; 3-digit height in hundreds of feet; Towering CUmulus or CumulonimBus in **METAR**; in **TAF**, only CB. Vertical Visibility for obscured sky and height "VV004". More than 1 layer may be reported or forecast. In automated **METAR** reports only, CLeaR for "clear below 12,000 feet."	**OVC010CB**
	Temperature: Degrees Celsius; first 2 digits, temperature "/" last 2 digits, dewpoint temperature; Minus for below zero, e.g., M06	**18/16**
	Altimeter setting: Indicator and 4 digits; in U.S., A: inches and hundredths; (Q: hectoPascals, e.g., Q1013)	**A2992**

Continued

Key to Aerodrome Forecast (TAF) and Aviation Routine Weather Report (METAR)

Forecast	Explanation	Report
WS010/31022KT	In U.S. **TAF**, nonconvective low-level (≤2,000 feet) Wind Shear; 3-digit height (hundreds of feet); "/"; 3-digit wind direction and 2–3 digit wind speed above the indicated height, and unit, KT	
	In **METAR**, ReMarK indicator and remarks. For example: Sea-Level Pressure in hectoPascals and tenths, as shown: 1004.5 hPa; Temp/dewpoint in tenths °C, as shown: temp. 18.2°C, dewpoint 15.9°C	**RMK SLP045 T01820159**
FM091930	FroM: Changes are expected at: 2-digit date, 2-digit hour, and 2-digit minute **beginning** time: indicates significant change. Each FM starts on a new line, indented 5 spaces	
TEMPO 0920/0922	TEMPOrary: Changes expected for <1 hour and in total, < half of the period between the 2-digit date and 2-digit hour **beginning**, and 2-digit date and 2-digit hour **ending** time	
PROB30 1004/1007	PROBability and 2-digit percent (30 or 40): Probable condition in the period between the 2-digit date and 2-digit hour **beginning** time, and the 2-digit date and 2-digit hour **ending** time	
BECMG 1013/1015	BECoMinG: Change expected in the period between the 2-digit date and 2-digit hour **beginning** time, and the 2-digit date and 2-digit hour **ending** time	

Table of Significant Present, Forecast and Recent Weather – Grouped in categories and used in the order listed below; or as needed in TAF, No Significant Weather

QUALIFIERS

Intensity or Proximity

"–" = Light **No sign** = Moderate "+" = Heavy

"VC" = Vicinity, but not at aerodrome. In the U.S. **METAR**, 5 to 10 SM from the point of observation. In the U.S. **TAF**, 5 to 10 SM from the center of the runway complex. Elsewhere, within 8000m.

Descriptor

BC Patches	**BL** Blowing	**DR** Drifting	**FZ** Freezing
MI Shallow	**PR** Partial	**SH** Showers	**TS** Thunderstorm

WEATHER PHENOMENA

Precipitation

DZ Drizzle	**GR** Hail	**GS** Small hail or snow pellets	
IC Ice crystals	**PL** Ice pellets	**RA** Rain	**SG** Snow grains
SN Snow	**UP** Unknown precipitation in automated observations		

Obscuration

BR Mist (≥5/8SM)	**DU** Widespread dust	**FG** Fog (<5/8SM)	**FU** Smoke
HZ Haze	**PY** Spray	**SA** Sand	**VA** Volcanic ash

Other

DS Dust storm	**FC** Funnel cloud	**+FC** Tornado or waterspout	
PO Well-developed dust or sand whirls		**SQ** Squall	**SS** Sandstorm

- Explanations in parentheses "( )" indicate different worldwide practices.
- Ceiling is not specified; defined as the lowest broken or overcast layer, or the vertical visibility.
- NWS **TAF**s exclude BECMG groups and temperature forecasts, NWS **TAF**s do not use PROB in the first 9 hours of a TAF; NWS **METAR**s exclude trend forecasts. U.S. Military **TAF**s include Turbulence and Icing groups.

Figure 18-8 ASA's METAR/TAF decoder table.

Pilot Weather Reports (PIREPs)

Pilot reports can be your best source—sometimes the only source—of information about what is going on between weather stations. Since the reports are voluntary, PIREPs may not be available to you on every flight, but you should still ask for them.

Pilot reports (PIREPs), identified by UA or by UUA if urgent, are often appended METARs. The form of a PIREP is UA followed by the mandatory items:

- /OV (over location);
- /TM (time);
- /FL (altitude or flight level);
- /TP (aircraft type); and then by the optional items /SK (sky cover);
- /WX (flight visibility and weather);
- /TA (temperature in degrees Celsius); /WV (wind velocity °M/kt);
- /TB (turbulence);
- /IC (icing); and
- /RM (remarks).

Example 18-3

A typical PIREP, decoded below, is:

```
UA/OV 12 NW MDB/TM 1540/FL 120/TP BE55/SK 026 BKN 034/044
BKN-OVC/TA –11/IC MDT RIME 060-080/RM R TURBC INCRS WWD
MH 270 TAS 185
```

"PIREP, 12 NM northwest of MDB, at time 1540 UTC, altitude 12,000 feet MSL, type Beech Baron, sky cover is first cloud layer base 2,600 feet MSL broken with tops at 3,400 feet MSL and second cloud layer base 4,400 feet MSL broken occasionally overcast with no reported tops, temperature minus 11 degrees Celsius, icing moderate rime between 6,000 and 8,000 feet MSL, remarks are turbulence increasing westward, magnetic heading 270, true airspeed 185 knots."

You can generally interpret the abbreviations without too much trouble. For example: FL080/SK INTMTLY BL means an airplane at 8,000 feet MSL is flying intermittently between layers; /TB MDT means turbulence moderate; /TP B727 means type Boeing 727; /SK OVC 075/085 OVC 150 means sky cover is an overcast layer with tops 7,500 feet MSL and no reported base, with a second overcast layer base 8,500 feet MSL and tops 15,000 feet MSL.

If the METAR at the place where the UA PIREP contained those last cloud details above also contained OVC009, then it is possible to calculate the thickness of the lower cloud layer. If the station elevation is say 2,300 feet MSL, then the cloud base is 3,200 feet MSL (elevation 2,300 feet MSL + ceiling 900 feet AGL). Since the pilot reported the tops of the lower layer at 7,500 feet MSL, the thickness of this layer is 4,300 feet (7,500 − 3,200).

Examples of typical PIREPs follow.

```
ONT UA/OV PDZ/TM 2109/FL 085/TP PA28/SK SCT–BKN 090/TA 05
```

"The report is from Ontario, California at 2109Z. The aircraft was over the Paradise (PDZ) VOR at 8,500 feet. It was a Piper Cherokee (or Warrior, the FAA uses the PA-28 designation for both). The pilot reported scattered to broken clouds with tops at 9,000 feet. The temperature at 8,500 feet was +5 degrees Celsius."

Example 18-4

```
SFO UUA/OV SFO 020030/TM 2100/FL 100/TP C130/IC MDT–SVR/
RM HAIL
```

"The aircraft was on the 020 radial from the San Francisco VOR, 30 miles out. The report was made at 2100 UTC. The airplane was at 10,000 feet. It was a C130 Lockheed Hercules. Under IC for icing, the pilot reported moderate to severe icing. Under remarks (RM), the pilot noted there was hail. While no comment is made on the weather, we can conclude that thunderstorms or violent towering cumulus clouds are around to generate the hail and, even though the pilot has not made a specific turbulence report, it probably exists—any cloud that can produce hailstones will be turbulent. The icing was probably caused by supercooled water in cloud updrafts hitting the airplane."

Example 18-5

```
AHN UA/OV AHN/TM 2038/FL DURGD/TP CE152/SK 055 SCT–BKN
080/TB MDT BLO 040
```

"The report is from Athens, Georgia, and the aircraft was over the Athens VOR at 2038 UTC. The DURGD under FL means the pilot reported during descent. ('During climb' is written DURGC.) Aircraft type Cessna 152. The pilot encountered a scattered to broken layer of clouds with the bases at 5,500 feet and the tops at 8,000 feet. Note that all altitudes in PIREPs are referenced to mean sea level (MSL), since the pilot will be making estimates of altitude with reference to the altimeter. The pilot also reported moderate turbulence below 4,000 feet."

See AIM Chapter 7 for more information on reporting turbulence.

When reporting turbulence, use standard criteria so that other pilots derive correct information from your PIREP.

Duration:

- *occasional* is less than one-third of the time;
- *intermittent* is one-third to two-thirds of the time; and
- *continuous* is more than two-thirds of the time.

Intensity:

- *light turbulence* causes slight, erratic changes in altitude and/or attitude, with the occupants feeling slight strain on their seatbelts. Rhythmic bumpiness, without appreciable changes in altitude and/or attitude, should be reported as "light chop" rather than light turbulence;
- *moderate turbulence* causes changes in altitude and/or attitude, and usually causes variations in indicated airspeed, but the aircraft remains in positive control at all times: the occupants will feel definite strains on their seatbelts and unsecured objects in the aircraft may be dislodged. Rapid bumps or jolts, without appreciable changes in altitude and/or attitude, should be reported as "moderate chop" rather than moderate turbulence;
- *severe turbulence* causes large, abrupt changes in attitude and/or altitude and usually large changes in indicated airspeed, and the aircraft may be momentarily out of control; the occupants will be forced violently against their seatbelts and unsecured objects in the aircraft will be tossed about; and
- *extreme turbulence* will toss the aircraft about violently and the aircraft may be practically impossible to control—structural damage may result.

Weather Forecasts

If you visit a FSS or Weather Service Office and check over the charts and reports described above, and also look at satellite photos, you should have a good idea of what the weather was doing at the time the information was gathered. Knowing what the weather is doing now, and what it has been doing in the last few hours, makes it easier to understand the forecasts of what it should be doing later on during your flight.

You need to develop a three-dimensional picture of current weather, and then judge how this picture will change with time. To take a single example: you are planning a two-hour trip to another airport; the weather is forecast to be good at the destination when you expect to arrive, and the weather is now good at your departure point. The forecast, however, predicts that thunderstorm activity will cease at your destination about an hour before your estimated time of arrival.

Obviously, you need to know more. What is the weather likely to be along your planned route? Will the thunderstorms be moving across your planned route? If the thunderstorms are moving away from both the destination and your route, are there any indications that they are in fact moving away as predicted by the forecast? What will you do if you arrive at your destination and find that the forecast is inaccurate and the storms have not ended? Having studied the recently observed weather, it is now time to study the forecasts of what the weather is predicted to do in the hours ahead.

Low-Level Significant Weather Prognostic Charts

Prognostic charts are *forecasts*, rather than observations, and are the only charts that can give you a good overall view of the expected weather. The low-level significant weather prognostic chart is a two-panel chart that shows the general conditions that are forecast to occur from the surface to 24,000 feet MSL (the 400 millibar (hPa) pressure level) at the valid time (VT) of the chart. The left panel shows the forecast for 12 hours from the issuance time, and the right panel shows the forecast for 24 hours from the issuance time. Prognostic charts are issued four times daily at 0000, 0600, 1200, 1800 UTC. (See figure 18-9, page 434).

Each chart depicts freezing levels, turbulence, and low cloud ceilings and/or restrictions to visibility (shown as contoured areas of MVFR and IFR conditions) during that forecast period. The chart will typically contain a legend of the depicted conditions (see figure 18-9). A solid red contour line represents ceilings less than 1,000 feet and/or visibility less than 3 miles (IFR). An area enclosed by scalloped blue lines represent ceilings 1,000 to 3,000 feet inclusive and/or visibility 3 to 5 miles inclusive (MVFR). Any area on the chart not outlined represents VFR conditions. Moderate or greater turbulence is shown on the chart by areas enclosed with long dashed orange lines. General freezing levels are also given in intervals of 4,000 feet as shown by short dashed teal lines with a corresponding altitude (wavy teal line when the freezing level is at the surface). Charts may be shown in either black and white or color.

Note. The method of outlining the IFR and MVFR areas differs from what is used on weather depiction charts.

The low-level significant weather prognostic chart, as shown in figure 18-9, can be used to determine which areas to avoid, those with non-VFR weather, turbulence, and the possibility of icing above the freezing level.

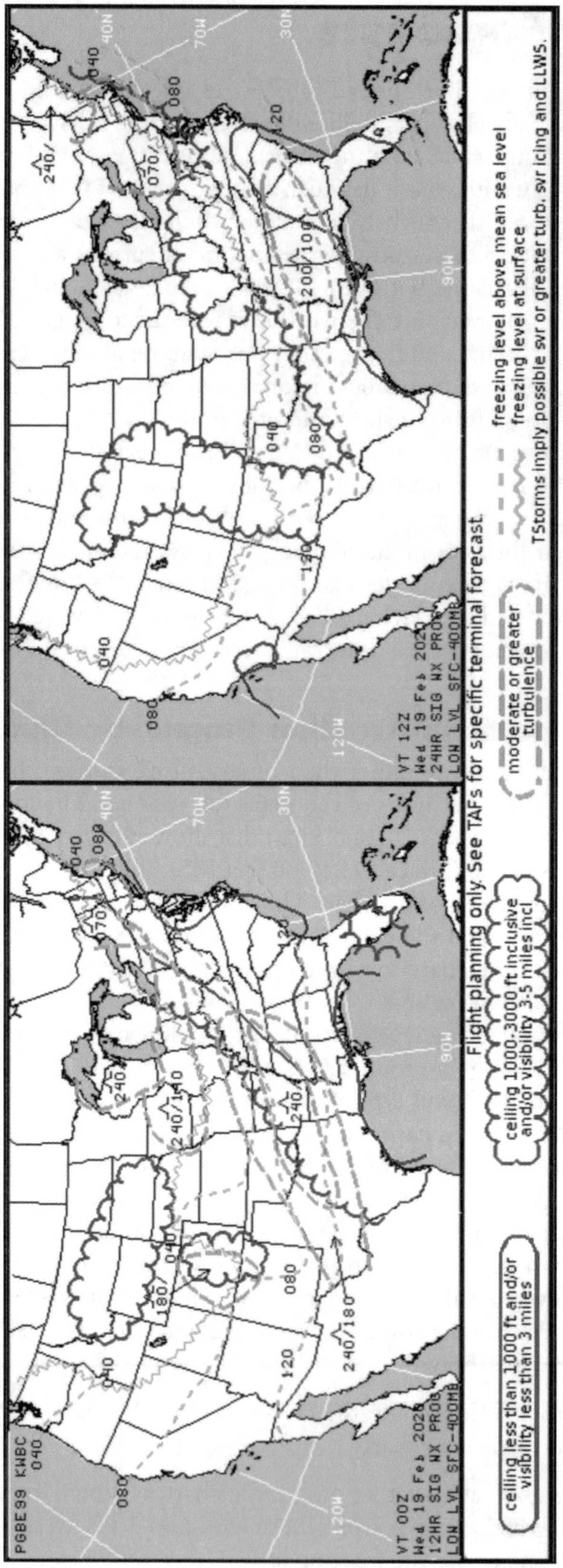

Figure 18-9 A typical low-level significant weather prognostic chart.

Surface Prognostic Chart

A surface prognostic chart is a snapshot of surface conditions generated by the weather prediction center (WPC). These forecast charts include surface pressure systems, fronts, and precipitation over the contiguous United States and coastal waters (see figure 18-11). Each forecast is divided into five forecasts periods: 12, 18, 24, 48, and 60 hours.

Areas of precipitation expected at the valid time of the forecast are shaded in colors depending on the type and likelihood of precipitation. The areas are derived from the National Digital Forecast Database grid for weather and shown in figure 18-10.

Note. In addition to surface and low-level significant weather prognostic charts there is also mid-level (FL100-450) and high-level (FL250-630) charts available. The mid-level and high-level (as seen in figure 18-12) charts are similar in presentation. The mid-level chart contains more detail in respect to icing and turbulence which are more likely to be encountered at altitudes below FL250.

NDFD Rain (Chance) - There is chance of measurable rain (≥0.01") at the valid time.

NDFD Rain (Likely) - Measurable rain (≥0.01") is likely at the valid time.

NDFD Snow (Chance) - There is chance of measurable snowfall (≥0.01" liquid equivalent) at the valid time.

NDFD Snow (Likely) - Measurable snow (≥0.01" liquid equivalent) is likely at the valid time.

NDFD Mix (Chance) - There is chance of measurable mixed precipitation (≥0.01" liquid equivalent) at the valid time. "Mixed" can refer to precipitation where a combination of rain and snow, rain and sleet, or snow and sleet are forecast.

NDFD Mix (Likely) - Measurable mixed precipitation (≥0.01" liquid equivalent) is likely at the valid time. "Mixed" can refer to precipitation where a combination of rain and snow, rain and sleet, or snow and sleet are forecast.

NDFD Ice (Chance) - There is chance of measurable freezing rain (≥0.01") at the valid time.

NDFD Ice (Likely) - Measurable freezing rain (≥0.01") is likely at the valid time.

NDFD T-Storm (Chance) - There is chance of thunderstorms at the valid time.
NOTE: Areas are displayed with diagonal hatching enclosed in a dark red border.

NDFD T-Storm (Likely and/or Severe) - Thunderstorms are likely and/or the potential exists for some storms to reach severe levels at the valid time.

Figure 18-10 Surface prognostic chart precipitation types.

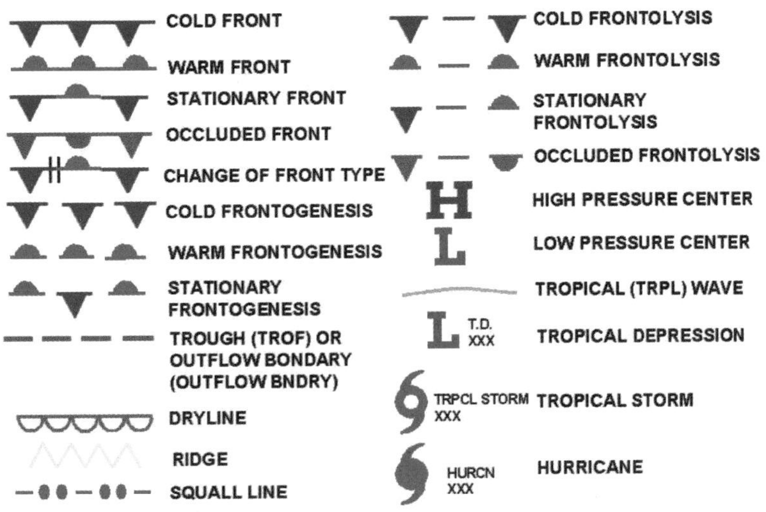

Figure 18-11 Surface prognostic chart symbols.

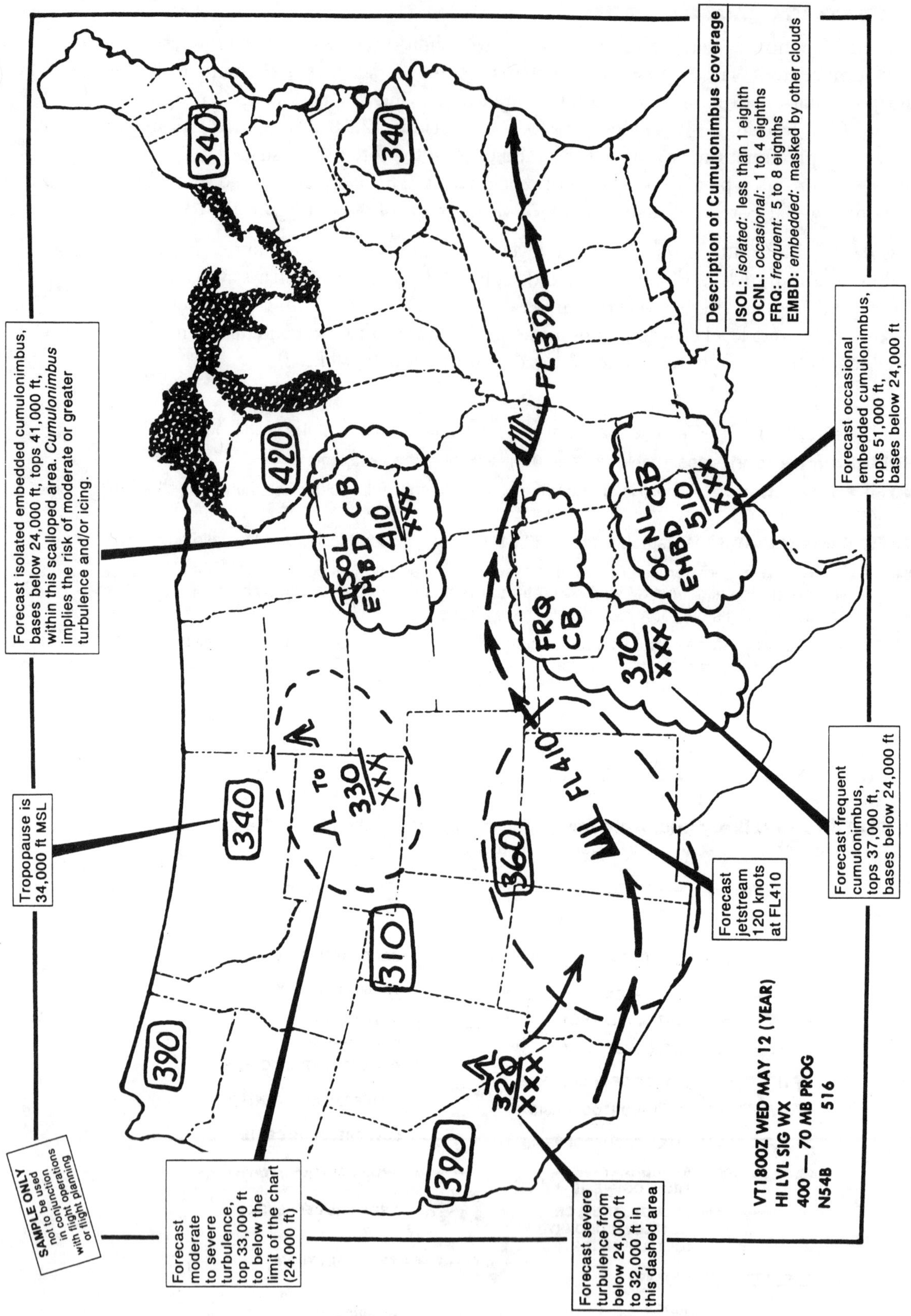

Figure 18-12 Extract of high-level significant weather prognosis panel.

Terminal Aerodrome Forecasts (TAF)

Aerodrome forecasts (TAF) are the ones most used by pilots.

As the name indicates, terminal aerodrome forecasts (TAF) predict the weather at particular airports. They are issued four times a day and are valid for a 24-hour period. If the weather changes significantly between scheduled forecasts, amendments are issued.

The forecast is for cloud heights and amounts, visibility, weather and wind that would affect flying within five miles of the airport's center. If the forecast uses the term VCNTY, an abbreviation for *vicinity*, it is referring to weather expected in the area from 5 to 25 miles from the airport that could affect flying there.

The format of the terminal aerodrome forecast is essentially that of the METAR, but a few examples will illustrate the differences. There will be a date-time group, such as 141730Z, which means that the forecast was issued on the 14th day of the month at 1730Z. Forecasts are given in UTC (Zulu time), but you can translate them into local times if it makes it easier for you. Eastern Daylight Time (EDT) is found by subtracting 4 hours from the UTC time.

Next come the valid times, 1418/1518, meaning, the 14th day, from 1800Z to the 15th day 1800Z. From there on out, the forecast reads much like a METAR, except with multiple levels.

For example:

```
TAF KRSW 141730Z 1418/1518 27008KT P6SM SCT0040 SCT200
BECMG 1421/1422 34007KT
BECMG 1402/1403 VRB04KT SCT150 SCT200
TEMPO 1410/1414 BKN150
FM140000 33007KT P6SM SCT035 SCT150
TEMPO 1414/1418 BKN150
```

"This terminal forecast is for Southwest Florida International Airport on the 14th day of the month, issued at 13:30 local time and valid from 14:00 local time until 14:00 local time on the 15th. The wind is forecast to be from 270 degrees at 8 knots, with a visibility of more than 6 miles, with a scattered layer of clouds (3–4 octas coverage) at 4,000 feet, and another scattered layer of clouds at 20,000 feet. This becomes, between 17:00 and 18:00 local time, a wind from 020 degrees, variable at 4 knots, with scattered clouds at 15,000 and 20,000 feet. Temporary changes are expected between 06:00 and 10:00 local time, when clouds are expected to be broken at 15,000 feet. From 10:00 local time, winds are forecast from 330 degrees at 7 knots, with scattered clouds at 3,500 feet. Temporary changes are forecast between 10:00 and 14:00 local time (1400–18002), when clouds are expected to be broken (BKN, 5/8–7/8) at 15,000 feet."

International Differences

Pilots who fly outside of the U.S. will notice that all METAR and TAF reports are not quite the same:

- international altimeter settings are given in hectopascals and noted as Q1013;
- wind may be reported in knots, meters per second (MPS) or kilometers per hour (KPH). Low-level windshear that is not associated with convective activity does not get reported outside of the U.S., Canada or Mexico;
- visibility is reported in thousands of meters, with reference to the lowest visibility in a geographic sector and a trend (for instance, 3000SWD, which means visibility of 3,000 meters to the southwest, reducing); and
- finally, in international METAR/TAF the code CAVOK means that there are no clouds below 1,500 meters (5,000 feet) or the lowest ATC sector altitude and the visibility is 10 kilometers or better.

Area Forecasts and the Convective Outlook

While TAFs provide detailed predictions for airports, they do not tell you what to expect between airports. When obtaining a weather briefing, it is a good idea to look at the forecasts for airports along and near your route for an indication of what to expect.

Area Forecasts (FA)

Area Forecasts are issued for Alaska, Hawaii, the Caribbean, and the Gulf of Mexico. Refer to the Graphical Forecast for Aviation (GFA) for forecasts over the continental United States (see page 444).

Area Forecasts—coded "FA"—are issued three times a day separately from the Aviation Weather Center in Kansas City for the Gulf of Mexico and the Caribbean, from the Alaska Aviation Weather Unit for Alaska, and from the Weather Service Forecast Office in Honolulu for Hawaii. They are valid for 12 hours plus a six-hour *outlook* period. The outlook gives a generalized forecast. Area forecasts are supplied in 4 sections. The first two contain:

- *communication and product header section*—shows where the FA was issued from, the date and time of its issue, the product name, valid times and the States the FA covers; and
- *a precautionary statement section*—lets the reader know immediately if and where any IFR conditions, mountain obscurations or thunderstorm hazards exist. It also warns the reader that heights, for the most part, are given in AGL.

Then, two weather sections contain:

- *a synopsis*—a brief summary of the location and movement of weather fronts, pressure systems and circulation patterns for the eighteen-hour period; plus
- *a statement of VFR clouds and weather*—a twelve-hour forecast, in broad terms, of clouds and weather significant to VFR flights, giving a summary of the sky condition, cloud heights, visibility, weather and/or obstructions to visibility, and surface winds of 30 knots or more. It concludes with a categorical outlook valid for 6 hours.

Pilots often have more trouble deciphering area forecasts than other reports and forecasts. This is because they use more contractions than plain English words and also because they describe the location of areas of turbulence and icing by referring to VORs—often VORs that are outside the area covered in the forecast. Practice, with a list of the most common contractions, is the only way to learn to read area forecasts.

When checking the turbulence and icing parts of the forecast, look for VORs along or within 100 miles or so on either side of your planned route. If you find such a VOR listed, then you can look closer to see if your flight is likely to be affected. A sample FA for Hawaii is shown in figure 18-13.

The Convective Outlook (AC)

The convective outlook (AC) forecasts the possibility for general, as well as severe, thunderstorm activity during the following 24 hours. The convective outlook chart is issued each morning and provides a preliminary 48-hour outlook for thunderstorm activity, tornadoes and watch areas. It is presented in two panels, the first for the time period of 24 hours, and the second for the next day. It is used for advanced planning only.

Convective Outlook Charts. These charts portray areas of probable convectivity. An area of forecast general thunderstorm activity is represented by a line with an arrowhead—when you face in the direction of the arrowhead, thunderstorm activity is expected to the right of that line. Forecast severe thunderstorms are shown by a single-hatched area, which may be labeled SLGT (slight risk), MDT (moderate risk) or SVR (high risk). Any tornado watches in effect at chart time are shown by crosshatched areas. Convective outlook charts are issued five times daily.

```
000
FAHW31 PHFO 181523
FA0HI

HNLC FA 181535
SYNOPSIS AND VFR CLD/WX
SYNOPSIS VALID UNTIL 190400
CLD/WX VALID UNTIL 182200...OUTLOOK VALID 182200-190400
.
SEE AIRMET SIERRA FOR IFR CLD AND MTN OBSC.
TS IMPLY SEV OR GREATER TURB SEV ICE LOW LEVEL WS AND IFR COND.
NON MSL HGT INDICATED BY AGL OR CEILING.
.
SYNOPSIS...SFC HIGH PRESSURE NORTH OF HAWAII WILL MAINTAIN A
STABLE AND WINDY/GUSTY TRADE WIND FLOW. ISOLATED SHOWERS ON WINDWARD
SLOPES OF THE ISLANDS.
.
ENTIRE AREA.
SFC WIND OVR MTN RIDGES AND THRU VALLEYS NE 20 TO 25 KT.
LOWER CLD AND WX FOLLOW.
.
BIG ISLAND INTERIOR ABV 070.
FEW-SCT120. OUTLOOK...VFR.
.
BIG ISLAND LOWER SLOPES...COAST AND ADJ WATERS FROM UPOLU POINT
TO CAPE KUMUKAHI TO APUA POINT.
BKN-SCT025 BKN-SCT040 TOPS 080 TEMPO BKN025 VIS 3-5SM -SHRA
ISOL BKN020 TOPS 090 VIS BLW 3SM SHRA. 17Z SCT025 SCT-BKN040
TOPS 080 ISOL BKN030 TOPS 100 VIS 5SM SHRA. OUTLOOK...VFR.
.
BIG ISLAND LOWER SLOPES AND COAST FROM APUA POINT TO SOUTH CAPE
TO UPOLU POINT.
FEW030 SCT050 ISOL -SHRA. 20Z FEW-SCT030 SCT-BKN050 TOPS 070 ISOL -SHRA.
OUTLOOK...VFR.
.
MTN...N THRU E SECTIONS AND ADJ WATERS OF MAUI MOLOKAI OAHU AND
KAUAI.
SCT025 BKN-SCT040 TOPS 070 ISOL BKN025 TOPS 090 VIS 5SM SHRA.
OUTLOOK...VFR.
.
REST OF AREA.
FEW030 FEW-SCT045 ISOL BKN030 TOPS 080 -SHRA. OUTLOOK...VFR.
```

AREA FORECAST (FA) VALIDITY & COVERAGE

REFERENCE TO IMPORTANT WEATHER

SYNOPSIS

SIGNIFICANT CLOUDS AND WEATHER

Figure 18-13 A sample FA for Hawaii.

Note. Any forecasted AIRMETs will follow the significant clouds and weather section of the FA report to include turbulence (T), IFR weather and mountain obscurations (S), and icing and freezing levels (Z).

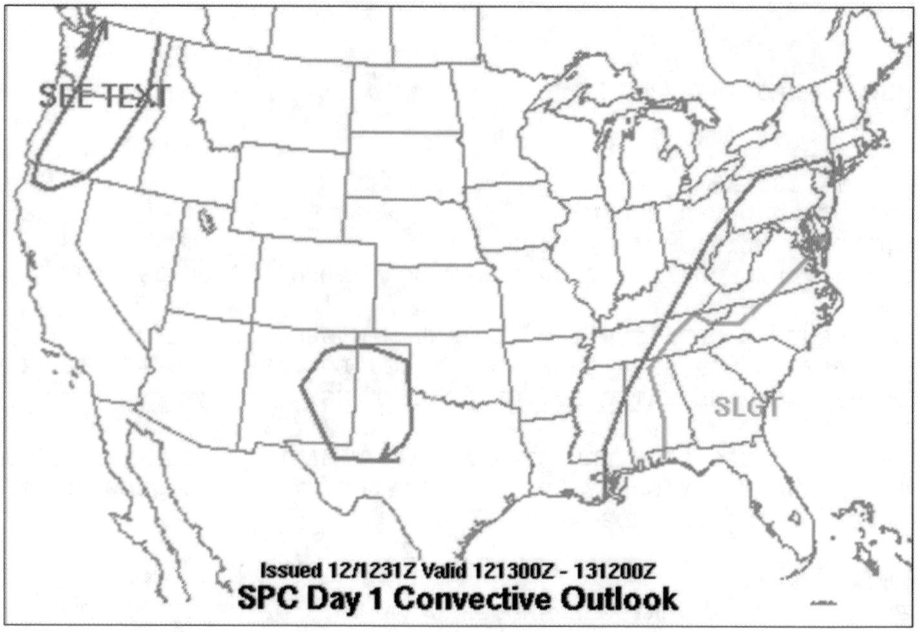

Figure 18-14 Example of a convective outlook chart.

Weather Advisories

AIRMETs (WA)

AIRMETs warn of hazards primarily to small aircraft; they are issued *every six hours beginning at 0245 UTC* with intermediate updates as needed. There are three types of AIRMETs: Tango, Sierra, and Zulu available in both textual form (WA) or graphics (G-AIRMET).

- AIRMET Tango—turbulence—a forecast of non-convective activity related to turbulence of moderate intensity, low-level wind shear, or sustained surface winds of 30 knots and greater;
- AIRMET Sierra—IFR Weather and Mountain Obscuration—a forecast that identifies aviation weather hazards that meet in-flight advisory criteria; and
- AIRMET Zulu—icing—a forecast of non-thunderstorm-related icing of moderate or greater intensity, often using VOR points to outline the area of icing (it sometimes extends beyond the FA boundary).

When checking the AIRMETs, look for VORs along or within 100 miles or so either side of your planned route. If you find such a VOR listed, then you can look closer to see if your flight is likely to be affected. An example of a typical area forecast and group of AIRMETs, with explanatory expansion, is shown in figure 18-13. Be aware that *hyphens* in weather data can be used for three purposes:

- to indicate a range—e.g., VSBY 3-5, "visibility 3 to 5 miles";
- for spacing—VSBY 3-F, "visibility 3 miles in fog"; and
- to condition a phenomenon as *lighter*—RW-, "light rain showers".

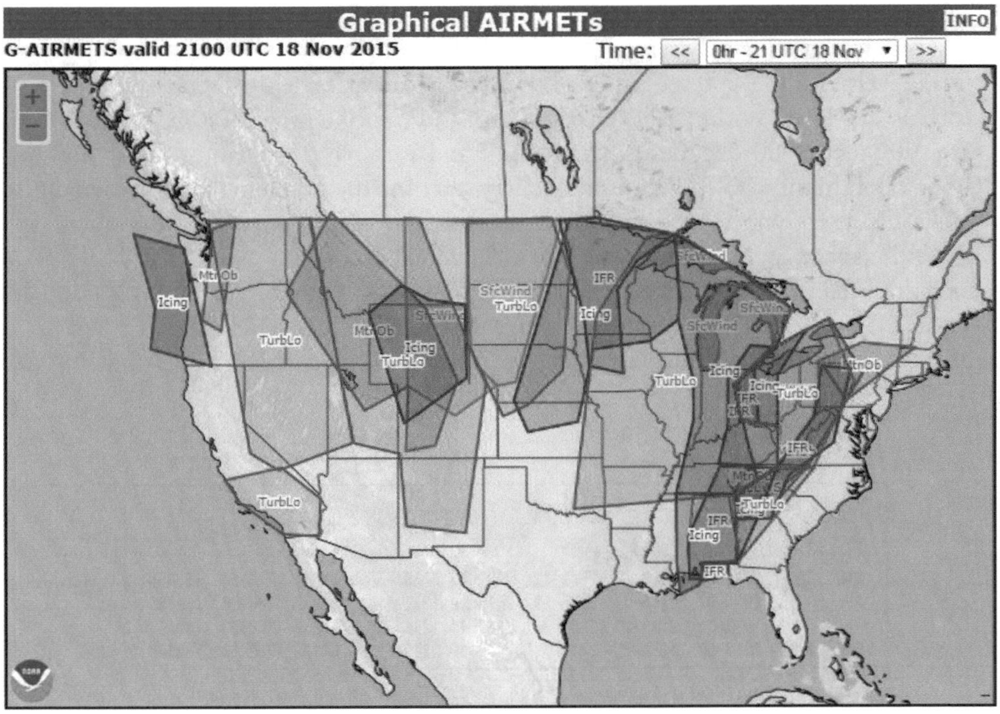

Figure 18-15 Example of G-AIRMET graphical advisory.

SIGMETs (WS) and Convective SIGMETs (WST)

SIGMETs warn of conditions that could be dangerous to all aircraft (severe icing, and severe/extreme turbulence). *Convective* SIGMETs are observations and/or forecasts that warn of conditions associated with thunderstorms that could be dangerous to all aircraft—tornados, large hail, embedded thunderstorms, large Cb areas (and with severe icing, severe turbulence and low-level windshear implied). They are issued when necessary to alert pilots of these conditions.

Center Weather Advisories (CWA)

Advice of the sudden development in the weather situation will often first be issued in the form of a Center Weather Advisory, for conditions beginning within 2 hours. This may be used to supplement an area forecast or prior to the issue of the appropriate AIRMET or SIGMET.

VFR Not Recommended (VNR)

When VFR flight operations are considered inadvisable, Flight Service will include a "VNR" statement in standard briefings.

Winds and Temperatures Aloft Forecasts (FB)

Winds and temperatures aloft forecasts contain forecast upper winds in degrees true and knots, and forecast upper temperatures in degrees Celsius. 2867–21 at 18,000 feet MSL decodes as a wind from 280° true (by adding a 0 after the first two digits) at 67 knots and temperature -21°C (+/– precedes temperature up to 24,000 feet, above this all temperatures will be below zero and so no signs need be given):

- at 3,000 feet, MSL 2308 decodes as a wind from 230° true at 8 knots with no forecast temperature (usually temperature is not forecast for the 3,000 feet MSL level or for a level within 2,500 feet AGL of the station elevation—also winds aloft are not forecast for levels within 1,500 feet AGL of the station elevation);
- at 6,000 feet, 9900 decodes as winds light and variable (less than 5 knots), and for winds aloft in the 100–199 knots range, to overcome the problem that only two digits are available for wind speed the forecaster adds 50 to the direction and subtracts 100 from the speed, which you need to reverse when decoding;
- at 34,000 feet, 760850 decodes as a wind from 260° true (76 − 50 = 26) at 108 knots (100 + 08 = 108) and temperature -50°C; and
- at 39,000 feet, 760559 decodes as a wind from 260° true at 105 knots and -59°C.

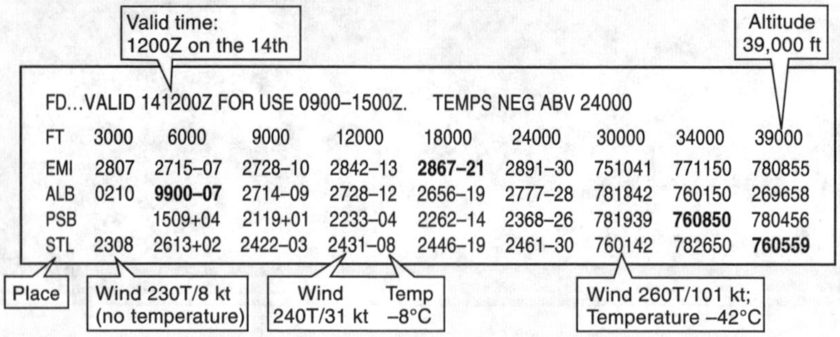

Figure 18-16 Winds and temperatures aloft forecast.

```
24000 ft 30000
2367-26 781938
```

You can *interpolate* to estimate the winds and temperatures at intermediate levels. For example, the winds and temperatures aloft forecast is as given opposite. You can estimate the conditions at FL270 by interpolating:

- FL240 is wind 230° at 67 knots and temperature -26°C;
- FL300 is wind 280° at 119 knots and temperature -38°C; and
- differences: 50°, 52 knots and 12°C.

Interpolating for FL270 (halfway between) gives differences of 25 in direction, 26 knots in speed, and 6°C in temperature. So the estimated values are wind from 255 degrees true (230 + 25) at 93 knots (67 + 26) and temperature -32°C (-26 − 6).

Temperatures may be asked for in the written test in °C, or as a deviation from the ISA standard (which is +15°C at MSL, decreasing at 2°C per 1,000 feet, and remaining constant at -57°C above approximately 36,000 feet). At 24,000 feet, ISA = 15 − (2 × 24) = 15 − 48 = -33°C. A temperature here of, say, -35°C (2°C cooler) is ISA–2, and a temperature of -26°C, which is 7°C warmer, is ISA+7.

Severe Weather Outlook Charts (AC)

The severe weather outlook chart is issued each morning and provides a *preliminary 24-hour outlook* for thunderstorm activity, tornados and watch areas. It is presented in two panels, the first for the time period 0000Z–1200Z, and the second for the period 1200Z–2400Z, and is used for advanced planning. An area of forecast *general thunderstorm activity* is represented by a line with an arrowhead—when you face in the direction of the arrowhead, thunderstorm activity is expected to the right of that line. Forecast *severe thunderstorms* are shown by a single-hatched area, which may be labeled SLGT (slight risk) or MDT (moderate risk). Any *tornado watches* in effect at chart time are shown by crosshatched areas.

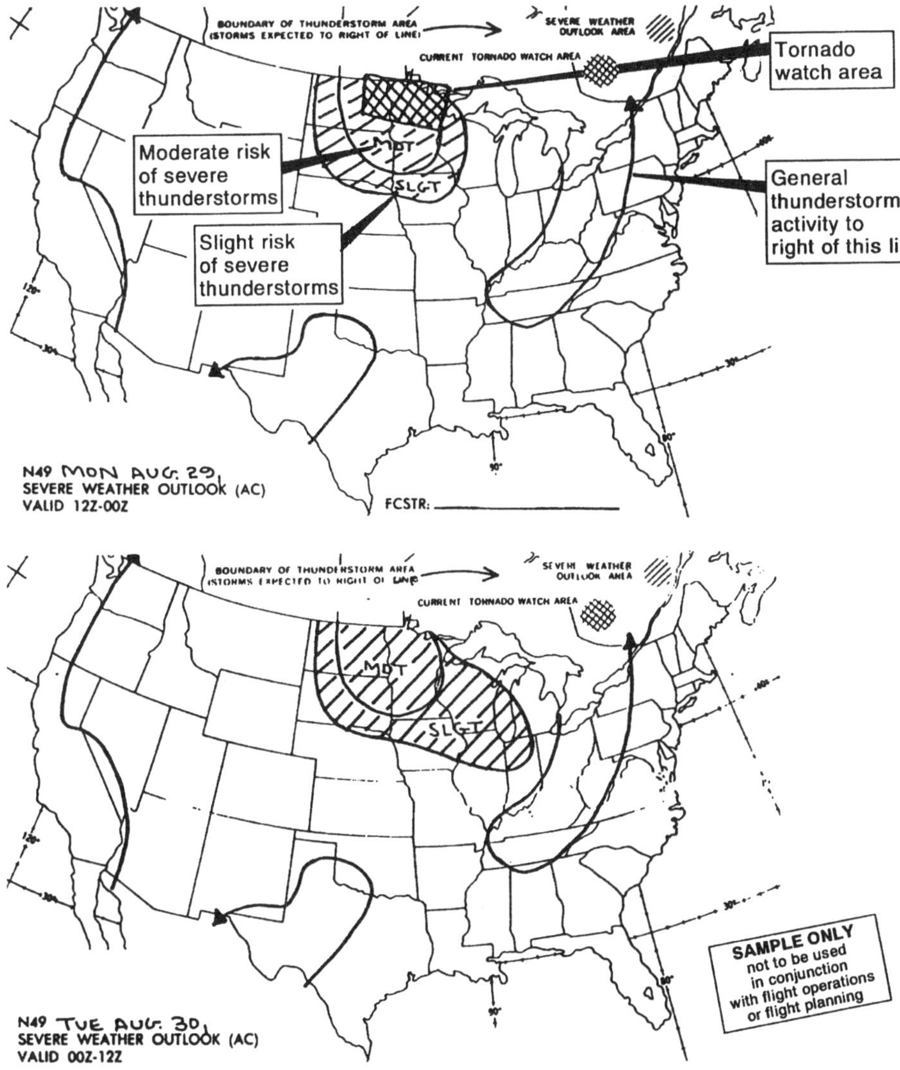

Figure 18-17 Example of a severe weather outlook chart.

Graphical Forecast for Aviation (GFA)

The aviation weather centers (AWC) GFA is an interactive web-based display providing continuously updated observed and forecasted weather information over the continental United States (CONUS). It is intended to give users a complete picture of weather critical to aviation safety. The GFA display shows user-selected weather categories, each containing multiple fields of interest at altitudes from the surface up to FL480. Depending on the field of interest chosen, weather information is available from -14 in the past (observed) to +18 hours in the future (forecasted). Table 18-5 shows the details for each of the eight weather categories.

Category	Layer	Data Displayed
Observations & Warnings	METARs	Station Model METARs; SIGMETs; all NWS Warnings impacting aviation; Satellite/Radar (Now -14 hours)
Observations & Warnings	Precipitation/Weather	Weather Symbols; Convective SIGMETs; tropical cyclone, tornado, severe thunderstorm, winter storm, freezing rain, ice, and lake effect snow warnings; Satellite/Radar (Now -14 hours)
Observations & Warnings	Ceiling/Visibility	Flight Category symbol/number; Convective SIGMETs; tropical cyclone warnings; blowing dust, blowing sand and volcanic ash SIGMETs; winter storm, blizzard, blowing dust warnings; dense fog/freezing fog/marine dense fog advisories; Satellite/Radar (Now -14 hours with selector for FLT CAT, CIG, VIS)
Observations & Warnings	PIREPs	PIREPs; all SIGMETs; Satellite/Radar (Now -14 hours with vertical slider)
Observations & Warnings	Radar/Satellite	Radar/Satellite; all SIGMETs; all NWS warnings impacting aviation (Now -14 hours)
Forecasts	TAFs	Station Model TAFs; all SIGMETs; all NWS warnings impacting aviation (+1 to +15 hours)
Forecasts	Ceiling/Visibility	LAMP Flight Category; ceiling & visibility with weather overlay including NDFD precipitation/weather type/intensity; IFR AIRMETs; Convective SIGMETs; tropical cyclone warnings; blowing dust, blowing sand, and volcanic ash SIGMETs; winter storm, blizzard, and blowing dust warnings; dense fog/freezing fog/marine dense fog advisories (+1 to +15 hours with selector for FLT CAT, CIG, VIS)
Forecasts	Clouds	RAP Clouds Coverage, Bases, and Tops; mountain obscuration AIRMETs; Convective SIGMETs; tropical cyclone warnings; volcanic ash SIGMETs (+1 to +15 hours with selector for TOPS/COV/BASE)
Forecasts	Precipitation/Weather	NDFD Precipitation Type/Chance/Intensity; NDFD Weather; Convective SIGMETs; tropical cyclone warnings; volcanic ash SIGMETs; tornado, severe thunderstorm, winter storm, ice, freezing rain, and lake effect snow warnings (+1 to +15 hours)
Forecasts	Thunderstorms	NDFD Thunderstorms Coverage/Type/Intensity; Convective SIGMETs; tropical cyclone warnings; tornado and severe thunderstorm warnings (+1 to +15 hours)
Forecasts	Winds	RAP/NDFD Wind Speed and Gust; low level wind shear and strong surface wind AIRMETs; Convective SIGMETs; tropical cyclone warnings; gale, high wind, lake wind, winter storm, blizzard, ice, storm, and blowing dust warnings (+1 to +15 hours; vertical slider)
Forecasts	Turbulence	Graphical Turbulence Guidance; turbulence AIRMETs; turbulence SIGMETs (+1 to +15 hours with vertical slider)
Forecasts	Ice	FIP; NDFD Winter Precipitation/Weather Type/Chance/Intensity; Icing AIRMETs; Icing SIGMETs; winter storm, blizzard, lake effect snow warnings; freezing fog advisories (+1 to +15 hours with vertical slider)

Table 18-5 Details of GFA weather categories.

The GFA is not considered a weather product but an aggregate of several existing weather products, many of which have been discussed throughout this chapter. The information and data from the various weather products are overlaid on a high-resolution basemap of the United States (see Figure 18-18). The user selects flight levels and current time period for either observed or forecasted weather information. Mouse clicking or hovering over the map provides additional information in textual format, such as current METAR or TAF for a selected airport. The GFA replaces the textual FA for the continental United States (CONUS) with a more modern digital solution for obtaining weather information.

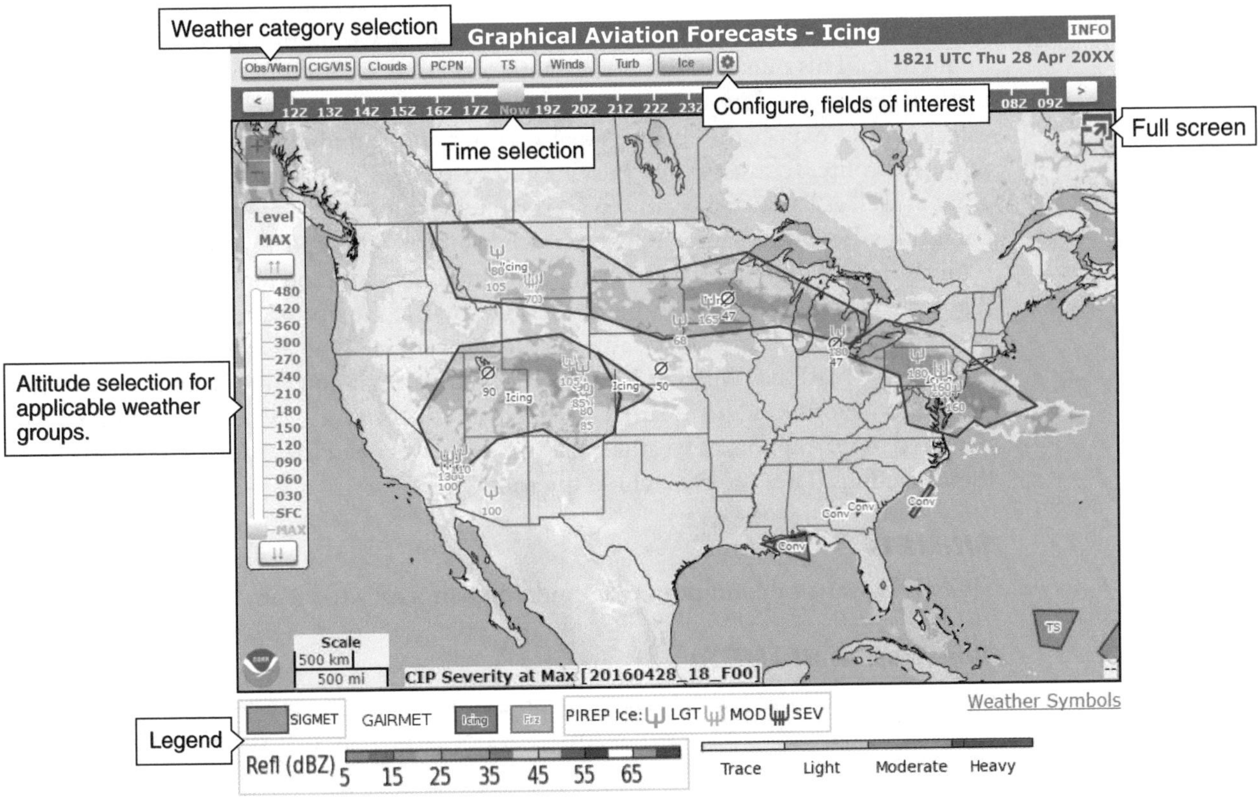

Figure 18-18 Example of a graphical forecast for aviation (GFA).

Staying Informed in the Air

After receiving a briefing and taking off, you should remain aware that weather forecasts are just that—forecasts. They are scientific estimates of what the weather will be like at various times in the future. Forecasts can and do go wrong. Stay alert to what you see as you fly. There is no real excuse for being caught by unforecast weather changes. If the weather shows any signs of turning out to be worse than you and your airplane are prepared to deal with, then you must devise an alternative plan of action. You may have to land short of your destination or divert to an alternate airport and wait out the weather.

Contact Flight Service on 122.2 or any RCO frequency.

RCOs extend the range of a Flight Service Facility and are unmanned and remotely operated.

The best source of weather information en route is available by contacting Flight Service common frequency on 122.2 and all Remote Communications Outlets (RCO) frequencies. This puts you in contact with someone at Flight Service who has immediate access to the latest weather information, including "live" weather radar. You can normally expect to receive actual weather and thunderstorm activity along your proposed route. To assist Flight Service and other pilots, you are encouraged to report good as well as bad weather, and to confirm expected conditions as well as unexpected conditions. Beyond weather, Flight Service Facilities offer updates to NOTAMs/TFRs, critical safety of flight information, flight planning services, and the ability to open/close flight plans. You can refer to Flight Service by the facility name and radio followed by your call sign (example—Seattle Radio, November One Two Three Four Alpha).

Also, the National Weather Service and Federal Aviation Administration issue and broadcast various kinds of weather alerts on various NAV-COM frequencies. These are designed to warn pilots of weather that may not have been forecast when they received their briefings. These alerts include the following.

SIGMETs

See AIM 7-1-6 for more information.

SIGMETs warn of conditions that could be dangerous to all aircraft.

Convective SIGMETs

Convective SIGMETs are observations and/or forecasts that warn of conditions associated with thunderstorms, such as tornadoes or large hail, that could be dangerous to all aircraft.

AIRMETs

AIRMETs warn of hazards primarily to small aircraft. Flight Service Stations broadcast SIGMETs and AIRMETs on receipt, and at periodic intervals thereafter (15 minutes past the hour and 45 minutes past the hour for the first hour after issuance).

Airport Weather Broadcasts

Automatic Terminal Information Service (ATIS)

The *automatic terminal information service* (ATIS) is a continuous broadcast of recorded noncontrol information at certain airports containing weather information, runway in use and other pertinent remarks. ATIS broadcasts are updated on the receipt of any official weather, regardless of content change and reported value. The ATIS may be broadcast on a discrete VHF frequency. ATIS frequencies are published on instrument charts and in the Chart Supplement U.S., which also includes their hours of operation. For example, Yakima Air Terminal ATIS operates between 1400–0600Z. Time conversion is GMT–8 (–7 DT), making the hours 0600–2200 local standard time. Weather at many airports is reported by automated weather observing equipment.

Automated Weather Observing System (AWOS)

The *automated weather observing system* (AWOS) transmits data over a COM or NAVAID frequency at the airport (see Chart Supplement U.S.).

- AWOS-A reports altimeter setting;
- AWOS-1 reports altimeter setting, wind data and usually temperature, dewpoint and density altitude;
- AWOS-2 reports the same as AWOS-1 plus visibility; and
- AWOS-3 reports the same as AWOS-1 plus visibility and cloud/ceiling data.

Automated Surface Observing System (ASOS)

The *automated surface observing system* (ASOS) reports the same as AWOS-3 plus precipitation (type and intensity) and freezing rain occurrence (a future enhancement). ASOS is a more sophisticated and newer system than AWOS and as well as being transmitted on radio frequencies, the observations are fed into the weather observation system METAR reports, which are appended with A02A (facility attended) and A02 (facility unattended) in the remarks. A METAR report that comes from a completely automated site may also be notated in the remarks section with the word AUTO.

Note. Automated observing equipment has fixed sampling paths, and unlike a human observer who can take into account variations that are evident, the automated equipment may observe readings of, say, cloud base and visibility which are significantly different (better or worse) than an arriving pilot may encounter at the end of an instrument approach to the airfield.

Constant Pressure Analysis Charts

CPL

A constant pressure analysis chart shows meteorological data at a particular *pressure level* in the atmosphere, rather than at a particular altitude. They are useful for determining winds and temperatures aloft. The upper air measurements are usually taken by radiosonde instruments carried aloft by balloon, with the information then radioed back to the ground station.

In contrast to constant pressure charts, surface charts, with which you are already familiar, are based on a constant altitude, with pressure variations being plotted. They show *isobars*, which are lines joining points of equal pressure, and allow you to estimate wind direction and strength near that level in the atmosphere, based on the pattern of high and low pressure systems and the closeness of the isobars. Once you are above the friction layer (more than about 2,000 feet AGL), the wind in the northern hemisphere flows clockwise around a high pressure system and counterclockwise around a low pressure system; it generally flows parallel to the isobars, but with a component towards the center of a low and away from the center of a high. The closer the isobars, the stronger the wind.

At upper levels in the atmosphere, however, the lower air density causes the relationship between the isobars and the wind to alter, and constant pressure charts become more useful than constant altitude charts. They are just a different means of plotting the same data to better describe the same meteorological situation. The pressure systems in the upper levels may differ from those shown on surface charts, and often they have more bearing on the actual flying weather.

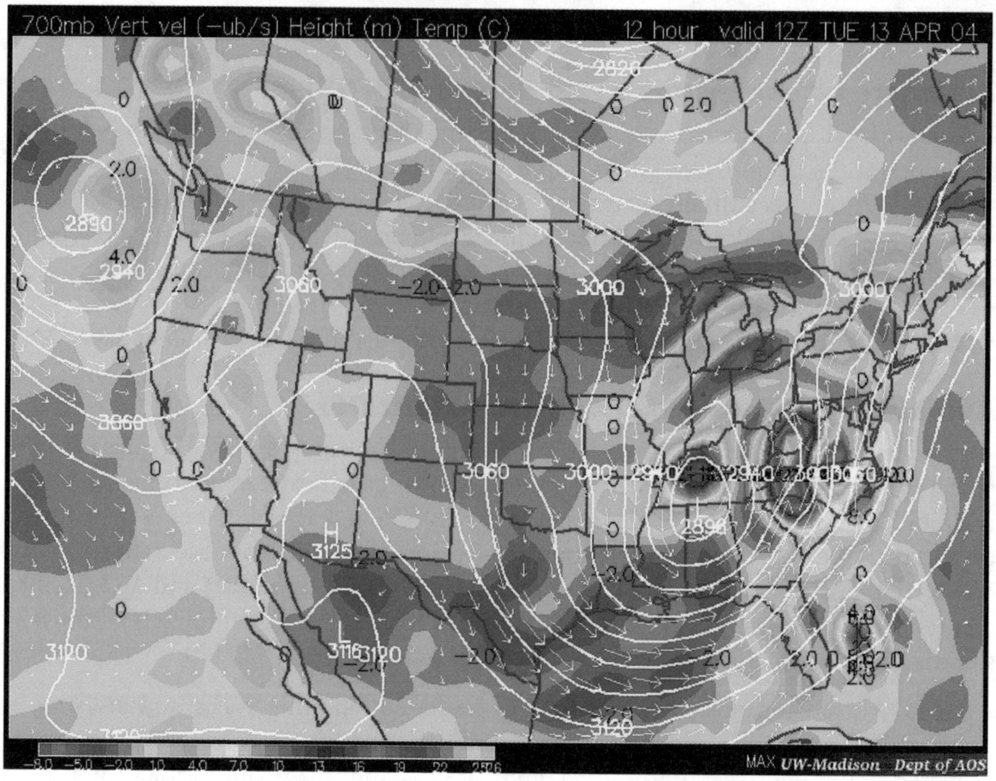

Figure 18-19 Part of a 700 mb constant pressure analysis chart (pressure alt. 10,000 feet).

The various constant pressure charts relate to approximate altitudes MSL:

- 850 mb/hPa and 5,000 feet—this chart is good for forecasting poor weather which often occurs in the lower levels, such as heavy clouds, thunderstorms, rain, snow, overcast, and fronts;
- 700 mb/hPa and 10,000 feet;
- 500 mb/hPa and 18,000 feet;
- 300 mb/hPa and 30,000 feet; and
- 200 mb/hPa and 39,000 feet.

If you plan on cruising at 10,000 feet MSL, you should look at the 700 mb/hPa chart especially. The 700 mb/hPa pressure level, which is equivalent to about 10,000 feet pressure altitude in the standard atmosphere, will vary in its height MSL in any real atmosphere. By plotting contour lines showing the altitudes MSL (in meters) at which the specified pressure level is found, 700 mb in this case, an upper air picture of pressure distribution is formed, in exactly the same way that variations in height are shown by contours on an ordinary survey map.

Plotted at each reporting station, at the level of the specified pressure, are:

- *height of that pressure surface* (in meters);
- *changes in this height over the past 12 hours;*
- *temperature;*
- *temperature/dewpoint spread* (useful in determining the possibility of cloud or fog formation); and
- *wind direction and speed.*

Height contours join places where the pressure level is at equal heights MSL, and these height pattern contours depict highs, lows, troughs and ridges in the upper atmosphere in a similar way to isobars on the surface charts. A *high height center* on a 700 mb/hPa constant pressure chart is analogous to a *high pressure center* at about 10,000 feet. Winds will parallel the contours, flowing clockwise around a *high* height center in the northern hemisphere and counterclockwise around a *low* above the friction layer. Fronts, if they reach as high as the specified pressure level, are depicted in the normal manner.

Isotherms are dashed lines joining places of equal temperatures, and these allow you to determine if you are flying toward warmer or cooler air. Temperatures near to and below freezing and a temperature/dewpoint spread of 5°C or less indicate a risk of structural icing.

Isotachs are short dashed lines joining places of equal wind strength. Strong wind areas are indicated by hatching. Areas with winds of 70–110 knots will be hatched, and these areas may include a clear area of stronger winds of 110–150 knots, and perhaps contain another hatched area of even stronger winds.

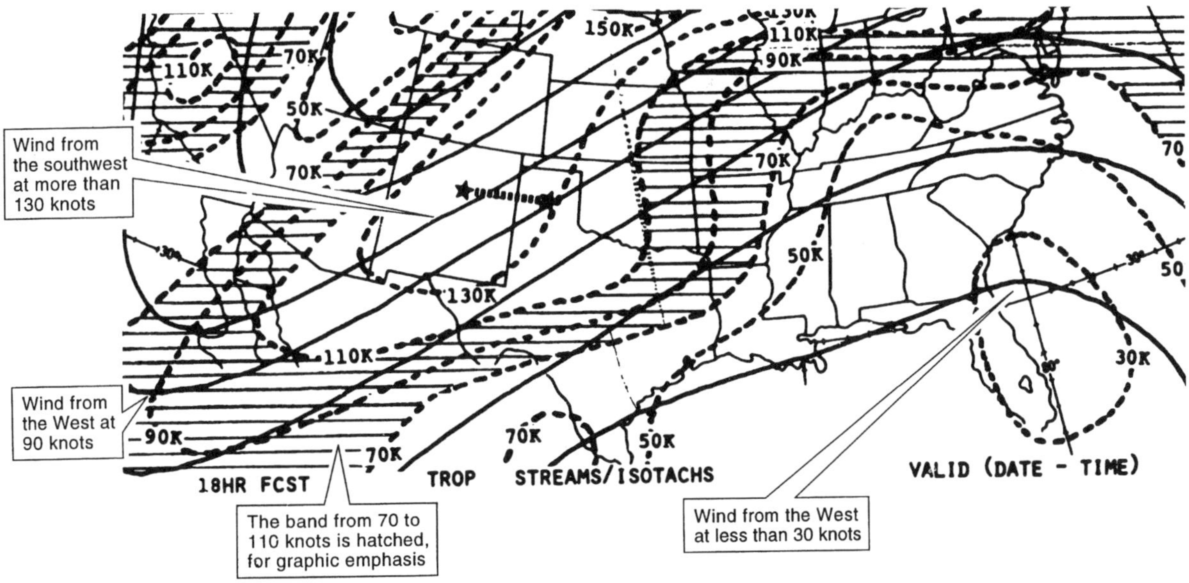

Figure 18-20 Extract from a chart showing isotachs (tropopause wind prognostic chart).

If the constant pressure level is high, then it has warm air beneath it. A consequence of this is that a parcel of warm air will not tend to rise through the already warm air, and so the weather in the vicinity of a *warm upper high* is likely to be typical of a high pressure system, good, although with a possibility of restricted visibility. Conversely, if the constant pressure level is low, then it has cool air beneath it. A parcel of warm air that starts to rise from the surface will tend to keep rising through the cooler air, an unstable situation, and so a *cold upper low* is an indicator of possible unstable conditions and poor flying weather.

CPL

Other Weather Information

RADAT

Sometimes freezing level data, obtained from upper air (radiosonde) observation stations and codified by the term RADAT, is provided in surface aviation weather reports. It includes:

- relative humidity at the freezing level in percent; and
- the height (in hundreds of feet above mean sea level) at which the upper air sounding passed through the 0°C isotherm (freezing level).

RADAT 86 0 55 decodes as relative humidity 86% at freezing level, and freezing level (0°C) was passed at 5,500 feet MSL.

Composite Moisture Stability Chart

The composite moisture stability chart has one panel which is an analysis of observed freezing level data from upper air observations.

Radar Weather Reports (SD)

Sometimes radar weather reports are available indicating the position and intensity of thunderstorm cells detected by a radar station. For example:

```
DFW 1735 LN 7TRW++/+ 75/30 160/50 170/110 12W C2520 MT470
AT 140/45
```

This decodes as: Dallas-Ft. Worth at 1735Z, a line of very heavy thunderstorms, increasing in intensity and covering 7/10 of the sky, in the area defined by 075 bearing from DFW radar site at a distance of 30 NM, 160 bearing 50 NM, 170 bearing 110 NM, 12 NM wide band, cells moving from 250° at 20 knots, maximum tops (MT) of 47,000 feet located on 140 bearing at 45 NM.

End CPL

Review 18
Weather Reports and Forecasts

Obtaining a Weather Briefing

1. What is a weather synopsis?
2. What is an outlook briefing?
3. What information should you give a weather briefer?

Weather Reports

4. *Refer to figure 18-3 (page 423).*
   - **a.** What is the ceiling in southeast New Mexico in the contoured area without shading?
   - **b.** What is the visibility?
   - **c.** Are conditions IFR?
   - **d.** What sort of front extends from New Mexico to Indiana?
   - **e.** What is the IFR weather in eastern Texas is due to?
   - **f.** What are the IFR conditions along the coast of Oregon and California caused by?
   - **g.** The weather for a flight from Arkansas to southeast Alabama will have broken to scattered clouds at what altitude?

METARs and PIREPs

5. *Refer to figure 18-21.*
   - **a.** Where is the turbulence reported by the pilot of moderate intensity?
   - **b.** Describe the report of icing in terms of intensity, type, and altitude band.
   - **c.** What time did the pilot make this PIREP?
   - **d.** What altitude did the pilot report from?
   - **e.** What type of aircraft was the pilot flying?
   - **f.** What wind did the pilot report?
   - **g.** What temperature did the pilot report?
   - **h.** If the terrain elevation is 1,295 feet MSL, what is the height above ground level of the base of the ceiling?
6. How often are routine aviation weather reports normally made?
7. Define "ceiling."
8. Translate the following routine aviation report from Great Falls, Montana (KGFT):

```
SPECI KGFT 251750Z 28004 4SM
BKN010 OVC015 10/09 A2989 RMKS
VIRGA VC
```

Refer to figure 18-22 (page 452) for questions 9 to 12.

9. Decode the METAR report for Boise, Indiana (KBOI):

```
METAR KBOI 041854Z 13004 30SM
SCT150 16/09 A3015 RMK SLP181
```

10. Decode the METAR report for Amarillo, Texas (KAMA):

```
METAR KAMA 041453Z 14007KT
M1/4SM FZFG OVC001 M03/M03
A2998 RMK A02 SLP164 T10281033
```

11. The remarks section in a METAR has "RAB12" listed. What does this mean?
12. What are the current conditions depicted for Chicago Midway Airport (KMDW)?

Weather Forecasts

13. Interpret the TAF forecast for KGAG:

```
TAF KGAG 041135Z 041212 06008KT
P6SM OVC003 FM1500 08008KT P6SM
OVC006 BECMG 1618 BKN010 FM1900
10010KT P6SM BKN012 OVC250
TEMPO 2024 SCT012 OVC250 FM0000
11008KT P6SM BKN012 BKN100
PROB30 0412 5SM -RA OVC010
```

```
UA /OV OKC—TUL /TM 1800 /FL 120 /TP BE90 /SK 018 BKN 055 /
/072 OVC 089 /CLR ABV /TA —9/WV 0921/TB MDT 055—072 /IC LGT—MDT
CLR 072—089
```

Figure 18-21 PIREP.

```
INK SA 1854 CLR 15 106/77/63/1112G18/000
BOI SA 1854 150 SCT 30 181/62/42/1304/015
LAX SA 1852 7 SCT 250 SCT 6HK 129/60/59/2504/991
MDW RS 1856 -X M7 OVC 11/2R+F 990/63/61/3205/980/RF2 RB12
JFK RS 1853 W5 X 1/2F 180/68/64/1804/006/R04RVR22V30 TWR VSBY 1/4
```

Figure 18-22 METARs.

14. What are the conditions for KTUL from 0200Z to 0000Z?

```
FM0200 04025G35KT SKC
```

15. What are the weather conditions at KMLC expected to be from 1200Z to 1500Z?

```
FM 1215 18010KT 3SM +TSRA
OVC010 BKN030
```

16. *Refer to the following TAF for KOKC.*

```
TAF KOKC 041135Z 041212 12008KT
P6SM OVC008 TEMPO 1215 4SM BR
OVC005 FM1500 23015G25KT 4SM RA
OVC010 BKN100 PROB40 1SM TSRA
FM2000 35020G35KT P6SM BKN250
FM0500 01010KT P6SM SKC
```

a. When should the cold front pass through?
b. What wind conditions are expected at KOKC at 1600Z?
c. What type conditions (i.e. VFR, IFR or MVFR) are forecast at KOKC from 1500Z to 2000Z?

17. *Refer to the following forecast.*

```
TAF KHVR 181818Z SCT003 BKN012
OVC030 —RA BECMG 0306Z PROB40
OVC003 —RA. BECMG 2000Z 35008
BKN015 OVC030 OCNL —RA. BECMG
0003Z 32008 SCT015 BKN035
PROB40 —RA. 0310Z SCT035 TEMPO
BKN035. BECMG 1012Z SCT010 1SM
FG. BCMG 1215Z VV005 FG. FM
1500Z SKC
```

You plan to arrive at Havre at noon MST on the first day of the forecast:

a. what time in UTC is this?
b. what is the ceiling forecast to be?
c. could it be lower?
d. what time is fog forecast to form? (Give your answer in both UTC and MST.)
e. when is it forecast to clear? (Give your answer in both UTC and MST.)
f. what is the ceiling forecast to be at 3 p.m. MST on the forecast's first day?
g. what is the wind forecast for this time?
h. is there a chance of rain forecast?

Refer to figure 18-9 (page 434) for questions 18 to 20.

18. Interpret the weather symbol depicted over southern Arkansas on the 12-hour significant weather prognostic chart.

19. What weather is forecast along the Gulf Coast on the 12-hour significant weather prognostic chart?

20. At what altitude is the freezing level over southern Arizona on the 24-hour significant weather prognostic chart?

21. What area around an airfield is a TAF forecast for?

22. What ceiling and/or visibility would you expect if you saw MVFR in the outlook section of an area forecast?

23. What are the primary methods to obtain the most current aviation weather information?

24. What does the term "VC" mean?

25. If the term "VC" is used, what is the extent of the area referred to?

26. How often are aerodrome forecasts normally issued in the contiguous United States?

27. How long are aerodrome forecasts valid for?

Forecasts and Advisories

28. What amount of time is covered in the main part of an area forecast?

29. How much additional time is covered in the outlook part of an area forecast?

30. If your destination does not have a terminal forecast, where can a general idea of the weather be obtained from?

Refer to figure 18-18 (page 444) for questions 31 to 33.

31. What information is shown over Utah?

32. What is the red symbol along the coast of Alabama (Gulf Shores)?

33. What is the valid time shown on the GFA?

Refer to figure 18-23 for questions 34 to 37.

34. What wind and temperature aloft is forecast for KSTL at 18,000 feet?

35. What wind and temperature aloft is forecast for KDEN at 30,000 feet?

36. What wind and temperature aloft is forecast for KMKC at 3,000 feet?

37. What is the coded group for light and variable winds less than 5 knots in winds aloft forecast?

38. What information is contained in a convective SIGMET?

39. What is indicated when a current convective SIGMET forecasts thunderstorms?

40. On what frequency can you contact Flight Service throughout the U.S.?

Commercial Review

41. In area forecasts (FA), what method is used to describe the location of each icing phenomenon?

42. What is the upper limit of the low-level significant weather prognostic chart?

43. What does hachuring (hatching) on a Constant Pressure Analysis Chart indicate?

44. What weather is implied on a "HI LVL SIG WX PROG" chart in an area enclosed by small scalloped lines?

45. What does a surface analysis chart provide?

46. A TAF gives a visibility entry of "P6SM." What does this imply?

47. The station originating the following METAR report has a field elevation of 3,500 feet MSL. If the sky cover is one continuous layer, what is its thickness?

```
OVC005 OVC075 1/2SM HZ 15/14
A3000
```

48. Describe the cloud coverage reported by a pilot in the following UA:

```
UA/OV15NW MOB 1355/SK OVC
025/045 OVC 090
```

49. What does the following mean in a RAREP?

```
MT 460 AT 140/55
```

50. The remarks section of the hourly aviation weather report contains the following coded information:

```
RADAT 87045
```

What is the meaning of this information?

FB WBC 151745
BASED ON 151200Z DATA
VALID 1600Z FOR USE 1800-0300Z. TEMPS NEG ABV 24000

FT	3000	6000	9000	12000	18000	24000	30000	34000	39000
ALS			2420	2635-08	2535-18	2444-30	245945	246755	246862
AMA		2714	2725+00	2625-04	2531-15	2542-27	265842	256352	256762
DEN			2321-04	2532-08	2434-19	2441-31	235347	236056	236262
HLC		1707-01	2113-03	2219-07	2330-17	2435-30	244145	244854	245561
MKC	0507	2006+03	2215-01	2322-06	2338-17	2348-29	236143	237252	238160
STL	2113	2325+07	2332+02	2339-04	2356-16	2373-27	239440	730649	731960

Figure 18-23 Questions 34 to 37.

Answers are given on page 701.

Flight Operations

Regulations 19

Chapter 14 of the Code of Federal Regulations (14 CFR) is designed to regulate aviation and to keep flying safe and efficient. These regulations are almost universally called the Federal Aviation Regulations (or FARs), although this is not the proper term. This chapter is a sample of paraphrased and abbreviated regulations relevant to private and commercial pilots. As a pilot, it is your responsibility to comply with each detail in some pretty complex regulations. Therefore, the discussion of regulations in this chapter is intended to introduce you, the beginning aviator, to the intricacies of the regulations in a manner that is understandable and puts regulations in some sort of context. As you begin flying, however, you should study and use the actual regulations. As a responsible pilot you should have in your personal library a copy of the current 14 CFR and the Aeronautical Information Manual (AIM), obtainable from the FAA and most pilot shops. These are the official documents on which aviation is based and they are updated continuously. Study these documents in conjunction with this chapter.

You can tackle the review questions piece-by-piece as you work your way through this chapter but, just prior to taking the FAA Knowledge Exam, it is a good idea to complete the review once more from start to finish.

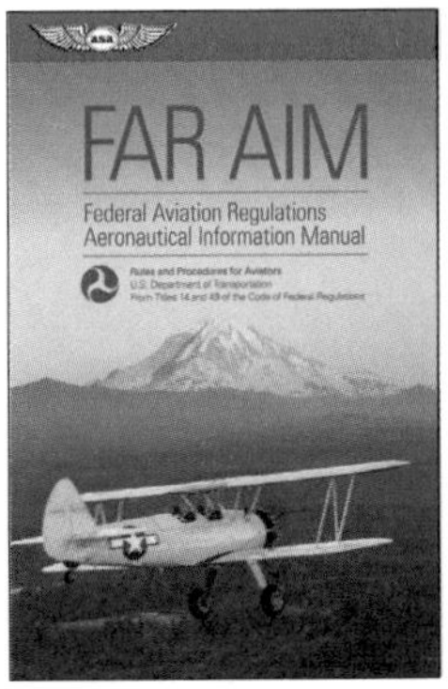

Figure 19-1 Example of FAR/AIM book.

Note. Commercial pilots are required to be familiar with certain regulations in addition to the PPL knowledge. You need to understand that the Regulations are set up to overlap each other. Depending on the type of operation you are participating in, you may be governed by several levels of Regulations, beginning with the most lenient, Part 91, and progressing through Parts 135, 125 and, if you become a pilot for a scheduled commercial operator, even Part 121.

Definitions and Abbreviations

To ensure that all aviators speak the same technical language it is necessary to define certain terms, such as aircraft, night and operator. Part 1.1 is the place to find the legal definitions of aviation terminology that are applicable to all of Chapter 14 of the CFR. Some terms, however, are further defined, and those definitions are applicable to a particular sub-part of the regulations. In other words, some words may mean more than one thing, depending upon which part of the rules you are applying. We will see an example of this in the discussion of "night" for different purposes.

Many commonly used aviation terms, such as *above ground level*, or *instrument landing system*, are abbreviated. Part 1.2 defines these abbreviations.

Some useful definitions from Part 1.1 are outlined in the following. Some definitions included are not necessarily found in Part 1.1:

- *night* is the time from the end of evening civil twilight through the hours of darkness until the beginning of morning civil twilight. As you know, darkness does not descend immediately at sunset, but rather after it following a period of twilight. Similarly, there is a period of twilight in the morning before the sun can actually be seen;

- an *air traffic clearance* means an authorization by air traffic control (ATC), for the purpose of preventing collision between known aircraft, to proceed under specified traffic conditions in Class A, B, C, D or E airspace;
- an *authorized instructor* is an instructor who has a valid ground instructor certificate or current flight instructor certificate with appropriate ratings issued by the Administrator, or any other person authorized by the Administrator to give instruction;
- an *airplane flight simulator* is a device that is a full-sized airplane cockpit replica of a specific type of airplane, or make, model, and series of airplane. It includes the hardware and software necessary to represent the airplane in ground and flight operations, including a force cueing system (motion sensations) and a visual cueing system. The simulator must be evaluated, qualified and approved by the Administrator;
- a *flight training device* is a full-sized replica of instruments, equipment, panels and controls of an airplane or rotorcraft in an open flight deck area or an enclosed cockpit. It includes the hardware and software necessary to simulate the airplane or rotorcraft in ground and flight operations, but it does not have a force cueing system or a visual cueing system. It must be evaluated, qualified and approved by the Administrator; and
- a *Basic Aviation Training Device (BATD)* is a flight training device that combines a personal computer, flight simulation software, and appropriate hardware to simulate an airplane in ground and flight operations. Some visual cues may be available, although no force cues are necessary. BATDs may be used in lieu of, and for not more than, 10 hours of time that ordinarily may be acquired in a flight simulator or flight training device authorized for use under Part 61 or Part 141 towards an initial instrument rating. However, the FAA has not authorized the use of BATDs for conducting practical tests nor for accomplishing recency of experience requirements. The device must be approved by the Administrator.

If you intend to log simulator or flight training device time as part of the time required for a certificate or rating, or as time required for maintaining your currency and proficiency, be sure you do so on a piece of equipment that has been approved by the Administrator.

CPL

The Operation of Aircraft

To operate an aircraft is to use an aircraft, to cause to use an aircraft, or to authorize to use an aircraft. Therefore, the term *operator* is primarily applied both to the pilot and to the person who authorizes the pilot's use of the aircraft, but could also be applied solely to the pilot. A *commercial operator* is a person, who for compensation or hire, engages in air commerce by the carriage of persons or property in an aircraft (other than as an air carrier). *Operational control* is the exercise of authority over initiating, conducting, or terminating a flight.

End CPL

Pilot Qualifications

Category and *class* are two terms that you will often hear, but they have different meanings depending on whether they are being used in reference to airmen (pilot certificates, ratings, privileges, and limitations), or in reference to the certification of aircraft.

Category

Category, when used for *pilot* qualification purposes (certification of airmen), is a broad classification of aircraft into families such as:

- airplane (fixed-wing and heavier-than-air);
- rotorcraft (heavier-than-air and supported by rotor-generated lift—for example, helicopters and gyroplanes);
- glider (heavier-than-air and not depending on an engine);
- lighter-than-air (airships and balloons supported by a gas weighing less than air); and
- powered-lift (such as a tilt rotor).

Unmanned aircraft systems (UAS) are another aircraft category. UAS come in a variety of shapes and sizes and serve diverse purposes. Many of these require specific FAA authorization including operator certifications. Regardless of size and mission, the responsibility to fly safely and legally within the National Airspace System (NAS) applies equally to manned and unmanned aircraft operations. UAS operators can learn more about this rapidly growing aviation segment by visiting the FAA website.

Class

Class, when used for *pilot* qualification purposes, is a further classification of aircraft within a category having similar operating characteristics. Examples of *airplane* class ratings (Part 61.5) that may be earned and placed on a pilot certificate are:

- single-engine land (SEL);
- multi-engine land (MEL);
- single-engine sea (SES); and
- multi-engine sea (MES).

Your pilot qualifications will be:
- *category—airplane*
- *class—single-engine land (SEL).*

Aircraft Certification

Category

Category, when used for *aircraft* certification purposes, is a grouping of aircraft based on *intended use* or *operating limitations*, such as:

- transport;
- normal (all maneuvers except aerobatics and spins);
- utility (normal category maneuvers plus limited aerobatics, including spins);
- acrobatic;
- limited;
- restricted; and
- provisional.

For an airplane to be flown, it must have a current Airworthiness Certificate (except in certain abnormal situations). An Airworthiness Certificate, once issued, remains in force as long as any maintenance or alteration of the aircraft is performed as required by the Regulations (Part 21). An airplane should only be flown in the permitted maneuvers. For instance, a *utility category* airplane may fly all normal maneuvers plus limited acrobatics, including spins, but may not fly acrobatic maneuvers such as loops and rolls (Part 23).

V_S	Stall speed or minimum steady flight speed at which the airplane is controllable.
V_{SO}	Stall speed or minimum steady flight speed in the landing configuration. (An easy way to remember this is to think of the "0" as "flaps Out").
V_{S1}	Stall speed or minimum steady flight speed in a specific configuration (for instance, flaps up and landing gear retracted).
V_{NO}	Maximum structural cruise speed (marked by intersection of green and yellow arcs on airspeed indicator).
V_{NE}	Never-exceed speed (red line on airspeed indicator).
V_{FE}	Maximum flap extended speed (high-speed end of the white arc on airspeed indicator)
V_F	Design flap speed.
V_{LO}	Maximum landing-gear operating speed.
V_{LE}	Maximum landing-gear extended speed (faster than V_{LO} in some airplanes because of the greater structural strength once the gear is lowered).
V_X	Speed for best angle of climb (used to clear obstacles by achieving the steepest possible climb-out gradient).
V_Y	The speed for best rate of climb (used to gain altitude as quickly as possible).

Table 19-1 V speeds.

Class

Class, when used for *aircraft* certification purposes, is a broad grouping of aircraft having similar characteristics of propulsion, flight, or landing, such as:

- airplane;
- balloon;
- rotorcraft;
- land plane;
- glider;
- seaplane; or
- powered-lift.

Abbreviations and Symbols

There are various airspeeds that are important when flying, some of which are target airspeeds to provide best performance, and others which are limit airspeeds to protect the structural integrity of the airplane. Many of these airspeeds are symbolized as *V-speeds*, and these are found in Part 1.2. Some examples are given in table 19-1.

Part 61—Pilot Certification

Requirement to Carry Pilot Certificate and Medical Certificate

To act as pilot-in-command (PIC) or as a required pilot flight crewmember, you must have in your personal possession or readily accessible in the aircraft a current pilot certificate issued under Part 61, a current medical certificate issued under Part 67, and a photo ID. You are required to present your pilot or flight instructor certificate and medical certificate for inspection on the request of the FAA Administrator or his representative, an authorized representative of the Safety Board (NTSB), or a law enforcement officer.

Certificates and Ratings

Pilot certificates that may be issued include:

- student pilot;
- sport pilot;
- recreational pilot;
- private pilot;
- commercial pilot;
- airline transport pilot; and
- remote pilot (sUAS).

A *flight instructor* and *ground instructor certificate* may also be issued. *Ratings* may be placed on pilot and flight instructor certificates as:

- an aircraft category rating (airplane, rotorcraft, glider, lighter-than-air, powered-lift);
- an airplane class rating (SEL, MEL, SES, MES); a rotorcraft class rating; or a lighter-than-air class rating;

- an aircraft type rating for advanced and/or large aircraft—examples: a B757 (Boeing 757) type rating; a CE500 (Cessna Citation) type rating; and
- an instrument rating.

Duration of Pilot and Flight Instructor Certificates

Flight Instructor Certificates are valid for a period of 24 months expiring at the end of the 24th month in which it was issued or renewed. All Pilot Certificates to include Student Pilot Certificates (issued after April 1, 2016) are issued with no expiration date and remain valid unless surrendered, suspended, or revoked.

Pilot certificates are issued with no expiration date.

Duration of Medical Certificates

A third-class (or higher) medical certificate, which is required for operations requiring a private, recreational, or student pilot certificate expires at the end of the 60th month after the month of the date of examination shown on the certificate if the holder is less than 40 years old on the date of the examination. If the pilot is 40 years old or older on the date of the examination, the certificate is only valid for 24 months.

The medical certificate for a Private Pilot Certificate lasts for 5 years to the end of the month for pilots less than 40 years.

A second-class (or higher) medical certificate, which is required for operations requiring a commercial pilot certificate, expires at the end of the 12th month after the month of the date of examination shown on the certificate. A first-class medical certificate, which is required of Airline Transport Pilots, expires at the end of the sixth month after the month of the examination shown on the certificate.

Higher class medical certificates can be used as a lower class after expiration of the certificate for its original level of authority; i.e. after 12 months, a 2nd class certificate can be used as a 3rd class certificate.

14 CFR Part 68: BasicMed

In place of a third-class (or higher) medical certificate, a private, recreational, or student pilot, flight instructor, or safety pilot when acting as pilot-in-command may choose to operate in compliance with 14 CFR Part 68, otherwise known as BasicMed. The pilot must meet and adhere to the requirements for operating certain small aircraft without a medical certificate outlined in Part 68 and AC 68-1.

To operate under BasicMed, a pilot must comply with the following requirements:

- Hold a valid U.S. driver's license and comply with all medical requirements or restrictions associated with that license.
- Hold or have held a medical certificate issued by the FAA at any point after July 14, 2016.
- Complete the comprehensive medical examination checklist (CMEC), FAA Form 8700-2, every 48 months.
- Have a physical examination by any State-licensed physician, and have that physician complete the CMEC. Once complete, the applicant is required to retain a copy of their CMEC. This must be completed every 48 months to maintain compliance.
- Take a BasicMed online medical education course every 24 months. The online course covers topics such as medical self-assessments, warning signs of serious medical conditions, and mitigating medical risk.

The Mayo Clinic and the Aircraft Owners and Pilots Association (AOPA) both offer a free online BasicMed medical education course.

A pilot operating under BasicMed will be restricted to the following limitations:

- The pilot may fly with no more than five passengers;
- Fly an aircraft with a maximum certificated takeoff weight of no more than 6,000 lbs;
- Fly an aircraft that is authorized to carry no more than 6 occupants, or 5 passengers plus the pilot;

- Fly within the United States, at an indicated airspeed of 250 knots or less, and at an altitude at or below 18,000 feet MSL; and
- The pilot may not fly for compensation or hire.

To operate beyond these limitations, a pilot must obtain an FAA Medical Certificate.

General Limitations

Unless you hold a *category and class rating* for that aircraft, you may not act as pilot-in-command of an aircraft that is carrying another person or is operated for compensation or hire. An exception is when you are taking a practical test with an examiner or when you hold a logbook or certificate endorsement for solo operations in training for a rating and you are supervised by an authorized instructor.

No person may act as pilot-in-command of a *tailwheel airplane* unless that person has received and logged flight training from an authorized instructor in a tailwheel airplane and received an endorsement in the person's logbook from an authorized instructor who found the person proficient in the operation of a tailwheel airplane. The flight training must include at least the following maneuvers and procedures:

- normal and crosswind takeoffs and landings;
- wheel landings (unless the manufacturer has recommended against such landings); and
- go-around procedures.

If you hold a private or commercial pilot certificate then, to act as pilot-in-command of a *high performance airplane*, you must receive and log ground and flight training from an authorized flight instructor who then certifies (endorses) in your logbook that you are proficient to fly airplanes with an engine of more than 200 horsepower. To act as pilot-in-command of a *complex airplane*, you must receive and log ground and flight training from an authorized flight instructor who then certifies in your logbook that you are proficient to fly airplanes with retractable landing gear, flaps, and a controllable propeller.

To act as pilot-in-command of a *pressurized airplane*, you must receive and log flight training from an authorized flight instructor in normal cruise flight operations while operating above 25,000 feet MSL; proper emergency procedures for simulated rapid decompression without actually depressurizing the aircraft; and emergency descent procedures. The ground training must include at least the following subjects:

- high-altitude aerodynamics and meteorology;
- respiration;
- effects, symptoms, and causes of hypoxia and any other high-altitude sickness;
- duration of consciousness without supplemental oxygen;
- effects of prolonged usage of supplemental oxygen;
- causes and effects of gas expansion and gas bubble formation;
- preventive measures for eliminating gas expansion, gas bubble formation, and high-altitude sickness;
- physical phenomena and incidents of decompression; and
- any other physiological aspects of high-altitude flight.

You must hold a specific *type rating* to act as pilot-in-command of:

- a large aircraft (more than 12,500 pounds certificated takeoff weight, other than lighter-than-air);
- a helicopter for operations requiring an airline transport pilot certificate; or
- a turbojet-powered airplane.

Equipment Required For Practical Tests

You must supply an aircraft appropriate and qualified for the practical test you are about to take. If the test is for a multi-engine rating, for example, you must supply a multi-engine airplane for the test. If the test is for a commercial rating, the airplane used must be complex. If you are taking the test for an instrument rating, be sure to arrive with a view limiting device. Required equipment for each practical test is listed in the *Practical Test Standards* (PTS) or *Airman Certification Standards* (ACS) for that rating or certificate.

Pilot Logbooks

Part 61 of the Regulations tells pilots how to log flight time. Flight time begins when an aircraft moves under its own power for the purpose of flight and ends when the aircraft comes to rest after landing.

The aeronautical training and experience used to meet the requirements for a certificate or rating, or the recent flight experience requirements must be logged. The *pilot-in-command* has final authority and responsibility for the operation and safety of the flight; has been designated as pilot-in-command before or during the flight; and holds the appropriate category, class, and type rating, if appropriate, for the conduct of the flight.

You may log as *pilot-in-command* only that flight time during which you are:

- the sole manipulator of the controls of an aircraft on which you are rated;
- flying solo; or
- when acting as pilot-in-command of an aircraft requiring more than one pilot.

You may log as *second-in-command* time all flight time during which you act as second-in-command of an aircraft requiring more than one pilot. You may log *solo time* only when you are the sole occupant of the aircraft. All time logged as instructional must be certified by the authorized instructor from whom it was received.

All instrument approaches logged must include the place and type of approach completed, whether conditions were simulated or actual, and, in the case of simulated conditions, the name of the safety pilot. When a flight simulator or flight training device is used, the type of device should be logged.

Flight Review

Flight reviews and proficiency checks are valid for 2 years to the end of the month.

To act as pilot-in-command, you must have, since the beginning of the 24th month prior to this flight, successfully completed, and had endorsed in your logbook, either:

- a (biennial) flight review (consisting of at least 1 hour of flight instruction and 1 hour of ground instruction); or
- a proficiency check for a pilot certificate or rating.

The flight review lasts for 2 years to the end of the month. Instrument proficiency checks are valid for six months, after which the pilot must meet currency requirements or receive another instrument proficiency check.

A flight simulator or flight training device may be used to meet the flight review or proficiency check requirements if:

- it has been approved for that purpose by the Administrator (FAA);
- it is being used in accordance with an approved course conducted by a training center that operates under Part 142 of the Regulations; and
- it represents an aircraft or set of aircraft for which the pilot is rated.

Recent Flight Experience: Pilot-in-Command

To carry passengers, you must have made three takeoffs and three landings within the preceding 90 days.

To carry passengers by day, you must have made three takeoffs and three landings within the preceding 90 days in an aircraft of the same *category* and *class* (or *type* if a type rating is required). For tailwheel airplanes, the landings must be to a full stop (because steering "taildraggers" on the ground is more difficult compared with steering nosewheel aircraft).

To carry passengers *at night*, you must have made three takeoffs and three landings to a full stop in the hours between 1 hour after sunset to 1 hour before sunrise within the preceding 90 days in an aircraft of the same category, class, and, if required, type. Note that for *recency of experience* the definition of night is different to that in Part 1.1 of the Regulations. The requirement for three *full-stop* landings at night applies to both nosewheel and tailwheel airplanes. The takeoffs and landings may be performed in an approved simulator at a Part 142 training facility.

Change of Address

Unless you notify the FAA Airman Certification Branch in Oklahoma City in writing of any change in your permanent mailing address, you may not exercise the privileges of your pilot certificate after 30 days from the date you moved.

Glider Towing

You must be properly qualified to tow gliders.

To act as pilot-in-command of an aircraft towing a glider, you must:

- hold a private pilot certificate or higher with a powered aircraft category rating;
- have an endorsement in your logbook from an authorized instructor certifying that you:
  - have received ground and flight instruction in gliders; and
  - are proficient in the techniques and procedures essential to the safe towing of gliders;
- have logged at least three flights as the sole manipulator of the controls of an aircraft towing a glider or simulating glider-towing flight procedures while accompanied by a suitably qualified pilot;
- have logged at least 100 hours of pilot-in-command time in the aircraft category, class, and type, if required, that the pilot is using to tow a glider; and
- within the preceding 12 months made at least 3 actual or simulated glider tows while being accompanied by a suitably qualified pilot, or made at least 3 flights as pilot-in-command of a glider towed by an aircraft.

Private Pilot Privileges and Limitations

A private pilot may not act as pilot-in-command of an aircraft that is carrying passengers or property for compensation or hire, nor may he be hired or compensated to act as pilot-in-command of any aircraft. But a private pilot may share operating expenses with a passenger, although he may not pay less than the *pro rata* (equal) share of the operating expenses of the flight. The expenses shared may involve only fuel, oil, airport expenditures, or rental fees. A private pilot can carry passengers on business trips if the flight is only incidental to that business or employment. A private pilot who is an aircraft salesman and who has at least 200 hours of logged flight time may demonstrate an aircraft in flight to a prospective buyer.

Under certain strict constraints, including FAA notification and a donation to the charitable organization concerned, a private pilot who has logged at least 200 hours may carry paying passengers on an airlift for a charitable organization.

Airplane Rating: Aeronautical Experience

CPL

The aeronautical experience requirements to obtain a commercial pilot certificate are found in Part 61. A commercial pilot without an instrument rating may not carry passengers for hire on cross-country flights of more than 50 nautical miles, or at night.

End CPL

Part 91—General Operating and Flight Rules

Responsibility and Authority of the Pilot-in-Command

The pilot is responsible for the operation of the aircraft.

The pilot-in-command of an aircraft is directly responsible for, and is the final authority as to, the operation of that aircraft.

In the event of an in-flight emergency requiring immediate action, the pilot-in-command may deviate from the Regulations to the extent required to meet that emergency. On the request of the Administrator (of the FAA), a written report of the deviation should be sent to the FAA.

Aircraft Airworthiness

Operate within the limitations of your aircraft.

The pilot-in-command is responsible for determining whether that aircraft is in condition for safe flight. The pilot-in-command shall discontinue the flight when unairworthy mechanical, electrical or structural conditions occur.

Flight Manual, Marking, and Placard Requirements

You must operate within the limitations specified in the approved Flight Manual, on markings and placards, or as otherwise prescribed. Within the aircraft, there should be an FAA-approved Flight Manual or Pilot's Operating Handbook (which should include weight-and-balance information).

Note. The required documents on board an aircraft can be remembered using the mnemonic AROW:

- **A** Airworthiness Certificate;
- **R** Registration Certificate;
- **O** Operating limitations (Flight Manual, POH, placards, etc.);
- **W** Weight-and-balance information (in the Flight Manual, POH, or separate).

Instrument and Equipment Requirements for Aircraft in the U.S. Standard Category

For *VFR flight by day*, a *standard category* aircraft requires:

- an airspeed indicator;
- an altimeter;
- a magnetic direction indicator;
- a tachometer (RPM) for each engine;
- a fuel gauge;
- shoulder harnesses (for relatively new model aircraft);
- an emergency locator transmitter (ELT) (if required by Part 91.207); and
- flotation gear and a pyrotechnic signal device(s) if beyond the power-off gliding distance from shore.

Additional items for *VFR flight by night* are:

- approved position (navigation) lights;
- an approved aviation red or white anticollision light;
- at least one electric landing light if the aircraft is operated for hire;
- an adequate source of electrical energy; and
- spare fuses that are accessible.

Other items are required for certain aircraft—for instance, those with altitude engines, or retractable landing gear.

Dropping Objects

No object should be dropped from an aircraft in flight that creates a hazard to persons or property. You may drop an object if reasonable precautions are taken to avoid injury or damage to persons or property.

Alcohol and Drugs

Alcohol and other drugs are not compatible with flying.

No person may act, or attempt to act, as a crewmember:

- within 8 hours after the consumption of any alcoholic beverage;
- while under the influence of alcohol;
- while using any drug that affects their faculties in any way contrary to safety; or
- while having 0.04% by weight or more of alcohol in the blood.

You may be asked by a law enforcement officer or by the Administrator to submit to a blood alcohol test if they suspect you are intoxicated. Except in an emergency, a pilot may not allow an intoxicated person, or one under the influence of drugs (other than a medical patient under proper care) to be carried on that aircraft.

There are several thousand medications currently approved by the U.S. Food and Drug Administration (FDA), not including over the counter (OTC) drugs. Virtually all medications have the potential for adverse side effects in some people. Additionally, herbal and dietary supplements, sport and energy boosters, and some other "natural" products are derived from substances often found in medications that could also have adverse side effects. While some individuals experience no side effects with a particular drug or product, others may be noticeably affected. The FAA regularly reviews FDA and other data to assure that medications found acceptable for aviation duties do not pose an adverse safety risk. Drugs that cause no apparent side effects on the ground can create serious problems at even relatively low altitudes. Even at typical general aviation altitudes, the changes in concentrations of atmospheric gases in the blood can enhance the effects of seemingly innocuous drugs that can result in impaired judgment, decision-making, and performance. In addition, fatigue, stress, dehydration, and inadequate nutrition can increase an airman's susceptibility to adverse effects from various drugs, even if they appeared to tolerate them in the past. If multiple medications are being taken at the same time, the adverse effects can be even more pronounced.

Some of the most commonly used OTC drugs, antihistamines and decongestants, have the potential to cause noticeable adverse side effects, including drowsiness and cognitive deficits. The symptoms associated with common upper respiratory infections, including the common cold, will often suppress a pilot's desire to fly, and treating symptoms with a drug that causes adverse side effects only compounds the problem. Particularly, medications containing diphenhydramine (e.g., Benadryl®) are known to cause drowsiness and have a prolonged half-life, meaning the drugs stay in one's system for an extended time, which lengthens the time that side effects are present.

Another important consideration is that the medical condition for which a medication is prescribed may itself be disqualifying. The FAA will consider the condition in the context of risk for medical incapacitation, and the medication as well for cognitive impairment, and either or both could be found unacceptable for medical certification.

Preflight Action

Prepare thoroughly for a flight.

Each pilot-in-command shall, before beginning a flight, become familiar with all available information concerning that flight. This information must include:

- for all flights:
  - runway lengths at the airports of intended use; and
  - the airplane's takeoff and landing distance data; and
- for any flight not in the vicinity of an airport:
  - weather reports and forecasts;
  - fuel requirements;
  - alternatives available if the planned flight cannot be completed; and
  - any known traffic delays.

Flight Crewmembers at Stations

When at your flight station, wear your safety belt.

During takeoff and landing, and while en route, each required flight crewmember shall be at their station with the safety belt fastened. The shoulder harness should be fastened during takeoff and landing, but is not required en route.

Crewmembers are permitted to leave their stations to attend to other duties in connection with the operation of the aircraft, or because of physiological needs.

Use of Safety Belts, Shoulder Harnesses, and Child Restraint Systems

The pilot must ensure that all persons on board are:

- briefed on how to fasten and unfasten their safety belt, and shoulder harness if fitted;
- notified that they must wear their safety belt, and shoulder harness if fitted, during taxi, takeoff and landing;
- wearing their safety belt, and shoulder harness if fitted, during taxi, takeoff and landing (except for infants under 2 years of age held on an adult's lap, parachutists sitting on the floor or someone aiding in floatplane operations on the water); and

- children under 2 not held by an adult should be occupying an approved child restraint system (such restraint system are placarded as approved for aircraft use) and must be accompanied during the flight by a designated guardian adult.

Operating Near Other Aircraft

Keep clear of other aircraft.

You must not operate an aircraft so close to another as to create a collision hazard. You must not operate an aircraft in formation flight except by arrangement with the pilot-in-command of each aircraft in the formation, and you must not carry passengers for hire when flying in formation.

Right-of-Way

Each person operating an aircraft should be vigilant so as to see and avoid other aircraft. If a rule gives another aircraft right-of-way, then you should give way to that aircraft, and not pass over, under, or ahead of it unless well clear:

- an aircraft in distress has right-of-way;
- when aircraft are approaching head-on, or nearly so, each shall turn right; and
- when two aircraft of different categories are converging at approximately the same altitude, the more maneuverable aircraft must give way to the less-maneuverable in this order: airplanes or rotorcraft, airships, gliders, balloons.

For instance, an airplane must give way to an airship, glider, or balloon. A glider must give way to a balloon, but has right-of-way over a powered airplane:

- when two aircraft of the same category are converging, the aircraft to the other's right has right-of-way. Airplanes and rotorcraft (for example, helicopters) are considered to be equally maneuverable, and so have equal rights. However, an aircraft that is towing or refueling other aircraft has the right-of-way over all other engine-driven aircraft;
- an airplane being overtaken has right-of-way, and the overtaking airplane shall alter course to the right to pass well clear; and
- an aircraft landing, or on final approach to land, has right-of-way over aircraft in flight or operating on the surface, but it should not take advantage of this rule to force an aircraft that has just landed off the runway. If two aircraft are approaching an airport for the purpose of landing, the lower aircraft has right-of-way, but it shall not take advantage of this rule to cut in front of another aircraft on final approach to land or to overtake that aircraft.

Similar right-of-way rules apply to *water operations*, with seaplanes and vessels on crossing courses giving way to the right.

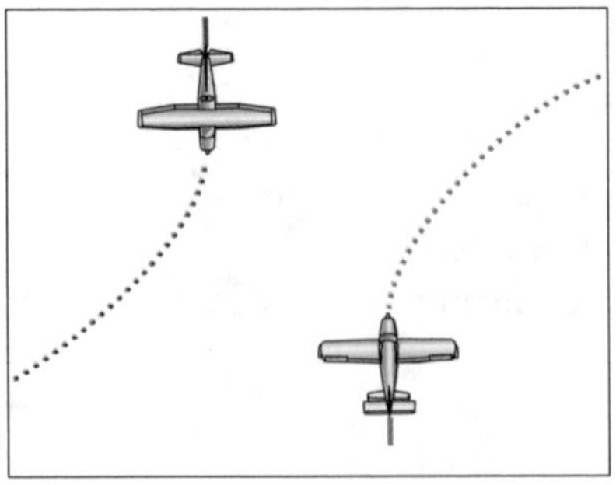

Figure 19-2
Approaching head-on, turn right.

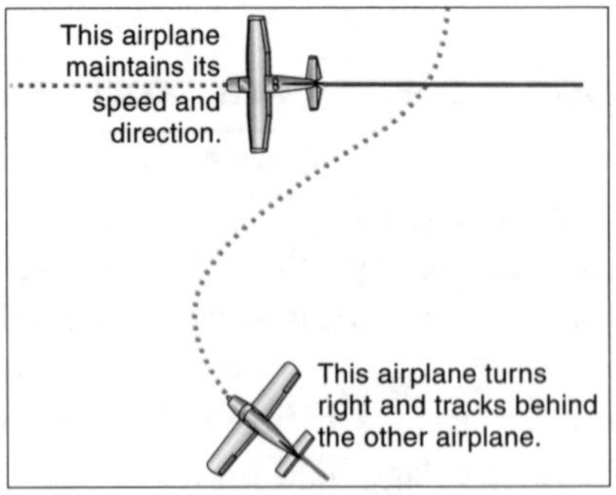

Figure 19-3
Give way to the right.

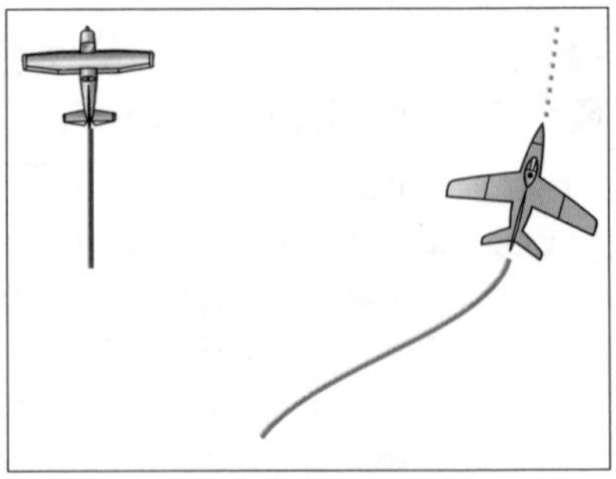

Figure 19-4
Overtaking, keep right.

Aircraft Speed

Maximum indicated airspeed below 10,000 feet MSL is 250 KIAS, or 288 mph (unless otherwise authorized). This speed also applies in Class B airspace. Maximum indicated airspeed at or below 2,500 feet AGL within 4 nautical miles of the primary airport of a Class C or Class D airspace area is 200 KIAS, or 230 mph (unless otherwise authorized or required by ATC, or unless the operation is within Class B airspace, in which case 250 KIAS applies). A maximum indicated airspeed limit of 200 KIAS also applies to the airspace underlying Class B airspace, or in a VFR corridor through Class B airspace. If minimum safe airspeed for your airplane exceeds these speeds, ATC should be notified and the aircraft should be operated at the minimum safe speed.

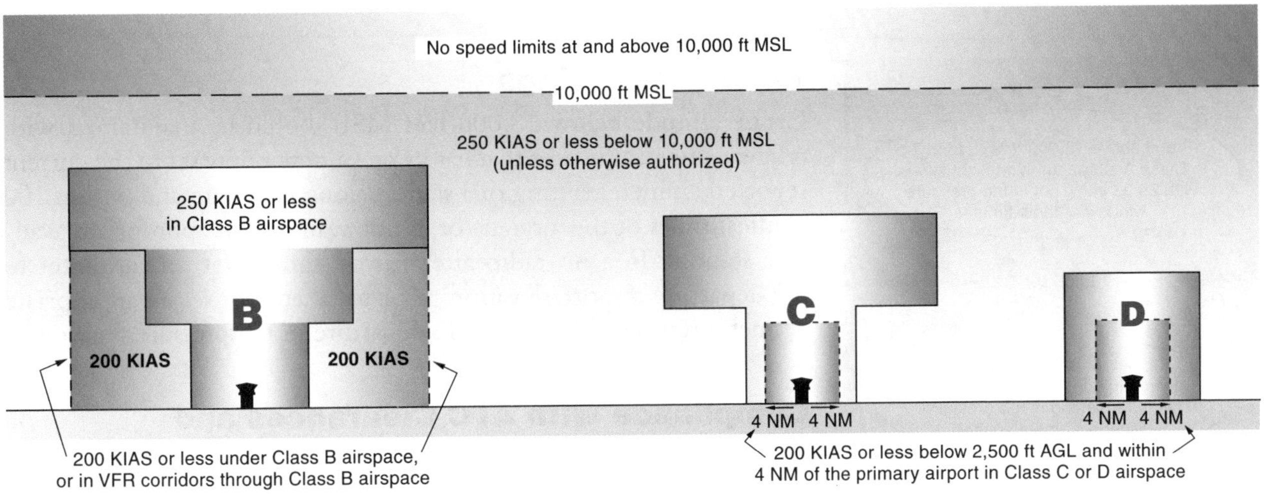

Figure 19-5 Speed limitations.

Minimum Safe Altitudes

Except when taking off or landing, no person may operate an airplane below the following altitudes:

- *anywhere*—an altitude allowing, if an engine fails, an emergency landing without undue hazard to persons or property on the surface;
- *over congested areas*—over any congested area of a city, town, or settlement, or over an open-air assembly of persons, an altitude of 1,000 feet above the highest obstacle within a horizontal distance of 2,000 feet of the aircraft; and
- *over other than congested areas*—an altitude of 500 feet above the surface, except over open water or sparsely populated areas (be careful the area is indeed not "congested"—less than a few buildings should be around). In those cases, the aircraft may not be operated closer than 500 feet to any person, vessel, vehicle, or structure.

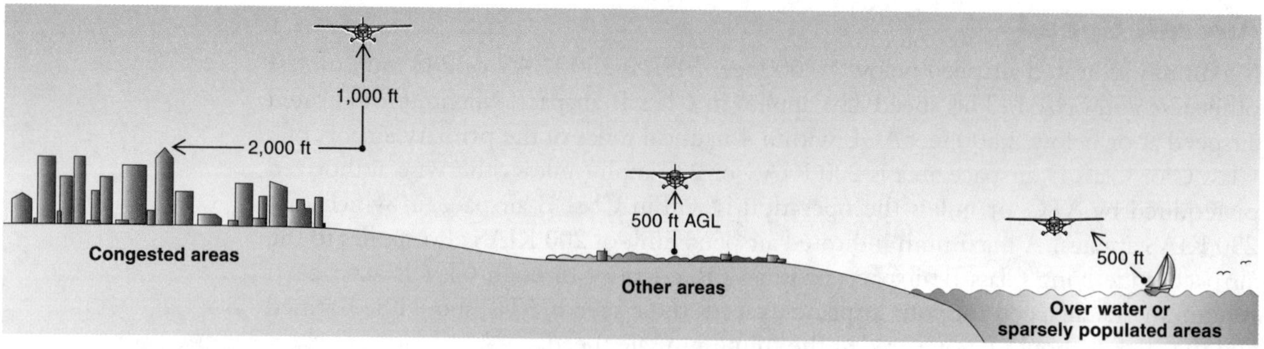

Figure 19-6 Minimum safe altitudes.

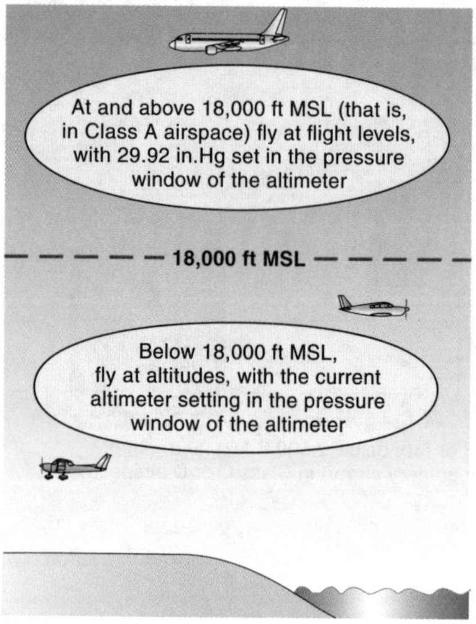

Figure 19-7
Use the current altimeter setting when flying below 18,000 feet MSL.

Altimeter Settings

Cruise altitude below 18,000 feet MSL should be maintained with reference to an altimeter that has its pressure window set to the current reported altimeter setting of a station along the route and within 100 nautical miles of the aircraft (or, if not available, an appropriate available station). In a no-radio aircraft, you should set the altimeter to the departure airport elevation prior to takeoff, or set an appropriate altimeter setting available before departure in the pressure window.

Compliance with ATC Clearances and Instructions

You shall not deviate from an ATC clearance except in an emergency or if the deviation is in response to a traffic alert and collision avoidance system resolution advisory. If you do deviate from an ATC clearance in an emergency, then you shall notify ATC of that deviation as soon as possible.

If you are given priority by ATC in an emergency (even though you may not have deviated from any rules), you shall, on request, submit a detailed report of that emergency to the manager of that ATC facility within 48 hours.

ATC Light Signals

If you experience radio communications failure, ATC may use light signals originating in the control tower to communicate basic commands.

Color and Type of Signal	Movement of Vehicles, Equipment and Personnel	Aircraft on the Ground	Aircraft in Flight
Steady green	Cleared to cross, proceed, or go	Cleared for takeoff	Cleared to land
Flashing green	Not applicable	Cleared for taxi	Return for landing (to be followed by steady green at the proper time)
Steady red	Stop	Stop	Give way to other aircraft and continue circling
Flashing red	Clear the taxiway/runway	Taxi clear of the runway in use	Airport unsafe, do not land
Flashing white	Return to starting point on airport	Return to starting point on airport	Not applicable
Alternating red and green	Exercise extreme caution!	Exercise extreme caution!	Exercise extreme caution!

Table 19-2 ATC light signals.

Operating on or in the Vicinity of an Airport in Class G Airspace

When approaching to land at an airport in Class G airspace, make all turns to the left, unless there are approved light signals or visual markings indicating that turns should be made to the right.

Operating on or in the Vicinity of an Airport in Class E Airspace

As for Class G (above), when approaching to land, and when departing, comply with any traffic patterns established by the FAA for that airport. Two-way radio communications must be established prior to 4 nautical miles from the airport, up to and including 2,500 feet AGL. If the aircraft radio fails in flight, the pilot-in-command may operate that aircraft and land if weather conditions are at or above basic VFR weather minimums, visual contact with the tower is maintained, and a clearance to land is received.

Class E airspace also includes *Federal airways* that exist between navigation facilities and/or intersections. Federal airways extend laterally 4 nautical miles either side of the centerline and extend from 1,200 feet AGL, or the floor of the Class E airspace if lower, up to but not including 18,000 feet MSL (but with no upper limit in Hawaii).

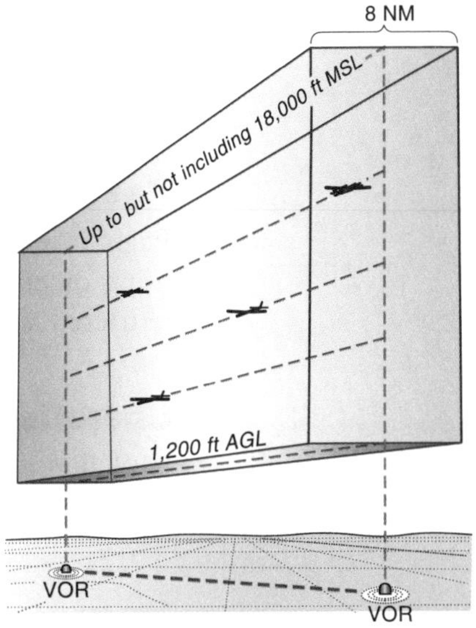

Figure 19-8 Federal airways.

Operating on or in the Vicinity of an Airport in Class D Airspace

Class D airspace generally exists around smaller controlled airports (one or more primary airports, or satellite airports).

To operate in Class D airspace:

- two-way radio communications must be established with ATC before entering the Class D airspace. Two-way radio communications must be established before taxiing at the primary airport on departure, and as soon as possible after departure from a satellite airport without an operating control tower;
- ATC clearances are required to taxi, take off, or land; and
- you must comply with other applicable Regulations unless otherwise authorized by ATC.

Operations in Class C Airspace

Class C airspace exists around certain large and busy airports. (Part 71)

To operate in Class C airspace, you must:

- comply with the Regulations for airspace already discussed; and
- use an altitude-encoding transponder.

Operations in Class B Airspace

Class B airspace exists around certain large and busy airports. (Part 71)

To operate in Class B airspace, you must:

- comply with Regulations for all other airspace;
- obtain an ATC clearance to operate in the Class B airspace;
- use an altitude-encoding altimeter in the Class B airspace and within 30 nautical miles of the primary airport for the Class B airspace area;
- have VOR available if operating IFR (not required for VFR); and
- satisfy certain pilot rating requirements:
  a. have a private pilot certificate or higher; or
  b. be a solo student pilot or recreational pilot seeking private pilot certification who has:
    - received both ground and flight instruction for that specific Class B airspace or airport;
    - logbook endorsement by an instructor within the previous 90 days for conducting solo flight in that specific Class B airspace or airport.

Student pilots may not take off or land at certain major airports (listed in Part 91).

Restricted and Prohibited Areas

Flight is not permitted in restricted or prohibited areas without the permission of the using or controlling agency (shown on Sectional charts). More information about restricted and prohibited areas is found in Part 73.

Operations in Class A Airspace (at and above 18,000 feet MSL)

Class A airspace exists at and above 18,000 feet MSL.

VFR flights are not permitted in Class A (controlled) airspace—only IFR flights with an ATC clearance.

Fuel Requirements for Flight in VFR Conditions

Always carry sufficient fuel.

After considering wind and forecast weather conditions, you must ensure that there is enough fuel to fly:

- to the first point of intended landing; plus
- sufficient reserve fuel to fly for an additional 30 minutes by day, or 45 minutes at night, at normal cruise speed.

Basic VFR Weather Minimums

The basic weather minimums required for you to fly VFR are stated in terms of flight visibility and distance from clouds (horizontally and vertically). For VFR operations within Class B, C, D and E surface areas around airports with an operating control tower, you require:

- cloud ceiling at least 1,000 feet AGL; and
- ground visibility at least 3 statute miles (usually measured by ATC but, if not available, flight visibility at least 3 statute miles as estimated by the pilot).

This can seem very confusing and not just to the beginning pilot. Yet it really is pretty simple for most general aviation pilots, because below 10,000 feet, the following rules comply with all airspace ceiling and visibility requirements—maintain 3 SM visibility:

- 500 feet below clouds;
- 1,000 feet above clouds; and
- at least 2,000 feet lateral separation from the clouds.

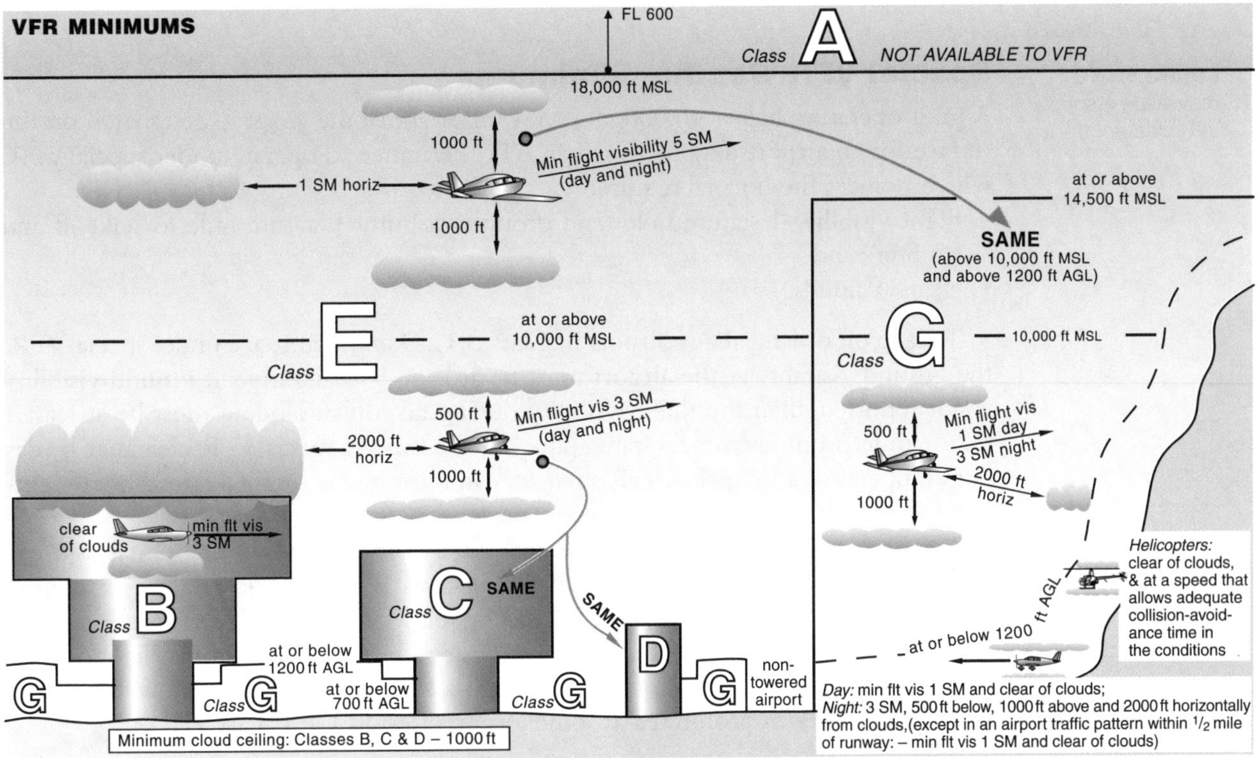

Figure 19-9 VFR weather minimums.

	Class A Airspace	Class B Airspace	Class C Airspace	Class D Airspace	Class E Airspace	Class G Airspace
VFR minimum visibility	Not applicable (IFR only)	3 statute miles	3 statute miles	3 statute miles	*3 statute miles	**1 statute miles
VFR minimum distance from clouds	Not applicable (IFR only)	Clear of clouds	500 feet below; 1,000 feet above; and 2,000 feet horizontal	500 feet below; 1,000 feet above; and 2,000 feet horizontal	*500 feet below; 1,000 feet above; and 2,000 feet horizontal	**500 feet below; 1,000 feet above; and 2,000 feet horizontal

**Different visibility minimums and distance from cloud requirements exist for operations above 10,000 feet MSL in Class E airspace.*

***Different visibility minimums and distance from cloud requirements exist for night operations, operations above 10,000 feet MSL, and operations below 1,200 feet AGL in Class G airspace.*

Table 19-3 VFR weather minimums.

Figure 19-10 ATC may issue a special VFR clearance.

The requirements are slightly less restrictive in Class G airspace, with a less-restrictive daytime visibility below 10,000 feet MSL (1 statute mile only) and, below 1,200 feet AGL by day a less-restrictive separation from clouds (clear of clouds, with no distance-from-cloud requirements). In Class B airspace aircraft are required to remain clear of clouds. In Class C, D, E and at night, Class G airspace, aircraft are required to maintain a minimum distance of 1,000 feet above, 500 feet below and 2,000 feet horizontal from clouds. Also, in Class G airspace, when the visibility is less than 3 statute miles but not less than 1 statute mile during night hours, an airplane may be operated clear of clouds if operated in an airport traffic pattern within one-half mile of the runway.

Special VFR Weather Minimums

A pilot operating below 10,000 feet MSL in or above the airspace designated on the surface for an airport may be issued an ATC clearance to operate under special VFR, which reduces the normal requirements down to:

- flight visibility 1 statute mile (and ground visibility 1 statute mile for takeoff and landing); and
- clear of clouds.

To take off or land at any airport in Class B, C, D and E airspace under special VFR, the ground visibility at the airport must be at least 1 statute mile. If ground visibility is not reported, then the flight visibility during takeoff or landing must be at least 1 statute mile. A noninstrument-rated pilot may be issued a special VFR clearance by day but, to operate under special VFR *at night*, you must be instrument-rated, instrument-current and flying in an IFR-equipped airplane.

Airports in Class B, C or D airspace have a control tower from which you can request a special-VFR clearance. Airports in Class E airspace do not have a control tower, but your request for special VFR can be relayed via Flight Service Station to the ATC facility responsible for that Class E airspace (only ATC, and not a Flight Service Station, can issue an ATC clearance, although a Flight Service Station may relay it to you). Special VFR is prohibited at some airports (see 14 CFR, Part 91).

VFR Cruise Altitude or Flight Level

VFR cruise altitudes or flight levels, when more than 3,000 feet AGL, are:

- on a magnetic course of magnetic north to magnetic 179: *odds+500 feet*—for example, 3,500 feet MSL, 15,500 feet MSL; and
- on a magnetic course of magnetic 180 to magnetic 359: *evens+500 feet*—for example, 4,500 feet MSL, 16,500 feet MSL.

  (You can memorize this as "West Evens, East Odds, plus 500 feet," or "WEEO+500.")

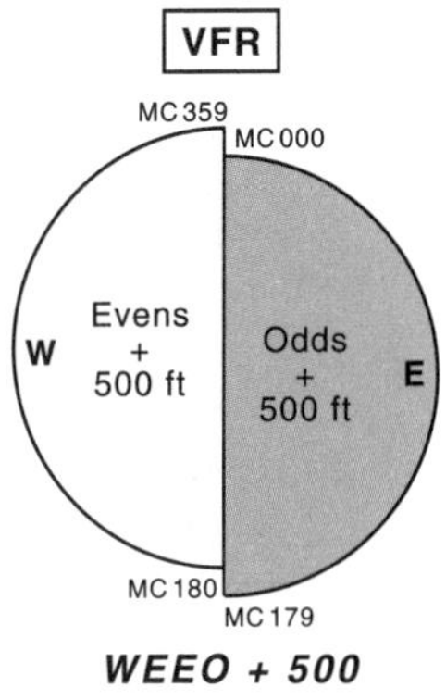

Figure 19-11
VFR cruise altitudes and flight levels above 3,000 feet AGL.

Civil Aircraft: Certifications Required

The aircraft should carry within it:

- the current Airworthiness Certificate clearly displayed; and
- the Registration Certificate.

Emergency Locator Transmitters

The batteries in an emergency locator transmitter (ELT) must be replaced, or recharged, when the ELT has been used for more than 1 cumulative hour or 50% of the battery's useful life. ELTs transmit an audible tone on the emergency frequencies 121.5 MHz and 243.0 MHz. A short ELT ground test should be conducted only in the first 5 minutes after any hour, and then for only 3 cycles. To check that an ELT has not been inadvertently activated, say by a hard landing, you should monitor the emergency frequency 121.5 MHz (see AIM for details). It is good airmanship to do this before normal engine shutdown at the conclusion of each flight.

Most aircraft are required to carry emergency locator transmitters. Refer to the regulation for exceptions and placarding rules.

Aircraft Lights

An aircraft operating on the ground or in flight between sunset and sunrise should have lighted *position lights* (sometimes called navigation lights). In Alaska, where twilight hours in summer can be long and bright, the lighting requirements are different.

U.S.-registered civil aircraft must have an approved aviation red or aviation white anticollision light system. If the anticollision light system fails you may continue to a location where repairs or replacement can be made. The anticollision lights need not be lighted when the pilot-in-command determines that, because of operating conditions, it would be in the interest of safety to turn the lights off.

Turn position lights on between sunset and sunrise.

Supplemental Oxygen

Crew oxygen requirements for operations under Part 91 Regulations:

- crew members are not required to use oxygen up to a cabin pressure altitude of 12,500 feet MSL;
- at cabin pressure altitudes above 12,500 feet up to and including 14,000 feet, the required minimum flight crew may fly without supplemental oxygen for up to 30 minutes. Supplemental oxygen must be provided and used for at least the time in excess of 30 minutes at these cabin pressure altitudes; and
- at cabin pressure altitudes above 14,000 feet, the required minimum flight crew must be provided with and use supplemental oxygen during the entire time at those cabin altitudes.

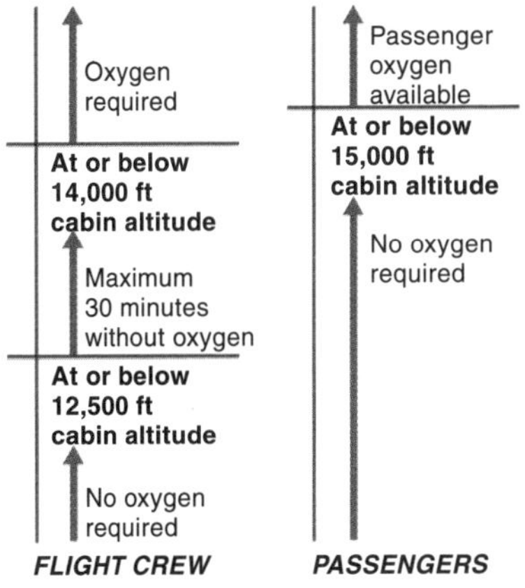

Figure 19-12
Oxygen requirements.

For passenger oxygen requirements, at cabin pressure altitudes above 15,000 feet, each occupant (flight crew and passengers) must be provided with supplemental oxygen.

ATC Transponder and Altitude Reporting Equipment and Use

A Mode C (Mode 3/A 4096 code capability, or the newer and more advanced Mode S) transponder is required to be turned on in all aircraft operating:

- in Class A airspace (at and above 18,000 feet MSL);
- in all airspace of the 48 contiguous states and the District of Columbia at and above 10,000 feet MSL, except at and below 2,500 feet AGL;
- in Class B airspace, and within 30 nautical miles of any airport listed in Part 91, Appendix D, Section 1, from the surface up to 10,000 feet MSL (this list contains most major U.S. airports—Class B airspace primary airports such as: Atlanta, Denver, Los Angeles, Miami, Minneapolis, both New York airports, San Francisco, St. Louis, and both Washington airports);
- in Class C airspace, and above it to 10,000 feet MSL; and
- from the surface to 10,000 feet MSL within a 10 NM radius of any airport listed in Part 91, Appendix D, Section 2, except the airspace below 1,200 feet AGL that is outside the lateral boundaries of the surface area of the airspace designated for that airport.

A functioning Mode C or Mode S transponder is not required in Class D, E or G airspace, unless one of the above applies—for example, operating within 30 nautical miles of San Francisco International but outside of the Class B and C airspace areas. Exceptions to this transponder-equipment regulation are also listed in Part 91—these include aircraft without original electrical systems, balloons and gliders in certain circumstances.

If your transponder fails in flight, and you are, or will be, operating in airspace where it is required equipment, you should notify ATC immediately. ATC may authorize deviation from the requirement to have an operating transponder to allow you to continue to the airport of your ultimate destination, including any intermediate stops, or to proceed to a place where suitable repairs can be made, or both. For a continuing waiver you should make a request to ATC at least one hour before the proposed flight.

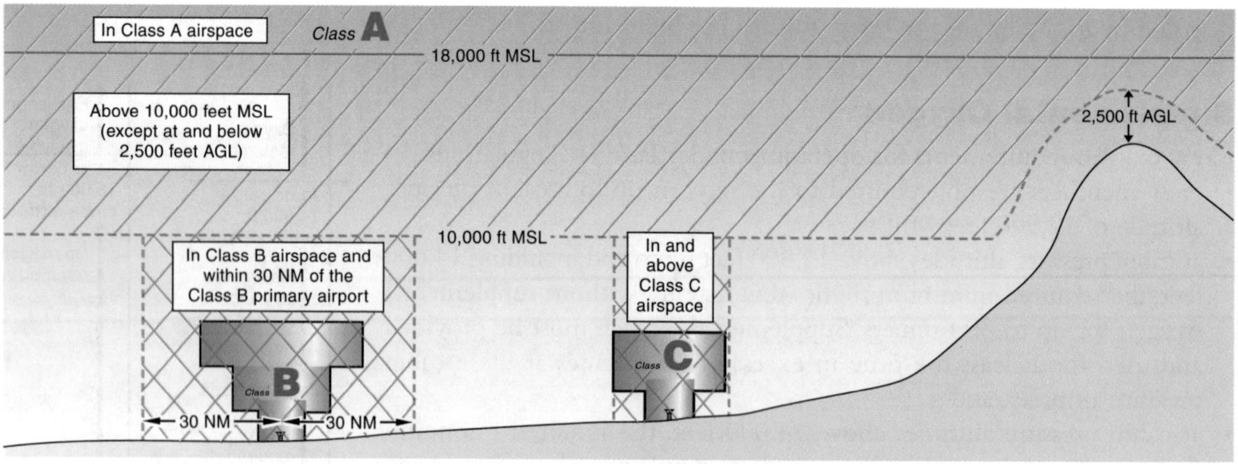

Figure 19-13 A transponder is required in the shaded airspace.

Automatic Dependent Surveillance – Broadcast Out (ADS-B Out)

As of January 1, 2020, all airspace requiring the use of a transponder will now require all aircraft to be equipped with an FAA approved ADS-B Out system. This system can be either a 1090ES (DO-260B) or a Universal Access Transceiver (DO-282B). Aircraft operating above FL180 (Class A airspace) must be equipped with the 1090ES system (a Mode S transponder-based ADS-B Transmitter). ADS-B Out is a function of the aircrafts onboard avionics that broadcasts the aircrafts 3-dimensional position and 3-dimentional velocity.

Guidelines on ADS-B equipment can be accessed by visiting faa.gov.

NextGen ADS-B technology is replacing the conventional radar-based surveillance of the past as the primary means for identifying and tracking all aircraft in the U.S. National Airspace System. If you fly in the following airspace your aircraft must be equipped with ADS-B Out:

- Class A;
- Class B, from the surface to 10,000 feet MSL including the airspace from portions of Class B that extend beyond the Mode C Veil up to 10,000 feet MSL;
- Class C, from the surface up to 4,000 feet MSL including the airspace above the horizontal boundary up to 10,000 feet MSL;
- Class E, above 10,000 feet MSL over the 48 states and Washington, D.C., excluding airspace at and below 2,500 feet AGL, and over the Gulf of Mexico at and above 3,000 feet MSL within 12 nautical miles of the coastline of the United States; and
- Within a Mode C Veil, the airspace within a 30 NM radius of any airport listed in Part 91, Appendix D, Section 1, from the surface up to 10,000 feet MSL.

Aircraft that were not originally certificated with an electrical system, such as balloons and gliders, are exempt from operations requiring ADS-B Out in certain specified airspace:

- Outside any Class B or Class C airspace area; and
- Below the altitude of the ceiling of a Class B or Class C airspace area designated for an airport, or 10,000 feet MSL—whichever is lower.

All aircraft equipped with ADS-B Out must operate in transmit mode at all times regardless of the airspace they are operating in, unless otherwise authorized by 14 CFR §91.225. Any deviation from the regulations must be approved by the ATC facility with jurisdiction over the airspace and must be requested at least 1 hour before the operation. Requests to ATC to fly an aircraft with inoperative ADS-B equipment may be made at any time.

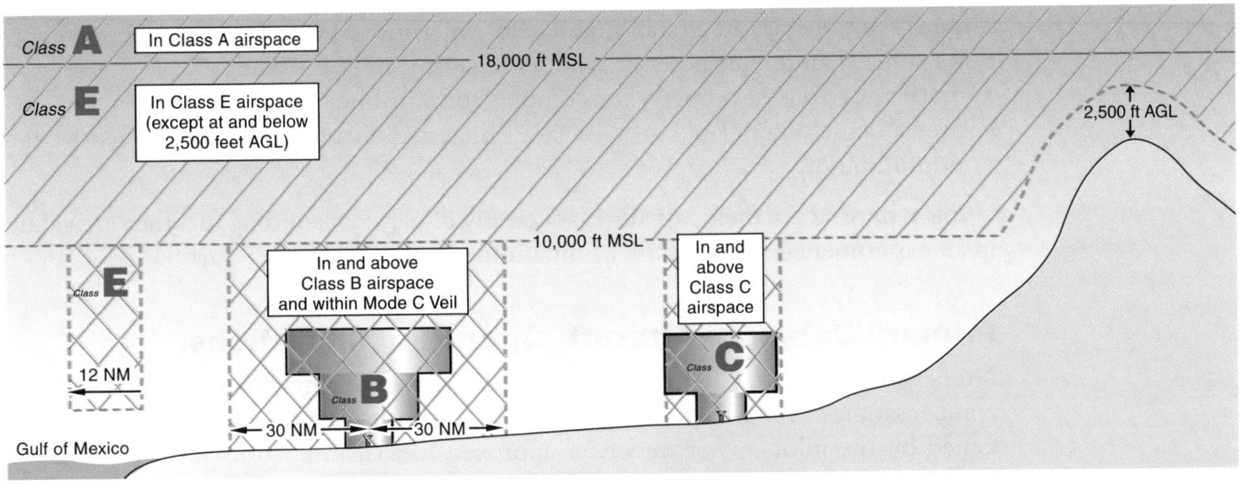

Figure 19-14 Controlled airspace requiring ADS-B Out.

Aerobatic Flight

Aerobatic flight means intentional maneuvers involving an abrupt change in aircraft attitude, an abnormal attitude, or abnormal acceleration, that is not necessary for normal flight. You may not perform aerobatics:

- over any congested area of a city, town, or settlement;
- over an open air assembly of persons;
- within or above the lateral boundaries of the surface areas of Class B, C, D or E airspace designated for an airport;
- within 4 nautical miles of the centerline of any Federal airway;
- below an altitude of 1,500 feet AGL; or
- when the flight visibility is less than 3 statute miles.

Parachutes and Parachuting

Each occupant of an aircraft must wear a parachute for maneuvers that exceed 60° bank angle, or 30° nose-up or nose-down. Parachutes are not required for spin training with a flight instructor, designated examiner or Airline Transport pilot. Modern parachutes (including chair-types) carried for emergency use must have been packed by a certificated and appropriately rated parachute rigger within the preceding 120 days.

Restricted Category Civil Aircraft: Operating Limitations

You may not operate a restricted category civil aircraft:

- for other than the special purpose for which it is certificated (for example, crop dusting, seeding, banner towing, and so on);
- to carry persons or property for compensation or hire;
- over a densely populated area;
- in a congested airway; or
- near a busy airport used by passengers.

You may not ride in a restricted category aircraft unless you are a required crewmember or crewmember trainee, or your skills are specially required for that flight. Other limitations may also apply (see Part 91).

Aircraft Having Experimental Certificates: Operating Limitations

You may not operate an aircraft that has an experimental certificate:

- for other than the purpose for which the certificate was issued;
- to carry persons or property for compensation or hire; or
- over a densely populated area, or in a congested airway, unless authorized by the Administrator.

Pilots must advise their passengers via clearly displayed placarding that they are riding in an experimental aircraft. Other limitations may also apply (see Part 91).

Primary Category Aircraft: Operating limitations.

No person may operate a primary category aircraft carrying persons or property for compensation or hire. You may not operate a primary category aircraft that is maintained by the pilot-owner under an approved special inspection and maintenance program unless you are the pilot-owner or a designee of the pilot-owner.

Maintenance, Preventive Maintenance, and Alterations (General)

The owner or operator of an aircraft is primarily responsible for maintaining that aircraft in an airworthy condition. Part 43 of the Regulations details what maintenance pilots may perform on their own aircraft.

Maintenance Required

Each owner or operator of an aircraft shall ensure that prescribed inspections and maintenance are carried out, and that maintenance personnel make appropriate entries in the aircraft maintenance records indicating that the aircraft has been approved for return to service.

Operations after Maintenance, Preventive Maintenance, Rebuilding or Alteration

After an aircraft has undergone maintenance, preventive maintenance, rebuilding or alteration, then for the Airworthiness Certificate to remain valid:

- applicable maintenance record entries in the aircraft logbooks must be made;
- the aircraft should not be operated until it has been approved for return to service by an authorized person; and
- if the flight characteristics or operation in flight have been altered appreciably, passengers may not be carried until the aircraft is test flown satisfactorily by an appropriately rated pilot with at least a private pilot certificate.

Inspections

You may not operate an aircraft unless within the preceding 12 calendar months it has had either:

Aircraft must be properly maintained and regularly inspected.

1. an annual inspection; or
2. an inspection for the issuance of an Airworthiness Certificate.

As a general rule, you may not operate an aircraft carrying persons for hire, or give flight instruction for hire, unless within the preceding 100 hours the aircraft has received:

A 100-hour inspection is not required if pilots want to hire an instructor to train them in their own airplane.

1. an annual inspection; or
2. an inspection for the issuance of an Airworthiness Certificate; or
3. a 100-hour inspection.

The *annual inspection* is a requirement, and is the normal inspection that is done during the life of the airplane following the initial airworthiness inspection. The annual inspection is more thorough than the 100-hour inspection and can replace it (but not vice versa). With FAA approval, a series of progressive checks through the year may replace the annual/100-hour inspections. People who own their own airplanes and operate them privately, and not for hire, typically do not have 100-hour inspections done.

An annual inspection is more thorough than a 100-hour inspection, and so can replace it.

The 100-hour limitation may be exceeded by not more than 10 hours while en route to reach a place where the inspection can be done, but this excess time must be included in computing the next 100 hours of service.

For example, if a 100-hour inspection is due when the tachometer reads 1,395.3, the next inspection is due at 1,495.3 hours. If the actual inspection is done at 1,497.3 hours (that is, 2 hours later than the due time) because of a 3-hour flight to the place where the inspection was done, the next 100-hour inspection will still be due at 1,595.3 hours (that is, the 2 hours overdue forms part of the next 100 hours, and the next 100-hour inspection is due 100 hours from the prior due time).

Annual inspections are valid for 1 year to the end of the month.

Annual inspections occur every 12 calendar months, so an aircraft that had an annual inspection performed on July 9 this year is due for another annual inspection no later than July 31 next year. Normally an Airworthiness Certificate remains in effect as long as the maintenance, preventive maintenance, and alterations are performed in accordance with the Regulations and are entered correctly in the maintenance records.

ATC Transponder Tests and Inspections

Transponder tests and inspections are valid for 2 years to the end of the month.

To be used, a transponder must have been tested and inspected satisfactorily within the preceding 24 calendar months. For example, if this is carried out on any day in November, it is valid until the last day of November, 24 months hence—that is, 2 years to the end of the month.

Maintenance Records

The owner or operator must keep detailed maintenance records.

The owner or operator of an aircraft shall keep records of:
- maintenance, preventive maintenance, alteration;
- 100-hour inspections, annual inspections, progressive inspections; and
- any other required or approved inspections.

Preventive maintenance is defined in Part 1.1 as simple or minor preservation operations and the replacement of small standard parts not involving complex assembly operations. Preventive maintenance items that the *pilot* may perform are found in Part 43, and include such items such as oil changes, replenishing hydraulic fluid, and servicing the landing gear wheel bearings. It does not include structural work on the airframe, or major adjustments to the engine.

Maintenance records apply to each aircraft (including airframe), each engine, each propeller, rotor, and each appliance of the aircraft. The records must include:
- a description of the work performed and the date of completion;
- the signature, and certificate number of the person approving the aircraft for return to service;
- total time in service of the airframe, engine and propeller;
- current status of life-limited parts;
- time since last overhaul of all items requiring overhaul on a specified time basis;
- current inspection status including time since the last inspection required;
- current status of applicable Airworthiness Directives (ADs), which must be complied with for the aircraft to remain airworthy; and
- copies of the forms prescribed by Part 43 for each major alteration.

Rebuilt Engine Maintenance Records

A rebuilt engine can be retuned to "zero time."

An aircraft engine rebuilt by the manufacturer or its agent may have a new maintenance record (that is, zero hours) without previous operating history, but it should specify date of rebuilding, and each change as required by Airworthiness Directives (ADs) and specified Service Bulletins.

Portable Electronic Devices

CPL

Portable electronic devices which may cause interference with the navigation or communication system may not be operated on aircraft being flown in commercial operations. Items excluded from this include portable voice recorders, hearing aids, heart pacemakers, electric shavers, or any other portable electronic device that the operator of the aircraft has determined will not cause interference.

Electronic Flight Bag (EFB)

EFB's are devices intended to be used in the cockpit or cabin to display a variety of aviation data including, navigation charts, Pilot Operating Handbook, and checklists. These devices can be either portable in nature like an iPad or built into the aircraft. They can be used in lieu of paper reference material at the discretion of the operator or pilot-in-command as long as certain criteria are meet. It is always recommended that a back-up source of information be available whether in the form of a secondary EFB or paper references.

Truth in Leasing

A copy of a lease for a large civil U.S. aircraft must be mailed to the FAA, Oklahoma City, within 24 hours of its execution.

Towing: Other Than Gliders

To tow anything other than a glider (for example, a banner) requires a *Certificate of Waiver* issued by the Administrator of the FAA.

Limited Category Civil Aircraft: Operating Limitations

You may not operate a limited category civil aircraft to carry persons or property for compensation or hire.

End CPL

Part 107—Small Unmanned Aircraft Systems (sUAS)

The FAA has adopted specific regulations to allow the operation of civil small unmanned aircraft systems (sUAS) in the NAS for purposes other than hobby and recreation. Part 107 specifically applies to the registration, airman certification, and operation of civil sUAS within the United States.

Remote pilots are required to demonstrate a level of aeronautical knowledge by passing an FAA knowledge test prior to earning certification to operate as remote pilot-in-command within the NAS. Having an understanding of the following operating rules pertaining to Part 107 will better help you identify where you might encounter sUAS operations and allow you to safely operate your manned aircraft within the same airspace.

The following are some of the operational limitations pertaining to sUAS operations:

- Must weigh less than 55 lbs (25 kg).
- Must operate within visual line-of-sight (VLOS). Unmanned aircraft must remain within the VLOS of the remote pilot-in-command and the person manipulating

the flight controls of the sUAS or a visual observer, without the aid of any device other than corrective lenses.

- May not be operated over any persons not directly participating in the operation, under a covered structure, or inside a covered stationary vehicle.
- Must operate during daylight hours or during civil twilight (30 minutes before official sunrise to 30 minutes after official sunset, local time) with appropriate anti-collision lighting.
- Must yield right of way to other aircraft.
- Maximum groundspeed of 100 mph (87 knots).
- Maximum altitude of 400 feet AGL or, if higher than 400 feet AGL, within 400 feet of a structure.
- Minimum weather visibility of 3 miles from control station.
- May operate in Class B, C, D and E airspace with required ATC permission. Operations in Class G airspace do not require ATC permission.
- No operations from a moving aircraft.
- No operations from a moving vehicle unless the operation is over a sparsely populated area.
- No careless or reckless operations.
- No carriage of hazardous materials.
- External load operations are allowed if the object being carried by the sUAS is securely attached and does not adversely affect the flight characteristics or controllability of the aircraft.

It is important to note that most of the restrictions discussed above are waivable if the applicant demonstrates that his or her operation can safely be conducted under the terms of a certificate of waiver.

National Transportation Safety Board

Document NTSB 830 refers to accidents and incidents.

The U.S. National Transportation Safety Board (NTSB) is charged with investigating aircraft accidents and incidents. The procedures that a pilot should use to report such matters are specified in document 49 CFR Part 830.

49 CFR Part 830

Report accidents immediately, followed by a written report to the NTSB within 10 days. Report serious incidents immediately, followed by a written report to the NTSB if requested.

NTSB Part 830 covers rules pertaining to the notification and reporting of aircraft accidents or incidents and overdue aircraft, and preservation of aircraft wreckage, mail, cargo, and records. An *accident* involves the death or serious injury of a person, or substantial damage to an aircraft, between the time any person boards the aircraft with the intention of flight and the time they disembark. An *incident* is an occurrence other than an accident, associated with the operation of an aircraft, which affects or could affect the safety of operations.

An accident must be reported immediately to the nearest NTSB field office, followed by a written report within 10 days. The following serious incidents must also be reported immediately, but a written report is only required on request from the NTSB:

- a flight control system malfunction or failure;
- the inability of a required flight crewmember to perform normal flight duties as a result of injury or illness;
- failure of a turbine (jet) engine;
- an in-flight fire;

- an aircraft collision in flight;
- significant damage to other property by the aircraft operation; and
- an overdue airplane believed to have been involved in an accident—(a written report is required after 7 days if an overdue airplane is still missing).

Prior to the time the NTSB (or its authorized representative) takes custody of aircraft wreckage, mail, cargo and records, it must not be disturbed or moved except to the extent necessary to remove persons injured or trapped, to protect the wreckage from further damage, or to protect the public from injury.

Only disturb aircraft wreckage and contents for good reasons.

CPL

Part 119

Certification: Air Carriers and Commercial Operators

Part 119 governs aircraft in commercial operations when common carriage is not involved, in operations of U.S.-registered civil airplanes with a seat configuration of 20 or more passengers, or a maximum payload capacity of 6,000 pounds or more. This part prescribes the types of air operator certificates issued by the Federal Aviation Administration, including:

- air carrier certificates and operating certificates;
- the certification requirements an operator must meet in order to obtain and hold a certificate authorizing operations under Part 121, 125, or 135 of this chapter and operations specifications for each kind of operation to be conducted and each class and size of aircraft to be operated under Part 121 or 135 of this chapter;
- the requirements an operator must meet to conduct operations under Part 121, 125, or 135 of this chapter and in operating each class and size of aircraft authorized in its operations specifications;
- requirements affecting wet leasing of aircraft and other arrangements for transportation by air;
- requirements for obtaining deviation authority to perform operations under a military contract and obtaining deviation authority to perform an emergency operation; and
- requirements for management personnel for operations conducted under Part 121 or Part 135 of this chapter.

Persons subject to this part must comply with the other requirements of this chapter, except where those requirements are modified by or where additional requirements are imposed by Part 119, 121, 125, or 135 of this chapter.

Part 125

Certification and Operations: Airplanes having a seating capacity of 20 or more passengers or a maximum payload capacity of 6,000 pounds or more.

Part 125 refers to aircraft operations where common carriage (such as scheduled operations or advertising or using agents—that is, *holding out* to furnish air transportation)—is not involved. Operating under Part 125 requires that you also operate under Part 91. A Part 125 certificate holder must display a true copy of the Part 125 in each aircraft. Part 125 operations include *nonscheduled* operations (that is, *not* an air carrier)

CPL

using an aircraft with 20 or more passenger seats or with a maximum payload of 6,000 pounds or more. A person authorized to operate airplanes under any *air carrier operating certificate* (such as, Part 121 for Air Carriers, Part 129 or Part 135) is not eligible to operate under Part 125.

The pilot-in-command of a Part 125 operation (nonscheduled) must hold at least a commercial pilot certificate, an appropriate category, class, and type rating, and an instrument rating and has had at least 1,200 hours of flight time as a pilot, including 500 hours of cross-country flight time, 100 hours of night flight time, including at least 10 night takeoffs and landings, and 75 hours of actual or simulated instrument flight time, at least 50 hours of which were actual flight.

The second-in-command must hold at least a commercial pilot certificate with appropriate category and class ratings, and a current instrument rating. Recent experience requirements can be met in the airplane, or by doing three takeoffs and three landings within the preceding 90 days in the type of airplane or in an approved visual simulator.

Part 135—Commuter and On-Demand Operators

Applicability of Part 135 to Air Taxi and Commercial Operators

Part 135 prescribes the rules governing:

- some commuter air taxi operations;
- the transportation of mail by aircraft under a postal services contract;
- the carriage of persons or property for compensation or hire as a commercial operator (not an air carrier) in aircraft having:
  - a maximum seating capacity of less than 20 passengers; or
  - a maximum payload capacity of less than 6,000 pounds; or
  - if within any one state of the U.S., 30 seats or less, or payload 7,500 pounds or less.

Some commuter and even some sightseeing operations (such as those operating in the Grand Canyon area) must also operate under Part 119 and Part 121 rules.

Part 135 does *not* apply to:

- student instruction;
- nonstop sightseeing flights within 25 statute miles (SM) of the airport;
- ferry or training flights; and
- aerial work operations (including crop dusting, banner towing, aerial photography or survey, fire fighting, and others).

Pilot-in-Command Qualifications

A pilot-in-command during Part 135 IFR operations must:

- hold at least a commercial pilot certificate with appropriate category and class ratings (and type rating if required);
- have at least 1,200 hours of flight time as a pilot, including 500 hours cross-country flight time, 100 hours night flight time, and 75 hours of actual or simulated instrument flight time (at least 50 of which were in actual flight); and
- for an airplane, hold an instrument rating, or an airline transport pilot certificate with an airplane category rating.

End CPL

Review 19
Regulations

Definitions and Pilot Qualifications

1. Define "night."
2. What does ATC clearance provide?
3. With respect to the certification of aircraft, what is:
   a. a *utility*?
   b. an *airplane*?
4. How long are airworthiness certificates valid for?
5. Where can you find the legal definitions of *air traffic control* and *air traffic clearance*?
6. What does V_{LE} stand for?
7. What does V_{FE} stand for?
8. Define V_{SO}.

Part 61—Pilot Certification

9. Name three documents that must be in your possession any time you fly as pilot-in-command.
10. Does a private pilot certificate have a specific expiration date?
11. For private pilot operations, a third-class or second-class medical certificate issued on July 15, this year is valid until midnight on which date?
12. What is the exception to the rule that a private pilot may not act as pilot-in-command of an aircraft carrying passengers or property for compensation or hire?
13. Describe the requirements for carrying passengers, including any special considerations for tailwheel aircrafts.
14. Recency of experience requirements for night flight have not been met and official sunset is 1830. What is the latest time passengers may be carried?
15. As one requirement to act as pilot-in-command of an aircraft towing a glider, at least how many actual or simulated glider tows do you need to have made while accompanied by a suitably qualified pilot within the previous 12 months?

Part 91—General Operating and Flight Rules

16. Who has final authority as to the operation of an airplane?
17. Who is responsible for determining if an aircraft is in condition for safe flight?
18. There is an in-flight emergency requiring immediate action. Can the pilot-in-command deviate from the regulations to the extent required to meet that emergency? If so, must a written report of the deviation be sent to the FAA?
19. Where may an aircraft's operating limitations be found?
20. Which documents should be carried onboard an aircraft?
21. What is the blood alcohol limit for a person to act as a crewmember even if they have not consumed alcohol in the previous 8 hours?
22. May a medical patient under the influence of drugs be carried on an aircraft?
23. May people under the influence of drugs or alcohol be carried on an aircraft?
24. During which phases of flight are flight crew members required by the regulations to keep their seat belts and shoulder harnesses fastened?
25. Which category of aircraft must give right-of-way to all others in normal circumstances?
26. Which aircraft has the right-of-way over all other air traffic?
27. Does an airplane refueling another have right-of-way over a glider?
28. What action is required when two aircraft of the same category converge, but not head-on?
29. An airplane is converging at an angle with a helicopter on its left. Which one has right-of-way?
30. A glider and an airplane are on a head-on collision course. What action should be taken?

31. An airship and an airplane are converging, with the airship left of the airplane's position. Which aircraft has the right-of-way?
32. When two or more aircraft are approaching an airport for the purpose of landing, the right-of-way belongs to which aircraft?
33. In an overtaking situation, does the aircraft being overtaken have right-of-way?
34. An aircraft being overtaken should expect to be passed on which side?
35. What is the maximum speed below 10,000 feet MSL for all aircraft?
36. What is the maximum speed in Class B airspace for all aircraft?
37. What is the maximum speed in Class C or D airspace within 4 nautical miles of the primary airport for all aircraft?
38. Except when necessary for takeoff or landing, an aircraft may not be operated closer than what distance from any person, vessel, vehicle, or structure?
39. Except when necessary for takeoff or landing, what is the minimum safe altitude for a pilot to operate an aircraft anywhere?
40. When would a pilot be required to submit a detailed report of an emergency which caused the pilot to deviate from an ATC clearance?
41. What does an alternating red and green light signal directed from the control tower to an aircraft in flight indicate?
42. What does a flashing white light directed from the control tower to an aircraft on the ground mean?
43. While on final approach for landing, the control tower directs an alternating red and green light at you, followed by a flashing red light. What actions should you take?
44. You are approaching to land at an airport in Class G airspace. All turns should be made in which direction (unless otherwise indicated)?
45. You are operating from a satellite airport located in Class D airspace. When must two-way radio communications be established with ATC?
46. Is an ATC clearance required to operate at an airport located in Class D airspace?
47. What minimum radio equipment is required to operate in Class C airspace?
48. Operations in which class(es) of airspace require an encoding altimeter?
49. What fuel is required for:
    - **a.** a VFR flight by day?
    - **b.** a VFR flight at night?
50. In what airspace may a special VFR clearance be issued by ATC?
51. What are the visibility and distance-from-clouds requirements for special VFR clearances?
52. What is the next higher appropriate cruise altitude or flight level to 5,000 feet MSL for a VFR flight along an airway whose magnetic course is MC 180?
53. How often do the batteries in an emergency locator transmitter (ELT) need to be replaced or recharged?
54. Except in Alaska, when should you display position lights?
55. When operating an aircraft at cabin pressure altitudes above 12,500 feet MSL up to and including 14,000 feet MSL, when should supplemental oxygen be used?
56. When must aircraft equipped with an ADS-B Out system must operate in transmit mode?
57. What is the minimum altitude and flight visibility for aerobatic flight?
58. An annual inspection was due at 1,259.6 hours, but was actually done at 1,261.2 hours. When is the next 100-hour inspection due?
59. Can the annual inspection replace a 100-hour inspection?
60. Where is the expiration date of the last annual aircraft inspection found?
61. May aircraft wreckage be moved prior to the time the NTSB takes custody?
62. If you undertake a forced landing because of piston-engine failure, does this need to be immediately reported to the nearest NTSB field office?
63. The operator of an aircraft has been involved in an accident. He or she is required to file an accident report within how many days?
64. An aircraft that is overdue for an inspection is involved in an accident. Does this fact need to be immediately reported to the nearest NTSB field office?

Commercial Review

65. Define "commercial operator."
66. What does "operational control" refer to?
67. Are you permitted to perform spins in a normal category aircraft?
68. For commercial pilot operations, when is a first- or second-class medical certificate issued on April 5 this year valid until?
69. If a pilot does not meet the recency of experience requirements for night flight and official sunset is 1800 CST, what is the latest time passengers should be carried?
70. At night, the pilot of aircraft A sees only the green light of aircraft B, which is converging from the left. Which aircraft has right-of-way?
71. You are a commercial pilot without an instrument rating.
    a. Can you carry passengers for hire on cross-country flights of more than 50 NM?
    b. Is carrying passengers at night prohibited?
72. You lease a large civil U.S. aircraft and must mail a copy of the lease to the FAA in Oklahoma. What time period must this be done within?
73. In addition to other preflight actions for IFR flight, regulations require that you, as pilot-in-command, become familiar with all available information concerning that flight, including runway lengths and takeoff and landing distance data for your aircraft. For IFR flights, or any flight not in the vicinity of an airport, four other items are specifically mentioned in the regulations. What are they?
74. If weather conditions at the destination require an alternate airport to be designated on your flight plan, what minimum fuel is required?
75. Normal day VFR reserve fuel is how many minutes?
76. Night VFR reserve fuel and IFR reserve fuel, day or night, is how many minutes?
77. No IFR minimum altitude is prescribed.
    a. What is the minimum IFR altitude for a route in designated mountainous terrain?
    b. What clearance is required above non-mountainous terrain?
78. An IFR flight on a westerly course should be planned at which of the following?
    a. Odd altitudes or flight levels, as appropriate.
    b. Odd+500 altitudes or flight levels, as appropriate.
    c. Even altitudes or flight levels, as appropriate.
    d. Even+500 altitudes or flight levels, as appropriate.
79. Which of the following is required equipment for powered aircraft during VFR night flights?
    a. Anticollision light system.
    b. Gyroscopic direction indicator.
    c. Gyroscopic bank-and-pitch indicator.
80. What type of ADS-B Out equipment is required for flight in class A airspace?
81. The due date for a transponder to be tested and inspected has passed. May it be used?
82. True or false? Part 135 applies to carriage of persons and property for compensation or hire in aircraft with less than 30 passenger seats or a maximum payload capacity of less than 8,000 pounds.
83. True or false? By day, you should fly VFR no lower than 500 feet AGL and at least 500 feet horizontally from any obstacle.
84. True or false? By night over terrain not designated as mountainous, you should fly VFR at an altitude of at least 1,000 feet above the highest obstacle within a horizontal distance of 5 miles from the intended course.
85. True or false? By night over designated mountainous terrain, you should fly VFR at an altitude of at least 1,000 feet above the highest obstacle within a horizontal distance of 4 miles from the intended course.

Answers are given on page 702.

Charts 20

If you want to navigate an airplane efficiently from one place to another over long distances or in poor visibility, you need to refer to some representation of the earth. This representation must be smaller in size than the earth portraying a picture of a "reduced earth."

The simplest and most accurate reduced representation of earth is a globe, which retains the spherical shape of the earth and displays the various oceans, continents, cities, and so on. A cumbersome globe is not the ideal navigation tool to have in a cockpit or to carry in a navigation bag, especially if detailed information is required, hence the need for maps or charts that can be folded and stowed away. The task of the "map-maker" or cartographer is to project a picture of a reduced-earth globe onto a flat surface and make a map or chart from this.

Maps represent the earth's surface, or parts thereof, on a flat surface; *charts* are maps which show additional information or special conditions, sometimes using only an outline of geographical features such as the coastline. Since most maps that pilots use show specific aeronautical and navigational data, they are referred to as charts.

The Form or Shape of the Earth

The exact shape of the earth's surface is constantly changing. Volcanoes erupt and grow, new islands form and others disappear, landslides and earthquakes cause large land movements, the ocean surface continually changes in height with the tides, and, on a very long-term basis, the continents gradually move.

The regular geometric shape that the earth resembles most is a sphere, but even when all the surface bumps are ironed out, the earth is still not a perfect sphere. It is slightly flat at the North and South Poles, forming a flattened (oblate) spheroid, the polar diameter being approximately 23 nautical miles (NM) less than the equatorial diameter (6,865 NM as against 6,888 NM). For the purposes of practical navigation, however, the earth can be treated as a sphere.

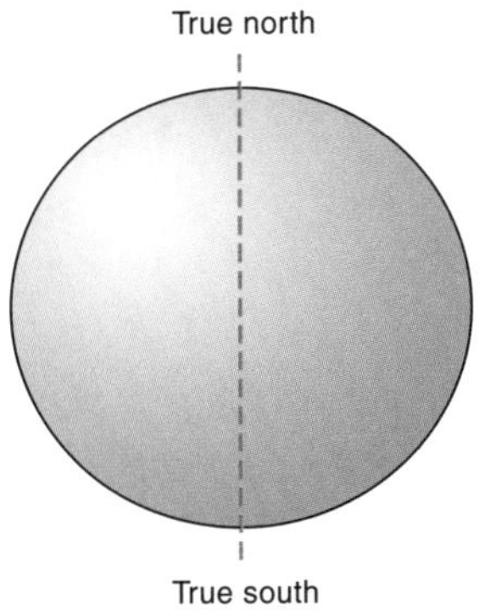

Figure 20-1
The earth is a slightly flattened (oblate) sphere.

The earth rotates on its own axis as well as moving in an orbit about the sun. This axis of rotation is called the geographic *polar axis*, and the two points where it meets the surface of the sphere are called:

- the northern geographic pole or *true north*; and
- the southern geographic pole or *true south*.

If you stand anywhere on earth and face toward the northern geographic pole, then you are facing true north.

Note. The earth's axis is tilted in relation to its orbital path around the sun. It is shown as vertical here for ease of explanation.

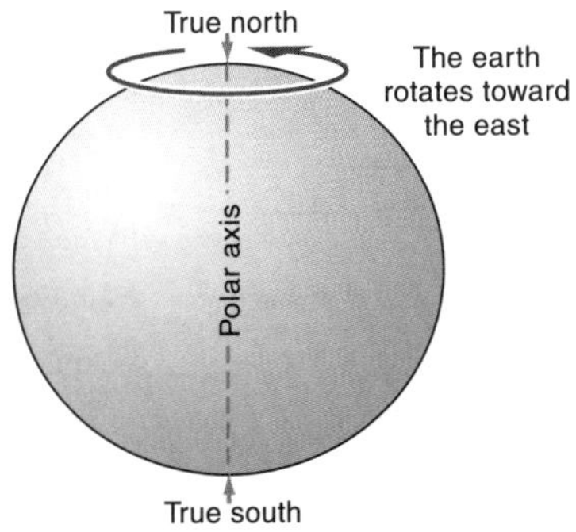

Figure 20-2
The earth rotates about on its own axis.

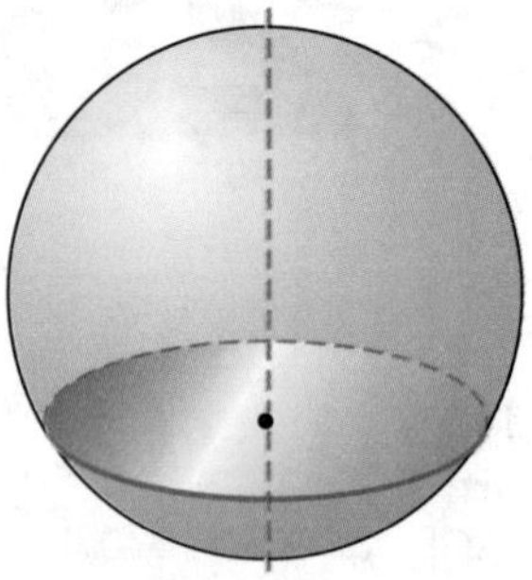

Figure 20-3
The plane of a small circle does not pass through the center of a sphere.

Imaginary Lines on the Earth's Surface

A *great circle* drawn on the earth's surface is one whose plane passes through the center of the earth. Great circles have some significant properties, including those in figure 20-4:

- a great circle is the largest circle that can be drawn on the surface of the earth or on any sphere;
- the shortest distance between any two points on the surface of a sphere is the arc of a great circle; and
- only one great circle can be drawn between two points on the surface of a sphere (unless the two points are diametrically opposed, as are the geographic poles).

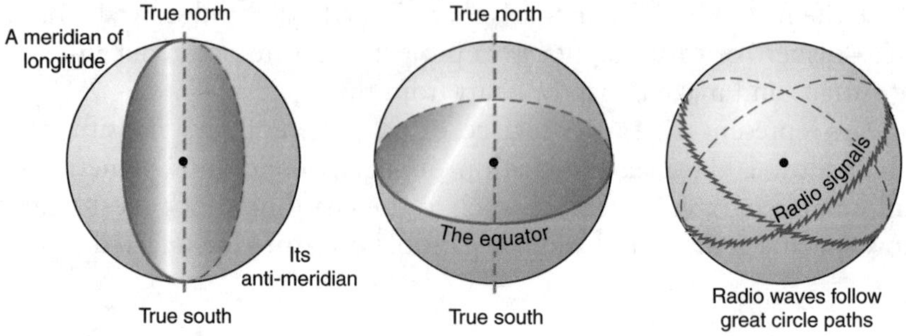

Figure 20-4 A great circle has the center of the earth as its axis.

Some examples of great circles are: meridians of longitude, the equator, and the paths that radio waves follow. A *small circle* is any circle on the surface of a sphere that is not a great circle and therefore the center of a small circle is not at the center of the earth. Parallels of latitude (other than the equator) are small circles.

Latitude and Longitude

A convenient way of specifying the position of any point on earth is to relate it to the imaginary lines that form the *latitude* and *longitude* grid on the surface of the earth.

Latitude

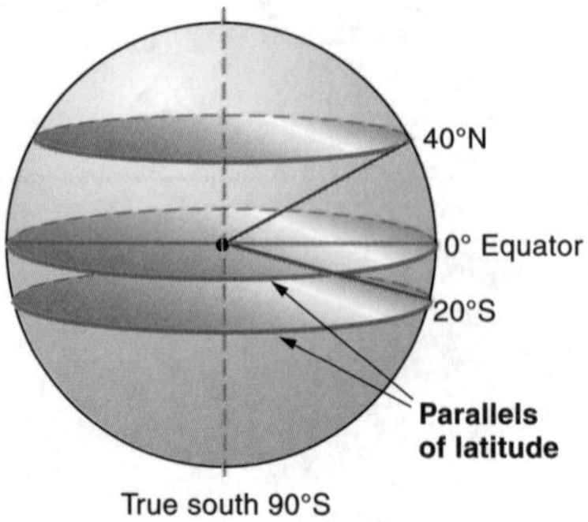

Figure 20-5
Latitude.

The reference for latitude is the plane of the *equator*, the great circle whose plane is perpendicular (at right angles, or 90 degrees) to the polar axis.

The *latitude* of a place is its angular distance in degrees from the equator, measured at the center of the earth and designated either north or south. For instance, Detroit, Michigan is at 42°N latitude.

A *parallel of latitude* joins all points of the same latitude and (except for the equator) is a small circle. Detroit, Boston, Barcelona in Spain, Rome in Italy, Istanbul in Turkey, Tashkent in Uzbekistan and Shenyang in China are all about 42° north of the equator, and therefore the line joining them is called the 42°N parallel of latitude.

Parallels of latitude are parallel to the equator and to each other.

The longest parallel of latitude is the equator (latitude 0°). The other parallels, as you move away from the equator toward the higher latitudes, progressively decrease in size until the 90° parallels of latitude become just points at the north and south geographic poles.

Longitude

The basic reference for longitude is the *Greenwich meridian*, which is also known as the *prime meridian*. It is that half of the great circle which contains the polar axis (about which the earth rotates), and passes through the Greenwich Observatory situated near London, England, as well as the north and south geographic poles. The prime meridian is designated as *longitude 0°*.

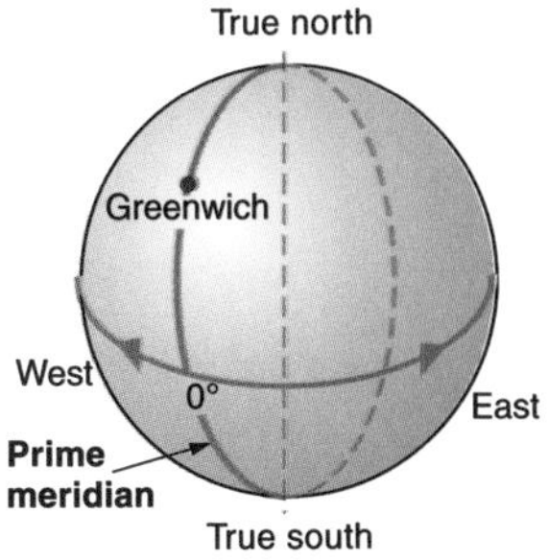

Figure 20-6
The prime meridian.

The other half of the same great circle that makes up the prime meridian is on the other side of the earth from Greenwich. It passes down the western side of the Pacific Ocean and is known as *longitude 180°*. It can be reached by traveling 180 degrees either east or west from the prime meridian. Therefore longitude 180° can be called either 180°E or 180°W. It is also called the *anti-meridian* of Greenwich:

- all of the great circles containing the polar axis (and therefore the north and south geographic poles) are called *meridians of longitude*; and
- meridians of longitude are specified by their angular difference in degrees east or west from the prime meridian.

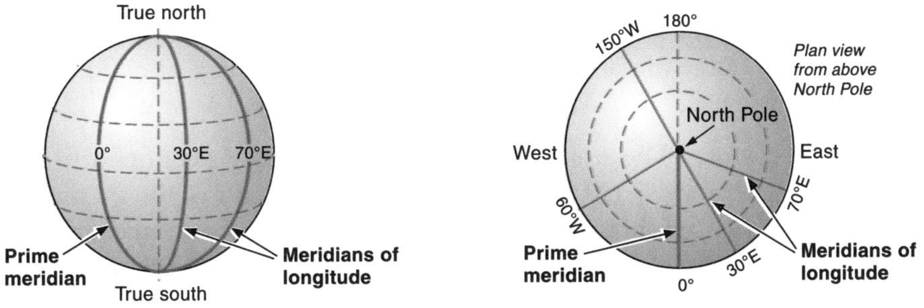

Figure 20-7 The longitutde of a place is the angle between its meridian of longitude and the prime (Greenwich) meridian, measured east or west from the prime meridian.

Specifying Position

The parallels of latitude and meridians of longitude form an imaginary grid over the surface of the earth. Position of any point on the earth can be specified by:

- its *latitude*—the angular position N or S of the plane of the equator; together with
- its *longitude*—the angular position E or W of the prime meridian.

It is usually sufficiently accurate to specify the latitude and longitude of a place in degrees and minutes (one minute is 1⁄60 of one degree). For more accuracy, each minute is divided into 60 seconds of arc. The symbols used are degrees (°), minutes ('), and seconds ("). For example, the position of Warren in Pennsylvania is 41°50'N, 079°08'W, accurate to the nearest minute.

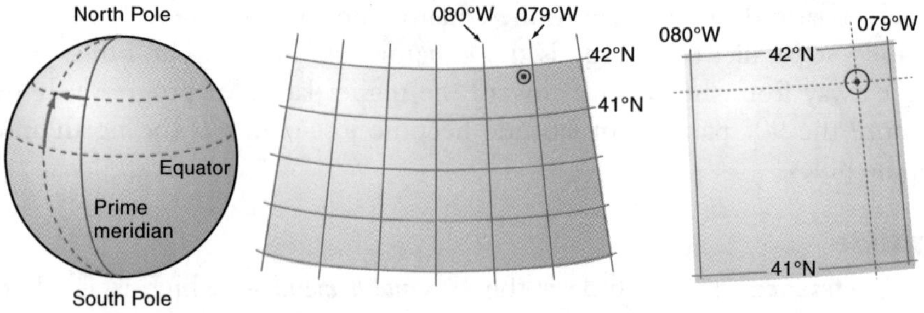

Figure 20-8 The position of Warren in Pennsylvania is 41°50'N, 79°08'W.

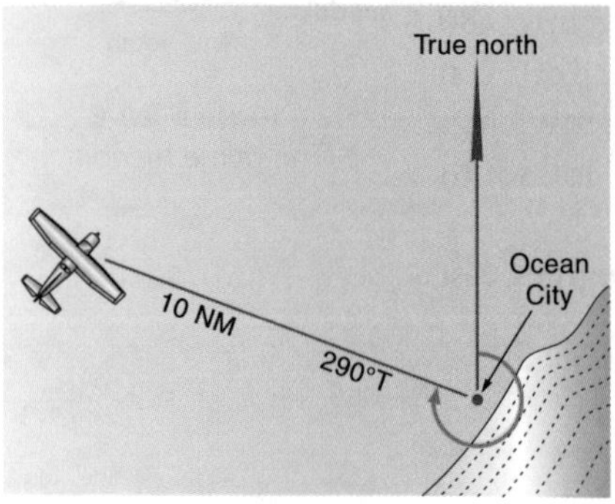

Figure 20-9
Specifying position on the earth by range and bearing.

Modern electronic navigation systems are very accurate, requiring latitude and longitude to be expressed to an accuracy of 0.1' of arc (6 seconds of arc is the same as 0.1' of arc). To cater for these systems, aeronautical charts and documents such as the Chart Supplement U.S. would show position N52°20'36", W105°25'6" as N52°20.6', W105°25.1'.

Latitude and longitude are the normal means to indicate a particular position on earth. They are most commonly used at the flight planning stage when preparing the charts and flight plan. Once in flight, however, there are other means of specifying the position of the aircraft, such as by position over or abeam a landmark or radio beacon (for instance, "*Over Tuscaloosa, Abeam Mansfield, Over Casa Grande VOR*") or by range (distance) and bearing from a landmark or radio beacon (for instance, "*10 NM on a bearing of 290°M from Ocean City*").

> **Note.** The use of place names needs to be confined to places that are likely to be known to the recipient of the message, and that are shown on the commonly used aeronautical charts. In the United States, place names are frequently duplicated and can be misleading.

Distances

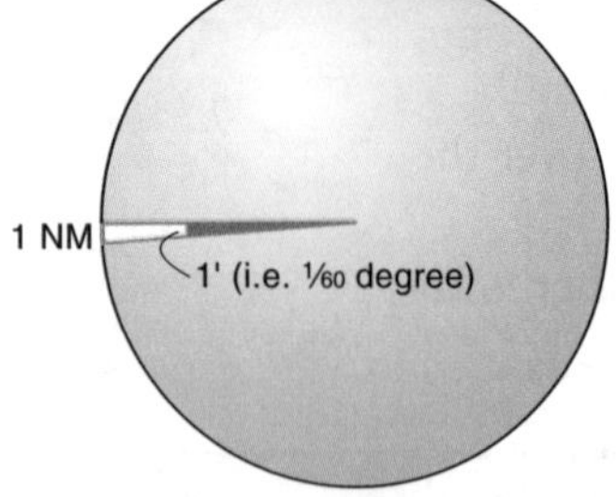

Figure 20-10
1 NM is the length of 1 minute of arc of a great circle on the earth.

The standard unit of distance in navigation is the *nautical mile* (NM), which is the length of 1 minute of the arc of any great circle on earth. There are 360 degrees in a circle and 60 minutes in a degree, making 60 × 360 = 21,600 minutes of arc in a circle. The circumference of the earth is therefore 60 × 360 = 21,600 minutes of arc, which is 21,600 NM.

Latitude (the angular distance north or south of the equator) is measured up and down a meridian of longitude (which is a great circle) and therefore:

- 1 minute of latitude at any point on earth = 1 nautical mile; and
- 1 degree of latitude at any point on earth = 60 nautical miles.

This is very useful for measuring distances on a chart, although the usual means of measuring distance is to use the scale line or a plotter.

Longitude is measured around the parallels of latitude (all small circles, except for the equator), and so 1 minute of longitude varies in length, depending on where it is on the earth's surface. The only place where 1 minute of longitude is equal to 1 NM is around the equator—the higher the latitude, the further away from the equator the place is, and the shorter the length of 1 minute of longitude in that region.

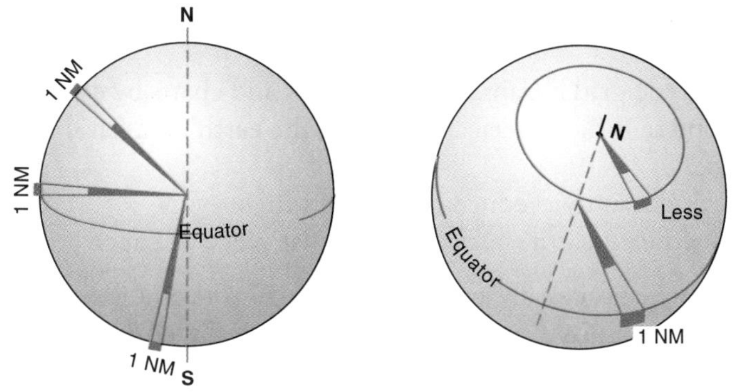

Figure 20-11 1 minute of latitude = 1 NM; 1 minute of longitude varies in length.

Angles

The most fundamental reference from which angles are measured is that of true north, from 000°T, through 090°T, 180°T, 270°T, to 360°T. As figure 20-12 shows, if an airplane follows a long-range great circle course, the course direction will gradually change. A great circle route will therefore cross successive meridians at a gradually changing angle. Sometimes it is convenient to fly a course whose direction remains constant when referred to true north, so that the course crosses all meridians of longitude at the same angle. This is known as a *rhumb line.*

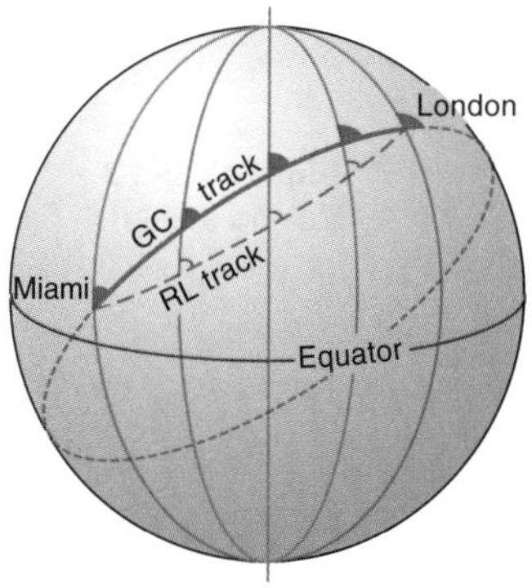

Figure 20-12
The great circle and the rhumb line tracks between two places.

The rhumb line and great circle between two places coincide only if the two places lie on either the same meridian of longitude (which is a great circle) or on the equator which is also a great circle. In practical terms, the great circle direction and the rhumb line direction may be considered to be the same over short distances of less than 200 NM.

Direction is the angular position of one point to another without reference to the distance between them. It is expressed as the angular difference from a specified reference direction. In air navigation this reference direction is either:

- north (for *true* or *magnetic* bearings); or
- the heading (or the nose) of the aircraft (for *relative* bearings).

You must always be very clear as to whether you are referring direction to true north or to magnetic north, the difference between the two being the magnetic variation. In this chapter, we are referring direction to true north.

A true course of 085°T (85° measured clockwise from true north) may be written as TC 085. A magnetic course of 130°M (130° measured clockwise from magnetic north) may be written as MC 130.

Direction is usually specified as a three-figure group.

It is usual to refer to direction as a three-figure group to prevent any misunderstanding. For example, north is referred to as 360 or 000, east is referred to as 090, south-west as 225.

Representing the Spherical Earth on Flat Charts

The latitude–longitude grid is translated onto maps and charts by cartographers whose major task is to represent the spherical surface of the earth on a flat sheet of paper. The process consists of:

- scaling the earth down to a reduced earth; and then
- projecting the reduced earth's surface onto a flat piece of paper.

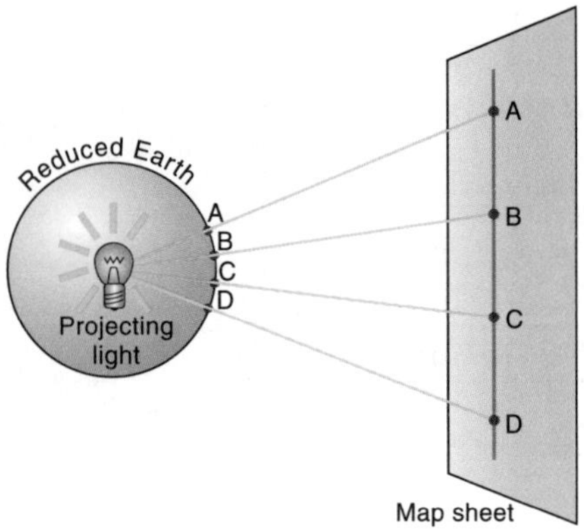

Figure 20-13
Making a chart.

The process always leads to some distortion of areas, distances, angles or shapes. By using certain mathematical techniques when projecting the spherical earth onto a flat chart, the cartographer can preserve some properties, but not all. Some property will always be distorted to a greater or lesser extent depending on how the points on the surface of the reduced spherical earth are transferred onto the flat chart.

Unlike a sphere, certain other curved surfaces (such as a cylinder or a cone) can be cut and laid out flat. By projecting points on the surface of the reduced earth onto either a conical or cylindrical surface (which can then be flattened out to form a sheet), less distortion occurs and a better chart results, compared with a projection onto an already flat sheet like that illustrated in figure 20-13.

A simplified view of chart-making is to think of a light projecting the shadows of the latitude–longitude grid of the reduced sphere onto a cone (Lambert conical projection) or onto a cylinder (Mercator cylindrical projection). The cone or cylinder is then laid out flat to form a chart.

Charts based on conic and cylindrical projections are widely used in aviation, mainly because they:

- *preserve shapes* (or at least minimize distortions);
- *preserve angular relationships* (in mathematical terminology, charts that exhibit this important property are said to be *conformal* or *orthomorphic*); and
- have a reasonably *constant scale* over the whole chart.

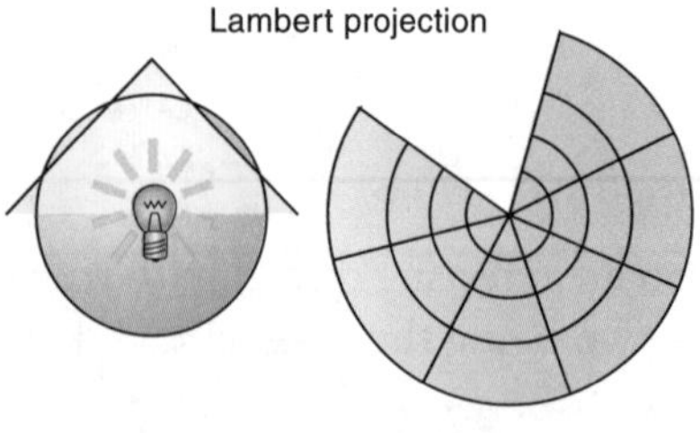

Figure 20-14
A conical projection (Lambert).

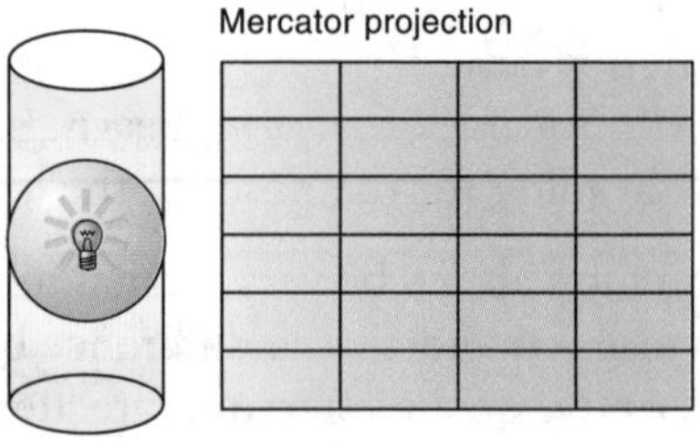

Figure 20-15
A cylindrical projection (Mercator).

Scale

There are various ways of describing just how much the earth is scaled down on a particular chart. Scale is defined as the ratio of the chart length compared to the earth distance that it represents.

$$\text{Scale} = \frac{\text{chart length}}{\text{chart distance}} \quad \text{(with both items in the same unit)}$$

Large scale charts cover small areas in detail.

The greater the chart length for a given earth distance, the *larger* the scale and the more detail that can be shown. A large-scale chart covers a small area in detail. For example, a 1:250,000 (one to one-quarter million) chart has a larger scale and can show more detail than a 1:500,000 (one to one-half million) aeronautical chart. The sample excerpts in figures 20-16 and 20-17 cover the same physical area.

Scale can be expressed in various ways:

- as a *representative fraction*. For instance, sectionals are 1:500,000 charts (one to one-half million), where 1 inch on the chart represents 500,000 inches (7 nautical miles) on the earth, or where 1 NM on earth is represented by 1 half-millionth of a nautical mile on the chart;
- as a *graduated scale line*, situated at the bottom of the chart. A graduated scale line allows you to measure off the distance between two points on the chart and match it against the scale line. Make sure that you use the correct scale line (usually nautical miles), since there may be various ones so that nautical miles, statute miles or kilometers can be measured; and
- in *words*—for instance, "1 inch equals 5 NM," which means that 5 NM on the earth's surface is represented by 1 inch on the chart.

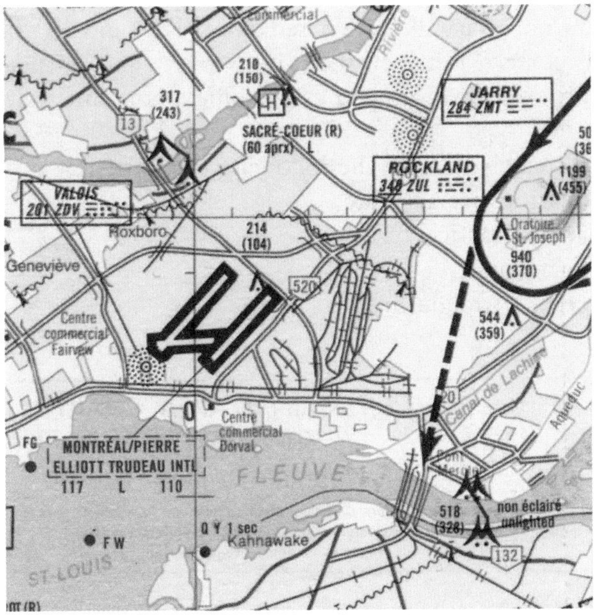

Figure 20-16
Sample except from 1:250,00 Terminal Area.

Figure 20-17
Sample excerpt from 1:500,000 Sectional VFR chart.

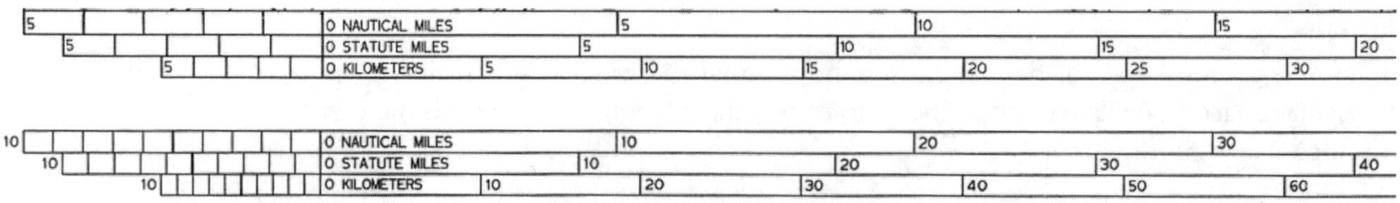

Figure 20-18 Scale lines from a 1:250,000 chart (top) and a 1:500,000 chart.

Topographical Charts

When navigating by visual reference to the ground, the pilot refers to land features. A *topographical* chart showing the surface features of the area in detail is therefore of great value. There are various topographical charts available for visual navigation in the United States, including (in order of importance):

- *Sectional Charts*, which are the most common charts used for visual navigation; their scale is 1:500,000 (half-million);
- *VFR Terminal Area Charts*, scale 1:250,000 (quarter-million), showing more detail around busy airports; and
- *1:1,000,000 Navigation Charts*, which have a small scale and are sometimes used for long-distance visual navigation.

Most aviation charts are based on the Lambert conformal conic projection. The chart sheet is formed from a cone that cuts the sphere representing the reduced earth at two standard parallels of latitude. Just which two parallels of latitude are chosen by the cartographer depends on which part of the earth, and how much of it, he wants to represent on that particular chart.

The standard parallels are usually mentioned on the title section of the chart—for example, on the Seattle Sectional the standard parallels are stated to be 41°20 and 46°40. The scale at the standard parallels is correct. Between them it contracts, and outside of them it expands. For practical purposes however, you can assume a constant scale over the whole chart.

The Sectional and VFR Terminal Area charts have the following properties:

- they are conformal—angles and bearings are accurate;
- constant scale over the whole chart in practical terms;
- shapes are preserved in practical terms; and
- the true course between two places is a straight line.

SEATTLE
SECTIONAL AERONAUTICAL CHART
SCALE 1:500,000
Lambert Conformal Conic Projection Standard Parallels 41° 20′ and 46° 40′
Horizontal Datum: North American Datum of 1983
Topographic data corrected to October 1993

VFR TERMINAL AREA CHART
SEATTLE
SCALE 1:250,000
Lambert Conformal Conic Projection Standard Parallels 33° and 45°
Horizontal Datum: North American Datum of 1983
Topographic data corrected to April 1993

Figure 20-19 Most charts are based on the Lambert conformal conic projection.

Sectional Charts

Sectionals are colorful charts that show significant ground details, such as height of terrain, position of rivers and lakes, cities, railroads, roads, and so on, as well as aeronautical details in the airspace above, including federal airways and airspace boundaries and altitudes. The aeronautical information also includes ground features such as airports, which are sometimes easy to see from an airplane and sometimes not, as well as the position of navigation aids.

Ground Features

Ground features may change with changing seasons.

Topographical information shown on sectionals is that considered to be of most value to visual navigation. Features shown on the chart will be evident on the ground. It is impossible to show everything. For example, an isolated rocky outcrop may not be considered significant by the cartographer and therefore will not be shown. You might spot it on the ground, yet not find it depicted on the chart.

If, however, there is an isolated rock shown on the chart, it will certainly exist on the ground. The same thing may be said about cultural features depicted on charts, such as radomes and golf courses. If they are shown on the chart, then they may be suitable as landmarks for visual navigation.

Drainage and Water Features

Drainage and water features (hydrographic features) are usually depicted in blue. Hydrographic features include creeks, streams, rivers, canals, lakes, reservoirs, swamps, marshes, shorelines, tidal flats, and so on. Just how they are depicted on the chart is explained by the chart legend, but bear in mind that after a flood, for instance, what might be shown as a small stream on the chart may have become a raging torrent.

Relief

There are various ways of bringing ground contours into relief so that an impression of hills, mountains, valleys, and so on, is obtained when you look at the chart. Sectionals charts show *contours*—lines joining places of equal elevation above mean sea level—to depict relief. The closer that the contour lines are together on the chart, the steeper the terrain.

The basic contour interval on sectionals is in 500-foot vertical steps, with 250-foot contour intervals in gently rolling areas—for example, 250 feet MSL, 500 feet MSL, 750 feet MSL.

Color or layer tinting in 1,000-foot steps up to 2,000 feet MSL, then in 2,000-foot steps, is used in conjunction with the contour lines to give even more relief. The colors or tints used for the various ground elevations are shown on a table on the chart legend. The shades of color start with light green for low land just above sea level, then go through shades of brown, gradually darkening as the ground becomes higher. Remember that a particular color may indicate ground elevation up to the level of the next contour above it. Refer to the legend and chart excerpts on pages 503–509.

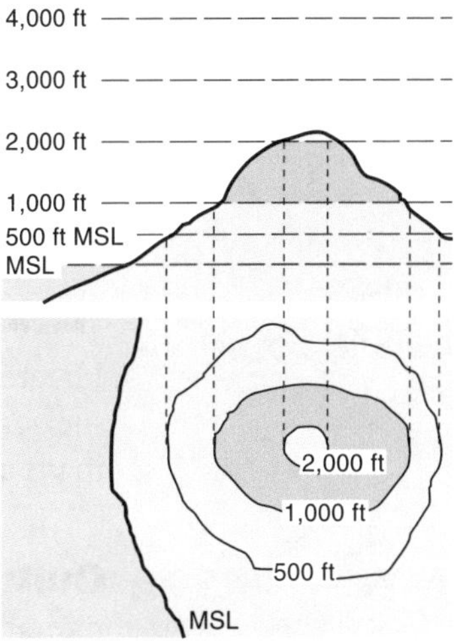

Figure 20-20
Contour lines represent changes in height MSL.

Hill Shading

Hill shading is used to give a three-dimensional effect on some aeronautical charts. Hill shading shows darkened areas on the low side of high ground where you would expect to see shadows with the light coming from the northwest (a graphic standard).

Spot Elevations

Spot elevations (or spot heights) are shown using a black spot with an adjacent number to indicate the elevation (height MSL—above mean sea level) in feet. These elevations are generally accurate (unless amended by NOTAM), or unless shown on the chart by an *x* instead of a •. Doubtful locations are indicated by omission of the • or *x*.

Spot elevations are normally used to show local peaks and other critical elevations that are significantly higher than the surrounding terrain. The spot heights may not be higher than all other terrain in the general area, so you should always check hypsometric tints as well as spot heights. The highest point on each chart has its elevation printed slightly larger than the rest. It also rates a mention on the color-tint table, and its position in latitude and longitude is specified there.

Obstructions

Obstructions are shown on sectionals using their own symbols, differing slightly for obstructions 1,000 feet above ground level (AGL) and higher, and for those below 1,000 feet AGL. A bold number gives the elevation MSL of the highest point on the obstruction, and a lighter number in parentheses gives its height AGL. Be aware that guy wires may extend outward from some structures. You can determine the elevation of the terrain at the base of the obstruction by subtracting the obstruction height AGL from its elevation MSL. Lighted obstructions have flash lines radiating from the top of their symbols.

Maximum Elevation Figures

MEFs concern the highest known feature including terrain and obstructions.

Maximum elevation figures (MEFs) for specified areas are shown on sectionals. Thousands of feet are shown as a large number, with the hundreds shown as a smaller number beside it—for example, 3^1 (3,100 feet MSL), and 5^6 (5,600 feet MSL). MEFs concern the highest known feature lying within the specified latitude–longitude quadrangle, and include terrain and obstructions. Elevations are rounded up to the next 100 feet, or higher if thought appropriate.

If you fly 500 feet higher than the MEF, you will clear all terrain and obstacles in that quadrangle by 500 feet vertically, which is normal minimum VFR clearance when flying over open terrain. Over congested areas, you are required by Part 91 of the Regulations to have a clearance of 1,000 feet vertically, in which case you would add 1,000 feet or more to the MEF.

Hazards to Aviation

Hazards to aviation information are also depicted. These include certain aerial activities such as parachuting and hang-gliding, as well as permanent obstructions such as radio masts and elevated cables.

Cultural Features

Cultural features are of great help in visual navigation. It is not possible to show every town or house on the chart, so a choice is made to show what is significant. A group of, say, 100 houses is obviously of little significance if it lies in the middle of a city the size of Los Angeles, and so will not be specifically depicted on the chart, yet in the western desert areas it may be extremely significant and will be shown.

Roads and railroads can be of great assistance for visual air navigation. Those that are most significant will be clearly shown on the chart. Distinctive patterns such as curves, roads running parallel to and crossing railroad lines, road or railroad junctions, forks, overpasses and tunnels, are especially useful.

Many other easily seen cultural features, such as isolated golf courses, hospitals, factories, microwave stations, ranches, sawmills, and so on, may also be shown. Pilots are requested to fly no lower than 2,000 feet AGL over national wildlife refuges, where there may be a lot of bird activity, and where a certain amount of tranquillity might be appreciated. Examine the chart legend carefully and become familiar with the symbols.

Pilots are requested to fly no lower than 2,000 feet AGL over national wildlife refuges.

Aeronautical Information on Sectionals

Most people are familiar with topographical and cultural information, since these are surface features which are shown on a road map and in an atlas. A pilot, however, operates in a three-dimensional environment and therefore requires information on the airspace above the surface of the earth as well.

Aeronautical information is vital information for a pilot, showing not only the position of airports on the ground, but also the division of airspace, the location on the ground of navigation aids such as VORs and NDBs, and of course other information such as special use airspace.

Sectional chart legends explain this information clearly and thoroughly, although sometimes you have to search for the information in the legend and its associated notes. It is a good idea to memorize the most commonly used symbols for airports, airspace, obstructions, and so on. If in doubt, check the legend.

Use the legend to explain chart information.

Airports

Airports are shown on sectionals as:

- circles, for airports with runways that are not hard-surfaced;
- shaded circles, showing hard-surfaced runways 1,500–8,000 feet long; or
- shaded runways, for hard-surfaced runways longer than 8,000 feet.

Blue indicates airports equipped with control towers. *Magenta* is used for all other airports. If fuel is available and the airport is attended in normal working hours, four small ticks are shown around the basic airport symbol. A star ☆ near the airport symbol indicates a rotating beacon from sunset to sunrise. Further information regarding airport lighting, navigation aids, and services may be found in the Chart Supplement U.S.

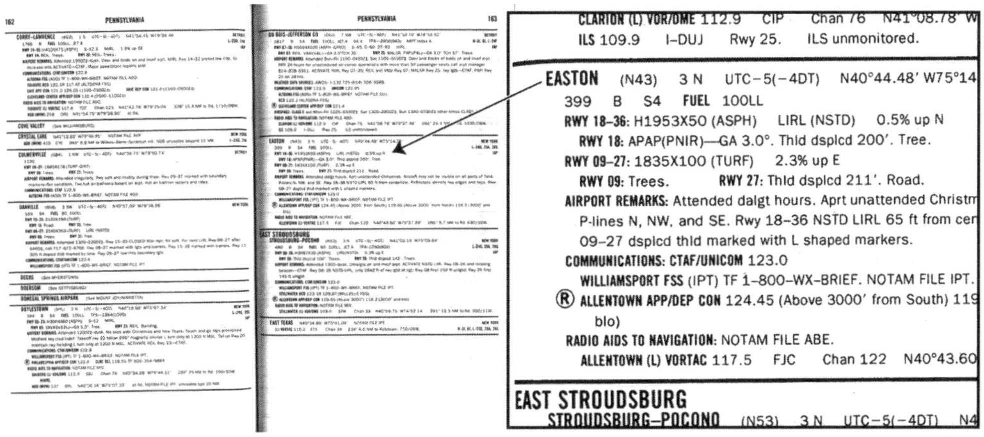

Figure 20-21 The Chart Supplement U.S.

The identifier for each airport shown on the Sectional chart will have the following where appropriate:

- the airport name—for example, Seattle Tacoma International (Intl), Boeing Field, King County Intl, Renton, McChord Air Force Base (AFB);
- the control tower frequency, for example, CT 120.1 (a star ★ indicates part-time, NFCT indicates a Non-Federal Control Tower, a C indicates the Common Traffic Advisory Frequency—CTAF);
- the ATIS frequency—for example, ATIS 134.85;
- field elevation, lighting, longest runway, UNICOM frequency—for example, *313L 115 122.95*, which means: field elevation 313 feet MSL, lighting in operation sunset to sunrise (★*L* if on-request, part-time, or pilot-controlled), longest runway 11,500 feet, and UNICOM frequency 122.95 MHz; and
- FSS above the airport name, where a Flight Service Station is at the airport (with advisory services available on 123.6 MHz if no tower in operation).

Radio Frequencies

When the control tower is operating, use tower frequency.

Communications boxes shown on sectional charts indicate frequencies to be used. At airports *with* operating control towers, you should use the control tower frequency. At airports *without* operating control towers, you should use the common traffic advisory frequency (CTAF), which may be:

Use CTAF frequency at airports without operating control towers.

- the FSS advisory frequency at airports without control towers but with FSS;
- the control tower frequency if there is a control tower, but it is not attended (in which case there may be no wind or runway-in-use information available, and you would have to use the UNICOM to obtain this information);
- the UNICOM frequency if there is no tower or FSS (UNICOM is a nongovernment frequency); or
- MULTICOM 122.9 MHz if there is no tower, FSS or UNICOM.

When inbound to or outbound from an airport *without* an operating control tower, you should communicate your position and monitor traffic on the CTAF within a 10-mile radius of the airport.

Navigation Facilities

Navigation facilities shown on sectionals include VORs, VORTACs, VOR/DMEs, and NDBs. NDBs are surrounded by a small circle lightly shaded with magenta-colored dots. VORs, VORTACs and VOR/DMEs are shown in blue, and have a large compass rose aligned with *magnetic* north centered on them to help in plotting radials where necessary.

The direction of true north is indicated by the meridians of longitude, and the angle between this and magnetic north on the VOR compass rose depends on the magnetic variation in that area.

Information on each radio facility is shown nearby in a NAVAID information box.

Position Information on Sectionals

The latitude/longitude grid is clearly marked on sectional charts. True bearings are measured from a meridian of longitude, which is the direction of true north. The east/west *parallels of latitude* indicate degrees north or south of the equator (north in the United States of course). They are labeled at either side of the 1:500,000 sectional chart in one-degree (1°) intervals, which are also 60 NM intervals. Each degree is divided into 60 minutes ('), with marks each 1' and 10', and a full line across the chart at 30'. In the northern hemisphere, latitude is measured up from the bottom of the chart (from the equator toward the pole).

The north–south *meridians of longitude* are labeled at the top and/or bottom of the chart in degrees east or west of the prime meridian. Each degree is divided into 60 minutes, with marks each 1' and 10', and a full line up the chart at 30'.

Magnetic Information

Isogonals are lines on a chart joining places of equal variation.

Isogonic lines, or *isogonals*, join places of equal magnetic variation. They are indicated on sectional charts by dashed magenta lines. Magnetic bearings can be found by applying the magnetic variation to the true bearing.

The *agonic line* (where true north and magnetic north are the same direction, and variation is zero) lies in between the areas experiencing west variation and those experiencing east variation. The agonic line passes through the eastern side of the United States.

VOR radials are magnetic courses away from a VOR.

Because the earth's magnetic poles are gradually moving, the amount of magnetic variation at a particular place will also gradually change over a period of years. Every year the isogonic information on the charts is updated. Compass roses aligned with *magnetic* north are shown around VORs, since VOR radials are magnetic courses away from a VOR.

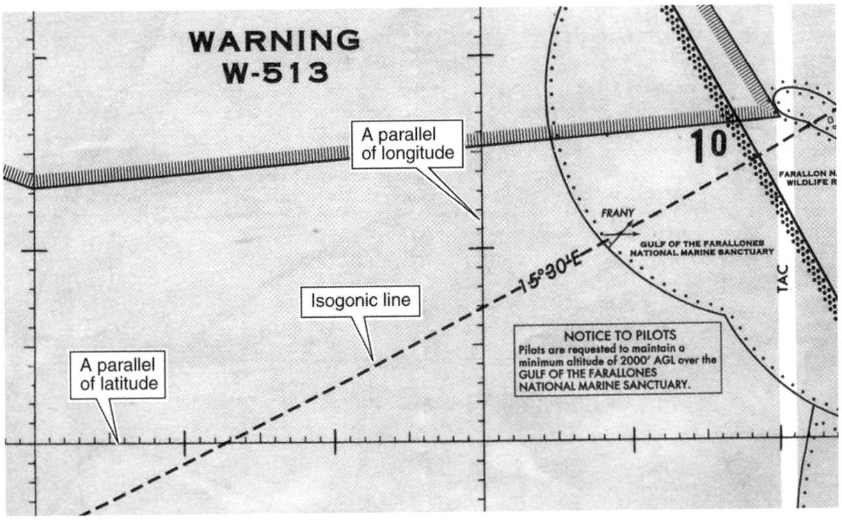

Figure 20-22 Grid of the 1:500,000 series.

VFR Terminal Area Charts

VFR Terminal Area Charts have a larger scale (1:250,000, or quarter-million) than Sectionals (1:500,000) and are used to show more detail around busy terminal areas. They look similar to sectional charts in that they also display both topographical and aeronautical information. On the rear face of many VFR Terminal Area Charts are *VFR Flyway Planning Charts*, which show suggested VFR flyways and altitudes designed to help VFR pilots avoid major controlled traffic flows in busy terminal areas. These charts are not to be used as your primary navigation chart. Ground references shown on the VFR Flyway Planning Charts only provide a guide for improved visual navigation. A sample excerpt of a VFR Terminal Area Chart is shown on page 508.

CPL

1:1,000,000 Navigation Charts

As you can imagine, charts having a scale of one to one million cover quite a lot of territory compared to the quarter- and half-million charts. This scale is often used when large distances are involved, to provide pilots mainly with topographical information (mountains, lakes, rivers, deserts, coastlines, and so on) and cultural information (cities, towns, highways, country roads, railroads, and so on). Aeronautical information is shown, but it is not as detailed as that shown on Sectionals or VFR Terminal Area Charts.

As of 2015 World Aeronautical Charts have been discontinued. The Operational Navigation Chart (ONC) series is still issued for areas covered in Figure 20-23.

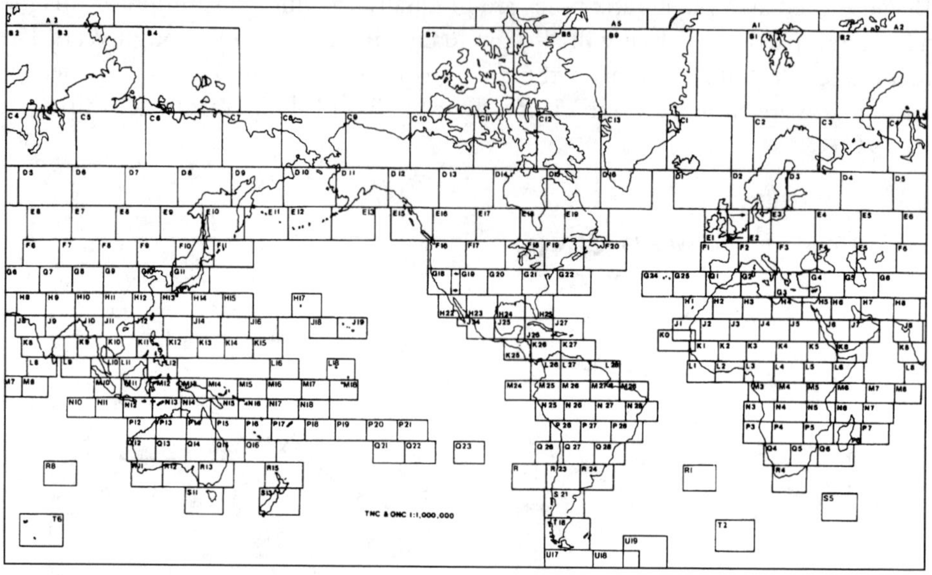

Figure 20-23 ONC world coverage.

This series uses much the same symbols and are based on the same projection as the half-million charts, the Lambert conformal conic projection.

Detail such as isogonic lines, restricted airspace, obstructions, irrigation channels, railroads and road systems change from time to time, and so the charts are reprinted regularly—about every two years for busy areas and every five or six years for more remote parts of the world. As with all aeronautical charts, ensure that you use only the latest edition and study the legend carefully prior to flight.

The ONC series originates from military sources but is available to civil pilots for most areas of the world.

End CPL

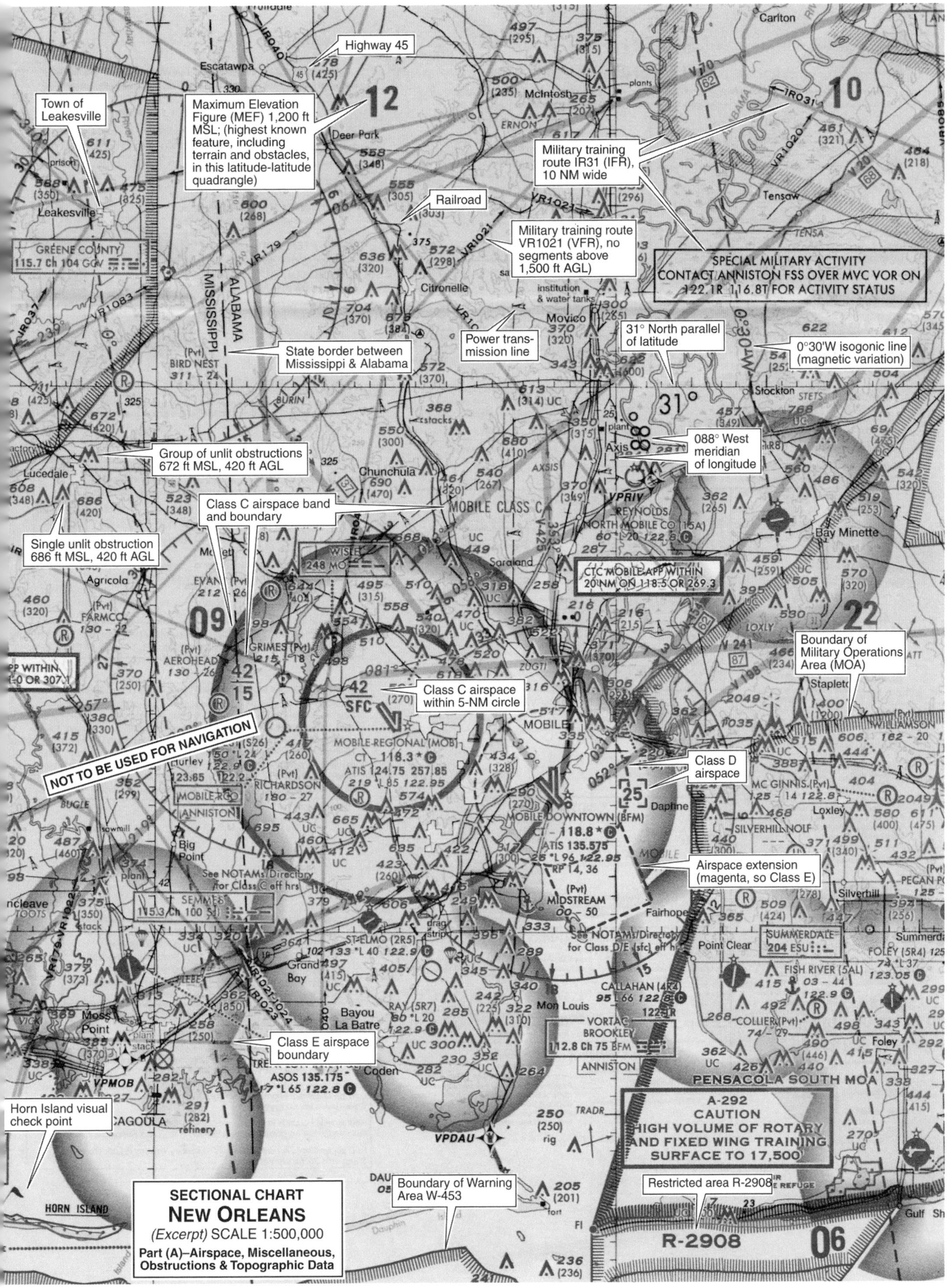

Figure 20-24 Sectional chart excerpt no. 1.

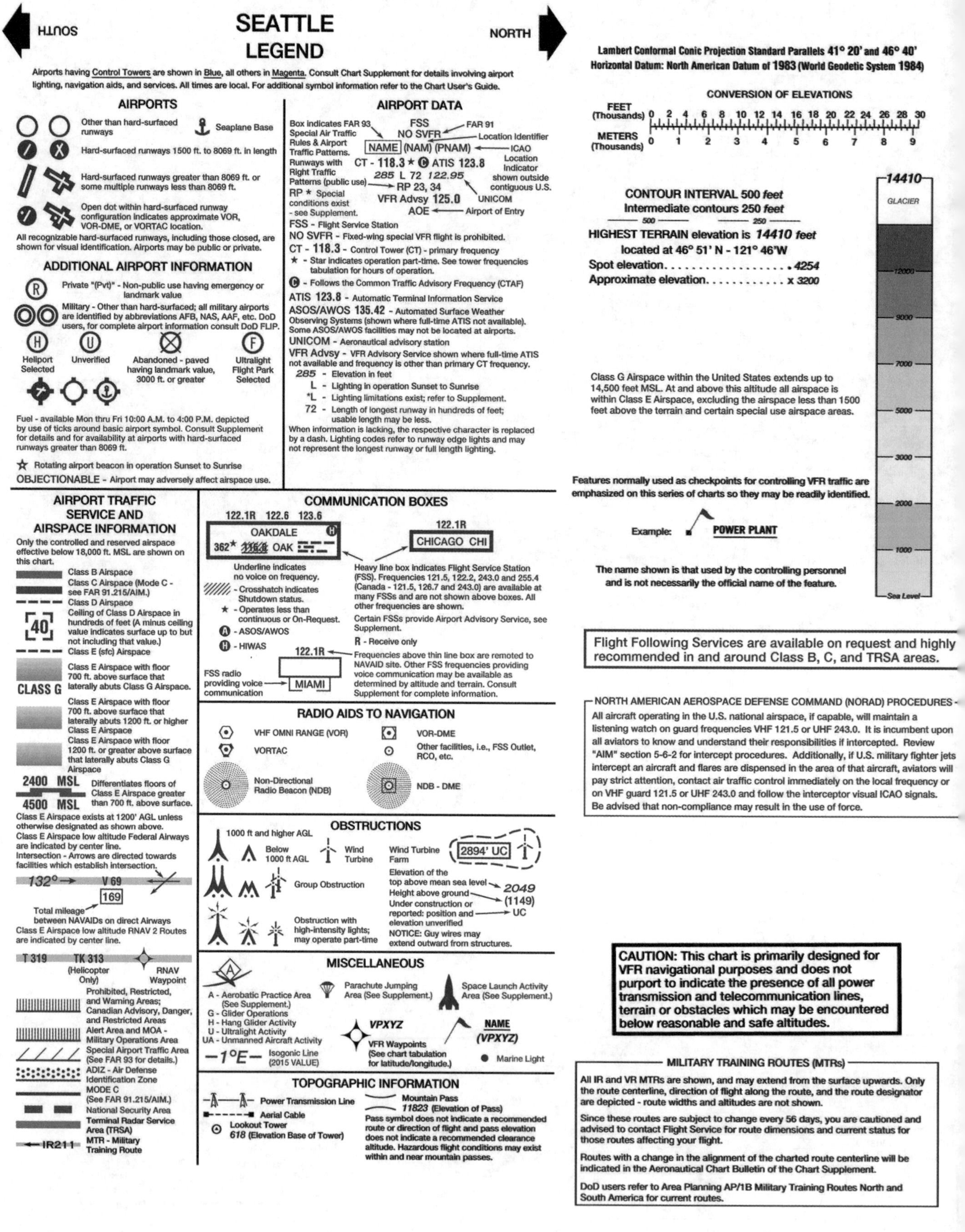
SOUTH
SEATTLE
LEGEND
NORTH
Airports having Control Towers are shown in Blue, all others in Magenta. Consult Chart Supplement for details involving airport lighting, navigation aids, and services. All times are local. For additional symbol information refer to the Chart User's Guide.
AIRPORTS
Other than hard-surfaced runways
Seaplane Base
Hard-surfaced runways 1500 ft. to 8069 ft. in length
Hard-surfaced runways greater than 8069 ft. or some multiple runways less than 8069 ft.
Open dot within hard-surfaced runway configuration indicates approximate VOR, VOR-DME, or VORTAC location.
All recognizable hard-surfaced runways, including those closed, are shown for visual identification. Airports may be public or private.
ADDITIONAL AIRPORT INFORMATION
Private "(Pvt)" - Non-public use having emergency or landmark value
Military - Other than hard-surfaced; all military airports are identified by abbreviations AFB, NAS, AAF, etc. DoD users, for complete airport information consult DoD FLIP.
Heliport Selected
Unverified
Abandoned - paved having landmark value, 3000 ft. or greater
Ultralight Flight Park Selected
Fuel - available Mon thru Fri 10:00 A.M. to 4:00 P.M. depicted by use of ticks around basic airport symbol. Consult Supplement for details and for availability at airports with hard-surfaced runways greater than 8069 ft.
Rotating airport beacon in operation Sunset to Sunrise
OBJECTIONABLE - Airport may adversely affect airspace use.
AIRPORT DATA
Box indicates FAR 93 Special Air Traffic Rules & Airport Traffic Patterns.
FSS
NO SVFR
FAR 91
Location Identifier
NAME (NAM) (PNAM)
ICAO Location Indicator shown outside contiguous U.S.
Runways with Right Traffic Patterns (public use)
CT - 118.3 ★ C ATIS 123.8
285 L 72 122.95
RP 23, 34
RP * Special conditions exist - see Supplement.
VFR Advsy 125.0
UNICOM
AOE
Airport of Entry
FSS - Flight Service Station
NO SVFR - Fixed-wing special VFR flight is prohibited.
CT - 118.3 - Control Tower (CT) - primary frequency
★ - Star indicates operation part-time. See tower frequencies tabulation for hours of operation.
C - Follows the Common Traffic Advisory Frequency (CTAF)
ATIS 123.8 - Automatic Terminal Information Service
ASOS/AWOS 135.42 - Automated Surface Weather Observing Systems (shown where full-time ATIS not available). Some ASOS/AWOS facilities may not be located at airports.
UNICOM - Aeronautical advisory station
VFR Advsy - VFR Advisory Service shown where full-time ATIS not available and frequency is other than primary CT frequency.
285 - Elevation in feet
L - Lighting in operation Sunset to Sunrise
*L - Lighting limitations exist; refer to Supplement.
72 - Length of longest runway in hundreds of feet; usable length may be less.
When information is lacking, the respective character is replaced by a dash. Lighting codes refer to runway edge lights and may not represent the longest runway or full length lighting.
AIRPORT TRAFFIC SERVICE AND AIRSPACE INFORMATION
Only the controlled and reserved airspace effective below 18,000 ft. MSL are shown on this chart.
Class B Airspace
Class C Airspace (Mode C - see FAR 91.215/AIM.)
Class D Airspace
Ceiling of Class D Airspace in hundreds of feet (A minus ceiling value indicates surface up to but not including that value.)
40
Class E (sfc) Airspace
Class E Airspace with floor 700 ft. above surface that laterally abuts Class G Airspace.
CLASS G
Class E Airspace with floor 700 ft. above surface that laterally abuts 1200 ft. or higher Class E Airspace
Class E Airspace with floor 1200 ft. or greater above surface that laterally abuts Class G Airspace
2400 MSL
4500 MSL
Differentiates floors of Class E Airspace greater than 700 ft. above surface.
Class E Airspace exists at 1200' AGL unless otherwise designated as shown above.
Class E Airspace low altitude Federal Airways are indicated by center line.
Intersection - Arrows are directed towards facilities which establish intersection.
132°
V 69
169
Total mileage between NAVAIDs on direct Airways
Class E Airspace low altitude RNAV 2 Routes are indicated by center line.
T 319
TK 313
(Helicopter Only)
RNAV Waypoint
Prohibited, Restricted, and Warning Areas; Canadian Advisory, Danger, and Restricted Areas
Alert Area and MOA - Military Operations Area
Special Airport Traffic Area (See FAR 93 for details.)
ADIZ - Air Defense Identification Zone
MODE C (See FAR 91.215/AIM.)
National Security Area
Terminal Radar Service Area (TRSA)
MTR - Military Training Route
IR211
COMMUNICATION BOXES
122.1R 122.6 123.6
OAKDALE
362★ 116.4 OAK
122.1R
CHICAGO CHI
Underline indicates no voice on frequency.
- Crosshatch indicates Shutdown status.
★ - Operates less than continuous or On-Request.
A - ASOS/AWOS
H - HIWAS
Heavy line box indicates Flight Service Station (FSS). Frequencies 121.5, 122.2, 243.0 and 255.4 (Canada - 121.5, 126.7 and 243.0) are available at many FSSs and are not shown above boxes. All other frequencies are shown.
Certain FSSs provide Airport Advisory Service, see Supplement.
R - Receive only
122.1R
MIAMI
FSS radio providing voice communication
Frequencies above thin line box are remoted to NAVAID site. Other FSS frequencies providing voice communication may be available as determined by altitude and terrain. Consult Supplement for complete information.
RADIO AIDS TO NAVIGATION
VHF OMNI RANGE (VOR)
VORTAC
VOR-DME
Other facilities, i.e., FSS Outlet, RCO, etc.
Non-Directional Radio Beacon (NDB)
NDB - DME
OBSTRUCTIONS
1000 ft and higher AGL
Below 1000 ft AGL
Wind Turbine
Wind Turbine Farm
2894' UC
Group Obstruction
Elevation of the top above mean sea level
Height above ground
Under construction or reported: position and elevation unverified
2049
(1149)
UC
Obstruction with high-intensity lights; may operate part-time
NOTICE: Guy wires may extend outward from structures.
MISCELLANEOUS
A - Aerobatic Practice Area (See Supplement.)
G - Glider Operations
H - Hang Glider Activity
U - Ultralight Activity
UA - Unmanned Aircraft Activity
Parachute Jumping Area (See Supplement.)
Space Launch Activity Area (See Supplement.)
VPXYZ
VFR Waypoints (See chart tabulation for latitude/longitude.)
NAME (VPXYZ)
-1°E- Isogonic Line (2015 VALUE)
Marine Light
TOPOGRAPHIC INFORMATION
Power Transmission Line
Aerial Cable
Lookout Tower 618 (Elevation Base of Tower)
Mountain Pass 11823 (Elevation of Pass)
Pass symbol does not indicate a recommended route or direction of flight and pass elevation does not indicate a recommended clearance altitude. Hazardous flight conditions may exist within and near mountain passes.
Lambert Conformal Conic Projection Standard Parallels 41° 20' and 46° 40'
Horizontal Datum: North American Datum of 1983 (World Geodetic System 1984)
CONVERSION OF ELEVATIONS
FEET (Thousands) 0 2 4 6 8 10 12 14 16 18 20 22 24 26 28 30
METERS (Thousands) 0 1 2 3 4 5 6 7 8 9
CONTOUR INTERVAL 500 feet
Intermediate contours 250 feet
500
250
HIGHEST TERRAIN elevation is 14410 feet located at 46° 51' N - 121° 46'W
Spot elevation . 4254
Approximate elevation x 3200
14410
GLACIER
12000
9000
7000
5000
3000
2000
1000
Sea Level
Class G Airspace within the United States extends up to 14,500 feet MSL. At and above this altitude all airspace is within Class E Airspace, excluding the airspace less than 1500 feet above the terrain and certain special use airspace areas.
Features normally used as checkpoints for controlling VFR traffic are emphasized on this series of charts so they may be readily identified.
Example: POWER PLANT
The name shown is that used by the controlling personnel and is not necessarily the official name of the feature.
Flight Following Services are available on request and highly recommended in and around Class B, C, and TRSA areas.
NORTH AMERICAN AEROSPACE DEFENSE COMMAND (NORAD) PROCEDURES
All aircraft operating in the U.S. national airspace, if capable, will maintain a listening watch on guard frequencies VHF 121.5 or UHF 243.0. It is incumbent upon all aviators to know and understand their responsibilities if intercepted. Review "AIM" section 5-6-2 for intercept procedures. Additionally, if U.S. military fighter jets intercept an aircraft and flares are dispensed in the area of that aircraft, aviators will pay strict attention, contact air traffic control immediately on the local frequency or on VHF guard 121.5 or UHF 243.0 and follow the interceptor visual ICAO signals. Be advised that non-compliance may result in the use of force.
CAUTION: This chart is primarily designed for VFR navigational purposes and does not purport to indicate the presence of all power transmission and telecommunication lines, terrain or obstacles which may be encountered below reasonable and safe altitudes.
MILITARY TRAINING ROUTES (MTRs)
All IR and VR MTRs are shown, and may extend from the surface upwards. Only the route centerline, direction of flight along the route, and the route designator are depicted - route widths and altitudes are not shown.
Since these routes are subject to change every 56 days, you are cautioned and advised to contact Flight Service for route dimensions and current status for those routes affecting your flight.
Routes with a change in the alignment of the charted route centerline will be indicated in the Aeronautical Chart Bulletin of the Chart Supplement.
DoD users refer to Area Planning AP/1B Military Training Routes North and South America for current routes.

Figure 20-25 Sectional chart legend.

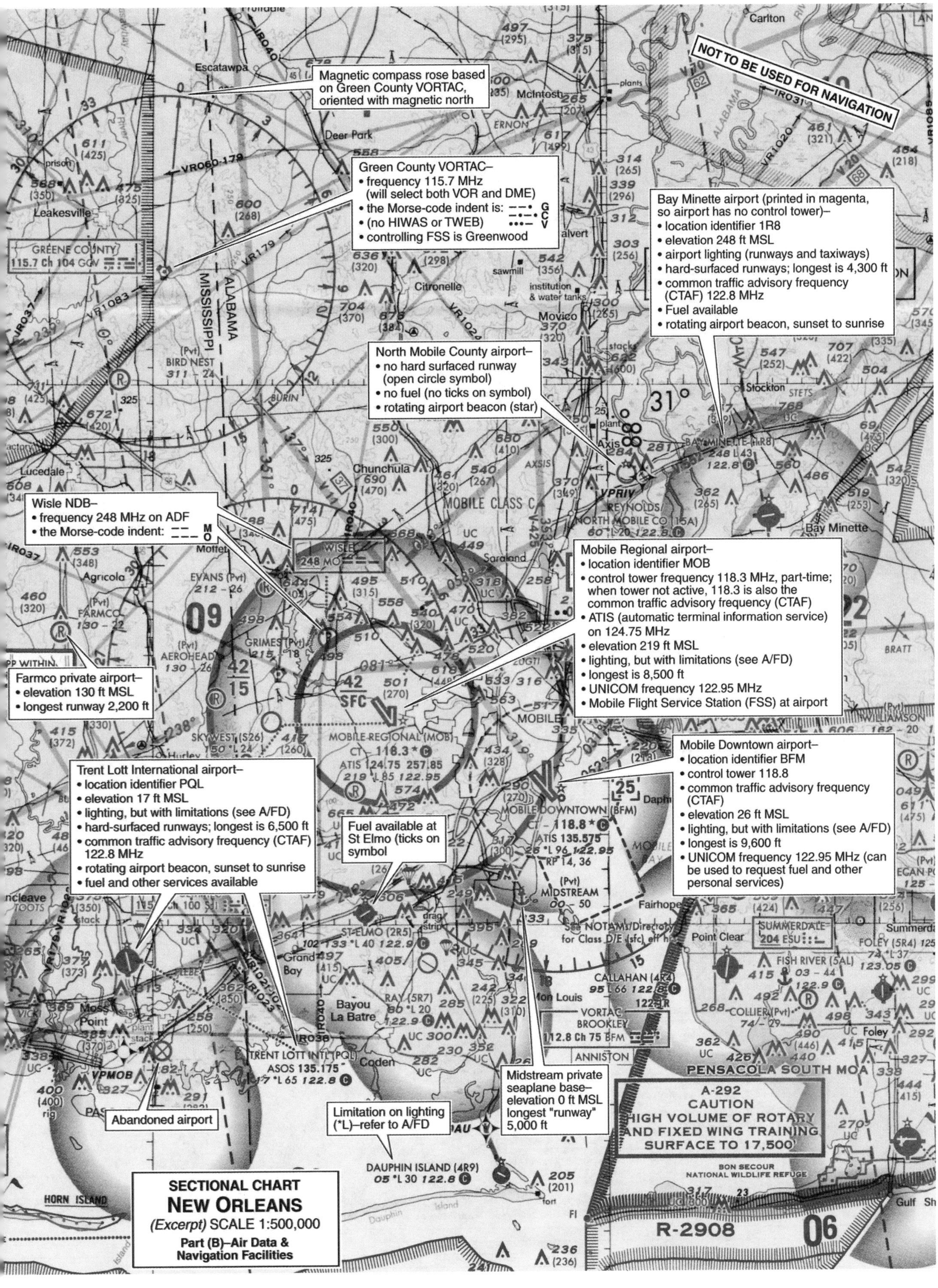

Figure 20-26 Sectional chart excerpt no. 2.

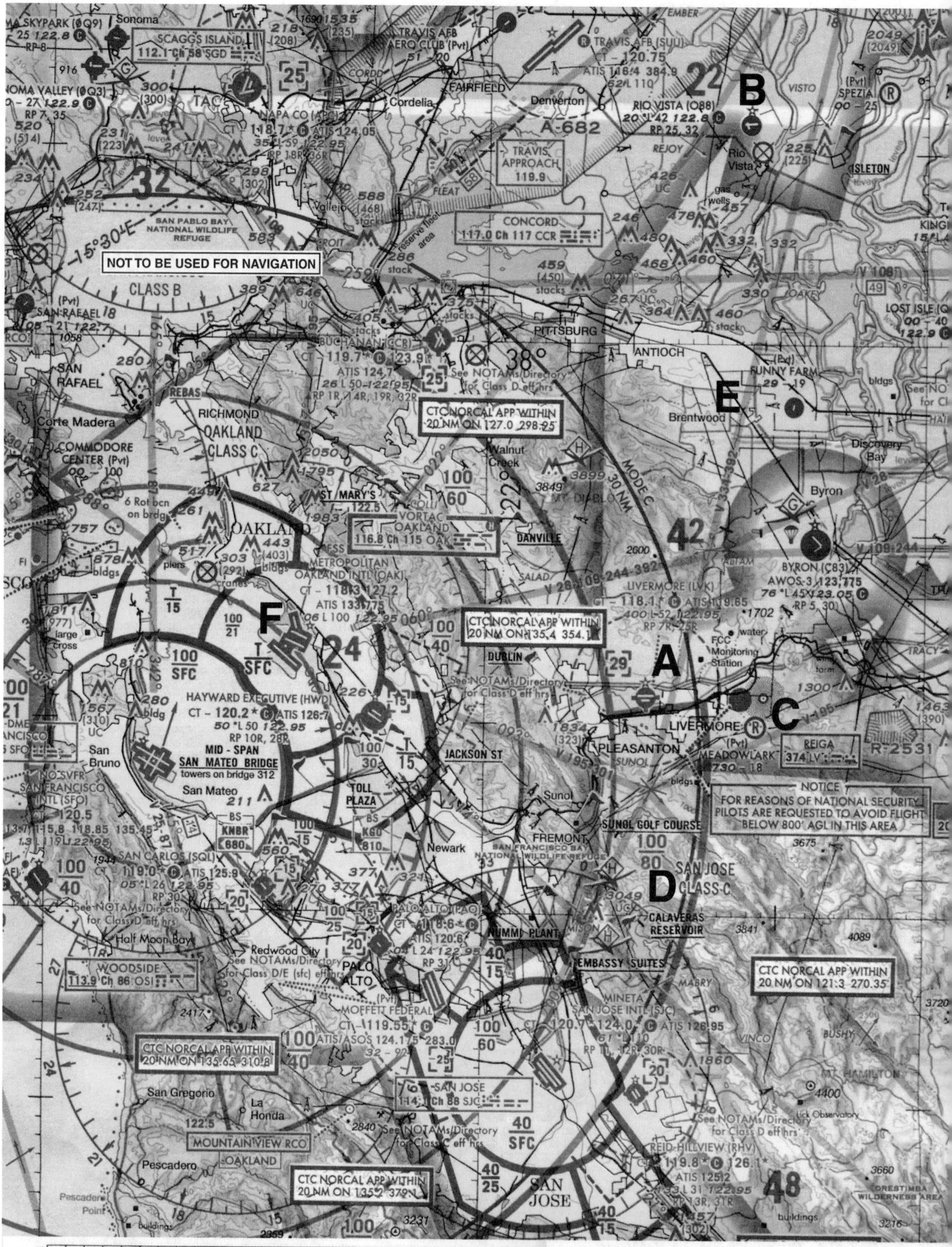

Figure 20-27 Sectional chart excerpt no. 3.

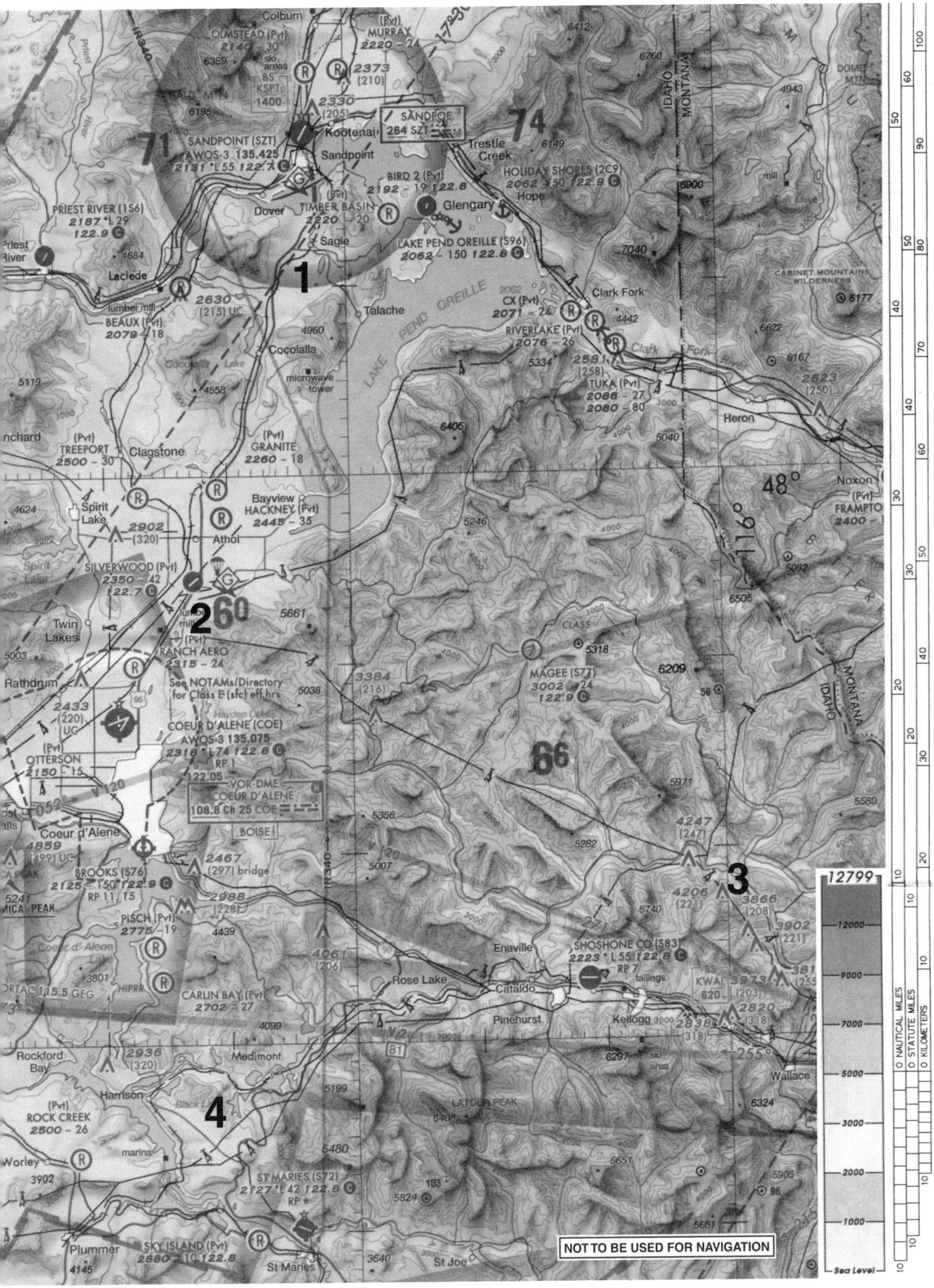

Figure 20-28 Sectional chart excerpt no. 4.

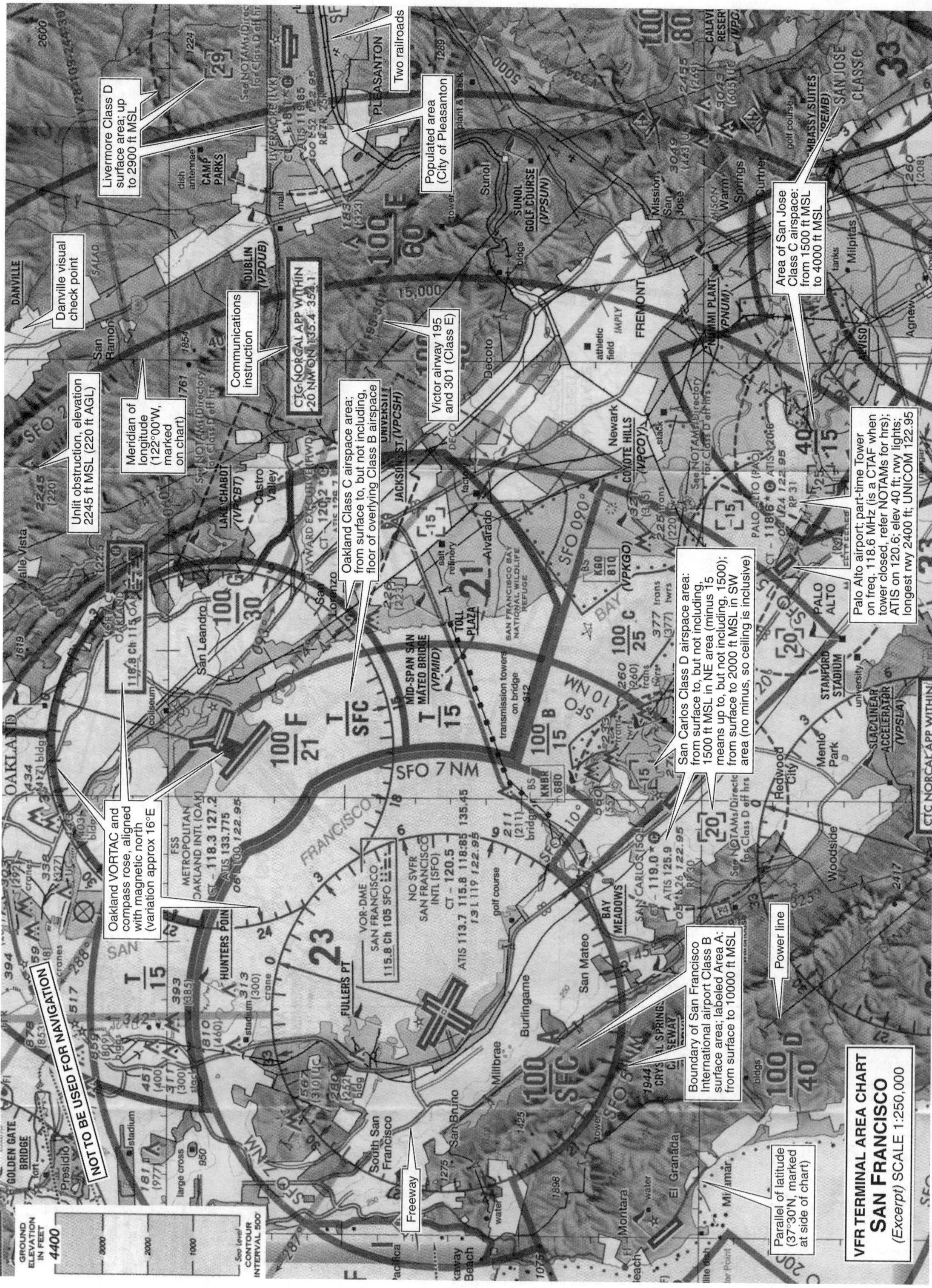

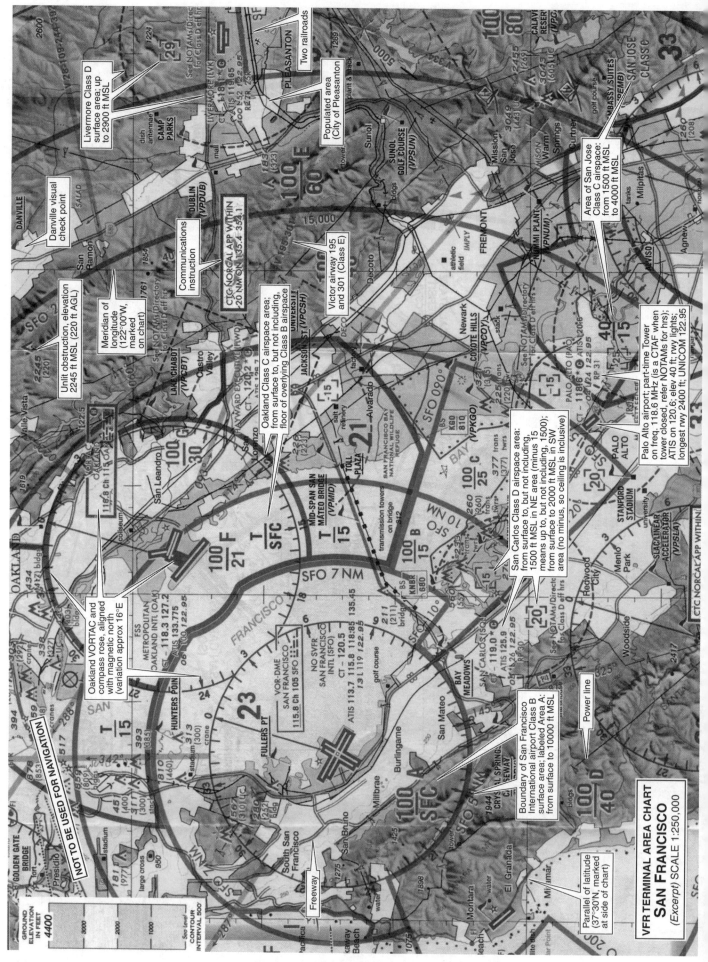

Figure 20-29 VFR Terminal area chart.

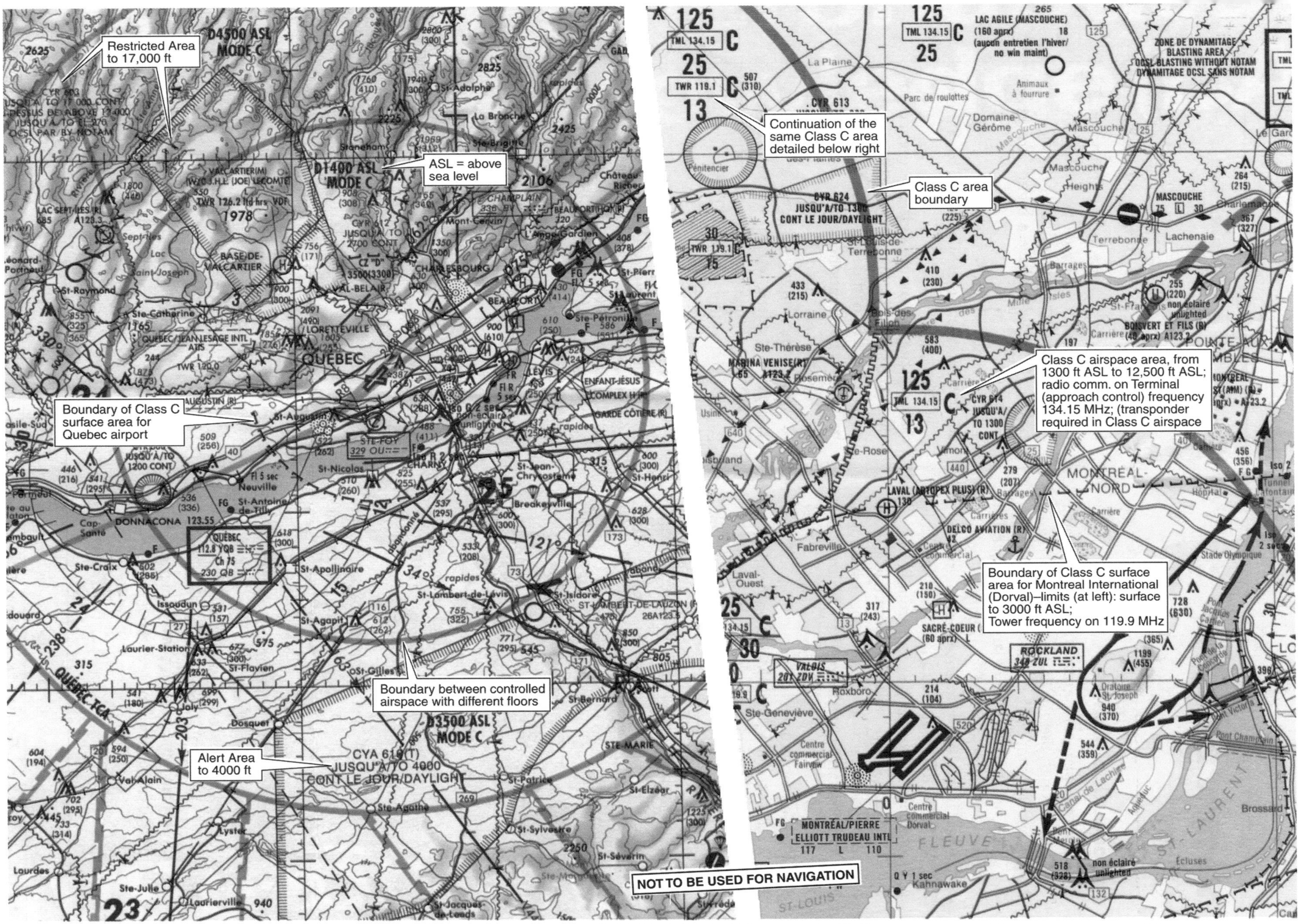

VFR NAVIGATION CHART (Montreal) SCALE 1:500,000

CANADA CHARTS

VFR TERMINAL AREA CHART (Montreal) SCALE 1:250,000

Figure 20-30 Canadian charts.

Review 20

Charts

Aeronautical Charts

1. Does the plane of a great circle on the earth pass through the center of the earth?
2. What is meant by the term "small circle?"
3. True or false? Parallels of latitude are parallel to the equator and to each other.
4. What is the basic reference for longitude?
5. What well-known landmark does the basic reference for longitude pass through?
6. True or false? Meridians of longitude all pass through the north and south geographic poles.
7. True or false? Meridians of longitude are small circles.
8. Define "longitude."
9. What is the length (NM) of one minute of arc of a great circle on the earth's surface?
10. 1 degree of latitude is equivalent to how many nautical miles?
11. With respect to topography, what is meant by the term "scale?"

VFR Charts

Refer to Sectional Chart Excerpt no. 2 (page 505).

12. What is the minimum altitude required to clear the single obstacle 6 NM to the SE of Mobile Regional Airport?

Refer to the Sectional Chart Excerpt no. 4 (page 507) and figure 20-31 (page 511) when required for questions 13 to 24.

13. The obstacle 4 NM northeast of Sandpoint is 210 feet AGL. What minimum altitude is necessary to clear it by 500 feet?
14. Which frequency should be used at Coeur d'Alene Tower to monitor airport traffic?
15. What UNICOM frequency is to be used at Coeur d'Alene Tower to request fuel?
16. What should you refer to for information about parachute jumping and glider operations at Silverwood Airport?
17. In comparing Silverwood airport (area 2) with Shoshone County Airport (area 3):
    - **a.** is Silverwood airport further north?
    - **b.** does Silverwood have a higher northerly latitude?
    - **c.** is Silverwood further east?
    - **d.** does this mean that Silverwood has a more easterly longitude?
18. Answer the following with reference to Shoshone County Airport (area 3).
    - **a.** What is the latitude and longitude?
    - **b.** What is its elevation?
    - **c.** Does it have lighting?
    - **d.** What is the runway surface like?
    - **e.** What is the length of the longest runway?
    - **f.** What does the color magenta indicate?
    - **g.** Which frequency is the CTAF on?
    - **h.** Which radio is used to select the CTAF?
19. Answer the following with reference to Silverwood airport (area 2).
    - **a.** What is the latitude and longitude?
    - **b.** What is its elevation?
    - **c.** Does it have lighting?
    - **d.** What is the runway surface like?
    - **e.** What length is the longest runway?
    - **f.** Which frequency is the CTAF on?
    - **g.** What aeronautical activity, apart from aircraft, can you expect in the vicinity?
    - **h.** Which document would you refer to for further information about this activity?
20. Give the following with reference to the airport located N48°18' W116°34' (approx).
    - **a.** What airport is this?
    - **b.** It lies in which direction from the town?
    - **c.** Is fuel available?
    - **d.** Is there an FSS located on the airport?
    - **e.** What navigation aid is situated near the airport?
    - **f.** What is its frequency?
    - **g.** What equipment could you use to select it?
    - **h.** How could you identify that you have selected it correctly?

21. Answer the following with reference to Coeur d'Alene airport.

- **a.** What is the latitude and longitude?
- **b.** It lies in which direction from the town?
- **c.** What does the color magenta indicate?
- **d.** What is its elevation?
- **e.** Does it have lighting?
- **f.** What are the runway surfaces like?
- **g.** What is the length of the longest runway?
- **h.** Which radio would you use to select this?
- **i.** Automatic weather information is available on which frequency?
- **j.** Which radio would you use to select this?
- **k.** Which class of airspace is this airport surrounded by?
- **l.** To clear the highest obstacle in the latitude-longitude quadrangle surrounding Coeur d'Alene airport by 500 feet, what altitude would you need to fly at?

22. You wish to fly from Shoshone County airport to Silverwood airport.

- **a.** What is the magnetic course?
- **b.** What is the distance?

23. What is the flag symbol at Mica Peak to the SW of Coeur d'Alene airport?

24. Which statement is true relating to the blue and magenta colors used to depict airports on Sectional Aeronautical Charts?

- **a.** Airports having control towers are shown in blue; all others are shown in magenta.
- **b.** Airports having runways capable of handling large aircraft are shown in blue; all others are shown in magenta.

Answers are given on page 704.

IDAHO 31

COEUR D'ALENE–PAPPY BOYINGTON FLD (COE) 9 NW UTC−8(−7DT)
N47°46.46′ W116°49.18′ **GREAT FALLS**
2320 B S4 **FUEL** 100, JET A OX 1, 2, 3, 4 Class IV, ARFF Index A NOTAM FILE COE **H–1C, L–13B**
RWY 05–23: H7400X100 (ASPH-GRVD) S–57, D–95, 2S–121, 2D–165 HIRL 0.6% up NE **IAP**
RWY 05: MALSR (NSTD). PAPI(P4R)—GA 3.0° TCH 56′.
RWY 23: REIL. PAPI(P4R)—GA 3.0° TCH 50′.
RWY 01–19: H5400X75 (ASPH) S–50, D–83, 2S–105, 2D–150
MIRL 0.3% up N
RWY 01: REIL. PAPI(P2L)—GA 3.0° TCH 39′. Rgt tfc.
RWY 19: PAPI(P2L)—GA 3.0° TCH 41′.

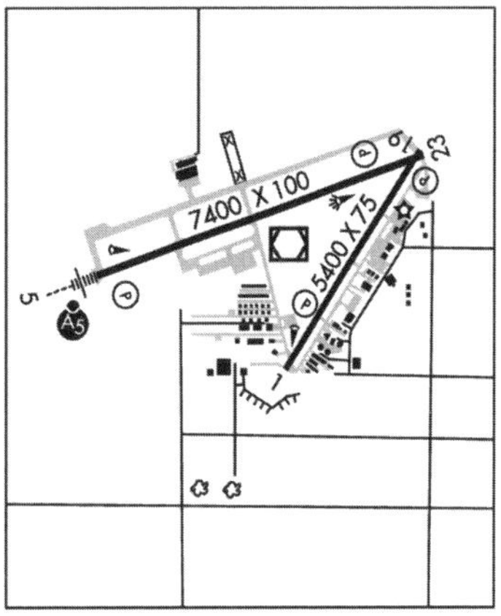

RUNWAY DECLARED DISTANCE INFORMATION

RWY 01:	TORA–5400	TODA–5400	ASDA–5400	LDA–5400
RWY 05:	TORA–7400	TODA–7400	ASDA–7400	LDA–7400
RWY 19:	TORA–5400	TODA–5400	ASDA–5400	LDA–5400
RWY 23:	TORA–7400	TODA–7400	ASDA–7400	LDA–7400

AIRPORT REMARKS: Attended Mon–Fri 1500–0100Z‡. For after hrs fuel-self svc avbl or call 208–772–6404, 208–661–4174, 208–661–7449, 208–699–5433. Self svc fuel avbl with credit card. 48 hr PPR for unscheduled ops with more than 30 passenger seats call arpt manager 208–446–1860. Migratory birds on and invof arpt Oct–Nov. Remote cntl airstrip is 2.3 miles west AER 05. Arpt conditions avbl on AWOS. Rwy 05 NSTD MALSR, thld bar extends 5′ byd rwy edge lgts each side. ACTIVATE MIRL Rwy 01–19, HIRL Rwy 05–23, REIL Rwy 01 and Rwy 23, MALSR Rwy 05—CTAF. PAPI Rwy 01, Rwy 19, Rwy 05, and Rwy 23 opr continuously.
WEATHER DATA SOURCES: AWOS–3 135.075 (208) 772–8215.
HIWAS 108.8 COE.
COMMUNICATIONS: CTAF/UNICOM 122.8
RCO 122.05 (BOISE RADIO)
® **SPOKANE APP/DEP CON** 132.1
AIRSPACE: CLASS E svc continuous.
RADIO AIDS TO NAVIGATION: NOTAM FILE COE.
(T) VORW/DME 108.8 COE Chan 25 N47°46.42′ W116°49.24′ at fld. 2320/19E. **HIWAS.**
DME portion unusable:
220°–240° byd 15 NM 280°–315° byd 15 NM blo 11,000′.
POST FALLS NDB (MHW) 347 LEN N47°44.57′ W116°57.66′ 053° 6.0 NM to fld.
ILS 110.7 I–COE Rwy 05 Class ID. Localizer unusable 25° left and right of course.

Figure 20-31 Coeur d'Alene Chart Supplement U.S. excerpt.

Airspace 21

United States airspace is organized into six classes (A, B, C, D, E and G), in line with the International Civil Aviation Organization (ICAO) airspace classification system. Airspace Classes A through E are allocated to controlled airspace where Class A is the most restrictive and Class E the least restrictive, being allocated to general controlled airspace. Uncontrolled airspace is Class G. (Class F, although available in the ICAO system, has not been allocated in the United States.) The airspace classification system links various parameters to each class, including:

- entry requirements (for example, radio contact for all aircraft in Class C airspace; ATC clearance for IFR flights in controlled airspace, and so on);
- minimum pilot qualifications;
- two-way communication and transponder equipment requirements;
- VFR weather minimums (where VFR is available); and
- aircraft separation, conflict resolution and traffic advisory services.

Airspace features	Class A Airspace	Class B Airspace	Class C Airspace	Class D Airspace	Class E Airspace	Class G Airspace
Flight Operations Permitted	IFR	IFR and VFR	IFR and VFR	IFR and VFR	IFR and VFR	IFR and VFR
Entry Prerequisites	ATC clearance	ATC clearance	IFR clearance/ VFR radio contact	IFR clearance/ VFR radio contact	Clearance/ radio for IFR	None
Minimum Pilot Qualifications	Instrument Rating	Private Plot Certificate/ *endorsed student	Student Certificate	Student Certificate	Student Certificate	Student Certificate
Two-Way Radio Commu-nications	Yes	Yes	Yes	Yes	IFR	No
VFR Minimum Visibility	Not applicable	3 statute miles	3 statute miles	3 statute miles	**3 statute miles	***1 statute miles
Aircraft Separation	All	All	IFR, SVFR and rwy operations	IFR, SVFR and rwy operations	IFR, SVFR	None
Conflict Resolution (collision avoidance)	Not applicable	Not applicable	Between IFR and VFR flights	No	No	No
Traffic Advisories	Not applicable	Not applicable	Yes	Workload permitting	Workload permitting	Workload permitting
Safety Advisories	Yes	Yes	Yes	Yes	Yes	Yes

**Operations at some class B airports require a minimum of a Private Pilot Certificate—see Part 91 of the regulations.*

***Visibility and cloud clearance requirements increase above 10,000 feet MSL.*

****Visibility and cloud clearance requirements decrease below 1,200 feet AGL; increase above 10,000 feet MSL, and at night—see Part 91 of the regulations or the AIM.*

Table 21-1 Summary of the United States airspace classification system.

Subdivision of Airspace

Class A Airspace

Class A airspace generally extends from 18,000 feet MSL up to and including FL600. Class A airspace is only available to aircraft operating on an IFR flight plan.

Class B Airspace

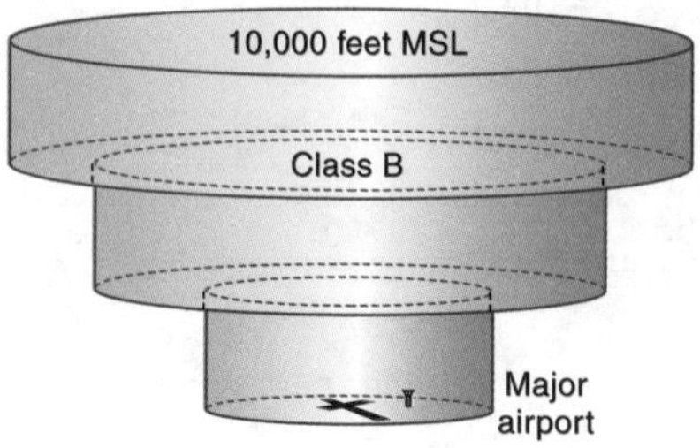

Figure 21-1 Class B airspace.

Class B airspace generally extends from the surface to 10,000 feet MSL surrounding the nation's major airports. The configuration of each Class B airspace is individually tailored and consists of a surface area with two or more larger radius layers above. Class B airspace is shown on sectional charts with a *thick blue solid line.*

To fly within Class B airspace the *minimum pilot qualification* is a private pilot certificate or an endorsed student pilot certificate for Class B airspace at a specific airport (see Part 61 of the regulations). The minimum required *airplane equipment* includes a two-way radio communication and a 4096-code transponder with Mode C capability (altitude reporting). IFR aircraft are required to carry VOR or TACAN equipment. VFR requirements are 3 SM visibility and clear of clouds.

Class B airspace *operating rules* include:

- ATC clearance must be obtained before entering or departing the airspace;
- fly on published VFR transition routes found on the back of VFR terminal area charts; and
- contact ATC at geographical fixes shown on the sectional charts by small flags to obtain a clearance prior to entering Class B airspace.

If possible avoid Class B airspace by using VFR corridors, Terminal Area VFR Routes, or by flying above or below the Class B airspace.

Class C Airspace

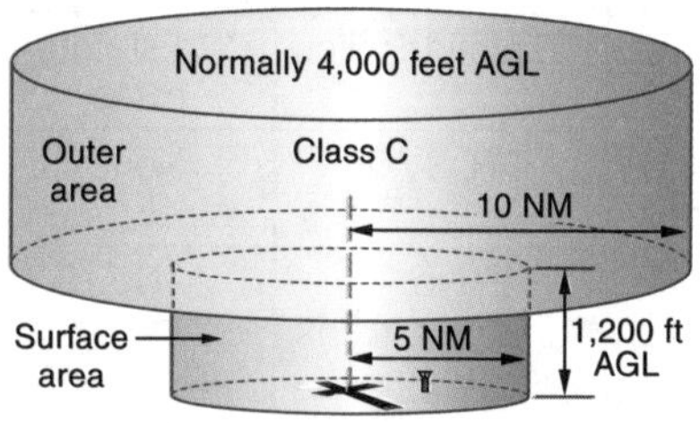

Figure 21-2 Class C airspace.

Class C airspace generally extends from the surface to 4,000 feet AGL around a busy airport which has:

- an operational control tower;
- a radar approach control; and
- a certain number of IFR operations or passenger enplanements.

Class C airspace areas are depicted by *solid magenta lines* on sectional charts. The configuration of each Class C airspace is individually tailored, usually with two tiers. The vertical limits of Class C airspace are indicated with the circle and are expressed in hundreds of feet MSL. The upper limit is shown above the straight line and the bottom limit (which may be SFC for surface area altitude) beneath the line. For example, refer to sectional chart excerpt no. 1 (page 503) and the Class C airspace around Mobile Regional Airport. The limits in the surface area are "$\frac{42}{SFC}$" which means that Class C airspace extends from the surface to 4,200 feet MSL. The limits for the outer area are 42/15 which means that the C Class airspace extends from 1,500 to 4,200 feet MSL.

To fly in Class C airspace no specific *pilot certification* is required and the minimum *airplane equipment* includes two-way communication and a 4096 transponder with Mode C (altitude reporting). Class C *operating rules* require the establishment of two-way radio communications with approach control before entering Class C airspace. In addition, unless otherwise authorized or required by ATC, airplanes below 2,500 feet AGL and within 4 NM of the primary airport must not exceed an indicated airspeed of 200 knots. Class C radar services are usually provided beyond Class C airspace out to 20 NM from the primary airport. The minimum *VFR weather requirements* for Class C airspace are shown in figure 21-4.

Class D Airspace

Class D airspace surrounds airports which have an operational control tower but are not associated with Class B or C airspace. Class D airspace generally extends from the surface to 2,500 feet AGL and is cylindrical in shape, plus extensions up to 2 NM necessary to include instrument approach and departure paths. On sectional charts Class D airspace is shown as a dashed or *segmented blue line*, with a blue segmented box showing the top of the Class D airspace in hundreds of feet MSL. For example on Sectional Excerpt No. 3 (page 506), Napa County is surrounded by Class D airspace with an upper limit of 2,500 feet MSL.

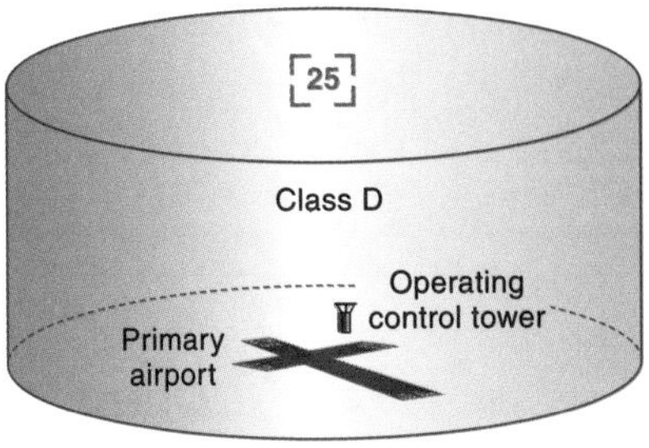

Figure 21-3
Class D airspace.

No specific *pilot certification* is required to fly in Class D airspace, and the minimum *airplane equipment* is an operational two-way radio. Class D *operating rules* include establishing two-way radio contact before entering Class D airspace and maintaining two-way radio contact while in Class D airspace. In addition, airplanes within 4 NM of the primary airport in the Class D airspace and at or below 2,500 feet AGL must not exceed 200 KIAS. The VFR minimums are the same as those for Class C airspace (figure 21-4). When the control tower is not operating, the Class D airspace reverts to Class E.

Class E Airspace

Class E airspace is controlled airspace that is not Class A, B, C or D. Class E airspace includes airspace around airports without control towers, airspace used to transit between terminal or en route environments, Federal Airways including Victor airways, plus unallocated airspace over the United States from 14,500 feet MSL up to Class A airspace beginning at 18,000 feet MSL, or any overlying Class B, C or D airspace. Class E airspace lower limits are:

- the surface around airports marked by *segmented magenta lines*;
- 700 feet AGL in areas marked by *light magenta shading*;
- 1,200 feet AGL in areas marked by *light blue shading*;
- as depicted numerically by a *blue staggered line*; and
- 14,500 feet MSL if none of the others apply.

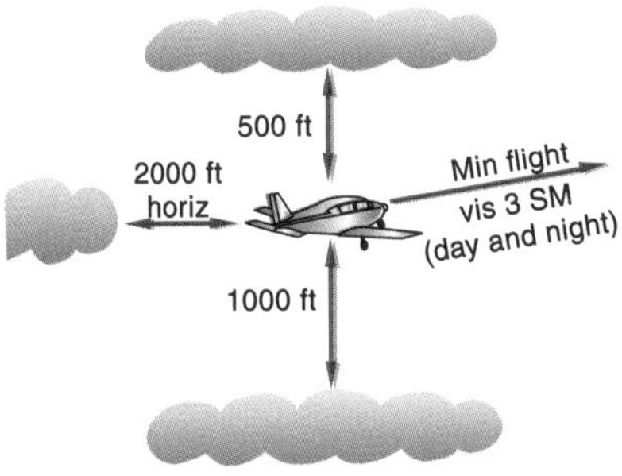

Figure 21-4
VFR requirements for Class C, D, and E airspace below 10,000 MSL.

To fly in Class E airspace, no specific pilot certification is required and there are no specific equipment or operating requirements. The minimum VFR requirements are the same as for Class C and D if operating below 10,000 feet MSL (figure 21-4). At or above 10,000 feet MSL, VFR conditions are increased to flight visibility 5 SM, with 1,000 feet vertical separation from clouds and 1 SM horizontal separation from clouds (figure 21-6). An ATC clearance is required to fly IFR in Class E airspace.

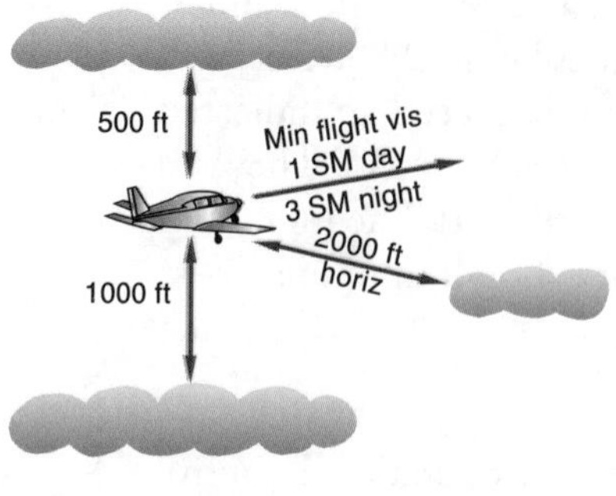

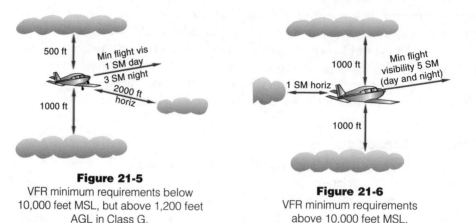

Figure 21-5
VFR minimum requirements below 10,000 feet MSL, but above 1,200 feet AGL in Class G.

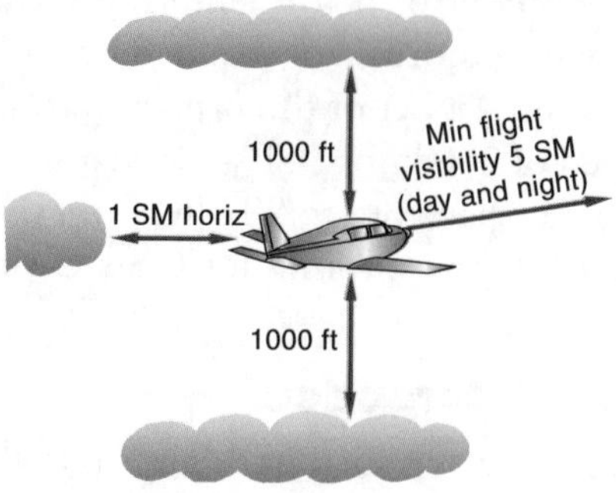

Figure 21-6
VFR minimum requirements above 10,000 feet MSL.

Class G Airspace

Class G airspace is the remaining airspace other than special use or restricted airspace. The minimum VFR requirements in Class G airspace depend on day or night and altitude above the surface. At or below 1,200 feet AGL by day, the minimum visibility is 1 statute mile (SM) and the airplane must remain clear of clouds. By day above 1,200 feet AGL but below 10,000 feet MSL, the minimum visibility is 1 SM and the airplane must remain at least 2,000 feet horizontally from, 500 feet below and 1,000 feet above clouds. For night VFR minimums, see Part 91. You do not need an ATC clearance to fly IFR in Class G airspace. Refer to Part 71 of the regulations for more detail on the airspace classes. Also, airspeed rules are contained in Part 91 (see chapter 19).

Terminal Radar Service Areas

Some airports offer optional radar advisory services in airspace known as *Terminal Radar Service Areas* (TRSAs). The primary airport of a TRSA is Class D. The boundaries are marked on sectionals with thick dark-gray lines. Pilots can choose whether or not to participate with ATC by squawking 1200 or an ATC assigned code while flying in TRSA airspace. There are very few TRSAs.

Victor Airways

Victor Airways are low-altitude federal airways connecting VORs along specified radials and are for use by both IFR and VFR aircraft. They are shown on sectionals by straight blue lines containing the airway designator and its magnetic direction (e.g. V31–348°). Any *intersections* fixed by NAVAIDs are indicated by fine blue arrows directed toward the relevant facilities. Victor airways are normally 8 NM wide and extend vertically from 1,200 feet AGL up to but not including 18,000 feet MSL. Unusually high floors will be marked. You should normally cruise at an appropriate altitude along Victor airways. For VFR aircraft, "odds+500 feet" on easterly routes, and "evens+500 feet" on westerly routes.

Airspace			Flight Visibility	Distance from Clouds
Class A			N/A	Not applicable
Class B			3 SM	Clear of clouds
Class C			3 SM	500 ft below, 1,000 ft above, 2,000 ft horizontal
Class D			3 SM	500 ft below, 1,000 ft above, 2,000 ft horizontal
Class E	Less than 10,000 ft MSL		3 SM	500 ft below, 1,000 ft above, 2,000 ft horizontal
	At or above 10,000 ft MSL		5 SM	1,000 ft below, 1,000 ft above, 1 SM horizontal
Class G	1,200 ft or less above the surface (regardless of MSL or altitude)	Day, except as provided in Part 91	1 SM	Clear of clouds
		Night, except as provided in Part 91	3 SM	500 ft below, 1,000 ft above, 2,000 ft horizontal
	More than 1,200 ft above the surface but less than 10,000 ft MSL	Day	1 SM	500 ft below, 1,000 ft above, 2,000 ft horizontal
		Night	3 SM	500 ft below, 1,000 ft above, 2,000 ft horizontal
	More than 1,200 ft above the surface and at or above 10,000 ft MSL		5 SM	1,000 ft below, 1,000 ft above, 1 SM horizontal

Table 21-2 Part 91 summary of basic VFR weather minimums.

Special Use Airspace

Special use airspace is not allocated a class. It consists of that airspace within which certain activities must be confined because of their nature such as military aerobatic training or missile firing. Special use airspace is shown on aeronautical charts (except for controlled firing areas where activity ceases when aircraft are spotted in the area either visually or by radar). Prohibited, Restricted and Warning Areas are outlined on sectionals by *blue lines with hachuring*.

Prohibited Areas contain airspace within which the flight of aircraft is prohibited for national security or other reasons. *Restricted Areas* contain airspace within which the flight of aircraft is subject to restrictions, but is not totally prohibited, because of hazards such as artillery firing, aerial gunnery or guided missiles. Penetrating Restricted Areas without authorization from the using or controlling authority may be extremely hazardous. *Warning Areas* are similar to restricted areas, except that they are beyond the 3-mile limit from the United States coastline and are therefore in international airspace. *Military Operations Areas* (MOAs) consist of airspace of defined vertical and lateral limits established to separate military training activities (usually involving aerobatic or abrupt flight maneuvers) from civil Instrument Flight Rules (IFR) traffic. Any FSS within 100 miles of the MOA should be able to advise if it is active or not and, if it is active, you should contact the controlling agency for traffic advisories. VFR pilots should exercise extreme caution when flying in an active MOA. *MOAs* are outlined on sectionals by *magenta lines with hachuring*. *Alert Areas* depicted on sectional charts by *blue boxes* show airspace within which there may be a lot of pilot training or unusual aerial activity.

Other Airspace

"Other airspace areas" is a general term referring to the majority of the remaining airspace. It includes:

- Local airport advisories (LAA);
- Military training routes (MTR);
- Temporary flight restrictions (TFR);
- Parachute jump aircraft operations;
- Published VFR routes;
- Terminal radar service areas (TRSA);
- National security areas (NSA);
- Air Defense Identification Zones (ADIZ)—land and water based, Defense VFR (DVFR) flight plan needed to operate VFR in this airspace;
- Intercept Procedures and use of 121.5 for communication (if not on ATC already);
- Flight Restricted Zones (FRZ) in vicinity of Capitol and White House;
- Special Awareness Training required by 14 CFR 91.161 for pilots to operate VFR within 60 NM of the Washington, D.C., VOR/DME;
- Wildlife Areas/Wilderness Areas/National Parks and request to operate above 2,000 AGL;
- National Oceanic and Atmospheric Administration (NOAA) Marine Areas off the coast with requirement to operate above 2,000 AGL; and
- Tethered Balloons for observation and weather recordings that extend on cables up to 60,000.

Military Training Routes

Military Training Routes (MTRs) are for military low-altitude high-speed training and may be flown by military aircraft either under the Instrument Flight Rules (indicated on the chart by IR), or under the Visual Flight Rules (VR). Military training routes are depicted with a *thin gray line*:

- MTRs at or below 1,500 feet AGL (with no segment above 1,500 feet AGL) are identified by 4-digit numbers, for instance, IR 1006, and VR 1007;
- MTRs above 1,500 feet AGL (with some segments possibly below 1,500 feet AGL) are identified by 3-digit numbers, for instance, IR 008, and VR 009; and
- alternate IR/VR military training routes are identified normally, but with a final letter suffix, such as IR 008A, or VR 009B.

Temporary Flight Restrictions (TFRs)

Airspace not defined on a chart may be activated by NOTAM (Notice to Airmen) and may temporarily restrict access or require special procedures. Such airspace is activated to allow activities such as fire fighting or disaster relief, where the operational aircraft must have free access, but access is denied to sightseeing aircraft that may impair operations. TFRs may be activated to prevent aircraft being exposed to hazards, such as volcanic ash, dense smoke, or high traffic density of a temporary nature.

TFRs may also be activated for purposes such as disaster relief, and temporarily prohibited for space flights, presidential flights, and so on.

Drones

Most airports are a "no drone zone" unless operators have obtained ATC authorization. It is common to see drones at and below 400 feet AGL in uncontrolled airspace. Drones operating in Class B, C, D, and the lateral boundaries of surface area Class E airspace require prior authorization from ATC. It is likely, although not assured, that when unmanned aircraft operations are taking place in controlled airspace that a NOTAM will be issued. These are often referred to as UOAs (unmanned aircraft system operating areas).

Review 21
Airspace

1. How is Class B airspace indicated on Sectional charts?
2. What minimum pilot certification is required for operation within Class B airspace?
3. What are the VFR minimum weather requirements for Class B airspace?
4. How is Class C airspace indicated on sectional charts?
5. How far out does the outer area of Class C airspace typically extend?
6. What is minimum radio equipment required for operation within Class C airspace?
7. Who should you make radio contact with on the published frequency before entering Class C airspace?
8. What is the speed limit when below 2,500 feet AGL and within 4 NM of the primary airport in the Class C surface area?
9. What are the basic VFR minimum weather conditions in Class C airspace?
10. What class of airspace does Class D airspace around an airport with a control tower revert to when the tower is not operating?
11. What are the basic VFR weather minimums in Class D airspace?
12. What is the lower limit of Class E airspace?
13. On sectional charts, what lower limit in Class E airspace is indicated by:
    a. magenta shading?
    b. blue shading?

Refer to Sectional Chart Excerpt no. 4 (page 507) for questions 14 to 17.

14. What are the regulation visibility and cloud requirements to operate at Standpoint Airport below 700 feet AGL?
15. Identify the airspace over Sandpoint Airport that exists from the surface up to 14,500 feet MSL.
16. Identify the airspace over Coeur d'Alene airport that exists from the surface up to 14,500 feel MSL.
17. What type of military operations would you expect along IR314 crossing Lake Pend Oreille?

Refer to Sectional Chart Excerpt no. 3 (page 506) for questions or questions 18 to 22.

18. What class of airspace surrounds San Francisco International?
19. What is the elevation of San Jose International airport?
20. What is the meaning of the flag symbol shown at Crown Sterling Suites (area D)?
21. Within what distance of San Francisco International airport is a Mode C transponder required?
22. Is Special VFR (SVFR) flight permitted in the airspace surrounding San Francisco International airport? State how this is indicated on the chart.
23. What are the VFR minimums for flight in Class E airspace below 10,000 feet MSL, day or night?
24. What are the VFR minimums for flight in Class G airspace at 1,200 feet or less AGL (regardless of MSL altitude) by day?
25. What are the VFR minimums for flight in Class G airspace at or above 10,000 feet and more than 1,200 feet AGL (regardless of MSL altitude), day or night?
26. What are the VFR minimums for flight in Class G airspace more than 1,200 feet above the surface (regardless of MSL altitude) by night?
27. An airplane may be operated at night, in the traffic pattern of an airport in Class G airspace under what conditions?
28. How are military operations areas outlined on sectional charts?
29. What action should a pilot take when operating under VFR in a Military Operations Area (MOA)?

Answers are given on page 704.

Airports and Airport Operations 22

Airports come in all shapes and sizes. Some have long, hard-surfaced runways, others have short, grass runways, some have operating control towers to regulate the flow of traffic in the airspace around the airport as well as on the ground (known as *controlled* airports, *towered* airports, or *tower-controlled* airports), and others have no active control tower (known as *uncontrolled* airports or *nontowered* airports), where the traffic is self-regulating according to specified FAA procedures.

An *ATC clearance* is authorization for a VFR aircraft to proceed under specified conditions in Class B, C or D airspace. An ATC clearance to takeoff at a controlled airport should be obtained from the control tower if it is in operation. Time references will be in UTC (Coordinated Universal Time).

An ATC clearance is required for you to operate in Class B, C or D controlled airspace.

A very good source of information for correct procedures is the *Aeronautical Information Manual* (AIM), which contains an entire chapter on airport operations.

Taxiway and Runway Markings

Study the airport chart prior to taxiing at an unfamiliar airport so that your taxi route from the parking area to the takeoff holding point follows the shortest and most expeditious route. The same applies when taxiing back to the parking area after landing.

Study the airport chart before operating at an unfamiliar airport.

Further airport information may be found in the Chart Supplement U.S., with a full explanation of all terms found at the front.

Runways are named according to their magnetic direction, rounded-off to the nearest 10°. For instance, a runway whose direction is 274°M is named RWY 27. When used in the opposite direction (094°M), it is named RWY 9.

Runway directions are rounded-off to the nearest 10°.

Taxiway Markings

Taxiway markings are *yellow*. The taxiway *centerline* may be marked with a continuous yellow line, and the *edges* of the taxiway may be marked by two continuous yellow lines 6 inches apart. Airplanes should taxi with their nosewheel on the yellow centerline.

Taxiway markings are yellow.

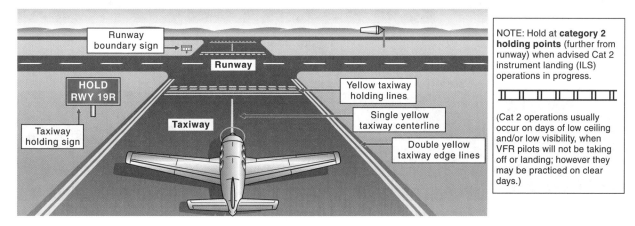

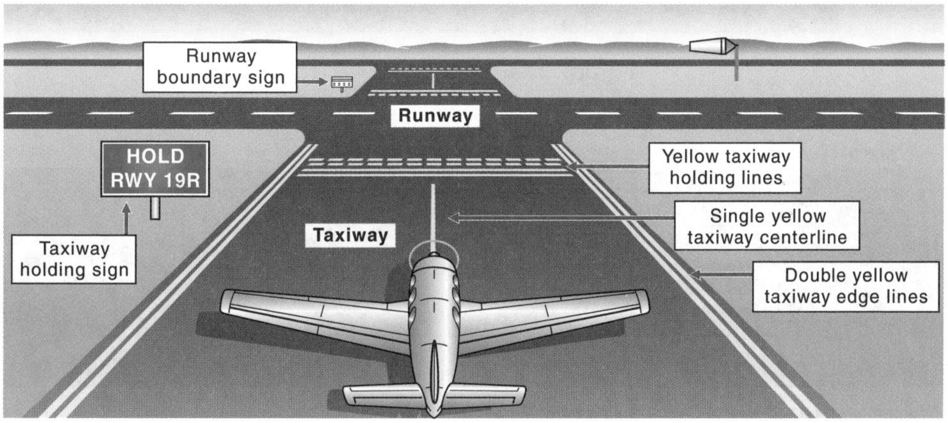

NOTE: Hold at **category 2 holding points** (further from runway) when advised Cat 2 instrument landing (ILS) operations in progress.

(Cat 2 operations usually occur on days of low ceiling and/or low visibility, when VFR pilots will not be taking off or landing; however they may be practiced on clear days.)

Figure 22-1 Taxiway markings are in yellow.

Figure 22-2
Runway holding position sign.

Figure 22-3 Runway boundary sign.

Figure 22-4 No-entry sign.

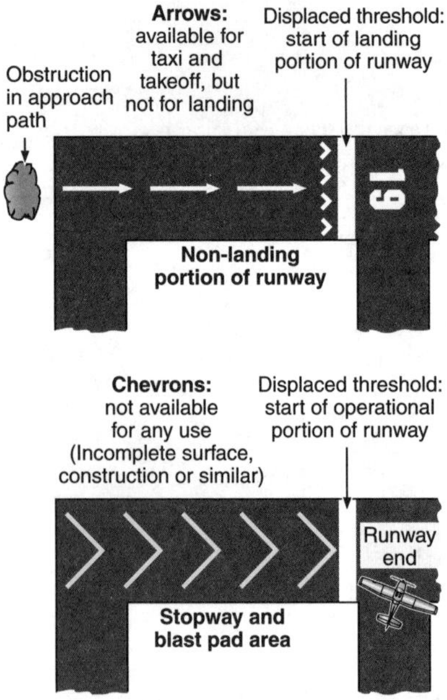

Figure 22-5
Displaced threshold markings.

Taxiway *holding lines*, across the width of the taxiway, consist of two continuous and two dashed yellow lines, spaced 6 inches between dashes. The two continuous lines are on the side from which an aircraft will approach a runway when taxiing, and if you are instructed to hold short of the runway or if you are not cleared onto the runway, you should stop with no part of the aircraft extending beyond the holding line.

Taxiway and Runway Signs

Next to the holding line at the edge of the taxiway there may be *runway holding position signs* with white characters on a red background. There may also be a runway boundary sign that faces the runway and is visible to pilots exiting the runway. It will also be adjacent to the holding position marked on the pavement and may even be painted on the rear face of the holding sign. The sign has black markings on a yellow background. After landing, you will be clear of the runway when your aircraft is completely past this sign and the holding lines on the pavement. A *no-entry sign* (red and white) prohibits the entry of an aircraft.

Runway Markings

Runway markings vary in complexity according to the operations likely to occur on that particular runway. To assist pilots landing and stopping at the conclusion of a successful precision instrument approach, some precision instrument runways have very specific markings, as shown in figure 22-7.

Ensure that you know whether the full length of the runway is available for landing or not. A *displaced threshold* showing the start of the landing portion of the runway will be indicated by white arrows pointing to a thick white solid line across the runway, or by yellow chevrons. If arrows are used, that part of the runway may be available for takeoff, but not for landing. If chevrons, rather than arrows are used, then that part of the runway is only suitable for use during an aborted takeoff (as a stopway). If the whole runway is totally unusable, it will have a large cross (×) at each end.

Figure 22-6 Closed runway (or taxiway).

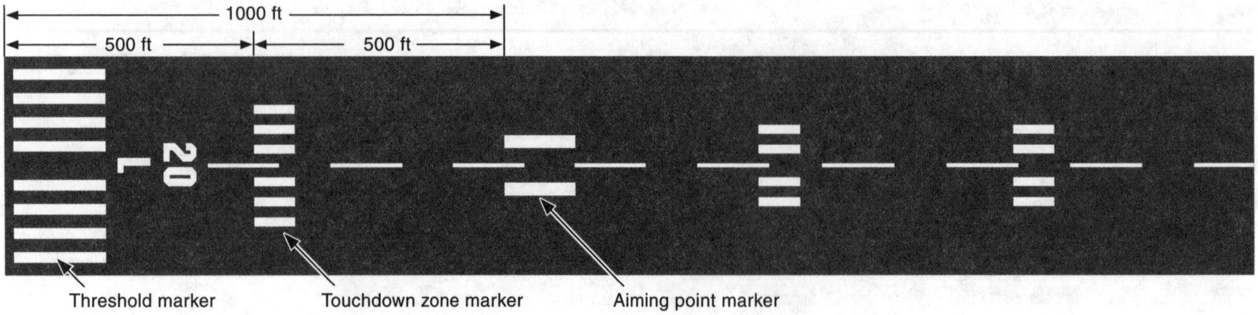

Figure 22-7 Markings on a precision instrument runway.

Airport Lighting

The main aeronautical lighting provided at an airport to assist pilots to maneuver their airplanes at night consists of:

- taxiway lighting;
- runway lighting;
- an airport beacon;
- approach lighting;
- visual approach slope indicators (VASI); and
- red warning lights on significant obstacles.

The approach lights and runway lights at an airport are controlled by:

- the control tower personnel (when the tower is active);
- the FSS, at some locations where no control tower is active; or
- the pilot (at certain airports).

The pilot may request ATC or FSS to turn the lights on (or off), or to vary their intensity if required. On a hazy day with restricted visibility, but with a lot of glare, maximum brightness might be necessary; on a clear dark night, a significantly lower brightness level will be required.

Pilot-Controlled Lighting Systems

At selected airports, when ATC and/or FSS facilities are not manned, *airborne* control of the lights is possible using the NAV-COM. The Chart Supplement U.S. specifies the type of lighting available, and the NAV-COM frequency used to activate the system. To use an FAA-approved *pilot-activated* lighting system, simply select the appropriate VHF frequency on the NAV-COM, and depress the microphone switch a number of times. Key the mike 7 times within 5 seconds, to activate the lights at maximum intensity, and then key it a further 5 or 3 times, for medium or low intensity lights respectively, if desired.

For pilot-controlled lights at maximum intensity, select the frequency and key the mike seven times within five seconds. Activation lasts 15 minutes.

All lighting is activated for 15 minutes from the time of the most recent transmission. If pilot-activated lights are already on as you commence an approach, it is good airmanship to reactivate them and thereby ensure good lighting throughout the approach and landing.

Taxiway Lights

Taxiways are lit in one of two ways for the guidance of pilots, with either:

- two lines of taxiway *blue edge* lights; or
- one line of *centerline green* taxiway lights.

Taxiway lights are either centerline green or blue edge.

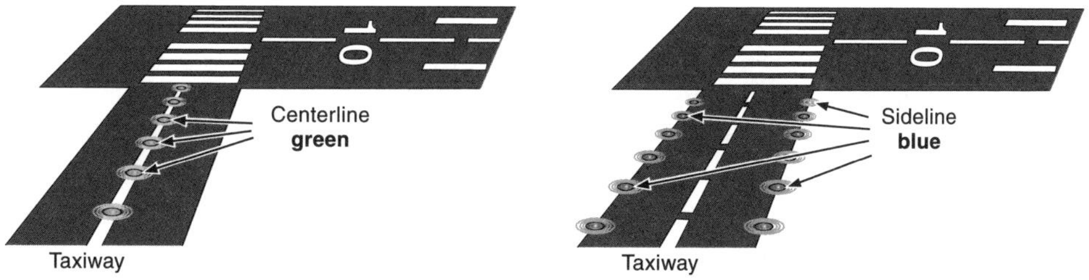

Figure 22-8 Taxiway lighting.

At some airports, there is a mixture of the two types, centerline green on some taxiways, and blue edge on others. Taxiway lights are omnidirectional, which means they shine in all directions, since a taxiing aircraft may be coming from any direction.

At certain points on the taxiway, there may be *red stop-bars* installed, to indicate the position where an airplane should hold position, for instance before entering or crossing an active runway.

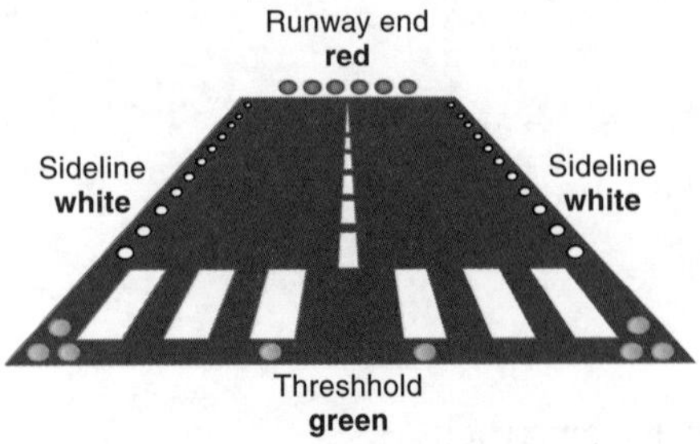

Figure 22-9
Basic runway lighting at night.

Runway Lighting

Runway lighting defines the boundaries of the actual landing area. Some advanced systems on precision instrument approach runways also provide you with distance-down-the-runway information.

Runway edge lights are white, and outline the edges of runways during periods of darkness or restricted visibility. The *runway end lights* each have two colors, showing green at the near end to aircraft on approach, and red to airplanes stopping at the far end.

> **Note.** Runway lighting is the extent of the airport lighting at basic airports.

Advanced runway edge lights are classified according to the intensity or brightness they are capable of producing:

- HIRL—high intensity runway lights;
- MIRL—medium intensity runway lights; and
- LIRL—low intensity runway lights.

Runway edge lights are white, except on instrument runways where amber replaces white for the last 2,000 feet (or last-half on runways shorter than 4,000 feet) to form a *caution* zone for landings in restricted visibility.

Runway End Identifier Lights (REIL)

Runway end identifier lights consist of a pair of synchronized white flashing lights located each side of the runway threshold at the approach end. They serve to:

- identify a runway end surrounded by many other lights;
- identify a runway end which lacks contrast with the surrounding terrain; and
- identify a runway end in poor visibility.

In-Runway Lighting

In-runway lighting is embedded in the runway surface of some precision approach runways. It consists of:

- *touchdown zone lighting* (TDZL)—bright white lights either side of the runway centerline in the touchdown zone (from 100 feet in from the landing threshold to 3,000 feet or the half-way point, whichever is the lower);
- *runway centerline lighting* (RCLS)—flush centerline lighting at 50 feet intervals, starting 75 feet in from the landing threshold to within 75 feet of the stopping end. RCLS also includes *runway-remaining lighting*, where the centerline lighting seen by a stopping airplane is:
  - initially all white;
  - alternating red and white from 3,000 feet-to-go point to 1,000 feet-to-go;
  - all red for the last 1,000 feet; and
- *taxiway turn-off lights*—a series of green in-runway lights spaced at 50 feet intervals defining a curved path from the runway centerline onto the taxiway.

Runway Status Lights (RWSL)

This enhanced advisory system is composed of two features *runway entrance lights* (REL) and *takeoff hold lights* (THL). RWSL is a fully automated system that provides runway status information to pilots and surface vehicle operators to indicate when it is unsafe to enter, cross, or takeoff from a runway. The system is installed at select airports across the U.S. to assist in preventing runway incursions. See figure 22-10.

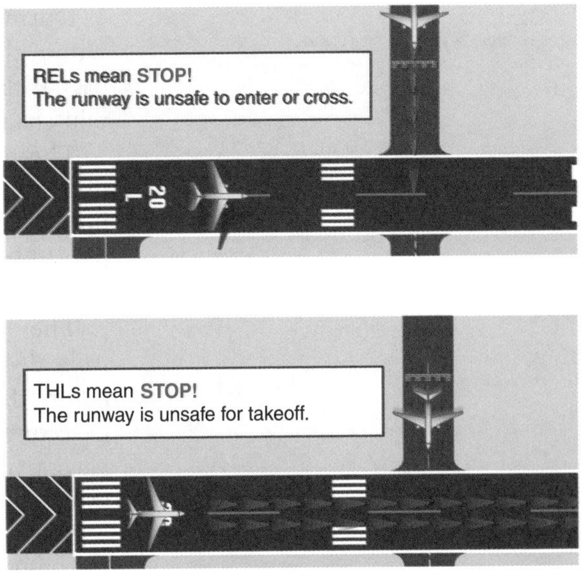

Figure 22-10
RWSL indicate when it is unsafe to enter, cross, or takeoff from a runway.

Approach Light Systems (ALS)

At many airports, an approach lighting system (ALS) extends out from the approach end of the runway to well beyond the physical boundaries of the airport, possibly into forested or built-up areas. Approach lights do *not* mark the boundaries of a suitable landing area—they simply act as a lead-in to a runway for a pilot on approach to land.

ALS lighting is a standardized arrangement of white and red lights, consisting basically of extended centerline lighting, with crossbars sited at specific intervals back along the approach path from the threshold before the runway is reached.

Visual Approach Slope Indicators (VASI)

In conditions of poor visibility and at night, when the runway environment and the natural horizon may not be clearly visible, it is often difficult for a pilot to judge the correct approach slope of the airplane toward the touchdown zone of the runway. A number of very effective visual approach slope indicators provide visual slope guidance to a pilot on approach.

Lateral guidance is provided by the runway, the runway lights or the approach light system. The slope guidance provided by a *visual approach slope indicator* (VASI) is to the touchdown zone, which will probably be some 1,000 feet in from the runway threshold. The VASI slope is typically 3°.

The typical 2-bar VASI has two pairs of wingbars alongside the runway, usually at 500 feet and 1,000 feet from the approach threshold. It is sometimes known as the *red-on-white* system, since these two colors are used to indicate to the pilot whether the airplane is on slope, too high or too low. The pilot will see:

- all bars white if high on approach;
- the near bars white and the far bars red if right on slope; and
- all bars red if low on slope.

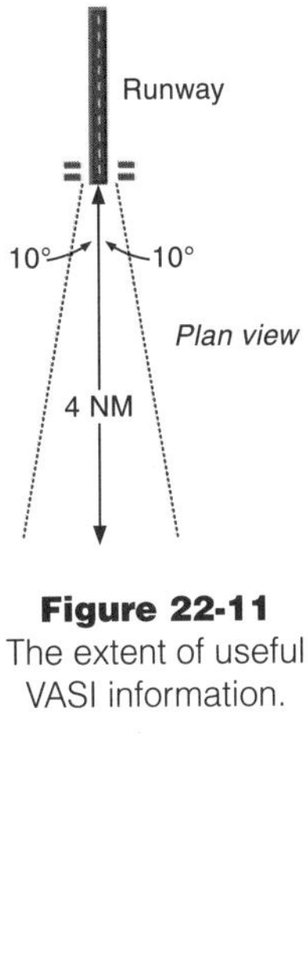

Figure 22-11
The extent of useful VASI information.

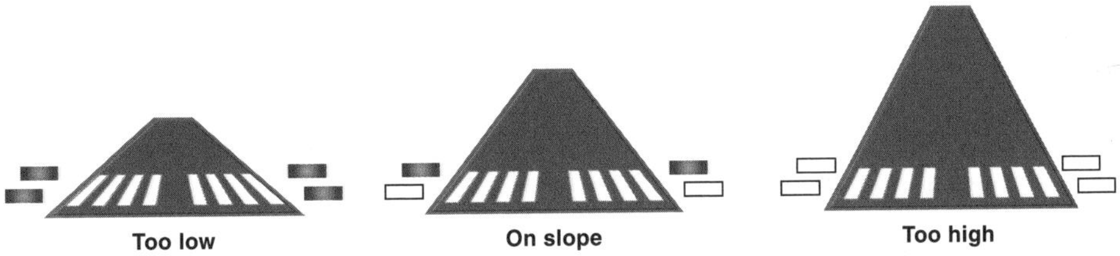

Figure 22-12 Perspectives on approach using a 2-bar VASI—fly "red-on-white."

During the approach, the airplane should be maintained on a slope within the *white* sector of the near bars and the *red* sector of the far bars. If the airplane flies above or below the correct slope, the lights will change color from white to pink, to red, or visa versa.

The plane of the VASI approach slope only provides guaranteed obstacle clearance in an arc 10° left or right of the extended centerline out to a distance of 4 nautical miles (NM) from the runway threshold, even though the VASI may be visible in good conditions out to 5 NM by day and 20 NM by night.

There are other operational considerations when using the *red-on-white* VASI. At maximum range, the white bars may become visible before the red bars, because of the nature of red and white light. In haze or smog, or in certain other conditions, the white lights may have a yellowish tinge about them. In addition, if water collects in or on the light lens false indications may occur.

When extremely low on slope, the two wingbars (all lights red) may appear to merge into one red bar—at close range to the threshold this would indicate a critical situation with respect to obstacle clearance, and the pilot must take urgent action.

Some VASI systems use a reduced number of lights, in which case they may be known as an *abbreviated VASI* or *AVASI.*

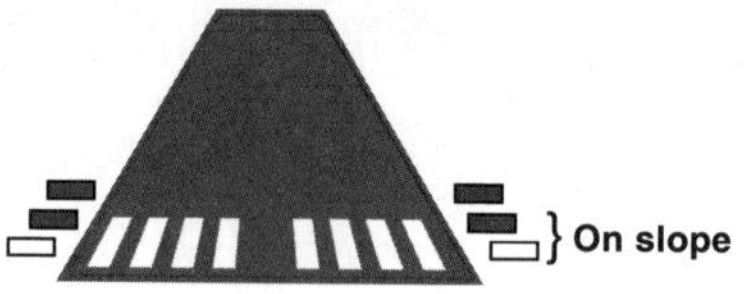

Figure 22-13
Correct view for the pilot of a smaller airplane using the 3-bar VASI.

The *3-bar VASI* has an additional wingbar at the far end, intended to assist the pilots of large passenger airliners. Pilots of such airplanes will use the second and third wingbars, and ignore the first to allow for the extra length of the airplane.

Pilots of smaller airplanes should refer only to the two nearer wingbars, and ignore the further "long-bodied" wingbar. On slope, the indications should be (top bar red and ignored), middle bar red and lower bar white.

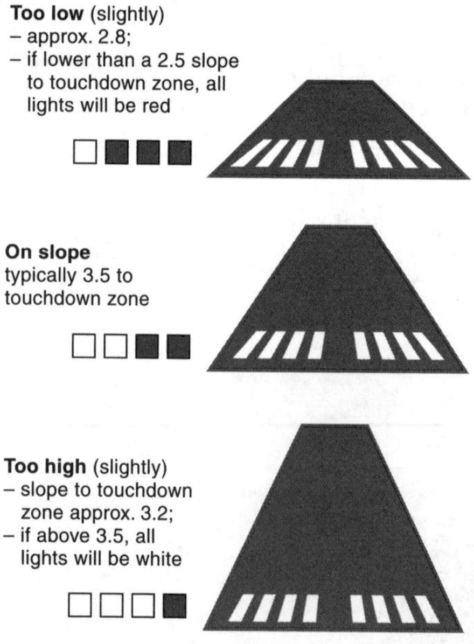

Too low (slightly)
– approx. 2.8;
– if lower than a 2.5 slope to touchdown zone, all lights will be red
On slope
typically 3.5 to touchdown zone
Too high (slightly)
– slope to touchdown zone approx. 3.2;
– if above 3.5, all lights will be white

Figure 22-14
Slope guidance using PAPI.

The *precision approach path indicator* (PAPI) is a development of the VASI, and also uses red/white light signals for guidance in maintaining the correct approach angle, but the lights are arranged differently and their indications must be interpreted differently. PAPI has a single wingbar, which will consist of four light units on one or both sides of the runway adjacent to the touchdown point. There is no pink transition stage as the lights change from red to white.

If the airplane is on slope, the two outer lights of each unit are white and the two inner lights are red. Above slope, the number of white lights increase, and below slope the number of red lights increase.

A *pulsating visual approach slope indicator* (PVASI) consists of a single light unit, positioned on the left side of a runway adjacent to the touchdown point, which projects three or four different "bands" of light at different vertical angles, only one of which can be seen by a pilot on approach at any one time.

The indications provided by a typical PVASI are:
- pulsing white—above glide slope;
- steady white—on glide slope (alternating red/white on some systems); and
- pulsing red—below glide slope.

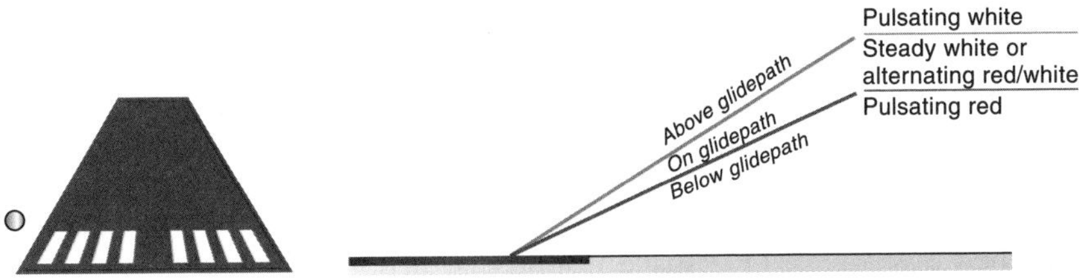

Figure 22-15 The PVASI.

The *tri-color VASI* is a short-range visual slope aid (½ mile by day, 5 miles by night), and consists of a single-light unit that indicates:

- amber if above slope;
- green if on slope; and
- red if below slope.

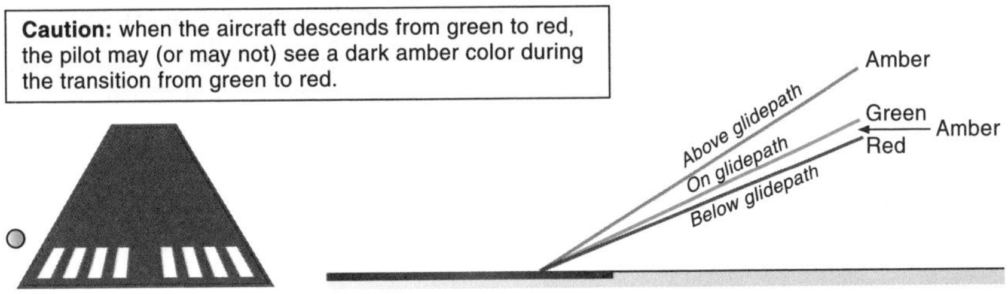

Figure 22-16 The tri-color VASI.

The *T-VASI* is a system that has a horizontal bar of white lights either side of the runway aiming point. If the airplane is right on slope, you will see the horizontal bar only. If you are high on slope, single lights will appear above this bar, forming an inverted-T, and indicating fly down. If you are low on slope, single lights will appear below the bar, forming a T, and indicating fly up. The number of vertical lights give an indication of how far off slope you are. If extremely low, the lights turn red.

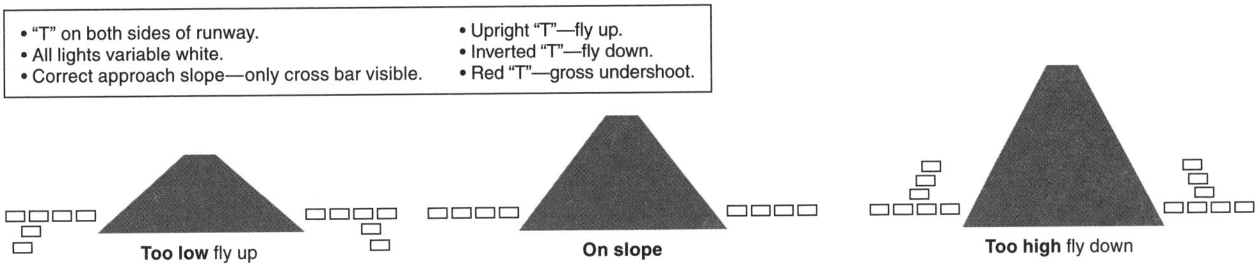

Figure 22-17 T-VASI.

Airport Beacon

The airport beacon is designed to help the pilot visually locate the airport from some distance away. Some airport beacons rotate, others transmit pulses of light, the effect being the same—flashes of one or two alternating colors, which are:

- green/white/green/white—at *civil land airports*;
- green/white-white/green/white-white—at *military land airports*;
- green/yellow/white—at *lighted heliports*; and
- white/yellow—at *lighted water ports*.

An airport rotating beacon that is operating during daylight hours indicates that weather in the Class B, C or D airspace around that airport, which will have an operating control tower, is below basic VFR weather minimums (ground visibility less than 3 miles and/or ceiling less than 1,000 feet). This is a good warning for VFR pilots.

Airport Operations

There are two types of airport:
- controlled; and
- uncontrolled.

A controlled airport has an active control tower and all movements must be approved. An uncontrolled airport relies on pilot-to-pilot communications for traffic awareness and safe separation. Radio procedures for each are defined.

Basic Communications Procedures for Uncontrolled Airports

The standard calls for a nontowered airport, or when the tower is closed, is described in table 22-1.

Facility at Airport	Frequency Use	Communication/Broadcast Procedures		
		Outbound	**Inbound**	**Practice Instrument Approach**
UNICOM (no tower or FSS).	Communicate with UNICOM station on published CTAF frequency (122.7, 122.8, 122.725, 122.975, or 123.0). If unable to contact UNICOM station, use self-announce procedures on CTAF.	Before taxiing and before taxiing on the runway for departure.	10 miles out. Entering downwind, base, and final. Leaving the runway.	
No tower, FSS, or UNICOM.	Self-announce on MULTICOM frequency 122.9.	Before taxiing and before taxiing on the runway for departure.	10 miles out. Entering downwind, base, and final. Leaving the runway.	Departing final approach fix (name) or on final approach segment inbound.
No tower in operation, FSS open.	Communicate with FSS on CTAF frequency.	Before taxiing and before taxiing on the runway for departure.	10 miles out. Entering downwind, base, and final. Leaving the runway.	Approach completed/ terminated.
FSS closed (no tower).	Self-announce on CTAF.	Before taxiing and before taxiing on the runway for departure.	10 miles out. Entering downwind, base, and final. Leaving the runway.	
Tower or FSS not in operation.	Self-announce on CTAF.	Before taxiing and before taxiing on the runway for departure.	10 miles out. Entering downwind, base, and final. Leaving the runway.	

Table 22-1 Recommended communication procedures.

Lost Communications Procedures

If a pilot experiences a radio failure, it may be the receiver only. The procedure is to remain outside or above Class D airspace if possible, advise the tower of the loss of reception, make the usual position calls, squawk 7600 on your transponder, join the standard traffic pattern, and look for light signals from the tower. If the transmitter fails but the pilot can receive, listen to the ATC frequency and join the pattern.

If all communications are lost, join the pattern after establishing landing direction and traffic, and look for light signals. The standard light signals to an aircraft in flight, are shown in figure 22-18.

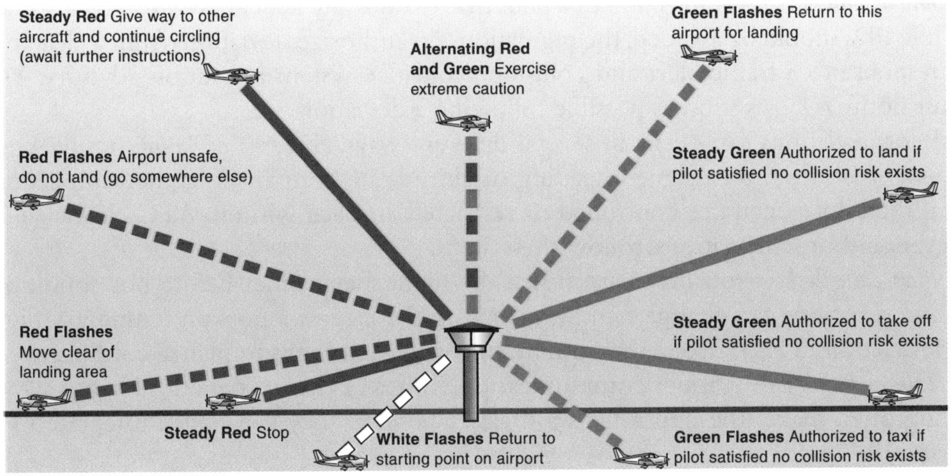

Figure 22-18 Standard light signals to aircraft.

Traffic Pattern and Wind Indicators

Landing direction—and therefore all legs of the traffic pattern—relate to wind direction. There are several types of wind indicators. In the absence of an active control tower, the pilot selects the pattern and landing direction in accordance with the traffic pattern indicators and the wind direction indicator. These are shown in figure 22-19.

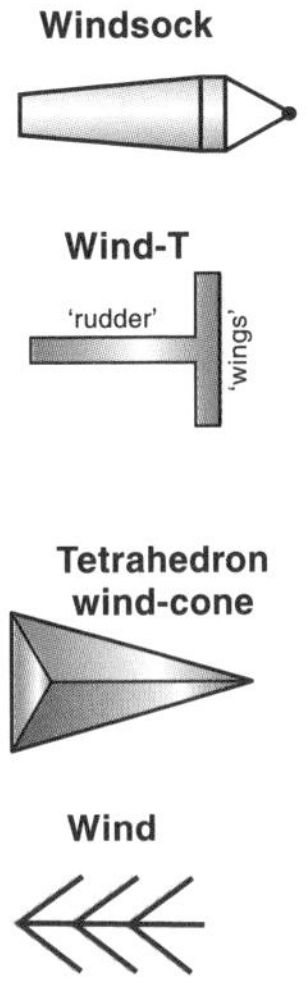

Figure 22-19 Wind and landing direction indicators.

Radar Traffic Information Service

Traffic advisories and air traffic control may provide additional services, such as safety alerts, traffic advisories vectoring if requested, and sequencing of traffic in higher density areas. In certain locations, a *terminal radar service area* (TRSA) may be implemented to provide separation for participating VFR and all IFR aircraft operating within its area. Class C or B service may be provided. Advisories take the form of a radio call, such as, *"You have traffic in your 11 o'clock, 3 miles, crossing left to right, Cessna, 3,000 feet ."*

> **Note.** The clock code from radar is based on your track and not your heading as it would be if you were reporting traffic to your instructor. Therefore, drift has an effect which must be considered.

Unmanned Aircraft Systems

Most airports are a "no drone zone" unless operators have obtained special FAA authorization. Visit faa.gov to stay informed of the rapidly changing rules and procedures associated with UAS, particularly relative to airport operations.

Collision Avoidance

Collision avoidance for VFR aircraft rests largely with the pilot. An effective scan pattern must be practiced, as the eyes tend to rest and not focus at a distance. Also, a continuous scan may miss traffic. It is necessary to scan a little and then pause, then scan a little further and pause again. This is called the *saccade/rest cycle*. It is also essential to scan by turning the head—not just sweep with eye movement. The aircraft has many blind spots. Therefore, the flight path may need to be varied to look under or over the nose or wings—don't forget that faster traffic can approach from behind.

Pilot Deviations (PD)

A *pilot deviation* (PD) is an action of a pilot that violates any Federal Aviation Regulation. While PDs should be avoided, the regulations do authorize deviations from a clearance in response to a traffic alert and collision avoidance system resolution advisory. You must notify ATC as soon as possible following a deviation.

Pilot deviations can occur in several different ways. *Airborne deviations* result when a pilot strays from an assigned heading or altitude or from an instrument procedure, or if the pilot penetrates controlled or restricted airspace without ATC clearance. To prevent airborne deviations, follow these steps:

- *Plan each flight*—you may have flown the flight many times before but conditions and situations can change rapidly, such as in the case of a pop-up temporary flight restriction (TFR). Take a few minutes prior to each flight to plan accordingly.
- *Talk and squawk*—Proper communication with ATC has its benefits. Flight following often makes the controller's job easier because they can better integrate VFR and IFR traffic.
- *Give yourself some room*—GPS is usually more precise than ATC radar. Using your GPS to fly up to and along the line of the airspace you are trying to avoid could result in a pilot deviation because ATC radar may show you within the restricted airspace.

Ground deviations (also called surface deviations) include taxiing, taking off, or landing without clearance, deviating from an assigned taxi route, or failing to hold short of an assigned clearance limit. To prevent ground deviations, stay alert during ground operations. Pilot deviations can and frequently do occur on the ground. Many strategies and tactics pilots use to avoid airborne deviations also work on the ground.

Pilots should also remain vigilant about *vehicle/pedestrian deviations* (V/PDs). A vehicle or pedestrian deviation includes pedestrians, vehicles, or other objects interfering with aircraft operations by entering or moving on the runway movement area without authorization from air traffic control. In serious instances, any ground deviation can result in a runway incursion. Best practices in preventing ground deviations can be found in the following section under runway incursion avoidance.

Prevent a runway incursion: read back all crossing and /or hold instructions, review airport layouts as part of preflight planning, know airport signage, review NOTAMs for runway/taxiway closures, and request progressive taxi instructions when unsure of taxi route.

Runway Incursion Avoidance

The most serious risk of collision is around and on an airport. Even on the ground, it is essential to be vigilant and scan for traffic—especially if approaching a runway or holding point, crossing another strip or taxiway, landing on a crossing runway, or landing behind another aircraft. Have lights on, and if in doubt, stop and ask the tower or another aircraft for directions. Never enter or cross a runway if there is any doubt about it being active or if there is an aircraft visible on that runway.

The Standard Traffic Pattern

To maintain some form of safe and orderly flow of traffic at an airport, and to allow easy and safe access to the active runway, aircraft are flown in a standard traffic pattern. For good operational reasons, the preferred direction of takeoff and landing is into the wind, therefore the same direction will generally be used by aircraft both taking off and landing.

The standard traffic pattern is left hand.

The traffic pattern is a rectangular ground path based on the runway in use. The *standard pattern* is to the left of the runway with all turns being made to the left. At some airports and on some particular runways, however, the patterns are right-hand to avoid built-up areas, high terrain or restricted airspace.

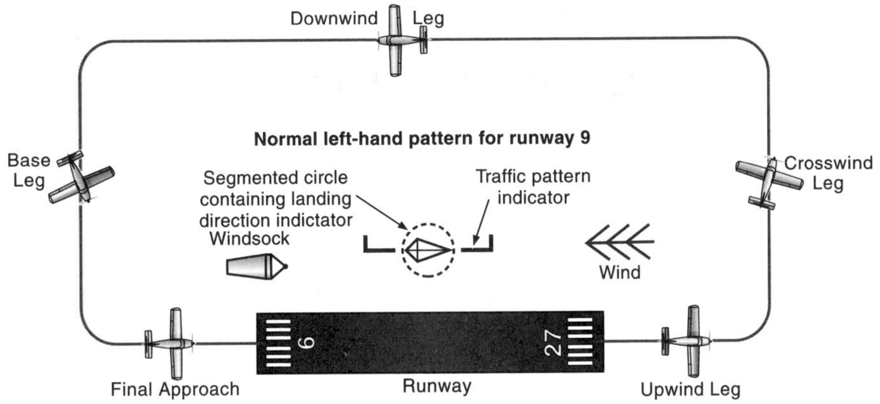

Figure 22-20 The traffic pattern is rectangular.

The tower will advise takeoff and landing direction.

At non-towered airports, comply with any FAA traffic pattern established for that particular airport.

At tower-controlled airports takeoff and landing directions will be advised from the tower or on the ATIS.

At airports *without* an operating control tower, make use of any *segmented circle* with its associated wind indicator and traffic pattern indicators to assist you in determining which runway to use and the direction of the traffic pattern. You should comply with any FAA traffic pattern established for a particular airport (see Chart Supplement U.S.).

Some airports have *parallel runways*, with a left traffic pattern off Runway Left, and a right traffic pattern off Runway Right, and with a "no transgression zone" between the two patterns.

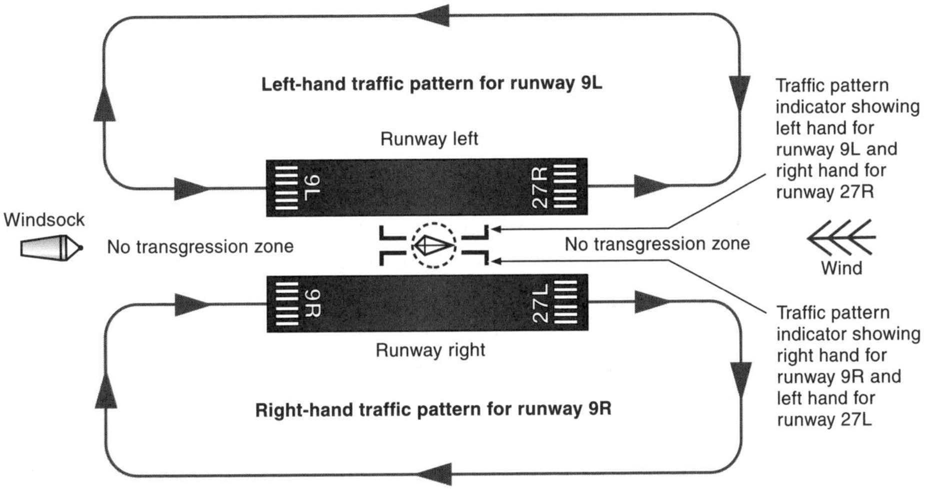

Figure 22-21 Left and right traffic patterns for parallel runways.

The traffic pattern is referenced to the runway on which it is based, for example, "left traffic for Runway 35" refers to the pattern based on Runway 35. The 35 indicates that the runway heading is somewhere in the range 345°–350°–355°.

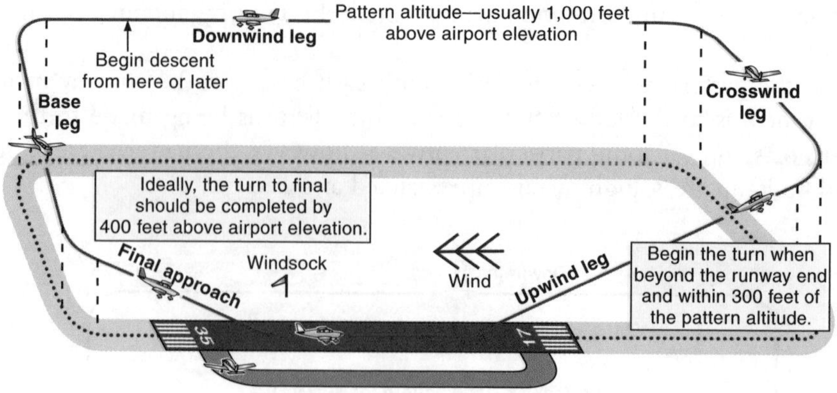

Figure 22-22 The normal traffic pattern.

Ensure that the current altimeter setting is set in the pressure window, so that the altimeter will read altitude above mean sea level (MSL). This enables you to accurately determine when you have reached pattern altitude. If the airport has an elevation of 890 feet, and the pattern is to be flown 1,000 feet above this, then traffic pattern altitude is reached when the altimeter indicates (890 + 1,000) = 1,890 feet MSL.

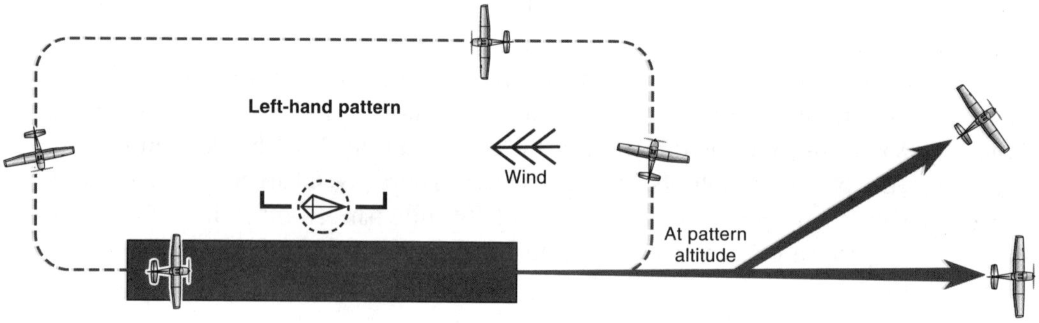

Figure 22-23 Departing the traffic pattern.

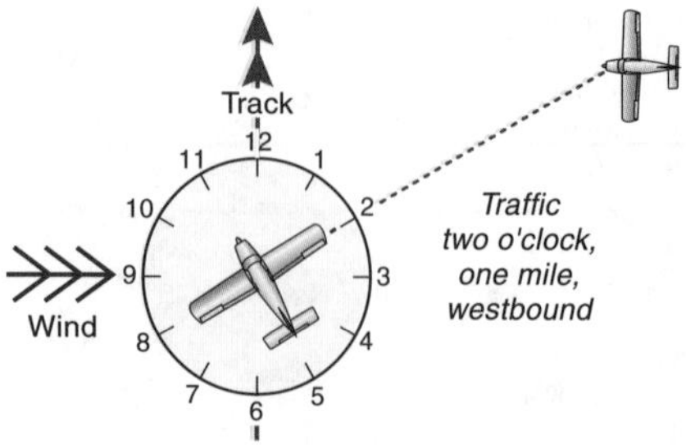

Figure 22-24
Radar traffic information service.

Airport Radar Services

Radar has greatly simplified ATC procedures by enabling the controller to see a picture on the radar screen of the air traffic in his area of responsibility. The transponder carried in the aircraft can provide the radar controller with further information on the screen, such as aircraft identification and altitude. Unless otherwise authorized, VFR aircraft should squawk transponder *code 1200*.

When passing traffic information to you, the radar controller will often use the clock system to specify the other aircraft's position relative to your track, and also give its distance in miles, direction of flight, and altitude. The controller sees your *track*, rather than your heading, and so you will have to allow for any wind drift angle when you look out the window and search for other traffic. Note that, even in a radar environment, the pilot has the ultimate responsibility to see and avoid other traffic.

Normal transponder code for VFR is 1200.

Various levels of radar service are available, depending on the particular airspace, the nature of the operation (IFR/VFR), and the controller's workload.

If you ever experience *radio failure*, you should squawk *7600* on your transponder. This will alert the tower controller to your radio communications failure. You should observe the traffic flow, enter the traffic pattern keeping a particularly good lookout, and watch for light signals from the tower (see figure 22-18). If the radio failure occurs on the ground, you would normally not takeoff but taxi back to a parking position for repairs or clarification.

Following radio communications failure, keep a good lookout, squawk code 7600, observe the traffic flow, enter the traffic pattern, and watch for light signals from the tower.

Basic Radar Service

Basic radar service can provide traffic advisories and limited radar vectoring on a workload-permitting basis to VFR aircraft arriving at Class D airports and occasionally at airports in Class E or G airspace. Basic radar service exists primarily to aid tower controllers sequencing arriving and departing traffic.

Traffic Sequencing for Pilots

Basic service with traffic sequencing is provided to adjust the flow of arriving VFR and IFR aircraft into the traffic pattern and to provide traffic information to departing VFR aircraft. VFR aircraft may be assigned specific headings to fly (vectors), as well as specific altitudes, to aid controllers in facilitating traffic separation.

ATC instruction "Line up and Wait" instructs the pilot to taxi onto the departure runway into position and wait for takeoff clearance.

Full Radar Services

Full service provides sequencing and separation for all participating VFR and IFR aircraft, and is typically encountered in and around busy Class B, C, and D airspace. IFR traffic is always accorded the highest level of radar service during all segments of flight.

In a radar environment, pilots of *arriving aircraft* should contact approach control on the published frequency, usually at approximately 25 miles, and give callsign, aircraft type, position, altitude, transponder code, destination, ATIS information received, and request traffic information. Approach control will issue wind and runway, except when the pilot states *"have numbers"* or *"have ATIS information."* Traffic information will be advised on a workload-permitting basis. Radar service is automatically terminated when approach control advises the pilot to contact the control tower for further landing instructions.

> **Note.** "Have numbers" does not mean "Have ATIS", it means you have wind, runway and altimeter information only.

Pilots of *departing* aircraft are encouraged, on initial contact with ground control, to request radar traffic information in the proposed direction of flight, for example:

> *San Carlos ground control, Mike seven three two, Cessna one seventy two, ready to taxi, VFR southbound at two thousand five hundred feet, have information Charlie, request radar traffic information.*

After receiving a takeoff clearance from the tower and becoming airborne, the tower will advise when to contact departure control.

When departing and being advised that the radar service is being terminated, you should set the *normal VFR code 1200* in your transponder. Be careful not to pass through any of the emergency codes when selecting 1200: 7500—unlawful interference, 7600—radio failure, or 7700—emergency.

Review 22

Airports and Airport Operations

Airports

1. In terms of runway orientation, what do the numbers 9 and 27 on a runway indicate?
2. *Refer to figure 22-25.*
   - **a.** What is area C on the airport depicted classified as?
   - **b.** Landing may be commenced at which position for runway 12?
   - **c.** What may the portion of runway 12 identified by the letter A be used for?

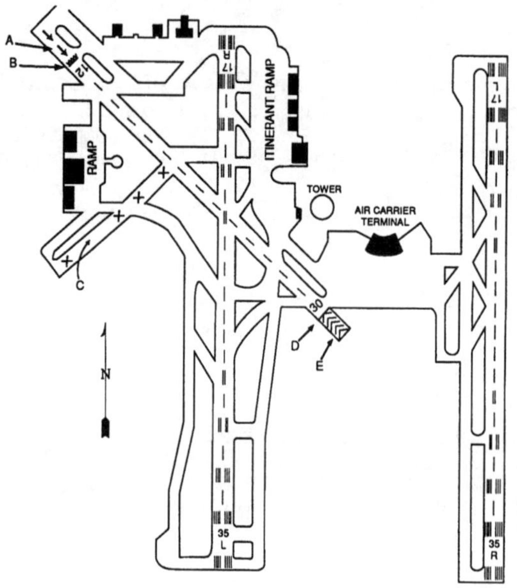

Figure 22-25 Question 2.

3. What does an airport's rotating beacon operated during daylight hours indicate?
4. How is PAL activated at maximum intensity?
5. How are airport taxiway edge lights identified at night?
6. What color are taxiway centerline lights?
7. When using PAPI, what do three white lights and one red light indicate?
8. What does a red light signal from a tri-color VASI indicate?
9. What is the below glide slope indication from a pulsating approach slope indicator?

Airport Operations

10. *Refer to figure 22-26.*
    - **a.** Which is the proper traffic pattern and runway for landing?
    - **b.** What does the segmented circle indicate?

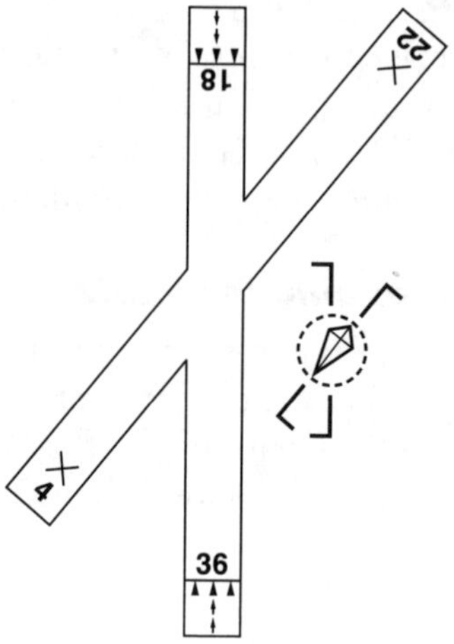

Figure 22-26 Question 10.

11. If two-way radio communication fails at an airport with a tower and cannot be restored, what is the recommended procedure?
12. What does a steady green light signal directed from the control tower to you while on the ground indicate?
13. What is indicated by the following directed to you in flight from the control tower:
    - **a.** an alternating red and green light?
    - **b.** a flashing red light signal?
    - **c.** a steady red light signal?

Refer to figure 22-27 (page 536) for questions 14 to 23. You may refer to the legend of any Chart Supplement U.S. to help you (the legend will be provided in the Knowledge Exam).

14. What is the three-letter identifying code for Lincoln Municipal Airport?

15. What is the elevation of Lincoln Municipal Airport?

16. What is the traffic pattern altitude (TPA) at Lincoln Municipal Airport? (Give your answer in feet MSL and feet AGL)

17. With respect to Runway 17 Right at Lincoln Municipal Airport:
- **a.** what sort of surface does it have?
- **b.** how long is it?
- **c.** how wide is it?

18. What is the CTAF at Lincoln Municipal Airport?

19. What frequency is the ATIS at Lincoln Municipal Airport on?

20. What is the recommended communications procedure for landing at Lincoln Municipal Airport during the hours when the tower is not in operation?

21. You approach Lincoln Municipal Airport at noon local time. What is this in UTC (or Z)?

22. When is Lincoln Municipal approach control active?

23. Which frequency would aircraft approaching Lincoln Municipal from the east use?

24. You require radar service when departing a primary airport in Class D airspace. When should you request this?

25. You are on a heading MH 090 and the ATC radar facility issues you the advisory: "Traffic 3 o'clock, 2 miles, westbound."
- **a.** Which way should you look?
- **b.** In which direction is this?

26. True or false? A clearance to taxi to the active runway at an airport with an operating control tower permits you to taxi via the taxiways, to cross intersecting nonactive runways, but not to enter the active runway.

27. An ATC radar facility issues the following advisory to a pilot flying north in a calm wind: "Traffic 9 o'clock, 2 miles, southbound..." Where should the pilot look for this traffic?

NEBRASKA **271**

LINCOLN (LNK) 4 NW UTC–6(–5DT) N40°51.05′ W96°45.55′ **OMAHA**
1219 B S4 **FUEL** 100LL, JET A TPA—See Remarks ARFF Index—See Remarks **H–5C, L–10I**
NOTAM FILE LNK **IAP, AD**

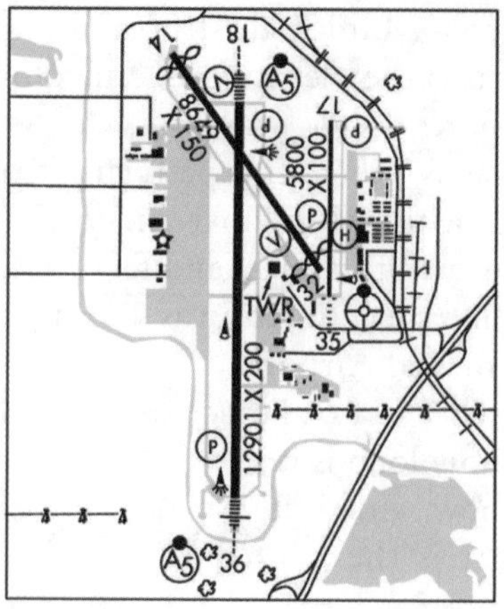

RWY 18–36: H12901X200 (ASPH–CONC–GRVD) S–100, D–200, 2S–175, 2D–400 HIRL
RWY 18: MALSR. PAPI(P4L)—GA 3.0° TCH 55′. Rgt tfc. 0.4% down.
RWY 36: MALSR. PAPI(P4L)—GA 3.0° TCH 57′.
RWY 14–32: H8649X150 (ASPH–CONC–GRVD) S–80, D–170, 2S–175, 2D–280 MIRL
RWY 14: REIL. VASI(V4L)—GA 3.0° TCH 48′. Thld dsplcd 363′.
RWY 32: VASI(V4L)—GA 3.0° TCH 50′. Thld dsplcd 470′. Pole. 0.3% up.
RWY 17–35: H5800X100 (ASPH–CONC–AFSC) S–49, D–60 HIRL 0.8% up S
RWY 17: REIL. PAPI(P4L)—GA 3.0° TCH 44′.
RWY 35: ODALS. PAPI(P4L)—GA 3.0° TCH 30′. Rgt tfc.
RUNWAY DECLARED DISTANCE INFORMATION

RWY 14:	TORA–8649	TODA–8649	ASDA–8649	LDA–8286
RWY 17:	TORA–5800	TODA–5800	ASDA–5400	LDA–5400
RWY 18:	TORA–12901	TODA–12901	ASDA–12901	LDA–12901
RWY 32:	TORA–8649	TODA–8649	ASDA–8286	LDA–7816
RWY 35:	TORA–5800	TODA–5800	ASDA–5800	LDA–5800
RWY 36:	TORA–12901	TODA–12901	ASDA–12901	LDA–12901

AIRPORT REMARKS: Attended continuously. Birds invof arpt. Rwy 18 designated calm wind rwy. Rwy 32 apch holdline on South A twy. TPA–2219 (1000), heavy military jet 3000 (1781). Class I, ARFF Index B. ARFF Index C level equipment provided. Rwy 18–36 touchdown and rollout rwy visual range avbl. When twr clsd MIRL Rwy 14–32 preset on low ints, HIRL Rwy 18–36 and Rwy 17–35 preset on med ints, ODALS Rwy 35 operate continuously on med ints, MALSR Rwy 18 and Rwy 36 operate continuously and REIL Rwy 14 and Rwy 17 operate continuously on low ints. VASI Rwy 14 and Rwy 32, PAPI Rwy 17, Rwy 35, Rwy 18 and Rwy 36 on continuously.
WEATHER DATA SOURCES: ASOS (402) 474–9214. LLWAS
COMMUNICATIONS: CTAF 118.5 **ATIS** 118.05 **UNICOM** 122.95
RCO 122.65 (COLUMBUS RADIO)
® **APP/DEP CON** 124.0 (180°–359°) 124.8 (360°–179°)
TOWER 118.5 125.7 (1130–0600Z‡) **GND CON** 121.9 **CLNC DEL** 120.7
AIRSPACE: CLASS C svc 1130–0600Z‡ ctc **APP CON** other times CLASS E.
RADIO AIDS TO NAVIGATION: NOTAM FILE LNK.
(H) VORTACW 116.1 LNK Chan 108 N40°55.43′ W96°44.52′ 181° 4.4 NM to fld. 1370/9E
POTTS NDB (MHW/LOM) 385 LN N40°44.83′ W96°45.75′ 355° 6.2 NM to fld. Unmonitored when twr clsd.
ILS 111.1 I–OCZ Rwy 18. Class IB OM unmonitored.
ILS 109.9 I–LNK Rwy 36 Class IA LOM POTTS NDB. MM unmonitored. LOM unmonitored when twr clsd.
COMM/NAV/WEATHER REMARKS: Emerg frequency 121.5 not available at twr.

LOUP CITY MUNI (ØF4) 1 NW UTC–6(–5DT) N41°17.20′ W98°59.41′ **OMAHA**
2071 B **FUEL** 100LL NOTAM FILE OLU **L–10H, 12H**
RWY 16–34: H3200X60 (CONC) S–12.5 MIRL
RWY 34: Trees.
RWY 04–22: 2040X100 (TURF)
RWY 04: Tree. **RWY 22:** Road.
AIRPORT REMARKS: Unattended. For svc call 308–745–1344/1244/0664.
COMMUNICATIONS: CTAF 122.9
RADIO AIDS TO NAVIGATION: NOTAM FILE OLU.
WOLBACH (H) VORTAC 114.8 OBH Chan 95 N41°22.54′ W98°21.22′ 253° 29.3 NM to fld. 2010/7E.

MARTIN FLD (See SO SIOUX CITY)

Figure 22-27 Questions 14 to 23.

Answers are given on page 705.

Visual Navigation Fundamentals 23

Air Navigation

Air navigation involves basic principles that apply to all airplanes, from the simplest trainers to the most sophisticated passenger jets. Our objective in *The Pilot's Manual* is to show you navigation techniques that will not increase your workload in the cockpit to an unacceptable degree, and still allow time to fix your position and navigate the airplane safely to your desired destination. We make the assumption that you already know how to fly the airplane; the objective here is to add the basic principles of air navigation to those flying skills. Other aspects that have a bearing on the conduct of a cross-country flight are covered in the chapters to follow.

This chapter concentrates on accurate navigation of a light aircraft, flown by a single pilot in VFR conditions. When flying cross-country you are the pilot, the navigator and the radio operator. You must:

- primarily fly the airplane safely and accurately;
- navigate correctly; and
- attend to the radio and other aspects of your duty in the cockpit.

In short, you must, "*Aviate, navigate, and communicate.*"

Remember the key words: "aviate, navigate, communicate" in that order.

To conduct a cross-country flight efficiently, the navigation tasks must be coordinated with (and not interfere with) the smooth flying of the airplane. It is most important that you, as pilot/navigator, clearly understand the basic principles underlying navigation so that correct techniques and practices can be applied quickly and accurately without causing too much distraction or apprehension.

Navigating an airplane, unlike a car or ship, is *three-dimensional*—you must think of *altitude* (vertical navigation) as well as *direction* (horizontal navigation). Also, you must think of *time*.

Horizontal Navigation

Types of Navigation

Visual Navigation

Pilotage is determining position by correlating chart information with what is seen on the ground.

The basic method of visual navigation, called *pilotage*, is chart-reading and correlating information from the chart with what is seen on the surface of the earth, and thus determining position. Pilotage requires more or less continuous visual reference to the ground, and the ability to chart-read is restricted in poor visibility or if above partial cloud cover, and at night. Pilotage involves comparing the chart to the ground features and determining your actual position relative to the planned course.

Pilotage is a skill learned by practice. Learning to match shapes of lakes and rivers as seen out the window from aloft to how they look on the chart (e.g. looking for railroad tracks in the right places, finding and using radio towers for correlation to towers marked on charts, discerning one town from another by the location of a water tower or how the railroad tracks come into and leave that town) are all skills acquired from practice. Teach yourself how to estimate distances over the ground between two objects seen on the ground by looking up how long a certain lake is, or how far apart two towns are on the chart, and then remembering what that distance looks like out the window. Learn to use section lines, a mile apart and laid out true north–south–east–west.

Dead reckoning is determining position by calculating headings, distances and times.

As a back-up to pilotage you can use deduced reckoning, commonly known as *dead reckoning* or *DR*. This allows you to apply current conditions of speed, direction, and wind to your latest known position (*a fix*) and thus predict where you should be at a certain time.

When navigating, pilotage and DR always go together. Using the two methods together always produces more accurate navigation than when only one of the two methods are used. DR solutions, figured out during preflight, tell you where (and when) you should be somewhere, and about when to be looking for a particular feature on the ground. Pilotage, on the other hand, tells you where you are at the moment. Learn to work the two together. Practice even when using electronic navigation systems, for the day will surely come when those systems will fail you. You may find yourself wishing to fly where there are no electronic NAVAIDs, or only one (GPS), which, if used by itself, can leave you *very* lost if it fails. As a pilot, it is your responsibility to improve and maintain your DR/pilotage skills by practice.

Navigation with Electronic Aids

Navigation may use electronic aids.

Navigation may use radio equipment installed in the airplane and tuned to ground-based or satellite radio beacons. This enables the pilot to fly along radio position lines, without visual reference to the ground, although pilotage should always be used to back up radio navigation when the ground can be seen. Typical navigation systems are VOR, NDB, and DME, with the more advanced area navigation systems of GPS (these are discussed in chapter 27). The VFR pilot may use these navigation aids to assist in visual navigation.

Before Flight

Flight plan carefully.

Being properly prepared is essential if a cross-country flight is to be successful. Always *flight plan* carefully and meticulously. This sets up an accurate base against which you can measure your in-flight navigation performance. Preflight consideration should be given to the following items:

- serviceability of your watch or aircraft clock. *Time* is vital to accurate navigation;
- contents of your "nav bag", including pencils, flight computer, protractor and scale (or a plotter), suitable aeronautical charts, and relevant flight information publications;
- preparation of the appropriate maps and charts;
- desired route;
- terrain en route;
- airspace en route (Class B, C, D, E, G, special use);
- suitability of the destination airport and any alternate airports;
- *forecast* weather en route and at the destination and alternate airports (plus any reports of *actual* weather that might be available);
- calculation of accurate headings, groundspeeds and estimated time intervals; and
- consideration of fuel consumption, and accurate fuel planning.

It sounds like a lot, but each item considered individually is simple to understand.

In Flight

Since you spent considerable time preparing an accurate flight plan, it is important to fly the plan accurately. Once the airplane is in flight, flying a reasonably accurate *heading* (which involves reference to both the heading indicator and outside cues) is essential if the airplane is to track toward the desired destination. Maintaining *cruise airspeed*, and comparing your progress and actual *times of arrival* at various fixes with those estimated at the flight planning stage will normally ensure a pleasant and drama-free journey.

Fly accurate headings, check times, and keep a flight log.

Speed

Speed is the rate at which distance is covered, or more precisely, *distance per unit time*. The standard unit for speed is the knot, (abbreviated kt). 1 knot equals 1 nautical mile per hour. The speed of the airplane through the air is its *true airspeed* (TAS), which may have to be calculated from the indicated airspeed (IAS) using a flight computer, or obtained from tabulated values in the Pilot's Operating Handbook (POH). TAS is the actual speed of the airplane relative to the air mass.

Because of the design of the airspeed indicator in the airplane, the airspeed that it indicates is usually *less* than the true airspeed because of the lower air density at altitude. The flight computer can be used to convert the indicated airspeed that you read in the cockpit into a true airspeed. Some airspeed indicators have a correction scale incorporated in their design (see figure 23-1).

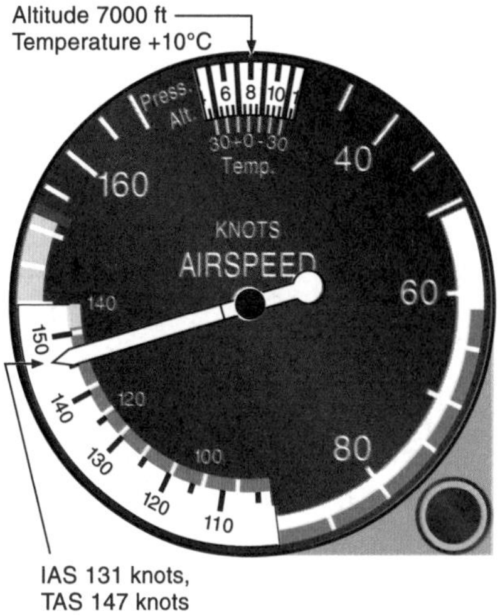

Figure 23-1 IAS and TAS indicator.

Direction and Speed Combined

An airplane flies in the medium of air. Its motion relative to the air mass is specified by its direction (known as *heading*) and its speed through the air mass (*true airspeed*). When considered together HDG/TAS constitute what is known as a *vector* quantity, which requires both *magnitude* (in this case *TAS*) and *direction* (here *HDG*) to be completely specified. HDG/TAS is the *vector* (direction and speed) of the airplane through the air. HDG/TAS is symbolized by a single-headed arrow ——>——. The direction of the arrow indicates the direction of movement along the vector line.

The HDG/TAS vector fully describes the motion of the airplane relative to the air mass.

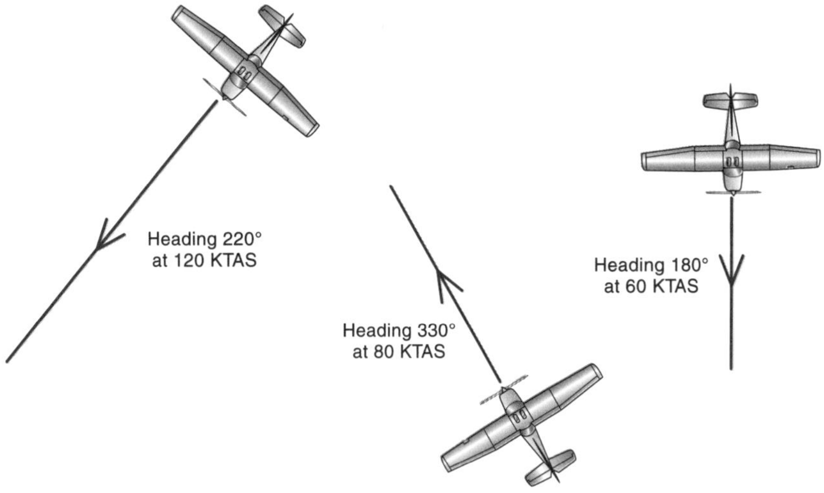

Figure 23-2 Examples of the HDG/TAS vector.

The Effect of Wind

Figure 23-3 Examples of W/V vector.

The general movement of air relative to the ground is called *wind vector* and is abbreviated to *W/V*. Like HDG/TAS, W/V is a *vector* quantity because both direction and magnitude are specified. By convention, the wind direction is expressed as the direction *from* which it is blowing. For example, a northerly wind blows from the north toward the south. W/V is symbolized by a triple-headed arrow.

With a W/V of 230/20, the air mass will be moving relative to the earth's surface from a direction of 230 degrees at a rate of 20 NM per hour. In a 6 minute period, for example, the air mass will have moved 2 NM (6 minutes = ¹⁄₁₀ hour; ¹⁄₁₀ of 20 NM = 2 NM) from a direction of 230 degrees (and therefore toward 230 − 180 = 050 degrees).

The motion of the airplane relative to the surface of the earth is made up of two velocities: the airplane moving relative to the air mass (HDG/TAS); and the air mass moving relative to the surface of the earth (W/V). Adding these two vectors together gives the resultant vector of the airplane moving relative to the surface of the earth. This is the track and groundspeed (TR/GS), which is symbolized by a double headed arrow. The angle between the HDG and the actual ground track (TR) is called the *drift angle*.

An airplane flying through an air mass is in a similar situation to a swimmer crossing a fast-flowing river. If you dive in at position A and head off through the water in the direction of B, the current will carry you downstream toward C. To an observer sitting overhead on a tree branch, you will appear to be swimming a little bit sideways as you get swept downstream, even though in fact you are swimming straight through the water.

Careful! Surface wind velocities are usually reported in statute miles per hour, not knots.

In the same way, it is quite common to look up and see an airplane flying somewhat sideways in strong-wind situations. Of course the airplane is not actually flying sideways through the air, rather it is flying straight ahead relative to the air mass and it is the wind velocity (W/V) which, when added to the airplane's motion through the air (HDG/TAS), gives it the resultant motion over the ground (TR/GS).

These three vectors form what is known as the *triangle of velocities*. It is a pictorial representation of the vector addition: HDG/TAS + W/V = TR/GS.

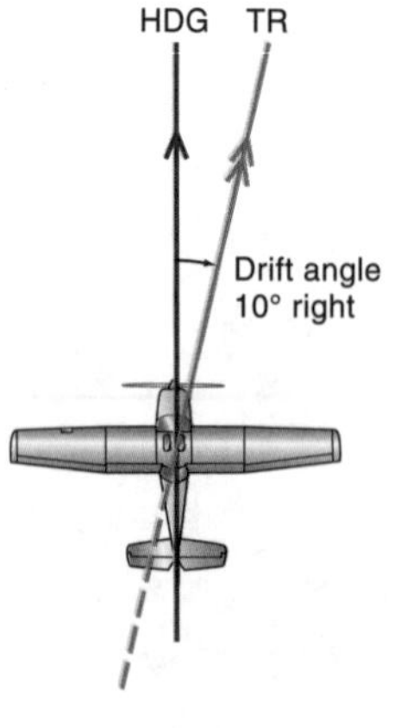

Figure 23-4 Drift is the angle between heading and ground track.

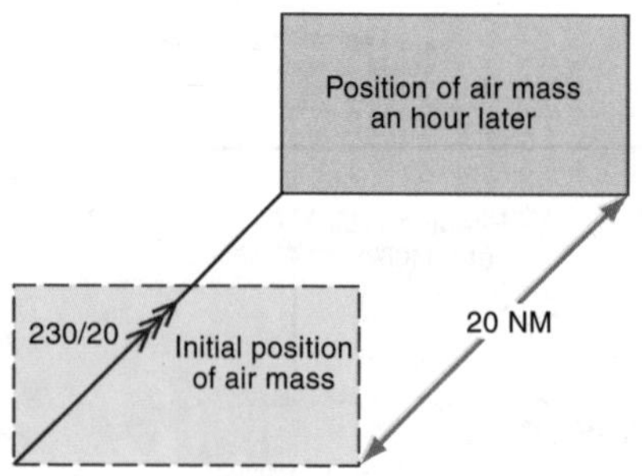

Figure 23-5 A wind of 230/20.

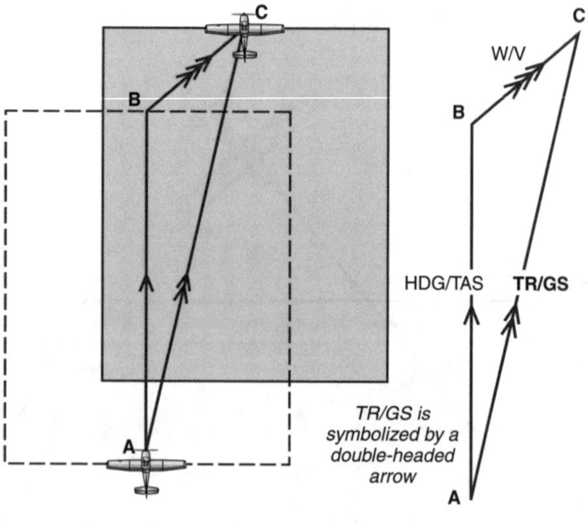

Figure 23-6 HDG/TAS + W/V = TR/GS— the triangle of velocities.

Achieving the Desired Course (CRS)

Apply a wind correction angle (WCA) to counteract drift, and thereby achieve the desired course.

Your objective during visual navigation is to steer a heading so that the *track* made good over the ground exactly overlies the desired *course*. At the flight planning stage you will know the desired course (also known as course required) and will have obtained a forecast wind velocity. Using the planned true airspeed, you will be able to calculate the *heading* required to "make good" the desired course by applying a *wind correction angle* (WCA) into the wind to counteract drift. You will also be able to calculate the expected groundspeed.

Later on during the flight you may find that, even though you have flown the HDG/TAS accurately, your *actual* ground track differs from the *desired* course; in other words there is a *tracking error*. This error could be specified as either distance off-course, or degrees off-course. The tracking error is most likely caused by the *actual* wind being different from the *forecast* wind that you used at the flight planning stage. You will then have to make adjustments to the HDG in order to achieve your desired course.

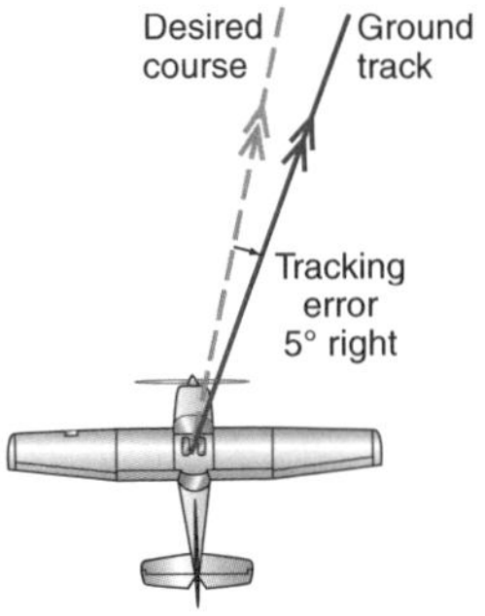

Figure 23-7 Tracking error is the angle between desired course and actual track.

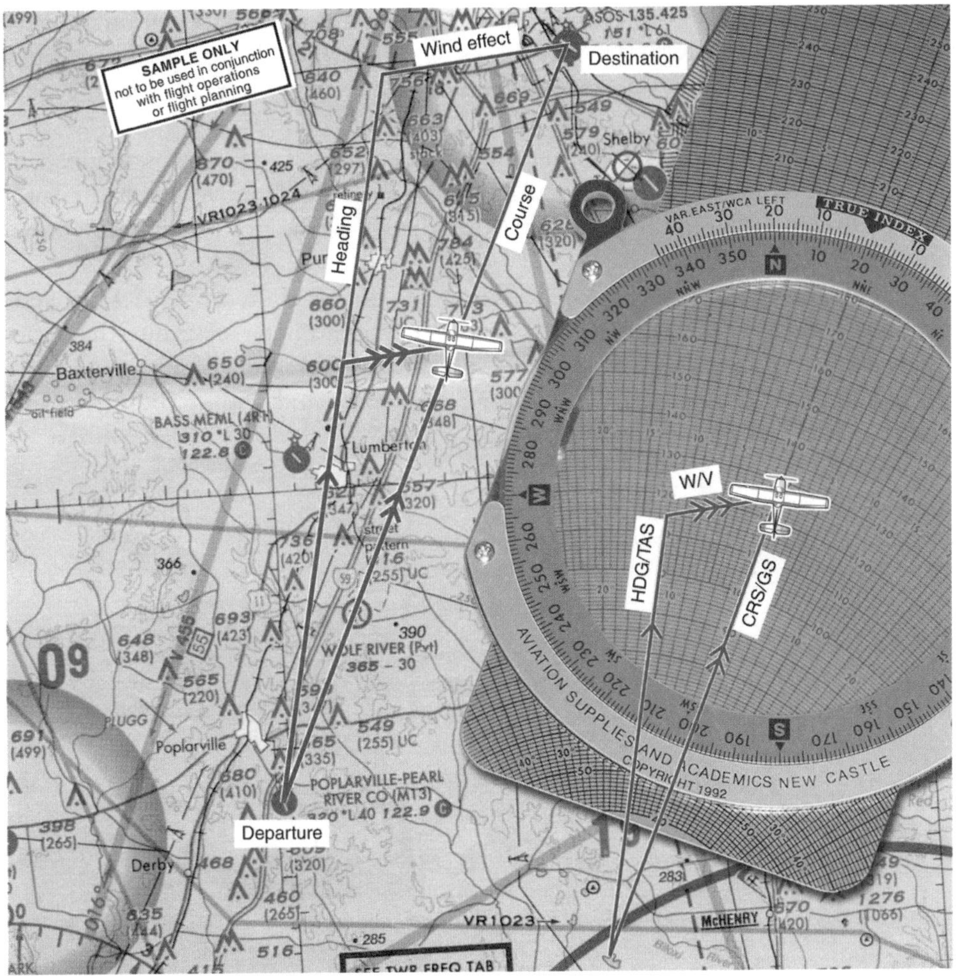

Figure 23-8 The triangle of velocities—calculating a heading to achieve the desired course.

Vertical Navigation

Navigating an airplane requires three-dimensional awareness. Correct vertical navigation using the altimeter is important for three basic reasons:

- for *terrain clearance*, to ensure that you will not collide with terrain or fixed obstacles on the ground;
- for *traffic separation*, to allow you to cruise at an altitude different from that of nearby aircraft, and so to ensure safe vertical separation; and
- to be able to calculate the *performance capabilities* of the aircraft and its engine, so as to operate safely and efficiently.

For aviation purposes, the standard unit of altitude is the *foot* in the United States and the western world. In other parts of the world, such as Eastern Europe and some of Asia, the unit used is the *meter*.

Terrain elevation is given as altitude in feet above mean sea level (MSL).

On maps and charts in the United States the altitude of terrain is given as altitude in feet above mean sea level (MSL). It is therefore essential that you know the aircraft's altitude above mean sea level so that you can compare this with the altitude of any terrain or obstructions and determine if there is sufficient vertical separation. Normally you would plan on at least 500 feet vertical separation when flying over open country, and at least 1,000 feet over congested and mountainous areas. Most cross-country flights occur much higher than this.

Mean sea level pressure varies from place-to-place, from day-to-day, and indeed from hour-to-hour, as the various high and low pressure systems move across the surface of the earth. This will require you to periodically adjust the pressure window in your altimeter.

Periodically update the altimeter setting.

Flying cross-country below 18,000 feet MSL in the United States, you need to periodically update the altimeter setting so that the altimeter continues to indicate altitude based on the *current* sea level pressure in that area. You should use a current reported altimeter setting of a station along your route and within 100 NM of your position (Part 91 of the regulations).

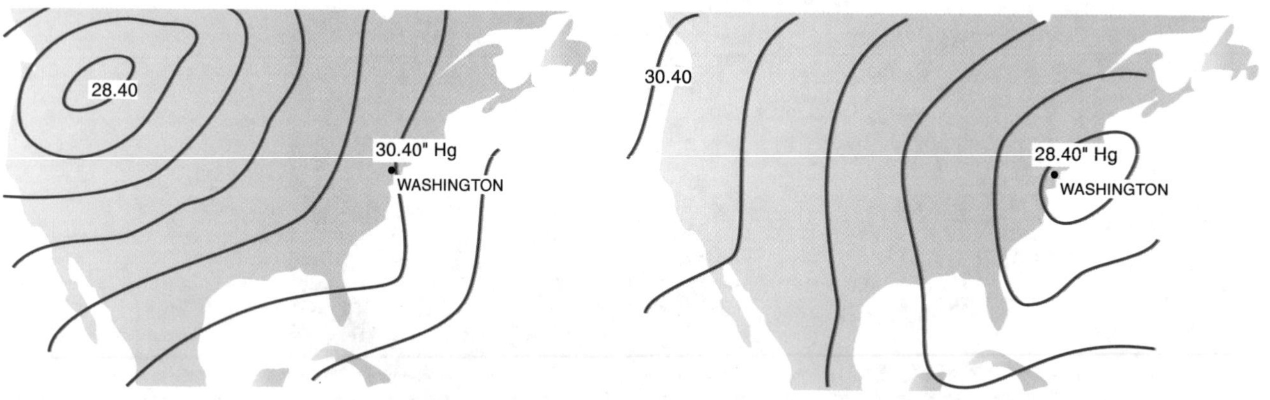

Figure 23-9 Two different synoptic situations at different times.

Flying higher than 18,000 feet MSL, separation from terrain is not a problem in the United States. All aircraft above 18,000 feet should be operating on standard pressure (29.92 in. Hg) so that their altimeters are all measuring altitude above the same datum. This will ensure vertical separation from other high-flying aircraft. An indication of 23,000 feet on the altimeter with 29.92 in. Hg set is called *flight level* 230, abbreviated as FL230.

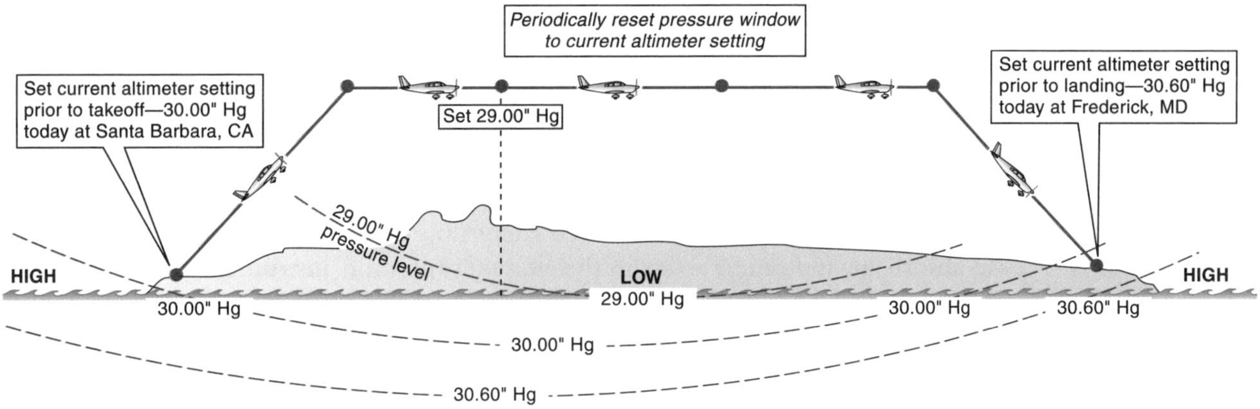

Figure 23-10 Periodically reset current reported altimeter setting.

VFR Cruise Altitude

To separate different types of traffic, Part 91 specifies that aircraft flying higher than 3,000 feet above the surface (AGL) according to the Visual Flight Rules (VFR) should cruise at "full thousands plus 500 feet."

To vertically separate VFR aircraft flying in opposing directions, VFR cruise altitudes are specified according to the direction in which they are flying:

- on a magnetic course of magnetic north to MC 179: *odds+500 feet* (for example 3,500 feet MSL, 5,500 feet MSL, 7,500 feet MSL); and
- on a magnetic course of MC 180 to MC 359: *evens+500 feet* (for example 4,500 feet MSL, 6,500 feet MSL, 8,500 feet MSL).

IFR traffic is operating at even and odd thousands, 500 feet above or below VFR traffic.

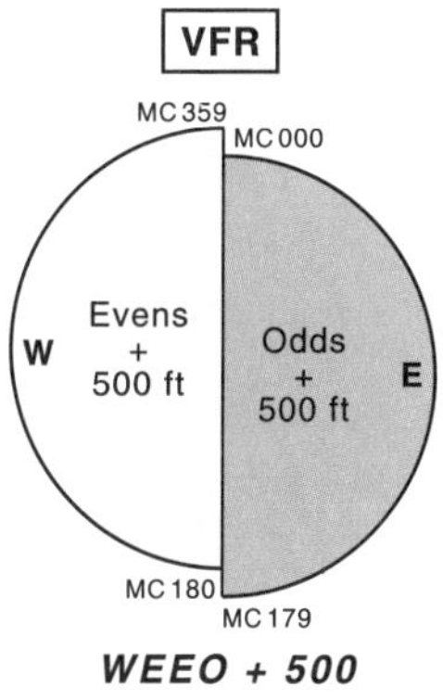

Figure 23-11
VFR cruise altitudes above 3,000 feet AGL.

Safety Altitude

Part 91 specifies *minimum safe altitudes* (MSA) which you must comply with. They are a minimum of 500 feet above the surface in noncongested areas, 1,000 feet above the highest obstacle within a 2,000 feet radius in congested and mountainous areas, and sufficient altitude to glide clear if an engine fails.

Where possible on cross-country operations, choose a suitable cruise level above these minimums that will ensure adequate terrain clearance and vertical separation from other aircraft. A suitable technique is to determine a *safety altitude* which will ensure adequate terrain clearance, then select an appropriate cruise level above this safety altitude according to your magnetic course.

Note. In certain circumstances it may not always be possible to cruise above the calculated safety altitude, for example due to overlying controlled airspace around a major airport. In such cases, extra care to avoid terrain and obstructions should be taken, particularly in minimum visibility, until it is possible to climb above the safety altitude.

To determine a safety altitude determine the highest obstacle en route to a set amount either side of course, then add a safety clearance altitude above this.

There are no hard and fast rules as to how far either side of course you should scrutinize, or how high above obstacles you should fly. Reasonable values are 1,000 feet or 1,500 feet above the highest obstacle within 5 NM or 10 NM either side of course. This allows for navigation errors. Over long distances or mountainous areas, 15 or 20 NM might be more appropriate.

To assist you in determining the highest obstacle, it is a good idea to mark in lines 5 NM (or 10 NM) either side of course. Another approach to finding a reasonable buffer is to add 10% to the elevation of the highest obstacle en route plus a further 1,500 feet.

If you remain above your calculated safety altitude, there should be sufficient buffer to absorb any indication errors in the altimeter (position, instrument and temperature errors) and to stay out of any turbulent areas near the ground, where a downdraft or windshear could be dangerous. In certain circumstances (such as in standing waves downwind of mountain ridges), it may be advisable to add more vertical clearance than usual to give sufficient safety margin.

Example 23-1

Elevation of the highest obstacle within 5 NM of course is 438 feet MSL. A reasonable safety altitude in good conditions would be 438 + 1,000 feet = 1,438 feet. If the highest obstacle within 10 NM of course is 798 feet, and you wish to be more conservative, then a reasonable safety altitude would be 798 + 1,000 = 1,798 feet. Because these are below 3,000 feet AGL, you do not need to apply the *WEEO + 500* rule.

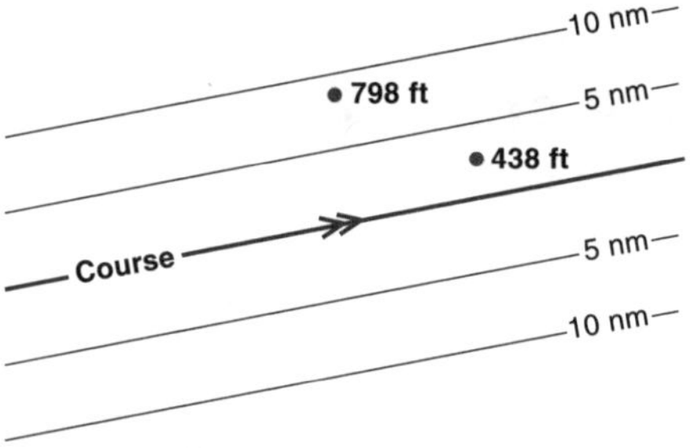

Figure 23-12 Example 23-1.

Example 23-2

Calculate a conservative safety altitude above an obstacle 2,117 feet MSL.

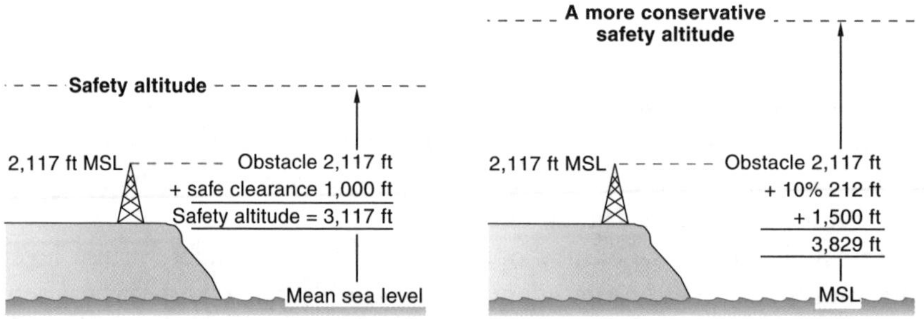

Figure 23-13 Example 23-2 using 1,000 feet clearance and using 10% plus 1,500 feet.

Time

Time is of great importance to the air navigator, and the clock is one of the basic instruments used in the cockpit. Time enables you to:

- regulate affairs on board your airplane;
- measure the progress of your flight;
- compute arrival time (ETA) at certain positions;
- calculate a safe endurance for flight and manage fuel consumption;
- estimate when weather conditions at the destination are likely to improve or get worse; and
- measure rest periods between flights.

For flight planning and navigation purposes we usually do not refer to the year or the month, but only the *day* of the month as the *date*, followed by the *time* in *hours and minutes*. As most air navigation occurs within a few hours, and only rarely in excess of 30 hours, we can be reasonably confident of which year and month we are talking about, and so there is no need to specify them. Seconds, which are 1⁄60 of a minute, are usually too short a time interval for us to be concerned with in practical navigation. It is usual to express date/time as a six-figure date/time group.

In the six-figure date/time group:

- the *date* is a two-figure group for the day of the month from 00 to 31; and is followed by
- the *time*, written as a four-figure group on a 24 hour clock—the first two figures representing the hours from 00 to 24, and the last two figures representing the minutes from 00 through to 59.

Example 23-3

Express September 13, 10:35 a.m. as a six-figure date/time group. (*Answer:* 131035.)

Date	Time	
13	10	35
day	hour	minute

Example 23-4

Express 3:21 p.m. on March 17, as a six-figure date/time group. (*Answer:* 171521.)

3:21 p.m. = 1200
+ 321
1521 on the 24 hour clock

In the eight-figure date/time group, to specify the *month,* the six-figure date/time group is preceded by two figures representing the month, and so is expanded into an eight figure time-group. This is often used in NOTAMs (Notices to Airmen):

- the first two numbers refer to month;
- the second two numbers refer to the date; and
- the last four numbers refer to the time.

Example 23-5

5:45 p.m. on September 30 may be written as:

- SEP 30 17 45;
- 09 30 17 45; or
- 09301745.

The Relationship Between Longitude and Time

In one day, the earth makes about one complete rotation of 360° with respect to the chosen celestial body, which is the sun. The time of day is a measure of this rotation and indicates how much of that day has elapsed or, in other words, how much of a rotation has been completed.

As observers on the earth, we do not feel its rotation about its own axis, but rather we see the sun apparently move around the earth. In one mean solar day the sun will appear to have traveled the full 360° of longitude around the earth. 360° of longitude in 24 hours is equivalent to *15° per hour.*

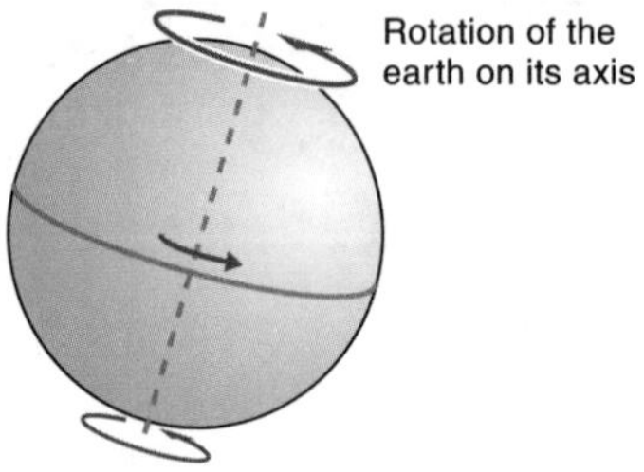

Figure 23-14
The earth rotates at 15° of longitude per hour.

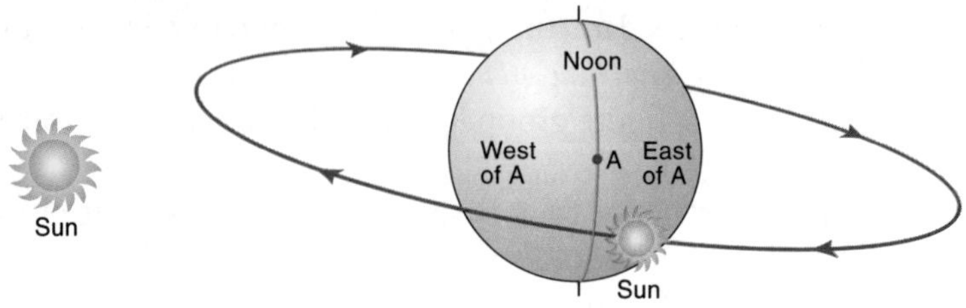

Figure 23-15
The apparent motion of the sun around the earth.

Local Time

Meridians of longitude further east are ahead in local time; meridians of longitude further west are behind in local time.

Time is a measure of the rotation of the earth, and any given time interval can be represented by a corresponding angle through which the earth turns. Suppose that the sun (the celestial reference point) is directly overhead at noon. For every point along that same meridian of longitude, the sun will be at its highest point in the sky for that day.

Example 23-6

Place A is 45° of longitude west of Place B. How much earlier or later will noon occur at A compared to B?

Answer: At the rate of 15° per hour, 45° arc of longitude = 3 hours, and because A is to the west of B, noon will occur three hours later at A.

Coordinated Universal Time (UTC)

Longitude east—Universal least; Longitude west—Universal best.

UTC is the local mean time at the 0° meridian of longitude that runs through the observatory at Greenwich, England, and is known as the *prime meridian.* Until recently the international time standard was the well known *Greenwich Mean Time* (GMT). This term has now been replaced by *Coordinated Universal Time* (UTC), which is also known as *Zulu* (Z). UTC is a universal time, and all aeronautical communications around the world are expressed in UTC. For this reason, you need to be able to convert quickly and accurately from local time to UTC, and vice versa. UTC is approximately equal to the old GMT.

Standard or Local Time

Standard times operate in a similar fashion to time zones in that all clocks in a given geographical area are set to the local mean time of a given standard meridian. This is known as *standard time* or *local time* for that area. When involved in flights between different time zones, it is easiest to work entirely in UTC and convert the answer at the end.

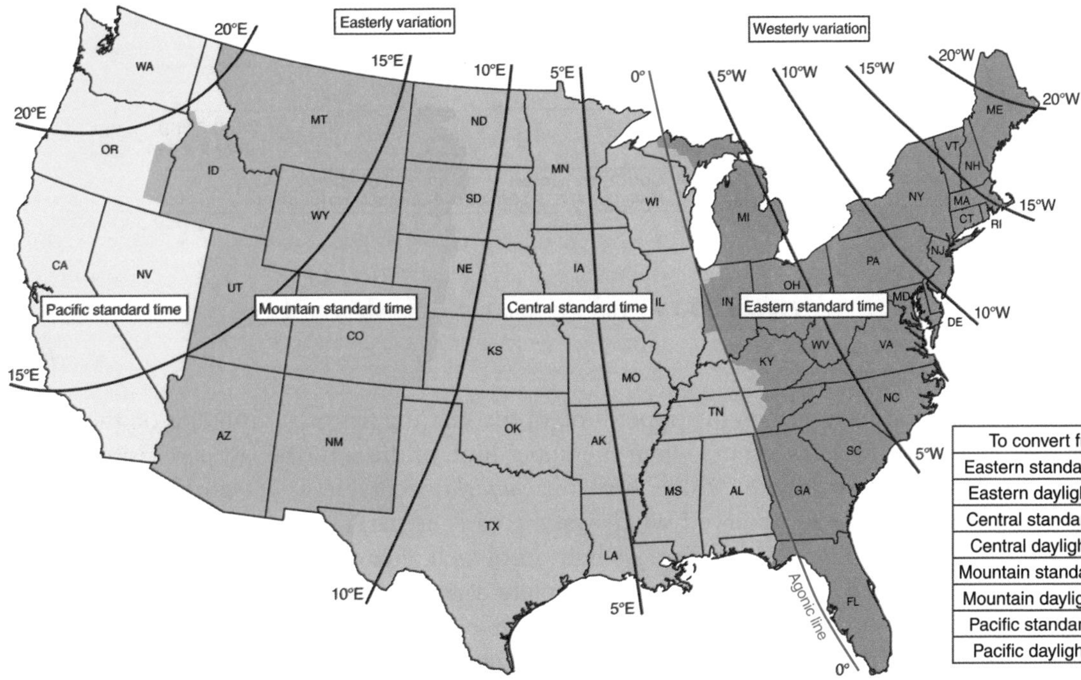

To convert from	To UTC
Eastern standard time	add 5 hours
Eastern daylight time	add 4 hours
Central standard time	add 6 hours
Central daylight time	add 5 hours
Mountain standard time	add 7 hours
Mountain daylight time	add 6 hours
Pacific standard time	add 8 hours
Pacific daylight time	add 7 hours

Figure 23-16 U.S. time zones and conversion table.

Example 23-7

You depart New York, NY at 0945 Eastern Standard Time on a flight of 6 hours 10 minutes duration to Denver, Colorado. At what time should your friends meet you in Denver?

Depart NY	09 45	EST
	+5	
	14 45	UTC
Flight time	6 10	
Arrive Denver	20 55	UTC
	−7	
	13 55	MST

Answer: 1355 Mountain Standard Time.

Light from the Sun

The sun's rays strike different parts of the earth at different angles depending on latitude and season.

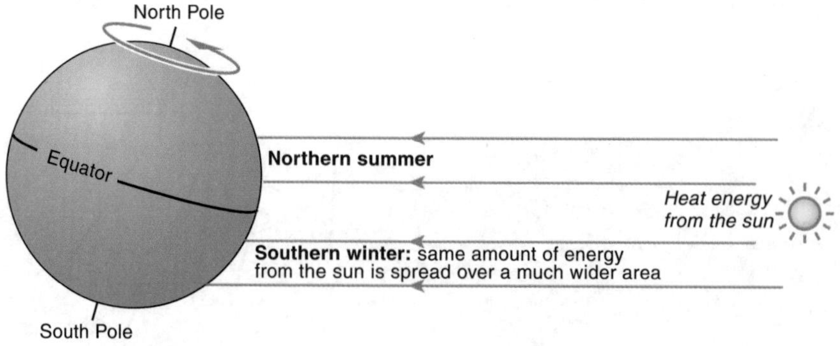

Figure 23-17 The sun does not shine evenly on the earth.

Sunrise occurs when the upper limb of the sun (the first part visible) is on the visible horizon and *sunset* occurs when the upper limb of the sun (the last part visible) is just disappearing below the visible horizon. *Sunlight* occurs between sunrise and sunset.

As we have all observed when waking early, it starts to become light well before the sun actually rises, and it stays light until well after the sun has set. This period of incomplete light, or if you like, incomplete darkness, is called *twilight.* Civil twilight is when the sun is 6° below the horizon. While the sun is less than 6° below the horizon, there is generally enough light to see significant objects on the ground, unless the overcast is heavy. Civil twilight is generally considered the end (evening) or beginning (morning) of when there is enough light to land on an unlit airstrip.

The period from the start of morning twilight until the end of evening twilight is called *daylight.* In the tropics the sun rises and sets at almost 90° to the horizon, which makes the period of twilight quite short, and the onset of daylight or night quite dramatically rapid.

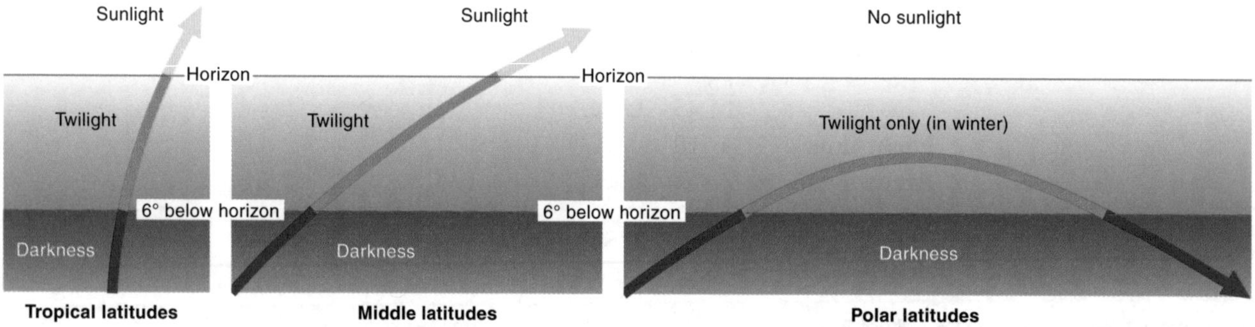

Figure 23-18 The higher the latitude, the longer the twilight.

In the higher latitudes, toward the North and South Poles, the sun rises and sets at a more oblique angle to the horizon, consequently the period of twilight is much longer and the onset of daylight or darkness far more gradual than in the tropics. At certain times of the year inside the Arctic and Antarctic Circles, the period of twilight occurs without the sun actually rising above the horizon at all during the day. This is the winter situation.

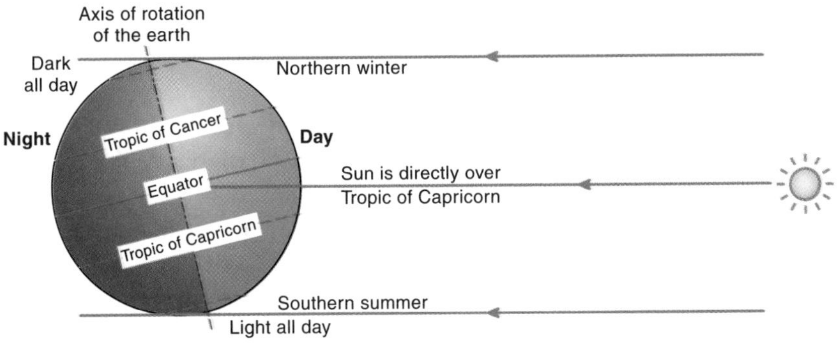

Figure 23-19 The sun does not shine evenly on the earth.

While to an observer at sea level the sun may appear to have set and the earth is no longer bathed in sunlight, an airplane directly overhead may still have the sun shining on it. In other words, the time at which the sun rises or sets will depend on the altitude of the observer. In fact, it is possible to take off after sunset at ground level and climb to an altitude where the sun appears to rise again and shine a little longer on the airplane. This is especially noticeable in polar regions when the sun might be just below the horizon, as seen from sea level, for long periods of time (twilight).

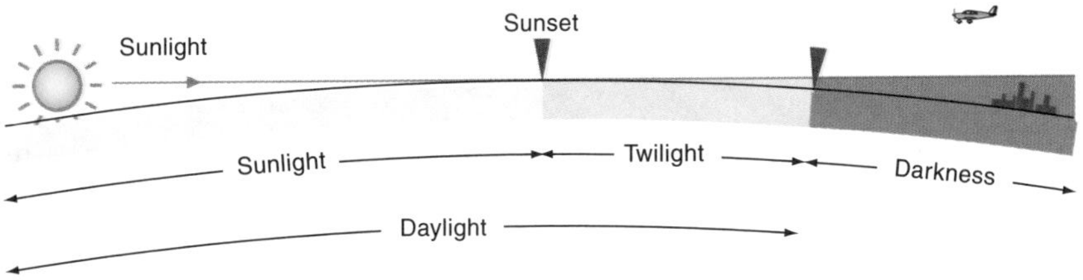

Figure 23-20 An airplane can be in sight of the sun after it has set on the earth below.

It is easy to be deceived by brightness at altitude only to find a few minutes later after a descent to near ground level, and possibly under some cloud cover, that it has become very dark. High ground to the west of an airport will also reduce the amount of light from the sun reaching the vicinity of the airport as night approaches (an important point to remember when flying). Good airmanship may dictate using an earlier arrival time than the end of daylight when planning a flight, if, for example, the destination airport has high ground to the west, or the weather forecast indicates poor visibility or cloud cover approaching from the west, as in a cold front. Another important consideration related to sunset is that many smaller airports close at sunset. This may also apply to the alternate airport(s) chosen for a flight.

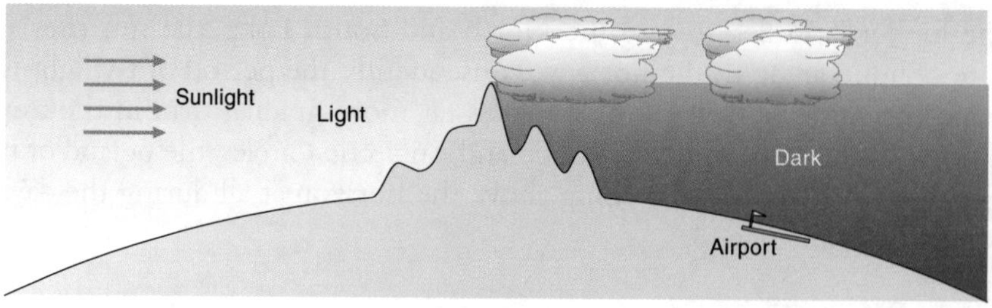

Figure 23-21 Local sunrise and sunset is affected by terrain.

The times at which sunrise and sunset occur depend on two things:

- the *date*—in summer sunrise is earlier and sunset later, therefore the daylight hours are longer in summer. The reverse occurs in winter; and
- the *latitude*—in the northern summer for instance, place B in the figure below is experiencing sunrise while place A is already well into the day, and it is still night at place C, yet all are on the same meridian of longitude. Because of this they all have the same local time, but are experiencing quite different conditions of daylight because they are on different latitudes.

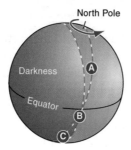

Figure 23-22 Places A, B & C, although on the same meridian, experience different sunrise and sunset times because they are on different latitudes.

The official source in the United States for times including sunrise, sunset, and beginning and end of daylight is the *Air Almanac.*

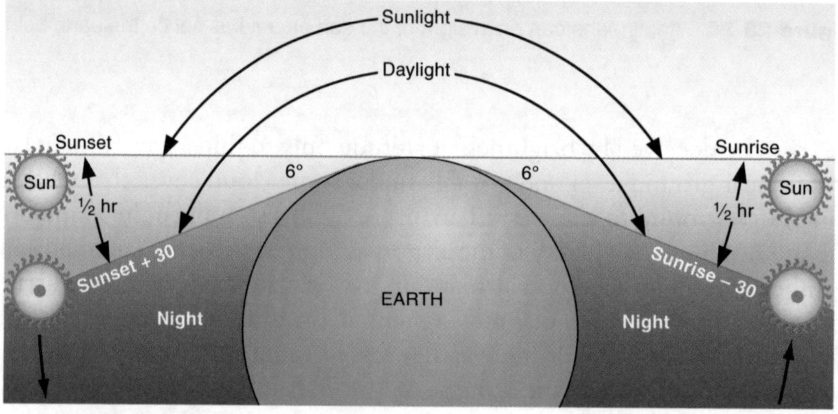

Figure 23-23 In the United States, official night commences at sunset approximately +30 minutes and night ends at sunrise approximately –30 minutes.

Daylight Time

To take advantage of the longer daylight hours and the better weather in summer, the clocks in many countries are put forward in the spring, usually by one hour, to give a new standard time known as *daylight time*. For example, in New York, 1200 EST becomes 1300 Eastern Daylight Time.

Spring, (clocks) forward. Fall, (clocks) back.

Make allowances for these when planning a flight that may end near the onset of darkness. It is good airmanship to plan on arriving well before the end of daylight. Common sense would encourage you to increase this margin on long journeys or on flights where it is difficult to estimate accurately your time of arrival. Remember also that the further south you are in the United States the shorter the twilight time.

The Dateline

Suppose that the time at the Greenwich meridian is 261200 (261200 UTC). Now, if you instantaneously travel *eastward* from Greenwich to the 180° east meridian, the local mean time there is 12 hours ahead of the local mean time at Greenwich, that is 262400 local mean time at 180°E, or midnight on the 26th local mean time at 180°E. If, however, you travel *westward* from Greenwich to the 180° west meridian, then the time there is 12 hours behind Greenwich, 260000 or, as it is usually written, 252400 at 180°W, midnight on the 25th. Note that the time is midnight in both cases but, on one side of the 180° meridian it is midnight on the 25th, and on the other side it is midnight on the 26th.

The 180°E and 180°W meridians are the same meridian, the anti-meridian to Greenwich. In its vicinity, midnight occurs on different dates, depending on which side of the 180° meridian you are on. Making a complete instantaneous trip around the world, you would lose a day traveling westward or gain a day traveling eastward.

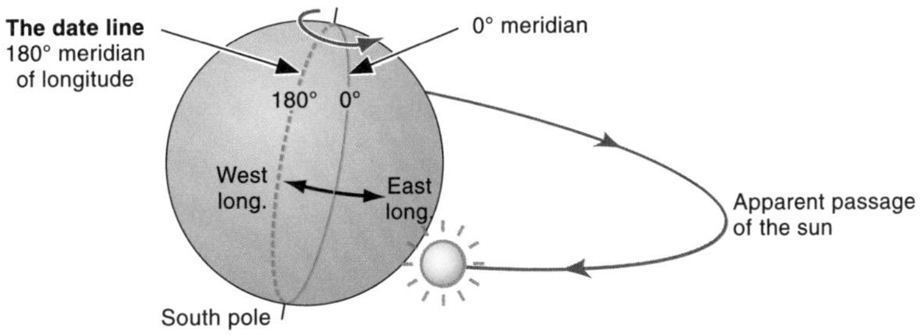

Figure 23-24 The dateline runs basically along the 180° meridian.

To prevent the date being in error and to provide a starting point for each day, a *dateline* has been fixed by international agreement, and it basically follows the 180° meridian of longitude, with minor excursions to keep groups of islands together. Crossing the dateline, you alter the date by one day—in effect changing your time by 24 hours to compensate for the slow change during your journey around the world.

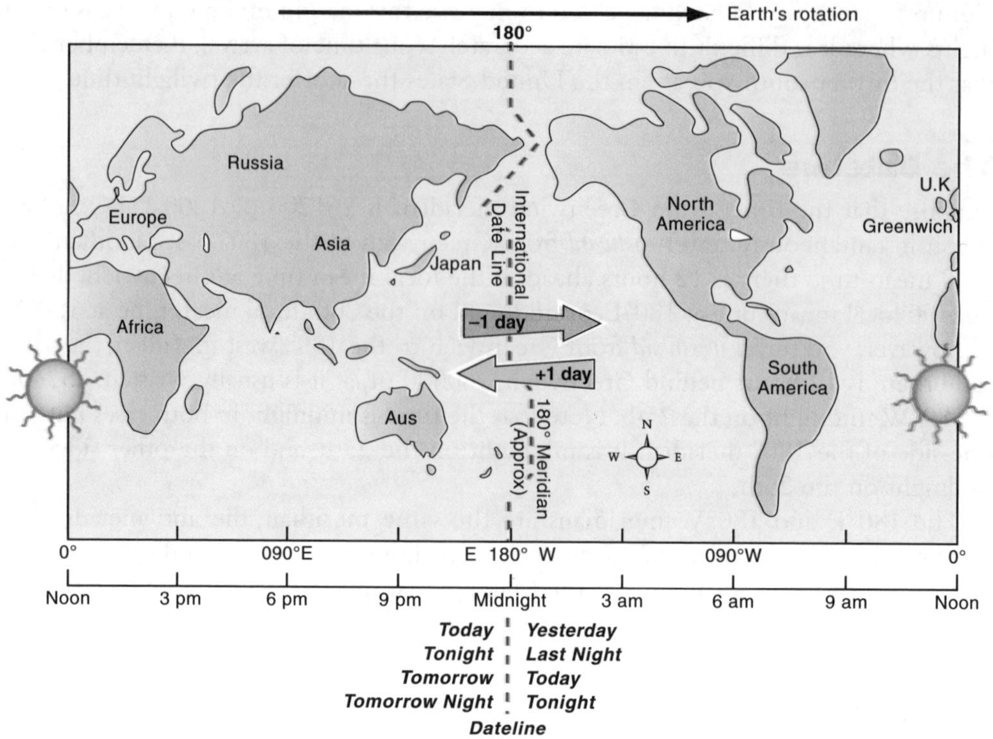

Figure 23-25 Crossing the dateline traveling eastward—subtract one day; traveling westward—add one day.

Review 23
Visual Navigation Fundamentals

Navigation

1. What is distance stated in for most navigation purposes?
2. What is the usual navigation unit for airspeed? (State how many nautical miles per hour this is equivalent to.)
3. What is the accepted unit of length for shorter distances, such as runway length?
4. What is the accepted unit for altitude?
5. How many feet are there in 1 nautical mile?
6. As a simple method of expressing direction, we divide a full circle into 360 degrees and number them from 000 through 090, 180, 270 to 360. Is this in a clockwise direction?
7. Define "true airspeed (TAS)."
8. What two things need to be specified in order to fully describe the motion of an airplane relative to an air mass?
9. How is the *heading/true airspeed* vector symbolized?
10. Define the following:
    - **a.** wind.
    - **b.** wind direction.
    - **c.** groundspeed.
    - **d.** heading.
    - **e.** track.
    - **f.** drift.
    - **g.** tracking error.

Refer to figure 23-26 for questions 11 and 12.

11. What is the shaded angle known as?
12. The drift in this figure is:
    - **a.** left.
    - **b.** right.

Refer to figure 23-27 for questions 13 and 14.

13. What is the shaded angle known as?
14. The tracking error in this figure is:
    - **a.** left.
    - **b.** right.

Refer to figure 23-28 for questions 15 and 16.

15. Label the vectors A and B and the angle D with their appropriate navigation terms.
16. Which statement best fits the situation in this figure?
    - **a.** TAS exceeds GS.
    - **b.** GS exceeds TAS.
    - **c.** Drift is left.
17. The earth rotates on its axis. What are the two points at which this axis meets the earth's surface?

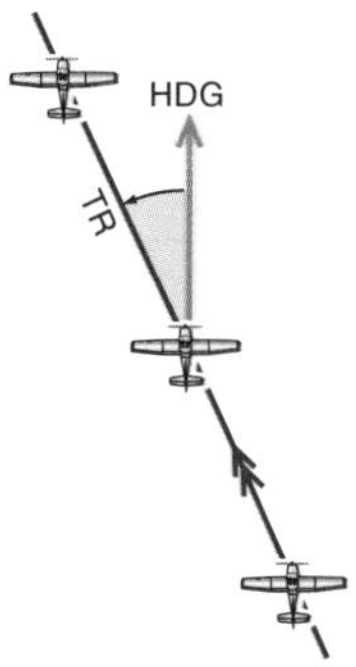

Figure 23-26 Questions 11 and 12.

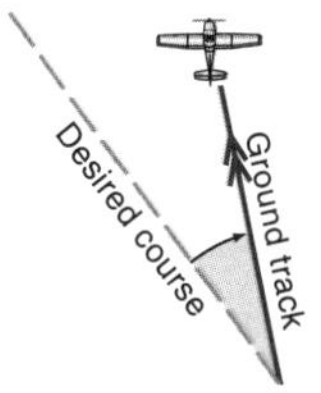

Figure 23-27 Questions 13 and 14.

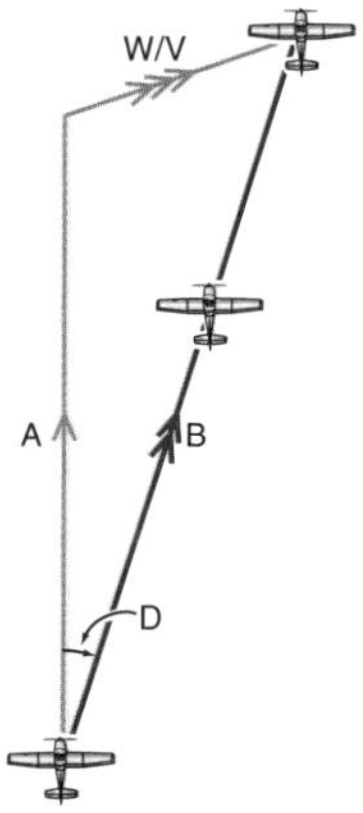

Figure 23-28 Questions 15 and 16.

Time

18. Express the following dates and times as a six-figure date/time group and as an eight-figure date/time group:
    - **a.** November 29, 10:15 a.m.
    - **b.** July 19, 3:17 p.m.
    - **c.** April 1, 5 p.m.
19. Convert the following time intervals to arc units:
    - **a.** 1 hour.
    - **b.** 9 hours 30 minutes.

20. It's 1200 Pacific Standard Time in Los Angeles. What time is it in New York? (Give your answer in both UTC and Eastern Standard Time.)

21. It's 0500 Mountain Daylight Time in Denver. What time is it in San Francisco? (Give your answer in Zulu and Pacific Daylight Time.)

Refer to figure 23-29 for questions 22 and 23.

22. An aircraft departs an airport in the central standard time zone at 0930 CST for a 2-hour flight to an airport located in the Mountain Standard Time zone. The landing should be at what time?

23. An aircraft departs an airport in the eastern daylight time zone at 0945 EDT for a 2-hour flight to an airport located in the Central Daylight Time zone. The landing should be at what coordinated universal time?

24. Convert 150° of arc to time.

25. You depart Santa Barbara, California at 0600 Pacific Standard Time for a 5 hour 30 minute flight to Denver, Colorado. What time do you expect to arrive? (Give your answer in UTC and MST.)

26. True or false? Traveling eastward across the dateline from Hong Kong to Hawaii, you would expect to gain 1 day.

27. What is the official source of sunrise and sunset times?

28. True or false? High ground to the west of an airport causes an earlier onset of darkness.

29. What two things do sunrise and sunset times vary with respect to?

30. For Daylight Time, clocks are advanced by how many hours?

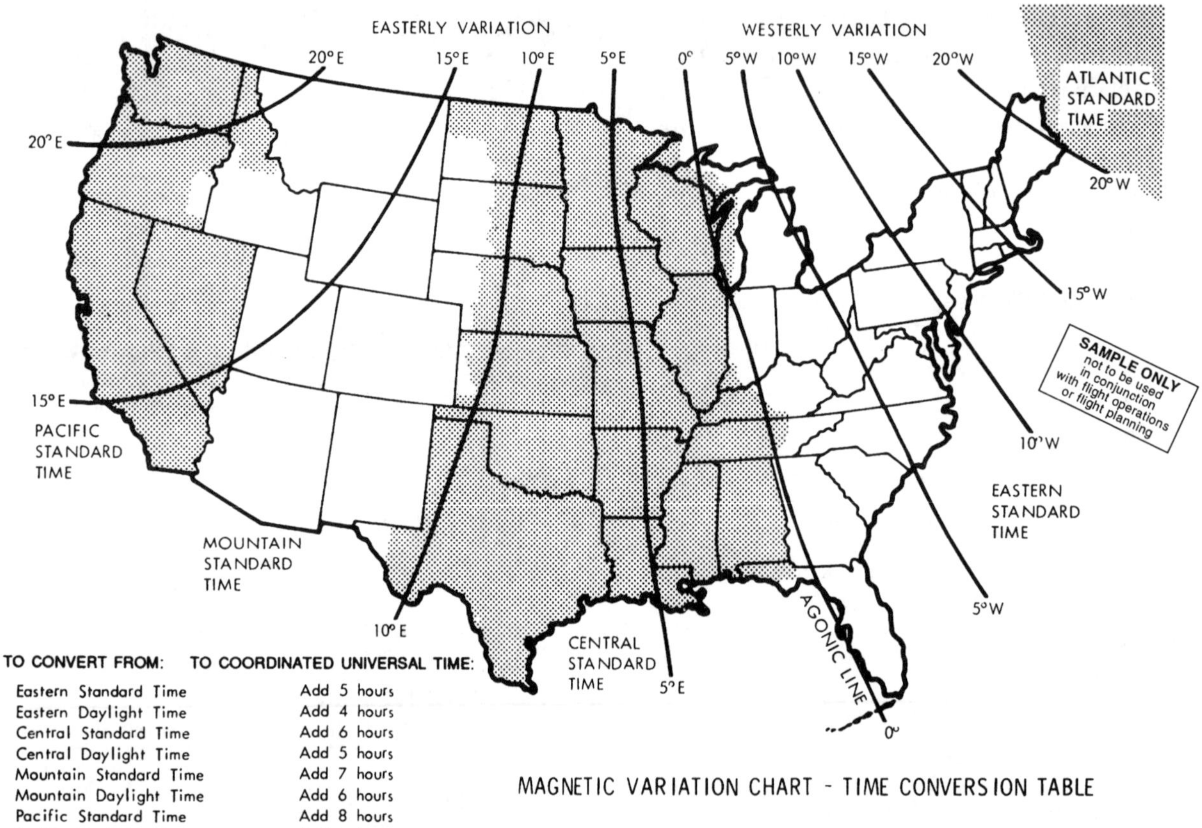

TO CONVERT FROM:	TO COORDINATED UNIVERSAL TIME:
Eastern Standard Time	Add 5 hours
Eastern Daylight Time	Add 4 hours
Central Standard Time	Add 6 hours
Central Daylight Time	Add 5 hours
Mountain Standard Time	Add 7 hours
Mountain Daylight Time	Add 6 hours
Pacific Standard Time	Add 8 hours
Pacific Daylight Time	Add 7 hours

Figure 23-29 Time conversion table.

Answers are given on page 705.

Using the Flight Computer 24

General Description

The mechanical flight computer is a wonderful invention that vastly simplifies navigation tasks. It consists of two circular sheets of metal or card through the center of which passes a movable grid. The flight computer has two sides:

- a *calculator side*—used for speed–distance–time–fuel computations (and many others); and
- a *wind side*—used to calculate headings to steer and groundspeeds resulting from the effect of any wind that is blowing.

A flight computer has a calculator side and a wind side.

The Calculator Side of the Flight Computer

The calculator side of the flight computer consists of two circular discs riveted together at the center so that the smaller top disc can rotate over the larger bottom disc. It may look complicated at first but you will soon become familiar with it.

The calculator side of a flight computer is used for simple math calculations.

The *outer* scale on the bottom disc and the *inner* scale on the top disc are used to represent speed, distance, fuel or other units. Although the scales are only numbered from 10 to 99, they can easily be used for any number. For example, "17" can stand for 0.17, 1.7, 17 or 170. In addition the spacing of the numbers is not equal. This causes you no problems except that you must be careful using the graduations. For example, the first graduations past 11, 30 and 70 are 11.1, 30.5 and 71 respectively.

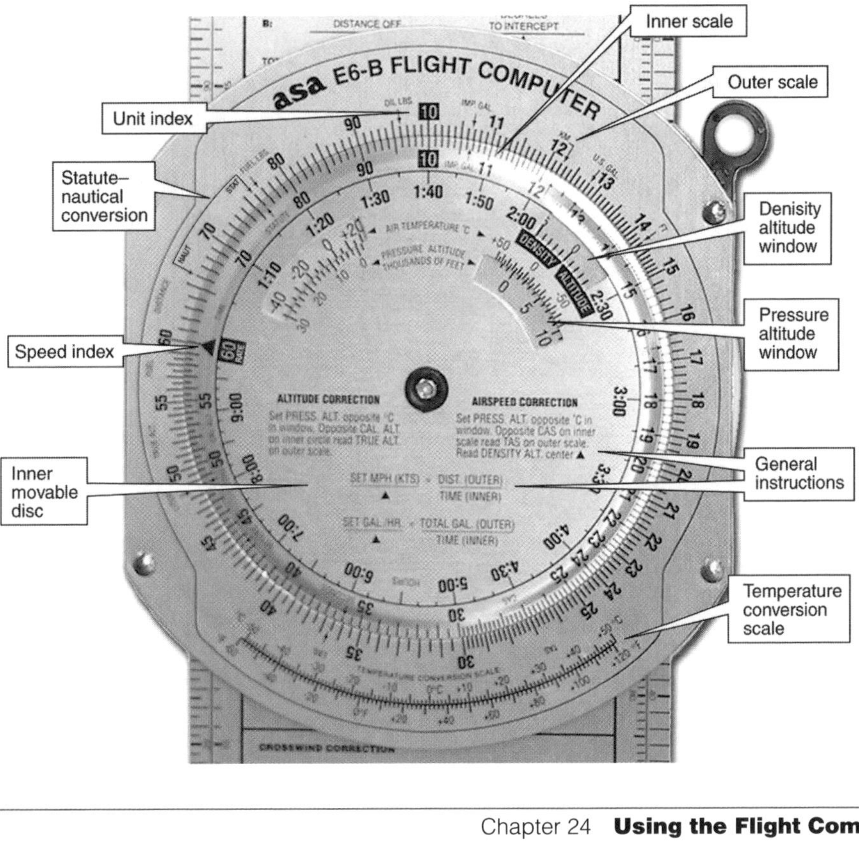

Figure 24-1
Calculator side of a typical flight computer.

The Wind Side of the Flight Computer

The wind side of a flight computer is used for 'triangle of velocities' navigation calculations.

The wind side of the flight computer allows you to handle navigation problems involving the *triangle of velocities* in a quick and accurate manner.

Components of the wind side are:

- circular, rotatable *compass rose* (or azimuth circle) set in a fixed frame which is marked with an *index* at the top;
- a transparent plastic *plotting disc* attached to the rotatable compass rose, marked with a *grommet* in the center and
- a *sliding grid* marked with radial lines which can be used to determine the *wind correction angle* (WCA). This plate slides through the frame and compass rose assembly, hence the term "slide" flight computer which is often used to refer to this type.

At higher altitudes, true airspeed (TAS) is greater than indicated airspeed (IAS).

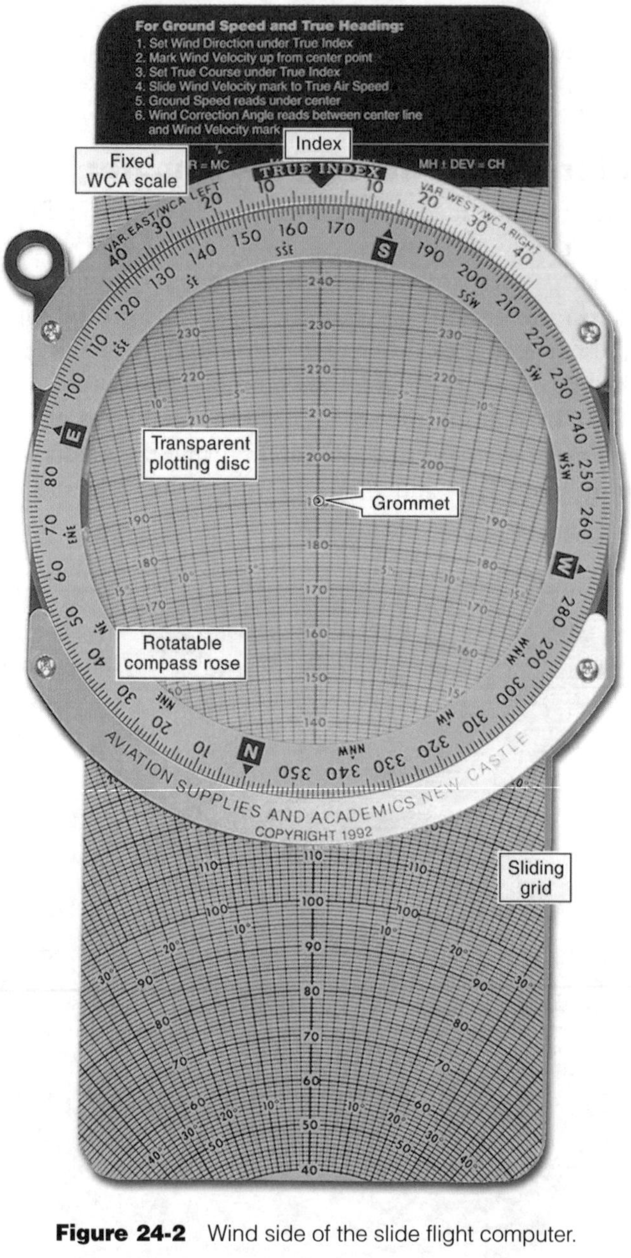

Figure 24-2 Wind side of the slide flight computer.

The Flight Computer and Flight Planning

The main use of the flight computer is for *flight planning*. You will know:

- the *planned course* and *ground distance* from the chart;
- the planned *indicated airspeed* (IAS) and *cruising altitude*; and
- the *forecast wind* and forecast *temperature* at cruise altitude.

You will want to find (in order):

- the *true airspeed* (TAS);
- the *heading* required to "make good" the required course; and
- the expected *groundspeed*, so that you can calculate the *time* en route and *fuel* requirements.

The following pages explain and demonstrate how you will do this using examples. Starting on page 564, we show that the flight computer is also very useful for conversions, such as nautical miles to statute miles and °F to °C.

Finding TAS

When flying en route you will fly at a certain IAS which you can read directly off the airspeed indicator. However from chapter 1 we know that IAS is related to dynamic pressure ($\frac{1}{2}\rho V^2$), which varies with both speed and air density. Therefore when an airplane climbs, to maintain the same IAS, while the air density reduces, the real speed or TAS must increase (see figure 7-11, page 166). TAS is important for navigation.

Although IAS is of aerodynamic importance, navigation requires a knowledge of the TAS. Provided you know your planned or actual IAS, your planned or actual pressure altitude, and the forecast or actual outside temperature, you can determine TAS quickly and easily using the flight computer. You can also find the TAS from your Pilot's Operating Handbook for specified conditions.

At higher altitudes, true airspeed (TAS) is greater than indicated airspeed (IAS).

Scenario A	
Planned Course	300°T
Distance	88 NM
Planned IAS	100 knots
Planned pressure altitude	6,500 feet
Forecast temperature at cruise altitude	+20°C
Forecast wind	160°T/30
Fuel flow	12 gph
Variation	9° West

Figure 24-3 Scenario A.

Scenario B	
Planned Course	172°T
Distance	384 NM
Planned IAS	145 knots
Planned pressure altitude	9,500 feet
Forecast temperature at cruise altitude	–5°C
Forecast wind	300°T/40
Fuel flow	18 gph
Variation	11° West

Figure 24-4 Scenario B.

Example 24-1

Find the TAS in scenario A (figure 24-3).

1. Allow for variation in air density: on the calculator side of your flight computer locate the pressure altitude window for airspeed correction shown in figure 24-5. The numbers in the pressure altitude window represent pressure altitude in thousands of feet. The 5 therefore represents 5,000 feet pressure altitude, and the first graduation to the right of the 5 represents 6,000 feet pressure altitude. Immediately above the pressure altitude window is the air temperature scale which extends from +50°C on the left to -70°C on the right. Rotate the inner disc to line up 6,500 feet against +20°C (the second long graduation to the left of the 0). This is shown in figure 24-5. Once correctly aligned do not rotate the inner disc further because you will disturb the air density correction.
2. Find TAS: using figure 24-5, locate the *outer* scale which represents TAS and the *inner* scale which represents IAS. Unlike the scales in figure 24-1 which are perfectly aligned (10 against 10, 11 against 11, and so on), the scales on your flight computer will be offset. This is because you have aligned 6,500 feet altitude against +20°C in step 1, which has allowed for the reduced density at your cruise altitude.
3. Now find the 10 on the inner scale which represents 100 knots IAS. See figure 24-5. Directly opposite the 10 on the inner scale is 11.4 on the outside scale which is used to represent TAS. The TAS is therefore 114 knots.

Answer: 114 KTAS.

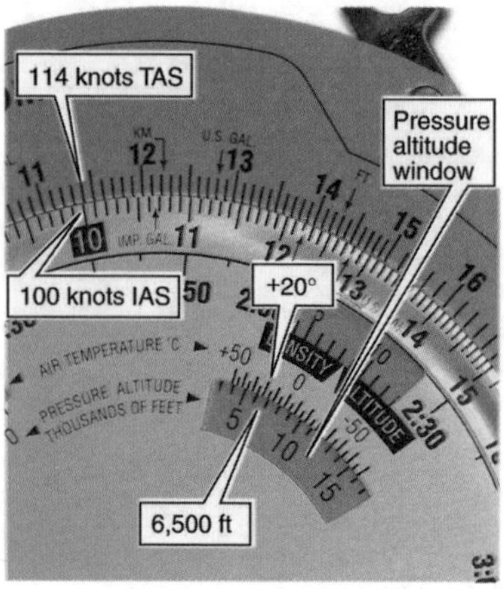

Figure 24-5 Example 24-1.

Example 24-2

What is the expected TAS in scenario B (figure 24-4)?

1. Line up -5°C against 9,500 feet in the pressure altitude window. See figure 24-6.
2. Locate 14.5 (for 145 knots) on the inner scale and read off 16.7 on the outer scale. The TAS is therefore 167 knots.

Answer: 167 KTAS.

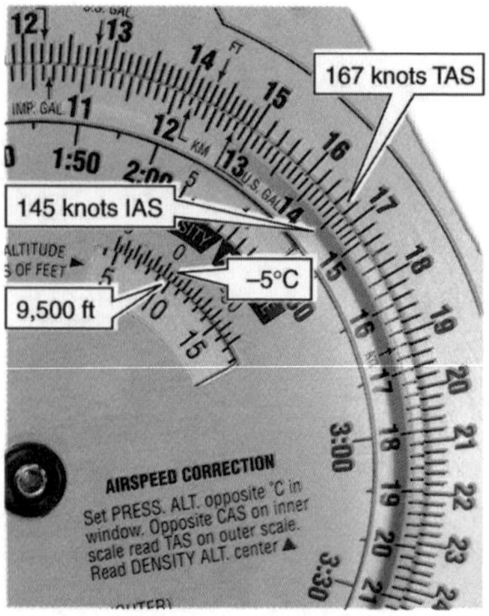

Figure 24-6 Example 24-2.

Finding Heading and Groundspeed

At this stage of flight planning you already know the intended course (CRS) in °T, measured on an aeronautical chart, the wind velocity (W/V) in °T/knots, obtained from the weather forecast and the expected true airspeed obtained by converting IAS to TAS (or from the Pilot's Operating Handbook). You can then calculate the heading (HDG) to steer and the groundspeed (GS) that should be achieved. See figure 23-8 (page 541).

Example 24-3

Find the HDG and GS in scenario A (figure 24-3, page 557).

Place the W/V on the plotting disc (figure 24-7).

1. Rotate the compass rose until the wind direction 160°T is under the true index.

2. Mark the start of the W/V vector 30 knots vertically *above* the grommet. At this stage in your training, it is a good idea to mark in the full W/V, showing the three arrowheads of the W/V vector pointing down toward the grommet. This will give you a very clear picture as the whole triangle of velocities is developed on the plotting disc. When you become familiar with the use of the computer, drawing each vector becomes unnecessary, and just one single mark, known as the *wind dot* or *wind cross*, to illustrate the extent of the wind velocity is all that is needed.

   Place the TR/GS vector on the plotting disc.

3. The desired course is known (having been measured on the chart); groundspeed is not known. Therefore, only one aspect of the TR/GS vector is known—its direction, but not its magnitude. Rotate the compass rose until the required CRS of 300°T is under the index.

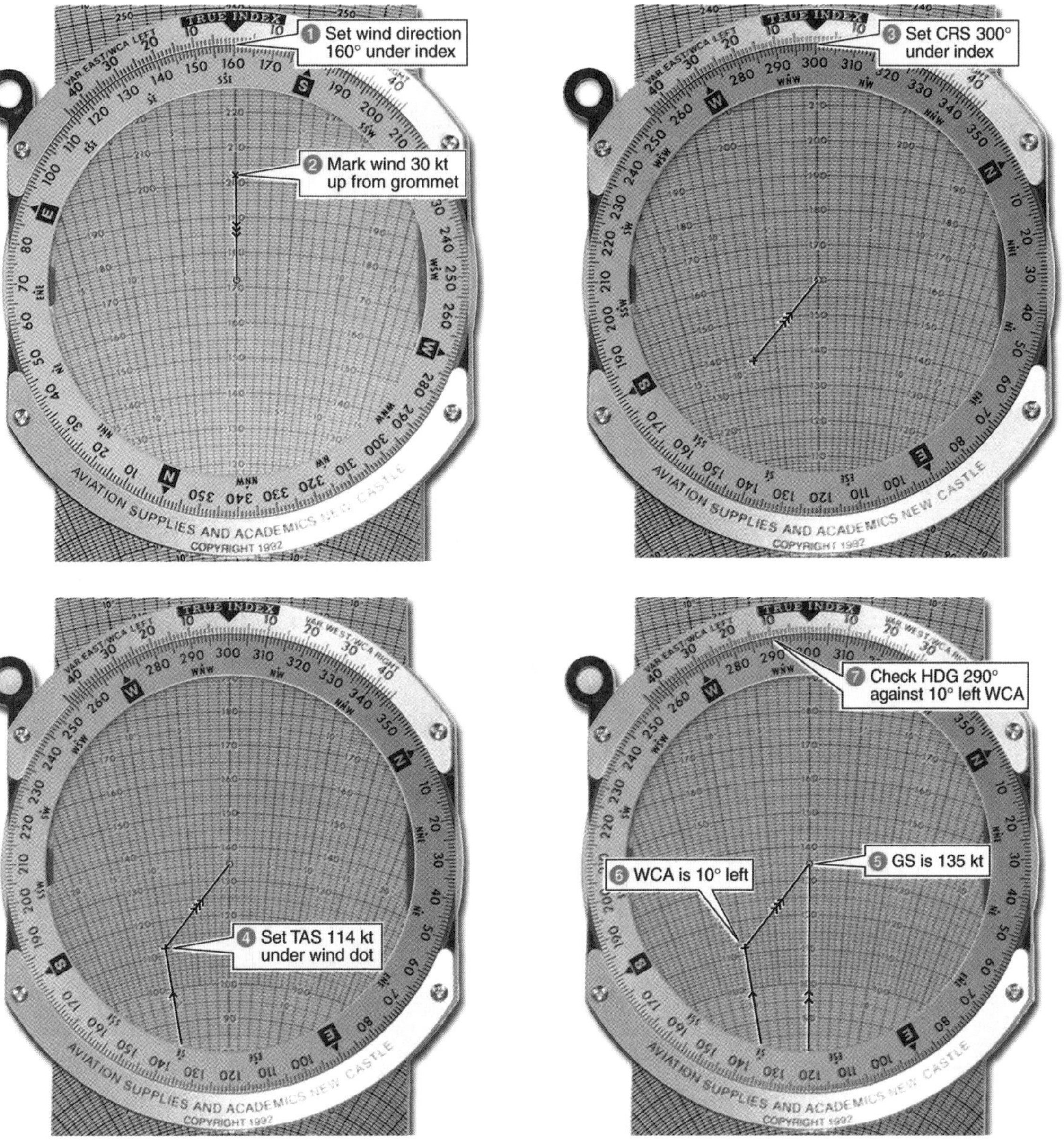

Figure 24-7 Example 24-3.

Place the HDG/TAS vector on the plotting disc.

4. True airspeed is known, but the heading is not. In this case, only one aspect of the HDG/TAS vector is known—its magnitude. Move the slide and place the TAS 114 (found in example 24-1) knots speed arc under the wind dot (which is the starting point of the W/V vector). Note that the end of the HDG/TAS vector is where the W/V begins.

   Read off the answers for HDG and GS.

5. The GS of 135 knots appears under the grommet.
6. From the drift lines, the wind correction angle is 10° to the left of the course. This means to achieve CRS 300T, the airplane must be headed 10 into the wind and flown on a HDG of 290°T to allow for the 10° right drift.
7. Finally, to find the magnetic heading, apply the variation. If variation is 9W, then 290°T is 299°M (variation west, magnetic best).

   Answer: Magnetic heading 299°M, groundspeed 135 knots.

Example 24-4

Find the HDG and GS in scenario B (figure 24-4, page 557).

1. Place the wind velocity vector on the disc by plotting the wind speed with the compass rose at 300° (figure 24-8). Then rotate the compass rose until the required CRS of 172°T is under the index.
2. Place the HDG/TAS vector on the plotting disc and read off the answers, which are GS 188 knots and WCA 11° right. (TAS of 167 knots was found in example 24-2). HDG is 172°T + 11°WCA = 183°T. Finally find magnetic heading by allowing for magnetic variation (11°E).

   Answer: MH 183 − 11°E = 172°M (variation east, magnetic least), GS 188 knots.

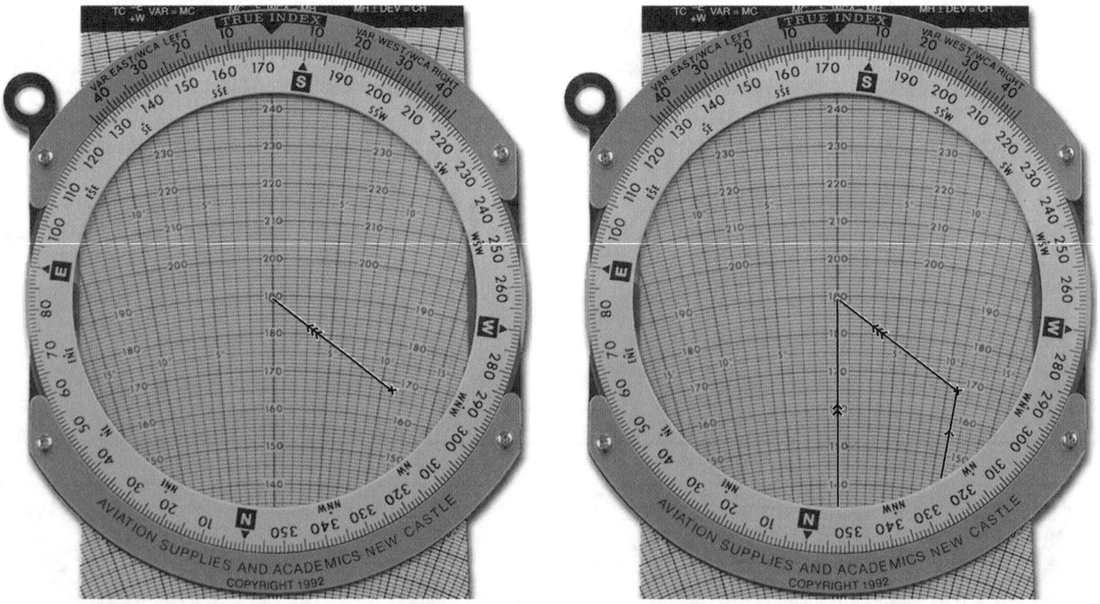

Figure 24-8 Example 24-4.

Finding the Time En Route and Fuel Requirements

The *time en route* and *fuel requirements* are found using the calculator side of the flight computer. The inner and outer scales, which you have already used to represent IAS and TAS respectively, can also be used for many other problems. When using the flight computer to solve *speed–time–distance* problems and *fuel calculations*, which are rate problems, the inner scale represents time and the outer scale represents distance or fuel. In rate problems:

> The inner scale represents time.
> The outer scale represents distance or fuel.

Speed–Time–Distance Problems

There are three basic problems.

1. How far will you travel at a given speed in a specified time?
2. How long will it take to fly a given distance at a known speed?
3. What is the groundspeed achieved knowing time and distance traveled?

You can solve these problems using the equations below with your electronic calculator, or by using your flight computer, as explained in the following examples.

$$\text{Speed} = \frac{\text{Distance}}{\text{Time}} \qquad \text{Time} = \frac{\text{Distance}}{\text{Speed}} \qquad \text{Distance} = \text{Time} \times \text{Speed}$$

Example 24-5

How long will the flight in scenario A (page 557) take?

Rough calculation: at 135 knots groundspeed (from example 24-3), the airplane will cover 135 GNM in 1 hour. Therefore it will take about ⅔ of an hour (40 minutes) to cover 88 GNM.

1. In 1 hour you will cover 135 NM (135 knots), therefore place 60 (to represent 60 minutes) on the inner scale, against 13.5 (to represent 135 NM) on the outer distance scale.
2. Now find 8.8 (88 NM) on the outer scale and read off the time it will take to cover this distance on the inner scale. See figure 24-9.

Answer: 39 minutes.

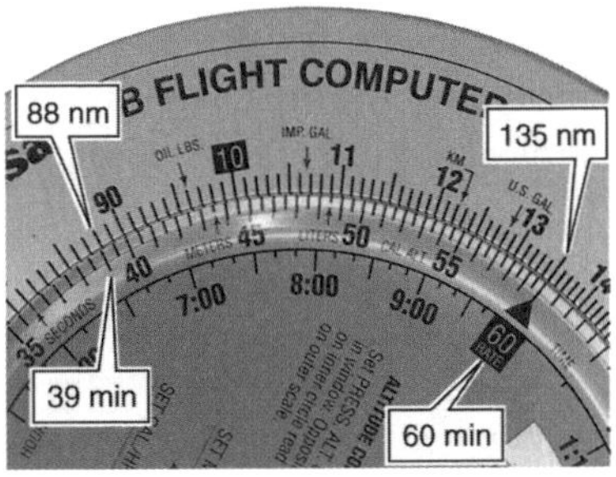

Figure 24-9 Example 24-5.

Example 24-6

How long will the flight in scenario B (page 557) take? Rough calculation: at 188 knots groundspeed (from example 24-4), the airplane will cover 188 GNM in 1 hour, so it will take approximately 2 hours to cover 384 NM.

Place 60 (60 minutes) on the inner scale against 18.8 (188 NM) on the outer distance scale. Now find 38.4 (384 NM) and read off the time it will take to cover this distance on the inner scale. The answer is 122 minutes (12.2 on the inner scale) which is also shown in hours, just over 2 hours (2:00), on the inner fixed scale (figure 24-10).

Answer: 122 minutes.

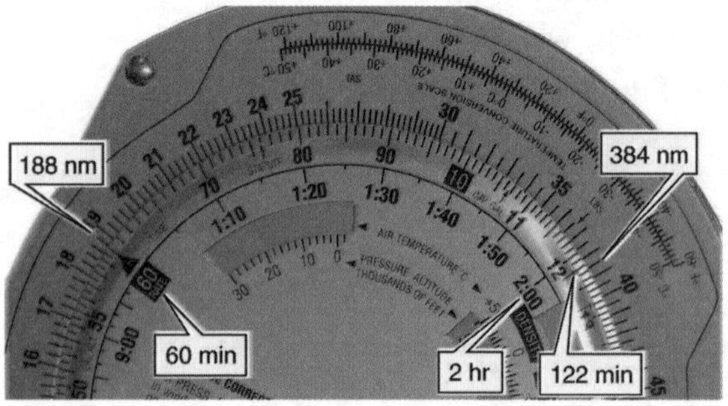

Figure 24-10 Example 24-6.

Fuel Consumption Problems

Example 24-7

In scenario A (page 557), how much fuel would you expect to use during the flight?

Rough calculation: at 12 gph, 12 gallons will be used in 60 minutes, therefore in 40 minutes you would use 8 gallons. Place 60 minutes opposite to 12 gallons and then read off 7.8 gallons opposite 39 minutes. See figure 24-11.

Answer: 7.8 gallons.

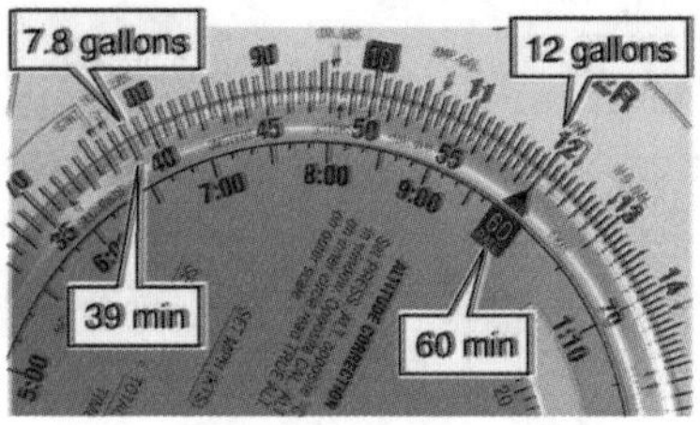

Figure 24-11 Example 24-7.

Example 24-8

In scenario B, how much fuel would you expect to use during the flight?

Rough calculation: 122 minutes is just over 2 hours, therefore at 18 gph you would expect to use approximately $18 \times 2 = 36$ gallons.

In 1 hour you will use 18 gallons, therefore place 60 on the inner fuel scale against 18 on the outer fuel scale. Look for 122 on the inner scale which is opposite 36.6, say 37 gallons (figure 24-12).

Answer: 37 gallons.

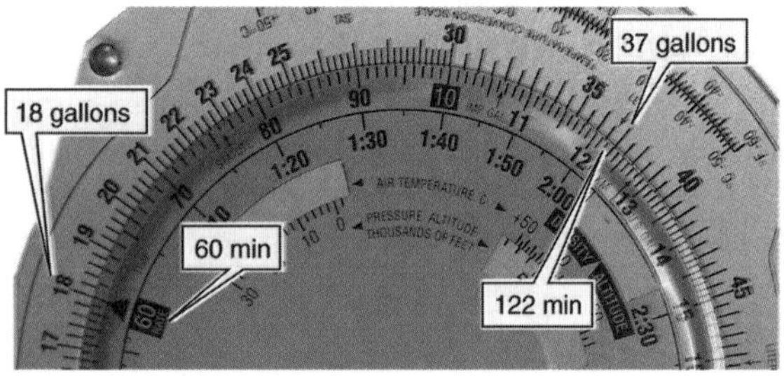

Figure 24-12 Example 24-8.

Example 24-9

In flight you may be faced with other fuel consumption problems. If you have burned 3.5 gallons in 10 minutes, how much fuel will you burn in the next 35 minutes?

Rough calculation: at 0.35 gal/min for 35 minutes is about (0.35×35) 12 gallons.

1. Set up 10 min on the inner time scale against 3.5 gallons on the outer scale.
2. Against 35 min on the inner time scale read off 12.25, say 12.3 gallons on the outer scale. See (a) in figure 24-13.

Answer: 12.3 gallons (not 1.23 or 123).

The circular slide rule is now set up to answer many other problems relevant to this situation, such as:

- what is the rate of fuel consumption in gallons/hr? (*Answer:* 21 gallons/hr. See (b) in figure 24-13); and
- how long would it take to burn 28 gallons? (*Answer:* 80 min. See (c) in figure 24-13).

Finding Wind Components

Quite often a wind needs to be broken down into its two components:

- the *headwind* or *tailwind* component; and
- the   component.

This is especially the case when taking off and landing, because:

- for *performance* reasons, you often need to know the headwind or tailwind component to determine the takeoff or landing distance required; and
- for reasons of *safe handling* of the airplane, you always need to know the approximate crosswind component on a particular runway that you intend using and not exceed the maximum crosswind specified in the Pilot's Operating Handbook.

Winds found on forecasts, and which are most likely to be used for flight planning purposes, are given in degrees true. The winds in takeoff and landing reports broadcast by Air Traffic Control however, are given in degrees magnetic, so that they can be easily related to runway direction, which is always in °M. This applies to the direction of the wind given to you by the control tower, or as broadcast on the automatic terminal information services (ATIS).

A runway whose centerline lies in the direction 074°M will be designated RWY 7 or RWY 07. A runway whose centerline lies in the direction 357°M will be designated RWY 36. A wind of 350°M/25 knots would favor RWY 36, which is almost directly into the wind. RWY 7 would experience a strong crosswind from the left; the pilot should determine just how strong the crosswind is before using this particular runway.

Since both wind direction from the tower and runway direction are measured from the same datum (magnetic north), there is no need to convert into degrees true for this particular computer manipulation. When using your computer, work either totally in true or totally in magnetic.

In chapter 9, we determined wind components mentally and on a chart. Here we show you how to do it using the wind side of your flight computer. An alternative technique is to use the crosswind correction table on the back of the sliding card on some flight computers. See figure 24-14.

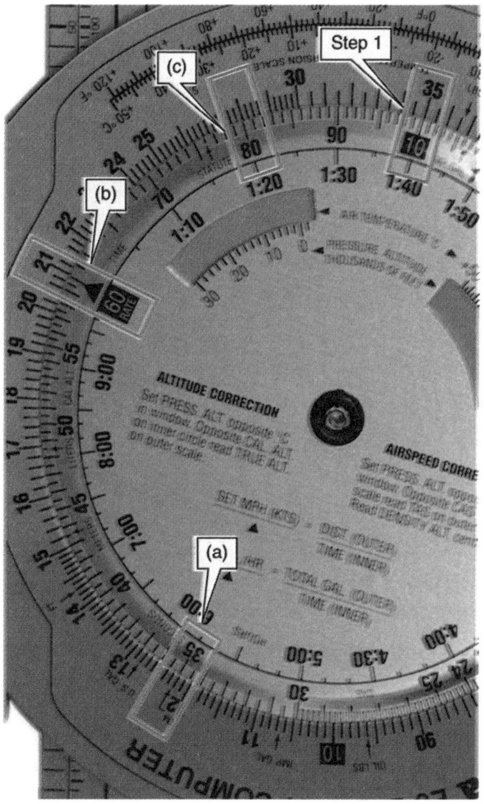

Figure 24-13 Example 24-9.

CROSSWIND CORRECTION

Angle Between Wind Direction and True Course

Wind Speed Knots	0°	10°	20°	30°	40°	50°	60°	70°	80°	90°
10	10/0	10/2	9/3	9/5	8/6	6/8	5/9	3/9	2/10	0/10
20	20/0	20/3	19/7	17/10	15/13	13/15	10/17	7/19	3/20	0/20
30	30/0	30/5	28/10	26/15	23/19	19/23	15/26	10/28	5/30	0/30
40	40/0	39/7	38/14	35/20	31/26	26/31	20/35	14/38	7/39	0/40
50	50/0	49/9	47/17	43/25	38/32	32/38	25/43	17/47	9/49	0/50
60	60/0	59/10	56/21	52/30	46/39	39/46	30/52	21/56	10/59	0/60
70	70/0	69/12	66/24	61/35	54/45	45/54	35/61	24/66	12/69	0/70

Headwind 0/0 Crosswind

Figure 24-14 Crosswind correction table.

Using a Crosswind Correction Table

To solve the problem in example 24-10 using a conventional crosswind correction table, refer to figure 24-14. Move vertically down the 60° column (the angle between wind direction and runway direction) until you meet the wind speed row of 30 knots. Directly read off 15 knots headwind and 26 knots crosswind.

Example 24-10

What crosswind and headwind components exist on Runway 18 if the wind broadcast by the Tower is 120°M/30? (Runway 18 means the runway direction is approximately 180°M.)

Set up the W/V on the sliding grid (see figure 24-15).

1. Set wind direction under index.
2. Mark the start of the W/V vector above the grommet.

Draw in headwind and crosswind components.

3. Rotate the compass rose until the runway direction 180°M is under the index.
4. Run a horizontal line from the wind dot across to the centerline and make a mark.
5. Read off the headwind (or tailwind) component, in this case 15 knots headwind.

Find the crosswind component.

6. Rotate the compass rose until the crosswind component is aligned with the grid.
7. Adjust the sliding grid (if necessary), and read off the crosswind component, in this case 26 knots crosswind from the left.

Answer: 15 knots headwind, 26 knots crosswind from the left.

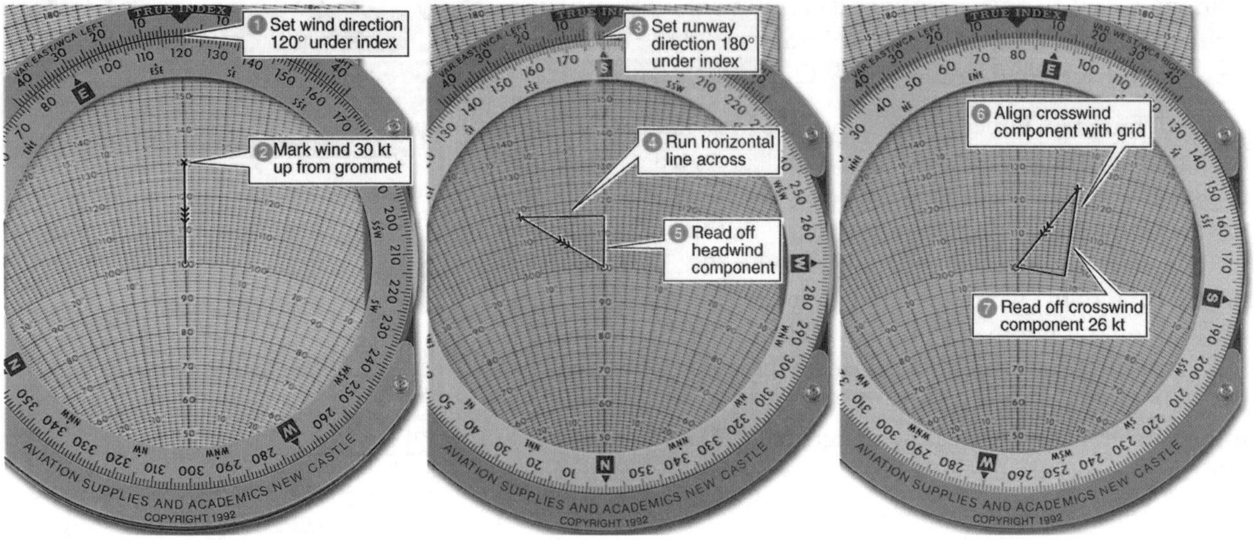

Figure 24-15 Example 24-10.

Conversions on the Flight Computer

As a pilot you will often have to convert from one unit of measurement to another. Some of the common conversions are labeled on the scales of the circular slide rule to help you, but which ones and precisely how it is done varies from computer to computer, so we suggest that you refer to your computer handbook as well as to this manual.

Temperature Conversions

Most flight computers have a temperature conversion scale where conversions from *Fahrenheit* to *Celsius* and vice versa can be read directly. See figure 24-16.

Example 24-11

What is +90°F in °C? *Answer:* 32°C. See figure 24-17.

Example 24-12

What is -10°C in °F? *Answer:* 14°F. See figure 24-18.

Distance Conversions

It is an unfortunate fact of life that we have to deal with the same physical distance being measured in different units. In day-to-day life in the United States, longer distances are measured in *statute miles*, which are smaller than nautical miles which are normally used in aviation navigation.

Nautical miles used in navigation are relevant because of their relationship to the *angular* measurement of latitude on the earth. One *minute* of latitude is equal to 1 nautical mile, and so 1 *degree* of latitude will equal 60 NM. We need to understand the relationship between these various units of distance and be able to convert from one to the other. One *meter* is $\frac{1}{10,000,000}$ (one ten millionth) of the distance from the equator to a pole, which makes one kilometer $\frac{1}{10,000}$ of the distance from the equator to a pole. Thus the average distance from the equator to a pole is 10,000 kilometers. A *kilometer* is much shorter than a nautical mile. The kilometer is the standard unit of distance in most of Europe and many other parts of the world. The relationship between the navigation, statute and metric units is:

1 NM = 1.15 SM = 1.852 km (1,852 meters)

Most flight computers can provide us with accurate conversions using indexes for nautical miles, statute miles and kilometers marked on the outer scale, making it quite straight forward to convert these units without having to remember the exact relationships.

How to Convert from One Unit to Another

As with all computer calculations, carry out a rough mental check. Then set the known quantity on the inner scale of the computer against its index on the outer scale. Against the index of the required unit on the outer scale, read off the answer on the inner scale.

Example 24-13

Convert 10 nautical miles to statute miles and kilometers.

Rough calculation: 1 NM is slightly under 1 SM and approximately equal to 2 km. Therefore 10 NM is a little over 10 SM and approximately equal to 20 km. For the method, refer to figure 24-19. (Note that this method may also be used to convert speeds.)

Answer: 10 NM = 11.5 SM = 18.5 km.

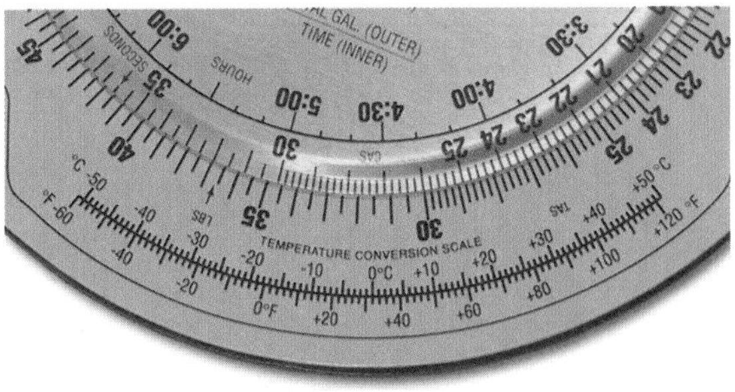

Figure 24-16 A typical temperature conversion scale.

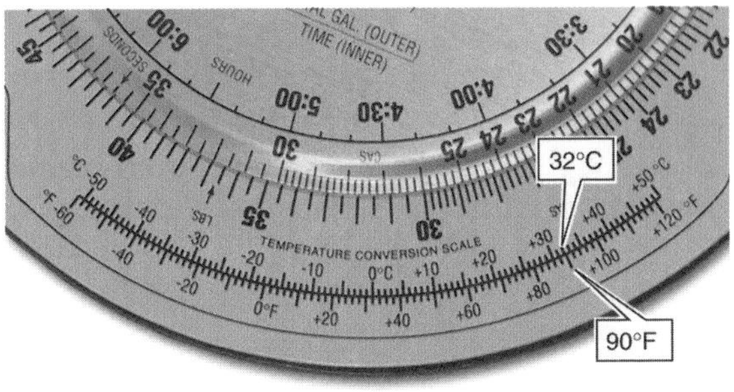

Figure 24-17 Example 24-11.

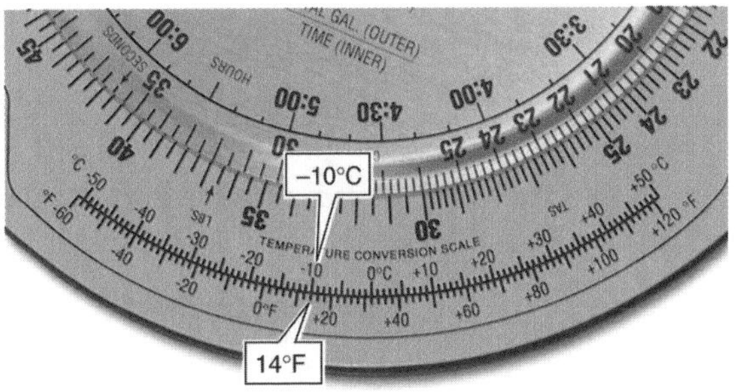

Figure 24-18 Example 24-12.

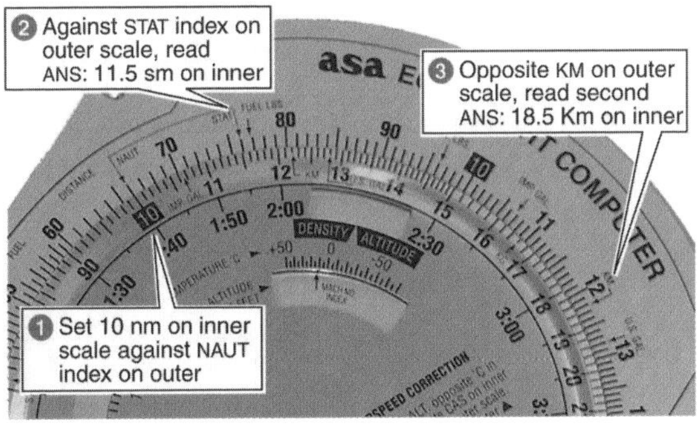

Figure 24-19 Example 24-13.

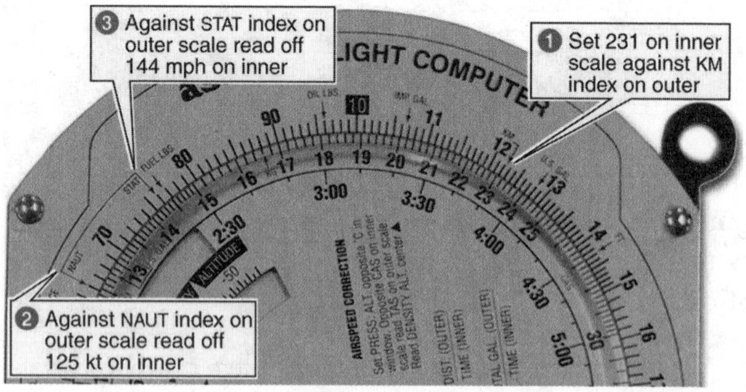

Figure 24-20 Example 24-14.

Example 24-14

Convert 231 kph to knots and mph.

Rough calculation: 1 km is about 0.5 NM and slightly over 0.5 SM. Therefore 230 kph is about 115 knots and slightly over 115 mph. For the method, refer to figure 24-20.

Answers. 231 kph = 125 knots = 144 mph.

Volume Conversions

In aviation worldwide we are faced with three different sorts of volumetric units—the *U.S. gallon*, the *imperial gallon*, and the *liter*. In most general aviation aircraft the fuel gauges are marked in U.S. gallons. However, you may find different units in other countries. There is a possibility of confusion here, so you must become very confident in converting fuel quantities and weights from one unit to another.

For rough calculations, the conversion factors are:

1 U.S. gallon = 0.8 imperial gallon = 4 liters

This calculation is very simple on the flight computer, which has indexes marked on the outer scale for U.S. GAL, IMP GAL and LITERS.

1. Set the known quantity on the inner scale against its index on the outer scale.
2. Against the desired index on the outer scale read off the answer on the inner scale.

Note. Imperial gallons are rarely used in the U.S., and in general, the "U.S." is dropped from U.S. gallons. Whenever "gallons" are mentioned, assume U.S. gallons, not imperial gallons. Flight computers normally have indexes for both U.S. and imperial gallons, so make sure that you use the correct ones in your conversions.

Example 24-15

Convert 24 U.S. gallons to liters and imperial gallons. See figure 24-21.

Rough calculation: 1 U.S. gallon is 4 liters and a little less than 1 imperial gallon. Therefore 24 U.S. gallons is 24 × 4 = 96 liters and a little less than 24 imperial gallons.

Answer: 24 U.S. gallons = 91 liters = 20 imperial gallons.

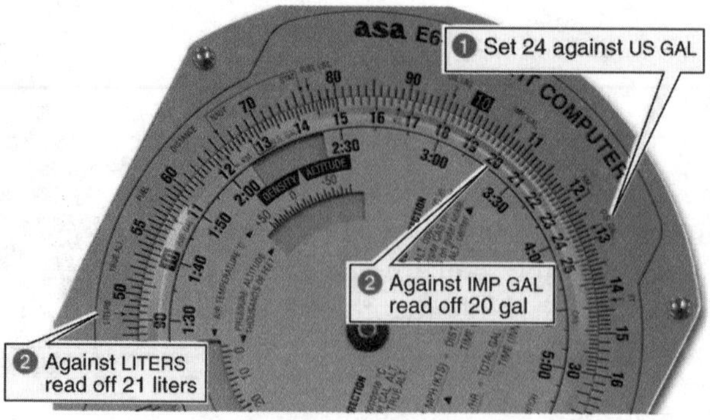

Figure 24-21 Example 24-15.

Volume to Weight Conversions

Converting *U.S. gallons* to *pounds* is made easy by the FUEL LBS index on the outer scale. For rough calculations remember that 1 U.S. gallon of aviation gasoline weighs 6 lb.

Example 24-16

What does 8 U.S. gallons of aviation gasoline weigh? (See figure 24-22.)

Rough calculation: 1 U.S. gallon weighs 6 pounds. Therefore 8 U.S. gallons weigh 8 × 6 = 48 pounds.

1. Set 8 on inner scale against U.S. GAL on outer scale.
2. Against FUEL LBS on outer scale, read off 48 on inner scale.

Answer: 8 U.S. gallons = 48 pounds.

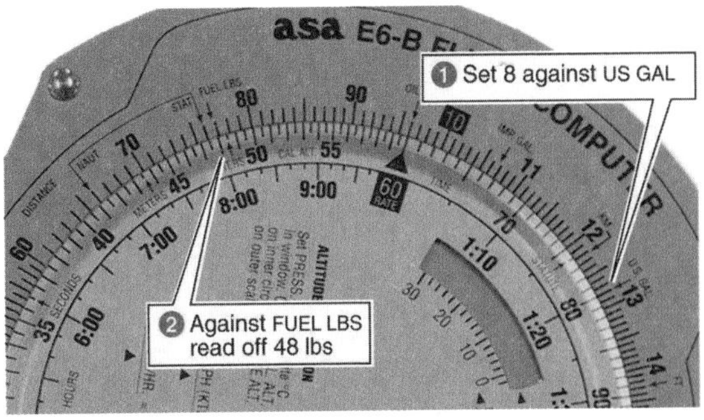

Figure 24-22 Example 24-16.

Weight Conversions

Converting between *kilograms* and *pounds* is made easy by the LBS index on the outer scale and the KG index on the inner scale. For rough calculations remember that 1 kg is about 2 lb.

Example 24-17

Convert 83 lb to kg. (See figure 24-23.)

Rough calculation: 1 lb is about 0.5 kg. Therefore 83 lb is approximately 40 kg.

1. Align LBS on the outer scale against KG on the inner scale.
2. Against 83 lb on the outer scale, read off 37.5 kg on the inner scale, which is the answer in kg.

Answer: 83 pounds = 37.5 kilograms.

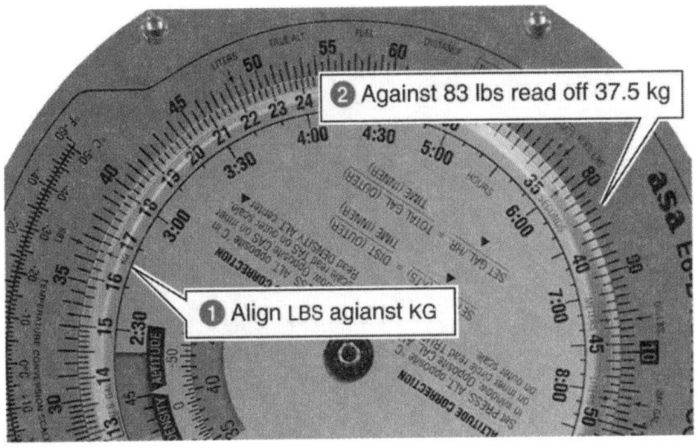

Figure 24-23 Example 24-17.

Calculating the Wind Velocity In Flight

CPL

After obtaining two position fixes en route, it is possible to determine the *actual* W/V, which can then be used in your further in-flight calculations rather than the less accurate forecast wind. The two position fixes enable you to determine the actual ground track (TR) and the actual groundspeed achieved between the two positions, assuming you have maintained a reasonably steady heading and true airspeed.

This problem can be summarized as:

Known	Find
HDG/TAS and TR/GS	W/V

Remember that in the United States it is usual for visual pilots to work in true.

CPL

Example 24-18

Finding a W/V in flight. Known:

- HDG 143°M;
- variation 5°W;
- TAS 120 knots; and
- TR 146°T, GS 144 knots.

Place the TR/GS vector under the grommet.

1. Rotate the compass rose and set track 146°T under the index.
2. Set the GS 144 knots under the grommet. See figure 24-24.

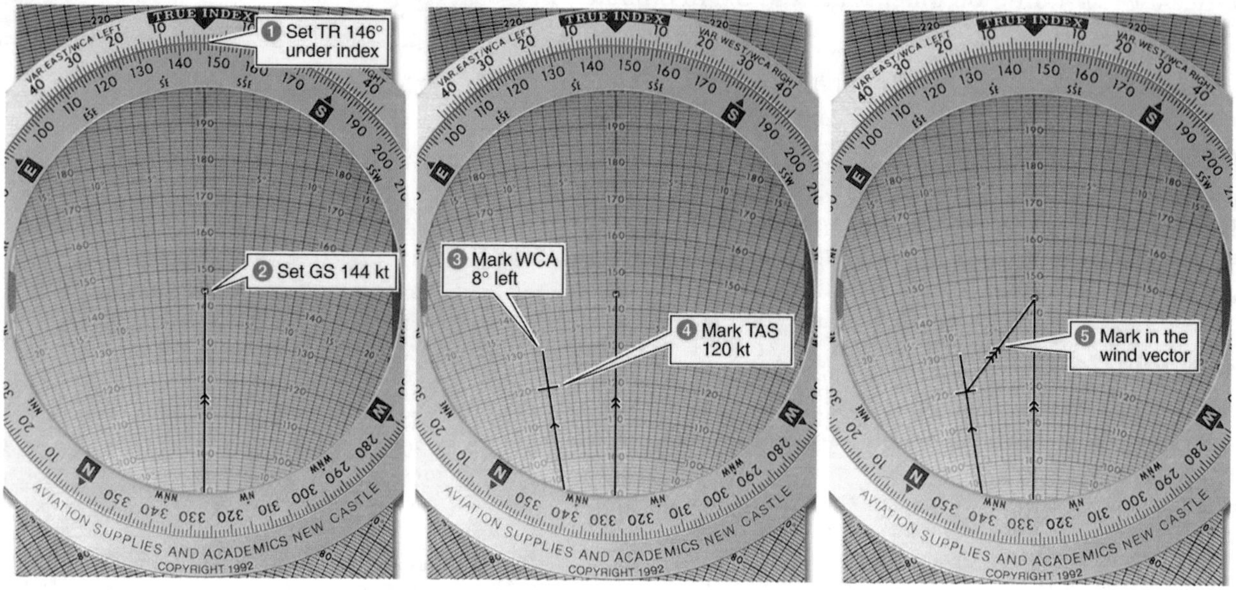

Figure 24-24 Example 24-18.

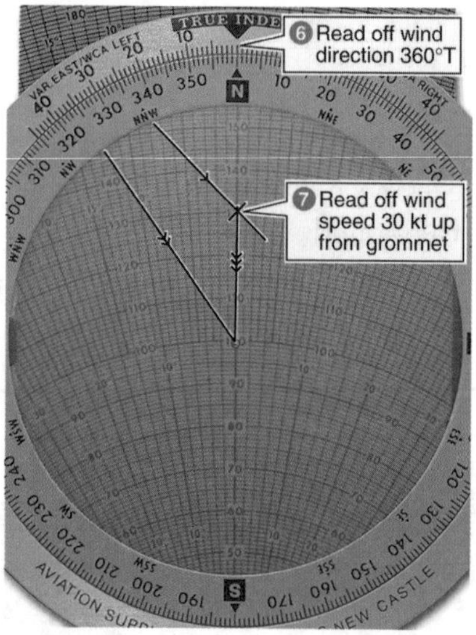

Figure 24-25 Example 24-18.

Place the HDG/TAS vector on the plotting disc.

3. From HDG 138°T (143°M − 5°W) and TR 146°T, the drift is 8° right; the HDG is 8° left of TR (the wind correction angle is 8° left). Mark in the HDG direction as the 8° drift line to the left of track.
4. Mark the TAS where the 120 knots speed arc intersects the drift line; this now indicates the HDG/TAS vector.
5. Mark in the wind vector. Remember, the W/V blows the aircraft from HDG to TR.

Determine the W/V.

6. Rotate the compass rose until the wind dot is on the index line with the arrows pointing down toward the grommet. The direction from which it is blowing, 360°T, is now indicated under the index.
7. Read off the wind strength 30 knots. (Setting a definite speed arc under the grommet, 100 knots in this case, makes the wind strength easier to read.) See figure 24-25.

Answer: W/V 360°T/30 knots.

End CPL

Review 24
Using the Flight Computer

The Flight Computer for Flight Planning

1. Label the sides marked A and B in figure 24-26.

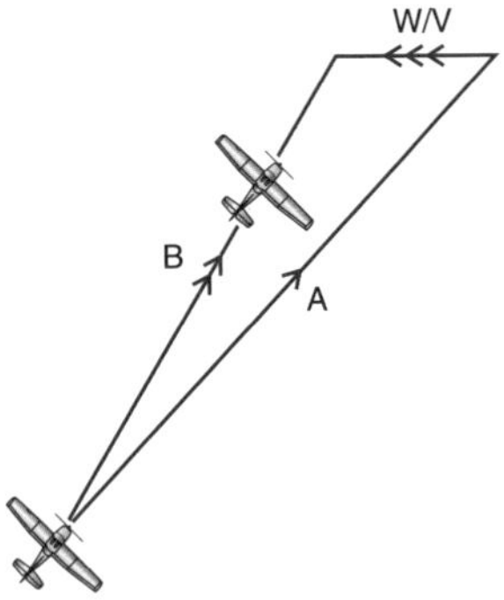

Figure 24-26 Question 1.

2. True or false? The wind blows an airplane from its heading to its ground track.
3. What information is necessary to calculate heading and groundspeed?
4. What is the expected TAS at 8,500 feet if the temperature is -10°C and the IAS 115 knots?
5. The planned course is 240°T and the forecast wind 140°T/30. If the expected TAS is 129 knots and the variation 8° East, what is the required magnetic HDG and expected GS?
6. How long will it take to fly 85 NM at a groundspeed of 131 knots?
7. How much fuel will you use in 39 minutes at a fuel flow of 15 gph?
8. Calculate the true heading and groundspeed for TAS 98 knots, W/V 280°T/35, and course 072°T.
9. At a GS of 183 knots, how far will you travel in 17 minutes?
10. At a GS of 120 knots, how far will you travel in 10 minutes?
11. If we cover 23 NM over the ground in 9 minutes, what is our GS?
12. To achieve a course of 300°T, calculate the magnetic heading and groundspeed if you plan to cruise at 10,000 feet where the forecast wind velocity and temperature is 280°T/25 and +6°C, at an indicated airspeed of 100 knots. Variation is 6°W.
13. We cover 22 GNM in 10 minutes.
    - **a.** What is our GS?
    - **b.** How long will it take us to reach the next checkpoint which is 73 NM further on in the same direction?
14. Distance is 57 NM, true course is 213°T, wind is 090°T/16, and TAS is 90 knots. Add 2 minutes for the climb-out. What is the time en route for the flight?
    - **a.** 33 minutes.
    - **b.** 37 minutes.
    - **c.** 41 minutes.
15. Refer to Sectional Chart excerpt no. 4 on page 507. The wind is 215°T/25 and the TAS is 125 knots. What is the estimated time en route from Sandpoint Airport (area 1) to St. Maries Airport (area 4)?
    - **a.** 27 minutes.
    - **b.** 30 minutes.
    - **c.** 34 minutes.
16. Refer to Sectional Chart excerpt no. 4 on page 507. The wind is 300°T/14 and the true airspeed is 90 knots. Add 3 minutes for climb-out. What is the estimated time en route from St. Maries Airport (area 4) to Priest River (area 1)?
    - **a.** 38 minutes.
    - **b.** 43 minutes.
    - **c.** 48 minutes.
17. You burn 5 gallons of fuel in 24 minutes.
    - **a.** What is your rate of fuel consumption?
    - **b.** How long would it take to burn 8 gallons?
18. Full tanks have 26 gallons of usable fuel, and the average consumption rate is 5.5 gal/hour. Calculate the safe endurance for flight if you wish to retain 1 hour's fuel as reserve.

Conversions

19. Convert +32°F to °C.
20. Convert +20°C to °F.
21. Convert 55 NM to kilometers.
22. Convert 50 knots to km/hour (or kph).
23. Convert 631 lb to kg.
24. Convert 80 kg to lb.
25. You wish to refuel from 16 gal to 45 gal. How many liters should you order?
26. What does 45 gal. of aviation gasoline weigh in pounds?

Commercial Review

27. Given the information below, determine the wind direction and speed:
    a. 020°T/32
    b. 030°T/38
    c. 200°T/32

True course	105°
True heading	085°
True airspeed	95 kt
Groundspeed	87 kt

28. If fuel consumption is 80 pounds per hour and groundspeed is 180 knots, how much fuel is required for an airplane to travel 460 NM?
    a. 205 pounds.
    b. 212 pounds.
    c. 460 pounds.
29. Given the information below, determine the time en route and fuel consumption:
    a. 1 hour 28 minutes and 73.2 pounds.
    b. 1 hour 38 minutes and 158 pounds.
    c. 1 hour 40 minutes and 175 pounds.

Wind	175°T/20
Distance	135 NM
True course	075°
True airspeed	80 kt
Fuel consumption	105 lb/hr

30. If fuel consumption is 14.7 gallons per hour and groundspeed is 157 knots, how much fuel is required for an airplane to travel 612 NM?
    a. 58 gallons.
    b. 60 gallons.
    c. 64 gallons.
31. An airplane departs an airport under the conditions given below. Determine the approximate time, compass heading, distance, and fuel consumed during the climb.
    a. 14 minutes, 234°, 26 NM, 3.9 gallons.
    b. 17 minutes, 224°, 36 NM, 3.7 gallons.
    c. 17 minutes, 242°, 31 NM, 3.5 gallons.

Airport elevation	1,000 ft
Cruise altitude	9,500 ft
Rate of climb	500 fpm
Average true airspeed	135 kt
True course	215°
Average wind velocity	290°T/20
Variation	3°W
Deviation	–2°
Average fuel consumption	13 gal/hr

32. An airplane descends to an airport under the conditions outlined below. Determine the approximate time, compass heading, distance, and fuel consumed during the descent.
    a. 16 minutes, 168°, 30 NM, 2.9 gallons.
    b. 18 minutes, 164°, 34 NM, 3.2 gallons.
    c. 18 minutes, 168°, 34 NM, 2.9 gallons.

Cruising altitude	7,500 ft
Airport elevation	1,300 ft
Descends to	800 ft AGL
Rate of descent	300 ft/min
Average true airspeed	120 kt
True course	165°
Average wind velocity	240°T/20
Variation	4°E
Deviation	–2°
Average fuel consumption	9.6 gal/hr

Answers are given on page 706.

Flight Planning 25

Flight Management

Cross-country flying is a significant step forward in your training. Up to this point, you have only been concerned with flying the aircraft. However, during cross-country flight, you will have to fly *and* navigate, which will significantly increase your workload. Careful preflight planning is paramount to safely managing the flight. Therefore, *flight management* applies to the preflight planning stage as well as to the actual flight.

Thorough preflight planning is paramount to flight safety.

Preflight planning includes preparing a detailed flight log, calculating weight and balance, filing a flight plan, obtaining a thorough weather briefing, securing the necessary aeronautical charts and airport data, and laying out your proposed route. The better the flight planning prior to flight, the easier the en route navigation!

Personal Navigation Equipment

A *flight case*, satchel, or nav bag that fits comfortably within reach in the cockpit should be used to hold your navigation equipment. A typical flight case should contain:

Keep the cockpit organized to reduce distractions.

- current aeronautical charts—typically Sectional Charts, together with Terminal Charts for nearby Class B airspace;
- a flight computer;
- a scale rule and protractor (or a plotter);
- pens and pencils;
- relevant documents (such as the Chart Supplement U.S. and logbook for student pilots);
- spare flight log forms;
- a flashlight; and
- sunglasses.

Note. Also consider a kneeboard and some type of small electronic timer.

Notice to Airmen (NOTAMs)

NOTAMs are an important and time-critical piece of aeronautical information that could affect a pilot's flight and should be checked as part of the flight planning process. NOTAMs are classified into categories:

- NOTAM (D) distant—includes information in regards to navigational facilities and public use airports listed within the Chart Supplement U.S. Issued for such things as taxiway or runway closures, airport taxiway lighting that may be out of service, or even construction equipment around the runway environment.
- FDC NOTAM—contains regulatory information pertaining to flight. Common examples include temporary flight restriction (TFR), an out of service VOR facility, or general changes to airspace and instrument flight procedures.
- Pointer NOTAM—issued by Flight Service Stations simply to point out another important NOTAM.

- SAA NOTAM—advises pilots when special activity airspace will be active outside the published and schedule times listed on aeronautical charts or other operational publications.
- Military NOTAM—pertains to military navigational aids and airports within the NAS.

```
!BFI 04/001 BFI AD AP ALL SFC WIP MOWING 1604010312-1609302359
!BFI 06/003 BFI OBST TOWER (ASR UNKNOWN) 473244N1222106W (2.22NM WNW BFI)
      390FT (80FT AGL) NOT LGTD 1606061345-1607061500
!BFI 06/008 BFI RWY 13R/31L CLSD TUE-SAT 0445-1015 1606140445-1607301015
!BFI 06/031 BFI TWY B EDGE MARKINGS BTN TWY B4 AND TWY B5 WEST SIDE NOT STD
      1606141455-1607312359
```

Figure 25-1 Typical NOTAM information for a selected airport.

Weather and Operational Considerations

TFRs are commonly issued over disaster areas, special events, or within the proximity of the President and other dignitaries.

Flight Service Stations can provide a standard, abbreviated, or outlook briefing.

You should obtain *weather information*, NOTAMs, and TFRs by the most convenient means available to you prior to your flight. Typically, this is accomplished via computer or by dialing 1-800-WX-BRIEF or visiting 1800wxbrief.com for the nearest Flight Service Station.

Flight Service Stations (FSS) can provide three basic types of preflight briefing:

- a *standard briefing*—a full briefing including adverse conditions, VFR flight recommended or not, weather synopsis, current conditions, en route forecast, destination forecast, winds aloft, relevant NOTAMs, known ATC delays; or
- an *abbreviated briefing*—to supplement information you already have; or
- an *outlook briefing*—for advanced planning purposes (for a flight 6 or more hours from the time of briefing).

```
KBFI 221653Z 00000KT 10SM FEW020 SCT120 BKN200 18/10 A3010 RMK AO2 SLP192 T01830100

KBFI 221135Z 2212/2312 00000KT P6SM BKN130
  FM221300 00000KT P6SM SCT019 BKN130
  TEMPO 2214/2216 BKN019
  FM221800 22006KT P6SM SCT040 BKN100
  TEMPO 2223/2303 31006KT
  FM230600 19003KT P6SM VCSH BKN045 OVC080
  FM231000 15005KT P6SM -SHRA OVC040
```

Figure 25-2 METAR and TAF for a selected airport.

The online GFA or FA will give cloud bases above mean sea level and the aerodrome forecast above ground level. From this information the most suitable cruising altitude can then be chosen. You should read and analyze the weather information so that you can make well-based judgments regarding your proposed flight, especially the "go/no-go" decision.

Analyze the weather reports and forecasts, weather charts, pilot weather reports, SIGMETs, AIRMETs, NOTAMs, windshear reports, and whatever other relevant information is available. Don't forget to walk outside and have a look at the sky yourself! It sounds like a lot, but the information will be presented to you in a logical manner—and the more practiced you become in planning a flight, the easier it will seem.

From this information, and from your knowledge of your own experience and capabilities, you can now make a firm, positive and confident "go/no-go" decision. This is a command decision, possibly the most important decision of the whole flight.

Make a sensible "go/no-go" decision based on your own personal weather minimums.

To help you make this critical decision objectively, establish your own personal weather minimums. For example: visibility 5 miles, ceiling 5000, wind < 15 KTS. If the weather at any point along your route exceeds, or is forecast to exceed, your personal minimums, *don't go.*

In addition, use your personal weather minimums while en route. If at any point the weather deteriorates below your personal minimums, consider an alternate course of action, such as making a 180 or landing at a different airport.

Preflight Planning

Start your planning by looking at the big picture. Select the route over which you want to fly. Note the nature of the terrain and the type of airspace along this route and to either side of it:

Use current charts, and check for terrain and airspace.

- *terrain*—check the height of any obstacles within (say) 10 miles either side of your proposed course; and
- *airspace*—check the route for:
  - different classes of airspace;
  - prohibited areas, restricted areas or warning areas; and
  - other airports.

Use the chart legend to decode the chart information.

It may be best to avoid particularly high or rugged terrain (especially if you are flying a single-engine airplane), areas of dense air traffic, and areas of bad weather such as coastal fog, low clouds, and thunderstorms.

Choose turning points and prominent checkpoints which will be easily identified in flight, and which cannot be confused with other nearby ground features. Remember you are sitting on the left-hand side of the airplane. Select appropriate en route navigation aids, and note the communications facilities. Allow for necessary fuel stops. Mark the route on your sectional chart, and enter a few prominent checkpoints on the flight log.

It is not necessary to list every checkpoint on your flight log.

Note any suitable *alternate airports* available on or adjacent to the route, in case an unscheduled landing becomes necessary. Information on airports is available in the Chart Supplement U.S.

Consider highlighting suitable en route alternate airports.

Altitude

Terrain awareness is vital.

It is good airmanship to calculate a *safety altitude* that provides adequate clearance above terrain and obstacles. A quick means of determining the height of the highest obstacle or terrain is to use the *maximum elevation figure* (MEF) published for each latitude–longitude quadrangle on Sectional charts.

To be less restricted, you could instead find the highest terrain or obstacle within 5 NM or 10 NM either side of track. Then apply a safety buffer, say of 1,000 feet or whatever your flight instructor suggests, to obtain a safety altitude. Enter this figure on your flight log. This is not a requirement, but it provides a safe minimum altitude to fly at if, for instance, cloud forces you down.

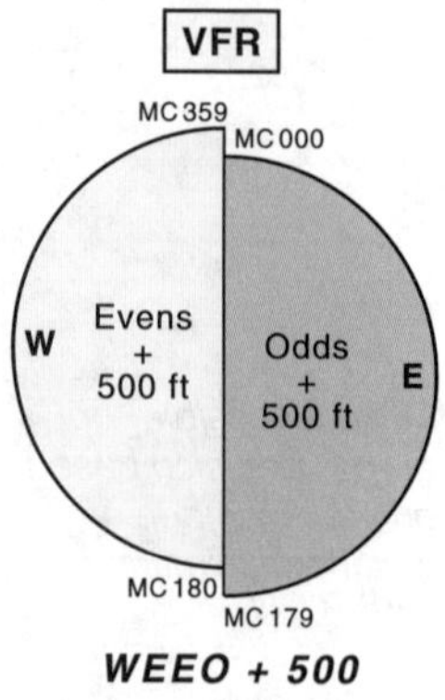

Figure 25-3
VFR cruise altitudes above 3,000 feet AGL.

Select a suitable *cruise altitude* for each leg and enter it in the flight log. Considerations should include:

- terrain;
- airspace restrictions;
- the cloud base; and
- VFR cruise altitudes.

The *VFR cruise altitudes*, when more than 3,000 feet above the surface, are:

- on a magnetic course 000° to 179° magnetic—*odd* thousands plus 500 (for example 3,500, 5,500, 7,500 feet MSL); and
- on a magnetic course 180° to 359° magnetic—*even* thousands plus 500 (for example 4,500, 6,500, 8,500 feet MSL).

Magnetic course is true course + or – variation.

Note. Cruise altitudes, as well as VOR radials, are based on *magnetic* course. A common mistake is to calculate VFR cruising altitudes based upon magnetic heading rather than magnetic course.

Courses and Distances

Estimating course and distance prior to actual measurement will avoid gross errors.

For each leg of the flight, mentally estimate the course direction and the distance in nautical miles before measuring it accurately (ensuring that you are using the correct scale). Insert the accurately measured figures on the flight log.

Measure true course against a meridian of longitude at the approximate midpoint of each leg. Add or subtract *magnetic variation* to the measured true course to find the magnetic course.

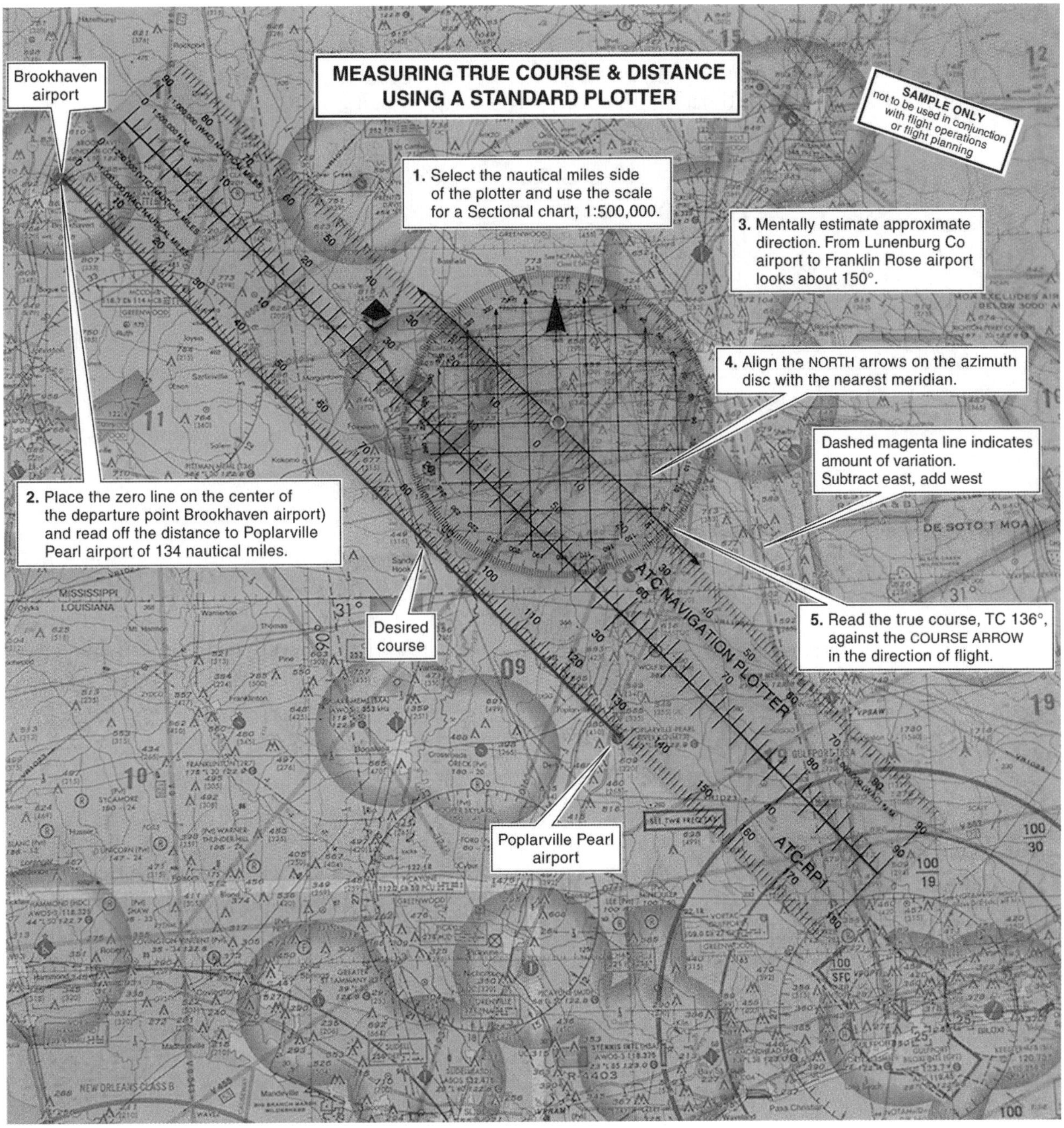

Figure 25-4 Measuring true course and distance on a standard plotter.

Distance Markers or Time Markers

To assist you in flight, it is suggested that each leg be subdivided using small marks placed at regular intervals along the course lines drawn on the chart. These may be:

- distance markers each 10 nautical miles (NM); or
- distance markers at the ¼, ½ and ¾ points; or
- time markers each 10 minutes; or
- time markers at the ¼, ½ and ¾ points.

Time markers have to wait until you have calculated groundspeeds and time intervals. Once in flight, these may vary from the flight planned values, unlike the distance markers. Engraving a pencil with 10 NM marks (in the correct scale for the chart) will help you estimating distances, particularly in flight.

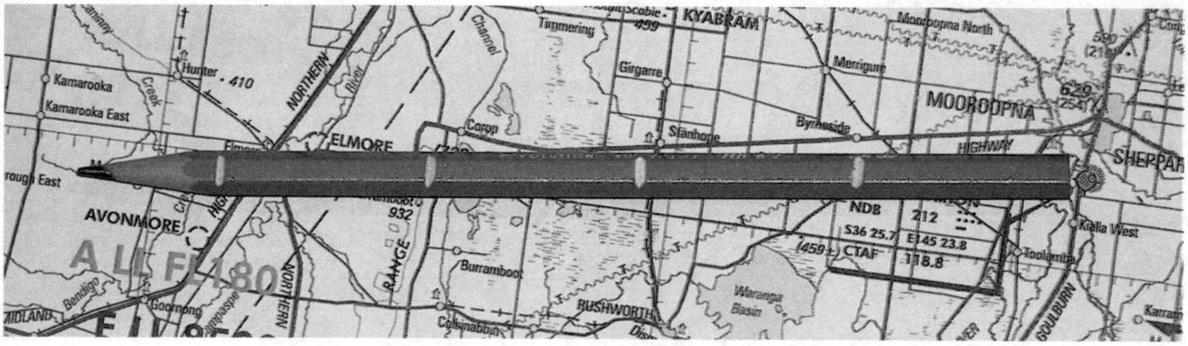

Figure 25-5 A pencil engraved (by yourself) with 10 NM nicks is very useful.

Speed, Time, and Heading Calculations

Once the route has been selected and the courses and distances measured, the flight plan may be completed. Calculations of headings, groundspeeds, time intervals and fuel consumption must all be made. For a full explanation of how to perform these calculations, refer to chapter 24 on the flight computer.

Completing the Flight Log

Insert the forecast winds, the selected cruise altitude, and the TAS for each leg onto the flight log. Remember that for a given indicated airspeed, the true airspeed will be greater at higher altitudes and temperatures because of the decreased air density. Converting IAS to TAS is easily done on the calculator side of the computer, but most Pilot's Operating Handbooks directly provide cruise TAS information in the published cruise tables.

On the wind side of the flight computer, use the forecast wind to set up the triangle of velocities and calculate wind correction angle, heading and groundspeed for each leg (see chapter 24).

> **Note.** It is most important when using the wind side of the computer that you work *completely* in degrees true (or *completely* in degrees magnetic).

Having measured the distance of each leg and calculated the expected groundspeed, determine the *estimated time interval* and insert it on the flight log. Then add all of the individual time intervals together and obtain the *total* time interval for the whole flight. Since climb to altitude will be at a lower airspeed (and higher fuel consumption) than cruising flight, some pilots add a climb allowance, say 2 minutes and 0.5 gallon, to the cruise-only figures calculated for the first leg. Check the POH for recommendations on fuel allowances for taxi and climb.

To check for gross errors, compare the total time en route with the total distance for the flight, considering the average GS expected. Also, confirm that you will arrive with adequate daylight remaining. You should plan to arrive with at least 30 minutes of daylight remaining. Ask your flight instructor for guidance. If diversion to an alter-

Flight Planner

Preflight

AIRCRAFT	N19630	TIME OFF	1400	BLOCK START		BLOCK END	
ATIS CODE	Bravo	SKY	10,000Sct	TEMP	23	WIND	
En Route		ALTIMETER	29.92	RUNWAY	28	EST GPH	8

TRUE COURSE (Planned)	ALTITUDE (Planned)	DIRECTION (Predicted Wind)	VELOCITY (Predicted Wind)	TEMP	PLAN TAS	WIND CORR ANGLE -L +R	TRUE HEADING / -E +W VAR	MAG HEADING / ± DEV	Checkpoints (DEPARTURE)	COMPASS HEADING	DIST LEG / REM	GS EST / ACT	ETE / ATE	ETA / ATA	FUEL USED / FUEL REM.	VOR FREQ / IDENT	VOR BEARING TO/FROM	TRANSPONDER CODES "SQUAWKS"
									KMYF									
84	3500	330	6	16°C	76	-4	80 / -12	68 / +2	Gillespie	70	8 / 85	78	06:09	14:06	0.8 / 42.2			1200
68	7500	305	20	8°C	76	-13	55 / -12	43 / +2	El Cap Reservoir	45	10 / 75	85	07:04	14:13	0.9 / 41.3			
34	7500	305	20	8°C	110	-11	23 / -12	11 / +1	Julian VOR	12	18 / 57	108	10:00	14:23	1.3 / 40	114.0	22 TO	
33	7500	305	20	8°C	110	-11	23 / -12	11 / +1	Cochran	12	36 / 21	108	20:00	14:43	2.7 / 37.3	114.0	21 FROM	
304	7500	305	20	8°C	110	0	304 / -12	292 / -1	KPSP	291	21 / 0	90	14:00	14:57	1.9 / 35.4	116.2	292 FROM	
									ARRIVAL	TOTALS	93							

Notes:

KPSP - TPA 1,500 msl
Runway 13R/31L 10,000 × 150 ft.
Runway 13L/31R 4,952 × 75 ft.

Terminal Information

Field	Elevation	Runways	Radio Frequencies
KMYF	427	10L/R 28L/R	Ⓖ 118.22 Ⓣ 119.2
KPSP	476	13L/R 31L/R	ATIS - 118.25
			Ⓖ 121.9 Ⓣ 119.7

 ASA-FP-3

Figure 25-6 Sample flight log; Montgomery Field Airport to Palm Springs Airport.

nate airport is a possibility, then you should plan for a departure time that will allow you to fly to the destination airport, then to the alternate airport and still arrive well before the end of daylight.

Fuel Calculations

The fuel consumption for various power settings is published in the Pilot's Operating Handbook. These figures assume *correct leaning* of the fuel/air mixture when cruising at 75% maximum continuous power or less. Leaning the mixture can decrease fuel consumption by up to 20%. From the estimated time interval for the whole flight and the published fuel consumption rate, calculate the expected flight fuel.

Surprisingly, running out of fuel is a leading cause of accidents.

Reserve fuel should also be carried to allow for in-flight contingencies such as diversions, fuel consumption poorer than that published and unexpected headwinds en route. A *fixed reserve fuel* of 45 minutes by night and 30 minutes by day is required. This fixed reserve is only intended to be used in an emergency. Any fuel over and above the minimum fuel required is known as *margin fuel*. Insert the fuel calculations onto the flight log.

Weight and Balance

Do not exceed weight-and-balance limitations.

At this stage of flight planning, when the fuel required and the passenger and baggage load is known, it is appropriate to consider weight and balance. For a flight to be legal, the airplane must not exceed any weight limitation, and must be loaded so that the center of gravity (CG) lies within the approved range throughout the flight. Complete a load sheet (if necessary) to verify that the requirements are met. See chapter 11 for more on weight and balance. Refer to figure 25-7.

SAMPLE ONLY
not to be used
in conjunction
with flight operations
or flight planning

SAMPLE LOADING PROBLEM	SAMPLE AIRPLANE			YOUR AIRPLANE		
	WEIGHT (LBS.)	ARM (IN.)	MOMENT (LB.-IN. /1000)	WEIGHT (LBS.)	ARM (IN.)	MOMENT (LB.-IN. /1000)
*1. Licensed Empty Weight (Typical)	1262	83.4	105.25	1267		105.05
2. Oil (8 qts.) 1 qt. = 1.875 lbs.	15	32.0	.48	15	32.0	.48
3. Fuel (in excess of unuseable) Standard Tanks (37 gal.)	222	90.9	20.18	222	90.9	20.18
Long Range Tanks (51 gal.)		94.81		—	94.81	—
4. Pilot and Co-Pilot	340	90.6	30.80	340	90.6	30.80
5. Rear Seat Passengers	340	126.0	42.84	—	126.0	—
*6. Baggage (in baggage compartment) Max. allowable 120 lbs.	21	151.0	3.17	45	151.0	6.80
7. Cargo Area Max. allowable 340 lbs.		116.4		20	116.4	2.32
8. Total Airplane Weight (loaded)	2200	92.17	202.72	1909		165.63

NOTE: Change in moment from upright to fold-down position of rear seat is negligible.

*Maximum allowable is 120 pounds if C.G. is within Center of Gravity Envelope. Refer to Cargo Loading and Weight and Balance Section for cargo loading instructions.

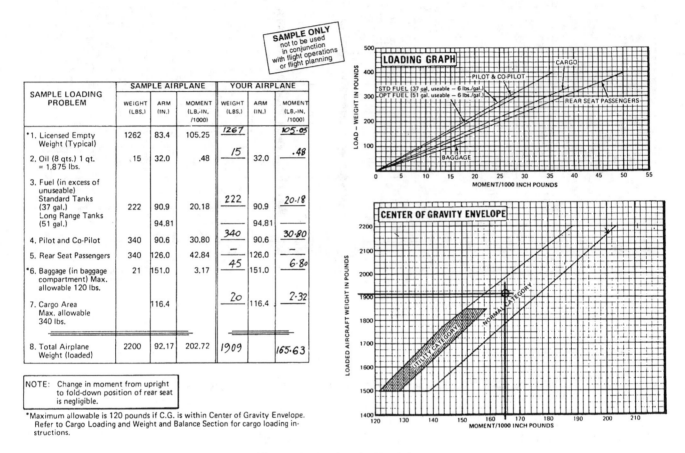

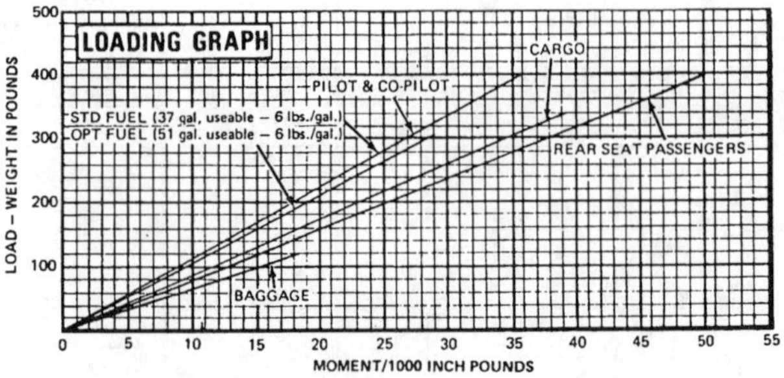

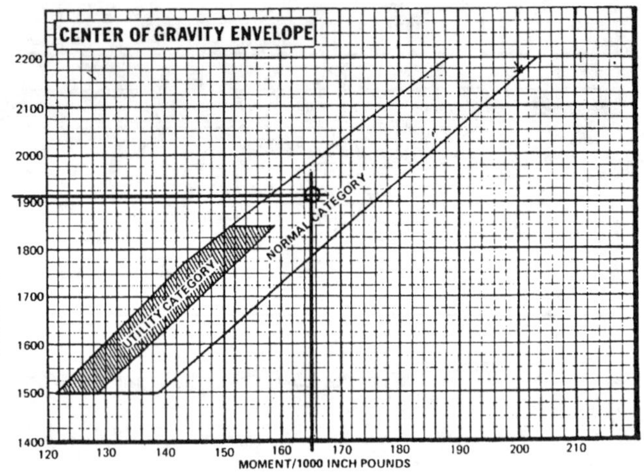

Figure 25-7 A typical load sheet.

Takeoff and Landing Performance

Having considered weight and balance, you will know the expected takeoff weight and landing weight of the airplane. If any doubt exists regarding the suitability of the departure, destination and alternate airports, then reference should be made to the takeoff and landing *performance charts* in the Pilot's Operating Handbook. The official source of *airport data* is the Chart Supplement U.S. *Weather data* (wind and temperature) affecting the performance can be obtained from the forecast. See chapter 9 for more on takeoff and landing performance. Refer to figures 25-8 and 25-9.

TAKEOFF DISTANCE

SHORT FIELD

SAMPLE ONLY
not to be used
in conjunction
with flight operations
or flight planning

CONDITIONS:
Flaps 10°
Full Throttle Prior to Brake Release
Paved, Level, Dry Runway
Zero Wind

NOTES:
1. Short field technique as specified in Section 4.
2. Prior to takeoff from fields above 3000 feet elevation, the mixture should be leaned to give maximum RPM in a full throttle, static runup.
3. Decrease distances 10% for each 9 knots headwind. For operation with tailwinds up to 10 knots, increase distances by 10% for each 2 knots.
4. For operation on a dry, grass runway, increase distances by 15% of the "ground roll" figure.

WEIGHT LBS	TAKEOFF SPEED KIAS		PRESS ALT FT	0°C		10°C		20°C		30°C		40°C	
	LIFT OFF	AT 50 FT		GRND ROLL FT	TOTAL FT TO CLEAR 50 FT OBS	GRND ROLL FT	TOTAL FT TO CLEAR 50 FT OBS	GRND ROLL FT	TOTAL FT TO CLEAR 50 FT OBS	GRND ROLL FT	TOTAL FT TO CLEAR 50 FT OBS	GRND ROLL FT	TOTAL FT TO CLEAR 50 FT OBS
1670	50	54	S.L.	640	1190	695	1290	755	1390	810	1495	875	1605
			1000	705	1310	765	1420	825	1530	890	1645	960	1770
			2000	775	1445	840	1565	910	1690	980	1820	1055	1960
			3000	855	1600	925	1730	1000	1870	1080	2020	1165	2185

Figure 25-8 Excerpt from a Cessna 152 takeoff performance chart.

LANDING DISTANCE

SHORT FIELD

SAMPLE ONLY
not to be used
in conjunction
with flight operations
or flight planning

CONDITIONS:
Flaps 30°
Power Off
Maximum Braking
Paved, Level, Dry Runway
Zero Wind

NOTES:
1. Short field technique as specified in Section 4.
2. Decrease distances 10% for each 9 knots headwind. For operation with tailwinds up to 10 knots, increase distances by 10% for each 2 knots.
3. For operation on a dry, grass runway, increase distances by 45% of the "ground roll" figure.
4. If a landing with flaps up is necessary, increase the approach speed by 7 KIAS and allow for 35% longer distances.

WEIGHT LBS	SPEED AT 50 FT KIAS	PRESS ALT FT	0°C		10°C		20°C		30°C		40°C	
			GRND ROLL FT	TOTAL FT TO CLEAR 50 FT OBS	GRND ROLL FT	TOTAL FT TO CLEAR 50 FT OBS	GRND ROLL FT	TOTAL FT TO CLEAR 50 FT OBS	GRND ROLL FT	TOTAL FT TO CLEAR 50 FT OBS	GRND ROLL FT	TOTAL FT TO CLEAR 50 FT OBS
1670	54	S.L.	450	1160	465	1185	485	1215	500	1240	515	1265
		1000	465	1185	485	1215	500	1240	520	1270	535	1295
		2000	485	1215	500	1240	520	1270	535	1300	555	1330
		3000	500	1240	520	1275	540	1305	560	1335	575	1360

Figure 25-9 Excerpt from a Cessna 152 landing performance chart.

The Flight Plan Form

AIM Chapter 5 provides an additional description of the International Flight Plan form.

Fill out the ICAO International Flight Plan form. This is the standardized form for both domestic and international flights. A typical domestic VFR flight will require the blue highlighted portions be filled in (see figure 25-10). It is to your benefit to fill in as much information about your flight as possible. Table 25-1 describes the minimum required items that must be filled in for a domestic VFR flight.

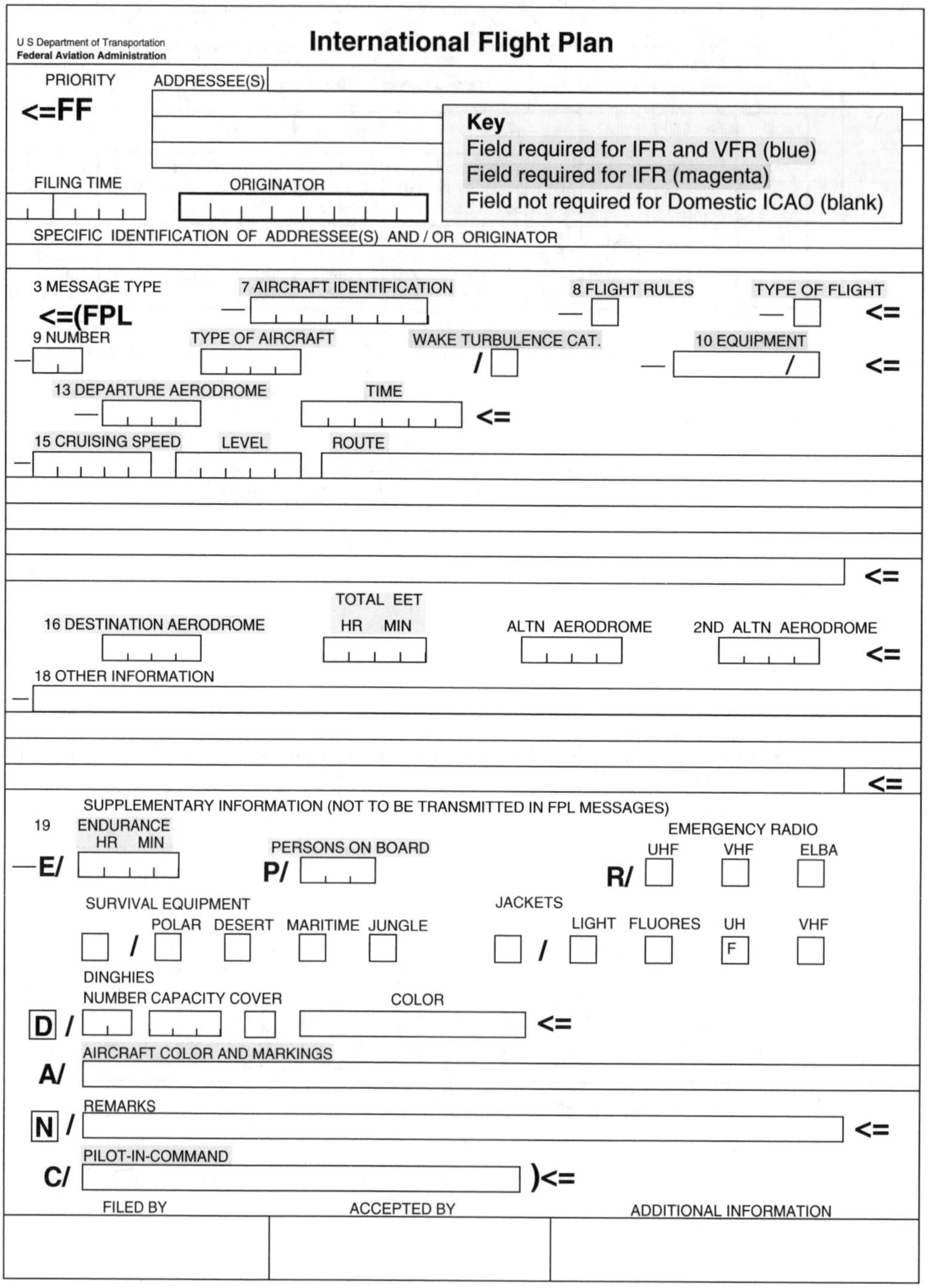

U S Department of Transportation
Federal Aviation Administration

International Flight Plan

PRIORITY
<=FF
ADDRESSEE(S)

Key
Field required for IFR and VFR (blue)
Field required for IFR (magenta)
Field not required for Domestic ICAO (blank)

FILING TIME
ORIGINATOR
SPECIFIC IDENTIFICATION OF ADDRESSEE(S) AND / OR ORIGINATOR

3 MESSAGE TYPE
<=(FPL
7 AIRCRAFT IDENTIFICATION
8 FLIGHT RULES
TYPE OF FLIGHT
<=
9 NUMBER
TYPE OF AIRCRAFT
WAKE TURBULENCE CAT.
/
10 EQUIPMENT
/
<=
13 DEPARTURE AERODROME
TIME
<=
15 CRUISING SPEED
LEVEL
ROUTE
<=
16 DESTINATION AERODROME
TOTAL EET
HR MIN
ALTN AERODROME
2ND ALTN AERODROME
<=
18 OTHER INFORMATION
<=

19
SUPPLEMENTARY INFORMATION (NOT TO BE TRANSMITTED IN FPL MESSAGES)
ENDURANCE
HR MIN
—E/
PERSONS ON BOARD
P/
EMERGENCY RADIO
UHF VHF ELBA
R/
SURVIVAL EQUIPMENT
POLAR DESERT MARITIME JUNGLE
/
JACKETS
LIGHT FLUORES UH VHF
/
F
DINGHIES
NUMBER CAPACITY COVER
COLOR
D /
<=
AIRCRAFT COLOR AND MARKINGS
A/
REMARKS
N /
<=
PILOT-IN-COMMAND
C/
)<=
FILED BY
ACCEPTED BY
ADDITIONAL INFORMATION

Figure 25-10 ICAO International Flight Plan form.

Item	Explanation of Item
7	AIRCRAFT IDENTIFICATION: Insert the full registration number of the aircraft ("N" number).
8	FLIGHT RULES: Enter one of the following letters to denote the category of flight rules with which the pilot intends to comply: V (VFR), I (IFR), Y (IFR to VFR), Z (VFR to IFR).
9	TYPE OF AIRCRAFT: Enter the aircraft type designator (i.e. C172, for a Cessna 172).
13	DEPARTURE AERODROME: Insert the ICAO four letter identifier of your departure airport. TIME: Enter estimated off-block time.
15	CRUISE SPEED: Insert the true airspeed for the first or the whole cruising portion of the flight, in terms of knots, expressed as N followed by 4 digits (e.g. N0125 for 125 knots). LEVEL: Insert the planned cruising altitude in hundreds of feet for the first or the whole portion of the route to be flown expressed as A followed by 3 figures (e.g. A075 for 7,500 feet MSL). ROUTE: Insert your intended route of flight.
16	DESTINATION AERODROME: Insert the ICAO identifier of your destination airport. TOTAL EET: Insert your total estimated elapsed time (your time en route).
19	ENDURANCE: Insert 4-digits group giving the fuel endurance in hours and minutes. PERSONS ON BOARD: Insert the total number of persons (passengers and crew) on board. AIRCRAFT COLOR AND MARKINGS: Insert color of aircraft and significant markings. PILOT-IN-COMMAND: Insert name of pilot-in-command.

Table 25-1 Description of required entries for a domestic VFR flight plan.

Flight Notification

Prior to flight, contact the FAA and file the flight plan by calling 1-800-WX-BRIEF or online at 1800wxbrief.com.

Airplane Documentation and Preparation for Flight

You should check that the required documents are carried:

- "AROW"—for the airplane (see page 465 for details); and
- pilot certificate and medical certificate (and logbook with endorsements if you are a student pilot)—for yourself as pilot-in-command.

"AROW"
- *Airworthiness Certificate*
- *Registration Certificate*
- *Operating limitations (Flight Manual, etc.)*
- *Weight-and-balance information*

You must be familiar with these airplane documents, any equipment list, weight-and-balance data, maintenance requirements and appropriate records.

Ensure that there is adequate fuel on board and complete your normal preflight duties, including the external (walk-around) inspection and internal inspection. Never hurry this aspect of the flight. It is most important that the preflight preparation is thorough and, even if you are running behind schedule because flight planning took longer than expected (a common reason), do not rush your normal preflight duties.

UNITED STATES OF AMERICA
DEPARTMENT OF TRANSPORTATION—FEDERAL AVIATION ADMINISTRATION
STANDARD AIRWORTHINESS CERTIFICATE

1 NATIONALITY AND REGISTRATION MARKS	2 MANUFACTURER AND MODEL	3 AIRCRAFT SERIAL NUMBER	4 CATEGORY
N620FT	American General Aircraft AG-5B	10009	Normal Utility

5 AUTHORITY AND BASIS FOR ISSUANCE
This airworthiness certificate is issued pursuant to the Federal Aviation Act of 1958 and certifies that as of the date of issuance the aircraft to which issued has been inspected and found to conform to the type certificate therefor to be in condition for safe operation, and has been shown to meet the requirements of the applicable comprehensive and detailed airworthiness code as provided by Annex 8 to the Convention on International Civil Aviation, except as noted herein
Exceptions

None

6 TERMS AND CONDITIONS
Unless sooner surrendered, suspended, revoked, or a termination date is otherwise established by the Administrator this airworthiness certificate is effective as long as the maintenance, preventative maintenance and alterations are performed in accordance with Parts 21, 43, and 91 of the Federal Aviation Regulations, as appropriate and the aircraft is registered in the United States

DATE OF ISSUANCE	FAA REPRESENTATIVE	DESIGNATION NUMBER
12-20-90	Emil F. Miehlke	CE-51

Any alteration, reproduction, or misuse of this certificate may be punishable by a fine not exceeding $1,000 or imprisonment not exceeding 3 years, or both. THIS CERTIFICATE MUST BE DISPLAYED IN THE AIRCRAFT IN ACCORDANCE WITH APPLICABLE FEDERAL AVIATION REGULATIONS.

FAA Form 8100-2 (8-82) U.S. GOVERNMENT PRINTING OFFICE: 1988-0-562-105

REGISTRATION NOT TRANSFERABLE

UNITED STATES OF AMERICA
DEPARTMENT OF TRANSPORTATION - FEDERAL AVIATION ADMINISTRATION
CERTIFICATE OF AIRCRAFT REGISTRATION

This certificate must be in the aircraft when operated.

NATIONALITY AND REGISTRATION MARKS N 620FT
AIRCRAFT SERIAL NO. 10009

MANUFACTURER AND MANUFACTURER'S DESIGNATION OF AIRCRAFT
AMERICAN GENERAL ACFT CORP AG5B
ICAO Aircraft Address Code: 52013314

ISSUED TO
FLORIDA INSTITUTE OF TECHNOLOGY
150 W UNIVERSITY BLVD
MELBOURNE FL 32901

CORPORATION

This certificate is issued for registration purposes only and is not a certificate of title. The Federal Aviation Administration does not determine rights of ownership as between private persons.

It is certified that the above described aircraft has been entered on the register of the Federal Aviation Administration, United States of America, in accordance with the Convention on International Civil Aviation dated December 7, 1944, and with the Federal Aviation Act of 1958, and regulations issued thereunder.

DATE OF ISSUE
FEB. 04, 1991

ADMINISTRATOR

U.S. Department of Transportation
Federal Aviation Administration

AC Form 8050-3(7/89) Supersedes previous editions

Figure 25-11 Examples of airworthiness and registration certificates.

Complete as much flight planning as possible a day or more in advance of your planned flight.

Settle into the cockpit and place your navigation equipment and charts where they are readily accessible. Ensure that the charts are folded so that at least 20 NM either side of course is visible. Ensure that no metallic or magnetic objects (like headsets) are placed near the magnetic compass. Check on the comfort of your passengers (at this stage your flight instructor), and carry out any necessary briefing.

These final checks are worthwhile since, once the engine starts, the noise level will be higher, communication will be slightly more difficult, and you will be busier with the normal workload of manipulating the airplane.

Route Segment	Safety Altitude	Altitude	Temp C	TAS	Course			Wind T	Heading						Speed/Distance/Time			
					TC (ref long)	Var	MC (VOR)		WCA	TH	Var	MH	Dev	CH	GS	Dist	ETA ATE	ETA ATE
Peter Ck R																		
Dermott	2800	5500	+10	107	062	4E	058	270/30	–9	053	4E	049	+1	050	132	65	30	
Kelly	1300	5500	+10	107	177	3E	174	270/30	+12	189	3E	186	+2	188	105	47	25	
															TOTAL	112	55	

DEVIATION CARD

FOR	N	30	60	E	120	150
STEER	001	031	060	089	118	149
FOR	S	210	240	W	300	330
STEER	181	213	242	271	301	330

ON ☒ RADIOS ☐ NO

Base your selection of cruise altitude on Magnetic Course (also use it when selecting VOR radials)

Calculate MH at flight-planning stage, and apply any deviation in flight (found on compass card in aircraft)

Figure 25-12 Flight log for a flight from Peter Creek to Kelly, via Dermott.

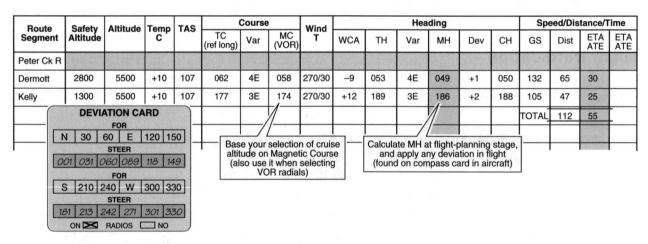

Review 25
Flight Planning

1. When planning a VFR flight, what weather information should you study?
2. Where is detailed airport information found?
3. True or false? You should normally plan a VFR flight to cruise at least 500 feet AGL over open country.
4. What are the minimum altitudes for the following?
   a. Flying above mountainous terrain.
   b. Clearing wildlife refuges.
5. True or false? If planning to fly more than 3,000 feet AGL, you should you base your VFR cruise altitude on magnetic heading.
6. True or false? VOR radials are based on true north.
7. Cloud bases in Area Forecasts are given in:
   a. feet MSL.
   b. feet AGL.
8. Cloud bases in Terminal Aerodrome Forecasts are given in:
   a. feet MSL.
   b. feet AGL.
9. What are suitable cruise altitudes at or above your safety altitude of 4,300 feet MSL if the cloud bases are at 7,000 feet MSL and your planned magnetic course is:
   a. MC 060.
   b. MC 250.
   c. MC 179.
   d. MC 180.
10. How is fuel information specified on a flight plan form submitted to FSS?

Refer to figure 25-10 on page 580 for questions 11 to 13.

11. If more than one cruising level is intended, which one should be entered?
12. What information should be entered under ENDURANCE?
13. What information should be entered under item 8?
14. How should a VFR flight plan be closed at the completion of the flight at a controlled airport?

Answers are given on page 707.

En Route Navigation 26

As the pilot/navigator of a light airplane operating in visual conditions, you must be able to fly the airplane accurately and safely, and at the same time carry out the necessary navigation activities which will ensure that you arrive at your planned destination.

Proper division of attention between flying and navigating is crucial.

The basis of successful navigation is proper *preflight planning*. You must ensure that you measure the intended courses and distances accurately, and then apply the correct forecast wind velocities and planned TAS so as to derive the headings and groundspeeds. Once airborne, you must be able to confirm the actual track of the airplane over the ground and, if this turns out to be different from your planned course, know how to make proper estimates of the alteration to your heading so as to regain the planned course.

The aim of this chapter is to show you how to go about the business of pilot/navigation in an effective manner, and with the minimum interruption to the main task—flying the airplane safely. There are several components to successful pilot/navigation:

Cross-country flying involves a combination of pilotage, dead reckoning, and radio navigation.

- *flight planning*;
- *chart-reading* (sometimes referred to as *pilotage*) which means determining your position over the ground by comparing the ground features with those marked on the chart;
- using *navigation aids* to assist and/or confirm your map-reading;
- *making corrections* to your flight path over the ground so as to regain your planned course and reach your destination; and
- using *dead reckoning* to back up your other visual navigation methods.

As explained in chapter 25, we need to work out a navigation plan for all flights. From this plan we will have established the headings, groundspeeds and time intervals between points on the route. We will also have preselected suitable ground features (or checkpoints) which we can use to assess the accuracy of our plan. To assist in the identification of these features, we can note the compass heading to fly and estimated elapsed time between them.

A fix is the geographical position of an aircraft at a specific time determined by visual reference to the surface of the earth, or by navigation equipment.

By flying your planned heading for an estimated time, you should arrive at or near the next checkpoint at the planned time. By comparing the chart to the ground, you will be able to *visually fix* your position without using navigation equipment.

Fixing the aircraft's position is not a continuous process second by second throughout the flight, but rather a regular process repeated every 10 or 15 minutes. (This may need to be reduced to a shorter interval in areas requiring very precise tracking like VFR Transition Routes through busy Class B airspace.)

A pinpoint is the ground position of an aircraft at a specific time determined by direct observation of the ground.

If you try to identify ground features to obtain a fix at shorter time intervals than this, then you may find yourself just flying from feature to feature without any time being available for the other important navigation tasks, such as planning ahead and monitoring the fuel situation, and looking for traffic.

For normal en route navigation you should fly the flight plan, fly accurately (by scanning the instruments and looking well ahead) and periodically identify landmarks.

Note. After each fix, use the ground track and groundspeed achieved to mentally plan ahead to the next feature, so that you can anticipate it appearing in your view.

Compensating for Wind Effect

Tracking error can be caused by changing wind, poorly calculated or flown headings, or a misaligned heading indicator.

Most navigation calculations are to compensate for wind effect, so if the wind differs in either speed or direction from the forecast wind, then a tracking error will probably result. If it is not possible to fix the position of the airplane, we can determine a DR position by plotting the calculated ground track and distance flown since the last fix, and mark this point on our chart.

At the flight planning stage, a forecast wind was used to calculate a HDG for the airplane to make good the desired course. This wind will almost certainly not be precisely the same as the actual wind experienced in flight. Whether your ground track in flight is left or right of the desired course will depend on whether you have allowed a wind correction angle that is greater or lower than the actual drift.

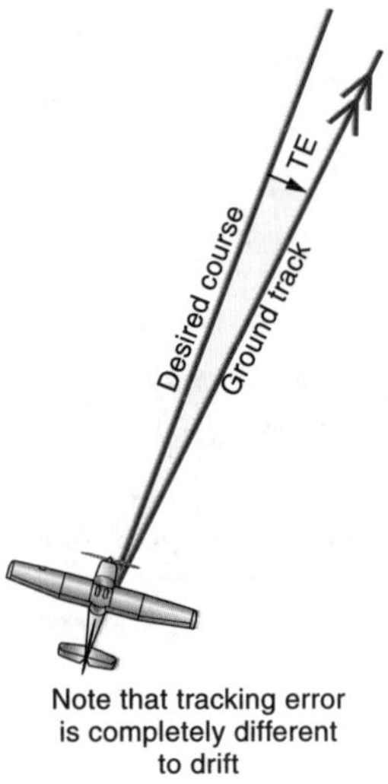

Figure 26-1 Tracking error is the angular difference between the desired course and the ground track.

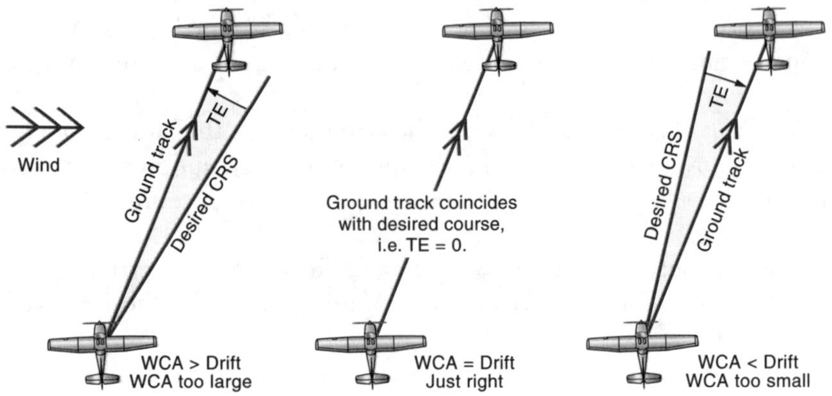

Figure 26-2 Tracking error results if WCA is greater or lesser than actual drift.

If we find that we are not maintaining the planned course, then we can counteract a tracking error by modifying the heading and so regain the original course. It is also usual to find that the actual in-flight groundspeed differs from that expected at the flight planning stage, when all we had at hand was the forecast winds. This means that the original *estimated times en route* (ETEs) to cover certain distances could be somewhat in error and may need to be modified once an accurate in-flight check of groundspeed is obtained. The *estimated time of arrival* (ETA) at any point can then be revised.

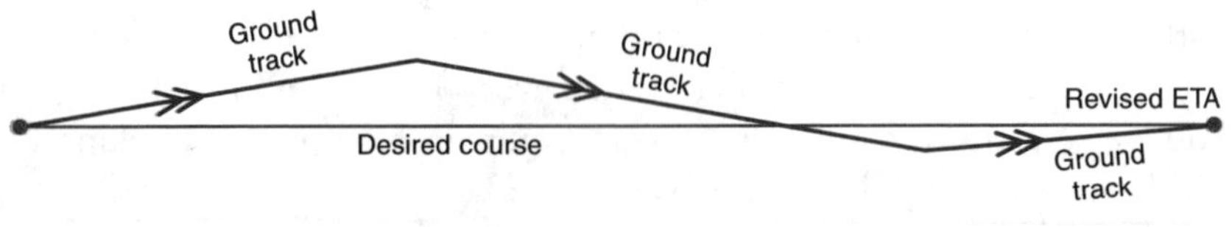

Figure 26-3 In-flight modification of HDGs and ETEs is usual in en route navigation.

First and foremost, the most important way to keep in-flight navigation workload to a minimum is to be thorough in your preflight preparation. For in-flight navigation, concentrate on simple mental calculations and simple flight computer operations. This will allow you to modify the headings and estimated times en route (ETEs) calculated at the flight planning stage without too much "head-down" work, and the methods that we discuss here will be adequate for most situations.

Airmanship

Airmanship is common sense. Fly the airplane accurately at all times (HDG ±5°; altitude ±100 feet; indicated airspeed ±5 knots). Even though you are looking out of the cockpit most of the time to monitor the attitude and heading of the airplane and to check for other traffic, you should periodically check the flight instruments to achieve precise heading, airspeed and altitude.

Flying improper headings is the leading cause of getting lost.

Setting the correct power and holding the attitude will result in the required performance in general terms but, to fly precisely, you will need to refer to the flight instruments and make suitable minor adjustments to the attitude and the power. This means take a quick look at the relevant flight instruments every 10 seconds or so throughout the flight. Strive to develop a rapid scan rate, which will assist accurate flying.

Check your heading indicator against the magnetic compass frequently.

Ensure that the airplane is in trim, and can fly itself accurately "hands-off"; not that you will actually fly it hands-off, but correct trimming will considerably lighten your task of maintaining altitude and heading. Check that the TAS used in your preflight calculations is within 5 knots of that actually being flown, and that the altitude is within 100 feet; if not, do something about it by adjusting the power and the attitude.

To reduce work load, keep the airplane trimmed so it will fly hands off.

Keep your paperwork in the cockpit neat and accessible. Do not work head-down for more than a few seconds at a time.

Keep a good lookout!

Continually *observe weather* conditions, not only ahead of you, but also to either side and behind (just in case you have to beat a hasty retreat). You must assess any deterioration in weather and modify your flight accordingly. Ask Flight Service for an update on the weather en route and at your destination airport if you desire this information. Their function is to provide a service to you.

Be aware of the total weather picture. Flight Service is available on 122.2 Mhz.

Take appropriate action to *avoid hazardous conditions*. For instance, it is good airmanship to divert around thunderstorms instead of flying near or under them, and to avoid areas of fog and reduced visibility, as well as dense smoke from fires because the visibility will be reduced and the air turbulent.

Obtain a position fix every 10 or 15 minutes and update your headings and ETAs (more frequently in poor visibility and/or congested airspace).

Periodically fix your position.

Also, carry out *regular en route checks* of the magnetic compass and heading indicator alignment, engine instruments, and electrical and other systems. This en route check can be remembered by a convenient mnemonic such as "*FREHA*:"

Periodically check the operation of your airplane.

F Fuel on and sufficient;
Fuel tank usage monitored;
Mixture, leaned as required for the cruise;
Fuel pump (if installed), as required.

R Radio frequency correctly selected, volume and squelch satisfactory, any required calls made.

E Engine: oil temperature and pressure within limits, carburetor heat if required, other systems checked, such as the electrical system, suction (if vacuum-driven gyroscopes are installed).

H Heading indicator (direction indicator or directional gyro) aligned with the magnetic compass, and your position checked on the chart.

A Altitude checked and the correct current altimeter setting in the pressure window.

If you encounter deteriorating weather, consider making a 180.

Constantly re-evaluate your go/no-go decision during the flight.

Maintain a *time awareness*, so you always know how much fuel you have left and how much further (in terms of time) you can go before refueling.

Time awareness = fuel awareness

The Flight Sequence

Departure from an Airport

On your initial exercises, the simplest method of departure may be to set your initial heading from directly over the top of the field at cruise speed and at the cruise altitude. The actual method of departing an airport will depend on the direction of the airport traffic pattern, and the nature of the airport and surrounding terrain.

Many airports have no restrictions placed on them, but this is not always the case. For instance, a number of airports lie within Class B, C, or D airspace, and have VFR Transition Routes which must be adhered to. Other airports may have local restrictions because of heavy traffic, high terrain or nearby built-up areas calling for special departure or arrival procedures. Refer to the Chart Supplement U.S., and to Terminal Area Charts.

If you depart by any means other than departing from over the top, then a simple calculation of *actual time of departure* (ATD) needs to be made. Your en route *estimated times of arrival* (ETAs) will be based on this (at least initially, until groundspeed checks allow you to update them).

We will consider *two* possible methods of departing on a course of, for example, 150°M from an airport where the appropriate runway to use is RWY 6 and the traffic pattern is left-handed. Assume airport elevation to be 1,200 feet MSL.

Since your compass will be experiencing acceleration and turning errors while setting course, ensure that the gyroscopic heading indicator is aligned with the magnetic compass prior to commencing your takeoff roll, and ensure that both the compass and the HI agree at least approximately with the runway direction.

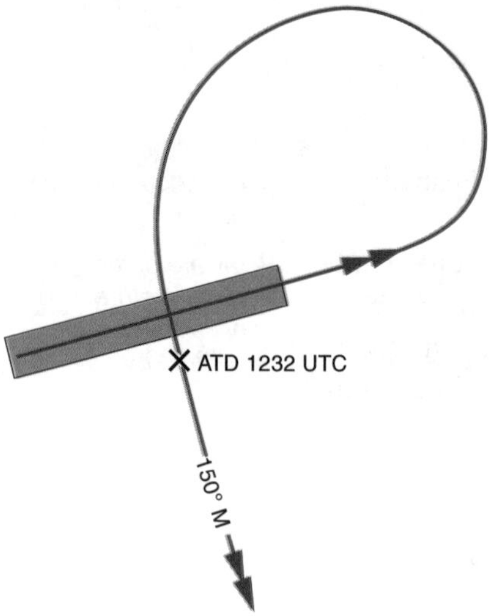

Figure 26-4
Method 1: Setting course overhead.

Method 1. Turning in the Direction of the Traffic Pattern

After takeoff, climb out straight ahead and turn in the direction of the traffic pattern. Continue turns in the pattern direction and set course *overhead* the field at a suitable altitude above other aircraft in the traffic pattern. Log the actual time of departure (ATD) in the appropriate place on the flight log. The ATD will be your time of setting course overhead the airport.

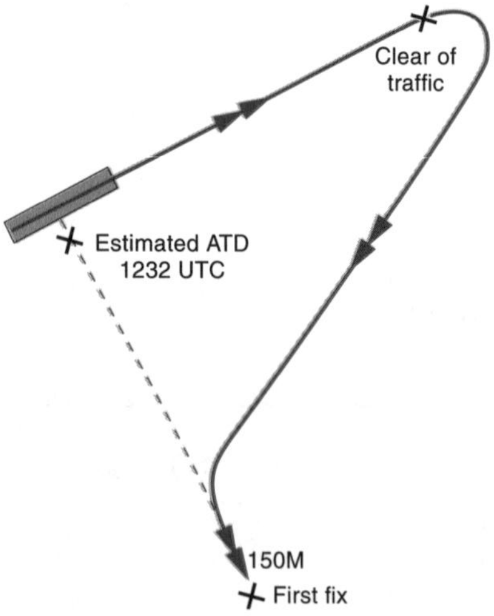

Figure 26-5
Method 2: Setting course en route and calculating ATD.

Method 2. Climbing Straight Ahead Until Well Clear of the Traffic Pattern Before Turning to Take Up the Desired Heading

This method is necessary when, after takeoff, flying directly overhead of the airport is not an option. This is most often the case at busier, towered airports.

After completing your run-up and prior to calling for takeoff clearance, make your best estimate of what your actual time of departure will be. Based on this estimate, and your previously calculated time en route, determine the time of arrival at your first checkpoint and make a note of it on your navigation log.

Making these estimates and calculations prior to departure will reduce your work load during the busy departure phase and allow you to concentrate fully on flying the aircraft and navigating to the first checkpoint. At a non-towered airport, you may be able to taxi into position on the runway and then quickly do these calculations just before you takeoff. At a towered airport, you will probably not have this luxury and will have to rely more on estimates.

Once cleared for takeoff, make a quick mental note of the actual takeoff time and how much, in whole minutes, it varies from your estimate. Once you get leveled off and headed toward your first checkpoint, you can add or subtract the difference to "fine tune" your estimated time of arrival at the first fix if needed. Just remember that, since you are not actually flying directly to your first checkpoint, you may be a minute or more late arriving at your first fix.

Example 26-1

You're number one ready for takeoff. You estimate that it will take you three more minutes for the tower to actually clear you for takeoff. The current time is 12:29. Therefore, you estimate your actual time of departure to be 12:32. Your previously completed flight log shows an estimate of 11 minutes to get to your first checkpoint at your computed climb groundspeed. Based on this information, you calculate that you will arrive at the first fix at 12:42, and you note this on your flight log. Once cleared for takeoff, you glance at the clock and notice it is now 12:35, three minutes past your estimate. As a result, you know that you will probably be approximately three minutes late arriving at your first checkpoint.

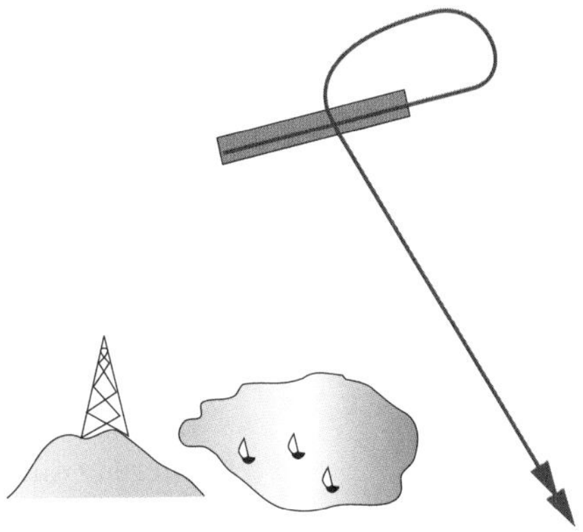

Figure 26-6
Check approximate course direction soon after departure.

Alternatively, if there is a laid down departure route via a specific point, then you can log your time of departure from that specific point. The main purpose is to have a starting point in time for your en route time calculations. Remember that fuel, however, is being burned from the moment the engine starts.

Immediately after setting course, you should log the actual time of departure (ATD) and insert your estimate overhead the first checkpoint, based on the ATD and the flight-planned ETE.

Rough Check of Departure Ground Track

On departure you should have in mind some ground feature en route which is within 10 or 15 NM of the airport, against which you can check that you are indeed tracking in approximately the right direction.

Example 26-2

After takeoff from a certain airport and taking up the calculated heading to achieve your desired course of say 150°, you should pass slightly left of a large lake about 8 NM from the airport. To confirm that it is the correct lake, the chart shows a large hill with a radio mast on its north-west side, so you should use these to confirm your identification of it.

Within the first few minutes you should ensure that you are making good the correct course by obtaining a fix. Use your flight-planned groundspeed to calculate the ETA at the next checkpoint. If you are in any doubt, check the heading indicator against the magnetic compass. For accuracy, apply the deviation correction found on the card in the cockpit to amend degrees magnetic to degrees compass.

Cruise

Check correct altimeter setting approximately every 100 miles.

On reaching the cruise level you should ensure that you have the correct local altimeter setting in the pressure window. Establish cruise speed and cruise power and trim the airplane. Scan all the vital instruments and systems for correct operation. Verify that the HI is aligned with the magnetic compass. Now is a good time to do a full FREHA en route check. It is good airmanship to check right away that you are achieving the desired heading and true airspeed (TAS) in cruise. This may be done very quickly by:

As soon as possible during the cruise, obtain a ground speed and heading check.

- setting the adjustable *temp/TAS* scale, if installed on your ASI, so as well as reading IAS on one scale, the other scale indicates TAS;
- using your flight computer (by setting pressure altitude against temperature, and reading off TAS on the outer scale against IAS on the inner); or
- approximation (at 5,000 feet TAS is about 8% greater than IAS, and at 10,000 feet TAS is about 17% greater than IAS);

If the achieved TAS is significantly different from that expected, then you should check:

- correct power set;
- correct airplane configuration—flaps up, and landing gear up and position of cowl flaps (if appropriate); and
- mixture properly leaded for cruising altitude.

From two position fixes separated by about 20 to 30 NM, you should be able to establish an accurate groundspeed and determine if your heading is achieving the desired course or not. Naturally, if you are about to fly over featureless terrain or water where position fixing will be difficult, there is nothing to stop you using fixes obtained on the climb. Good airmanship is just a matter of common sense.

If the actual GS is significantly different from that calculated, then you will have to revise your ETAs. If your actual ground track differs significantly from the desired course, then you will have to make a HDG change. Make use of the best available information to estimate a suitable heading. Techniques of calculating the amount of HDG change are discussed later in this chapter. To get good fixes you need to select good checkpoints and make use of your map-reading skills.

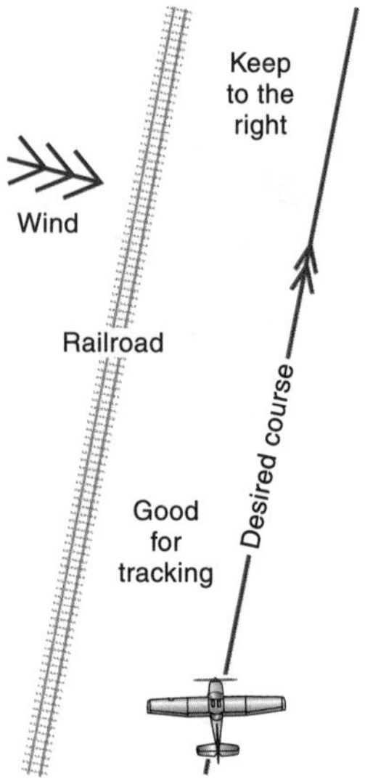

Figure 26-7
Long, narrow features are particularly useful to parallel.

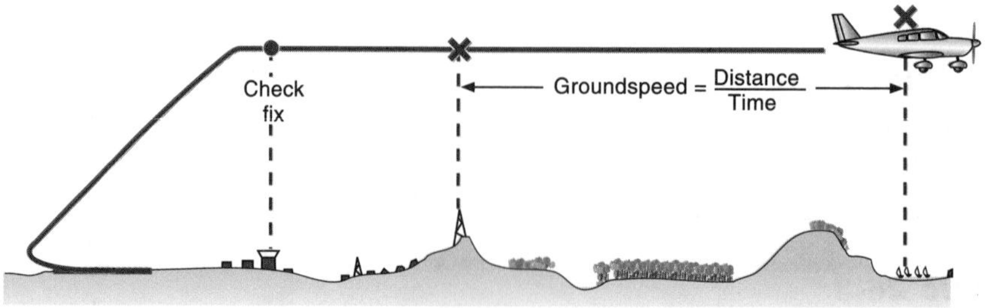

Figure 26-8 Obtain a check on GS and tracking early in the cruise.

Chart-Reading In Flight

The success of map-reading depends on four basic factors:

- a knowledge of *direction*;
- a knowledge of *distance*;
- a knowledge of *groundspeed*; and
- the selection and identification of *landmarks* and *checkpoints*.

Select good checkpoint features. Landmarks and checkpoints that can be easily identified, and which will be within your range of visibility when you pass by them, are best. Just how conspicuous a particular feature may be from the air depends on:

- the flight visibility;
- the dimensions of the feature;
- the relationship of your selected feature to other features; the angle of observation;
- the plan outline of the feature if you are flying high; and
- the elevation and side appearance of the feature if you are flying low.

Preferably the feature should be unique in that vicinity so that it cannot be confused with another nearby similar feature. A feature that is long in one dimension and quite sharply defined in another is often useful, because:

- if a long feature (such as a railroad, canal or road) runs *parallel* to your planned course, it can assist in maintaining accurate tracking; and
- if a long feature *crosses* the course it can be used as a position line to aid in determining an updated groundspeed (GS).

The relationship between your selected feature and other nearby ground features is very important for a positive confirmation of your position. For example, there may be two small towns near each other, but you have chosen as a feature the one that has a single-track railroad to the west of the town and with a road that crosses a river on the north side of the town, whereas the other town has none of these features. This should make positive identification fairly easy.

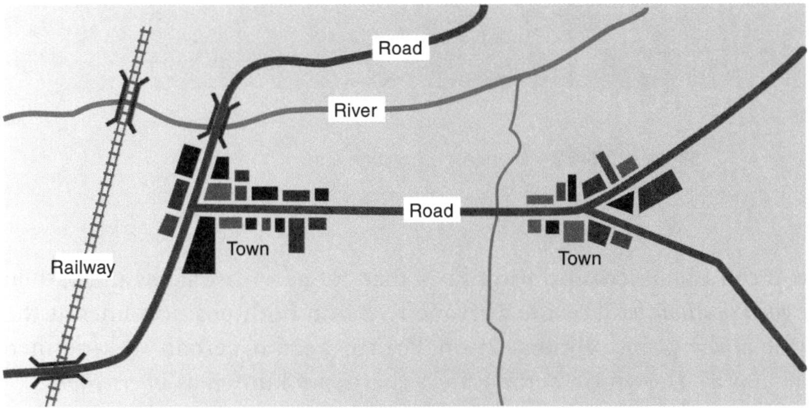

Figure 26-9 Confirm identification of your selected feature by its relationship with other features.

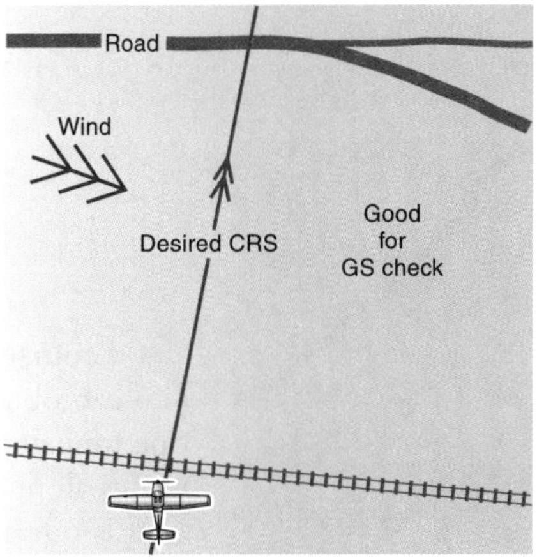

Figure 26-10 Long, narrow features are particularly useful for groundspeed checks.

Position Lines

A position line is an extended straight line joining two points, somewhere along which the airplane was located at a particular time.

Don't be afraid to mark your chart.

A *position fix* is obtained when you can positively identify the position of the airplane relative to the ground. A *position line* is not as specific as a fix because you can only identify the position of the airplane as being somewhere along that line, and not actually fixed at a particular point. You may see a position line referred to as a *PL line of position* (LoP). Position lines can be obtained:

- from long narrow features such as railroads, roads, highways, and coastlines;
- from two features that line up as the airplane passes them (known as *transit bearings*); and
- from magnetic bearings to (and from) a feature—this need not only be visual, it can also be a radio position line (a magnetic bearing from an NDB or VOR).

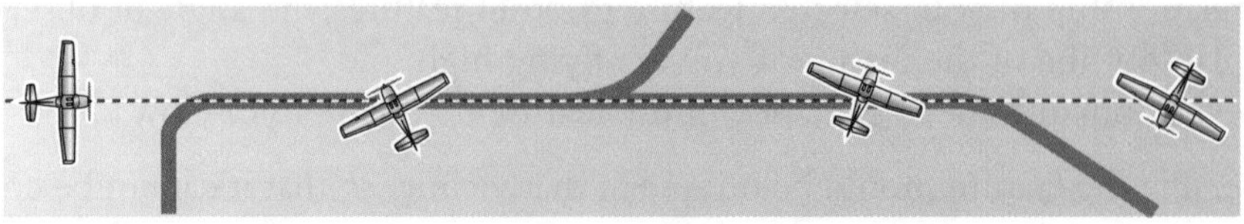

Figure 26-11 Each of these airplanes is on the same position line.

It is normal to show a position line on your chart as a straight line with an arrowhead at either end, and with the time written in UTC at one end.

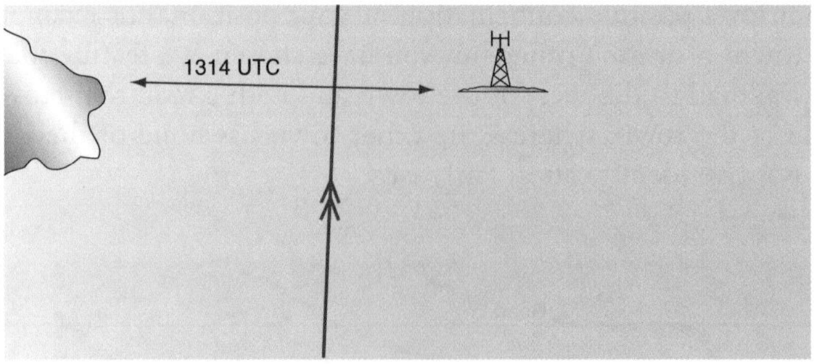

Figure 26-12 Marking a position line.

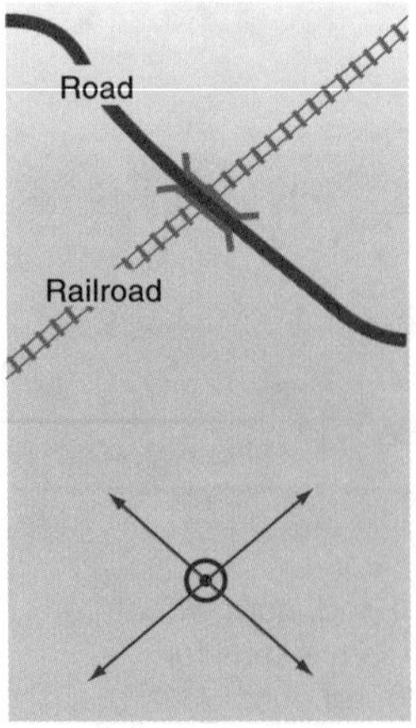

Figure 26-13 Two position lines with a good cut can give you a fix.

Of course, if you can obtain two position lines that cut at a reasonable angle, then you can obtain a *good position fix*. For the airplane to be on both position lines at the one time, it must be at the point of intersection. For this reason, certain well-defined points along *Victor airways*, shown on aeronautical charts, are known as *intersections*.

It is often possible to select two different VORs and determine which radials you are on. By marking these two radials (which are magnetic bearings from the VOR) on the chart using the compass roses centered on each of the VORs, the two position lines will intersect at your position. Navigation aids (such as VOR, NDB and DME) are discussed in detail later.

Feature Selection

Do not choose a multitude of landmarks and checkpoints. Just one good checkpoint every 15 or 20 minutes is sufficient. At a groundspeed (GS) of 120 knots, this puts them 20 to 30 NM apart. Using fixes any closer together than this can introduce significant errors in your calculations. Knowing direction, distance and groundspeed, you can think ahead, and anticipate the appearance of a landmark.

Example 26-3

From a chart, the pilot chooses a small hill with a radio mast as a suitable checkpoint about 4 NM right of the desired course and about 20 NM ahead. If the groundspeed is 120 knots the pilot will expect to be abeam of this feature in 10 minutes. If the present time is 1529 UTC, the estimated time en route (ETE) of 10 minutes gives an estimate at, or abeam, the checkpoint at 1539 UTC. He will, of course, be keeping an eye out for it for some minutes prior to this.

Begin looking for checkpoints several minutes prior to ETA.

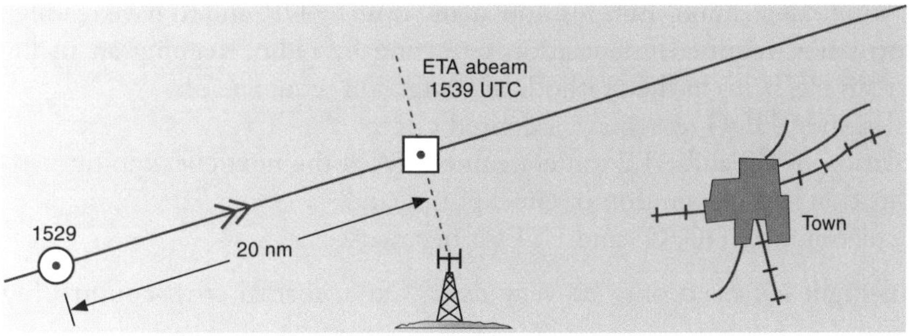

Figure 26-14 Look for a definite feature at a definite time.

If, instead of passing 4 NM abeam of the feature as expected, the airplane passes directly overhead, the pilot recognizes from this fix that the airplane is off-course. It is appropriate to confirm that the feature is indeed the selected feature and not another nearby similar one. This can be done by checking the surrounding area for additional ground detail, say a small nearby town with a railroad junction. Strive to take in the whole picture. Once certain of the position of the airplane at a particular time, the pilot can estimate a new heading to achieve the desired course.

Chart-reading is used to confirm your flight planning.

Chart Orientation in the Airplane

In flight, you should relate the land features and their relative bearing from the airplane to their representations on the chart. To do this it is best to place the chart so that your desired course runs from bottom to top. If, according to the chart, a landmark is 30° off-course to the right from the present position of the airplane, then you should be able to spot it by looking out of the airplane window approximately 30° to the right of course. (Note: It may not be 30° to the right of the heading of the airplane because the heading may differ from the course, depending on the wind correction angle applied.)

With the chart oriented correctly in the cockpit, the features shown to the right of the course drawn on your chart will appear on the right of the airplane's ground track as you fly along. The only disadvantage is that it may be difficult to read what is printed on the chart, unless you happen to be flying north.

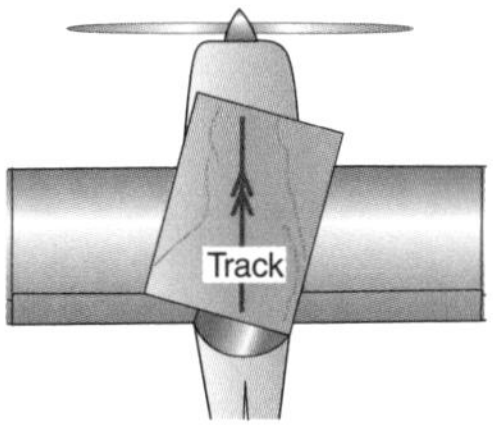

Figure 26-15 Fold and orient the chart in the cockpit prior to departure.

Select a suitable feature on the chart 10 minutes or so ahead of your present position, calculate an ETA at, or abeam, it and then at the appropriate time (two or three minutes before the ETA) start looking for the actual feature on the ground. Do not expect the feature to be dead ahead. You should include a lookout 30° either side of the nose, and beneath the aircraft to several miles ahead. Your chosen landmark need not be in view at the time you choose it, but you should anticipate it coming into view at the appropriate time. If you have flown the plan accurately, and the weather forecast has been correct, then the feature should be where you expect it to be.

Note. If your ETA has arrived and you cannot locate your fix, it may be located directly below the aircraft, out of sight.

Log Keeping

The purpose of keeping an in-flight log is to record and organize flight data. This enables you to determine your position at any time by DR and to have readily at hand the information required for position reporting by radio. Keeping an in-flight log, however simple, helps in the methodical navigation sequence of:

- calculation of HDG to achieve a desired CRS;
- calculation of GS and ETE to determine ETA at the next checkpoint;
- anticipation and recognition of checkpoints; and
- recalculation of HDG, GS and ETEs if necessary.

An in-flight log need only be very basic. On a normal cross-country flight you should log:

- takeoff time;
- actual time of departure (ATD);
- a few prominent fixes for groundspeed checks;
- ground track;
- changes of HDG (and airspeed), and time of making them;
- calculated GS;
- ETEs and revised ETAs at checkpoints;
- altitudes; and
- fuel burn data and any required ATC or FSS frequencies.

This may sound like a lot, but it isn't. Indicating ground track and fixes on the chart simplifies things for you, as these cover the two fundamentals of your progress toward your destination.

Navigation Techniques

Position Lines

Groundspeed Checks

You should update your groundspeed (GS) as the opportunities arise. *Time* is of vital importance in navigation and your time of arrival anywhere will depend on the GS that you achieve. Position lines that are approximately at right angles to your course can assist in updating your GS. Noting the amount of time it takes to cover the distance between the two position lines allows you to calculate the GS.

Example 26-4

1351 UTC—Crossing a railroad perpendicular (at right angles) to course.

1359 UTC—Transit bearing of a radio mast and a bend in a river perpendicular to course 18 NM further on. 18 NM in 8 minutes = *GS 135 knots.*

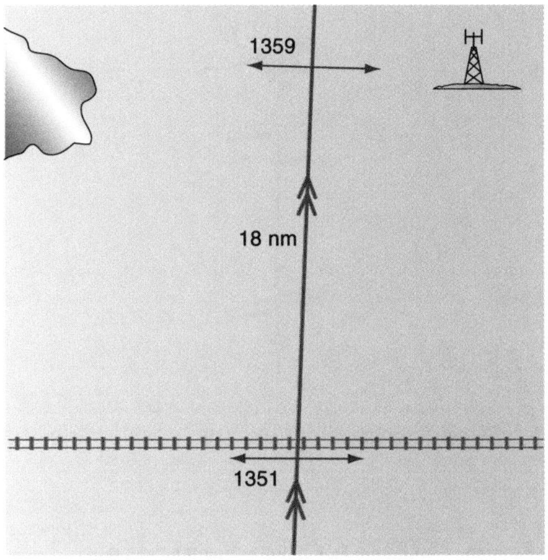

Figure 26-16 Groundspeed check using position lines perpendicular to track.

These position lines need not only be visual. You could also make use of radio position lines from an abeam NDB or VOR navigation station.

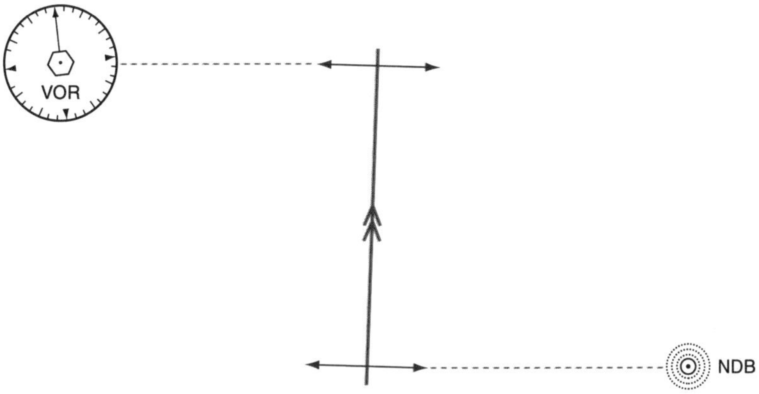

Figure 26-17 GS check using radio position lines from abeam navigation beacons (NDBs and VORs).

Estimating Drift

If you have a position line roughly parallel to course you can use it to estimate the drift angle. Tracking directly overhead a long straight railroad makes a visual estimate of your drift angle quite easy, as does tracking along a radio position line to (or from) an NDB or VOR navaid station.

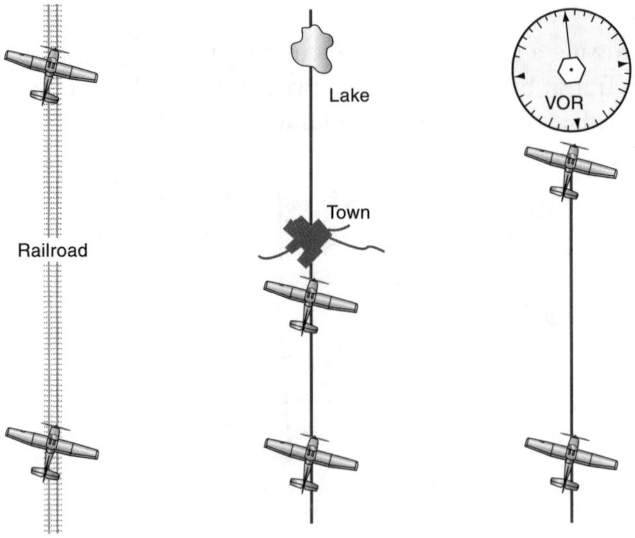

Figure 26-18 Determining drift angle from position lines parallel to track.

Off-Course Heading (HDG) Corrections

It is usual to find that the actual ground track differs from the desired course that you plotted on the chart at the flight planning stage. If this is the case, then you will have to make some precise corrections to the heading so that you can return to course at some point further on. Since the in-flight workload for the pilot/navigator can be quite high, we will concentrate on quick methods of mentally calculating course corrections.

The angle between the ground track and the required course is called *tracking error* (TE). The angle at which you want to close on your required course is known as the closing angle (CA). The size of the CA will depend on how much further down the ground track you wish to rejoin course. The sooner you want to rejoin the desired course the greater the CA will have to be.

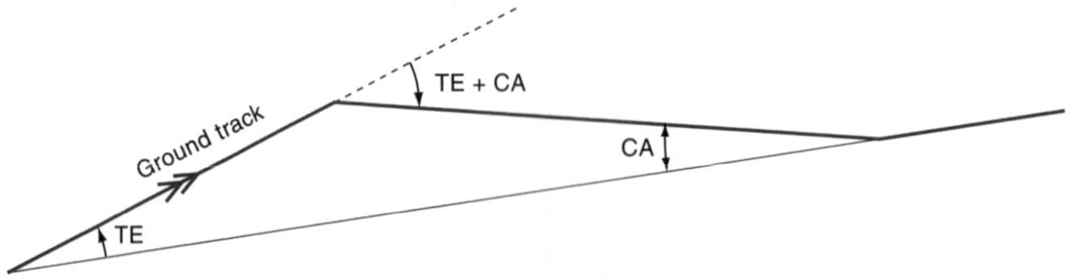

Figure 26-19 Tracking error and closing angle.

Figure 26-19 shows that to rejoin the desired course at the chosen position will involve a *course change* equal to *TE* + *CA*. (This equation makes use of a theorem of geometry that says the external angle of a triangle equals the sum of the two interior opposite angles.)

For angles up to about 15°, we can assume that a course change can be achieved by an equal heading change.

It is at this point that we make an approximation that simplifies our in-flight calculations. We assume that a *course change* of, say, 15° can be achieved by a *heading change* of the same 15°. This is not perfectly accurate because the effect of the wind may cause a different drift angle after making a significant heading change, but within limits it is accurate enough for visual navigation.

The big advantage for pilot/navigators in doing this is that it allows us to make course corrections without having to calculate the actual wind velocity.

Diversions

En Route Diversions

Occasionally, en route, you have the need to divert around a thunderstorm, a heavy rain shower, or a town. If there are suitable landmarks you can use these to assist you to divert around the "obstacle" and then to return to course.

If there are no suitable landmarks, then it is a good idea to follow a simple procedure such as:

- divert 60° to one side of the desired course for a suitable time (and note the HDG and time flown);
- parallel course for a suitable time (and note the time flown);
- return at 60° for the same time to return to course; and
- take up a suitable HDG to maintain course.

Note. A 60° diversion is convenient because an equilateral (equal-sided) triangle's three angles are each 60°. However, depending on circumstance, a different angle can be flown.

With a 60° diversion followed immediately by a 60° return to course, the actual distance flown on the diversion is *double* the on-course distance. In nil-wind conditions this will take *double* the time.

If the initial 60° diversion HDG is flown for 2 minutes, and the "return to course leg" is flown for 2 minutes then the dogleg has therefore taken 4 minutes, which means the direct on-course time interval has been exceeded by 2 minutes. Our ETA at the next checkpoint will therefore be 2 minutes later than previously estimated. If we had flown 5 minute diversion legs, then it would add 5 minutes to our ETA. The length of the leg flown parallel to course will not affect the ETA.

Note. We have assumed no-wind conditions in this discussion. If a significant wind is blowing, then you have to make appropriate allowances for it.

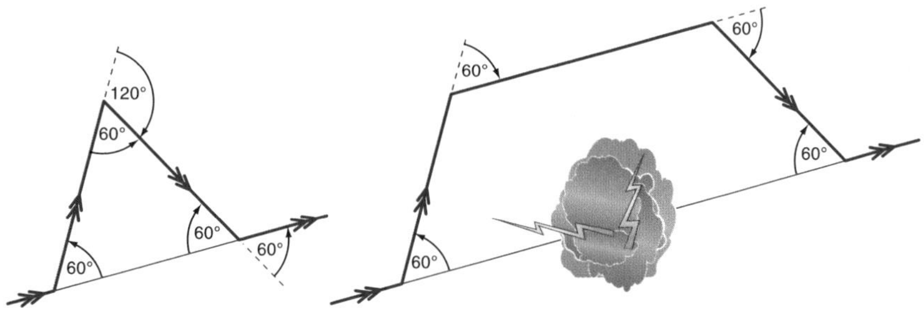

Figure 26-20 The angles of an equal-sided triangle are each 60°.

Diversion to an Alternate Airport

Sometimes it may be necessary to divert from our planned destination. This may be because of deteriorating weather at the destination, the possibility of running out of daylight if you continue the flight to your original destination, or a suspected mechanical problem that suggests an early landing would be advisable.

Some Practical Hints on Diversions

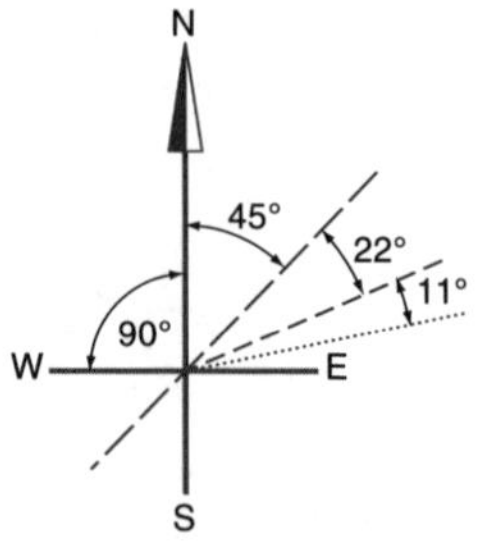

Figure 26-21 Halving angles as a means of estimating track.

Diversions sometimes become necessary at the most inopportune moments, possibly when you have other problems on your hands. It therefore pays to have a few tricks up your sleeve to allow you to make quick and practical diversions without having to get your computer out and go "head-down" in the cockpit.

If you can estimate direction and distance by eyeballing, then your diversion will be easier. Once you have taken up an approximate diversion heading and settled into the diversion course, you can calculate an accurate heading, distance to go, groundspeed and ETE in a more relaxed atmosphere.

Use pilotage for your diversions. Sometimes, the simplest thing to do is to follow a road or railroad track or other feature or combination of features to your alternate destination. Use radio navigation to proceed to your alternate. Many times, there is an NDB or VOR right on the field.

When established on your diversion, inform the nearest FSS and do not forget to *close your flight plan* when you arrive at the diversion airport. Pilots usually close flight plans after landing by telephoning the nearest FSS, or by requesting the controllers in the tower to relay the cancellation to FSS.

Eyeballing Course

Estimation of course is surprisingly easy and, with a bit of practice, you can achieve a ±5° accuracy. In fact, you should *always* estimate your course before measuring it with a protractor or plotter—this will avoid making 180° or 90° errors. Estimating before measuring will also help you develop faith in your ability to estimate to a practical degree of accuracy.

"Halving known angles" is the simplest means of estimating angles. Halving the angle between a quadrantal point and a cardinal point will give you an angle of 22.5°, say 22°, and halving this again will give you 11°. An accuracy of ±5° will be achieved with practice.

Estimating Distance

The average adult top thumb-joint will cover about 10 NM on a 1:500,000 Sectional chart (and 5 NM on 1:250,000 VFR Terminal Chart). Check yours!

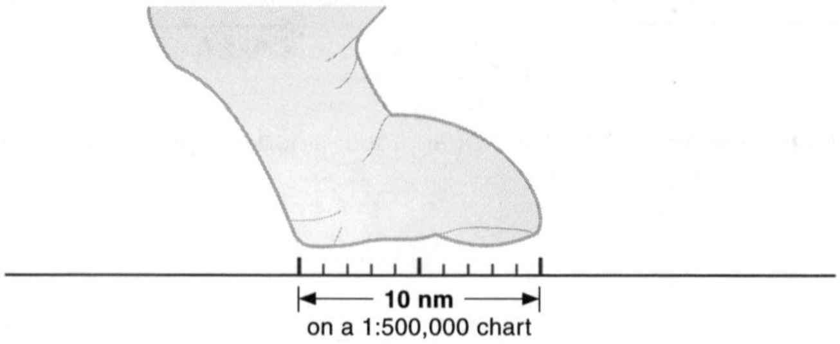

Figure 26-22 The top thumb-joint covers approximately 10 NM at 1:500,000.

A full hand span might measure 60 NM on a 1:500,000 chart. Check yours!

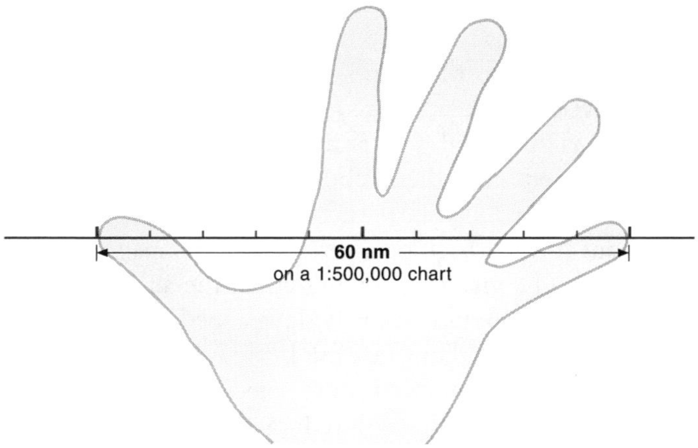

Figure 26-23 A full hand span is approximately 60 NM on a 1:500,000 chart.

If you have a 60 NM span and a 10 NM top thumb-joint, then you have built-in 1:60 measuring device, ideally designed to measure 10°.

10 NM in 60 NM = 10°, by the 1-in-60 rule.

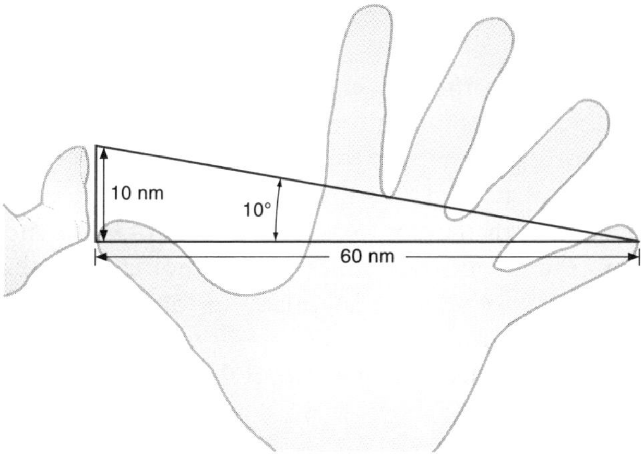

Figure 26-24 The built-in personal 1-in-60 measuring device for 10°.

Navigation Operations

Visibility

As a VFR pilot, you should only conduct cross-country flights in visual meteorological weather conditions that are forecast to permit continual observations of the ground. You should generally be able to spot each check feature at an appropriate time prior to reaching or passing abeam it.

Poor Visibility

Poor visibility may be caused by smoke, haze, mist, rain, or smog. It makes the handling of the airplane more difficult since the lack of a natural horizon makes holding an attitude more difficult. Poor visibility also means that checkpoints may not come into view until you are almost upon them and, if the checkpoints are some distance off-course, you may not even see them.

Good visibility decreases the workload on the VFR pilot/navigator.

Sooner or later you will be faced with reduced visibility. If you feel that VFR conditions cannot be maintained, or if the visibility (even if in excess of VFR minimum requirements) is not adequate for your particular flight and your particular experience, you should think about turning back or diverting to a destination with better weather. Consideration should also be given to slowing down the airplane and even extending some flap in a precautionary configuration. A slower speed gives you more time to see things, as well as reducing your radius of turn if maneuvering is required.

Poor visibility increases workload dramatically.

If you are expecting poor visibility en route, select more en route checkpoints that are closer to your desired course. This will reduce the time between fixes and reduce the anxiety you feel if you do not spot one of the check features, but the next one comes up on time shortly thereafter. If several checkpoints fail to appear, you could have reason to feel uncertain of position.

Uncertain of Position

If you have flown for some time without obtaining a fix (say 20 or 30 minutes), you may feel a little uncertain of your precise position. You will be able to calculate a DR position (using expected TR and GS), but you may feel a little anxious that you cannot back this up with a positive fix over or abeam some ground feature. Don't panic, you are not yet lost.

If a checkpoint does not come into view at the expected time, log HDG (compass and heading indicator readings) and time. If the heading indicator is incorrectly set, then you have the information needed to make a fair estimate of your actual position, so reset the HI and calculate a HDG and ETE to regain the desired course; or if the HI is aligned correctly with the compass, then the non-appearance of a landmark, while it will perhaps cause you some concern, need not indicate that you are grossly off-course. You may not have seen the landmark for some perfectly legitimate reason, such as bright sunlight obscuring your vision, poor visibility, a change in the ground features not reflected on the chart (such as removal of a TV mast or the emptying of a reservoir), or if you are navigating above even a small amount of cloud, the inconvenient positioning of some clouds may have obscured your check point.

If uncertain of your position, consider a radio call to FSS or ATC or a VOR radial crosscheck to pinpoint position.

If you consider the situation warrants it, make a radio call to FSS or ATC. They may be able to fix your position by radar or VHF/DF. If you obtain a fix, or if the next checkpoint comes up on time, the flight can continue and normal navigation procedures apply once again. If still unable to fix your position, follow the procedure below.

Procedure When Lost

Becoming lost is usually the result of some human error. Being lost is totally different from being *temporarily uncertain* of your position, where you can determine a reasonably accurate DR position. It is impossible to lay down a set of hard and fast rules on what to do, except to give you the advice that careful preflight planning and in-flight attention to the normal, simple en route navigation tasks will ensure that you will not get lost. Also, using navigation aids (discussed shortly) to back up your visual navigation will help to keep you oriented.

If you change your thinking from one of being *uncertain of position* to one of being *lost*, then make use of a nearby ATC or FSS and any radar or position-fixing service if available. If you are still lost, maintain HDG (if terrain, visibility and what you know of the proximity of controlled airspace permit) and carry out a *sequence of positive actions*. If a vital checkpoint is not in view at your ETA, then continue to fly for 10% of the time since your last positive fix. Decide what your last positive fix was, and *check the headings flown since that last fix*, ensuring that:

If lost, you must formulate a plan of action.

- the magnetic compass is not being affected by outside influences such as a camera, portable radio, headset or other magnetic material placed near it;
- the HI is aligned with the magnetic compass correctly;
- magnetic variation and drift have been correctly applied to obtain your HDGs flown; and
- an estimate of course direction on the chart against that shown on the flight plan is correct.

Read from ground to chart. Look for *significant ground features* or combinations of features and try to determine their position on the chart. Establish a "*most probable area*" in which you think you are. There are several ways in which this can be done, and we recommend that you consult your flight instructor for his or her preferred method. Two suggested methods for establishing a "most probable area" are described below.

Method 1: estimate the distance flown since the last fix and apply this distance, plus or minus 10%, to an arc 30° either side of what you estimate the probable ground course to be.

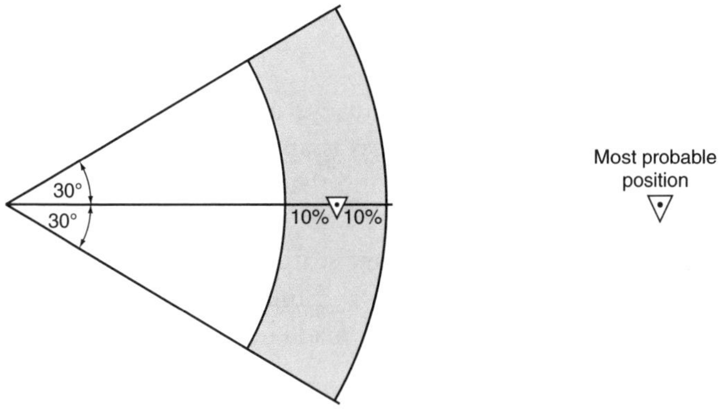

Figure 26-25 Method 1: estimating the "most probable area" that you are in.

Method 2: estimate your "most probable position" and draw a circle around it of radius equal to 10% the distance flown since the last fix.

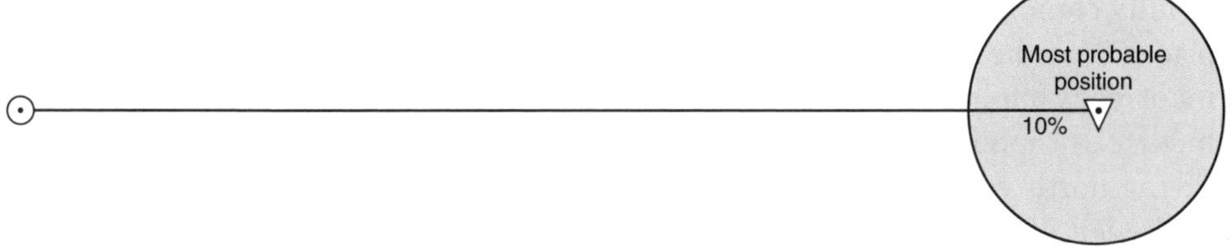

Figure 26-26 Method 2 for estimating "most probable position".

Establish a *safety altitude* at which to fly in order to ensure adequate clearance of all obstacles in what you consider the general area to be. Use MEF to determine the highest terrain or obstruction in the area as a basis from which to establish a safety altitude. Be especially careful in conditions of poor visibility or low clouds.

Check *large features* within this area of the chart with what can be seen on the ground. Try to relate those features seen on the ground with those shown on the chart. Confirm the identification of any feature by closely observing secondary details around the feature. For instance, a small irregular lake may be confirmed by the position of a small town on a bend in the railroad as it turns from west to south. Double check any fix. Water towers with city names are also helpful.

When you do positively establish a fix, recheck your HI and recommence normal navigation activity. Calculate the HDG, GS and ETE for the next check feature and set course for it. If you are still unable to fix your position, you should consider taking one of the following actions:

- inform ATC and request assistance;
- increase the "most probable area" by 10, 15 or even 20% of the distance flown from the last fix;
- climb to a higher altitude to increase your range of vision;
- turn toward a known prominent line feature, such as a coastline, large river, railroad or road, and then follow along it to the next town where you should be able to obtain a fix; and
- steer a reciprocal heading and attempt to return to your last fix.

Note the following important points of airmanship:

- if you want to cover as much ground as possible with the fuel you have available, you should fly the airplane for *best range*;
- keep a *navigation log* going;
- remain positively *aware of time*. Keep your eye on the fuel and on the time remaining until the end of daylight. If darkness is approaching, remember that it will be darker at ground level than at altitude, and that it becomes dark very quickly in the tropics; and
- if you decide to carry out a precautionary search and landing (a forced landing with the use of power), allow sufficient time and fuel to do this on the assumption that two or three inspections might have to be made before finding a suitable landing area.

Why Did You Become Lost?

A properly operating heading indicator will not precess more than 3° in 15 minutes.

If at any stage you became lost, you should systematically try to determine the reason (either in flight or post flight) so that you can learn from the experience. Common reasons for becoming lost include:

- incorrectly calculated HDGs, GSs, and ETEs (hence the need for you always to make *mental estimates* of approximate answers to these items);
- incorrectly synchronized HI—remember to check that the gyroscopic HI is aligned correctly with the magnetic compass every 10 or 15 minutes;
- a faulty compass reading (caused by transistor radios, cameras and other metal objects placed near the compass);
- incorrectly applied variation (*variation west, magnetic best; variation east, magnetic least*);
- incorrectly applied drift (compared with CRS, the HDG should be into the wind. Flying north with a westerly wind blowing would mean that the HDG should be to the left of course and into the wind);
- a wind velocity significantly different from that forecast, and not allowed for in flight by the pilot;

- a deterioration in weather, reduced visibility, increased cockpit workload;
- an incorrect fix, such as mis-identification of a check feature;
- a poorly planned diversion from the original desired course; and
- not paying attention to carrying out normal navigation tasks throughout the flight.

With regular checks of HI alignment with the magnetic compass, reasonably accurate flying of HDG, and with position fixes every 10 or 15 minutes, none of these errors should put you far off-course. It is only when you are slack and let things go a bit too far, that you become lost.

Mental Navigation Checks

If you develop the skill of carrying out mental navigation checks in flight, then it will be less likely that you will ever make a gross navigational error. Each time you are flying, not only on cross-countries but also out in the local training area, practice estimating tracks, distances and altitudes.

Making mental navigation checks will help you avoid gross navigational errors.

Wind Components

When flight planning and also en route, it is a good idea to keep a mental check on all your heading and GS calculations. Remember the following:
- a headwind component reduces groundspeed to less than true airspeed;
- a tailwind component increases groundspeed to more than true airspeed; and
- to achieve the desired course, the airplane must be headed somewhat into wind.

Example 26-5

Your desired course is west and the wind is from 220°. Having a headwind component, your GS should be less than TAS. Your heading must be into the wind compared to desired course and so will be to the left of west, a heading less than 270°. With this in mind, you check that your flight plan and en route calculations reflect this, with GS less than TAS, and HDG less than the course in this case.

Estimating Distances

Keep in mind that a *sight-down* angle of 45° from the horizon gives an approximate horizontal distance equal to your altitude AGL—either ahead or to the side. This will also help you estimate visibility while airborne.

Example 26-6

If you are 6,000 feet AGL (approximately 1 NM), a sight-down angle of 45° gives a horizontal distance of 1 NM. At 12,000 feet AGL, a sight-down angle of 45° gives 2 NM. At 3,000 feet AGL, a sight-down angle of 45° gives 0.5 NM.

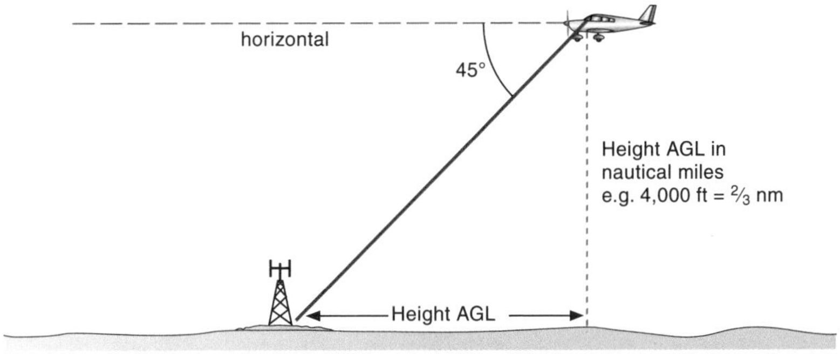

Figure 26-27 Estimating distances using sight-down angle 45° below the horizon.

The Emergency Locator Transmitter (ELT)

In remote areas visual searches can be difficult. The emergency locator transmitter (ELT), if properly used, can allow the search area to be reduced quickly so that the visual search can be concentrated in a small area.

ELT is a generic (family) term covering devices known as crash locator beacons or emergency locator beacons. They all operate on both 121.5 and 243.0 MHz.

A few common sense points on the use of the ELT are:

- know how to use the ELT and how to gain access to it if it is not remotely controlled. Review the operating instructions for your particular beacon prior to flight;
- ensure that the battery is fully charged;
- ensure that the ELT is capable of operating properly. An ELT may be tested by tuning the aircraft radio to the emergency frequency 121.5, then activating the ELT and listening for the signal. However, this type of test can only be conducted within the first five minutes of the hour and must be limited to three audible sweeps; and
- if you are forced down, do not be reluctant to activate the ELT at an appropriate time.

Review 26
En Route Navigation

1. What is meant by the term "fix?"
2. What does normal en route visual navigation consist of?
3. You cross a small town at 0325 UTC followed by a railroad junction some 27 NM further on at 0340 UTC. What is your groundspeed?
4. What is meant by the term "track error"?
5. List the situations a pilot should read from chart to ground and from ground to chart.
6. What are two essential requirements for successful navigation?
7. You have held a steady heading but observe that you are 4 NM left of track 30 NM from departure. The next turning point (TP) is 60 NM ahead. What heading correction would you make to arrive on track at the next TP?
8. To lose time, you divert 60° off track for 3 minutes, and then turn 120° to regain track. Assuming no wind and a negligible time for the turns, how much time will you lose?
9. What is the angular difference between heading and track called?
10. If you are 3 NM off track to the right in 20 NM, what is your track error?
11. You are 2 NM left of track after travelling 15 NM.
    - **a.** What is the track error?
    - **b.** To regain track in another 15 NM, what is the closing angle (CA)?
    - **c.** To regain track in another 30 NM, what is the CA?
12. You are 4 NM right of track after travelling 20 NM. By how many degrees should you change your heading to regain track in another 20 NM?
13. You are steering 293°M and 4 NM right of track after 34 NM.
    - **a.** What is the TE?
    - **b.** What is the CA to regain track in another 48 NM?
    - **c.** What heading should you take up to regain track?
    - **d.** Once on track, what would you expect your heading to be?
14. You want to descend 3,500 ft at 500 FPM rate of descent. How long will that take?

Answers are given on page 707.

Navigation Aids 27

VOR

The VOR is a very high frequency (VHF) NAVAID that is extensively used in instrument flying. Its full name is the *very high frequency omni-directional radio range*, commonly abbreviated to the VOR, VHF omni range, or omni.

The VOR has been largely supplanted by GPS in the real world of IFR with the FAA shifting to a VOR MON. Although the VOR remains an important element of navigation, it is no longer the primary NAVAID.

Each VOR ground station transmits on a specific VHF frequency between 108.00 and 117.95 megahertz (MHz), which is immediately below the frequency range used for VHF communications. A separate NAV-COM radio is required for navigation purposes, but is usually combined with the NAV-COM in a NAV-COM set.

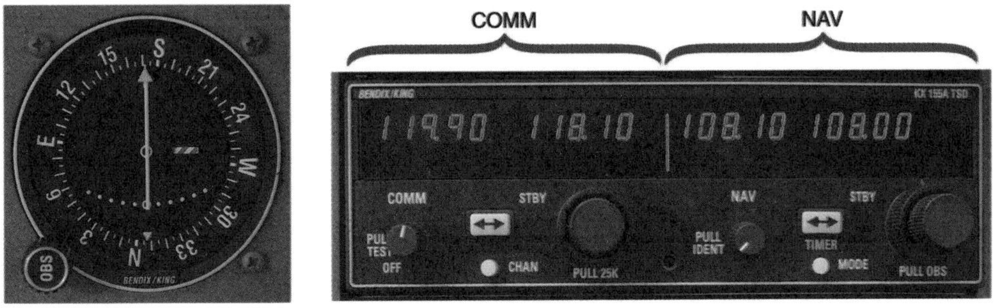

Figure 27-1 VOR display and NAV-COM controller.

The VOR was developed in the U.S. during the late 1940s, and was adopted by the International Civil Aviation Organization (ICAO) as the standard short-range radio navigation aid in 1960. When introduced, it offered an immediate improvement over previously existing aids such as the ADF/NDB combination, most of which operated in lower frequency bands than the VOR and suffered significant limitations such as night effect, mountain reflections and interference from electrical storms.

Principal advantages of the VOR over the NDB include:

- a reduced susceptibility to electrical and atmospheric interference (including thunderstorms);
- the elimination of night effect, since VHF signals are line-of-sight and not reflected by the ionosphere (as are NDB signals in the low and medium frequency band); and
- VOR is more accurate than NDBs.

Many VORs are paired with distance measuring equipment (DME). Selection of the VOR on the NAV-COM set in the cockpit also selects the paired DME, thereby providing both tracking and distance information.

VORs are often paired with a DME.

VOR Minimum Operational Network (VOR MON)

In 2011, the FAA began gradually reducing the VOR network to a Minimum Operational Network that would shift the National Airspace System towards performance-based navigation as part of the Next Generation Air Transportation System (NextGen) project. This has resulted in the establishment of the VOR MON which provides a conventional navigational backup service in the event of a global navigation satellite system (GNSS) disruption or loss of GPS signal.

The VOR MON will provide nearly continuous VOR signal coverage for aircraft operating at 5,000 feet AGL across the NAS (except within the Western U.S. Mountainous Area where coverage is not guaranteed). The VOR MON is primarily intended for IFR flights but VFR flights may still navigate using the VOR MON as desired.

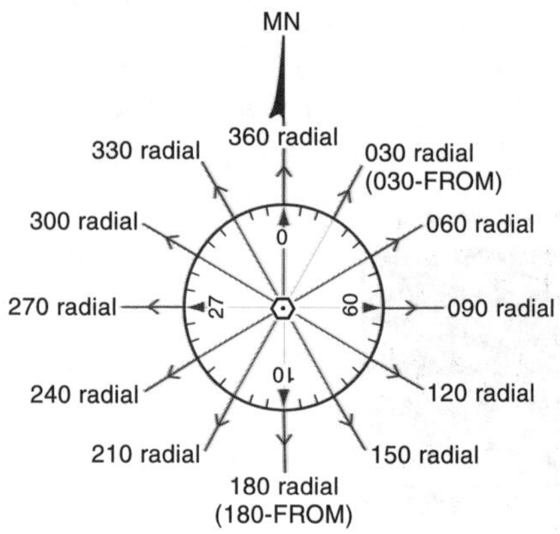

Figure 27-2
A radial is a magnetic bearing outbound *from* a VOR ground station.

VOR Radials

As its name *omni* suggests, a VOR ground transmitter radiates signals in all directions. Its most important feature, however, is that the signal in any particular direction differs slightly from its neighbors. These individual directional signals can be thought of as ground tracks or position lines radiating out from the VOR ground station, in much the same way as spokes from the hub of a wheel.

By convention, 360 different tracks away from the VOR are used, each separated from the next by 1°, and each with its direction related to magnetic north. Each of these 360 VOR tracks or position lines is called a *radial*. The 075 radial may be written R-075. A radial is the magnetic bearing outbound from a VOR.

An airplane tracking outbound on the 060 radial will diverge from an airplane tracking outbound on the 090 radial. Conversely, if they both reverse direction and track inbound on the 060 radial (240-TO the VOR) and the 090 radial (270-TO), their tracks will converge.

When a VOR is operating normally, the radials are transmitted to an accuracy of ±2° or better.

How the VOR Works

The VOR ground station transmits two VHF radio signals:

1. the *reference phase* signal, which is omni-directional (the same in all directions); and
2. the *variable phase* signal, which rotates uniformly at a rate of 1,800 rpm, with its phase varying at a constant rate throughout the 360°.

The antenna of the VOR airborne receiver picks up the signals, whose *phase difference* (the difference between the wave peaks) is measured, this difference depending on the bearing of the airplane from the ground station. In this manner, the VOR can determine the magnetic bearing of the airplane from the VOR ground station.

The two signals transmitted by the VOR ground station are:

- in-phase on magnetic north, which is the reference for VOR signals;
- 90° out of phase at magnetic east 090°M;
- 180° out of phase at magnetic south 180°M;
- 270° out of phase at magnetic west 270°M; and
- 360° out of phase (back in-phase) at magnetic north 360°M, or 000°M.

Figure 27-3 A VOR ground station.

Figure 27-4 VOR antennas.

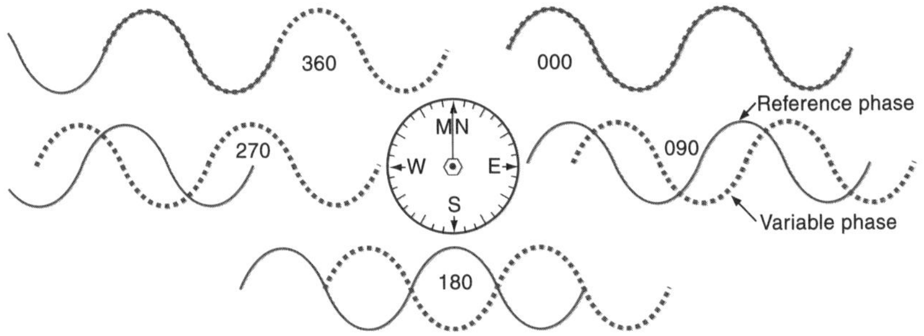

Figure 27-5 The VOR transmits two VHF signals with a phase difference between them.

Every 10 seconds or so a Morse code identifier signal (or *ident*) is transmitted, modulated at 1,020 Hz, allowing the pilot to positively identify the VOR. The coded identifier for the Redmond VOR is RDM (*dit-dah-dit dah-dit-dit dah-dah*). Any associated DME will have a coded identifier broadcast about every 30 seconds, modulated at 1,350 Hz, about one DME ident at a higher pitch tone for every three or four VOR idents.

Some VORs transmit voice messages.

Some VORs may also carry voice transmissions either identifying them (for example, "Linden VOR," alternating with the coded identifier), or carrying a message such as a relevant *automatic terminal information service* (ATIS).

Check the Morse code ident before using a VOR.

The voice identifier of the VOR must have the word VOR or VORTAC stated after its name for the VOR to be considered identified. If the VOR ground station is undergoing maintenance, the coded identifier is not transmitted, but it is possible that navigation signals will still be received. Sometimes a coded *test* signal (*dah dit dit-dit-dit dah*) is transmitted. Do not use these aids for navigation. No NAVAID signal should be used until positive identification is made.

VOR Distance

The VOR is a very high frequency aid operating in the frequency band 108.0 to 117.95 MHz. It allows high quality "line-of-sight" reception because there is relatively little interference from atmospheric noise in this band. Reception may be affected by the terrain surrounding the ground station, the height of the VOR beacon, the altitude of the airplane and its distance from the station.

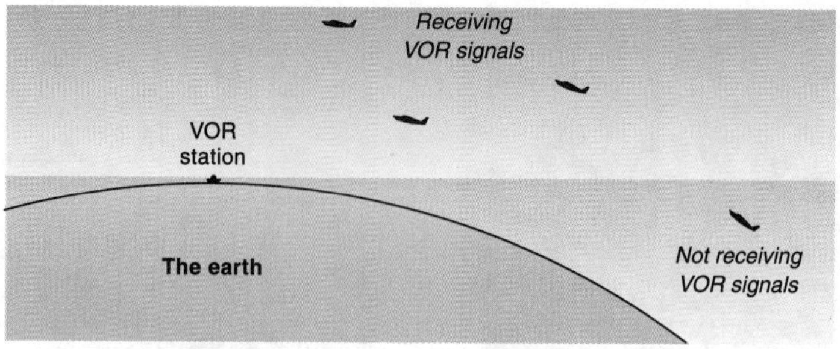

Figure 27-6 VHF line-of-sight signals.

Radio navigation aids are classified according to their Standard Service Volume (SSV)—refer to AIM, paragraph 1-1-8. This determines the maximum range at which they may be used for specified altitude bands. VORs are classified as:

- terminal (TVOR);
- low altitude (LVOR); and
- high altitude (HVOR).

Note the following:

- TVOR is usable out to 25 NM (aircraft at 1,000 to 12,000 feet AGL);
- LVOR is usable out to 40 NM (aircraft at 1,000 to 18,000 feet AGL); and
- HVOR is usable out to:
  - 40 NM (aircraft at 1,000 to 14,500 feet AGL);
  - 100 NM (aircraft at 14,500 to 60,000 feet); and
  - 130 NM (aircraft at 18,000 to 45,000 feet).

TACAN and DME are also classified in the same way.

The VOR signal is line-of-sight.

Different VORs may operate on the same frequency, but they will be well separated geographically so that there is no interference between their VHF line-of-sight signals. The higher the airplane's altitude, however, the greater the possibility of interference.

VORs on Aeronautical Charts

Most aeronautical charts show the position, frequency and Morse code *ident* of each VOR ground station. Information on a particular VOR may be found in the Chart Supplement U.S., and any changes in this information will be referred to in NOTAMs (to which a pilot should refer prior to flight). You should take time to read the Directory Legend at the front of the Chart Supplement U.S. regarding Radio Aids to Navigation.

VOR radials are based on magnetic north.

A VOR ground station may be represented in various ways on a chart, the common forms are shown in figure 27-7. Since magnetic north is the reference direction for VOR radials, a magnetic north arrowhead usually emanates from the VOR symbol, with a compass rose heavily marked each 30° and the radials shown in 10° intervals. This is generally adequate for in-flight estimation of an off-airway course to an accuracy of ±2°, however, when flight planning prior to flight, it is advisable to be more accurate than ±2°.

Most routes are published on the en route charts as airways, with the courses marked in degrees *magnetic*, thereby making it easy for the pilot to plan without having to use a protractor or plotter. If, for some reason, the pilot measures the course in true using a protractor, then variation needs to be applied to convert to magnetic ("Variation west, magnetic best" or "East is least, west is best").

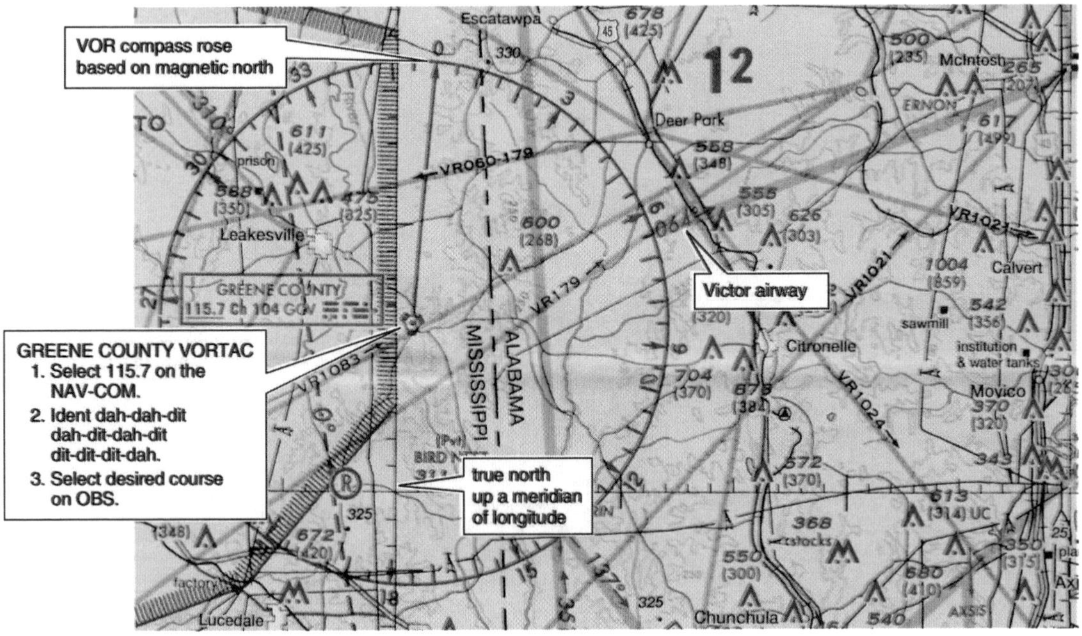

Figure 27-7 A VOR and its radials represented on a sectional chart.

The *Victor airways* between VORs shown on the low-altitude en route charts are marked at either end with the radial out of that VOR. These radials are not always exact reciprocals of each other, especially on east–west tracks, because:

- great circles (which the airways are) cross the north–south meridians of longitude at different angles; and
- magnetic variation changes slightly across the country (and this affects the calculation of the magnetic course, which a radial is, from the true course).

VOR/DME, TACAN and VORTAC

A civil pilot can use only DME information from a TACAN.

Most civil VORs have an associated DME, providing both azimuth and distance information, and are known as VOR/DMEs. The VOR operates in the VHF range, but the DME, even though automatically selected along with the VOR selection, operates in the UHF range.

The military has developed a different navigation system, called TACAN (Tactical Air Navigation system), which operates in the UHF band, and also provides both azimuth and distance information. It requires special airborne equipment (installed only in military aircraft) for the azimuth information to be received, however civil aircraft can receive the TACAN distance information using the DME. When a TACAN ground station has been integrated with a VOR/DME ground station, the combined facility is known as a VORTAC. The end result for a civil pilot using a VORTAC is the same as using a VOR/DME—both VOR and DME information are available.

VOR Cockpit Instruments

There are various types of VOR cockpit displays, however they are all reasonably similar in terms of operation. The VOR cockpit display, or VOR indicator, or omni bearing indicator (OBI), displays the omni bearing selected by the pilot on the course card using the *omni bearing selector* (OBS), a small knob that is geared to the card. The omni bearing selector is also known as the course selector.

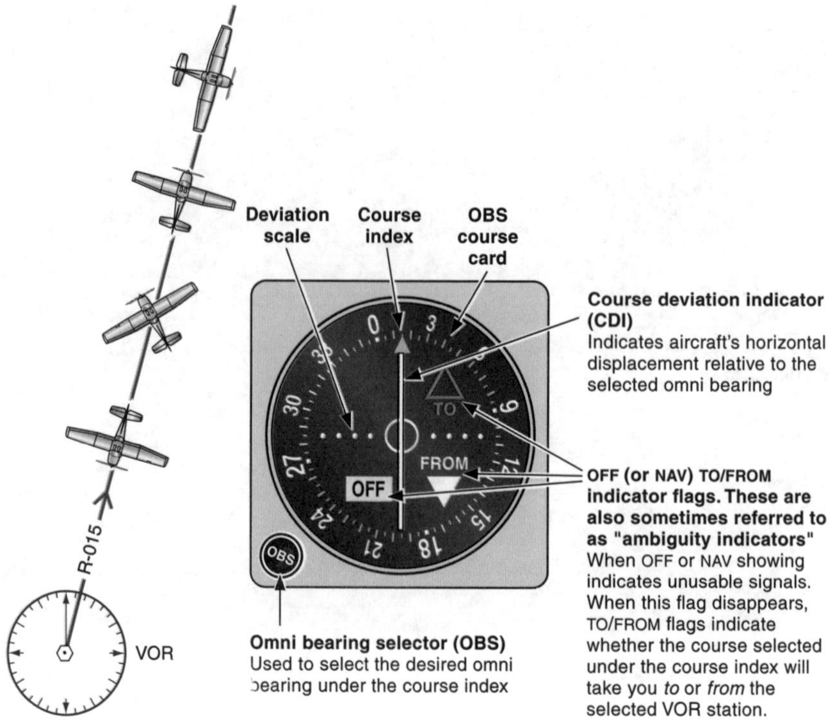

Figure 27-8 The VOR cockpit display (OBI) for airplanes on the 015 radial.

Course Deviation

If the airplane is on the selected radial, then the VOR needle, known as the *course deviation indicator* (CDI), is centered. If the airplane is not on the selected course, then the CDI will not be centered.

Whether the selected course would take the airplane *to* or *from* the VOR ground station is indicated by the TO/FROM flag, removing any ambiguity.

The VOR is only to be used for navigation if:

- the red OFF warning flag is hidden from view;
- the correct Morse code or voice *ident* is heard; and
- the CDI is not moving erratically.

The red OFF flag showing indicates that the signal strength received is not adequate to operate the airborne VOR equipment, which may be the case if the airplane is too far from the VOR ground facility, too low for line-of-sight reception, or directly overhead where there is no signal. Also, it will show OFF if the equipment is switched off.

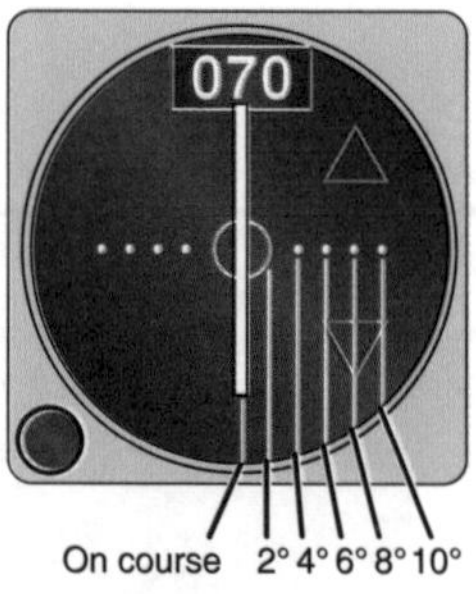

Figure 27-9 Course deviation in 2° increments.

Course Deviation Indicator

The course deviation indicator (or CDI) in the VOR cockpit instrument indicates off-course deviation in terms of angular deviation from the selected course. At all times, the reference when using the VOR is the selected course under the course index. (This is a totally different principle to that of the ADF needle which simply points at an NDB ground station and indicates its relative bearing.)

The amount of angular deviation from the selected course is referred to in terms of dots, there being 5 dots either side of the central position. The inner dot on both sides is often represented by a circle passing through them. Each dot is equivalent to 2 degrees course deviation:

- if the airplane is on the selected course, the CDI is centered;
- if the airplane is 2° off the selected course, the CDI is displaced 1 dot from the center (on the circumference of the inner circle);
- if the airplane is 4° off the selected course, the CDI is displaced 2 dots; and
- if the airplane is 10° or more off the selected course, the CDI is fully deflected at 5 dots.

Deviation "dots" on the CDI match up with the 1-in-60 rule: 1 NM off-course in 60 NM = 1° course error, therefore 2 NM off-course in 60 NM = 2° course error, or 1 dot on the VOR.

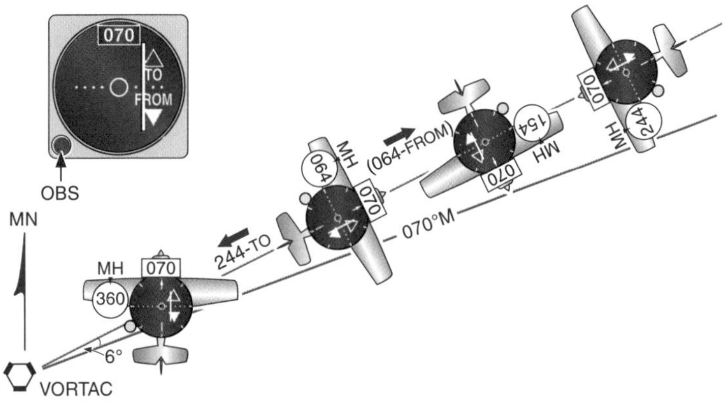

Figure 27-10 Each of these airplanes is displaced 6° from the 070 radial.

Since the CDI indicates angular deviation, the actual distance off-course for a given CDI indication will be smaller the closer the airplane is to the ground station. In a manner of speaking, airplanes tracking inbound are funneled in toward the VOR ground station.

Each dot on the VOR is equivalent to 2° course deviation.

At 1 NM distance from the VOR ground facility, a one-dot deviation from the selected course is a lateral deviation of approximately 200 feet, so:

- at 1 NM, one dot on the VOR indicator = 200 feet laterally;
- at 2 NM, one dot on the VOR indicator = 2 × 200 = 400 feet;
- at 30 NM, one dot on the VOR indicator = 30 × 200 = 6,000 feet = 1 NM;
- at 60 NM, one dot on the VOR indicator = 60 × 200 = 12,000 feet = 2 NM.

Full-scale deflection of the CDI at 5 dots indicates a course deviation of 10° or more.

TO or FROM

The 090 radial, which is a magnetic bearing of 090 away *from* the station, is the same position line as 270-to the station. If an airplane is on this position line, then the CDI will be centered when either 090 or 270 is selected with the OBS. Any ambiguity in the pilot's mind regarding the position of the airplane relative to the VOR ground station is resolved with the TO/FROM indicator.

The TO or FROM flags or arrows indicate to the pilot whether the selected omni bearing will take the airplane to the VOR ground station, or away *from* it. In the case shown in figure 27-11, the pilot can center the CDI by selecting either 090 or 270 (which are reciprocals) with the OBS. A course of 090 would take the airplane *from* the VOR, whereas a course of 270 would lead it *to* the VOR.

A VOR does not care or change with an aircraft heading change.

Note. In this manual, the active direction is indicated by the white arrow, triangle.

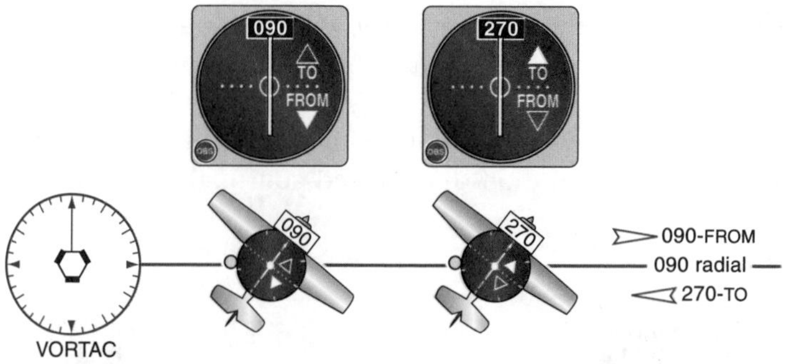

Figure 27-11 Using the TO/FROM flag.

The Radio Magnetic Indicator (RMI)

The radio magnetic indicator (RMI) combines a remote indicating compass and a relative bearing indicator into the one instrument. The RMI is a remote indicating compass with one or two ADF/VOR needles, but without a CDI.

The RMI compass card is continually being aligned so that it indicates magnetic heading, and the RMI needles point at the ground stations to which they are tuned. These ground stations, on many RMIs, may be either an NDB or a VOR, the selection of either ADF or VOR being made with small switches at the base of the RMI.

In figure 27-12, the pilot has selected RMI needle 1 to the ADF, hence:

- the head of needle 1 indicates magnetic bearing *to* the NDB; and
- the tail of needle 1 indicates magnetic bearing *from* the NDB.

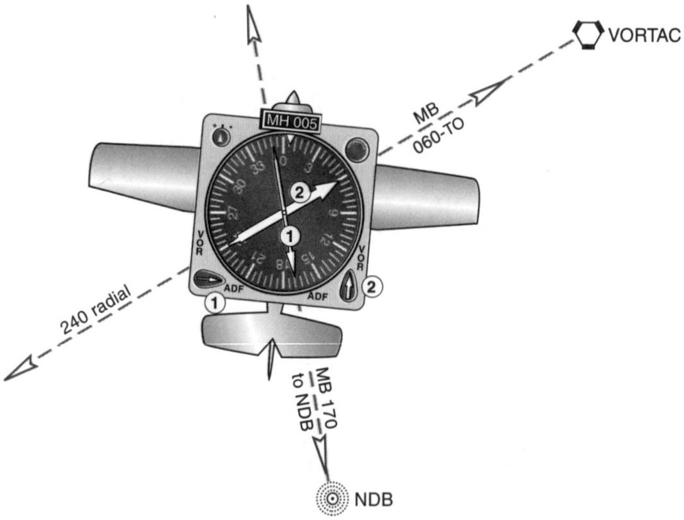

Figure 27-12 RMI needle 1 indicating NDB; RMI needle 2 indicating VOR.

RMI needle 2 has been selected to the VOR, hence:

- the head of needle 2 indicates magnetic bearing *to* the VOR; and
- the tail of needle 2 indicates magnetic bearing *from* the VOR (radial).

Using the RMI with one needle selected to a VOR allows the VOR to be used as if it were an NDB for orientation and tracking purposes.

The Horizontal Situation Indicator (HSI)

The HSI is a remote indicating compass with a VOR indicator superimposed on it. It provides an easily understood pictorial display and is one of the most popular navigation instruments ever devised. It shows the magnetic heading and the position of the airplane relative to the selected course. Figure 27-13 shows the airplane on MH 175, about to intercept 205-TO the VOR.

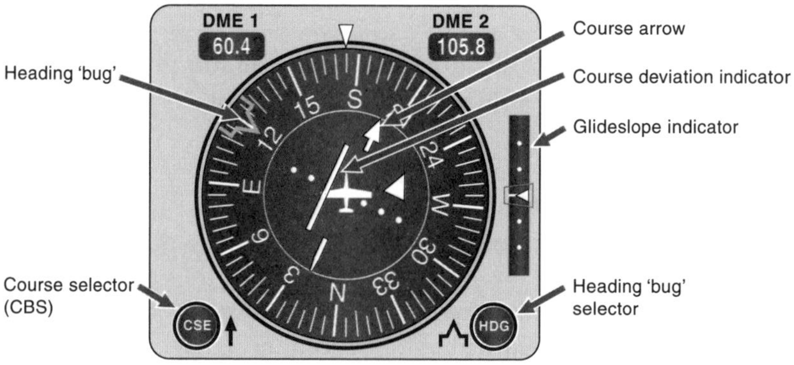

Figure 27-13 The horizontal situation indicator is always a command instrument.

An outstanding benefit of the HSI over the traditional VOR indicator is that the HSI is always a command instrument. If the airplane turns, the remote indicating compass card turns, carrying the VOR display with it, and so the HSI will always show the pilot a CDI deflection toward the selected course. In figure 27-13, the selected course is out to the left. If the airplane turns 180°, to MH 355, the HSI will show the selected course 205 out to the right of the airplane, which it actually is. There is no reverse sensing with an HSI.

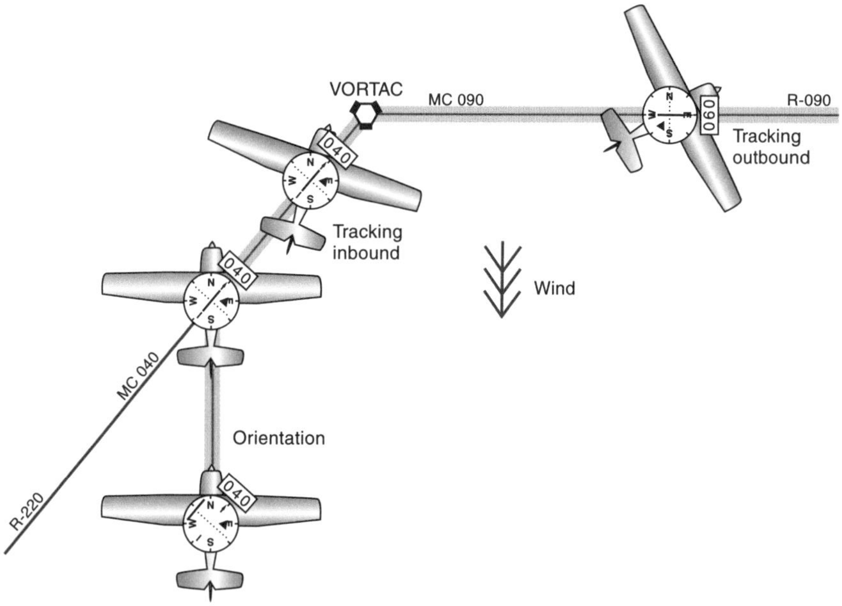

Figure 27-14 Tracking using an HSI.

Operational Use of the VOR

Preparing the VOR Equipment for Use

Always select, tune and identify the VOR before use.

Prior to using the VOR, a pilot must:
- ensure that the VOR has been checked as suitable for IFR flight (see The VOR Receiver Check below);
- ensure electrical power is available, and switch the NAV-COM on;
- select the desired frequency (as found on the en route charts or in the Chart Supplement U.S.);
- identify the VOR (the coded identifier is specified on the charts); and
- check that the OFF flag is not showing (the signal is usable, otherwise the OFF flag would be visible).

The VOR Receiver Check

Figure 27-15 Logbook with VOR check.

It is required that, for a pilot to use the VOR for IFR flight, the VOR equipment of that aircraft either:
- is maintained, checked and inspected under an approved procedure; or
- has been operationally checked within the preceding 30 days as specified below, and is within the limits of the permissible indicated bearing error.

There are five ways in which the VOR receiver may be checked for accuracy prior to IFR flight. The regulations require this check to be logged or for there to be other records, but this doesn't necessarily need to be carried in the airplane.

1. VOT. FAA VOR test facility, or a radiated test signal from an appropriately rated radio repair station (usually on 108.0 MHz). These are test signals which allow the VOR to be tested for accuracy on the ground. To use the VOT service:
- tune the VOT frequency (found in the Chart Supplement U.S. or on the A/G Communications panel of the Enroute Low Altitude Chart). The VOT radiates the 360 radial (360-FROM) in all directions; and
- center the CDI by turning the OBS; the omni bearing indicator (OBI) should read 360-FROM or 180-TO, with an acceptable accuracy of ±4° (356-FROM to 004-FROM, or 176-TO to 184-TO is acceptable). Should the VOR operate an RMI, its needle should point to 180°±4° with any OBI setting, between 176° and 184° is acceptable.

2. FAA Certified Ground Checkpoint. (Specified in the Chart Supplement U.S.). This is a certified radial that should be received at specific points on the airport surface.

a. Position the airplane on the ground checkpoint at the airport—try to center the VOR antenna over the ground check point circle.

b. Tune the VOR and select the designated radial with the OBS. The CDI must be within ±4° of the radial, with the FROM flag showing (since it is a radial), for the accuracy of the VOR receiver to be acceptable.

3. FAA Certified Airborne Checkpoint. (Specified in the Chart Supplement U.S.). This is a certified radial that should be received over specific landmarks while airborne in the immediate vicinity of the airport.

a. Tune the VOR and select the designated radial with the OBS.

b. Visually position the airplane over the landmark, and center the CDI with the OBS. The course reading on the OBI must be within ±6° of the designated radial for the accuracy of the VOR receiver to be acceptable.

4. Dual System VOR Check. If a dual system VOR (units independent of each other except for the antenna) is installed in the aircraft, one system may be checked against the other.

- **a.** Tune both systems to the same VOR ground facility and center the CDI on each indicator using the OBS.
- **b.** The maximum permissible variation between the two indicated bearings is 4°, and this applies to tests carried out both on the ground and in the air.

5. Course Sensitivity Check. This is not a required check.

- **a.** Center the CDI and note the indicated bearing.
- **b.** Turn the OBS until the CDI lies over the last (5th) dot which, ideally, indicates a bearing difference of 10°. Between 10° and 12° is acceptable sensitivity.

Orientation

Using the VOR to Obtain a Position Line

Orientation means "to determine an airplane's approximate position." The first step in orientation is to establish a position line along which the airplane is known to be at a particular moment.

To obtain a position line using the VOR:

- rotate the OBS (omni bearing selector) until the CDI (course deviation indicator) is centered; and
- note whether the TO or FROM flag is showing.

Example 27-1

A pilot rotates the OBS until the CDI is centered, which occurs with 334 under the course index and the TO flag showing. Illustrate the situation. Could another reading be obtained with the CDI centered?

In this location, the CDI will be centered with either 334-TO or 154-FROM.

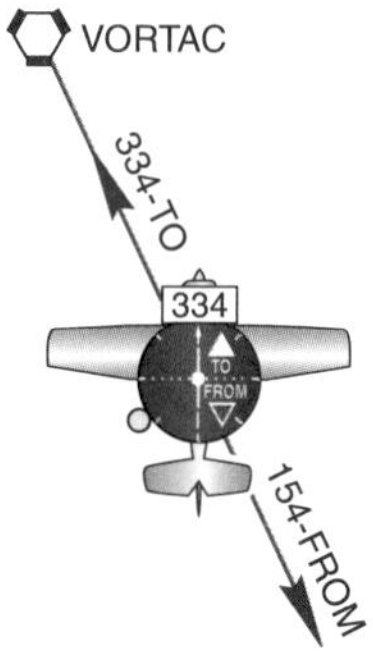

Figure 27-16 Example 27-1: on the 154 radial.

Using Two Position Lines to Fix Position

One position line alone does not allow a pilot to positively fix the position of the airplane; it only provides a line somewhere along which the airplane lies. It requires two or more position lines to positively fix the position of an airplane.

To be of any real value for position fixing, the two position lines need to cut, or intersect, at an angle of at least 45°; any cut less than this decreases the accuracy of the fix. Position lines can be provided by any convenient NAVAIDs, including VORs, NDBs and DMEs. Positions defined on charts by this means are known as *intersections*.

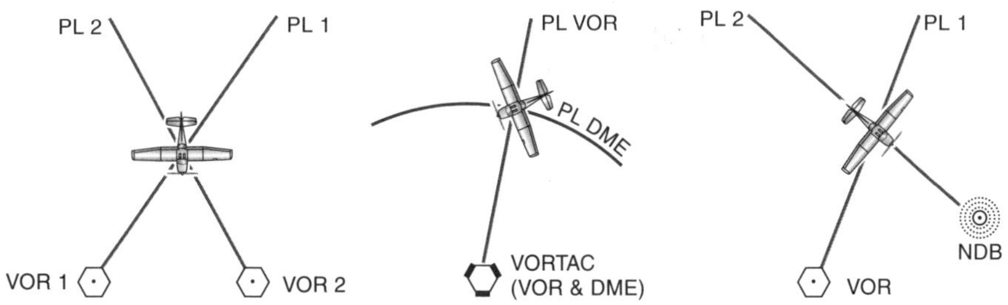

Figure 27-17 Fixing position requires two position lines with a good intersection.

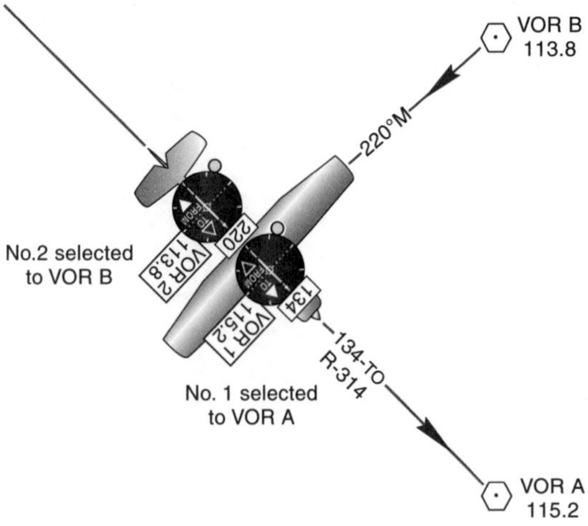

Figure 27-18 Fixing position using two VORs.

Fixing Position Using Two VORs

Most IFR airplanes are fitted with two independent NAV-COM systems, enabling two different VORs to be tuned at the same time. Two position lines from two different VOR ground stations can then be obtained simultaneously. In an airplane with only one NAV-COM set, a pilot can, if he or she so desires, obtain two position lines using the one NAV-COM by retuning it from one VOR to another—a bit tedious, and an increased workload, but still satisfactory.

Example 27-2

An airplane fitted with two NAV-COMs is tracking MC 134-TO to VOR-A. The pilot obtains these indications:

- *VOR 1*—VOR-A 115.2 is selected, the *tracking* VOR, and the CDI centers with 134-TO; and
- *VOR 2*—VOR-B 113.8 is selected, the *crossing* VOR, and the CDI centers with 220-FROM.

The two VOR position lines intersect at a good angle, and the pilot has a fairly positive indication of where the airplane is. The pilot has a VOR/VOR *fix*. Often an intersection of two radials from two VORs is used to define a position on the route, and such a position is known as an intersection. These intersections are clearly marked on the en route charts by triangles, with a five-letter name such as CISSI, GLADD, MUSKS, RADEX and ADOBE.

Fixing Position Using a VOR and a DME

A common form of en route position fixing between aids is the VOR/DME fix, based on a ground station where the DME (distance measuring equipment) is co-located with the VOR ground station. This is also the case with a VORTAC.

The VOR can provide a straight position line showing the radial that the airplane is on (CDI centered), and the DME can provide a circular position line showing the distance that the airplane is from the ground station. The intersection of the lines is the position of the airplane.

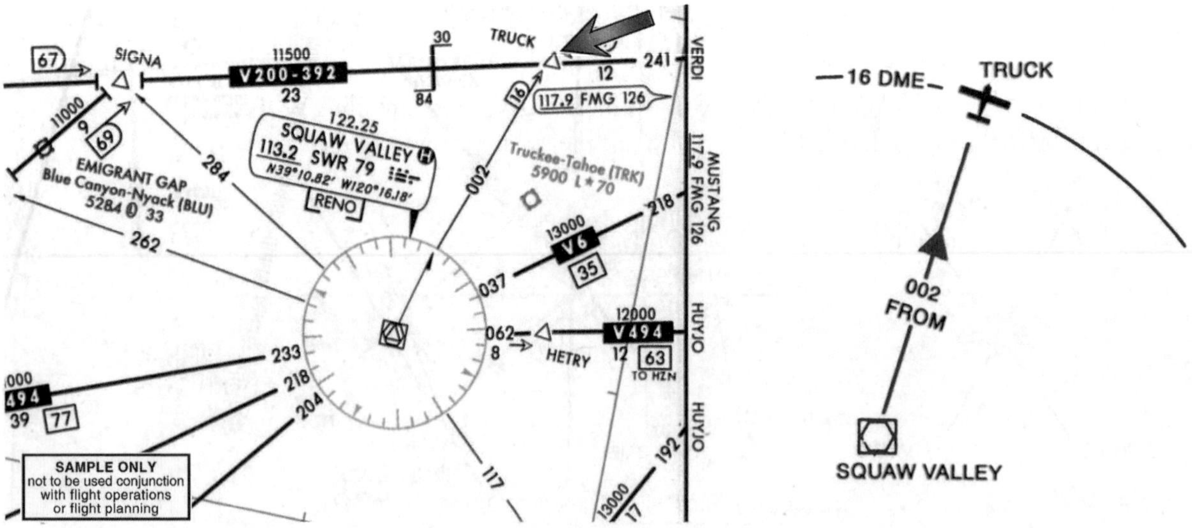

Figure 27-19 Fixing position at TRUCK using a co-located VOR and DME.

Example 27-3

An airplane tracking north from Squaw Valley (SWR 113.2) has the cockpit indications of SWR VOR 002-FROM, and SWR DME 16 NM. Where is the airplane?

As the en route chart extract in figure 27-19 shows, the airplane is at the TRUCK position, an in-flight position determined purely by NAVAIDs.

Fixing Position Over a VOR

As an airplane approaches a VOR, the CDI will become more and more sensitive as the ±10° funnel either side of course becomes narrower and narrower.

As the airplane passes through the *zone of confusion* over the VOR ground station, the CDI may flick from side to side, before settling down again as the airplane moves away from the VOR. The flag will also change from TO to FROM (or vice versa), and the red OFF flag may flicker in and out of view because of the unusable signal. The zone of confusion can extend in an arc of 70° over the station, so it may take a minute or so for the airplane to pass through it before the CDI and the FROM flag settle down, and the OFF flag totally disappears. VOR *station passage* is indicated by the first positive complete reversal of the TO/FROM flag.

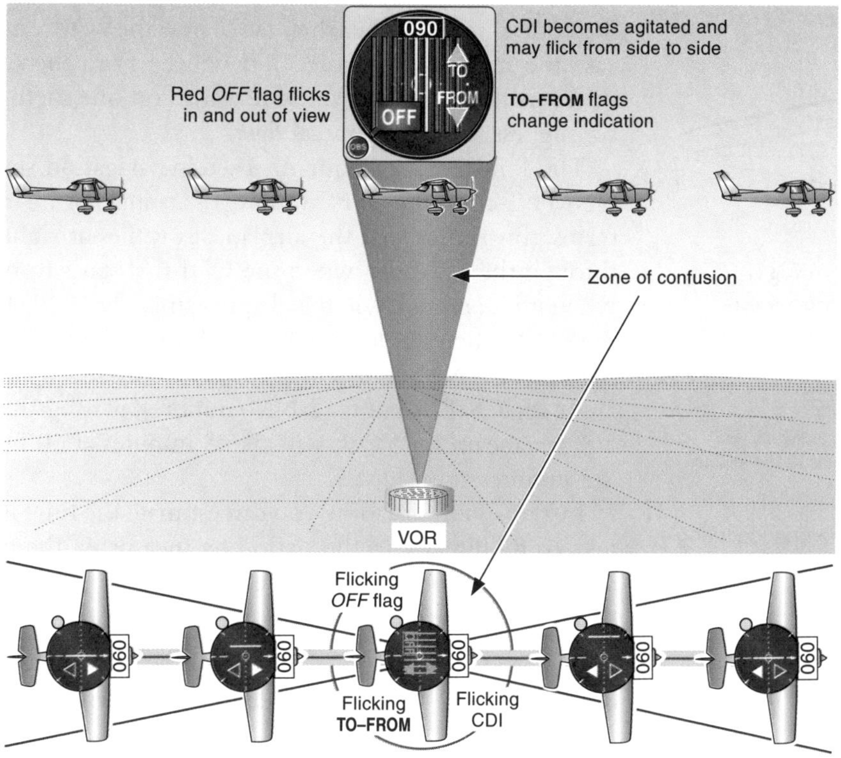

Figure 27-20 Fixing position over a VOR.

Fixing Position Passing Abeam a VOR

A common means of checking flight progress is to note the time passing *abeam* (to one side of) a nearby VOR ground station. The most straightforward procedure is to:

- select and identify the VOR; and
- under the course index, set the radial perpendicular (at 90°) to your course.

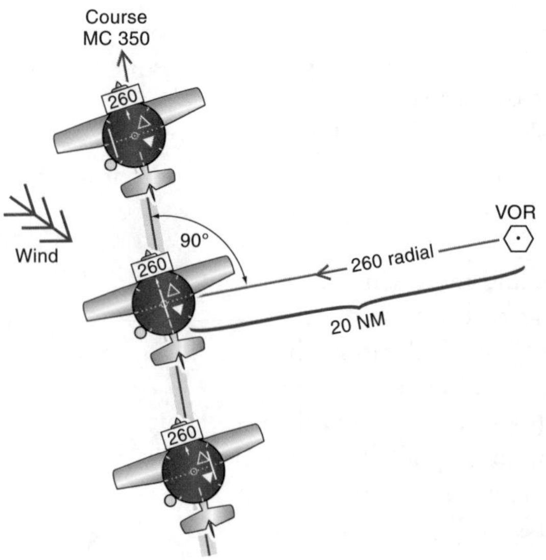

Figure 27-21 Passing abeam a VOR.

$$\text{Time to station} = \frac{\text{Time from A to B (seconds)}}{\text{Bearing change}(°)}$$
$$\text{(minutes)}$$

$$T \text{ (min)} = \frac{t \text{ (sec)}}{\text{degrees}}$$

$$= \frac{60 \text{ seconds}}{10 \text{ degrees}}$$

$$= 6 \text{ minutes to the station}$$
$$\text{@ 120 knots (2 NM/minute)}$$

$$= 12 \text{ NM}$$

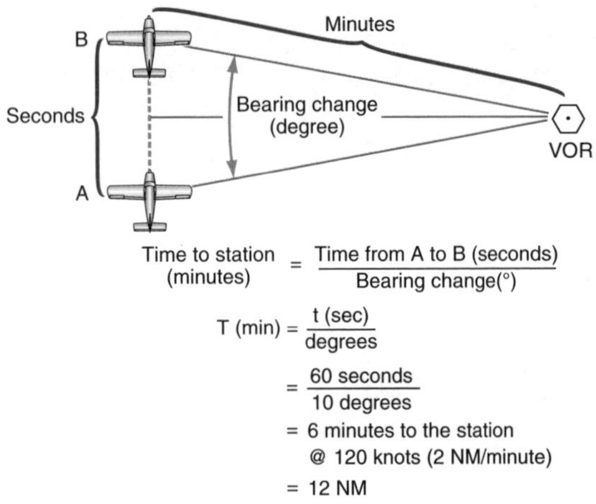

Figure 27-22 Principle of bearing change triangle.

$$T \text{ (min)} = \frac{t \text{ (sec)}}{\text{degrees}}$$

$$= \frac{300 \text{ seconds}}{10 \text{ degrees}}$$

$$= 30 \text{ minutes to the station}$$
$$\text{@ 120 knots}$$

$$= 60 \text{ NM}$$

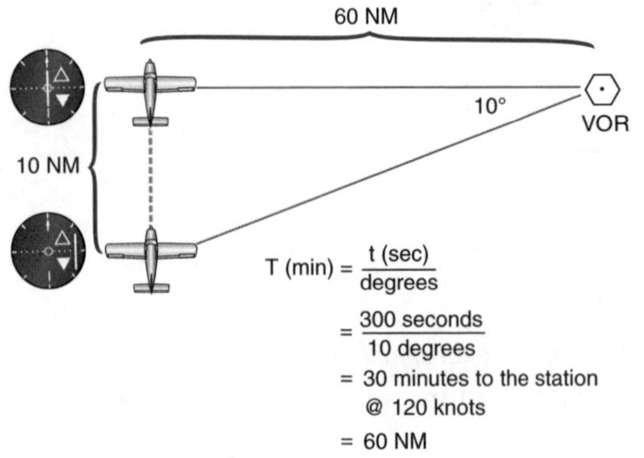

Figure 27-23 Sample calculation.

Example 27-4

An airplane is tracking MC 350, and will pass approximately 20 nautical miles abeam a VOR ground station out to its right. The VOR radial perpendicular to course is the 260 radial, and so 260 should be set with the OBS.

The CDI will be fully deflected to one side if the airplane is well away from the abeam position, and will gradually move from full deflection one side to full deflection on the other side as the airplane passes through the ±10° arc either side of the selected radial. The airplane is at the abeam position when the CDI is centered.

It is suggested that you set the radial (the bearing *from*) the off-course VOR on the OBI, in which case the CDI will be on the same side as the VOR until you have passed the radial. In figure 27-21, the VOR is off-course to the right, and before passing abeam the ground station, the CDI will be out to the right. It will center to indicate the abeam position, and then move to the other side. The abeam position can also be identified by setting the bearing *to* the VOR under the course index (rather than radial *from* the VOR), in which case the movement of the CDI will be from the opposite side. It is better practice to standardize on one method, and we suggest setting the radial *from*.

The 1–in–60 rule, frequently used in navigation, states that 1 NM off-course in 60 NM subtends an angle of 1°. In rough terms, this means that the airplane, as it flies at right angles through the 10° from when the CDI first starts to move to when it is centered, will travel approximately 10 NM abeam the VOR when it is located 60 DME from the VOR ground station (or 5 NM at 30 DME).

At say GS 120 knots (2 NM/minute), passing through a 10° arc abeam the VOR will take 5 minutes at 60 DME, or 2.5 minutes at 30 DME.

In a no-wind situation, you can estimate the time it would take to fly directly to the station by measuring the time for a bearing change as you fly abeam the station, and using the simple expression:

$$\text{Minutes to the station} = \frac{\text{seconds between bearings}}{\text{degrees of bearing change}}$$

Example 27-5

A 10° bearing change abeam a VOR takes 5 minutes. By turning and flying direct to the VOR, the time required to reach the station is:

$$\text{Minutes to VOR} = \frac{300 \text{ Seconds}}{10°} = 30 \text{ minutes}$$

At a groundspeed of 120 knots (2 NM/minute), this would mean that you are: $2 \times 30 = 60$ NM from the station.

Orientation Without Altering the OBS

It is possible, without altering the omni bearing selector, to determine which quadrant the airplane is in with respect to the selected course. In figure 27-24, the selected omni bearing is 340:

- the CDI is deflected left, which indicates that, when looking in direction 340, the airplane is out to the right (of the line 340–160); and
- the FROM flag indicates that tracking 340 would take the airplane from the VOR ground station. The airplane is ahead of the line 250–070 when looking in the direction 340.

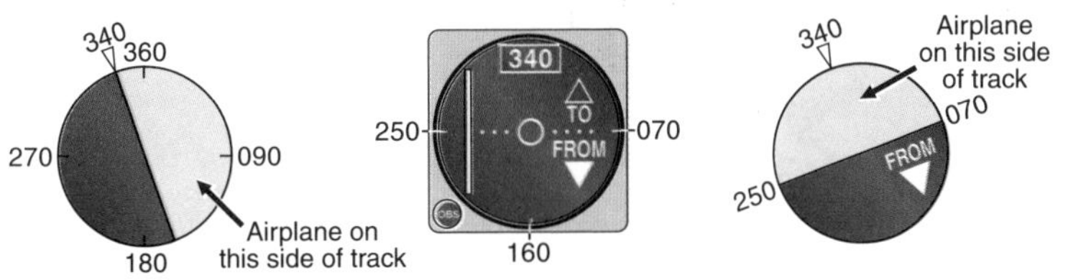

Figure 27-24
Using the CDI and the TO/FROM flag for orientation without moving the omni bearing selector.

This puts the airplane in the quadrant:

- away from the CDI; and
- away from the TO/FROM flag.

So it is between the 340 and 070 radials (omni bearings from the VOR ground station). See figure 27-25.

Note. Remember, no information is available from the VOR cockpit display regarding airplane heading. Heading information in degrees magnetic must be obtained from the heading indicator.

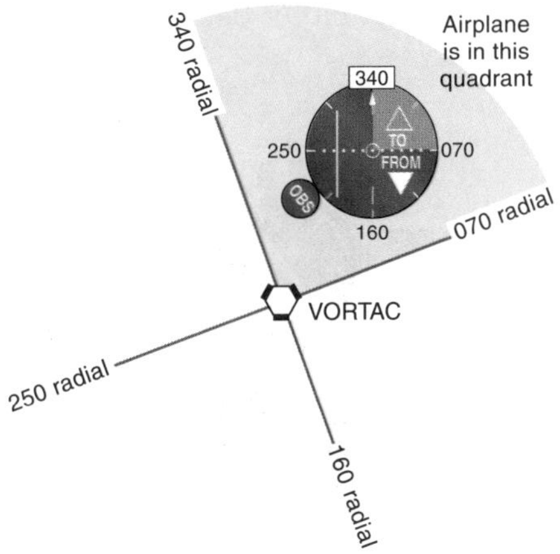

Figure 27-25
The airplane is in the quadrant away from the CDI and TO/FROM flag.

Example 27-6

With 085 under the course index, the VOR indicator shows CDI deflected right with the TO flag showing. Position the airplane with respect to the VOR. This method is just a quick means of determining the approximate position of the airplane with respect to the VOR ground station.

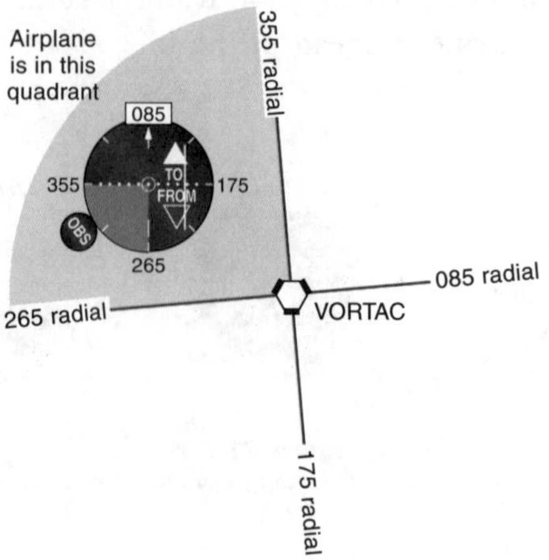

Figure 27-26
The airplane is between the 355 and 265 radials.

Orientation with VOR Selected to One Needle on the RMI

This makes orientation with the VOR easy, and it does not involve altering the OBI (omni bearing indicator). In figure 27-27, RMI needle 2 indicates that the magnetic bearing *to* the VOR is MB 043 (so the airplane is on the 223 radial).

> **Note.** There is no need to alter the OBI to determine this, as would be necessary if an RMI were not installed. Without an RMI, the pilot would have had to alter the OBI until the CDI centered at either 043-TO or 223-FROM.

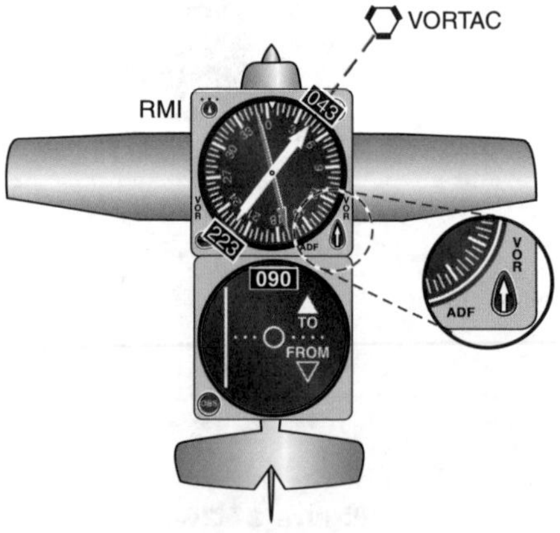

Figure 27-27
The RMI indicates 043 to the VOR.

Tracking

Tracking to a VOR

To track to a VOR:

- *tune* the VOR frequency;
- *identify* the station (Morse code ident as shown on the chart, or voice ident with VOR stated after the name);
- *check* that the red OFF warning flag is not displayed; and
- *select* the omni bearing of the desired course with the OBS.

Orient the airplane with respect to the desired course, and then take up a suitable *intercept heading* using the heading indicator (aligned with the magnetic compass). If the airplane is heading approximately in the direction of the desired course, the center circle will represent the airplane, and the CDI the desired course; to intercept course in this case, the pilot would turn toward the CDI. This is using the VOR indicator as a *command instrument*, commanding the pilot to turn toward the CDI to regain course. Be aware, however, that this only applies when the airplane's heading is in roughly the same direction as the selected omni bearing. On intercepting the course, the pilot should steer a reasonable heading to maintain the course, allowing a suitable wind correction angle to counter any wind effect. Remaining on course is indicated by the CDI remaining centered.

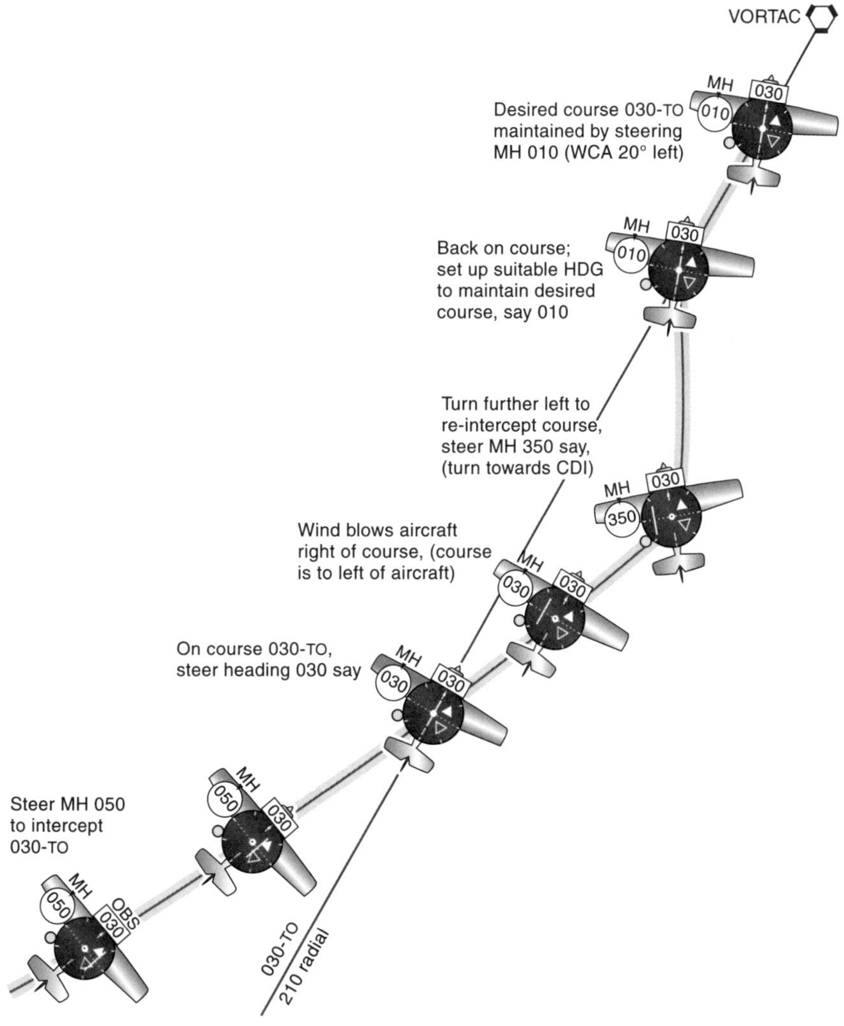

Figure 27-28
Using the CDI as a command instrument (by following its commands).

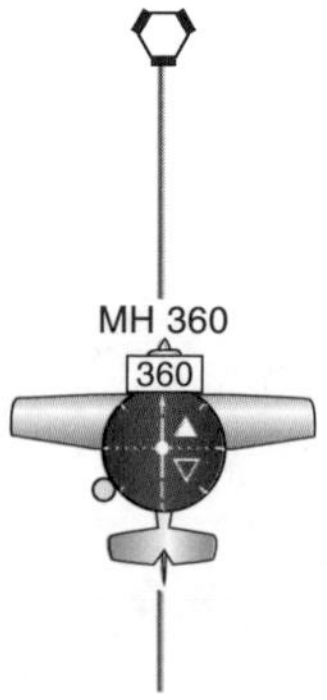

Example 27-7

In figure 27-28, with the desired course 030 set under the course index, the CDI is out to the right. Since the airplane's initial heading agrees approximately with the course of 030, the pilot concludes that the course is out to the right of the airplane. The CDI out to the right commands the pilot to turn right to regain track and center the CDI. The pilot has taken up a heading of MH 050 to intercept a course of 030-TO the VOR, which will give the pilot a 20° intercept. This shallow intercept is satisfactory if the airplane is close to the course.

If the airplane is well away from the course, then a 60° or 90° intercept might be more appropriate. This would be MH 090 or MH 120.

Determining Wind Correction Angle when Tracking on the VOR

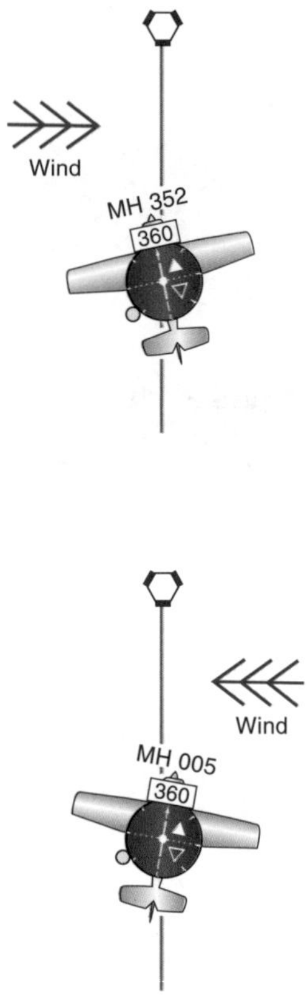

Drift angles exaggerated

Figure 27-29
Tracking inbound and allowing for drift.

When tracking inbound on 360-TO a VOR with 360 set under the course index, MH 360 will allow the airplane to maintain course provided there is no crosswind component. If, however, there is a westerly wind blowing, then the airplane will be blown to the right of course unless a wind correction angle (WCA) is applied and the airplane steered on a heading slightly into wind. This is MH 352 in figure 27-29.

If, on the other hand, there is an easterly wind blowing, the airplane will be blown left of course, unless a wind correction angle is applied and the airplane steered on a heading slightly into wind, such as MH 005 in figure 27-29.

Just how great the WCA needs to be is determined in flight by trial and error (preflight calculations using the flight computer may suggest a starting figure for WCA). If the chosen WCA is not correct, and the airplane gradually departs from course causing the CDI to move from its central position, the heading should be altered to regain the course (CDI centered) and a new magnetic heading flown with an improved estimate of WCA. This process of achieving a suitable WCA by trial and error is known as *bracketing.*

In the real world the wind frequently changes in both strength and direction, and so the magnetic heading required to maintain course will also change from time to time. This becomes obvious by gradual movements of the CDI away from its central position, which the pilot will notice in regular scan of the navigation instruments, and which the pilot will correct by changes in magnetic heading using the heading indicator.

Tracking From a VOR

To track *from* a VOR (assuming the VOR has not already been selected and identified):

- *select* the VOR frequency;
- *identify* the station (Morse code ident or voice ident);
- *check* that the red OFF warning flag is not displayed; and
- select the *omni bearing* of the desired course with the OBS.

Orient the airplane with respect to the course, and then take up a suitable intercept heading using the heading indicator (aligned with the magnetic compass). If the airplane is heading approximately in the direction of the course, the center circle will represent the airplane, and the CDI will represent the course.

To intercept course in this case, the pilot would turn toward the CDI. This is using the CDI as a command instrument, commanding the pilot to turn toward the CDI to regain course. Be aware, however, that this only applies when the heading is roughly in

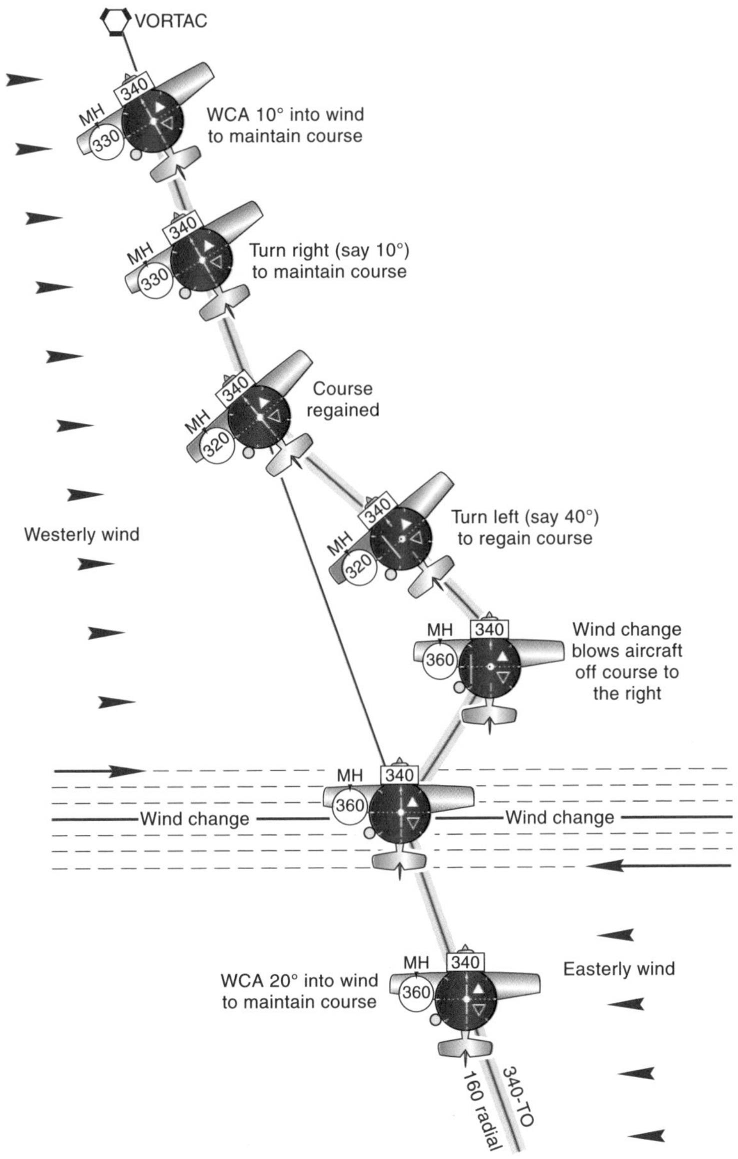

Figure 27-30 Tracking inbound through a wind change.

the same direction as the selected omni bearing. On intercepting course, the pilot steers a suitable heading to maintain it, keeping in mind the wind direction and strength. If the course is maintained, the CDI will remain centered.

Example 27-8

In figure 27-31, with the course 140 set with the omni bearing selector (OBS), the CDI is out to the right. Since the airplane's initial heading agrees approximately with the course of 140, the pilot concludes that the course is out to the right of the airplane (or, in this case, straight ahead and to the right).

The pilot steers MH 220 to intercept a course of 140-FROM the VOR, which will give an 80° intercept. This is satisfactory if the airplane is well away from the course. If the airplane is close to course, then a 60° or 30° intercept might be more suitable which, in this case, would be MH 200 or MH 170.

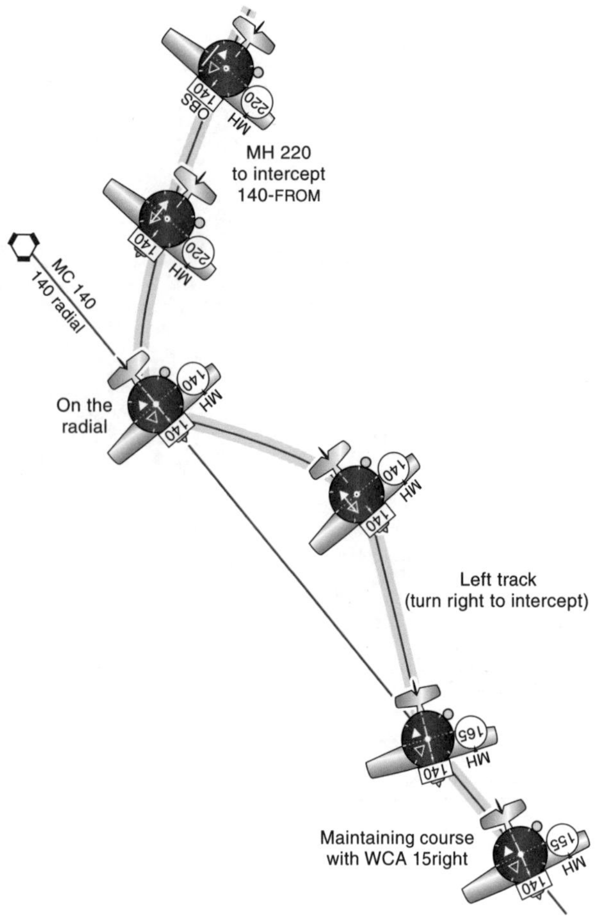

Figure 27-31
Using the CDI as a command instrument (example 27-8).

Using the CDI as a Command Instrument

With the course set on the OBI, and the airplane headed at least roughly in the same direction as the selected course, the CDI will act as a command instrument. By flying toward the deflected CDI, the pilot can center it, and thereby regain course. For example, tracking 060-TO the VOR, set 060 under the course index, and tracking 030-FROM the VOR, set 030 under the course index. See Figure 27-32.

A minor complication arises when the airplane is steered on a heading approximating the reciprocal of the course selected on the OBI. Under these circumstances, the CDI is *not* a command instrument. This situation is called *reverse sensing*.

Example 27-9

Suppose a pilot has been tracking 140-FROM a VOR, with 140 selected on the OBI and by steering MH 140. The airplane has drifted left of course, and so the CDI will be deflected to the right of center. Examine figure 27-33—to regain the 140-FROM course, the pilot must turn toward the needle, in this case to the right. Heading and OBI selection are similar, so it is used as a command instrument.

Suppose now that the pilot wants to return to the VOR ground station on the reciprocal course, which is 320-TO the VOR, and so turns through approximately 180° to MH 320 without altering the 140 set under the course index. The VOR indicator, because it is not heading sensitive, indicates exactly as it did before the turn, with the CDI out to the right of center.

To regain course on this reciprocal heading, the pilot would turn, not toward the CDI, but away from it.

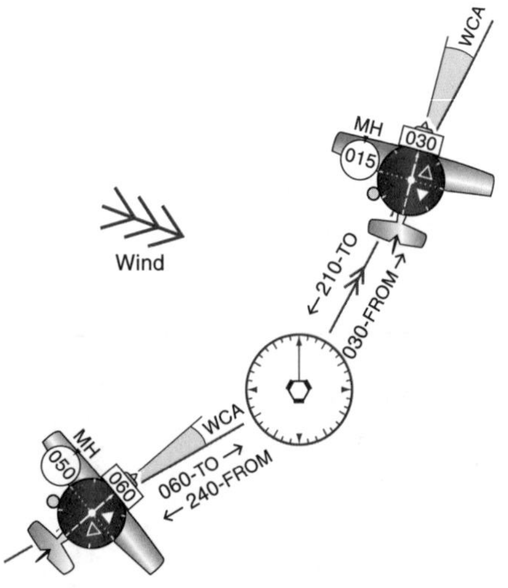

Figure 27-32
Use the CDI as a command instrument.

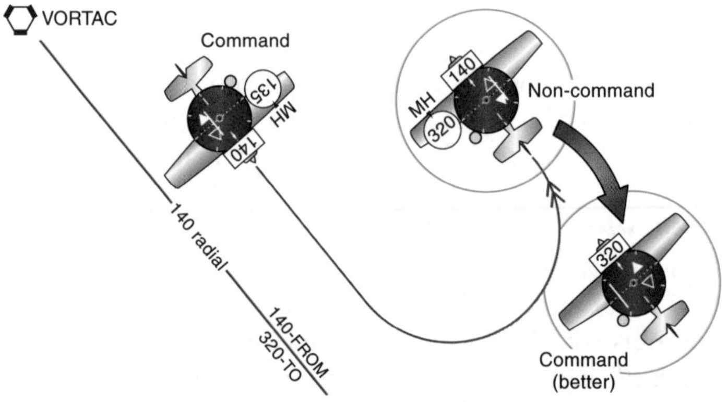

Figure 27-33
For ease of operation, use the CDI as a command instrument.

Turning toward the CDI on this reciprocal heading to the selected course would take the pilot further away from the selected course and the VOR is no longer a command instrument. This inconvenience can be easily removed, and the OBI returned to being a command instrument, by setting the new course under the course index of MC 320, which approximates the heading being flown. The immediate effect will be for the TO flag to appear, replacing the FROM flag, and the CDI to swing across to the other side. The CDI will now be out to the left, and a turn toward it will bring the airplane back toward the selected course. The VOR indicator is once again a command instrument, easier to understand, and easier to fly.

The NDB and the ADF

The *nondirectional beacon* (NDB) is the simplest NAVAID used by aircraft. It is a ground-based transmitter which transmits radio energy in all directions, hence its name—the *nondirectional beacon*. The ADF, or *automatic direction finder*, installed in an airplane has a needle that indicates the direction from which the signals of the selected NDB ground station are being received. NDBs are rare in today's cockpit, ADF procedures are no longer prevalent throughout the U.S. and this subject is no longer tested on in the FAA Knowledge Exam, however, this information will be useful if your aircraft and/or location uses NDB equipment and ADF procedures.

Flying to an NDB in an airplane is similar to following a compass needle to the north pole—fly the airplane toward where the needle points, and eventually you will arrive overhead. Flying away from the north pole, however, with the magnetic compass needle pointing behind, could take the airplane in any one of 360 directions. Similarly, flying away from an NDB using only the ADF needle will not lead the airplane to a particular point (unlike flying to an NDB). The airplane could end up anywhere! Further information is required.

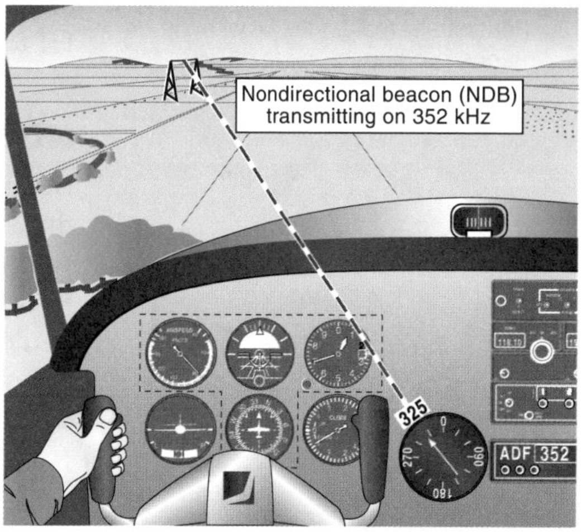

Figure 27-34 A correctly tuned ADF indicates the direction of the selected NDB from the aircraft.

NDBs in the NAS are an obsolete NAVAID and quickly disappearing, as are ADF-equipped aircraft. However, there are still a handful of NDBs spread across the United States and north and south of the border.

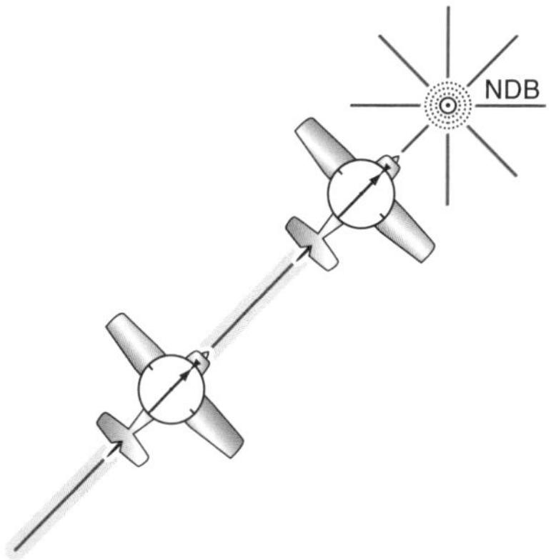

Figure 27-35 Flying to a station is straightforward.

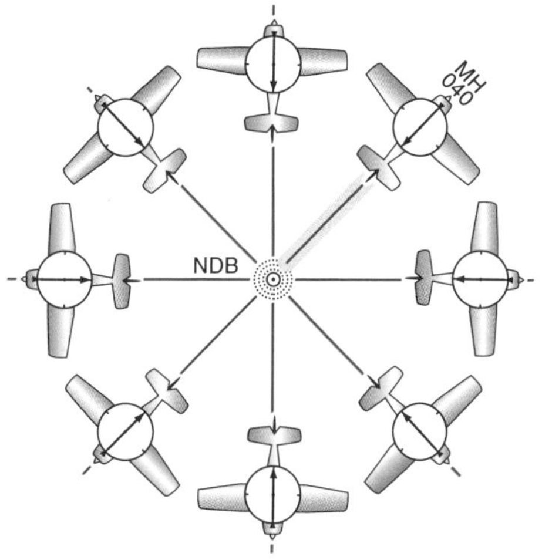

Figure 27-36 Flying away from a station requires further information than just the needle on the tail.

ADF and the HI

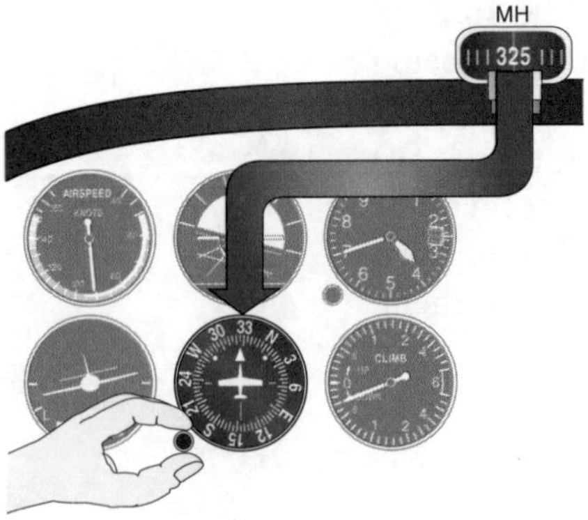

Figure 27-37
Periodically realign the HI with the magnetic compass in steady flight.

The extra information required by the pilot, in addition to that supplied by the ADF needle, comes from the magnetic compass or, more commonly, from the heading indicator (which is kept manually aligned with the compass by the pilot, and is easier to use). Accurate navigation can be carried out using these two references:

- an *ADF needle* that points at an NDB ground station; plus
- a *heading indicator* that indicates the airplane's magnetic heading (MH).

Since a heading indicator will slowly drift out of alignment, it is vital that you periodically realign it with the magnetic compass in straight flight at a steady speed, say every 10 minutes or so. A drift out of alignment of 3° in 15 minutes is the maximum acceptable for the HI to be considered serviceable.

NDB/ADF Combination

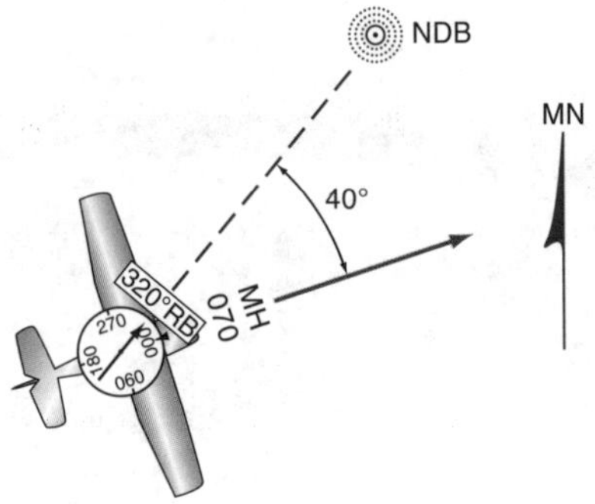

Figure 27-38
A diagrammatic representation.

Before using an ADF's indications of the bearing to a particular NDB, the airplane must be within the operational range of the NDB and you must have:

- correctly selected the NDB frequency;
- identified its Morse code ident; and
- tested the ADF needle to ensure that it is indeed "ADFing."

Also, the HI should have been aligned with the magnetic compass (plus or minus the deviation correction, as given on the compass card).

If the NDB bears 40 degrees to the left of the airplane's magnetic heading, say MH 070, then the situation can be illustrated as in figure 27-38. Since the NDB is 40 degrees left of the nose or, if you prefer, on a *relative bearing* of 320 (RB 320), it will have a magnetic bearing of 030 (MB 030) from the airplane. This gives you some idea of where the airplane is, and in what direction to travel to reach the NDB.

The ADF/NDB combination, in conjunction with the heading indicator, can be used by the pilot:

- *to track* to the NDB on any desired course, pass over the NDB, and track outbound on whatever course is desired; or
- *to fix* the airplane's position.

The ADF is selected to an NDB relevant to the desired path of the airplane. If tracking en route between two NDBs, the changeover point from one NDB to the next would reasonably be the halfway point, depending of course on their relative power.

If the NDB is ahead, the ADF needle will point up the dial; if the NDB is behind, the ADF needle will point down the dial. As the airplane passes over the NDB, the ADF needle will become quite sensitive and will swing from ahead to behind. The ADF can also be used for more advanced procedures such as:

- flying an accurate "racetrack" holding pattern based on the NDB; and
- using the NDB for guidance when maneuvering in the vicinity of an airport, either as a nonprecision approach aid in its own right, or as a lead-in to a precision approach aid such as an ILS (instrument landing system).

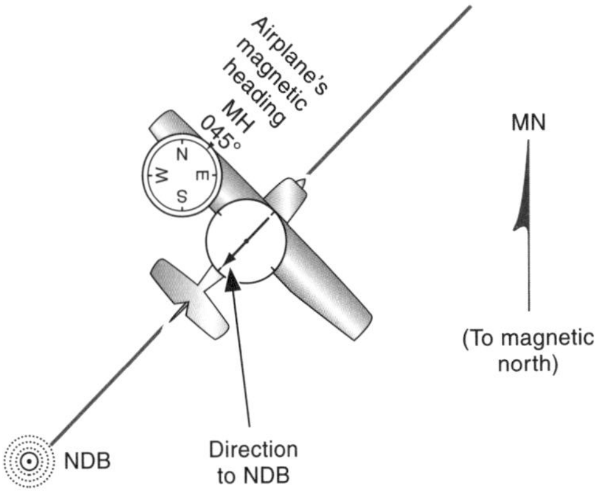

Figure 27-39a
To be really useful for navigation, the ADF/NDB combination needs support from a magnetic compass (or from a HI).

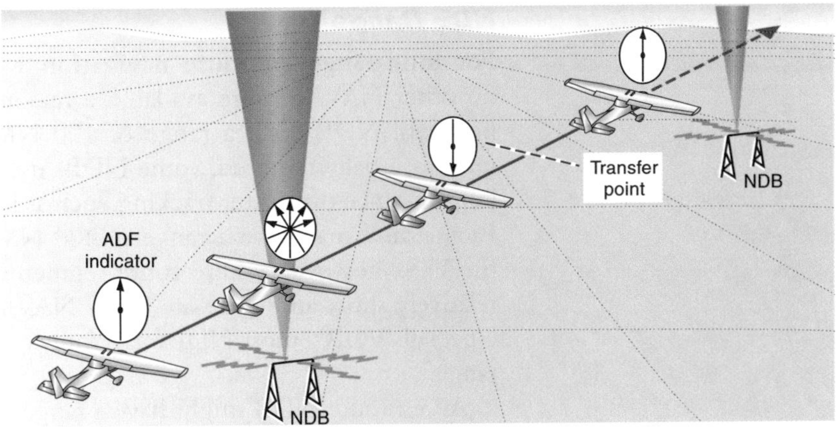

Figure 27-39b
Flying toward, over, and past an NDB, and then on to the next one.

The NDB

The nondirectional beacon (NDB) is the ground-based part of the combination. It is referred to as nondirectional because no particular direction is favored in its transmissions; the NDB radiates identical electromagnetic energy in all directions.

The NDB is a ground-based transmitter.

Each NDB transmits on a given frequency in the low-frequency or medium-frequency LF/MF band (somewhere between 200 and 1,750 kHz), the transmission mast being either a single mast or a large T-antenna strung between two masts.

To avoid confusion between various NDBs, and to ensure that the pilot is using the correct beacon, each NDB transmits its own particular identification signal (or *ident*) in the form of a two- or three-letter Morse code signal, which should be checked by the pilot before using the NDB for navigation. If the NDB is the only NAVAID being used for navigation, for instance during a typical NDB approach, the ident should be continuously monitored in the cockpit by the pilot, since the ADF has no failure flag to indicate a faulty signal or, indeed, no signal at all.

Identify an NDB before using it for navigation.

Figure 27-40 NDB transmission antennas.

NDB Range

Class	Range
MH	25 NM
H	50 NM*
HH	75 NM

The range of individual H-class NDB stations may be less than 50 NM—such restrictions will be published in NOTAMs, and in the Chart Supplement U.S.

The distances are the same at all altitudes. The classification (and range) for an individual NDB can be checked in the Chart Supplement U.S.

Table 27-1 NDB SSV radii.

For long-range en route navigation where no other NAVAIDs are available, a reasonably powerful NDB with a range of 100 NM or more is usually required. Some NDBs used for long-distance overwater tracking, such as in the Pacific area, may have a range of 400 NM. In the U.S., however, where route segments are relatively short and there are many NAVAIDs, especially VORs, most NDBs have only a short range.

An en route NDB might have a range of 75 NM. The range of an NDB depends on:
- the power of transmission (10–2,000 watts);
- the frequency of transmission;
- atmospheric conditions existing at the time—electrical storms, which can generate spurious signals, and periods of sunrise and sunset, which can distort or reflect the signals from an NDB; and
- the nature of the earth's surface over which the signals travel.

In the U.S., NDBs are classified according to their range, or *standard service volume* (SSV) radius, as given in table 27-1.

NDB Signal Accuracy

An ideal NDB signal received at an airplane may be accurate to ±2°, however various factors may reduce this accuracy considerably. These factors include:
- *thunderstorm effect*, which causes the ADF needle to be deflected toward a nearby electrical storm (cumulonimbus cloud) and away from the selected NDB;
- *night effect*—at night, NDB signals can be refracted by the ionosphere and then return to earth as strong skywaves, causing interference with the normal NDB surface waves, and resulting in a fading signal and a wandering ADF needle (most pronounced at dawn and dusk);
- *interference* from other NDBs transmitting on similar frequencies can be particularly significant at night;
- *mountain effect*, which is caused by reflections of the NDB signals from mountains; and
- *coastal effect*, which is caused by the NDB signal bending slightly toward the coastline when crossing it at an angle.

NDB Identification

Each NDB is identifiable by a three-letter Morse code identification signal that is transmitted along with its normal signal. This is known as its *ident*.

You must identify an NDB before using it for any navigational purposes within its operational range and, if using it for some length of time, then it should be periodically re-identified. During an NDB approach, the NDB or compass locator ident should be monitored continuously.

If a test or incorrect ident is heard, the NDB must not be used.

The lack of an ident may indicate that the NDB is out of service, even though it may still be transmitting (say for maintenance or test purposes), and it must not be used for navigation. When under test, the coded word *test* may sometimes be transmitted: *dah dit dit-dit-dit dah*. If an incorrect ident is heard, then those signals must not be used.

To identify most NDBs and compass locators, simply select AUDIO on the ADF, listen to the Morse code signal, and confirm that it is indeed the correct one. All NDBs in the U.S. can be identified with the ADF mode selector in the ADF position.

Burnet NDB
B —•••
M ——
Q ——•—

Figure 27-41 Typical NDB idents.

Many NDBs carry voice transmissions, such as the *automatic terminal information service* (ATIS) at some airports. It is also possible, in a situation where the communications radio (NAV-COM) has failed, for ATC to transmit voice messages on the NDB frequency, and to receive them on the ADF if AUDIO is selected. Those that do not have a voice capability will have "W," which stands for *without voice*, included in their class designator in the Chart Supplement U.S., for instance as "HW."

Note. Broadcast stations may also be received by an ADF, since they transmit in the LF/MF bands. It is not good airmanship, however, to use broadcast stations as NAVAIDs, since they are difficult to identify precisely. Even if an announcer says "*This is the Memphis Country Hour*," it is possible that the transmission is coming, not from the main transmitter, but from an alternative or emergency transmitter located elsewhere, or even a relay station many miles away from the main transmitter.

To use information from a broadcast station, you must be certain of its geographical position—something which is difficult to determine. Listening to broadcast stations in flight is also distracting from your main operational tasks. Broadcast stations are not used for IFR navigation in the United States—they are not required to have standby generators and do not have to advise the FAA if they are not transmitting for some reason.

The ADF

The ADF is an airborne receiver.

The airborne partner of the ground-based NDB is the automatic direction finder, usually referred to as the ADF. It operates on the radio compass principle whereby the ADF needle indicates the direction from which the signals are coming. Under ideal conditions, the ADF needle will point directly at the NDB antenna; under less-than-ideal conditions, the signals from the NDB antenna may not follow a straight path, and so the direction indicated by the ADF needle will be somewhat in error.

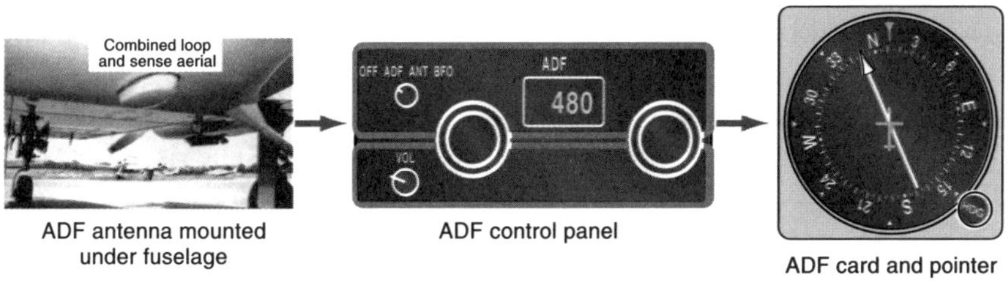

Figure 27-42 The airborne ADF equipment.

The automatic direction finder has three main components:

- the ADF receiver;
- the antenna system; and
- the ADF cockpit display.

The ADF receiver is installed in the cockpit radio panel, which the pilot tunes to the frequency of the desired NDB and verifies with the ident. The antenna system comprises a loop antenna and a sense antenna (or their modern equivalent, a single combined unit) which together determine the signal direction. The ADF cockpit display is either a fixed-card or a rotatable-compass-card, with a pointer or needle indicating the signal direction. The ADF cockpit instrument is usually installed to the right of the attitude flight instruments, with the top of the dial representing the nose of the airplane and the bottom of the dial representing its tail. Ideally, the ADF needle will point continually and automatically toward the NDB ground station.

The ADF Control Panel

There are various types of ADF that may be fitted to an airplane and, prior to flight, you must be familiar with the set that you will use. You must be able to select and positively identify the NDB that you wish to use, and then verify that the ADF needle is indeed responding to the signals from that NDB. The correct procedure, any time a new NDB is to be used, is to confirm (verbally if so desired):

- *selected*;
- *identified*; and
- *ADFing* (active needle, giving a sensible bearing to the NDB).

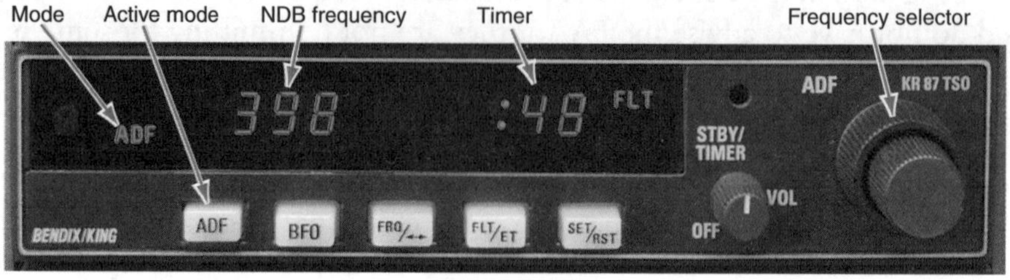

Figure 27-43 Typical ADF control panel.

The ADF mode selector is usually selected to ADF.

The mode selector switches between ADF modes of operation.

- *OFF*—use the OFF to switch the ADF off;
- *ADF*—ADF is the normal position when the pilot wants bearing information to be displayed automatically by the needle. Most NDBs can be identified with the mode selector in this position (and the volume knob adjusted suitably);
- *ANT* or *REC*—these are the abbreviations for antenna or receiver. In this position, only the signal from the sense antenna is used, and no satisfactory directional information is available to the ADF needle. This function position gives the best audio reception to allow easier identification, and better understanding of any voice messages. Never leave the mode selector in this position if you are navigating using the ADF—the ADF needle will remain stationary with no obvious indication that it is not responding! It is possible, however, to identify most NDBs with the mode selector in the ADF position (which is a safer position), and for the ANT position to be avoided;
- *BFO* or *CW*—these are the abbreviations for beat frequency oscillator or continuous wave. This position, rarely required in the United States, is selected when identifying the few NDBs that use A0/A1 or A1 transmissions, which are unmodulated carrier waves whose transmission is interrupted to provide the NDB's Morse code iden-

tification. Since no audio message is carried on an unmodulated carrier wave, the BFO (as part of the airborne equipment) imposes a tone onto the carrier wave signal to make it audible to the pilot so that the NDB signal can be identified. Again, do not leave the mode selector switch in this position when navigating using the ADF;
- *TEST*—placing the mode selector into the TEST position will deflect the ADF needle from its current position. Placing the mode selector back to ADF should cause the needle to swing back and indicate the direction of the NDB. This function should be tested every time as part of the selected, identified, ADFing tuning procedure. Some ADF sets have a separate TEST button which only needs to be pressed to deflect the needle, and then released to check the return of the needle. You only have to deflect the needle approximately 30°, and watch the return, for the test to be satisfactory; and (Note that on some ADF equipment, the TEST function is achieved using the ANT/REC position, which drives the needle to the 090 position. Returning the mode selector to ADF should see the needle start ADFing again.)
- *VOL*—the volume knob will probably be separate to the mode selector. With audio selected to the pilot's headset or to the cockpit speakers, the volume should be adjusted so that the ident or any voice messages on the NDB or compass locator may be heard. If signal reception is poor in ADF, then try ANT/REC; if there is no signal reception, try BFO/CW. Remember to return the mode selector to ADF!

NDBs transmit on frequencies in the range 200–1,750 kilohertz, the most common band being 200–400 kHz. To allow easier and accurate selection of any particular frequency, most modern ADFs have knobs that allow digital selection, in 100, 10 and 1 kHz steps. Some ADFs may have a band selector (200–400; 400–800; 800–1,600 kHz), with either a tuning knob or digital selection for precise tuning.

ADF Cockpit Displays

The basic purpose of an automatic direction finder (ADF) in an airplane is for its needle to point directly toward the selected NDB ground station. The ADF cockpit display is a card or dial placed vertically in the instrument panel so that:

Remember, with an ADF, the needle always points to the NDB station.

- if the ADF needle points up, the NDB is ahead;
- if the ADF needle points down, then the NDB is behind; and
- if the ADF needle points to one side, then the NDB is located somewhere to that side of the fore–aft axis of the airplane.

To convey this information to the pilot, various presentations are used, three of which we will consider:
- the fixed-card ADF, also known as the relative bearing indicator (RBI);
- the rotatable-card ADF (the "poor man's" RMI); and
- the radio magnetic indicator (RMI).

Fixed-Card ADF or Relative Bearing Indicator (RBI)

A fixed-card display has an ADF needle that can rotate against the background of a fixed-azimuth card of 360°, with 000 (360) at the top, 180 at the bottom, etc. The fixed-card ADF is also known as the relative bearing indicator (RBI), and is common in many general aviation aircraft. On the fixed-card ADF, the needle indicates the relative bearing (RB) of the NDB from the airplane. The *relative bearing* of the NDB from the aircraft is the angle between the aircraft's heading and the direction of the NDB. Relative bearings are usually described clockwise from 000 to 360; however, it is

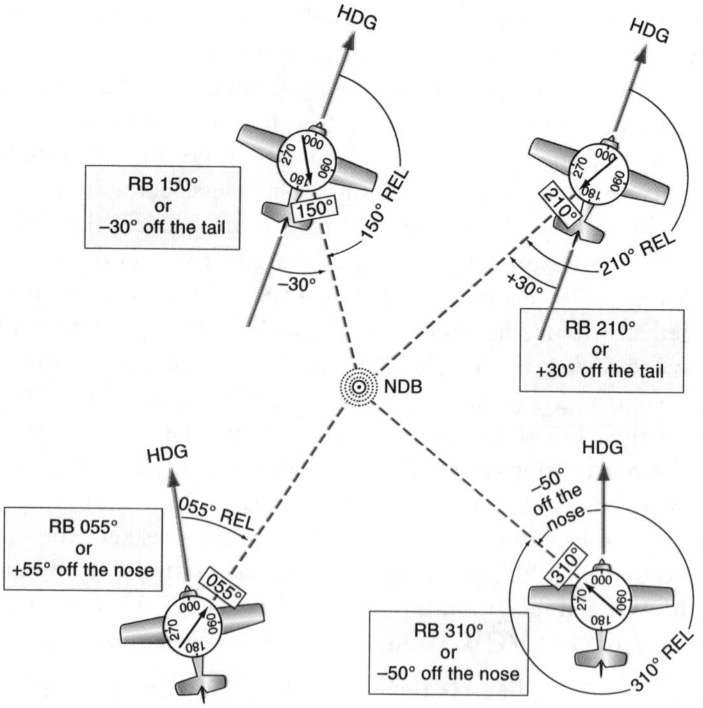

Figure 27-44 The RBI or fixed-card ADF shows relative bearings.

sometimes convenient to describe the bearing of the NDB relative to the nose or tail of the airplane. Each time the airplane changes its magnetic heading, it will carry the fixed card with it. Therefore, with each change of magnetic heading, the ADF needle will indicate a different relative bearing (RB).

It is not the needle that moves, but rather the fixed-card—the needle continues to point at the station. The principle is easily understood if you stand, point at an object, and then turn and face another direction while continuing to point at the object. Your arm indicates the same direction to the object, but it makes a different angle with your body because you have changed your heading. The relative bearing of the object has changed because your heading has changed.

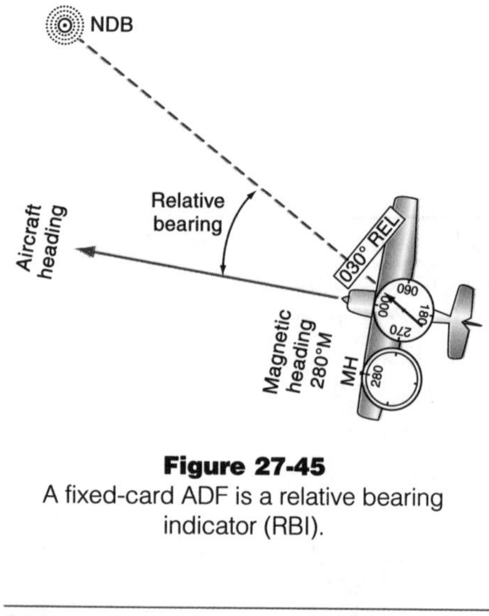

Figure 27-45
A fixed-card ADF is a relative bearing indicator (RBI).

Orientation Using the RBI or Fixed-Card ADF. The airplane can be oriented with respect to the NDB knowing:

- the magnetic heading (MH) of the airplane (from the magnetic compass or heading indicator); plus
- the relative bearing (RB) of the NDB from the airplane.

In practice, magnetic heading is flown using the heading indicator, which should be realigned with the magnetic compass in steady flight every 10 minutes or so. The illustrations will therefore display the heading indicator instead of the magnetic compass. In figure 27-45, the pilot is steering MH 280, and the ADF indicates RB 030 to the NDB.

$$\text{MH } 280 + \text{RB } 030 = \text{MB } 310 \text{ to NDB}$$

$$\begin{pmatrix}\text{Aircraft}\\ \text{Magnetic}\\ \text{Heading}\end{pmatrix} + \begin{pmatrix}\text{Relative Bearing}\\ \text{of NDB}\\ \text{from Aircraft}\end{pmatrix} = \begin{pmatrix}\text{Magnetic Bearing}\\ \text{of NDB}\\ \text{from Aircraft}\end{pmatrix}$$

Visualizing Magnetic Bearing To the NDB (MB). A quick pictorial means of determining MB to an NDB, using a relative bearing indicator and a heading indicator, is to translate the ADF needle onto the HI by paralleling a pencil or by using your imagination. MH + RB = MB to ground station.

Visualizing Magnetic Bearing From the NDB. The magnetic bearing of the aircraft from the NDB is the reciprocal of the magnetic bearing to the NDB. In figure 27-46, this is MB 130 from the NDB. MB from can be visualized as the tail of the pencil (or needle) when it is transferred from the RBI onto the HI.

> **Note.** An easier method of finding reciprocals than adding or subtracting 180°, is to either add 200 and subtract 20 or subtract 200 and add 20.

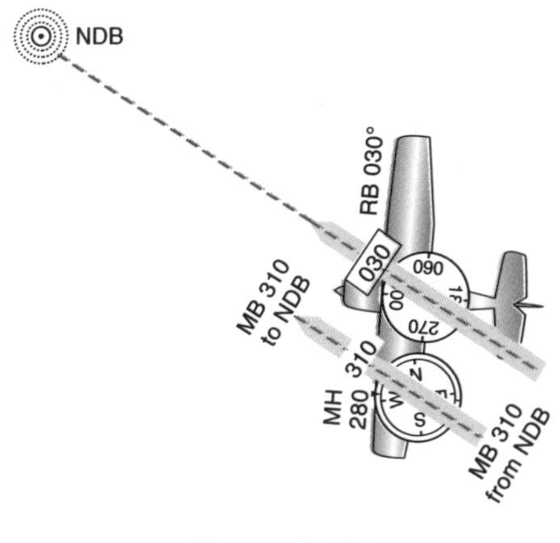

Figure 27-46
A pictorial (albeit clumsy) method of finding MB.

Example 27-10

MB 310 to NDB	MB 270 to NDB	MB 085 to NDB
−200	−200	+200
+ 20	+ 20	− 20
MB 130 from NDB	MB 090 from NDB	MB 265 from NDB

The Rotatable-Card ADF

The rotatable-card ADF is an advance on the fixed-card ADF, because it allows the pilot to rotate the card so that the ADF needle indicates, not relative bearing, but magnetic bearing to the NDB. The pilot does this by aligning the ADF card with the HI compass card each time the airplane's magnetic heading is changed.

To align a manually rotated ADF card:

- note magnetic heading on the heading indicator; then
- rotate the ADF card, setting magnetic heading under the index.

When the ADF card is aligned with the HI, the ADF needle will indicate the magnetic bearing to the NDB. This eliminates the need for mental arithmetic—an obvious advantage. Note also that the tail of the needle, 180° removed from its head, indicates the magnetic bearing of the airplane from the NDB. Any time the aircraft

Figure 27-47 A rotatable-card ADF.

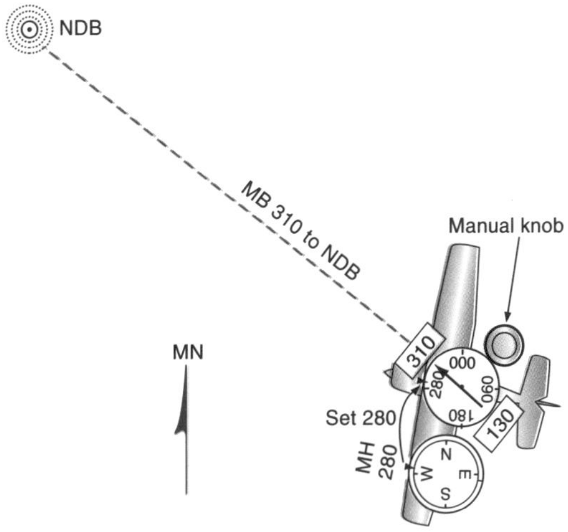

Figure 27-48 Using a rotatable-card ADF.

Figure 27-49
The HSI is an RMI with a superimposed course deviation indicator (CDI).

changes magnetic heading, the pilot should manually align the ADF card with the HI (after ensuring, of course, that the HI is aligned with the magnetic compass).

If desired, the rotatable-card can still be used as a fixed-card simply by aligning 000 with the nose of the airplane and not changing it. The next step up from a rotatable-card ADF is an instrument with a card that remains aligned automatically. This instrument is known as the radio magnetic indicator, or RMI.

The Radio Magnetic Indicator (RMI)

The RMI display has the ADF needle superimposed on a card that is continuously and automatically being aligned with magnetic north. It is, if you like, an automatic version of the rotatable-card ADF—an automatic combination of the heading indicator and RBI. The RMI is the best ADF presentation, and the easiest to use:

- the RMI needle will always indicate the magnetic bearing *to* the NDB; and
- the tail of the RMI needle will indicate the magnetic bearing *from* the NDB.

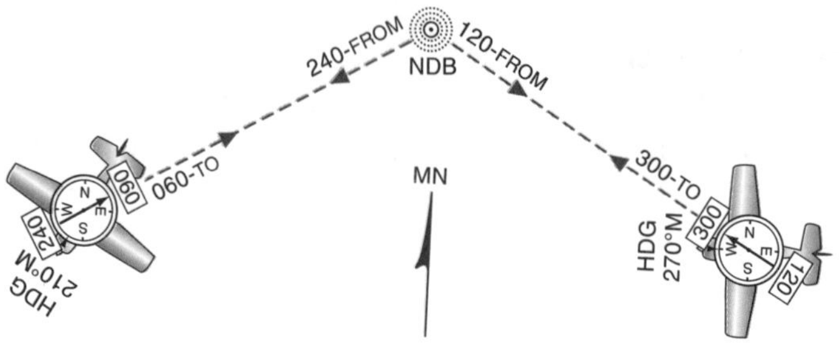

Figure 27-50 The RMI compass card remains aligned with magnetic north.

The RMI instrument is shown in figure 27-51. As an airplane turns and its magnetic heading alters, the RMI card (which automatically remains aligned with magnetic north) will appear to turn along with the ADF needle. In reality, of course, it is the compass card and the RMI needle that remain stationary while the airplane turns about them. Before, during and after the turn, the RMI's needle will continue to indicate the current MB to the NDB.

Figure 27-51
The RMI compass card is driven by a fluxvalve and a gyroscope.

Gyro-Stabilized Compass Equipment. In most airplanes fitted with an RMI, the initial magnetic north reference for the RMI card is provided by a *fluxgate* or *fluxvalve*, a detector that is sensitive to magnetic north, and situated in a fairly nonmagnetic part of the airplane such as in a wingtip. A heading indicator is electrically slaved to this magnetic reference so that the gyroscope is continually being aligned with magnetic north, and it is this heading indicator that drives the RMI compass card in a process known as slaving. Most gyro-stabilized compasses have an annunciator near the compass card. This contains a small needle, often triangular in shape, that oscillates when automatic slaving is in process (which should be all the time). When the annunciator needle is hard over to one side, it indicates that the compass card is a long way out of alignment. This can usually be remedied using a manual knob to quickly realign the compass card with the magnetic heading of the airplane, after which the slower, automatic slaving should be sufficient to maintain alignment. If slaving is not occurring because of some fault in the system (indicated by the annunciator being stationary and not oscillating) then the pilot can revert to using the RMI as a rotatable-card ADF ("poor man's RMI") or as a fixed-card ADF (relative bearing indicator).

Indicators with Two Pointers. Some airplanes are fitted with two ADF receivers, and have two needles superimposed on the one indicator (which may be a fixed-card twin-ADF indicator, or a dual-pointer RMI). Most RMIs have function switches that allow you to select either an NDB or a VOR ground station for the RMI needle to point at. This gives you more flexibility in using NAVAIDs, since you can select the RMI to any suitable NDB or VOR within range or, with two needles, select one to ADF and the other to VOR.

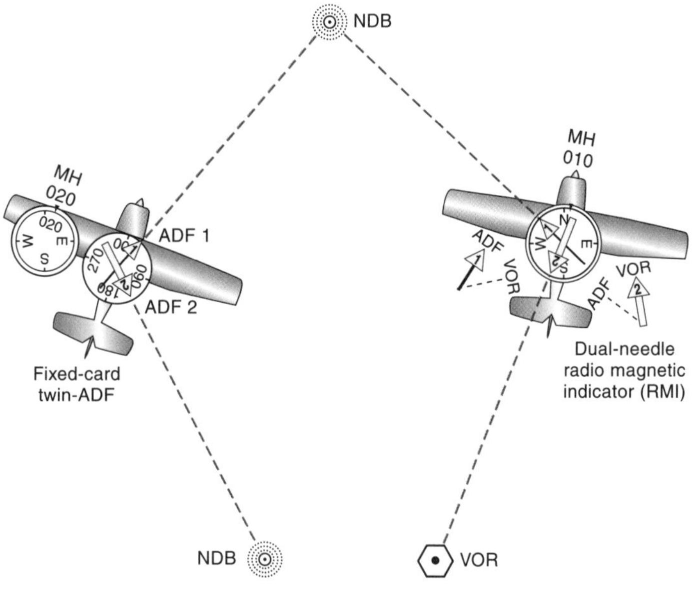

Figure 27-52 An indicator with two needles.

Figure 27-53
The manually rotatable ADF card.

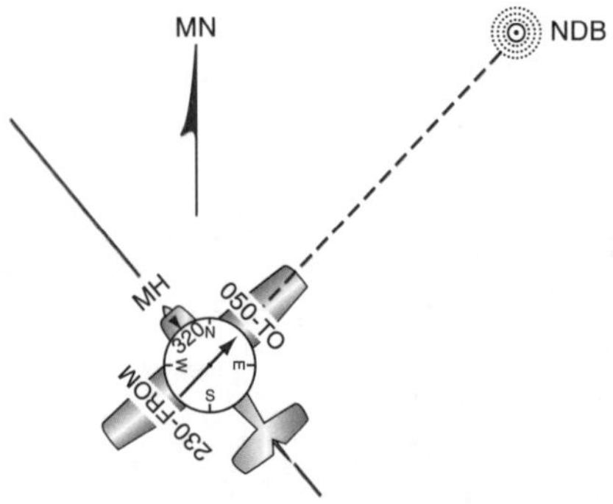

Figure 27-54
Orientation with an RMI is quite straightforward.

Figure 27-55
Typical radio magnetic indicators (courtesy Allied Signal Aerospace).

Operational Use of the ADF

The principles of using the ADF are the same whether the airplane is equipped with an RBI or an RMI display. Early models of the ADF were primarily of the fixed-card ADF design, with the rotatable-card ADF coming as a later improvement to the instrument. Many airplanes are still equipped with this instrument, which, although being more difficult to use than the more modern RMI design, is still an excellent aid.

The rotatable-card ADF will allow you to manually align the ADF card with magnetic north. This can be done whenever the aircraft heading is changed. Once aligned, this will also reduce your workload by reducing the amount of visualization and mental arithmetic required.

The RMI combines the RBI and the HI into the one instrument, where the ADF card is aligned automatically with magnetic north. This considerably reduces your workload by reducing the amount of visualization and mental arithmetic required.

Whatever ADF instrument is installed in your airplane, the same principles of operation apply. The discussion that follows applies to both the RBI, RMI and the manually rotatable-card ADF, except that:

- the fixed-card ADF requires you to visualize and mentally transfer the indicated relative bearing to the NDB ground station across to the airplane HI;
- the manually rotatable-card RBI must be realigned with the heading indicator by hand following every heading change (and of course the HI must be realigned with the magnetic compass by hand every 10 minutes or so); and
- the RMI is continuously and automatically aligned with magnetic north.

An RMI gives a graphic picture of where the airplane is:

- the *head* of the RMI needle displays magnetic bearing *to* the ground station; and
- the *tail* of the RMI needle displays magnetic bearing *from* the ground station.

One significant advantage of the RMI over the RBI is that you can select it to either an NDB or a VOR ground station. Some RMIs have two needles which allow two stations to be selected. The method of use is the same in each case. If the head of the RMI needle indicates 030, then we write this as RMI 030. It tells us that the magnetic bearing *to* the ground station from the airplane is 030 degrees magnetic. The bearing *from* the ground station to the airplane is, of course, the reciprocal 210 degrees magnetic.

Orientation

A *position line*, also known as a *line of position* (LoP), is a line along which the airplane is known to be at a particular moment. A line of position may be obtained either visually or by radio means as shown in figure 27-56. Two lines of position that cut at a reasonable angle, ideally close to 90°, are needed for a *fix*. For the airplane to be on both lines of position simultaneously, it must be at their point of intersection.

A *radio fix* can be obtained using two NDBs in an airplane fitted with two ADFs. It is possible to fix position using a combination of radio aids including NDBs, VORs and DMEs. Figure 27-57 shows that these position lines can be considered from two perspectives:

- *to the NDB* from the airplane. This is the line of position to the NDB that a pilot would see from the airplane as either a *relative* bearing (RB 030 *to* NDB 1), or as a *magnetic* bearing to the NDB (MB 360 *to* NDB 1); and
- *from the NDB* to the airplane, as a *magnetic* bearing from the station (MB 180 *from* NDB 1). The magnetic bearing from the NDB may be converted to a *true* bearing by applying magnetic variation, if for instance you wanted to plot the airplane's position on a chart.

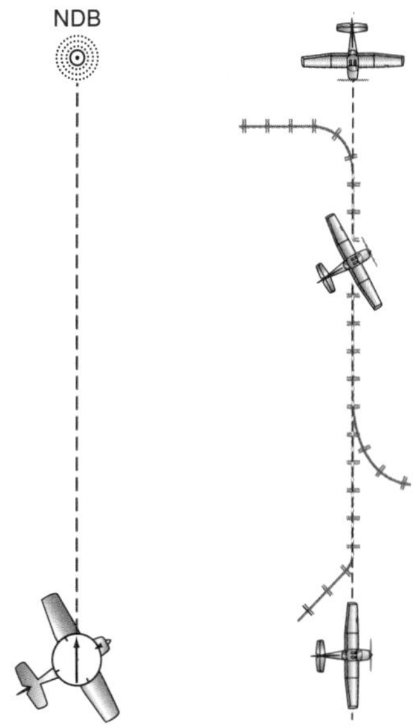

Figure 27-56
A radio position line (left) and a visual position line.

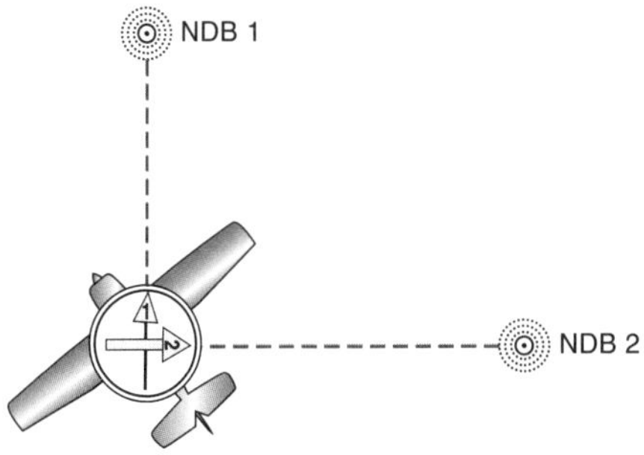

Figure 27-57
Two lines of position with a good "cut" can provide a fix.

Example 27-11

The airplane in figure 27-58 is steering MH 015. Its ADF needle points toward a nondirectional beacon 75° to the right of the nose on a relative bearing indicator (also known as a fixed-card ADF). Magnetic variation is 5°W. Calculate:

a. the relative bearing (RB) to the NDB from the airplane;
b. the magnetic bearing to the NDB from the airplane;
c. the magnetic bearing from the NDB to the airplane; and
d. the true bearing from the NDB to the airplane.

While it is possible to calculate all of this mentally, at this early stage it is a good idea to sketch a clear diagram to help visualize the situation.

1. Sketch the airplane on MH 015.
2. Indicate RB 075.
3. Draw in the position line to the NDB.

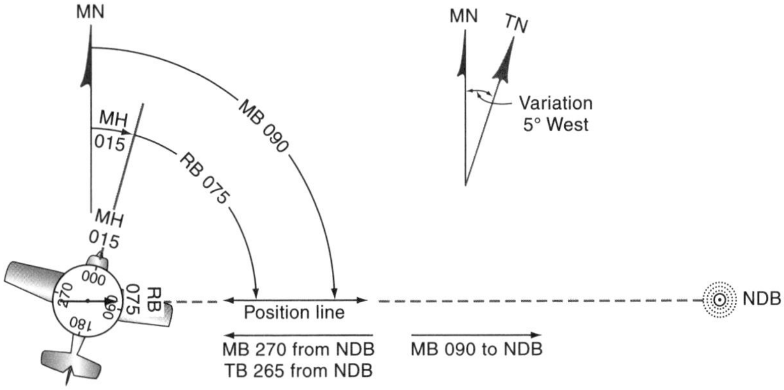

Figure 27-58 Magnetic heading MH 015; relative bearing RB 075.

MH 015	MB 090 to NDB	MB 270 from NDB
RB 075	+ 180	Westerly variation − 5
MB 090 to NDB	MB 270 from NDB	TB 265 from NDB

Answers: a. RB 075; b. MB 090 to NDB; c. MB 270 from NDB; d. TB 265 from NDB.

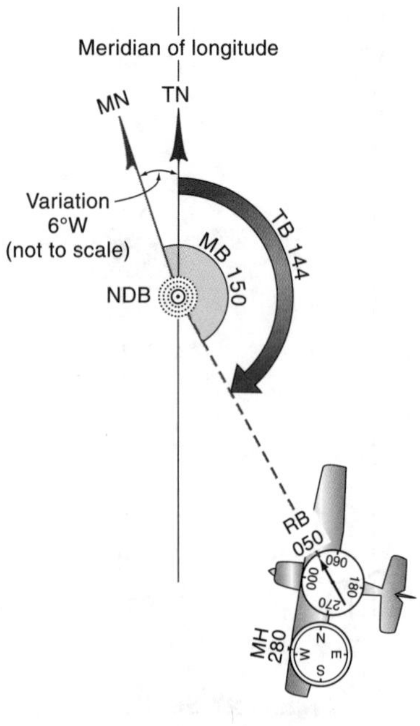

Figure 27-59
Finding true bearing from an NDB.

True Bearings From an NDB

To plot your position relative to an NDB on a sectional chart, you will need to determine your true bearing from the NDB—your bearing from the NDB related to *true north.* True north is indicated on the chart by the meridians of longitude that run north-south. You can then plot your straight true bearing position line from the NDB.

> **Note.** It is possible to plot *magnetic* bearings from a VOR, known as *radials,* since each VOR shown on a chart has a compass rose around it oriented to *magnetic* north—NDBs do not. True bearing = magnetic bearing plus east variation (minus west variation).

Example 27-12

MH is 280. RB is 050. What is the true bearing (TB) from the NDB? Magnetic variation in the area is 6°W.

MH 280 + RB 050 = MB 330 to NDB
−2
+2
MB 150 from NDB
−6 °W Var'n
TB 144 from NDB

An Easier Method of Visualizing MB

A relative bearing, as well as being specified using the 360° method clockwise from the nose of the airplane, can be specified as either *left* or *right* of the nose (or the tail). For instance, a RB of 290 may be thought of as -70, since the corresponding MB will be 70° *less* than the current MH. Similarly, RB 030 may be thought of as +30, since the corresponding MB to the NDB will be 30° *greater* than the MH.

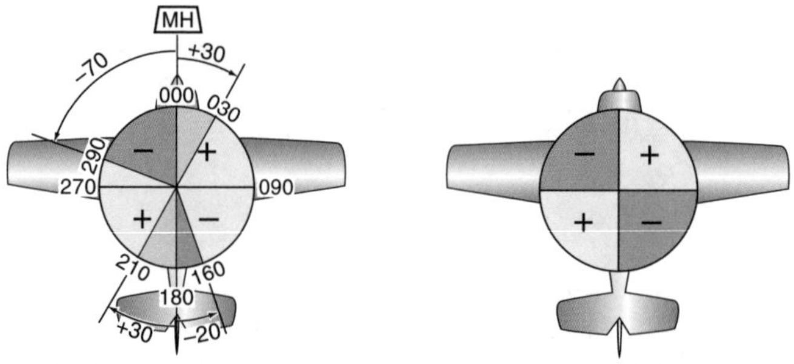

Figure 27-60 Quadrants for converting relative bearings to magnetic bearings.

Relative bearings off the *tail* of the airplane may be treated in a similar shorthand fashion. For instance, RB 160 may be thought of as -20 off the tail; and RB 210 as +30 off the tail. This *quadrantal* approach to RB and MB problems can simplify your in-flight visualization.

Example 27-13

An airplane is steering MH 340. The ADF needle shows RB 010. Determine the MB to the NDB.

MH	340	
	+10	off the nose (RB 010)
MB	350	to NDB

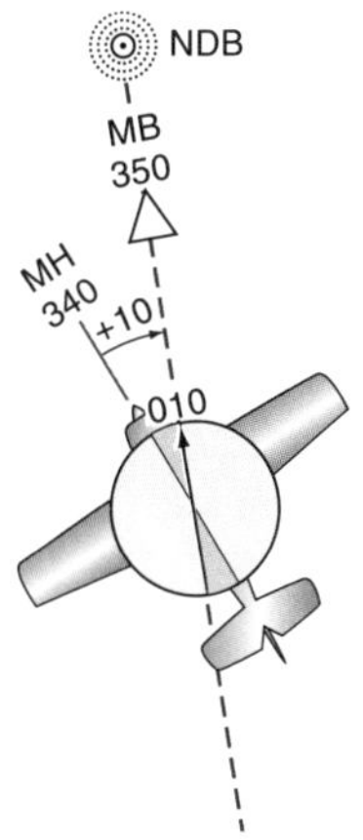

Figure 27-61 Example 27-13: MH 340 + 10 off the nose = MB 350.

Visualizing Position on the Heading Indicator

Mentally transferring the RBI needle onto the HI allows quick visualization of MB *to* NDB on the head of the needle, and MB *from* NDB on its tail.

If you now imagine a model airplane attached to the tail of the needle, with the model airplane oriented with the actual heading, you have a very good picture of the whole situation.

Mentally transferring the RBI onto the HI is the norm when flying the airplane and is considerably easier than performing mental calculations and flying at the same time.

Example 27-14

Visualize the situation of MH 070 and RB 260. See figure 27-62.

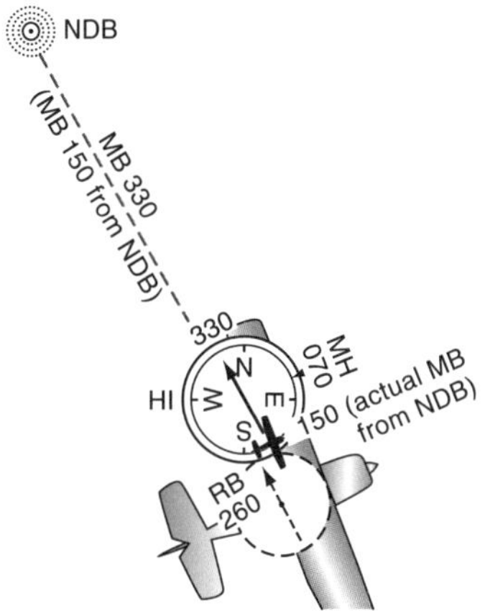

Figure 27-62
Visualizing position on the HI; MH 070 and MB 330.

Changing Heading

The ADF needle points directly at the selected NDB (see figure 27-63). If the aircraft heading is changed, the ADF needle will continue to point at the NDB, but the relative bearing between the ADF needle and the nose of the aircraft will alter by the same number of degrees. For example, if the aircraft heading increases by 45° by turning right, the RB will decrease (by 45°).

Example 27-15

With reference to the instrument indications in figure 27-64, what would be the relative bearing if the aircraft was turned onto a MH of 355°?

1. MH 300 + RB 040 to NDB = MB 340 to NDB.
2. Changing heading to MH 355 will *not* alter the MB to the NDB, but will alter the RB. The heading will change by +55°, and the RB will change by -55°. See figure 27-63.

$$
\begin{aligned}
MB &= MH + RB \\
340 &= 355 + RB \\
RB &= 340 - 355 \\
&= -015 \ (360 - 15 = 345)
\end{aligned}
$$

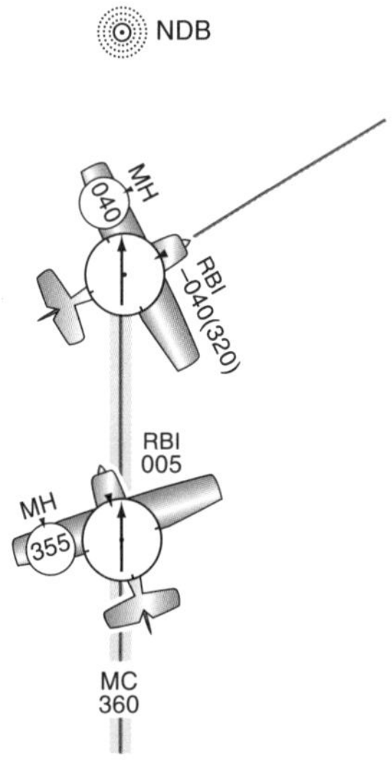

Figure 27-63
Changing heading alters relative bearing.

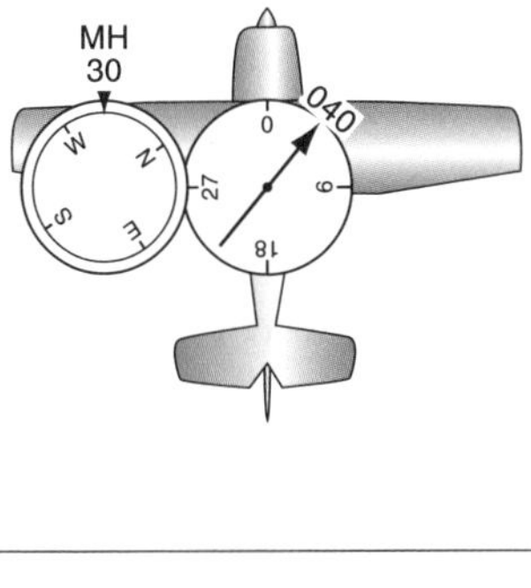

Figure 27-64
Typical heading and ADF indications.

Intercepting Course

Having oriented yourself with respect to an NDB, you know the answer to the question, "Where am I?" You now may ask, "Where do I want to go?" and "How do I get there?" This is accomplished by:

- *orienting the airplane* relative to the NDB, and to the desired course;
- *turning to take up a suitable intercept heading*, after considering where you want to join the desired course;
- *maintaining the intercept heading and wait*:
  - for the *head* of the needle to fall if inbound; or
  - for the *tail* of the needle to rise if outbound; and
- *just before the desired course is reached*, commencing a turn to complete the intercept, and applying a suitable *wind correction angle* to maintain it.

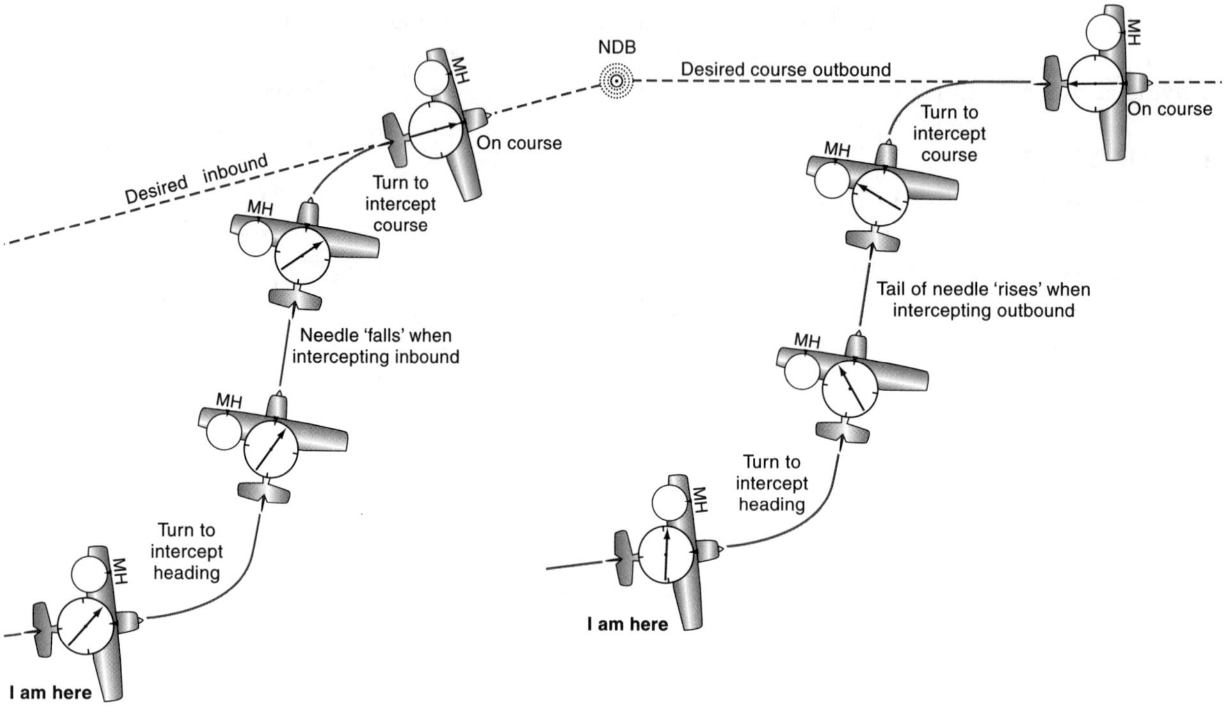

Figure 27-65 Visualizing: Where am I? Where do I want to go? How do I get there?

The HI can assist greatly in visualizing the situation. In example 27-15 (figure 27-62), the situation MH 070 and RB 260 was visualized, with MB 330 to the NDB.

Now what if you wish to intercept a magnetic course (MC) 270 to the NDB? All that you need to do is visualize the desired course on the HI. With a model airplane on the tail of the needle tracking as desired, it becomes quite clear what turns are necessary to intercept the desired course. First turn left to a suitable intercept heading, say MH 360 for a 90° intercept of MC 270 to the NDB.

> **Note.** If you become disoriented, a simple procedure is to take up the heading of the desired course. Even though not on course, the airplane will at least be parallel to it, and the ADF needle will indicate which way to turn to intercept it.

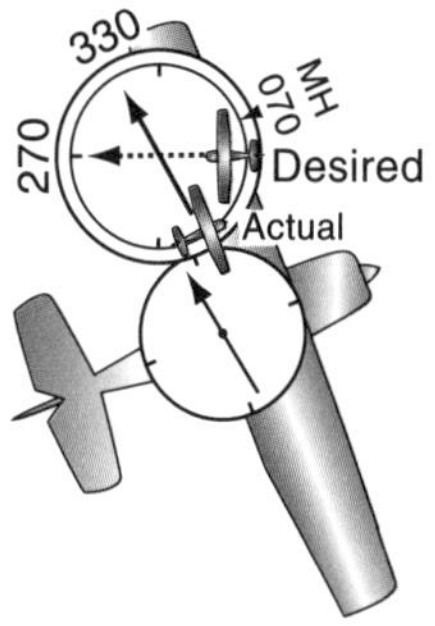

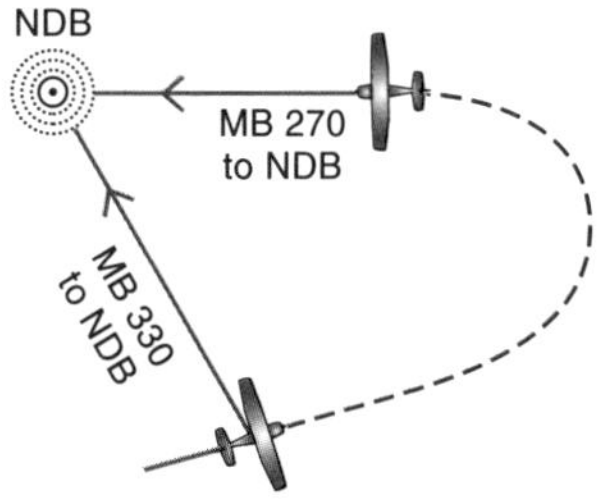

Figure 27-66 Visualizing an intercept on the HI.

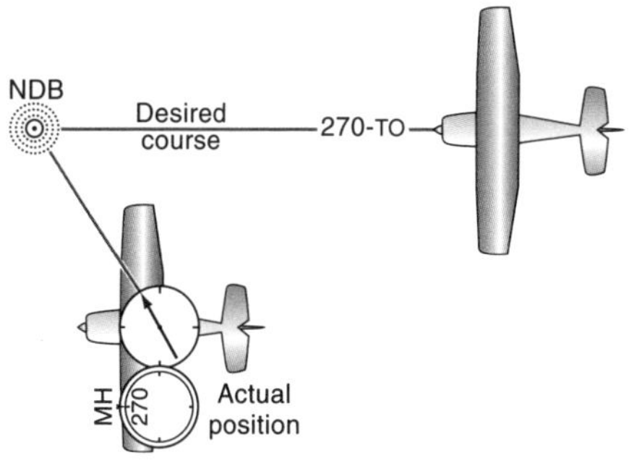

Figure 27-67
Paralleling course to help in visualization.

"When in doubt, parallel out."

Suppose the situation is MH 340, RB 080 (shown in figure 27-68), and you wish to intercept a course MC 090 to the NDB. The current magnetic bearing to the NDB is easily found to be MB 060 (MH 340 + RB 080). By continuing to steer MH 340 (shown in figure 27-69), the airplane will eventually intercept MC 090 to the NDB, but it would be a rather untidy intercept, with the airplane tracking somewhat away from the NDB, and with an intercept turn of 110° being required.

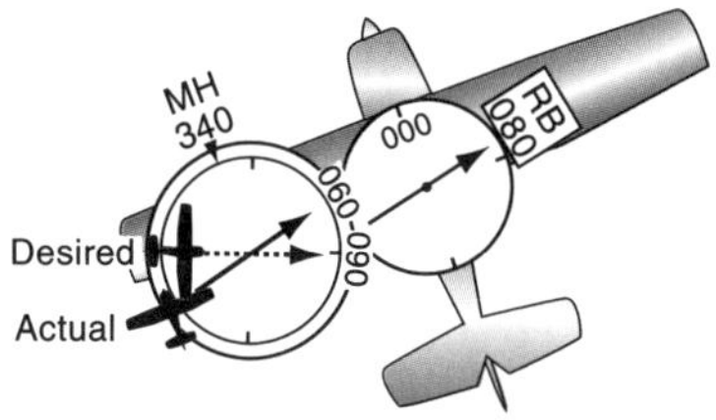

Figure 27-68
Visualizing the intercept.

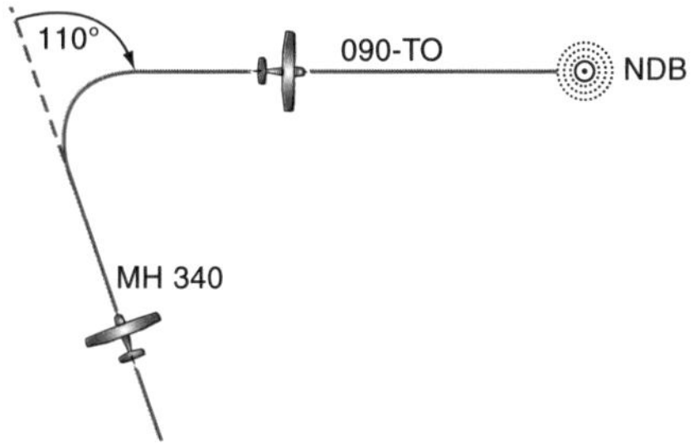

Figure 27-69
An inefficient intercept of course.

A tidier and more efficient intercept may be achieved by turning to an initial heading of MH 360 for a 90° intercept (shown in figure 27-70); or MH 030 for a 60° intercept. Turning further right to MH 060 would of course point the airplane at the NDB, and MC 090 to the NDB would not be intercepted.

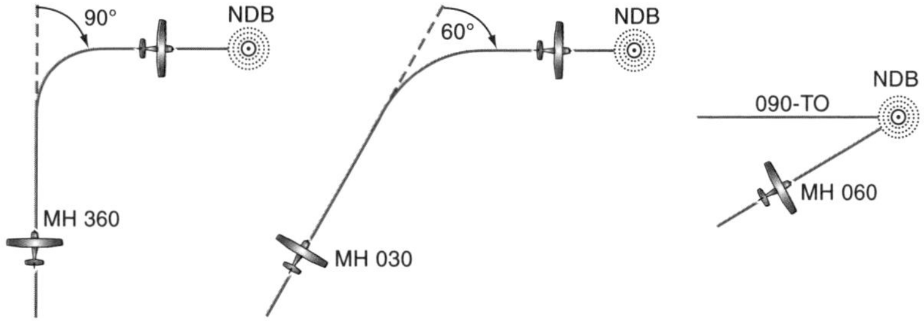

Figure 27-70 Different intercepts of course.

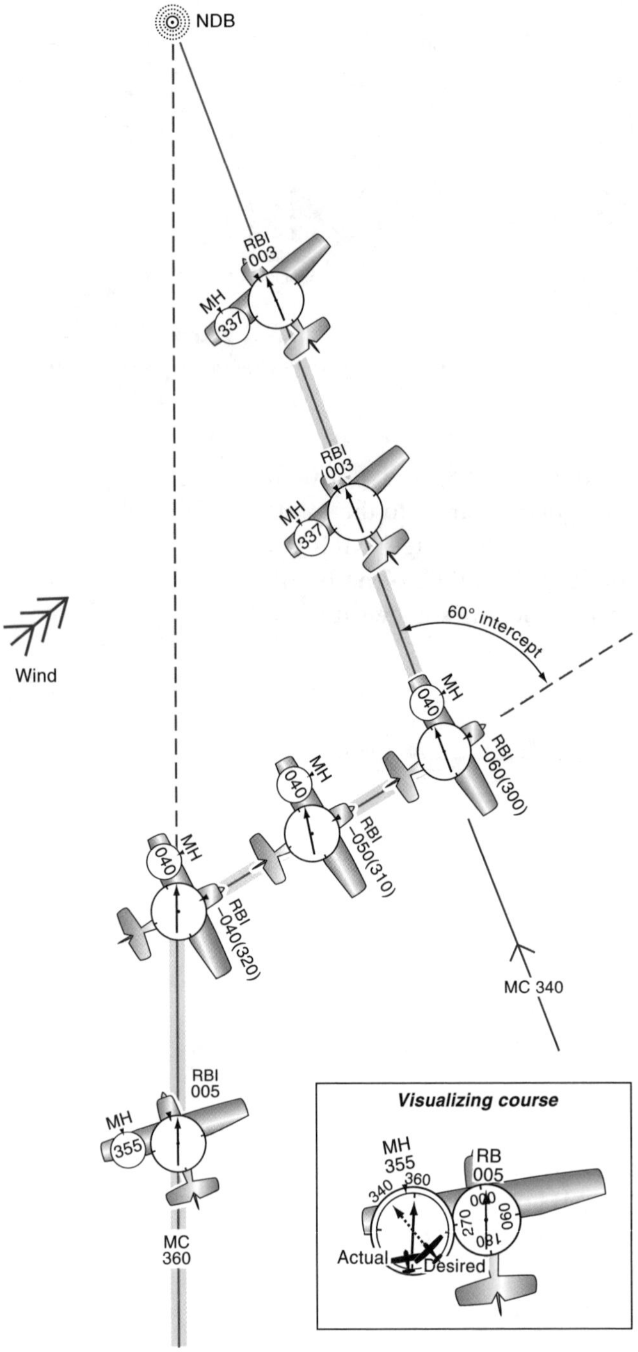

Figure 27-71
Intercepting MC 340 inbound from the south of the station.

Intercepting an Inbound Course

Fixed-Card ADF. An airplane is steering MH 355, and the RBI indicates RB 005 when tuned to a particular NDB. The pilot is requested to track inbound on course MC 340 to the station, intercepting the course at 60°. See figure 27-71.

Initially, orient the airplane. MH 355 + RB 005 = MB 360 to NDB, or MB 180 from NDB. The airplane is south of the NDB and heading MH 355. The desired course is MC 340 to the NDB (which is on the line of position MB 160 from the NDB), to the right of the airplane.

Second, to intercept the course MC 340 from the left at 60°, the airplane should steer (340 + 60 = 400) MH 040. As the airplane's heading alters, the ADF needle will continue to point *at* the NDB and so the *relative* bearing will change (in this case, even though it is not an important calculation, from RB 005 to RB 320, or -40 off the nose, with the 45° right turn).

Third, maintain MH 040 and periodically observe the RBI as the head of the needle falls. Since it is a *plus 60* intercept, wait until the head of the needle falls to *minus 60* (or RB 300). You are steering *course plus 60, waiting for minus 60.*

Finally, at MB 340 to the NDB, and as the needle is falling to RB -60, turn left to take up the desired course to the NDB, allowing for the estimated crosswind effect on tracking. In this case, a wind correction angle (WCA) of 3° left is used. Maintain the desired course of MC 340 to the station by continually checking that MH + RB = MB 340, for example: MH 337 + RB 003 = MB 340.

> **Note.** An airplane takes some distance to turn, and so you should anticipate the desired course by commencing the turn onto course just before MB 340 is reached. You can do this by observing the *rate* at which the ADF needle falls toward -060, and commence the turn accordingly.

Example 27-16

RMI. An airplane has a MH 340 and the RMI indicates 030. You are requested to intercept a course of 090 to the NDB.

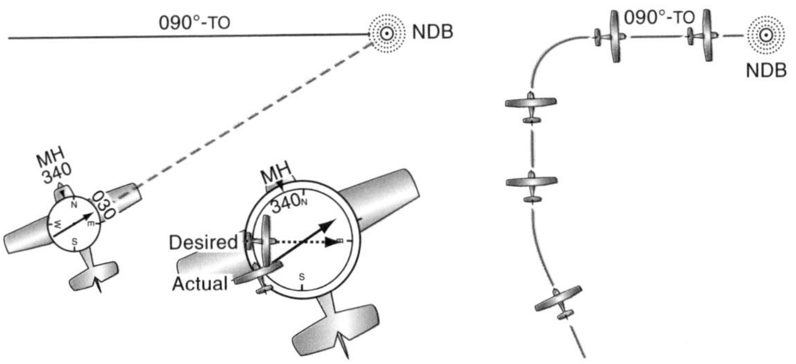

Figure 27-72 Visualizing course on an RMI.

First, orient the airplane with the RMI. The magnetic bearing to the NDB from your present position is 030. If you now imagine a model airplane attached to the *tail* of the needle, with the airplane on the actual heading (which in this case is MH 340), then you have a very good picture of the situation.

The desired course of 090 *to* the NDB is ahead of the present position of the airplane. If you visualize the desired course on the RMI, with the model airplane on the *tail* of the needle tracking as desired, it becomes quite clear what turns are required to intercept the desired course.

Second, intercept course MC 090 to the NDB. Turn to a suitable intercept heading, such as one of those illustrated in figure 27-73.

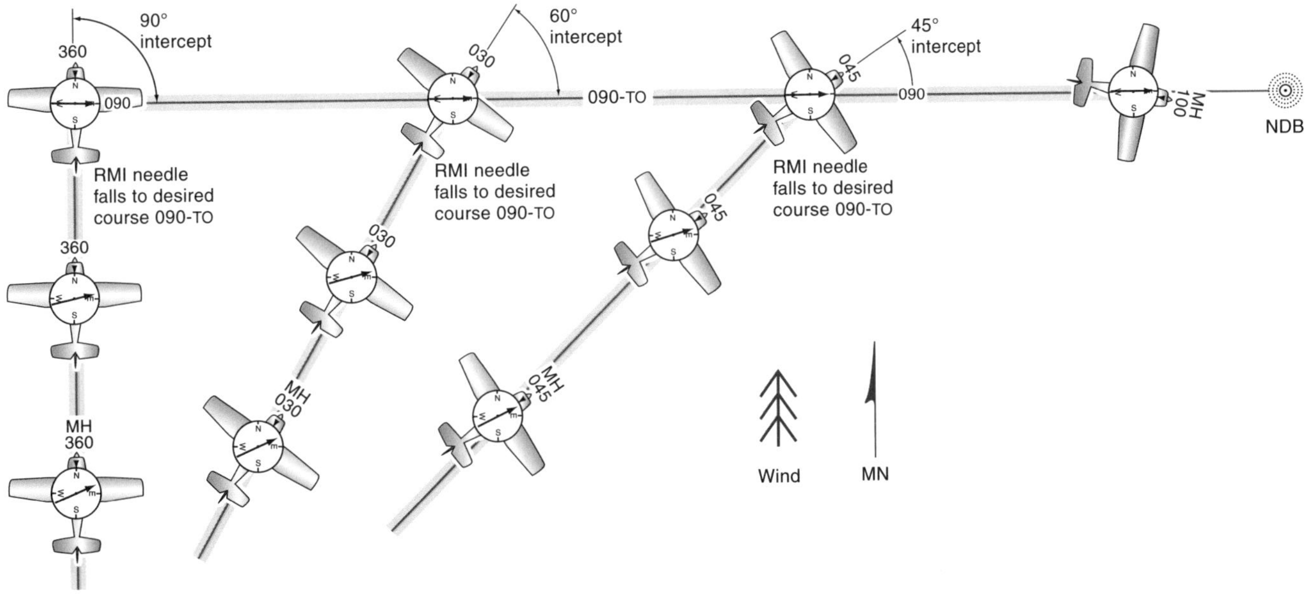

Figure 27-73 Intercepting course at 90°, 60°, or 45°.

Third, maintain the chosen intercept heading and periodically observe the RMI needle as it falls toward the desired inbound course of 090.

Finally, as MC 090 to the NDB is approached, indicated by the RMI needle approaching 090, turn right to take up the desired course to the NDB, allowing for any estimated crosswind effect on tracking. In this case, a WCA of 10° right has been used. With MH 100, and the RMI steady on 090, the airplane now tracks MC 090 to the NDB.

Intercepting an Outbound Course

Example 27-17

Fixed-card ADF. The radar controller gives you a radar vector of 340 to intercept an outbound course of 280. See figure 27-74.

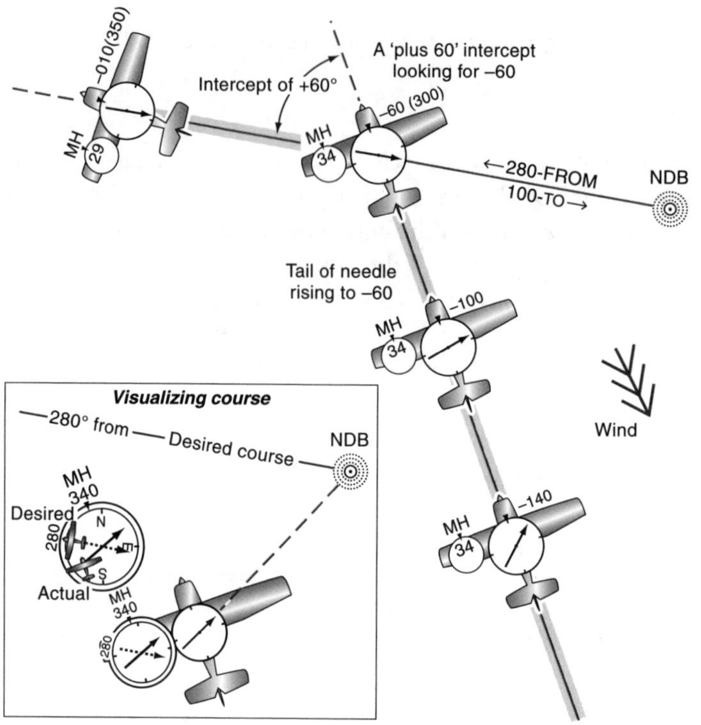

Figure 27-74 Radar vector 340 to intercept MC 280 outbound.

Initially, orient the airplane. It must be south of the outbound course.

Second, consider the intercept. A radar vector of 340 to intercept MC 280 outbound means a +60° intercept.

Third, monitor the intercept by steering a steady MH 340 and periodically checking the RBI to see the tail of the needle rising to -60 (RB 300). You are steering *course plus 60, waiting for minus 60.*

Finally, as MC 280 outbound is approached, indicated by the tail of the needle rising to -60, turn left to pick it up, in this case allowing a WCA of 10° for a wind from the right—MH 290.

Periodically check that MH ADF tail = MB from NDB. In this case, the tail of the ADF needle should be -10 off the nose (on RB 350), so that MH 290 − 10 = MC 280 from NDB.

Example 27-18

RMI. You are given a radar vector of 340 to intercept 280 outbound from an NDB. See figure 27-75.

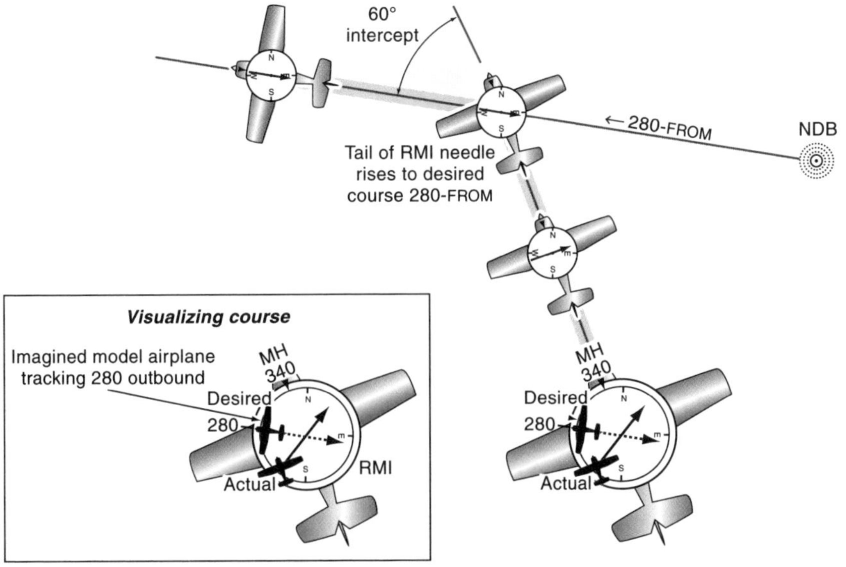

Figure 27-75 Intercepting 280 outbound off radar vector 340.

Initially, orient the airplane.

Second, consider the intercept, 60° in this case (340 − 280 = 60). Visualize the situation. Again, the model airplane imagined on the tail of the needle helps.

Third, monitor the intercept by steering a steady MH 340 and periodically checking the *tail* of the RMI needle rising to 280.

Finally, as the desired course 280 outbound is approached, and as the tail of the needle approaches 280, turn left to pick up the MC 280, in this case allowing no WCA, since you expect no crosswind effect.

Tracking

The ADF/NDB combination is often used to provide guidance for an airplane to fly from a distant position to a position overhead the NDB ground station. This is known as *tracking*. Just how this is achieved depends to a certain extent on the prevailing wind direction and speed.

Tracking Inbound with no Crosswind

When tracking toward an NDB, the head of the ADF needle will lie toward the top of the dial. With no crosswind, a direct inbound course can be achieved by simply pointing the airplane directly *at* the NDB, by steering a heading that keeps the *fixed-card ADF* needle on the nose (RB 000). Since the MH will, in this case, be the same as the desired course, the *RMI* needle will also be on the nose indicating the course.

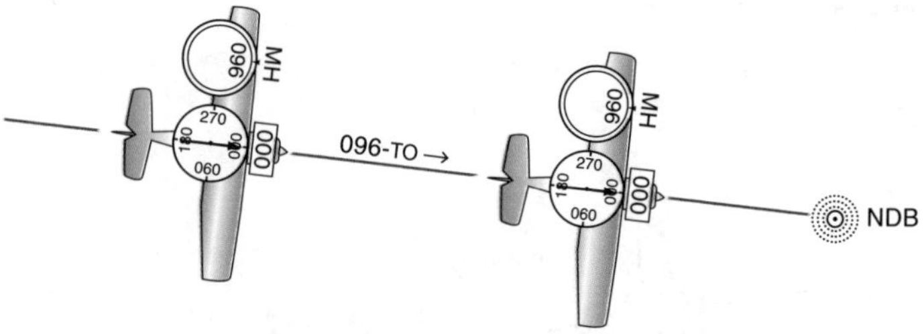

Figure 27-76 Tracking inbound, with no crosswind.

If there is no crosswind to blow the airplane off course, then everything will remain constant as shown in figure 27-76—the MH 096, the RB 000, and the MB 096 to the NDB will all remain constant. This can only occur in:

- no-wind conditions;
- a direct headwind; or
- a direct tailwind.

Tracking Inbound with a Crosswind

If no wind correction angle (WCA) is applied, and the airplane is pointed directly at the NDB, so that the ADF needle indicates RB 000, then any crosswind will cause the airplane to be blown off course.

In the case illustrated in figure 27-77, a wind with a northerly component has blown the airplane to the right of course. This is indicated by the ADF needle starting to move down the left of the dial. To return to course, the airplane must be turned toward the left, toward the direction in which the head of the needle is moving.

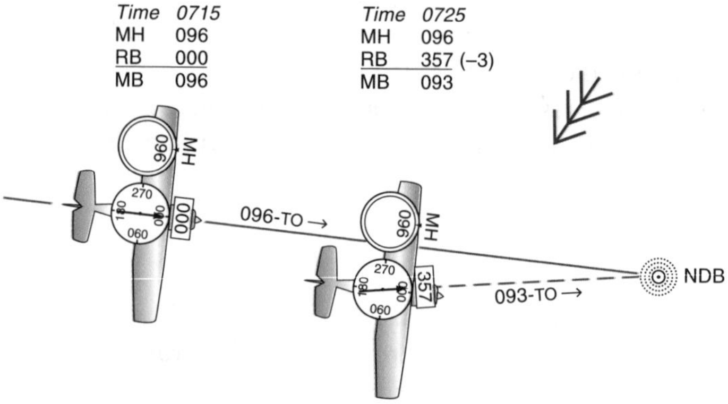

Figure 27-77 Crosswind causes drift.

If you turn left to put the NDB on the nose again, so that the RB is 000, then after a short while the airplane will again have been blown to the right of course, and the ADF needle will again move to the left of the nose. A further turn to the left will be required—and the process will need to be repeated again and again.

In this way, the ground track to the NDB will be curved, and the airplane will finally arrive overhead the NDB heading roughly into the wind. This rather inefficient means of tracking over the NDB is known as *homing* (keeping the NDB on the nose).

It will involve traveling a greater distance than that required to fly a direct course to the NDB from the original position. With the correct WCA applied, the airplane will track directly toward the ground station in a straight line. This is known as *tracking* and is a far better procedure than homing. If 5° left is indeed the correct WCA, you can achieve a course of MC 096 direct to the NDB by steering MH 091 (figure 27-78).

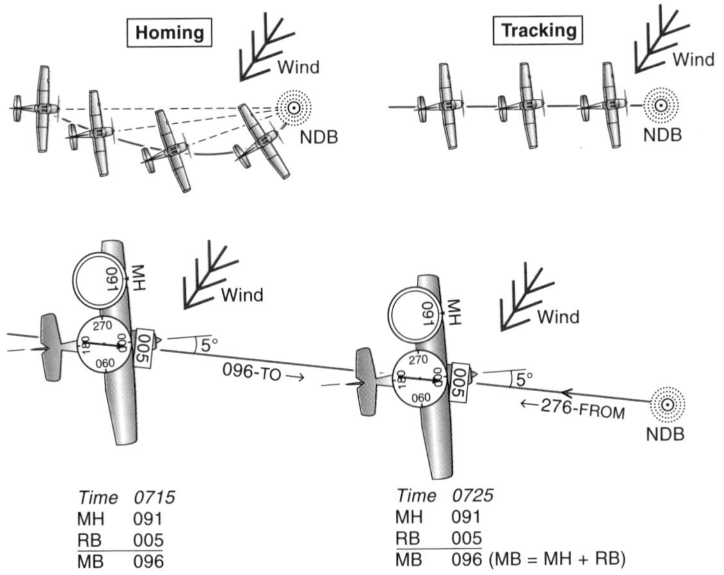

Figure 27-78 Tracking direct to the NDB.

Different winds will require different WCAs. An airplane is on course when the RB is equal-and-opposite to the difference between the actual MH and the desired MC. This is illustrated in figure 27-79. In each situation, the airplane is on the desired course of MC 010, but using a different WCA to counteract the drift under different wind conditions. The head of the ADF needle will point at the NDB and, with the current WCA applied, the nose of the aircraft will point upwind of this.

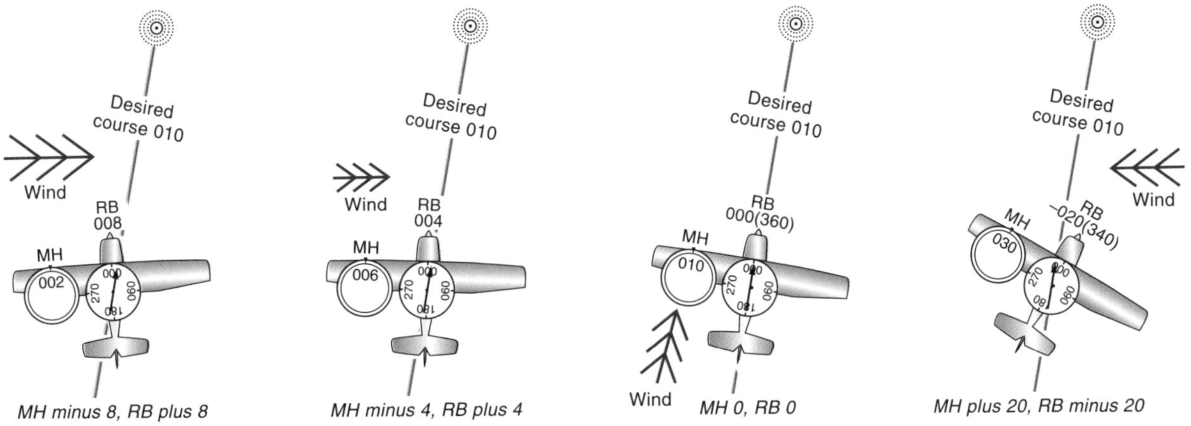

Figure 27-79 Laying off drift to achieve the desired course.

If the precise wind effect is not known, then initially use a *best-guess* WCA estimated from the available information. For the same crosswind, slower airplanes will need to allow a greater WCA than faster airplanes. See how the estimated WCA works, then make an adjustment to heading if required.

It is possible that the wind effect will change as an airplane tracks toward an NDB, so regular adjustments to the heading may be required. This is often the case as an airplane descends while using the NDB as the tracking aid, as changes in wind speed and/or direction may occur during the descent.

If an incorrect drift correction is made, then the airplane will move off the desired course. The RB indication, and the MB to the NDB, will change. If a steady heading is being flown, then any divergence from course will become obvious through a gradually changing RB, with the ADF needle moving left or right down the dial.

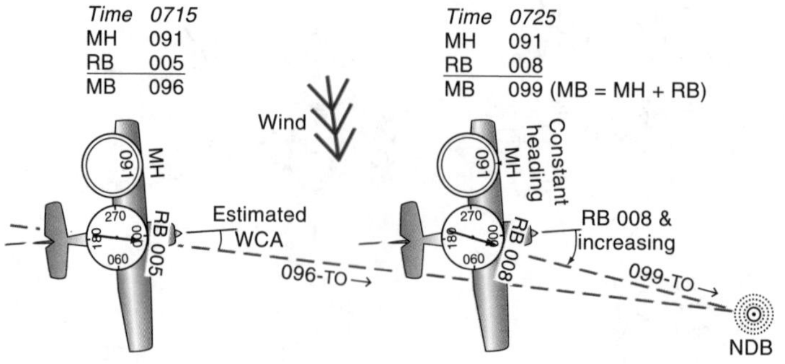

Figure 27-80 An incorrect wind correction angle causes MB to change.

Modify the wind correction angle to maintain course by altering heading.

Suppose, for instance, you fly a heading with a 5° WCA to the left to counteract the effect of a wind from the left. If the wind effect turns out to be less than expected, then the airplane will gradually move to the left of the desired course to the NDB, and the RB will gradually increase (naturally, the MB to the NDB will also increase).

The head of the ADF needle falling away to the right indicates that a turn right must be made to track to the NDB. Conversely, the head of the ADF needle falling away to the left indicates that a left turn must be made to track to the NDB. Just how great each correcting turn should be depends on the deviation from course.

Note. Be careful of terminology. *Drift* is the angle between heading and the *ground track*, which may not be the desired course. The perfect wind correction angle will counteract any drift exactly, and the actual ground track will follow the desired course, which is usually the aim of tracking.

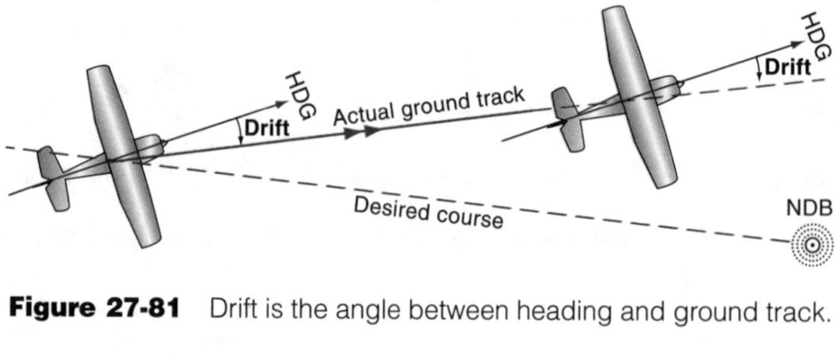

Figure 27-81 Drift is the angle between heading and ground track.

Maintaining Course

In reality, *flying level* is a series of small and gentle climbs and descents made in an attempt to maintain the desired altitude perfectly. Similarly, *tracking* is a series of small turns made in an attempt to maintain the desired course perfectly.

Reintercepting a course, having deviated from it, involves the same procedure as the initial intercept of a new course, except that the intercept angles will be smaller (provided you are vigilant and do not allow large deviations to occur). Realizing that the airplane is diverging from the direct course to the NDB, you have several options. You may either:

- track direct from the present position (along a new course); or
- regain the original course.

To track direct from your present position to the NDB (even though the present position is not on the originally desired course), turn slightly right (say 3° in this case), and track direct to the NDB from the present position. Normally, this technique is used only when within one or two miles from the NDB, when there is insufficient distance remaining to regain the original course.

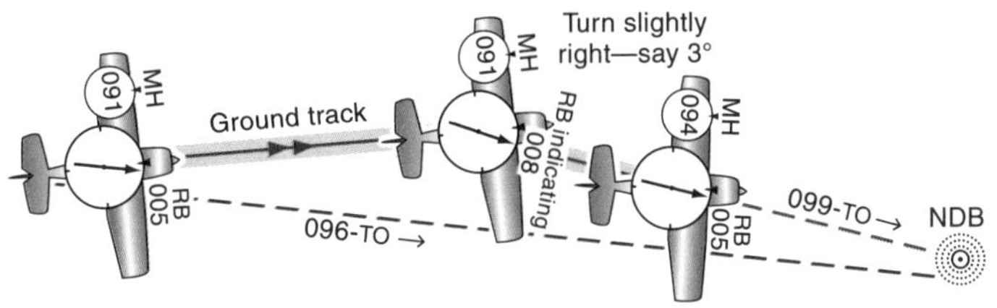

Figure 27-82 Needle head falling right; turn right.

To regain the original course, turn further right initially (say 5° to MH 096), and reintercept the original course by allowing the wind to blow the airplane back onto it. Once the desired course is regained, turn left and steer a heading with a different WCA, (say WCA 3° left instead of 5° left), MH 093 instead of MH 091. This is a relatively minor correction.

If MH + RB = desired MB constantly, then ADF tracking is good.

Attempting to maintain the desired course (by remaining on a constant MB to the NDB) is the normal navigational technique when at some distance from the NDB. If, when steering a steady MH, the ADF needle indicates a constant RB near the top of the dial, then the airplane is tracking directly to the NDB, and no correction to heading is necessary.

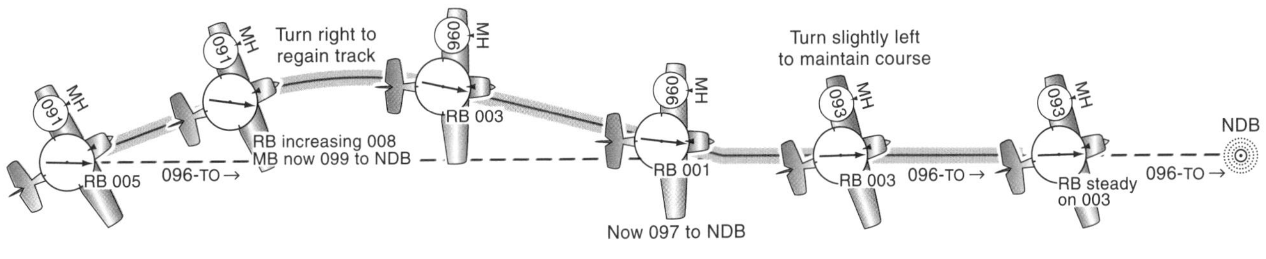

Figure 27-83 Regain the desired course.

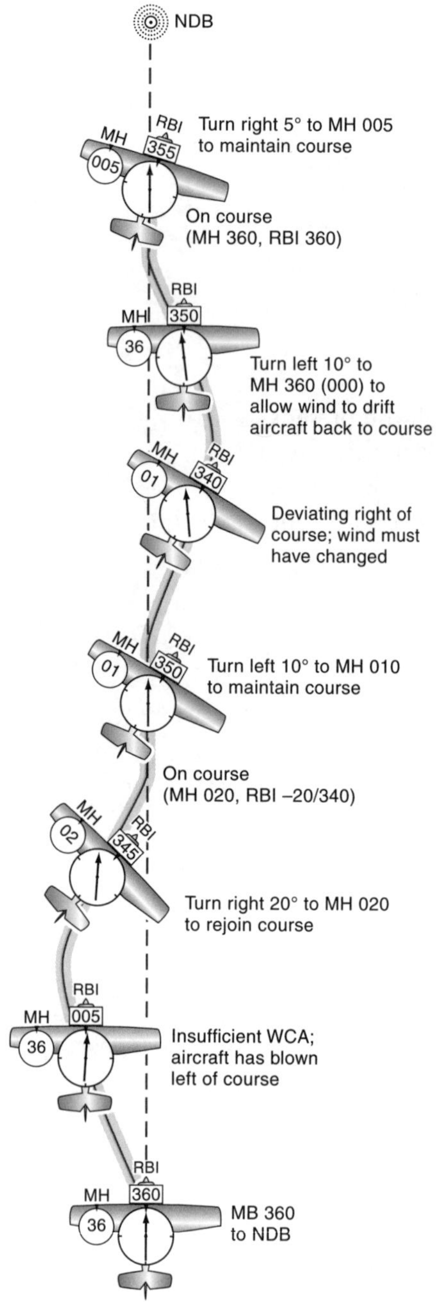

Figure 27-84
Bracketing the course: Head of needle falling right—turn right. Head of needle falling left—turn left.

Bracketing Course

In practice, an absolutely perfect direct course is difficult to achieve. The actual ground track flown will probably consist of a series of short segments either side of the desired course, which corresponds to minor corrections similar to those described above. This technique is known as *bracketing* the course, and involves making suitable heading corrections, left or right as required, to regain and maintain the desired course. The aim of bracketing is to find the precise WCA needed to maintain course. If, for instance, a WCA of 10° right is found to be too great and the airplane diverges to the right of course, and a WCA of only 5° right is too little and the wind blows the airplane to the left of course, then try something in between, say WCA 8° right.

You should monitor the tracking of the airplane on a regular basis, and make corrections earlier rather than later, resulting in a number of small corrections rather than just one big correction. However, if a big correction *is* required as may be the case in strong winds, make it. Be positive in your actions!

Wind Effect

If the wind direction and strength is not obvious, then the best technique is to initially steer course as heading and make no allowance for drift. The effect of the wind will become obvious as the ADF needle moves to the left or right. Observe the results, and then make appropriate heading adjustments to bracket course.

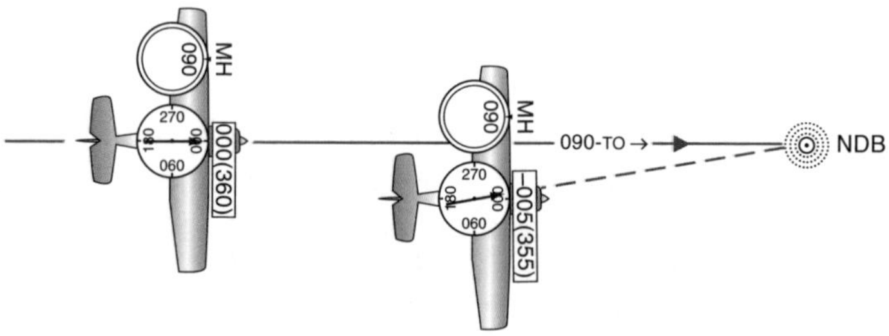

Figure 27-85 If uncertain of wind, initially steer course as heading.

Tracking Over an NDB

The closer you get to an NDB, the more sensitive the ADF needle becomes. Minor displacements left or right of course will cause larger and larger changes in RB and MB. For a precise course to be achieved, you must be prepared to increase your scan rate as the NDB is approached, and to make smaller corrections more frequently.

Close to the station and just prior to passing over the NDB, the ADF needle will become sensitive and agitated. You should, at this point, relax a little and steer a steady heading until the airplane passes over the NDB, indicated by the ADF needle moving from the top toward the bottom of the dial.

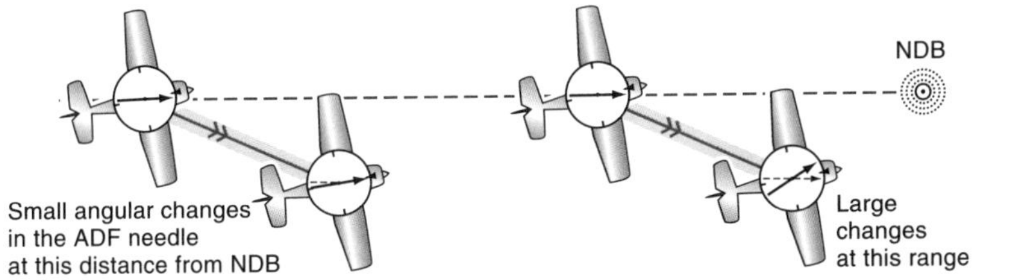

Figure 27-86 Approaching the NDB, the ADF needle becomes more sensitive.

Having passed over the NDB, tracking *from* the NDB should be checked and suitable adjustments made to heading. If the course outbound is different from that inbound, then a suitable heading change estimated to make good the new desired course could be made as soon as the ADF needle falls past the 090 or 270 position on its way to the bottom of the dial.

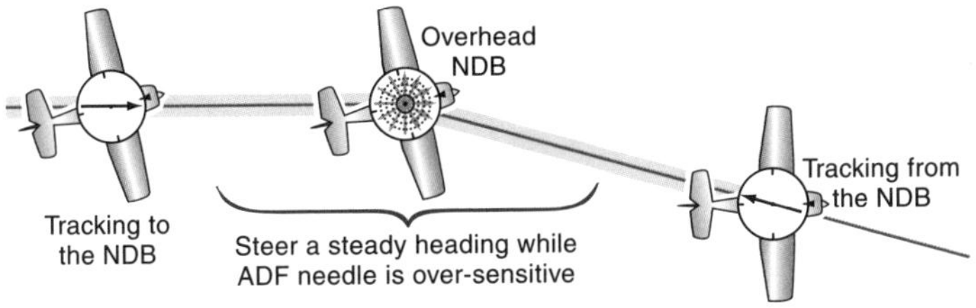

Figure 27-87 Do not overcorrect when close to the station.

The ADF needle becoming extremely active, and then falling rapidly to the bottom of the dial, indicates that the airplane has passed directly over the NDB.

The ADF needle moving gradually to one side, and slowly falling to the bottom of the dial indicates that the airplane is passing to one side of the beacon, the rate at which the needle falls being an indication of the airplane's proximity to the NDB. If it falls very slowly, then possibly the tracking could have been better.

Time over (or abeam) the NDB with no WCA can be taken as the needle falls through the approximate 090 or 270 position.

Time over (or abeam) the NDB with a WCA 10° right can be taken as the needle falls through the approximate 080 (090 – WCA 10) or 260 (270 – WCA 10) position.

Tracking Outbound with no Crosswind

When tracking away from an NDB, the *head* of the ADF needle will lie toward the bottom of the dial and the *tail* of the ADF needle will be toward the top of the dial (figure 27-88). If the pilot tracks over the NDB and then steers course as heading, the airplane will track directly away from the NDB with the head of the fixed-card ADF needle steady on 180, and the tail of the fixed-card ADF needle steady at the top of the dial on 000. The tail of the *RMI* equipped airplane will also lie towards the top of the dial and will indicate the MB from the station.

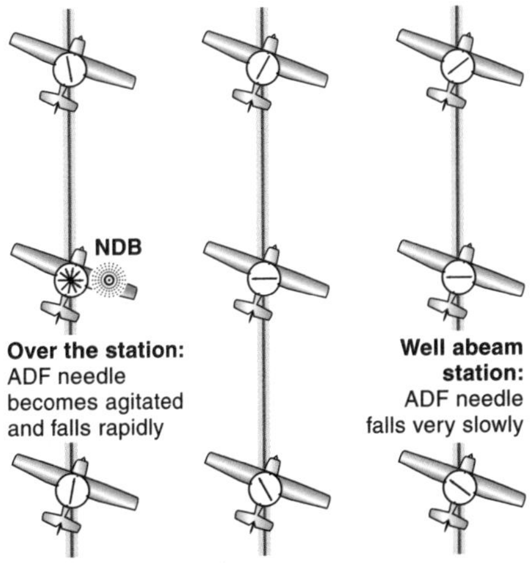

Figure 27-88
Good ADF tracking (left); reasonable tracking (center); poor tracking (right).

Since we are considering the outbound course, in both cases it is the tail of the needle that is of more use. The airplane in figure 27-89 has MB 040 from the NDB, and MB 220 to the NDB.

Tracking Outbound with a Crosswind

Suppose that the desired course outbound from an NDB is MC 040, and the pilot estimates that a WCA of 5° to the right is necessary to counteract a wind from the right. To achieve this, he steers MH 045, and hopes to see the *tail* of the ADF needle stay on -5 off the nose (RB 355). The MC away from the station is found from MB from NDB = MH deflection of the *tail* of the needle.

In this case, MH 045 − 005 tail = MB 040 from NDB, and so the chosen WCA and magnetic heading to steer are *correct* (figure 27-90).

If the estimated WCA is *incorrect*, then the actual ground track made by the airplane will differ from the desired course. If, in the previous case, the wind is stronger than expected, the airplane's ground track may be 033, and to the left of the desired course of MC 040 (figure 27-91).

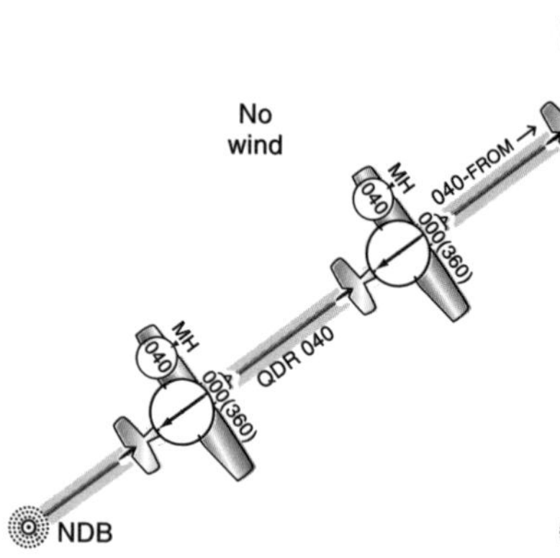

Figure 27-89
Tracking from an NDB with no crosswind effect.

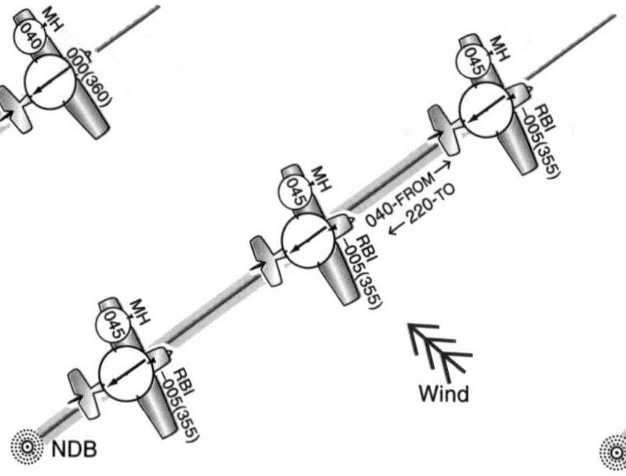

Figure 27-90
Tracking away from an NDB, with a WCA of 5° into wind.

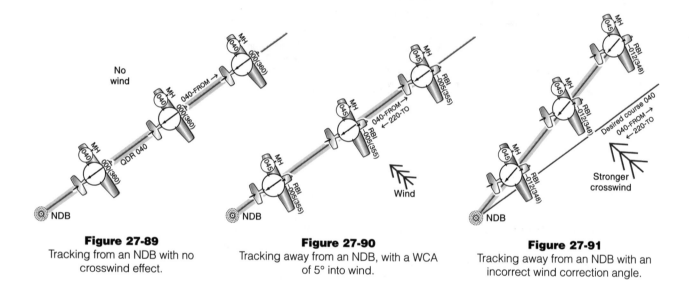

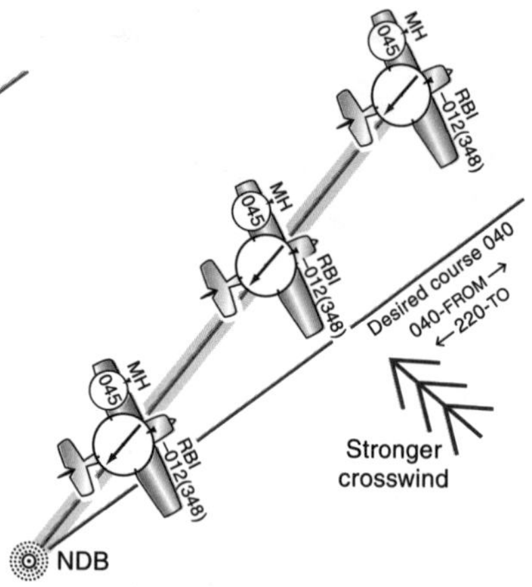

Figure 27-91
Tracking away from an NDB with an incorrect wind correction angle.

Whereas inaccurate tracking *to* an NDB is indicated by the ADF needle falling, incorrect tracking *away* from an NDB can occur with the ADF needle indicating a steady reading. Having passed overhead the NDB, an airplane can track away from it in any of 360 directions. You must always ensure that you are flying away from the NDB along the correct course, and the easiest means to do this is to calculate MB from the NDB using the HI and the RBI.

Radar

VFR pilots often fly near or within a radar environment, so an understanding of radar is useful. An in-depth knowledge is required for the IFR certificate and this is fully covered in Volume 3 of the Pilot's Manual, *Instrument Flying*.

In the high-volume traffic environment of today's airspace, *radar* is the primary tool used by Air Traffic Control to provide many vital services to airplanes, such as radar vectoring, radar separation and sequencing. The air traffic controller is presented with an electronic map of his area of responsibility, showing the position of airplanes within it.

FAA radar units operate continuously at the locations shown in the Chart Supplement U.S. Their primary role is to provide positive direction and coordination for IFR flights, but they are also used to provide a varying level of service to VFR flights, depending on the facilities available, the type of airspace, and controller workload.

The radar controller can also provide a *radar traffic information service* to alert pilots to other nearby and possibly conflicting traffic. Even if in receipt of this service, you are still responsible for continual vigilance to *see and avoid* other traffic. The radar controller will pass what he considers relevant information using the clock system to specify the position of the other traffic relative to your track. He sees your *track* on his screen rather than your heading, so you will have to allow for the drift angle due to the wind effect when you look out the window for the other traffic.

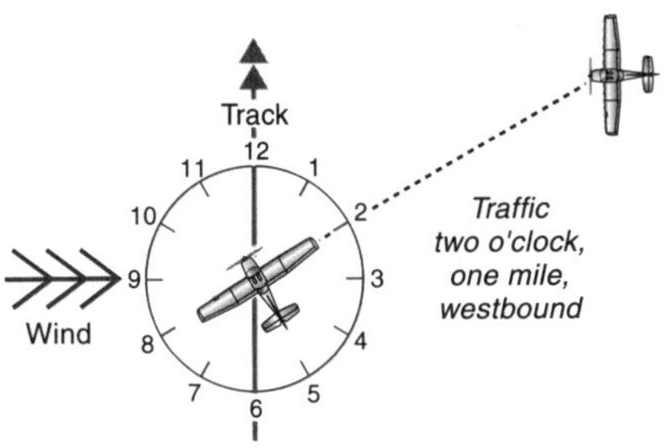

Figure 27-92 A radar traffic information service report of conflicting traffic.

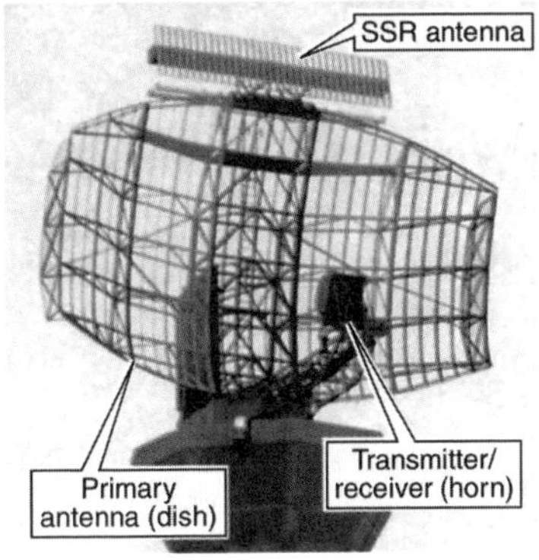

Figure 27-93 A typical radar head.

Radar Vectoring

Radar vectoring is a procedure in which a radar controller passes a *heading* to steer to a pilot, with an instruction like:

Seven zero seven four delta
Turn left heading two five zero

The aim of the controller when issuing these headings is to get the aircraft to follow a particular *course* over the ground. Because the radar controller will not know precisely the actual wind at your level, or the amount of drift it is causing, he or she will occasionally issue modified vectors to achieve the desired course.

No navigation instruments other than the compass and altimeter are required in the aircraft to follow radar vectoring, but radio communication is essential. The pilot concentrates on attitude flying (maintaining the desired heading, altitude and airspeed), while the radar controller concentrates on getting the aircraft to follow the desired course. This does not, however, relieve the pilot of the responsibility to be aware of the aircraft's approximate position at all times, especially in the vicinity of high terrain or obstructions—such an awareness is essential in the event of a communications failure, or controller error.

Primary Radar

The detection of reflected radio waves back at the point from which they were originally transmitted is the fundamental basis of radar. The basic operating principles of radar were first developed during the late 1920s, and subsequent rapid improvements in the ability to detect objects, such as aircraft, and to measure their range, was often a decisive factor during World War II (1939–45). The term *radar* was derived from *ra*dio *d*etection *a*nd *r*anging.

A typical radar system consists of a combined transmitter-receiver unit, which is equipped with a parabolic dish antenna that is designed to be efficient both in the transmission of a focused beam of radio signals, and in the reception of any reflected signals from the same direction. The dish can be rotated slowly, so that the whole sky can be scanned systematically, if desired.

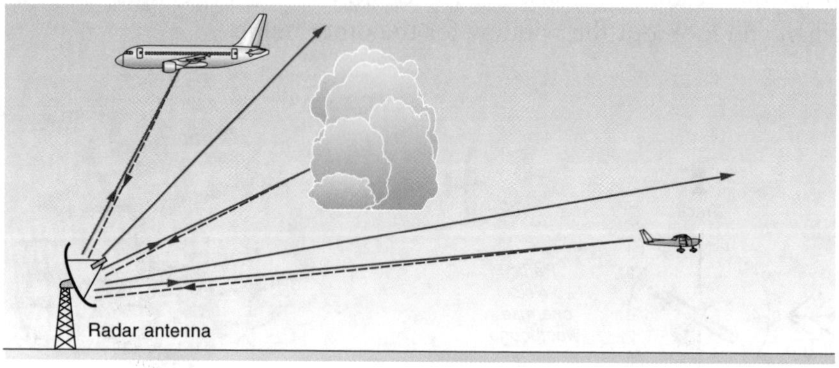

Figure 27-94 Radar is the transmission of electromagnetic radio energy and the detection of some of the reflected energy back at the point of transmission.

The properties and behavior of radio waves (their reflectivity and range) depends on their frequency. Radio signals from the upper range of the radio frequency spectrum, with very short wavelengths, are the most suitable for use in radar systems. Radars usually operate in the UHF (ultra-high frequency) and SHF (super-high frequency) bands.

Secondary Surveillance Radar (SSR) or Air Traffic Control Radar Beacon System (ATCRBS)

Secondary surveillance radar overcomes most of the limitations of primary radar simply by ensuring that a conspicuous, high-energy return pulse is produced by any aircraft that is equipped with a *transponder*.

Primary radar detects radar energy passively reflected from a target and displays it as a blip, or fading series of blips, on a screen; this is similar to seeing an aircraft reflected in the beam of a searchlight at night.

Secondary radar is much more than this, and involves an active response by the aircraft every time it is interrogated by a ground-based radar. It is as if each time a searchlight strikes a target, the target is triggered to light itself up very brightly in response, rather than just passively reflect some of the light energy transmitted from the ground site. Secondary radar actually consists of two sets of radar "talking" to each other.

The strength of the reflected signals received by a primary radar system is usually only a tiny fraction of the energy of the original pulse transmissions. Consequently, primary radars need powerful transmitters and large antennas.

As only a small amount of radio energy transmitted from the ground is required to trigger a response from an airborne SSR transponder, the ground-based secondary radar transmitter and antenna systems tend to be quite compact in comparison. In fact, the typical long, narrow SSR antenna is small enough to be mounted above the larger primary radar dish at many radar ground sites.

The SSR ground equipment consists of:

- an interrogator that provides a coded signal asking a transponder to respond;
- a highly directional rotating radar antenna that transmits the coded interrogation signal, then receives any responding signals, and passes them back to the interrogator; and
- a decoder, which accepts the signals from the interrogator, decodes them and displays the information on a radar screen.

The SSR airborne equipment consists of a transponder carried in each individual aircraft. The original interrogation pulses transmitted from the ground station trigger an automatic response from the aircraft's transponder. It transmits strong coded reply pulses, which are then received back at the ground station. These reply pulses are much, much stronger than the simple reflected signals used in primary radar. Even a very weak interrogation pulse received at the aircraft will trigger a strong response from the transponder.

The secondary responding pulse sent by a transponder not only enhances the basic positional information available to a controller, but can also carry coded information that will help distinguish that aircraft from all others on the same radar screen.

Depending on the type, or *mode*, of the transponder, and the *code* selected on it by the pilot (as requested by ATC), it can convey additional information such as:

- the specific identity of an aircraft;
- its altitude (if Mode C has been selected by the pilot); and
- any abnormal situation affecting the aircraft, such as radio failure, distress, emergency, etc.

Other significant advantages of SSR systems include:

- they are not degraded to the same extent as primary radar by weather or ground clutter;
- they present targets of the same size and intensity to the controller, regardless of the relative reflectivity of individual aircraft; and
- they minimize blind spots.

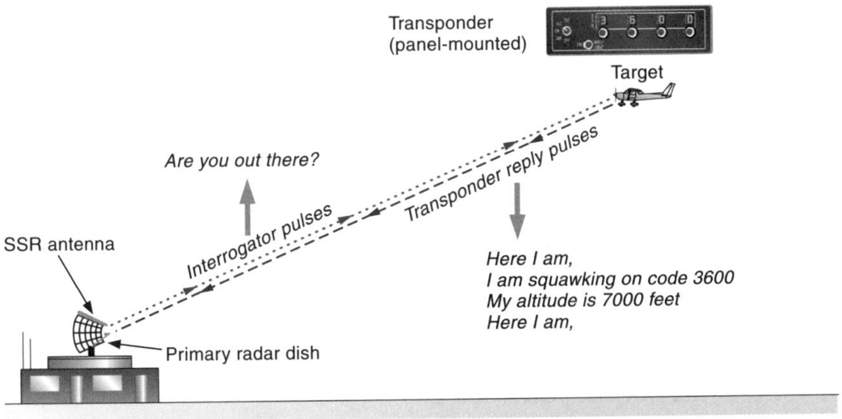

Figure 27-95 SSR is two radars talking to each other.

The Transponder

A transponder makes it easier for a radar controller to positively identify your airplane.

Most aircraft are equipped with a transponder (XPDR) that transmits a strong responding signal to a secondary ground radar, which can provide ATC with additional information such as aircraft identification and altitude. The theory of secondary surveillance radar (SSR or ATCRBS) is discussed in detail at the end of this chapter. The operating techniques are considered here.

The transponder is usually warmed-up in the standby (SBY) position during start-up prior to taxi. It should also go to SBY at the end of a flight before the master avionics switch is moved to OFF. The four-figure discrete code to be used for VFR flight is 1200. Air Traffic Control will advise if they require a different code (separate transponder codes are given for IFR flights).

A Mode C transponder allows the radar controller to see your altitude.

The transponder should be selected to the ON position, or the ALT position if it is a Mode C system, prior to the aircraft entering the airport movement area. If your airplane is equipped with a serviceable transponder, then it must be used in flight, even when you are operating in airspace where its carriage is not mandatory.

Even though transponders produced by various manufacturers vary slightly in design, they are all operated in basically the same manner. However, as a responsible pilot, you should become thoroughly familiar with your particular transponder. The POH for the transponder is required to be carried in the aircraft, within easy reach of the pilot.

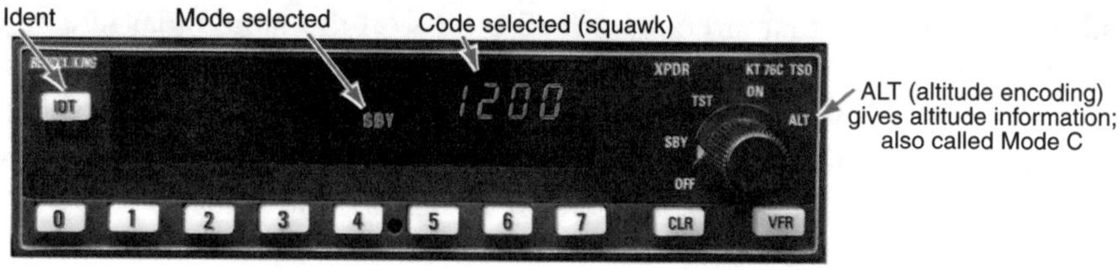

Figure 27-96 Typical transponder panel.

The Function Selector Knob

This enables you to select the transponder on and off, and to operate it in one of its various modes. Typical transponder operating modes include the following.

OFF

The transponder is deactivated completely.

STANDBY

The transponder is warmed up and ready for immediate use. This is the normal position during start-up and prior to shut down. Select ALT or ON just before entering the airport movement area. "Squawk standby" may be requested by the radar controller to prevent overly strong blips appearing on the screen from aircraft close to the interrogating antenna.

ON

The transponder transmits the selected code in Mode 3/A (to assist with aircraft identification only) at the normal power level.

ALT

This is the altitude-reporting mode (Mode C), which may be used if the aircraft is fitted with a suitable altitude encoding device, either an encoding altimeter or a blind encoder. These feed the current pressure altitude to the transponder for transmission onto the ATC radar screen. The ATC radar computer adjusts pressure altitude to read out actual altitude on the radar screen. (If not installed, the transponder still transmits in Mode A aircraft identification without altitude reporting).

TST

This mode tests the transponder by causing it to generate an internal self-interrogation signal—correct operation is indicated by illumination of the reply monitor light.

> **Note.** This tests only the transmitter section of the transponder, so is no guarantee the transponder and encoder are working correctly. The only true test is to confirm what ATC is seeing on the radar screen.

Code Selection

Suitable knobs are provided to allow selection of the required code on the transponder, the selected code being prominently displayed in digital form. Whenever codes are selected or altered, it is important to avoid passing through such vital codes as 7700 (for emergencies), 7600 (for radio failure) and 7500 (for hijack) when the transponder is switched ON, as these codes will activate unnecessary alarms in nearby ATC radar facilities. This can be prevented by making it your standard procedure to select SBY while the transponder code is being changed.

The Reply-Monitor Light

The reply light flashes to indicate that the transponder is replying to an interrogation pulse from a ground station. The reply-monitor light will glow steadily when you:

- press the TEST button, or move the function switch to the TEST position (depending on the design of your particular transponder), to confirm correct functioning;
- transmit an *ident* pulse (when requested by ATC); or
- are in a very busy terminal area.

The IDENT Switch or Button

The IDENT button is pressed whenever the radar controller requests the pilot to "*squawk ident*." A special reply pulse is transmitted by the transponder to the interrogating ground station, which causes a special symbol to appear for a few seconds on the radar screen alongside the normal return from your aircraft, thus allowing positive identification by the radar controller.

> **Note.** Your particular transponder may have minor variations to the functions described above, but will certainly be fundamentally the same. It may, for instance, have a separate mode selector to select Mode A (position reporting) or Mode C (position and altitude reporting).

Radio Terminology for Transponder Operation

The term *squawk* that is commonly used by ATC in connection with transponder operation is basically intended to mean "transmit." It is usually followed by an instruction describing the type of transmission required by the controller, for instance: squawk ident, squawk code 4000, squawk mayday (7700).

ATC: "... (callsign) squawk code 4000."

Pilot response is to read back: "... (callsign) code 4000," and to select the transponder to that code.

ATC: "... (callsign) squawk code... and ident."

Pilot response is to change the code and then press the IDENT button, allowing the radar controller to identify you positively on the screen.

ATC: "... (callsign) squawk standby."

Pilot response is to move the function switch from ALT or ON to the STANDBY position, for a temporary suspension of transponder operation (maintaining present code).

ATC: "... (callsign) squawk normal."

Pilot response is to reactivate the transponder from STANDBY to ON, or to ALT if it is a Mode C system, retaining the existing code.

ATC: "... (callsign) stop squawk."

Pilot response is to select the transponder to OFF or stand by.

ATC: "... (callsign) stop altitude squawk."

Pilot response is to move the function selector from ALT to ON, so that the altitude information is removed from the transponder's reply signals. Further information on transponder operating procedures may be found in the Aeronautical Information Manual (AIM).

Transponder Modes

Two different types, or modes, of transponder equipment are fitted in civil aircraft:

- Mode 3/A: the basic transponder type, with 4,096 different codes selectable by the pilot; and
- Mode C: the same as Mode 3/A sets, but with an automatic altitude-reporting capability (provided the aircraft is fitted with an encoding altimeter, or a "blind" encoder). This sends altitude information to the controller based on 29.92 in. Hg regardless of what the pilot has set in the pressure window.

So that a radar controller can distinguish a particular aircraft from others operating in its vicinity, ATC will usually assign a discrete transponder code to each aircraft, using the phraseology "*Squawk code* ...." When this code is selected by the pilot, the aircraft's alphanumeric identification (N number or flight number, whatever the controller desires) is displayed on the radar screen next to its position symbol.

If the aircraft is fitted with a Mode C transponder, then its current altitude will be automatically displayed (to the nearest 100 feet), no pilot or controller input being necessary. If the radar display is an automated type, then the current groundspeed, as calculated by the radar's digital processor, can also be called up and displayed by the controller. All this information assists the controller in the rapid interpretation of the situation presented on a radar screen, and eases the task in separating aircraft and maintaining a safe and efficient traffic flow.

You may be specifically requested by ATC to "squawk ident," when they want positive identification of an aircraft. This is the only time that you should touch the ident button on your transponder. Pressing this button once will cause a special "ID" symbol to appear adjacent to the aircraft's position on the screen. The ident button should not be held in, just firmly pressed once and released.

Transponder Codes

A total of 4,096 different codes can be selected on a transponder, but not all of them are available to be assigned as discrete codes to assist with identification.

There are certain standard codes allocated for military and civilian use. For instance, all transponder-equipped VFR aircraft should squawk Code 1200, unless they are assigned another discrete code. Other standard codes are allocated for use in emergencies only, and will trigger visual and aural alarms in ATC facilities:

- emergency situations—7700;
- radio communications failure—7600; and
- hijack—7500.

Mandatory Transponder Requirements

The regulations require carriage and use of a transponder with *altitude-reporting* capability in a considerable amount of U.S. airspace. This is primarily to assist in reducing the risk of midair collisions in congested airspace where the old "see-and-avoid" system of traffic separation is considered inadequate.

A Mode C transponder must be carried (and be operational) by all aircraft operating:

- in Class A airspace, Class B airspace and Class C airspace, and, within the lateral boundaries of Class B and C airspace areas designated for an airport, up to 10,000 feet MSL;
- from the surface up to 10,000 feet MSL when operating within 30 NM of an airport listed in Appendix D, Section 1, of 14 CFR Part 91 (list contains most major U.S. airports, including Atlanta, Denver, Los Angeles, Miami, Minneapolis, both New York airports, St. Louis, Seattle and both Washington airports);
- in all airspace of the 48 contiguous states and the District of Columbia at or above 10,000 feet MSL (except when flying at or below 2,500 feet AGL); and
- from the surface to 10,000 feet MSL within a 10-NM radius of any airport in 14 CFR Part 91 Appendix D, section 2, except the airspace below 1,200 feet outside the lateral boundaries of the surface area of the airspace designated for that airport; (currently no airport meets this criterion, so there is none listed in section 2 of Appendix D).

Mode S

A new type of transponder, known as Mode S, and also referred to as the *discrete address beacon system*, has been developed to reduce the workloads of both controllers and pilots, as well as reducing the congestion on normal radio communications frequencies.

In addition to the altitude information provided by Mode C systems, Mode S transponders can automatically transmit an aircraft's registration and type whenever it is interrogated by ground-based radar. This eliminates the need for the controller to enter the identification of each aircraft manually into the ATC computer, and means that a pilot does not have to select a discrete code. This improvement is significant enough on its own, but fully optioned Mode S installations will provide further benefits.

By a process known as *select addressing*, it is possible for ATC to transmit other information, such as weather reports, ATIS, and clearances to a specific aircraft, which can then be displayed on a suitable screen or printer in the cockpit. This promises to decrease the volume of radio transmissions considerably.

ADS-B

Automatic dependent surveillance – broadcast (ADS-B) was briefly discussed in Chapter 19 in terms of regulatory requirements. ADS-B was established as part of NextGen which is the modernization of the U.S. National Airspace System. The primary focus of the system is to provide a higher level of safety and efficiency both in the air and on the ground. It consists of two components which are both functions of the aircraft's avionics: ADS-B Out, which is required for operations in most controlled airspace; and ADS-B In which is an optional capability.

ADS-B Out

ADS-B Out is replacing radar technology with the use of satellites. Radar relies on radio signals and antennas that can take 5 to 12 seconds to determine an aircraft's position, whereas ADS-B uses satellite signals which provide a quicker and more precise way to track an aircraft's movement.

Aircraft equipped with ADS-B Out broadcast transmissions containing the aircraft's position, velocity, and identifying information (ascertained by the global navigation satellite system), which is received by ground-based transceivers and by ADS-B In equipped aircraft (see figure 27-97). These ground-based transceivers, or ADS-B ground stations, are much more adaptable than a typical radio tower and can be placed in harder to reach areas therefore providing better aircraft visibility regardless of terrain or altitude.

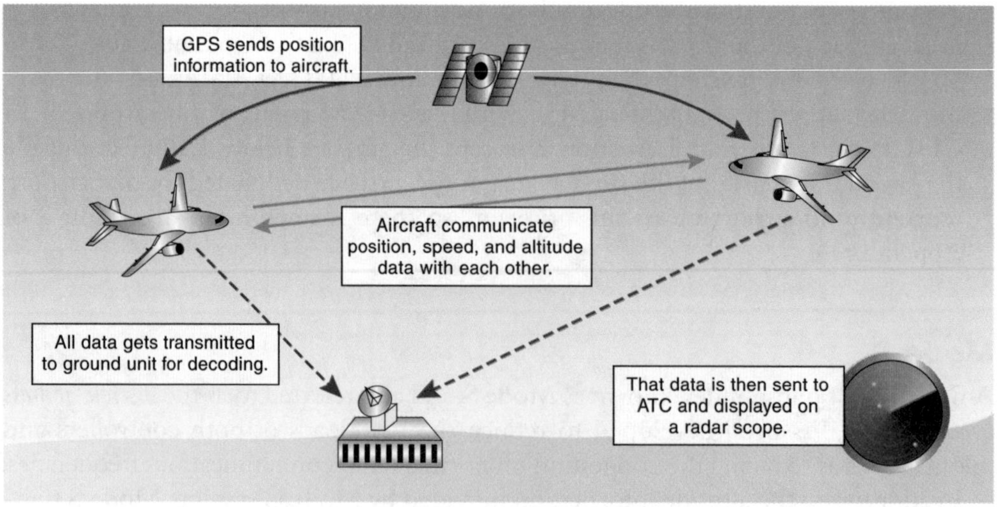

Figure 27-97 ADS-B network.

ADS-B In

As noted earlier, ADS-B In is an optional capability that provides aircraft with traffic information (TIS-B) and weather (FIS-B) delivered directly to the cockpit, enhancing both situational awareness and safety.

Traffic information service – broadcast (TIS-B) is a free service which broadcasts relevant traffic position reports to properly equipped aircraft flying within the ADS-B coverage area below FL240. It allows pilots to see air-to-air traffic from within the cockpit and displays radar targets sent from ground stations allowing for enhanced situational awareness of conflicting traffic.

Flight information system – broadcast (FIS-B) is also a free service for properly equipped aircraft flying within the ADS-B coverage area, allowing the automatic transmission of a wide range of weather products. Table 27-2 lists of some of the aeronautical information and weather products available through FIS-B. Additional products are constantly being added and updated.

Note. FIS-B information, including weather, NOTAMs, and TFR areas, is intended only for advisory use for the sole purpose of assisting in long- and near-term planning and decision making. The oldest weather radar data on the display can be up to 20 minutes older than the display's indicated age for that weather radar data.

Product	Description
AIRMET	Airman's Meteorological Information. An advisory issued every six hours for low-level weather that is potentially hazardous to aircraft with limited capability. AIRMETs cover less-severe weather than SIGMETs: moderate turbulence, icing, surface winds of 30 knots or greater, and widespread restricted visibility.
Cloud Tops	A forecast of cloud tops over the CONUS given in mean sea level based on the National Weather Service's High Resolution Rapid Refresh Model.
CWA	Center Weather Advisory. Unscheduled bulletins warning of previously unforecast AIRMETS, SIGMETS, or Convective SIGMETS.
Convective SIGMET	Convective Significant Meteorological Information. Issued for severe thunderstorms with the potential for tornadoes, large hail, and winds 50 knots or greater; embedded thunderstorms; a line of thunderstorms; and for thunderstorms producing precipitation affecting 40% or more of a 3,000 square mile area. All convective SIGMETs imply severe or greater turbulence, severe icing, and low-level windshear.
G-AIRMET	Graphical AIRMET. A graphical depiction of AIRMET advisories.
Icing	A forecast of icing probability, severity, and presence of supercooled large water droplets. Information is available in intervals of 2,000 feet up to 24,000 feet MSL over the CONUS.
Lightning	A graphical depiction of recent cloud-to-ground lighting strikes over the CONUS.
SIGMET	Significant Meteorological Information. A weather advisory that contains meteorological information concerning the safety of all aircraft: severe or greater turbulence, severe or greater icing, and IMC conditions due to dust, sand, or volcanic ash over a 3,000 square mile area.
METAR	Aviation routine weather report. Contains data for temperature, dew point, wind speed and direction, precipitation, cloud cover and heights, visibility, and barometric pressure. Reports are typically generated hourly.
SPECI	A Special METAR generated if conditions change significantly within the hour.
National NEXRAD	Continental United States Next Generation Radar. NEXRAD detects precipitation and atmospheric movement or wind. Data can be displayed in a mosaic map which shows patterns of precipitation and its movement.
Regional NEXRAD	Regional Next Generation Radar.

Table 27-2 Products available through FIS-B. *(Continued on next page.)*

Turbulence	A forecasted graphical depiction of maximum intensity turbulence from 2,000 feet MSL up to 24,000 feet MSL over the CONUS.
NOTAM (D)	Distant Notice to Airmen. Information pertaining to navigational facilities and public use airports. Issued for things like taxiway or runway closures, inoperative taxiway lighting, or construction equipment around the runway environment.
FDC NOTAM	Flight Data Center Notice to Airmen. Regulatory information pertaining to changes to charts, procedures, and airspace usage.
PIREP	Pilot report. A report of actual weather conditions encountered by an aircraft in flight.
SUA Status	Special Use Airspace status.
TAF	Terminal aerodrome forecast. Issued four times per day, contains the predicted weather at an airport.
AMEND	Amended TAF. Issued when the current TAF no longer adequately describes the ongoing weather or the forecaster feels the TAF is not representative of the current or expected weather.
Winds & Temperature Aloft	Computer-prepared forecasts of winds & temperatures aloft.
TIS-B Service Status	Provides periodic status of TIS-B service via FIS-B UAT uplink.

Table 27-2 Products available through FIS-B. *(Continued from previous page.)*

DME

Distance measuring equipment operates using the secondary radar principle, except that the *airborne transmitter* is the *interrogator* sending out a stream of radio pulses in all directions on the receiving frequency of the DME ground beacon which acts as a *transponder* (receives and responds 11 seconds later).

The airborne DME equipment detects the answering signal and measures the *time* between the transmission of the interrogating pulse from the airplane and the reception of the ranging reply pulse from the DME ground station. It converts this time to a *distance in nautical miles*. The DME indicator, when it displays this distance, is said to have *latched on* or *locked on*.

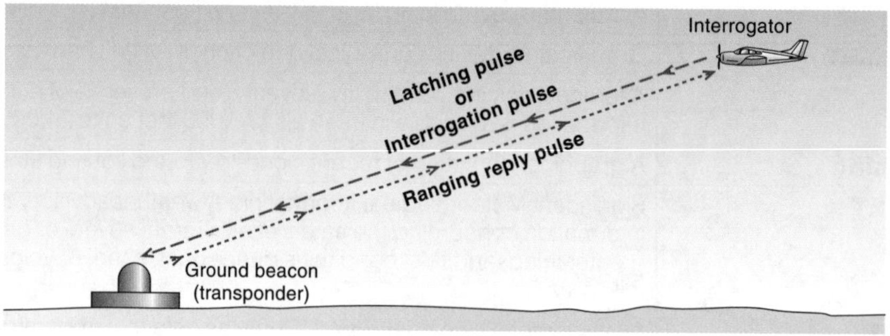

Figure 27-98 Operation of the DME.

DME Measures Slant Distance

Distance measuring equipment (DME) provides pilots with extremely useful information: their distance from a DME ground station. This distance is the *slant* distance in nautical miles, rather than the *horizontal* distance (or range).

For most practical purposes, the DME distance can be considered as range, except when the airplane is near the DME ground station. As a general rule of thumb, the DME distance may be considered as an accurate horizontal distance (with negligible slant range error) if the airplane is 1 NM or more from the DME ground facility for each 1,000 feet above the facility. For instance, if the airplane is 12,000 feet higher than the elevation of the DME ground station, DME distances greater than 12 NM will provide an accurate range. The greatest errors occur at high altitudes close to the DME ground station.

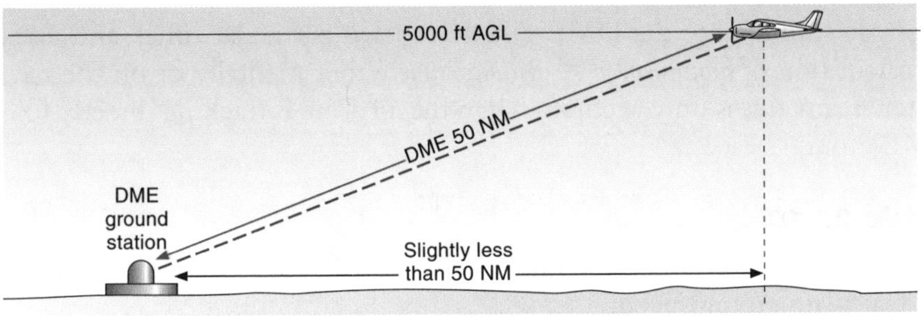

Figure 27-99 DME measures slant distance.

Passing directly over the ground station, the DME indicator in the cockpit will either show the altitude of the airplane above the ground in nautical miles (1 NM = 6,000 feet approximately), or the DME indication will drop out.

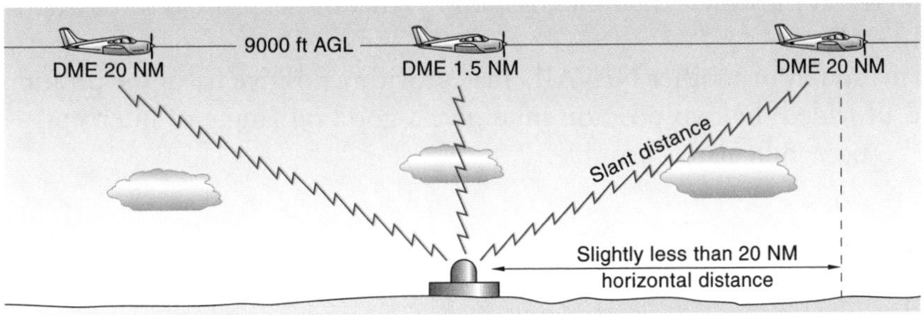

Figure 27-100 Passing over a DME ground station at 9,000 feet AGL.

DME Cockpit Displays

DME distance may be displayed in the cockpit as either a digital read-out, or by a pointer that moves around a calibrated scale. The pilot selects the DME by selecting the VOR or ILS frequency on the NAV-COM radio (since DMEs are paired with a VOR frequency or a localizer frequency). Once the DME is locked on, and a DME reading and available ident obtained, the DME indications can be used for distance information regardless of whether the VOR (or localizer) is used for tracking or orientation purposes.

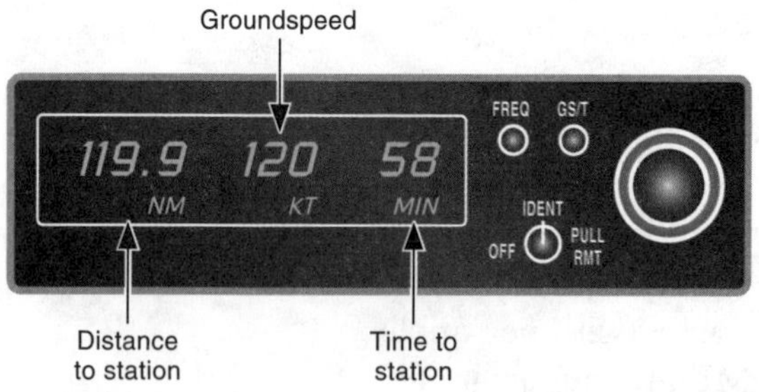

Figure 27-101 A digital DME panel.

Most airborne DME equipment is capable of computing and displaying the rate of change of DME distance (the *rate of closure* of the airplane with the DME ground station). If it is assumed that slant distance equals horizontal distance, and that the airplane is tracking either directly toward or directly away from the DME ground station, then the rate of closure read-out will represent groundspeed, a useful piece of information.

Most DME indicators can also display *time to the station* (TTS) in minutes at the current rate of closure, by comparing the groundspeed with the DME distance. If the airplane is not tracking directly toward or away from the DME ground station, then these readings will not represent groundspeed and TTS.

If the DME equipment in the airplane does not give a groundspeed read-out, then the pilot can simply note the DME distance at two particular times, and carry out a simple calculation of *groundspeed = distance/time* either mentally or on the navigation computer. Again, this is only accurate when the airplane is tracking directly to or from the DME ground beacon.

Example 27-19

A pilot notes DME distance and time as the aircraft tracks directly toward a DME station. Calculate groundspeed:

DME 35	Time 0215 UTC	
DME 25	Time 0220 UTC	
10 NM	in 5 minutes	= 120 NM in 60 minutes
		= 120 kt GS

Circular Lines of Position (LOP)

The DME provides a circular line of position (referred to as a DME arc). If the DME reads 35 NM, for instance, then the pilot knows that the airplane is somewhere on the 35 NM DME arc.

Information from another NAVAID may provide a positive fix of the position of the airplane, provided the two position lines give a good *cut* (angle of intercept)—ideally as close to perpendicular as possible.

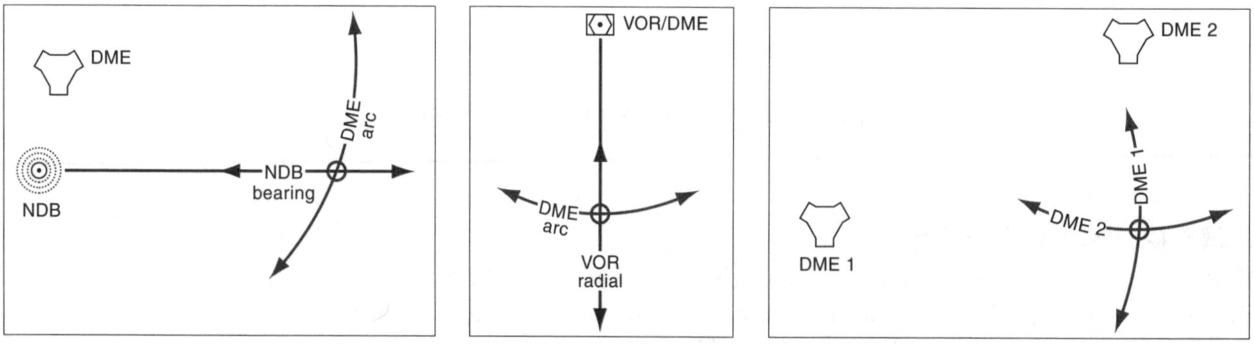

Figure 27-102 Using two NAVAIDs to fix a position.

VOR/DME Pairing

Each VOR frequency has a specific DME channel paired with it (VORTAC). For instance, VOR frequency 112.10 MHz has DME Channel 58 paired with it, so that the VOR's associated DME will automatically be interrogated when the pilot selects the VOR frequency 112.10 on the NAV-COM. The purpose of this pairing is to reduce the pilot's workload in the cockpit, with only one selection instead of two required, and to reduce the risk of a pilot selecting the right VOR but the wrong DME station.

Co-located VORs and DMEs are frequency paired, and each will have the same Morse code *ident*, the VOR identifier modulated on 1,020 Hz and broadcast about every 10 seconds, and the DME identifier modulated on 1,350 Hz and broadcast about every 30 seconds, which is about one DME ident for every three VOR idents, with the DME ident being heard with a higher-pitched tone.

A single coded identifier received only once every 30 seconds, and not mixed in with another identifier broadcast every 10 seconds, means that the DME component of the VORTAC station is operative, but the VOR component is not.

VOR ground stations are often combined with TACAN installations (Tactical Air Navigation system), which provide azimuth and distance information to military aircraft on UHF frequencies. The combined VOR/TACAN facility is known as a VORTAC. Civil aircraft obtain azimuth (course) information from the VOR, and distance information from the DME component of the TACAN. In a few cases, a DME station may exist by itself, in which case the associated VOR frequency will be shown so the pilot can tune in the DME station. A paired VOR and DME (or VORTAC) can provide a very good position fix, consisting of:

- the *radial* from the VOR; and
- the *distance* from the DME.

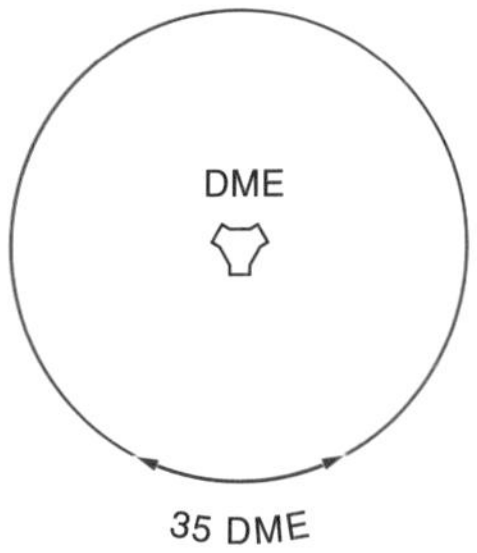

Figure 27-103
A circular position line from a DME.

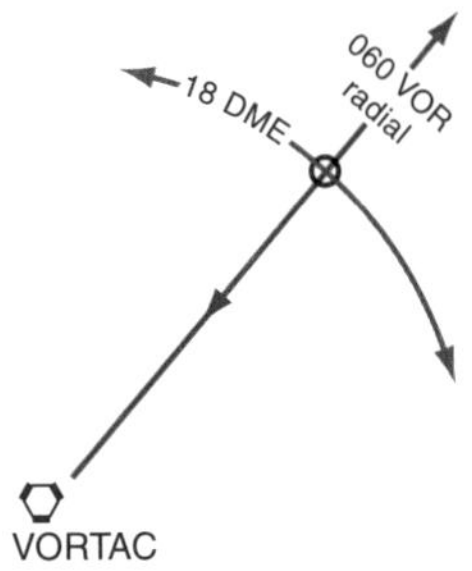

Figure 27-104
Fixing position with VOR and DME.

RNAV—Area Navigation

A waypoint is a geographical position used to define a route.

Area navigation (RNAV) allows you to fly point to point on a direct course without having to overfly ground-based NAVAIDs. Instead of flying from VORTAC to VORTAC along Victor airways on what might be a circuitous route, you can fly direct from your departure airport to the destination airport, or from waypoint to waypoint, using RNAV. A *waypoint* is a predetermined geographical position usually specified by latitude and longitude, or by radial and distance from a VORTAC, and used to define an RNAV route or instrument approach.

Some RNAV systems can define a waypoint internally by the pilot inserting latitude and longitude into the computer. These systems include GPS, inertial navigation systems (INS), VLF/Omega systems, and Doppler radar. Other RNAV systems define waypoints relative to a VORTAC, using radial and distance (or latitude and longitude) to create "phantom" VORTACs, known as pseudo-VORTACs.

Pseudo-VORTACs

Some general aviation aircraft have a course line computer system which, when used in conjunction with the NAV radio selected to a VORTAC, can electronically *relocate* that VORTAC, so that a pseudo-VORTAC (an offset VORTAC) is created at any desired waypoint. It does this by electronically adding a vector (radial and distance) to the position of the actual VORTAC.

You can locate pseudo-VORTACs wherever you like, provided they are within signal reception range of the parent VORTAC, and thereby create a series of waypoints along your desired route.

The normal NAV-COM receiver is selected to the parent VORTAC, and the RNAV computer is programmed to electronically add the vector (radial and distance) to receive VORTAC signals. How this is done depends on the actual equipment in the cockpit—refer to equipment information in the Pilot Operating Handbook for the RNAV unit.

The *course deviation indicator* (CDI) receives its input via the computer, and indicates deviation from course between the waypoints—not an angular deviation as for normal VOR flying, but a lateral deviation in nautical miles, or fractions thereof. A one-dot deviation of the CDI might be 1 NM off course during the en route phase; in the approach mode, a 1 dot deviation might be 0.25 NM off course (see the POH to clarify this).

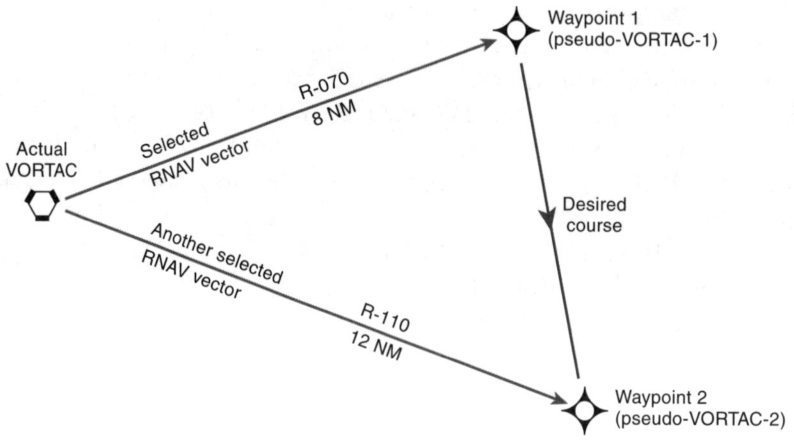

Figure 27-105 Electronically creating "pseudo" VORTACs.

The course between waypoints is maintained by keeping the CDI centered. Because it indicates *lateral* deviation in nautical miles, known as *crosstrack deviation*, rather than *angular* deviation, there is no "funneling" effect using the RNAV CDI. Distance to the waypoint is shown on the DME indicator.

The waypoints can normally be preset on the RNAV equipment, and then instantaneously recalled as you need them. As the flight progresses, you will proceed through the waypoints in order, keeping within signal range of each parent VORTAC by flying at a suitable altitude and distance from it. If the usable signal range is exceeded, the CDI OFF flag will show.

Typical RNAV systems can provide:

- crosstrack deviation from the selected course in nautical miles with TO/FROM information;
- distance to the waypoint in nautical miles;
- groundspeed in knots; and
- time-to-waypoint in minutes.

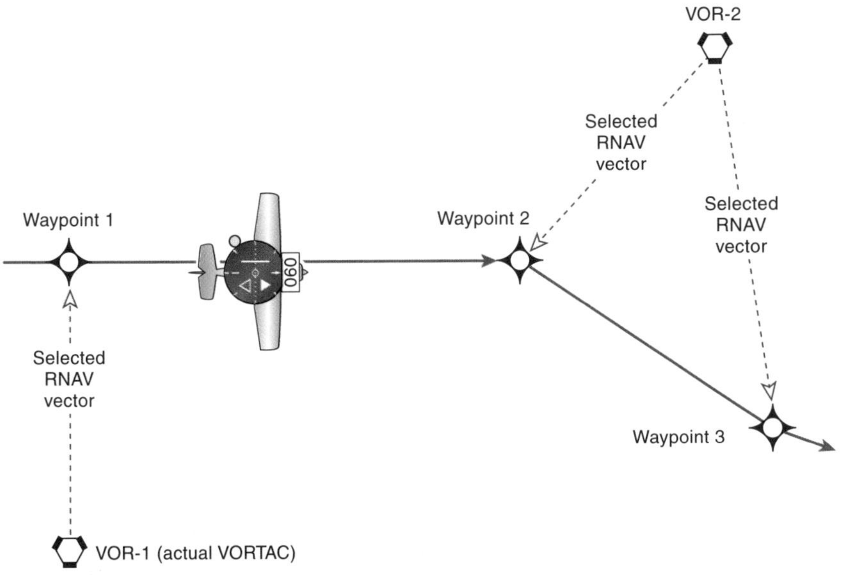

Figure 27-106 Tracking between waypoints.

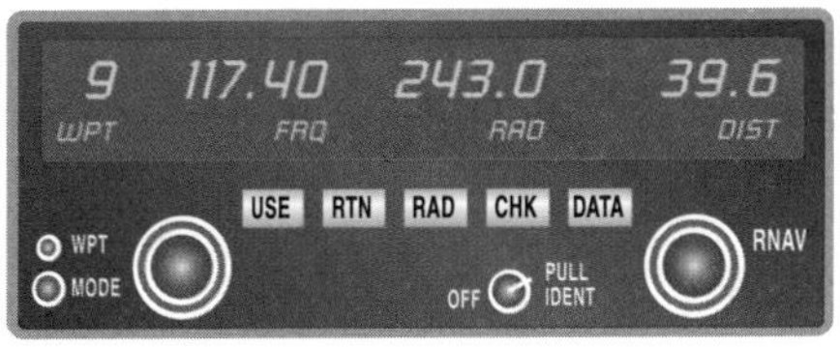

Figure 27-107
A typical RNAV display.

Global Positioning System (GPS)

Precise point-to-point navigation is possible using satellite navigation systems that can compute aircraft position and altitude accurately by comparing signals from a global network of navigation satellites. The first global positioning systems (GPS) were designed for the U.S. Department of Defense, but in the early 1990s, GPS was made available for civil use. Later, full system accuracy was also made available.

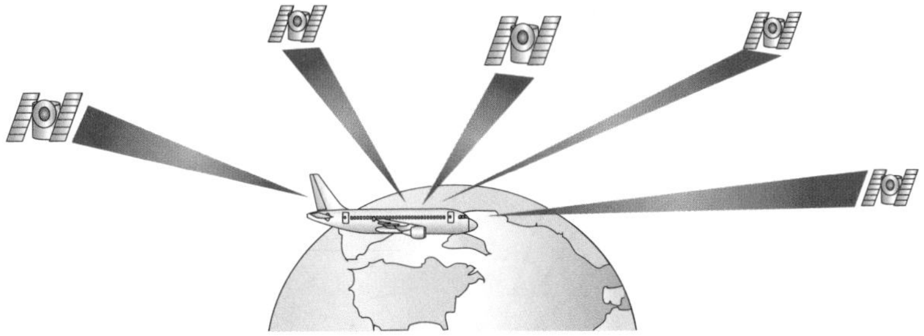

Figure 27-108 Signals from satellites are received to establish an aircraft's position.

Each satellite transmits its own computer code packet on frequency 1,575.42 MHz (for civilian use) 1,000 times a second. The satellite constellation typically guarantees that at least four satellites are in view and usable for positioning at any one time from any position on earth. GPS equipment pinpoints an aircraft's horizontal position in lat.-long. coordinates, similar to other long-range navigation systems, such as VLF/Omega; in the case of most aviation units, it then turns the information into a graphical moving map display of the aircraft's position in relation to surrounding airspace on an LCD or CRT screen. Most GPS receivers can also display a CDI presentation, along with track, pres-

GPS can be used for situational awareness in VFR operations.

ent position, actual time (to an accuracy of a few nanoseconds), groundspeed, time and distance to the next waypoint, and the current altitude of the aircraft.

GPS units have been approved for both en route and approach navigation, but, not all units are approved for anything other than situational awareness. IFR units must have their databases updated on a regular basis to remain IFR certified.

Nonprecision GPS approaches are available at most U.S. airports today. Precision GPS approaches using a ground station to augment the satellite signals is coming soon. This *wide area augmentation system* (WAAS) will allow GPS to be used as the primary NAVAID from takeoff through to approach.

Some manufacturers have produced *multi-function displays* (MFDs), which combine data from conventional flight instruments and on-board fuel/air data sensors for light aircraft. Typical GPS panels are shown in figure 27-109.

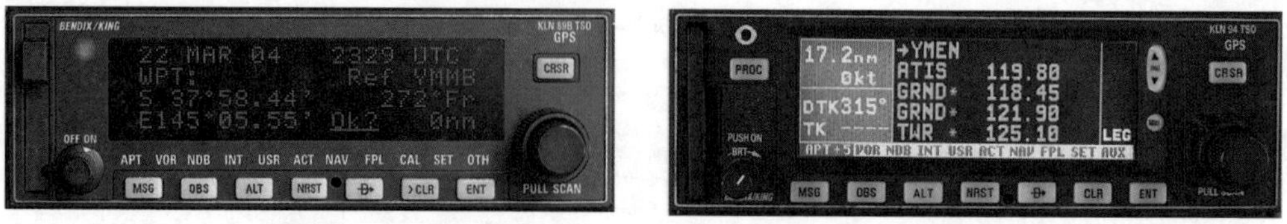

Figure 27-109 GPS and NAV management receivers.

The GPS has three functional elements:

- a space segment;
- a control segment; and
- a user segment (the airborne receivers).

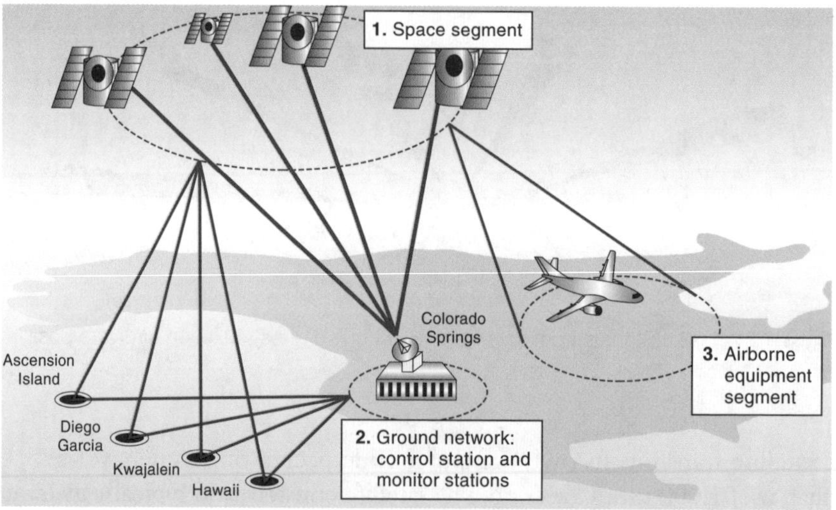

Figure 27-110 The GPS consists of three basic segments.

Space Segment

The space segment consists of a constellation of an expanding number of satellites orbiting the earth at an altitude of just over 20,200 km (10,900 NM) in several, strategically defined orbital planes. The objective of the GPS satellite configuration is to provide a window of at least four satellites in view from any point on earth. The satellites orbit at an inclination angle of 55° (they cross the equator northeast bound at an angle of 55°), taking approximately 12 hours to complete an orbit, and the orbital position of each satellite is known precisely at all times.

As a point of interest, the GPS space segment consists of so-called Block II and IIA satellites and upgraded versions known as Block IIR satellites. The service they provide is identical as far as a user is concerned. They will be the basis of the system for at least the next decade.

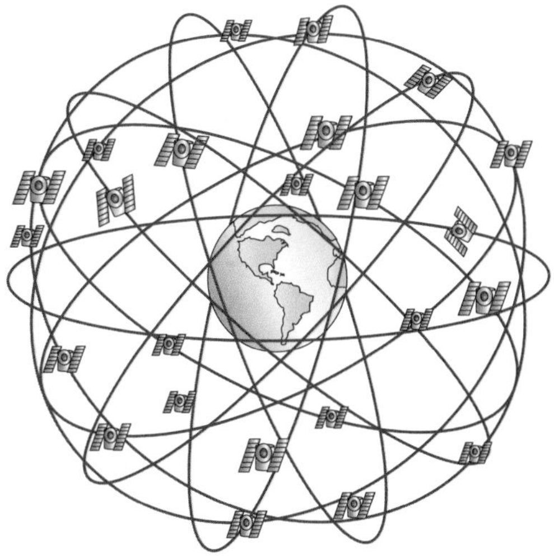

Figure 27-111
The relative orbital positions of GPS satellites.

Pseudo-Random Code

Each satellite transmits its position and precise time of transmission, and a separate signal is used by the receiver to establish range from the satellite. This is achieved by the satellite RF carrier transmissions being modulated with a 50 bit/second navigation message and a unique encoded signal known as a *pseudo-random code*. It repeats itself every millisecond and is used by the GPS receivers to recognize and track individual satellites for ranging purposes. There are two types of pseudo-random code:

- a *coarse acquisition* (C/A) *code* (also called the *standard positioning service* (SPS)) available for general civilian use, which provides accuracy in the order of 100 meters in position and 140 feet in altitude with a 95% probability given a quality receiver; and
- a *precision* (P) *code* (or the *precise positioning service* (PPS)), which permits extremely precise position resolution (primarily available for authorized military use only).

As will be discussed, a minimum of three satellites is required to determine a two-dimensional fix if altitude is known. For a three-dimensional fix, four satellites are required. The navigation message contains information on satellite ephemeris (where it is in space), GPS time reference, clock corrections, almanac data, and information on system maintenance status.

Control Segment

The controlling authority is the United States Department of Defense. By letter of agreement between the United States Government and ICAO, civilian access via the C/A code only is permitted on a no-cost basis for the foreseeable future. The deliberate degrading of the accuracy of the system for civilian users, i.e. the standard positioning service (SPS) accessed via the C/A code, is known as *selective availability* (SA).

Note. In early 2000, the U.S. Department of Defense turned SA off, but it could be re-activated in case of national defense.

The control segment includes monitoring stations at various locations around the world, ground antennas and up-links, and a master station. The stations track all satellites in view, passing information to a master control station, which controls the satellites' clock and orbit states and the currency of the navigation messages.

Satellites are frequently updated with new data for the compilation of the navigation messages transmitted to system users. Assuming the current level of space vehicle technology, the planned life span of a GPS satellite is around seven to eight years, but many function long after that.

User Segment (the Receiver)

As previously mentioned, the receiver identifies each satellite being received by its unique pseudo-random code, i.e. the C/A code for civilian operations. It then starts to receive and process navigation information. Ephemeris data takes about 6 seconds to transmit, but almanac data takes about 13 seconds. For this reason, almanac data is stored in the receiver's memory. During operation, almanac data in the receiver is changed on a continuous basis. On start-up, the receiver recalls the data that was last in memory on the preceding shutdown. From this information and the stored almanac data, the receiver determines which satellites should be in view and then searches for their respective C/A codes. It then establishes ranges to the satellites, and by knowing their position, computes aircraft position, velocity, and time. This process is known as *pseudoranging*.

Receiver Design

Receiver autonomous integrity monitoring (RAIM) is a special receiver function which analyses the signal integrity and relative positions of all satellites which are in view, so as to select only the best four or more, isolating and discarding any anomalous satellites.

The capability of making range calculations to three, four or more satellites has an impact on the design, cost, and accuracy of GPS receivers, namely, whether they are single-channel receivers operating sequentially or the more expensive and accurate receivers providing multiple channels operating simultaneously. GPS receivers approved as a supplemental- or primary-means navigation aid have multiple channels and come under the provisions of an FAA Technical Service Order (TSO C129). IFR/primary navigation certification specifications for GPS equipment include a requirement for multiple receiver channels and a navigation integrity monitoring system, known as *receiver autonomous integrity monitoring* (RAIM).

Receiver Displays

Displays for the pilot vary from one GPS unit to another. Flight planning data is usually entered via an appropriate keypad on a control display unit (CDU) or control panel. The usual navigation information—i.e. position (POS), track (TRK), groundspeed (GS), EET, and, with TAS and MH input, wind direction and velocity—is displayed. The unit must also be capable of showing satellite status, satellites in view and being tracked, the value of PDOP, RAIM status, and signal quality.

Review 27
Navigation Aids

VOR

1. Many VORs are coupled with a:
   a. ILS.
   b. DME.
   c. NDB.
2. What is VORTAC?
3. What is a radial?
4. You are instructed by ATC to track outbound on the 070 radial from a VOR. The more suitable heading is:
   a. 070.
   b. 250.
5. You are instructed to track inbound on the 050 radial. The more suitable heading is:
   a. 050.
   b. 230.
6. What is a particular VOR identified by?
7. How many degrees of displacement from the selected course are indicated by the following deviations of the CDI on the VOR:
   a. 1 dot deviation?
   b. 5 dot deviation?
8. A VOR ground station should transmit to what accuracy (±°)?
9. The CDI is centered with 090 selected in the OBS. What radial is the airplane on if:
   a. the FROM flag is showing?
   b. the TO flag is showing?
   c. the CDI is 2 dots right and the TO flag is showing?
   d. the CDI is 1 dot left and the FROM flag is showing?
10. You are flying MH 080, with the OBS selected to 080, CDI needle showing 2 dots right, and the FROM flag showing. The desired course is the 080 radial outbound. The desired course is out to your:
   a. left.
   b. right.
11. You are flying MH 300, with the OBS selected to 300, the CDI needle showing 3 dots left, and the TO flag showing. If the airplane is now turned to the reciprocal heading of MH 120, would the indications in the VOR cockpit display change in any way (assuming the OBS is left unaltered)?
12. Specify which VOR indication in figure 27-113 corresponds to which aircraft in figure 27-112.
13. The position of VOR receiver checkpoint(s) are given in which document?
14. A VOR is undergoing maintenance.
   a. Is its identification removed?
   b. Can it still transmit navigation signals?
15. If a single coded identification from a VORTAC is received only once approximately every 30 seconds:
   a. can the VOR be used for navigation?
   b. can the DME be used for navigation?
16. How can you check the sensitivity of a VOR receiver?
17. What does an RMI combine the functions of?
18. What does an HSI combine the functions of?

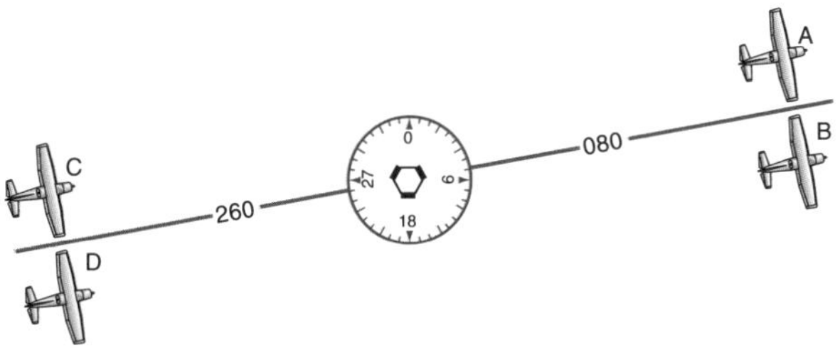

Figure 27-112 Question 12.

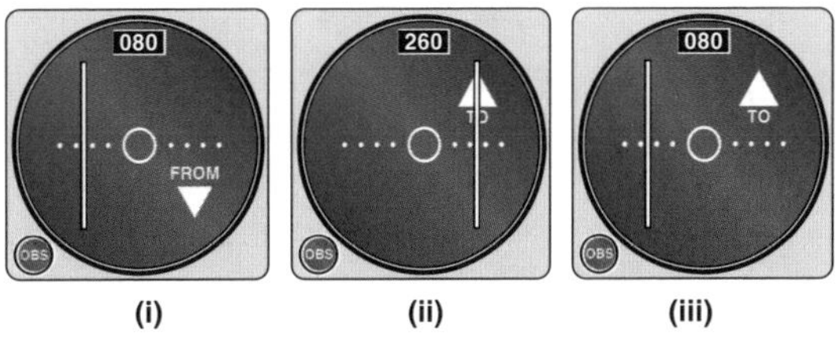

Figure 27-113 Question 12.

Refer to figure 27-114 for question 19.

19. When checking a dual VOR system by use of a VOT, which illustration indicates that the VORs are satisfactory?

20. VOR station passage is indicated by:
- **a.** the first full-scale deflection of the CDI.
- **b.** the first movement of the CDI as the airplane enters the zone of confusion.
- **c.** the first positive, complete reversal of the TO-FROM indicator.

21. After overflying a VOR ground station, you select the desired radial and fly a heading estimated to keep you on that course. If, however, there is a steady half-scale deflection of the CDI as you fly some miles away from the station, where will you be in relation to the radial?

Refer to figure 27-115 for question 22.

22. The aircraft is located:
- **a.** northwest of the VORTAC.
- **b.** northeast of the VORTAC.
- **c.** southwest of the VORTAC.
- **d.** southeast of the VORTAC.

Refer to figure 27-116 for questions 23 to 28.

23. No. 1 NAV is a:
- **a.** VOR.
- **b.** HSI.

24. No. 2 NAV is a:
- **a.** VOR.
- **b.** HSI.

25. The aircraft as indicated by the No. 1 NAV is on which radial?

26. Which OBS selection on the No. 1 NAV would center the CDI and change the ambiguity indication to a TO?

27. Which OBS selection on the No. 2 NAV would center the CDI?

28. Which OBS selection on the No. 2 NAV would center the CDI and change the ambiguity indication to a TO?

29. What is meant by the term "reverse sensing?"

30. What is the recommended procedure for the following?
- **a.** Tracking outbound on the 030 radial of a VOR station.
- **b.** Tracking inbound on the 030 radial of a VOR station.

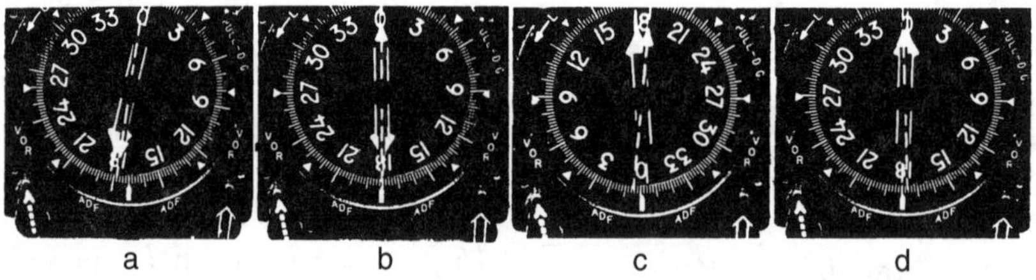

Figure 27-114 Question 19.

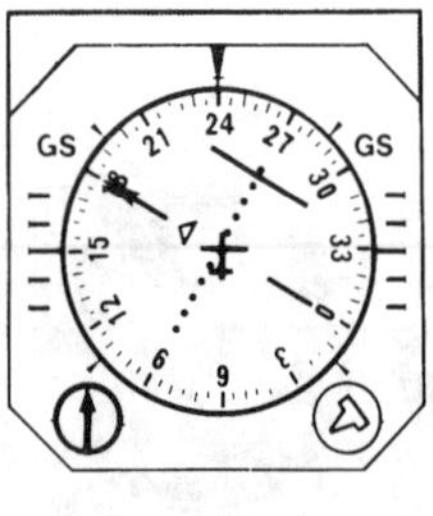

Figure 27-115 Question 22.

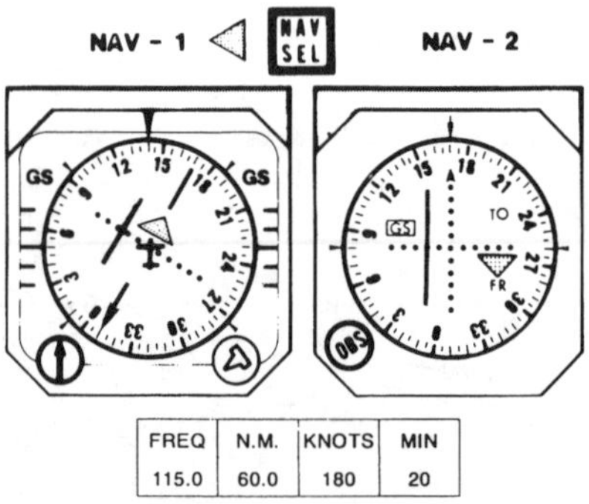

Figure 27-116 Questions 23 to 28.

Refer to figure 27-117 for questions 31 to 33.

31. Which aircraft position does HSI presentation E correspond to?
- **a.** 5.
- **b.** 6.
- **c.** 15.
- **d.** 17.

32. Which aircraft position does HSI presentation F correspond to?
- **a.** 2.
- **b.** 10.
- **c.** 14.
- **d.** 16.

33. Which aircraft position does HSI presentation A correspond to?
- **a.** 1.
- **b.** 8.
- **c.** 11.
- **d.** 18.

NDB and ADF

34. What is an NDB?

35. How is a particular NDB identified?

36. What three basic steps should a pilot follow before using a particular NDB?

37. What is an ADF?

38. What effect can the following have on NDB signals?
- **a.** Atmospheric conditions.
- **b.** Mountains.

ADF Displays

39. An airplane steering MH 250 has a reading of 030 on its RBI (RB030). What is:
- **a.** the magnetic bearing to the NDB from the airplane?
- **b.** the magnetic bearing of the airplane from the NDB?

40. What is the MB to the NDB:
- **a.** on MH 020 with RB 010?
- **b.** on MH 020 with RB 000?
- **c.** on MH 020 with RB 355?

41. You are steering MH 340 with RB 180.
- **a.** What is the MB to the NDB?
- **b.** What is the MB from the NDB?

42. An airplane steering MH 250 has a reading of RB 350 on its RBI. Calculate:
- **a.** the magnetic bearing to the NDB from the airplane.
- **b.** the magnetic bearing of the airplane from the NDB.

43. An airplane is steering MH 035. Its RBI indicates 040. Magnetic variation in the area is 4°W. Calculate:
- **a.** MB to the NDB.
- **b.** MB from the NDB.
- **c.** true bearing from the NDB.

44. If the head of the RMI needle reads RMI 070, what is the magnetic bearing to the ground station from the airplane?

45. If the head of the RMI needle reads RMI 010, which radial are you on?

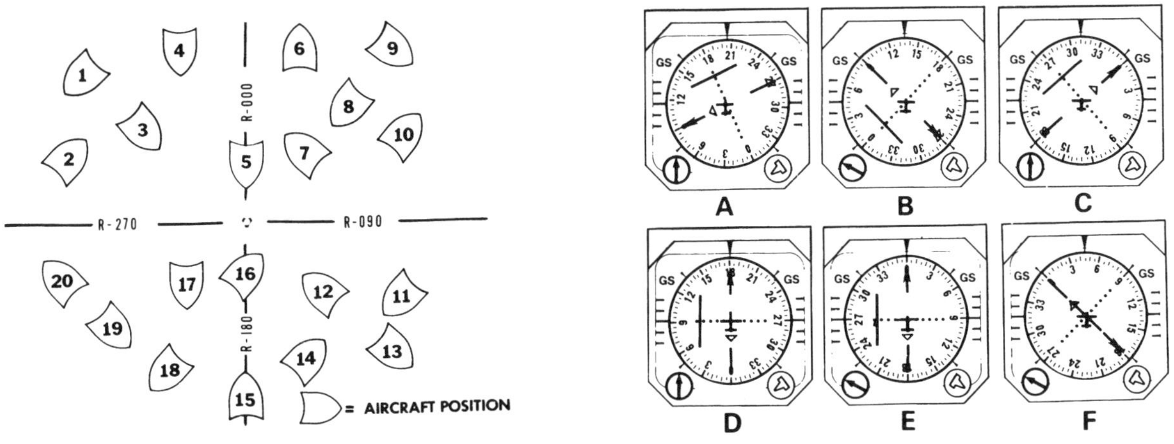

Figure 27-117 Questions 31 to 33.

46. If the tail of the RMI needle reads 089, which radial are you on?
47. If the head of the RMI needle reads RMI 070, what is the magnetic bearing from the ground station to the airplane?
48. An airplane steers MH 035. Its RMI indicates RMI 075. Calculate:
    a. MB to the NDB.
    b. MB from the NDB.
    c. RB to the NDB.

Intercepting Course and Tracking

49. Given MH 070 and RBI 010, which way would you turn to intercept MC 075 to the NDB?
50. Given MH 080 and RBI 000:
    a. what heading would you steer to make a 90° intercept of a course of MC 040 to the NDB?
    b. what would the RBI indicate at the point of intercept?
51. Is homing to an NDB in a crosswind an efficient procedure? Explain your answer.
52. What is the desired MC if you are tracking toward an NDB with the following ADF readings?
    - Time 1: MH 055, RBI 005 and on course.
    - Time 2: MH 055 and RBI 002.
53. You are tracking toward an NDB on MC 340 with an expected crosswind from the right causing 5 of drift.
    a. What magnetic heading would you steer?
    b. What would you expect the RBI to indicate?
54. You wish to track MC 360 in no-wind conditions.
    a. What magnetic heading would you steer?
    b. What would the RBI indicate as you pass abeam an NDB 10 NM to the right of course (i.e. when the NDB is on magnetic bearing MB 090 to the course)?
55. You wish to track MC 360 and expect 10° of drift caused by a wind from the east.
    a. What magnetic heading would you steer?
    b. What would the RBI indicate as you pass abeam an NDB 10 NM to the right of course?
56. You are tracking to an NDB in a crosswind. What needs to be applied in order for you to achieve a straight path to the station?

Transponder and ADS-B

57. What is radar vectoring?
58. True or false? Primary surveillance radar can detect airplanes, even if they carry no airborne equipment.
59. ATC report the position of a possibly conflicting airplane as "two o'clock northbound." What does the "two o'clock" relate to?
60. What is "Mode C?"
61. When ATC requests you to "*squawk ident*," what should you do?
62. What is the standard transponder code for an emergency?
63. What are the two components of ADS-B and which is required for most aircraft operating in controlled airspace as of January 2020?
64. What is the purpose of TIS-B and FIS-B?

DME

65. What does DME measure?
66. The DME is selected on which radio?
67. How often is the coded identifier of the DME transmitted?
68. Which frequency is the coded identifier of the DME modulated to?
69. How often is the coded identifier of the VOR transmitted?
70. True or false? For each time you hear the DME identifier, you should hear the VOR identifier about 6 times.
71. What will happen to the DME indicator if an airplane flies 12,000 feet directly above a DME ground beacon?
72. An airplane is tracking directly away from a DME at 22 DME at time 1223, and at 32 DME at time 1230. What is its GS?
73. DME can provide a:
    a. circular position line.
    b. straight position line.

RNAV

74. What is a pseudo-VORTAC?
75. How is a pseudo-VORTAC created?
76. What does the CDI display when being used as part of an RNAV system?
77. What are waypoints?

GPS

78. True or false? Approved IFR GPS aircraft systems may be used for VFR navigation.
79. At least how many satellites are needed in order to determine aircraft position?

Commercial Review

80. On MH 035 you are passing east of an NDB. If you continue on MH 035, what magnetic bearing outbound would you intercept at 40°? (Sketch a diagram.)
81. On MH 340 you are passing west of an NDB. If you continue on MH 340, what magnetic bearing outbound would you intercept at 30°? (Sketch a diagram.)

Refer to figure 27-118 for questions 82 to 84.

82. Which illustration indicates that the airplane will intercept the 360 radial at a 60° angle inbound, if the present heading is maintained?
    - **a.** C.
    - **b.** A.
    - **c.** B.
83. Which statement is true regarding illustration C, if the present heading is maintained?
    - **a.** The airplane will cross the 240 radial at a 60° angle.
    - **b.** The airplane will intercept the 240 radial at a 45° angle.
    - **c.** The airplane will intercept the 060 radial at a 60° angle.
84. Which illustration indicates that the airplane will intercept the 060 radial at a 75° angle outbound, if the present heading is maintained?
    - **a.** A.
    - **b.** B.
    - **c.** C.
85. While maintaining a constant heading, a relative bearing of 15° doubles in 6 minutes.
    - **a.** What is the time to the station?
    - **b.** If the speed is 100 knots and the rate of fuel consumption is 8 gal/hour, what will be the distance to the station?
    - **c.** How much fuel would be burned?
86. The relative bearing on an ADF changes from RB 090 to RB 100 in 3 minutes of elapsed time. If you turned and tracked direct to the NDB, approximately how many minutes would it take, assuming no change to groundspeed?
87. The relative bearing of an ADF changes from RB 265 to RB 260 in 2 minutes of elapsed time. If the groundspeed is 145 knots:
    - **a.** what is the time to the station?
    - **b.** what is the distance to the station?

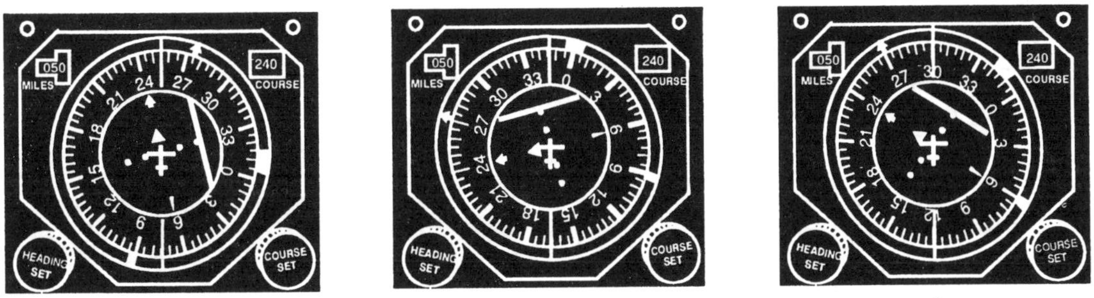

A B C

Figure 27-118 Questions 82 to 84.

88. On MH 035, the selected NDB is at RB 340. You wish to intercept a magnetic bearing of 240° from the NDB at a 30° angle (while outbound).
a. Which direction should you turn in?
b. How many degrees should you turn?
c. What will be your MH?

Refer to figure 27-119 for questions 89 and 90.

89. If an aircraft has the indications shown in instrument group C, then makes a 180° turn to the left and continues straight ahead, it will intercept which radial?
a. 135 radial.
b. 270 radial.
c. 360 radial.

90. Which instrument shows the aircraft in a position where a 180° turn would result in the aircraft intercepting the 120 radial?
a. B.
b. C.
c. D.

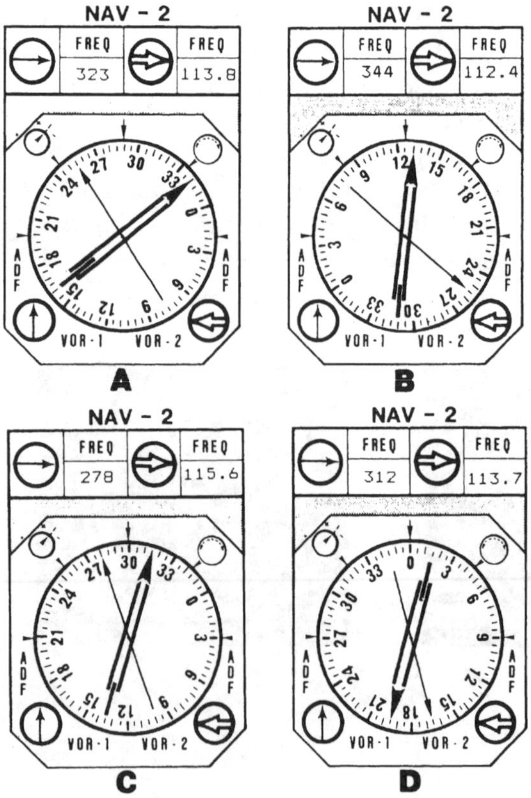

Figure 27-119 Questions 89 and 90.

91. On MH 300, the selected NDB is at RB 040. You wish to intercept a magnetic bearing of 330° from the NDB at a 30° angle (while outbound).
a. Which direction should you turn in?
b. How many degrees should you turn?
c. What will be your MH?

92. On MH 330, the selected NDB is at RB 270. What will the ADF indicate when the aircraft reaches MB 030 FROM the NDB?

93. On MH 330, the selected NDB is at RB 040. What would be the relative bearing if the aircraft were turned to MH 090?

Refer to figure 27-120 for questions 94 and 95.

94. With respect to ADF dial N, the relative bearing TO the station is:
a. 090°.
b. 180°.
c. 270°.

95. With respect to ADF dial O, on a magnetic heading of 320°, the magnetic bearing TO the station is:
a. 005°.
b. 185°.
c. 225°.

96. True or false? When tracking outbound from an NDB in crosswind conditions on the desired track with the proper drift correction established, the tail of the ADF pointer will be deflected to the downwind side of the tail position and the head of the ADF pointer will be deflected to the downwind side of the nose position.

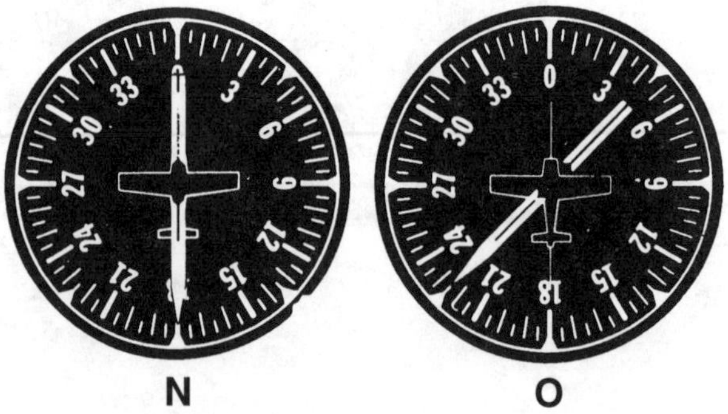

Figure 27-120 Questions 94 and 95.

97. True or false? When tracking inbound from an NDB in crosswind conditions on the desired track with the proper drift correction established, the tail of the ADF pointer will be deflected to the windward side of the tail position and the head of the ADF pointer will be deflected to the downwind side of the nose position.

98. An airplane steers MH 010 and its RMI indicates RMI 030. To track to the NDB in no-wind conditions:

a. which way would you turn?

b. what MH would you steer?

Refer to figure 27-121 for question 99.

99. At the position indicated by instrument group A, what would be the RB if the aircraft were turned to a magnetic heading of 090°?

100. An airplane steers MH 330 and its RMI indicates RMI 210.

a. Which outbound bearing is it crossing?

b. What approximate heading would you steer to track outbound on this bearing?

c. What approximate heading would you steer to track inbound to the NDB?

101. You fly on MC 239 with 7° of left drift. What will the RMI read at a position directly abeam an NDB to the left of course?

102. Given MH 080 and RMI 080:

a. what heading would you steer to make a 90° intercept of a course of MC 040 to the NDB?

b. what heading would you steer to make a 60° intercept of MC 040 to the NDB?

c. what would the RMI indicate at the point of intercept?

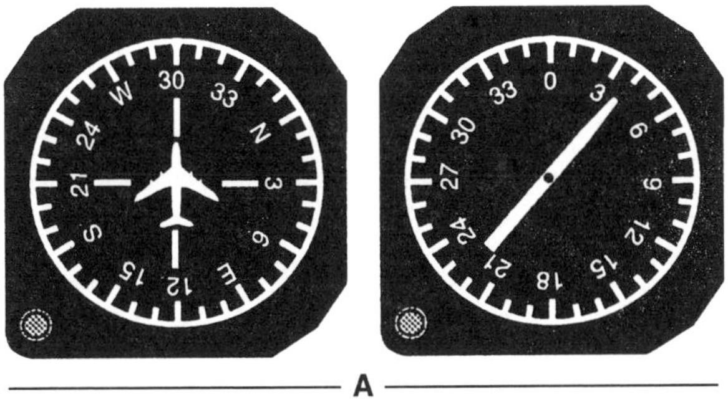

Figure 27-121 Question 99.

103. What course is the airplane maintaining to the NDB if you are tracking toward an NDB and the RMI readings are as follows?

- Time 1: MH 055, RMI 060.
- Time 2: MH 055, RMI 060.

104. You are tracking away from an NDB on MC 120 with an expected crosswind from the right causing 8° of drift.

a. What magnetic heading would you steer?

b. What would you expect the RMI to indicate?

105. You wish to track MC 360 and expect 10° of drift caused by a wind from the east.

a. What magnetic heading would you steer?

b. What would the RMI indicate as you passed abeam an NDB 10 NM to the right of course?

Refer to figure 27-122 for questions 106 to 107.

106. Determine the magnetic bearing TO the station as indicated by ADF dial A.

107. What is the relative bearing TO the station depicted by ADF dial A?

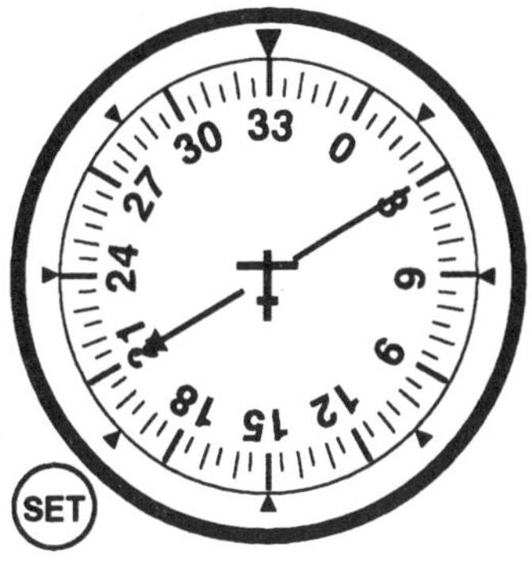

Figure 27-122 Questions 106 and 107.

Answers are given on page 707.

Appendices

Appendix 1
Abbreviations

Note. Refer also to the Pilot/Controller Glossary in the Aeronautical Information Manual or the Index to the Federal Aviation Regulations.

α: symbol for angle of attack
ρ: symbol for air density
AD: Airworthiness Directive
ADF: automatic direction finder
ADS-B: automatic dependent surveillance – broadcast
AFM: Approved Flight Manual
agl or AGL: above ground level
AH: artificial horizon (see AI)
AI: attitude indicator
AIM: Aeronautical Information Manual
AIRMET: Airman's Meteorological Information
ALS: approach light system
ALT: altitude; altimeter
A&P: airframe and powerplant
APG: adverse pressure gradient
ASI: airspeed indicator
ASOS: automated surface observing system
ATC: Air Traffic Control
ATCO: Air Taxi and Commercial Operators
ATCRBS: ATC Radar Beacon System
ATD: actual time of departure
ATIS: automatic terminal information service
ATP: airline transport pilot
AVASI: abbreviated VASI
AVGAS: aviation gasoline
AWOS: automated weather observing system
BDC: bottom-dead-center
BFO: beat frequency oscillator (ADF mode)
BHP: brake horsepower
C: Celsius (formerly centigrade) degrees
CA: closing angle
CAT: clear air turbulence
CD: coefficient of drag
CDI: course deviation indicator
CFI: certified flight instructor
CG: center of gravity
CHT: cylinder head temperature
CL: coefficient of lift
CMEC: comprehensive medical examination checklist
CO: carbon monoxide
CO_2: carbon dioxide
CONUS: continental or contiguous United States
CP: center of pressure
CRS: course
CST: Central Standard Time
CTAF: common traffic advisory frequency
CW: continuous wave (ADF mode)
D: drag
DA: density altitude
DALR: dry adiabatic lapse rate
DC: direct current
DME: distance measuring equipment
DR: dead (deduced) reckoning
EDT: Eastern Daylight Time
EGT: exhaust gas temperature
ELT: emergency locator transmitter
ELR: environmental lapse rate
EST: Eastern Standard Time
ETA: estimated time of arrival
ETD: estimated time of departure
ETE: estimated time en route
ETI: estimated time interval
F: Fahrenheit degrees
FA: area forecasts
FAA: Federal Aviation Administration
FB: winds aloft forecast
FBO: fixed base operator
FCU: fuel control unit
FIS-B: flight information service – broadcast
FL: flight level (hundreds of feet, e.g. FL210 is 21,000 feet)
fpm or FPM: feet per minute
FSS: Flight Service Station
ft or FT: feet (distance or altitude)
ft/min: feet per minute
g or G: the gravity force
GFA: graphical forecast for aviation
GMT: Greenwich Mean Time or "Z" Zulu time (now UTC)
GNSS: global navigation satellite system
gph: gallons per hour
GPS: global positioning system
GS: groundspeed; glide slope
GW: gross weight
HAA: height above airport
HDG: heading
HI: heading indicator
HIRL: high intensity runway lights
HP: horsepower
hPa: hectopascal (unit of pressure used internationally)
HSI: horizontal situation indicator
HWC: headwind correction
Hz: Hertz (cycles per second)
IAS: indicated airspeed
ICAO: International Civil Aviation Organization
IFR: instrument flight rules
ILS: instrument landing system
IMC: instrument meteorological conditions
in. Hg or Hg: inches of mercury (unit of pressure)
in-lb: inch-pounds
IOAT: indicated outside air temperature
ISA: international standard atmosphere
KCAS: knots calibrated airspeed
kg-mm: kilogram-millimeters
kHz: kilohertz (1,000 cycles per second)
KIAS: knots indicated airspeed
km: kilometer (1,000 meters)
kt: knots
KTAS: knots true airspeed
L: lift
lb: pounds
lb-in: pound-inches
L/D: lift/drag ratio
L–W: lift–weight couple
LDA: landing distance available
LIRL: low intensity runway lights
LoP: line of position
LW: landing weight
m or M: meters (distance)

M: degrees magnetic
MAC: mean aerodynamic chord (in weight and balance)
MAYDAY: (repeated three times) international distress radio signal
mb: millibars (unit of pressure, replaced by hPa)
MC: magnetic compass; magnetic course
MCP: maximum continuous power
MEF: maximum elevation figure
METAR: aviation routine weather forecast
METO: maximum except takeoff power
MH: magnetic heading
MHz: megahertz (million cycles per second)
MIRL: medium intensity runway lights
MLS: microwave landing system
MLW: maximum certificated landing weight
MOA: Military Operations Area
MSA: minimum safe altitude
msl or MSL: mean sea level
MST: Mountain Standard Time
MTOW: maximum certificated takeoff weight
MTR: Military Training Route
MULTICOM: a self-announce radio frequency
MVFR: marginal VFR
MZFW: maximum zero fuel weight
NDB: nondirectional radio beacon
NM: nautical mile(s)
NOTAM: Notice To Airmen
NTSB: National Transportation Safety Board
NWS: National Weather Service
OAT: outside air temperature
OBI: omni bearing indicator (on VOR cockpit instrument)
OBS: omni bearing selector (on VOR cockpit instrument)
OMNI: VHF omnidirectional radio range (same as VOR)
ONC: Operational Navigation Charts
PA: pressure altitude
PAN-PAN: (repeated three times) international urgency radio signal
PAPI: precision approach path indicator
PATWAS: pilots' automatic telephone weather answering service
PCL: pilot controlled lighting
PD: pilot deviation
PDT: Pacific Daylight Time
P-factor: asymmetric propeller blade effect
PIC: pilot-in-command
PIREP: pilot weather report
PL: position line
POH: Pilot's Operating Handbook
PRV: pressure relief valve
PST: Pacific Standard Time
PVASI: pulsating VASI
QNH: international term for *altimeter setting*
RAIL: runway alignment indicator lights
RB: relative bearing
RBI: relative bearing indicator
RCLS: runway centerline light system
RCO: remote communications outlet
REIL: runway end identifier lights
RMI: radio magnetic indicator
RNAV: area navigation
RoC: rate of climb
RPM: revolutions per minute
RWY: runway
SAE: Society of Automotive Engineers
SALR: saturated adiabatic lapse rate
SAR: specific air range; search and rescue
SD: radar weather reports
SFL: sequenced flashing lights
SGR: specific ground range
SIGMET: Significant Meteorological Information
SM: statute mile(s)
SSR: secondary surveillance radar
SSV: standard service volume
sUAS: small unmanned aircraft system
SVFR: Special Visual Flight Rules
T: thrust
T: degrees true
TACAN: military navigation station (see VORTAC)
TAF: terminal aerodrome forecast
TAS: true airspeed
TC: true course; turn coordinator
TCA: Terminal Control Area
T/D: thrust–drag couple
TDC: top-dead-center
TDZL: touchdown zone lights
TE: tracking error
TH: true heading
TIS-B: traffic information service – broadcast
TOSS: takeoff safety speed
TOW: takeoff weight
TPA: traffic pattern altitude
TR: track
TRSA: Terminal Radar Service Area
TTS: time to the station
T-VASI: T-form VASI
UAS: unmanned aircraft systems
UNICOM: aeronautical advisory radio communications unit (non-government)
UTC: coordinated universal time (previously GMT) or "Z" Zulu time (ATC reference to UTC)
V_A: design maneuvering speed
V_B: turbulence penetration speed
VASI: visual approach slope indicator
V_F: design flap speed
V_{FE}: maximum flaps-extended speed
VFR: visual flight rules
VHF: very high frequency
V_{LE}: maximum landing gear extended speed
V_{LO}: maximum speed, landing gear operating
V_{MAN}: design maneuvering speed
VMC: visual meteorological conditions
V_{NE}: never-exceed speed
V_{NO}: normal-operating limit speed
VNR: VFR not recommended
VOR: VHF omnidirectional radio range
VORTAC: co-located and integrated VOR and TACAN* (*used for distance measuring)
V/PD: vehicle/pedestrian deviation
V_{RA}: rough-air speed
V_S: stall speed
V_{S0}: stall speed in landing configuration
V_{S1}: stall speed clean
VSI: vertical speed indicator
V_{TURB}: turbulence penetration speed
V_X: best angle-of-climb speed
V_Y: best rate-of-climb speed
W: weight
WAC: World Aeronautical Charts
WCA: wind correction angle
WSFO: National Weather Service Forecast Office
WSO: National Weather Service Office
W/V: wind velocity
WX: weather
Z: Zulu (ATC reference to UTC)
ZFW: zero fuel weight

Appendix 2
Answers to Review Questions

Review 1: Forces Acting on an Airplane

Four Forces in Flight

1. Lift.
2. Thrust.
3. Drag.
4. 10 times.
5. Lift = weight; thrust = drag.

Airfoil Lift

6. An airfoil.
7. Streamline flow.
8. At the separation point.
9. Static pressure in the air is exerted in all directions.
10. Dynamic pressure.
11. Static pressure + dynamic pressure.
12. It will decrease.
13. Dynamic pressure.
14. The mean camber line.
15. The lifting ability of the wing.
16. True.
17. Relative airflow is parallel to the flight path of the airplane and flows in the opposite direction.
18. The angle between the wing chord line and the relative airflow.
19. It will increase.
20. Answer b.
21. Distribution of positive and negative pressure on the wing.
22. It moves forward on the wing.
23. True.
24. Frost will disrupt the smooth flow of air over the wing, adversely affecting its lifting ability.

Drag

25. Drag is the component of relative airflow which is parallel to the relative airflow.
26. True.
27. The two basic groups of drag are induced drag, which comes about in the production of lift, and parasite drag which is not associated with the production of lift.
28. False. As airspeed increases, drag caused by skin friction increases.
29. To reduce form drag, separation of the boundary layer airflow from the wing surface should be delayed by streamlining.
30. True.
31. At high angles of attack and low airspeeds.
32. At medium speed where the parasite drag and induced drag are equal.
33. Because of the greater parasite drag.
34. True.
35. The lift/drag ratio describes the aerodynamic efficiency of the wing.

Wing Flaps

36. It increases the camber of the wing.
37. Drag.
38. No, flaps decrease the lift/drag ratio.
39. True.
40. False. With flaps extended, the nose attitude of the airplane is lower.
41. True.

Thrust from the Propeller

42. Thrust.
43. False. At high altitudes, when the air is less dense, a propeller will be less efficient.
44. To ensure that it operates at its most efficient angle of attack along its full length.
45. True.
46. True.
47. Answer a.
48. P-factor causes the airplane to yaw left at high angles of attack of the wing.
49. Because of the propeller torque reaction.
50. Torque effect is greatest in a single-engine airplane at high power and low airspeed.
51. By applying right rudder.

Commercial Review

52. It decreases.
53. $C_L \frac{1}{2} \rho V^2 S$. C_L is the coefficient of lift, ρ is air density, V is the airspeed, and S is the wing surface area.
54. The center of pressure will not move.
55. Wing loading is the weight supported per unit area of wing.
56. 20 pounds per square feet.
57. **a.** 2,850 pounds.
b. 19 pounds per square feet.
58. Wings of high aspect ratio, washout, or wingtip modification.
59. False. A high aspect ratio wing has a long span and a short chord.
60. Yes.
61. 12:1.
62. Because of increased parasite drag.

63. Because of increased induced drag.
64. True.
65. The ratio of useful power output to actual power output, or thrust horsepower to brake horsepower.
66. You would select a lower RPM that would provide a greater propeller blade angle.
67. The blade angle to maintain the selected RPM.
68. **a.** $C_L = 0.32$.
b. $C_D = 0.028$.
c. $C_L/C_D = 0.32 \div 0.028 = 11.4$.
d. L/D = 11.4.
69. **a.** 6° angle of attack.
b. L/D = 12.5.
70. **a.** L/D = 7.5.
b. 16.5° angle of attack.

Review 2: Stability and Control

Stability

1. Yes.
2. A nose-down pitching moment.
3. A nose-up pitching moment.
4. It would pitch down.
5. The center of pressure is behind the CG.
6. A downward force.
7. These will cause the nose to drop.
8. Answer b.
9. Pitching.
10. Yawing.
11. The horizontal stabilizer.
12. Yes.
13. False. An airplane loaded with the CG too far aft will be unstable at all speeds, and if stalled will be difficult to recover.
14. No (a forward CG location will cause an airplane to be more stable at all speeds).
15. With a large vertical stabilizer.
16. Answer b.
17. Lateral stability.
18. Roll.

Control

19. The elevators.
20. The pitching plane.
21. Lateral axis.
22. Up.
23. **a.** The airplane will be excessively stable, which may make it difficult to flare on landing.
b. The airplane will be excessively unstable, which may make it difficult to fly smoothly.
24. The ailerons.
25. The longitudinal axis.
26. Left.
27. True.
28. False. One aileron will rise by an amount greater than the other aileron is lowered.
29. Yes.
30. The vertical (normal) axis.
31. It will tend to yaw the nose away from the turn.
32. By the use of differential ailerons, or by Frise-type ailerons.
33. Rudder.
34. Yes, lift increases. This leads to a roll.
35. Yes.
36. Yes.
37. Yes.
38. To reduce the control pressures (or "stick load") on the pilot.
39. Servo tab, horn balance, and inset hinge.
40. Answer a.
41. Answer b.
42. To prevent control-surface flutter in flight.

Commercial Review

43. Positive static stability.
44. By pitch oscillations becoming progressively steeper.
45. Answer d.
46. Answer a.
47. Answer a.
48. Answer a.

Review 3: Aerodynamics of Flight

Straight-and-Level Flight

1. Answer b.
2. Zero.
3. It must be increased.
4. High angles of attack and a high nose attitude.
5. This is achieved by decreasing the angle of attack or decreasing airspeed.
6. It disrupts the smooth airflow over the wings, decreasing the lifting ability.

Climb and Descent

7. Yes.
8. Answer a.
9. 350 FPM.
10. Answer c.
11. 600 FPM.
12. Answer b.
13. The vertical speed indicator.
14. True.
15. The altitude at which the climb performance of an airplane falls to zero.
16. Answer b.
17. Answer b.
18. Lift and drag.
19. It will decrease the rate and angle of decent.
20. False. The descent becomes steeper.
21. False. Flying faster than the correct descent speed will steepen the descent angle through the air.
22. No, it will glide the same distance.

23. Airspeed must be lowered.
24. 6 minutes (wind does not affect rate of climb or descent).
25. 8,000 feet.
26. 528 feet.

Turning and Load Factor

27. Load factor is the ratio of lift to weight.
28. Centripetal force.
29. Centripetal force is provided by the horizontal component of lift.
30. False. The pilot must apply power to overcome the increased induced drag.
31. Answer a.
32. **a.** Load factor is 2.
    b. 2 times.
33. Approximately 3,795 pounds (3,300 × 1.15).
34. Approximately 9,180 pounds (5,400 × 1.7).

Stalling and Spinning

35. Control buffet.
36. 16°.
37. Answer b.
38. Answer d (stall IAS is not affected by air density).
39. False. It will stall at the same angle of attack.
40. The inner section.
41. No, power-on stall speed is less than the power-off stall speed.
42. It must be stalled.
43. Answer a.
44. Frost and ice on the wing may delay the takeoff to a higher airspeed than normal.

Commercial Review

45. Maximum-range cruise airspeed is minimum thrust airspeed, and maximum-endurance airspeed is minimum power airspeed.
46. Endurance.
47. True.
48. It reduces.
49. When it is above the minimum-drag airspeed.
50. 500 FPM.
51. Excess power.
52. Excess thrust.
53. No, it is worse.
54. You would glide it at the airspeed for 6° angle of attack, where the L/D ratio is at its maximum value.
55. 11:1.
56. 480 feet (L/D = 11:1 ∴ 5280 ÷ 11 = 480).
57. 1,320 feet (L/D = 12 ∴ (3 × 5280) ÷ 12 = 1,320).
58. **a.** Bank angle needs to be increased.
    b. Bank angle needs to be increased.
59. **a.** Airspeed needs to be reduced.
    b. Airspeed needs to be reduced.
60. Rate of turn would increase.
61. It would remain constant.
62. Bank angle.
63. **a.** 40 seconds.
    b. 15°.
64. 80 lb.
65. **a.** 54 KIAS.
    b. 58 KIAS.
    c. 77 KIAS.
    d. 62 KIAS.
66. Maintain the bank and decrease airspeed.
67. Answer b.
68. Answer a.
69. Answer c.
70. Answer b.
71. Answer b.

Review 4: Airframe

1. The spar.
2. The vertical stabilizer, the rudder, the horizontal stabilizer, and the elevator.
3. Ribs.
4. Monoplanes.
5. Semi-monocoque.
6. Yes.
7. Oil.
8. False. The oleo strut will extend further in flight than on the ground.
9. To avoid rapid wearing of the seals during taxiing and ground maneuvers as the strut telescopes in and out.
10. A torque link.
11. A shimmy-damper.
12. Creep.
13. Castoring.
14. Answer a.
15. Answer b.
16. Answer b.
17. No.
18. Yes.
19. Answer c.

Review 5: Engine

The Engine

1. Intake (or induction), compression, power (or expansion), and exhaust.
2. No.
3. No.
4. No.
5. Yes.
6. Valve overlap.
7. By a high-voltage spark just prior to top-dead-center and the commencement of the power stroke.
8. Yes.
9. True.
10. No.

11. Answer b.
12. There is a broken magneto ground wire.
13. Answer c.
14. By impulse coupling.

Carburetor and Fuel Injection

15. The principle of a simple carburetor is to decrease the pressure as air flows through a venturi throat and draw fuel into the passing airstream.
16. The ratio between the weight of the fuel and the weight of the air entering the carburetor.
17. With the mixture control.
18. Excess fuel.
19. Excess air.
20. An idling jet.
21. The fuel/air ratio which provides the most power for any given throttle setting.
22. By using the mixture control, which is usually a red colored knob.
23. Fouling of the spark plugs.
24. Answer a.
25. True.
26. Answer c.
27. Answer c.
28. Answer b.
29. Preignition.
30. The expansion of air as it accelerates through the carburetor venturi causes it to drop in temperature, and if it contains moisture carburetor ice can form.
31. Carburetor heat.
32. A loss of power (indicated by a decrease in RPM).
33. Yes.
34. It will increase the ground roll.
35. Yes.
36. True.
37. Answer c.
38. The fuel/air mixture may become excessively lean.
39. Detonation is an explosive combustion of the fuel/air mixture in the cylinders.
40. By using a lower than specified grade of fuel and/or excessively high engine temperatures. Detonation may also be caused by the mixture being too lean.
41. Preignition.
42. Answer c.
43. Because the hot air source is unfiltered.
44. Answer a.

The Oil System

45. Oil lowers friction between moving parts and so prevents high temperatures, and what heat is formed can to some extent be carried away by circulating oil.
46. False—oil grades may not be mixed.
47. With the oil filter.
48. You may observe a high oil temperature and/or a low oil pressure.
49. It is forced through an oil filter bypass valve.
50. True.

The Cooling System

51. To increase the exposed surface area in order to allow better cooling.
52. Answer c.
53. Reduce rate of climb and increase airspeed.
54. Answer b.

Engine Operation

55. Only prior to startup.
56. Oil pressure.
57. 30 seconds.
58. Yes.
59. **a.** RPM.
    b. Manifold pressure and RPM.
60. True.
61. True.
62. Increase RPM first, then manifold pressure.
63. Decrease manifold pressure first, followed by RPM.
64. **a.** The throttle.
    b. The manifold pressure gauge.
65. Answer b.
66. **a.** RPM will stay the same.
    b. MP will decrease by about 1 in. Hg per 1,000 ft.
67. True.
68. Answer b.
69. Answer a.
70. It means reducing the amount of fuel to match the reduced weight of air.
71. Answer b.
72. In a carbureted engine, moving the mixture to idle cut-off clears the induction manifold and engine cylinders of fuel. With a fuel-injected engine, this clears fuel lines and cylinders of fuel. Not answer a—stopping the engine by removing the spark ignition would leave fuel in the fuel lines and engine. Not answer c—this would only turn off aircraft electrical services such as lighting, or radios, but would have no effect at all on the engine or engine ignition.
73. The oil temperature gauge.
74. **a.** You should suspect a serious loss of oil.
    b. You should consider an immediate landing.
75. Answer b.

Review 6: Systems

The Fuel System

1. To provide fuel at the required pressure, to purge the fuel lines of any vapor, to prime a fuel-injected engine for start-up, and to supply fuel if the engine-driven fuel pump fails.
2. The next higher octane aviation gas.
3. Because it could lead to detonation and engine damage.
4. No.
5. Prior to the first flight of the day and after each fueling.

6. False. Water tends to collect at the lowest points in the fuel system.
7. By color and smell.
8. Green.
9. Blue.
10. Answer c.
11. AVGAS is colored blue, and the decal labels are red.
12. Jet fuel is clear, and the decal labels are black.
13. Air being drawn into the fuel lines and causing a vapor lock.

The Electrical System

14. The alternator or generator.
15. The battery.
16. Answer c.
17. To provide electrical power for start-up and to act as an emergency source of electrical power.
18. A center-zero ammeter measures current in and out of the battery.
19. A left-zero ammeter measures only the battery of the alternator.
20. True.
21. Excessive electrical current.
22. 3 hours.
23. Typically, answers e, g, and i. The ASI, altimeter and VSI are pitot-static instruments and are not typically electrically powered (although there may be an electrical pitot heater to avoid icing). The gyroscopic instruments (AI, TC and HI) may be electrically powered or powered from the vacuum system—a typical arrangement is a vacuum-powered AI and HI with an electrical TC. The fuel quantity gauges and oil temperature gauge (if installed) will probably be electrically powered. The RPM gauge (tachometer) is self-powered directly off the engine. (Check the POH for your airplane.)

The Vacuum System

24. Answer b.
25. By the vacuum relief valve.
26. True.

Review 7: Flight Instruments

Pressure Instruments

1. The static vent.
2. Total pressure.
3. As a precaution against ice forming in the pitot tube.
4. The rate of change of static pressure.
5. Pitot and static pressures.
6. The airspeed indicator only.
7. No.
8. Yes.
9. The airspeed indicator, the altimeter, and the VSI.
10. The same altitude.
11. **a.** The yellow or amber arc.
    b. The green arc.
    c. The white arc.
12. The red radial line.
13. Lower limit of the white arc.
14. The low-speed end of the white arc.
15. The low-speed end of the green arc.
16. Yes.
17. False. The maximum flaps-extended speed corresponds to the high-speed end of the white arc.
18. Yes.
19. 165 to 208 mph.
20. 60 to 100 mph.
21. 100 mph.
22. 29.92 in. Hg/1,013.2 hPa.
23. The height of the airplane above the 30.05 in. Hg pressure level.
24. The height of the airplane above mean sea level.
25. Field elevation (approximately).
26. The vertical distance of the aircraft above the surface.
27. The pressure altitude corrected for non-standard temperature.
28. The correct local altimeter setting.
29. The local altimeter setting is set in the pressure window. This is done so the altimeter will read height above sea level.
30. **a.** 10,500 feet.
    b. 14,500 feet.
    c. 9,500 feet.
31. Answer b.
32. 150 feet higher.
33. Indicated altitude will increase by approx. 60 feet.
34. 6,100 feet.
35. A pressure altitude of 23,000 feet.
36. False. The airplane will be lower than the indicated altitude.
37. The indicated altitude to be less than the true altitude.
38. Standard atmospheric conditions must exist.
39. In warmer than standard temperature.
40. False. The altimeter will indicate a lower altitude than actually flown when the air temperature is higher than standard.
41. It will increase.
42. A transponder.

Gyroscopic Instruments

43. Yes.
44. Below it.
45. Turn information.
46. Turn and roll information.
47. No.
48. 3° per second.
49. The magnetic compass.
50. The AI, the HI, and the turn coordinator.
51. Coordination ball.

52. Answer b.
53. To guard against a simultaneous loss of all gyroscopic instruments.
54. The attitude indicator.
55. The turn coordinator (or turn indicator).
56. Answer c.

Magnetic Compass

57. The geographic or true north and south poles.
58. The magnetic north and south poles.
59. Magnetic variation.
60. No, it varies.
61. 10° east variation.
62. **a.** MH 080 (variation east—magnetic least).
    b. MH 086.
    c. MH 095.
63. The isogonic lines.
64. An agonic line.
65. MH 180.
66. MH 225.
67. The earth's magnetic poles being positioned away from the true geographic poles.
68. Magnetic fields within a particular airplane distorting the lines of magnetic force.
69. Airplane heading.
70. Answer a.
71. The magnetic heading of the airplane.
72. Answer b.
73. Acceleration errors occur on easterly or westerly headings, and do not occur on northerly or southerly headings.
74. You should undershoot this heading on the magnetic compass, and roll out wings-level when the compass initially indicates 320, because the compass will lag behind the actual turn.
75. You should overshoot this heading on the magnetic compass, and roll out wings-level when the compass initially indicates 140, because the compass will be ahead of the actual turn.
76. Latitude.
77. Because of the greater magnetic dip.
78. Answer c.
79. Only in unaccelerated flight.
80. Answer c.

Review 8: Airplane Performance Factors

Airworthiness

1. Yes.
2. **a.** Sections 1 and 2.
   b. Section 3.
   c. Section 5.
   d. Section 7.
   e. Section 9.
3. Limited acrobatics, including spins.
4. Operator or owner of the aircraft.

Airframe Limitations

5. The limit load factor may be exceeded.
6. **a.** MLW is the maximum gross weight, according to the Flight Manual and approved weight-and-balance documents at which that airplane is permitted to land.
   b. V_{NE} is the absolute maximum speed at which the airplane may be flown.
   c. Recommended target speeds for flying through turbulence.
7. Red line.
8. Positive limit load factor.
9. Green arc.

Air Density

10. Density altitude.
11. Air pressure and air temperature.
12. No, a water molecule weighs less than the average air molecule.
13. No, less air is processed.
14. No, this decreases efficiency.
15. Set 29.92 in. Hg in the pressure window and then read the altimeter.
16. 15°C and 29.92 in. Hg.
17. Answer b.
18. 4,000 feet.
19. Answer c.
20. ISA+8.
21. 3,526 feet pressure altitude (3,563 − 37).
22. 2,991 feet pressure altitude (1,380 + 1,611) Interpolation:

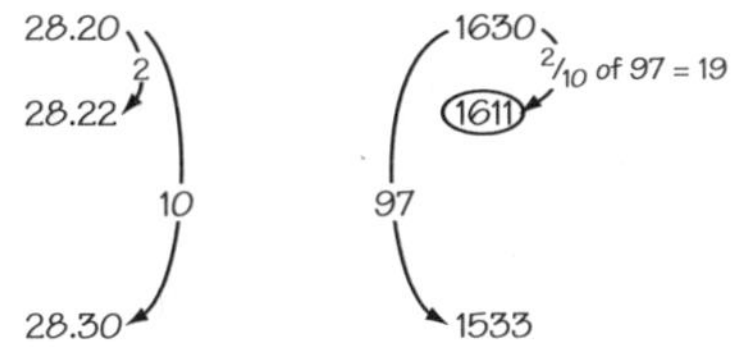

Figure A2-1 Review 8, question 22.

23. 3,298 feet pressure altitude (pressure less than standard, so add 298 feet conversion factor found from table).
24. **a.** 5,000 feet.
    b. 5,500 feet.
    c. 4,850 feet.
    d. 6,800 feet.
25. 1,950 feet increase (6,150 − 4,200).
26. 1,850 feet decrease (2,300 to 450 feet, a decrease of 1,850 feet).
27. 8,500 feet (pressure altitude = 5,250 + 626 = 5,876).
28. Answer c.
29. Answer b.

30. 7,700 feet.

Indicated altitude	=	5,000
Correction (figure 9-16)	=	+1,533
Therefore PA	=	6,533
ISA temperature at PA 6,500 ft	=	15 − (2 × 6.5)
	=	+2°C
Temperature deviation	=	+10
∴ ISA temperature at PA 6,500 ft	=	+12°C

Calculation methods:

- using figure 8-15, DA = 7,700 feet;
- using 120 feet/1°C difference from ISA:

Correction	=	12 × 10
	=	1,200
PA	=	6,500
Therefore DA	=	7,700 ft

- using flight computer: 7,500 feet (approx).

31. 12,600 feet.

ISA	=	15 − (2 × 15) = − 15°C
∴ −35°C at PA 15,000 ft	=	ISA−20
Correction	=	−20 × 120 = −2,400
PA	=	15,000
DA	=	12,600 ft

32. 16,000 feet.

ISA	=	15 − (2 × 15) = − 15°C
∴ −5°C at PA 15,000 ft	=	ISA+10
Correction	=	10 × 120 = +1,200
PA	=	15,000
DA	=	16,200 ft

Review 9: Takeoff and Landing Performance

Takeoff Performance

1. Yes.
2. 10 knots.
3. Answer a.
4. **a.** 25 knots.
b. 22 knots.
5. **a.** It increases takeoff distance.
b. It increases takeoff distance.
c. It decreases takeoff distance.
6. Takeoff distance is measured from the start point on the runway to the point where the airplane reaches 50 feet above the runway.
7. Flaps up.
8. 10,000 feet.
9. 2,950 pounds.
10. Liftoff speed is 61 KIAS and takeoff speed is 66 KIAS.
11. -5°C; +23°F.
12. **a.** Takeoff distance to 50 feet is 1,800 feet.
b. Ground roll is 1,100 feet.
c. Liftoff is at 64 KIAS, reaching 50 feet at takeoff speed 70 KIAS.
13. **a.** 1,750 feet.
b. 1,050 feet.
c. 64 KIAS.
d. 70 KIAS.
e. 7°C and 46°F.
14. 650 feet.

Landing Performance

15. Flaps down.
16. **a.** 2,750 feet.
b. 1,900 feet.
c. 68 KIAS.
17. 1,725 feet.
18. 1,440 feet.
19. Flaps lowered to 40°.
20. **a.** 968 feet (1,075 reduced by 10% = 1,075 × 0.9 = 967.5).
b. 401 ft (445 reduced by 10% = 445 × 0.9 = 400.5).
21. **a.** 908 feet (1,135 × 0.8).
b. 376 feet (470 × 0.8).
22. **a.** 815 feet (3,750 feet is halfway between 2,500 feet and 5,000 feet, so distance is halfway between 1,135 and 1,195, i.e. 1,135 + ½ of 60 = 1,135 + 30 = 1,165, multiplied by 0.7 to allow for 12 knots HWC = 815).
b. 338 ft (470 + ½ of 25 = 470 + 12.5 = 482.5, multiplied by 0.7 to allow for 12 knots HWC = 338).
23. **a.** 929 ft (pressure altitude correction 1,075 + ½ of 60 = 1,075 + 30 = 1,105, wind correction 1,105 × 0.7 = 774, dry grass runway correction—add 20% of 774 = 774 + 155 = 929).
b. 476 feet (pressure alt. correction 445 + ½ of 25 = 445 + 13 = 458, wind correction 458 × 0.7 = 321, dry grass runway correction = 321 + 20% of 774 = 321 + 155 = 476).
24. 956 feet.

Wake Turbulence

25. **a.** Wingtip vortices.
b. Wake turbulence.
26. Down and outward.
27. Answer c.
28. Below its flight path.
29. By maneuvering your airplane above and upwind of its flight path.
30. By being airborne prior to reaching the jet's flight path until able to turn clear of its wake.
31. Beyond its touchdown point.

32. You should make sure you are slightly above the path of the jet.
33. Answer c.

Ground Effect

34. Ground effect is the result of the interference of the surface of the earth with the air-flow patterns about an airplane.
35. Answer b.
36. Answer a.
37. When within 1 wingspan height above the ground.
38. Answer a.
39. Answer b.

Windshear

40. Any change in the wind speed and/or the wind direction as you move from one point to another.
41. The effect of a windshear that causes an airplane to fly above the desired flight path and/or to increase its speed.
42. This term describes the overall influence of the windshear on the airplane when the initial effect of a windshear is reversed as the airplane travels further along its flight path (say on approach to land).
43. Yes.
44. Answer a.
45. Answer a.

Commercial Review

46. Flaps 20°.
47. By taking 73% of the takeoff distance to 50 feet found on the performance graph.
48. 1,460 feet.
49. **a.** 1,400 feet.
    b. 1,020 feet.
    c. liftoff speed is 62 KIAS, and takeoff speed is 62 KIAS.
50. Liftoff speed is 64 KIAS, and takeoff speed is 64 KIAS.
51. 1,500 feet.
52. 1,450 feet (73% of takeoff distance 2,000 feet).
53. Flaps down.
54. 78 KIAS.
55. A paved, level, dry surface.
56. 636 feet (53% of landing distance 1,200 feet).
57. 1,125 feet.

Review 10: En Route Performance

Cruise Altitude and Power Setting

1. TAS 157 knots or 181 mph.
2. TAS 159 knots or 183 mph (interpolate between the TAS values for 8,000 and 10,000 feet).
3. 20.1 in. Hg.
4. Answer a.
5. **a.** 11.5 gph.
   b. 163 KTAS.
6. **a.** 111.5 gph.
   b. 163 KTAS.
7. Answer c.
8. 36.2 gallons (fuel flow 11.5 gph, 500 NM @ 159 KTAS = $^{500}/_{159}$ hour = 3.14 hours @ 11.5 gph = 36.2 gallons).
9. 32.1 gallons (10.9 gph, TAS 163 knots, headwind 10 knots = GS 153 knots for 450 NM = 2.94 hours @ 10.9 gph = 32.1 gal).
10. 73.3 gallons (fuel flow 11.5 gph, TAS 157 knots for 1,000 NM = $^{1,000}/_{157}$ hours = 6.37 hours @ 11.5 gph = 73.24, say 73.3 gal).

Commercial Review

11. Answer b.
12. +13°C (ISA at 6,000 feet is [15 – (2 × 6)] = 3°C, therefore ISA+10 = 13°C).
13. True.
14. False. Higher gross weights will decrease climb performance.
15. 3.89 ANM/pound.
16. **a.** 24.4 ANM/gallon.
    b. 19.8 GNM/gallon.
    c. 28.9 GNM/gallon.
17. Answer b.
18. **a.** 2,500 RPM, 30 in. Hg MP.
    b. 110 KIAS.
    c. open.
    d. 16 pounds.
19. By multiplying through using a factor of 1.2.
20. **a.** 22 minutes, 44 pounds, 43 NM and 43 NM.
    b. 22 minutes, 44 pounds, 43 NM and 34 NM ($^{22}/_{60}$ × 24 = 8.8, say 9; 43 – 9 = 34).
    b. 60 pounds (engine start, taxi, takeoff allowance 16 pounds + climb fuel 44 pounds).
21. 69 pounds (44 pounds to 12,000 feet; 62 pounds to 16,000 feet; by interpolation, use ½ of the 18 pounds difference to climb ½ of the 4,000 feet difference; i.e. 44 + 9 = 53 pounds to climb + 16 pounds start, taxi and takeoff allowance).
22. 46 pounds (21°C = ISA+14, therefore apply 20% correction to climb fuel from 4,000 feet to 12,000 feet, (37 – 12) = 25 × 1.2 = 30 + 16 pounds start and taxi = 46 pounds).
23. 82.5 lb/hour.
24. **a.** 4 hours 31 minutes (370 lb @ 82 lb/hour = 4.51 hours = 4 hours 31 minutes).
    b. 3 hours 46 minutes (4 hours 31 minutes minus 45 minutes = 3 hours 46 minutes).
25. **a.** 5 hours 48 minutes (505 lb @ 87 lb/hour = 5.80 hours = 5 hours 48 minutes).
    b. 5 hours 03 minutes (5 hours 48 minutes minus 45 minutes = 5 hours 03 minutes).

26. a. 166 KTAS, 87 lb/hour, 1.91 ANM/lb.
b. 164 KTAS, 85 lb/hour, 1.93 ANM/lb.
c. 159 KTAS, 79 lb/hour, 2.01 ANM/lb.
d. 155 KTAS, 75 lb/hour, 2.07 ANM/lb.

27. a. 6 hours 12 minutes (465 lb @ 75 lb/hour = 6.2 hours = 6 hours 12 minutes).
b. 5 hours 27 minutes (6 hours 12 minutes minus 45 minutes = 5 hours 27 minutes).

28. 4 hours 01 minute (425 lb @ 94 lb/hour = 4.52 hours = 4 hours 31 minutes, minus day VFR reserve 30 minutes = 4 hours 01 minute).

29. 2 hours 28 minutes (318 lb @ 99 lb/hour = 3.21 hours = 3 hours 13 minutes, minus night VFR reserve 45 minutes = 2 hours 28 minutes).

30. a. 5 hours 20 minutes (344 lb @ 59 lb/hour = 5.83 hours = 5 hours 50 minutes, minus VFR day reserve 30 minutes = 5 hours 20 minutes).
b. 5 hours 59 minutes (for best fuel economy at 70% power or less, operate at 6 lb/hour leaner, i.e. at 53 lb/hour. Therefore 344 lb @ 53 lb/hour = 6.49 hours = 6 hours 29 minutes − 30 minutes = 5 hours 59 minutes).

31. a. 28″ MP.
b. 182 KIAS.
c. 99 lb/hour.

32. 2.9 gallons (by interpolation on graph, fuel flow = 17.3 gph for 10 minutes = $17.3 \times {}^{10}\!/_{60}$ = 2.9 gallons).

33. 3 hours 22 minutes (from graph, fuel flow is 11.4 gph. Total time = 47 gallons ÷ 22.4 gph = 4.12 hours = 4 hours 7 minutes − 45 minutes reserve = 3 hours 22 minutes flight time).

34. 4 hours 30 minutes (from graph, fuel flow is 13.0 gph. Total time = 65 gallons ÷ 13.0 gph = 5.0 hours, minus 30 minutes reserve = 4 hours 30 minutes flight time).

35. 2 hours 35 minutes (from graph, fuel flow = 11.4 gph ∴ total time = 38 gallons ÷ 11.4 gph = 3.33 hours = 3 hours 20 minutes, minus 45 minutes reserve = 2 hours 35 minutes flight time).

36. 16.7 gph.

37. 2 ANM/lb.

38. a. 4.07 ANM/lb (6.6 gph = 39.6 lb/hour).
b. 3.31 GNM/lb.
c. 4.82 GNM/lb.

Review 11: Weight and Balance

Weight and Balance

1. Maximum takeoff weight.
2. True.
3. True.
4. a. airframe.
b. powerplant.
c. permanently installed equipment.
d. unusable fuel.
e. unusable oil (unless it is specifically stated that full oil is included).
f. hydraulic fluid.
5. a. 6 pounds.
b. 156 pounds.
6. 18.4 gallons.
7. False. If the CG is located at the rear limit, the airplane be less stable longitudinally.
8. True.
9. Answer b.
10. 17,600 lb-in.
11. Answer b.
12. 273 lb (2,400 − 2,127), 45.5 gal.

Empty weight	1,432 lb
Front seat	320
Rear seat	340
Baggage	20
Oil	15
ZFW	2,127*
MTOW	2,400
Fuel	273 lb

**This is the zero fuel weight for these conditions. Note that it is not a limiting weight.*

13. 43 lb.

Basic empty weight (incl. oil)	2,015 lb
Front seat	369
Rear seat	267
Fuel (36 gal @ 6 lb/gal)	216
ZFW	2,867
Max allowed TOW	2,910
Therefore, max. baggage is:	43 lb

14. Answer b.

	Weight (lb)	Arm (in)	Moment (lb-in)
Empty weight	1,495.0	101.4	151,593.0
Pilot and passenger	380.0	64.0	24,320.0
Full fuel (30 gal usable)	180.0	96.0	17,280.0
Total	2,055.0	94.1	193,193.0

Weight-and-Balance Calculations

15. a. 80.8.
b. Using the center of gravity moment envelope 1,999 lb and 80.8 inches lie just within the envelope in the utility category.

Item	Weight (lb)	Moment (mom/1,000)
Empty weight	1,350	51.5
Pilot and front passenger	310	11.5
Rear passengers	96	7.0
Fuel (38 gal)	228	11.0
Oil (8 quarts)	15	–0.2
Gross weight	1,999	80.8

16. **a.** 79.2, 38.9 inches aft of datum. The weight and moment index of the oil is given in the graph at Note 2.

b. Using the center of gravity moment envelope, 2,033 lb and 79.2 lie within the envelope in the normal category.

c.

$$\text{CG position} = \frac{\text{total moment}}{\text{total weight}}$$

$$= \frac{79{,}200}{2{,}033}$$

$$= 38.9 \text{ inches aft of datum}$$

Item	Weight (lb)	Moment (mom/1,000)
Empty weight	1,350	51.5
Pilot and front passenger	380	14.2
Fuel (48 gal = 288 lb)	288	13.7
Oil (8 qt)	15	–0.2
Gross weight	2,033	79.2

17. Answer c.

- fill in the table as far as possible;
- calculate weight and moments as far as possible—without the fuel, since it is an unknown quantity;
- add up the actual weights and, from the known maximum gross weight (2,300 lb shown on CG envelope for the normal category), calculate the maximum possible fuel from a weight point of view (no balance as yet), and check that it does not exceed fuel tank limits (48 gal = 288 lb);
- add the fuel weight and moment to table, find new totals, and check they lie inside the CG envelope; and
- convert pounds of fuel to gallons (1 gal = 6 lb).

Item	Weight (lb)	Moment (mom/1,000)
Empty weight	1350	51.5
Pilot and front passenger	340	12.5
Rear passengers	310	22.5
Baggage	45	4.0
Oil (8 qt)	15	–0.2
ZFW	2060	90.3
Maximum fuel (2300 – 2060)	240	11.5
Maximum gross weight (from CG envelope)	2300	101.8 OK

18. 45 lb.

Note. The empty weight and moment is stated in figure 11-21 (page 264).

Item	Weight (lb)	Moment (mom/1,000)
Empty weight	1350	51.5
Front seats (200 +187)	387	330 (170 + 160)
Rear seats (140 + 153)	293	355 (169 + 186)
Fuel (35 gal)	210	158
Gross weight (no baggage)	2905	2397
Baggage	45	63
Gross weight (with baggage)	2950	2460
Maximum weight	2950 OK	2422-2499 OK

19. **a.** Weight is 2,927 lb.

b. CG is 83.39 inches aft of datum. To calculate the CG position:

$$\text{Mom}/100 = 2{,}441$$

$$\text{Moment} = 244{,}100 \text{ lb-in}$$

$$= 2{,}927 \text{ lb} \times \text{CG arm}$$

$$\text{CG arm} = \frac{79{,}200}{2{,}033}$$

$$= 83.39 \text{ inches aft of datum}$$

Note. "Determine weight and balance" means: "calculate the weight, calculate the moments, and also calculate the position of the CG."

c. Weight and balance is within limits (i.e. within the range 2399–2483 at the very close weight of 2930 lb.

Item	Weight (lb)	Mom/100
Empty weight	2015	1554
Front seats (200 + 150)	350	298 (170 + 128)
Rear seats (200 + 125)	325	393 (242 + 151)
Baggage	27	38
Fuel (35 gal)	210	158
Gross weight	2927 OK	2441 OK

20. The weight is within limits (right on maximum), but the CG is out of limits (because the mom/100 lies outside the allowable range at that weight—2422–2499 is the CG range at 2950 lb).

Item	Weight (lb)	Mom/100
Empty weight	2015	1554
Front seats (215 + 200)	415	353 (183 + 170)
Rear seats	110	133
Baggage	32	45
Fuel (mains 44 gal aux 19 gal)	264 114	198 107
Gross weight	2950 OK (max wt)	2390 NOT OK

Weight Shift Calculations

21. Answer b.
Drain 9 gallons of fuel. You need to reduce gross weight by (3,004 – 2,950) = 54 lb = $^{54}/_{6}$ gal = 9 gal. Shifting fuel changes the CG, but not the weight. Balance is not the problem, but weight is, so answer c is not correct.

Item	Weight (lb)	Mom/100
Empty weight	2015	1554
Front seats (225 + 200)	425	362 (192 + 170)
Rear (150 + 150)	300	364 (182 + 182)
Fuel (mains 44 gal)	264	198
Gross weight	3004 NOT OK, max wt 2950 lb	2478

Answer a and answer b are correct from the weight point of view, since draining 9 or more gallons of fuel will bring the weight within limits. So now we need to check the balance. Try the 9 gal first, since the less we have to drain the better, and if this doesn't work, try the balance after draining 12 gal. In these workings, we have shown how the weight values (and associated mom/100) have been subdivided and necessary interpolations made. With practice, you will be able to do this without having to lay out your workings in this way. Remember, you can always use weight arm to derive the moment.

Item	Weight (lb)	Mom/100
Empty weight	2015	1554
Front seats (225 + 200)	425	362 (192 + 170)
Rear seats (150 + 150)	300	364 (182 + 182)
Fuel (mains 35 gal)	210	158
Gross weight	2959 OK	2438 OK 2422-2499 is allowable range

22. Answer a.
This question is best solved by following the tabulation method shown in example 11-9 on page 255. The following is the sequence of steps:

- deduct the front passenger and derive the new gross weight and moment;
- deduct the rear passenger and derive the new gross weight and moment;
- add rear passenger (204 lb) to front seat and derive final gross weight and moment;
- check that weight and moment are within limits; and
- calculate original and new CG locations and determine the CG movement; and
- original CG = 84.01 in. aft of datum (226,000/2,690). New CG = 81.00 in. aft of datum (203,300/2,510). CG movement 84.01 – 81.00 = 3.01 inches forward (say 3 inches).

Item	Wt (lb)	Arm (in)	Mom/100
Gross weight	2690	84.01	2260
Front seat (OUT)	–180		–153
New GW	2510	–	2107
Rear seat (OUT)	–204		–247
New GW	2306	–	1860
Front seat (IN)	+204		+173
Final GW	2510	81.00	2033

Both GW and moment (mom/100) are within limits.

23. **a.** Yes, you can carry 100 lb but must move one passenger to front seat. As loaded initially, CG is outside aft limits of 2,393 mom/100 (by interpolation). So, 1 passenger must move from rear seat to front seat (rear arm 121, front arm 85). CG limits for 2,815 lb are 2,271 – 2,393 mom/100, so the new CG location is well within.

b. Final CG is at 82.84 inches aft of datum.

$$\text{CG location} = 2{,}332 \text{ index} = \frac{233{,}200 \text{ lb-in}}{2{,}815} = 82.84 \text{ inches aft of datum}$$

(See table on next page.)

Item	Weight (lb)	Mom/100	
Empty weight	2015	1554	
Pilot (front seat)	180	153	
2 × rear seat @ 170 lb	340	412	
Baggage	100	140	
Minimum fuel (30 gal)	180	135	
Gross weight	2815	2394	CG outside aft limit
1 × rear passenger OUT	–170	–206	to move CG fwd
New GW	2645	2188	
1 × passenger to front	+170	+144	
Final GW	2815	2332	OK

24. Answer a.
Burning 35 gallons will reduce gross weight by 210 lb, which will reduce the mom/100 by 158 (find this on table, or work it out as 210 lb arm 75 in. = 15,750 lb-in = 157.5 mom/100, say 158). New gross weight = 2,890 – 210 = 2,680 lb. New mom/100 = 2,452 – 158 = 2,294, but allowable limits are 2,123 to 2,287. Therefore, weight is OK, but mom/100 is too great, which means CG is aft of limits.

25. **a.** Yes, takeoff is permitted and no ballast is required.
b. Landing weight is 2,699 lb and CG is 82.25 inches aft of datum:

$$\text{CG at landing} = \frac{222{,}000 \text{ lb-in}}{2{,}699 \text{ lb}}$$
$$= 82.25 \text{ inches aft of datum}$$

Item	Wt (lb)	Mom/100
Empty weight	2015	1554
Front seat	300	256
Rear seat	180	218
Baggage	60	84
ZFW	2555	2112 OK (1990 limit)
Fuel (mains 44 gal aux 15 gal)	264 90	198 85
Planned TOW	2909 OK	2395 OK (2377 limit)
Burn-off (aux 15 gal) mains 20 gal	–90 2819 –120	–85 2310 OK –90
Landing weight	2699	2220 OK (2144 limit)

Commercial Review

26. CG is 117.9 inches aft of datum.

	Weight (lb)	Arm (in. aft of datum)	Moment (lb-in)
A	165	135.0	22275
B	125	115.0	14375
C	75	85.0	6375
Totals	365	117.9	43025

27. CG is 15.05 inches aft of datum (at +15.05 in.)

	Weight (lb)	Arm (in. aft of datum)	Moment (lb-in)
Empty weight	857	29.07	24913.0
Pilot (fwd)	145	–45.30	–6568.5
Passenger (aft)	175	+1/60	+280.0
Ballast	15	–45.30	–679.5
Totals	1,192	+15/05	+17945.0

28. Answer a.
Plotting 2,133 lb against 187.04 index units on the bottom graph, it falls within the envelope in the normal category.

Item	Weight	Moment/1,000
Empty weight	1271	102.04
Pilot and copilot	400	36.0
Rear seat passenger	140	17.5
Cargo	100	11.5
Fuel (37 gal)	222	20.0
Gross weight	2,133	187.04

29. Answer a.
Fuel remaining is 37 gal (start) – 30 gal (burned) = 7 gal = 7 × 6 lb = 42 lb. The intersection of total weight of 2,013 lb and total moment of 178.04 in-lb is within the CG moment envelope.

Item	Weight	Moment/1,000
Empty weight	1271	102.04
Pilot and copilot	360	32.50
Cargo	340	39.50
Fuel (7 gal × 6 lb/gal)	42	4.00
Gross weight	2,013	178.04

30. 96 in aft of datum.

	Weight (lb)	Arm (in)	Moment (lb-in)
Original tools	5000	98	490000
Rear baggage OUT	–100	145	–14500
Front baggage IN	+100	45	4500
New tools	5000	96	48000

31. 67.79 inches aft of datum.

Weight change = fuel burn in 1 hour 45 minutes

$$= \frac{105}{60} \text{ hours} \times 14.7 \text{ gph} \times 6 \text{ lb/gal}$$
$$= 154.35 \text{ lb}$$

	Weight (lb)	Arm (in)	Moment (lb-in)
Original tools	4037.00	67.80	273708.6
Fuel change	–154.35	68.00	–10495.8
New tools	3882.65	67.79	263212.8

32. Answer a.

Weight change = 1.5 hours @ 13. 6 lb/gal 123.3 lb from aft of original CG, which will move the CG forward:

$$\text{Change in individual moments} = \text{change in total moment}$$

$$\text{weight change} \times \text{arm} = \text{change in total moment}$$

$$123.3 \times (68 - 67.8) = (4{,}137 - 123.3) \times \text{CG shift}$$

$$= \frac{123.3 \times 0.2}{4{,}013.7}$$

$$= 0.006 \text{ fwd}$$

$$\text{new CG position} = 67{,}800 - 0.006$$

$$= 67.794$$

33. Answer a.

$$\text{Weight shifted} \times \text{distance shifted} = \text{GW} \times \text{CG shift}$$

$$\text{weight shifted} \times (180 - 40) = 3{,}650 \times (94 - 92)$$

$$\text{weight shifted} \times 140 = 3{,}650 \times 2$$

$$\text{weight shifted} = \frac{23.3 \times 0.2}{140}$$

$$= 52.14$$

34. Fwd limit 11% MAC, rear limit 25.73% MAC. From figure 11-22 (page 265), for GW 2,700 lb the total moments lie between 2,144 mom/100 and 2,303 mom/100.

The forward limit of the CG is therefore:

$$\frac{214{,}400}{2{,}700} = 79.4''$$

The aft limit is at:

$$\frac{230{,}300}{2{,}700} = 85.3''$$

The forward limit is therefore (79.4 –75) inside the leading edge, which gives:

$$\frac{(79.4 - 75)}{40} \times \frac{100}{1} \% \text{ MAC} = 11\% \text{ MAC}$$

The aft limit is at:

$$\frac{(85.3 - 75)}{40} \times \frac{100}{1} \% \text{ MAC} = 25.75\% \text{ MAC}$$

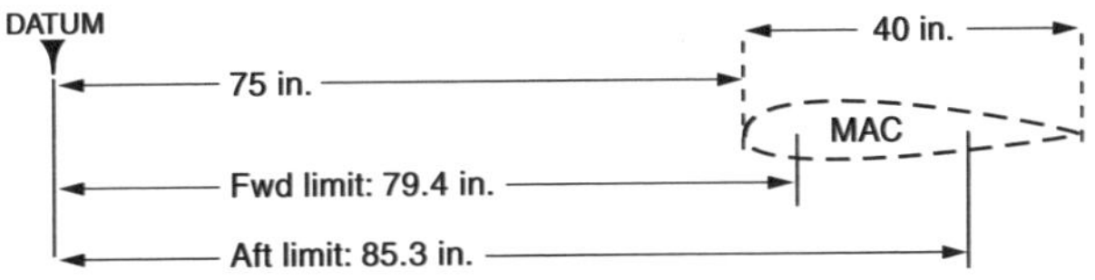

Figure A2-2 Review 11, question 34.

35. 50.43 lb. Add "w" lb as ballast, to shift CG aft to at least 60 in.:

$$\text{Weight change} \times \text{distance from CG} = \text{new CG} \times \text{CG shift}$$

$$w \times (120 - 58.5) = (2{,}017 + w) \times (60 - 58.5)$$

$$w \times 61.5 = (2{,}017 \times 1.5) \times 1.5$$

$$= (2{,}017 \times 1.5) \times 1.5\ w$$

$$61.5\ w - 1.5\ w = 2{,}017 \times 1.5$$

$$60\ w = 2{,}017 \times 1.5$$

$$w = \frac{2{,}017 \times 1.5}{60}$$

$$= 50.43 \text{ lb}$$

36. Fwd limit 80.50 inches, rear limit 85.03 inches.

Review 12: The Human in the Cockpit

Am I Fit to Fly?

1. 8 hours.

2. Hypothermia is when a person suffers from an abnormally low temperature.

3. DECIDE, which stands for: Detect, Estimate, Choose, Identify, Do, Evaluate. The six-step process is a logical way to make decisions while flying or flight planning.

4. Know your personal limits; use all available resources, avoid hazardous attitudes, learn to modify your behavior, and develop methods to assess risk.

Respiration

5. A state of oxygen deficiency in the body.

6. Hyperventilation is overbreathing.

7. Hyperventilation causes low carbon dioxide levels in the blood.

8. Stress.

9. Tingling sensations in the hands and feet.

10. Because of the possibility of carbon monoxide poisoning.

11. Answer c.

Balance

12. Spatial disorientation is a state of temporary confusion resulting from misleading information being sent to the brain by various sensory organs.
13. The flight instruments.
14. Answer c.

Vision

15. Cones are concentrated around the central section of the retina. Rods are concentrated in the outer parts of the foveal area.
16. False. Cones are most effective in the day.
17. No. They only see in black-and-white.
18. Rods.
19. Using successive eye movements.
20. True.
21. Yes.
22. False. They are most clearly seen in your peripheral vision.
23. Answer c.
24. There will be no apparent relative motion between your aircraft and the other aircraft.
25. Yes.
26. 30 minutes.
27. The other aircraft is crossing to the left.
28. The illusion that the correct approach path is too steep and that the runway is shorter than it is.
29. The illusion that you are higher than you really are, resulting in the airplane flying into the runway.

Review 13: Heating Effects in the Atmosphere

The Atmosphere

1. Temperature.
2. The troposphere.
3. **a.** The stratosphere.
   b. The tropopause.
4. Abrupt change in temperature lapse rate.
5. Nitrogen (78%), oxygen (21%), other gases (1%), and a variable amount of water vapor.
6. Troposphere.
7. Answer b.
8. Maritime air.
9. *Temperature lapse rate* is the rate of decrease of temperature with altitude in the actual atmosphere.
10. 15°C (59°F) and 29.92 in. Hg (1013.2 hPa).

Heat Exchange Process

11. In the tropics.
12. A heat exchange.
13. The re-radiation of heat from the earth.
14. False. The sea heats less rapidly than land and cools less rapidly than land.
15. Cloud coverage reduces it.
16. By the terrestrial re-radiation of heat.
17. **a.** Radiation is the process of transfer of heat as electromagnetic waves.
    b. Conduction is the process of transfer of heat from body to body by direct contact.
    c. Convection is the transfer of heat by the vertical motion of an air mass.
    d. Advection is the transfer of heat by the horizontal motion of an air mass.
18. Solar heating.
19. True.
20. Cumuliform clouds.
21. Answer c.
22. Katabatic wind is the wind that flows down mountain slopes at night due to cooling.
23. Anabatic wind is the wind that flows up mountain slopes by day due to heating.
24. Yes, because of the force of gravity.
25. The temperature increases as altitude increases.
26. A temperature inversion describes conditions whereby air at the earth's surface is cooler than that above.
27. Answer a.
28. **a.** Yes.
    b. No.
29. Smooth with poor visibility.

Review 14: Wind

1. Differences in pressure.
2. Answer a.
3. Answer b.
4. True.
5. False. A wind will initially tend to flow from a high pressure area to a low pressure area before it is turned by the Coriolis force.
6. Answer a.
7. The Coriolis force tends to counterbalance the horizontal pressure gradient.
8. The Coriolis force.
9. Yes, winds are usually weaker than winds at 2,000 feet AGL because of friction.
10. True.
11. Answer b.
12. Friction between the wind and the surface.

Commercial Review

13. Because of the reduced Coriolis force caused by friction.
14. True.
15. A jet stream is a wind of 60 knots or greater.
16. 36,000 feet.
17. Near breaks in the tropopause.
18. Troughs of low pressure in the upper atmosphere.
19. False. The jet stream is generally weaker but further north in the summer compared with in the winter.
20. Answer b.

21. Answer a.
22. Answer c.
23. Answer a.
24. Answer b.

Review 15: Clouds and Thunderstorms

Clouds

1. When water vapor condenses.
2. Height range.
3. High-level clouds, middle-level clouds, low-level clouds, and clouds with extensive vertical development.
4. Low-level clouds.
5. Rain-bearing cloud.
6. Fractus.
7. Evaporation and sublimation.
8. Evaporation is the process of liquid water altering its state to water vapor.
9. Sublimation is the process of solid ice altering its state to water vapor.
10. Its temperature.
11. The temperature to which air must be cooled to become saturated.
12. Dew.
13. The dewpoint must be below freezing, and the collecting surface must be below freezing.
14. Steady precipitation and little or no turbulence.
15. Towering cumulus.
16. **a.** 3°C per 1,000 feet.
    b. 1.5°C per 1,000 feet.
    c. 2°C/1,000 feet.
17. Stratiform cloud with little vertical development.
18. Clouds with considerable vertical development and associated turbulence.
19. **a.** Cumuliform clouds.
    b. Turbulent flying conditions.
    c. Good visibility.
20. Ice crystals.
21. Cumulonimbus clouds.
22. Conditions are often smoother above fair weather cumulus clouds compared with below them.
23. Lenticular clouds are almond or lens-shaped clouds that appear stationary but may contain winds of 50 knots or more.
24. Rain that evaporates before it reaches the ground.
25. No, it will cause the air temperature to decrease.
26. Yes.
27. A microburst is a very dangerous and localized downflow of air that may be quite narrow in extent.
28. 4.4°F; 2.5°C.
29. 6,000 feet MSL:

$$\frac{70-48}{4.4} = \frac{22}{4.4} = 5$$

$$\text{cloud base} = 1{,}000 \text{ feet MSL} + 5{,}000 \text{ feet} = 6{,}000 \text{ feet MSL}$$

30. **a.** 10,000 feet AGL:

$$\frac{82-38}{4.4} = \frac{44}{4.4} = 10$$

    b. 11,500 feet MSL.

Thunderstorms

31. Cumulonimbus cloud.
32. Yes.
33. High humidity, lifting force, and unstable conditions.
34. The lapse rate is high, and rising air will tend to keep rising.
35. Cumulus stage, mature stage, and dissipating stage.
36. **a.** Updrafts.
    b. Updrafts and downdrafts.
    c. Downdrafts.
37. That downdrafts have developed, and that the mature stage in the storm's life cycle has started.
38. The mature stage.
39. Embedded thunderstorms are thunderstorms that grow out of a massive cloud layer that possibly obscures them.
40. Answers c and d (windshear and turbulence).
41. A nonfrontal narrow band of active thunderstorms that often develops ahead of a cold front.

Commercial Review

42. It increases and the air becomes more saturated.
43. 6,000 feet MSL.
44. 10,000 feet AGL:

$$\frac{89-45}{4.4} = \frac{44}{4.4} = 10$$

45. A parcel of air that is warmer than the environmental air surrounding it and will tend to rise.
46. The stability of the air before lifting occurs.
47. Unstable air.
48. Strong updrafts and cumulonimbus clouds.
49. Cumulonimbus cloud.
50. Unstable, moist air and orographic lifting.
51. By detecting water drops.
52. Answer a.

53. The minimum distance that should exist between these two storms is 40 miles. This is so that each storm can be avoided by at least 20 miles.
54. No.
55. Answer b.
56. The ambient lapse rate.
57. Answer c.
58. Answer c.
59. Answer c.

Review 16: Air Masses and Frontal Weather

1. An air mass is an extensive body of air with fairly uniform temperature and moisture content.
2. False. A polar maritime air mass will be cold and moist.
3. Yes.
4. No, unstable air tends to rise.
5. Cumuliform clouds.
6. True.
7. False. A tropical continental air mass will be warm and dry.
8. True.
9. Yes.
10. A front.
11. Answer a.
12. Answer c.
13. A temperature change.
14. A warm front occurs when warm air replaces cold air at the surface with the warm air tending to slide over the cold air.
15. A cold front occurs when cold air replaces warm air at the surface with the cold air tending to undercut the warm air.
16. A cold front is usually steeper than a warm front, and faster moving.
17. Cumuliform clouds.
18. An occluded front occurs when a cold front overtakes a warm front.
19. A front with little or no movement.

Commercial Review

20. An area of descending air, i.e. stable air.
21. An area of ascending air, i.e. unstable air.
22. Answer a.
23. Answer b.
24. Answer b.
25. Answer c.
26. There exists a layer of warmer air above.
27. A stationary front.
28. A cold front.
29. Slow moving cold fronts or stationary fronts.
30. As or just after the cold front passes.

Review 17: Operational Weather Factors

Icing

1. Visible moisture and the temperature at or below freezing.
2. Frost may prevent the airplane from becoming airborne at normal takeoff speed.
3. Freezing rain.
4. 4,500 feet MSL.
5. Visible moisture.
6. High-level clouds.
7. Frost spoils the smooth flow of air over the wings, thereby decreasing lifting capability.
8. The carburetor heat control.
9. **a.** The airspeed indicator.
   b. The airspeed indicator, the altimeter, and the vertical speed indicator.
10. Answer a.
11. True.
12. True.
13. By recycling the gear (if in accordance with manufacturer's procedures).
14. Because they are susceptible to being clogged by ice from crankcase vapors that have condensed and subsequently frozen.

Visibility

15. False. Poor visibility is more likely to result with stable air.
16. True.
17. Typically, there is smooth air and poor visibility.
18. Fog is formed when the air is cooled to its dewpoint temperature.
19. Because of the prevalence of condensation nuclei as a result of the combustion process.
20. Answer a.
21. Fog or low clouds.
22. A mixture of smoke and fog.
23. An air mass moving inland from the coast in winter.
24. False.
25. True.
26. Steam fog.

Turbulence

27. Moderate.
28. 6 knots/1,000 feet.
29. It can be present at any level and can exist in both a horizontal and vertical direction.
30. The turbulent areas in and above rotor clouds.
31. Very strong turbulence.
32. Stronger Coriolis force at the surface.
33. Answer b.
34. True.
35. After the front has passed.
36. Answer c.

Commercial Review

37. Answer c.
38. True.
39. Answer a.
40. Answer a.
41. Answer c.
42. Answer c.
43. Answer c.
44. Precipitation-induced fog.
45. Answer b.
46. False. Ice pellets encountered during flight normally mean there is a layer of warmer air above.
47. Clear ice.

Review 18: Weather Reports and Forecasts

Obtaining a Weather Briefing

1. A weather synopsis is a brief statement explaining the causes of the weather.
2. An outlook briefing is a weather briefing provided when the information requested is 6 or more hours in advance of the proposed departure time.
3.
- The fact that you are a pilot;
- whether you are VFR or IFR;
- the N-number of aircraft;
- the aircraft type;
- your departure point;
- your route;
- your destinations;
- your en route altitude;
- your time of departure; and
- your time en route.

Weather Reports

4. **a.** 6,000 feet.
b. 4 miles.
c. No, conditions are MVFR.
d. A stationary front.
e. Fog.
f. Low ceilings of 300 feet with fog and drizzle.
g. 25,000 feet.

METARs and PIREPs

5. **a.** 5,500 feet MSL to 7,200 feet MSL.
b. Light to moderate clear ice from 7,200 feet MSL to 8,900 feet MSL.
c. 1800Z.
d. 12,000 feet.
e. BE 90.
f. 090°T/21 knots.
g. -9°C.
h. 505 feet AGL.
6. Hourly.
7. Ceiling is the height above the earth's surface of the lowest layer of clouds or obscuring phenomena reported as broken, overcast, and not classified as thin or partial.
8. Record special on the 25th day of the month at 1750Z. Winds from 280 degrees true at 4 knots. 4 miles visibility. 1,000 feet broken clouds. An overcast layer at 1,500 feet. 10°C temperature. 09°C dewpoint. Altimeter setting 29.89. Virga seen in the vicinity.
9. METAR for KBOI (VFR conditions) taken on the 4th day of the month at 1854Z. Wind 130°T/4 knots. Visibility 30 miles. 15,000 feet base of scattered clouds. Temperature 16°C. Dewpoint 09°C. Altimeter setting 30.15 in. Hg. Remarks: sea level pressure 1018.1 hectopascals.
10. Aviation routine weather report for Amarillo (IFR conditions) the 4th day of the month at 1453Z. Wind from 140 degrees at 7 knots. Visibility measured one-quarter mile in freezing fog. Ceiling of clouds 100 feet overcast. Temperature -3°C. Dewpoint -3°C. Altimeter 29.98 in. Hg. Remarks: automated system with precipitation detection, sea level pressure 1001.64 hectopascals, temperature 2.8°C, dewpoint 3.3°C.
11. Rain began at 12 minutes past the hour.
12. Sky partially obscured, measured ceiling 700 overcast, visibility 1½, heavy rain, and fog.

Weather Forecasts

13. KGAG aerodrome forecast valid on 4th day of month from 1200Z until 1200Z the following day. Initial time period from 1200Z: wind from 60° at 8 knots, visibility better than six miles, and 300 feet overcast cloud layer. From 1500Z: wind from 80° at 8 knots, better than six miles visibility, and ceiling of 600 ft. Overcast clouds, becoming from 1600Z to 1800Z: broken clouds at 1000 ft. From 1900Z the wind shifts to 100° at 10 knots, visibility better than six miles, with a ceiling of broken clouds at 1200 ft and another overcast layer of clouds at 25,000 ft. Temporary conditions from 2000Z to 2400Z are a scattered layer of clouds at 1200 ft and an overcast layer of clouds at 25,000 ft. From 0000Z expect winds from 110° at 8 knots and visibility better than six miles with broken clouds at 1200 ft and 10,000 ft, with a probability of 30% that between 0400Z and 1200Z there will be 5 miles visibility in light rain with overcast clouds at 1000 ft.
14. VFR and windy.
15. Ceilings 1,000 and 3,000 feet with thunderstorms and rain showers.

16. **a.** By 2000Z.
b. 230°T/15 knots gusting to 25 knots.
c. MVFR conditions with chance of IFR (ceiling 1,000 ft overcast with 4 miles visibility and rain so MVFR, with a 40% probability of one mile visibility and thunderstorms with rain so a chance of IFR.)

17. **a.** 1900Z.
b. 1,200 feet.
c. Yes—300 feet.
d. 1000 UTC or 3 a.m. MST.
e. 1500 UTC or 8 a.m. MST.
f. 1500 broken.
g. 350°T/8 knots.
h. Yes, there is a 40% probability of light rain.

18. Moderate turbulence from the surface up to FL240.
19. IFR conditions, ceilings less than 1,000 feet, and/or visibility less than 3 miles.
20. 12,000 feet MSL.
21. Within five miles of the airport center.
22. You would expect a ceiling from 1000 to 3000 feet and visibility from 3 to 5 miles.
23. By calling FSS (1-800-WX-BRIEF) or visiting the NWS website (nws.noaa.org).
24. Vicinity.
25. 5 miles to 25 miles.
26. 4 times daily.
27. 24 hours.

Forecasts and Advisories

28. 12 hours.
29. 6 hours.
30. From the graphical forecast for aviation (GFA) or area forecast (FA).
31. PIREPs for light to moderate icing conditions for various altitude ranging from 8,000 to 10,500 feet MSL.
32. Convective SIGMET for icing associated with a thunderstorm.
33. 1821 UTC Thursday, April 28.
34. 230°T/56 knots, -16°C.
35. 230°T/53 knots, -47°C.
36. 050°T/7 knots, no temperatures forecast for 3,000 feet MSL or within 2,500 feet AGL.
37. 9900.
38. Tornados, embedded thunderstorms, and hail ¾ inch or greater in diameter.
39. Thunderstorms obscured by massive cloud layers.
40. 122.2 MHz.

Commercial Review

41. VOR points are used to outline the area of icing, including VOR points outside the designated FA boundary, if necessary.
42. 24,000 feet.
43. Wind speed 70 knots to 110 knots.
44. Cumulonimbus clouds and the associated icing and moderate or greater turbulence.
45. A ready means of locating observed frontal positions and pressure centers.
46. The surface visibility is expected to be more than 6 miles.
47. 3,500 feet thick (base MSL = elevation 3,500 + ceiling 500 = 4,000 ft MSL tops MSL = 7,500 ft MSL; therefore thickness = tops 7,500 ft MSL — base 4,000 ft MSL = 3,500 ft).
48. The pilot reports the sky as overcast with the top of the lower overcast layer at 2,500 feet MSL, and a second overcast layer with base at 4,500 feet MSL and tops at 9,000 feet MSL.
49. Maximum tops of thunderstorm cells is 46,000 feet, located on a bearing of 140°M from the station at 55 NM.
50. Relative humidity was 87% and the freezing level (0°C) was at 4,500 feet MSL.

Review 19: Regulations

Definitions and Pilot Qualifications

1. Night is defined as starting at the end of evening civil twilight and ending at the beginning of morning civil twilight.
2. Authorization to proceed under specified traffic conditions in Class A, B, C, D and E airspace.
3. **a.** A category of aircraft.
b. A class of aircraft.
4. An airworthiness certificate remains valid provided the aircraft is maintained and operated according to the regulations.
5. Part 1.1.
6. Maximum landing gear extended speed.
7. Maximum flap extended speed.
8. Stalling speed or minimum steady flight speed in the landing configuration.

Part 61—Pilot Certification

9. A current pilot certificate, a current medical certificate, and photo ID.
10. No.
11. July 31, 3 years later, if the pilot was younger than 40 on the date of the examination.
12. During an airlift for a charitable organization, when the FAA has been notified and a donation made to the charitable organization.
13. You must have made 3 takeoffs and 3 landings within the preceding 90 days in an aircraft of the same category and class, or type. For tailwheel airplanes, the landings must be to a full stop.
14. 1929.
15. Three.

Part 91—General Operating and Flight Rules

16. The pilot-in-command.
17. The pilot-in-command.

18. Yes, the pilot-in-command may deviate from the regulations to the extent required to meet the emergency. A written report of the deviation should be sent to the FAA on request.
19. In the current, FAA-approved flight manual, approved manual material, markings, and placards, or any combination thereof.
20. Airworthiness certificate, registration certificate, operating limitations (Flight Manual, POH, placards, etc.), and weight-and-balance information (in the Flight Manual, POH, or separate). These can be remembered using the mnemonic "AROW."
21. 0.04% by weight.
22. Yes.
23. No.
24. During takeoffs and landings.
25. Airplane.
26. An aircraft in distress.
27. No (it only has right-of-way over other engine-driven aircraft).
28. The aircraft on the left shall give way.
29. The airplane.
30. Both should turn right.
31. The airship.
32. An aircraft at the lower altitude, but it shall not take advantage of this rule to cut in front of or to overtake another.
33. Yes.
34. The right.
35. 250 KIAS.
36. 250 KIAS.
37. 200 KIAS.
38. 500 feet.
39. An altitude allowing, if a power unit fails, an emergency landing without undue hazard to persons or property on the surface.
40. When requested by ATC.
41. Exercise extreme caution.
42. Return to the starting point on the airport.
43. Exercise extreme caution, then on seeing flashing red (only) abandon the approach because the airport is unsafe and the ATC message is "*do not land.*"
44. Left.
45. As soon as possible after departure.
46. Yes.
47. Two-way radio communication equipment and an ADS-B Out approved system.
48. Class B and C.
49. **a.** Flight fuel plus 30 minutes at normal cruise speed.
    b. Flight fuel plus 45 minutes at normal cruise speed.
50. Class B, C, D or E surface areas, except at the airports listed in Part 91, Appendix D, Section 3.
51. Visibility 1 SM and clear of clouds.
52. 6,500 feet MSL.
53. When the ELT has been used for more than 1 hour cumulative, or 50% of the battery's useful life.
54. During the period from sunset until sunrise.
55. That flight time in excess of 30 minutes at those altitudes.
56. At all times.
57. 1,500 feet AGL and 3 statute miles.
58. 1,359.6 hours.
59. Yes (note that the reverse does not apply).
60. In the maintenance records.
61. Yes, but only to protect the wreckage from further damage.
62. No.
63. 10 days.
64. Yes.

Commercial Review

65. A commercial operator is a person, who, for compensation or hire, engages in air commerce by the carriage of persons or property in an aircraft, other than as an air carrier.
66. Operational control refers to the exercise of authority over initiating, conducting, or terminating a flight.
67. No.
68. On April 30 one year later.
69. 1859 CST.
70. Aircraft A.
71. **a.** No.
    b. Yes.
72. 24 hours.
73. Weather reports and forecasts, fuel requirements, alternatives available if the planned flight cannot be completed, and any known traffic delays.
74. Flight fuel from departure airport to destination airport, plus flight fuel from destination airport to alternate airport, plus 45 minutes reserve at normal cruise speed.
75. 30 minutes.
76. 45 minutes.
77. **a.** 2,000 feet above the highest obstacle within 4 nautical miles of the route.
    b. 1,000 feet.
78. Answer c.
79. Answer a.
80. 1090ES.
81. No.
82. False. Part 135 applies to carriage of persons and property for compensation or hire in aircraft with less than 20 passenger seats or a maximum payload capacity of less than 6,000 pounds.
83. True.
84. True.
85. False. By night over designated mountainous terrain, you should fly VFR at an altitude of at least 2,000 feet above the highest obstacle within a horizontal distance of 5 miles from the intended course.

Review 20: Charts

Aeronautical Charts

1. Yes.
2. A parallel of latitude that joins all points of the same latitude with the exception of the equator.
3. True.
4. The prime meridian.
5. The Greenwich Observatory just outside London, England.
6. True.
7. False. Meridians of longitude are great circles.
8. Angular position east or west of the prime meridian.
9. 1 NM.
10. 60 NM.
11. Scale is the ratio of chart length to earth distance.

VFR Charts

12. 1,434 feet (434 + 1,000 because of being in a congested area).
13. 2,873 feet MSL.
14. 122.8, the CTAFs.
15. 122.8 MHz.
16. Chart Supplement U.S. (check contents).
17. **a.** Yes.
    b. Yes.
    c. No, it is further west.
    d. No, it has a more westerly longitude.
18. **a.** N47°33′ W116°12′.
    b. 2,223 feet MSL.
    c. It has some lighting.
    d. Hard.
    e. 5,500 feet.
    f. This airport does not have a control tower.
    g. 122.8 MHz.
    h. NAV-COM.
19. **a.** N47°54 W116°43′.
    b. 2,350 feet MSL.
    c. No.
    d. Hard.
    e. 4,200 feet.
    f. 122.7 MHz.
    g. Parachuting.
    h. Chart Supplement U.S.
20. **a.** Sandpoint.
    b. North.
    c. Yes.
    d. No.
    e. SANDPOE NDB.
    f. 264 kHz.
    g. Automatic direction finder (ADF).
    h. Morse code ident SZT (dit-dit-dit dah-dit-dit-dit dah).
21. **a.** N47°47' W116°49'.
    b. North.
    c. This airport does not have a control tower.
    d. 2,318 feet MSL.
    e. It has some lighting.
    f. Hard.
    g. 7,400 feet.
    h. NAV-COM.
    i. 135.075 MHz.
    j. NAV-COM.
    k. Class E.
    l. 6,500 feet MSL.
22. **a.** 299°M (316°T − 17°E variation).
    b. 30 NM.
23. A visual checkpoint to identify position for initial call up.
24. Answer a.

Review 21: Airspace

1. By a blue, solid line surrounding the primary airport.
2. A private pilot certificate, or a student pilot certificate which has the appropriate logbook endorsements.
3. 3 SM and clear of clouds.
4. By thick magenta, solid lines.
5. 10 NM.
6. Two-way radio communications equipment and a 4096-code transponder with an encoding altimeter (mode C).
7. Approach control.
8. 200 KIAS.
9. 3 SM and a distance from clouds of 500 feet below clouds, 1,000 feet above clouds, and 2,000 feet horizontally from clouds.
10. Class E.
11. Visibility 3 SM and distance from clouds 500 feet below clouds, 1,000 feet above clouds, 2,000 feet horizontally from clouds.
12. 14,500 feet MSL but is often designated lower.
13. **a.** 700 feet AGL.
    b. 1,200 feet AGL.
14. Visibility 1 mile and clear of clouds (since the airspace around the airport is Class G below 700 feet).
15. Class G airspace from surface to 699 feet, Class E airspace starting at 700 feet.
16. Class E airspace.
17. Low altitude high-speed military training, under IFR, above 1,500 feet AGL but with some sectors possibly below 1,500 feet AGL.
18. Class B.
19. 61 feet MSL.
20. Visual checkpoint for initial radio call prior to entering the San Jose Class C airspace.
21. 30 NM (see 30 NM arc and Part 91).

22. No SVFR is not permitted. It is indicated on the chart by "NO SVFR."
23. Flight visibility 3 SM, and distance from clouds 500 feet below, 1,000 feet above, and 2,000 feet horizontal.
24. Flight visibility 1 SM and clear of clouds.
25. Flight visibility 5 SM, and distance from clouds 1,000 feet below, 1,000 feet above, and 1 SM horizontal.
26. Flight visibility 3 SM, and distance from clouds 500 feet below, 1,000 feet above, 2,000 feet horizontal.
27. In a flight visibility of 1 SM and clear of clouds, if flown within ½ mile of the runway.
28. By magenta lines with hachuring.
29. Exercise extreme caution when military activity is being conducted.

Review 22: Airports and Airport Operations

Airports

1. 090° and 270° magnetic.
2. **a.** A closed runway.
   b. B.
   c. Taxiing and takeoff.
3. The weather in the control zone is below basic VFR minimums (i.e. visibility less than 3 miles and/or ceiling less than 1,000 feet).
4. By clicking the NAV-COM microphone 7 times within 5 seconds.
5. By blue omnidirectional lights.
6. Green.
7. You are slightly high on glide slope.
8. You are below glide slope.
9. A pulsating red light.

Airport Operations

10. **a.** Right-hand traffic and Runway 18.
    b. The traffic patterns are left-hand for Runway 22, and right-hand for Runway 4. Runway 22 and Runway 4 are not available for use.
11. Observe the traffic flow, enter the traffic pattern, and look for a light signal from the tower. Squawk transponder code 7600.
12. You are cleared for takeoff.
13. **a.** You should exercise extreme caution.
    b. The airport is not safe and you should not land there.
    c. You should give way to other aircraft and continue circling.
14. LNK.
15. 1,214 feet MSL.
16. 3,414 feet MSL; 2,200 feet AGL.
17. **a.** A hard surface.
    b. 12,901 feet.
    c. 200 feet.
18. 118.5 MHz.
19. 118.05 MHz.
20. Monitor the airport traffic, and announce your position and intentions on frequency 118.5 MHz.
21. 1800Z (1200 local + 6 hours).
22. 1200Z to 0600Z.
23. 124.8 MHz.
24. On initial contact with ground control.
25. **a.** Right.
    b. South.
26. True.
27. West.

Review 23: Visual Navigation Fundamentals

Navigation

1. Nautical miles.
2. Knot (= 1 NM per hour).
3. Foot.
4. Foot.
5. 6,076 feet.
6. Yes.
7. The speed of the airplane relative to the air mass.
8. Heading and true airspeed.
9. By a single-headed arrow.
10. **a.** The movement of an air mass relative to the ground.
    b. By convention, the direction that the wind blows from.
    c. The speed of an airplane relative to the ground.
    d. The direction in which an airplane points.
    e. The airplane's direction of travel over the ground.
    f. The angle between the direction an airplane is pointing (its heading) and the direction in which it is traveling over the ground (its ground track).
    g. The difference between desired course and the ground track.
11. The drift angle.
12. Answer a.
13. Tracking error.
14. Answer b.
15. • A: HDG/TAS;
    • B: TR/GS; and
    • D: drift.
16. Answer b.
17. The physical north pole and the physical south pole (otherwise known as true north and true south.)

Time

18. **a.** 291015, 11291015.
    b. 191517, 07191517.
    c. 011700, 04011700.
19. **a.** 15°.
    b. 142.5° (142°30').
20. 2000 UTC, 1500 EST.

21. 1100Z; 0400 PDT.
22. 1030 MST.
23. 1545Z.
24. 10 hours.
25. 1930 UTC, 1230 MST.
26. False. You would expect to lose one day.
27. American Air Almanac (a publication not required by pilots).
28. True.
29. Latitude and date.
30. One hour.

Review 24: Using the Flight Computer

The Flight Computer for Flight Planning

1.
- A: HDG/TAS; and
- B: TR/GS.

2. True.
3. The forecast wind velocity in knots and true, and the true airspeed expected from the airplane at the selected altitude.

Figure A2-3 Review 24, question 4.

4. 129 KTAS.
5. True heading 240 − 13 = 227°T ∴ magnetic heading is 227 − 8 = 219°M, and groundspeed = 131 knots.
6. 39 minutes (remember the rough check).
7. Approximately 10 gallons.
8. HDG 062°T, GS 127 knots.
9. 52 NM.
10. 20 NM.
11. 153 knots.
12. TAS 119 knots, HDG 296°T and 302°M, GS 95 knots.
13. **a.** 132 knots.
b. ETE 33 minutes.
14. Answer b.
15. Answer c.
34 minutes (distance 59 NM, course 181°T, GS 104 knots).

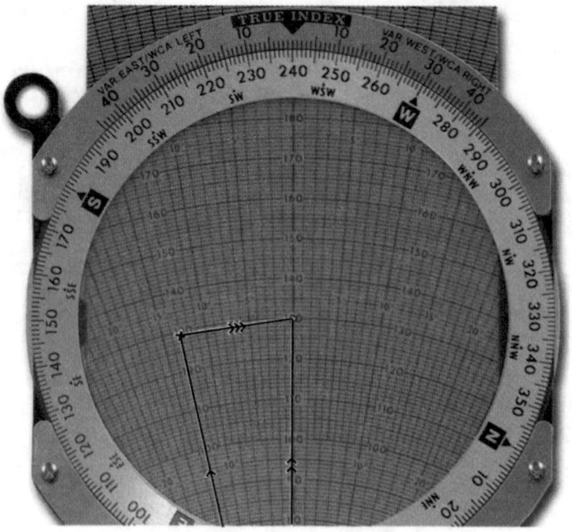

Figure A2-4 Review 24, question 5.

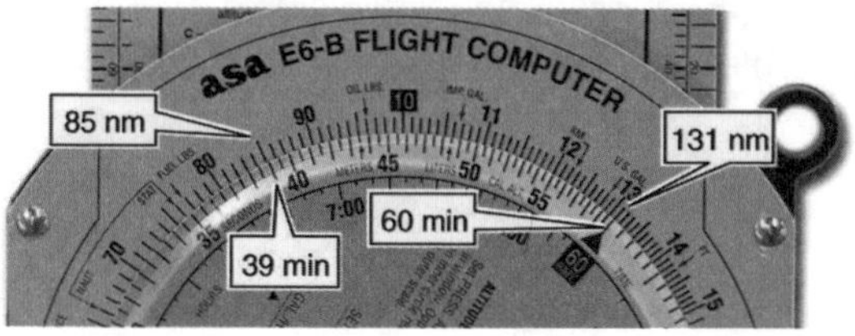

Figure A2-5 Review 24, question 6.

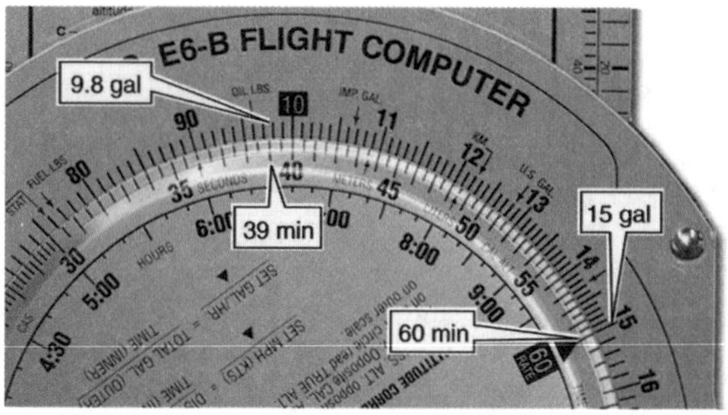

Figure A2-6 Review 24, question 7.

16. Answer b.
Total time including climb-out 43 minutes (distance 54 NM, course 346°T, GS 80 knots, time 40 minutes).
17. **a.** 12.5 gallons/hour.
b. 38 minutes.
18. 224 minutes or 3 hours 44 minutes (20.5 gal of flight fuel available).

Conversions

19. 0°C.
20. +68°F.
21. 102 km.
22. 92.5 km/hour.
23. 287 kg.
24. 176 lb.
25. 29 gal = 110 liters.
26. 270 lb.

Commercial Review

27. Answer a.
(True heading 085° with 20° left WCA.)
28. Answer a.
Approximately 205 pounds (time 153 minutes).
29. Answer c.
30. Answer a.
31. Answer b.
Climb 8,500 feet at 500 fpm will take 17 minutes. At 13 gal/hour, the fuel used is 3.7 gal. Use wind side of flight computer to calculate °T. Convert to °M, then allow for deviation. Use the ground-speed to find distance.
32. Answer c.
5,400 feet descent at 300 fpm takes 18 minutes. At 9.6 gal/hour, the fuel used is 2.9 gallons. Use a flight computer to calculate °T. Convert to °M and allow for deviation. Use the groundspeed from the computer to find the distance.

Review 25: Flight Planning

1. Meteorological forecasts and NOTAMs.
2. In the Chart Supplement U.S. (previously called the Airport/Facility Directory).
3. True.
4. **a.** 2,000 feet AGL.
b. 2,000 feet AGL.
5. False. When planning to fly more than 3,000 feet AGL, you should base your VFR cruise altitude on magnetic course.
6. False. VOR radials are based on magnetic north.
7. Answer a.
8. Answer b.
9. **a.** 5,500 feet MSL.
b. 4,500 feet MSL or 6,500 feet MSL.
c. 5,500 feet MSL.
d. 4,500 feet MSL or 6,500 feet MSL.
10. In hours and minutes.
11. Enter the planned cruising level for the first or the whole portion of the route to be flown.
12. A 4-figure group giving the fuel endurance in hours and minutes.
13. The category of flight rules for which the pilot intends to fly, VFR, IFR or a combination of both.
14. The pilot must close the flight plan with the nearest FSS or other FAA facility on landing.

Review 26: En Route Navigation

1. A known position of an airplane at a given time (also called pinpoint).
2. Flying accurate headings and identifying landmarks.
3. 108 knots.
4. The angular difference between planned track and track made good.
5. For normal en route navigation, read from chart to ground; when lost or uncertain of position, read from ground to chart.
6. Good flight planning; flying accurate headings and airspeeds.
7. 12° right (TE 8° + CA 4°).
8. 3 minutes.
9. Drift.
10. 9° right.
11. **a.** TE 8° left.
b. CA 8°.
c. CA 4°.
12. 18° left.
13. **a.** TE 7°.
b. CA 5°.
c. HDG 281°M.
d. HDG 286°M.
14. 7 min.

Review 27: Navigation Aids

VOR

1. Answer b.
2. VORTAC refers to when a military TACAN ground station is integrated with a VOR/DME ground station.
3. A radial is the magnetic bearing from a VOR ground station.
4. Answer a.
5. Answer b.
6. Its Morse code ident or voice ident.
7. **a.** 2°.
b. 10° or more.
8. ±2°.
9. **a.** 090 radial.
b. 270 radial.
c. 274 radial (094-TO).
d. 092 radial.
10. Answer b.
11. No (the VOR cockpit display is not heading sensitive).
12.
- VOR indication (i) corresponds to Airplane B;
- VOR indication (ii) corresponds to Airplane B and
- VOR indication (iii) corresponds to Airplane D.

13. Chart Supplement U.S.
14. **a.** Yes.
b. It may still transmit navigation signals.

15. **a.** No.
    b. Yes.
16. If you change the OBS to move the CDI from the center position to overhead the last dot, this should cause a bearing change of between 10° and 12°.
17. A remote indicating compass and ADF/VOR needles.
18. A remote indicating compass and a VOR indicator.
19. Illustration a.
20. Answer c.
21. You will be diverging from the radial.
22. Answer b.
23. Answer b.
24. Answer a.
25. R-345 (2.5 dots = 5° before reaching the selected R-350 FROM).
26. 165 (345-FROM to center the CDI = 165-TO).
27. 174 (aircraft is 2 dots = 4° to the right of the selected R-170.
28. 354 (174-FROM to center the CDI = 354-TO).
29. The result of flying a heading approximately the reciprocal of the VOR bearing selected on the OBS.
30. **a.** Set 030 in the OBS and make heading corrections toward the CDI (note that the FROM flag would be in the window).
    b. Set 210 in the OBS and make heading corrections toward the CDI (note that the TO flag would be in the window).
31. Answer b.
32. Answer d.
33. Answer a.

NDB and ADF

34. A ground-based receiver.
35. By its Morse code *ident*.
36. Select the NDB frequency, identify the NDB, and check that the needle is indeed "ADFing."
37. An airborne receiver.
38. **a.** Atmospheric conditions, such as electrical storms or the periods of sunrise and sunset, distort NDB signals, making ADF indications less reliable.
    b. Mountains reflect and distort NDB signals, making ADF indications less reliable.

ADF Displays

39. **a.** MB 280 to the NDB.
    b. MB 100 from the NDB.
40. **a.** MB 030 to NDB.
    b. MB 020 to NDB.
    c. MB 015 to NDB.
41. **a.** MB 160 to NDB.
    b. MB 340 from NDB.
42. **a.** MB 240 to the NDB.
    b. MB 060 from the NDB.
43. **a.** MB 075 to the NDB.
    b. MB 255 from the NDB.
    c. TB 251 from the NDB.
44. MB 070 to ground station.
45. 190 radial.
46. 089 radial.
47. MB 250 from ground station (the reciprocal of 070).
48. **a.** MB 075 to the NDB.
    b. MB 255 from the NDB.
    c. RB 040 to the NDB.

Intercepting Course and Tracking

49. Right.
50. **a.** right turn to MH 130.
    b. RBI 270.
51. No, it is inefficient, because it will result in a curved path.
52. MC 060 inbound to the NDB.
53. **a.** MH 345.
    b. RB 355.
54. **a.** MH 360.
    b. RB 090.
55. **a.** MH 010.
    b. RB 080.
56. A wind correction angle.

Transponder and ADS-B

57. The process of separating airplanes and positioning them by ATC passing headings to steer.
58. True.
59. The track of your airplane.
60. The altitude-reporting capability of a transponder.
61. Press the ident button once.
62. 7700.
63. ADS-B Out and ADS-B In. ADS-B Out is required.
64. TIS-B allows pilots to see air-to-air traffic on the cockpit as well as radar targets from ground stations to enhance situational awareness. FIS-B provides aeronautical information and weather in the cockpit to enhance safety.

DME

65. Slant distance.
66. NAV-COM (usually along with a collocated VOR).
67. About once every 30 seconds.
68. 1350 Hz.
69. 10 seconds.
70. False. For each time you hear the DME identifier, you should hear the VOR identifier about 3 times.
71. The DME indicator will either drop out or show 2 NM.
72. 10 NM in 7 minutes = GS 86.
73. Answer a.

RNAV

74. A phantom VORTAC.
75. By electronically adding a vector to the position of the real VORTAC.
76. Crosstrack error.
77. Fixes along an off-airways route.

GPS

78. True.
79. Three.

Commercial Review

80. MB 075 from the NDB.
81. MB 310 from the NDB.
82. Answer a.
83. Answer c.
84. Answer b.
85. **a.** 6 minutes.
b. 10 NM.
c. 0.8 gals.
86. 18 minutes ((60 × 3) ÷ 10).
87. **a.** 24 minutes.
b. 58 NM.
88. **a.** Left.
b. 125°.
c. MH 270.
89. Answer a.
(The double-arrowed needle is selected to a VOR, hence "radial" refers to the tail of this needle.)
90. Answer c.
(This refers to RMI "D." It would take some time on MH 180 to intercept the 120 radial, depending on how close you are to the VOR, but you would eventually intercept it off this heading.)
91. **a.** Right.
b. 60°.
c. MH 360.
92. RB 240.
93. RB 250.
94. Answer b.
95. Answer b.
96. False. The tail of the ADF pointer will be deflected to the downwind side of the tail position and the head of the ADF pointer will be deflected to the windward side of the nose position.
97. True.
98. **a.** Right.
b. MH 030.
99. 250°.
100. **a.** 030.
b. MH 030.
b. MH 210.
101. RMI 149.
102. **a.** Right turn to MH 130.
b. Right turn to MH 100.
c. RMI 040.
103. MC 060.
104. **a.** MH 128.
b. RMI 300, RMI tail 120.
105. **a.** MH 010.
b. RMI 090.
106. 210°.
107. 240°.

Index

A

B

C

D

E

F

G

H

M

N

O

P

T

U

V

W

Y

Z